Family World Atlas

An Illustrated and Informative View of the Earth

American Map Corporation

New York, N.Y.

Photographic Credits

Cover illustrations
(Small photographs – from left to right)
Carlo Lauer, Rainer Kiedrowski, Erik Lieber-mann, Rainer Kiedrowski, (World map)
ZEFA/IMTEK IMAGINEERING

Inside illustrations
H. Abernathy/H. Armstrong Roberts: 138
B & U Int. Picture Service/ Herman Schol-ten, Huizen (NL): 98/99
Prof. Dr. Jürgen Bähr: 117, 122, 125, 136, 139, 140/141, 144/145, 146, 148/149, 150/151
Battman: 138/139

Dr. Ambros Brucker: 93, 96, 104
Ron Calamia: 139
California Division of Tourism: 140
Deutsche Forschungs- und Versuchsanstalt für Luft- und Raumfahrt e.V., Oberpfaffen-hofen: 82/83
Ingrid Eckhardt-Heinert: 133
Prof. Dr. Eckart Ehlers: 116
Ina Grill: 146
Prof. Dr. Hartwig Haubrich: 122
Hans-Georg Herrnleben: 102, 107, 113, 120, 151
Hungarian Pictures/Kossuth: 95
Dr. Jörg Janzen: 130/131, 132
Rainer Kiedrowski: 84, 88/89, 99, 102, 111, 116, 121, 123, 125, 126, 130
Dr. Werner Klohn: 142

Prof. Dr. Heinrich Lamping: 117, 120
Carlo Lauer: 102, 128, 129, 134, 135, 136, 140, 141
Erik Liebermann: 99, 106
Christoph Lutze: 93
New York State Department of Economic Development: 141
Photo Press: 92/93, 96
97; Brucker: 114; Pago: 99;
Pape: 95, 100; Schweitzer:
108, 109, 112/113
Prof. Dr. Ulrich Pietrusky: 84, 88/89, 94, 95, 110, 124, 125, 126, 128, 129, 130/131, 132, 143, 144, 146, 148/149, 150/151, 152
Prisma Fotoservice/Gartung: 129
Québec Tourism: 140

Erika Rieger: 135
Peer Schmidt-Walther: 83, 90, 115, 117
Prof. Dr. Wulf-D. Schmidt-Wulffen: 82, 92/93, 124/125, 132
Ernst Schneider: 86
Prof. Dr. Fred Scholz: 110, 111
Urs Schweitzer: 87, 101, 102/103, 104, 106, 107, 108, 110/111, 118, 120/121, 145, 148, 149, 151
S. Sieb/H. Armstrong Roberts: 138
State of Washington Tourism Division: 142
Dr. Christoph Stein: 131
ZEFA/Damm: 94/95

Aerial photograph (88/89) by permission of the regional council of Düsseldorf
38 V 10

© by RV Reise- und Verkehrsverlag GmbH
Berlin · Gütersloh · Leipzig · Munich · Potsdam/Werder · Stuttgart 1994

American edition 1994 published and distributed by
American Map Corporation, New York, NY

Cartography: Kartographisches Institut Bertelsmann, Gütersloh
Text and photograph editor: Carlo Lauer
American Editor: Vera Benson, American Map Corporation
Cover design: Bärbel Jehle
Texts to »The Earth — Its Continents and Countries«: Dr. Ambros Brucker, Munich
Translation: GAIA Text (Lonnie Legg), Munich
English text for »North and Central America – People and Culture«: Donald Olson
Book design and production: Hubertus Hepfinger, Freising

Typesetting: Buchmacher Bär, Freising
Reproduction: Repro Ludwig, Zell am See
Printing and bookbinding: Mohndruck Graphische Betriebe GmbH, Gütersloh
Printed in Germany
ISBN 0–8416–2025–3

Introduction

With its combination of superlative maps, informative essays and memorable photographs, the Family World Atlas brings the global family of humankind – and the Earth we all share – to *your* family's fingertips. Designed for years of use, this unique atlas will quickly become an indispensable home reference tool and guide to today's fast-changing world.

To be effective, an atlas must reflect the changes taking place all around the globe. Each of the full-color maps in the Family World Atlas has been painstakingly researched to ensure that it is accurate and up to date. Clear and crisply detailed cartography, the result of meticulous European craftsmanship and state-of-the-art production techniques, makes each map easy to read and beautiful to look at.

In the Family World Atlas you'll find physical reference overview maps of the entire Earth and of each continent, as well as regional maps that depict a wealth of topographical details such as mountain ranges, rivers, lakes, and marshlands. Major cities and the political boundaries of sovereign states, including the new republics of the former Soviet Union and Yugoslavia, have of course been included. A comprehensive index makes it easy to locate any corner of the Earth in seconds.

But the Family World Atlas does far more than show you places on a map. To enhance and increase your knowledge of Planet Earth and its inhabitants, it takes you on a fascinating round-the-world journey. The unique natural environment of each continent and the diverse cultures of the peoples who live there spring vividly to life in special photographs, thematic maps, and descriptive essays. Below the flags of every nation are the pertinent facts of that nation – its capital, land area, population, primary languages, and currency.

Each and every family member can learn and benefit from this comprehensive and authoritative new volume. Let the Family World Atlas be your experienced guide to all the familiar and mysterious corners of this beautiful planet we call Earth.

Contents

Abbreviations used in the Maps

A....;...	Alpes, Alpen
ad.	adasi
Ág.	Ágia, -ios
Aig.lle	Aiguille(s)
AK	Alaska
Akr.	Akreotérion
AL	Alabama
AO	Autonome Oblast
AR	Arkansas
Arch.	Archipelago
Arr.	Arroyo
Austr.	Australia
Aut.	Autonomous
AZ	Arizona
B.	Bad, Basin, Bay
Ban.	Banjaran
Bat.	Batang
-b.	-bach
Bel.	Belyi, -aja-, -oje, -yje
Bg(e).	Berg(e)
-bg(e).	-berg(e)
-bǧ.	-burg
B.io	Balneario
Bol.	Bol'šoj, -aja, -oje, -ije
Bos.	Bosanski, -a, -e
Bras.	Brazil
-br(n).	-brücke(n)
B.t	Bukit
C.	Cape
Č.	Český, -ká, -ké
CA	California
Can.	Canal
C.bo	Cabo
C.d	Ciudad
Chan.	Channel
Chin.	China
chr.	chrebet
C.l(e)	Coll(e)
C.ma	Cima
CO	Colorado
Col.	Colombia
Coll.s	Collines
Cor.	Coronel
Cord.	Cordillera
C.po	Capo
Cr.	Creek
C.Rica	Costa Rica
C.ro	Cerro
ČSFR	Czech Rep. and Slovakia
CT	Connecticut
Cuch.	Cuchilla
D.	Danau
Dağl.	Dağlari
DC	District of Columbia
DE	Delaware
Den.	Denmark
Dép.	Département
-df.	-dorf
Ea.	East
Ec.	Ecuador
E.ción	Estación
E. G.	Equatorial Guinea
f.	fontein
Fd.	Feld
-fd(e)	-felde(e)
-fdn.	-felden
Fed.	Federal
F.êt	Forêt
Fj.	Fjord
-fj.	-fjord
FL	Florida
Fr.	France, French
F.rte	Fuerte
F.t	Fort
F.tin	Fortín
G.	Gölü (lakes); Gulf (bays, gulfs)
GA	Georgia
G.a	Gora
G.d	Grand
G.de(s)	Grande(s)
-geb.	-gebirge
G.fe	Golfe
Gl.	Glacier
-gl.	-gletscher
-gn.	-ingen
G.ng	Gunung
G.ng-g.ng	Gunung-gunung
Gr.	Groß, -er, -e, -es
-gr.	-gruppe (mountains); -graben (waters)
G.ral	General
G.t	Great
-h.	-hafen
-hav.	-haven
H.d	Head
-hfn.	-hofen
-hgn.	-hagen
HI	Hawaii
-hm.	-heim
-h.n	-horn
Hon.	Honduras
H.s	Hills
-hsn.	-hausen
Htr.	Hinter
-hvn.	-hoven
...I.	Insel, Island
I....	Isle
Î	Île
IA	Iowa
I.a	Ilha
Î.a	Ísola
ID	Idaho
IL	Illinois
I.la(s)	Isla(s)
IN	Indiana
Ind.	India
I.s	Islands
Î.s	Îles
Isr.	Israel
It., Ital.	Italy
J.	Jabal
-j.	joch; joki
Jap.	Japan
Jord.	Jordans
Juž.	Južnyj, -aja, -oje
-K.	-kopf
-kan.	-kanal
-kchn.	-kirchen
Kep.	Kepulauan
-kfl.	-kofel
Kgl.	Kogel
-kgl.	-kogel
km.	Kilómetro
Kl.	Klein
Kör.	Körfezi
Kr.	Krasno, -yj, -aja, -oje
KS	Kansas
KY	Kentucky
L.	Lake
LA	Lousiana
-lbn.	-leben
L.d	Land
-l.d	-land
Lim.	Limnē
L.le	Little
L.oa	Lago(a)
L.una(s)	Laguna(s)
M.	Monte
MA	Massachusetts
Mal.	Malyj, -aja, -oje
M.as	Montanhas
Mc.	Mac
MD	Maryland
ME	Maine
Mex.	Mexico
M.gne(s)	Montagne(s)
MI	Michigan
MN	Minnesota
MO	Missouri
MS	Mississippi
MT	Montana
Mt.	Mount
M.t	Mont
M.ti	Monti
Mt.n	Mountain
Mt.s	Mountains
M.t(s)	Mont(s)
n.	nos
Nat.	National-
Nat.-P(ark)	Nationalpark
NC	North Carolina
ND	North Dakota
N.do	Nevado
Ndr.	Nieder
NE	Nebraska
Neth.	Netherlands
NH	New Hampshire
Nic.	Nicaragua
Niž.	Nižnij, -'aja, -eje, -ije
nizm.	nizmenost'
NJ	New Jersey
NM	New Mexico
Norw.	Norway
Nov.	Novo, -yj, -aja, -oje
NV	Nevada
N.va	Nueva
NY	New York
N. Z.	New Zealand
o.	ostrov
Ob.	Ober
Obl.	Oblast
OH	Ohio
OK	Oklahoma
OR	Oregon
Ou	Ouèd
o-va	ostrova
oz.	ozero
P.	Port (cities, towns); Paß (passes); Pulau (islands)
PA	Pennsylvania
Pan.	Panama
Pass.	Passage
P.c	Pic
P.co	Pico
Pen.	Peninsula
per.	pereval
P.it(e)	Petit(e)
P.k(s)	Peak(s)
Pl.a	Planina
Pl.au	Plateau
-pl.au	-plateau
Port.	Portugal
p-ov	poluostrov
P.-p.	Pulau-pulau
Pr.	Prince
Prov.	Province, Provincial
P.rto	Puerto
P.so	Passo
P.t	Point
P.t(e)	Point(e)
P.ta	Punta
P.to	Porto
P.zo	Pizzo
R	Rio
Ra.	Range
Ra.s	Ranges
R.ca	Rocca
Reg.	Region
Rep.	Republic
Res.	Reservat
RI	Rhode Island
Riv.	River
-riv.	-rivier
S.	San
...(-)S.	(-see) See
S. Afr.	South Africa
S.ai	Sungai
SC	South Carolina
Sd.	Sund
S.d	Sound
SD	South Dakota
S.ei	Sungei
Sev.	Severnyj, -aja, -oje
S.i	Sidi
Sl.	Slovenski, -a, -e
S.nia	Serrania
Sp.	Spitze
-sp.	-spitze (mountains); -sperre (waters)
S.ra(s)	Sierra(s)
Sred.	Sredne, -ij, -'aja, eje
S.rra	Serra
St.	Sankt
S.t	Saint
-st.	-stadt (cities, towns); -stein (mountains)
S.ta	Santa
Star.	Staryj, -aja, -oje
S.te	Sainte
S.th	South
-stn.	-stetten
st.n	stein
S.to	Santo
Str.	Street
Tel.	Teluk
Ter.	Territory
TN	Tennessee
T.ng	Tanjung
TX	Texas
U. K.	United Kingdom
Unt.	Unter, -ere
USA	United States
UT	Utah
V.	Volcán
V.a	Vila
VA	Virginia
V.an	Volcán
vdchr.	vodochranilišče
Vel.	Veliki, -aja, -oje
Ven.	Venezuela
Verch.	Verchne, -ij, -'aja, -eje, -ije
V.ey	Valley
V.la	Villa
vozvyš.	vozvyšenost'
VT	Vermont
W.	West
(-)W.	(-wald) Wald
-w	-witz
WA	Washington
-wd(e).	-wald(e)
W.di	Wadi
WI	Wisconsin
-wlr.	weiler
WV	West Virginia
WY	Wyoming
zal.	zaliv
Zap.	Zapadnaja
zapov.	zapovednik

Conversion diagram

meters	0	10	20	30	40	50	60	70	80	90	100
feet	0	32.8	65.6	98.4	131.2	164.0	196.8	229.6	262.4	295.2	328.0

meters	0	100	200	300	400	500	600	700	800	900	1,000
feet	0	328	656	984	1,312	1,640	1,968	2,296	2,624	2,952	3,280

meters	0	1,000	2,000	3,000	4,000	5,000	6,000	7,000	8,000	9,000	10,000
feet	0	3,280	6.560	9,840	13,120	16,400	19,680	22,960	26,240	29,520	32,800

UNITED STATES

8

1 : 5,000,000

One inch to 79 miles   conversion meters-feet see page 6

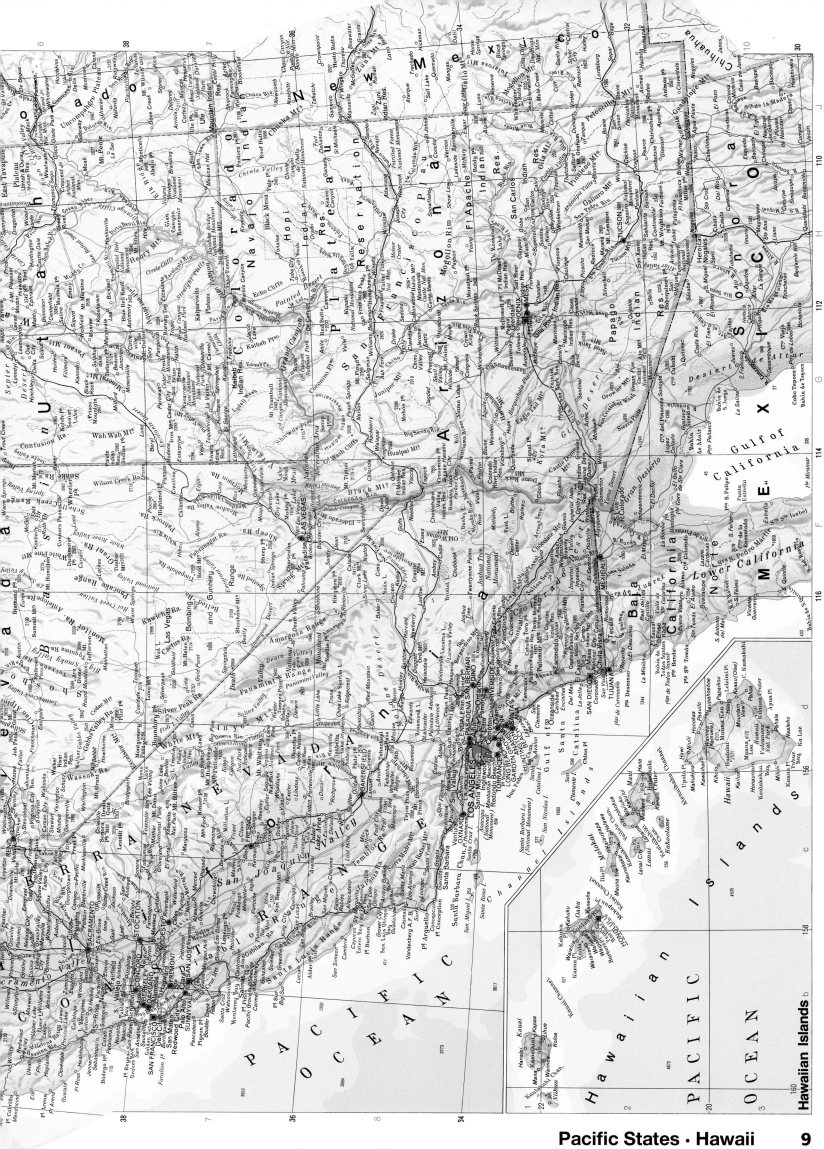

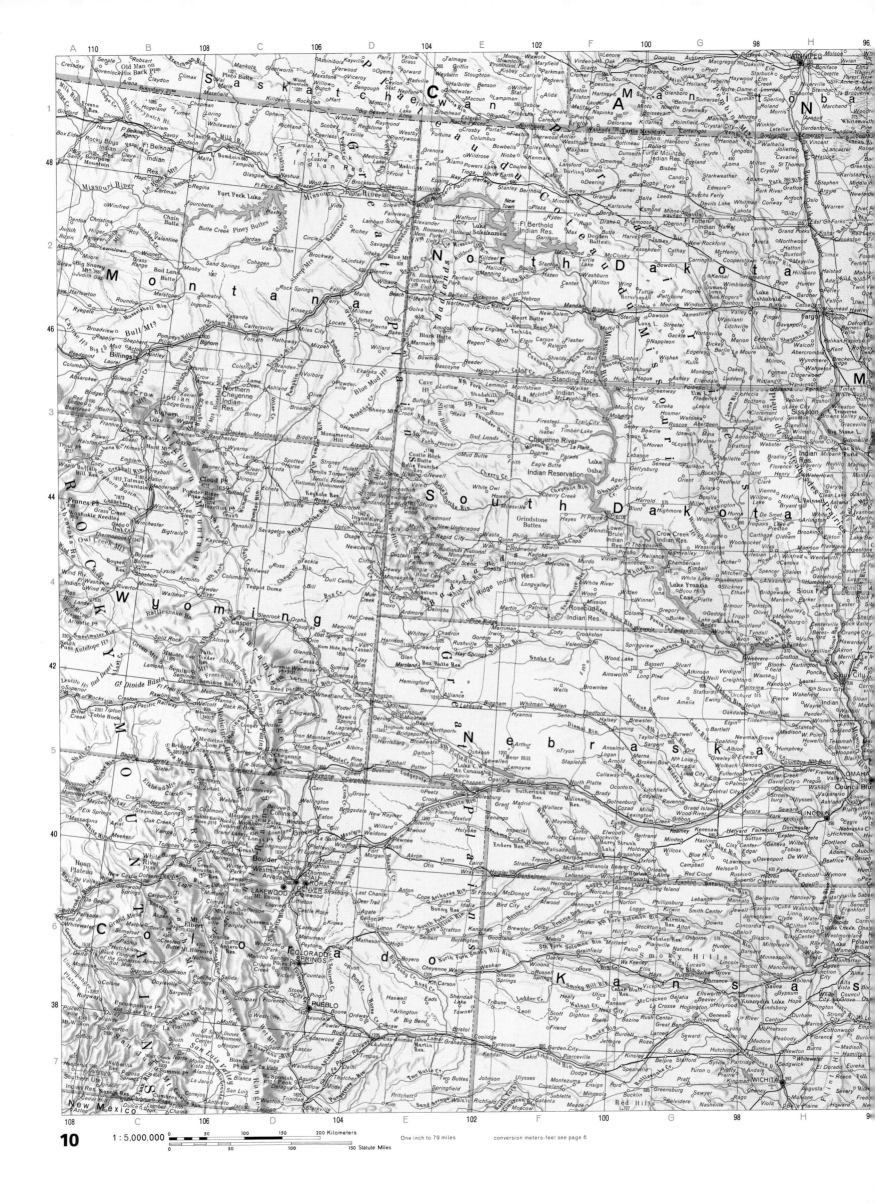

1 : 5,000,000

0   50   100   150   200 Kilometers

One inch to 79 miles   conversion meters-feet see page 6

0   50   100   150 Statute Miles

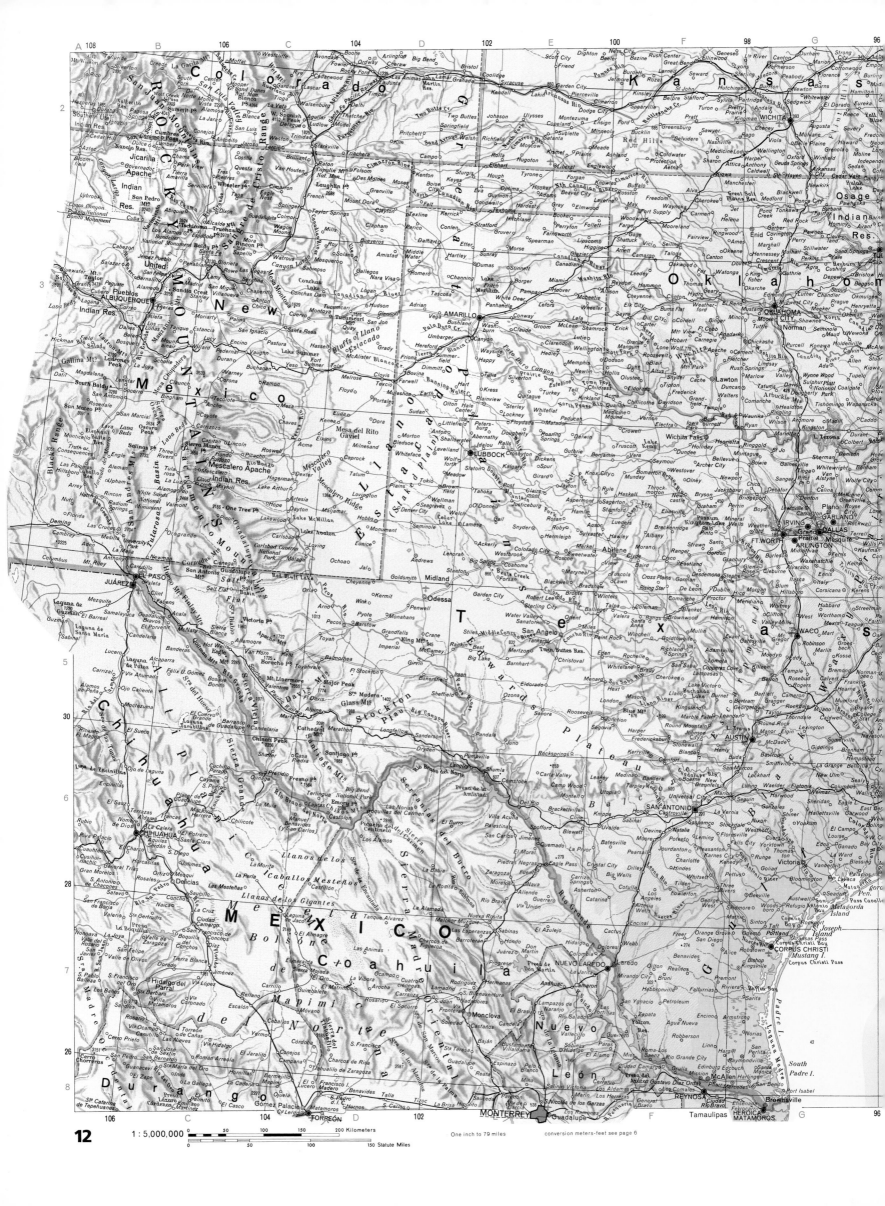

14   1 : 5,000,000

0   50   100   150   200 Kilometers

0   50   100   150 Statute Miles

One inch to 79 miles   conversion meters-feet see page 6

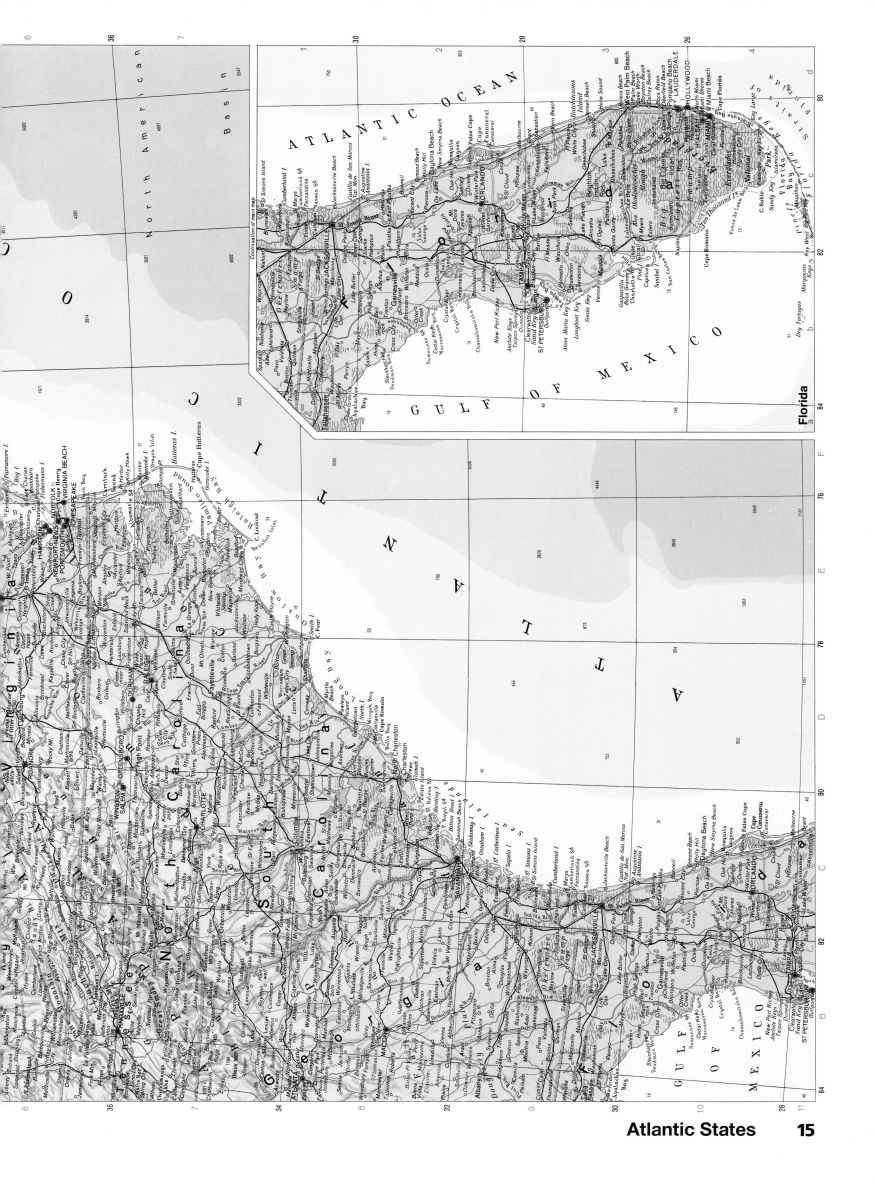

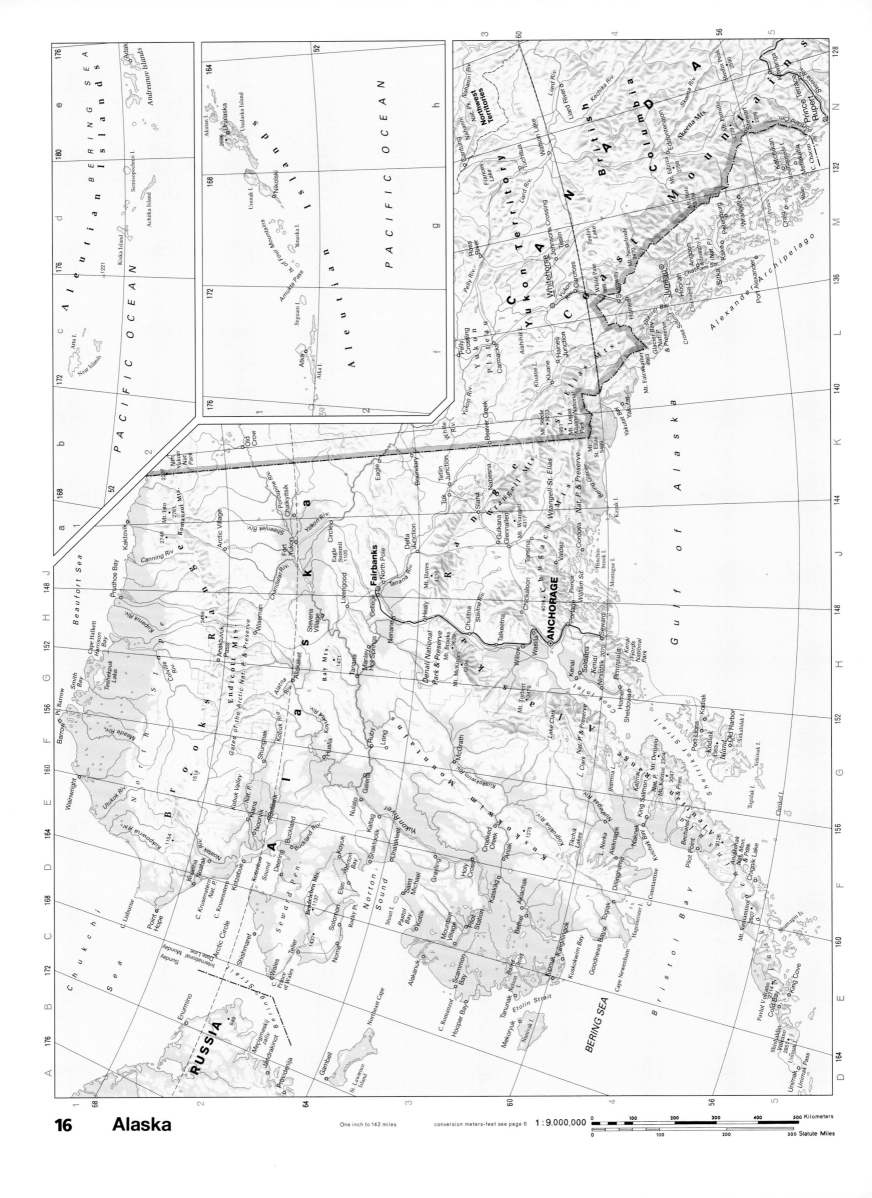

16   Alaska

One inch to 142 miles   conversion meters-feet see page 6   1 : 9,000,000

THE EARTH

Symbols

～～	River, stream		————	Railroad
～～	Drying river, stream		▬▬▬	Primary railroad
～～	Intermittent river, stream		————	Secondary railroad

on larger scale maps

·········	Canal		++++++++	Suspended cable car
- - - -	Canal under construction		– – – –	Railroad under construction
～	Waterfall, rapids		·············	Train ferry
～	Dam		⊣–⊢⊣–⊢	Tunnel
	Fresh-water or salt-water lake with permanent shore line		————	Major highway
	Fresh-water or salt-water lake with variable or undefined shore line		————	Expressway
	Intermittent lake		====	Expressway under construction

on larger scale maps

∪	Well in dry area		– – – –	Caravan route, path, track
	Swamp, Bog		·············	Ferry
	Salt marsh		⋈	Pass
	Flood area		⊕ ✛	Airport, Airfield
	Mud flat			
+	Reef, Coral reef			
	Glacier		▬▬▬▬	International boundary
	Average pack ice limit in summer		▬▬▬▬	Boundary of autonomous area
	Average pack ice limit in winter		– – – –	Boundary of subsidiary administrative unit
	Shelf ice		MADRID	National capital
	Sand desert, gravel desert, etc.		Salem / Nachičevan'	Principal cities of subsidiary administrative units

	Place					Locality			
◖	LONDON	over 1,000,000 Inhabitants			⬦	L.-HARROW		•	Inhabited spot, station
◼	BRISBANE	500,000 -1,000,000 Inhabitants			▪	BR.-IPSWICH		∴	Ruins
◉	ROSTOCK	100,000 - 500,000 Inhabitants			▫	R.-WARNEMÜNDE		♂	Castle, fort
◎	Segovia	50,000 - 100,000 Inhabitants						♁	Monastery, church
⊙	Douglas	10,000 - 50,000 Inhabitants						⊥	Monument
○	Ansó	unter 10,000 Inhabitants						☼ ⚓	Lighthouse
								◌	Nature reserve

Type Styles

VENEZUELA	Independent country		*G O B I* / *Mallorca* / *Devon*	Physical regions and islands
T i r o l	Subordinate administrative unit			
(Port.) *(Port.)*	Political affiliation		*OCÉANO* / *North Sea* / *Volga*	Hydrography
VALENCIA / Cáceres / *Dover*	Places		*Devil's Hole*	Ocean basin, trench, ridge etc.
ATLAS / Causses	Mountain		2834	Altitude and depth in meters
Snowdon	Mountain, cape, pass, glacier		*164*	Depth of lakes below surface

Altitudes and Depths

1:15,000,000 and smaller	>10000	10000	8000	6000	4000	2000	200	0 Depr. 0	200	500	1000	2000	3000	4000	5000	>5000 m
	>32809	32809	26247	19685	13124	6562	656	0 Depr. 0	656	1640	3281	6562	9843	13124	16405	>16405 ft

1:5,000,000 to 1:7,500,000	>10000	10000	8000	6000	4000	2000	200	0 Depr. 0	100	200	500	1000	2000	3000	4000	5000	>5000 m
	>32809	32809	26247	19685	13124	6562	656	0 Depr. 0	328	656	1640	3281	6562	9843	13124	16405	>16405 ft

1:1,000,000			>200	200	100	40	20	0 Depr. 0	100	200	300	500	700	1000	1500	2000	2500	3000	>3000 m
			>656	656	328	131	66	0 Depr. 0	328	656	984	1640	2297	3281	4921	6562	8202	9843	>9843 ft

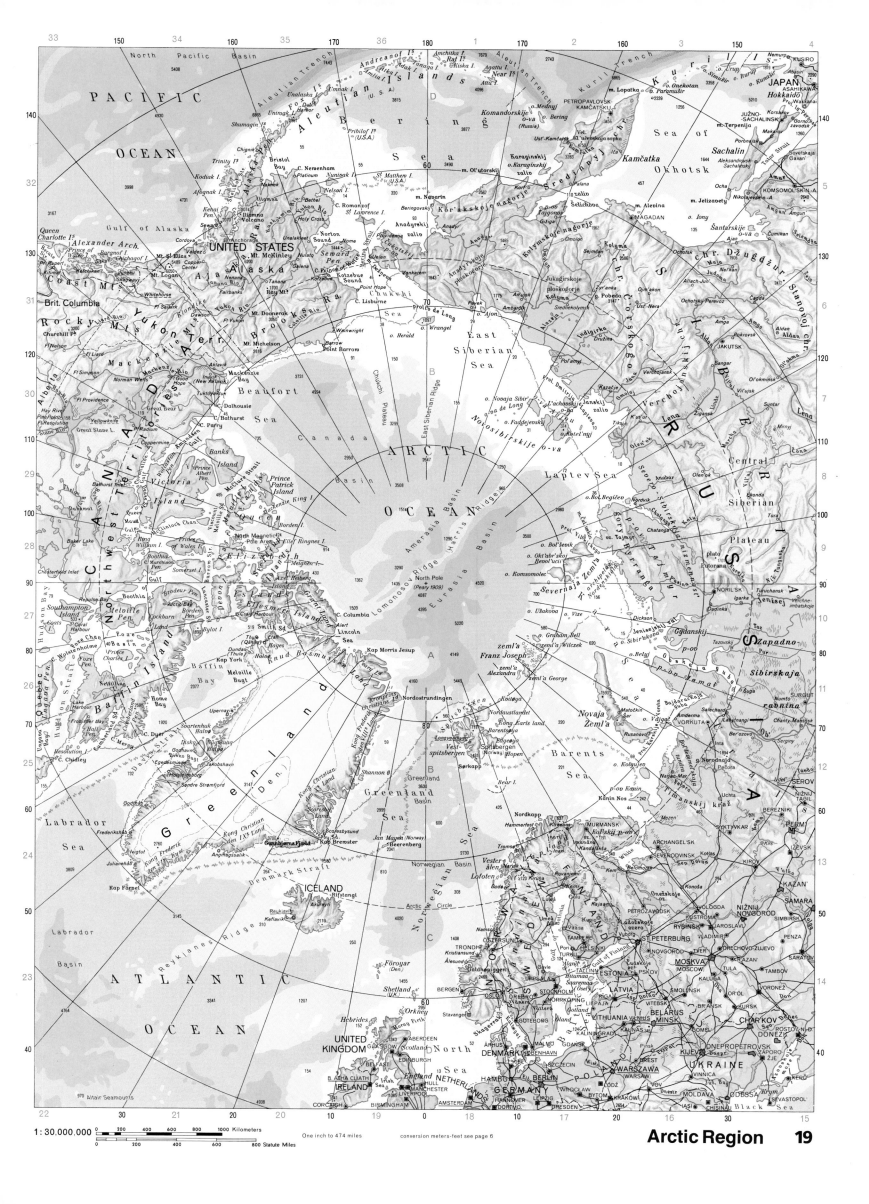

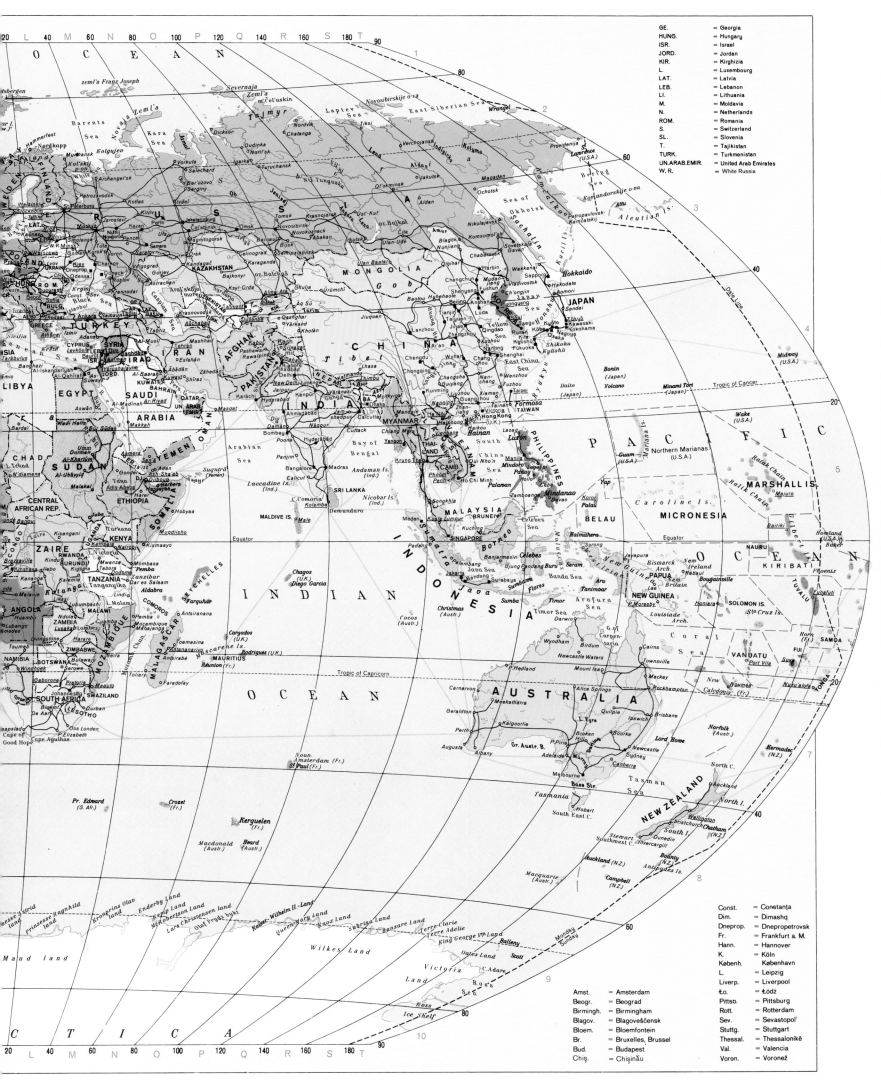

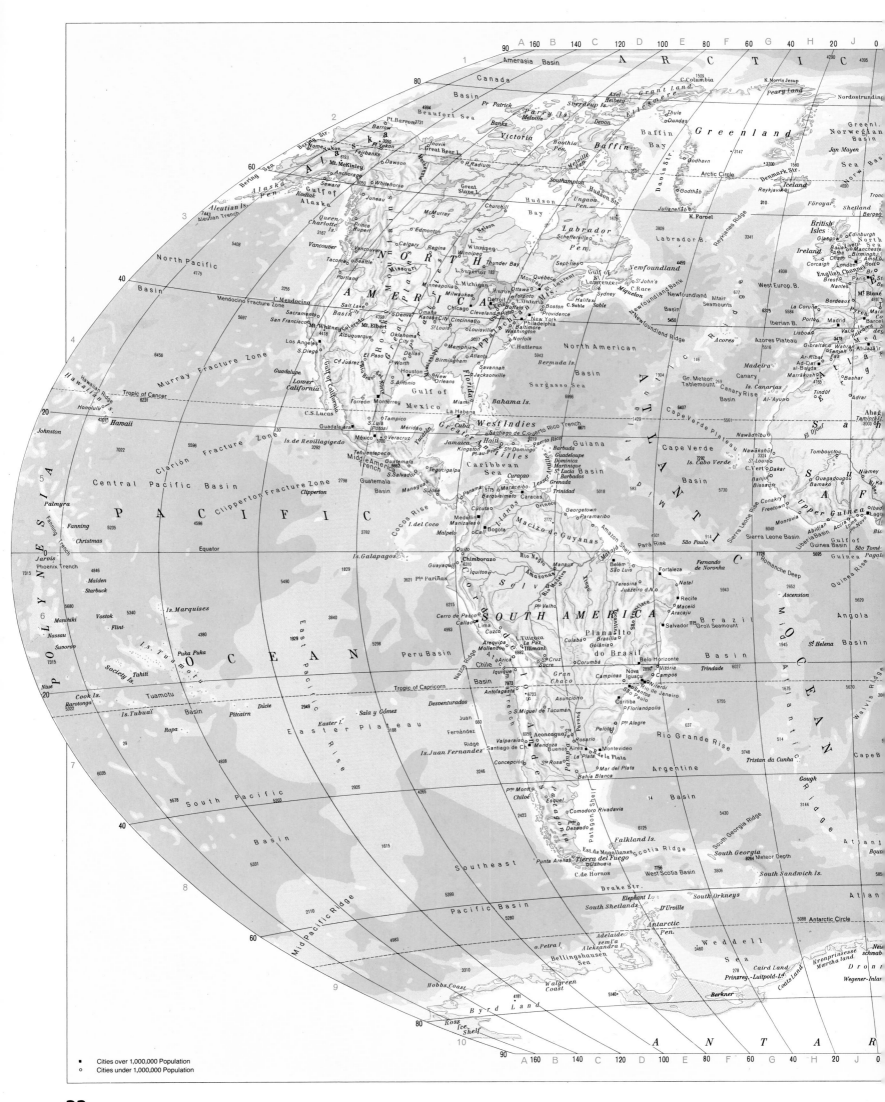

Cities over 1,000,000 Population
Cities under 1,000,000 Population

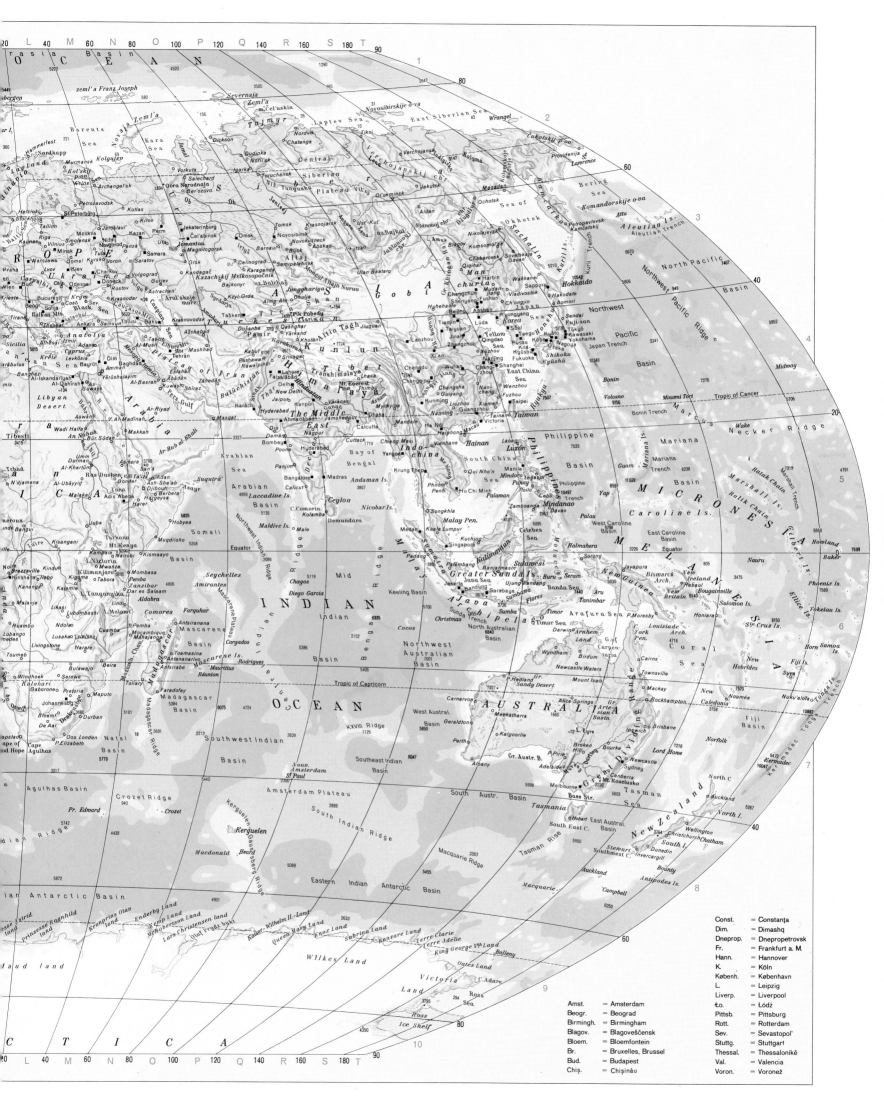

Const. = Constanța
Dim. = Dimashq
Dneprop. = Dnepropetrovsk
Fr. = Frankfurt a. M.
Hann. = Hannover
K. = Köln
København. = København
L. = Leipzig
Liverp. = Liverpool
Ło. = Łódź
Pittsb. = Pittsburg
Rott. = Rotterdam
Sev. = Sevastopol'
Stuttg. = Stuttgart
Thessal. = Thessalonikē
Val. = Valencia
Voron. = Voronež

Amst. = Amsterdam
Beogr. = Beograd
Birmingh. = Birmingham
Blagov. = Blagoveščensk
Bloem. = Bloemfontein
Br. = Bruxelles, Brussel
Bud. = Budapest
Chiș. = Chișinău

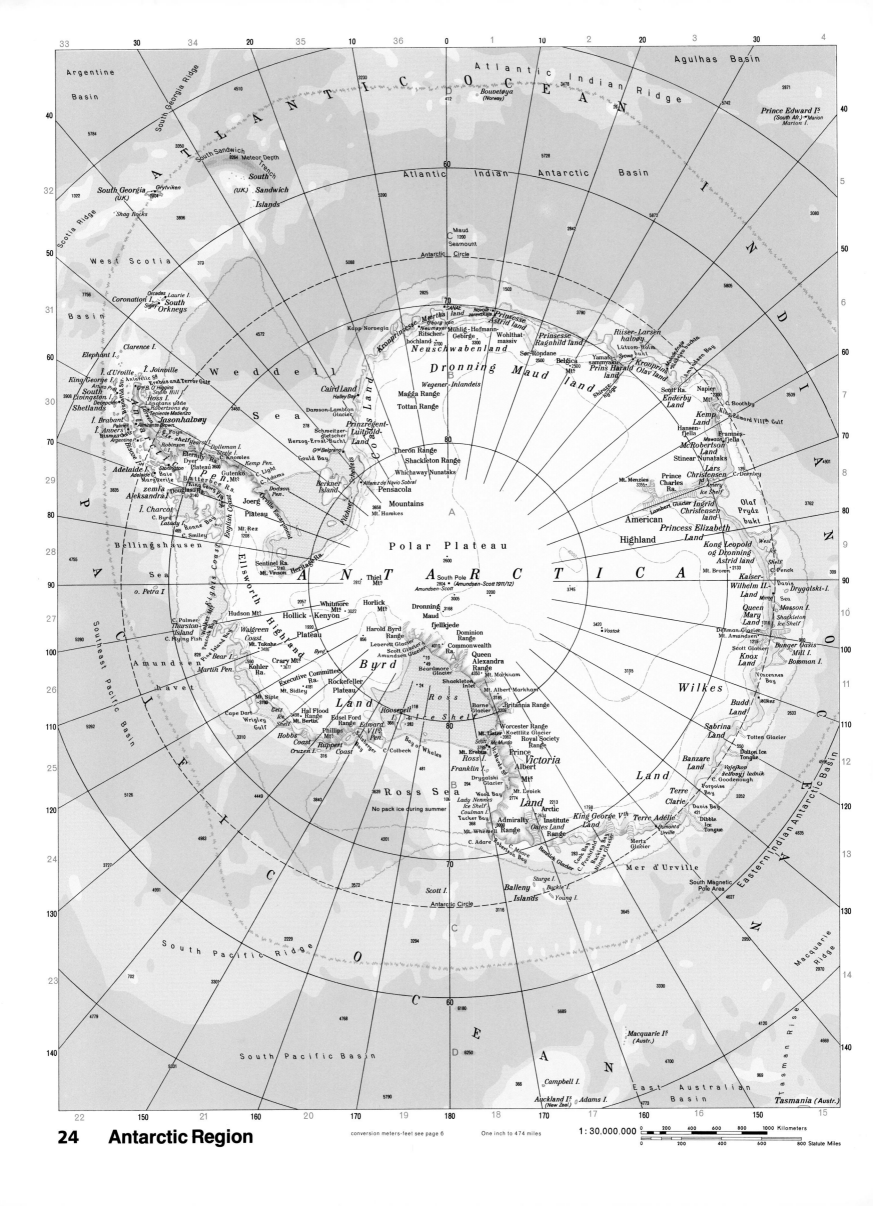

Agulhas Basin

Argentine
Basin

ATLANTIC OCEAN

Atlantic Indian Ridge

3230

4510

412

Bouvetøya
(Norway)

3478

5742

2871

South Georgia Ridge

60

Atlantic Indian Antarctic Basin

Prince Edward Is.
(South Afr.) Marion
Marion I.

40

5784

3350

8264 Meteor Depth
South Sandwich Trench

5728

5390

5872

3080

5

South
(UK.) Sandwich
Islands

A T L A N T I C

32

1322

South Georgia
(UK.)

Grytviken
2934

3806

Shag Rocks

Maud
1200
Seamount

5805

Antarctic Circle

50

Scotia Ridge

373

5088

1503

C

B

A

6

West Scotia

7756

Orcades Laurie I.
Signy I.

Coronation I. South
Orkneys

2825

70

SANAE

Novolazarevskaya
Norvegia

Prinsesse
Astrid land

3780

31

Basin

Clarence I.

Kapp Norvegia

Kronprinsesse Martha
Georg von
Neumayer

Mühlig-Hofmann
Gebirge

Wohlthat-
massiv

Prinsesse
Ragnhild land

Riiser-Larsen
halvøya

Lützow-Holm
bukt

Syowa

Amundsen Bay

60

Elephant I.

Î. d'Urville Î. Joinville
King George I.
South
Shetlands

Ritscher-
hochland

2700

3300

Sør-Rondane

2500

Belgica
Mts.
2500

Kronprins
Olav land

Yamato-
sammyaku
Prins Harald
land

Scott Ra. Napier
Mts.

C. Boothby

King Edward VIIth Gulf

3539

7

Livingston I.
Decepción I.
I. Brabant
Palmer
Î. Anvers
Bismarck

Caird Land

Halley Bay

Wegener-Inlandeis

Neuschwabenland

Dronning Maud land

Enderby
Land

Kemp
Land

Hansen-
fjella

Frammes-
fjella

3080

30

3908

Antarctic St.
Arturo Prat
G.B. O'Higgins
Langtans udde
Robertson ø
Teniente Matienzo

Magga Range

Tottan Range

Shinze
Nunge

McRobertson
Land

Scott Ra.

3539

Jasonhalvøy

3460

278

Prinzregent-
Luitpold-
Land

Schweitzer-
gletscher

Stinear Nunataks

Foyn
Robinson
Dolleman I.
Steele I.
Eternity Ra. Knowles

Schmeitzer-
gletscher
Herzog-Ernst-
Bucht

Theron Range

Lars
Christensen
Land

3762

Adelaide I.

Dyer
Plateau

C. Light
C. Adams

Gen. Belgrano

Shackleton Range

Whichaway Nunataks

Mt. Menzies
3355

Prince
Charles
Ra.

Amery
Ice Shelf

139

C. Darnley

4901

A

80

Battorbee Ra.

Gutenko
Mts.
3600

Berkner
Island

Pensacola

Lambert Glacier

Olaf
Prydz
bukt

80

Aleksandra I.
Î. Charcot

Douglass Ra.
3140

Joerg
Plateau

Orville Escarpment

3658
Mt. Harokes

Mountains

American

Ingrid
Christensen
land

Princess Elizabeth
Land

Kong Leopold
og Dronning
Astrid land

West
Ice
Shelf

3762

C. Byrd Latady I.
Mt. Rex
1208
C. Smiley

Ronne Bay

Bellingshausen
Sea

English Coast

Polar Plateau

Highland

Mt. Brown
2133

C. Penck

309

90

o. Petra I

Sentinel Ra.
5140
Mt. Vinson

Heritage Ra.

Thiel
Mts.
2812

South Pole
2804 (Amundsen-Scott 1911/12)
Amundsen-Scott
3005

2600

3200

3745

Vostok

Kaiser-
Wilhelm II.-
Land

Davis
Sea

Mirny

Drygalski-I.

90

4755

P A C I F I C

Whitmore
Mts.
3022

Horlick
Mts.

Dronning
Maud
fjellkjede

3668

Queen
Mary
Land

Masson I.
1316

Shackleton
Ice Shelf

27

Eights Coast

Hollick-Kenyon
Plateau

Harold Byrd
Range

Dominion
Range

3420

3135

Denman Glacier
1219

Mt. Amundsen

10

Hudson Mts.

1920

856

Leverett Glacier
Scott Glacier
Amundsen Glacier

4010
49

Commonwealth
Ra.

Scott Glacier
Mill I.

C. Palmer
Thurston
Island
C. Flying Fish

Walgreen
Coast

Mt. Takahe
3460

Bear I.
550

Crary Mts.
3677

Byrd

Beardmore
Glacier

Queen
Alexandra
Range
4350 Mt. Markham

Knox
Land

Bowman I.

100

5280

828

Kohler
Ra.

Byrd
Land

Shackleton
Inlet

Wilkes

Vincennes
Bay

2633

Amundsen
havet

Martin Pen.

Executive Committee
Ra.
Mt. Sidley
4181

Rockefeller
Plateau

24

Ross
Ice Shelf

Mt. Albert Markham

Barne
Glacier

Britannia Range
3209

3185

Budd
Land

Wilkes

11

5262

Cape Dart
Wrigley
Gulf

Getz
Ice
Shelf

Hal Flood
Range
Mt. Berlin
3498

Roosevelt
I.

118

Worcester Range
Mt. Lister
3662

Koettlitz Glacier
Royal Society
Range

Sabrina
Land

Totten Glacier

110

25

Hobbs
Coast

Phillips
Mts.

Edsel Ford
Range

Edward
VIIth
Pen.

366

283

Mt. Erebus
3795
Ross I.

McMurdo
Scott

Prince
Albert
Mts.

Banzare
Land

Dalton Ice
Tongue

4596

12

Ruppert
Coast

Cruzen I.
316

Saunders
B

Bay of Whales
C. Colbeck

481

Franklin I.

Victoria

Terre
Clarie

Vojejkov
ledinoj lednik
C. Goodenough

Porpoise
Bay

3352

5126

4449

3840

3639

No pack ice during summer

Drygalski Glacier
Wood Bay

294

Mt. Levick
2774

Land

2213

King George Vth
Land

Davis Bay

Dibble
Ice
Tongue

120

Ross Sea

106

Lady Newnes
Ice Shelf
Coulman I.

Arctic
Institute
421

1798

Terre Adélie

Mertz Glacier

24

4201

Tucker Bay
368

Admiralty
Range
3000
Mt. Whemell

Oates Land

Dumont
d'Urville

Mer d'Urville

4835

13

3727

4983

3572

Scott I.

C. Adare

Robertson Bay

Moore

Rennick Glacier

C. Prudhomme
C. Frautlay Cape
Buckley Bay
Ninnis Glacier

South Magnetic
Pole Area

4627

70

4991

Balleny
Islands

Sturge I.
Buckle I.
Young I.

3645

2950

N

130

Antarctic Circle

3116

South Pacific Ridge

2229

3294

5689

6180

3330

Macquarie
Ridge

2970

14

702

5790

Campbell I.

East Australian
Basin

Macquarie Is.
(Austr.)

4120

140

4779

O C E A N

South Pacific Basin

6250

D

Auckland Is.
(New Zeal.) Adams I.

366

4773

4669

Tasman Rise

969

Tasmania (Austr.)

24   Antarctic Region

conversion meters-feet see page 6   One inch to 474 miles   1 : 30,000,000

0   200   400   600   800   1000 Kilometers

0   200   400   600   800 Statute Miles

EUROPE

1:15,000,000

0 100 200 300 400 500 Kilometers

0 100 200 300 400 Statute Miles

One inch to 237 miles   conversion meters-feet see page 6

Komi-Permyak Aut. Area
Udmurt A.R.
Mari A.R.
Chuvash A.R.

5 Mordovian A.R.
6 Tatar A.R.
7 Bashkir A.R.
8 Kalmyk A.R.

9 Adygei Aut. Reg.
10 Karachayevo-Cherkess Aut. Reg.
11 Kabardino-Balkar A.R.
12 North Ossetian A.R

13 South Ossetian Aut. Reg.
14 Checheno-Ingush A.R.
15 Dagestan A.R.
16 Abkhaz A.R.

17 Adjarian A.R.
18 Nakhichevan -part of Azerbaijan
19 Nagorno-Karabagh Aut. Reg.

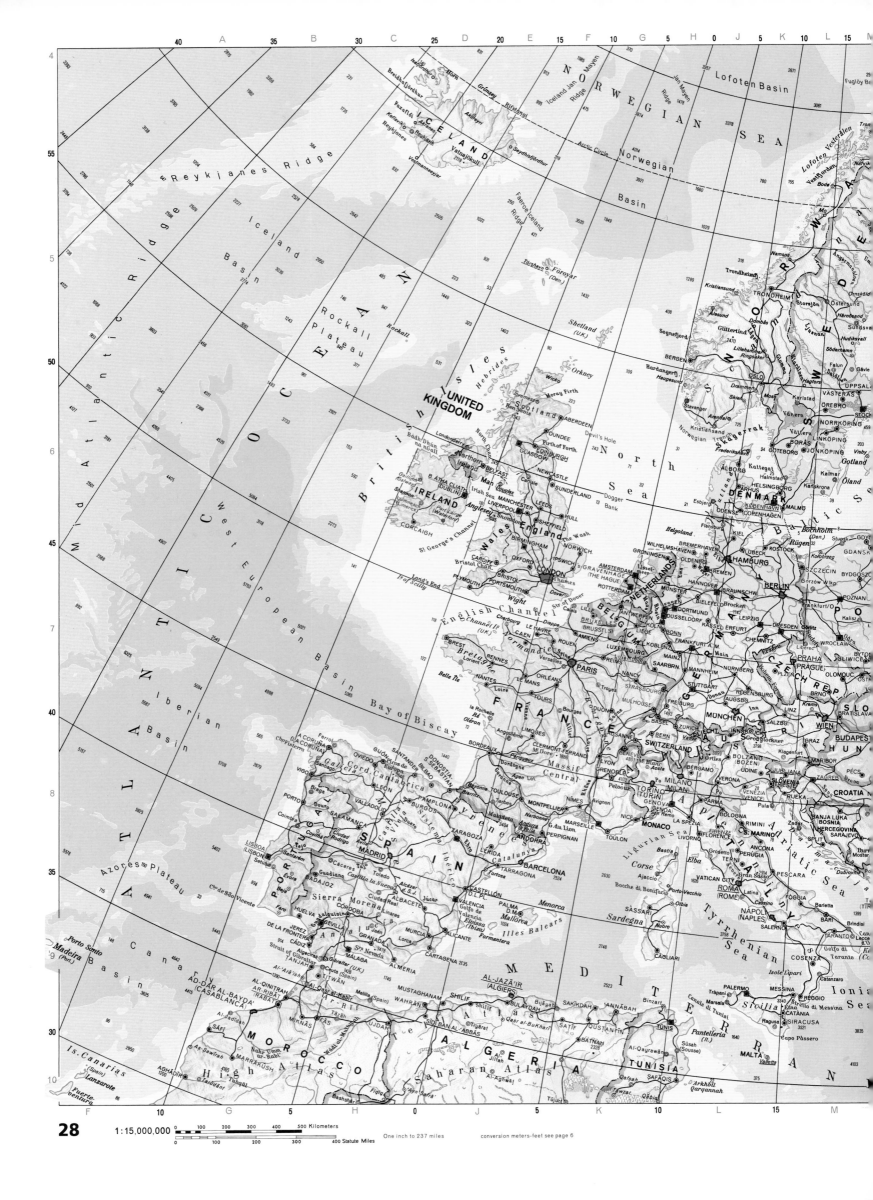

1:15,000,000

0 100 200 300 400 500 Kilometers

0 100 200 300 400 Statute Miles

One inch to 237 miles   conversion meters-feet see page 6

1 Part of Russia   2 Nakhichevan-part of Azerbaijan

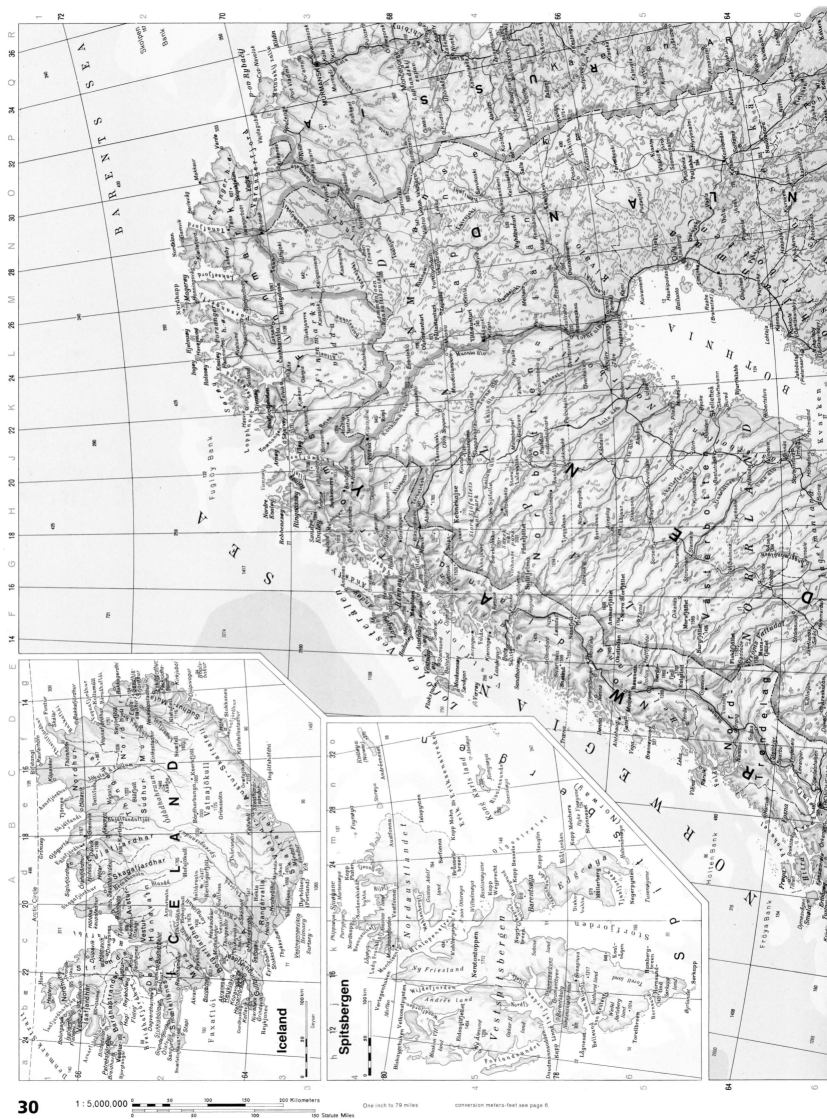

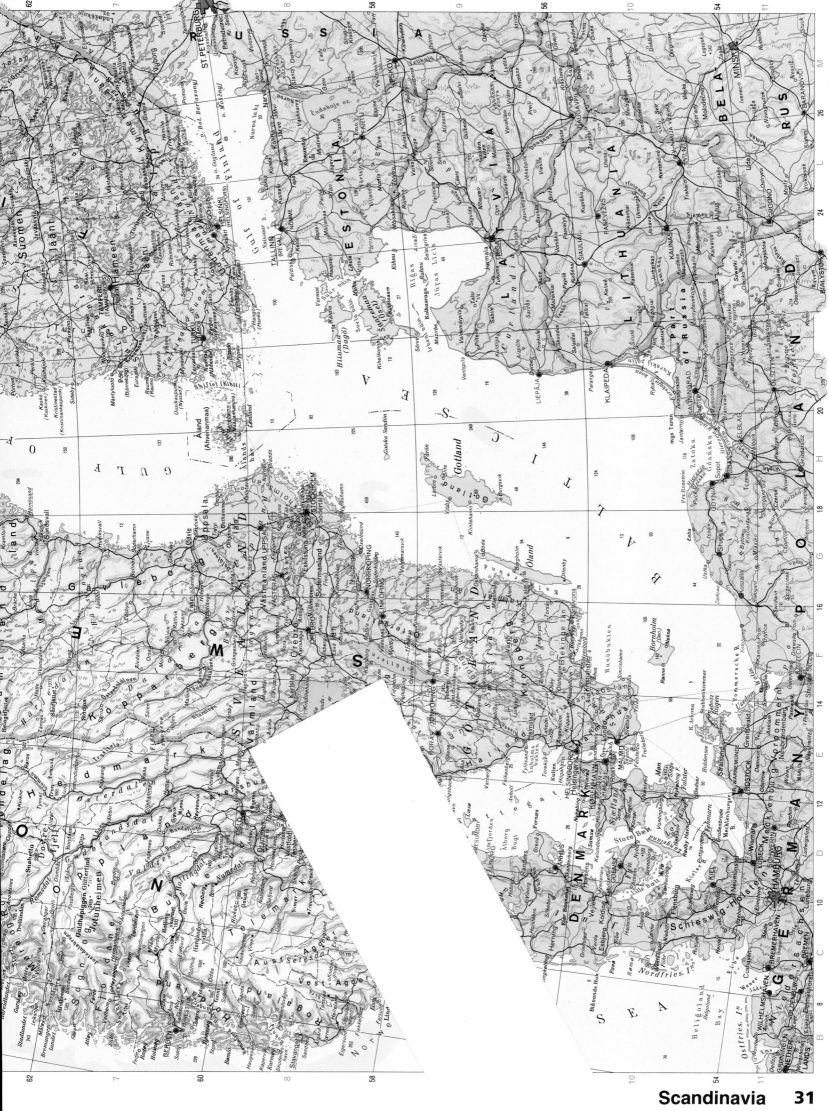

conversion meters-feet see page 6

One inch to 79 miles

1 : 5,000,000

0   50   100   150   200 Kilometers

0   50   100

150 Statute Miles

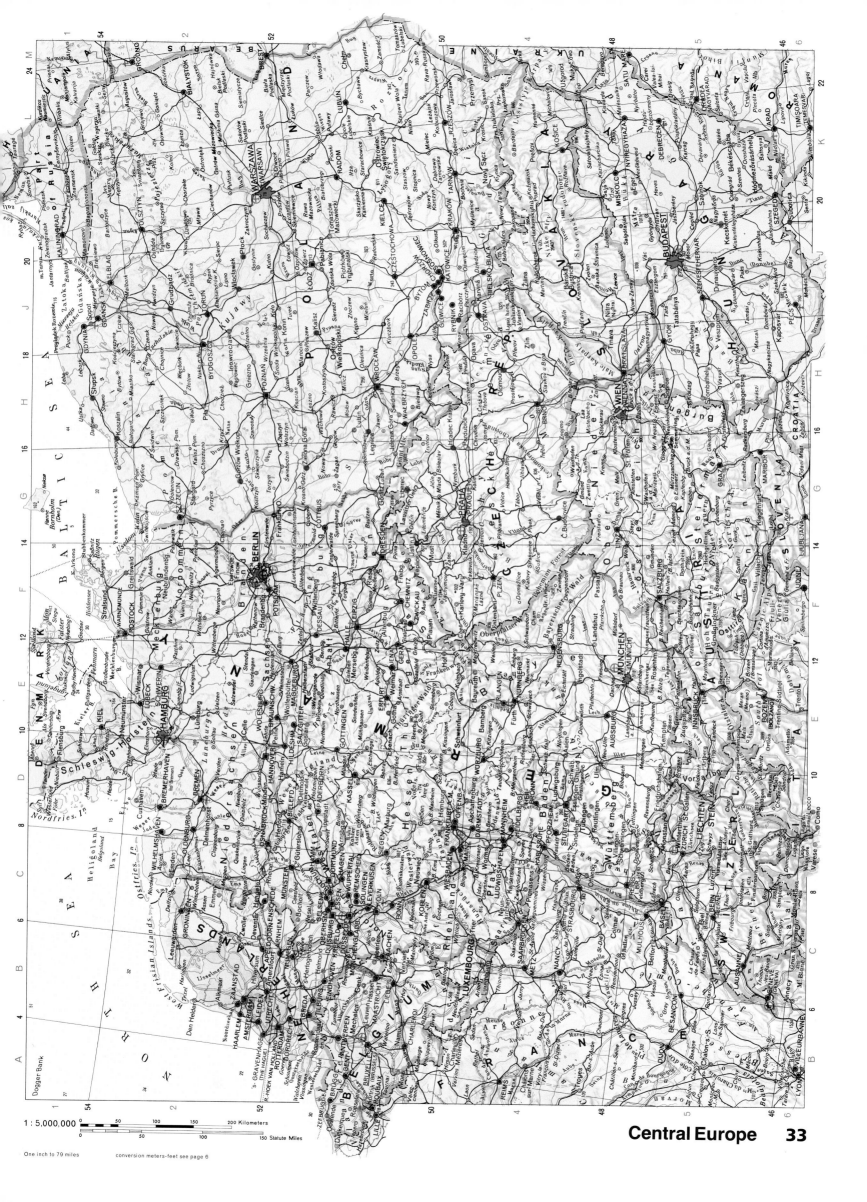

1 : 5,000,000

50   100   150   200 Kilometers

50   100   150 Statute Miles

One inch to 79 miles   conversion meters-feet see page 6

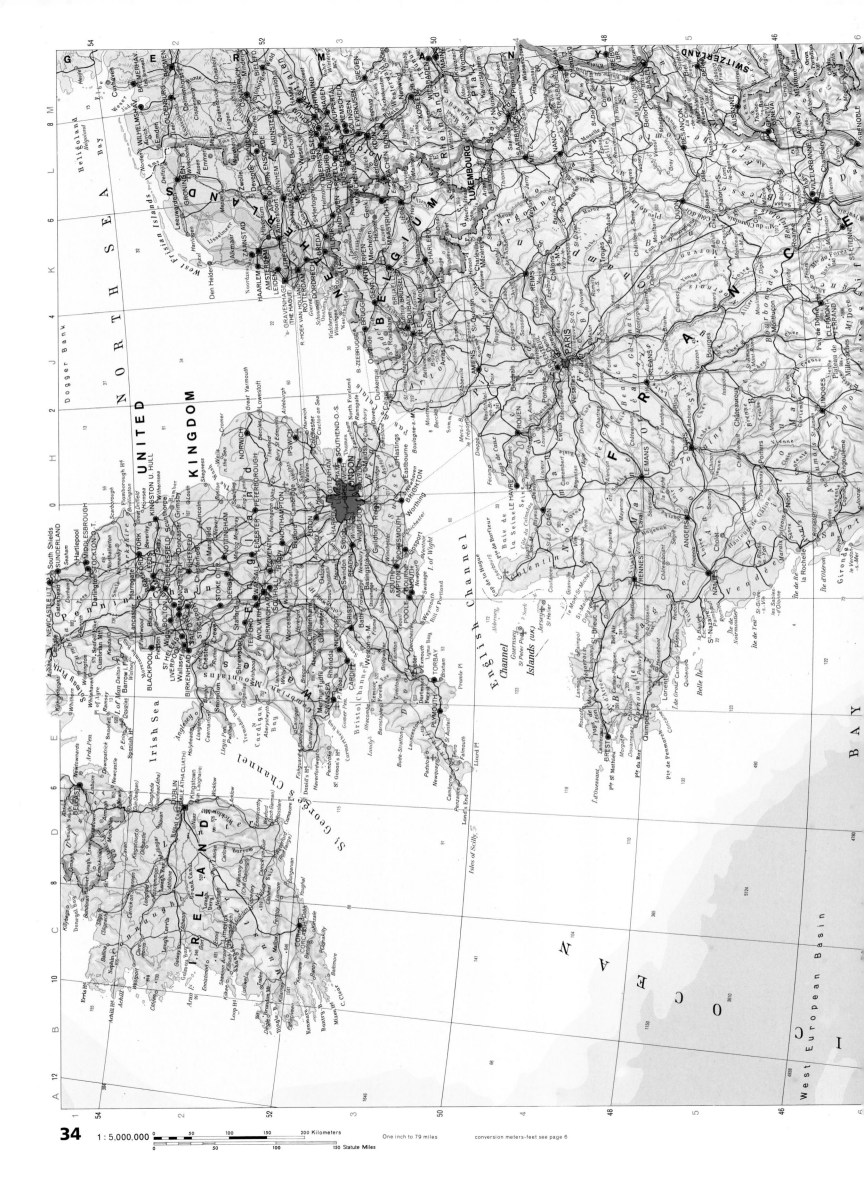

34 1:5 000 000

One inch to 79 miles   conversion meters-feet see page 6

200 Kilometers

150 Statute Miles

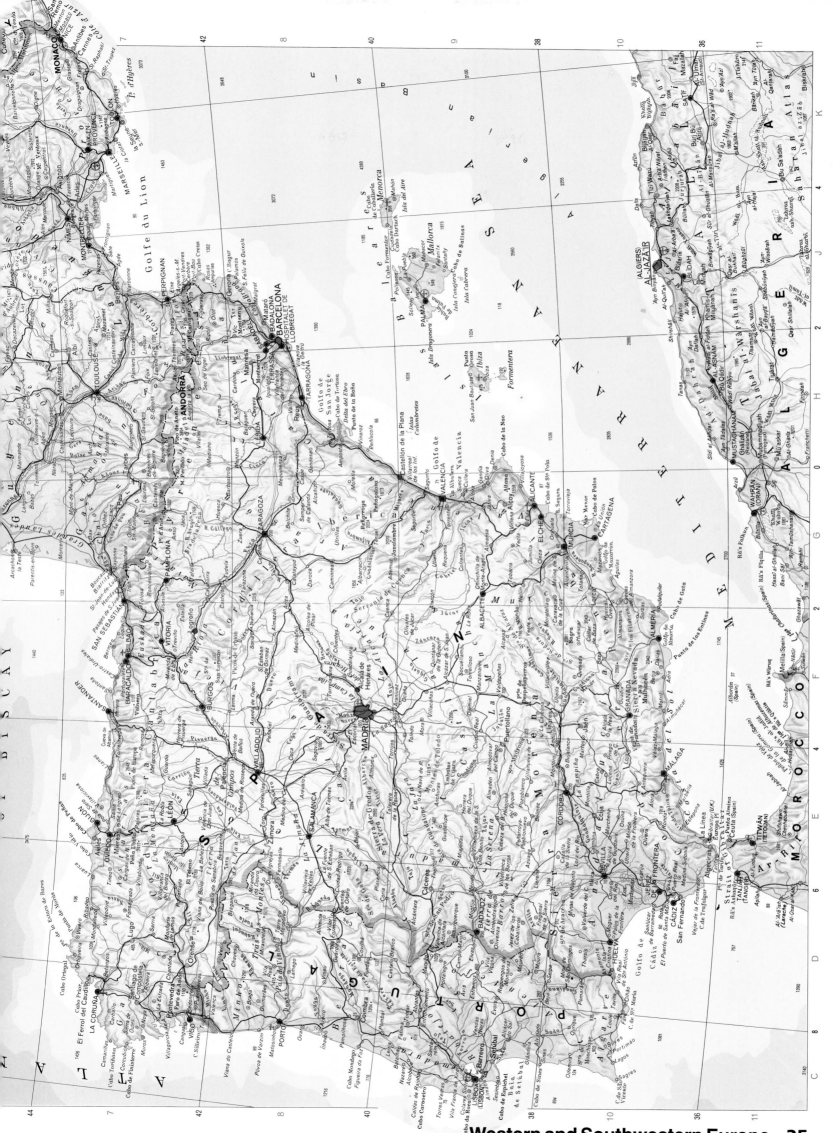

1 : 5,000,000

50   100   150   200 Kilometers

0   50   100   150 Statute Miles

One inch to 79 miles   conversion meters-feet see page 6

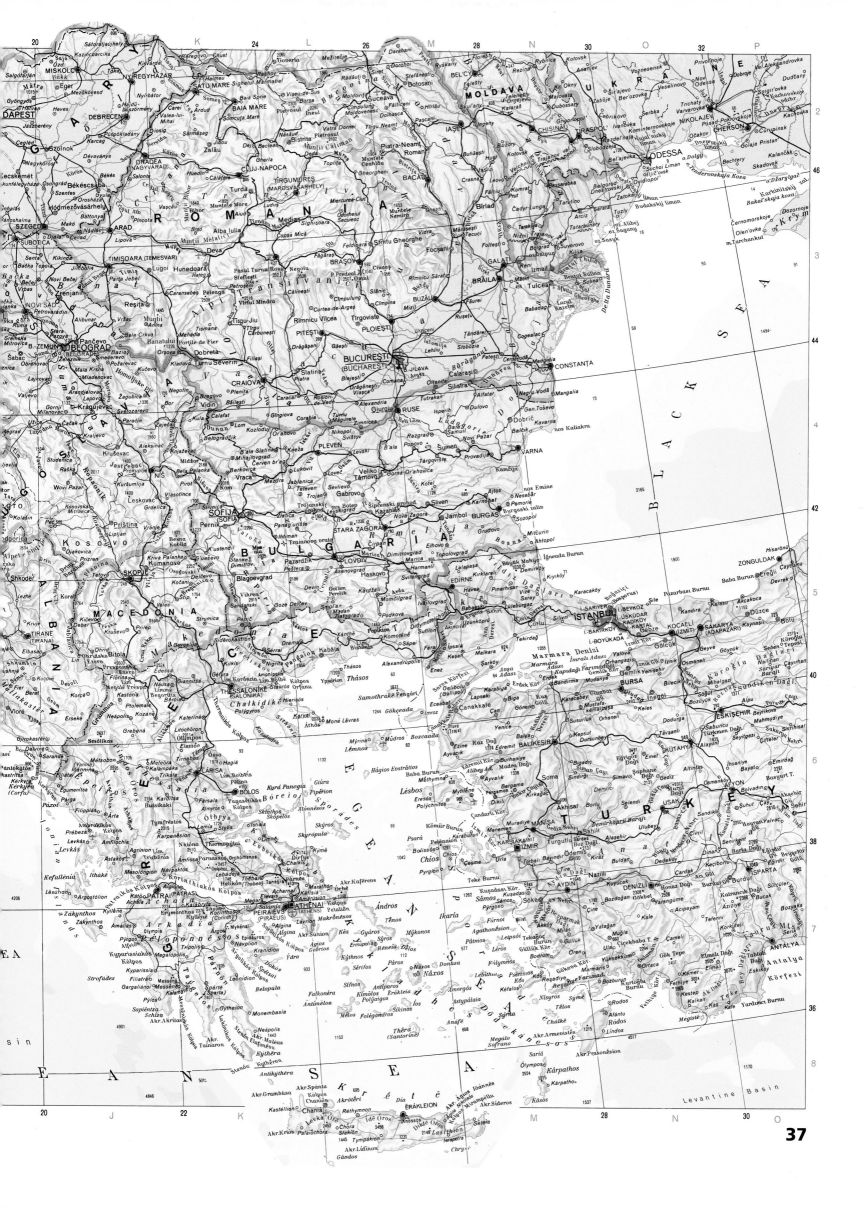

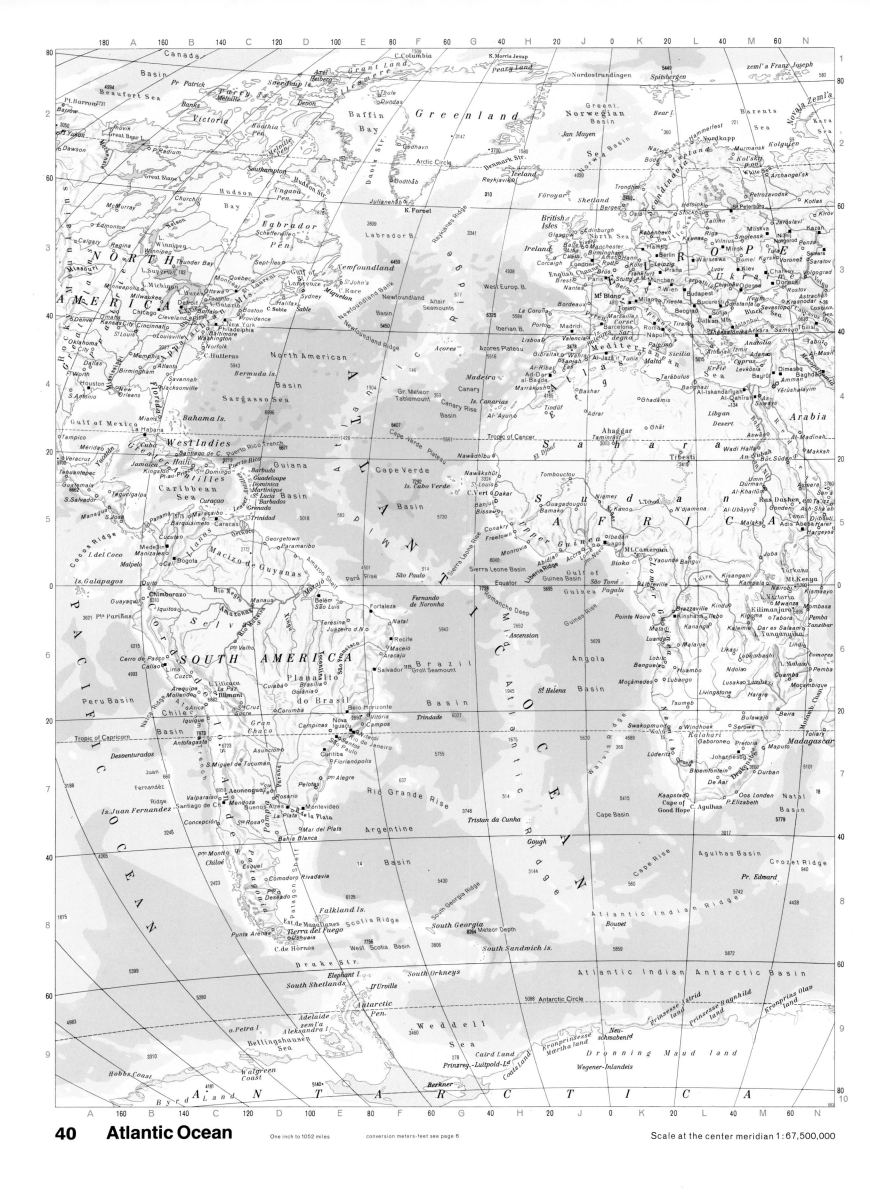

One inch to 1052 miles   conversion meters-feet see page 6   Scale at the center meridian 1:67,500,000

ASIA

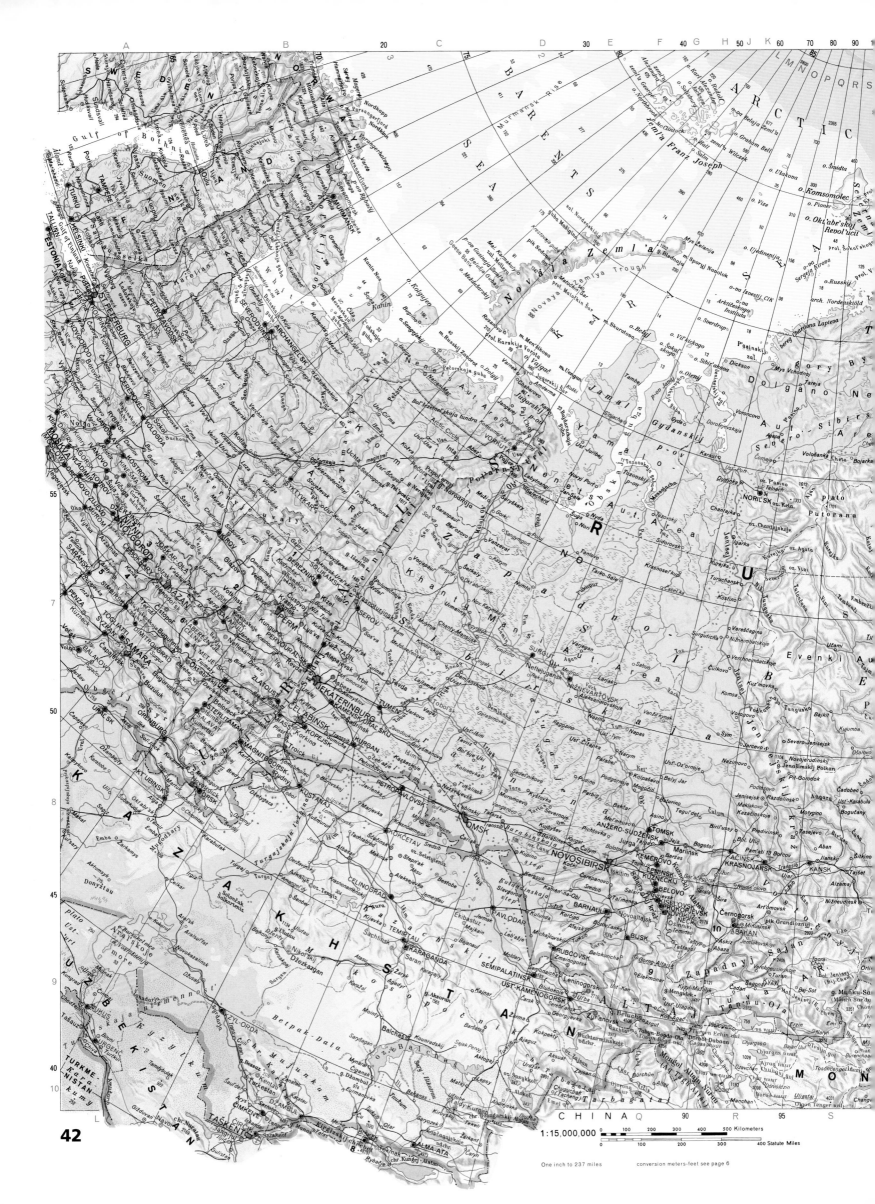

1:15,000,000

One inch to 237 miles   conversion meters-feet see page 6

Administrative units in the former Soviet Union :   1 Komi- Permyak Aut. Area   4 Chuvash A.R.   7 Bashkir A.R.   10 Khakass Aut. Reg.   13 Jewish Aut. Reg.
2 Udmurt A.R.   5 Mordovian A.R.   8 Kirgizia   11 Ust- Ordynsky- Buryat Aut. Area
3 Mari A.R.   6 Tatar A.R.   9 Gorno- Altai Aut. Reg.   12 Aginsky-Buryat Aut. Area

1 : 5,000,000

50   100   150   200 Kilometers

0   50   100   150 Statute Miles

One inch to 79 miles   conversion meters-feet see page 6

a Nakhichevan-part of Azerbaijan

Administrative units in Lebanon 1 Lubnān ash-Shimālī 2 Jabal Lubnān
3 Lubnān al-Janūbī 4 Al-Biqā'

1:15,000,000

0   100   200   300   400   500 Kilometers

0   100   200   300   400 Statute Miles   One inch to 237 miles

conversion meters-feet see page 6

Administrative units in China:

A Linxia Huizu Zizhizhou
B Dêqên Zangzu Zizhizhou
C Nujiang Lisuzu Zizhizhou

D Dehong Daizu Zizhizhou
E Xishuangbanna Daizu Zizhizhou
F Bortala Monggol Zizhizhou

Administrative units in Mongolia:

1 Bajan Ölgij	4 Dzavchan	7 Archangaj	10 Övörchangaj	13 Dundgov
2 Uvs	5 Gov'altaj	8 Bajan Chongor	11 Selenge	14 Ömnogov'
3 Chovd	6 Chövsgöl	9 Bulgan	12 Tov	15 Chentij

16 Dornogov
17 Suchbaatar
18 Dornod

1 : 5,000,000

| 0 | 50 | 100 | 150 | 200 Kilometers |

One inch to 79 miles   conversion meters-feet see page 6

| 0 | 50 | 100 |
150 Statute Miles

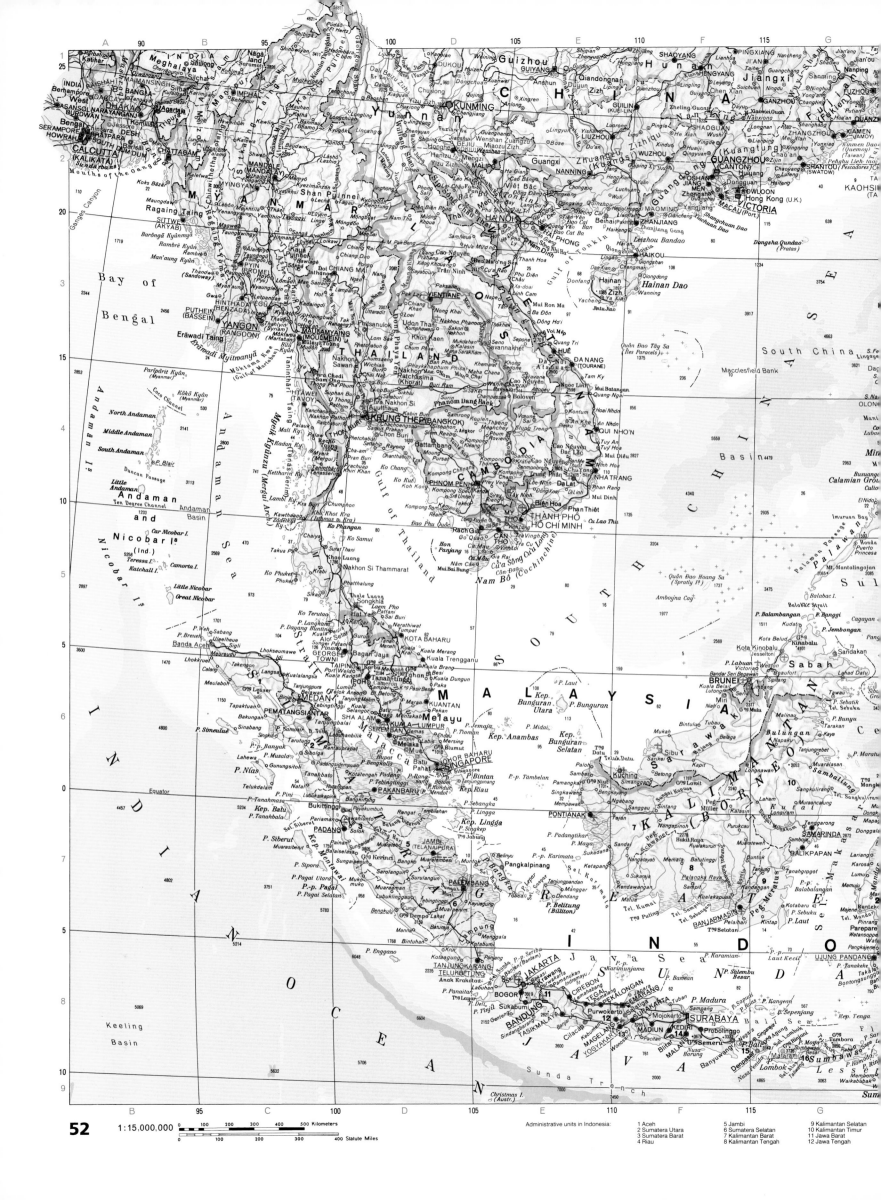

1:15,000,000

100 200 300 400 500 Kilometers

100   200   300   400 Statute Miles

Administrative units in Indonesia:

1 Aceh	5 Jambi	9 Kalimantan Selatan
2 Sumatera Utara	6 Sumatera Selatan	10 Kalimantan Timur
3 Sumatera Barat	7 Kalimantan Barat	11 Jawa Barat
4 Riau	8 Kalimantan Tengah	12 Jawa Tengah

East China Sea / **Pacific Ocean**

TAIWAN (Formosa)

Okinawa, Nansei-shotō (Ryūkyū), NAHA

Tropic of Cancer

LUZÓN

PHILIPPINES

MANILA, QUEZON CITY

Philippine Basin

Philippine Trench

Cape Johnson Depth

MINDANAO

DAVAO

Moro Gulf

Sulu Archipelago

Celebes Sea

MANADO

Halmahera

Molucca Sea

Ceram Sea

Banda Sea

South Banda Sea

Banda Basin

Timor Sea

Timor Trough

Arafura Sea

INDONESIA

Fiji Islands / PACIFIC OCEAN

Vanua Levu

Viti Levu, Suva

TONGA

Koro Sea

Lau Group (Eastern Group)

Tonga Trench

Fiji–Samoa

SAMOA

Upolu, Apia

Î? Horn (Fr.), Futuna, Alofi

Î? Wallis (Fr.)

Hawaii

PACIFIC OCEAN

Tropic of Cancer

Hawaiian Islands (U.S.A.)

Kauai, Oahu, HONOLULU, Pearl Harbor

Molokai, Lanai, Maui, Kahoolawe

Mauna Kea, Mauna Loa, Hawaii, Hilo

Ka Lae

Solomon Islands

PACIFIC OCEAN

Bismarck Sea

Bismarck Archipelago

New Hanover, New Ireland, Kavieng

New Britain, Rabaul

Gazelle Pen.

PAPUA NEW GUINEA

Bougainville, Kieta

Buka I.

Choiseul

Santa Isabel

New Georgia Group

SOLOMON IS.

Guadalcanal, Honiara

Malaita

San Cristóbal

Santa Cruz I?

Solomon Sea

Solomon Basin

New Guinea

Trobriand I? (Kiriwina I?)

Woodlark I.

d'Entrecasteaux I?

Owen Stanley Ra.

Milne Bay

Louisiade Archipelago

Rossel I.

Yap I?

Ngulu

Babelthuap, Koror

BELAU

Palau I?

Caroline Islands

MICRONESIA

West Caroline Basin

East Caroline Basin

Equator

New Guinea Ridge

Admiralty I?, Manus

Saint Matthias Group

New Hanover

Wuvulu

Ninigo Group

Hermit I?

BISMARCK

PAPUA NEW GUINEA

Irian Jaya

(Vogelkop)

Sorong, Manokwari

P. Biak, P. Yapen

Geelvink Bay

Jayapura (Hollandia), Vanimo

Wewak, Madang

Mount Hagen, Mt. Wilhelm

Maoke, Peg. Jayawijaya

Lae, Huon Gulf, Salamaua

Gulf of Papua

PORT MORESBY

Owen Stanley Ra.

Torres Strait, Cape York

AUSTRALIA

Coral Sea

13 Yogyakarta
14 Jawa Timur
15 Bali
16 Nusa Tenggara Barat
17 Nusa Tenggara Timur
18 Sulawesi Utara
19 Sulawesi Tengah
20 Sulawesi Tenggara
21 Sulawesi Selatan
22 Maluku
23 Timor Timur

conversion meters-feet see page 6   One inch to 237 miles

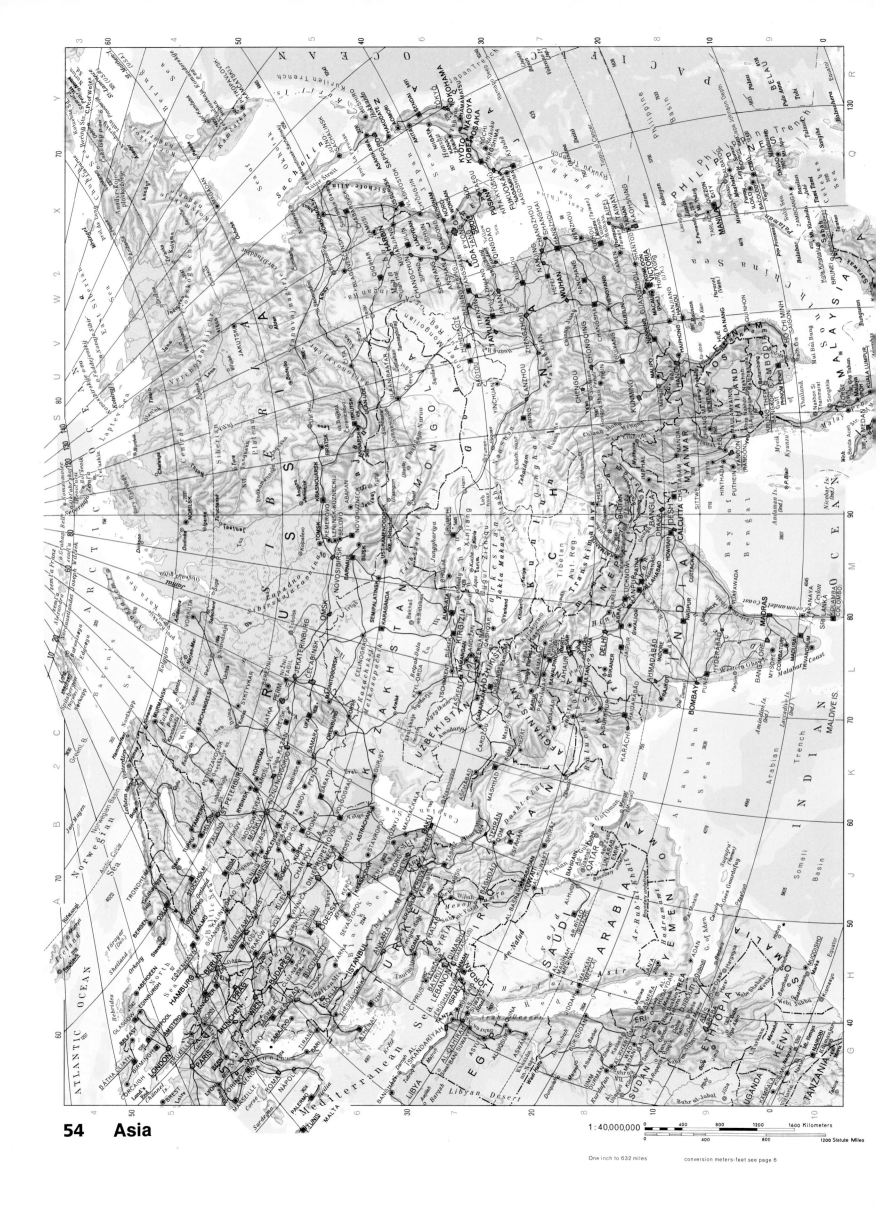

54   Asia

1 : 40,000,000

One inch to 632 miles   conversion meters-feet see page 6

AUSTRALIA

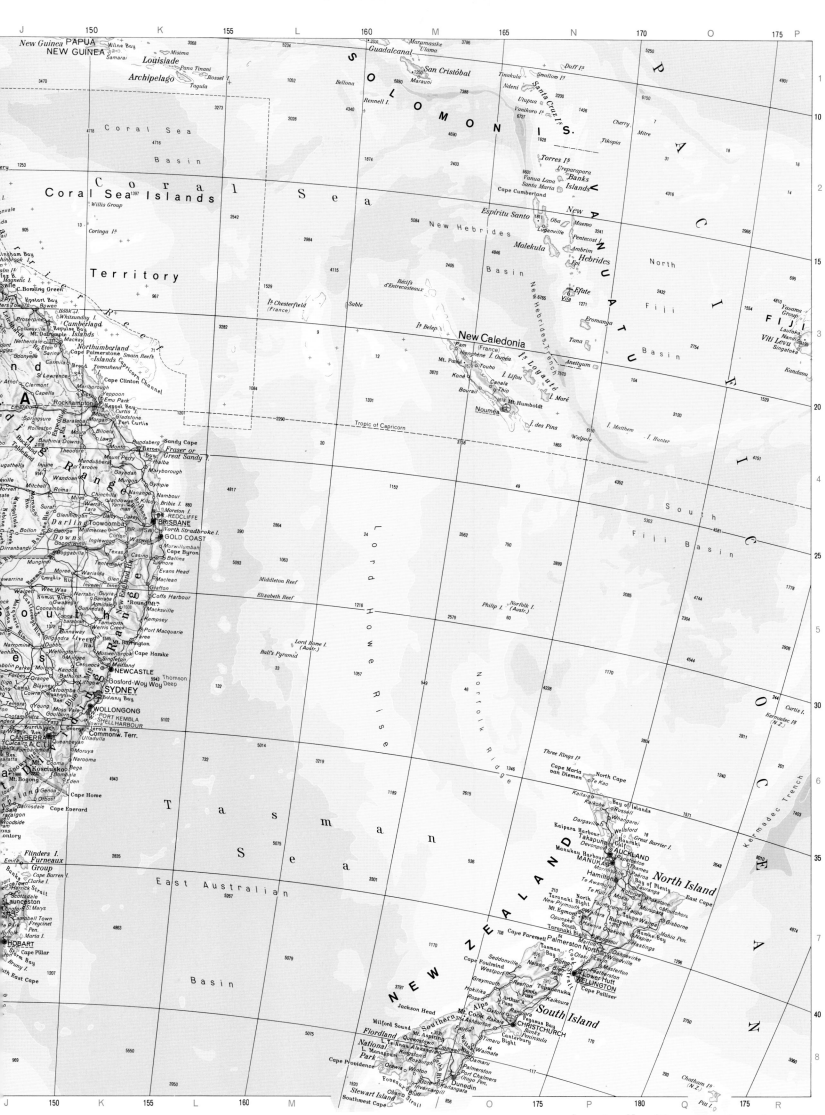

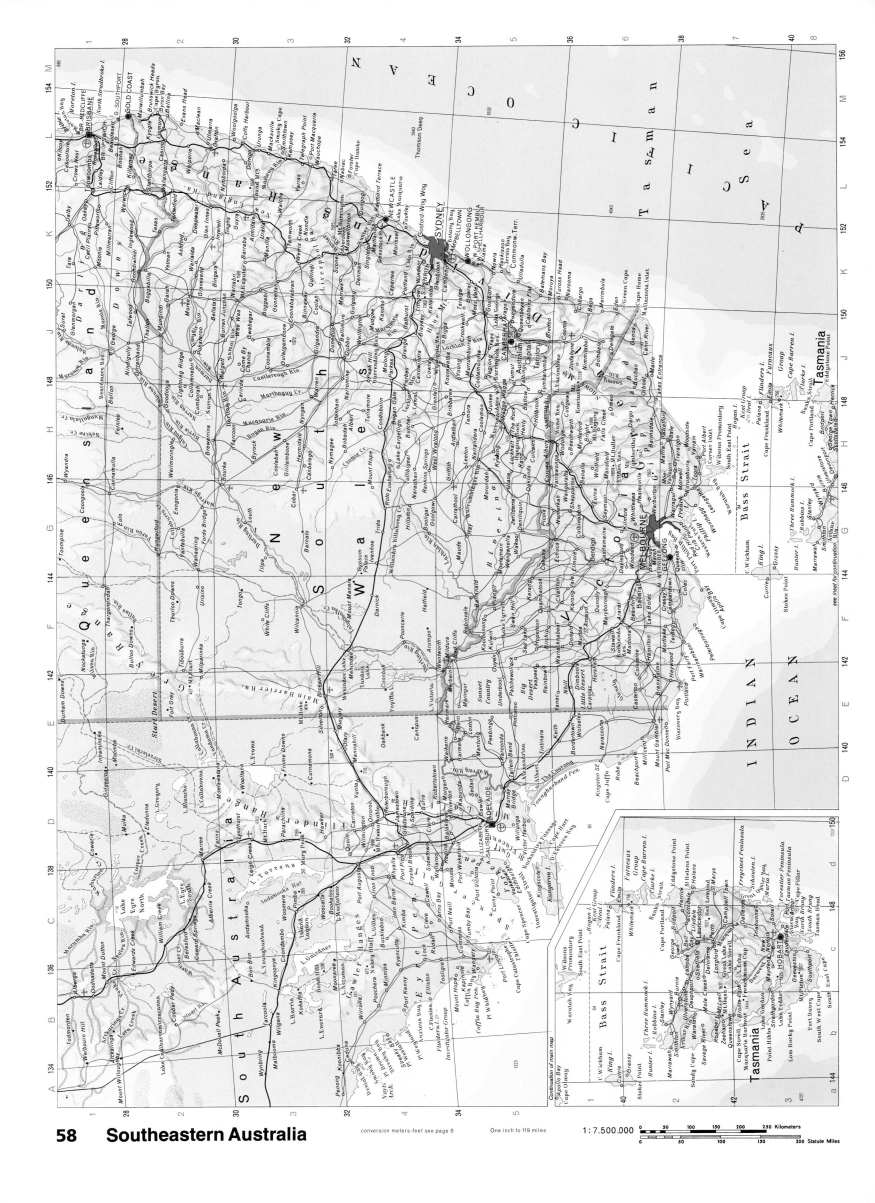

conversion meters-feet see page 6

One inch to 119 miles

1 : 7,500,000

50   100   150   200   250 Kilometers

50   100   150   200 Statute Miles

AFRICA

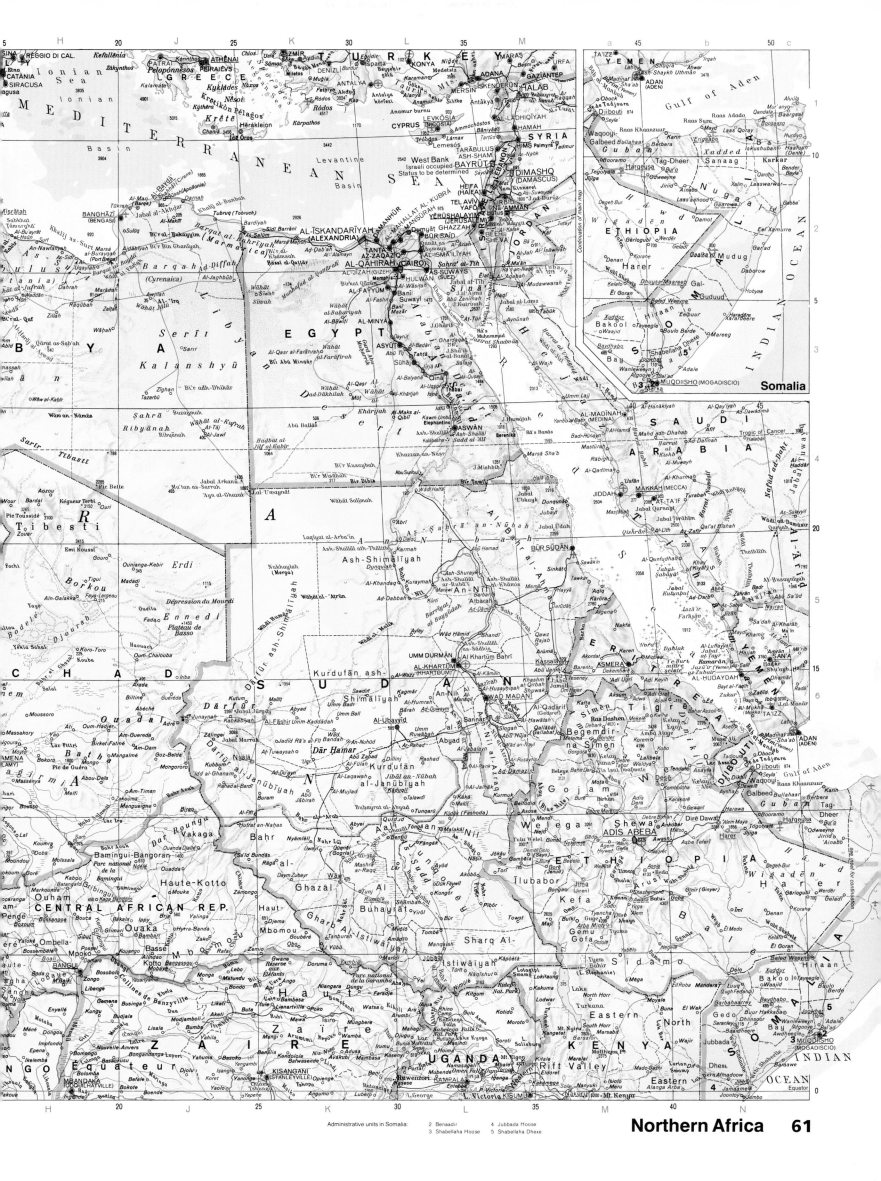

Administrative units in Somalia: 2 Benaadir   4 Jubbada Hoose
                                           3 Shabellaha Hoose   5 Shabellaha Dhexe

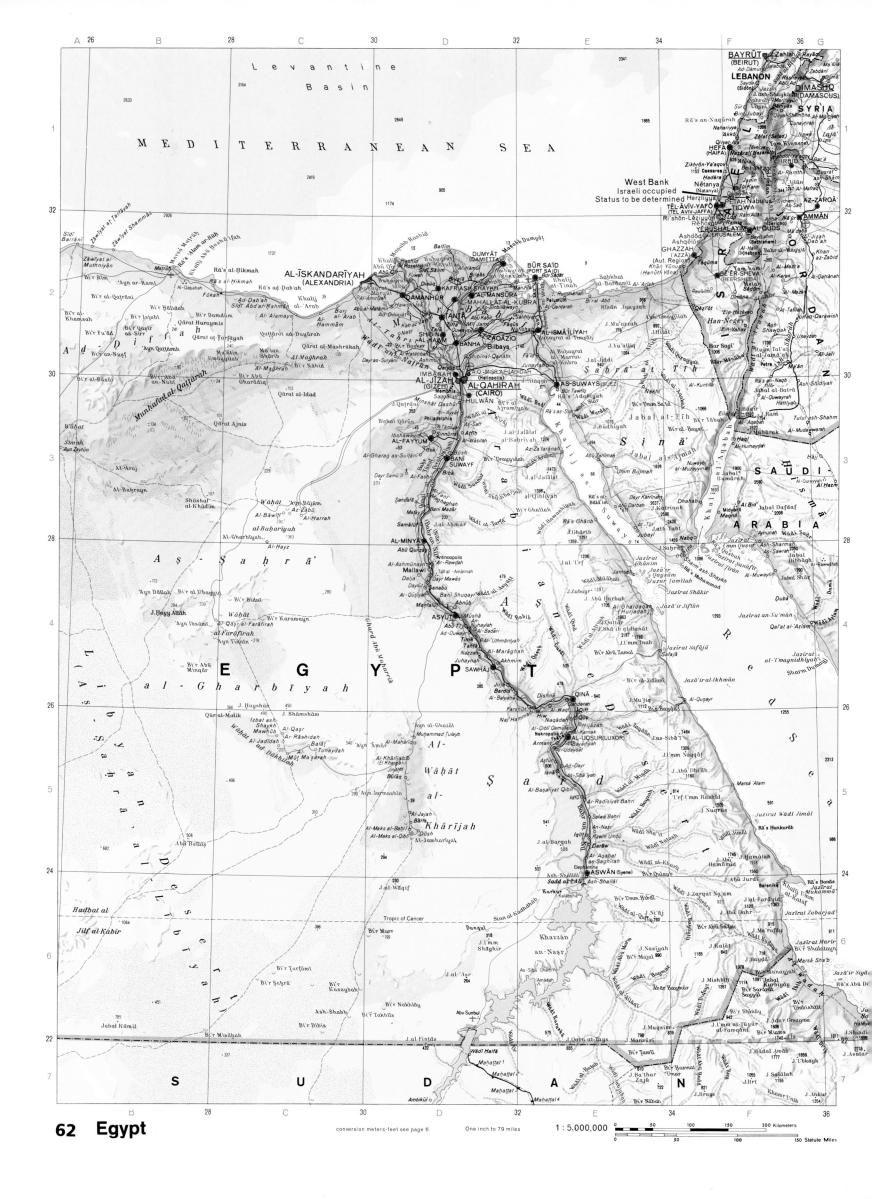

conversion meters-feet see page 6

One inch to 79 miles

1 : 5,000,000

50   100   150   200 Kilometers

50   100   150 Statute Miles

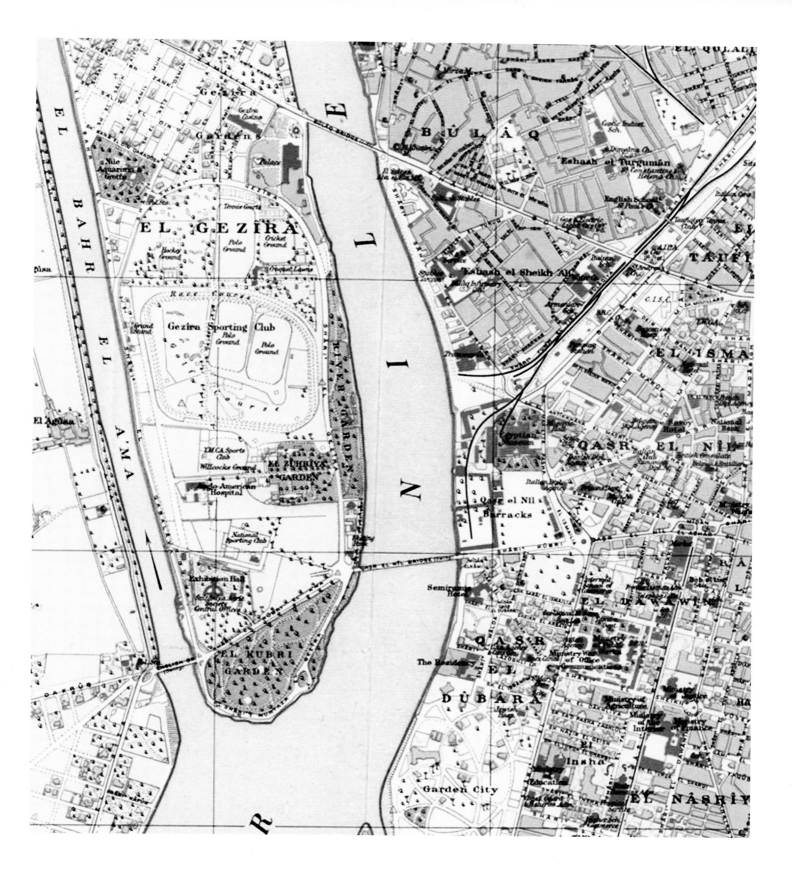

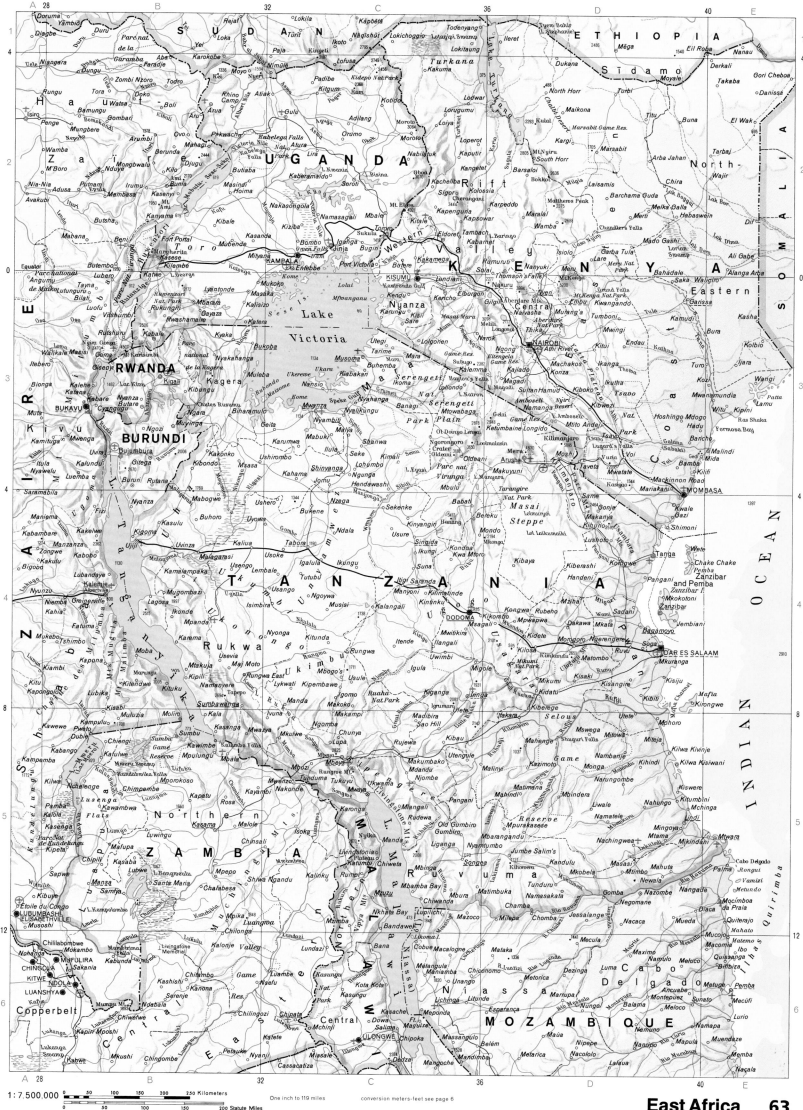

East Africa 63

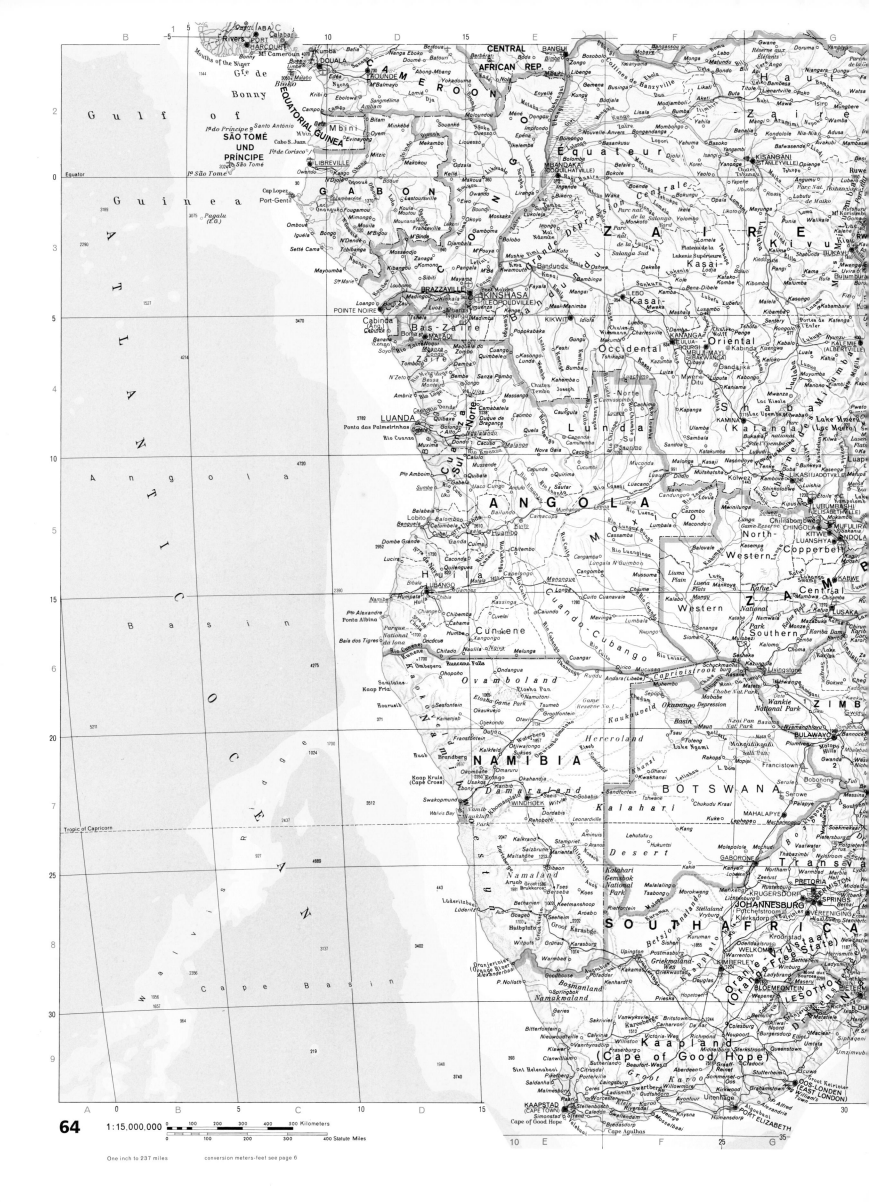

1:15,000,000

100 200 300 400 500 Kilometers

100 200 300 400 Statute Miles

One inch to 237 miles   conversion meters-feet see page 6

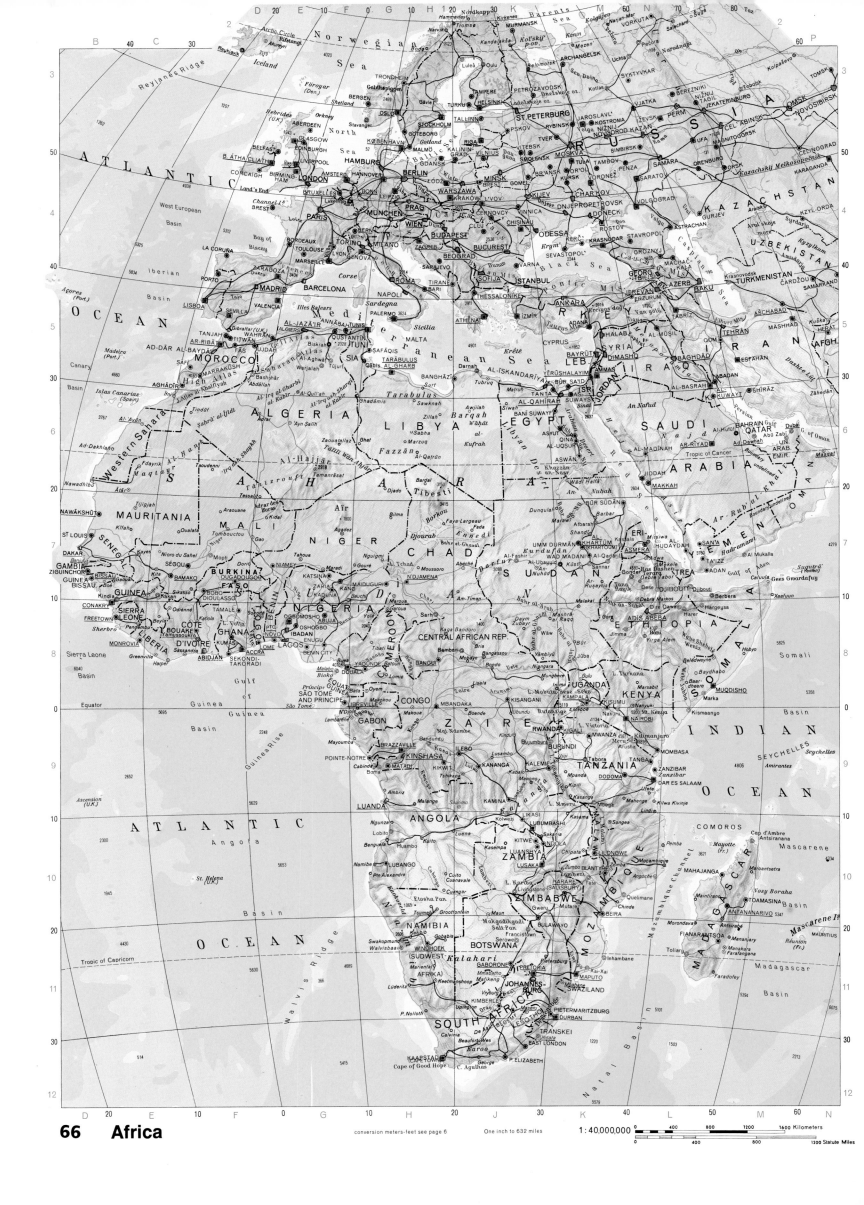

66   Africa

conversion meters-feet see page 6

One inch to 632 miles

1:40,000,000

AMERICA

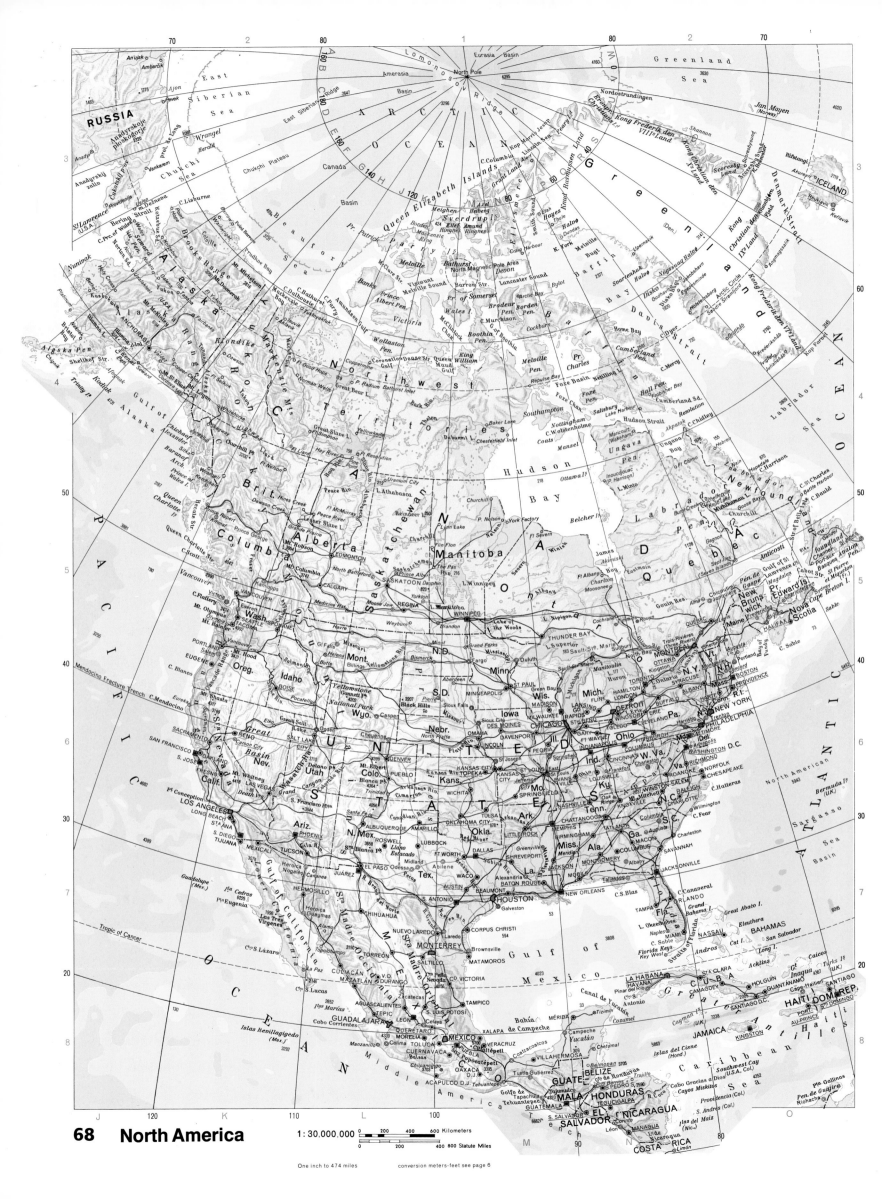

1 : 30,000,000

0 200 400 600 Kilometers
0 200 400 800 Statute Miles

One inch to 474 miles   conversion meters-feet see page 6

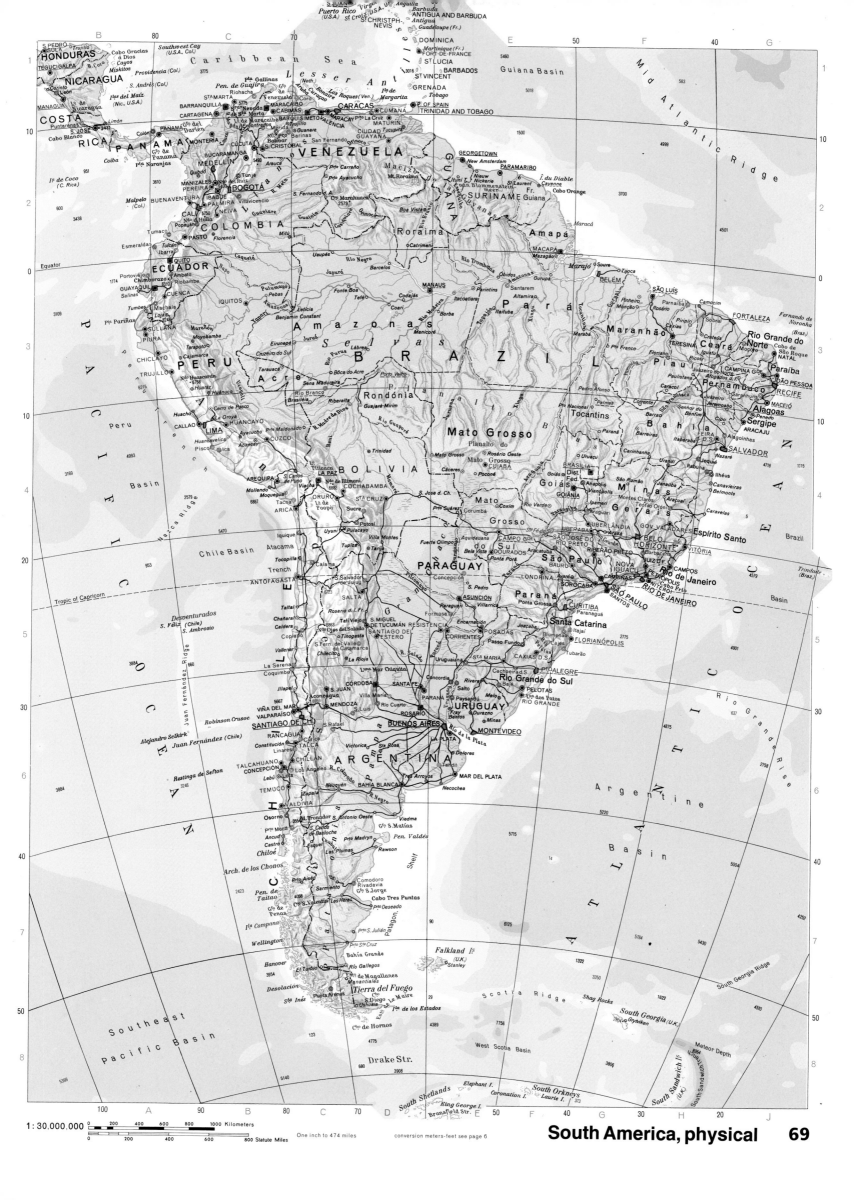

South America, physical 69

Northern North America 71

Panama Canal
1:900,000

72   1:15,000,000

Southern North America 73

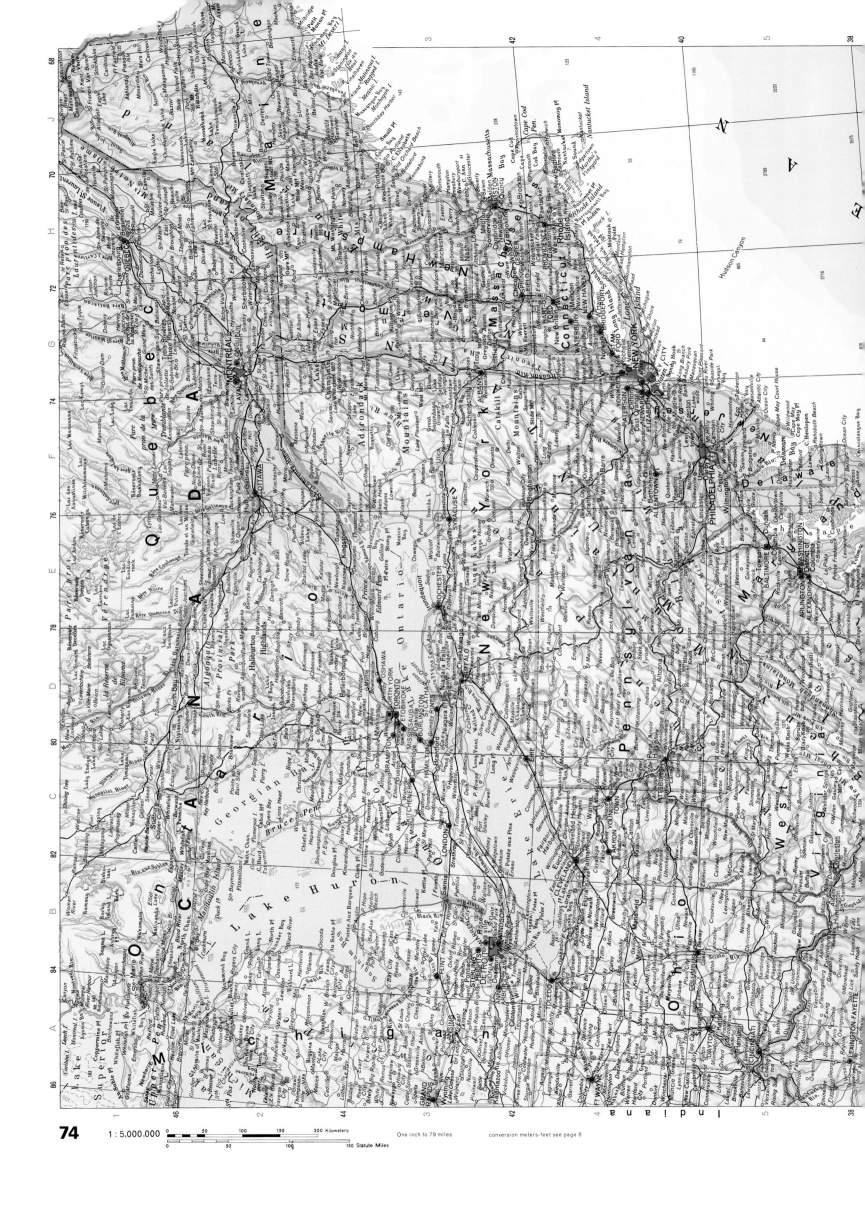

1 : 5,000,000

50   100   150   200 Kilometers

50   100   150 Statute Miles

One inch to 79 miles   conversion meters-feet see page 6

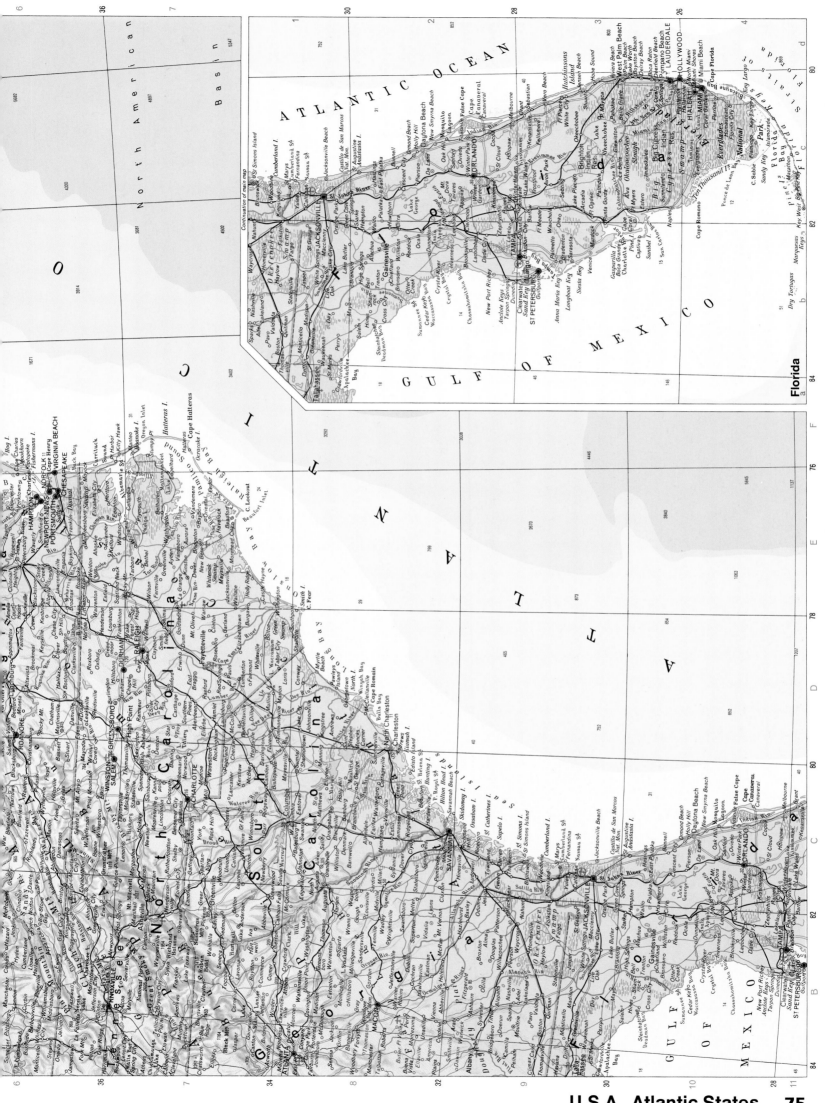

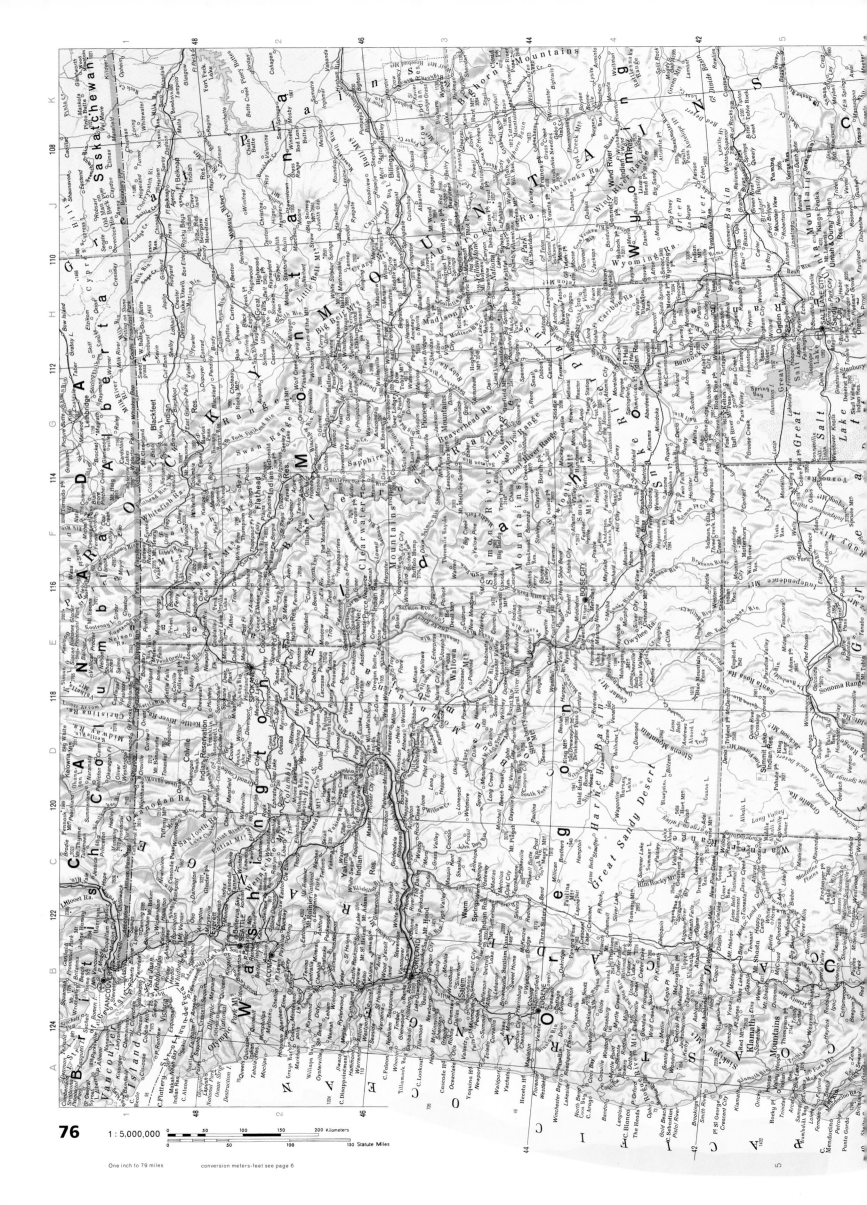

1 : 5,000,000

50   100   150   200 Kilometers

50   100   150 Statute Miles

One inch to 79 miles   conversion meters-feet see page 6

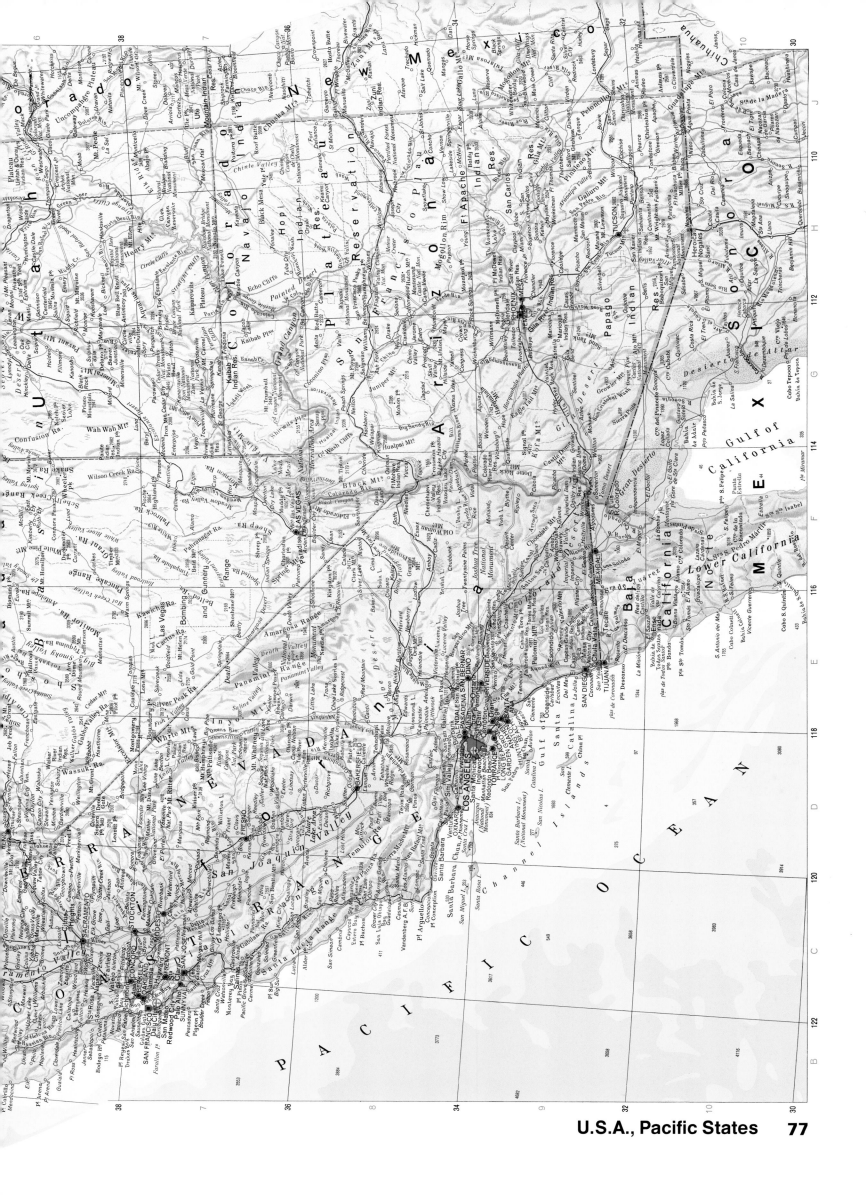

Northern South America   79

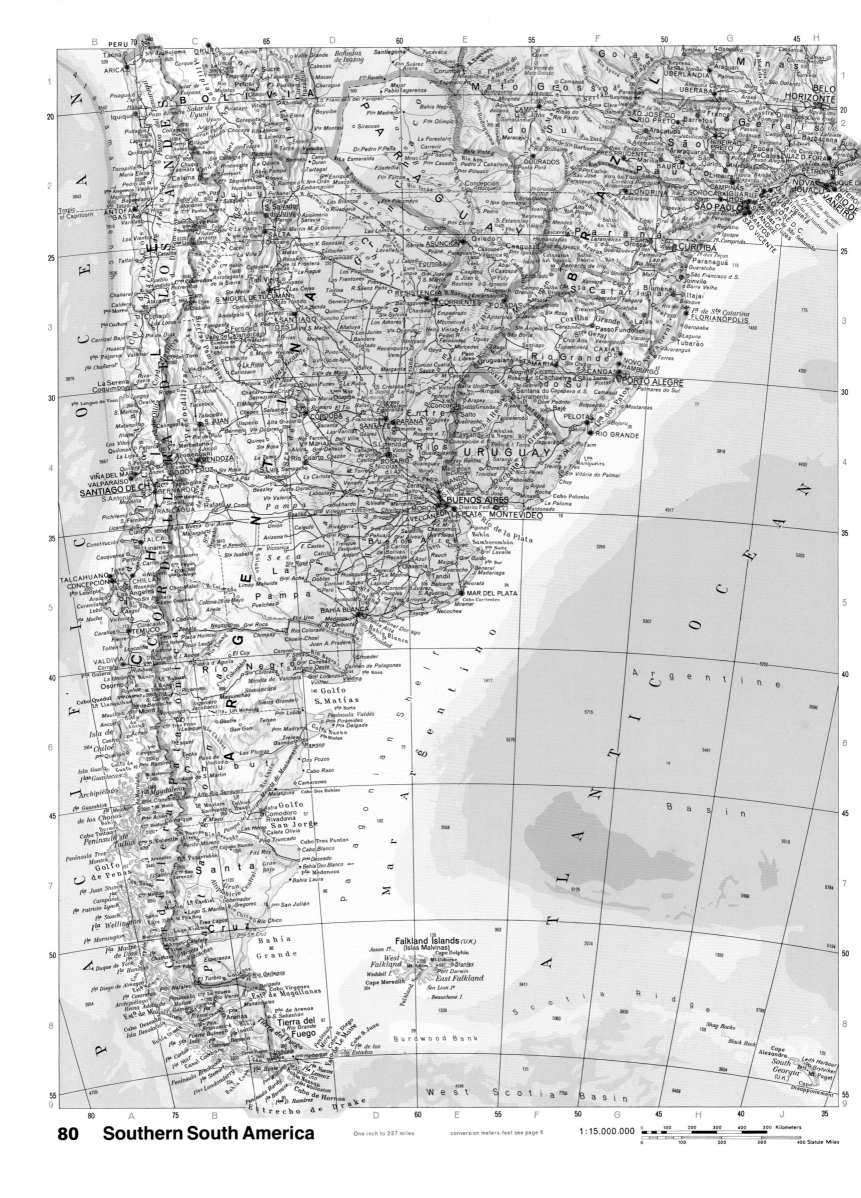

One inch to 237 miles   conversion meters-feet see page 6   1:15,000,000

THE EARTH

Its Continents and Countries

The Earth
NATURAL ENVIRONMENT AND BIOSPHERE

Unique in every respect, our planet earth is the only planet in our solar system with an atmosphere containing water. Thus, it alone provides a suitable environment for organic life.

The continents and the surrounding oceans give our planet earth its unmistakable face. The water masses cover around 71 per cent of the total surface area – with oceans taking up 60 per cent of the northern hemisphere and 81 percent of the southern hemisphere. The Pacific alone is larger than all the land masses on earth. Although the individual oceans constitute a single continuous body of water, they vary considerably in terms of salt content, tem-perature and ocean currents, as well as in the topography of their ocean floors. This submarine land-scape consists of vast seabed plains at a depth of approx. 5,000 meters (16,400 ft.), includes deep-sea trenches ringing the Pacific (the deepest point being the Wit-jas Deep at -11,034 meters (-36,200 ft.) within the Mariana Trench), and features the largest continuous system of mountain ranges on earth, the Midoceanic Ridges. Wherever these ridges rise above sea-level, we find signs of volcanic activity – such as on Iceland.

The most prominent contours in the ever changing topography of the land masses are also produced

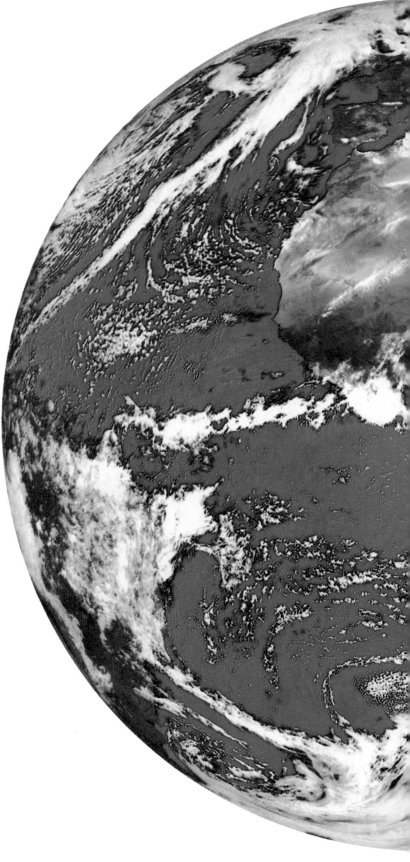

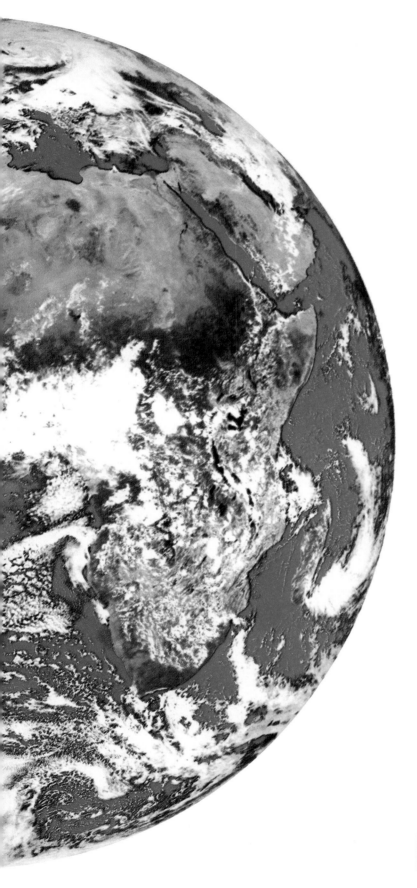

by various configurations of mountain ranges. Here we distinguish two major forms. On the one hand, the latitudinal chain of mountain ranges that stretches from the Pyrenees via the Alps, the Caucasus and the Himalayas to the Southeast Asian chains; on the other hand, the circumpacific mountain ranges interlinked with the alpine mountain chains in Southeast Asia. Compared with the horizontal dimensions of the earth surface, the mountain ranges and trenches are but faint wrinkles on the face of the planet – the greatest difference in elevation being only some twenty kilometers (6,500 ft.). The Dead Sea is the lowest visible depression on

our planet (-403 m/-1,322 ft.), whereas the bed of Lake Baykal (-1,158 m/-3,799 ft.) is actually the lowest point on any continent. The Himalayas rise to an elevation of 8,848 meters (29,029 feet) at Mount Everest, the highest place on earth; but in terms of absolute elevation, the highest mountain is the Chimborazo in Ecuador, rising from an ocean depth of 6,600 meters to 6,310 meters (21,653 feet to 20,702 ft.) above sea-level. The largest mountain in terms of its surface area is the Kilimanjaro (5,895 m/ 19,341 ft.) in Africa. Enclosed by these high mountain ranges, or flanking them, are highlands and lowlands of varying di-

Center: »The earth is a shining oasis amidst the infinite vastness of space,« proclaimed one of the astronauts on his return flight from the moon. Without warmth or water, however, that same earth remains desolate, as in the Sahara Desert.

Left: The middle latitudes with their moderate climate are the granaries of the earth. Today industrial farming is a widely practiced form of agriculture in this part of the world.

Right: The German research ship »Polarstern« plowing its way through the earth's ›icy desert‹.

mensions. They are covered by the planet's major belts of vegetation, such as the northern coniferous forests, the vernally greening deciduous forests and the tropical rainforests. This is where the large river systems arise. Here also are the regions, that were the original habitat of that adaptable species, homo sapiens.

The human population distribution, largely due to regional climatic and topographic differences, is highly uneven. Extremely cold or arid climates make some regions virtually uninhabitable; whereas others with damp, mild climates and fertile soil are densely populated. Latter conditions exist within the moderate or subtropical zones, and in large oases along the major rivers. Initially, a thriving agriculture was responsible for the early development of advanced civilizations in these regions. Although they make up only seven per cent of the total land area, these zones of dense population are inhabited by three quarters of the over five billion human beings. This is also where most of the cities with over a million inhabitants are located: in southern and eastern Asia, in Europe and the eastern half of the United States. Compared to the other centers of agglomeration, the European zone lies remarkably far to the north. This shift can be largely attributed to the favorable influence of the warm North Atlantic stream on the climate of Western Eurasia.

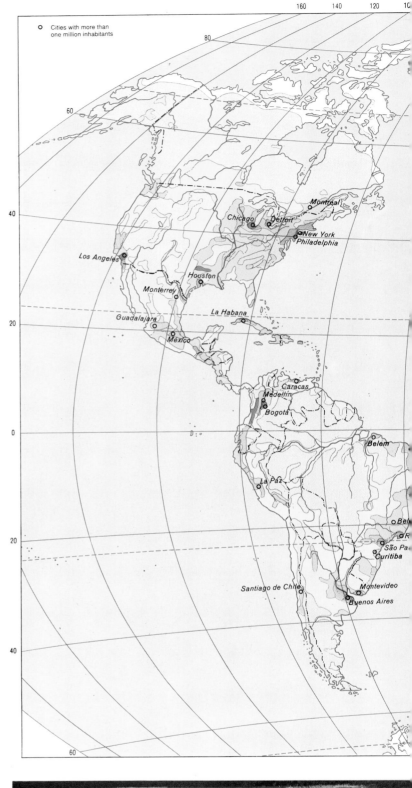

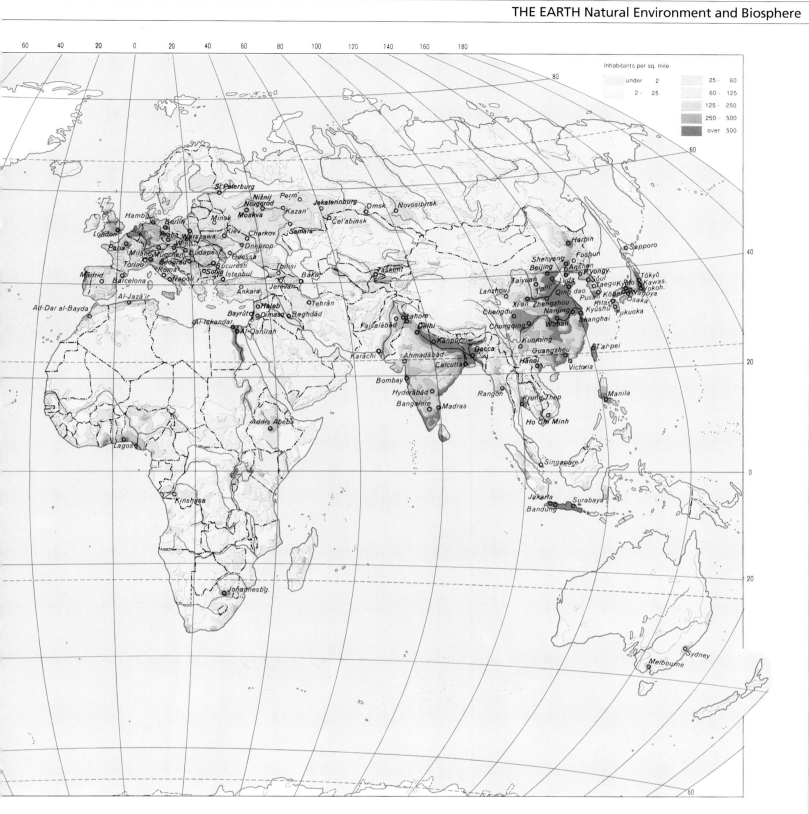

Inhabitants per sq. mile

under 2	25 - 60
2 - 25	60 - 125
	125 - 250
	250 - 500
	over 500

Left: Tulip fields near Amsterdam (Netherlands).

Center: Rice terraces in Southeast Asia. Rice is the major agricultural crop in the world – feeding around a third of the human population.

Right: The Paraguay flows through a forested flood savanna, the Pantanal, a huge swamp area in Southern Brazil.

85

With conditions less favorable to settlement at higher altitudes, some nine tenths of the world population is crowded into the elevation range between zero and 1,000 meters/3,280 feet. Conversely, it is only in the tropics that population densities increase at higher altitudes – where the air is less sultry. Due to the wide range of natural conditions prevailing within individual countries – such as the USA, Russia, India, Australia, and Egypt – there is also great variance in population density between regions. Generally, industrial nations are more densely populated than developing countries, but there are exceptions like India and China. The populations of these two most populous countries in the world alone make up two thirds of the human race.

Since population growth is not linear but exponential – that is, the human race doubles in number within shorter and shorter intervals – the development of the human population is one of mankind's most urgent problems. In order to meet their growing needs – e.g. for food and raw materials – human beings continue to tamper more and more extensively with nature. We do not yet know how far we can tax this planet's resilience – how much more strain the earth can bear.

Left: Vast areas of Canada and Alaska in northern North America are deserted. The summers are too short for higher plants to develop.

Earth Statistics

Surface area: 197,000,000 sqmiles

Equatorial circumference: 40,902 miles

Meridial circumference: 24,860 miles

Equatorial diameter: 7,927 miles

Equatorial radius: 3,963 miles

Polar radius: 3,950 miles

Volume: 672,976,200,000 miles³

EUROPE

On a world map Europe looks like a subcontinent of the huge land mass of Eurasia. Due to its independent historical and cultural development and distinctive topographic features, Europe is nevertheless considered a separate continent. Europe is distinguished by tightly interlocking contours of land and sea, highly differentiated topography, a predominately temperate and mild climate and its central location with respect to the other populated continents. It is heir to strong political fragmentation and cultural differentiation — manifest, for example, in the former division of the continent into two opposing political and ideological blocs.

Europe
NATURAL ENVIRONMENT

The second smallest continent on earth is also the lowest, with an average elevation of only 300 meters (984 feet). The marginal seas of the Atlantic, such as the North Sea, the Baltic Sea and the Mediterranean penetrate deeply into the continent. Europe, due to the large number of peninsulas and islands, has nearly 40,000 kilometers (24,850 miles) of coastline.

The traditional demarcation line separating Europe and Asia runs from the Ural Mountains along the Ural River and the northern edge of the Caucasus, through the Bosporos to the Dardanelles. The topography of the continent is characterized by a diversity of landscapes within a small area. A chain of mountains stretching from the Pyrenees via the Alps (Montblanc, 4,807 m/15,771 ft.) to the Balkans separates Southern Europe from the rest of the continent.

From time immemorial, however, people have discovered numerous passes, using these chinks in the wall of mountains to maintain close ties with the inhabitants on the other side. Enclosed within the young mountain chains of the

Mediterranean region, we find old continental masses like the mesetas in Spain and young lowlands like the Po Plain. The western and central European peneplain spreading out north of the Alps is made up of disintegrated bevelled uplands. This landscape's abundance of forms is further enhanced by the various manifestations of former volcanic activity: the volcanic columns in the French central massif, the volcanic lakes in the Eifel Mountains, the lava caps in Vogelsberg and the rounded basaltic cupolas in the Rhön.

The western, central and eastern European lowland, the most uniform and expansive landscape in Europe, fans out to the east. Its broad glacial valleys, the chains of hilly terminal moraines and the rounded ground moraines were all caused by the glaciers which reshaped the region during the Ice Ages (approx. 600,000 to 12,000 years ago).

Scandinavia's sharply indented fjord coastline, the Scandinavian »fjells« (Glittertind 2,472 m/8,110 ft.), the skerry coast and the Finnish lake-filled lowland plain are

also products of ice-age remodelling. During the Ice Ages over half of the European region was reshaped by glacial activity!

Located within the Northern Temperate Zone with exposure to the Atlantic Ocean, Europe – with the exception of the north – has an extraordinarily favorable climate. Besides providing Europe with sufficient moisture, the Atlantic Stream with its northernmost branch, the Gulf Stream, and the west-wind drift have the effect of ›shifting‹ the cool-to-warm Variable Zone northward to include the continent. There are nevertheless noticeable differences in climate between the north and the south, the east and the west. The seasonal temperature variation increases as one moves east: from the even Atlantic climate of Western Europe with its mild winters and cool summers to the continental climate of Eastern Europe with its typical hot summers and very cold winters. Hot, predominately dry summers and mild, damp winters are characteristic of the subtropical climate in southern Europe.

One remarkable feature of Europe-

Page 87: Schönbrunn Palace, the 18th-century imperial summer residence in Vienna, surrounded by a splendid palace park.

Above: North Sea lighthouse amidst mud-flats which dry up each time the tide goes out. The mud-flats are scored with an even grid of ditches.

Far left: Tuscany, one of the most colorful landscapes in the world.

Top left: View of Mount Watzmann (2,713 m/8,901 ft.) in the Salzburg Alps.

Bottom left: Iceland, the Island of Fire and Ice, is composed entirely of volcanic rock. Hot springs are scattered throughout the island.

Right: Since prehistoric time men have been cutting the fine-grained stone in the famous Carrara (Tuscany) marble quarries at the foot of the Apuanic Alps.

an climates is distinctive local winds; e.g. the Alpine föhn, the mistral of the Lower Rhone Valley or the bora in Yugoslavia and the etesia in the Aegean region. Before humans began to settle here, the continent was largely covered by forests. Today, the only uninterrupted belt of coniferous forest lies north of the 60th parallel – where the unfavorable climate prevents any other utilization of the land. Land cultivation has displaced the mixed woodlands throughout the rest of Europe except on the wooded mountain ranges. In the Mediterranean region, however, these ranges generally bear a secondary vegetation of sclerophyllous evergreens.

Although not the longest European river, the Rhine is certainly the major economic artery, because it connects several industrial areas before emptying into the North Sea; whereas the Danube flows into the »remote« Black Sea.

Above: Rügen, the largest German island in the Baltic Sea, is surrounded on all sides by steep, chalky cliffs battered by the sea.

Cultivated land (arable land, plantations and irrigated land)

Grassland of the temperate zone

Forest of the temperate zone (predominant exploitation of forest)

Mediterranean scrub (Maquis; partly low trees with leathery leaves)

Semi-desert and desert

Tundra, fell and swamp taiga

Rock, snow and ice areas of mountain regions

1:15 000 000

Europe
PEOPLE AND CULTURE

Unlike all other continents, Europe is very evenly populated. With an average of 171 inhabitants per square mile, it is one of the most densely populated regions in the world. Europe includes numerous unique geographic areas – which explains the variety of different peoples inhabiting the region. 120 languages are spoken across this small continent – forty of them in the Caucasus alone. Over thirty countries have evolved in Europe. The powerful forces emanating from this »hotbed of human activity« have had a crucial effect on all the other continents: the colonization of nearly all the so-called southern continents; the settlement of the »New World«; industrialization and mechanization; and the dissemination of religions, ideologies and European civilization. In the course of discovering and conquering the world, the Europeans spread their languages to all parts of the globe. 95 per cent of all Europeans speak Romance, Germanic or Slavic languages. Seven of these – English, French, Spanish, Russian, German, Portuguese and Italian – are world languages spoken by over 350 million Europeans. Even after their independence many former colonies have kept English or French as their official languages. Portuguese or Spanish are spoken throughout South and Central America.

The europeanization of the earth has been closely connected with the spreading of European religions. In Europe proper (without the former Soviet Union) about half the population belongs to the Roman Catholic Church, around a quarter to the Protestant and about one tenth to one of the various Orthodox Churches. As the center of world Catholicism, Rome is the site of both the politically independent Vatican State and St. Peter's, the largest ecclesiastical building in the world. Church buildings from various architectural periods distinguish the unmistakeable skylines of many European cities. Villages, and cities are the typical forms of settlement in Europe. Some were erected on ancient foundations. Others simply evolved out of trading settlements, grew in the shelter of forts or were established by royal incorporation during the Middle Ages – then expanded and changed during the period of industrialization. They have always, however, served as the economic and cultural centers of the various states. They also cover a considerable portion, nearly three per cent, of the entire land area of Europe.

For centuries Europe was the dominant economic center of the world. With fertile soils and a mild climate favorable to intensive cultivation, a large portion of the total land area could be made agriculturally productive. Other assets were abundant mineral resources, convenient means of transportation and a population trained in

Top left: Prague with the former royal castle, Hradschin, (now the seat of the President of Czechoslovakia) and the Gothic St. Vitus Cathedral overlooking the Vitava River.

Lower left: Malbork (German: Marienburg) on the Nogat. The castle, once occupied by the Teutonic Order, dominates the town.

Top right: St. Petersburg is famous for its baroque (here: Smolny Cloister) and classical architecture.

Bottom right: The 16th-century Basilius Cathedral dominates the southern end of the Red Square in Moscow, the capital of Russia.

Netherlands
Koninkrijk der Nederlanden

Amsterdam

41,548 sqkm/ 16,042 sqm

Pop.: 15,158,000

Dutch (in Friesland Province: Frisian)

Dutch Guilder

Belgium
Royaume de Belgique Koninkrijk België

Brussels

30,518 sqkm/ 11,783 sqm

Pop.: 9,910,000

French, Dutch, German

Belgian Franc

Luxembourg
Grand-Duché de Luxembourg Grousherzogdem Letzebuerg

Luxembourg

2,586 sqkm/ 998 sqm

Pop.: 378,000

Luxembourgian, French, German

Luxembourgian Franc

France
République Française

Paris

547,026 sqkm/ 211,207 sqm (incl. Corsica, w/o overseas territories)

Pop.: 57,182,000

French (German, Breton, Basque Corsican and other regional languages)

French Franc

Germany
Bundesrepublik Deutschland

Berlin

357,040 sqkm/ 137,853 sqm

Pop.: 80,570,000

German (partially school language in Schleswig-Holstein: Danish; by a regional minority: Sorbian)

Deutsche Mark

Slovak Republic
Solvenská Republika

Bratislava

49,036 sqkm/ 18,933 sqm

Pop.: 5,274,000

Slovak

Slovak koruna

Poland
Rzeczpospolita Polska

Warsaw

312,683 sqkm/ 120,727 sqm

Pop.: 38,417,000

Polish

Zloty

Czech Republic
Česká Republika

Prague

127,869 sqkm/ 49,370 sqm

Pop.: 10,302,000

Czech

Czech koruna

93

a tradition of skilled craftsmanship. These factors all contributed to the evolution of the first major center of industrial production in the world, located within the triangle between the English Midlands, Paris and the Ruhr area. Other industrial centers were to follow, such as Ukraine, Upper Silesia and Northern Italy.

The various European countries are grouped into regions according to geographic location.

Central Europe includes the German-speaking countries Germany, Switzerland and Austria. As a whole this area, with its high degree of industrialization and increasing urbanization, is comparable to the Northeastern United States or Japan.

Because of their location and historic development Hungary, the Czech Republic, Slovakia and Poland are considered part of Eastern Central Europe, which also includes the Baltic states Estonia, Latvia and Lithuania – now that they have broken away from the former Soviet Union.

The Western European countries are all strongly oriented toward the Atlantic and the adjoining seas. They largely owe their former status, in fact, as mother countries of colonial empires to this geographic blessing. France, the Benelux states (Belgium, the Netherlands and Luxembourg), Great Britain and Ireland make up this »Atlantic Europe«. The cosmopolitan cities Paris and London have remained important centers of culture, the insurance business, commerce and major finance to this day.

Southern Europe comprises the so-called Mediterranean countries: Portugal and Spain on the Iberian Peninsula, Italy on the Apennine Peninsula and Greece. Owing to the favorable Mediterranean climate and the physical heritage of their rich past, mass and educational tourism together are a dominant economic factor in these countries.

In Southern Europe there is a marked contrast between population centers with their urban culture and the agrarian regions with open and concealed unemployment. In Italy this has given rise to a conflict between the industrial north and the agrarian Mezzogiorno in the south – the upshot being the migration of workers to the industrial areas in

Estonia	Latvia	Lithuania	Russia	White Russia	Ukraine	Moldavia
Eesti Vabariik	Latvijas	Lietuva	Rossija	Belaruš	Ukraïna	Moldova
Tallinn	*Riga*	*Vilnius* (Vilna)	*Moscow*	*Minsk*	*Kiev*	*Kishinev*
45,100 sqkm/ 17,413 sqm	64,500 sqkm/ 24,903 sqm	65,200 sqkm/ 25,174 sqm	17,075,000 sqkm/ 6.592.658 sqm	207,600 sqkm/ 80,154 sqm	603,700 sqkm/ 233,090 sqm	33,700 sqkm/ 13,012 sqm
Pop.: 1,582,000	Pop.: 2,679,000	Pop.: 3,755,000	Pop.: 149,003,000	Pop.: 10,295,000	Pop.: 52,158,000	Pop.: 4,362,000
Estonian, Russian	Latvian, Russian	Lithuanian, Russian	Russian	Byelorussian, Russian	Ukrainian, Russian	Romanian, Russian
Kroon	Lats	Litas	Ruble	Ruble	Ruble	Ruble

Top: One result of German Unification: the Reichstag Building in Berlin (built by Paul Wallot) is again available for sessions of the Bundestag, the German parliament.

Center left: Even today Iceland lives to a large extent from fishing and whaling.

Center right: Istanbul (Constantinople, Byzantium) sprawls on the hills to either side of the Bosporus.

Top right: 384 meters (420 yards) long and built from 1840-49, this chain bridge in Budapest is still considered a technical masterpiece. It connects Buda on the right bank of the Danube with the newer district, Pest.

Lower right: The Holstentor in the old Hanseatic city of Lübeck – located in the Holstein-Mecklenburg hills country. The gate, erected from 1466-78, is a typical example of Northern German brick Gothic architecture.

Northern Italy and Central Europe.

Southeastern Europe is a diverse mosaic of peoples, religions and states. As a result, the region is considered the »European powderkeg« – where hatred and prejudice keep rekindling century-old conflicts. The collapse of Communist rule in Yugoslavia, Albania, Bulgaria and Rumania in 1989/1990 sparked the revival of ancient Balkan conflicts: the most dramatic example being the civil war between Serbs, Croatians and Slovenes, and the resulting disintegration of the Yugoslavian multi-national state. The border between Slovenia and Bosnia-Herzegovena marks an old cultural boundary: the region to the north and west was proselytized by Rome and then, as part of the Austro-Hungarian Empire was under Central European influence

Right: The Campanile (12th century), or »Leaning Tower« of Pisa, is over four meters askew.

Sunflowers are grown as a source of oil, as green fodder and as ornamental plants. The plant attains heights of up to 3,5 meters (11,5 feet). Its seeds contain lecithin and cholesterine, as well as protein and fat.

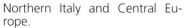

Great Britain and Northern Ireland	Ireland	Iceland	Norway	Sweden	Finland	Denmark
United Kingdom of Great Britain and Northern Ireland	Poblacht Na h'Eire-ann Irish Republic Eire	Lýdveldid Ísland	Kongeriket Norge	Konungariket Sverige	Suomen Tasavalta	Kongeriget Danmark
London	Dublin (Baile Atha Cliath)	Reykjavík	Oslo	Stockholm	Helsinki	Copenhagen
245,000 sqkm/ 94,595 sqm	70,283 sqkm/ 27,136 sqm	102,829 sqkm/ 39,702 sqm	323,883 sqkm/ 125,051 sqm	449,964 sqkm/ 173,731 sqm	338,107 sqkm/ 130,543 sqm	43,092 sqkm/ 16,638 sqm
Pop.: 57,649,000	Pop.: 3,486,000	Pop.: 260,000	Pop.: 4,288,000	Pop.: 8,652,000	Pop.: 5,008,000	Pop.: 5,158,000
English, (rudiments of Celtic languages)	Irish, English	Icelandic	Norwegian	Swedish	Finnish, Swedish, Lapp	Danish, (in North Schleswig: German)
Pound sterling	Irish pound	Icelandic krone	Norwegian krone	Swedish krone	Markkaa	Danish krone

until the last century. Initially under Eastern Roman rule, the region to the south and east later fell to the Islamic Ottoman Empire. To fend off this Ottoman threat, fortified farms were set up along the wide corridor between the two spheres of control – farmed by armed Croatian and Serbian refugees. Even today a diverse array of separate social groups lives side by side within this small area.

During the national wars of liberation against the Turks which began in 1804, Orthodox Christians fought against Moslems; during the Balkan Wars of 1912/1913 the Serbs and Bulgarians battled on opposing sides, and during the Second World War the Catholic Croatians clashed with Orthodox Serbs. Today, the bloody rifts crisscrossing the Balkans seem insurmountable.

Top right: Sevilla, the southern Spanish port on the Guadalquivir and the old capital of Andalusia, was once the center of trade with America.
The heritage of that period includes an array of prestigious buildings – like these here on Plaza de España at the edge of the expansive Parque de Maria Luisa.

Below: The Tower of Belém is the symbol of Lisbon, the capital of Portugal. To defend the entrance to the harbor, it was built in Emanuel style from 1515-21.

Spain	**Andorra**
Reino de España	Principat d'Andorra Principauté d'Andorra Principado de Andorra
Madrid	*Andorra la Vella*
504,782 sqkm/ 194,896 sqm	453 sqkm/ 175 sqm
Pop.: 39,092,000	Pop.: 47,000
Spanish (Castilian), Catalan, Galician, Basque	Catalan, French, Spanish
Peseta	Peseta, French Franc

97

Rumania, Albania and Bulgaria have their own smouldering minority conflicts. Is a disintegrating Yugoslavia merely the first in a series of regional conflicts to shake the Balkans?

Eastern Europe encompasses the area of Belarus, Ukraine, Moldova and Russia – whose remaining territory also makes up all of northern Asia. Prior to the tremendous upheavals in Eastern Europe in 1989/1990, the largest state in the world was controlled from Moscow with the Kremlin being the central seat of Soviet power. Moscow was also the headquarters of a number of central authorities both of the former Soviet Union and of the former »Eastern bloc« countries.

Before the »Silent Revolution« and the overthrow of the Communist Party in 1990, a monolithic

An old city in the province of North Holland, Alkmaar is known for the long tradition of its cheese market, which is held at the old town scales every Friday from ten to twelve a.m. (May through September).

Portugal	Monaco	Italy	San Marino	Vatican State	Malta	Switzerland	Austria
República Portuguesa	Principauté de Monaco	Repubblica Italiana	Repubblica di San Marino	Status Civitatis Vaticanae Stato della Cittá del Vaticano	Repubblica ta'Malta Republic of Malta	Schweizerische Eidgenossenschaft Confédération Suisse Confederazione Svizzera	Republik Österreich
Lisbon	*Monaco*	*Rome*	San *Marino*		*Valletta*	*Berne*	*Vienna*
91,791 sqkm/ 35,510 sqm	1,95 sqkm/ 0,75 sqm	301,277 sqkm/ 116,320 sqm	61 sqkm/ 24 sqm	0,44 sqkm/ 0,17 sqm	316 sqkm/ 122 sqm	41,293 sqkm/ 15,940 sqm	83,854 sqkm/ 32,376 sqm
Pop.: 9,866,000	Pop.: 28,000	Pop.: 57,782,000	Pop.: 23,000	Pop.: 1,000	Pop.: 359,000	Pop.: 6,813,000	Pop.: 7,776,000
Portuguese	French, Monegasque	Italian, (regionally: German, Ladin, French, Slowenian)	Italian, Roma	Latin, Italian	Maltese, English	German, French, Italian, Rheato-Romanic	German, (regional minority: Croatian)
Escudo	French Franc	Italian lira	Italian lira, lira of San Marino	Vatican lira, Italian lira	Maltese lira	Swiss franc	Austrian shilling

political and economic system had held the former Soviet Union together. Since its disintegration the republics of the former state have declared their independence and united to form the Community of Independent States (CIS). The location of one of the oldest industrial regions in Russia on both sides of the Ural Mountain Range – the European and the Asian slopes – clearly demonstrates that the boundary between Europe and Asia was as immaterial in the former Soviet Union, as it is in the Russia of today. Northern Europe includes the countries Norway, Sweden, Finland and, because of its old historic affiliation, Denmark. It is the most sparsely populated portion of Europe. Until recently rich deposits of iron ore, an abundance of wood and rich fishing grounds were the lifeblood of this

Top: These neat town houses are typical of Flanders. In the Middle Ages its textile industry and trade made this Belgian province on the North Sea Coast one of the wealthiest regions in Europe.

Bottom: Snowbound alpine cabins. The buildings are only used during the summer when the cattle is driven up to the alpine pastures.

Lower right: Loch Maree in Scotland (loch meaning 'lake' or 'bay' in Scottish Gaelic). The lake fills a basin enclosed by softly rounded ridges.

Liechtenstein	Hungary	Macedonia	Slovenia	Croatia	Bosnia-Herzegovina	Yugoslavia
Fürstentum Liechtenstein	Magyar Köztársaság	Republika Makedonija	Republika Slovenija	Republika Hrvatska	Republika Bosna i Hercegowina	Federativna Republika Jugoslawija (International recognition in dispute)
Vaduz	Budapest	Skopje	Ljubljana	Zagreb	Sarajevo	Belgrade
160 sqkm/ 62 sqm	93,032 sqkm/ 35,920 sqm	25,713 sqkm/ 9,928 sqm	20,251 sqkm/ 7,819 sqm	56,538 sqkm/ 21,829 sqm	51,129 sqkm/ 19,741 sqm	102,173 sqkm/ 39,449 sqm
Pop.: 28,000	Pop.: 10,512,000	Pop.: 2,034,000	Pop.: 1,966,000	Pop.: 4,784,000	Pop.: 4,365,000	Pop.: 10,406,000
German	Madjarish (Hungarian)	Macedonian, Serbian, Croatian, Albanian	Slovenian	Croatian	Serbian, Croatian	Serbian, Croatian, Albanian, Hungarian
Swiss Franc	Forint	MacedonianDinar	Tolar	Dinar	Dinar	New Yugoslavian Dollar

On its lower reaches in the Rhône-Alpes region, the Ardèche (a right tributary of the Rhône) has carved deeply into the massive layers of limestone, creating this picturesque gorge. The Ardèche is popular with canoers.

region. Today, however, the inhabitants have come to depend more and more on Norway's oil reserves and on the processing industries. For the inhabitants of Iceland, the »Island of Fire and Ice«, fishing still provides the main livelihood.

Istanbul and its hinterland are actually located on the European continent – with a bridge only recently connecting them to Asia Minor. Because of its cultural differences, however, Turkey is not generally considered a part of Europe.

Albania	**Rumania**	**Bulgaria**	**Greece**	**Cyprus**
Republika Shqipërisë	Republica România	Republika Bălgarija	Helleniki Demokratia	Kypriaki Dimokratia Kibris Cumhuriyeti Republik of Cyprus
Tirana	*Bukarest*	*Sofia*	*Athens*	*Nicosia*
28,748 sqkm/ 11,100 sqm	237,500 sqkm/ 91,699 sqm	110,912 sqkm 42,823 sqm	131,957 sqkm/ 50,949 sqm	9,251 sqkm/ 3,572 sqm
Pop.: 3,315,000	Pop.: 23,327,000	Pop.: 8,952,000	Pop.: 10,182,000	Pop.: 716,000
Albanian	Rumanian, (colloquial minority languages)	Bulgarian, (colloquial minority languages)	Greek (modern Greek)	Greek, Turkish, English
Lek	Leu	Lew	Drachme	Cypriot pound

ASIA

This »Giant among the Continents« covers almost a third of the earth's land surface. More people live here than on all other continents combined. From the western to the eastern end of Asia, there are eleven time zones. Its territory includes every type of climatic and vegetation zone: from perpetual ice to tropical rain forests. Asia is a continent of superlatives – boasting the mightiest mountain range and the highest peak, the area most distant from an ocean, and the largest area undrained by rivers. It includes a unique diversity of peoples, religions and cultures; the most populous country in the world, wealthy industrial nations, and miserably poor developing countries.

Asia
NATURAL ENVIRONMENT

At an average elevation of 925 meters (3,035 feet), Asia is the highest continent on earth. With islands and peninsulas making up a quarter of its total surface area, it has over 70,000 kilometers (43,500 miles) of coastline. Asia stretches 11,000 kilometers (6,835 miles) from west to east, 8,500 (5,282 miles) from north to south. Piercing the isthmus between the Mediterranean and the Red Sea, the Suez Canal is considered the boundary between Asia and Africa. The dividing line between Asia and Europe runs along the Ural Mountains, the Ural River, the Caspian Sea, the northern edge of the Caucasus, the Black Sea through the Bosporos and the Dardanelles to the Aegean Sea. This boundary, however, is relatively meaningless, since large parts of Northern Asia have strong political and cultural ties with Eastern Europe. For the better part of this century, in fact, these countries – now members of the Community of Independent States (CIS) – were parts of one nation: the Soviet Union.

The European mountain chains extend by way of the Mediterranean islands to Asia, where they converge at the Ararat (5,156 m/16,916 feet)) and in the clusters of mountains in the Hindukush and Pamir (7,495 m/24,590 feet) – enclosing the highlands of Anatolia, Iran and Tibet – before finally extending into the Indo-Chinese Peninsula. Covering some eight million square kilometers (3,089,000 sqm), the inner Asian mountain block – including the Himalayas with the tallest mountain in the world, Mount Everest (8,848 m/29,029 feet) – is the largest raised land mass on earth. To the south the topography changes, giving rise to the tablelands of Arabia and Southeast Asia. To the east, the continent drops off in several wide steps to the Pacific. The arched garlands of islands fringing the coast are bordered by deep-sea trenches (Mariana Trench: -11,022 m/-36,161 feet). Separating individual seas from the open Pacific, the Kurils, Japan, the Ryukyu (Nansei) Islands, the Philippines and Indonesia are all part of the Pacific »Ring of Fire«. The earthquakes and volcanic eruptions (Fujisan 3,776 m/12,388 feet) caused by the shifting earth's crust in this tectonically active zone are a threat to human life. East of the Ural extend the western Siberian lowland, the Central Siberian Plateau, and the eastern Siberian mountain ranges.

Mighty rivers issuing from the Central Asian mountains flow in all directions. In most of these rivers, the discharge fluctuates con-

Page 101: Indian street scene at sunset. The sari, a wrapped garment frequently made of silk, is the typical dress of Indian women.

Lower left: The cones and spires of the karst landscape along the Li River near Guilin in subtropical southern China.

Center: Blossom and multiple fruits (bunches); this is how bananas grow in tropical countries all over the world.

Lower right: The harvesting of natural latex, the thickened milky liquid of the rubber tree, which grows to a height of 30 meters (98 feet).

siderably throughout the year. The rivers of Siberia (Ob/Irtysch, Jenissej, Lena) drain into the Arctic Sea. With thaws setting in earlier in the south than in the north, huge floods are regular events. The Amur, the Huang, the Chang Jiang (or Yangtze) and the Mekong empty into the Pacific; the Brahmaputra, Ganges and Indus rivers, the Euphrates and Tigris flow into the Indian Ocean. With an area of 370,000 square kilometers (142,857 sqm), the Caspian Sea is the largest undrained lake on earth. The Dead Sea is the lowest visible point on earth (-400 m/-1,312 feet), and Lake Baykal is the largest freshwater lake in Asia with a depth of 1,620 meters (5,315 feet).The distance from the ocean and the

Top: Nepal, a kingdom on the southern slope of the Himalayas, is the country with the largest number of mountains over 8,000 meters (26,246 feet).

Lower left: Ladakh, the mountainous region between the Himalayas and the Karakorum, lies on either side of the upper Indus. Livestock is the main source of livelihood, since irrigated agriculture is only possible in some of the lower valleys.

Lower right: Palm grove in Malaysia.

location in the lee of huge chains of mountains gave rise to the deserts at the edge of or within the Central Asian Massif; e.g., the Kyzyl-Kum, the Gobi (or Shamo) or the Taklamakan in the Tarim Basin. The deserts of Arabia, by comparison, are tropical deserts that owe their existence to atmospheric conditions. Whereas winter rains are features of Asia Minor's Mediterranean climate, the climate in southern and eastern Asia is dominated by monsoons: the southwestern monsoon bringing summer rains, the northeastern monsoon winter dryness.

Corresponding with climatic conditions, Asia is covered by various belts of vegetation: northern Asia with its distinctly continental climate is covered with tundra in the North, followed by a belt of coniferous forests, then by steppes and desert areas. Large areas of Indonesia are still covered with rain forest.

Top: Loess landscape near Yenan in northern China. The river has gouged deep valleys with steep walls, whereas the higher slopes have been terraced. Erosion is a major problem in China.

Bottom: Camel market in Rajastan (India).

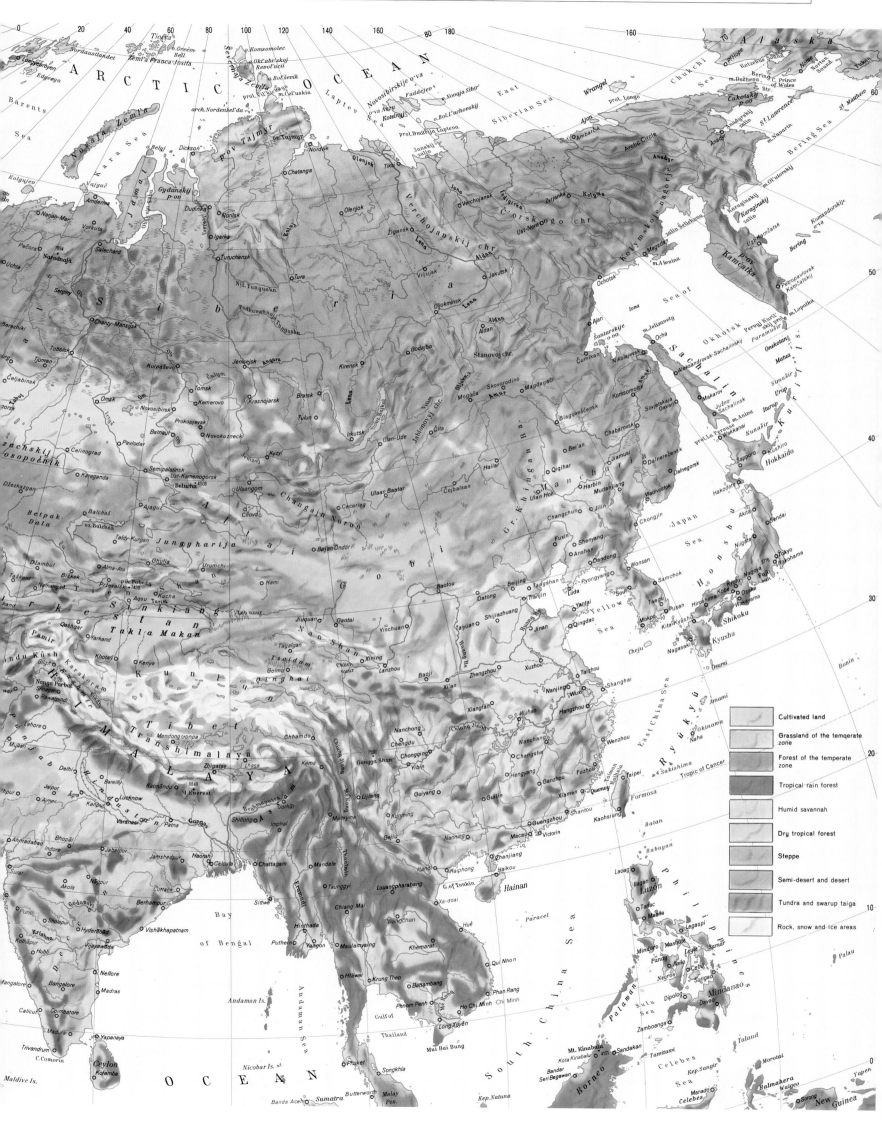

Cultivated land

Grassland of the temperate zone

Forest of the temperate zone

Tropical rain forest

Humid savannah

Dry tropical forest

Steppe

Semi-desert and desert

Tundra and swamp taiga

Rock, snow and ice areas

Asia
PEOPLE AND CULTURE

Asia's cultural diversity and its colorful mosaic of ethnic and racial groups are the result of a long historical process. In Asia one can encounter almost every cultural stage in the history of human evolution: from the game hunters in the subarctic north (Archaic Siberians), and the nomads in the arid regions, to the land-cultivating peoples of Mesopotamia, India, East Asia and the East Indies.

In Asia, the average population density is 168 inhabitants per square mile. On a continent with such varied topography, however, this does not tell us very much about the actual population distribution. In the tundra or taiga with their permafrost, in the vast desert regions of India and Central Asia, in the mountainous regions or rain forests of Southeast Asia, for example, the population density is extremely low. Yet Asia is also the continent with the largest densely-populated agricultural regions in the world. 90

Georgia	**Armenia**	**Azerbaijan**	**Kazakhstan**	**Uzbekistan**	**Turkmenistan**	**Kirgiziya**	**Tadzhikistan**
Sakhartwelos Republikas	Hajkh	Azärbajcan	Kazakstan	Üzbekiston	Türkmenistan	Kyrgyzstan	Toçíkiston
Tbilisi (Tiflis)	Erevan	Baku	Alma Ata	Tashkent	Ashkhabad	Pishpek (Frunze)	Dushanbe
69,700 sqkm/ 26,911 sqm	29,800 sqkm/ 11,506 sqm	86,600 sqkm/ 33,436 sqm	2,717,300 sqkm/ 1,049,150 sqm	447,400 sqkm/ 172,741 sqm	488,100 sqkm/ 188,455 sqm	198,500 sqkm/ 76,641 sqm	143,100 sqkm/ 55,251 sqm
Pop.: 5,471,000	Pop.: 3,489,000	Pop.: 7,283,000	Pop.: 17,048,000	Pop.: 21,453,000	Pop.: 3,861,000	Pop.: 4,400,000	Pop.: 5,587,000
Georgian, Russian	Armenian, Russian	Azerbaijani, Russian	Kazak, Russian	Uzbek, Russian	Turkoman, Russian	Kirgisian, Russian	Tadzhik, Uzbek, Russian
Ruble	Ruble	Ruble	Ruble	Ruble	Ruble	Ruble	Ruble

per cent of all Asians – that is, nearly three fifths of the world population – live on a mere third of the continent's surface area: the fertile plains and estuaries of the large rivers between the Indus and the Huang. In the last 300 years alone, the population here has grown to five times its size. This silent »explosion« – the combined result of traditionally high birth rates and advances in medical care – is so dramatic that by the year 2000 this region will be inhabited by some 3,5 billion Asians! So far family-planning programs have been successful only in Japan, Singapore and, to some extent, in China. There are already 70 cities in Asia with populations of over a million – compared with 13 in 1935. The majority of population, however, still subsists on agriculture and, hence, lives in the country. Only around one fifth of the total area

of Asia is cultivated – the alpine regions, deserts, tundras, marshes and forests are all non-arable land.

Struggling with the elements, farmers were forced to irrigate fields artificially or control flooding, to organize and intensify their efforts. This process gave rise to Asia's first advanced civilizations, (around 4000 B.C.) wherever soils were good and climates favorable: within the Near Eastern »fertile crescent« – including the extensive oases along the Euphrates and Tigris rivers – that crescent-shaped arc joining Asia and Africa, which stretches from the Persian Gulf via Mesopotamia, Syria and Palestine to the Nile Valley. Or in the Indian subcontinent which is separated from the rest of Asia by towering mountain ranges where the monsoon-belt agriculture is dictated by the biannual succession of dry and rainy sea-

Far left: Buddhism, the world religion, was founded by Buddha (560-480 B.C.) in northern India. It then spread to China and Japan, Ceylon and Southeast Asia, as well as to the Himalayan countries.

Top center: Female tea pickers.

Center: A boy at a candy stand in Sri Lanka (Ceylon).

Top right: A cremation in India. Hindus believe that the soul continues to roam about after death until it has found redemption through purification.

Lower right: The Omar Mosque or Rock Dome, finished in 691. To followers of Islam, it is one of the most important shrines in Jerusalem – the Holy City of Jews, Christians and Moslems alike.

Turkey	Syria	Lebanon	Israel	Jordan	Iraq	Iran
Türkiye Cumhuriyeti	El Dschamhurija el Arabija es Surija	El Dschumhurija el Lubnanija	Medinat Yisrael	Al Mamlakah Al Urdunniyah Al Hashimiyah	Al Dschumhurijah al Iraqija ad Dimukratija asch-Sha'abija	Dschumhuri-i-Islami Iran
Ankara	Damascus	Beirut	Jerusalem	Amman	Bagdad	Teheran
780,576 sqkm/ 301,380 sqm	185,180 sqkm/ 71,498 sqm	10,400 sqkm/ 4,015 sqm	20,770 sqkm/ 8,019 sqm	97,740 sqkm/ 37,737 sqm	438,446 sqkm/ 169,284 sqm	1,648,000 sqkm/ 636,293 sqm
Pop.: 57,237,000	Pop.: 13,276,000	Pop.: 2,838,000	Pop.: 5,131,000	Pop.: 4,291,000	Pop.: 19,290,000	Pop.: 61,565,000
Turkish, (colloquial languages of other nationalities)	Arabic, (Kurdish, Armenian)	Arabic, English, French, (Kurdish, Armenian)	New Hebrew, Arabic	Arabic	Arabic, Kurdish (additional colloquial languages)	Persian (Farsi), (various Iranian dialects)
Lira	Pound	Pound	Shekel	Jordan Dinar	Iraq Dinar	Rial

sons. Above all, in China, where rice, the most important crop throughout the monsoon belt, is grown in fields cultivated as in India, by the plow.

These spheres of cultural progress not only fostered the development of numerous languages, but also the cultivation of a variety of alphabets. Chinese, now spoken by one out of three Asians, has become the most important language in Asia. Written Chinese, with its ideographic system of representation, has exerted a formative influence far beyond the borders of China – in Japan, in particular. Asia as a whole has played a pre-eminent role in the history of religion as the continent which spawned and nurtured such major world religions as Islam, Buddhism, Hinduism, Judaism and Christianity. It is only with some reservation that Chinese Universalism – including Confucianism and Taoism – with its roots in nature worship can be considered a religion. A strong link between religion and all aspects of daily life and culture

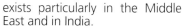

exists particularly in the Middle East and in India.

In spite of all the cultural differences between the various larger Asian regions, since World War II, the combined influence of industrialization and western civilization has succeeded in bringing them closer together – these influences being more pronounced, however, in urban centers than in rural areas.

In the former socialist republics of the Soviet Union people have begun to resist any form of ideological, cultural or economic control or »levelling« – having suffered all that for nearly 70 years. The demise of communism brought on by politics of openness and restructuring (»Perestroyka« and »Glasnost«; introduced around 1985), was sealed in 1990 when all the republics of the former Soviet Union formally declared their independence.

As early as the 16th century, Cossacks in the service of the Czar began conquering that sparsely populated »sleeping land«, Siberia. During the 18th and 19th

Top left: The Gilgit Valley, near the Kashmir town of the same name, is 1,500 meters (4,921 feet) above sea level. The lofty mountain ranges framing it on both sides, the Hindukush, Karakorum and Himalayas, ascend to elevations of above 8,000 meters (26,246 feet).

Top: At the top of Swayambhunath Hill we find the oldest and most important shrine in Nepal: the main stupa Chaitya. Resting on the white dome representing the vault of heaven there is a square tower bearing the pairs of Buddha eyes and the golden point with the 13 heavens.

Bottom left: Russian-style houses in Irkutsk, the regional capital of South Siberia, located on the Transsiberian Railway and the Angara River.

Below: A detail of Permual Temple in Singapore. The »City of Lions« is situated on an island off the southern tip of the Malay Peninsula. The numerous Chinese temples, mosques and churches are a typical feature of the city's Old Town.

Bottom right: Saddhu in Nepal. This Hindu holy man lives off the alms he receives from the faithful.

centuries the Czar signed defensive treaties with the kings of Georgia and Azerbaijan, annexing these territories to his empire. At the outset of the 20th century, Russia ruled both the Black Sea and the Caspian Sea. In 1847 the Cossacks began conquering the area around the Aral Sea and Lake Balkhash. By the turn of the century they had reached the borders of India and Afghanistan. In the aftermath of the October Revolution of 1917, the Russian Empire converted into the Union of Soviet Socialist Republics, the most diverse multi-national state on earth. Although the individual union republics were promised cultural self-administration, the central policy was actually one of across-the-board Russianization. The Asian portions of the former Soviet Union were radically transformed by the systematic development of industrial complexes; e.g., in the Ural, the Kuzneck Basin, along the upper Angara and in the Fergana Basin. Local industrial centers were set up along the 7,525 kilometers (4,676 miles) of Transsiberian Railway, built from 1891 to 1904, and along the Baykal-Amur Magistral (BAM). Another major step, accomplished by developing more resistent varieties of grains, was the creation of a new granary: the Siberian Grain Belt. So far, only a fraction of the area's tremendous hydroelectric potential has been harnessed.

In addition to cultural self-determination, the peoples of Georgia, Armenia, Azerbaijan, Uzbekistan, Kazakhstan, Kyrgystan, Tadzhikistan and Turkmenistan have demanded jurisdiction to plan the expansion of their economies and infrastructures. In claiming the rights of disposal, they will also have the opportunity to end the rampant over-exploitation of natural resources. In Uzbekistan, for example, water was diverted from rivers to irrigate vast cotton fields, thus causing the Aral Sea to dry up – threatening the entire region with an ecological disaster of horrendous proportions.

In the autonomous regions within Russia, voices are growing, demanding more freedom – evidence that this part of the world has far from settled down. Benefitting from its highly developed traditions of agriculture and craftsmanship Japan managed to overcome its two main handicaps – the crippling damage it suffered during the Second World War, and its lack of

Saudi-Arabia	Yemen Yemen Arabic Republic	Oman	United Arab Emirates	Bahrain	Qatar	Kuwait
Al Mamlaka Al 'Arabiya As-Sa'udiya	Al Dschumhurija al Jamanija	Saltanat aman	Al- Imārāt al-'ArabTya al-Muttahida United Arab Emirates	Dawlat al-Bahrain	Dawlat al Qatar	Dawlat al Kuwait
Riyadh	Sanaa	Maskat	Abu Dhabi	Manama	Doha	Kuwait
2,149,690 sqkm/ 829,995 sqm	527,968 sqkm/ 203,848 sqm	212,457 sqkm/ 82,030 sqm	83,600 sqkm/ 32,278 sqm	622 sqkm/ 240 sqm	11,437 sqkm/ 4,416 sqm	17,818 sqkm/ 6,880 sqm
Pop.: 15,922,000	Pop.: 12,535,000	Pop.: 1,637,000	Pop.: 1,670,000	Pop.: 533,000	Pop.: 453,000	Pop.: 1,970,000
Arabic	Arabic	Arabic, Persian, Urdu	Arabic, English (commercial language)	Arabic, English (commercial language)	Arabic, Persian, English (com.language)	Arabic, English (commercial language)
Saudi Riyal	Yemen-Rial	Rial Omani	Dirham	Bahrain Dinar	Katar-Riyal	Kuwait Dinar

Top: The Taj Mahal in Agra (India). Built from 1630 to 1652, this mosque-like marble mausoleum was erected by a king in memory of his favorite wife.

Center: Natural gas being burnt off an oil well in the United Arab Emirates on the Persian Gulf.

Top right: Terraced rice fields in northern Luzon (Philippines). Created some 2,000 years ago, these »sky terraces« can comprise up to 80 tiers of paddies.

Lower right: Irrigated seedlings in the United Arab Emirates.

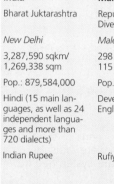

Afghanistan

De Afghánistán Djamhuriare

Kabul

647,497 sqkm/ 249,999 sqm

Pop.: 19,062,000

Pashto, Dari (Persian)

Afghani

Pakistan

Islamic Republic of Pakistan Islami Jamhuriya-e-Pakistan

Islamabad

803,943 sqkm/ 310,402 sqm

Pop.: 124,773,000

Urdu, English, regional languages

Pakistan Rupee

India

Bharat Juktarashtra

New Delhi

3,287,590 sqkm/ 1,269,338 sqm

Pop.: 879,584,000

Hindi (15 main languages, as well as 24 independent languages and more than 720 dialects)

Indian Rupee

Maledives

Republic of Maledives Divehi raajje

Malé

298 sqkm/ 115 sqm

Pop.: 227,000

Devehi, English

Rufiyaa

Sri Lanka

Sri Lanka Janarajaya

Colombo

65,610 sqkm/ 25,332 sqm

Pop.: 17,666,000

Sinhalese, Tamil, English

Sri Lanka Rupee

Nepal

Nepal Adiradscha Sri Nepalá Sarkár

Kathmandu

140,797 sqkm/ 54,362 sqm

Pop.: 20,577,000

Nepali, (additional languages and dialects)

Nepalese Rupee

Bhutan

Druk-Yul

Thimphu

47,000 sqkm/ 18,147 sqm

Pop.: 1,612,000

Dzongkha, (additional regional languages)

Ngultrum

Bangladesh

Ghana Praja Tantri Bangla Desh

Dhaka

143,998 sqkm/ 55,598 sqm

Pop.: 119,288,000

Bengali (additional regional languages)

Taka

coal and iron – accomplishing a rapid process of extensive industrialization. The region also includes several upwardly mobile economies gradually emerging from Japan's shadow; particularly the four »Little Tigers«: South Korea, Taiwan, Hong Kong and Singapore. Obviously, close international trade relations are vitally important in an area which has become the hub not only of the Pacific realm, but of the entire world economy.

Although still mainly an agricultural society, the People's Republic of China has begun to accelerate industrialization – capitalizing especially on its abundant reserves of hard coal. Back in colonial days, in fact, the western powers had already begun to set up heavy industry in Manchuria, as well as textile mills and other light industrial plants in the major ports. Currently, the main priorities are the improvement of the deficient transportation infrastructure and the exploitation of China's abundant mineral resources. Initially, the state was entirely in charge of planning and administering the economy. As of 1978, however, »systems of autonomous responsibility« were introduced – first in the country, then in the cities – coupled with free-market elements. This has created a widening, unbridgeable rift be-

Burma (Myanmar)	Laos	Vietnam	Cambodia (Kampuchea)	Thailand	Malaysia	Singapore	Brunei
Union Myanmar	République démocratique populaire Lao Sāthālamalid Pasāthu'paait Pasāsīm Lao	Công Hóa Xa Hôi Chu Nghĩa Viêt Nam	Ravax Samaki Songkruos Cheat Kampuchea	Prathet T'hai Muang T'hai	Persekutuan Tanah Malaysia	Majulah Singapura Republic of Singapore	Negara Brunei Darussalam
Rangoon	Vientiane	Hanoi	Phnom Penh	Bangkok	Kuala Lumpur	Singapore	Bandar Seri Begawan
678,528 sqkm/ 261,980 sqm	236,800 sqkm/ 91,428 sqm	332,556 sqkm/ 128,400 sqm	181,035 sqkm/ 69,898 sqm	513,115 sqkm/ 198,114 sqm	329,749 sqkm 127,316 sqm	618,1 sqkm/ 239 sqm	5,765 sqkm/ 2,226 sqm
Pop.: 43,668,000	Pop.: 4,469,000	Pop.: 69,485,000	Pop.: 8,774,000	Pop.: 56,129,000	Pop.: 18,792,000	Pop.: 2,769,000	Pop.: 270,000
Burmese	Lao, colloquial languages of various ethnic groups	Vietnamese, (dialects of various ethnic groups)	Khmer	Thai, colloquial languages of other groups	Malay, Chinese, Tamil, Iban, English	English, Malay Chinese, Tamil	Malay, English, Chinese, Iban
Kyat	New Kip	Dong	Riel	Baht	Malaysian Ringgit	Singapore dollar	Brunei dollar

Top left: Coastal fishermen spreading their catch out to dry near the port of Puttalam on the west coast of Sri Lanka. Fish and rice are basic foodstuffs on Sri Lanka.

Right above: A torii, a Japanese Shinto monument. Positioned 160 meters (525 ft.) off the coast, it is part of the Miyajima Island Temple Shrine in the Bay of Hiroshima.

Lower left: The city of Amritsar in Punjab (India) is the religious capital of the Sikhs. The Golden Temple, the tallest Sikh shrine, towers over the Pool of Immortality, where Sikhs come to cleanse themselves.

tween the political and economic systems. Unable to participate in the achievements of the new economic system, the Chinese intellectual class, for example, is at a disadvantage. There are also islands of industrial development within the agricultural societies of Indonesia, the Indo-Chinese peninsula and India – with their huge ›dormant‹ reserves of manpower and vast mineral resources. Some of these countries are western-influenced, while others have an eastern, communist orientation. The communists have gained the upper hand in Vietnam, Laos and Cambodia. India is the most populous democracy on earth.

The Arab states pursue a course of industrialization based on their abundant oil reserves. Striking contrasts between intensively cultivated arable land and desert, between traditional craftsmanship and modern industry are characteristic features of the Near Eastern economies.

38 meters (125 feet) tall, the Heavenly Temple is one of the symbols of both Beijing and China. The most beautiful temple in China, it was first erected in 1420. A gilded sphere tops the three-tiered roof. The wooden temple was built without a single nail.

Indonesia	Philippines	Taiwan	China	Mongolian People's Republic	Democratic Peoples Republic of Korea	Republic of Korea	Japan
Republic of Indonesia	Republika Ňg Philipinas República de Filipinas	Chung-Hua Min-Kuo	Zhonghua Renmin Gonghe Guo	Bügd Nairamdach Mongol Ard Uls	Tschosson Mintschu tschu-i-Jinmin Konghwa-Guk	Dähan-Minkuk Han Kopk	Nihon-Koku Nippon
Jakarta	*Manila*	*Taipeh*	*Beijing*	*Ulaan baatar*	*P'yong yang*	*Seoul*	*Tokyo*
1,919,443 sqkm/ 741,097 sqm	300,000 sqkm/ 115,830 sqm	36,188 sqkm/ 13,972 sqm	9,560,779 sqkm/ 3,691,417 sqm	1,565,000 sqkm/ 604,247 sqm	120,538 sqkm/ 46,540 sqm	98,484 sqkm/ 38,025 sqm	372,313 sqkm/ 143,750 sqm
Pop.: 191,170,000	Pop.: 65,186,000	Pop.: 20,455,000	Pop.: 1,160,017,000	Pop.: 2,310,000	Pop.: 22,618,000	Pop.: 44,163,000	Pop.: 124,491,000
Bahasa Indonisia (Malay), (Indonesian regional languages)	Filipino, Cebuano, Tagalog, Ilocano, Panay Hiligayon, Bicol et al	Mandarin Chinese, Fukien (Amoy) dialects	Mandarin Chinese, (regional official languages)	Khalkah Mongolian	Korean	Korean	Japanese
Rupiah	Philippine Peso	New Taiwan dollar	Renminbi Yuan	Tugrik	Won	Won	Yen

AUSTRALIA OCEANIA

The smallest continent on earth is also the furthest removed from the others. Moreover, it is the only inhabited continent located entirely in the southern hemisphere – an island continent within the earth's watery hemisphere. This geographic separation from the other continents is responsible for the independent development of its unique flora and fauna.

One of the reasons for its late discovery is its antipodal location with respect to Europe. The »empty continent« is home to less than half of one per cent of the world population.
Due to its favorable climate, over three quarters of its some 16 million inhabitants live in the metropolitan areas of Australia's southeast.

Australia/Oceania
NATURAL ENVIRONMENT

Surrounded on three sides by »empty« oceans, this southernmost continent is 13,000 kilometers (8,078 miles) from South America and 9,000 kilometers (5,593 miles) from Africa. The Southeast Asian archipelago to the north, the only ›connection‹ to another continent, was an actual land bridge to Asia at an earlier stage of the earth's development. Australia owes its relatively short coastline (20,000 km/ 12,428 miles) to its compact form – the only indentation being the Carpentaria Gulf to the north. Off the eastern and northeastern shores of Australia there are coral reefs; the most important being the Great Barrier Reef off the eastern coast.

The average elevation of Australia is similar to that of Europe, but otherwise there are considerable topographic differences. The continent of wide open spaces, Australia is basically a vast tableland ringed almost entirely by raised rims bordering narrow coastal plains. The western Australian plateau covers over two thirds of the surface area, rising to elevations between 200 and 500 meters (650–1,640 feet) – punctuated only by individual worndown mountain ranges or by »mountain islands«, isolated mountains rising abruptly from the plains. The most striking of these mountain islands is Ayers Rock in the center of Australia, the eroded sandstone remains of a larger ancient geological formation.

The central Australian lowland surrounds the salt-flat-ringed depression of Lake Eyre at 12 m (39 ft.) below sea level. Eastern Australia and Tasmania are covered by the Australian cordillera, the Great Dividing Range. The only rugged formations in this low, eroded range are the Australian Alps (Mount Kosciusko, 2,228 m/ 7,310 feet). During the summer, the north of Australia is part of a

Page 115: The »road trains« on Australia's highways can be over 50 meters (164 ft.) long. Most of them haul livestock (sheep, cattle) to the coast.

Lower left: The scrub, or brushland, in the interior of this dry continent.

Top right: Coral reefs and islands in the Pacific.

Right: The Great Barrier Reef off the eastern coast of Australia is 2,000 kilometers (1,243 miles) long and 300 to 2,000 meters (984–6,652 ft.) wide. For a long time this coral barrier represented a major obstacle to the exploration of Australia.

zone with tropical rains. The resulting narrow strip of marshy mangrove along the northern coast borders on evergreen rain forest. Further south, this gives way to the so-called »scrub« or brushland, a dry savanna covered with thorny brushwood.

The southeasterly trade wind sheds abundant rain on the slopes of the mountains in the southeast. The typical plant of this subtropical forest, the eucalyptus tree, can grow to heights of up to

Top: Ayers Rock in the center of Australia. The largest monolith on earth, it is a sacred site to the Aborigines.

Center: The elements have carved this hollow out of Ayers Rock, which rises 350 meters (1,148 feet) above the plain with a circumference of 9,000 meters (29,527 feet).

Lower left: Devil's Marbles in the Australian interior. These ›bales of wool‹ are also products of erosion.

Lower right: A herd of sheep in the Australian Alps.

160 meters (525 feet). The only area with considerable winter precipitation is the extreme south-western tip of the continent. Here, the typical vegetation consists of sclerophyllous evergreens. The rest of the area between the slope of the cordillera and the west coast, however, is part of a dry region. Nevertheless, aside from the »dead heart« of the continent, there is hardly any actual sandy desert. The Australian fauna includes mammals of the lowest orders, such as marsupials (kangaroos, opossums) and the egg-laying, duckbilled platypus. The koala, a tree-climbing marsupial indigenous to eastern Australia, feeds on eucalyptus leaves. Some rivers contain lungfish, creatures which survive the dry season buried in sand, using their swimming bladders as a sort of lung to breathe with. Domestic animals did not exist before the arrival of the Europeans, yet recently the semi-wild dingo and the rabbit have begun to reproduce at an unpleasant rate.

The groups of Pacific islands to the north and east of the Australian continent are known as Oceania. Oceania is made up of an inner and an outer arc of islands – the inner one comprising New Zealand and Melanesia, whereas the outer one includes Micronesia and Polynesia. From a geological point of view, New Guinea, the second largest island in the world (2,100 km/1,305 miles long, up to 800 km/497 miles wide), is considered part of Australia because it rises from the same continental shelf. The remaining islands are composed of either vulcanic rock or coral limestone. They mark the edges of the submarine rises, which are staggered in wide, sweeping arcs across the South Pacific.

The most distinctive features of the twin islands of New Zealand are their young chains of mountains (Mount Cook, 3,764 m/ 12,349 feet), the active volcanoes on the North Island (Ruapehu, 2,797 m/9,176 feet), the deep fjords, and the U-shaped valleys.

Above: Tree ferns in New Zealand – one of numerous species which owe their unique evolution to the isolated conditions on this island.

Cultivated land (arable land, plantations and irrigated land)

Grassland of the temperate zone

Forest of the temperate zone

Tropical rain forest

Humid savannah (open eucalyptus forests in Australia)

Dry savannah

Scrub

Semi-desert and desert

Rock, snow and ice areas of mountain regions

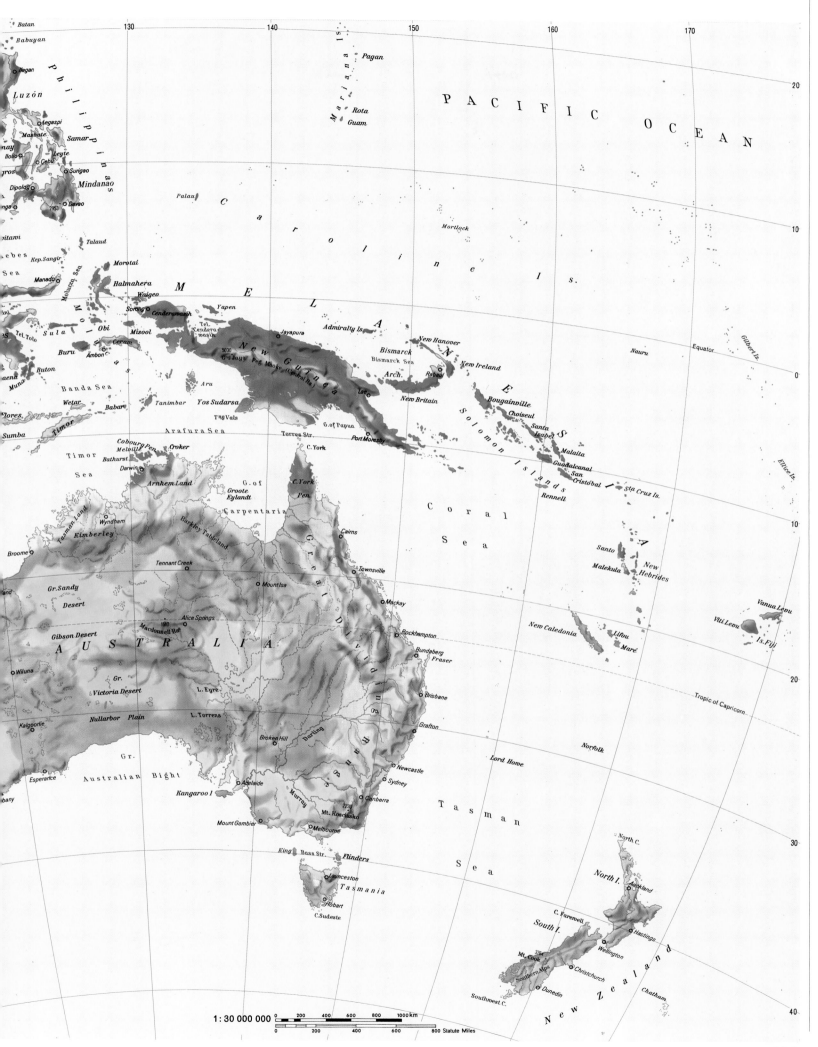

PACIFIC OCEAN

Batan
Babuyan

Ilagan
Luzón
Legaspi
Masbate
Samar
Leyte
Iloilo
Cebu
gros
Surigao
Dipolog
Mindanao
Davao
2953

Pagan

Mariana Is.

Rota
Guam

Mortlock

tawi
Kep.Sangir
Talaud

ebes
Morotai

Sea

Manado
Molucca Sea
Halmahera

M E L

Palau

C a r o l i n e   I s.

Waigeo
Sorong
Cenderawasih
Yapen
Admiralty Is.

Sula
Obi
Misool
Tel.Cenderawasih

Buru
Ceram
3030
Jayapura
New Guinea
Bismarck
New Hanover
Nauru

Equator

Ambon
G.Jaya
Peg.Maoke (Central ha)
Bismarck Sea
New Ireland

aena
Banda Sea
Aru
Lae
Rabaul

Muna
Buton
Arch.

Wetar
Tanimbar
Yos Sudarsa
New Britain
Bougainville

ores
Babar
Tng Vals
G.of Papua
Choiseul

Sumba
Timor
Arafura Sea
Torres Str.
Port Moresby
Santa Isabel

Gilbert Is.

Ellice Is.

Timor
Cobourg Pen.
Croker
C.York
Malaita

Sea
Melville
Bathurst
Groote
C.York
Guadalcanal
San Cristóbal
Sta Cruz Is.

Darwin
Eylandt
Pen.
Rennell

Arnhem Land
G.of
Carpentaria

C o r a l

Tasman Land
Wyndham
Kimberley
Barkley Tableland
Cairns

Broome
Townsville
Santo
Malekula
New Hebrides

Gr.Sandy Desert
Tennant Creek
Mount Isa

Sea

Vanua Levu

Mackay
Viti Levu
Alice Springs
Is.Fiji
Gibson Desert
Macdonnell Ra.
1990
Rockhampton
New Caledonia
Lifou
Maré

A U S T R A L I A
Bundaberg
Fraser

Wiluna
Gr.
Victoria Desert
L.Eyre
Brisbane

Tropic of Capricorn

Kalgoorlie
Nullarbor Plain
L.Torrens
Grafton
Norfolk

Gr.
Broken Hill
Darling
Lord Howe

Esperance
Australian Bight
Newcastle
bany
Adelaide
Sydney

T a s m a n

Kangaroo I
Murray
Canberra
Mount Gambier
Mt. Kosciusko
2230

Melbourne

S e a

North C.

King
Bass Str.
Flinders

Launceston
North I.
Auckland

Tasmania

Hobart
C.Sudeste
C.Farewell
South I.
Hastings

Mt.Cook
Wellington
3764

1:30 000 000
Christchurch

Southern Alps
Dunedin
Southwest C.
Chatham

0   200   400   600   800   1000 km
0   200   400   600   800 Statute Miles

N e w   Z e a l a n d

119

Australia/Oceania
PEOPLE AND CULTURE

Australia was not discovered and opened up to colonization until quite late, in the early 17th century. Aside from being extremely far from Europe, in the era of seafaring exploration, Australia's largely inaccessible coastline posed a major obstacle.

Prior to its invasion by whites, the vast continent was populated solely by Native Australians, today generally called »Aborigines«. At the time of their ›discovery‹, they still lived in the manner of stone-age hunters and gatherers, equipped with a simple array of implements (spear, boomerang, bone and stone tools). After a long period of persecution had finally reduced their population to around 7,000, they were assigned reservations in the arid interior. In the meantime, their numbers have increased to 50,000, or 160,000 including those of mixed ancestry.

Today Australia is a continent populated mostly by whites with strict immigration laws designed to make sure it remains that way. The Briton James Cook was the first white to set foot on this southern continent. Subsequently the British used the remote island continent for a while as a penal colony. In the middle of the 19th century the discovery of gold near Coolgardie and Kalgoorlie brought droves of settlers to the country. When the pay dirt proved to be poorer than expected, many a prospector settled down as a farmer. Finally one began to discover the continent's economic potential. Within a few decades the population grew from one to over ten million. Around 95 per cent of the inhabitants are Australians of British ancestry, a fifth of the population was born abroad – an indication that Australia still draws a large number of immigrants. In 1988 the white population celebrated the 200th anniversary of the first European settlement in Australia – despite protests from the Aborigines. Today the Commonwealth of Australia, comprising six states and

Australia	New Zealand	Papua New Guinea	Vanuatu	Fiji	Tonga	Samoa	Tuvalu
The Commonwealth of Australia	New Zealand	Papua New Guinea	Republic of Vanuatu République de Vanuatu	Fiji Matanitu Ko Viti	Kingdom of Tonga Pule' anga Tonga	Malotutuo' atasi o Samoa i Sisifo	Tuvalu
Canberra	*Wellington*	*Port Moresby*	*Port Vila*	*Suva*	*Nuku' alofa*	*Apia*	*Vaiaku*
7,686,420 sqkm/ 2,967,727 sqm	269,063 sqkm/ 103,885 sqm	461,691 sqkm/ 178,259 sqm	14,763 sqkm 5,700 sqm	18,272 sqkm/ 7,055 sqm	699 sqkm/ 270 sqm	2842 sqkm/ 1,097 sqm	24,6 sqkm/ 9,5 sqm
Pop.: 17,596,000	Pop.: 3,455,000	Pop.: 4,056,000	Pop.: 157,000	Pop.: 739,000	Pop.: 97,000	Pop.: 158,000	Pop.: 12,000
English	English, Maori	English, Melanesian Pidgin, various Papua-languages	Bislama, English, French	English, Fiji, Hindi	Tonga, English	Samoan, English	Tuvalu
Australian dollar	New Zealand dollar	Kina	Vanuatu franc, Australian dollar	Fiji dollar	Pa'anga	Tala	Australian dollar

two territories, is still a constitutional monarchy and part of the British Commonwealth – with the English Queen as chief-of-state. The seat of government is Canberra. Founded in 1927, the city is purely an administrative center. Five sixths of Australia's inhabitants live within the narrow fringe along the southwestern and southeastern coasts – the areas where the first whites settled. The vast interior, on the other hand, is almost entirely uninhabited.

Due to the arid climate, large portions of the continent can only be used for grazing sheep. As the basis for its wool production and meat exports, however, sheep breeding brought the country considerable wealth until a few decades ago. »Australia rides to prosperity on the back of a sheep,« was a frequently quoted slogan. As one approaches the moister edges of the continent, sheep farms give way to cattle ranches.

The main areas for cultivating wheat, fruit, and other agricultural products are in the southeast and southwest where land has been made arable through irrigation. The most important irrigation project was carried out in the Australian Alps. The purpose of the Snowy Mountains Scheme was to rechannel unused water flowing off the damp east side of the range to the dry west side.

Although Australia still produces considerable amounts of wool and other animal products for the world market, the importance of agricultural products as export items has been dwindling ever since the discovery of Australia's rich mineral deposits. Several mountains of ore are currently being stripped in open-pit mining

Top left: In the dry interior, reservations were set up for the Aborigines, the original inhabitants of Australia. Many of them find work on cattle ranches.

Lower left: The Polynesian inhabitants of Samoa, a group of islands in the Pacific, raise coconuts (copra) as their staple commodity.

Top center: Most Australians live in their own homes in vast housing areas in the southeast of the continent. The moving of entire homes is one expression of the population's high mobility.

Center: This geothermal power station on New Zealand harnesses the forces at work in the bowels of the earth – steaming evidence of volcanic, tectonic and thermal activity.

Right: This view of Sydney shows the modern opera building erected at the entrance to the harbor. Its principal architectural elements symbolize the hulls of ships.

Solomon Islands	Kiribati	Nauru
Solomon Islands	Republic of Kiribati	Republic of Nauru Naoero
Honiara	*Tarawan (Bairiki)*	*Yaren*
28,446 sqkm/ 10,983 sqm	886 sqkm/ 342 sqm	21,3 sqkm/ 8,2 sqm
Pop.: 342,000	Pop.: 74,000	Pop.: 10,000
English, Pidgin, (Polynesian and Melanesian dialects)	Kiribati (Gilbertese), English	Nauruan, English
Solomon dollar	Australian dollar, Kiribati	Australian dollar

121

operations in the Kimberley District in the northwest.

Initially, the textile industry and the food, beverage and tobacco industries (mills, canning) played a major role, but for some time heavy industry, processing plants, and the consumer goods industry have been gaining importance. The latter industries are concentrated in the metropolitan regions around Sydney, Melbourne and Adelaide.

New Zealand is one of the major exporters of agricultural products for the world market. Its inhabitants are almost entirely of English, Scotch or Irish ancestry. In addition, there are around 300,000 Aborigines. Some 80 percent of the New Zealand population lives in the cities. Whereas the western portion of New Guinea is under the political jurisdiction of Indonesia, the eastern section, Papua New Guinea is independent. The island is inhabited by pygmy tribes and by the dark-skinned Papua.

In 1959 Hawaii, the most important group of islands in Micronesia and Polynesia, became the 50th state of the USA. Three quarters of the population (totalling around one million, mainly Polynesian, inhabitants) live in the capital city, Honolulu.

Huge plantations – mainly sugar cane, coffee and pineapple – take advantage of the fertile, weathered soil of the mightiest volcanoes in the world – rising from a depth of 5,000 meters (16,404 feet) below sea level to an elevation of 4,000 meters (13,123 feet). Hawaii also flourishes on its revenues from tourism and as a major naval base.

Top: Native Australian rock paintings inspire the bark paintings of contemporary Aborigine artists, in which they represent episodes from their tribal history.

Below: Coober Pedy in Southern Australia, where opals were first found in 1915. To escape from the unbearable heat many of the 4,000 local inhabitants live in underground dwellings.

Islands under United States Trusteeship

Palau	Micronesia	Marshall Islands
Republic of Palau	Federated States of Micronesia	Republic of the Marshall Islands
Koror	*Kolonia*	*Uliga*
458 sqkm/ 177 sqm	720,6 sqkm/ 278 sqm	181 sqkm/ 70 sqm
Pop.: 15,122	Pop.: 105,000	Pop.: 48,000
English, Micronesian dialects	English, Micronesian dialects	English, Micronesian dialects
US dollar	US dollar	US dollar

AFRICA

In contrast to Eurasia with its complex contours, Africa is often called a »giant torso without limbs«. The second largest continent on earth, it covers a fifth of the entire land mass – but is inhabited by only a tenth of the world population. This »torrid continent without winters« lies almost entirely within the Tropics. The largest desert on earth, the Sahara, separates »White Africa«, the oriental Islam-influenced north, from »Black Africa« in the south. Nearly all the 52 sovereign African states are considered developing countries. The exception in every respect is South Africa, where the Apartheid rule of a white minority had, until recently, excluded the black majority from government.

Africa
NATURAL ENVIRONMENT

Africa has the shape of a trapezium to the north resting on an upside-down triangle to the south – with the equator marking the dividing line between them. The continent extends 8,000 kilometers (4,971 miles) from the north to the south and 7,300 kilometers (4,536 miles) from east to west. Not counting Madagascar, islands and peninsulas make up only two per cent of the total area, so that the largely unindented coastline measures only about 30,000 kilometers (18,642 miles).

The Suez Canal severs the land bridge between Africa and Asia at its narrowest point and is considered the demarcation line between the two continents. At its nearest point, the Straights of Gibraltar, Africa is only 14 kilometers (8,7 miles) from Europe.

With the exception of the young ridges at the very northern and southern ends of the continent, it is composed almost entirely of primitive rock strata. Thus, the continent not only lacks the long chains of mountains which normally create meteorological and cultural barriers, but also sizable lowlands. Instead, the topography comprises extensive, gently undulating basins – such as the Western Sahara basin, the had, Zaire and Kalahari basins – interrupted by dividing rises and sweeping highlands. The rises ringing the entire continent reduce the navigability of most rivers. Where they overcome rises like the Asande and the Lunda rises, the rivers often form waterfalls – the most famous being the Victoria Falls on the Sambesi with a drop of 120 meters (394 feet).

The chains of volcanoes in East Africa are part of the extensive East African/Syrian system of rifts and faults. The highest point in Africa is the Kilimanjaro rising to 5,895 meters (19,341 feet). Lying in the recess of a rift valley, Lake Tanganyika reaches a depth of 1,435 meters (4,708 feet). The Ethiopian highland (Ras Daschan

4,620 m/15,157 feet) with its deep gorges is also largely of volcanic origin. A line drawn from Port Sudan on the Red Sea to Luanda on the Atlantic Ocean roughly divides the continent into ›Low Africa‹ to the north and ›High Africa‹ to the south. Bisected virtually in the middle by the equator, Africa comprises an

Page 123: These two Bantus illustrate what is meant by »world-wide Europeanization«.

Top left: The baobab or monkey-bread tree is a typical savanna plant. It loses its leaves in the summer. The natives cook its young leaves as a vegetable and make oil from its seeds.

Lower left: These basalt columns, once the chimney fillings of active volcanoes, jut up from the Tassili Highland – the natural environment of the Tuareg.

Top : The approaching front of a Saharan sandstorm.

Center: Once covered with tropical mountain forest, these steep slopes have been cleared and cultivated by mountain farmers in eastern Zaire.

Far right: Deep canyons gouged out of the East African highland plateau.

Lower right: A sailboat near Assuan on the Nile, the main artery of Egypt.

almost archetypal sucession of climatic and vegetation zones. The equatorial areas typically have two rainy seasons, spring and autumn – in addition to precipitation in other months – with high humidity and little variation in average monthly temperatures. Thus, one refers to the climate in the ever-humid equatorial tropics as being diurnal. The characteristic regional vegetation is tropical rain forest with its abundance of species. To the north and to the south, this zone borders on the tropics characterized by periodical changes in humidity: with a marked dry season following a distinct period of (northern or southern) summer rains. Beyond the tropical rain forest, there are the well-watered savannas, giving way to dry savannas, followed by thorny savannas. The wildlife preserves – famous for their big game (antilopes, zebras, giraffes, elephants, rhinoceros, lions, etc.), lie in the East African savannas. In the region of the

Tropics, there are also large arid areas, including the Kalahari salt and clay basins in South Africa and, in the north, the largest desert on earth: the Sahara. The Namib, a desert along the coast of southwestern Africa, is caused by offshore trade winds and the cold upward currents from the Benguela Stream.

A third of the African continent is covered by desert-like terrain – yet even in the Sahara itself, no more than about one fifth of the area is actual sandy desert. Predominately one finds a gravel and rock desert etched with deep dry valleys, or wadis, produced during earlier pluvial periods. Oases are found either where ground water surfaces, or where exotic rivers bring in water from rainier regions.

Top: Smoke from fire-clearing in the Zaire Basin in Central Africa. More and more tropical rain forest goes up in flames to create arable land where tropical fruits can be grown for personal consumption and trade – temporarily relieving the strain of a growing population.

Bottom: The East African savanna is the only remaining animal paradise on earth. Extensively protected, major parts serve as national parks.
From left to right: Elephants, the largest mammals on earth; a bufallo herd at a watering hole; long-nosed rhinoceros, hunted for the medicinal powder from their horns and thus threatened with extinction; lions; a leopard; and zebras.

Cultivated land (arable land, plantations, oasis and irrigated land)

Grassland of the temperate zone and of the tropical highlands

Forest of the temperate zone and of the tropical higlands

Tropical rain forest

Humid savannah

Dry tropical forest (Miambo) and dry sahannah

Steppe

Semi-desert and desert

1 : 30 000 000

0   200   400   600   800   1000 km

0   200   400   600   800 Statute Miles

Africa
PEOPLE AND CULTURE

2,000 kilometers (1,243 miles) wide, the hostile range of the Sahara Desert acts as a natural barrier, separating White Africa in the north from Black Africa to the south. The population to the north of this region is made up of light-skinned peoples – predominately Hamites and Arabs – belonging to the large Caucasian race, whereas the South is populated by Negro peoples. The Ethiopians of Eastern Africa, on the other hand, are unique in that they bear traits of both these major races. Then there are the few remaining survivors of the original African native peoples: the pygmy tribes of the Zaire (Congo) basin, and the bushmen of the South African Kalahari. The Hamite and Negro races have been mingling ever since the Hamites began moving south into the northern fringe of Black Africa, conquering the Negro population. The resulting tribes, the cattle-breeding Fulbe (Fulah) and the trade-oriented Hausa built mighty empires long before the arrival of the Europeans.

Distinguishing according to language, there are two major groups of black-skinned Africans: Sudanese Negros and Bantu Negros. Each individual African belongs to one of many nations or tribes – each having their own characteristic forms of industry and commerce, types of settlement, language and culture, customs and religion. Generally speaking, the animistic religions are on the wane, whereas Islam – considered to be free of any association with the former colonial rulers – continues its triumphal sweep through the Sahel Zone south of the Sahara. Based on its black-majority population, South Africa is also considered a part of Black Africa – even though until recently a white minority controlled the political and economic system.

Until about 500 years ago, Europeans thought of Africa as the »Dark Continent« – having explored only the narrow strip along the Mediterranean coast. They did not reach the Cape of Good Hope until 1487. Operating from support bases along the coast, the Europeans then began to extend their influence into the hinterland. Even today, several sections of the West African coast still bear the names of the fundamental commodities which once lured the colonial powers: the Pepper, Ivory, Gold and Slave Coasts. After the discovery of the Americas, slave labor was needed there to work the fields. The resulting slave hunts in Black Africa lasted well into the middle of the 19th century. Entire regions were brutally depopulated. The Portuguese and Spanish, but above all the English, French and Belgians and, for a while, the Germans and Ital-

Morocco	Algeria	Tunesia	Libya	Egypt	Sudan	Ethiopia	Eritrea
Al Mamlakah al Maghrebia	Rép. Algérienne Démocratique et Populaire El Dschamhurija el Dschasarija el demokratija escha'abija	El Dschumhuri ja et Tunusija République Tunisienne	Al-Jamahiriyah Al-Arabiya Al-Libya Al-Shabiya Al-Ishtirakiya	El Dschumhurija Misr El Arabija	El Dchumhurijat ed Demokratijat es Sudan Jamhuriyat as Sudan Al Demokratia	Ye Ethiopia Hizebawi Democraciyawi Republic	Eritrea
Rabat	*Algiers*	*Tunis*	*Tripoli*	*Cairo*	*Khartoum*	*Addis Ababa*	*Asmara*
458,730 sqkm/ 177,116 sqm	2,381,741 sqkm/ 919,590 sqm	164,150 sqkm/ 63,378 sqm	1,759,540 sqkm/ 679,358 sqm	1,001,449 sqkm/ 386,660 sqm	2,505,813 sqkm/ 967,494 sqm	1,221,900 sqkm/ 471,776 sqm	124,000 sqkm/ 47,876 sqm
Pop.: 26,318,000	Pop.: 26,346,000	Pop.: 8,401,000	Pop.: 4,875,000	Pop.: 54,842,000	Pop.: 26,656,000	Pop.: 52,981,000	Pop.: 3,500,000
Arabic, Berber dialects, French, Spanish	Arabic, French, Berber dialects	Arabic, French, Tunesian (Arabic dialect)	Arabic, Berber dialects	Arabic, (English, French)	Arabic, English, Hamitic, Nilotic and Sudanic languages	Amharic, English, Italian, ca. 50 additional languages	Tigrinya, Arabic, English)
Dirham	Algerian dinar	Tunesian dinar	Libyan dinar	Egyptian pound	Sudanese pound	Birr	Birr

Far left: Massai women with their typical jewelry and clothing. The huts are built by flinging cow dung onto frames of interwoven branches and twigs.

Top: A tannery in Fez (Morocco). The animal hides are tanned by dipping them in the various vats filled with diluted vegetable tanning agents.

Center: A tradition since the Middle Ages – the caravan of a Tuareg tribe transports salt from the north of Niger, across the Ténéré desert, to the south of the country.

Right: A native village, or kral, in Uganda.

ians, divided up Africa with a ruler – not taking into consideration the tribal boundaries. These arbitrary borders have been maintained to this day.

Up to 1950 the only independent countries were Liberia and Ethiopia. In the years from 1956 to 1961, the »African era« reached its climax as 30 countries gained their independence. Today Africa has more UN members than any other continent. Seeking combined solutions to their political and economic difficulties, most African states have joined the »Organization for African Unity« (OAU).

The African national borders of today – and thus the mixture of peoples in each country – are a legacy of the colonial era. As a result, many countries are fraught with deeply-rooted tribal conflicts. Many of these nations are headed by military regimes or are ruled by a single party.

European influence and the resulting spread of western civilization gave rise to radical changes and has set off tremendous upheavals in the economy and medical care, as well as in social and cultural matters. Efforts to improve the infrastructure – designed, as they were, mainly to promote the export of mining and plantation products to European industrial countries – were originally focussed on the coastal regions – thus leaving the interiors of the various countries undeveloped. In a continent of this tremendous size, the lack of infrastructure facilities, particularly the lack of roads, is an acute problem. The slums of the modern cities are inhabited by a new urban proletariat: masses living outside the traditional forms of tribal order without education or employment. The search for work caused huge streams of migrant workers to pour into the cities – losing those original tribal ties which constitute both a network of mutual social security as well as a family defence alliance. Aside from the ports, the main population magnets are industrial regions like the Copper Belt in Zambia and Zimbabwe, Katanga/Shaba in Zaire, or the industrial

Djibouti	Cape Verde	Mauretania	Senegal	The Gambia
République de Djibouti	República de Cabo Verde	République Islamique de Mauritanie El Dschumhurija el Muslimija el Mauretanija	République du Sénégal	Repúblic of the Gambia
Djibouti	Praia	Nouakchott	Dakar	Banjul (Bathurst)
22,000 sqkm/ 8,494 sqm	4,033 sqkm/ 1,557 sqm	1,030,700 sqkm/ 397,953 sqm	196,192 sqkm/ 75,750 sqm	11,295 sqkm/ 4,361 sqm
Pop.: 467,000	Pop.: 384,000	Pop.: 2,143,000	Pop.: 7,736,000	Pop.: 908,000
French, Arabic, Kushitic languages (of the Afar and Issa tribes)	Portuguese, Crioulo	Arabic, French, (Hassanya, Ful,Berber and Sudanic languages)	French, Wolof, (Sudanic languages)	English, Mandinka, Wolof, Ful, Arabic
Djibouti franc	Cape Verde escudo	Ouguiya	CFA-Franc	Dalasi

129

centers in the Republic of South Africa. The transition from a self-reliant subsistence economy to a free market economy and the attendant social revolution have caused the disintegration of the traditional tribal society. With a small educated leadership, on the one hand, and an unstructured proletarian mass, on the other, what is largely missing is a middle class. There is a lack of skilled labor in agriculture, industry and the administration. Thus, the fight against illiteracy is one of the major goals in all African coun-tries. The high birth rates characteristic of all African states, moreover, literally eat up any increase in productivity.

Compared with the two other major developing regions, Latin America and Southern Asia, Africa is at the lowest level of economic development.

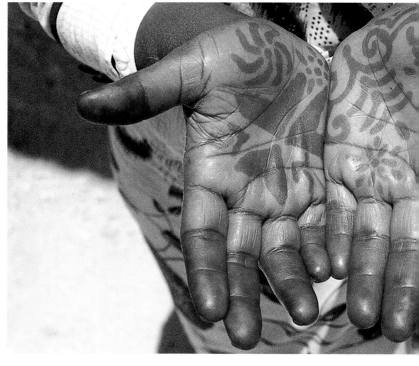

Mali	**Burkina Faso (Upper Volta)**	**Niger**	**Chad**	**Guinea-Bissau**	**Guinea**	**Sierra Leone**	**Liberia**
République du Mali	Burkina Faso	République du Niger	République du Tschad Djoumhourîyat Tschâd	República da Guiné-Bissau	République de Guinée	Republic of Sierra Leone	Republic of Liberia
Bamako	Ougadougou	Niamey	N'djamena	Bissau	Conakry	Freetown	Monrovia
1,240,142 sqkm/ 478,819 sqm	274,200 sqkm/ 105,869 sqm	1,267,000 sqkm/ 489,189 sqm	1,284,000 sqkm/ 495,752 sqm	36,125 sqkm/ 13,948 sqm	245,857 sqkm/ 94,925 sqm	71,740 sqkm/ 27,699 sqm	111,369 sqkm/ 43,000 sqm
Pop.: 9,818,000	Pop.: 9,513,000	Pop.: 8,252,000	Pop.: 5,846,000	Pop.: 1,006,000	Pop.: 6,116,000	Pop.: 4,376,000	Pop.: 2,751,000
French, Bambara, Songhai Djerma, Arabich, Ful	French, Volta semi Bantu languages, Foulani, western sudanic languages	French, Songhai Djerma, Arabic dialects, Foulani, Hausa, Tamashagh	French, Arabic, Chad-Arabic	Portuguese, Sudanic languages	French, Mandinka languages, Foulani	English, Sudanic languages, Krio	English, Mande, Kru, Golla, Kpelle
CFA franc	CFA franc	CFA franc	CFA franc	Guinea peso	Guinea-Franc	Leone	Liberian dollar

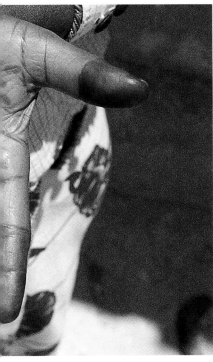

Far left: This Massai woman is wearing typical glass beaded jewelry. The Massai, a nomadic cattle-herding people, live in the savannas of Kenya and Tanzania.

Top: A view out over the roofs of Cairo. On top of its crippling traffic and housing problems, the Egyptian capital is plagued by extreme environmental pollution.

Center: An ancient African cosmetic application: henna-painted hands.

Right: The harvesting of long-fibred sisal leaves on a plantation in East Africa.

Ivory Coast	**Ghana**	**Togo**	**Benin**	**Nigeria**	**Cameroon**	**Gabon**	**Congo**
République de Côte d'Ivoire	Republic of Ghana	République Togolaise	République Populaire du Bénin	Federal Republic of Nigeria	République du Cameroun Republic of Cameroon	République Gabonaise	République Populaire du Congo
Abidjan	*Accra*	*Lomé*	*Porto-Novo*	*Lagos*	*Yaoundé*	*Libreville*	*Brazzaville*
322,463 sqkm/ 124,503 sqm	238,537 sqkm/ 92,099 sqm	56,785 sqkm/ 21,925 sqm	112,622 sqkm/ 43,483 sqm	923,768 sqkm/ 356,667 sqm	475,442 sqkm/ 183,568 sqm	267,667 sqkm/ 103,346 sqm	342,000 sqkm/ 132,046 sqm
Pop.: 12,910,000	Pop.: 15,959,000	Pop.: 3,763,000	Pop.: 4,918,000	Pop.: 115,664,000	Pop.: 12,198,000	Pop.: 1,237,000	Pop.: 2,368,000
French, Kwa	English, Twi, Fante, Ga, Ewe, Foulani and other west African languages	French, (native languages and dialects)	French, (and over 60 African dialects)	English, Sudanic and Bantu languages, (in the North; Foulani and Hausa))	French, English, Bantu,Semi-Bantu, Sudanic languages	French, Bantu languages	French, Lingala Kikongo, Teke, Sanga, Ubangi
CFA franc	Cedi	CFA franc	CFA franc	Naira	CFA franc	CFA franc	CFA franc

Left: The rich palette of African peoples ranges from the light-skinned Arabs in the North to ebony-skinned Negros in Black Africa. The continent also abounds with languages and cultures, religions, customs and traditions; and supports a wide variety of archetypal forms of industry and commerce. – Self-adornment is one of the human being's primal instincts.

Equatorial Guinea

República de Guinea Ecuatorial

Malabo

28,051 sqkm/ 10,830 sqm

Pop.: 369,000

Spanish, Bubi, Fang

CFA franc

São Tomé and Principe

República Democrática de São Tomé e Principe

São Tomé

964 sqkm/ 372 sqm

Pop.: 124,000

Potuguese, Crioulo

Dobra

Central African Republic

République Centralafricaine

Bangui

622,984 sqkm/ 240,534 sqm

Pop.: 3,173,000

French, Sangho, Bantu and Sudanic languages

CFA franc

Zaire

République du Zaïre

Kinshasa

2,345,409 sqkm/ 905,562 sqm

Pop.: 39,882,000

French, Tshiluba, Kikongo, Lingala, Suaheli

Zaïre

Rwanda

Republica y'u Rwanda République Rwandaise

Kigali

26,338 sqkm/ 10,169 sqm

Pop.: 7,526,000

French, Kinyarwanda, Kiswahili

Rwanda franc

Burundi

Republika y'Uburundi République du Burundi

Bujumbura

27,834 sqkm/ 10,747 sqm

Pop.: 5,823,000

Kirundi, French, Kiswahili

Burundi franc

Tanzania

United Republic of Tanzania Jamhuriya Mwungano wa Tanzania

Dar es Salaam

945,087 sqkm/ 364,898 sqm

Pop.: 27,829,000

Swahili, English, Bantu and Hamitic languages

Tanzania franc

Uganda

Republic of Uganda

Kampala

236,036 sqkm/ 91,133 sqm

Pop.: 18,674,000

English, Kiswahili,

Uganda shilling

Kenya

Republic of Kenya Dschamhuri ja Kenia

Nairobi

582,646 sqkm/ 224,960 sqm

Pop.: 25,230,000

Swahili, English, languages of the Bantu and Nilotic tribes

Kenya shilling

Somalia

Al-Jumhouriya As Somaliya Al-Domocradia

Mogadishu

637,657 sqkm/ 246,199 sqm

Pop.: 9,204,000

Somali, Arabic, English, Italian

Somalia shilling

Seychelles

Republic of Seychelles République des Seychelles

Victoria

280 sqkm/ 108 sqm

Pop.: 72,000

Creole, English, French

Seychelles rupee

Comores

Republique fédérale et islamique des Comores

Moroni

1,862 sqkm/ 719 sqm

Pop.: 585,000

French, Comoran Arabic

Comoran franc

Madagascar

Repoblika Demokratika Malagasy République Démocratique de Madagascar

Antananarivo

587,041 sqkm/ 226,657 sqm

Pop.: 12,827,000

French, Malagasy, (native idioms like Howa)

Madagascar franc

Mauritius

Mauritius

Port Louis

2,045 sqkm/ 790 sqm

Pop.: 1,098,000

English, Creole, French, East Indian languages

Mauritius rupee

Angola

República Popular de Angola

Luanda

1,246,700 sqkm/ 481,351 sqm

Pop.: 9,888,000

Portuguese, Bantu languages

Kwanza

Zambia

Republic of Zambia

Lusaka

752,614 sqkm/ 290,584 sqm

Pop.: 8,638,000

English, Bantu languages

Kwacha

Malaŵi

Republic of Mala^wi

Lilongwe

118,484 sqkm/ 45,747 sqm

Pop.: 10,356,000

English, Chichewa, Nyanja, Chitumbuca, Chiyao

Malaŵi Kwacha

Moçambique

República Popular de Moçambique

Maputo

799,380 sqkm/ 308,641 sqm

Pop.: 14,872,000

Potuguese, Bantu languages

Metical

Botswana

Republic of Botswana

Gaborone

600,372 sqkm/ 231,804 sqm

Pop.: 1,313,000

Setswana, Bantu languages, English

Pula

Zimbabwe

Republic of Zimbabwe

Harare

390,622 sqkm/ 150,819 sqm

Pop.: 10,583,000

English, Bantu languages

Simbabwe dollar

South Africa

Republic of South Africa

Pretoria

1,221,037 sqkm/ 471,442 sqm

Pop.: 39,818,000

Afrikaans, English, Bantu languages, East Indian languages

Rand

Swaziland

Umbuso we Swantini Ngwane

Mbabane

17,364 sqkm/ 6,704 sqm

Pop.: 792,000

Si-Swati (Isi-Zulu), English

Lilangeni

Lesotho

Kingdom of Lesotho Muso oa Lesotho

Maseru

30,335 sqkm/ 11,712 sqm

Pop.: 1,836,000

Southern Sotho, English

Maloti

Namibia

Republic of Namibia

Windhuk

823,168 sqkm/ 317,825 sqm

Pop.: 1,534,000

Afrikaans, English, German, Bantu languages

NORTH AND CENTRAL AMERICA

The continents of the Americas stretch 16,000 kilometers (9,942 miles) from north to south. Together they constitute the world's second largest land mass (40 million square kilometers/15,4 million square miles). The two continents are connected by the narrow land bridge of Central America, as well as semi-connected by the ›bridge piles‹ of the West Indian Islands.

The natural demarcation line between North and South America is the Isthmus of Panama.
Canada, the second largest country in the world, and the USA, the leading economic power, together make up the Anglo-American portion of the »New World«. Latin America, the Iberian-influenced part begins at the northern border of Mexico.

North and Central America
NATURAL ENVIRONMENT

With islands and peninsulas making up a quarter of its surface area, this continent has the longest coastal circumference of any continent: 75,000 kilometers (46,600 miles). Greenland is also considered part of this northern land mass. At the Bering Straight there are only 92 kilometers (57 miles) separating North America from Asia. The continent stretches 6,000 kilometers (3,728 miles) from Alaska in the west to Novia Scotia in the east and measures 8,700 kilometers (5,406 miles) from north to south.

Mountain ranges basically divide the continent meridionally into three parts: the Atlantic maritime region to the east of the low Appalachian Mountains, a central lowland including the Canadian Shield in the middle, with the high mountain region of the western cordillera to the west.

The Appalachians, a soft, rolling range of parallel ridges, rise to their highest point at Mount Mitchell (2,037 m/6,683 feet). The slopes are still largely covered with their original vegetation of mixed and summer-green deciduous forest.

On the adjoining plains to the west, however, the natural flora has been largely decimated. The woodlands of this temperate zone were cleared by the early settlers who proceeded to till the inland plains. In Florida and on the coastal plain along the Gulf, parts of the subtropical moist forests and marshlands (Everglades) have been protected as national parks. The Mississippi, the third longest river in the world, drains the central lowland, before emptying into the Gulf of Mexico. The Cana-

dian Shield with the Hudson Bay in the middle is the tectonic keystone of North America. It gets its name from the shield-like bulge running around its edges. The glaciated valleys and fjords, terrain featuring smoothly rounded rockmasses, and the long chains of lateral moraines provide visible evidence that this region was once covered by glaciers. The string of lakes running along the rim of the shield starts at the

Great Lakes, the largest freshwater lakes in the world, and stretches up to Great Bear Lake in the far North. With the exception of the icy desert of the Arctic archipelago and the lichen and moss-covered tundra in the marshy permafrost areas, the North is covered by vast boreal coniferous forests. To this day, trappers and hunters continue to stalk the animals of these woodlands for their fur.

The Rocky Mountains (Mount McKinley, 6,193 m/20,320 feet), a young range of longitudinal ridges, make up the Continental Divide, the mighty watershed dividing the areas draining into the Pacific and the Atlantic Ocean. The twin chains of the Rockies are separated by vast elevated basins, such as the Colorado Plateau, the Great Basin and the Mexican highland. In the rain shadow of the Rockies, highland steppes and

even semi-deserts and deserts have evolved (Mojave Desert). Cutting their way through the mountains and highland plateaus of this range, rivers have created spectacular ravines, or canyons. Due to low precipitation, there are no major lakes, and except in Alaska, no major glaciers. The Mexican highland, bounded by a mighty string of volcanoes to the south, is typical cactus country. It was from here that these prickly

Page 133: To find an outlet, the Colorado River carved its way 1,800 meters (5,904 feet) deep through 350 kilometers /217 miles) of plateau, creating the Grand Canyon.

Top left: Calc-sinter terraces formed by the geysers in Yellowstone National Park.

Far left: Moose in Yellowstone National Park.

Left: Originally indigenous only to the Americas, the triumphant cactus has spread around the world.

Top: The Canyon de Chelly in Arizona (»arida zona«; Spanish = arid area).

Center: Alpine landscape in the Canadian Rocky Mountains.

Right: Redwood National Park in the Sierra Nevada. These giant Sequoia trees, which can grow to a height of 100 meters (329 feet), yield a fine-grained soft timber valued by the furniture industry.

plants began their successful proliferation around the world. Parallelling the coast and flanked by the Pacific Mountains, the long Californian valley marks the position of the earth-quake-prone San Andreas Fault. In fact, all of western North America makes up part of the circumpacific »Ring of Fire«. This was dramaticly demonstrated by the eruptions of Mount St. Helen (1980).

With its arching chains of mountains, its strings of volcanoes, and lowlands opening out onto the Caribbean, the Central American land bridge comprises highly varied topography within a small area. 4,000 kilometers (2,486 miles) long, the curved string of islands including the Greater Antilles (Cuba, Jamaica, Hispaniola, Puerto Rico), the Lesser Antilles and the Bahamas is partially of volcanic origin and partially evolved from karstified limestone tables or coral limestone deposits.

The Cayman Trench and the Puerto Rico Trench (-8,605 m/-28,232 ft), mark the Atlantic edge of Central America. The natural vegetation on the windward slopes consists of rain forests, whereas the leeward sides are covered with dry savanna. Both types of vegetation have been reduced through chop-and-burn clearing for plantations.

North America owes much of the temperateness of its climate to the meridional structure of its tectonic elements. Mountain ranges along the coasts limit the areas affected by oceanic influences. Well on into late spring, cold air sweeps in from the arctic north, reaching as far as the southern coast. In the summer, conversely, hot, damp air floods north from the Gulf of Mexico, spreading a blanket of unbearable humidity all the way up into Canada. Nothing stands in the way of tornadoes racing north. The cold Labrador Stream lowers temperatures as far south as the New York area, and the Hudson Bay functions like an ice cellar. The 100th meridian marks the beginning of an arid zone where rain crops fail to grow.

On the whole, North America's climate is more typically continental than Europe's.

Top: Mesas and spires in Bryce Canyon National Park. The splendid array of rugged forms was produced by the erosion of red clays and marl in this elevated, arid zone.

Left: Monument Valley in Arizona.

Lower right: With its 50-meter-(164 feet)-high steaming spout, Old Faithful is one of the largest geysirs in Yellowstone National Park.

Cultivated land (arable land, plantations, irrigated land)

Grassland and grassland farming

Forest of the temperate Zone

Tropical forest

Savannah

Steppe

Semi-desert, desert

Boreal forest

Tundra

Rock, snow and ice areas of mountain and polar regions

1:30 000 000

0 200 400 600 800 1000 km

0 200 400 600 800 Statute Miles

North and Central America
PEOPLE AND CULTURE

The ethnic diversity of its people makes North America a truly multicultural continent. This enormous land mass, which includes Central America, the United States, Canada, and the Caribbean islands is home to many different races and nationalities.

Not surprisingly, then, no one language or culture can be said to represent all the people living in North America. Spanish predominates in Central America, but Indian dialects are also used. The residents of the various Caribbean islands may use English, Spanish, French, or Creole. Although Canada and the United States are primarily English-speaking, millions of Canadians speak French and the number of non-English-speaking residents in the U.S. is growing.

The human history of North America by no means begins with the sighting of Newfoundland by the Viking Leif Ericsson in 1000 A.D., or the landing of the Italian Christopher Columbus on San Salvador in 1492. By the time the first European explorers arrived in the New World, the continent had been inhabited for thousands of years by various Indian tribes, each with its own history, territory, religion, and culture.

The first people to »discover« North America came from Asia by way of a now-vanished land bridge in the Bering Strait. Today's Native American Indians of Canada, the U.S., and Central America are descended from these ancient Paleoindians. The Eskimos of northernmost Canada, who still lead a semi-aboriginal way of life, are distinct from American Indians and closely re-

lated to the Mongolian peoples of eastern Asia.

In Mesoamerica, today called Central America, native Indian groups such as the Olmecs, the Mayans, the Toltecs, and the Aztecs developed agriculture and glyph writing; created intricate mathematical, astronomical, and calendrical systems; and built magnificent cities.

The exploration, conquest, and settlement of North America by white Europeans, beginning in the late 15th century, laid the groundwork for the ethnic mix of people inhabiting the continent today. Seeking new markets and new resources, the first colonists arrived from Spain, England, Holland, France, and Sweden.

The transplanted cultures of Europe brought new ideas, values, religions, agricultural methods, and technology to the New World. They also brought new viruses, which had a devastating effect on the in-

Top left: Farm amidst cornfields in Iowa. Located in the fertile heart of the American Midwest, Iowa is a leader in grain and livestock production.

Lower left: Historic Portsmouth, New Hampshire, the gateway to the New Hampshire and Maine, is a typical New England fishing community.

Top right: Virginia City (Nevada), once a center of commerce and of the livestock trade, is now a museum town.

Center: Lower Manhattan, New York City, as seen from the Hudson River. This part of the city is home to the most important financial center and stock market in the world. The 110-story twin towers of the World Trade Center are 427 meters (1,400 feet) high.

Far right: Jazz musicians entertain visitors on Bourbon Street, in the historic French Quarter of New Orleans (Louisiana), the birth place of Jazz.

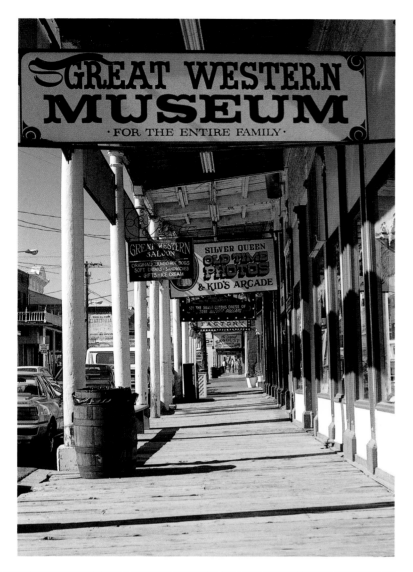

digenous population. Epidemics, and increasing waves of European settlers, displaced the native Amerindians from their ancient lands and ways of life.

In Central America, where the Spanish were concentrated, the conquered native cultures gradually became Hispanicized. The Spanish conquerors and their creole descendants formed the apex of a social and economic hierarchy that excluded Indians, mestizos and the Africans transported to work as slaves. The population of Central America and many of the Caribbean islands stems in large part from this mixture of Indian, Spanish, and African peoples.

There was less cultural assimilation between Indians and whites in the United States and Canada, where westward expansion by English, Dutch, and French colonists pushed the Native Americans from their traditional home-

lands to Indian reservations. As the U.S. grew, so grew its influx of immigrants, all of whom contributed to its multi-ethnic culture. Between 1815 and 1920 some 5.5 million Irish came to work in factories, construction, and as domestic help. The annexation of Texas, the southwest, and California also annexed many of the Spanish-speaking residents in those areas. Mexican-American vaqueros, the original cowboys, taught the newcomers how to rope, brand, and handle cattle. Mexicans served as an important work force in railroad construction, as did the Chinese, who began arriving in 1849. Chinese labor transformed farming in California from wheat to fruit, paving the way for an enormous agricultural industry built with the help of Japanese farmers. Protestant Germans and Scandinavians established towns and farming communities in the Midwest. Bur-

geoning Roman Catholic Italian enclaves within larger cities became known as »Little Italys.« Seeking asylum from ethnic persecution, Jews from Russia and Eastern Europe began to immigrate to the U.S. in the 1880s. Working primarily in the garment industry, German and Russian Jews in New York revolutionized the way clothes were made and worn.

Currently, about 10% of the total population of the United States is of African-American ancestry. In the early 17th century their ancestors were forcibly brought from Africa to work as slaves on sugar cane, cotton, and tobacco plantations in the West Indies and the southern U.S. Granted their freedom in 1863, many black Americans migrated from the south to the industrial cities of the north. Over the ensuing decades, and especially following important civil rights legislation of recent times, black Americans have made important contributions in many areas of U.S. society. The number of blacks elected to state, city, and federal political offices has grown steadily, as has recognition of their contributions to the arts.

The United States, with nearly 250 million people, is the most highly populated nation in North America today and also the most visible in terms of its worldwide influence. The continuing growth of non-Englisch-speaking residents in the U.S. – 14% of the nation now speaks a language other than English – represents a general trend. By 2056, according to current projections, the majority

Top left: From the eleventh to thirteenth centuries, the Anasazi, precolumbian Pueblo Indians, built these cliff dwellings into the sandstone rock (Mesa Verde, Colorado).

Left center: Changing of the guard at the Citadel, overlooking the historic Château Frontenac in Québec, Canada.

Lower left: The beautiful Golden Gate Bridge is one of the longest suspension bridges in the world (1,966 meters/ 6,450 feet). Symbolic of San Francisco, it connects the city with Marin County to the north.

of U.S. residents will no longer trace their ancestry to white Europe, but to Asia, the Hispanic world, and Africa.

Americans of German ancestry currently represent the largest of the 65 ancestry groups in the U.S. population, followed by Irish, English, African-American, and Italian. Asian-Americans and Chicanos (Mexican-Americans), who together represent 80% of all new immigrants, are the fastest-growing ethnic groups. Chicanos have visibly transformed regional culture in southern California, Texas, and the southwest. The Asian immigrant population of the U.S. tends to be concentrated in dense urban areas such as the »Chinatowns« of New York, San Francisco, and Los Angeles.

Canada, with an area larger than that of the United States, is much less densely populated than the U.S. and Central American countries. The settlement of New France, as Canada was originally called, began in 1604. By the mid-18th century its colonial population was almost entirely French, and French explorers and fur traders had penetrated beyond the Great Lakes and south along the Mississippi all the way to the Gulf of Mexico. French culture has strongly influenced not only Canada, but portions of the southern U.S. as well. After England gained control of New France in 1763, thousands of colonists from the British Isles and the British colonies in America emigrated to the British Dominion of Canada. Today Canada is an independent nation, but its ten pro-

Top center: An Indian woman working her loom in Mexico City. She sells her hand-crafted products to tourists.

Center: With its splendid mosaic façades, the Central Library in Mexico City is the symbol of the university.

Top right: A show in Disneyland, the fantasy and adventure park for young and old built in 1955. The film producer Walt Disney (1901-1966) invented Mickey Mouse and Donald Duck.

Lower right: School children typically reflect the mosaic of people and cultures that is the United States.

Canada	United States of America	Mexico	Guatemala	Belize	El Savador	Honduras	Nicaragua
Canada	United States of America	Estados Unidos Mexicanos	República de Guatemala	Belize	República de El Salvador	República de Honduras	República de Nicaragua
Ottawa	*Washington*	*México*	*Guatemala*	*Belmopan*	San *Salvador*	*Tegucigalpa*	*Managua*
9,976,139 sqkm/ 3,851,787 sqm	9,363,123 sqkm/ 3,615,102 sqm	1,958,128 sqkm/ 756,033 sqm	108,889 sqkm/ 42,042 sqm	22,963 sqkm/ 8,866 sqm	21,041 sqkm/ 8,124 sqm	112,088 sqkm/ 43,277 sqm	130,000 sqkm/ 50,193 sqm
Pop.: 27,367,000	Pop.: 255,159,000	Pop.: 88,153,000	Pop.: 9,745,000	Pop.: 198,000	Pop.: 5,396,000	Pop.: 5,462,000	Pop.: 3,955,000
English, French	English	Spanish, Indian languages	Spanish, Maya-Quiche dialects	English, Spanish Creole, Carib, Maya	Spanish, Indian dialects	Spanish, English, Indian dialects	Spanish, English, Chibcha
Canadian dollar	US dollar	Mexican peso	Quetzal	Belize dollar	El Salvador Colón	Lempira	Córdoba

vinces and two territories remain bound to England by an allegiance to the British monarch. Except for the province of Quebec, where French language and culture prevails, English customs are generally observed.

The people of North America today are thus many different people from many different backgrounds. The continent they share includes some of the largest and most densely populated cities in the world – Mexico City, New York, and Los Angeles – along with vast wilderness areas of jungle, desert and ice.

The 1993 North American Free Trade Agreement ushered in a new era of economic cooperation between Canada, the United States, and Mexico by creating the largest common market in the World. As national trade barriers disappear, and new groups of immigrants arrive, North America's future, like its past, will be multi-ethnic in character and multi-cultural in outlook.

Top left: Bananas, one of the main agricultural and export products of Central America.

Lower left: Indian children in Mexico.

Top right: Fruit plantations (orange groves) in California, the »fruit garden« of North America.

Lower right: The vineyards in the State of Washington produce some of the finest wines in the United States.

Costa Rica	**Panama**	**Cuba**	**Bahamas**	**Jamaica**	**Haiti**	**Dominican Republic**	**Antigua and Barbuda**
República de Costa Rica	República de Panamá	República de Cuba	The Commonwealth of the Bahamas	Jamaika	République d'Haïti	República Dominicana	Antigua and Barbuda
San José	*Panamá*	*Havanna*	*Nassau*	*Kingston*	*Port-au-Prince*	*Santo Domingo*	*St. John's*
50,700 sqkm/ 19,575 sqm	75,650 sqkm/ 29,208 sqm	114,524 sqkm/ 44,218 sqm	13,935 sqkm/ 5,380 sqm	10,991 sqkm/ 4,244 sqm	27,750 sqkm/ 10,714 sqm	48,734 sqkm/ 18,816 sqm	443 sqkm/ 171 sqm
Pop.: 3,192,000	Pop.: 2,515,000	Pop.: 10,811,000	Pop.: 264,000	Pop.: 2,469,000	Pop.: 6,755,000	Pop.: 7,471,000	Pop.: 66,000
Spanish	Spanish, English, Indian dialects	Spanish	English	English	French	Spanish	English, Creole
Costa Rica Colón	Balboa	Cuban peso	Bahama dollar	Jamaican dollarr	Gourde	Dominican peso	East Caribbean dollar

Saint Cristopher and Nevis	**Dominica**	**Saint Lucia**	**Saint Vincent and the Grenadines**	**Barbados**	**Grenada**	**Trinidad and Tobago**
Federation of Saint Cristopher and Nevis	Commonwealth of Dominica	St. Lucia Sainte-Lucie	St. Vincent and the Grenadines	Barbados	State of Grenada	Republic of Trinidad and Tobago
Basseterre	*Roseau*	*Castries*	*Kingstown*	*Bridgetown*	*Saint George's*	*Port of Spain*
262 sqkm/ 101 sqm	751 sqkm/ 290 sqm	616 sqkm/ 238 sqm	389 sqkm/ 150 sqm	431 sqkm/ 166 sqm	344 sqkm/ 133 sqm	5,128 sqkm/ 1,980 sqm
Pop.: 42,000	Pop.: 72,000	Pop.: 137,000	Pop.: 108,000	Pop.: 259,000	Pop.: 91,000	Pop.: 1,265,000
English	English, Creole French	English, Patois (Creole French)	English, Creole English	English	English, Creole English or French	English
East Caribbean dollar	East Caribbean dollar	East Caribbean dollar	East Caribbean dollar	Barbados Dollar	East Caribbean dollar	Trinidad and Tobago dollar

SOUTH AMERICA

South America is the most tropical continent with a corresponding climate and vegetation. It has the world's largest river basin and the most complex river system. There is great disparity in the levels of economic development among the South American countries. The fourth largest continent is one of the world's major developing zones with all the familiar characteristics: from exploding populations migrating to expanding city slums to unemployment, housing shortages and national debt. The unbalanced population distribution – its heterogenous population crowding into the Atlantic coastal region while large portions of the interior remain nearly deserted – is an inheritance of South America's colonial past.

South America
NATURAL ENVIRONMENT

The triangular southern continent has a very regular, unindented outline without a single major bay. With islands and peninsulas making up only one per cent of its total surface area, its coastline measures a mere 28,700 kilometers (17,834 miles). Its maximum width is 5,100 kilometers (3,169 miles), its maximum length 7,500 kilometers (4,661 miles). The Central American land bridge connects it to North America to the north; it is joined with the Antarctic by the South Antilles and South Georgia to the south. Whereas deep ocean trenches (Peru Trench, Atacama Trench: -8,066 m/ -26,463 feet) parallel the Pacific coastline, on the Atlantic side the continent slopes gradually, spreading out to form a broad shelf base – upon which the Islas Malvinas (Falkland Islands) rest.

The surface of South America displays a structure similar to that of its continental neighbor, North America.

Like the North American Rocky Mountains, the Andes are a part of the circumpacific fault zone and include several chains of volcanoes, such as the Cotopaxi (5,897 m/19,347 feet), the Chimborazo (6,310 m/20,702 feet) and the Aconcagua (6,958 m/22,831 feet). This young mountain range, consisting of an east and a west cordillera, has been frequently shaken by earthquakes. The coastal chain and the eastern chain are separated – e.g. in the central Andes – by highlands (the Bolivian Altiplano) at elevations of 3,500 to 4,000 metres (11,480 – 13,120 feet). Lying in the rain shadow of the coastal ridges, these highlands are very arid. As a result,

most of the lakes, with the exception of Lake Titicaca, have a very high salt content. In Patagonia the Cordilleras lose some of their height, taking on the more subdued forms of secondary mountains. The fjords penetrating the western coastline and the finger-shaped lakes surrounded by moraines are signs of Patagonia's glacial past.

Over half the surface of South America is covered by lowlands. The largest, the Amazon lowland, was built up out of alluvium from rivers and lakes. With a drainage area of over seven million square kilometers (2,7 million square-miles), it is comparable only to the Zaire (Congo) basin. Most of this lowland is at an elevation below 200 metres (656 feet) above sea-level. The Amazon carries more water than any other river and, measuring 250 kilometers (155 miles) at the mouth, it is also the widest river in the world.

Parts of the broad fluvial plains of the Orinoco (Llanos) and the Parana/Rio de la Plata are as flat as a table. Benchlands (cuestas) and lava plateaus (Mato Grosso) are characteristic features of the highlands in the eastern mountainous regions of Guyana (Pico da Neblina, 3,014 m/9,888 ft.) and Brazil (Pico da Bandeira, 2,890 m/9,482 ft.). In Brazil the Atlantic coastline rises sharply like a wall to meet the eastern edge of the Planalto,

Page 143: The floodplain of the Rio Negro, just above where it empties into the Amazon.

Top left: Ravaged tropical rain forest: robbed of its protective vegetation, the soil of this sloping terrain is totally exposed to erosion.

Lower left: To the Incas, Lake Titicaca in the central Andean highland was a holy lake. Today, it is not only the largest standing body of water in South America, but also the highest lake (3,812 meters/12,500 feet) in the world on which steamboats ply.

Top: This sort of barren mountain steppe is typical of the »tierra helada« in the Peruvian Andes.

Center: South America's Cordilleras rise to an elevation of 6,958 meters (22,831 feet) at Mt. Aconcagua. Unlike high mountain regions in temperate zones, in the tropics they are islands of aridity.

Right: Iguacu Falls: shortly before flowing into the Rio Parana, the roaring Iguacu River plunges over basalt steps into the depths 60 to 80 meters (200–260 feet) below.

which then descends gradually toward the interior.

South America's tropical climate manifests itself in average monthly temperatures which never vary more than one degree (»diurnal climate«) from the annual temperature average (in Manaus: 27 °C / 81 °F). Another tropical ›blessing‹ is year-round precipitation. On the northwestern flank of the Colombian Cordillera northeasterly and southeasterly trade winds shed an average of over 8,500 millimeters (335 inches) of rain per year. The meridional arrangement of the cordilleras blocks major air currents. There are regions affected by periodic aridity beginning just above and below the equator; such as the Mato Grosso (1,300-1,400 mm/51–55 inches) and the Gran Chaco (less than 500 mm/18 inches). On the western side of the continent where the cold waters of the Humboldt Stream rise to the surface, the air currents shed their moisture before reaching land. As a result, the central Pacific coast includes one of the most arid deserts in the world, the Atacama. In the continent's remote South, the distribution of rainfall is just the opposite with westerly winds blessing the Pacific maritime region with plenty of rain, while Patagonia to the east remains dry. A third of the continent is covered with tropical rain forests (»selva« or »hyläa«), which are bordered by savannas with scattered forest formations, like the Venezuelan »llano«, the Brazilian »caatinga« and »campo«, as well as the Argentinean Gran Chaco and »pampa«.

Among the abundant species of South American wildlife, the most spectular varieties are the some 200 types of hummingbirds and multi-hued parrots. Another of this continent's characteristic animals is the llama, the tamed version of the South American camel.

Top: In tropical rain forests, the various plants compete for what little light there is – and even it rarely reaches the forest floor.

Center: Settlers set up homesteads along the new roads, burning down the rain forest, only to reap a meagre harvest for a few years before moving on – leaving behind irreparably destroyed terrain.

Lower left: With its long limbs and prehensile tail, the death's-head monkey is well-adapted to the conditions of its environment.

Lower right: Sheep grazing on the vast Patagonian pampa.

Cultivated land (arable land, plantations and irrigated land)

Grassland of the temperate zone

Forest of the temperate zone

Tropical forest (predominant tropical rain forest)

Savannah (Campos and Llanos)

Dry tropical forest and dry savannah (Chaco and Caatinga)

Steppe (Grassland and shrub; Pampa)

Semi-desert and desert

Alpine vegetation (Puna and Paramo); Subantarctic shrub and moss tundra

Rock, snow and ice areas of mountain regions

1 : 30 000 000

South America
PEOPLE AND CULTURE

The dominant influence of the discoverers and conquerors from the Iberian Peninsula – and of their Spanish and Portuguese descendants – still pervades all forms of South American culture particularly in the use of their Romance languages. Because of this influence South America, along with Central America, is considered part of the cultural sphere called Latin America, or Ibero-America.

Only few remaining countries, such as Ecuador, Peru, and Bolivia have a strong Indian influence. Mestizos, the ›mixed-blooded‹ offspring of European and American Indian parentage, make up 24 per cent of the Latin American population. 43 per cent are whites – who in the so-called »white countries«, Argentina, Uruguay and Chile, in fact, make up the majority. Twelve per cent are mulattoes, of mixed European and African extraction, and eight per cent are blacks. The some 100,000 Brazilian Indians live in isolated groups – with probably no long-term prospects of preserving their cultural identities. Once they had discovered America in 1492, the Spanish and Portuguese powers set about exploiting their overseas wealth. Destroying the advanced Indian civilizations, they divided up the continent between them; Portugal claimed Brazil, leaving the rest to Spain. As a result, Spanish is spoken in all the countries of Latin America except in Brazil where Portuguese is spoken. The vernacular versions spoken in the various countries of course vary to a greater or lesser degree from the language spoken in their respective mother country. Since mission-

aries were busy spreading their faith wherever the European colonists settled, today, South America is the Roman Catholic continent – with only five million Protestants. A more recent trend, however, is the proliferation of cults mixing African traditions with elements of Christian religion.

The European powers divided their colonies into vicekingdoms

and provinces, distributing the land among wealthy aristocrats, merchants or military leaders in the form of latifundia, or large estates; thus preventing peasant colonization from the outset. Until 1888, when slavery was abolished, blacks were brought in as slave labor from Africa.

Here, unlike in North America, the dominance of large haciendas

made it difficult for immigrants to settle as farmers. So even the mass immigration of Italians, Spanish and Portuguese during the 19th century was no real stimulus to agricultural development in Latin America. Hampered by this barrier to mass settlement, the colonies were reduced to suppliers of raw materials (sugar, tobacco, cotton, gold, diamonds, etc.) and markets for European goods. This established South America's economic and political dependence upon the industrial countries. Foreign investment policies reinforced this development, with Europeans and Americans pouring capital into the cattle industry in the Rio de la Plata district, as well as into sugar, cotton and coffee production,

Top left: The Copacabana, the famous bathing beach of Rio de Janeiro. The buildings in the background belong to the upper class.

Lower left: In Latin America, the Catholic continent, devout Christian religiousness mingles with traditional Indian customs.

Top center: This view of Brasilia from the television tower shows the business and entertainment center in the midground with the crown-shaped cathedral (to the right) and the congressional high-rises and government buildings

behind it, on either side of the Square of the Three Powers.

Lower center: A road through the Pantanal, a vast marshland in southern Brazil.

Top right: Picturesque painted façades, such as these in a poor quarter in Buenos Aires, often distract from the misery of the inhabitants.

Lower right: The tango, originally a West Indian folk dance, was turned into a social dance in Argentina prior to its introduction in Europe in 1911.

149

and Andean mining ventures – investments geared exclusively toward promoting the export of raw materials and agricultural products.

In the early 19th century, the South American colonies gained their independence, within national borders largely adhering to the lines of the former Spanish-American administrative districts. Independence did nothing, however, to change the traditional social order. Feudal and semi-feudal social structures, large-scale land-holding and slavery remained as sources of the extreme social tension still unresolved today – and particularly evident in the visual contrast between the manor houses of rural landlords and the miserable hovels of their tenant farmers. The military continues to play a crucial role in the power structures of these countries. Since the early sixties alone, military juntas have gained power through coup d'états: in Brazil in 1964, in Peru and Panama in 1968, in Bolivia in 1969, in Ecuador in 1972, in Chile in 1973 and in Argentina in 1976 – some of them still in power today. Alternately, the heads of state are frequently authoritarian rulers, so-called caudillos, supported by loyal members of the military forces.

All South American countries have one factor in common: a growing population. Once a result of the large influx of immigrants (around 13 million since 1850), this growth is now due to high birth rates – which, in turn, can be partly attributed to high il-

Top left: São Salvador da Bahia, the capital of Bahia State (Brazil).

Bottom: A market on Antigua, one of the Lesser Antilles with a predominately mestizo population.

Top center: The opera house of Manaus – the capital of the Brazilian state of Amazon. Its gilded cupola testifies to the city's former wealth as a center of the rubber trade.

Center: A small holding in the rain forest of the Amazon basin. Once the jungle has been burnt down and stripped, it takes but a few crops to deplete the forest soil.

Top right: São Salvador da Bahia, with its array of baroque churches, is the seat of a Catholic archbishop.

Lower right: Rio de Janeiro sprawls around the Bay of Guanabara (left). The unmistakable Sugar Loaf Mountain (center) separates the bay from the open Atlantic to the right.

literacy rates: over fifty per cent in Bolivia, Brazil, Peru and Ecuador; just under ten per cent in the ›white‹ South American countries. The gross disparity in the distribution of property between the rural poor and the landed class has caused many of the landless to emigrate to the cities in search of work, better living conditions and a more promising life. Today, therefore, nearly half the South American population lives in the cities, i.e. in the major centers of commerce and industry. Cities like Rio de Janeiro, São Paulo, Montevideo, Buenos Aires, Santiago de Chile, Caracas, Bogotá and Lima; cities with skylines dominated by the huge skyscrapers of multinational corporations. Instead of solving the problems, though, this migration has merely shifted them.

The result: growing slums within the principal cities, as well as at the edges of metropolises – with all their negative symptoms, such as crime, poverty, unemployment, undernourishment, chronic lack of education, prostitution, etc.

Half the South American population still subsists on agriculture – under property and market conditions equivalent to those prevailing under the old colonial plantation systems. Economic development is impeded by the uneven population distribution, which in turn counteracts attempts to improve the transport and communications infrastructure. South America lacks efficient transportation systems, with the large, navigable rivers

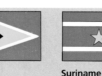

Colombia	Venezuela	Guyana	Suriname
República de Columbia	República de Venezuela	Cooperative Republic of Guyana	Republiek van Suriname
Bogotá	*Caracas*	*Georgetown*	*Paramaribo*
1,138,914 sqkm/ 439,735 sqm	912,050 sqkm/ 352,143 sqm	214,969 sqkm/ 83,000 sqm	163,265 sqkm/ 63,037
Pop.: 33,424,000	Pop.: 20,186,000	Pop.: 808,000	Pop.: 438,000
Spanish, Indian languages	Spanish, Indian languages	English	Dutch, Sranan Tongo (Creole) Saramaccan (mixed languages) English
Colombian peso	Bolívar	Guyana dollar	Suriname guilder

151

often the only access to the remote interior. The population is concentrated along the coastal fringe; particularly within the maritime provinces ›facing‹ Europe, i.e. along the Atlantic coast, where the extensive industrial regions around São Paulo and along the Rio de la Plata developed.In a largely failed attempt to focus the attention of the public and industry upon the development of the interior, Brasil resorted to building its new capital, Brasilia, inland!

South America is still heavily dependent on foreign capital for all major endeavors – whether they be Venezuelan or Colombian oil drilling operations; mineral-mining in the Guyanan mountains; extracting copper, zinc, lead or silver from the Peruvian or Bolivian Indian highlands, or farming in the Argentinian pampas.

In spite of deeply rooted national differences, culturally, the countries of South America have a great deal in common, particularly the pervasive Iberian influences. Among these shared characteristics are the checker-board layout of Latin American cities around central squares, as well as the dominant ecclesiastical and secular buildings in the ubiquitous baroque style. Like Anglo-American jazz, Latin American folk music – along with such rhythmically accentuated dances as the rumba, samba and tango – has become popular throughout the world.

Left: This road cutting straight through the tropical rain forest gets its rich red color from laterite – an iron-rich deposit typical of many tropical soils.

Ecuador	Peru	Bolivia	Chile	Brazil	Paraguay	Argentina	Uruguay
República del Ecuador	República del Perú	República Bolivia	República de Chile	República Federativa do Brasil	República del Paraguay	República Argentina	República Oriental del Uruguay
Quito	Lima	Sucre	Santiago de Chile	Brasilia	Asunción	Buenos Aires	Montevideo
283,561 sqkm/ 109,483 sqm	1,285,216 sqkm/ 496,222 sqm	1,098,581 sqkm/ 424,162 sqm	756,626 sqkm/ 292,133 sqm	8,511,965 sqkm/ 3,286,470 sqm	406,752 sqkm/ 157,047 sqm	2,767,889 sqkm/ 1,068,682 sqm	177,508 sqkm/ 68,536 sqm
Pop.: 11,055,000	Pop.: 22,451,000	Pop.: 7,524,000	Pop.: 13,600,000	Pop.: 154,113,000	Pop.: 4,519,000	Pop.: 33,100,000	Pop.: 3,130,000
Spanish, Quetchua	Spanish, Quetchua	Spanish, Quetchua	Spanish	Portuguese	Spanish, Guaranî	Spanish	Spanish
Sucre	Inti	Boliviano, (Peso?)	Chilean peso	Cruzado	Guaranî	Austral	New peso

Index

The index contains all the names that appear within the international map section (p. 9-14 and p. 16-80). It is ordered alphabetically. The umlauts ä, ö and ü have been treated as the letters a, o and u, and the ligatures æ, œ, as ae and oe.

The first figure after the name entry is the page number of the single or double page where the name being looked up is to be found. The letters and figures after the page reference refer to the grid in which the name is located or those grid sections through which the name extends. In the case of places (cities and towns), the positions of the place symbols are also included in the grid coordinates given.

The names that have been abbreviated on the maps are listed unabbreviated in the index. Only with U.S. place names have the official abbreviations been inserted accorded to common U.S. practice, e.g. Washington, D.C. The alphabetical sequence includes also prefixes, e.g. Fort, Saint. The determinative element of geographical names follows behind, e.g. Mexico, Gulf of –; Wight, Isle of – or the name of the city behind that of a suburb, e.g. Fremantle, Perth –. Official supplements to place names are included in the alphabetization. They may follow the name proper, e.g. Châlons-sur-Marne or be added in parenthesis, particularly in German speaking areas, e.g. Kempten (Allgäu).

To a certain extend official second name forms, linguistic variants, renamed places and other secondary designations are listed in the index with reference to the name form used in the map, e.g. Kamien Pomorski = Cammin in Pommern; Meran = Merano; Siam = Thailand.

To differentiate identical name forms mainly motor vehicle nationality letters for the respective countries have been added in brackets following these names:

A	Austria	ET	Egypt	N	Norway	SD	Swasiland
AFG	Afghanistan	ETH	Ethiopia and Eritrea	NA	Netherlands Antilles	SF	Finland
AL	Albania	F	France	NIC	Nicaragua	SGP	Singapore
AND	Andorra	FJI	Fiji	NL	Netherlands	SME	Suriname
AUS	Australia	FL	Liechtenstein	NZ	New Zealand	SN	Senegal
B	Belgium	GB	United Kingdom	P	Portugal	SP	Somalia
BD	Bangladesh	GCA	Guatemala	PA	Panama	SU	former
BDS	Barbados	GH	Ghana	PAK	Pakistan		Sovjet Union
BG	Bulgaria	GR	Greece	PE	Peru	SY	Seychelles
BH	Belize	GUY	Guyana	PL	Poland	SYR	Syria
BOL	Bolivia	H	Hungary	PNG	Papua New Guinea	T	Thailand
BR	Brazil	HK	Hong Kong	PY	Paraguay	TG	Togo
BRN	Bahrein	HY	Burkina Faso	Q	Qatar	TJ	China
BRU	Brunei	I	Italy	RA	Argentina	TN	Tunisia
BS	Bahamas	IL	Israel	RB	Botswana	TR	Turkey
BUR	Burma	IND	India	RC	Taiwan	TT	Trinidad and Tobago
C	Cuba	IR	Iran	RCA	Central African	USA	United States
CDN	Canada	IRL	Ireland		Republic	VN	Vietnam
CH	Switzerland	IRQ	Iraq	RCB	Congo	WAG	Gambia
CI	Ivory Coast	IS	Iceland	RCH	Chile	WAL	Sierra Leone
CL	Sri Lanka	J	Japan	RFC	Cameroun	WAN	Nigeria
CO	Colombia	JA	Jamaika	RH	Haiti	WD	Dominica
CR	Costa Rica	JOR	Jordan	RI	Indonesia	WG	Grenada
CS	Czech Rep. and	K	Cambodia	RIM	Mauritania	WL	Saint Lucia
	Slovakia	KWT	Kuwait	RL	Lebanon	WS	Samoa
CY	Cyprus	L	Luxembourg	RM	Madagascar	WV	Saint Vincent
D	Germany	LAO	Laos	RMM	Mali	Y	Yemen
DK	Denmark	LAR	Libya	RN	Niger	YU	Yugoslavia including
DOM	Dominican Republic	LB	Liberia	RO	Romania		Slowenia, Croatia,
DY	Benin	LS	Lesotho	ROK	South Korea		Bosnia Herzegowina
DZ	Algeria	M	Malta	ROV	Uruguay		and Macedonia
E	Spain	MA	Morocco	RP	Philippines	YV	Venezuela
EAK	Kenya	MAL	Malaysia	RSM	San Marino	Z	Zambia
EAT	Tanzania	MC	Monaco	RU	Burundi	ZA	South Africa
EAU	Uganda	MEX	Mexico	RWA	Rwanda	ZRE	Zaire
EC	Ecuador	MS	Mauritius	S	Sweden	ZW	Zimbabwe
ES	El Salvador	MW	Malawi	SCV	Vatican City		

To differentiate identical name forms among others the following symbols are used					
▲	Mountain	⊙	Island	∅	Ruin
∪	Bay, Gulf	∧	Cape	≈	Lake
~	River	≅	Landscape, Region	★	State
▲▲	Mountain Range	●	City, Town, Locality	☆	administrative Unit
∩	Peninsula	⇄	Pass		

153

A

Aachen 33 C 3
Aalen 33 E 4
A'âlî an-Nîl 60-61 KL 7
Äänekoski 30-31 L 6
Aar, De – 64-65 F 9
Aarau 33 D 5
Aare 33 D 5
Aavasaksa 30-31 KL 4

Aba [WAN] 60-61 F 7
Aba [ZRE] 64-65 GH 2
Abā' al-Qūr, Wādī – 46-47 J 7
Abā ar-Rūs, Sabkhat – 44-45 GH 6
Abad 48-49 E 3
Ābādān 44-45 F 4
Ābādān, Jazīreh – 46-47 N 7-8
Ābādeh 44-45 G 4
Abagnar Qi = Xilin Hot 48-49 M 3
Abai 80 E 3
Abajo Peak 76-77 J 7
Abakan 42-43 R 7
Aban 42-43 S 6
Abancay 78-79 E 7
Abanrherit, I-n- 60-61 F 5
Abā Sa'ūd 44-45 EF 7
Abashiri 48-49 RS 3
Abashiri-wan 50-51 d 1-2
Abasiri = Abashiri 48-49 RS 3
Abau 52-53 N 9
Abay 60-61 M 6
Abaya Hayik 60-61 M 7
Abaza 42-43 R 7
Aba Zangzu Zizhizhou 48-49 J 5
Abbeville 34-35 HJ 3
Abbeville, GA 74-75 B 8-9
Abbeville, SC 74-75 B 7
Abbottabad = Ebuṭṭābād 44-45 L 4
Abchasische Autonome Republik = 6 ◁ 38-39 H 7
Abchaska, AR - 38-39 H 7
Abchazische Autonome Republiek = 6 ◁ 38-39 H 7
'Abd al-'Azīz, Jabal – 46-47 HJ 4
'Abd al Kūrī 44-45 G 8
'Abdāllah 60-61 D 2
'Abd Allāh, Khawr – 46-47 N 8
'Abd Allāh, Khawr – 46-47 N 8
Ābdānān 46-47 M 6
Ābdānān, Rūdkhāneh-ye – 46-47 M 6
Abd an-Nabī, Bi'r – 62 B 2-3
Abdulino 42-43 J 7
'Abdullah = Minā' 'Abd Allāh 46-47 N 8
Abéché 60-61 J 6
Abécher = Abéché 60-61 J 6
Abed-Larache, El – = Al-Ādib al-'Arsh 60-61 F 3
Abeg, I-n- 60-61 D 4
Abeløya 30-31 n 5
Abengourou 60-61 D 7
Åbenrå 30-31 C 10
Abeokuta 60-61 E 7
Abercorn = Mbala 64-65 H 4
Aberdare Mountains 64-65 J 2-3
Aberdare National Park 63 D 3
Aberdeen [AUS] 58 K 4
Aberdeen [GB] 32 EF 3
Aberdeen [ZA] 64-65 F 9
Aberdeen, ID 76-77 G 4
Aberdeen, MD 74-75 E 5
Aberdeen, NC 74-75 D 7
Aberdeen, SD 72-73 G 2
Aberdeen, WA 72-73 B 2
Aberdeen Lake 70-71 R 5
Abergavenny 32 E 6
Abert, Lake – 76-77 CD 4
Aberystwyth 32 D 5
Abessinien = Äthiopien 60-61 MN 7
Abesszinia = Etiópia 60-61 MW 7
Abez' 42-43 L 4
Abhā 44-45 E 7
Ābhār 46-47 N 4
Abház Autonóm Köztársaság 38-39 H 7
Abhē Bid Hayik 60-61 N 6
Abchazská AR 38-39 H 7
Abiad, Râss el – = Rā's al-Abyaḍ 60-61 FG 1
Ābīd al-'Arsh, Al- 60-61 F 3
Abidjan 60-61 CD 7
Abilene, TX 72-73 FG 5
Abingdon, VA 74-75 BC 6
Abingdon = Isla Pinta 78-79 A 4
Abisko 30-31 H 3
Abisynia = Etiopia 60-61 MN 7
Abitibi, Lake – 70-71 UV 8
Abitibi River 70-71 U 7-8
Abjasia, República Autonóma de – = 6 ◁ 38-39 H 7
Abkhaz Autonomous Republic = 6 ◁ 38-39 H 7
Abkhazie, République Autonome d' = 6 ◁ 38-39 H 7
Abnūb 62 D 4
Åbo = Turku 30-31 K 7
Abomé = Abomey 60-61 E 7
Abomey 60-61 E 7
Abong-Mbang 60-61 G 8
Aborigen, pik ⤳ 42-43 cd 5
Abou-Deïa 60-61 H 6
Aboû ed Douhoûr = Abū aẓ-Ẓuhūr 46-47 G 6
'Abr, Al- 44-45 F 7
Abrantes 34-35 CD 9
Abra Pampa 80 CD 2
Abreojos, Punta – 72-73 CD 6
'Abrī 60-61 L 4
Abrolhos, Arquipélago dos – 78-79 M 8
Abruzzen = Appennino Abruzzese 36-37 E 4-F 5
Abruzzes = Appennino Abruzzese 36-37 E 4-F 5
Abruzzi 36-37 EF 4
Absaroka Range 72-73 D 2-E 3
Abu 44-45 L 6
Abū 'Ajāj = Jalib Shahab 46-47 M 7
Abū al-Ḥaṣīb 46-47 MN 7
Abū al-Maṭāmīr 62 CD 2
Abū 'Aweiqīla = Abū 'Uwayjīlah 62 EF 2
Abū aẓ-Ẓuhūr 46-47 G 5
Abū Ballāṣ 60-61 K 4
Abū Ḍahr, Jabal – 62 F 6
Abū Dārah, Rā's – 62 G 6
Abū Darbah 62 E 3
Abū Dhi'āb, Jabal – 62 F 5
Abū Durba = Abū Darbah 62 E 3
Abu Gharādiq, Bi'r – 62 C 2-3
Abū Ghashwah, Rā's – 44-45 G 8
Abū Ḥadd, Wādī – 62 F 7
Abū Ḥaggāg = Rā's al-Ḥikmah 46-47 BC 7
Abū Ḥajār, Khawr – 46-47 L 7
Abū Ḥamad 60-61 L 5
Abū Ḥamāmīd, Jabal – 62 F 5
Abū Ḥammān 46-47 J 5
Abū Ḥarbah, Jabal – 62 E 4
Abū Ḥashūifah, Khalīj – 62 BC 2
Abū Ḥjār, Hōr – = Khawr Abū Ḥajār 46-47 L 7
Abū Hujar 60-61 LM 6
Abuja 60-61 F 7
Abū Jābirah 60-61 K 6
Abū Jahaf, Wādī – 46-47 K 6
Abū Jamal 60-61 M 5
Abū Jamal, Jabal – 60-61 M 6
Abū Jīr 46-47 K 6
Abū Jīr, Wādī – 46-47 K 6
Abū Jurdī, Jabal – 62 F 6
Abū Kabīr 62 D 2
Abū Kamāl 44-45 DE 4
Abū Khārga, Wādī – = Wādī Abū Kharjah 62 DE 3
Abū Kharjah, Wādī – 62 DE 3
Abukuma-sammyaku 50-51 N 4
Abū Marīs, Sha'īb – 46-47 L 7
Abū Marw, Wādī – 62 E 6
Abū Minqār, Bi'r – 60-61 K 3
Abū Muḥarrik, Ghurd – 60-61 KL 3
Abunā 78-79 FG 6
Abuná, Rio – 78-79 F 7
Abū Qīr 62 D 2
Abū Qīr, Khalīj – 62 D 2
Abū Qurqāṣ 62 D 4
Abū Rijmayn, Jabal – 46-47 H 5
Abū Sa'fah, Bi'r – 62 F 6
Abū Ṣaida = Abū Ṣaydat Ṣaghīrah 46-47 L 6
Abū Salmān 46-47 M 7
Abū Ṣaydat Ṣaghīrah 46-47 L 6
Abū Shalīl 46-47 K 5
Abū Shīlī = Abū Shalīl 46-47 K 5
Abū Sinbil = Abu Sunbul 60-61 L 4
Abū Ṣkhair = Abū Ṣuhayr 46-47 L 7
Abū Ṣuhayr 46-47 L 7
Abu Sunbul 60-61 L 4
Abū Tīj 60-61 L 3
Abū 'Uwayjīlah 62 EF 2
Abū Zabad 60-61 K 6
Abū Ẓabī 44-45 G 6
Abū Zanīmah 60-61 L 3
Abū Zawal, Bi'r – 62 E 4
Abū Zenīma = Abū Zanīmah 60-61 L 3
Abyad 60-61 K 6
Abyaḍ, Ar-Rā's al- 60-61 A 4
Abyaḍ, Rā's al- 60-61 FG 1
Abyay 60-61 K 7
Abymes, les – 72-73 O 8
Abyssinie = Éthiopie 60-61 MN 7

Acadia = Acadie 70-71 XY 8
Acadia National Park 74-75 J 2
Acadie 70-71 XY 8
Acajutla 72-73 HJ 9
Acámbaro 72-73 FG 7
Acandí 78-79 D 3
Acaponeta 72-73 EF 7
Acapulco de Juárez 72-73 FG 8
Acará 78-79 K 5
Acaraí, Serra – 78-79 H 4
Acaraú 78-79 LM 5
Acarigua 78-79 F 3
Accomac, VA 74-75 F 6
Accra 60-61 DE 7
Aceh = 1 ◁ 52-53 C 6
Achacachi 78-79 F 8
Achaguas 78-79 F 3
Achaïa 36-37 JK 6
Achalciche 38-39 H 7
Achao 80 B 6
'Achârâ, El – = Al-'Asharah 46-47 J 5
Acharnai 36-37 K 6
Achegour 60-61 G 5
Achelôos 36-37 J 6
Acheng 48-49 O 2
Acherusia = Zonguldak 44-45 C 2
Achigh Köl 48-49 F 4
Achill 32 A 5
Achill Head 32 A 4-5
Achter-Indië 22-23 OP 5
Achtuba 38-39 J 6
Achtubinsk 38-39 J 6
Achtyrka 38-39 F 5
Aci Göl 46-47 CD 4
Ačinsk 42-43 R 6
Acıpayam 46-47 C 4
Acireale 36-37 F 7
Acklins Island 72-73 LM 7
Acomayo 78-79 E 7
Aconcagua [RCH, ▲] 80 C 4
Acopiara 78-79 M 6
Açores 66 D 5
Açores, Seuil des – 22-23 HJ 4
Àcqui Terme 36-37 C 3
Acraman, Lake – 56-57 FG 6
Acre 78-79 EF 6
Acre = 'Akkō 46-47 F 6
Acre, Rio – 78-79 F 6
Acri 36-37 G 6
Acton 74-75 C 3
Acton, CA 76-77 D 8
Açú, Rio – = Rio Piranhas 78-79 M 6
Acworth, GA 74-75 A 7

Ačinsk 42-43 R 6

Achacachi 78-79 F 8
Achaguas 78-79 F 3
Achaïa 36-37 JK 6
Achalciche 38-39 H 7
Achao 80 B 6
'Achârâ, El – = Al-'Asharah 46-47 J 5
Acharnai 36-37 K 6
Achegour 60-61 G 5
Achelôos 36-37 J 6
Acheng 48-49 O 2
Acherusia = Zonguldak 44-45 C 2
Achigh Köl 48-49 F 4
Achill 32 A 5
Achill Head 32 A 4-5
Achter-Indië 22-23 OP 5
Achtuba 38-39 J 6
Achtubinsk 38-39 J 6
Achtyrka 38-39 F 5

Ada [GH] 60-61 E 7
Ada, OK 72-73 G 5
'Adabīyah, Rā's – 62 E 3
Adado, Raas – = Raas Cadcadde 60-61 b 1
Adafir 60-61 BC 5
Adakale = Ardanuç 46-47 K 2
Adak Island 19 D 36
Adale = Cadale 60-61 b 3
Adalia = Antalya 44-45 C 3
Ādam 44-45 H 6
Adam, Monte – = Mount Adam 80 DE 8
Adam, Mount – 80 DE 8
Adama = Nazrēt 60-61 M 7
Adamana, AZ 76-77 HJ 8
Adamantina 78-79 JK 9
Adamaoua 60-61 G 7
Adamaua = Adamaoua 60-61 G 7
Adamello 36-37 D 2
Adamovka 38-39 LM 5
Adam Peak 76-77 E 5
Adampol = Polonezköy 46-47 C 2
Adams, MA 74-75 G 3
Adams, NY 74-75 EF 3
Adams, Cape – 24 B 30-31
Adams, Mount – 72-73 B 2
Adams Island 24 D 17
Adam's Peak = Samānalakanda 44-45 N 9
'Adan 44-45 F 8
Adana 46-47 F 4
Adapazarı = Sakarya 44-45 C 2
Adare, Cape – 24 B 18
Adavale 56-57 HJ 5
Adda 36-37 C 3
Addār, Râss – = Rā's aṭ-Ṭīb 60-61 G 1
Addis Alem = Alem Gena 60-61 M 7
Addison, NY 74-75 E 3
Addison = Webster Springs, WV 74-75 C 5
Addiss Abeba = Adīs Abeba 60-61 M 7
Addy, WA 76-77 E 1
Adel, GA 74-75 B 9
Adel, OR 76-77 D 4
Adelaide [AUS] 56-57 GH 6-7
Adelaide Island 24 C 29-30
Adelaide Peninsula 70-71 R 4
Adelaide River 56-57 F 2
Adelanto, CA 76-77 E 8
Adélie, Terre – 24 C 14-15
Adélie Land = Terre Adélie 24 C 14-15
Adelsberg = Postojna 36-37 F 3
Ademuz 34-35 G 8
Aden = 'Adan 44-45 EF 8
Aden, Golfe d' 44-45 F 8
Adén, Golfo de – 44-45 F 8
Aden, Golf van – 44-45 F 8
Aden, Golf von – 44-45 F 8
Aden, Gulf of – 44-45 F 8
Ádeni-öböl 44-45 F 8
Adeńska, Zatoka – 44-45 F 8
Adenský záliv 44-45 F 8
Adghar = Adrār 60-61 DE 3
Ādhār, Rā's – 60-61 G 1
Ādharbayejān-e- Bākhtarī 44-45 EF 3
Ādharbāyejān-e-Khāvarī 44-45 EF 3
Adi, Pulau – 52-53 K 7
Adib al-'Arsh, Al- 60-61 F 3
Adige 36-37 D 3
Adige Autonóm Terület 38-39 H 7
Adigej Autonome Oblast = 1 ◁ 38-39 H 7
Adīgrat 60-61 MN 6
Adiguey, Oblast Autónoma de – = 1 ◁ 38-39 H 7
Adī Keyih 60-61 MN 6
Adilang 63 C 2
Adilcevaz 46-47 K 3
Adin, CA 76-77 C 5
Adiriyāt, Jabal al- 46-47 G 7
Adirondack Mountains 72-73 M 3
Adīs Abeba 60-61 M 7
Adīs Dera = Dirē 60-61 M 6
Adī Ügrī 60-61 M 6
Adıyaman 46-47 H 4
Adjarian Autonomous Region = 8 ◁ 38-39 H 7
Adjarie, République Autonome d' = 8 ◁ 38-39 H 7
Adler, Soči- 38-39 G 7
Adler, Soči- 38-39 G 7
Admar, Irq – 60-61 F 4
Admer, Erg d' = 'Irq Admar 60-61 F 4
Admiralicji, Wyspy – = Admiralty Islands 52-53 N 7
Admiralitätsinseln = Admiralty Islands 52-53 N 7
Admiralitni ostrovy = Admiralty Islands 52-53 N 7
Admiralty Gulf 56-57 DE 2
Admiralty Inlet [CDN] 70-71 TU 3
Admiralty Inlet [USA] 76-77 B 1-2
Admiralty Island 70-71 K 6
Admiralty Islands 52-53 N 7
Admiralty Range 24 B 17
Admont 33 G 5
Adonara, Pulau – 52-53 H 8
Ādoni 44-45 M 7
Adour 34-35 G 7
Adra 34-35 F 10
Adramúttion = Edremit 44-45 B 3
Ādrār 60-61 DE 3
Adraskan, Daryā-ye – = Hārūt Rōd 44-45 J 4
Adré 60-61 J 6
Adrī = Idrī 60-61 G 3
Àdria 36-37 E 3
Adrian, OR 76-77 E 4
Adrianopel = Edirne 44-45 B 2
Adriatic Sea 36-37 E 3-H 5
Adriatisches Meer 36-37 E 3-H 5
Adriatische Zee 36-37 E 3-H 5
Adriatyckie, Morze - 36-37 E 3-H 5
Adscharische Autonome Republik = 8 ◁ 38-39 H 7
Adua 52-53 J 7
Adua = Adwa 60-61 M 6
Adusa 64-65 G 2
Adventura, Banco – 36-37 DE 7
Adventure Bank 36-37 DE 7
Adventurebank 36-37 DE 7
Adwa 60-61 M 6
Adyča 42-43 a 4
Adyča 42-43 a 4
Adygei Autonomous Region = 1 ◁ 38-39 H 7
Adygejsk AR 38-39 H 7
Adygejski, Ob.A - 38-39 H 7
Adyghéens, Région Autonome des – = 1 ◁ 38-39 H 7
Adygische Autonome Oblast = 1 ◁ 38-39 H 7
Adž Bogd uul 48-49 GH 3
Adzharia, República Autónoma de – = 8 ◁ 38-39 H 7
Adzjarische Autonome Republiek = 8 ◁ 38-39 H 7
Adžarská AR 38-39 H 7
Adž Bogd uul 48-49 GH 3
Adžarska, AR - 38-39 H 7

Adzsár Autonóm Köztársaság 38-39 H 7

Aegean Sea 36-37 L 5-M 7
Ærø 30-31 D 10
'Afag 46-47 L 6
Afallah 60-61 B 5
Afántu 36-37 N 7
Afars et Issas = Djibouti 60-61 N 6
Afganistán 44-45 J 4-L 3
Afganistan 44-45 J 4-L 3
Afganisztán 44-45 J 4-L 3
Afghánistán 44-45 J 4-L 3
Afghanistan 44-45 J 4-L 3
Afgooye 60-61 ab 3
Āfhjalar = Āqchalar 46-47 L 5
'Afif 44-45 E 6
Afikpo 60-61 F 7
Aflāj, Al- 44-45 F 6
Afmadow 60-61 N 8
Afogados da Ingàzeira 78-79 M 6
Afognak Island 70-71 F 6
Afrēra Ye-Tyew Hayik 60-61 N 6
Afrēra Ye-Tyew Hayik 60-61 N 6
Africa 22-23 J-L 5
África 22-23 J-L 5
África del Sudoeste = Namibia 64-65 E 7
African Island 64-65 M 3
Afrika 22-23 J-L 5
'Afrīn 46-47 G 4
Āfrīneh 46-47 M 6
Afrique 22-23 J-L 5
Afrique du Sud 64-65 F-H 8
Afryka Południowo-Zachodnia = Namibia 64-65 E 7
Afşin 46-47 G 3
Afton, WY 76-77 H 4
Afuá 78-79 J 5
'Afūla 46-47 F 6
Afyon 44-45 C 3

Aga = Aginskoje 42-43 VW 7
Ağaçören 46-47 EF 3
Agadem 60-61 G 5
Agades = Agadez 60-61 F 5
Agadez 60-61 F 5
Agādīr = Aghādīr 60-61 BC 2
Ägadische Inseln = Ìsole Ègadi 36-37 DE 6
Agadyr' 42-43 N 8
Agai Burját Autonóm Körzet 42-43 V 7
Agaie 60-61 F 7
Ägäis = Ägäisches Meer 36-37 L 5-M 7
Ägäisches Meer 36-37 L 5-M 7
Agalega Island 64-65 N 5
Agalta, Sierra de – 72-73 J 8-9
Agan 42-43 O 5
Agapa 42-43 Q 3
Agarā = Agra 44-45 M 5
Agartala 44-45 P 6
Agata, ozero – 42-43 R 4
Agathonēsion 36-37 M 7
Agats 52-53 L 8
Agatti Island 44-45 L 8
Agattu Island 19 D 1
Agboville 60-61 D 7
Agdam 38-39 J 7-8
Agde 34-35 J 7
Agen 34-35 H 6
Agere Ḥiywer = Hagerē Hiywet 60-61 M 7
Aghādīr 60-61 BC 2
Aghā Jārī 44-45 FG 4
Aghwāṭ, Al- 60-61 E 2
Ağın 46-47 H 3
Agin-Boerjatmongolen, Autonome Gebied der – 42-43 V 7
Agin-Burjatmongolen, Nationalkreis der – 42-43 V 7
Agiński Buriacki Okręg Autonomiczny 42-43 V 7
Aginskoje 42-43 VW 7
Aginský burjatský autonomní okruh 42-43 V 7
Aginsky-Buryat Autonomous Area 42-43 V 7
Ágios Geṓrgios 36-37 KL 7
Ágios Iōánnēs, Akrōtḗrion – 36-37 LM 8
Ágios Nikólaos 36-37 LM 8
Ağlasun 46-47 D 4
Agnew 56-57 D 5
Agnone 36-37 F 5
Agochi = Aoji 50-51 H 1
Agout 34-35 J 7
Agra 44-45 M 5
Agrachanskij poluostrov 38-39 J 7
Agram = Zagreb 36-37 FG 3
Ağrı [TR] 44-45 E 3
Agrigento 36-37 E 7
Agrínion 36-37 J 6
Agròpoli 36-37 F 5
Agryz 42-43 J 6
Agua Caliente Indian Reservation 76-77 E 9
Água Clara [BR] 78-79 J 9
Agua Fria River 76-77 G 8-9
Aguán, Río – 72-73 J 8
Agua Nueva 80 BC 4-5
Agua Prieta 72-73 DE 5
Aguascalientes [MEX, ●] 72-73 F 7
Aguascalientes [MEX, ☆] 72-73 F 7
Águas Formosas 78-79 L 8
Águeda, Rio – 34-35 D 8
Aguga 63 C 2
Aguila, AZ 76-77 G 9
Águilas 34-35 G 10
Aguja, Punta – 78-79 C 6
Agujas, Cabo – 64-65 F 10
Agujas, Cuenca de – 22-23 L 8
Agulhas, Cape – 64-65 F 10
Agulhas, Kaap – 64-65 F 10
Agulhas Basin 22-23 L 8
Agulhasbecken 22-23 L 8
Agulhasbekken 22-23 L 8
Agulhas Negras 78-79 K 9
Agung, Gunung – 52-53 G 8
Agusan 52-53 J 5
Ägypten 60-61 KL 3

Ahaggar = Al-Hajjār 60-61 EF 4
Ahaggar, Tassili Oua n' = Tāsīlī Wān al-Hajjār 60-61 E 5-F 4
Ahar 46-47 M 3
Ahar Chāy 46-47 M 3
Ahar Chāy 46-47 M 3
Ahar Chāy 46-47 M 3
Ahır Dağı 46-47 G 4
Ahırlı = Karaburun 46-47 B 3
Ahlat 46-47 K 3
Ahlat = Yusufeli 46-47 J 2
Ahmadabad [IND] 44-45 L 6
Aḥmadābād [IR] 46-47 M 4
Aḥmadī, Al- = Mīnā' al-Aḥmadī 46-47 N 8
Ahmadnagar 44-45 LM 7
Aḥmadpūr Sharqī 44-45 L 5
Aḥmar, Jabal al- 62 D 3
Ahmednagar = Ahmadnagar 44-45 LM 7
Ahogayegua, Sierra de – 72-73 b 2-3
Ahoskie, NC 74-75 E 6
Ahtopol 36-37 MN 4
Āhūrān 46-47 M 6
Åhus 30-31 F 10
Ahvāz 44-45 F 4
Ahvenanmaa = Åland 30-31 HJ 7
Āhwar 44-45 F 8
Ahwaz = Ahvāz 44-45 F 4

Achacachi 78-79 F 8
Achaguas 78-79 F 3
Achaïa 36-37 JK 6
Achalciche 38-39 H 7
Achao 80 B 6
'Achârâ, El – = Al-'Asharah 46-47 J 5
Acharnai 36-37 K 6
Achegour 60-61 G 5
Achelôos 36-37 J 6
Acheng 48-49 O 2
Acherusia = Zonguldak 44-45 C 2
Achigh Köl 48-49 F 4
Achill 32 A 5
Achill Head 32 A 4-5
Achter-Indië 22-23 OP 5
Achtuba 38-39 J 6
Achtubinsk 38-39 J 6
Achtyrka 38-39 F 5

Āībak = Samangān 44-45 K 3
Aibetsu 50-51 c 2
Aichi 50-51 L 5
Aidin = Aydın 44-45 B 3
Aigina [GR, ⊙] 36-37 K 7
Aigina [GR, ●] 36-37 K 7
Aigion 36-37 JK 6
Aigle, Chaîne de l' 33 GH 3
Aigle, Chaîne de l' 33 GH 3
Aigle, Chaîne de l' 33 GH 3
Aigle, l' 34-35 H 4
Aiguá 80 F 4
Aigues-Mortes 34-35 JK 7
Aiguilles, Bassin des – 22-23 L 8
Aiguilles, Cap des – 64-65 F 10
Aigun = Aihun 48-49 O 1
Ai He 50-51 E 2
Ai Ho = Ai He 50-51 E 2
Aihsien = Yacheng 48-49 K 8
Aihui 48-49 O 1
Aija 78-79 D 6
Aikawa 50-51 LM 3
Aiken, SC 72-73 K 5
Aileron 56-57 F 4
'Ailī, Sha'īb al- = Sha'īb al- 'Aylī 46-47 H 7
Aim 42-43 Z 6
Aimorés 78-79 L 8
Aimorés, Serra dos – 78-79 L 8
Ain 34-35 K 5
'Ain, Wādī al- = Wādī al-'Ayn 44-45 H 6
'Ainabo = Caynabo 60-61 b 2
'Ain al Mugshin, Al- = Al'Ayn al-Muqshin 44-45 GH 7
Ainaži 30-31 KL 9
Ainaži 30-31 KL 9
Aïn-Beïda = 'Ayn Bayḍā' 60-61 F 1
Aïn-ben-Tili = 'Ayn Bin Tīlī 60-61 C 3
'Aïn Dîouâr = 'Ayn Dīwār 46-47 K 4
Aïn Galakka 60-61 H 5
Aïn-Salah = 'Ayn Ṣāliḥ 60-61 E 3
Aïn-Sefra = 'Ayn Ṣafrā 60-61 DE 2

154 Aache

Aïn-Témouchent = 'Ayn Tamūšhanat 60-61 D 1
Aioi 50-51 K 5
Aiquile 78-79 F 8
Aïr 60-61 F 5
Airan Köl = Telijn nuur 48-49 F 2
Aire, Isla del – 34-35 K 9
Air Force Island 70-71 W 4
Aisch 33 E 4
Aisega 52-53 g 6
Aishihik 70-71 J 5
Aisne 34-35 J 4
Aitana 34-35 G 9
Aitape 52-53 M 7
Aiud 36-37 K 2
Aiun, El – = Al-'Ayūn 60-61 B 3
Aix-en-Provence 34-35 KL 7
Aix-les-Bains 34-35 KL 6
Āizāl = Aizawal 44-45 P 6
Aizawal 44-45 P 6
Aizpute 30-31 J 9
Aizu-Wakamatsu 48-49 QR 4
Aizu-Wakamatu = Aizu-Wakamatsu 48-49 QR 4

Aj 38-39 L 4
Ajā, Jabal – 44-45 E 5
'Ajabshīr 46-47 L 4
Ajaccio 36-37 C 5
Ajaguz 42-43 P 8
Ajaj, Wādī – 46-47 J 5
'Ajājā 46-47 J 4
'Ajam, Al- 46-47 G 6
'Ajam, El- = Al-'Ajam 46-47 G 6
Ajan [SU, ~] 42-43 R 4
Ajan [SU, ● Pribrežnyj chrebet] 42-43 a 6
Ajan [SU, ● Sibirskoje ploskogorje] 42-43 U 6
Ajana 56-57 BC 5
Ajanka 42-43 g 5
Ajanta Range 44-45 M 6
Ajax Mountain 76-77 G 3
Ajdābīyah 60-61 J 2
Ajedabya = Ajdābīyah 60-61 J 2
Ājī Chāi = Rūd-e Āqdogh Mīsh 46-47 M 4
Ājī Chāi = Rūd-e Āqdogh Mīsh 46-47 M 4
Ajigasawa 50-51 MN 2
Ājī Chāi = Rūd-e Āqdogh Mīsh 46-47 M 4
Ājīn 46-47 M 5
Ajjer, Tassili n' = Tāsīlī Wan Ahjār 60-61 F 3
Ajkino 38-39 J 3
'Ajlūn 46-47 FG 6
'Ajlūn, Jabal – 46-47 FG 6
'Ajmah, Jabal al- 60-61 L 3
'Ajmān 44-45 GH 5
'Ajmī 46-47 L 5-6
Ajnis, Qārat – 62 BC 3
Ajo, AZ 76-77 G 9
Ajo Mountains 76-77 G 9
Ajon, ostrov – 42-43 g 4
Ajrag nuur 48-49 GH 2
'Ajramīyah, Bi'r al- 62 DE 3
Ajtos 36-37 M 4

Akabira 50-51 c 2
Akademii, zaliv – 42-43 a 7
Akadien = Acadie 70-71 XY 8
Akaishi-sammyaku 50-51 LM 5
Akalkot 44-45 M 7
Akan ko 50-51 cd 2
Akantarer, I-n- 60-61 E 5
Akanyaru 63 B 3
Akasaki 50-51 J 5
'Akāsh, Wādī – = Wādī 'Ukāsh 46-47 J 5-6
Akashi 50-51 K 5
Akasi = Akashi 50-51 K 5
Äkäsjoki 30-31 KL 4
Akayu 50-51 N 3
Akbulak 38-39 L 5
Akcaabat 46-47 H 2
Akçadağ 46-47 GH 3
Akçakale 46-47 H 4
Akçakoca 46-47 D 2
Akçakoyumla 46-47 G 4
Akçan = Sakavi 46-47 J 3
Ak Çay 46-47 C 4
Akchar = Āqshar 60-61 B 4
Ak Dağlar 44-45 BC 3
Akdağlar 46-47 FG 3
Akdağmadeni 46-47 F 3
Akershus 30-31 D 7-8
Aketi 64-65 F 2
Akhḍar, Jabal al- [LAR] 60-61 J 2
Akhḍar, Jabal al- [Oman] 44-45 H 6
Akhisar 46-47 BC 3
Akhmīm 62 DE 4
Aki 50-51 J 6
Akik = 'Aqīq 60-61 M 5
Akimiski Island 70-71 UV 7
Akıncı Burnu 46-47 F 4
Akıncılar 46-47 B 2
Akita 48-49 QR 4
Akjoujt = Aqjawajat 60-61 B 5
Akkajaure 30-31 G 4
Akka-mori 50-51 N 2
Akkeshi 50-51 d 2
Akkeshi wan 50-51 d 2
'Akkō 46-47 F 6
Akköy 46-47 B 4
Akku = Çaldere 46-47 G 2
Akkuş 46-47 G 2
Aklavik 70-71 J 4
Akmal'-Abad = Gižduvan 42-43 L 9
Ak-Mečet' = Kzyl-Orda 42-43 M 9
Ak-Mečet' = Kzyl-Orda 42-43 M 9
Akmolinsk = Celinograd 42-43 MN 7
Akō 50-51 K 5
Akōbō = Akūbū 60-61 L 7
Akola 44-45 M 6
Akonolinga 60-61 G 8
Akordat 60-61 M 5
Akören 46-47 E 4
Akpatok Island 70-71 X 5
Akpınar = Çınar 46-47 J 4
Akranes 30-31 bc 2
Akrar 30-31 b 2
Akre = 'Āqrah 46-47 K 4
Akrítas, Akrōtḗrion – 36-37 JK 7
Akron, OH 72-73 K 3
Akrōtḗri 36-37 L 8
Akrōtḗriu, Kólpos – 46-47 E 5
Akša 42-43 V 7
Akşar 46-47 K 2
Aksaray 46-47 EF 3
Akşehir 44-45 C 3
Akşehir Gölü 46-47 D 3
Akseki 46-47 D 4
Aks'onovo-Zilovskoje 42-43 VW 7
Aksoran, gora – 42-43 O 8
Aksu [SU] 42-43 N 7
Aksu [TR] 46-47 G 4
Aksu = Aqsu 48-49 E 3
Aksuat 42-43 P 8
Aksu Çay 46-47 D 4
Aksum 60-61 M 6
Akša 42-43 V 7
Aktogaj 42-43 O 8
Akt'ubinsk 42-43 K 7
Aktumsyk 42-43 K 8
Akūbū 60-61 L 7
Akulurak, AK 70-71 CD 5
Akune 48-49 OP 5
Akure 60-61 F 7
Akureyri 30-31 de 2
Akwizgran = Aachen 33 C 3
Akyab = Sittwe 52-53 B 2
Akyaka 46-47 K 2
Akyazı 46-47 D 2

Ål 30-31 C 7
Alabama 72-73 J 5
Alabama River 72-73 J 5
Alaca 46-47 F 2
Alacadağ 46-47 DE 4
Alacahan 46-47 G 3
Alacahöyük 46-47 F 2
Alaçam 46-47 F 2
Alachua, FL 74-75 b 2
Aladağ 46-47 K 3
Ālādāgh, Reshteh – 44-45 H 3
Ala Dağlar [TR, ▲▲] 46-47 F 4
Alagoas 78-79 M 6-7
Alagoinhas 78-79 M 7
Alagón 34-35 D 9
Alag Šan Gov' 48-49 J 4
Alag Šan Gov' 48-49 J 4
Alajuela 72-73 K 9-10
Alakol', ozero – 42-43 P 8
Alalaú, Rio – 78-79 G 5
'Alamar-Rūm, Rā's – 62 B 2
'Alamayn, Al- 60-61 K 2
Alameda, CA 76-77 BC 7
Alameda, ID 76-77 G 4
Alamo, NV 76-77 F 7
Alamo, Cerro – 76-77 EF 10
Álamo, El – [MEX, Baja California] 76-77 EF 10
Alamogordo, NM 72-73 E 5
Alamo Lake 76-77 G 8
Alamo River 76-77 F 9
Alamos 72-73 E 6
Alamosa, CO 72-73 E 4
Ālāmūt 46-47 O 4
Åland [SF, ⊙] 30-31 HJ 7
Åland [SF, ☆] 30-31 HJ 7
Åland, Fosa de – 30-31 H 7
Åland, Fosse d' 30-31 H 7
Åland-mélység 30-31 H 7
Ålandsdiep 30-31 H 7
Ålands hav 30-31 H 7-8
Ålandstief 30-31 H 7
Alanga Arba 64-65 JK 2
Ālanmyō 52-53 C 3
Alanya 44-45 C 3
Alaotra, Lac – 64-65 L 6
Alapaha, GA 74-75 B 9
Alapaha River 74-75 B 9
Alapajevsk 42-43 L 6
Alaplı 46-47 D 2
Ālappi = Alleppey 44-45 M 9
Alāq 60-61 B 5
Alarcón 34-35 FG 9
Alas, Selat – 52-53 G 8
Alaşehir 46-47 C 3
Alašejev buchta 24 C 5
Alashtar 46-47 MN 6
Alaska 70-71 F-H 4
Alaska, Golfe d' 70-71 GH 6
Alaska, Golfo de – 70-71 GH 6
Alaska, Golf van – 70-71 GH 6
Alaska, Golf von – 70-71 GH 6
Alaska, Gulf of – 70-71 GH 6
Alaska, Zatoka – 70-71 G-J 6
Alaska Highway 70-71 H 5
Alaska Peninsula 70-71 DE 6
Alaska Range 70-71 F-H 5
Alàssio 36-37 C 3-4
Alašejev buchta 24 C 5
Alaszka 70-71 E-H 4
Alaszkai-öböl 70-71 G-J 6
Alatri 36-37 E 5
Alatyr' [SU, ●] 42-43 H 7
Alausi 78-79 D 5
Alava, Cape – 76-77 A 1
Alaverdi 38-39 H 7
Alayunt 46-47 D 3
Alazani 38-39 J 7
Alazeja 42-43 d 3-e 4
Alazejskoje ploskogorje 42-43 c 4
Alba 36-37 C 3
Albacete 34-35 FG 9
Alba de Tormes 34-35 E 8
Alba Iulia 36-37 K 2
Albanese Alpen = Alpet e Shqipërisë 36-37 HJ 4
Albania 36-37 H 4-5
Albania 36-37 J 5
Albánia 36-37 J 5
Albanië 36-37 H 4-5
Albanie 36-37 H 4-5
Albánie 36-37 J 5
Albanien 36-37 H 4-5
Albany 56-57 C 6-7
Albany, CA 76-77 B 7
Albany, GA 72-73 K 5
Albany, NY 72-73 LM 3
Albany, OR 72-73 B 3
Albany River 70-71 U 7
Albarracin 34-35 G 8
Albatros Island 64-65 NO 6
Albatross Bay 56-57 H 2
Albayrak 46-47 KL 3
Albemarle, NC 74-75 C 7
Albemarle = Isla Isabela 78-79 A 5
Albemarle Sound 74-75 EF 6
Albenga 36-37 C 3
Alberche 34-35 E 8
Alberga 58 B 1
Alberga, The – 56-57 FG 5
Alberrie Creek 58 C 2
Albert [AUS] 58 H 4
Albert, Lake – 56-57 GH 7
Albert, Parc national – = Parc national Virunga 64-65 G 2-3
Alberta 70-71 NO 6
Alberta, VA 74-75 E 6
Albertkanaal 34-35 J 3
Albert Lea, MN 72-73 H 3
Albert Markham, Mount – 24 AB 17-15
Albert Nile 64-65 H 2
Alberton, MT 76-77 F 2
Albertville 34-35 L 6
Albertville = Kalemie 64-65 G 4
Albi 34-35 J 7
Albina 78-79 J 3
Albino 36-37 CD 3
Albion, NY 74-75 DE 3
Alborán 34-35 F 11
Ålborg 30-31 CD 9
Ålborg Bugt 30-31 D 9
Alborz, Reshteh Kūhhā-ye – 44-45 G 3
Albufera, La – 34-35 GH 9
Albuquerque, NM 72-73 EF 4
Alburquerque 34-35 D 9
Albury-Wodonga 56-57 J 7
Alcácer do Sal 34-35 C 9
Alcalá de Guadaira 34-35 E 10
Alcalá de Henares 34-35 F 8
Alcalá la Real 34-35 F 10
Àlcamo 36-37 E 7
Alcañiz 34-35 G 8
Alcántara 34-35 D 9
Alcântara [BR] 78-79 L 5
Alcantarilla 34-35 G 10
Alcañiz 34-35 G 8
Alcaraz 34-35 F 9
Alcaraz, Sierra de – 34-35 F 9
Alcarria, La – 34-35 F 8
Alcázar de San Juan 34-35 F 9
Alcázarquivir = Al-Qaṣr al-Kabīr 60-61 C 1
Alcester Island 52-53 h 6
Alcira 34-35 G 9
Alcira [RA] 80 D 4
Alcobaça 34-35 C 9
Alcobaça [BR] 78-79 M 8
Alcolea del Pinar 34-35 FG 8
Alcoota 56-57 F 4
Alcoy 34-35 G 9
Aldabra Islands 64-65 L 4
Aldağ [TR, ▲] 46-47 F 4
Aldağ [TR, ●] 46-47 F 4
Aldan [SU, ~] 42-43 Z 6
Aldan [SU, ●] 42-43 XY 6
Aldano-Učurskij chrebet 42-43 Y 6
Aldano-Učurskij chrebet 42-43 Y 6
Aldanskoje nagorje 42-43 X-Z 6
Aldeburgh 32 GH 5
Alder, MT 76-77 GH 3
Alderney 32 E 7
Alder Peak 76-77 C 8
Alduş = Temsiyas 46-47 H 3
Aleg = Alaq 60-61 B 5
Alegrete 80 E 3-4
Aleï, I-n- 60-61 D 5
Alejandra, Cabo – = Cape Alexandra 80 J 8
Alejandría = Al-Iskandarīyah 60-61 KL 2
Alejandro Selkirk 69 B 6
Alejsk 42-43 P 7
Aleksandra, mys – 42-43 ab 7
Aleksandra I, zeml'a 24 C 29
Aleksandria = Al-Iskandarīyah 60-61 KL 2
Aleksandrov 38-39 GH 4
Aleksandrov Gaj 38-39 J 5
Aleksandrovsk = Belogorsk 42-43 YZ 7
Aleksandrovskoje [SU, Zapadno-Sibirskaja nizmennost'] 42-43 OP 5
Aleksandrovsk-Sachalinskij 42-43 bc 7
Aleksandrów Kujawski 33 J 2
Aleksandry, zeml'a – 42-43 FG 1
Aleksejevka [SU, Kazachskaja SSR] 42-43 N 7
Aleksejevsk = Svobodnyj 42-43 YZ 7
Aleksinac 36-37 JK 4
Ålem 30-31 G 9
Alem Gena 60-61 M 7
Alem Maya 60-61 N 7
Além Paraíba 78-79 L 9
Alençon 34-35 H 4
Alenquer [BR] 78-79 HJ 5
Alentejo 34-35 C 10-D 9
Alenuihaha Channel 52-53 ef 3
Alenuihaha Channel 52-53 ef 3
Alenuihaha Channel 52-53 ef 3
Alenz 46-47 J 4
Aleoetentrog 11 D 35
Aléoutiennes, Fosse des – 19 D 35
Alert 19 A 25
Alerta 78-79 E 7
Alès 34-35 K 6
Alessàndria 36-37 C 3
Ålesund 30-31 AB 6
Aleucki, Rów – 19 D 35
Aleut-árok 19 D 35
Aleutengraben 19 D 35
Aleuten Trench 19 D 35
Aleutianas, Fosa de las – 19 D 35
Aleutian Islands 19 D 35-1
Aleutian Range 70-71 E 6-F 5
Aleutka 48-49 T 2
Aleutský příkop 19 D 35
Alevina, mys – 42-43 cd 6
Alevisik = Samandağ 46-47 F 4
Alexander, Kap – 70-71 WX 2
Alexander, Point – 56-57 G 2
Alexander Archipelago 70-71 J 6-K 7
Alexanderbaai 64-65 DE 8
Alexandra [NZ] 56-57 N 9
Alexandra, Cape – 80 J 8
Alexandra, zeml'a – = zeml'a Aleksandry 42-43 FG 1
Alexandra Fiord 70-71 VW 2
Alexandra land = zeml'a Aleksandry 42-43 FG 1
Alexandretta = İskenderun 44-45 D 3
Alexandrette = İskenderun 44-45 D 3
Alexandria [AUS] 56-57 G 3
Alexandria [BR] 78-79 M 6
Alexandria [R] 36-37 L 4
Alexandria [ZA] 64-65 G 9
Alexandria, LA 72-73 H 5
Alexandria, VA 72-73 L 4
Alexandria = Al-Iskandarīyah 60-61 KL 2
Alexandrie = Al-Iskandarīyah 60-61 KL 2
Alexandrië = Al-Iskandarīyah 60-61 KL 2
Alexandrie = Al-Iskandarīyah 60-61 KL 2
Alexandrina, Lake – 56-57 GH 7
Alexandrúpolis 36-37 L 5
Alfambra 34-35 G 8
Alfarez de Navio Sobral 24 A 32-35
Alfatar 36-37 M 4
Alfeiós 36-37 J 7
Alföld 33 J 5-L 4
Ålfotbreen 30-31 A 7
Alfred, ME 74-75 H 3
Alga 42-43 K 8
Ålgård 30-31 A 8
Algarve 34-35 CD 10
Algeciras 34-35 E 10
Algena 60-61 M 5
Alger = Al-Jazā'ir 60-61 E 1
Algéria 60-61 D-F 3
Algeria 60-61 D-F 3
Algerian Basin 28-29 J 8-K 7
Algérie 60-61 D-F 3
Algerien 60-61 D-F 3
Algerisch-Provenzialisches Becken 28-29 J 8-K 7
Algerije 60-61 D-F 3
Algerijns-Provençaals Bekken 28-29 J 8-K 7
Alghero 36-37 C 5
Algier = Al-Jazā'ir 60-61 E 1
Algieria 60-61 D-F 3
Algiers = Al-Jazā'ir 60-61 E 1
Algiersko-Prowansalski, Basen – 34-35 J 10-L 8
Algír = Al-Jazā'ir 60-61 E 1
Algoabaai 64-65 G 9
Algoa Bay = Algoabaai 64-65 G 9
Algodones 76-77 F 9
Algoma, OR 76-77 C 4
Algonquin Provincial Park 70-71 V 8
Alhambra, CA 76-77 DE 8
Alhucemas = Al-Ḥusaymah 60-61 D 1
Alhucemas, Islas de – 34-35 F 11
'Ālī, Sadd al- 60-61 L 4
Aliákmon 36-37 JK 5
'Alī al-Garbī 46-47 M 6
Ali-Bajramly 38-39 J 8
Alibardak = Mermer 46-47 J 3
Alibej, ozero – 36-37 O 3
Alibey Adası 46-47 B 3
Alibunar 36-37 J 3
Alicante 34-35 GH 9
Alice, TX 72-73 G 6
Alice, Punta – 36-37 G 6
Alice Springs 56-57 FG 4
Alicudi 36-37 F 6
Ali Gabe 63 E 2
Aligar = Aligarh 44-45 M 5
Aligarh 44-45 M 5
Alīgūdarz 46-47 NO 6
Alihe 48-49 N 1
Alima 64-65 DE 3
Alindao 60-61 J 7-8
Alingsås 30-31 E 9
Alipur Duar 44-45 O 5
Aliquippa, PA 74-75 C 4
Alisal, CA 76-77 C 7
Aliwal-Noord 64-65 G 9
Aliwal Suid = Mosselbaai 64-65 G 9
Aljaška 70-71 E-H 4
Aljašský záliv 70-71 G-J 6
Alkali Desert 76-77 EF 5-6
Alkali Flat 76-77 DE 5
Alkali Lake 76-77 D 5
Alkmaar 34-35 K 2
Allach-Jun' 42-43 a 5
Allada 60-61 E 7
Allagash, ME 74-75 J 1
Allagash River 74-75 J 1
Allahabad [IND] 44-45 N 5
Allaire, Banc – 72-73 BC 7
Allaire, mělčina – 72-73 BC 7
Allairebank 72-73 BC 7
Allaire-pad 72-73 BC 7
Allakaket, AK 70-71 F 4
Allahüekber Dağları 46-47 K 2
Allanmyo = Ālanmyō 52-53 C 3
'Allāqī, Wādī al- 62 E 6
Alleghenies = Allegheny Mountains 72-73 K 4-L 3
Allegheny Mountains 72-73 K 4-L 3
Allegheny Plateau 74-75 C 5-F 3
Allegheny River 74-75 D 4
Allemagne 33 D-F 2-4
Allemagne, Baie d' 33 C 1
Allendale, SC 74-75 C 8
Allenstein = Olsztyn 33 K 2
Allentown, PA 72-73 L 3
Alleppey 44-45 M 9
Aller 33 D 2
Allerheiligenbaai = Baia de Todos os Santos 78-79 M 7
Allerheiligenbai = Baia de Todos os Santos 78-79 M 7
Alliance, NE 72-73 F 3
Alliance, OH 74-75 C 4
Allier 34-35 J 6
Alligator Sound 74-75 EF 7
Alliston 74-75 D 2
Alma [CDN, Quebec] 70-71 W 8
Alma, GA 74-75 B 9
Alma-Ata 42-43 O 9
Almada 34-35 C 9
Almadén 34-35 E 9
Almalyk 44-45 KL 2
Almanor, Lake – 76-77 C 5
Almansa 34-35 G 9
Almanzora 34-35 F 10
Almazán 34-35 F 8
Almeida 34-35 D 8
Almeidia Campos 78-79 K 8
Almeirim [BR] 78-79 J 5
Almenara [BR] 78-79 LM 8
Almendralejo 34-35 D 9
Almería 34-35 F 10
Almería, Golfo de – 34-35 F 10
Al'metjevsk 42-43 J 7
Älmhult 30-31 F 9
Almirante Brown [Antarktika] 24 C 30-31
Almo, ID 76-77 G 4
Almodóvar del Campo 34-35 E 9
Almonte [CDN] 74-75 E 2
Almorox 34-35 E 8
Almota, WA 76-77 E 2
Almuñécar 34-35 F 10
Almuñécar 34-35 F 10
Almus 46-47 G 2
Almyrós 36-37 K 6
Alnwick 32 F 4
Alofi 52-53 b 1
Aloha, OR 76-77 B 3
Alonnēsos 36-37 KL 6
Alor, Pulau – 52-53 HJ 8
Álora 34-35 E 10
Alor Setar 52-53 CD 5
Alotau 52-53 NO 9
Aloysius, Mount – 56-57 E 5
Alpen 28-29 KL 6
Alpena, MI 72-73 K 2
Alpercatas, Rio – 78-79 KL 6
Alpes 28-29 KL 6
Alpes Albaneses = Alpet e Shqipërisë 36-37 HJ 4
Alpes Cárnicos 36-37 E 2
Alpes Carniques 36-37 E 2
Alpes Cottiennes 34-35 G 6
Alpes Dolomíticos = Dolomiti 36-37 DE 2
Alpes Graies 34-35 L 6
Alpes Julianos 36-37 EF 2
Alpes Juliennes 36-37 EF 2
Alpes Maritimes 34-35 L 6
Alpet e Shqipërisë 36-37 HJ 4
Alpha 56-57 J 4
Alphonse Island 64-65 M 4
Alpine, AZ 76-77 J 9
Alpine, ID 76-77 H 4
Alpine, TX 72-73 F 5
Alpi Transilvanici 36-37 KL 3
Alps 28-29 KL 6
Alpu 46-47 D 3
Alpy 36-37 A 3-E 2
Alpy 36-37 A 3-E 2
Alpy Australijskie = Snowy Mountains 56-57 J 7
Alqūsh 46-47 K 4
Alroy Downs 56-57 G 3
Als 30-31 C 10
Alsace 34-35 L 4-5
Alsasko 34-35 L 4-5
Alsasua 34-35 FG 7
Alsea, OR 76-77 B 3
Alstahaug 30-31 DE 5
Alta 30-31 K 3
Altaelv 30-31 K 3
Alta Gracia [RA] 80 CD 4
Altagracia [YV] 78-79 E 2
Altaï = Altaj 48-49 EF 1
Altai = Altaj 42-43 PQ 7
Altair, Cima del – 22-23 H 2-3
Altairkuppe 22-23 H 3
Altair-Ondiepte 22-23 H 2-3
Altair Seamounts 22-23 H 2-3
Altaj [MVR, Altaj] 48-49 H 2
Altaj [MVR, Chovd] 48-49 G 2
Altaj [SU] 42-43 PQ 7
Altaj-hegyvidéki Autónom Terület 42-43 Q 7
Altaj Mongolski = Mongol Altajn Nuruu 48-49 H-L 2
Altajn Nuruu = Mongol Altajn Nuruu 48-49 F-H 2
Altajská republika = 8 ◁ 42-43 Q 7
Altamaha River 72-73 K 5
Altamira [BR] 78-79 J 5
Altamira, Cueva de – 34-35 EF 7
Altamont, OR 76-77 BC 4
Altamont, WY 76-77 H 5
Altamura 36-37 G 5
Altanbulag 48-49 K 1-2
Altar Valley 76-77 H 10
Altavista, VA 74-75 D 6
Altay 48-49 F 2
Altdorf 33 D 5
Altenburg 33 F 3
Alter do Chão [BR] 78-79 HJ 5
Alter do Chão [BR] 78-79 HJ 5
Alter do Chão [BR] 78-79 HJ 5
Altevatn 30-31 H 3
Altınekin 46-47 E 3
Altınhisar 46-47 F 4
Altınkaya Barajı 46-47 F 2
Altınözü 46-47 G 4
Altin Tagh 48-49 EF 4
Altıntaş 46-47 CD 3
Altiplanicie Mexicana 72-73 E 5-F 7
Altiplano 78-79 F 8
Altkastilien = Castilla la Vieja 34-35 E 8-F 7
Altmühl 33 E 4
Alto Anapu, Rio – 78-79 J 5
Alto Egipto = Aṣ-Ṣa'īd 60-61 L 3-4
Alto Garças 78-79 J 8
Alto Longá 78-79 L 6
Alto Molócuè = Molócuè 64-65 J 6
Alton, IL 72-73 HJ 4
Altoona, PA 72-73 L 3
Alto Parnaíba 78-79 K 6
Alto Piquiri 80 F 2
Alto Rio Senguerr 80 BC 6-7
Altsohl = Zvolen 33 J 4
Altunhisar = Ortaköy 46-47 F 4
Āltūn Kūprī 46-47 L 5
Alturas, CA 76-77 C 5
Altus, OK 72-73 G 5

Altus 155

Altyn Tagh = Altin tagh 48-49 EF 4
Alucra 46-47 H 2
Alūksne 30-31 M 9
Aluminė 80 B 5
Alung Gangri 48-49 E 5
'Aluula = Caluula 60-61 c 1
Alva, FL 74-75 c 3
Alvalade 34-35 C 9-10
Alvand, Kūh-e – 44-45 FG 4
Alvar = Alwar 44-45 M 5
Alvarado 72-73 GH 8
Alvarães 78-79 G 5
Álvaro Obregón = Frontera 72-73 H 8
Alvdal 30-31 D 6
Älvdalen 30-31 F 7
Alvesta 30-31 F 9
Alvord Lake 76-77 D 4
Älvsborgs län 30-31 E 8-9
Älvsbyn 30-31 J 5
Alwar 44-45 M 5
Alys = Kızılırmak 44-45 D 3
Alytus 30-31 L 10
Alzacja 34-35 L 4-5
Alzamaj 42-43 S 6
Alžir = Al-Jazā'ir 60-61 E 1
Alžirsko 60-61 D-F 3

Ałtaj = Altaj 48-49 PQ 7

Allach-Jun' 42-43 a 5
Allada 60-61 E 7
Allagash, ME 74-75 J 1
Allagash River 74-75 J 1
Allahabad [IND] 44-45 N 5
Allaire, Banc – 72-73 BC 7
Allaire, Banco – 72-73 BC 7
Allakaket, AK 70-71 F 4
Allaküekber Dağları 46-47 K 2
Allanmyo = Alanmyô 52-53 C 3
'Allāqī, Wadī al- 62 E 6
Alleghenies = Allegheny Mountains 72-73 K 4-L 3
Allegheny Mountains 72-73 K 4-L 3
Allegheny Plateau 74-75 C 5-F 3
Allegheny River 74-75 D 4
Allemagne 33 D-F 2-4
Allemagne, Baie d' 33 C 1
Allemania 33 D-F 2-4
Allendale, SC 74-75 C 8
Allentown, PA 72-73 L 3
Alleppey 44-45 M 9
Aller 33 D 2
Allerheiligenbaai = Baia de Todos os Santos 78-79 M 7
Alliance, NE 72-73 F 3
Alliance, OH 74-75 C 4
Allier 34-35 J 6
Alligator Sound 74-75 EF 7
Alliston 74-75 D 2

Amada = 'Amādah 62 E 6
Amadabad = Ahmadabad 44-45 L 6
'Amādah 62 E 6
Amadeus, Lake – 56-57 F 4
Amādī 60-61 KL 7
'Amādīyah, Al- 46-47 K 4
Amadjuak Lake 70-71 W 4-5
Amagasaki 50-51 K 5
Amahai 52-53 J 7
Amakusa nada 50-51 G 6
Amakusa-rettō 48-49 O 5
Amakusa syotô = Amakusa-rettō 48-49 O 5
Åmål 30-31 E 8
Amalfi 36-37 F 5
Amaliás 36-37 J 7
Amalyk 42-43 W 6
Amami-guntō 48-49 O 6
Amami-ō-shima 48-49 O 6
Amami-Ō sima = Amami-ō-shima 48-49 O 6
Amandola 36-37 E 4
Amangel'dy 42-43 M 7-8
Amanos Dağları = Nur Dağları 46-47 G 4
Amantea 36-37 FG 6
Amapá [BR, Amapá ●] 78-79 J 4
Amapá [BR, Amapá ☆] 78-79 J 4
Amara 60-61 M 6
'Amārah, Al- 44-45 F 4
Amaramba, Lagoa – = Lagoa Chiuta 64-65 J 5
Amarante [BR] 78-79 L 6
Amaravati = Amravati 44-45 M 6
Amargo, CA 76-77 E 8
Amargosa Desert 76-77 E 7
Amargosa Range 76-77 E 7-8
Amargosa River 76-77 E 8
Amarillo, TX 72-73 F 4
'Amarina, Tel el- = Tall al- 'Amārinah 62 D 4
'Amārinah, Tall al- 62 D 4
Amarna, Tell el – = Tall al- 'Amārinah 62 D 4
Amaro Leite 78-79 JK 7
Amarume 50-51 M 3
Amarúsion 36-37 KL 6-7
Amasra 46-47 E 2
Amasya 44-45 D 2
Amatique, Bahía de – 72-73 J 8
Amauã, Lago – 78-79 G 5

Amazon = Amazonas 78-79 F-H 5
Amazonas [BR] 78-79 F-H 5
Amazonas, Estuário do Rio – 78-79 JK 4
Amazonas, Plataforma del – 22-23 G 5-6
Amazonas, Rio – [BR] 78-79 HJ 5
Amazonas, Rio – [PE] 78-79 E 5
Amazonasschelf 22-23 G 5-6
Amazone, Plateau Continental de l' 22-23 G 5-6
Amazoneplat 22-23 G 5-6
Amazonka = Rio Amazonas 78-79 HJ 5
Amazon Shelf 22-23 G 5-6
Amba Alagê 60-61 MN 6
Amba Alaji = Amba Alagê 60-61 MN 6
Ambajogai 44-45 M 7
Ambala 44-45 M 4
Ambalavao 64-65 L 7
Ambam 60-61 G 8
Ambanja 64-65 L 5
Ambarčik 42-43 fg 4
Ambarčik 42-43 fg 4
Ambaro, Baie d' 64-65 L 5
Ambato 78-79 D 5
Ambatoboeny 64-65 L 6
Ambatolampy 64-65 L 6
Ambatondrazaka 64-65 L 6
Ambatosoratra 64-65 L 6
Ambelau, Pulau – 52-53 J 7
Amber, WA 76-77 E 2
Amberg 33 EF 4
Ambergris Cay 72-73 J 8
Ambikapur 44-45 N 6
Ambilobe 64-65 LM 5
Ambodifototra 64-65 LM 6
Ambohibe 64-65 K 7
Ambohimahasoa 64-65 L 7
Amboina = Pulau Ambon 52-53 J 7
Amboise 34-35 H 5
Amboland = Ovamboland 64-65 DE 6
Ambon 52-53 J 7
Ambon, Pulau – 52-53 J 7
Amboseli, Lake – 63 D 3
Amboseli Game Reserve 64-65 J 3
Ambositra 64-65 L 7
Ambovombe 64-65 L 8
Amboy, CA 76-77 F 8
Amboyna Cay 52-53 F 5
Ambrakikòs Kólpos 36-37 J 6
Ambre, Cap d' 64-65 LM 5
Ambre, Montagne d' 64-65 L 5
Ambridge, PA 74-75 CD 4
Ambrim 56-57 N 3
Ambriz 64-65 D 4
Ambrizete = N'Zeto 64-65 D 4
Amchitka Island 19 D 1
Am Dam 60-61 J 6
Amderma 42-43 L 4
Ameca 72-73 F 7
Amedabad = Ahmadabad 44-45 L 6
Amelia Court House, VA 74-75 DE 6
Aménas, In – = 'Ayn Umannâs 60-61 F 3
Amenia, NY 74-75 G 4
Amer, Lac – = Al-Buhayrat al-Murrat al-Kubrá 62 E 2
Amerasia Basin 19 A
América, Meseta de – 22-23 DE 3
American Highland 24 B 8
América del Norte 22-23 DE 3
América del Sur 22-23 FG 6
American Falls, ID 76-77 G 4
American Falls Reservoir 76-77 G 4
American Fork, UT 76-77 H 5
American Highland 24 B 8
American River North Fork 76-77 C 3
Americus, GA 72-73 K 5
Amerikai Egyesült Államok 72-73 D-K 4
Amerikai-magasföld = American Highland 24 B 8
Amerikanisches Hochland = American Highland 24 B 8
Amérique du Nord 22-23 DE 3
Amérique du Nord, Bassin de l' 22-23 FG 4
Amérique du Sud 22-23 FG 6
Amersfoort 34-35 K 2
Amery Ice Shelf 24 BC 7-8
Amerykański, Płaskowyż – American Highland 24 B 8
Ames, IA 72-73 H 3
Amesbury, MA 74-75 H 3
Amfilochía 36-37 J 6
Ámfissa 36-37 K 6
Amga [SU, ~] 42-43 X 6
Amga [SU, ●] 42-43 Z 5
Am Gérêda 60-61 J 6
Amghar, Al- = Al-Amgar 46-47 L 8
Amgu 42-43 a 8

Amguèma 42-43 k 4
Amgun' [SU, ~] 42-43 a 7
Amgun' [SU, ●] 42-43 a 7
Amhara = Amara 60-61 M 6
Amherst 70-71 XY 8
Amherst, MA 74-75 G 3
Amherst, VA 74-75 D 6
Amhurst, Mount – 56-57 E 3
Ami, Mont – 63 B 2
Amiata, Monte – 36-37 D 4
Amiens 34-35 J 4
Amik Gölü 46-47 G 4
Amindivi Islands 44-45 L 8
Amino 64-65 E 7
Aminuis 64-65 E 7
Amirantes 64-65 M 4
Amirauté, Îles de l' = Admiralty Islands 52-53 N 7
'Amīrīyah, Al- 62 CD 2
Amisós = Samsun 44-45 D 2
Amlia Island 19 D 36
'Ammān 44-45 D 4
Ammarfjället 30-31 FG 4
Ammersee 33 E 5
Amnok-kang 48-49 O 3
Amnyemachhen Gangri 48-49 HJ 5
Amol 38-39 K 8
Amores, Los – 80 DE 3
Amorgós 36-37 LM 7
Amos 70-71 V 8
'Āmoûdâ = 'Āmudâ 46-47 J 4
Amoy = Xiamen 48-49 M 7
Ampanihy 64-65 K 7
Ampasindava, Baie d' 64-65 L 5
Ampato, Nevado de – 78-79 E 8
Amphipolis 36-37 K 5
Amposta 34-35 H 8
Ampurias 34-35 J 7
Amravati 44-45 M 6
Amritsar 44-45 LM 4
Amroha 44-45 M 5
Amsīd, Al- 60-61 J 5
Amsterdam 34-35 K 2
Amsterdam, NY 74-75 FG 3
Amsterdam, Plateau d' 22-23 NO 8
Amsterdamdrempel 22-23 NO 8
Amsterdam Plateau 22-23 NO 8
Amsterdamplateau 22-23 NO 8
Amstetten 33 G 4
Amt'ae-do 50-51 EF 5
'Āmudâ 46-47 J 4
Amudarja 44-45 J 2
Amund Ringnes Island 70-71 RS 2
Amundsen, Mount – 24 BC 11
Amundsen Bay 24 C 5
Amundsen Glacier 24 A 23-20
Amundsen Gulf 70-71 L-N 3
Amundsen havet 24 BC 25-26
Amundsen-Scott 24 A
Amur 42-43 Z 8
Amur = Heilong Jiang 48-49 P 2
'Āmūr, 'Ayn – 62 CD 5
Amurang 52-53 H 6
Amursk 42-43 a 7
Amurskij zaliv 50-51 H 1

Anabar 42-43 V 3
Anâbîb an-Naft 44-45 DE 4
Ana Branch 56-57 H 6
Anabuki 50-51 K 5-6
Anacapa Island 76-77 D 9
Anaconda, MT 72-73 D 2
Anaconda Range 76-77 G 2-3
Anacortes, WA 76-77 B 1
Ana Deresi 46-47 B 2
Anadyr' [SU, ~] 42-43 hj 5
Anadyr' [SU, ●] 42-43 j 5
Anadyrskaja nizmennost' 42-43 j 4-5
Anadyrskij zaliv 42-43 j-l 5
Anadyrskoje ploskogorje 42-43 h 4
Anáfē 36-37 LM 7
Anagni 36-37 E 5
Anaheim, CA 76-77 DE 9
Anáhuac, Mesa de – 72-73 FG 7
Anaiza, Jebel – = Jabal Unayzah 44-45 DE 4
Anajás 78-79 JK 5
Anak 50-51 E 3
Anakapalle 44-45 N 7
Anakápaḷḷi = Anakapalle 44-45 N 7
Anak Krakatau, Pulau – 52-53 DE 8
Analalava 64-65 L 5
Anamã 78-79 G 5
Anambas, Kepulauan – 52-53 E 6
Anamur 44-45 C 3
Anamur Burnu 44-45 C 3
Anan 50-51 K 6
Ananjev 36-37 NO 2
Anantapur 44-45 M 8
Anantnag 44-45 M 4
Anápolis 78-79 K 8
Anâr 44-45 GH 4

Anarak 38-39 K 9
Anárak 44-45 G 4
Anârdara 44-45 J 4
Anastasia Island 74-75 c 2
Anatolia 44-45 C 3
Anatolia 36-37 NO 6
Anatóliai-magasföld 44-45 C 3
Anatólie 44-45 CD 3
Anatolie 44-45 C 3
Anatolie 44-45 C 3
Anatolie 36-37 NO 6
Anatolien 44-45 C 3
Anatone, WA 76-77 E 2
Añatuya 80 D 3
Anbâr, Al- 46-47 J 6
Anbyŏn 50-51 F 3
Ancenis 34-35 G 5
Anceny, MT 76-77 H 3
An-ching = Anqing 48-49 M 5
Anchorage, AK 70-71 FG 5
Anchuras 34-35 E 9
Anclote Keys 74-75 b 2
Ancober = Ankober 60-61 MN 7
Ancona 36-37 E 4
Ancuabe 64-65 J 5
Ancud 80 B 6
Ancud, Golfo de – 80 B 6
Ancyra = Ankara 44-45 C 3
Anda 48-49 NO 2
Andalgalá 80 C 3
Andalousie = Andalucia 34-35 D-F 10
Åndalsnes 30-31 BC 6
Andalucia 34-35 D-F 10
Andalusien = Andalucia 34-35 D-F 10
Andaman, Bassin des – 52-53 BC 4-5
Andamán, Cuenca de – 52-53 BC 4-5
Andamán, Mar de – 52-53 C 4-5
Andaman, Mer des – 52-53 C 4-5
Andaman and Nicobar Islands 44-45 OP 8
Andaman Basin 52-53 BC 4-5
Andamanbecken 52-53 BC 4-5
Andamán Dvīp = Andaman Islands 44-45 P 8
Andamanenbekken 52-53 BC 4-5
Andamanen und Nikobaren = Andaman and Nicobar Islands 44-45 OP 8
Andaman Islands 44-45 P 8
Andamán-medence 52-53 BC 4-5
Andaman Sea 52-53 C 4-5
Andamanse moře 52-53 C 4-5
Andamańskie, Morze – 52-53 C 4-5
Andamán-tenger 52-53 C 4-5
Andaman et Nicobar = Andaman and Nicobar Islands 44-45 OP 8
Andaman Islands 44-45 P 8
Andaman-medence 52-53 BC 4-5
Andamanse Zee 52-53 C 4-5
Andamanské moře 52-53 C 4-5
Andamańskie, Morze – 52-53 C 4-5
Andamán y Nicobar = Andaman and Nicobar Islands 44-45 OP 8
Andamenensee 52-53 C 4-5
Andamooka 56-57 G 6
Andamoaka Ranges 58 C 3
Andant 80 D 5
Andara 64-65 F 6
Andarāb, Al- 46-47 G 5
Andarin, Al- 46-47 G 5
Andelys, les – 34-35 H 4
Anden = Cordillera de los Andes 78-79 3-F 9
Andermatt 33 D 5
Anderson, CA 76-77 BC 5
Anderson, IN 72-73 J 3
Anderson, SC 72-73 K 5
Anderson Ranch Reservoir 76-77 F 4
Anderson River 70-71 L 4
Andes 78-79 D 3
Andes, Cordillera de los – 78-79 3-F 9
Andes, Los – 80 B 4
Andhra 44-45 M 8-N 7
Andhra Pradesh 44-45 M 8-N 7
Andidanob, Jebel – = Jabal Asūtarībah 62 G 7
Andīmashk 46-47 N 6
Andırın 46-47 G 4
Andižan 44-45 L 2
Andižan 44-45 L 2
Andkhoy 44-45 JK 3
Andoas 78-79 D 5
Andok = Cordillera de los Andes 78-79 3-F 9
Andong 48-49 O 4
Andong = Dandong 48-49 N 3
Andora 34-35 H 7
Andorja 30-31 GH 3
Andorra 34-35 H 7
Andorra la Vella 34-35 H 7
Andover, OH 74-75 C 4
Andøy 30-31 FG 3
Andra = Andhra 44-45 M 8-N 7

Andradina 78-79 J 9
Andreanof Islands 19 D 36
Andrêba = Ambatosoratra 64-65 L 6
Andrée land 30-31 j 5
Andrêeneset 30-31 n 4
Andrejevka [SU, Kazachskaja SSR] 42-43 OP 8
Andrews, OR 76-77 D 4
Andrews, SC 74-75 D 8
Andrews, TN 74-75 B 7
Àndria 36-37 FG 5
Andriba 64-65 L 6
Andringitra 64-65 L 7
Androka 64-65 K 8
Àndros 36-37 L 7
Androscoggin River 74-75 H 2
Andros Island 72-73 L 7
Androth Island 44-45 L 8
Andújar 34-35 EF 9
Andulo 64-65 E 5
Andy = Cordillera de los Andes 78-79 3-F 9
Anegada 72-73 O 8
Anegada Passage 72-73 O 8
Aného 60-61 E 7
Aneityum 56-57 N 4
Añelo 80 C 5
Aneto, Pico de – 34-35 H 7
Aney 60-61 G 5
An-fu = Linli 48-49 L 6
Angamos, Punta – 80 B 2
Ang-ang-ch'i = Ang'angxi 48-49 N 2
Ang'angxi 48-49 N 2
Angara 42-43 S 6
Angarsk 42-43 T 7
Angarskij kr'až 42-43 S-U 6
Angarskij kr'až 42-43 S-U 6
Ánge 30-31 F 6
Angel, Salto – 78-79 G 3
Ángel de la Guarda, Isla – 72-73 D 6
Ángeles, Los – [RCH] 80 B 5
Ängelholm 30-31 E 9
Ångermanälven 30-31 G 5-6
Ångermanland 30-31 GH 6
Angermünde 33 FG 2
Angers 34-35 G 5
Ängesån 30-31 K 4
Angka, Doi – = Doi Inthanon 52-53 C 3
Angkor 52-53 D 4
Anglesey 32 D 5
Angleterre 32 E-G 5
Anglia 32 E-G 5
Anglia 32 E-G 5
Anglie 32 E-G 5
Angmagssalik = Angmagssaliq 70-71 de 4
Angmagssaliq 70-71 de 4
Ango 64-65 G 2
Angoche 64-65 JK 6
Angoche, Ilhas – 64-65 JK 6
Angol 80 B 5
Angola 64-65 EF 5
Angola, NY 74-75 D 3
Angola, Bassin de l' 64-65 BC 5-6
Angola, Cuenca de – 64-65 BC 5-6
Angola Basin 64-65 BC 5-6
Angolabecken 64-65 BC 5-6
Angolai-medence 64-65 BC 5-6
Angolská pánev 64-65 BC 5-6
Angolski, Basen – 64-65 BC 5-6
Angora = Ankara 44-45 C 3
Angostura = Ciudad Bolívar 78-79 G 2
Angostura I, Salto de – 78-79 E 4
Angostura II, Salto de – 78-79 E 4
Angosturas 78-79 E 5
Angoulême 34-35 H 6
Angoumois 34-35 GH 6
Angrapa 33 KL 1
Angra Pequena = Lüderitzbaai 64-65 DE 6
Angren 44-45 KL 2
Angrenšachtstroj = Angren 44-45 KL 2
Angrenšachtstroj = Angren 44-45 KL 2
Anguila = Anguilla 72-73 O 8
Anguilla 72-73 O 8
Angumu 64-65 G 3
Anholt 30-31 D 9
An-hsi = Anxi 48-49 H 3
An-hui = Anhui 48-49 M 5
Anhui 48-49 M 5
Anhumas 78-79 HJ 8
Ani 50-51 N 2-3
Aniaï = Ani 50-51 N 2-3
Anie, Pic d' 34-35 G 7
Animas, NM 76-77 J 10
Animas Peak 76-77 J 10
Anina 36-37 JK 3
Anita, AZ 76-77 G 8
Aniva, mys – 42-43 b 8
Aniva, zaliv – 42-43 b 8
Anjar 44-45 KL 6
Anjou 34-35 G 5

Anjou, ostrova – = ostrova Anžu 19 B 4-5
Anjouan = Ndzuwani 64-65 KL 5
Anju 48-49 O 4
Ankara 44-45 C 3
Ankara Çayı 46-47 DE 3
Ankaratra 64-65 L 6
Ankazoabo 64-65 K 7
An Khe 52-53 E 4
Anklam 33 F 2
Ankober 60-61 MN 7
Ankûr, Jabal – 62 FG 7
Anlong 48-49 JK 6
Anlung = Anlong 48-49 JK 6
Anma-do 50-51 E 5
Ann, Cape – 74-75 H 3
Annaba = 'Annābah 60-61 F 1
'Annābah 60-61 F 1
Annai 78-79 H 4
Annam = Trung Bô 52-53 D 3-E 4
Annan 32 E 4
Annapolis, MD 72-73 L 4
Annapolis Royal 70-71 XY 9
Ann Arbor, MI 72-73 K 3
Annecy 34-35 L 6
An Nho'n 52-53 E 4
Anna Maria Key 74-75 b 3
Annan 32 E 4
Annapolis, MD 72-73 L 4
Annecy 34-35 L 6
Anniston, AL 72-73 JK 5
Anqing 48-49 M 5
Anşâb 44-45 F 8
Anşâb = Nişâb 44-45 EF 5
Anşârīyah, Jabal al- 46-47 G 5
Ansbach 33 E 4
Anshun 48-49 K 6
Ansó 34-35 G 7
Anson Bay 56-57 EF 2
Anşong 50-51 F 4
Ansongo 60-61 E 5
Ansonia, CT 74-75 G 4
Ansted, WV 74-75 C 5
Anta [PE] 78-79 E 7
An-ta = Anda 48-49 NO 2
Antabamba 78-79 E 7
Antakya = Hatay 44-45 D 3
Antália = Antalya 44-45 C 3
Antalya 44-45 C 3
Antalya Körfezi 44-45 C 3
Antananarivo 64-65 L 6
Antarctica 24 B 28-9
Antarctic Peninsula 24 BC 30-31
Antarctic Sound 24 C 31
Antarctique 24 B 28-9
Antarktika 24 B 28-9
Antarktis 24 B 28-9
Antarktisz 24 B 28-29
Antarktyda 24 B 28-9
Antártida 24 B 28-9
Antelope, OR 76-77 C 3
Antelope Hills 76-77 J 4
Antelope Island 76-77 G 5
Antelope Range 76-77 E 6
Antequera 34-35 E 10
Anthony Lagoon 56-57 FG 3
Anti-Atlas = Al-Aţlas aş-Şaghīr 60-61 C 2-3
Anti Atlas = Al-Aţlas aş-Şaghīr 60-61 C 2-3
Antiatlas = Al-Aţlas aş-Şaghīr 60-61 C 2-3
Anti-Atlasz = Al-Aţlas aş-Şaghir 60-61 C 2-3
Antibes 34-35 L 7
Anticosti, Île d' 70-71 Y 8
Antigua 72-73 O 8
Antigua a Barbuda 72-73 OP 8
Antigua and Barbuda 72-73 OP 8
Antigua en Barbuda 72-73 OP 8
Antigua és Barbuda 72-73 OP 8
Antigua et Barbuda 72-73 OP 8
Antigua Guatemala 72-73 H 9
Antigua i Barbuda 72-73 OP 8
Antigua und Barbuda 72-73 OP 8
Antigua y Barbuda 72-73 OP 8
Antikýthera 36-37 K 8
Anti Lebanon = Jabal Lubnân ash-Sharqî 46-47 G 5-6
Anti Liban = Jabal Lubnân ash-Sharqî 46-47 G 5-6
Antilibanon = Jabal Lubnân ash-Sharqî 46-47 G 5-6
Antilibanon = Jabal Lubnân ash-Sharqî 46-47 G 5-6
Antilibanon = Jabal Lubnân ash-Sharqî 46-47 G 5-6
Antilla-tenger = Karib-tenger 72-73 K-N 8
Antilles, Mer des – 72-73 K-N 8
Antilles du Sud, Bassin des – 22-23 G 8
Antillas 72-73 LM 7
Antimélos 36-37 KL 7
Antimony, UT 76-77 H 6
Antinopolis 62 D 4
Antioch, CA 76-77 C 6-7
Antióchia = Antakya 46-47 G 4
Antiokia = Antakya 46-47 FG 4
Antioquia [CO, ●] 78-79 D 4
Antiparos 36-37 L 7
Antitauro = Güneydoğu Toroslar 44-45 DE 3
Anti Taurus = Güneydoğu Toroslar 44-45 DE 3
Antofagasta [RCH, ●] 80 B 2
Antofagasta de la Sierra 80 C 3

Antongila, Helodrano – 64-65 LM 6
Antonibe 64-65 L 5-6
Antrim 32 C 4
Antrim Mountains 32 CD 4
Antsalova 64-65 K 6
Antsirabé 64-65 L 6
Antsiranana 64-65 LM 5
Antsla 30-31 M 9
Antsohihy 64-65 L 5
An Tuc = An Khe 52-53 E 4
Antung = Dandong 48-49 N 3
Antwerpen 34-35 J 3
Antyatlas = Al-Aṭlas aṣ-Ṣaghir 60-61 C 2-3
Antyliban = Jabal Lubnān ash-Sharqī 44-45 G 5-6
Anŭi 50-51 F 5
An'ujsk 42-43 f 4
An'ujskij chrebet 42-43 fg 4
Anuradhapura = Anuradhapuraya 44-45 MN 9
Anuradhapuraya 44-45 MN 9
Anvers = Antwerpen 34-35 J 3
Anvers, Île – 24 C 30
Anxi [TJ, Gansu] 48-49 H 3
Anxious Bay 56-57 F 6
Anyang [ROK] 50-51 F 4
Anyang [TJ] 48-49 LM 4
Anzá [CO] 78-79 D 3
Anzarān, Bi'r – 60-61 B 4
'Anz ar-Ruḥaymāwī 46-47 K 7
Anžero-Sudženska 42-43 PQ 6
Ànzio 36-37 E 5
Anžu, ostrova – 42-43 a-d 2
Anžero-Sudžensk 42-43 PQ 6
Anžu, ostrova – 42-43 a-d 2

Añatuya 80 D 3
Añelo 80 C 5

Aoba = Oba 56-57 N 3
Aoga-shima 48-49 Q 5
Aoga sima = Aoga-shima 48-49 Q 5
Aoji 50-51 H 1
Äolische Inseln = Ìsole Eòlie 36-37 F 6
Aomen = Macau 48-49 L 7
Aomori 48-49 QR 3
Aonae 50-51 a 2
Aosta 36-37 B 3
Aouk, Bahr – 60-61 HJ 7
Aouker = Āwkār 60-61 BC 5
Aoya 50-51 JK 5
Aozou 60-61 H 4

Apa, Rio – 80 E 2
Apache, AZ 76-77 J 10
Apalachee Bay 72-73 K 6
Apaporis, Rio – 78-79 EF 5
Aparri 52-53 H 3
Apat 70-71 ab 4
Apatity 42-43 EF 4
Apatzingan de la Constitución 72-73 F 8
Apeldoorn 34-35 KL 2
Apeninos 28-29 K 7-M 8
Apeniny 36-37 C 3-G 5
Apeniny 36-37 C 3-G 5
Apennine 28-29 K 7-M 8
Apenninen 28-29 K 7-M 8
Apennins 28-29 K 7-M 8
Apennijnen 28-29 K 7-M 8
Apenrade = Åbenrå 30-31 C 10
Apex, NC 74-75 D 7
Api [ZRE] 64-65 G 2
Apia 52-53 c 1
Apiacás, Serra dos – 78-79 H 6-7
Apiai 80 G 3
Apiaú, Serra do – 78-79 G 4
Apo, Mount – 52-53 HJ 5
Apodi, Chapada do – 78-79 M 6
Apodi, Chapada do – 78-79 M 6
Apodi, Chapada do – 78-79 M 6
Apolda 33 E 3
Apolinario Saravia 80 D 2
Apollo Bay 58 F 7
Apollonia = Sūsah 60-61 J 2
Apolo 78-79 F 7
Apolyont Gölü = Uluabat Gölü 46-47 C 2
Apopka, FL 74-75 c 2
Aporé, Rio – 78-79 J 8
Apostle Islands 72-73 HJ 2
Apóstoles 80 E 3
Apostolovo 38-39 F 6
Apoteri 78-79 H 4
Appalache-hegység = Appalachian Mountains 72-73 K 5-N 2
Appalachen = Appalachian Mountains 72-73 K 5-N 2
Appalaches = Appalachian Mountains 72-73 K 5-N 2
Appalachia, VA 74-75 B 6
Appalachian Mountains 72-73 K 5-N 2
Appalachy = Appalachian Mountains 72-73 K 5-N 2
Appalačské pohoří = Appalachian Mountains 72-73 K 5-N 2
Appennino Abruzese 36-37 E 4-F 5
Appennino Toscano 36-37 D 3-4
Appennino Umbro-Marchigiano 36-37 E 4
Appleton, WI 72-73 J 3
Appomattox, VA 74-75 D 6
Apposai 44-45 K 4
Apšeronsk 38-39 G 7
Apšeronskij poluostrov 38-39 K 7
Apsley Strait 56-57 EF 2
Apšeronsk 38-39 G 7
Apšeronskij poluostrov 38-39 K 7
Apucarana 80 F 2
Apucarana, Serra de – 80 F 2
Apulien = Pùglia 36-37 FG 5
Apure, Rio – 78-79 F 3
Apurimac, Rio – 78-79 E 7

'Aqabah, Al- [IRQ] 46-47 KL 7
'Aqabah, Al- [JOR] 44-45 CD 5
'Aqabah, Khalīj al- 44-45 C 5
'Aqabah, Wādī al- 62 EF 2-3
'Aqabat aṣ-Ṣaghīrah, Al- 62 E 5
Āqā Jarī = Āghā Jarī 44-45 FG 4
Āqchalar 46-47 L 5
Āq Chāy 46-47 L 3
Āq Chāy 46-47 L 3
Āqdogh Mīsh, Rūd-e – 46-47 M 4
'Aqeila, el – = Al-'Uqaylah 60-61 H 2
Āq Chāy 46-47 L 3
'Aqīq 60-61 M 5
Aqjawajat 60-61 B 5
'Aqrah 46-47 K 4
Aqshār 60-61 B 4
Āq Sū [IRQ] 46-47 L 5
Aqsu [TJ] 48-49 E 3
Aq Tagh altai = Mongol Altajn Nuruu 48-49 F-H 2
Aquarius Plateau 76-77 H 6-7
Äquatorial-Guinea 60-61 FG 8
Aquidauana 78-79 H 9
Aquila, L' 36-37 E 4

Ārā = Arrah 44-45 N 5
'Arab, Bahr al- 60-61 K 6-7
'Arab, Khalīj al- 62 C 2
'Arab, Shaṭṭ al- 44-45 F 4
'Arabah, Wādī – 62 E 3
'Arabah, Wādī al- 46-47 F 7
Araban 46-47 G 4
Arabatskaja Strelka, kosa – 38-39 FG 6
Arab Emirségek 44-45 G 6-H 5
'Arabestān = Khūzestān 44-45 F 4
Arabi, GA 74-75 B 9
'Arabī, Al-Khalīj al- 46-47 N 8
Arabia 22-23 LM 4
Arabian Basin 22-23 N 5
Arabian Desert 60-61 L 3-4
Arabian Sea 44-45 JK 7
Arabia Saudí 44-45 D 5-F 6
Arabia Saudyjska 44-45 D 5-F 6
Arabië 22-23 LM 4
Arabie 22-23 LM 4
Arabie, Bassin d' 22-23 N 5
Arabie, Mer d' 44-45 JK 7
Arabien 22-23 LM 4
Arabie Saoudite 44-45 D 5-F 6
Arabisch Bekken 22-23 N 5
Arabisches Becken 22-23 N 5
Arabisches Meer 44-45 JK 7
Arabische Woestijn 60-61 L 3-4
Arabische Wüste 60-61 L 3-4
Arabische Zee 44-45 JK 7
Arabistan = Khūzestān 44-45 F 4
Arab-sivatag 60-61 L 3-4
Arab-sivatag = Ar-Rub' al-Khālī 44-45 F 7-G 6
Arabska, Pustynia – 60-61 L 3-4
Arabská poušť 60-61 L 3-4
Arabské moře 44-45 JK 7
Arabskie, Morze – 44-45 JK 7
Arab-tenger 44-45 JK 7
Araç 46-47 E 2
Aracaju 78-79 M 7
Aracati 78-79 M 5
Araçatuba 78-79 JK 9
Araceli = Dumaran Island 52-53 GH 4
Aracena, Sierra de – 34-35 D 10
Arachthós 36-37 J 6
Araçuai 78-79 L 8
Arad 36-37 J 2
Arada 60-61 J 5-6
Arafura, Mar de – 56-57 FG 2
Arafura, Mer d' 56-57 FG 2
Arafura, Morze – 56-57 FG 2
Arafura Sea 56-57 FG 2
Arafurasee 56-57 FG 2
Arafura-tenger 56-57 FG 2
Arafurazee 56-57 FG 2
Arafurské moře 56-57 FG 2
Arago, Cape – 76-77 A 4
Aragón 34-35 G 7-8
Aragón, Río – 34-35 G 7
Aragonien = Aragón 34-35 G 7-8
Araguacema 78-79 K 6
Aragua de Barcelona 78-79 G 3
Araguaia, Parque Nacional do – 78-79 JK 7
Araguaia, Rio – 78-79 J 7
Araguari 78-79 K 8
Araguari, Rio – [BR, Amapá] 78-79 J 4
Araguatins 78-79 K 6
Arai 50-51 M 4
'Araîch, el – = Al-'Arā'ish 60-61 C 1
Araioses 78-79 L 5
'Arā'ish, Al- 60-61 C 1
Araito = ostrov Altasova 42-43 de 7
'Araiyida, Bîr – = Bi'r 'Urayyiḍah 62 DE 3
'Araj, Al- 62 B 3
Arak [DZ] 60-61 E 3
Arāk [IR] 44-45 F 4
Arakamčečen, ostrov – 42-43 I 5
Arakamčečen, ostrov – 42-43 I 5
Arakan = Ragaing Pyinnei 52-53 B 2
Arakawa 50-51 M 3
Araklı 46-47 HJ 2
Araks 38-39 J 8
Araks = Rūd-e Aras 46-47 L 3
Aral, Mar de – = Aral'skoje more 42-43 KL 8-9
Aral, Mer de – = Aral'skoje more 42-43 KL 8-9
Aralık 46-47 L 3
Aralmeer = Aral'skoje more 42-43 KL 8-9
Aral Sea = Aral'skoje more 42-43 KL 8-9
Aralsee = Aral'skoje more 42-43 KL 8-9
Aral'sk 42-43 L 8
Aralské jezero = Aral'skoje more 42-43 KL 8-9
Aralskie, Jezioro – = Aral'skoje more 42-43 KL 8-9
Aral'skoje more 42-43 KL 8-9
Aralsul'fat 42-43 L 8
Aral-tó = Aral'skoje more 42-43 KL 89
Aramac 56-57 HJ 4
'Aramah, Al- 44-45 F 5-6
Aran 32 B 4
Aranda de Duero 34-35 F 8
Arandjelovac 36-37 J 3
Aran Islands 32 AB 5
Aranjuez 34-35 F 8-9
Arany-part 60-61 DE 8
Arao 50-51 H 6
Araouane 60-61 D 5
Arapey 80 E 4
Arapkir 46-47 H 3
Arapongas 80 F 2
'Ar'ar 46-47 J 7
'Ar'ar, Wādī – 46-47 J 7
Araranguá 80 G 3
Araraquara 78-79 K 9
Araras [BR, Pará] 78-79 J 6
Araras [BR, São Paulo] 78-79 K 9
Araras, Serra das – [BR, Mato Grosso] 78-79 J 8
Araras, Serra das – [BR, Paraná] 80 F 2-3
Ararat [AUS] 56-57 H 7
Ararat = Büyük Ağrı Dağı 44-45 E 2-3
Arari, Cachoeira do – 78-79 K 5
Araripe, Chapada do – 78-79 LM 6
Araripe, Chapada do – 78-79 LM 6
Araripe, Chapada do – 78-79 LM 6
Arariúna = Cachoeira do Arari 78-79 K 5
Aras, Rūd-e – 46-47 L 3
Ārāsanj 46-47 O 5
Aras Nehri 44-45 E 2
Arato = Shirataka 50-51 MN 3
Arauan = Araouane 60-61 D 5
Arauca [CO, ●] 78-79 E 3
Arauca, Río – 78-79 F 3
Arauco 80 B 5
Aravaipa Valley 76-77 H 9
Arāvalā Parvata = Aravalli Range 44-45 L 6-M 5
Aravalli Range 44-45 L 6-M 5
Arawa 52-53 j 6
Araxá 78-79 K 8
Araxes = Rūd-e Aras 46-47 L 3
Arba Jahan 63 D 2
Arbaj Cheere = Arvajcheer 48-49 J 2
Arbaj Cheere = Arvajcheer 48-49 J 2
Arbaj Cheere = Arvajcheer 48-49 J 2
Arba Minch = Arba Minty 60-61 M 7
Arba Minty 60-61 M 7
Arbat 46-47 L 5
Arbīl 44-45 E 3
Arboga 30-31 F 8
Arbon, ID 76-77 G 4
Arbroath 32 E 3
Arbuckle, CA 76-77 B 6
Arcachon 34-35 G 6
Arcadia, FL 74-75 c 3
Arcadie = Arkadía 36-37 JK 7
Arcata, CA 76-77 A 5
Arc Dome 76-77 E 6
Archangaj = 7 ◁ 48-49 J 2
Archangel'sk 42-43 G 5
Archenŭ, Gebel – = Jabal Arkanū 60-61 J 4
Archer River 56-57 H 2
Arches National Monument 76-77 J 6
Arciz 36-37 N 3
Arckaringa 56-57 FG 5
Arckaringa Creek 58 B 1-2
Arco 36-37 D 3
Arco, ID 76-77 G 4
Arctic Bay 70-71 TU 3
Arctic Institute Range 24 B 16
Arctic Ocean 19 C 19-B 17
Arctic Ocean 19 AB 32-5
Arctic Red River [CDN, ~] 70-71 K 4
Arctic Red River [CDN, ●] 70-71 K 4
Archipiélago Malayo 22-23 O 5-Q 6
Ard, Rā's al- 46-47 N 8
Arda 36-37 L 5
Ardabīl 44-45 F 3
Ardahan 46-47 K 2
Ardakān 44-45 G 4
Ardakān = Ardekān 44-45 GH 4
Årdalstangen 30-31 BC 7
Ardanuç 46-47 K 2
Ardar Gwagwa, Jabal – 62 F 6
Ardasa = Torul 46-47 H 2
Ardebil = Ardabīl 44-45 F 3
Ardèche 34-35 K 6
Ardekān 44-45 GH 4
Arden, NV 76-77 F 7
Ardennes 34-35 K 4-L 3
Ardennes, Canal des – 34-35 K 4
Ardeşen 46-47 J 2
Ardestān 44-45 G 4
Ardila 34-35 D 9
Ardlethan 58 H 5
Ardmore, OK 72-73 G 5
Ards Peninsula 32 D 4
Ardud 36-37 K 2
Åre 30-31 E 6
Arecibo 72-73 N 8
Areia Branca 78-79 M 5-6
Arena, Point – 76-77 AB 6
Arenales, Cerro – 80 B 7
Arenas, Punta de – 80 C 8
Arendal 30-31 C 8
Arequipa [PE, ●] 78-79 E 8
Arere 78-79 J 5
Åreskutan 30-31 E 6
Arévalo 34-35 E 8
Arezzo 36-37 DE 4
Arfayyāt, Al- 46-47 K 8
Arğa = Akçadağ 46-47 GH 3
Argachtach 42-43 d 4
Arga-Muora-Sise, ostrov – 42-43 XY 3
Argel = Al-Jazā'ir 60-61 E 1
Argelès-sur-Mer 34-35 J 7
Argelia 60-61 D-F 3
Argenta 36-37 D 3
Argentan 34-35 GH 4
Argenteuil 34-35 J 4
Argentia 70-71 Za 8
Argentina 80 C 7-D 2
Argentina 80 C 7-D 3
Argentine 80 C 7-D 3
Argentine, Bassin d' 22-23 GH 7-8
Argentine Basin 22-23 GH 7-8
Argentine Islands 24 C 30
Argentinië 80 C 7-D 3
Argentinien 80 C 7-D 3
Argentinisches Becken 22-23 GH 7-8
Argentyna 80 C 7-D 3
Argentijns Bekken 22-23 GH 7-8
Argeş 36-37 M 3
Arghandāb Rōd 44-45 K 4
Argolikós Kólpos 36-37 K 7
Argonne 34-35 K 4
Árgos 36-37 K 7
Argostólion 36-37 J 6
Arguello, Point – 76-77 C 8
Argun' [SU, ~ ◁ Amur] 42-43 WX 7
Argungu 60-61 EF 6
Argut 42-43 Q 8
Arguvan 46-47 H 3
Arhavi 46-47 J 2
Arhli 60-61 F 5
Århus 30-31 D 9
Ariake kai = Ariakeno-umi 50-51 H 6
Ariakeno-umi 50-51 H 6
Ariake-wan = Shibushi-wan 50-51 H 7
Ariano Irpino 36-37 F 5
Aribinda 60-61 D 6
Arica [CO] 78-79 E 5
Arica [RCH] 80 B 1
'Ārid, Al- 44-45 F 6-7
Arid, Cape – 56-57 D 6
Ariège 34-35 H 7
Ariel, WA 76-77 B 3
Arīha 46-47 F 7
Arikawa 50-51 G 6
Arimã [BR] 78-79 G 6
Arimo, ID 76-77 GH 4
Arinos 78-79 K 8
Arinos, Rio – 78-79 H 7
Aripuanã, Rio – 78-79 G 6
Ariquemes 78-79 G 6
'Arīsh, Al- 60-61 L 2
'Arīsh, Wādī al- 62 E 2-3
Arismendi 78-79 F 3
Arita 50-51 K 5
Arivaca, AZ 76-77 H 10
Ariza 34-35 FG 8
Arizaro, Salar de – 80 C 2
Arizona [RA] 80 C 5
Arizona [USA] 72-73 D 5
Årjäng 30-31 E 8
Arjeplog 30-31 GH 4
Arjona [CO] 78-79 D 2
Arka 42-43 b 5
Arkadak 38-39 H 5
Arkadía 36-37 JK 7
Arkadien = Arkadiia 36-37 JK 7
Arkalyk 42-43 M 7
Arkansas 72-73 H 4
Arkansas River 72-73 F 4
Arkanū, Jabal – 60-61 J 4
Arkenu, Jebel – = Jabal Arkanū 60-61 J 4
Arklow 32 CD 5
Arkona, Kap – 33 F 1
Arktičeskogo Instituta, ostrova – 42-43 OP 2
Arktičeskogo Instituta, ostrova – 42-43 OP 2
Arktyczne, Morze – 19 AB 32-5
Arlanzón 34-35 EF 7
Arlberg 33 E 5
Arlee, MT 76-77 F 2
Arles 34-35 K 7
Arlington, OR 76-77 CD 3
Arlington, VA 72-73 L 4
Arlington, WA 76-77 BC 1
Arlit = Arhli 60-61 F 5
Arlon 34-35 K 4
Armadale 56-57 C 6
Armagh 32 C 4
Armagnac 34-35 GH 7
Armand, Rivière – 70-71 W 6
Armant 62 E 5
Armavir 38-39 H 6-7
Armenia 38-39 H 7-J 8
Armenië 38-39 H 7-J 8
Arménie 38-39 H 7-J 8
Armenien 38-39 H 7-J 8
Armentières 34-35 J 3
Armero 78-79 E 3
Armevistēs, Akrōtērion – 36-37 M 7
Armidale 56-57 K 6
Armstead, MT 76-77 G 3
Armuña, La – 34-35 DE 8
Armuña, La – 34-35 DE 8
Arnarfjördhur 30-31 ab 2
Arnarvatn 30-31 cd 2
Arnávtē, Akrōtērion – 46-47 DE 5
Årnes 30-31 cd 2
Arnheim = Arnhem 34-35 K 2-3
Arnhem 34-35 KL 2-3
Arnhem, Cape – 56-57 G 2
Arnhem Bay 56-57 G 2
Arnhem Land 56-57 FG 2
Arno 36-37 D 4
Arno Bay 58 C 4
Arnold, PA 74-75 D 4
Arnøy 30-31 J 2
Arnsberg 33 D 3
Arnstadt 33 E 3
Arnswalde = Choszczno 33 GH 2
Aroab 64-65 E 8
Arōmā = Arūmā 60-61 M 5
Aroostook River 70-71 X 8
Arpaçay 46-47 K 2
Arpa Çayı 46-47 K 2
Arqa tagh 48-49 FG 4
'Arqūb, Al- 60-61 AB 4
Arrah [IND] 44-45 N 5
Arraias 78-79 K 7
Arraiján 72-73 b 3
Arran 32 D 4
Arras 34-35 J 3
Arrecife 60-61 B 3
Arrecifes, Gran Barrera de – = Great Barrier Reef 56-57 H 1-K 4
Arrée, Monts d' 34-35 EF 4
Arriaga 72-73 H 8
Ar-Rijad = Ar-Riyāḍ 44-45 F 6
Arriola, CO 76-77 J 7
Arroyo Grande, CA 76-77 CD 8
Arroyo Seco [USA] 76-77 F 9
Arša Nuur = Chagan nuur 48-49 L 3
Arsenjev 42-43 Z 9
Arsī 60-61 M 7
Arsuz = Uluçınar 46-47 F 4
Arša Nuur = Chagan nuur 48-49 L 3
Árta 36-37 J 6
Artaki = Erdek 46-47 B 2
Arṭāwīyah, Al – 44-45 EF 5
Artesia, CO 76-77 J 5
Artesia, NM 72-73 EF 5
Arthur 74-75 C 3
Arthur River 58 b 2
Arthur's Pass 56-57 O 8
Arti 38-39 L 4
Ártico Central, Cuenca del – 19 A
Artigas [ROU, ●] 80 E 4
Artjärvi 30-31 LM 7
Artois 34-35 J 3
Art'om 42-43 Z 9
Art'omovsk [SU, Rossijskaja SFSR] 42-43 R 7
Art'omovskij [SU ↗ Bodajbo] 42-43 VW 6
Art'omovskij [SU ↗ Sverdlovsk] 42-43 L 6
Artova 46-47 G 2
Artur de Paiva = Capelongo 64-65 E 5
Arturo Prat 24 C 30-31
Artvin 44-45 E 2
Aru 64-65 H 2
Aru, Kepulauan – 52-53 KL 8
Arua 64-65 H 2
Aruab 64-65 E 8
Aruanã 78-79 J 7
Aruba 72-73 N 9
Arumã [BR] 78-79 G 5
Arūmā [Sudan] 60-61 M 5
Arumbi 64-65 G 2
Arumpo 58 F 4
Aruṇ 44-45 O 5
Arunachal Pradesh 44-45 P Q 5
Arunta Desert = Simpson Desert 56-57 G 4-5
Arusha 64-65 J 3
Arusī = Arsī 60-61 M 7
Aruwimi 64-65 G 2
Arvajcheer 48-49 J 2
Arvidsjaur 30-31 H 5
Arvika 30-31 E 8
Arvin, CA 76-77 D 8
Arys' 42-43 M 9
Arzamas 42-43 GH 6
Arzgir 38-39 H 6

Åsa [S] 30-31 E 9
Aša [SU] 38-39 L 4
Asadābād [AFG] 44-45 L 4
Asadābād [IR] 46-47 MN 5
Aşağıçıgıl 46-47 DE 3
Aşağı Pınarbaşı 46-47 E 3
Asahi 50-51 N 5
Asahi dake [J, Hokkaidō] 48-49 R 3
Asahi dake [J, Yamagata] 50-51 M 3
Asahigava = Asahikawa 48-49 R 3
Asahi gawa 50-51 J 5
Asahikawa 48-49 R 3
Asalē [ETH, ●] 60-61 MN 6
Asalē [ETH, ≈] 60-61 N 6
Asam 44-45 P 5
Asángaro = Azángaro 78-79 EF7
Asansol 44-45 O 6
Asante = Ashanti 60-61 D 7
Åsarna 30-31 F 6
'Asayr 44-45 G 8
Asayta 60-61 N 6
Asben = Azbine 60-61 F 5
Asbest 42-43 L 6
Asbe Teferī 60-61 N 7
Asbury Park, NJ 74-75 FG 4
Ascensión [BOL] 78-79 G 8
Ascension [GB] 66 E 9
Ascensión, Bahía de la – 72-73 J 8
Aschabad 44-45 HJ 3
Aschaffenburg 33 D 4
Àscoli-Piceno 36-37 E 4
Aseb 60-61 N 6
Asela 60-61 M 7
Åsele 30-31 G 5
Aselle = Asela 60-61 M 7
Asenovgrad 36-37 L 4-5
Aserbaidschan 38-39 J 7
Aşfī = Şāfī 60-61 C 2
Aşfūn 62 E 5
Ashanti 60-61 D 7
Ashāqif, Tulūl al- 46-47 G 6
'Asharah, Al- 46-47 J 5
Ashburn, GA 74-75 B 9
Ashburton 56-57 O 8
Ashburton River 56-57 C 4
Ashdōd 46-47 F 7
Asheboro, NC 74-75 CD 7
Asheville, NC 72-73 K 4
Ashe Yōma 52-53 C 3
Ashford 32 G 6
Ashford [AUS] 58 K 2
Ashford, WA 76-77 BC 2
Ash Fork, AZ 76-77 G 8
Ashibetsu 50-51 c 2
Ashikaga 50-51 M 4
Ashizuri-zaki 50-51 J 6
Ashkelon = Ashqĕlōn 46-47 F 7
Ashland, KY 72-73 K 4
Ashland, ME 74-75 J 1
Ashland, OH 74-75 BC 4
Ashland, OR 76-77 B 4
Ashland, VA 74-75 E 6
Ashland, WI 72-73 H 2
Ashland, Mount – 76-77 B 4
Ashmūn 62 D 2
Ashmūnayn, Al- 62 D 4
Ashqĕlōn 46-47 F 7
Ashshur = Assur 44-45 E 3
Ashtabula, OH 74-75 C 3-4
Ashton, ID 76-77 H 3
Ashuanipi Lake 70-71 X 7
'Āshūrīyah, Al- 46-47 K 7
'Āṣī, Al- 46-47 G 4
'Āṣī, Nahr al- 46-47 G 5
Asia 22-23 N-P 3
Asia, Kepulauan – 52-53 K 6

Asie 22-23 N-P 3
Asien 22-23 N-P 3
Asike 52-53 LM 8
Asinara 36-37 BC 5
Asinara, Golfo dell' 36-37 C 5
Asi Nehri 46-47 G 4
Asino 42-43 PQ 6
'Asīr 44-45 E 7
Asiut = Asyūṭ 60-61 L 3
Aşkale 46-47 J 3
Askalon = Ashqēlōn 46-47 F 7
Asker 30-31 D 8
Askersund 30-31 F 8
Askī Muşil 46-47 K 4
Askja 30-31 e 2
Aşlāndūz 46-47 M 3
Asmaca = Feke 46-47 F 4
Asmara = Asmera 60-61 M 5
Asmera 60-61 M 5
Asnām, Al- = Shilif 60-61 E 1
Asosa 60-61 LM 6
Asotin, WA 76-77 E 2
Asowsches Meer = Azovskoje more 38-39 G 6
Aso zan 50-51 H 6
Aspen Hill, MD 74-75 E 5
Aspiring, Mount - 56-57 N 8
Aspromonte 36-37 FG 6
'Aşr, Jabal al- 62 D 6
Assab = Aseb 60-61 N 6
Assaitta = Asaita 60-61 N 6
Assal, Lac - = Asalē 60-61 N 6
Assale = Asalē 60-61 MN 6
Assam = Asam 44-45 P 5
Assam Hills 44-45 P 5
Assam Himâlaya 44-45 OP 5
Assateague Island 74-75 F 5
Assen 34-35 L 2
Assens 30-31 CD 10
Assiniboine, Mount - 70-71 NO 7
Assiniboine River 70-71 Q 7
Assis 78-79 J 9
Assisi 36-37 E 4
Assiut = Asyūṭ 60-61 L 3
Assuan = Aswān 60-61 L 4
Assumption Island 64-65 L 4
Assur 44-45 E 3
Asszuán = Aswān 60-61 L 4
Astakós 36-37 J 6
Āstāneh 46-47 N 6
Astara 38-39 J 8
Āstārā [IR] 46-47 N 3
Astorga 34-35 DE 7
Astoria, OR 72-73 B 2
Astove Island 64-65 L 5
Astra 80 C 7
Astrachan 38-39 J 6
Astrida 64-65 G 3
Astrolabe Bay 52-53 N 7-8
Asturias 34-35 DE 7
Astypálaia 36-37 LM 7
Asunción [PY] 80 E 3
Asunción, La - 78-79 G 2
Asūtarībah, Jabal - 62 G 7
Aswa 64-65 H 2
Aswān 60-61 L 4
'Aswān, Sad el - = Sadd al-'Ālī 60-61 L 3
Asyūṭ 60-61 L 3
Asyūṭī, Wādī al- 62 D 4

Aša [SU] 38-39 L 4
Aščhabad 44-45 HJ 3

Aszjút = Asyūṭ 60-61 L 3

Atacama [RA] 80 BC 3
Atacama, Desierto de - 80 B 3-C 2
Atacama, Fosa de - 22-23 F 6-7
Atacama, Fosse d' 22-23 FG 7
Atacama, Salar de - 80 C 2
Atacamagraben 22-23 F 6-7
Atacama Trench 22-23 F 6-7
Atacamatrog 22-23 F 6-7
Atakor = Atākūr 60-61 F 4
Atakora, Chaîne de l' 60-61 E 6-7
Atakora, Chaîne de l' 60-61 E 6-7
Atakpamé 60-61 E 7
Atákūr 60-61 F 4
Atalaya [PE, ●] 78-79 E 7
Ataleia 78-79 L 8
Atami 50-51 M 5
Ataniya = Adana 44-45 D 3
Ataouat, Day Nui - 52-53 E 3
Atapupu 52-53 H 8
'Atāqah, Jabal - 62 E 2-3
Āţâr 60-61 B 4
Atarque, NM 76-77 J 8
Atascadero, CA 76-77 C 8
Atasu 42-43 N 8
Atatürk Baraji 46-47 H 4
'Aţbarah 60-61 L 5
'Aţbarah, Nahr - 60-61 LM 5
Atbasar 42-43 M 7
Ātbu Şāliḥ 46-47 M 7
Atenas = Athēnai 36-37 KL 7
Ateny = Athēnai 36-37 KL 7
Atény = Athēnai 36-37 KL 7

Atessa 36-37 F 4-5
Atfârītī 60-61 B 3
Aţfiḥ 62 D 3
Athabasca 70-71 O 7
Athabasca, Lake - 70-71 OP 6
Athabasca River 70-71 O 6
'Athāmīn, Al- 46-47 K 7
Athen = Athēnai 36-37 KL 7
Athena, OR 76-77 D 3
Athēnai 36-37 KL 7
Athēn = Athēnai 36-37 KL 7
Athene = Athēnai 36-37 KL 7
Athènes = Athēnai 36-37 KL 7
Athenry 32 B 5
Athens, GA 72-73 K 5
Athens, OH 74-75 B 5
Athens, PA 74-75 E 4
Athens = Athēnai 36-37 KL 7
Atherton 56-57 HJ 3
Athi 64-65 J 3
Äthiopien 60-61 MN 7
Athi River 63 D 3
Athlone 32 C 5
Athol, ID 76-77 E 2
Áthos 36-37 L 5
Ati 60-61 H 6
Atiak 63 BC 2
Atico 78-79 E 8
Atil 76-77 H 10
Atitlán, Volcán - 72-73 H 9
Atka 42-43 d 5
Atka Island 19 D 36
Atkarsk 38-39 H 5
Atlanta, GA 72-73 K 5
Atlanta, ID 76-77 F 4
Atlantic City, NJ 72-73 M 4
Atlantic Coastal Plain 72-73 K 5-L 4
Atlantic Indian Antarctic Basin 22-23 J-M 9
Atlantic Indian Trench 22-23 J-L 8
Atlantic Ocean 22-23 G 4-J 7
Atlántico Norte, Dorsal del - 22-23 J-L 5
Atlántico Sur, Dorsal del - 22-23 J 6-8
Atlantische Oceaan 22-23 G 4-J 7
Atlantischer Ozean 22-23 G 4-J 7
Atlantisch-Indischer Rücken 22-23 J-L 8
Atlantisch-Indische Rug 22-23 J-L 8
Atlantisch-Indisches Südpolarbecken 22-23 J-M 9
Atlantisch-Indisch Zuidpolarbekken 22-23 J-M 9
Atlas 22-23 JK 4
Atlas al-Khalfīyah, Jabal- 60-61 C 2-3
Atlas al-Wasṭī, Jabal- 60-61 CD 2
Atlas as-Şaghīr, Al- 60-61 C 2-3
Atlas Medio = Al-Aṭlas al-Mutawassiṭ 60-61 CD 2
Atlasova, ostrov - 42-43 de 7
Atlas Sahariano 60-61 D 2-F 1
Atlas Saharien 60-61 D 2-F 1
Atlas Saharyjski 60-61 D 2-F 1
Atlas Šrední = Al-Aṭlas al-Mutawassiṭ 60-61 CD 2
Atlas Tellien 60-61 D 2-E 1
Atlas Tellski 60-61 D 2-E 1
Atlas Telliano 60-61 D 2-E 1
Atlas Wysoki 60-61 CD 2
Atlin 70-71 K 6
Atlin Lake 70-71 K 6
Atlixco 72-73 G 8
Atløy 30-31 A 7
Atomic City, ID 76-77 G 4
Atouat, Massif d' = Day Nui Ataouat 52-53 E 3
Aträk 38-39 K 8
Aţrash, Wādī al- 62 E 4
Atrato, Rio - 78-79 D 3
Atrek 38-39 K 8
'Aţrūn, Al- 60-61 K 5
Atsumi 50-51 M 5
Atsumi-hantō 50-51 L 5
Atsunai 50-51 cd 2
Atsuta 50-51 b 2
Atsutoko 50-51 d 2
Attalea = Antalya 44-45 C 3
Attaléia = Antalya 44-45 C 3
Attawapiskat River 70-71 TU 7
Attopo' = Attopu 52-53 E 3-4
Attopu 52-53 E 3-4
Attu Island 19 D 1
Atûwi, Wâd - 60-61 B 4
Atwater, CA 76-77 C 7

Auati Paraná, Rio - 78-79 F 5
Aubagne 34-35 K 7
Aube 34-35 K 4
Aubrac, Monts d' 34-35 J 6
Auburn, AL 72-73 J 5
Auburn, CA 76-77 C 6
Auburn, ME 74-75 H 2
Auburn, NY 74-75 E 3
Auburn, WA 76-77 B 2
Auburndale, FL 74-75 c 2-3
Aucanquilcha, Cerro - 80 C 2
Auce 30-31 K 9
Auch 34-35 H 7
Auckland 56-57 OP 7
Auckland, Ramal de - 24 D 17
Auckland, Seuil des - 24 D 17

Aucklanddrempel 24 D 17
Auckland Islands 24 D 17-18
Auckland-küszöb 24 D 17
Aucklandschwelle 24 D 17
Aude 34-35 J 7
Aue 33 F 3
Auenat, Gebel - = Jabal al-'Uwaynāt 60-61 K 4
Auf, Ras el- = Rā's Banās 60-61 M 4
Augathella 56-57 J 5
Àugila = Awjilah 60-61 J 3
Augrabies Falls = Augrabiesval 64-65 EF 8
Augrabiesval 64-65 EF 8
Augsburg 33 E 4
Augusta [AUS] 56-57 BC 6
Augusta [I] 36-37 F 7
Augusta, GA 72-73 K 5
Augusta, ME 72-73 N 3
Augusta, MT 76-77 G 2
Augustów 33 L 2
Augustus, Mount - 56-57 C 4
Augustus Downs 56-57 GH 3
Augustus Island 56-57 D 3
Auja = Qēẓī'ôt 46-47 F 7
Auk = Bahr Aouk 60-61 HJ 7
Auki 52-53 k 6
Aulander, NC 74-75 E 6
Auld, Lake - 56-57 D 4
Aunis 34-35 G 5
Auob 64-65 E 8
Aurangabad [IND, Maharashtra] 44-45 LM 6-7
Aurich 33 C 2
Aurignac 34-35 H 7
Aurillac 34-35 J 6
Aurlandsvangen 30-31 B 7
Aurora [CDN] 76-77 D 2-3
Aurora, IL 72-73 J 3
Aurora, NC 74-75 E 7
Aurora, OH 74-75 A 5
Aurukun 56-57 H 2
Aus 64-65 E 8
Ausangate = Nudo Ausangate 78-79 E 7
Ausangate, Nudo - 78-79 E 7
Auschwitz = Oświęcim 33 J 3-4
Ausiait 70-71 Za 4
Aussig = Ústí nad Labem 33 FG 3
Aust-Agder 30-31 BC 8
Austerlitz = Slavkov u Brna 33 H 4
Austfonna 30-31 m 4
Austin, MN 72-73 H 3
Austin, NV 76-77 E 6
Austin, OR 76-77 D 3
Austin, TX 72-73 G 5
Austin, Lake - 56-57 C 5
Australia 56-57 C-J 4
Australia Meridional, Cuenca de - 22-23 PQ 8
Australia Noroccidental, Cuenca de - 22-23 OP 6
Australia Occidental, Cuenca de - 22-23 P 7
Australia Oriental, Cuenca de - 22-23 RS 8
Australia Septentrional, Cuenca de - 56-57 C 2
Australie 56-57 C-J 4
Australië 56-57 C-J 4
Australie 56-57 C-J 4
Australien 56-57 C-J 4
Australische Alpen = Snowy Mountains 56-57 J 7
Australské Alpy = Snowy Mountains 56-57 J 7
Austrálie 56-57 C-J 4
Ausztrália 56-57 C-J 4
Ausztria 33 E-G 5
Aután de Navarro 72-73 EF 8
Autriche 33 E-G 5
Autun 34-35 K 5
Auvergne 34-35 J 6
Auvergne [AUS] 56-57 EF 3
Auxerre 34-35 J 5
Auyuittuq National Park 70-71 XY 4

Aversa 36-37 EF 5
Avery, ID 76-77 F 2
Avesta 30-31 G 7
Avezzano 36-37 E 4-5
Avignon 34-35 K 7
Ávila 34-35 E 8
Avilés 34-35 DE 7
Avión, Faro de - 34-35 CD 7
Avis 34-35 D 9
Avlije-Ata = Džambul 42-43 MN 9
Avola 36-37 F 7
Avon, MT 76-77 G 2
Avondale, AZ 76-77 G 9
Avon Downs 56-57 G 4
Avon Park, FL 74-75 c 3
Avranches 34-35 G 4
Avşa Adası 46-47 B 2

Awadh = Avadh 44-45 N 5
Awādī 60-61 B 4
Awaji-shima 50-51 K 5
'Awānah 60-61 C 5
Awasa 60-61 M 7
Awasa Hayik 60-61 M 7
Awash [ETH, ~] 60-61 M 7
Awash [ETH, ●] 60-61 MN 7
Awaso 60-61 D 7
Awaya 50-51 K 5
Awbārī 60-61 G 3
Awbārī, Dahnā' - 60-61 G 3
Awdah, Hawr - 46-47 M 7
Awdheegle 60-61 N 8
Awe, Loch - 32 D 3
Aweil = Uwayl 60-61 K 7
'Awjā', Al- 46-47 M 8
Awjilah 60-61 J 3
Āwkār 60-61 BC 5
Awlaytīs, Wād - 60-61 B 3
Awsart 60-61 B 4
Awsaţ, Al- 60-61 L 6
Awul 52-53 h 6

Axarfjördhur 30-31 e 1
Axel Heiberg Island 70-71 ST 1-2
Axim 60-61 D 8
Ax-les-Thermes 34-35 HJ 7

Ayabaca 78-79 CD 5
Ayabe 50-51 K 5
Ayacucho [RA] 80 E 5
Ayacucho [PE, ●] 78-79 E 7
Ayagh Qum köl 48-49 F 4
Ayamonte 34-35 D 10
Ayancik 46-47 F 2
Ayas 72-73 GH 2
'Ayāshī, Jabal - 60-61 CD 2
Ayaviri 78-79 E 7
Aybastī 46-47 G 2
Ayden, NC 74-75 E 7
Aydin 44-45 B 3
Aydincik 46-47 E 4
Aydin Dağları 46-47 B 4-C 3
Aydinkent 46-47 D 4
Aydin köl 48-49 F 3
Aydinlik Dağları 46-47 J 3
Ayers Rock 56-57 F 5
'Aylay 60-61 L 5
Aylesbury 32 F 6
'Aylī, Sha'īb al- 46-47 H 7
Aylmer [CDN, Ontario] 74-75 C 3
'Ayn, Wādī al- 44-45 H 6
Aynabo 60-61 O 7
'Ayn al-Ghazal [LAR] 60-61 J 4
'Ayn al-Muqshin, Al- 44-45 GH 7
'Ayn 'Ayssah 46-47 H 4
'Ayn Azzān 60-61 G 4
'Ayn Dīwār 46-47 K 4
'Ayn Qazzān 60-61 EF 5
'Ayn Şafrā 60-61 DE 2
'Ayn Şālih 60-61 E 3
'Ayn-Umannās 60-61 F 3
Aynunāh 42-43 D 5
'Ayn Zālah 46-47 K 4
Ayöd = Ayūd 60-61 L 7
Ayr 32 D 4
Ayr [AUS] 56-57 J 3
Ayrancı 46-47 E 4
Ayre, Point of - 32 DE 4
Ayrig Nur = Ajrag nuur 48-49 GH 2
Aysha 60-61 N 6
Ayu, Kepulauan - 52-53 K 6
Ayūd 60-61 L 7
'Ayun, Al- 60-61 B 3
'Ayūn al-'Atrūs 60-61 C 5
Ayvacık [TR, Çanakkale] 46-47 B 3
Ayvalık 46-47 B 3
'Ayyāţ, Al- 62 D 3

Azafal 60-61 AB 4
'Azair, Al- = Al-'Uzayr 46-47 M 7
'Azamīyah, Baghdad-Al- 46-47 L 6
Azaoua, I-n- 60-61 F 4
Azaouâd 60-61 D 5
Azaouak, Vallée de - 60-61 E 5
Azare 60-61 FG 6
Āzar Shahr 46-47 LM 4
Azawak, Wadi = Azaouak 60-61 E 5
A'zāz 46-47 G 4
Azbine 60-61 F 5

Azdavay 46-47 E 2
Azéfal = Azafal 60-61 AB 4
Azerbaïdjan 38-39 J 7
Azerbaijan 38-39 J 7
Azerbajdžan 38-39 J 7
Āzerbāydjān 38-39 J 7
Āzerbāydžan 38-39 J 7
Azerbajdzjan 38-39 J 7
Azerbejdžan 38-39 J 7
Aziē 22-23 N-P 3
'Azīzīyah, Al- [IRQ] 46-47 L 6
'Azīzīyah, Al- [LAR] 60-61 G 2
Aẓlam, Wādī - 62 FG 4
'Azmāṭī, Sabkhat - 60-61 DE 3
Aznā 46-47 N 6
Azoren = Açores 66 D 5
Azorendrempel 22-23 HJ 4
Azorenschwelle 22-23 HJ 4
Azores = Açores 66 D 3
Azores, Plataforma de - 22-23 HJ 4
Azores Plateau 22-23 HJ 4
Azov 38-39 G 6
Azov, Mar de - = Azovskoje more 38-39 G 6
Azov, Mer d' = Azovskoje more 38-39 G 6
Azov, Sea of - = Azovskoje more 38-39 G 6
Azovskoje more 38-39 G 6
Azraq, El- = Azraq ash-Shīshān 46-47 G 7
Azraq ash-Shīshān 46-47 G 7
Azroū = Azrū 60-61 CD 2
Azrū 60-61 CD 2
Aztec, AZ 76-77 G 9
Azuaga 34-35 E 9
Azucar, Pan de - 78-79 D 4
Azuero, Península de - 72-73 K 10
Azul [RA] 80 E 5
Azuma-yama 50-51 MN 4
Azurduy 78-79 G 8-9
Azza = Ghazzah 44-45 C 4
'Azzān 44-45 F 8
Azzel Matti, Sebkra = Sabkhat 'Azmāṭī 60-61 DE 3

B

Baa 52-53 H 9
Ba'abdâ 46-47 F 6
Baalbek = Ba'labakk 46-47 G 5-6
Ba'an = Batang 48-49 H 6
Baardheere 60-61 N 8
Bâb, Al- 46-47 G 4
Baba Burun [TR, Çanakkale] 44-45 B 3
Baba Burun [TR, Zonguldak] 46-47 D 2
Babadag 36-37 N 3
Babadag, gora - 38-39 J 7
Babaeski 46-47 B 2
Baba Hatim 48-49 E 4
Babahoyo 78-79 CD 5
Babar, Kepulauan - 52-53 JK 8
Babati 63 C 4
Babb, MT 76-77 G 1
Babbit, NV 76-77 D 6
Babel = Babylon 44-45 EF 4
Babelthuap 52-53 KL 5
Babia Góra 33 J 4
Bābil 46-47 L 6
Bābil = Babylon 44-45 EF 4
Babinda 56-57 J 3
Babine Lake 70-71 L 6-7
Babine Range 70-71 L 6-7
Bābol 44-45 G 3
Baboquivari Peak 76-77 H 10
Baboua 60-61 G 7
Bābul = Bābol 44-45 G 3
Babuškin 42-43 U 7
Babuškin, zaliv - 42-43 de 6
Babuškin 42-43 U 7
Babuškina, zaliv - 42-43 de 6
Babuyan Channel 52-53 H 3
Babuyan Channel 52-53 H 3
Babuyan Islands 52-53 H 3
Babuyan Islands 52-53 H 3
Babylon 44-45 EF 4
Babylon, NY 74-75 G 4
'Ayun, Al- 60-61 B 3
Bacan, Pulau - 52-53 J 7
Bacău 36-37 M 2
Bacchus Marsh 58 G 6
Bacerac 76-77 J 10
Bachardem 44-45 H 3
Bachchar = Bashshār 60-61 D 2
Bachkirs, République Autonome des - = 42-43 K 7
Bachmač 38-39 F 5
Bachu = Maral Bashi 48-49 D 3-4
Bačka 36-37 H 3
Bačka Palanka 36-37 H 3
Bačka Topola 36-37 HJ 3
Back Bay 74-75 F 6
Back River 70-71 R 4

Backstairs Passage 56-57 G 7
Bac Lio' = Vinh Lo'i 52-53 E 5
Bacoachi 76-77 J 10
Bacolod 52-53 H 4
Bacuit = El Nido 52-53 G 4
Bačka 36-37 H 3
Bačka Palanka 36-37 H 3
Bačka Topola 36-37 HJ 3
Bad', Wādī - 62 E 3
Badahsan-hegyvidéki Autonóm Terület 44-45 L 3
Badajos, Lago - 78-79 G 5
Badajoz 34-35 D 9
Badakhshān 44-45 L 3
Badalona 34-35 J 8
Badanah 44-45 E 4
Badārī, Al- 60-61 L 3
Badayun = Budaun 44-45 M 5
Baddūzzah, Rā's al- 60-61 BC 2
Bad Ems 33 C 3
Baden [A] 33 H 4
Baden [CH] 33 D 5
Baden-Baden 33 D 4
Baden-Württemberg 33 D 4
Badgastein 33 F 5
Bad Hersfeld 33 D 3
Bad Homburg 33 D 3
Bādī, Al- [IRQ] 46-47 J 5
Badī', Al- [Saudi-Arabien] 44-45 F 6
Badīn 44-45 K 6
Badin, NC 74-75 C 7
Bad Ischl 33 F 5
Bad Kissingen 33 E 3
Bad Kreuznach 33 CD 4
Badlands [USA, North Dakota] 72-73 F 2
Badlands [USA, South Dakota] 72-73 F 3
Bad Mergentheim 33 DE 4
Bad Nauheim 33 D 3
Bad Neuenahr 33 C 3
Baḍodēñ = Vadodara 44-45 L 6
Ba Đôn 52-53 E 3
Badong [TJ] 48-49 KL 5
Badr 44-45 E 7
Badrah 46-47 L 6
Badr Ḥunayn 44-45 D 6
Bad Reichenhall 33 F 5
Bad Tölz 33 E 5
Badu Danan = Denan 60-61 N 7
Badu Island 56-57 H 2
Badulla 44-45 N 9
Bad Wildungen 33 D 3
Bafang 60-61 G 7-8
Baffin, Bahía de - 70-71 W-Y 3
Baffin, Baie - 70-71 W-Y 3
Baffin, District of - 70-71 T-V 3-4
Baffina, Morze - 70-71 W-Y 3
Baffinbaai 70-71 W-Y 3
Baffinbai 70-71 W-Y 3
Baffin Bay 70-71 W-Y 3
Baffin Island 70-71 V 3-X 5
Baffin Island National Park 70-71 XY 4
Baffinland = Baffin Island 70-71 V 3-X 5
Baffin-öböl 70-71 W-Y 3
Baffinŭvo moře 70-71 W-Y 3
Bafia 60-61 G 8
Bafing 60-61 B 6
Bafoulabé 60-61 BC 6
Bafoussam 60-61 G 7
Bâfq 44-45 GH 4
Bafra 46-47 FG 2
Bafra Burnu 46-47 G 2
Bafwasende 64-65 G 2
Bagabag Island 52-53 N 7
Bâgalakôṭṭē = Bagalkot 44-45 LM 7
Bagalkot 44-45 LM 7
Bagalpur = Bhagalpur 44-45 O 5-6
Bagamojo = Bagamoyo 64-65 J 4
Bagamoyo 64-65 J 4
Bagan Jaya = Butterworth 52-53 D 5
Bagase Burnu = İncekum Burnu 46-47 EF 4
Bagdad, AZ 76-77 G 8
Bagdad = Baghdād 44-45 EF 4
Bagdad = Baghdād 44-45 EF 4
Bagdād = Baghdād 44-45 EF 4
Bagdarin 42-43 VW 7
Bağgöze 46-47 JK 4
Baghdād 44-45 EF 4
Baghdad = Baghdād 44-45 EF 4
Baghdādī, Rās - = Rā's Ḥunkurāb 62 F 5
Baghelkhand 44-45 N 6
Bagheria 36-37 E 6
Baghlân 44-45 K 3
Baghrash köl 48-49 F 3
Bagirmi = Baguirmi 60-61 H 6
Bağlum 46-47 E 2
Bagnères-de-Bigorre 34-35 H 7
Bagnères-de-Luchon 34-35 H 7
Bagoé 60-61 C 6
Bagrationovsk 33 K 1
Baguio 52-53 H 3
Bagur, Cabo - 34-35 J 8
Bagzane, Monts - 60-61 F 5

Bahadale 63 D 2-3
Bahamas 72-73 L 6-M 7
Bahamas, Banc des – 72-73 L 6-7
Bahamas, Gran Banco de las – 72-73 L 6-7
Bahama-szigetek 72-73 L 6-M 7
Bahamy 72-73 L 6-M 7
Bāhār 46-47 N 5
Baharāich = Bahraich 44-45 N 5
Baharampur 44-45 O 6
Bahar Assoli = Beraisolē 60-61 N 6
Baḥarīyah, Wāḥāt al- 60-61 K 3
Bahāwalpur 44-45 L 5
Bahçe 46-47 G 4
Bahçesaray 46-47 K 3
Bahia 78-79 LM 7
Bahia = Salvador 78-79 M 7
Bahía, Islas de la – 72-73 J 8
Bahía Blanca [RA, ◡] 80 D 5
Bahía Blanca [RA, ●] 80 D 5
Bahía de Caráquez 78-79 CD 5
Bahía Grande 80 C 8
Bahía Laura 80 CD 7
Bahía Negra 80 E 2
Bahía Oso Blanco 80 CD 7
Bahía Solano [CO, ●] 78-79 D 3
Bahir Dar 60-61 M 6
Baḥrah, Al- 46-47 MN 8
Bahraich 44-45 N 5
Bahrain 44-45 G 5
Bahrajn 44-45 G 5
Baḥrayn, Al- 62 B 3
Bahr Dar Giorgis = Bahir Dar 60-61 M 6
Baḥreh, Āb-e – 46-47 N 7
Baḥr-e 'Ommān, Banāder va Jazāyer-e – = 6 ◁ 44-45 H 5
Bahrgān, Ra's-e – 46-47 N 7-8
Baḥrīyah, Barqat al- 60-61 JK 2
Bahu-mbelu 52-53 H 7
Bachmač 38-39 F 5
Bai 48-49 E 3
Baía = Salvador 78-79 M 7
Baía dos Tigres 64-65 D 6
Baia Mare 36-37 KL 2
Baião 78-79 JK 5
Baia Sprie 36-37 KL 2
Baïbokoum 60-61 H 7
Baibū = Baybū 46-47 KL 4
Bai Bung, Mui – 52-53 D 5
Baicheng 48-49 N 2
Baicheng = Bai 48-49 E 3
Baihe [TJ, ●] 48-49 KL 5
Ba'ijī 46-47 K 5
Baïkal, Lac – = ozero Bajkal 42-43 U 7
Baikal, Lake – = ozero Bajkal 42-43 U 7
Baikalmeer = ozero Bajkal 42-43 U 7
Baikalsee = ozero Bajkal 42-43 U 7
Baile Átha Cliath = Dublin 32 CD 5
Băileşti 36-37 K 3
Bailundo 64-65 E 5
Baing = Tanahkadu Kung 52-53 H 9
Bain-Tumen = Čojbalsan 48-49 L 2
Baiqibao = Baiqipu 50-51 D 2
Baiqipu 50-51 D 2
Bā'ir 44-45 D 4
Bā'ir, Wādī – 46-47 G 7
Baird Mountains 70-71 DE 4
Bairnsdale 56-57 J 7
Baïse 34-35 H 7
Baitou Shan 50-51 FG 2
Baitou Shan = Changbai Shan 48-49 O 3
Baituchangmen 50-51 CD 2
Baja 33 J 5
Bājā [Sudan] 63 C 1-2
Baja California 76-77 F 10
Baja California Norte 72-73 CD 6
Baja California Sur 72-73 D 6
Bājah 60-61 F 1
Bajan [MVR] 48-49 K 2
Bajan Adraga 48-49 KL 2
Bajanaul 42-43 O 7
Bajan Char uuul 48-49 H 5
Bajan Chongor = 8 ◁ 48-49 HJ 2
Bajan Choto 48-49 JK 4
Bajan Char uuul 48-49 H 5
Bajan Chongor = 8 ◁ 48-49 HJ 2
Bajan Choto 48-49 JK 4
Bajandaj 42-43 U 7
Bajandalaj 48-49 J 3
Bajangol [MVR] 48-49 K 2
Bajan Gol [TJ] 48-49 K 3
Bajan Char uuul 48-49 H 5
Bajan Chongor = 8 ◁ 48-49 HJ 2
Bajan Choto 48-49 JK 4
Bajan Obo 48-49 K 3
Bajan Ölgij = 1 ◁ 48-49 FG 2
Bajan Öndör 48-49 H 3
Bajan Ölgij = 1 ◁ 48-49 FG 2
Bajan Öndör 48-49 H 3
Bajan Sum = Bajan 48-49 K 2
Bajanteeg 48-49 J 2
Bajan Tümen = Čojbalsan 48-49 L 2
Bajan Ulaa = Bajan Uul 48-49 H 2
Bajan Uul [MVR, Dornod] 48-49 L 2
Bajan Uul [MVR, Dzavchan] 48-49 H 2
Bajawa 52-53 GH 8
Bajčunas 38-39 K 6
Bajčunas 38-39 K 6
Bajdarackaja guba 42-43 M 4
Bajé 80 F 4
Bajio, El – 72-73 F 7
Bajirge = Esendere 46-47 L 4
Bajkal, jezero – = ozero Bajkal 42-43 U 7
Bajkal, ozero – 42-43 U 7
Bajkal'skij chrebet 42-43 U 6-7
Bajkal'skoje 42-43 UV 6
Bajkál-tó = ozero Bajkal 42-43 U 7
Bajkał, Jezioro – = ozero Bajkal 42-43 U 7
Bajkit 42-43 S 5
Bajkonur 42-43 M 8
Bajmak 42-43 K 7
Bajo Baudo 78-79 D 3
Bajram-Ali 44-45 J 3
Bajšint = Chongor 48-49 L 2
Baj-Sot 42-43 S 7
Bajšint = Chongor 48-49 L 2
Bajtag Bogd uul 48-49 G 2-3
Bājūm, 'Ayn – 62 C 3
Bakal 42-43 K 6-7
Bakala 60-61 HJ 7
Bakal'skaja kosa 36-37 P 3
Bakanas 42-43 O 8-9
Bakčar 42-43 P 6
Bakčar 42-43 P 6
Bakel [SN] 60-61 B 6
Baker, CA 76-77 E 8
Baker, ID 76-77 G 3
Baker, NV 76-77 FG 6
Baker, OR 72-73 C 3
Baker, Canal – 80 B 7
Baker, Mount – 76-77 C 1
Baker Foreland 70-71 ST 5
Baker Lake [CDN, ●] 70-71 R 5
Baker Lake [CDN, ≈] 70-71 R 5
Bakersfield, CA 72-73 C 4
Bakhmah, Sadd al- 46-47 L 4
Bākhtarān [IR, ●] 44-45 F 4
Bākhtarān = 1 [IR, ☆ ◁] 44-45 F 4
Bakhtegān, Daryācheh – 44-45 G 5
26 Bakinskich Komissarov 38-39 K 8
Bakır Çayı 46-47 B 3
Bakırdağı 46-47 F 3
Bakırköy, İstanbul- 46-47 C 2
Bakkafjördhur 30-31 fg 1
Bakkaflói 30-31 f 1
Bakkagerdhi 30-31 g 2
Baklan 46-47 C 4
Bakongan 52-53 C 6
Bakony 33 HJ 5
Bakool 60-61 a 3
Baku 38-39 JK 7
Bakwanga = Mbuji-Mayi 64-65 F 4
B'ala 36-37 L 4
Bala [CDN] 74-75 D 2
Balâ [TR] 46-47 E 3
Bala, Cerros de – 78-79 F 7-8
Balabac Island 52-53 G 5
Balabac Strait 52-53 G 5
Balabaia 64-65 D 5
Ba'labakk 46-47 G 5-6
Balabalangan, Kepulauan – 52-53 G 7
Balachna 38-39 H 4
Balad 46-47 L 5-6
Bal'ad = Balcad 60-61 b 3
Balad'ok = Bolod'ok 42-43 Z 7
Balad Rūz 46-47 L 6
Balagansk 42-43 T 7
Balaghat 44-45 N 6
Balaguer 34-35 H 8
Balā'im, Rā's al- 62 E 3
Balaiselasa 52-53 CD 7
Balaklava 56-57 G 6
Balakovo 42-43 HJ 7
Balama 63 D 6
Balambangan, Pulau – 52-53 G 5
Balangan, Kepulauan – = Kepulauan Balabalangan 52-53 G 7
Ba Lang An, Mui – = Mui Batangan 52-53 EF 3
Balangir 44-45 N 6
B'ala Slatina 36-37 K 4
Balasore = Baleswar 44-45 O 6
Balašov 38-39 H 5
Balašov 38-39 H 5
Balāṭ 62 C 5
Balaton 33 HJ 5
Balau 52-53 KL 5
Balboa 72-73 b 3
Balboa Heights 72-73 b 3
Balcad 60-61 b 3
Balcanes 36-37 K-M 4
Balcarce 80 E 5
Balchaš 42-43 N 8
Balchaš, ozero – 42-43 NO 8
Balchaschsee = ozero Balchaš 42-43 NO 8
Balčik 36-37 MN 4
Balcones Escarpment 72-73 F 6-G 5
Balčik 36-37 MN 4
Bald Butte 76-77 D 4
Bald Head 56-57 C 7
Bald Knob, WV 74-75 C 6
Bald Mountain 76-77 F 7
Baldwinsville, NY 74-75 E 3
Baldy, Mount – 76-77 H 2
Baldy Peak [USA, Arizona] 72-73 DE 5
Balē 60-61 N 7-8
Bâle = Basel 33 C 5
Balearen = Illes Balears 34-35 H 9-K 8
Baléares, Îles – = Illes Balears 34-35 H 9-K 8
Baleares, Islas – 34-35 H 9-K 8
Balej 42-43 W 7
Bālēshvara = Baleswar 44-45 O 6
Baleswar 44-45 O 6
Balḥāf 44-45 F 8
Balhas-tó = ozero Balchas 42-43 NO 8
Balchaš 42-43 N 8
Balchaš, jezero – = ozero Balchaš 42-43 NO 8
Balchaš, ozero – 42-43 NO 8
Bali = 15 ◁ 52-53 F 8
Bali, Mar de – 52-53 FG 8
Bali, Mer de – 52-53 FG 8
Bali, Pulau – 52-53 FG 8
Balīh, Nahr – 46-47 H 4
Balijské moře 52-53 FG 8
Balijskie, Morze – 52-53 FG 8
Balikesir 44-45 B 3
Balikpapan 52-53 G 7
Balintang Channel 52-53 H 3
Balintang Channel 52-53 H 3
Balintang Channel 52-53 H 3
Bali Sea 52-53 FG 8
Balisee 52-53 FG 8
Bali-tenger 52-53 FG 8
Balizee 52-53 FG 8
Balkan 36-37 K-M 4
Balkán 36-37 K-M 4
Balkan Mountains 36-37 K-M 4
Balkans 36-37 K-M 4
Balkh 44-45 K 3
Balkh Āb 44-45 K 3
Balkhach, Lac – = ozero, Balchaš 42-43 NO 8
Balla Balla = Mbalabala 64-65 GH 7
Balladonia 56-57 D 6
Ballarat 56-57 H 7
Ballard, Lake – 56-57 D 5
Ballāri = Bellary 44-45 M 7
Ballé 60-61 C 5
Balleine, Rivière à la – 70-71 X 6
Balleny Islands 24 C 17
Ballimore 58 J 4
Ballina 32 B 4
Ballina 56-57 K 5
Ball's Pyramid 56-57 L 6
Ballstad 30-31 EF 3
Ballymena 32 C 4
Balmoral 32 E 3
Balombo 64-65 D 5
Balovale 64-65 F 5
Balqā 46-47 F 6-7
Balranald 56-57 H 6
Balsas [BR] 78-79 K 6
Balsas, Río – 72-73 F 8
Balsfjord 30-31 HJ 3
Balta 36-37 MN 3
Baltic Sea 30-31 G 10-J 8
Baltijsk 33 J 1
Balṭīm 62 D 2
Baltimore [GB] 32 B 6
Baltimore, MD 72-73 L 4
Bāltistān 44-45 M 3-4
Bāltit 44-45 L 3
Balti-tenger 30-31 G 10-J 8
Baltské moře 30-31 G 10-J 8
Balūchistān 44-45 J 5-K 4
Balvi 30-31 M 9
Balwin Aboriginal Reserve 56-57 E 3-4
Balya 46-47 B 3
Balyanā, Al- 60-61 L 3
Balygyčan 42-43 d 5
Balygyčan 42-43 d 5
Bałchasz, Jezioro – = ozero Balchaš 42-43 NO 8
Bałkany 36-37 K-M 4
Bałtyckie, Morze - 30-31 G 10-J 8
Ballenas, Dorsal de las – 22-23 K 7
Bam 44-45 H 5
Bama 60-61 G 6
Bamaco = Bamako 60-61 C 6
Bamako 60-61 C 6
Bamba [EAK] 63 D 3
Bamba [ZRE] 64-65 E 4
Bambari 60-61 J 7
Bamberg 33 E 4
Bamberg, SC 74-75 C 8
Bambesa 64-65 G 2
Bambinga 64-65 E 3
Bambui 78-79 K 8-9
Bamenda 60-61 G 7
Bamingui 60-61 HJ 7
Bamingui, Parc national de la – 60-61 HJ 7
Bamingui-Bangoran 60-61 HJ 7
Bāmiyān 44-45 K 4
Bampūr, Rūd-e 44-45 HJ 5
Ba mTsho 48-49 G 5
Bamum = Foumban 60-61 G 7
Bamungu 63 B 2
Bana [MW] 63 C 6
Baña, Punta de la – 34-35 H 8
Banaadir [SP, ≅] 60-61 ab 3
Banaadir [SP, ☆ = 2 ◁] 60-61 O 8
Banāder va Jazāyer-e Baḥr-e 'Ommān = 6 ◁ 44-45 H 5
Banāder va Jazāyer-e Khalīj-e Fārs = 5 ◁ 44-45 G 5
Banadia 78-79 E 3
Banagi 63 C 3
Banalia 64-65 FG 2
Banámichi 76-77 H 10
Banana 64-65 D 4
Bananal, Ilha do – 78-79 J 7
Bananeiras 78-79 M 6
Banat 36-37 J 3
Banatului, Munţii – 36-37 JK 3
Banaz 46-47 C 3
Banaz Çayı 46-47 C 3
Banbury 32 F 5
Banco, El – 78-79 E 3
Bancroft 74-75 E 2
Bancroft, ID 76-77 H 4
Banda = Sainte-Marie 64-65 D 3
Banda, Cuenca Meridional de – 52-53 J 8
Banda, Cuenca Septentrional de – 52-53 HJ 7
Banda, Kepulauan – 52-53 J 7
Banda, La – 80 D 3
Banda, Mar de – 52-53 JK 8
Banda, Mer de – 52-53 JK 8
Banda, Morze – 52-53 JK 8
Banda, Punta – 72-73 C 5
Banda Aceh 52-53 BC 5
Bandama 60-61 CD 7
Banda Méridional, Bassin de – 52-53 J 8
Bandar = Machilipatnam 44-45 N 7
Banḍāra = Machilipatnam 44-45 N 7
Bandar Banhâ = Banhā 62 D 2
Bandarbeyla 60-61 c 2
Bandar-e 'Abbās 44-45 H 5
Bandar-e Anzalī 44-45 FG 3
Bandar-e Būshehr 44-45 G 5
Bandar-e Chāh Bahār 44-45 HJ 5
Bandar-e Chāh Bahār 44-45 HJ 5
Bandar-e Chāh Bahār 44-45 HJ 5
Bandar-e Khomeynī 44-45 FG 4
Bandar-e Lengeh 44-45 GH 5
Bandar-e Māhshar 46-47 N 7
Bandar-e Shāh 44-45 G 3
Bandar Lampung 52-53 DE 8
Bandar Maharani = Muar 52-53 D 6
Bandar Murcaayo 60-61 bc 1
Bandar Penggaram = Batu Pahat 52-53 D 6
Bandar Seri Begawan 52-53 FG 5-6
Banda Sea 52-53 JK 8
Bandasee 52-53 JK 8
Banda Septentrional, Bassin de – 52-53 HJ 7
Banda-tenger 52-53 JK 8
Bandawe 64-65 H 5
Bandazee 52-53 JK 8
Band Bābā, Kuh-i- 44-45 J 4
Bandeira, Pico da – 78-79 L 9
Bandeirante 78-79 JK 7
Band-e Qir 46-47 N 7
Bandera 80 D 3
Banderas, Bahía de – 72-73 E 7
Bänd-e Turkestān = Selselae-i-Band-i-Turkestān 44-45 JK 3
Bandiagara 60-61 D 6
Bandırma 44-45 B 2
Band-i-Turkestān, Selselae-i- 44-45 JK 3
Bandjarmasin = Banjarmasin 52-53 F 7
Bandon 32 B 6
Bandon, OR 76-77 A 4
Bāndra, Bombay- 44-45 L 7
Bandské moře 52-53 JK 8
Bandundu [ZRE, ●] 64-65 E 3
Bandundu [ZRE, ☆] 64-65 E 3-4
Bandung 52-53 E 8
Bāneh 46-47 L 4-5
Banes 72-73 L 7
Bañeza, La – 34-35 DE 7
Banff [CDN] 70-71 NO 7
Banff [GB] 32 E 3
Banff National Park 70-71 NO 7
Banfora 60-61 D 6
Bangāl Khārī = Bay of Bengal 44-45 N-P 7
Bangalore 44-45 M 8
Bangassou 60-61 J 8
Bangassu = Bangassou 60-61 J 8
Bangfou = Bengbu 48-49 M 5
Banggai 52-53 H 7
Banggai, Kepulauan – 52-53 H 7
Banggai, Pulau – 52-53 H 7
Banggala Au = Bay of Bengal 44-45 N-P 7
Banggi, Pulau – 52-53 G 5
Banghāzī 60-61 HJ 2
Bangka, Pulau – 52-53 E 7
Bangka, Selat – 52-53 E 7
Bangkinang 52-53 D 6
Bangko 52-53 D 7
Bangkok = Krung Thep 52-53 D 4
Banglades 44-45 OP 6
Bangladesch 44-45 OP 6
Bangladesh 44-45 OP 6
Bangladesz 44-45 OP 6
Bangladéš 44-45 OP 6
Bangor 32 DE 5
Bangor, ME 72-73 N 3
Bangor, PA 74-75 F 4
Bangui [RCA] 60-61 H 8
Bangui [RP] 52-53 GH 3
Bangweulu, Lake – 64-65 GH 5
Banhā 62 D 2
Bani [DOM] 72-73 M 8
Bani [RMM] 60-61 C 6
Banī, Jabal – 60-61 C 2-3
Banī 'Abbās 60-61 D 2
Baniara 52-53 NO 8
Banī Mallīlah 60-61 C 2
Banī Mazār 60-61 L 3
Banī Sa 'd 46-47 L 6
Banī Shuqayr 62 D 4
Banī Suwayf 60-61 L 3
Banī Walīd 60-61 G 2
Banī Wanīf 60-61 D 2
Bāniyās [SYR, Al-Lādhiqīyah] 44-45 D 3
Bāniyās [SYR, Dimashq] 46-47 FG 6
Banjak, Kepulauan – 52-53 C 6
Banja Luka 36-37 G 3
Banjar 52-53 E 8
Banjarmasin 52-53 F 7
Banjermassin = Banjarmasin 52-53 F 7
Banjo = Banyo 60-61 G 7
Banjul 60-61 A 6
Banjuwangi = Banyuwangi 52-53 F 8
Bank 38-39 J 8
Banka = Pulau Bangka 52-53 E 7
Banks, ID 76-77 E 3
Banks, OR 76-77 B 3
Banks Island [CDN, British Columbia] 70-71 KL 7
Banks Island [CDN, District of Inuvik] 70-71 MN 3
Banks Islands 56-57 N 2
Banks Lake 76-77 D 2
Banks Peninsula 56-57 O 8
Banks Strait 56-57 J 8
Banks Strait = MacClure Strait 70-71 MN 2-3
Banmau 52-53 C 2
Ban Me Thuôt 52-53 E 4
Ban Muang = Pong 52-53 CD 3
Bannack, MT 76-77 G 3
Banning, CA 76-77 E 9
Banningville = Bandundu 64-65 E 3
Bannockburn [CDN] 74-75 DE 2
Bannockburn [ZW] 64-65 GH 7
Bannock Range 76-77 G 4
Bannū 44-45 KL 4
Ban Phai 52-53 D 3
Banská Bystrica 33 J 4
Banská Štiavnica 33 J 4
Banská Štiavnica 33 J 4
Banta Eng 52-53 GH 8
Bantam = Banten 52-53 E 8
Banten 52-53 E 8
Bantry 32 B 6
Bantry Bay 32 AB 6
Bantyū 60-61 KL 7
Banyak, Pulau-pulau – = Kepulauan Banjak 52-53 C 6
Banyo 60-61 G 7
Banyuwangi 52-53 F 8
Banzaburō-dake 50-51 M 5
Banzare Land 24 C 13
Banzystad = Yasanyama 64-65 F 2
Banzyville = Yasanyama 64-65 F 2
Banzyville, Collines des – 64-65 F 2
Baña, Punta de la – 34-35 H 8
Bañeza, La – 34-35 DE 7
Baoding 48-49 LM 4
Baoji 48-49 K 5
Baojing 48-49 K 6
Baoqing 48-49 P 2
Baoshan [TJ, Yunnan] 48-49 HJ 6
Baotou 48-49 KL 3
Baoulé 60-61 C 6
Baoying 48-49 M 5
Baptiste 74-75 DE 2
Bāqir, Jabal – 46-47 F 8
Ba'qūbah 44-45 EF 4
Baquedano 80 BC 2
Bar 36-37 H 4
Baraawe 60-61 N 8
Barabinsk 42-43 OP 6
Barabinskaja nizmennost' 42-43 O 6-7
Baracaldo 34-35 F 7
Bărăganul 36-37 M 3
Bārah 60-61 L 6
Barahī = Barhi 44-45 O 6
Barahona [DOM] 72-73 M 8
Barāīj, Al- 46-47 G 5
Barak = Karkamış 46-47 G 4
Baraka 60-61 M 5
Barakī [AFG] 44-45 K 4
Baralaba 56-57 JK 4
Bārāmūlā 44-45 L 4
Barā Nikōbār = Great Nicobar 44-45 P 9
Baranof Island 70-71 JK 6
Baranoviči 38-39 E 5
Baranoviči 38-39 E 5
Barão de Grajaú 78-79 L 6
Barbacena 78-79 L 9
Barbade 72-73 OP 9
Barbados 72-73 OP 9
Barbar 60-61 L 5
Barbastro 34-35 GH 7
Barberton 64-65 H 8
Barberton, OH 74-75 C 4
Barborá = Berbera 60-61 O 6
Barbosa [CO, Boyacá] 78-79 E 3
Barca = Al-Marj 60-61 J 2
Barcaldine 56-57 HJ 4
Barcellona Pozzo di Gotto 36-37 F 6
Barcelona [E] 34-35 J 8
Barcelona [YV] 78-79 G 2
Barcelone = Barcelona 34-35 J 8
Barcelonnette 34-35 L 6
Barcelos [BR] 78-79 G 5
Barchama Guda 63 D 2
Barchöl Choto = Bar köl 48-49 G 3
Barcoo River 56-57 H 4-5
Barchöl Choto = Bar köl 48-49 G 3
Bardaï 60-61 H 4
Bardarash 46-47 K 4
Bardawīl, Sabkhat al- 62 E 2
Barddhmān = Burdwan 44-45 O 6
Bardejov 33 K 4
Bårdharbunga 30-31 e 2
Bardīs 62 D 4
Bardīyah 60-61 K 2
Bardiz = Gaziler 46-47 K 2
Barduba 72-73 O 8
Bareilly 44-45 MN 5
Barēlī = Bareilly 44-45 MN 5
Bäreninsel 19 B 16-17
Barents, Mar de – 19 B 14-15
Barents, Mer de – 19 B 14-15
Barentsa, Morze – 19 B 14-15
Barentsburg 30-31 jk 5
Barentska, Morze - 38-39 E-J 1
Barentsovo moře 19 B 14-15
Barentsøya 30-31 l 5
Barents Sea 19 B 14-15
Barentssee 19 B 14-15
Barents-tenger 19 B 14-15
Barents-tenger 38-39 E-J 1
Barentszzee 19 B 14-15
Barentu 60-61 M 5
Barfleur, Pointe de – 34-35 G 4
Barga [TJ] 48-49 M 2
Barguzin 42-43 UV 7
Barguzinskij chrebet 42-43 U 7-V 6
Barhampura = Berhampur 44-45 NO 7
Bar Harbor, ME 74-75 J 2
Barhi [IND, Bihar] 44-45 O 6
Barchöl Choto = Bar köl 48-49 G 3
Bari [I] 36-37 G 5
Bari [SP] 60-61 bc 1
Baricho 63 DE 3
Barīm 44-45 E 8
Barinas [YV, ●] 78-79 EF 3
Baring, Cape – 70-71 MN 3
Baringo, Lake – 63 D 2
Bāris 62 D 5
Barisal 44-45 OP 6
Barīt, Al- 46-47 K 7
Barito, Sungai – 52-53 F 7
Barkā' 44-45 H 6
Barka = Al-Marj 60-61 J 2
Barka = Baraka 60-61 M 5
Barkan, Rās-e – = Ra's-e Bahrgān 46-47 N 7-8
Barkly Tableland 56-57 FG 3
Bar Köl [TJ, ●] 48-49 G 3
Bar köl [TJ, ≈] 48-49 G 3
Barla Dağı 46-47 D 3-4
Bar-le-Duc 34-35 K 4
Barlee, Lake – 56-57 C 5
Barletta 36-37 G 5
Barlovento, Islas de – 72-73 OP 8-9
Barma 52-53 BC 2
Barmer 44-45 L 5
Barmera 56-57 H 6
Barnabus, WV 74-75 BC 6
Barnato 58 G 3
Barnaul 42-43 P 7
Barnegat Bay 74-75 FG 5
Barne Glacier 24 A 17-18
Barnesville, OH 74-75 C 4-5
Barney Top 76-77 GH 7
Barnstable, MA 74-75 H 4
Barnstaple 32 D 6
Barnwell, SC 74-75 C 8
Baro 60-61 F 7

Baroda = Vadodara 44-45 L 6
Barôngã Kyûnmya 52-53 B 3
Barpeta 44-45 P 5
Barqa = Al-Marj 60-61 J 2
Barqah [LAR] 60-61 J 2
Barqah, Jabal al- 62 E 5
Barquisimeto 78-79 EF 2-3
Barra 32 C 3
Barra [BR, Bahia] 78-79 L 7
Barraba 56-57 K 6
Barracão do Barreto 78-79 H 6
Barra do Bugres 78-79 H 7-8
Barra do Corda 78-79 KL 6
Barra do Garças 78-79 J 8
Barra do São Manuel 78-79 H 6
Barrage 60-61 C 6
Barra Head 32 BC 3
Barra Islands 32 C 3
Barranca [PE] 78-79 D 5
Barrancabermeja 78-79 E 3
Barrancas [YV, Monagas] 78-79 G 3
Barranqueras 80 DE 3
Barranquilla 78-79 DE 2
Barra Velha 80 G 3
Barre, VT 74-75 G 2
Barreiras 78-79 KL 7
Barreirinha 78-79 H 5
Barreirinhas 78-79 L 5
Barreiro 34-35 C 9
Barreiros 78-79 MN 6
Barren Grounds 70-71 O 4-S 5
Barrenland = Barren Grounds 70-71 O 4-S 5
Barren Sage Plains 76-77 E 4
Barretos 78-79 K 9
Barrie 70-71 UV 9
Barrier Range 56-57 H 6
Barrington Tops 56-57 K 6
Barro Colorado, Isla – 72-73 b 2
Barros, Tierra de – 34-35 D 9
Barrow [IRL] 32 C 5
Barrow, AK 70-71 E 3
Barrow, Point – 70-71 EF 3
Barrow Creek 56-57 FG 4
Barrow in Furness 32 E 4
Barrow Island 56-57 BC 4
Barrow Strait 70-71 RS 3
Barşā' 46-47 H 4
Barsakel mes, ostrov – 42-43 KL 3
Barsaloi 64-65 J 2
Bârshī = Barsi 44-45 M 7
Barsi 44-45 M 7
Barstow, CA 72-73 C 4-5
Bar-sur-Aube 34-35 K 4
Barşātas 42-43 O 8
Barţallah 46-47 K 4
Bartenstein = Bartoszyce 33 K 1
Bartica 78-79 H 3
Bartın [TR] 46-47 E 2
Bartın çayı = Koca ırmak 46-47 E 2
Bartle, CA 76-77 C 5
Bartlesville, OK 72-73 G 4
Bartolomeu Dias 64-65 J 7
Bartoszyce 33 K 1
Bartow, FL 74-75 bc 3
Barú, Volcán – 72-73 K 10
Barun-Šabartuj, gora – 42-43 UV 8
Barun-Šabartuj, gora – 42-43 UV 8
Baruun Urt 48-49 L 2
Barwon River 56-57 J 5
Barwon River = Darling River 56-57 H 6
Barykova, mys – 42-43 jk 5
Barylas 42-43 Z 4
Barzanja = Barzinjah 46-47 L 5
Barzas 42-43 Q 6
Barzinjah 46-47 L 5
Başaliyat Qibli, Al- 62 E 5
Basankusu 64-65 EF 2
Baschkirische Autonome Republik = 7 ◁ 66-67 K 7
Basco 48-49 N 7
Basel 33 C 5
Basharrī 44-45 CD 4
Bashi Haixia = Pashih Haihsia 48-49 N 7
Bâshim = Bâsim 44-45 M 5
Bashkir Autonomous Republic = 7 ◁ 42-43 K 7
Bashkiria, República Aútonoma de – = 7 ◁ 42-43 K 7
Bash Kurghan = Bash Qurghan 48-49 G 4
Bash Malghun 48-49 F 4
Bash Qurghan 48-49 G 4
Bashshār 60-61 D 2
Basiano 52-53 H 7
Basilan Island 52-53 H 5
Basilan Strait 52-53 H 5
Basilicata 36-37 FG 5
Basílio 80 F 4
Basim 44-45 M 5
Basin, MT 76-77 G 2
Basingstoke 32 F 6
Basīţ, Râ's al- 46-47 F 5
Basjkiren, Autonome Republiek – = 7 ◁ 42-43 K 7
Başkale 46-47 KL 3
Baskil 46-47 H 3

Baskír Autonóm Köztársaság 42-43 K 7
Başköy = Aralık 46-47 L 3
Bâsmenj 46-47 M 4
Basoko [ZRE, Haute Zaïre] 64-65 F 2
Başrah, Al- 44-45 F 4
Bass, Détroit de = Bass Strait 56-57 HJ 7
Bassa, Cieśnina – = Bass Strait 56-57 HJ 7
Bassac = Champasak 52-53 DE 4
Bassano del Grappa 36-37 D 3
Basse Californie 76-77 F 10
Basse-Guinée 22-23 K 5-6
Bassein = Puthein 52-53 B 3
Basseterre [Saint Kitts und Nevis] 72-73 O 8
Basse Kotto 60-61 J 7-8
Basse-Terre [Guadeloupe, ●] 72-73 O 8
Bassett, VA 74-75 C 6
Bassin Algéroprovençal 28-29 J 8-K 7
Bassin Antarctico-Indien 22-23 O-Q 8
Bassin Arctique Central 19 A
Bassin Atlantique Indien Antarctique 22-23 J-M 9
Bassin Australien Méridional 22-23 PQ 8
Bassin Australien Occidental 22-23 P 7
Bassin Australien Oriental 22-23 RS 8
Bassin Australien Septentrional 56-57 C 2
Bassin Brésilien 22-23 H 6
Bassin Canadien 19 AB 32-33
Bassin Caraïbe 72-73 MN 8
Bassin Central Indienne 22-23 NO 6
Bassin Chinois Méridional 52-53 FG 3-4
Bassin Corallien 56-57 K 2
Bassin Chinois Méridional 52-53 FG 3-4
Bassin Eurasiatique 19 A
Bassin Chinois Méridional 52-53 FG 3-4
Bassin Ibérique 22-23 HJ 3
Bassin Ionien 36-37 GH 7
Bassin Islandais 28-29 CD 4
Bassin Norvégien 22-23 JK 2
Bassin Océanique japonais 50-51 J-L 2
Bassin Rouge = Sichuan Pendi 48-49 JK 5-6
Bass Strait 56-57 HJ 7
Bass-Straße = Bass Strait 56-57 HJ 7
Bass-szoros = Bass Strait 56-57 HJ 7
Bassův průliv = Bass Strait 56-57 HJ 7
Bastia 36-37 C 4
Bastianøyane 30-31 I 5
Bastogne 34-35 KL 3-4
Bastrop, LA 72-73 H 5
Bastuträsk 30-31 HJ 5
Bâsūr, Bi'r al- 62 AB 3
Basutoland = Lesotho 64-65 G 8
Basutos 64-65 G 6
Basyurt Tepesi 46-47 D 3
Bas-Zaïre 64-65 DE 4
Baszkirska Autonomiczna Republika = 7 ◁ 42-43 K 7
Baškirskaja Avtonomnaja Sovetskaja Socialisticeskaja Respublika = Baschkirische Autonome Republik = 7 ◁ 42-43 K 7
Baškortostán = 7 ◁ 42-43 K 7
Baszra = Al-Basrah 44-45 F 4
Bata 60-61 F 8
Batabanó, Golfo de – 72-73 K 7
Batac 52-53 GH 3
Batagaj 42-43 Za 4
Batagaj-Alyta 42-43 YZ 4
Batajsk 38-39 FG 4
Batala 44-45 M 4
Batalha 34-35 C 9
Batam, Pulau – 52-53 D 6
Batamaj 42-43 YZ 5
Batang [TJ] 48-49 H 6
Batangafo 60-61 H 7
Batangan, Mui – 52-53 EF 3
Batangas 52-53 H 4
Batan Island 48-49 N 7
Batan Islands 48-49 N 7
Batanta, Pulau – 52-53 JK 7
Batatchatu = Chulaq Aqqan Su 48-49 G 4
Batavia, NY 74-75 DE 3
Batavia = Jakarta 52-53 E 8
Batbakkara = Amangel'dy 42-43 M 7
Batemans Bay 58 K 5
Batesburg, SC 74-75 C 8
Batesville, OH 74-75 A 5
Bath 32 E 6
Bath, ME 74-75 J 3
Bath, NY 74-75 E 3
Batha 60-61 H 6

Baţha, Al- 46-47 L 7
B'athar Zajú, Jabal – 62 E 7
Bathurst [AUS] 56-57 JK 6
Bathurst [CDN] 70-71 XY 8
Bathurst = Banjul 60-61 A 6
Bathurst, Cape – 70-71 KL 3
Bathurst Inlet [CDN, ∪] 70-71 P 4
Bathurst Inlet [CDN, ●] 70-71 P 4
Bathurst Island [AUS] 56-57 EF 2
Bathurst Island [CDN] 70-71 R 2
Batié 60-61 D 6-7
Bâtin, Al- [IRQ ↙ As-Salmân] 46-47 K 7-L 8
Bâtin, Al- [IRQ ↘ As-Salmân] 46-47 M 8
Bâtin, Humrat al- 46-47 KL 8
Bâtin, Wâdî al- 44-45 F 5
Bâţinah, Al – 44-45 H 6
Batlow 58 HJ 5
Batman 44-45 E 3
Batna = Batnah 60-61 F 1
Batnah 60-61 F 1
Batoche 70-71 PQ 7
Baton Rouge, LA 72-73 H 5
Batouri 60-61 G 8
Batrâ, Jabal al- 46-47 F 8
Batrûn, Al- 46-47 F 5
Battambang 52-53 D 4
Batterbee Range 24 BC 30
Batticaloa = Maḍakalapūwa 44-45 N 9
Battle Creek, MI 72-73 J 3
Battle Creek [USA ◁ Owyhee River] 76-77 E 4
Battle Harbour 70-71 Za 7
Battle Mountain, NV 76-77 E 5
Battle River 70-71 OP 7
Battonya 34-35 K 5
Batu 60-61 M 7
Batu, Kepulauan – 52-53 C 7
Batu Arang 52-53 D 6
Batumi 38-39 H 7
Batu Pahat 52-53 D 6
Baturi = Batouri 60-61 G 8
Baturino 42-43 Q 6
Baturité 78-79 M 5
Batutinggi = Kasongan 52-53 F 7
Batvand 46-47 N 6-7
Baubau 52-53 H 8
Bauchi [WAN, ●] 60-61 FG 6
Baudh 44-45 N 6
Baudouinville = Moba 64-65 G 4
Baudwin 52-53 C 2
Bauhinia 56-57 J 4
Baukau 52-53 J 8
Baúl, El – 78-79 F 3
Bauld, Cape – 70-71 Za 7
Baule-Escoublac, la – 34-35 F 5
Bâ'ūrah, Sabkhat – 46-47 J 5
Baures 78-79 G 7
Bauru 78-79 K 9
Bauska 30-31 L 9
Bautzen 33 G 3
Bauya 60-61 B 7
Bavispe, Río de – 76-77 J 10
Bawean, Pulau – 52-53 F 8
Bâwiţi, Al- 60-61 K 3
Bawku 60-61 D 6
Bawlagê 52-53 C 3
Baxter State Park 74-75 J 1-2
Bay 60-61 a 3
Bayâd, Al- [DZ] 60-61 E 2
Bayâd, Al- [Saudi-Arabien] 44-45 F 6
Bayâḍiyah, Al- 62 E 5
Bay al-Kabîr, Wâdî – 60-61 GH 2
Bayamo 72-73 L 7
Bayat [TR, Afyon] 46-47 D 3
Bayat [TR, Çorum] 46-47 F 2
Bayâzeh 38-39 KL 9
Baybay 52-53 HJ 4
Bayboro, NC 74-75 E 7
Baybü 46-47 J 5
Bayburt 44-45 E 2
Bay City, MI 72-73 K 3
Bayḍâ', Al- [LAR] 60-61 J 2
Bayḍâ', Al- [Y] 44-45 EF 8
Bayḍâ', 'Ayn al- 46-47 GH 7
Bayḍâ', Barqat al- 60-61 HJ 2-3
Bayḍâ', Bi'r – 62 FG 4
Bayḍâ', Jabal – 62 E 7
Baydâh, 'Ayn al- 46-47 GH 5
Baydhabo 60-61 a 3
Bayerischer Wald 33 F 4
Bayern 33 E 4
Bayeux 34-35 G 4
Bayhân al-Qasab 44-45 F 8
Bay Hasan 46-47 L 5
Bayındır 46-47 B 3
Bayingolin Monggol Zizhizhou 48-49 FG 4
Baykan 46-47 J 3
Bay Mountains 74-75 B 6
Bayonne 34-35 G 6
Bayraktar = Karayazı 46-47 JK 3
Bayramiç 46-47 B 3
Bayreuth 33 E 4
Bayrût 44-45 CD 4
Bays, Lake of – 74-75 D 2
Bayt al-Faqîh 44-45 E 8
Bayt Laḥm 46-47 F 7
Baytown, TX 72-73 GH 6

Bayyûd, Bi'r al- 46-47 H 5
Bayyûah, Sahrâ' – 60-61 L 5
Bayzah, Wâdî – 62 E 5
Baza 34-35 F 10
Bazar Dere 48-49 D 4
Bazar'duzi, gora – 38-39 J 7
Bazargân 44-45 F 3
Bazaruto, Ilha do – 64-65 J 7
Bazas 34-35 G 6
Bâzdar 44-45 JK 5
Bazias 36-37 J 3
Beachport 56-57 G 7
Beacon, NY 74-75 G 4
Beagle, Canal – 80 C 8
Beagle Bay 56-57 D 3
Bealanana 64-65 L 4
Beara 52-53 MN 8
Bearcreek, MT 76-77 J 3
Beardmore Glacier 24 A 20-18
Beardmore Reservoir 58 HJ 1
Beardsley, AZ 76-77 G 9
Bear Island [Arctica] 19 B 16-17
Bear Island [Antarctica] 24 B 26
Bear Lake [USA] 72-73 D 3
Bearpaw Mountain 76-77 J 1
Bear River [USA] 72-73 D 3
Bear River Bay 76-77 G 5
Beata, Isla – 72-73 M 8
Beatrice 64-65 H 6
Beatrice, NE 72-73 G 3
Beatrice, Cape – 56-57 G 2
Beatty, NV 76-77 E 7
Beaucaire 34-35 K 7
Beauce 34-35 HJ 4
Beauchene Island 80 E 8
Beaudesert 58 L 1
Beaufort [AUS] 58 F 6
Beaufort, NC 74-75 E 7
Beaufort, SC 74-75 C 8
Beaufort, Mar de – 19 B 32-33
Beaufort, Mer de – 19 B 32-33
Beauforta, Morze – 19 B 32-33
Beaufort Inlet 74-75 E 7
Beaufortovo moře 19 B 32-33
Beaufort Sea 19 B 32-33
Beaufortsee 19 B 32-33
Beaufort-tenger 19 B 32-33
Beaufort-Wes 64-65 F 9
Beaufort West = Beaufort-Wes 64-65 F 9
Beaufortzee 19 B 32-33
Beauharnois 74-75 FG 2
Beaujolais 34-35 K 5
Beauly 64-65 L 7
Beaumont, CA 76-77 E 9
Beaumont, TX 72-73 GH 5
Beaune 34-35 K 5
Beauvais 34-35 HJ 4
Beaver, UT 76-77 G 6
Beaver Creek [USA ◁ Milk River] 76-77 J 1-K 2
Beaverdam, VA 74-75 DE 6
Beaver Falls, PA 74-75 C 4
Beaverhead Mountains 76-77 G 3
Beaverhead River 76-77 G 3
Beaverton 74-75 D 2
Beawar 44-45 LM 5
Beazley 80 C 4
Bebedouro 78-79 K 9
Bebra 33 D 3
Beccles 32 G 5
Bečej 36-37 HJ 3
Béchar = Bashshâr 60-61 D 2
Becharof Lake 70-71 EF 6
Bechtery 36-37 P 2
Beckley, WV 72-73 K 4
Beclean 36-37 KL 2
Bečki 36-37 H 3
Bečuánsko = Botswana 64-65 F 7
Bécs 33 H 4
Becsuánaföld = Botswana 64-65 FG 7
Beda 60-61 M 7
Beddington, ME 74-75 JK 2
Bedele 60-61 M 7
Bedford 32 F 5
Bedford [CDN, Quebec] 74-75 F 2
Bedford, PA 74-75 D 4
Bedford, VA 74-75 D 6
Bedirli 46-47 G 3
Bedourie 56-57 GH 4
Bedshar 38-39 K 8
Beech Creek, OR 76-77 D 3
Beechworth 58 H 6
Beegum, CA 76-77 B 5
Beerenberg 19 B 19
Bê'êr-Mênûḥa 46-47 F 7
Beersheba = Bê'er-Sheva' 44-45 C 4
Bê'er-Sheva' 44-45 C 4
Beeville, TX 72-73 G 6
Befale 64-65 F 2
Befandriana-atsimo 64-65 K 7
Befandriana-avavatva 64-65 L 6
Bega [AUS] 56-57 JK 7
Bega, Canal – 36-37 J 3
Begemdir-na Simen = Gonder 60-61 M 6

Begičeva, ostrov – = ostrov Bol'šoj Begičev 42-43 VW 3
Begičeva, ostrov – = ostrov Bol'šoj Begičev 42-43 VW 3
Begna 30-31 C 7
Begorītis, Limnē – 36-37 JK 5
Behagle, De – = Laï 60-61 H 7
Behara 64-65 L 7
Behbahân 44-45 G 4
Behn, Mount – 56-57 E 3
Bei'an 48-49 O 2
Beibei 48-49 K 6
Beibu Wan 48-49 K 7-8
Beiḍa, Bîr – Bi'r Baydâ' 62 EF 4
Beiḍâ', El – = Al-Baydâ' 60-61 J 2
Beida, Gebel – = Jabal Baydâ' 62 E 6
Beihai [TJ, Guangxi Zhuangzu Zizhiqu] 48-49 K 7
Beijing 48-49 LM 3-4
Beijingzi 50-51 DE 3
Beipa'a 52-53 N 8
Beipiao 50-51 C 2
Beira 64-65 HJ 6
Beira [P] 34-35 CD 8
Beiroet = Bayrût 44-45 CD 4
Beiroût = Bayrût 44-45 CD 4
Beisan = Bêt Shêan 44-45 F 6
Bei Shan 48-49 GH 3
Beitbridge 64-65 GH 7
Beit Laḥm = Bayt Laḥm 46-47 F 7
Beit Shê'an 44-45 F 6
Beizah, Wâdî – = Wâdî Bayzaḥ 62 E 5
Beizhen [TJ, Liaoning] 50-51 C 2
Beja 34-35 D 9-10
Béja 34-35 D 9-10
Bêja = Bâjah 60-61 F 1
Bejaia = Bijâyah 60-61 EF 1
Béjar 34-35 E 8
Bejestân 44-45 H 4
Bejneu 44-45 CD 4
Bejrut = Bayrût 44-45 CD 4
Bejrût = Bayrût 44-45 CD 4
Bejrut = Bayrût 44-45 CD 4
Bekabad 44-45 KL 2
Bekasi 52-53 E 8
Bek-Budi = Karši 44-45 K 3
Bekdaš 44-45 G 2
Bekdaš 44-45 G 2
Békés 33 K 5
Békéscsaba 33 K 5
Bekily 64-65 L 7
Belâ [PAK] 44-45 K 5
Bela Crkva 36-37 J 3
Belaga 52-53 F 6
Belagâm = Belgaum 44-45 LM 7
Bela = Beleye 60-61 b 2-3
Bel Air 34-35 F 4
Bel Air, MD 74-75 E 5
Belaja [SU, ~] 42-43 J 6
Belaja Cerkov 38-39 F 6
Belaja Glina 38-39 H 6
Belaja Zeml'a, ostrova – 42-43 L-N 1
Bel'ajevka 36-37 O 2
Belang 52-53 HJ 6
Bela Palanka 36-37 K 4
Belau 52-53 KL 5
Bela Vista [BR, Mato Grosso do Sul] 78-79 H 9
Bela Vista [Moçambique] 64-65 H 8
Bela Vista, Cachoeira – 78-79 J 5
Bela Vista de Goiás 78-79 K 8
Belawan 52-53 C 6
Belcher Channel 70-71 RS 2
Belcher Islands 70-71 U 6
Belchite 34-35 G 8
Belcik = Yavi 46-47 G 3
Bel'cy 38-39 E 6
Belcher Channel 70-71 RS 2
Belden, CA 76-77 C 5
Beldibi 46-47 D 4
Beled 60-61 M 7
Belek 52-53 G 6
Belém [BR, Pará] 78-79 K 5
Belém [Moçambique] 63 CD 6
Belen, NM 72-73 E 5
Belep, Îles – 56-57 M 3
Beleye 60-61 b 2-3
Belfair, WA 76-77 B 2
Belfast 32 CD 4
Belfast, ME 74-75 J 2
Bêlfodyo 60-61 LM 6
Belfort 34-35 L 5
Bêlgâ'ên = Belgaum 44-45 LM 7
Belgaon = Belgaum 44-45 LM 7
Belgard (Persante) = Białogard 33 GH 1-2
Belgaum 44-45 LM 7
Belgia 34-35 JK 3
Bélgica 34-35 JK 3
Belgien 34-35 JK 3
Belgique 34-35 JK 3
Belgium 34-35 JK 3
Belgorod 38-39 G 5
Belgorod-Dnestrovskij 38-39 EF 6

Belgrad = Beograd 36-37 J 3
Belgrád = Beograd 36-37 J 3
Belgrade, MT 76-77 H 3
Belgrade = Beograd 36-37 J 3
Belgrado = Beograd 36-37 J 3
Belhaven, NC 74-75 E 7
Belcher Channel 70-71 RS 2
Belikh, Nahr – = Nahr Balîh 46-47 H 4
Beli Lom 36-37 LM 4
Belinyu 52-53 E 7
Beli Timok 36-37 K 4
Belitung, Pulau – 52-53 E 7
Belize [BH, ●] 72-73 J 8
Belize [BH, ★] 72-73 J 8
Bel'kovskij, ostrov – 42-43 Za 2
Bell, FL 74-75 b 2
Bella Coola 70-71 L 7
Bellaire, OH 74-75 C 4-5
Bellary 44-45 M 7
Bellata 58 J 2
Bella Unión 80 E 3
Bella Vista [BOL] 78-79 G 8
Bella Vista [RA, Corrientes] 80 E 3
Bell Bay 58 c 2
Bellefonte, PA 74-75 DE 4
Belle Glade, FL 74-75 c 3
Belle Île 34-35 F 5
Belle Isle 70-71 Za 7
Belle Isle, Strait of – 70-71 Z 7
Bellemont, AZ 76-77 GH 8
Belleville [CDN] 70-71 V 9
Bellevue, WA 76-77 BC 2
Bellin [CDN] 70-71 WX 5
Bellingham, WA 76-77 BC 1
Bellinzona 33 D 5
Bellona 52-53 j 7
Bellota, CA 76-77 C 6
Bellows Falls, VT 74-75 G 3
Bell Peninsula 70-71 U 5
Bell Ville [RA] 80 D 4
Belluno 36-37 DE 2
Belmez 34-35 E 9
Belmont, NY 74-75 DE 3
Belmonte [BR] 78-79 M 8
Belmopan 72-73 J 8
Belogorsk [SU, Krym'] 38-39 FG 6
Belogorsk [SU, Rossijskaja SFSR] 42-43 YZ 7
Belogradčik 36-37 K 4
Belo Horizonte [BR, Minas Gerais] 78-79 L 8
Beloit, WI 72-73 J 3
Beloje, ozero – 42-43 F 5
Belokuricha 42-43 PQ 7
Belomorsk 42-43 EF 5
Belomorsko-Baltijskij kanal 38-39 F 3
Belopolje 38-39 F 5
Belopúla 36-37 K 7
Beloreck 42-43 K 7
Belören 46-47 G 4
Belorussia 38-39 EF 5
Belorussija 38-39 EF 5
Belo Tsiribihina 64-65 K 6
Bel'ov 38-39 G 5
Belovo 42-43 Q 7
Belpre, PH 74-75 B 5
Belső-Mongólia 48-49 K 3-M 2
Belsund 30-31 j 6
Belt, MT 76-77 H 2
Belted Range 76-77 E 7
Belton, SC 74-75 B 7
Belucha, gora – 42-43 Q 8
Beluchistan = Balûchistân 44-45 J 5-K 4
Belumut, Gunung – 52-53 D 6
Belušja Guba 42-43 HJ 3
Belušja Guba 42-43 HJ 3
Belyj, ostrov – 42-43 MN 3
Belyj Byčok = Čagoda 42-43 EF 6
Belyj Byček = Čagoda 42-43 EF 6
Belyj Jar 42-43 Q 6
Bemaraha 64-65 KL 6
Bembe 64-65 DE 4
Bembêrêkê 60-61 E 6
Bemidji, MN 72-73 GH 2
Benâb = Bonâb 46-47 M 4
Bena-Dibele 64-65 F 3
Benadir = Banaadir 60-61 ab 3
Benalla 56-57 J 7
Benares = Varanasi 44-45 N 5
Benas, Ras – = Râ's Banâs 60-61 M 4
Benátky = Venedig 36-37 E 3
Benavente 34-35 DE 7
Benbecula 32 BC 3
Bend, OR 72-73 B 3
Bendel 60-61 EF 6
Bender Abas = Bandar 'Abbâs 44-45 H 5
Bender Bayla = Bandarbeyla 60-61 c 2
Bendery 38-39 EF 6
Bendigo 56-57 HJ 7

Beneden Egypte = Aṣ-Ṣa'īd 60-61 L 3-4
Beneden Trajanuswal = Nižnij Trajanov val 36-37 N 3
Benevento 36-37 F 5
Benga 64-65 H 6
Bengal, Bay of – 44-45 N-P 7
Bengala, Dorsal de – 22-23 O 5-6
Bengala, Golfo de – 44-45 N-P 7
Bengale, Dorsale du – 22-23 O 5-6
Bengale, Golfe du – 44-45 N-P 7
Bengalen, Golf van – 44-45 N-P 7
Bengalen, Golf von – 44-45 N-P 7
Bengalenrug 22-23 O 5-6
Bengalischer Rücken 22-23 O 5-6
Bengalore = Bangalore 44-45 M 8
Bengál-öböl 44-45 N-P 7
Bengal Ridge 22-23 O 5-6
Bengalska, Zatoka – 44-45 N-P 7
Bengálský záliv 44-45 N-P 7
Bengaḷūru = Bangalore 44-45 M 8
Ben Gania, Bir – = Bi'r Bin Ganīyah 60-61 J 2
Bengasi = Banghāzī 60-61 HJ 2
Bengbu 48-49 M 5
Benge, WA 76-77 D 2
Benghazi = Banghāzī 60-61 HJ 2
Bengkalis, Pulau – 52-53 D 6
Bengkayang 52-53 EF 6
Bengkulu [RI, ●] 52-53 D 7
Benguela 64-65 D 5
'Ben Guerīr = Bin Gharīr 60-61 C 2
Beni [ZRE] 64-65 G 2
Beni, Rio – 78-79 F 7
Beni-Abbès = Banī 'Abbās 60-61 D 2
Benicia, CA 76-77 BC 6
Benī Mazâr = Banī Mazār 60-61 L 3
'Benī Mellâl = Banī Mallīlah 60-61 C 2
Benin 60-61 E 7-8
Bénin 60-61 E 7-8
Bénin, Baie de – 60-61 E 7-8
Benin, Bight of – 60-61 E 7-8
Benin City 60-61 F 7
Benī Shigeir = Banī Shuqayr 62 D 4
Béni Souef = Banī Suwayf 60-61 L 3
Benī Suêf = Banī Suwayf 60-61 L 3
Benito Juárez 80 DE 5
Benjamim Constant 78-79 EF 5
Benkulen = Bengkulu 52-53 D 7
Bennett, Lake – 56-57 EF 4
Bennetta, ostrov – 42-43 cd 2
Bennettsville, SC 74-75 D 7
Bennington, VT 74-75 G 3
Bénoué 60-61 G 7
Benqi = Benxi 48-49 N 3
Bensheim 33 D 4
Benson, AZ 76-77 H 10
Bentinck Island 56-57 GH 3
Bentiū = Bantyū 60-61 KL 7
Bent Jebaïl = Bint Jubayl 46-47 F 6
Benton, CA 76-77 D 7
Benton City, WA 76-77 D 2
Benué = River Benue 60-61 F 7
Benue, River – 60-61 F 7
Benue Plateau 60-61 F 7
Benxi 48-49 N 3
Beograd 36-37 J 3
Beppu 50-51 H 6
Beqâ', El- = Al-Biqā' 46-47 FG 5-6
Beraïje = Al-Barāij 46-47 G 5
Beraisolê 60-61 N 6
Berat 36-37 H 5
Berau, Teluk – 52-53 K 7
Berber = Barbar 60-61 L 5
Berbera 60-61 b 1
Berbérati 60-61 a 1
Berch 48-49 L 2
Berchtesgaden 33 F 5
Berck 34-35 H 3
Berd'ansk 38-39 G 6
Berdičev 38-39 E 6
Berdičev 38-39 E 6
Berdigest'ach 42-43 XY 5
Berea, OH 74-75 C 4
Beregovo 33 L 4
Bereku 63 CD 4
Berenda, CA 76-77 CD 7
Bereneiland 19 B 16-17
Berenike 60-61 LM 4
Berens River [CDN, ~] 70-71 R 7
Berens River [CDN, ●] 70-71 R 7
Berent = Kościerzyna 33 HJ 1
Beresford 58 C 2
Beresniki = Berezniki 42-43 JK 6
Beretău 36-37 JK 2
Berezina 38-39 E 5
Bereznik 38-39 H 3
Berezniki [SU, Perm'] 42-43 JK 6
Bergama 44-45 B 3
Bèrgamo 36-37 CD 3
Bergbadachschanen, Autonome Oblast der – 44-45 L 3
Bergen [D] 33 F 1
Bergen [N] 30-31 A 7
Bergerac 34-35 H 6
Bergkarabachen, Autonome Oblast der – = 9 ◁ 38-39 J 7-8
Bergslagen 30-31 F 7-8
Berhampore = Baharampur 44-45 O 6
Berhampur 44-45 NO 7
Berhampur = Baharampur 44-45 O 6
Béring, Détroit de – 70-71 B 5-C 4
Bering, Estrecho de – 70-71 B 5-C 4
Bering, Mar de – 19 D 35-1
Béring, Mer de – 19 D 35-1
Bering, mys – 42-43 k 5
Bering, Straat – 70-71 B 5-C 4
Beringa, Cieśnina – 70-71 B 5-C 4
Beringa, Morze – 19 D 35-1
Beringa, ostrov – 42-43 fg 7
Bering Glacier 70-71 H 5
Beringmeer 19 D 35-1
Beringovo moře 19 D 35-1
Beringovskij 42-43 j 5
Bering Sea 19 D 35-1
Bering Strait 70-71 B 5-C 4
Beringstraße 70-71 B 5-C 4
Bering-szoros 70-71 B 5-C 4
Bering-tenger 19 D 35-1
Beringův průliv 70-71 B 5-C 4
Beringzee 19 D 35-1
Beris = Bârîs 62 D 5
Berja 34-35 F 10
Berjozovo = Ber'ozovo 42-43 LM 5
Berkeley, CA 72-73 B 4
Berkner Island 24 B 31-32
Berkovica 36-37 K 4
Berlevåg 30-31 N 2
Berlin 33 FG 2
Berlin, MD 74-75 F 5
Berlin, NH 72-73 M 3
Berlin = Berlin 33 FG 2
Berlin, Mount – 24 B 23
Berlin = Berlin 33 FG 2
Berlijn = Berlin 33 FG 2
Bermejo [BOL] 78-79 G 9
Bermejo [RA] 80 C 4
Bermejo, Rio – [RA ◁ Rio Paraguay] 80 D 2
Bermeo 34-35 F 7
Bermuda Islands 72-73 NO 5
Bern 33 C 5
Bernardo de Irigoyen 80 F 3
Bernburg 33 EF 3
Berne, WA 76-77 C 2
Berne = Bern 33 C 5
Berner Alpen 33 C 5
Bernier Bay 70-71 ST 3
Bernier Island 56-57 B 4
Bernina 33 D 5
Bĕroia 36-37 JK 5
Beroroha 64-65 KL 7
Beroun 33 FG 4
Berounka 33 F 4
Ber'oza 38-39 DE 5
Ber'ozovka 36-37 O 2
Ber'ozovo 42-43 LM 5
Berri 58 E 5
Berry 34-35 HJ 5
Berryessa, Lake – 76-77 B 6
Berryville, VA 74-75 DE 5
Bersâ' = Barṣâ' 46-47 H 4
Bersabee = Bĕer Sheva' 44-45 C 4
Berseba 64-65 E 8
Bertiskos 36-37 K 5
Bertolinia 78-79 L 6
Bertoua 60-61 G 8
Bertua = Bertoua 60-61 G 8
Berunda 63 B 2
Beruni 42-43 L 9
Beruri 78-79 G 5
Berwick, PA 74-75 E 4
Berwick-upon-Tweed 32 EF 4
Beryl, UT 76-77 G 7
Berytus = Bayrūt 44-45 CD 4
Besalampy 64-65 K 6
Besançon 34-35 L 5
Besarabia = Bessarabija 38-39 E 6
Beşīrê, El- = Buṣayrah 46-47 J 5
Beşiri 46-47 J 4
Beskiden = Beskidy 33 JK 4
Beskidy 33 JK 4
Beşkonak 46-47 D 4
Besna Kobila 36-37 K 4
Besni 44-45 D 3
Beşparmak Dağı 46-47 BC 4
Bessa Monteiro 64-65 D 4
Bessarabie = Bessarabija 38-39 E 6
Bessarabien = Bessarabija 38-39 E 6
Bessarabija 38-39 E 6
Bessarabka 38-39 E 6
Bessaz gora 42-43 M 9
Bessels, Kapp – 30-31 lm 5
Bessemer, AL 72-73 J 5
Bessemer City, NC 74-75 C 7
Besshi 50-51 J 6
Bessšoky, gora – 44-45 G 2
Bessšoky, gora – 44-45 G 2
Bestamak 38-39 L 6
Bestobe 42-43 N 7
Bēṭ = Okha 44-45 K 6
Betaf 52-53 L 7
Betafo 64-65 L 6
Betanzos 34-35 CD 7
Bétare-Oya 60-61 G 7
Betchouanaland = Botswana 64-65 FG 7
Bethal 64-65 G 8
Bethanië = Bethanien 64-65 E 8
Bethanien 64-65 E 8
Bethel, AK 70-71 D 5
Bethel, ME 74-75 H 2
Bethel, NC 74-75 E 7
Bethel, VT 74-75 G 3
Bethlehem 64-65 G 8
Bethlehem, PA 74-75 F 4
Beth Shaan = Beit Shĕ'ān 44-45 F 6
Bethulie 64-65 G 9
Béthune 34-35 J 3
Betioky 64-65 K 7
Betische Kordillere = Cordillera Penibética 34-35 E 9-G 8
Betlehem = Bayt Laḥm 46-47 F 7
Betlejem = Baytlaḥm 46-47 F 7
Betlém = Bayt Laḥm 46-47 F 7
Betpak-Dala 42-43 MN 8
Betroka 64-65 L 7
Betschuanaland = Botswana 64-65 FG 7
Bêt Shĕ'ān = Beit Shĕ'ān 44-45 F 6
Betsiboka 64-65 L 6
Betsjoeanaland 64-65 F 8
Bette, Pic – 60-61 HJ 4
Bettyhill 32 DE 2
Betvâ = Betwa 44-45 M 6
Betwa 44-45 M 6
Beulah, OR 76-77 D 4
Beuthen = Bytom 33 J 3
Beverley 32 F 5
Beverly, MA 74-75 H 3
Beverly, WA 76-77 D 2
Beyābān, Kūh-e- 44-45 H 5
Beyce = Orhaneli 46-47 C 3
Bey Dağları 46-47 D 4
Beydili 46-47 D 2
Beykoz, İstanbul- 46-47 C 2
Beyla 60-61 C 7
Beylikova 46-47 D 3
Beypazarı 46-47 DE 2
Beypınarı 46-47 G 3
Beyrouth = Bayrūth 44-45 CD 4
Beyşehir 46-47 DE 4
Beyşehir Gölü 44-45 C 3
Beyt = Okhā 44-45 K 6
Beytişebap = Elki 46-47 K 4
Bežeck 38-39 G 4
Beziers 34-35 J 7
Bezwada = Vijayavada 44-45 N 7
Bežeck 38-39 G 4

Bhadrak 44-45 O 6
Bhagalpur 44-45 O 5-6
Bhairab Bazar 44-45 P 6
Bhamo = Banmau 52-53 C 2
Bhandāra 44-45 MN 6
Bharatpur [IND, Rajasthan] 44-45 M 5
Bharuch 44-45 L 6
Bhāṭgāṅv = Bhātgaon 44-45 O 5
Bhatgaon 44-45 O 5
Bhatinda 44-45 L 4
Bhātpara 44-45 O 6
Bhaunagar = Bhavnagar 44-45 L 6
Bhawānīpāṭnā = Bhawānipatna 44-45 N 7
Bhavnagar 44-45 L 6
Bhawānipatna 44-45 N 7
Bhelsā = Vidisha 44-45 M 6
Bhilainagar 44-45 N 6
Bhilsa = Vidisha 44-45 M 6
Bhima 44-45 M 7
Bhīr = Bir 44-45 M 7
Bhivānī = Bhiwani 44-45 M 5
Bhiwani 44-45 M 5
Bhopal 44-45 M 6
Bhor 44-45 L 7
Bhoutan 44-45 OP 5
Bhubanēshvara = Bhubaneswar 44-45 O 6
Bhubeneswar 44-45 O 6
Bhuj 44-45 KL 6
Bhusāvaḷ = Bhusawal 44-45 M 6
Bhusawal 44-45 M 6
Bhutān 44-45 OP 5
Bhután 44-45 OP 5
Bhûtân 44-45 OP 5
Bhutan 44-45 OP 5

Biābān, Kūh-e – = Kūh-e Beyābān 44-45 H 5
Biak, Pulau – 52-53 L 7
Biała Podlaska 33 L 2-3
Białobrzegi 33 K 3
Białogard 33 GH 1-2
Białystok 33 L 2
Biała Podlaska 33 L 2-3
Białe, Morze – 42-43 FG 4
Białobrzegi 33 K 3
Białogard 33 GH 1-2
Białoruś 38-39 EF 5
Białystok 33 L 2
Biar = Bihar 44-45 NO 6
Biaro, Pulau – 52-53 J 6
Biarritz 34-35 G 7
Biasso = Bissau 60-61 A 6
Bibā 62 D 3
Bibai 50-51 bc 2
Bibala 64-65 D 5
Biberach 33 D 4
Bībūr 60-61 L 7
Bībūr, Nahr – 60-61 L 7
Bicaner = Bikaner 44-45 L 5
Bickerton Island 56-57 G 2
Bickleton, WA 76-77 CD 2-3
Bicknell, UT 76-77 H 6
Biḍ = Bir 44-45 M 7
Bid', Al- 62 F 3
Bida 60-61 F 7
Bidar 44-45 M 7
Bidara = Bidar 44-45 M 7
Biddeford, ME 72-73 MN 3
Bidele Depression = Djourab 60-61 H 5
Bidnī, Bi'r – 62 C 4
Biè = Kuito 64-65 E 5
Bieber, CA 76-77 C 5
Biebrza 33 L 2
Biegun północny 19 A
Biegun południowy 24 A
Biel 33 C 5
Bielawa 33 H 3
Bielefeld 33 D 2
Biele Karpaty 33 HJ 4
Bielitz-Biala = Bielsko-Biała 33 J 4
Biella 36-37 BC 3
Bielorrusia 38-39 EF 5
Biélorussie 38-39 EF 5
Bielsko-Biała 33 J 4
Bielsko-Biała 33 J 4
Bielsk Podlaski 33 L 2
Biên Hoa 52-53 E 4
Bienne = Biel 33 C 5
Bienville, Lac – 70-71 W 6
Bifuka 50-51 c 1
Biga 46-47 B 2
Bigadiç 46-47 C 3
Big Arm, MT 76-77 FG 2
Big Baldy 76-77 F 3
Big Bell 56-57 C 5
Big Belt Mountains 76-77 H 2
Big Bend, CA 76-77 C 5
Big Bend National Park 72-73 F 6
Big Chino Wash 76-77 G 8
Big Creek, ID 76-77 F 3
Big Cypress Indian Reservation 74-75 c 3
Big Cypress Swamp 74-75 c 3-4
Big Chino Wash 76-77 G 8
Big Delta, AK 70-71 GH 5
Big Desert 58 E 5
Big Falls 76-77 E 1
Bigfork, MT 76-77 FG 1
Bigga 58 J 5
Biggar [CDN] 70-71 P 7
Bigge Island 56-57 DE 2
Biggs, OR 76-77 C 3
Bigha = Biğa 46-47 B 2
Big Hole River 76-77 G 3
Bighorn Mountains 72-73 E 2-3
Big Chino Wash 76-77 G 8
Big Island [CDN, Baffin Island] 70-71 WX 5
Big Lost River 76-77 G 4
Bigobo 63 A 4
Big Pine, CA 76-77 DE 7
Big Pine Key, FL 74-75 c 4
Big Piney, WY 76-77 HJ 4
Biğrān 44-45 G 6
Big Salmon Range 70-71 K 5
Big Sandy, WY 76-77 J 4
Big Sandy River 76-77 G 8
Big Smoky Valley 76-77 E 6
Big Spring, TX 72-73 F 5
Big Springs, ID 76-77 H 3
Big Stone Gap, VA 74-75 B 6
Big Sur, CA 76-77 BC 7
Big Timber, MT 76-77 J 3
Big Trout Lake [CDN, ≈] 70-71 T 7
Big Wood River 76-77 F 4
Bihar [IND, ●] 44-45 O 6
Bihar [IND, ☆] 44-45 NO 6
Biharamulo 64-65 H 3
Bihor 36-37 K 2
Bihor, Munţii – 36-37 K 2
Bihoro 50-51 d 2
Bijagós, Arquipélago dos – 60-61 A 6
Bijapur [IND, Karnataka] 44-45 LM 7
Bijāpura = Bijapur 44-45 LM 7
Bijār 44-45 F 3
Bij-Chem = Bol'šoj Jenisej 42-43 S 7
Bij-Chem = Bol'šoj Jenisej 42-43 S 7
Bij-Chem = Bol'šoj Jenisej 42-43 S 7
Bijie 48-49 K 6
Bījistān = Bejestān 44-45 H 4
Bijnoṭ 44-45 L 5
Bijrān 44-45 G 6
Bijsk 42-43 Q 7
Bikaner 44-45 L 5
Bikin [SU, ~] 42-43 a 8
Bikin [SU, ●] 42-43 Za 8
Bikoro 64-65 E 3
Bilaspur [IND, Madhya Pradesh] 44-45 N 6
Bilati 63 B 3
Bilbao 34-35 F 7
Bilbays 62 D 2
Bildudalur 30-31 ab 2
Bileća 36-37 H 4
Bilecik 46-47 C 2
Bílé moře 42-43 FG 4
Bili [ZRE, ~] 64-65 FG 2
Bili [ZRE, ●] 64-65 FG 2
Bilibiza 63 E 6
Biliran Island 52-53 H 4
Billefjord 30-31 k 5
Billings, MT 72-73 E 2
Billiton = Pulau Belitung 52-53 E 7
Bill Williams River 76-77 FG 8
Bilma 60-61 G 5
Biloela 56-57 K 4
Bilo gora 36-37 G 2-3
Biloxi, MS 72-73 J 5
Bilqās 62 D 2
Bilqas Qism Auwal = Bilqās 62 D 2
Biltine 60-61 J 6
Bilugyn = Bīlū Kyūn 52-53 C 3
Bīlū Kyūn 52-53 C 3
Bimbéréké = Bembèrèkè 60-61 E 6
Bimbo 60-61 H 8
Bimlipatam 44-45 M 7
Binalbagan 52-53 H 4
Binboğa 46-47 G 3
Bindloe = Isla Marchena 78-79 AB 4
Bin Ganīyah, Bi'r – 60-61 J 2
Bingara 58 K 2
Bingen 33 C 4
Bingerville 60-61 D 7
Bingham, ME 74-75 J 2
Bingham Canyon, UT 76-77 GH 5
Binghamton, NY 72-73 LM 3
Bin Gharīr = Bin Jarīr 60-61 C 2
Bingo Bay = Hiuchi-nada 50-51 J 5
Bingöl 46-47 J 3
Bingöl Dağları 46-47 J 3
Binjai 52-53 C 6
Bin Jarīr 60-61 C 2
Binnaway 56-57 JK 6
Binnen-Mongolië 48-49 K 3-M 2
Binnenzee = Seto-naikai 48-49 P 5
Bintan, Pulau – 52-53 DE 6
Bint Jubayl 46-47 F 6
Bintuan 52-53 D 7
Bintulu 52-53 F 6
Bintuni 52-53 K 7
Binzart 60-61 FG 1
Binzert = Binzart 60-61 FG 1
Bio Bio, Rio – 80 B 5
Biograd 36-37 F 4
Bioko 60-61 F 8
Biola, CA 76-77 CD 7
Bionga 63 AB 3
Biqā', Al- = 4 ◁ 46-47 G 6
Biqā', Al- = RL [≅] 46-47 FG 5-6
Biqā', Al- = Sahl al-Biqā' 46-47 FG 5-6
Bir 44-45 M 7
Bira 42-43 Z 8
Birāk 60-61 G 3
Bi'r al-Abd 62 E 2
Bi'r 'Alī 44-45 F 8
Birao 60-61 J 6
Birchip 58 F 5
Birch Mountains 70-71 O 6
Birdsville 56-57 G 5
Birecik 46-47 GH 4
Birganj 44-45 NO 5
Birhan Terara 60-61 M 6
Birigui 78-79 J 9
Biril'ussy = Novobiril'ussy 42-43 QR 6
Birimşe = Sincik 46-47 H 3
Bīrjand 44-45 H 4
Birkenhead 32 E 5
Birket Fatimé 60-61 HJ 6
Birkīm 46-47 L 4
Bîrlad [R, ~] 36-37 M 2-3
Bîrlad [R, ●] 36-37 M 2
Birma 52-53 BC 2
Birma = Mianma 52-53 BC 2
Birmania 52-53 BC 2
Birmanie 52-53 BC 2
Birmingham [GB] 32 EF 5
Birmingham, AL 72-73 J 5
Birnin Kebbi 60-61 EF 6
Birni N'konni 60-61 EF 6
Birobidžan 42-43 Z 8
Birobidžan 42-43 Z 8
Birrie River 58 H 2
Birrindudu 56-57 EF 3
Birsk 42-43 K 6
Birskij = Obluč'e 42-43 Z 8
Birtavarre 30-31 J 3
Bī'r Umm Qarayn 60-61 B 3
Biruni = Beruni 42-43 L 9
Bir'usa 42-43 S 6
Biržai 30-31 L 9
Biržai 30-31 L 9
Bisa, Pulau – 52-53 J 7
Bisaliya, El – = Al-Başalīyat Qiblī 62 E 5
Bisbee, AZ 76-77 HJ 10
Biscaje, Golf van – 34-35 EF 6
Biscay, Bay of – 34-35 EF 6
Biscaya, Golf von – 34-35 EF 6
Biscayne Bay 74-75 c 4
Biscéglie 36-37 G 5
Bischofshofen 33 F 5
Biscoe Islands 24 C 30
Biscra = Biskrah 60-61 F 2
Biševo 36-37 F 4
Bīshah, Wādī – 44-45 E 6-7
Bīsheh, Īstgāh-e – 46-47 N 6
Bishenpur 44-45 P 6
Bishop, CA 76-77 D 7
Bishopville, SC 74-75 C 7
Bishrī, Jabal al- 46-47 H 5
Bisina, Lake – 64-65 HJ 2
Biskajska, Zatoka – 34-35 EF 6
Biskajský záliv 34-35 EF 6
Biskayerhuken 30-31 hj 5
Biškek 42-43 NO 9
Biškek 42-43 NO 9
Biskrah 60-61 F 2
Bisling 52-53 J 5
Bismarck, ND 72-73 F 2
Bismarck, Archipel – 52-53 NO 7
Bismarck, Archipiélago de – 52-53 NO 7
Bismarck, Mar de – 52-53 NO 7
Bismarck, Mer de – 52-53 NO 7
Bismarcka, Archipelag – 52-53 NO 7
Bismarckarchipel 52-53 NO 7
Bismarck Archipel 52-53 NO 7
Bismarckburg = Kasanga 64-65 H 4
Bismarckovo moře 52-53 NO 7
Bismarckovo souostroví 52-53 NO 7
Bismarck Range 52-53 M 7-N 8
Bismarck Sea 52-53 NO 7
Bismarcksee 52-53 NO 7
Bismarckstraße 24 C 30
Bismarck-szigetek 52-53 NO 7
Bismarck-tenger 52-53 NO 7
Bismarckzee 52-53 NO 7
Bismil 46-47 J 4
Bīsotūn 46-47 M 5
Bissau 60-61 A 6
Bissau-Guinea 60-61 AB 6
Bistcho Lake 70-71 N 6
Bistōnis, Limnē – 36-37 L 5
Bistriţa [R, ~] 36-37 M 2
Bistriţa [R, ●] 36-37 L 2
Biševo 36-37 F 4
Biškek 42-43 NO 9
Biškek 42-43 NO 9
Bitam 64-65 D 2
Bitlis 44-45 E 3
Bitlis Dağları 46-47 JK 3
Bitola 36-37 J 5
Bitonto 36-37 G 5
Bitter Creek 76-77 J 5
Bitterfeld 33 F 3
Bitterfontein 64-65 E 9
Bittermeer = Al-Buḥayrat al-Murrat al-Kubrá 62 E 2
Bitterroot Range 72-73 C 2-D 3
Bitterroot River 76-77 F 2
Bitung 52-53 J 6
Biu 60-61 G 6
Biviraka 52-53 M 8
Biwa-ko 48-49 Q 4
Biyāḍ, Al- = Al-Bayāḍ 44-45 F 6
Biyalā 62 D 2
Bizerta = Binzart 60-61 FG 1
Bizerte = Binzart 60-61 FG 1

Bjargtangar 30-31 a 2
Bjelovar 36-37 G 3
Bjelowo = Belovo 42-43 Q 7
Bjelucha = gora Belucha 42-43 Q 8
Björkholmen 30-31 H 4
Björna 30-31 H 6
Björneborg = Pori 30-31 J 7
Bjuröklubb 30-31 JK 5

Blackall 56-57 HJ 4
Black Belt 72-73 J 5
Blackburn 32 EF 5
Blackburn, Mount – 70-71 H 5
Black Canyon 76-77 F 8
Black Diamond, WA 76-77 BC 2
Black Duck 70-71 ST 6
Black Eagle, MT 76-77 H 2
Blackfeet Indian Reservation 76-77 G 1
Blackfoot, ID 76-77 GH 4
Blackfoot, MT 76-77 G 1
Blackfoot Reservoir 76-77 H 4
Blackfoot River 76-77 G 2
Black Hills 72-73 F 3
Blackleaf, MT 76-77 G 1
Black Mesa 76-77 H 7
Black Mountain [USA] 74-75 A 7
Black Mountain, NC 74-75 BC 7

Black 161

Black Mountains [USA] 72-73 D 4-5
Black Pine Peak 76-77 G 4
Blackpool 32 E 5
Black River [USA ◁ Henderson Bay] 74-75 F 3
Black River [USA ◁ Salt River] 76-77 HJ 9
Black Rock 80 H 8
Black Rock, UT 76-77 G 6
Black Rock Desert 72-73 C 3
Blacksburg, VA 74-75 C 6
Black Sea 38-39 E-G 7
Blackshear, GA 74-75 BC 9
Black Springs, NM 76-77 J 9
Blackstone, PA 74-75 DE 6
Blackville, SC 74-75 C 8
Black Volta 60-61 D 7
Black Waxy Prairie 72-73 G 5
Bláfjall 30-31 e 2
Blåfjorden 30-31 lm 5
Blagodarnoje 38-39 H 6
Blagoevgrad 36-37 K 4-5
Blagoveščensk [SU, Belaja] 38-39 KL 4
Blagoveščensk [SU, Rossijskaja SFSR] 42-43 YZ 7
Blagoveščenskij proliv 42-43 c 2-d 3
Blagoveščensk [SU, Belaja] 38-39 KL 4
Blagoveščensk [SU, Rossijskaja SFSR] 42-43 YZ 7
Blagoveščenskij proliv 42-43 c 2-d 3
Blaine, WA 76-77 B 1
Blainville 74-75 FG 2
Blair Athol 56-57 J 4
Blairsden, CA 76-77 C 6
Blairsville, PA 74-75 D 4
Blanca Peak 72-73 E 4
Blanche, Lake — [AUS, South Australia] 56-57 GH 5
Blanche, Lake — [AUS, Western Australia] 56-57 GH 5
Blancos, Los — [RA] 80 D 2
Blandá 30-31 d 2
Blanding, UT 76-77 J 7
Blankaholm 30-31 FG 9
Blantyre 64-65 HJ 4
Blåvands Huk 30-31 BC 10
Blavet 34-35 F 4-5
Blaye 34-35 G 6
Blayney 56-57 J 6
Blaze, Point — 56-57 EF 2
Blazon, WY 76-77 H 5
Blednaja, gora — 42-43 M 2
Blejești 36-37 L 3
Blekinge län 30-31 F 9
Blenheim [CDN] 74-75 C 3
Blenheim [NZ] 56-57 O 8
Blida = Bulaydah 60-61 E 1
Blīdah = Bulaydah 60-61 E 1
Bliss, ID 76-77 F 4
Blitar 52-53 F 8
Blitong = Pulau Belitung 52-53 E 7
Blitta 60-61 E 7
Blitzen, OR 76-77 D 4
Block Island 74-75 H 4
Block Island Sound 74-75 GH 4
Bloemfontein 64-65 G 8
Blois 34-35 H 5
Blönduós 30-31 cd 2
Bloody Falls 70-71 NO 4
Bloomington, IL 72-73 HJ 3
Bloomington, IN 72-73 J 4
Bloomsburg, PA 74-75 E 4
Blosseville Kyst 70-71 ef 4
Bloxom, VA 74-75 F 6
Blūdān 46-47 G 6
Blue Bell Knoll 76-77 H 6
Blue Creek, UT 76-77 G 5
Bluefield, VA 74-75 C 6
Bluefield, WV 74-75 C 6
Bluefields 72-73 K 9
Bluejoint Lake 76-77 D 4
Blue Knob 76-77 D 5
Blue Lake, CA 76-77 B 5
Blue Mountain [USA, Pennsylvania] 74-75 EF 4
Blue Mountain Pass 76-77 E 4
Blue Mountains [USA, Maine] 74-75 H 2
Blue Mountains [USA, Oregon] 72-73 C 2-3
Blue Mud Bay 56-57 G 2
Blue Nile = Abay 60-61 M 6
Bluenose Lake 70-71 N 4
Blue Ridge [USA, New York] 74-75 F 3
Blue Ridge [USA, North Carolina] 72-73 KL 4
Blue Ridge, GA 74-75 A 7
Blue River 76-77 J 9
Bluff 56-57 N 9
Bluff, UT 76-77 J 7
Bluffton, IN 74-75 A 4
Blumenau [BR] 80 FG 3
Bly, OR 76-77 C 4
Blythe, CA 76-77 F 9
Blytheville, AR 72-73 HJ 4

Bo [WAL] 60-61 B 7
Boali 60-61 H 8
Boa Nova [BR, Bahia] 78-79 LM 7
Boardman, OR 76-77 D 3
Boa Vista [BR, Roraima] 78-79 G 4
Bobadah 58 H 4
Bobbili 44-45 N 7
Böbbio 36-37 C 3
Bobo-Dioulasso 60-61 D 6
Bobo-Dioulasso = Bobo-Dioulasso 60-61 D 6
Bobonong 64-65 G 7
Bóbr 33 G 3
Bobrujsk 38-39 E 5
Boca, La — 72-73 b 3
Boca del Pao 78-79 FG 3
Boca do Acre 78-79 F 5
Boca do Jari 78-79 J 5
Boca do Tapauá = Tapauá 78-79 FG 6
Boca Grande, FL 74-75 b 3
Bocaiuva 78-79 L 8
Bocaranga 60-61 H 7
Boca Raton, FL 74-75 cd 3
Bochina 33 K 4
Bocholt 33 C 3
Bochum 33 C 3
Böda 30-31 G 9
Boda [RCA] 60-61 H 8
Bodajbo 42-43 VW 6
Bodega Head 76-77 B 6
Bodêlé 60-61 H 5
Boden 30-31 JK 5
Bodensee 33 D 5
Bodø 30-31 EF 4
Bodoquena 78-79 H 8
Bodoquena, Serra — 78-79 H 9
Bodrog 33 K 4
Bodrum 46-47 B 4
Boé 60-61 B 6
Boedapest = Budapest 33 J 5
Boekarest = Bucureşti 36-37 LM 3
Boende 64-65 F 3
Boerjatien Autonome Republiek 42-43 T 7-V 6
Boerundi 64-65 GH 3
Boffa 60-61 B 6
Bôfu = Hôfu 50-51 H 5-6
Bogalusa, LA 72-73 HJ 5
Bogandé 60-61 DE 6
Bogan Gate 58 H 4
Bogan River 56-57 J 6
Bogarnes 30-31 bc 2
Boğazici 44-45 BC 2
Boğazkale 46-47 F 2-3
Boğazköprü 46-47 F 3
Boğazlıyan 46-47 F 3
Bogd 48-49 J 2
Bogdanovič 38-39 M 4
Bogdanovič 38-39 M 4
Bogdo uul 48-49 FG 3
Bogd uul, Ich — 48-49 J 3
Bogd uul, Ich — 48-49 J 3
Bogd uul, Ich — 48-49 J 3
Boggabilla 56-57 JK 5
Boggabri 58 JK 3
Boggai, Lak — 63 D 2
Bogham, Al- 46-47 J 5
Boghari = Qasr al-Bukharī 60-61 E 1
Bogia 52-53 MN 7
Bogo [RP] 52-53 H 4
Bogong , Mount — 56-57 J 7
Bogor 52-53 E 8
Bogorodick 38-39 G 5
Bogotá 78-79 E 4
Bogotol 42-43 Q 6
Bogučany 42-43 S 6
Bogučany 42-43 S 6
Bo Hai 48-49 M 4
Bohai Haixia 48-49 N 4
Bohême = Čechy 33 FG 4
Bohemen = Čechy 33 FG 4
Bohemia = Čechy 33 FG 4
Böhmen = Čechy 33 FG 4
Böhmerwald 33 FG 4
Bohol 52-53 H 5
Boibeïs, Limně — 36-37 K 6
Boigu Island 52-53 M 8
Boim 78-79 H 5
Bois, Lac des — 70-71 M 4
Bois Blanc Island 74-75 A 2
Boise City, ID 72-73 G 3
Boise River 76-77 E 4
Bois-le-Duc = 's-Hertogenbosch 34-35 KL 3
Bojador, Cabo — — Râ's Bujdûr 60-61 AB 3
Bojarka 42-43 S 3
Bojnûrd 44-45 H 3
Bojuru 80 F 4
Boké 60-61 B 6
Bokhona River 58 J 1
Bokkol 63 D 2
Boknfjord 30-31 A 8
Bokoro 60-61 H 6
Bokote 64-65 F 2-3
Bokovskaja 38-39 H 6
Bokungu 64-65 F 3
Bolaiti 64-65 FG 3
Bolama 60-61 A 6
Bolān, Kotal — 44-45 K 5
Bolangir = Balāngīr 44-45 N 6

Bolan Pass = Kotal Bolān 44-45 K 5
Bólbě, Limně — 36-37 K 6
Bolbec 34-35 H 4
Bole 60-61 D 7
Bole, MT 76-77 GH 2
Boles, ID 76-77 F 3
Bolesławiec 33 GH 3
Bolesławiec 33 GH 3
Bolgatanga 60-61 D 6
Bolgrad 38-39 E 6
Boli [TJ] 48-49 P 2
Boli [ZRE] 63 B 2
Boliden 30-31 J 5
Bolissós 36-37 L 6
Bolívar [PE] 78-79 D 6
Bolívar, Pico — 78-79 E 3
Bolivia 78-79 FG 8
Bolivia 78-79 FG 8
Boliviai-fennsik = Altiplano 78-79 F 8
Bolivie 78-79 FG 8
Bolivie 78-79 FG 8
Bolivien 78-79 FG 8
Bolivien, Hochland von — = Altiplano 78-79 F 8
Boliwia 78-79 FG 8
Bolkar Dağları 46-47 F 4
Bollnäs 30-31 G 7
Bollon 56-57 J 5
Bolobo 64-65 E 3
Bolod'ok 42-43 Z 7
Bologna 36-37 D 3
Bologne = Bologna 36-37 D 3
Bologoje 42-43 EF 6
Bolomba 64-65 E 2
Bolonia = Bologna 36-37 D 3
Bolonia = Bologna 36-37 D 3
Bolor = Bâltistân 44-45 M 3-4
Bolo-retto = Penghu Lieh-tao 48-49 N 7
Bólos 36-37 K 6
Bolotnoje 42-43 P 6
Bol'šaja = Velikaja 42-43 h 5
Bol'šaja Višera 38-39 F 4
Bol'šaja, ostrov — 42-43 T-V 2
Bol'šije Uki 42-43 N 6
Bol'šoj An'uj 42-43 fg 4
Bol'šoj Balchan 38-39 K 8
Bol'šoj Ber'ozovyj, ostrov — 30-31 MN 7
Bol'šoj Jenisej 42-43 S 7
Bol'šoj Oloj = Oloj 42-43 f 4
Bol'šoj Šantar, ostrov — 42-43 ab 7
Bol'šoj Uluj 42-43 R 6
Bol'šoj Uzen' 38-39 J 5-6
Bol'šaja Višera 38-39 F 4
Bol'ševik, ostrov — 42-43 T-V 2
Bol'šezemel'skaja tundra 42-43 JK 4
Bol'šije Uki 42-43 N 6
Bol'šoj An'uj 42-43 fg 4
Bol'šoj Ber'ozovyj, ostrov — 30-31 MN 7
Bol'šoj Jenisej 42-43 S 7
Bol'šoj Oloj = Oloj 42-43 f 4
Bol'šoj Šantar, ostrov — 42-43 ab 7
Bol'šoj Uzen' 38-39 J 5-6
Bolton 32 E 5
Bolton, NC 74-75 D 7
Bolu 46-47 D 2
Bolucan 46-47 GH 3
Bolukâbâd 46-47 M 4
Bolungarvík 30-31 ab 1
Bolvadin 46-47 D 3
Bolzano 36-37 D 2
Boma 64-65 D 4
Bômba, Khalig — = Khalīj al-Bunbah 60-61 J 2
Bombaim = Bombay 44-45 L 7
Bombala 56-57 JK 7
Bombay 44-45 L 7
Bomberai 52-53 K 7
Bombetoka, Baie de — 64-65 KL 6
Bombo 63 C 2
Bom Comércio 78-79 F 6
Bom Despacho 78-79 KL 8
Bomi Hills = Tubmanburg 60-61 B 7
Bom Jesus [BR, Piauí] 78-79 L 6
Bom Jesus da Gurguéia, Serra — 78-79 L 6
Bom Jesus da Lapa 78-79 L 7
Bømlafjord 30-31 A 8
Bømlo 30-31 A 8
Bomokandi 64-65 G 2
Bomongo 64-65 E 2
Bomu 64-65 F 2
Bônâb [IR ↖ Tabrīz] 46-47 LM 3
Bonâb [IR ↙ Tabrīz] 46-47 M 4
Bonaire 72-73 N 9
Bonancita 76-77 GH 10
Bonanza, ID 76-77 F 3
Bonaparte, Mount — 76-77 D 1

Bonaparte Archipelago 56-57 DE 2
Bonavista 70-71 a 8
Bon Bon 58 BC 3
Bondeno 36-37 D 3
Bond Hill 58 B 3
Bondo [ZRE] 64-65 F 2
Bondoc Peninsula 52-53 H 4
Bondoukou 60-61 D 7
Bondurant, WY 76-77 HJ 4
Bône = 'Annâbah 60-61 F 1
Bone = Watampone 52-53 GH 7
Bone, Teluk — 52-53 H 7
Bonga 60-61 M 7
Bongandanga 64-65 F 2
Bongo 64-65 CD 3
Bongolave 64-65 L 6
Bongor 60-61 H 6
Bonifacio 36-37 C 5
Bonifacio, Bocche di — 36-37 C 5
Bonin 54 RS 7
Boningraben 22-23 R 4
Bonin Trench 22-23 R 4
Bonintrog 22-23 R 4
Bonita, AZ 76-77 HJ 9
Bonitas, Las — 78-79 FG 3
Bonn 33 C 3
Bonne-Espérance, Cap de — 64-65 E 8
Bonner, MT 76-77 G 2
Bonners Ferry, ID 76-77 E 1
Bonneville, OR 76-77 C 3
Bonneville Salt Flats 76-77 G 5
Bonnie Rock 56-57 C 6
Bonny 60-61 F 8
Bonny, Golfe de — 60-61 F 8
Bonnyville 70-71 O 7
Bô-no misaki 50-51 GH 7
Bonthe 60-61 B 7
Bontongsunggu = Jeneponto 52-53 G 8
Bookabie 56-57 F 6
Bookaloo 56-57 G 6
Booligal 56-57 H 6
Boonah 58 L 1-2
Böön Cagaan nuur 48-49 HJ 2
Boone, NC 74-75 C 6
Boonville, NY 74-75 F 3
Boorama 60-61 N 7
Boosaaso 60-61 bc 1
Boothbay Harbor, ME 74-75 J 3
Boothby, Cape — 24 C 6-7
Boothia, Gulf of — 70-71 ST 3-4
Boothia Isthmus 70-71 S 4
Boothia Peninsula 70-71 RS 3
Boouê 64-65 D 2-3
Boqueirão [BR, Rio Grande do Sul] 80 F 4
Boqueirão, Serra do — [BR, Bahia] 78-79 L 7
Bor 36-37 K 3
Bor [TR] 46-47 F 4
Bôr = Bûr 60-61 L 7
Boraha, Nosy — 64-65 M 6
Borah Peak 72-73 D 3
Borås 30-31 EF 9
Borâzjân 44-45 G 5
Borba [BR] 78-79 H 5
Borba = Karadeniz Boğazici 44-45 BC 2
Borborema, Planalto da — 78-79 M 6
Bor Chadyn uul 48-49 EF 3
Bor Choro uul 48-49 E 3
Borçka = Yeniyol 46-47 JK 2
Borcu = Borkou 60-61 HJ 5
Bor Chadyn uul 48-49 EF 3
Bor Choro uul 48-49 E 3
Bordeaux 34-35 G 6
Borden Island 70-71 NO 2
Borden Peninsula 70-71 U 3
Bordertown 58 E 6
Bordighera 36-37 BC 4
Bordzongijn Gov' 48-49 K 3
Bóreioi Sporádes 36-37 KL 6
Bóreion Stenòn Kerkýras 36-37 HJ 6
Borg̊å 30-31 LM 7
Borgarfjardhar 30-31 c 2
Børgefjell 30-31 EF 5
Borger, TX 72-73 F 4
Borgholm 30-31 G 9
Borgomanero 36-37 BC 3
Borgoña = Bourgogne 34-35 K 5-6
Bor Chadyn uul 48-49 EF 3
Bor Choro uul 48-49 E 3
Borisoglebsk 38-39 H 5
Borisov 38-39 E 5
Borisova, mys — 42-43 a 6
Borja [PE] 78-79 D 5
Borkou 60-61 H 5
Borku = Borkou 60-61 H 5
Borlänge 30-31 FG 7
Borlu 46-47 C 3
Bòrmida 36-37 BC 4
Bormio 36-37 D 2
Borned = Kalimantan 52-53 F 7-G 6
Borneo = Kalimantan 52-53 F 7-G 6
Borneó = Kalimantan 52-53 F 7-G 6
Borneo = Kalimantan 52-53 F 7-G 6
Bornholm 30-31 F 10
Borno = Bornu 60-61 G 6
Bornou = Borno 60-61 G 6

Bornu 60-61 G 6
Borogoncy 42-43 Z 5
B'or'ol'och = Susuman 42-43 cd 5
Boron, CA 76-77 E 8
Borovići 42-43 EF 6
Borovići 42-43 EF 6
Borovl'anka 42-43 P 7
Borovskoj 42-43 LM 7
Borroloola 56-57 G 3
Borşa 36-37 L 2
Borščovočnyj chrebet 42-43 W 7
Bors-part 60-61 B 7-C 8
Borščovočnyj chrebet 42-43 W 7
Bortala Monggol Zizhizhou = F ◁ 48-49 E 2-3
Bor Talijn gol 48-49 E 3
Borto 42-43 V 7
Borûjerd 44-45 FG 4
Borz'a 42-43 W 7
Bosa 36-37 C 5
Bosanska Gradiška 36-37 G 3
Bosanska Gradiška 36-37 G 3
Bosanska Krupa 36-37 G 3
Bosanski Novi 36-37 FG 3
Bosanski Petrovac 36-37 G 3
Bose 48-49 K 7
Bosfor = Boğaziçi 44-45 BC 2
Bosfor = Boğaziçi 36-37 N 5
Bósforo = Boğaziçi 44-45 BC 2
Boshan 48-49 M 4
Bosmanland 64-65 E 8
Bosna [BG] 36-37 M 4
Bosna [YU] 36-37 GH 3
Bosna a Hercegovina 36-37 GH 3-4
Bosna i Hercegovina 36-37 GH 3-4
Bósnia i Herzegowina 36-37 G 3-H 4
Bosnia y Hercegovina 36-37 GH 3-4
Bosnie-Herzégovine 36-37 GH 3-4
Bosnien und Herzegowina 36-37 GH 3-4
Bosobolo 64-65 E 2
Bosphore = Boğaziçi 44-45 BC 2
Bospor, úž. - = Boğaziçi 36-37 N 5
Bospor, úžina — = Boğaziçi 44-45 BC 2
Bosporus = Boğaziçi 44-45 BC 2
Bossangoa 60-61 H 7
Bossembélé 60-61 H 7
Bosso 60-61 G 6
Bostân [IR] 46-47 MN 7
Bostânâbâd 46-47 M 4
Boston [GB] 32 FG 5
Boston, GA 74-75 B 9
Boston, MA 72-73 MN 3
Boston Mountains 72-73 H 4
Bosveld 64-65 G 7
Bosznia és Hercegovina 36-37 GH 3-4
Boszporusz = Karadeniz Boğaziçi 44-45 BC 2
Botan Çayı 46-47 K 4
Botany Bay 56-57 K 6
Botev 36-37 L 4
Bothia Golfo de — 30-31 H 7-K 5
Botletle 64-65 F 7
Botnica, Zatoka — 30-31 H 7-K 5
Botnicka, Zatoka - 30-31 H 7-K 5
Botnický záliv 30-31 H 7-K 5
Botnický záliv 30-31 H 7-K 5
Botnische Golf 30-31 H 7-K 5
Botoşani 36-37 M 2
Botswana 64-65 FG 7
Botte Donato 36-37 G 6
Botteni-öböl 30-31 H 7-K 5
Botteni-öböl 30-31 H 7-K 5
Bottnie, Golfe de — 30-31 H 7-K 5
Bottnischer Meerbusen 30-31 H 7-K 5
Botucatu 78-79 K 9
Botulu 42-43 W 5
Bouaflé 60-61 C 7
Bouaké 60-61 CD 7
Boû 'Amaroû = Bu 'Amarû 46-47 HJ 5
Bouar 60-61 H 7
Bouca 60-61 H 7
Boucau 34-35 G 7
Boudeuse Cay 64-65 M 4
Boudewijnstad = Moba 64-65 G 4
Boû Djébéha 60-61 D 5
Bougainville 52-53 j 6
Bougainville, Cape — [AUS] 56-57 E 2
Bougainville, Fosse de — 52-53 h 6
Bougainville, Rów — 52-53 h 6
Bougainvilleský příkop 52-53 h 6
Bougainvilletrog 52-53 h 6
Bougie = Bijâyah 60-61 EF 1
Bougouni 60-61 C 6
Bougtob = Bû Kutub 60-61 E 2
Boukân = Bûkân 46-47 LM 4

Bou-Ktoub = Bû Kutub 60-61 E 2
Boulder, CO 72-73 EF 3-4
Boulder, MT 76-77 GH 2
Boulder, WY 76-77 HJ 4
Boulder City, NV 72-73 CD 4
Boulder Creek, CA 76-77 B 7
Boulder Dam = Hoover Dam 72-73 D 4
Boulia 56-57 G 4
Boulogne-sur-Mer 34-35 H 3
Boumba 60-61 H 8
Bouna, Réserve de Faune de — Parc national de la Komoé 60-61 D 7
Boundary Mountains 74-75 H 2
Boundary Peak 72-73 C 4
Bounday, WA 76-77 E 1
Boundiali 60-61 C 7
Boundji 64-65 E 3
Boundou 60-61 B 6
Bountiful, UT 76-77 H 5
Bourail 56-57 MN 4
Bourbonnais 34-35 J 5
Bourem 60-61 DE 5
Bourg-en-Bresse 34-35 K 5
Bourges 34-35 J 5
Bourgogne 34-35 K 5-6
Bourgogne, Canal de — 34-35 K 5
Bouriates, District Nacional des — — 11 ◁ 42-43 T 7
Bouriates, République Autonome des — 42-43 T 7-V 6
Bouriates-Mongols, District National des — 42-43 V 7
Bourke 56-57 J 6
Bouse, AZ 76-77 FG 9
Boușrá ech Châm = Bușrat ash-Shâm 46-47 G 6
Boușrá ech Châm = Bușrat ash-Shâm 46-47 G 6
Boușrá ech Châm = Bușrat ash-Shâm 46-47 G 6
Bousso 60-61 H 6
Boutilimit = Bû Tilimît 60-61 B 5
Bouvard, Cape — 56-57 BC 6
Bouvetøya 24 D 1
Boven = Lake Superior 72-73 HJ 2
Bovill, ID 76-77 F 3
Bow Bridge 56-57 C 6-7
Bowdoin, ME — 76-77 K 1
Bowen [AUS] 56-57 J 3-4
Bowie, AZ 76-77 J 9
Bowling Green, KY 72-73 J 4
Bowling Green, VA 74-75 E 5-6
Bowling Green, Cape — 56-57 J 3
Bowman Island 24 C 11
Bowmanville 74-75 D 3
Bowral 58 JK 5
Bow Rover 70-71 O 7
Bo Xian 48-49 LM 5
Boyabat 46-47 F 2
Boyalık = Çiçekdağı 46-47 F 3
Boydton, VA 74-75 D 6
Boykins, VA 74-75 E 6
Boynton Beach, FL 74-75 cd 3
Boyuibe 78-79 G 9
Bozburun 46-47 C 4
Bozcaada [TR, ⊙] 46-47 AB 3
Boz Dağ [TR, ▲▲] 46-47 D 2-3
Boz Dağlar 46-47 C 3
Bozdoğan 46-47 C 4
Bozeman, MT 72-73 D 2
Bozen = Bolzano 36-37 D 2
Bozkır 46-47 E 4
Bozkurt 46-47 F 1-2
Bozok Yaylâsı 46-47 F 2-3
Bozoum 60-61 H 7
Bozova 46-47 H 4
Bozqūsh, Kūh-e — 46-47 M 4
Bozüyük 46-47 CD 3
Bożego Narodzenia, Wyspa — = Christmas Island 52-53 E 9
Bra 36-37 B 3
Brabant, Île — 24 C 30
Brač 36-37 G 4
Bracciano, Lago di — 36-37 DE 4
Bracebridge 74-75 D 2
Bräcke 30-31 F 6
Braço Menor de Aragua 78-79 JK 7
Brač 36-37 G 4
Brad 36-37 K 2
Brådano 36-37 G 5
Bradenton, FL 72-73 K 6
Bradford [GB] 32 F 5
Bradford [CDN] 74-75 D 2
Bradford, PA 74-75 D 4
Bradley, CA 76-77 C 8
Brady, MT 76-77 H 1-2
Braga 34-35 D 8
Bragança [BR, Pará] 78-79 K 5
Bragança 34-35 D 8
Bragança Paulista 78-79 K 9
Brahestad = Raahe 30-31 L 5

Brahmani 44-45 O 6
Brahmaputra 44-45 P 5
Brăila 36-37 M 3
Brainerd, MN 72-73 H 2
Bramaputra = Brahmaputra 44-45 P 5
Brampton 74-75 CD 3
Branchville, SC 74-75 C 8
Brandberg 64-65 D 7
Brandenburg [D, ≅] 33 FG 2
Brandenburg [D, ●] 33 F 2
Brandon [CDN] 70-71 Q 8
Brandon, FL 56-57 b 3
Brandon, VT 74-75 G 3
Brandon Mount 32 AB 5
Brandywine, MD 74-75 E 5
Branford, FL 74-75 b 1-2
Braniewo 33 JK 1
Bransfield Strait 24 C 30-31
Br'ansk 38-39 FG 5
Brantford 74-75 CD 3
Branxholme 58 EF 6
Brâsc = Birâk 60-61 G 3
Bras d'Or Lake 70-71 YZ 8
Brasil 78-79 F-L 6
Brasil, Macizo da – = Planalto Brasileiro 78-79 KL 8
Brasiléia 78-79 F 7
Brasilia 78-79 K 8
Brasília Legal 78-79 H 5
Brasilianisches Becken 22-23 H 6
Brasilianisches Bergland = Planalto Brasileiro 78-79 KL 8
Brasilien 78-79 F-L 6
Brașov 36-37 L 3
Brassó = Brașov 36-37 L 3
Bråsvellbreen 30-31 lm 5
Braszów = Brașov 36-37 L 3
Brašov = Brașov 36-37 L 3
Bratislava 33 H 4
Bratsk 42-43 T 6
Bratskoje vodochranilišče 42-43 T 6
Bratskoje vodochranilišče 42-43 T 6
Brattleboro, VT 74-75 G 3
Bratysława = Bratislava 33 H 4
Braunau 33 F 4
Braunsberg = Braniewo 33 JK 1
Braunschweig 33 E 2
Brawley, CA 72-73 C 5
Bray, CA 76-77 C 5
Bray Island 70-71 V 4
Brazil 78-79 F-L 6
Brazil Basin 22-23 H 6
Brazil-hegyvidék = Planalto Brasileiro 78-79 KL 8
Brazília 78-79 F-M 6
Braziliaans Bekken 22-23 H 6
Brazilian Plateau = Planalto Brasileiro 78-79 KL 8
Brazilie 78-79 F-L 6
Brazilië 78-79 F-L 6
Brazilská vysočina = Planalto Brasileiro 78-79 KL 8
Brazos River 72-73 G 5-6
Brazylia 78-79 F-L 6
Brazylijska, Wyżyna – = Planalto Brasileiro 78-79 KL 8
Brazzaville 64-65 DE 3
Brčko 36-37 H 3
Brčko 36-37 H 3
Brdy 33 FG 4
Brechin [CDN] 74-75 D 2
Brecknock, Peninsula – 80 B 8-9
Břeclav 33 H 4
Brecon 32 E 5-6
Breda 34-35 K 3
Bredasdorp 64-65 F 9
Bredbo 58 J 5
Bredy 42-43 KL 7
Bregalnica 36-37 K 5
Bregenz 33 DE 5
Bregovo 36-37 K 3
Breidhafjördhur 30-31 ab 2
Breidhavik 30-31 a 2
Brejinho do Nazaré 78-79 K 7
Brekstad 30-31 C 6
Bremangerlandet 30-31 A 7
Brême = Bremen 33 D 2
Bremen 33 D 2
Bremerhaven 33 D 2
Bremerton, WA 72-73 B 2
Brěmy = Bremen 33 D 2
Brenne 34-35 H 5
Brenner 33 E 5
Brennero = Brenner 33 E 5
Brennevinsfjord 30-31 k 4
Brèscia 36-37 D 3
Brésil 78-79 F-L 6
Breslau = Wrocław 33 H 3
Bressanone 36-37 DE 2
Bressay 32 F 1
Bresse 34-35 K 5
Bressuire 34-35 G 5
Brest [F] 34-35 E 4
Brest [SU] 38-39 D 5
Bretagne 34-35 F 4-G 5
Breton, Cape – 70-71 Z 8
Breton Sound 72-73 J 6
Breueh, Pulau – 52-53 B 5
Brevard, NC 74-75 B 7
Breves 78-79 J 5
Brevik 30-31 C 8
Brewarrina 56-57 J 5
Brewer, ME 74-75 J 2
Brewster, WA 76-77 CD 1
Brewster, Kap – 19 BC 20-21
Bria 60-61 J 7
Briançon 34-35 L 6
Brian Head 76-77 G 7
Briare 34-35 J 5
Bribbaree 58 HJ 5
Bribie Island 56-57 K 5
Briceland, CA 76-77 AB 5
Brickaville = Vohibinany 64-65 LM 6
Bridge, ID 76-77 G 4
Bridgeboro, GA 74-75 AB 9
Bridgeport, CA 76-77 D 6
Bridgeport, CT 72-73 M 3
Bridger Basin 76-77 HJ 5
Bridgeton, NC 74-75 E 7
Bridgeton, NJ 74-75 F 5
Bridgetown [AUS] 56-57 C 6
Bridgetown [BDS] 72-73 OP 9
Bridgton, ME 74-75 H 2
Bridgwater 32 E 6
Bridlington 32 FG 4
Bridport [AUS] 58 c 2
Brie 34-35 J 4
Brieg = Brzeg 33 H 3
Brig 33 CD 5
Brigham City, UT 72-73 D 3
Bright 58 H 6
Brighton 32 FG 6
Brighton [CDN] 74-75 DE 2
Brighton, NY 74-75 E 3
Brighton Indian Reservation 74-75 c 3
Brijuni 36-37 E 3
Brilon 33 D 3
Brindakit 42-43 a 5-6
Brindisi 36-37 GH 5
Brisbane 56-57 K 5
Brisbane River 56-57 K 5
Bristol 32 EF 6
Bristol, RI 74-75 H 4
Bristol, TN 74-75 B 6
Bristol, VA 72-73 K 4
Bristol Bay 70-71 DE 6
Bristol Channel 32 DE 6
Bristol Channel 32 DE 6
Bristol Channel 32 DE 6
Bristol Lake 76-77 EF 8
Britannia Range 24 AB 15-16
Brit Columbia = British Columbia 70-71 L 6-N 7
Britische Inseln 28-29 F 5-G 4
Britisch-Kolumbien = British Columbia 70-71 L 6-N 7
British Columbia 70-71 L 6-N 7
British Isles 28-29 F 5-G 4
British Mountains 70-71 HJ 4
Britse Eilanden 28-29 F 5-G 4
Britská Kolumbie = British Columbia 70-71 L 6-N 7
Britstown 64-65 F 9
Brive-la-Gaillarde 34-35 H 6
Brixen = Bressanone 36-37 DE 2
Brixham 32 E 6
Brno 33 H 4
Broach = Bharuch 44-45 L 6
Broadford 32 CD 3
Broad Law 32 E 4
Broad River 74-75 C 7
Broad Sound 56-57 JK 4
Brochet 70-71 Q 6
Brocken 33 E 3
Brock Island 70-71 N 2
Brockman, Mount – 56-57 C 4
Brockport, NY 74-75 DE 3
Brockton, MA 74-75 H 3
Brockville 70-71 V 9
Brockway, PA 74-75 D 4
Brodeur Peninsula 70-71 T 3
Brodnax, VA 74-75 DE 6
Brodnica 33 J 2
Brody 38-39 E 5
Brogan, OR 76-77 E 3
Broken Hill 56-57 H 6
Broken Hill = Kabwe 64-65 G 5
Brokopondo 78-79 HJ 3
Bromberg = Bydgoszcz 33 HJ 2
Brønderslev 30-31 CD 9
Brønnøysund 30-31 DE 5
Bronson, FL 74-75 b 2
Bronte 36-37 F 7
Bronte Park 56-57 J 8
Brookings, OR 76-77 A 4
Brookings, SD 72-73 G 3
Brookline, MA 74-75 H 3
Brookneal, VA 74-75 D 6
Brooks Range 70-71 E-H 4
Brooksville, FL 74-75 b 2
Brookton 56-57 C 6
Brookville, OH 74-75 A 5
Brookville, PA 74-75 D 4
Broome 56-57 D 3
Brotas de Macaúbas 78-79 L 7
Brothers, OR 76-77 C 4
Brothers, The – = Jazā'ir al-Ikhwān 62 F 4
Brothers, The – = Samḥah, Darsah 44-45 G 8
Brown, Mount – 24 BC 9
Brown, Point – 58 A 4
Browning, MT 76-77 G 1
Brownsville, OR 76-77 B 3
Brownsville, PA 74-75 CD 4-5
Brownsville, TX 72-73 G 6
Brownsweg 78-79 H 3-4
Brownville Junction, ME 74-75 J 2
Brownwood, TX 72-73 G 5
Broxton, GA 74-75 B 9
Bruay-en-Artois 34-35 J 3
Bruce, Mount – 56-57 C 4
Bruce Rock 56-57 C 6
Bruchsal 33 D 4
Bruck an der Leitha 33 H 4
Bruck an der Mur 33 G 5
Bruges = Brugge 34-35 J 3
Brugge 34-35 J 3
Bruin Peak 76-77 H 6
Bruja, Cerro – 72-73 b 2
Brukkaros, Mount – = Groot Brukkaros 64-65 E 8
Bruksel = Bruxelles 34-35 JK 3
Brumado 78-79 L 7
Bruneau, ID 76-77 F 4
Bruneau River 76-77 F 4
Brunei 52-53 F 6
Brunei = Bandar Seri Begawan 52-53 FG 5-6
Brunej 52-53 F 6
Brünn = Brno 33 J 4
Brunswick, GA 72-73 K 5
Brunswick, MD 74-75 E 5
Brunswick, ME 74-75 HJ 3
Brunswick, Peninsula – 80 B 8
Brunswick Bay 56-57 D 3
Brunswick Heads 58 LM 2
Bruny Island 56-57 J 8
Bruselas = Bruxelles 34-35 JK 3
Brusel = Bruxelles 34-35 JK 3
Brushy Mountains 74-75 C 6-7
Brusque 80 G 3
Brussel 34-35 JK 3
Brüssel = Bruxelles 34-35 JK 3
Brussel = Bruxelles 34-35 JK 3
Brussels = Bruxelles 34-35 JK 3
Brüx = Most 33 F 3
Bruxelles 34-35 JK 3
Brüsszel = Bruxelles 34-35 JK 3
Bryan, TX 72-73 G 5
Bryan, WY 76-77 J 5
Bryce Canyon National Park 76-77 GH 7
Brykalansk 38-39 KL 2
Bryson City, TN 74-75 B 7
Brzeg 33 H 3
Břeclav 33 H 4
Bșaiya, Al- = Al-Bușaiyah 44-45 EF 4
Bsharri = Basharrī 46-47 G 5
Btaymān, Bi'r – 46-47 H 4
Bua 63 C 6
Buake = Bouaké 60-61 CD 7
Buala 52-53 jk 6
Bū'Amarū 46-47 HJ 5
Bu'ayrāt al-Ḥsūn 60-61 H 2
Būbīyan, Jazīrat – 44-45 FG 5
Bubu 63 C 4
Bucaale 60-61 N 8
Bucak 46-47 D 4
Bucakkışla 46-47 E 4
Bucaramanga 78-79 E 3
Bucarest = București 36-37 LM 3
Buccaneer Archipelago 56-57 D 3
Buchan [AUS] 58 J 6
Buchanan [LB] 60-61 B 7
Buchanan, VA 74-75 CD 6
Buchans 70-71 Z 8
Buchara 44-45 JK 3
Buchardo 80 D 4
Bucharest = București 36-37 LM 3
Buchon, Point – 76-77 C 8
Buchtarma 42-43 Q 8
Buchtarminskoje vodochranilišče 42-43 PQ 8
Buchyn Mangnaj uul 48-49 EF 4-5
Buckeye, AZ 76-77 G 9
Buckhannon, WV 74-75 C 5
Buckhaven 32 E 3
Buckhorn Lake 74-75 D 2
Buckie 32 E 3
Buckland Tableland 56-57 J 4-5
Buckleboo 56-57 G 6
Buckle Island 24 C 16-17
Buckley, WA 76-77 BC 2
Buckley Bay 24 C 15-16
Bucksport, ME 74-75 J 2
Bucovina 36-37 LM 2
Buco Zau 64-65 D 3
București 36-37 LM 3
Budakskij liman 36-37 O 3
Budapest 33 J 5
Budapeszt = Budapest 33 HJ 5
Budapešť 33 J 5
Budaun 44-45 M 5
Budayr, Al- 46-47 L 7
Budd Land 24 C 12
Bude-Stratton 32 D 6
Budhardalur 30-31 c 2
Būdhīyah, Jabal – 62 E 3
Budjala 64-65 EF 2
Budva 36-37 H 4
Budweis = České Budějovice 33 G 4
Budyšin = Bautzen 33 G 3
Buea 60-61 F 8
Buena Esperanza, Cabo de – 64-65 E 9
Buenaventura [CO] 78-79 D 4
Buenaventura, Bahía de – 78-79 D 4
Buena Vista [MEX] 76-77 E 10
Buena Vista, VA 74-75 D 6
Buena Vista Lake Bed 76-77 D 8
Buenos Aires [PA] 72-73 b 2
Buenos Aires [RA, ●] 80 E 4
Buenos Aires [RA, ☆] 80 DE 5
Buenos Aires, Lago – 80 B 7
Buen Retiro 72-73 b 3
Buffalo, NY 72-73 L 3
Buffalo, WV 74-75 C 5
Buffalo Hump 76-77 F 3
Buffalo Lake 70-71 NO 5
Bug 33 L 2
Buga 78-79 D 4
Bugant 48-49 K 2
Bugária 36-37 K-M 4
Bugdajly 38-39 KL 8
Bugiri 63 C 2
Bugorkan 42-43 U 5
Bugrino 42-43 H 4
Bugt 48-49 N 2
Bugul'ma 42-43 J 7
Buguruslan 42-43 J 7
Buhăești 36-37 M 2
Buḥayrat al-Abyaḍ 60-61 KL 6
Buhemba 63 C 3
Buhl, ID 76-77 F 4
Buhoro 63 B 4
Buchtarminskoje vodochranilišče 42-43 PQ 8
Buin [PNG] 52-53 j 6
Bū'īn-e Zahrā' 46-47 O 5
Buir Nur 48-49 M 2
Buitenzorg = Bogor 52-53 E 8
Buj 42-43 G 6
Bujalance 34-35 EF 10
Bū Jaydūr, Rā's – 60-61 AB 3
Buji 52-53 M 8
Bujnaksk 38-39 J 7
Bujumbura 64-65 G 3
Bukačača 42-43 W 7
Bukačača 42-43 W 7
Buka Island 52-53 hj 6
Bukama 64-65 G 4
Būkān 46-47 LM 4
Bukarest = București 36-37 LM 3
Bukareszt = București 36-37 L 3
Bukavu 64-65 G 3
Bukene 64-65 H 3
Bukit Besi 52-53 D 6
Bukit Betong 52-53 D 6
Bukittinggi 52-53 CD 7
Bükk 33 K 4-5
Bukoba 64-65 H 3
Bukurešt = București 36-37 L 3
Bū Kutub 60-61 E 2
Bula [RI] 52-53 K 7
Bulagan = Bulgan 48-49 J 2
Bulan 52-53 H 4
Bulancak 46-47 GH 2
Bulanık 46-47 K 3
Būlāq 62 D 5
Bulawayo 64-65 G 7
Bulaydah 60-61 E 1
Buldan 46-47 C 3
Bulgan [MVR, ● Bulgan] 48-49 J 2
Bulgan [MVR, ● Chovd] 48-49 G 2
Bulgan [MVR, ☆ = 9 ◁] 48-49 J 2
Bulgaria 36-37 K-M 4
Bulgarie 36-37 K-M 4
Bulgarien 36-37 K-M 4
Bulgarije 36-37 K-M 4
Bulharsko 36-37 K-M 4
Buli, Teluk – 52-53 J 6
Bulkī 60-61 M 7
Bullaxaar 60-61 a 1
Buller, Mount – 58 H 6
Bullfinch 56-57 C 6
Bulloo Downs 56-57 H 5
Bulloo River 56-57 H 5
Bulls Bay 74-75 D 8
Bulu 52-53 J 6
Buluan 52-53 H 5
Bulucan = Emirhan 46-47 GH 3
Bulukumba 52-53 GH 8
Bulungan 52-53 G 6
Buluntou Hai = Ojorong nuur 48-49 F 2
Bulu Rantekombola 52-53 GH 7
Bułgaria 36-37 K-M 4
Bumba [ZRE, Bandundu] 64-65 E 4
Bumba [ZRE, Équateur] 64-65 F 2
Bumba = Boumba 60-61 H 8
Buna [EAK] 64-65 J 2
Buna [PNG] 52-53 N 8
Bunbah, Khalīj al- 60-61 J 2
Bunbury 56-57 BC 6
Bundaberg 56-57 K 4
Bundelkhand 44-45 MN 6
Bundi 44-45 M 5
Bundooma 56-57 FG 4
Bundoran 32 B 4
Bunge, zemľa – 42-43 b 2-3
Bungendore 58 JK 5
Bunger Oasis 24 C 11
Bungo-suidō 48-49 P 5
Bungotakada 50-51 H 6
Bunguran, Pulau – = Pulau Natuna Besar 52-53 E 6
Bunia 64-65 GH 2
Bunkeya 64-65 G 5
Bunnell, FL 74-75 c 2
Bunta 52-53 H 7
Buntok 52-53 FG 7
Bünyan 46-47 F 3
Bunyu, Pulau – 52-53 G 6
Bunzlau = Bolesławiec 33 GH 3
Buol 52-53 H 6
Buolkalach 42-43 W 3
Buôn Ma Thuôt = Ban Mê Thuôt 52-53 E 4
Buor-Chaja, guba – 42-43 Z 3
Buor-Chaja, mys – 42-43 Z 3
Buor-Chaja, guba – 42-43 Z 3
Buor-Chaja, mys – 42-43 Z 3
Buor-Chaja, guba – 42-43 Z 3
Buor-Chaja, mys – 42-43 Z 3
Buqaliq tagh 48-49 G 4
Buquq 48-49 E 3
Būr 60-61 L 7
Bura 64-65 JK 3
Bur Acaba = Buur Hakkaba 60-61 N 8
Buram 60-61 K 6
Burao = Bur'o 60-61 O 7
Bur'atskaja Avtonomnaja Sovetskaja Socialističeskaja Respublika = Burjatische Autonome Sozialistische Sowjetrepublik 42-43 T 7-V 6
Būr Atyan = Nawādhību 60-61 A 4
Buraydah 44-45 E 5
Buraymī, Al- 44-45 H 6
Burbank, CA 76-77 DE 8
Burchanbuudaj 48-49 H 2
Burcher 58 H 4
Burchun 48-49 F 2
Burco 60-61 b 2
Burdeau = Mahdīyah 60-61 E 1
Burdekin River 56-57 J 4
Burdur 44-45 BC 3
Burdur Gölü 46-47 CD 4
Burdwan 44-45 O 6
Burdwood, Banc de – 80 DE 8
Burdwood, Banco de – 80 DE 8
Burdwoodbank 80 DE 8
Burdwood Bank 80 DE 8
Burdwood-pad 80 DE 8
Burē [ETH, Gojam] 60-61 M 6
Burē [ETH, Īlubabor] 60-61 M 7
Bureå 30-31 J 5
Büreen = Büren 48-49 K 2
Bureinskij chrebet 42-43 Z 7-8
Bureja 42-43 Z 7
Büren [MVR] 48-49 K 2
Burenchaan [MVR, Chentij] 48-49 L 2
Burenchaan [MVR, Chövsgöl] 48-49 H 2
Bürencogt 48-49 L 2
Būr Fu'ād = Būr Sādāt 62 E 2
Burg 33 EF 2
Būr Gābo = Buur Gaabo 64-65 K 3
Bur Gao = Buur Gaabo 64-65 K 3
Burgas 36-37 M 4
Burgaski zaliv 36-37 MN 4
Burgaw, NC 74-75 DE 7
Burg el-'Arab = Burj al-'Arab 46-47 C 7
Burgenland 33 H 5
Burgersdorp 64-65 G 9
Burgfjället 30-31 F 5
Burghersdorp = Burgersdrop 64-65 G 9
Bùrgio 36-37 E 7
Burgos 34-35 F 7
Burgsvik 30-31 H 9
Burgund = Bourgogne 34-35 K 5-6
Burhaniye 46-47 B 3
Burhanpur 44-45 M 6
Buriacka Autonomiczna Republika 42-43 T 7-V 6
Burias Island 52-53 H 4
Buriatos, República Autónoma de los – 42-43 T 7-V 6
Buriatos de Aguinsk, Circunscripción Nacional de los – 42-43 V 7
Buriatos de Ust-Orda, Circunscripción Nacional de los – = 11 ◁ 42-43 T 7
Burica, Punta – 72-73 K 10
Burin Peninsula 70-71 Z 8
Burinšik 38-39 K 6
Burinšik 38-39 K 6
Buri Ram 52-53 D 3-4
Buriti [BR, Maranhão] 78-79 L 5
Buriti Bravo 78-79 L 6
Buriti dos Lopes 78-79 L 5
Burī Ye-Midir Selatē 60-61 M 5
Burj al-'Arab 62 C 2
Burj al-Haṭṭabah 60-61 F 2
Burját Autonóm Köztársaság 42-43 T 7-V 6
Burjatische Autonome Republik 42-43 T 7-V 6
Burjatská autonomní republika 42-43 T 7-V 6
Burj Ban Būl'īd = Qal'at Makmāhūn 60-61 E 3
Burjing = Burchun 48-49 F 2
Burj Luṭfī 60-61 F 3-4
Burj 'Umar Idrīs = Qal'at Flātarz 60-61 EF 3
Burketown 56-57 GH 3
Burkeville, VA 74-75 DE 6
Burkina 60-61 DE 6
Burley, ID 76-77 G 4
Burlingame, CA 76-77 B 7
Burlington 74-75 D 3
Burlington, IA 72-73 H 3
Burlington, NC 74-75 D 6
Burlington, VT 72-73 M 3
Burlington, WA 76-77 BC 1
Burma 52-53 BC 2
Burma = Myanmar 52-53 BC 2
Burma = Myanmar 52-53 BC 2
Burney, CA 76-77 C 5
Burnie 56-57 HJ 8
Burns, OR 76-77 D 4
Burns Lake 70-71 LM 7
Burnsville, WV 74-75 C 5
Burnt Creek 70-71 X 6-7
Burnt River 76-77 DE 3
Burnt River Mountains 76-77 DE 3
Burqah, Khahrat – 46-47 GH 6
Burqān 46-47 M 8
Burra 56-57 G 6
Burrendong Reservoir 58 J 4
Burren Junction 58 J 3
Burrinjuck Reservoir 56-57 J 7
Burro, Serranías del – 72-73 F 6
Burruyacú 80 CD 3
Bursa 44-45 B 2-3
Būr Sādāt 62 E 2
Būr Safāga = Safājah 60-61 L 3
Būr Sa'īd 60-61 L 2
Būr Sūdān 60-61 M 5
Būr Tawfīq 62 E 3
Buru, Pulau – 52-53 J 7
Burullus, Buḥayrat al- 62 D 2
Burūm 44-45 F 8
Burundi 64-65 GH 3
Burun-Šibertuj, gora – = gora Barun-Šabartuj 42-43 UV 8
Burun-Šibertuj, gora – = gora Barun-Šabartuj 42-43 UV 8
Bururi 64-65 G 3
Buryat Autonomous Region 42-43 T 7-V 6
Burye = Burē 60-61 M 6
Bury Saint Edmunds 32 G 5
Bușaīyah, Al- 44-45 EF 4
Bușayrah 46-47 J 5
Busayṭā', Al- 46-47 G 7-H 8
Būs Cagaan Nuur = Böön Cagaan nuur 48-49 HJ 2
Būsh 62 D 3
Bushehr 44-45 G 5
Bushire = Bushehr 44-45 G 5
Businga 64-65 F 2
Busira 64-65 E 2-3
Buskerud 30-31 C 7-D 8
Bușrat ash-Shām 46-47 G 6
Busselton 56-57 BC 6
Busto Arsizio 36-37 C 3
Busuanga Island 52-53 G 4
Busuluk = Buzuluk 42-43 J 7
Buta 64-65 F 2
Bután 44-45 OP 5
Butare 63 B 3
Butembo 63 B 2
Butere 63 C 2
Butha Qi 48-49 N 2
Butiaba 64-65 H 2
Bū Tilimīt 60-61 B 5
Butler, PA 74-75 D 4
Butmah 46-47 K 4
Buton, Pulau – 52-53 H 7-8
Butsha 63 B 2
Butsikáki 36-37 J 6
Butte Meadows, CA 76-77 BC 5
Butterworth 52-53 D 5
Butterworth = Gcuwa 64-65 G 9
Butte-Silver Bow, MT 72-73 D 2
Butuan 52-53 HJ 5
Buturlinovka 38-39 GH 5
Buulobarde 60-61 b 3
Buur Gabo 64-65 K 3
Buurhakaba 60-61 N 8
Buur Hakkaba 64-65 K 2
Buwārah, Jabal – 62 F 3
Büyükada, İstanbul- 46-47 C 2
Büyük Ağrı Dağı 44-45 E 2-3
Büyük Köhne 46-47 F 3
Büyük Mahya 46-47 B 2
Büyük Menderes Nehri 44-45 B 3
Buzači, poluostrov – 44-45 G 1-2
Buzači, poluostrov – 44-45 G 1-2
Buzău [R, ~] 36-37 M 3
Buzău [R, ●] 36-37 M 3
Buzaymah 60-61 J 4
Bužory 36-37 N 2
Buzuluk 42-43 J 7
Buzzards Bay 74-75 H 4
Bužory 36-37 N 2
Byam Martin Channel 70-71 PQ 2
Byam Martin Channel 70-71 PQ 2
Byam Martin Channel 70-71 PQ 2
Byam Martin Island 70-71 Q 2-3
Byāvar = Beawar 44-45 LM 5
Byawar = Beawar 44-45 LM 5

Byawa 163

Býblos = Jubayl 46-47 F 5
Bychawa 33 L 3
Bychov 38-39 EF 5
Bydgoszcz 33 HJ 2
Bydhošt' = Bydgoszcz 33 H 2
Bygdin 30-31 C 7
Bygland 30-31 BC 8
Byk 36-37 N 2
Bykovo 38-39 J 6
Bylot Island 70-71 V 3
Byrd 24 AB 25
Byrd, Cape – 24 C 29
Byrd Land 24 AB 23-22
Byrock 56-57 J 6
Byron, CA 76-77 C 7
Byron, Cape – 56-57 K 5
Byron Bay 58 LM 2
Byrranga, gory – 42-43 Q 3-V 2
Byske 30-31 J 5
Byssa 42-43 Z 7
Bytom 33 J 3
Bytów 33 H 1

Bzěmá = Buzaymah 60-61 J 4
Bzura 33 J 2

C

Caacupé 80 E 3
Caaguazú [PY, ●] 80 EF 3
Caaguazú, Cordillera de – 80 E 3
Cáala 64-65 DE 5
Caapucú 80 E 3
Caatinga 78-79 K 8
Caatingas 78-79 L 7-M 6
Caazapá [PY, ●] 80 E 3
Caballeria, Cabo de – 34-35 K 8
Caballococha 78-79 E 5
Cabanatuan 52-53 H 3
Cabedelo 78-79 N 6
Cabeza del Buey 34-35 E 9
Cabezas 78-79 G 8
Cabimas 78-79 E 2
Cabinda [Angola, ●] 64-65 D 4
Cabinda [Angola, ☆] 64-65 D 4
Cabinet Mountains 76-77 E 1-F 2
Cabo, Cuenca del – 22-23 K 7
Cabo, Ramal del – 22-23 K 8
Cabo Alto = Cape Dolphin 80 E 8
Cabo Blanco [CR] 72-73 J 10
Cabo Blanco [RA] 80 CD 7
Cabo Branco 78-79 N 6
Cabo Delgado [Moçambique, ∧] 64-65 K 5
Cabo Delgado [Moçambique, ☆] 64-65 JK 5
Cabo Falso [MEX] 72-73 D 7
Cabo Frio [BR, ∧] 78-79 L 9
Cabo Frio [BR, ●] 78-79 L 9
Caboolture 58 L 1
Cabo Pantoja = Pantoja 78-79 DE 5
Cabo Pasado 78-79 C 5
Cabora Bassa 64-65 H 6
Cabo Raso [RA, ●] 80 CD 6
Cabo Raso = Cabo Norte 78-79 K 4
Caborca Heroica 72-73 D 5
Cabo Rojo [MEX] 72-73 G 7
Cabot Strait 70-71 YZ 8
Cabo Verde, Cuenca de – 22-23 GH 4-5
Cabo Verde, Islas – 22-23 H 5
Cabo Verde, Umbral de – 22-23 H 4-5
Cabra 34-35 E 10
Cabra, Monte – 72-73 b 3
Cabrera, Isla – 34-35 J 9
Cabriel 34-35 G 9
Cabrillo, Point – 76-77 AB 6
Cabul = Kābul 44-45 K 4
Cabullona 76-77 J 10
Caçador 80 F 3
Čačak 36-37 J 4
Caçapava do Sul 80 F 4
Cáccia, Capo – 36-37 BC 5
Cacequi 80 F 3
Cáceres [BR] 78-79 H 8
Cáceres [CO] 78-79 D 3
Cáceres [E] 34-35 D 9
Cachar [TJ] 48-49 M 3
Cachegar = Qāshqār 48-49 CD 4
Cachemire = Kashmir 44-45 LM 4
Cache Peak 76-77 G 4
Cacheu 60-61 A 6
Cachi 80 C 3
Cachi, Nevado de – 80 C 2
Cachimbo, Serra do – 78-79 HJ 6
Cachimo 64-65 F 4
Cachoeira [BR ↓ Feira de Santana] 78-79 M 7
Cachoeira do Sul 80 F 3-4
Cachoeiro de Itapemirim 78-79 LM 9
Cachos, Punta – 80 B 3
Caçiporé, Cabo – 78-79 JK 4
Caçiporé, Rio – 78-79 J 4
Çacmak 46-47 F 4
Cacolo 64-65 E 4-5

Caconda 64-65 DE 5
Cactus Range 76-77 E 7
Caculê 64-65 L 7
Cacuso 64-65 E 4
Čačak 36-37 J 4
Cadale 60-61 b 3
Čadan 42-43 R 7
Cadcadde, Raas – 60-61 b 1
Cadena Costera = Coast Mountains, Coast Range 70-71 K 6-M 9
Cadibarrawirracanna, Lake – 58 AB 2
Cádiz 34-35 D 10
Cadiz, CA 76-77 F 8
Cádiz, Golfo de – 34-35 D 10
Čadobec [SU, ~] 42-43 S 6
Čadobec [SU, ●] 42-43 S 6
Čadyr-Lunga 36-37 N 2
Caen 34-35 G 4
Caernarfon 32 D 5
Caesarea 46-47 F 6
Caesarea = Kayseri 44-45 D 3
Caesarea Philippi = Bāniyās 46-47 FG 6
Caetité 78-79 L 7
Cafayate 80 C 3
Cafta = Kafta 60-61 M 6
Cagaan Cherem = Wanli Changcheng 48-49 K 4
Cagaan Cherem = Wanli Changcheng 48-49 K 4
Cagaan Cherem = Wanli Changcheng 48-49 K 4
Cagayan de Oro 52-53 HJ 5
Cagayan Islands 52-53 H 5
Cagayan Sulu Islands 52-53 GH 5
Čagda 42-43 Z 6
Caggan nuur 48-49 FG 2
Caguán, Rio – 78-79 E 4
Cagliari 36-37 C 6
Čágliari, golfo di – 36-37 C 6
Čagoda 42-43 EF 6
Čágrankaya = İkizdere 46-47 J 2
Cag Sum = Dzag 48-49 H 2
Cahama 64-65 DE 6
Cahirciveen 32 AB 6
Cahors 34-35 H 6
Cahuapanas 78-79 D 6
Cahuilla Indian Reservation 76-77 F 9
Cahungula = Caungula 64-65 E 4
Cáchy = Aachen 33 C 3
Caia [Moçambique] 64-65 J 6
Caiabis, Serra des – 78-79 H 7
Caiambé 78-79 FG 5
Cai Ban, Đao – 52-53 E 2
Caibarién 72-73 L 7
Caicara [YV] 78-79 F 3
Caicos Islands 72-73 M 7
Caicos Passage 72-73 M 7
Caimito 72-73 b 3
Caimito, Rio – 72-73 b 3
Cairari 78-79 K 5
Caird Land 24 B 33-34
Caire, le – = Al-Qâhirah 60-61 KL 2
Cairns 56-57 J 3
Cairo, IL 72-73 J 4
Cairo = Al-Qâhira 60-61 KL 2
Cairo, El – = Al-Qâhira 60-61 KL 2
Caiundo 64-65 E 6
Cajabamba 78-79 D 6
Cajamarca [PE, ●] 78-79 D 6
Cajapió 78-79 KL 5
Cajatambo 78-79 D 7
Cajdam nuur 48-49 M 2
Cajdamyn nuur, Ich – 48-49 GH 4
Cajdamyn nuur, Ich – 48-49 GH 4
Cajdamyn nuur, Ich – 48-49 GH 4
Čajek 44-45 L 2
Cajon Pass 76-77 E 8
Cajuás, Ponta dos – 78-79 M 5
Çakıralan 46-47 F 2
Çal = Demirciköy 46-47 C 3
Calabar 60-61 F 7-8
Calabogie 74-75 E 2
Calabozo 78-79 F 3
Calabre = Calàbria 36-37 FG 6
Calàbria 36-37 FG 6
Calada, CA 76-77 F 8
Calafat 36-37 K 3-4
Calafate 80 B 8
Calagua Islands 52-53 H 4
Calahari = Kalahari Desert 64-65 EF 7
Calahorra 34-35 G 7
Calais 34-35 H 3
Calais, Pas de – 34-35 HJ 3
Calalaste, Sierra de – 80 C 2-3
Calama [BR] 78-79 G 6
Calama [RCH] 80 C 2
Calamar [CO ↘ Bogotá] 78-79 E 4
Calamian Group 52-53 G 4
Calamian Islands 52-53 H 4
Calang 52-53 C 6
Calapan 52-53 H 4
Călăraşi 36-37 M 3
Calatayud 34-35 G 8
Calate = Qālāt 44-45 K 5
Călăţele 36-37 K 2
Calayan Island 52-53 H 3
Calbayog 52-53 HJ 4

Calca 78-79 E 7
Calcanhar, Ponta do – 78-79 N 6-N 5
Calçoene 78-79 J 4
Calcuta = Calcutta 44-45 O 6
Calcutta 44-45 O 6
Caldas da Rainha 34-35 C 9
Caldera 80 B 2
Çaldıran 46-47 K 3
Caldwell, ID 76-77 E 4
Caldwell, OH 74-75 C 5
Calecute = Calicut 44-45 LM 8
Caledon 64-65 DE 8
Caledon Bay 56-57 G 2
Caledonia [CDN, Ontario] 74-75 D 3
Caledonian Canal 32 D 3
Caledonrivier 64-65 G 8-9
Caleta de Vique 72-73 b 3
Caleta Olivia 80 C 7
Caleufú 80 D 5
Calexico, CA 76-77 F 9
Çalgan 46-47 H 4
Calgary 70-71 O 7
Calhoun, TN 74-75 A 7
Calhoun Falls, SC 74-75 B 7
Cali 78-79 D 4
Caliente, CA 76-77 D 8
Caliente, NV 72-73 CD 4
California [USA] 72-73 B 3-C 5
California, Golfo de – 72-73 D 5-E 7
California, Gulf of – 72-73 D 5-E 7
Californie = California 72-73 B 3-C 5
Californie, Golfe de – 72-73 D 5-E 7
Californië, Golf van – 72-73 D 5-E 7
Çáliman, Munţii – 36-37 L 2
Calimere, Point – 44-45 MN 8
Cálineşti 36-37 L 3
Calingasta 80 BC 4
Calipatria, CA 76-77 F 9
Calispell Peak 76-77 E 1
Calistoga, CA 76-77 B 6
Calkini 72-73 H 7
Callabonna, Lake – 56-57 G 5
Callahan, FL 74-75 c 1
Callahan, Mount – 76-77 E 6
Callao 78-79 D 7
Calmucos, República Autónoma de los – 38-39 HJ 6
Caloosahatchee River 74-75 c 3
Caltagirone 36-37 F 7
Caltanissetta 36-37 EF 7
Calulo 64-65 DE 4-5
Calva, AZ 76-77 HJ 9
Calvados, Côte du – 34-35 G 4
Calvi 36-37 C 4
Calvinia 64-65 DE 8
Calypso, Fosse de la – 28-29 N 8
Calypso, Sima del – 28-29 N 8
Calypsodiep 28-29 N 8
Calypsotiefe 28-29 N 8
Camabatela 64-65 E 4
Camacupa 64-65 E 5
Camagüey 72-73 L 7
Camagüey, Archipiélago de – 72-73 L 7
Çamalan 46-47 F 4
Camaná 78-79 E 8
Camapuã 78-79 J 8
Camapuã, Sertão de – 78-79 J 8-9
Camaquã 80 F 4
Camarat, Cap – 46-47 F 4
Camarillo, CA 76-77 D 8
Camariñas 34-35 C 7
Camariñas 34-35 C 7
Camarón [PA] 72-73 b 3
Camarones 80 CD 6
Camas, ID 76-77 G 3
Camas, WA 76-77 B 3
Camas Creek 76-77 GH 3
Camataquí = Villa Abecia 78-79 FG 9
Ca Mau 52-53 DE 5
Ca Mau, Mui – = Mui Bai Bung 52-53 D 5
Cambaia = Khambhat 44-45 L 6
Cambay = Khambhat 44-45 L 6
Cambay, Gulf of – 44-45 L 6
Cambing = Pulau Atauro 52-53 J 8
Cambodia 52-53 DE 4
Camborne 32 D 6
Camboya 52-53 DE 4
Cambrai 34-35 J 3
Cambria, CA 76-77 C 8
Cambrian Mountains 32 D 5-E 6
Cambridge [GB] 32 FG 5
Cambridge, ID 76-77 E 3
Cambridge, MA 74-75 NM 3
Cambridge, MD 74-75 D 5
Cambridge, OH 74-75 BC 4
Cambridge Bay 70-71 PQ 4

Cambridge City, OH 74-75 A 5
Cambridge Gulf 56-57 E 2-3
Camden 58 K 5
Camden, AR 72-73 H 5
Camden, ME 74-75 J 2
Camden, NJ 72-73 LM 4
Camden, SC 74-75 C 7
Cameia = Lumeje 64-65 F 5
Cameron, AZ 76-77 H 8
Cameron, WV 74-75 C 5
Cameron, Tanah Tinggi – 52-53 D 6
Cameroon 60-61 G 7-8
Camerota 36-37 F 5-6
Cameroun 60-61 G 7-8
Cameroun, Mont – 60-61 F 8
Cameroun Occidental 60-61 FG 7
Cameroun Oriental 60-61 G 7
Camerún 60-61 G 7-8
Cametá [BR ✓ Belém] 78-79 JK 5
Camiguin Island [RP, Babuyan Channel] 52-53 H 3
Camiguin Island [RP, Mindanao Sea] 52-53 H 4
Camiling 52-53 GH 3
Camino, CA 76-77 C 6
Caminreal 34-35 G 8
Camira = Camiri 78-79 G 9
Camiranga 78-79 K 5
Camiri 78-79 G 9
Camissombo 64-65 EF 4
Çamlıbel 46-47 G 3
Çamlıbel Dağları 46-47 G 3
Çamlıdere [TR, Ankara] 46-47 E 2
Çamlıdere [TR, Sanlı Urfa] 46-47 H 4
Cammin in Pommern = Kamień Pomorski 33 G 2
Camocim 78-79 L 5
Camooweal 56-57 G 3
Camorta Island 44-45 P 9
Campagna 36-37 F 5
Campana, Isla – 80 A 7
Campanario, Cerro – 80 BC 5
Campania 36-37 F 5
Campanie = Campania 36-37 F 5
Campanquiz, Cerros de – 78-79 D 5-6
Campbell, OH 74-75 C 4
Campbellford 74-75 E 2
Campbell Island 24 D 17
Campbell River 70-71 L 7
Campbellton 70-71 X 8
Campbell Town 56-57 J 8
Campeche 72-73 H 8
Campeche, Bahía de – 72-73 GH 7
Campeche, Banc – 72-73 HJ 7
Campechebank 72-73 HJ 7
Campeche Bank 72-73 HJ 7
Campeche-pad 72-73 HJ 7
Campeche, Banco de – 72-73 HJ 7
Campechská lavice 72-73 HJ 7
Camperdown [AUS] 58 F 7
Campidano 36-37 C 6
Campiña, La – 34-35 E 10
Campina Grande [BR, Amapá] 78-79 MN 6
Campinas 78-79 K 9
Campiña, La – 34-35 E 10
Campiña del Henares, La – 34-35 F 8
Campli 36-37 E 4
Camp Nelson, CA 76-77 D 7
Campo, CA 76-77 E 9
Campo [RFC, ~] 60-61 G 8
Campo [RFC, ●] 60-61 F 8
Campobasso 36-37 F 5
Campo Belo 78-79 KL 9
Campo de Diauarum 78-79 J 7
Campo Duran 80 D 2
Campo Grande [BR] 78-79 J 9
Campo Grande [RA] 80 EF 3
Campo Indian Reservation 76-77 E 9
Campo Maior 34-35 D 9
Campo Maior [BR] 78-79 L 5
Campos [BR, ≅] 78-79 L 7
Campos [BR, ●] 78-79 L 9
Campos, Tierra de – 34-35 E 7-8
Campos Altos [BR, Mato Grosso] 78-79 HJ 9

Canadian National Railways 70-71 PQ 7
Canadian Pacific Railway 70-71 OP 7
Canadian River 72-73 F 4
Çanakkale 44-45 B 2
Çanakkale Boğazı 44-45 B 2-3
Canala 56-57 N 4
Canal du Midi 34-35 HJ 7
Canal Número 11 80 E 5
Canal Viejo de Bahama 72-73 L 7
Canandaigua, NY 74-75 E 3
Cananea 72-73 DE 5
Cananor = Cannanore 44-45 LM 8
Cañar [EC, ●] 78-79 D 5
Canarias, Cuenca de las – 22-23 HJ 4
Canárias, Ilha das – 78-79 L 5
Canarias, Islas – 60-61 A 3
Canarias, Umbral de las – 22-23 HJ 4
Canaries, Bassin des – 22-23 HJ 4
Canaries, Seuil des – 22-23 HJ 4
Canarisch Bekken 22-23 HJ 4
Canarische Drempel 22-23 HJ 4
Canarreos, Archipiélago de los – 72-73 K 7
Canary Basin 22-23 HJ 4
Canary Rise 22-23 HJ 4
Canastota, NY 74-75 EF 3
Canastra, Serra da – [BR, Minas Gerais] 78-79 K 9
Canaveral, FL 74-75 c 2
Canaveral, Cape – 72-73 KL 6
Canavieiras 78-79 M 8
Canbelego 58 H 3
Canberra 56-57 J 7
Canby, CA 76-77 C 5
Canby, OR 76-77 B 3
Canchenjunga = Gangchhendsönga 44-45 O 5
Çandarlı Körfezi 46-47 B 3
Candi = Maha Nuwara 44-45 N 9
Cândido Mendes 78-79 KL 5
Çandili Tepe 46-47 G 3
Candon 52-53 GH 3
Canelos 78-79 D 5
Cañete [PE] 78-79 D 7
Cangallo [PE] 78-79 DE 7
Cangamba 64-65 E 5
Cangas 34-35 C 7
Cangas de Narcea 34-35 D 7
Cangombe 64-65 E 5
Canguaretama 78-79 MN 6
Cangxien = Cangzhou 48-49 M 4
Cangzhou 48-49 M 4
Caniapiscau, Rivière – 70-71 X 6
Canicatti 36-37 E 7
Canigou, Mont – 34-35 J 7
Canik Dağları 46-47 G 2
Canindé [BR, Ceará] 78-79 M 5
Canisteo, NY 74-75 E 3
Cannae 36-37 G 5
Cannanore 44-45 LM 8
Cannes 34-35 L 7
Canning Desert 56-57 D 3
Cann River 58 J 6
Cano = Kano 60-61 F 6
Canoas 80 F 3
Canobie 56-57 H 3
Canon City, CO 72-73 EF 4
Canopus 58 E 4
Caño Quebrado, Rio – [PA, Colón] 72-73 a 2
Caño Quebrado, Rio – [PA, Panamá] 72-73 b 2-3
Canora 70-71 Q 7
Canowindra 58 J 4
Canso 70-71 Y 8
Canso, Strait of – 70-71 YZ 8
Cansu = Gansu 48-49 G 3-J 4
Canta 78-79 D 7
Cantábrica, Cordillera – 34-35 D-F 7
Cantal 34-35 J 6
Cantal, Plomb du – 34-35 J 6
Cantaura 78-79 G 3
Canterbury 32 G 7
Canterbury Bight 56-57 O 8
Cân Tho' 52-53 E 4
Cantil, CA 76-77 DE 8
Cantilan 52-53 J 5
Canto do Buriti 78-79 L 6
Canton, GA 74-75 A 7
Canton, MA 74-75 H 3
Canton, NC 74-75 B 7
Canton, NY 74-75 F 2
Canton, OH 72-73 K 3
Canton, PA 74-75 E 4
Canton = Guangzhou 48-49 LM 7
Cantù 36-37 C 3
Canumã 78-79 H 5
Canumã, Rio – = Rio Sucunduri 78-79 H 6
Canuri = Kanouri 60-61 G 6
Čany, ozero – 42-43 O 7
Canyon, WY 76-77 H 3
Canyon City, OR 76-77 D 3

Canyon de Chelly National Monument 76-77 J 7-8
Canyon de Chelly National Monument 76-77 J 7-8
Canyon de Chelly National Monument 76-77 J 7-8
Canyon Ferry Dam 76-77 GH 2
Canyon Ferry Reservoir 76-77 H 2
Canyonville, OR 76-77 B 4
Cañada de Gómez 80 D 4
Cañar [EC, ●] 78-79 D 5
Caño Quebrado, Rio – [PA, Colón] 72-73 a 2
Caño Quebrado, Rio – [PA, Panamá] 72-73 b 2-3
Cao Băng 52-53 E 2
Caombo 64-65 E 4
Caoshi 50-51 E 1
Cap, Bassin du – 22-23 K 7
Cap, le – = Kaapstad 64-65 E 9
Cap, Seuil de – 22-23 K 8
Čapajev 42-43 J 7
Čapakçur = Bingöl 44-45 E 3
Capanema [BR, Mato Grosso] 78-79 H 7
Capanema [BR, Pará] 78-79 K 5
Capão Bonito 80 G 2
Caparaó, Serra do – 78-79 L 8-9
Cap Blanc = Ar-Râ's al-Abyaḍ 60-61 G 1
Cap Bon = Râ's Ādhār 60-61 G 1
Cap-de-la-Madeleine 70-71 W 8
Cape Barren Island 56-57 JK 8
Cape Basin 22-23 K 7
Cape Blanco 72-73 AB 3
Cape Breton Island 70-71 X-Z 8
Cape Charles, VA 74-75 EF 6
Cape Clear 32 B 6
Cape Coast 60-61 D 7
Cape Cod Bay 74-75 H 3-4
Cape Cod Peninsula 72-73 N 3
Cape Coral, FL 74-75 bc 3
Cape Charles, VA 74-75 EF 6
Cape Dorset 70-71 VW 5
Cape Fear River 72-73 L 4-5
Cape Girardeau, MO 72-73 HJ 4
Cape Charles, VA 74-75 EF 6
Cape Johnson, Fosa de – 52-53 J 4
Cape Johnson, Fosse – 52-53 J 4
Cape Johnson Depth 52-53 J 4
Cape Johnsondiep 52-53 J 4
Cape-Johnson-mélység 52-53 J 4
Cape-Johnson-Tiefe 52-53 J 4
Capella 56-57 J 4
Capelongo 64-65 E 5
Cape May, NJ 72-73 M 4
Cape May Court House, NJ 74-75 F 5
Cape Rise 22-23 K 8
Cape Town = Kaapstad 64-65 E 9
Cape Verde = Cap Vert 60-61 A 6
Cape Verde Basin 22-23 GH 4-5
Cape Verde Plateau 22-23 H 4-5
Cape Vincent, NY 74-75 EF 2
Cape York Peninsula 56-57 H 2
Cap-Haïtien 72-73 M 8
Capibara 78-79 F 4
Capim, Rio – 78-79 K 5
Capital Territory 56-57 J 7
Capitan Grande Indian Reservation 76-77 E 9
Capitol Peak 76-77 E 5
Capitol Reef National Monument 76-77 H 6
Capivara, Cachoeira – 78-79 J 6
Capiz = Roxas 52-53 H 4
Capodi, Chapada do – 78-79 M 6
Capodi, Chapada do – 78-79 M 6
Capodi, Chapada do – 78-79 M 6
Capoeiras, Cachoeira das – 78-79 H 6
Cápria 36-37 CD 4
Caprera 36-37 C 5
Capri 36-37 EF 5
Capricorn Channel 56-57 K 4
Capricorn Channel 56-57 K 4
Capricorn Channel 56-57 K 4
Caprivistrook 64-65 F 6
Captains Flat 58 JK 5
Captiva, FL 74-75 b 3
Cápua 36-37 EF 5
Capunda 64-65 E 5
Cap Vert 60-61 A 6
Cap Vert, Bassin du – 22-23 GH 4-5
Cap-Vert, Îles du – 22-23 H 5
Cap-Vert, Seuil du – 22-23 H 4-5
Cantin, Cap – = Râ's al-Baddūzah 60-61 BC 2
Caquetá, Rio – 78-79 E 5
Čara [SU, ●] 42-43 W 6
Carabaya, Cordillera de – 78-79 E 7
Caracal 36-37 KL 3
Caracarai 78-79 G 4
Caracaraí, Cachoeira – 78-79 G 4
Caracas 78-79 F 3
Carachi = Karāchi 44-45 K 6
Caracol [BR, Piauí] 78-79 L 6

Caracórum = Karakoram 44-45 L 3-M 4
Carahue 80 B 5
Carajás, Serra dos – 78-79 J 5-6
Caransebeş 36-37 K 3
Caratasca, Laguna de – 72-73 K 8
Caratinga 78-79 L 8
Caratunk, ME 74-75 HJ 2
Carauari 78-79 F 5
Caraúbas [BR, Ceara] 78-79 M 6
Caravaca de la Cruz 34-35 FG 9
Caravelas 78-79 M 8
Caraveli 78-79 E 8
Carazinho 80 F 3
Carballo 34-35 C 7
Carbonara, Capo – 36-37 CD 6
Carbondale, PA 74-75 F 4
Carbonear 70-71 a 8
Carbónia 36-37 C 6
Carcajou Mountains 70-71 L 4-5
Carcar 52-53 H 4-5
Carcassonne 34-35 J 7
Carcross 70-71 K 5
Çardak 46-47 C 4
Cardamum Island = Kadmat Island 44-45 L 8
Cárdenas [C] 72-73 K 7
Cárdenas [MEX] 72-73 G 7
Çardı = Harmancık 46-47 C 3
Cardiel, Lago – 80 B 7
Cardiff 32 E 6
Cardigan 32 D 5
Cardigan Bay 32 D 5
Cardona 34-35 H 8
Cardston 70-71 O 8
Čardžou 44-45 J 3
Carei 36-37 K 2
Careiro 78-79 H 5
Carelia 28-29 P 2-3
Carelia, República Autónoma de – 42-43 E 4-5
Carélie 28-29 P 2-3
Carélie, République Autonome de – 42-43 E 4-5
Carevokokšajsk = Joškar-Ola 42-43 H 6
Carevokokšajsk = Joškar-Ola 42-43 H 6
Carey, ID 76-77 G 4
Carey, Lake – 56-57 D 5
Careysburg 60-61 BC 7
Cargados 22-23 N 6
Cargados Carajos Islands 64-65 N 6
Carhaix-Plouguer 34-35 F 4
Cariaco 78-79 G 2
Caribana, Punta – 78-79 D 3
Caribbean Basin 72-73 MN 8
Caribbean Sea 72-73 K-N 8
Caribe, Cuenca del – 72-73 MN 8
Caribe, Mar del – 72-73 K-N 8
Caribisch Bekken 72-73 MN 8
Caribische Zee 72-73 K-N 8
Cariboo Mountains 70-71 M 7
Caribou, ME 74-75 JK 1
Caribou, Lac du – 70-71 Q 6
Caribou Mountains 70-71 NO 6
Caribou Range 76-77 H 4
Carinda 58 HJ 3
Caripito 78-79 G 2
Carleton Place 74-75 EF 2
Carlin, NV 76-77 EF 5
Carlisle 32 E 4
Carlisle, PA 74-75 E 4
Carlisle, SC 74-75 C 5
Carlos, Isla – 80 B 8
Carlos Chagas 78-79 LM 8
Carlos Chagas 78-79 LM 8
Carlos Chagas 78-79 LM 8
Carlota, La – [RA] 80 D 4
Carlow 32 C 5
Carlsbad, CA 76-77 E 9
Carlsbad, NM 72-73 F 5
Carlsberg, Dorsal de – 22-23 N 5-6
Carmacks 70-71 J 5
Carmagnola 36-37 BC 3
Carmánia = Kermán 44-45 H 4
Carmarthen 32 D 6
Carmarthen Bay 32 D 6
Carmaux 34-35 J 6
Carmel, CA 76-77 BC 7
Carmen, Isla – 72-73 DE 6
Carmen de Bolívar, El – 78-79 DE 3
Carmen de Patagones 80 D 6
Carmila 56-57 J 4
Carmona 34-35 E 10
Carmona = Uíge 64-65 E 4
Carnac 34-35 F 5
Carnamah 56-57 C 5
Carnarvon [AUS] 56-57 B 4
Carnarvon [ZA] 64-65 F 9
Carnatic 44-45 M 8-9
Carnegie, PA 74-75 C 4
Carnegie, Lake – 56-57 D 5
Carnic Alps 36-37 E 2
Car Nicobar Island 44-45 P 9
Carnot 60-61 H 8
Carnot Bay 56-57 D 3
Carnsore Point 32 CD 5
Carolina [BR] 78-79 K 6
Carolina [ZA] 64-65 H 8

Carolina, La – 34-35 F 9
Carolinas, Cuenca Occidental de las – 22-23 QR 5
Carolinas, Cuenca Oriental de las – 22-23 QR 5
Carolinas, Islas – = Caroline Islands 22-23 R 5
Caroline Islands 22-23 R 5
Carolinas Occidentales, Bassin du – 22-23 QR 5
Carol Spring, FL 74-75 c 3
Caroni, Rio – 78-79 G 3
Carora 78-79 EF 2
Carp 74-75 EF 2
Carp, NV 76-77 F 7
Carpates 36-37 L 2-3
Carpatians 36-37 L 2-3
Cárpatos 36-37 L 2-3
Carpentaria, Gulf of – 56-57 GH 2
Carpentariagolf = Gulf of Carpentaria 56-57 GH 2
Carpentaria-öböl = Gulf of Carpentaria 56-57 GH 2
Carpentaria, Golfe de – = Gulf of Carpentaria 56-57 GH 2
Carpentarský záliv = Gulf of Carpentaria 56-57 GH 2
Carpentras 34-35 K 6
Carpi 36-37 D 3
Carpina 78-79 M 6
Carpolac 56-57 H 7
Carrara 36-37 D 3
Carrathool 58 G 5
Carrbridge 32 E 3
Carreria 80 E 2
Carrick on Shannon 32 BC 5
Carrick-on-Suir 32 C 5
Carrieton 58 D 4
Carrión 34-35 E 7
Carrizal Bajo 80 B 3
Çarşamba 46-47 G 2
Çarşamba Suyu 46-47 DE 4
Caršanga 44-45 K 4
Čarsk 42-43 P 8
Carson City, NV 72-73 C 4
Carson Sink 76-77 D 6
Cartagena [CO, Bolívar] 78-79 D 2
Cartagena [E] 34-35 G 10
Cartago 60-61 G 1
Cartago [CO] 78-79 D 4
Cartago [CR] 72-73 K 10
Cartago, CA 76-77 DE 7
Carter, MT 76-77 H 2
Carter, WY 76-77 H 3
Carthage 60-61 G 1
Carthage, MO 72-73 H 4
Carthage, NC 74-75 D 5
Carthage, NY 74-75 F 2-3
Carthago 60-61 G 1
Cartier Island 56-57 D 2
Cartum = Al-Kharṭūm 60-61 L 5
Cartwright 70-71 Z 7
Caruaru 78-79 M 6
Carúpano 78-79 G 2
Carutapera 78-79 K 5
Carvoeiro, Cabo – 34-35 C 9
Cary, NC 74-75 D 7
Čaryn 42-43 OP 9
Čaryš 42-43 P 7
Çafihrad = İstanbul 44-45 BC 2
Çafihrad = İstanbul 44-45 BC 2
Casablanca = Ad-Dâr al-Bayḍâ' 60-61 BC 2
Casa Grande, AZ 76-77 H 9
Casal di Principe 36-37 EF 5
Casale Monferrato 36-37 C 3
Casalmaggiore 36-37 CD 3
Casanare, Rio – 78-79 E 3
Casa Nova [BR, Paraná] 80 F 2
Casas Grandes, Rio – 72-73 E 5-6
Cascadas, Las – 72-73 b 2
Cascade, ID 76-77 EF 3
Cascade, MT 76-77 GH 2
Cascade Head 76-77 A 3
Cascade Pass 76-77 C 1
Cascade Range 72-73 B 2-3
Cascade Reservoir 76-77 EF 3
Cascade Tunnel 76-77 C 2
Cascavel [BR, Paraná] 80 F 2
Casco Bay 74-75 HJ 3
Čašel'ka 42-43 P 4-5
Caserta 36-37 F 5
Casetas 34-35 G 8
Cashmere, WA 76-77 C 2
Casilda 80 D 4
Casino 56-57 K 5
Casiquiare, Rio – 78-79 F 4
Casita 76-77 H 10
Casitas, Cerro las – 72-73 E 7
Casma 78-79 D 6
Casmalia, CA 76-77 C 8
Caspe 34-35 GH 8
Casper, WY 72-73 E 3
Caspian Sea 42-43 G 2-3
Cass, WV 74-75 CD 5
Cassacatiza 63 C 6
Cassai = Kasai 64-65 E 3
Cassai, Rio – 64-65 EF 5
Cassamba 64-65 F 5
Cassiar Mountains 70-71 KL 6
Cassinga = Kassinga 64-65 E 6

Cassino 36-37 EF 5
Castaic, CA 76-77 D 8
Castanhal [BR, Pará] 78-79 K 5
Castanheiro 78-79 F 5
Castejón 34-35 FG 7
Castelfranco Veneto 36-37 DE 3
Castella, CA 76-77 B 5
Castellammare, Golfo di – 36-37 E 6
Castellammare del Golfo 36-37 E 6
Castellammare di Stàbia 36-37 EF 5
Castellana Grotte 36-37 G 5
Castelli = Juan José Castelli 80 DE 3
Castellón de la Plana 34-35 GH 9
Castelnaudary 34-35 HJ 7
Castelrosso = Mégistē 46-47 C 4
Castelsarrasin 34-35 H 7
Castelvetrano 36-37 E 7
Casterton 56-57 H 7
Castilla la Nueva 34-35 E 8-F 7
Castilla la Vieja 34-35 E 8-F 7
Castilletes 78-79 E 2
Castillo, Pampa del – 80 C 7
Castillo de San Marcos National Monument 74-75 c 1
Castle Dale, UT 76-77 H 6
Castle Dome Mountains 76-77 FG 9
Castle Gate, UT 76-77 H 6
Castle Hayne, NC 74-75 E 7
Castlemaine 56-57 HJ 7
Castle Peak [USA, Idaho] 76-77 F 3
Castlereagh Bay 56-57 FG 2
Castlereagh River 56-57 J 6
Castle Rock, WA 76-77 B 2
Castle Valley 76-77 H 6
Castres 34-35 J 7
Castries 72-73 O 9
Castro [BR] 80 F 2
Castro [RCH] 80 B 6
Castro-Urdiales 34-35 F 7
Castrovillari 36-37 G 6
Castroville, CA 76-77 C 7
Castrovirreyna 78-79 DE 7
Casuarinenkust 52-53 L 8
Çat 46-47 J 3
Çatak 46-47 K 3-4
Catalina 80 C 3
Catalogne = Cataluña 34-35 H 8-J 7
Cataluña 34-35 H 8-J 7
Cataluña 34-35 H 8-J 7
Çatalzeytin 46-47 F 1-2
Catamarca = San Fernado del Valle de Catamarca 80 C 3
Catandica 63 H 6
Catanduanes Island 52-53 HJ 4
Catanduva 78-79 K 9
Catània 36-37 F 7
Catanzaro 36-37 G 6
Çatar = Katar 44-45 G 5
Catarina, Gebel – = Jabal Katrīnah 60-61 L 3
Catarman 52-53 HJ 4
Catbalogan 52-53 HJ 4
Catena Costiera = Coast Mountains 70-71 K 6-M 7
Cathedral Peak [USA] 72-73 B 2-3
Cathkin Peak 64-65 GH 8
Cathlemet, WA 76-77 B 2
Catiaeum = Kütahya 44-45 BC 3
Catinzaco 80 C 3
Catió 60-61 AB 6
Cativá 72-73 b 2
Catlettsburg, KY 74-75 B 5
Catmandu = Katmāndū 44-45 NO 5
Catoche, Cabo – 72-73 J 7
Catrimani 78-79 G 4
Catrimani, Rio – 78-79 G 4
Catskill, NY 74-75 FG 3
Catskill Mountains 74-75 F 3
Cattaraugus, NY 74-75 D 3
Catumbela 64-65 D 5
Cauca, Rio – 78-79 E 3
Caucaia 78-79 M 5
Cáucaso 38-39 HJ 7
Caucasia 78-79 D 3
Caucasus Mountains 38-39 HJ 7
Cauldcleuch Head 32 E 4
Caungula 64-65 E 4
Caunpore = Kanpur 44-45 MN 5
Čaunskaja guba 42-43 gh 4
Caupolicán 78-79 F 7
Caura, Rio – 78-79 G 3
Cauquenes 80 B 5
Causses 34-35 J 6
Cauterets 34-35 G 8
Caux, Pays de – 34-35 H 4
Cavalcante 78-79 K 7
Cavally, River – 60-61 C 7-8
Cavan 32 C 4-5
Caviana, Ilha – 78-79 K 4
Cavite 52-53 H 4
Cavtat 36-37 GH 4

Çavuşçu Gölü 46-47 DE 3
Cawnpore = Kanpur 44-45 MN 5
Caxias [BR, Maranhão] 78-79 L 5
Caxias do Sul 80 F 3
Caxito 64-65 D 4
Caxiuana, Baia de – 78-79 J 5
Çay 46-47 D 3
Cayambe [EC, ▲] 78-79 D 5
Cayambe [EC, ●] 78-79 D 4
Cayar, Lac = Ar-R'kïz 60-61 AB 5
Çaybaşı = Çayeli 46-47 J 2
Cayes, Les – 72-73 M 8
Çaycuma 46-47 E 2
Çayeli 46-47 J 2
Cayenne [Französisch-Guyana, ●] 78-79 J 3-4
Çayıralan = Çayırşehri 46-47 F 3
Çayırbaşı 46-47 K 2
Çayırhan 46-47 DE 2
Çayırlı 46-47 HJ 3
Çayırlıahmetçiler = Yığılca 46-47 D 2
Çayırşehri 46-47 F 3
Çaykara 46-47 J 2
Caymán, Fosa de las – 72-73 KL 8
Cayman Brac 72-73 L 8
Caymangraben 72-73 KL 8
Caymans, Tranchée des – 72-73 KL 8
Cayman Trench 72-73 KL 8
Caymantrog 72-73 KL 8
Caynabo 60-61 b 2
Cayucos, CA 76-77 C 8
Cayuga Lake 74-75 E 3
Cayungo = Nana Candundo 64-65 F 5
Cazalla de la Sierra 34-35 E 10
Cazombo 64-65 F 5
Cchinvali 38-39 H 7
Cea 34-35 E 7
Ceahláu, Muntele – 36-37 LM 2
Ceará [BR, ☆] 78-79 LM 6
Ceará = Fortaleza 78-79 M 5
Čebarkul 38-39 M 5
Čeboksary 42-43 H 6
Cebrikovo 36-37 O 2
Cebú [RP, ⊙] 52-53 H 4
Cebú [RP, ●] 52-53 H 4
Çeceli 46-47 F 4
Cecen = Grozny 42-43 H 2
Cecerleg 48-49 J 2
Čechov [SU, Sachalin] 42-43 b 8
Cecil Plains 58 K 1
Čečina 36-37 D 4
Čečujsk 42-43 U 6
Cedar Breaks National Monument 76-77 G 7
Cedar City, UT 72-73 D 4
Cedar Creek [USA, Virginia] 74-75 D 5
Cedar Island [USA, North Carolina] 74-75 E 7
Cedar Island [USA, Virginia] 74-75 F 6
Cedar Key, FL 74-75 b 2
Cedar Lake [CDN] 70-71 Q 7
Cedar Mountains [USA, Nevada] 76-77 E 6
Cedar Mountains [USA, Oregon] 76-77 E 4
Cedar Rapids, IA 72-73 H 3
Cedarville, CA 76-77 C 5
Cederek 46-47 F 2
Cedro 78-79 M 6
Cedros, Isla – 72-73 C 6
Ceduna 56-57 F 6
Ceel 48-49 H 2
Ceel Buur 60-61 b 3
Ceel Xamure 60-61 bc 2
Cefalù 36-37 F 6
Cega 34-35 E 7
Čegdomyn 42-43 Z 7
Cegléd 33 J 5
Ceiba, La – [Honduras] 72-73 J 8
Ceiba, La – [YV] 78-79 E 3
Ceilán = Sri Lanka 44-45 N 9
Čekanovskogo, kr'až – 42-43 XY 3
Çekerek = Hacıköy 46-47 F 2
Çekerek Irmağı 46-47 F 3-G 2
Cela = Uaco Cungo 64-65 DE 5
Čel'abinsk 42-43 L 6
Celaya 72-73 F 7
Celebes = Sulawesi 52-53 G 7-H 6
Célebes, Mar de – 52-53 GH 6
Célèbes, Mer des – 52-53 GH 6
Celebes, Morze – 52-53 GH 6
Celebeské moře 52-53 GH 6
Celebeszee 52-53 GH 6
Celebesz = Sulawesi 52-53 G 7-H 6
Celebesz-tenger 52-53 GH 6
Celeken 44-45 G 3
Celikhan 46-47 H 3
Çeşme 46-47 B 3

Celinograd 42-43 MN 7
Celje 36-37 F 2
Čeljuskin, Cabo – = mys Čel'uskin 42-43 UV 2
Celle 33 E 2
Celovec = Klagenfurt 33 G 5
Çeltik 46-47 D 3
Çeltikçi = Aziziye 46-47 D 4
Celtyckie, Morze – 32 C 6
Celuo = Chira Bazar 48-49 DE 4
Čel'uskin, mys – 42-43 T-V 2
Çemişgezek 46-47 HJ 4
Çemlidere = Mecrihan 46-47 H 4
Cenad 36-37 J 2
Cenderawasih 52-53 K 7
Cenderawasih, Teluk – 52-53 KL 7
Centerfield, UT 76-77 H 6
Centinela, Picacho del – 72-73 F 6
Centraalafrikans Republiek 60-61 HJ 7
Centraalindisch Bekken 22-23 N 5-7
Centraalindische Drempel 22-23 N 5-7
Centraal Arctisch Bekken 19 A
Centraalpacifisch Bekken 22-23 BC 5
Central [EAK] 64-65 J 3
Central [MW] 63 C 6
Central [Z] 64-65 G 5
Central, NM 76-77 JK 9
Central African Republic 60-61 HJ 7
Central Australia Aboriginal Reserve 56-57 E 4-5
Central Falls, RI 74-75 H 4
Centralia, IL 72-73 J 4
Centralia, WA 76-77 B 2
Central Indian Ridge 22-23 N 5-7
Central Karroo = Groot Karoo 64-65 F 9
Central Mount Stuart 56-57 F 4
Central'nojakutskaja ravnina 42-43 WX 5
Central Pacific Basin 22-23 BC 5
Central Point, OR 76-77 B 4
Central Valley, CA 76-77 BC 5
Centreville, MD 74-75 EF 5
Čepca 38-39 K 4
Ceram = Seram 52-53 JK 7
Ceram Sea 52-53 JK 7
Cerbatana, Serrania de la – 78-79 F 3
Cerbère 34-35 J 7
Cercen = Chärchän 48-49 F 4
Cerdeña = Sardegna 36-37 C 5
Čerdyn 38-39 L 3
Čeremchovo 42-43 T 7
Čerepanovo 42-43 P 7
Čerepovec 42-43 F 6
Céres [BR] 78-79 JK 8
Ceres [ZA] 64-65 E 9
Ceres, CA 76-77 C 7
Céret 34-35 J 7
Čerevkovo 38-39 J 3
Cerf Island 64-65 M 4
Cerignola 36-37 F 5
Čerkassy 38-39 F 6
Čerkessk 38-39 H 7
Çerkeş 46-47 E 2
Čerlak 42-43 N 7
Čermik 46-47 H 3
Čern'achovsk 33 K 1
Černavodă 36-37 MN 3
Cernavoade 36-37 DE 4
Černigov 38-39 F 5
Černigovka 42-43 Z 9
Černogorsk 42-43 R 7
Černomorskoje 36-37 OP 3
Černoreče = Dzeržinsk 42-43 GH 6
Černovskije Kopi, Čita- 42-43 V 7
Černovskoje 38-39 J 4
Černovcy 38-39 DE 6
Černyševskij 42-43 V 5
Černyševskoje 33 KL 1
Cerralvo, Isla – 72-73 E 7
Cerrigeado 60-61 b 1
Cerritos 72-73 FG 7
Cerro, El – 78-79 G 8
Cerro Colorado [MEX] 76-77 F 10
Cerro de Pasco 78-79 D 7
Čerskij 42-43 f 4
Čerskogo, chrebet – 42-43 V 7
Certaldo 36-37 D 4
Čertež 38-39 L 4
Cervati, Monte – 36-37 F 5
Cervera 34-35 H 8
Cervéteri 36-37 E 4
Cérvia 36-37 DE 3
Cesareia = Caesarea 46-47 F 6
Cesena 36-37 DE 3
Cēsis 30-31 L 9
Česká Třebova 33 G 4
České Budějovice 33 G 4
České země 33 F-H 4
Českomoravská vrchovina 33 GH 4

Cessford 70-71 O 7
Cessnock-Bellbird 56-57 K 6
Cestos River 60-61 C 7
Cetinje 36-37 H 4
Çetinkaya 46-47 GH 3
Cetraro 36-37 F 6
Ceuta 60-61 CD 1
Cevennes 34-35 JK 6
Cevizlik = Maçka 46-47 H 2
Ceyhan 46-47 FG 4
Ceyhan Nehri 46-47 G 4
Ceylan = Sri Lanka 44-45 N 9
Ceylanpinar 46-47 HJ 4
Ceylon = Sri Lanka 44-45 N 9
Ceylon = Sri Lanka 44-45 N 9

Chaaltyn gol 48-49 GH 4
Cha-am [T] 52-53 CD 4
Chaba 48-49 F 2
Chabarovo 42-43 L 4
Chabarovsk 42-43 a 8
Chablis 34-35 J 5
Chachapoyas 78-79 D 6
Châchâran 72-73 K 4
Chachoengsao 52-53 D 4
Chachmas 38-39 J 7
Chaco 80 D 3
Chaco Austral 80 DE 3
Chaco Boreal 80 DE 2
Chaco Central 80 D 2-E 3
Chaco River 76-77 J 7
Chadasan 48-49 J 2
Chadchal = Chatgal 48-49 HJ 1
Chadum 64-65 F 6
Chadzaar 48-49 G 4
Chaeryŏng 50-51 EF 3
Chagang-do 50-51 EF 2
Chagan nuur 48-49 L 3
Chaghcharân 44-45 K 4
Chagny 34-35 K 5
Chagos 22-23 N 6
Chagres [PA, ~] 72-73 ab 2
Chagres [PA, ●] 72-73 b 2
Chagres, Brazo del – 72-73 b 2
Chagres, Río – 72-73 bc 2
Chagres Arm = Brazo del Chagres 72-73 b 2
Chahâr Burjak 44-45 J 4
Chahâr Burjak = Chahâr Burjak 44-45 J 4
Chahâr Maḥâl-e Bakhteyârī = 3 ◁ 44-45 G 4
Chahbâ = Shahbâ' 46-47 G 6
Châh Bahâr = Bandar-e Châh Bahâr 44-45 HJ 5
Ch'aho 50-51 G 2
Chaidamu Pendi = Tsaidam 48-49 GH 4
Ch'ail-bong 50-51 F 2
Chai Nat 52-53 D 3
Chaîne Pontique 44-45 C-E 2
Chaîne Rocheuse = Rocky Mountains 70-71 L 5-P 9
Chaiya 52-53 C 5
Chajari 80 E 4
Chajdag gol 48-49 EF 3
Chajlar 48-49 M 2
Chajlar = Hailar 48-49 M 2
Chajlar gol = Hailar He 48-49 MN 2
Chajpudyrskaja guba 38-39 LM 2
Chajrchan 48-49 e 6
Chajr'uzovo 42-43 e 6
Chaka Nor = Chöch nuur 48-49 H 4
Chakasische Autonome Oblast 42-43 R 7
Chakaski Obwód Autonomiczny = 9 ◁ 42-43 R 7
Chake Chake 63 DE 4
Chäl = Shâl 46-47 N 5
Chala 78-79 E 8
Chalabesa 63 B 5
Cha-lan-tun = Yalu 48-49 N 2
Chalbi Desert 63 D 2
Chalchyn gol 48-49 M 2
Chaleur Bay 70-71 XY 8
Chalhuanca 78-79 E 7
Cha-ling Hu = Kyaring Tsho 48-49 H 5
Chálkē 36-37 M 7
Chalkidikē 36-37 K 3
Chalkis 36-37 K 4
Challapata 78-79 F 8
Challis, ID 76-77 F 3
Chal'mer-Ju 42-43 L 4
Chalmer-Sede = Tazovskij 42-43 OP 4
Châlons-sur-Marne 34-35 JK 4
Chalon-sur-Saône 34-35 K 5
Chalosse 34-35 G 7
Chalturin 42-43 H 6
Cham 33 F 4
Chama 44-45 K 4
Chamba [EAT] 63 D 5
Chamba [IND] 44-45 M 4
Chambal [IND ◁ Kali Sindh] 44-45 M 5-6
Chambal [IND ◁ Yamuna] 44-45 M 5-6
Chamberlain Lake 74-75 J 1
Chambersburg, PA 74-75 DE 4-5
Chambéry 34-35 K 6
Chambeshi 64-65 H 5
Chamchamâl 46-47 L 5

Chiporiro 64-65 H 6
Chiputneticook Lakes 74-75 JK 2
Chiquimula 72-73 HJ 9
Chiquitos, Llanos de – 78-79 G 8
Chira 63 D 2
Chira Bazar 48-49 DE 4
Chiraz = Shīrāz 44-45 G 5
Chiredzi 64-65 H 7
Chirfa 60-61 G 4
Chiricahua National Monument 76-77 J 9-10
Chiricahua Peak 76-77 J 10
Chirikof Island 70-71 EF 6
Chiriquí, Golfo de – 72-73 K 10
Chiriquí, Laguna de – 72-73 K 9-10
Chiri-san 50-51 F 5
Chiromo 64-65 J 6
Chirripó Grande, Cerro – 72-73 K 10
Chirundu 64-65 G 6
Chisamba 64-65 G 5-6
Chisel Lake 70-71 QR 7
Chi-shih Shan = Amnyemachhen Gangri 48-49 HJ 5
Chishtian Mandi = Chishtiyân Maṇḍī 44-45 L 5
Chishtiyân Maṇḍī 44-45 L 5
Chisimaio = Kismaayo 64-65 K 3
Chişinău 38-39 E 6
Chitado 64-65 D 6
Chita-hantō 50-51 L 5
Ch'i-t'ai = Qitai 48-49 FG 3
Chitambo 63 B 6
Chitembo 64-65 E 5
Chitogarh = Chittaurgarh 44-45 L 6
Chitose 50-51 b 2
Chitradurga 44-45 M 8
Chitrâl 44-45 L 3
Chitré 72-73 K 10
Chittagong = Châṭṭagâm 44-45 P 6
Chittaldurga = Chitradurga 44-45 M 8
Chittaorgarh = Chittaurgarh 44-45 L 6
Chittaurgarh 44-45 L 6
Chittoor 44-45 M 8
Chittoor = Chittor 44-45 M 8
Chiuchuan = Jiuquan 48-49 H 4
Chiulezi, Rio – 63 D 5-6
Chiumbe, Rio – 64-65 F 4
Chiume 64-65 F 5-6
Ch'iung-chou Hai-hsia = Qiongzhou Haixia 48-49 KL 7
Chiungshan = Qiongshan 48-49 L 8
Ch'iung-tung = Qionghai 48-49 L 8
Chiuta, Lagoa – 64-65 J 5
Chiva [SU] 42-43 L 9
Chivasso 36-37 B 3
Chivay 78-79 E 8
Chivilcoy 80 DE 4
Chivu 64-65 H 6
Chiwanda 64-65 HJ 5
Chiwefwe 63 B 6
Chiweta 64-65 H 5
Chixoy, Río – 72-73 H 8
Chjargas 48-49 G 2
Chjargas nuur 48-49 GH 2
Chloride, AZ 76-77 F 8
Chmeiţiyé = Shmayṭīyah 46-47 H 5
Chmelnickij 38-39 E 6
Chobe 64-65 F 6
Chobe National Park 64-65 FG 6
Chocaya 78-79 F 9
Chocca 78-79 D 7
Chochiang = Charqiliq 48-49 F 4
Choch'iwŏn 50-51 F 4
Chöch nuur 48-49 H 4
Chöch Šili 48-49 G 4
Chöch Šili uul 48-49 FG 4
Chociebuż = Cottbus 33 G 3
Chocolate Mountains 76-77 F 9
Chocontá 78-79 E 3
Ch'o-do [Nordkorea] 50-51 E 3-4
Ch'o-do [ROK] 50-51 F 5
Chodžambas 44-45 JK 3
Chodžejli 42-43 K 9
Chodžent = Leninabad 44-45 KL 2-3
Chodzież 33 H 2
Choele-Choel 80 CD 5
Choibalsan = Čojbalsan 48-49 L 2
Choiseul 52-53 j 6
Chojna 33 G 2
Chojnice 33 HJ 2
Chōkai-zan 50-51 MN 3
Chōḷamaṇḍala = Coromandel Coast 44-45 N 7-8
Cholame, CA 76-77 CD 8
Chold = Chuld 48-49 K 2-3
Cholet 34-35 G 5
Cholgwan 50-51 E 3
Chŏlla-namdo 50-51 F 5
Chŏlla-pukto 50-51 F 5
Cholm 38-39 F 4
Cholmogory 42-43 G 5
Cholmsk 42-43 b 8
Cholodnoje 38-39 N 3
Cholos nuur 48-49 H 4
Ch'ŏlsan 50-51 E 3
Choluteca 72-73 J 9
Choma 64-65 G 6
Chomba 63 D 5
Ch'ŏnan 50-51 F 4
Chon Buri 52-53 D 4
Chŏnch'ŏn 50-51 F 2
Chone 78-79 CD 5
Ch'ŏng'chŏn-gang 50-51 EF 2-3
Chongdjin = Ch'ŏngjin 48-49 OP 3
Chŏnggŏ-dong 50-51 E 3
Ch'ŏngha 50-51 G 4
Ch'ŏngjin 48-49 OP 3
Chongjin = Ch'ŏngjin 48-49 OP 3
Chŏngju 48-49 O 4
Chongming 48-49 N 5
Chongor 48-49 L 2
Chongor = Bajan Adraga 48-49 KL 2
Chongor Oboo Sum = Bajandalaj 48-49 J 3
Chongor Tagh = Qungur tagh 48-49 D 4
Ch'ŏngp'yŏngch'ŏn 50-51 FG 4
Chongqing 48-49 K 6
Ch'ŏngsan-do 50-51 F 5
Chongshan = Chongzuo 48-49 K 7
Ch'ongsŏktu-ri 50-51 EF 3
Chongsŏng 50-51 GH 1
Chŏngŭp 50-51 F 5
Ch'ŏngyang [ROK] 50-51 F 4
Chongzuo 48-49 K 7
Chŏnju 48-49 O 4
Chonos, Archipiélago de los – 80 AB 6-7
Chonuu 42-43 b 4
Chooloj Gov' 48-49 H 3
Chop'or 38-39 H 5-6
Chor 42-43 Za 8
Chorasan = Khorāsān 44-45 H 3-4
Chŏra Sfakíon 36-37 L 8
Chordogoj 42-43 W 5
Chor He 48-49 N 2
Chorinsk 42-43 U 7
Chorog 44-45 L 3
Chorrera, La – [PA] 72-73 b 3
Chorsabad = Khorsabad 46-47 K 4
Chorwacja 36-37 F-H 3
Chŏrwŏn 50-51 F 3
Chŏryŏng-do = Yŏng-do 50-51 G 5
Chorzele 33 K 2
Chorzów 33 J 3
Chosedachard 38-39 L 2
Chŏsen-kaikyō 48-49 O 5
Chōshi 50-51 N 5
Chos-Malal 80 BC 5
Chosŏn-man = Tonghan-man 48-49 O 4
Choszczno 33 GH 2
Chota 78-79 D 6
Chota Nāgpur 44-45 NO 6
Choteau, MT 76-77 G 2
Chotin 38-39 E 6
Chou Shan = Zhoushan Dao 48-49 N 5-6
Chou-shan Ch'ün-tao = Zhoushan Qundao 48-49 N 5
Chovd [MVR, ●] 48-49 G 2
Chovd [MVR, ☆ = 3 ◁] 48-49 G 2
Chovd gol 48-49 G 2
Chövsgöl [MVR, ●] 48-49 KL 3
Chövsgöl [MVR, ☆ = 6 ◁] 48-49 J 1
Chövsgöl nuur 48-49 J 1
Chowan River 74-75 E 6
Chowchilla, CA 76-77 C 7
Christchurch [NZ] 56-57 OP 8
Christian Island 74-75 C 2
Christiansburg, VA 74-75 CD 6
Christianshåb = Qasigiánguir 70-71 ab 4
Christie Bay 70-71 O 5
Christmas Creek 56-57 E 3
Christmas Island [AUS] 52-53 E 9
Chromtau 42-43 K 7
Chrudim 33 GH 4
Chrysê 36-37 LM 8
Chrysochûs, Kólpos – 46-47 E 5
Chuang-ho = Zhuanghe 50-51 D 3
Chubb Crater = New Quebec Crater 70-71 VW 5
Chubbuck, CA 76-77 F 8
Chubisgalt = Chövsgöl 48-49 KL 3
Chubsugul = Chövsgöl nuur 48-49 J 1
Chūbu 50-51 LM 4-5
Chubut 80 BC 6
Chubut, Río – 80 C 6
Chucheng = Zhucheng 48-49 MN 4
Chu-chi = Zhuji 48-49 N 6
Ch'ü-ching = Qujing 48-49 J 6
Ch'ü-chou = Qu Xian 48-49 M 6
Chu-chou = Zhuzhou 48-49 L 6
Chuchow = Zhuzhou 48-49 L 6
Ch'üeh-shan = Queshan 48-49 L 5
Chugach Mountains 70-71 GH 5
Chugoku 50-51 HJ 5
Chūgoku-sammyaku 50-51 JK 5
Chuguchak 48-49 E 2
Chūgūchak = Tarbagataj 48-49 EF 2
Chuhsien = Qu Xian 48-49 M 6
Ch'u-hsiung = Chuxiong 48-49 J 7
Chü-hua Tao = Juhua Dao 50-51 C 2
Ch'uja-do 50-51 F 6
Chukchi Plateau 19 B 35
Chukchi Sea 19 BC 35-36
Chuki = Zhuji 48-49 N 6
Chukot Autonomous Area 42-43 g-j 4
Chukudu Kraal 64-65 F 7
Chūl, Gardaneh-ye – 46-47 MN 6
Chulaq Aqqan Su 48-49 G 4
Chula Vista, CA 72-73 C 5
Chuld 48-49 K 2-3
Chulga 38-39 M 3
Chū-liu-ho = Juliuhe 50-51 D 1
Chulp'o 50-51 F 5
Chulucanas 78-79 CD 6
Chulumani 78-79 F 8
Chumbicha 80 C 3
Chum Phae 52-53 D 3
Chumphon 52-53 CD 4
Chumsaeng 52-53 D 3
Chumunjin 50-51 G 4
Ch'unch'ŏn 48-49 O 4
Chungam-ni 50-51 G 5
Ch'ungch'ŏng-namdo 50-51 F 4
Ch'ungch'ŏng-pukto 50-51 FG 4
Chüngges 48-49 E 3
Chunghwa 50-51 EF 3
Ch'ungju 50-51 FG 4
Chungking = Chongqing 48-49 K 6
Ch'ung-ming = Chongming 48-49 N 5
Ch'ungmu 50-51 G 5
Chūngsan 50-51 E 3
Chungshan = Zhongshan 48-49 L 7
Chung-tien = Zhongdian 48-49 HJ 6
Chüngüj gol 48-49 GH 2
Chung-wei = Zhongwei 48-49 JK 4
Chunya 64-65 H 4
Chuquibamba 78-79 E 8
Chuquicamata 80 C 2
Chuquisaca = Sucre 78-79 FG 8
Chur 33 D 5
Churchill [CDN] 70-71 RS 6
Churchill, ID 76-77 FG 4
Churchill, Cape – 70-71 S 6
Churchill Falls 70-71 XY 7
Churchill Peak 70-71 LM 6
Churchill River [CDN, Manitoba] 70-71 RS 6
Churchill River [CDN ◁ Hamilton Inlet] 70-71 Y 7
Churu 44-45 LM 5
Chusei-hokudō = Ch'ungch'ŏng-pukto 50-51 FG 4
Chusei-nandō = Ch'ungch'ŏng-namdo 50-51 F 4
Chu-shan = Zhushan 48-49 KL 5
Chusistan = Khūzestān 44-45 F 4
Chuska Mountains 76-77 J 7-8
Chust 38-39 D 6
Chutag 48-49 J 2
Chuučnar 48-49 G 5
Chuŭronjang 50-51 GH 2
Chuvash Autonomous Republic = 4 ◁ 42-43 H 6
Chuwārtah 46-47 L 5
Chuxiong 48-49 J 7
Chuxiong Yizu Zizhizhou 48-49 J 6
Chuy 80 F 4
Chu Yang Sin 52-53 E 4
Chužand 44-45 K 2-L 3
Chužir 42-43 U 7
Chvalynsk 38-39 J 5
Chwārta = Chuwārtah 46-47 L 5
Chypre 44-45 C 3
Čibit 42-43 Q 7
Cibola, AZ 76-77 F 9
Cibuta 76-77 H 10
Çiçekbaba Tepesi 46-47 C 4
Çiçekdağı 46-47 F 3
Cicero Dantas 78-79 M 7
Cicladas 36-37 L 7
Cide 46-47 E 2
Ciechanów 33 K 2
Ciego de Ávila 72-73 L 7
Ciénaga 78-79 DE 2
Cienfuegos 72-73 K 7
Cieza 34-35 G 9
Çifteler 46-47 D 3
Çiftlik = Camlibel 46-47 G 2
Çiftlik = Kelkit 46-47 H 2
Cifuentes 34-35 F 8
Čiganak 42-43 N 8-9
Çığlı 46-47 K 4
Cihanbeyli 46-47 E 3
Cihanbeyli Yaylâsı 46-47 E 3
Čiili 42-43 M 9
Cijara, Embalse de – 34-35 E 9
Cilacap 52-53 E 8
Çıldır 46-47 K 2
Çıldır Gölü 46-47 K 2
Cilli = Celje 36-37 F 2
Cilo dağı 46-47 KL 4
Cima, CA 76-77 F 8
Cimaltepec 72-73 G 8
Čimbaj 42-43 KL 9
Čimkent 42-43 M 9
Ciml'ansk 38-39 H 6
Ciml'anskoje vodochranilišče 38-39 H 6
Ciml'anskoje vodochranilišče 38-39 H 6
Cimmarron River 72-73 F 4
Cimone, Monte – 36-37 D 3
Cîmpina 36-37 LM 3
Cîmpulung 36-37 L 3
Cîmpulung Moldovenesc 36-37 LM 2
Çınar 46-47 J 4
Cinca 34-35 H 8
Cincinnati, OH 72-73 K 4
Çine 46-47 BC 4
Cingaly 42-43 MN 5
Cinnabar Mountain 76-77 E 4
Cinta, Serra da – 78-79 K 6
Cinto, Mont – 36-37 C 4
Cintra = Sintra [BR] 78-79 G 6
Ciotat, la – 34-35 K 7
Čiovo 36-37 G 4
Cipikan 42-43 V 7
Cipó 78-79 M 7
Ciprus 44-45 C 3
Circeo, Monte – 36-37 E 5
Čirčik 42-43 M 9
Circle, AK 70-71 H 4
Circle Cliffs 76-77 H 7
Circleville, UT 76-77 G 6
Cirebon 52-53 E 8
Cirenaica = Barqah 60-61 J 2
Cirene = Shaḥḥāt 60-61 J 2
Ciri, Rio – 72-73 a 3
Cirò Marina 36-37 G 6
Čirpan 36-37 L 4
Cisa, Passo della – 36-37 CD 3
Cisco, UT 76-77 J 6
Cisne, Ilhas del – = Swan Islands 72-73 K 8
Cisneros 78-79 DE 3
Cisterna di Latina 36-37 E 5
Cisternino 36-37 G 5
Čistopol' 42-43 HJ 6
Čita 42-43 V 7
Citlaltépetl 72-73 G 8
Citra, FL 74-75 bc 2
Citrusdal 64-65 EF 9
Citrus Heights, CA 72-73 B 4
Cittanova 36-37 FG 6
Ciucaş 36-37 LM 3
Ciudad Bolívar 78-79 G 3
Ciudad Bolivia 78-79 E 3
Ciudad Camargo = Camargo 72-73 E 6
Ciudad del Carmen 72-73 H 8
Ciudad Delicias = Delicias 72-73 E 6
Ciudadela 34-35 J 8-9
Ciudad Guayana 78-79 G 3
Ciudad Guzmán 72-73 F 8
Ciudad Juárez = Juárez 72-73 E 5
Ciudad Lerdo 72-73 EF 6
Ciudad Linares = Linares 72-73 G 7
Ciudad Madero 72-73 G 7
Ciudad Mante 72-73 G 7
Ciudad Obregón 72-73 DE 6
Ciudad Ojeda 78-79 E 2-3
Ciudad Piar 78-79 G 3
Ciudad Real 34-35 EF 9
Ciudad-Rodrigo 34-35 DE 8
Ciudad Trujillo = Santo Domingo 72-73 MN 8
Ciudad Valles 72-73 G 7
Ciudad Victoria 72-73 G 7
Civa Burnu 46-47 G 2
Civita Castellana 36-37 E 4
Civitanova Marche 36-37 EF 4
Civitavècchia 36-37 D 4
Çivril 46-47 C 3
Čiža 42-43 G 4
Cizre 44-45 E 3
Čkalov = Orenburg 42-43 JK 7
Clacton on Sea 32 G 6
Clain 34-35 H 5
Claire, Lake – 70-71 O 6
Clairton, PA 74-75 CD 4
Clamecy 34-35 J 5
Clan Alpine Mountains 76-77 DE 6
Clanwilliam 64-65 E 9
Clara River 56-57 H 3
Clare [AUS] 56-57 G 6
Claremont, NH 74-75 GH 3
Claremorris 32 B 5
Clarence, Cape – 70-71 S 3
Clarence, Isla – 80 B 8
Clarence Island 24 C 31
Clarence Strait [AUS] 56-57 F 2
Clarion, PA 74-75 D 4
Clarion, Fosse – 22-23 B-D 5
Clarión, Fractura de – 22-23 B-D 5
Clarionbreukzone 22-23 B-D 5
Clarión-Bruchzone 22-23 B-D 5
Clarion Fracture Zone 22-23 B-D 5
Clarkdale, AZ 76-77 G 8
Clarke City 70-71 X 7
Clarke Island 56-57 J 8
Clark Fork, ID 76-77 E 1
Clark Fork River 72-73 CD 2
Clark Hill Lake 74-75 B 8
Clarkia, ID 76-77 EF 2
Clark Mountain 76-77 F 8
Clarksburg, WV 72-73 K 4
Clarksdale, MS 72-73 HJ 5
Clarkston, WA 76-77 E 2
Clarksville, TN 72-73 J 4
Clarksville, VA 74-75 D 6
Claxton, GA 74-75 BC 8
Clay, WV 74-75 C 5
Clay Belt 70-71 T-V 7
Claymont, DE 74-75 F 5
Claypool, AZ 76-77 H 9
Clayton, GA 74-75 B 7
Clayton, ID 76-77 F 3
Clayton, NC 74-75 D 7
Clayton, NY 74-75 EF 2
Clearcreek, UT 76-77 H 6
Clearfield, PA 74-75 D 4
Clearfield, UT 76-77 GH 5
Clear Hills 70-71 N 6
Clear Lake 76-77 B 6
Clear Lake Reservoir 76-77 C 5
Clearwater, FL 72-73 C 6
Clearwater Mountains 76-77 F 2-3
Clearwater River [USA] 76-77 E 2
Cleburne, TX 72-73 G 3
Cle Elum, WA 76-77 C 2
Clendenin, WV 74-75 C 5
Clermont [AUS] 56-57 J 4
Clermont, FL 74-75 bc 2
Clermont-Ferrand 34-35 J 6
Cleve 58 C 4
Cleveland, OH 72-73 K 3
Cleveland, TN 72-73 K 4
Cleveland, Mount – 72-73 D 2
Cleveland Heights, OH 74-75 C 4
Clewiston, FL 74-75 c 3
Clifden 32 A 5
Cliff, NM 76-77 J 9
Cliff Lake, MT 76-77 H 3
Cliffs, ID 76-77 E 4
Clifton 56-57 K 5
Clifton, AZ 76-77 J 9
Clifton, NJ 74-75 F 4
Clifton Forge, VA 74-75 D 6
Clifton Hills 56-57 G 5
Clinchco, VA 74-75 B 6
Clinch Mountains 74-75 B 6
Clinch River 74-75 B 6
Clinton [CDN, Ontario] 74-75 C 3
Clinton, IA 72-73 H 3
Clinton, MT 76-77 G 2
Clinton, NC 74-75 D 7
Clinton, SC 74-75 C 7
Clinton, Cape – 56-57 K 4
Clipperton, Fosse de – 22-23 CD 5
Clipperton, Fractura de – 22-23 CD 5
Clipperton, Île – 72-73 E 9
Clippertonbreukzone 22-23 CD 5
Clipperton-Bruchzone 22-23 CD 5
Clipperton Fracture Zone 22-23 CD 5
Clisham 32 C 3
Cloates, Point – 56-57 B 4
Clonakilty 32 B 6
Cloncurry 56-57 H 4
Cloncurry River 56-57 H 3
Clonmel 32 BC 5
Cloppenburg 33 CD 2
Cloucester, VA 74-75 E 6
Cloud Peak 72-73 E 3
Clover, VA 74-75 D 6
Cloverdale, CA 76-77 B 6
Cloverdale, NM 76-77 J 10
Clovis, CA 76-77 D 7
Clovis, NM 72-73 F 5
Cluj-Napoca 36-37 KL 2
Cluny 34-35 K 5
Clutha River 56-57 N 9
Clyde 70-71 X 3
Clyde, Firth of – 32 D 4
Clyde Park, MT 76-77 H 3
Clyo, GA 74-75 C 8
Coa 34-35 D 8
Coachella, CA 76-77 E 9
Coachella Canal 76-77 EF 9
Coahuila 72-73 F 6
Coaldale, NV 76-77 E 6
Coalinga, CA 76-77 C 7
Coalville, UT 76-77 H 5
Coari 78-79 G 5
Coari, Rio – 78-79 G 5-6
Coast Mountains 70-71 K 6-M 7
Coast Range 72-73 B 2-C 5
Coatá, Cachoeira do – 78-79 G 6
Coatepec 72-73 G 8
Coatesville, PA 74-75 EF 4-5
Coaticook 74-75 GH 2
Coats Island 70-71 U 5
Coats Land 24 B 33-34
Coatzacoalcos 72-73 H 8
Cobán 72-73 H 8
Çobandede 46-47 JK 3
Cobar 56-57 J 6
Cobargo 58 JK 6
Cobbo = Kobo 60-61 MN 6
Cobe = Kōbe 48-49 PQ 5
Cobh 32 B 6
Cobija 78-79 F 7
Cobleskill, NY 74-75 F 3
Coboconk 74-75 D 2
Cobourg 74-75 DE 3
Cobourg Peninsula 56-57 F 2
Cobre, NV 76-77 F 5
Cobue 63 C 6
Coburg 33 E 3
Coburg, OR 76-77 B 3
Coburg Island 70-71 V 2
Coca 34-35 E 8
Cocanada = Kakinada 44-45 N 7
Cochabamba [BOL, ●] 78-79 F 8
Cochem 33 C 3
Cochi = Kōchi 48-49 P 5
Cochim = Cochin 44-45 M 9
Cochin 44-45 M 9
Cochinchina = Nam Bô 52-53 DE 5
Cochise, AZ 76-77 J 9
Cochran, GA 74-75 B 8
Cochrane [CDN, Ontario] 70-71 U 8
Cochrane River 70-71 Q 6
Cockburn, Canal – 80 B 8
Cockburn Land 70-71 UV 3
Cockeysville, MD 74-75 E 5
Coco, El – 72-73 b 3
Coco, Isla del – 78-79 B 3
Coco, Río – 72-73 K 9
Cocoa, FL 74-75 c 2
Coco Channel 52-53 B 4
Coco Channel 52-53 B 4
Coco Channel 52-53 B 4
Coco Island 64-65 NO 6
Cocolalla, ID 76-77 E 1
Coconino Plateau 76-77 G 7-8
Cocos [AUS] 22-23 O 6
Cocos = Isla del Coco 78-79 B 3
Coco Solo 72-73 b 2
Cocos Rise 22-23 E 5
Cocuy, El – 78-79 E 3
Cod, Cape – 72-73 N 3
Codajás 78-79 G 5
Codera, Cabo – 78-79 F 2
Codihue 80 BC 5
Codó 78-79 L 5
Coen 56-57 H 2
Coesfeld 33 C 3
Coetivy Island 64-65 N 4
Coeur d'Alene, ID 72-73 C 2
Coeur d'Alene Indian Reservation 76-77 E 2
Coeur d'Alene Lake 76-77 E 2
Coffeyville, KS 72-73 G 4
Coffin Bay 56-57 FG 6
Coffin Bay Peninsula 56-57 FG 6
Coffs Harbour 56-57 K 6
Cofrentes 34-35 G 9
Cofu = Kōfu 48-49 Q 4
Cogealac 36-37 N 3
Cognac 34-35 G 6
Çoğun 46-47 F 3
Cohoes, NY 74-75 G 3
Cohuna 56-57 HJ 7
Coi, Sông – = Sông Nhi Ha 52-53 D 2
Coiba, Isla – 72-73 K 10
Coihaique 80 B 7
Coimbatore 44-45 M 8
Coimbra 34-35 C 8
Coin 34-35 E 10
Coipasa, Salar de – 78-79 F 8
Čojbalsan = 18 48-49 L 2
Čojbalsangijn Ajmag = Dornod = 18 ◁ 48-49 LM 2
Cojimies 78-79 C 4
Cojudo Blanco, Cerro – 80 BC 7
Çokak 46-47 G 4
Cokeville, WY 76-77 H 4
Čokurdach 42-43 cd 3
Colac 56-57 H 7
Colapur = Kolhapur 44-45 L 7
Cólar = Kolar Gold Fields 44-45 M 8
Colares 34-35 C 9
Colbeck, Cape – 24 B 20-21
Colbert, WA 76-77 E 2
Colbinabbin 58 G 6
Colca, Río – 78-79 E 8
Colchester 32 G 6
Coldwater 74-75 D 2
Colebrook, NH 74-75 H 2
Colégio = Porto Real do Colégio 78-79 M 6-7
Coleman River 56-57 H 2-3
Çölemerik = Hakkârı 46-47 K 4
Coleraine 32 C 4
Coleraine [AUS] 58 EF 6
Coles, Punta de – 78-79 E 8
Colesburg 64-65 FG 9
Colesville, CA 76-77 D 6
Colfax, CA 76-77 C 6
Colfax, WA 76-77 E 2
Colhué Huapi, Lago – 80 C 7
Colima 72-73 F 8
Colima, Nevado de – 72-73 EF 8
Colinas 78-79 L 6
Coll 32 C 3

Collaguasi 80 C 2
Collarenebri 58 HJ 2
College, AK 70-71 G 4-5
Collie 56-57 C 6
Collier Bay 56-57 D 3
Collingwood [CDN] 74-75 CD 2
Collins, MT 76-77 H 2
Collinson Peninsula 70-71 Q 3-4
Collinsville 56-57 J 4
Colmar 34-35 L 4
Colnett, Bahía – 76-77 E 10
Cologne = Köln 33 C 3
Cololo, Nevado – 78-79 F 7
Colomb-Béchar = Bashshār 60-61 D 2
Colombia 78-79 D-F 4
Colômbia [BR] 78-79 K 9
Colombie 78-79 D-F 4
Colombo = Kolamba 44-45 M 9
Colón [C] 72-73 K 7
Colón [PA, ●] 72-73 b 2
Colón [PA, ☆] 72-73 ab 2
Colón, Archipiélago de – 78-79 AB 5
Colona 56-57 F 6
Colonia = Köln 33 C 3
Colonia del Sacramento 80 E 4
Colonia 25 de Mayo 80 C 5
Colonia Las Heras = Las Heras 80 C 7
Colonial Beach, VA 74-75 E 5
Colonial Heights, VA 74-75 E 6
Colonia Morelos 76-77 J 10
Colonne, Capo delle – 36-37 G 6
Colonsay 32 C 3
Colorado [USA] 72-73 EF 4
Colorado, Río – [MEX] 72-73 CD 5
Colorado, Río – [RA, La Pampa] 80 C 5
Colorado, Río – [RA, Neuquén] 80 D 5
Colorado, Río – [RA, Río Negro] 80 CD 5
Colorado Desert 76-77 EF 9
Colorado National Monument 76-77 J 6
Colorado Plateau 72-73 DE 4
Colorado River [USA, Colorado] 72-73 E 4
Colorado River [USA, Texas] 72-73 G 5
Colorado River Aqueduct 76-77 F 8
Colorado River Indian Reservation 76-77 F 9
Colorados, Cerros – [RA] 80 C 6
Colorados, Cerros – [RCH] 80 C 3
Colorado Springs, CO 72-73 F 4
Colo River 58 K 4
Colton, UT 76-77 H 6
Columbia, MD 74-75 E 5
Columbia, MO 72-73 H 4
Columbia, NC 74-75 E 7
Columbia, PA 74-75 E 4
Columbia, SC 72-73 K 5
Columbia, Cape – 19 A 25-26
Columbia, District of – 74-75 E 5
Columbia, Mount – 70-71 N 7
Columbia Basin 76-77 D 2
Columbia Británica = British Columbia 70-71 L 6-N 7
Columbia Falls, MT 76-77 FG 1
Columbia Plateau 72-73 C 2-3
Columbia River 72-73 BC 2
Columbia River, WA 76-77 C 2
Columbretes, Islas – 34-35 H 9
Columbus, GA 72-73 K 5
Columbus, MS 72-73 J 5
Columbus, NE 72-73 G 3
Columbus, OH 72-73 K 3-4
Colusa, CA 76-77 BC 6
Colville, WA 76-77 E 1
Colville Indian Reservation 76-77 D 1
Colville River 70-71 EF 4
Comàcchio 36-37 E 3
Comàcchio, Valli di – 36-37 E 3
Comana 36-37 LM 3
Comayagua 72-73 J 9
Combourg 34-35 G 4
Comeau, Baie – 70-71 X 8
Come By Chance 58 J 3
Come By Chance 58 J 3
Come By Chance 58 J 3
Comer, GA 74-75 B 7
Comilla = Komillā 44-45 P 6
Comino, Capo – 36-37 CD 5
Comiso 36-37 F 7
Comitán de Domínguez 72-73 H 8
Commerce, GA 74-75 B 7
Committee Bay 70-71 T 4
Commonwealth Range 24 A
Commonwealth Territory 56-57 K 7
Como 36-37 C 3
Como, Lago di – 36-37 C 2-3
Comodoro Rivadavia 80 C 7
Comoé = Komoe 60-61 D 7
Comore-medence 64-65 L 5
Comores 64-65 KL 5
Comores, Archipel des – 64-65 KL 5
Comores, Bassin des – 64-65 L 5
Comores, Cuenca de – 64-65 L 5
Comore-szigetek 64-65 KL 5
Comorin, Cape – 44-45 M 9
Compiègne 34-35 J 4
Comprida, Cachoeira – = Treze Quedas 78-79 H 4
Comprida, Ilha – [BR, São Paulo] 80 G 2-3
Comprida, Lago – = Lagoa Nova 78-79 J 4
Compton, CA 76-77 DE 9
Čona 42-43 V 5
Conakry 60-61 B 7
Conca = Cuenca 78-79 D 5
Concarneau 34-35 EF 5
Conceição [BR, Mato Grosso] 78-79 H 6
Conceição da Barra 78-79 M 8
Conceição do Araguaia 78-79 JK 6
Concelho = Inhambane 64-65 J 7
Concepción [BOL] 78-79 G 8
Concepción [CO, Putumayo] 78-79 DE 4
Concepción [RA, Tucumán] 80 C 3
Concepción [RCH] 80 AB 5
Concepcion, CA 76-77 C 8
Concepción [PY, ●] 80 E 2
Concepción, Canal – 80 AB 8
Concepción, La – 78-79 E 2
Concepción, Río – 76-77 G 10
Concepción del Oro 72-73 F 7
Concepción del Uruguay 80 E 4
Conception, Point – 72-73 B 5
Conchi [RCH, Antofagasta] 80 C 2
Concho, AZ 76-77 J 8
Conchos, Río – 72-73 EF 6
Concord, CA 76-77 BC 7
Concord, NC 74-75 C 7
Concord, NH 72-73 M 3
Concordia [RA] 80 E 4
Côn Đao 52-53 E 5
Conde 78-79 M 7
Condobolin 56-57 J 6
Condon, OR 76-77 C 3
Conejera, Isla – 34-35 J 9
Confusion Range 76-77 G 6
Congo 64-65 D 3-F 2
Congo = Zaïre 64-65 E 3
Congress, AZ 76-77 G 8
Cônia = Konya 44-45 C 3
Conjeeveram = Kanchipuram 44-45 MN 8
Connaught 32 B 4-5
Conneaut, OH 74-75 C 3-4
Connecticut 72-73 M 3
Connecticut River 74-75 G 3-4
Connell, WA 76-77 D 2
Connellsville, PA 74-75 D 4
Conner, MT 76-77 FG 3
Conner, Mount – 56-57 F 5
Connersville, OH 74-75 A 5
Connors Pass 76-77 F 6
Conrad, MT 76-77 H 1
Conselheiro Lafaiete 78-79 L 9
Constância dos Baetas 78-79 G 6
Constanța 36-37 M 3
Constantina = Qusanțīn 60-61 F 1
Constantine, Cape – 70-71 DE 6
Constantinopla = İstanbul 44-45 BC 2
Constanza = Constanța 36-37 N 3
Constitución 80 B 5
Contact, NV 76-77 F 5
Contamana 78-79 DE 6
Contas, Rio de – 78-79 L 7
Continental, AZ 76-77 H 10
Contratación 78-79 E 3
Contreras, Isla – 80 AB 8
Contwoyto Lake 70-71 OP 4
Conway, NH 74-75 H 3
Conway, SC 74-75 D 8
Coober Pedy 56-57 F 5
Cook 56-57 F 6
Cook, Bahía – 80 B 9
Cook, Mount – [NZ] 56-57 NO 8
Cook Bay 24 C 16
Cooke City, MT 76-77 J 3
Cook Inlet 70-71 F 5-6
Cook Strait 56-57 O 8
Cooktown 56-57 HJ 3
Coolabah 58 H 3
Coolah 58 J 3
Coolamon 58 H 5
Coolgardie 56-57 CD 6
Coolidge, AZ 76-77 H 9
Coolidge Dam 76-77 H 9
Coolin, ID 76-77 E 1
Cooma 56-57 J 7
Coonabarabran 56-57 JK 6
Coonamble 56-57 J 6
Coonana 56-57 D 6
Coonbah 58 EF 4
Coondambo 58 BC 3
Coondapoor 44-45 L 8
Coongoola 56-57 HJ 5
Cooper Creek 56-57 G 5
Cooperstown, NY 74-75 F 3
Coorong, The – 56-57 G 7
Coos Bay 76-77 A 4
Coos Bay, OR 72-73 AB 3
Cootamundra 56-57 J 6
Čop 38-39 D 6
Copahue, Paso – 80 BC 5
Copán 72-73 J 9
Copco, CA 76-77 B 4-5
Copenhagen = København 30-31 DE 10
Copenhague = København 30-31 DE 10
Copiapó 80 BC 3
Copparo 36-37 DE 3
Copperbelt 64-65 G 5
Copper Center, AK 70-71 G 5
Coppermine 70-71 N 4
Coppermine River 70-71 NO 4
Copper River 70-71 GH 5
Copșa Mică 36-37 L 2
Coquilhatville = Mbandaka 64-65 E 2-3
Coquille, OR 76-77 AB 4
Coquille River 76-77 AB 4
Coquimbo [RCH, ●] 80 B 2
Corabia 36-37 L 4
Coracora 78-79 E 7-8
Corail, Grande Barrière de – 56-57 H 1-K 4
Corail, Mer de – 56-57 K-M 3
Coral, Cuenca del – 56-57 K 2
Coral, Mar del – 56-57 K-M 3
Coral Gables, FL 72-73 KL 6
Coral Harbour 70-71 U 5
Coral Sea 56-57 K-M 3
Coral Sea Basin 56-57 K 2
Coral Sea Islands Territory 56-57 JK 3
Coral Springs, FL 56-57 c 3
Corantijn 78-79 H 4
Corato 36-37 G 5
Corbeil-Essonnes 34-35 HJ 4
Corbières 34-35 J 7
Corbin, KY 72-73 K 4
Corcaigh = Cork 32 B 6
Córcega = Corse 36-37 C 4
Corcoran, CA 76-77 D 7
Corcovado, Volcán – 80 B 6
Corcubión 34-35 C 7
Cordele, GA 74-75 AB 8
Cordillera Azul 78-79 D 6
Cordillera Blanca 78-79 D 6
Cordillera Central [BOL] 78-79 F 8-G 9
Cordillera Central [CO] 78-79 D 4-E 3
Cordillera Central [DOM] 72-73 M 8
Cordillera Central [PE] 78-79 D 6
Cordillera Central [RP] 52-53 H 3
Cordillera Ibérica 34-35 F 7-G 8
Cordillera Negra 78-79 D 6
Cordillera Occidental [CO] 78-79 D 3-4
Cordillera Occidental [PE] 78-79 D 6-E 8
Cordillera Oriental [BOL] 78-79 FG 8
Cordillera Oriental [CO] 78-79 D 4-E 3
Cordillera Oriental [DOM] 72-73 N 8
Cordillera Oriental [PE] 78-79 D 5-E 7
Cordillera Penibética 34-35 E 9-G 8
Cordillera Real [EC] 78-79 D 5
Cordillère Bétique = Cordillera Penibética 34-35 E 9-G 8
Córdoba [E] 34-35 E 10
Córdoba [MEX, Veracruz] 72-73 G 8
Córdoba [RA] 80 D 4
Córdoba, Sierra de – [RA] 80 C 4-D 3
Córdova 78-79 DE 7
Cordova, AK 70-71 G 5
Corea del Norte 48-49 O 3-4
Corea del Sur 48-49 OP 4
Corée du Nord 48-49 O 3-4
Corée du Sud 48-49 OP 4
Core Sound 74-75 E 7
Corfield 56-57 H 4
Corfou = Kérkyra 36-37 H 6
Corfu = Kérkyra 36-37 H 6
Coria 34-35 D 8-9
Coria del Río 34-35 D 10
Coringa Islands 56-57 K 3
Corinne, UT 76-77 G 5
Corinth = Kórinthos 36-37 K 7
Corinthe = Kórinthos 36-37 K 7
Corinto [BR] 78-79 KL 8
Corinto [NIC] 72-73 J 9
Corinto = Kórinthos 36-37 K 7
Corisco, Isla de – 60-61 F 8
Cork 32 B 6
Corleone 36-37 E 7
Corleto Perticara 36-37 FG 5
Çorlu 46-47 B 2
Çorlusuyu Deresi 46-47 B 2
Cormoranes, Rocas – = Shag Rocks 80 H 8
Čormož 38-39 L 4
Čornaja 38-39 L 2
Čornaja [SU, Tajmyrskaja AO] 42-43 Q 3
Cornélio Procópio 80 FG 2
Corner Brook 70-71 Z 8
Corner Inlet 58 H 7
Corning, CA 76-77 B 6
Corning, NY 74-75 E 3
Cornouaille 34-35 EF 4
Cornwall [GB] 32 D 6
Cornwall [CDN] 70-71 VW 8
Cornwallis Island 70-71 RS 2-3
Cornwall Island 70-71 RS 2
Corny Point 58 C 5
Coro 78-79 EF 2
Coroatá 78-79 L 5
Corocoro 78-79 F 8
Coroico 78-79 F 8
Coromandel, Côte de – = Coromandel Coast 44-45 N 7-8
Coromandel Coast 44-45 N 7-8
Coromandelküste = Coromandel Coast 44-45 N 7-8
Coromandel-part = Coromandel Coast 44-45 N 7-8
Corona, CA 76-77 E 9
Coronado, CA 76-77 E 9
Coronado, Bahía de – 72-73 K 10
Coronados, Islas de – 76-77 E 9
Coronation Gulf 70-71 OP 4
Coronation Island [South Orkneys] 24 CD 32
Coronation Islands 56-57 D 2
Coronel Dorrego 80 DE 5
Coronel Fabriciano 78-79 L 8
Coronel Francisco Sosa 80 CD 5-6
Coronel Galvão = Rio Verde de Mato Grosso 78-79 HJ 8
Coronel Oviedo 78-79 E 2-3
Coronel Pringles 80 D 5
Coronel Rosales 80 D 5
Coronel Suárez 80 D 5
Coropuna, Nudo – 78-79 E 8
Corowa 58 H 5-6
Corozal [BH] 72-73 J 8
Corpus Christi, TX 72-73 G 6
Corpus Christi, TX 72-73 G 6
Corpus Christi, TX 72-73 G 6
Corque 78-79 F 8
Corral [RCH] 80 B 5
Corregidor Island 52-53 GH 4
Corrente 78-79 KL 7
Corrente, Rio – [BR, Bahia] 78-79 L 7
Correntes [BR, Mato Grosso] 78-79 HJ 8
Correntina 78-79 KL 7
Corrib, Lough – 32 B 5
Corrientes, Cabo – [CO] 78-79 D 3
Corrientes, Cabo – [MEX] 72-73 E 7
Corrientes, Cabo – [RA] 80 E 5
Corrigin 56-57 C 6
Corry, PA 74-75 D 4
Corse 36-37 C 4
Corse, Cap – 36-37 C 4
Corsica = Corse 36-37 C 4
Corsicana, TX 72-73 G 5
Č'orskogo, chrebet – 42-43 a 4-c 5
Corte 36-37 C 4
Cortez, CO 76-77 J 7
Cortez Mountains 76-77 E 5
Cortina d'Ampezzo 36-37 E 2
Čortkov 38-39 E 6
Cortland, NY 74-75 EF 3
Cortona 36-37 D 4
Çoruh = Artvin 44-45 E 2
Çoruh Nehri 46-47 J 2
Çorum 44-45 CD 2
Corumbá 78-79 H 8
Corumbá, Rio – 78-79 K 8
Coruña, La – 34-35 C 7
Coruña, La – 34-35 C 7
Corvallis, MT 76-77 FG 2
Corvallis, OR 72-73 B 3
Corwin Springs, MT 76-77 H 3
Cosenza 36-37 FG 6
Coshocton, OH 74-75 BC 4
Cosigüina, Punta – 72-73 J 9
Cosigüina, Volcán – 72-73 J 9
Cosmoledo Islands 64-65 L 4
Cosmopolis, WA 76-77 B 2
Cosmos Newberry Aboriginal Reserve 56-57 D 5
Č'ošskaja guba 42-43 H 4
Costa, Cordillera de la – [RCH] 80 B 2-3
Costa, Cordillera de la – [YV] 78-79 FG 3
Costa Brava 34-35 J 8
Costa de Marfil [★] 60-61 CD 7
Costa Grande 72-73 F 8
Costa Rica [CR] 72-73 JK 9-10
Costa Smeralda 24 B 3
Costermansville = Bukavu 64-65 G 3
Cotabato 52-53 H 5
Cotagaita [BOL] 78-79 F 9
Cotahuasi 78-79 E 8
Cotati, CA 76-77 B 6
Coteau des Prairies, Plateau du – 72-73 G 2-3
Coteau du Missouri, Plateau du – 72-73 FG 2
Côteau-Station 74-75 F 2
Côte d'Azur 34-35 L 7
Côte d'Ivoire [★] 60-61 CD 7
Côte Française = French Shore 70-71 Z 7-8
Cotentin 34-35 G 4
Cotonou 60-61 E 7
Cotonu = Cotonou 60-61 E 7
Cotopaxi [EC, ▲] 78-79 D 5
Cotswold Hills 32 EF 6
Cottage Grove, OR 76-77 B 4
Cottageville, SC 74-75 C 8
Cottbus 33 G 3
Cottica 78-79 J 4
Cottonwood, AZ 76-77 GH 8
Cottonwood, CA 76-77 B 5
Cottonwood, ID 76-77 E 2
Cottonwood Creek 76-77 B 5
Cottonwood Wash 76-77 HJ 8
Coudersport, PA 74-75 DE 4
Coulee City, WA 76-77 D 2
Coulee Dam, WA 76-77 D 1-2
Coulman Island 24 B 18
Council, ID 76-77 E 3
Council Bluffs, IA 72-73 GH 3
Council Mountain 76-77 E 3
Courlande 30-31 JK 9
Courtenay [CDN] 70-71 LM 8
Courtrai = Kortrijk 34-35 J 3
Coutances 34-35 G 4
Coveñas 78-79 D 3
Coventry 32 F 5
Coveñas 78-79 D 3
Covilhã 34-35 D 8
Covington, KY 72-73 JK 4
Covington, VA 74-75 CD 6
Cowal, Lake – 56-57 J 6
Cowan, Lake – 56-57 D 6
Cowansville 74-75 G 2
Coward Springs 56-57 G 5
Cowarie 56-57 G 5
Cowell 58 C 4
Cowen, Mount – 76-77 H 3
Cowlitz River 76-77 B 2
Cowra 56-57 J 6
Coxilha Grande 80 F 3
Coxim 78-79 J 8
Cox River 56-57 FG 3
Cox's Bazar = Koks Bāzār 44-45 P 6
Coyote, Arroyo el – 76-77 G 10
Coyotes Indian Reservation, Los – 76-77 E 9
Cozumel 72-73 J 7
Cozumel, Isla de – 72-73 J 7
Crab Creek 76-77 D 2
Cradock 64-65 G 9
Craig, MT 76-77 GH 2
Craig Harbour 70-71 UV 2
Craigmont, ID 76-77 E 2
Craiova 36-37 K 3
Crampel = Ra's al-Mā' 60-61 D 2
Cranbrook 70-71 NO 8
Crane, OR 76-77 D 4
Crane Mountain 76-77 CD 4
Cranston, RI 74-75 H 4
Crary Mountains 24 B 25
Crasna [R, ~] 36-37 K 2
Crasna [R, ●] 36-37 M 2
Crater Lake 72-73 B 3
Crater Lake, OR 76-77 BC 4
Crater Lake National Park 76-77 BC 4
Crateús 78-79 LM 6
Crato [BR] 78-79 M 6
Crau 34-35 K 7
Crauford, Cape – 70-71 TU 3
Cravo Norte 78-79 EF 3
Crawford, GA 74-75 B 8
Crawfordville, FL 74-75 AB 8
Crazy Mountains 76-77 H 2-3
Crazy Peak 76-77 HJ 3
Creedmoor, NC 74-75 D 6
Cree Lake [CDN, ≈] 70-71 P 6
Creil 34-35 J 4
Crema 36-37 C 3
Cremona 36-37 CD 3
Cres [YU, ⊙] 36-37 F 3
Cres [YU, ●] 36-37 F 3
Crescent, OR 76-77 C 4
Crescent, Lake – 76-77 B 1
Crescent City, CA 76-77 A 5
Crescent City, FL 74-75 c 2
Crescent Junction, UT 76-77 J 6
Crescent Lake, OR 76-77 C 4
Cressy 58 F 7
Crestline, NV 76-77 F 7
Creswell, OR 76-77 B 4
Creta = Krētē 36-37 L 8
Crete = Krētē 36-37 L 8
Crète = Krētē 36-37 L 8
Creus, Cabo – 34-35 J 7
Creuse 34-35 H 5
Creusot, le – 34-35 K 5
Crewe 32 E 5
Crewe, VA 74-75 D 6
Cribi = Kribi 60-61 F 8
Crib Point 58 G 7
Crichna = Krishna 44-45 M 7
Crikvenica 36-37 F 3
Crillon, mys – = mys Kriljon 42-43 b 8
Crimea = Krym' 38-39 F 6
Crimée = Krym' 38-39 F 6
Crișana 36-37 JK 2
Crisfield, MD 74-75 F 5-6
Cristobal 72-73 b 2
Crișul Alb 36-37 J 2
Crișul Negru 36-37 JK 2
Crna Gora 36-37 H 4
Crna Gora 36-37 H 4
Crna Reka 36-37 J 5
Croacia 36-37 F-H 3
Croatia 36-37 F-H 3
Croatie 36-37 F-H 3
Crocodile Islands 56-57 FG 2
Croker Island 56-57 F 2
Cromer 32 G 5
Cromwell 56-57 NO 8-9
Crooked Creek 76-77 DE 4
Crooked Island 72-73 M 7
Crooked Island Passage 72-73 LM 7
Crooked River [USA] 76-77 C 3
Crooksville, OH 74-75 B 5
Crookwell 58 J 5
Cross, Cape – = Kaap Kruis 64-65 D 7
Cross City, FL 74-75 b 2
Crossen (Oder) = Krosno Odrzańskie 33 G 2-3
Crossman Peak 76-77 FG 8
Cross River 60-61 F 7-8
Cross Sound 70-71 J 6
Crotone 36-37 G 6
Crowie Creek 58 H 4
Crowley, LA 72-73 H 5-6
Crowley, Lake – 76-77 D 7
Crown King, AZ 76-77 G 8
Crownpoint, NM 76-77 JK 8
Crows Nest 58 L 1
Croydon 56-57 H 3
Croydon, London- 32 FG 7
Crozet 22-23 M 8
Crozet, Dorsal de – 22-23 M 8
Crozet, Seuil des – 22-23 M 8
Crozetdrempel 22-23 M 8
Crozet Ridge 22-23 M 8
Crozetschwelle 22-23 M 8
Crucero, CA 76-77 EF 8
Cruces, Las – 72-73 b 2
Cruz, Cabo – 72-73 L 8
Cruz Alta [BR] 80 F 3
Cruz del Eje 80 CD 4
Cruzeiro 78-79 L 9
Cruzeiro do Sul 78-79 E 6
Cruzen Island 24 B 22-23
Crystal Bay 74-75 b 2
Crystal Brook 58 CD 4
Crystal River, FL 74-75 b 2
Csongrád 33 K 5
Ctesiphon = Ktesiphon 46-47 L 6
Ču 42-43 N 9
Cuamba 64-65 J 5
Cuando, Rio – 64-65 F 6
Cuando-Cubango 64-65 E 5-F 6
Cuangar 64-65 E 6
Cuango 64-65 E 4
Cuango, Rio – 64-65 E 6
Cuan Long 52-53 DE 5
Cuanza Norte 64-65 DE 4-5
Cuanza Sul 64-65 D 4-5
Cu'a Rao 52-53 DE 3
Cuauhtémoc 72-73 C 6
Cuba 72-73 KL 7
Cubabi, Cerro – 76-77 G 10
Cubal 64-65 D 5
Cubango, Rio – 64-65 E 6
Čubartau = Baršatas 42-43 O 8
Cubuk 46-47 E 2
Cuchi, Rio – 64-65 E 5-6
Cuchilla Grande [ROU] 80 EF 4
Cucuí 78-79 F 4
Cucumbi 64-65 E 5
Cucunor = Chöch nuur 48-49 H 4
Cucurpe 76-77 H 10
Cúcuta 78-79 E 3
Cuddalore 44-45 MN 8
Cuddapah 44-45 M 8
Cudgewa 58 HJ 6
Cudi Dağı 46-47 K 4
Čudovo 42-43 E 6
Čudskoje ozero 42-43 O 6
Cue 56-57 C 5
Cuenca [E] 34-35 FG 8
Cuenca [EC] 78-79 D 5
Cuenca, Serranía de – 34-35 F 8-G 9
Cuenca Arábiga 22-23 N 5
Cuenca Argelinoprovenzal 28-29 J 8-K 7
Cuenca Argentina 22-23 GH 7-8
Cuenca Atlántico-Índico Antártica 22-23 J-M 9
Cuenca Brasileña 22-23 H 6
Cuenca Canadiense 19 AB 32-33
Cuenca Euroasiática 19 A
Cuenca Ibérica 22-23 HJ 3
Cuenca Índico-Antártica 22-23 O-Q 8
Cuenca Jónica 36-37 GH 7
Cuenca Levantina 44-45 BC 4
Cuenca Mexicana 72-73 HJ 6
Cuenca Norteamericana 22-23 FG 4
Cuenca Pacífico-Antártica 22-23 DE 8-9
Cuenlum = Kunlun Shan 48-49 D-H 4
Cuernavaca 72-73 FG 8

168 Colla

Cuesta Pass 76-77 C 8
Cuevas del Almanzora 34-35 G 10
Cufra, Wáhát el – = Wāḥāt al-Kufrah 60-61 J 4
Čugujev 38-39 G 6
Cuiabá [BR, Amazonas] 78-79 H 6
Cuiabá [BR, Mato Grosso] 78-79 H 8
Cuiabá, Rio – 78-79 H 8
Cuillin Sound 32 C 3
Cuilo, Rio – 64-65 E 4
Cuima 64-65 E 5
Cuipo 72-73 a 2
Cuito, Rio – 64-65 EF 6
Cuito Cuanavale 64-65 EF 6
Čukotskij, mys – 42-43 I 5
Čukotskij poluostrov 42-43 kl 4
Çukurca 46-47 K 4
Culcairn 56-57 J 7
Culebra [PA] 72-73 b 2
Culgoa River 56-57 J 5
Culiacán 72-73 E 6-7
Culiacán Rosales = Culiacán 72-73 E 6-7
Culion Island 52-53 G 4
Čulkovo 42-43 Q 5
Cúllar de Baza 34-35 F 10
Cullera 34-35 GH 9
Čul'man 42-43 XY 6
Culpeper, VA 74-75 DE 5
Culuene, Rio – 78-79 J 7
Čuluut gol 48-49 J 2
Culver, Point – 56-57 DE 6
Čulym [SU, ~] 42-43 Q 6
Čulym [SU, ●] 42-43 P 6
Cum = Qom 44-45 G 4
Cumae 36-37 EF 5
Cumamoto = Kumamoto 48-49 P 5
Cumaná 78-79 G 2
Cumassia = Kumasi 60-61 D 7
Cumberland, KY 74-75 B 6
Cumberland, MD 72-73 L 4
Cumberland, VA 74-75 DE 6
Cumberland, Cape – 56-57 N 2
Cumberland, Lake – 74-75 A 6
Cumberland Island 74-75 C 9
Cumberland Islands 56-57 JK 4
Cumberland Peninsula 70-71 XY 4
Cumberland Plateau 72-73 J 5-K 4
Cumberland River 72-73 J 4
Cumberland Sound [CDN] 70-71 X 4-Y 5
Cumberland Sound [USA] 74-75 c 1
Cumborah 58 H 2
Cumbre, Paso de la – 80 BC 4
Cumbria 32 F 4
Cumbrian Mountains 32 E 4
Čumikan 42-43 Za 7
Cuminá, Rio – 78-79 H 5
Cummings, CA 76-77 B 6
Cummins 56-57 G 6
Cumpas 76-77 J 10
Çumra 46-47 E 4
Čuna [SU ◁ Angara] 42-43 S 6
Čun'a [SU ◁ Podkamennaja Tunguska] 42-43 ST 5
Cunani 78-79 J 4
Cunco 80 B 5
Cunene 64-65 E 6
Cunene, Rio – 64-65 D 6
Cùneo 36-37 B 3
Çüngüş 46-47 H 3
Cunnamulla 56-57 HJ 5
Cunningham, WA 76-77 D 2
Čuokkarašša 30-31 KL 2
Cupica, Golfo de – 78-79 D 3
Cuprum, ID 76-77 E 3
Curaçá [BR, Amazonas] 78-79 G 6
Curaçá [BR, Bahia] 78-79 LM 6
Curaçao 72-73 N 9
Curacautin 80 B 5
Curanilahue 80 B 5
Čurapča 42-43 Z 5
Curaray, Rio – 78-79 D 5
Curdistán = Kordestān 44-45 F 3
Curiapo 78-79 G 3
Curicó 80 B 4
Curitiba 80 G 3
Curlandia 30-31 JK 9
Curlew, WA 76-77 D 1
Curnamona 56-57 GH 6
Currais Novos 78-79 M 6
Currant, NV 76-77 F 6
Currie 56-57 H 7-8
Currie, NV 76-77 F 5
Currituck Sound 74-75 F 6
Curtea-de-Argeş 36-37 L 3
Curtin Springs 56-57 F 5
Curtis Island [AUS] 56-57 K 4
Curtis Island [NZ] 56-57 Q 6
Curuá, Rio – [BR ◁ Rio Iriri] 78-79 J 6
Curuai 78-79 H 5
Curuçá 78-79 K 5
Curup 52-53 D 7
Čurupinsk 36-37 P 2
Cururú 78-79 G 8
Cururupu 78-79 L 5
Curuzú Cuatiá 80 E 3
Curva Grande 78-79 K 5
Curvelo 78-79 L 8
Curych = Zürich 33 C 5
Čusovaja 38-39 L 4
Čusovoj 42-43 K 6
Čust 44-45 L 2
Cut Bank, MT 76-77 GH 1
Cutch = Kutch 44-45 K 6
Cutervo 78-79 D 6
Cutler, CA 76-77 D 7
Cuttaburra Creek 58 G 2
Cuttack 44-45 NO 6
Cu'u Long, Cu'a Sông – 52-53 E 5
Cuvašská, AR- 38-39 J 4
Cuvelai 64-65 E 6
Cuvier, Cape – 56-57 B 4
Cuvo, Rio – 64-65 D 5
Cuxhaven 33 D 2
Cuy, El – 80 C 5
Cuyahoga Falls, OH 74-75 C 4
Cuyama River 76-77 C 8
Cuyo Islands 52-53 H 4
Cuyuni River 78-79 G 3
Cuzco [PE, ●] 78-79 E 7

Cyangugu 63 B 3
Cyclades 36-37 L 7
Cyklady 36-37 L 6
Cyp-Navolok 30-31 PQ 3
Cypr 44-45 C 3
Cypress Hills 70-71 OP 8
Cyprus 44-45 C 3
Cyrenaica = Barqah 60-61 J 2
Cyrénaïque = Barqah 60-61 J 2
Cyrenajka = Barqah 60-61 J 2

Czad 60-61 HJ 5
Czad, Jezioro – = Lac Tchad 60-61 G 6
Czarne, Morze - 36-37 N 4-P 3
Czarne, Morze - 38-39 E-G 7
Czarnogóra 36-37 H 4
Czech Republic 33 F-H 4
Czeczeńsko-Inguska, AR - 38-39 J 7
Czeluskin, Przylądek – = mys Čel'uskin 42-43 UV 2
Czersk 33 J 2
Czerwone, Morze – 44-45 D 5-7
Czeska, Republika – 42-43 B-E 7
Czeska, Republika - 33 FH 4
Częstochowa 33 JK 3
Czingis-chana, Wały – 48-49 LM 2
Czomolungma 48-49 F 6
Czukockie, Morze – 19 BC 35-36
Czukockie, Wzniesienie – 19 B 35
Czukocki Okręg Autonomiczny 42-43 g-j 4
Czuwaska, AR - 38-39 J 4
Czuwaska Autonomiczna Republika = 4 ◁ 42-43 H 6

Č

Čad 60-61 HJ 5
Čadan 42-43 R 7
Čadobec [SU, ~] 42-43 S 6
Čadobec [SU, ●] 42-43 S 6
Čadyr-Lunga 36-37 N 2
Čagda 42-43 Z 6
Čagil 38-39 L 7
Čagoda 42-43 EF 6
Čajek 44-45 L 2
Čany, ozero – 42-43 O 7
Čapajev 42-43 J 7
Čapajevsk 42-43 HJ 7
Čara [SU, ~] 42-43 W 6
Čara [SU, ●] 42-43 W 6
Čardžou 44-45 J 3
Čarsk 42-43 P 8
Čaršanga 44-45 K 4
Čaryn 42-43 OP 9
Čaryš 42-43 P 7
Časel'ka 42-43 P 4-5
Čaunskaja guba 42-43 gh 4

Čebarkul 38-39 M 5
Čeboksary 42-43 H 6
Čečensko-ingušská AR 38-39 J 7
Čečujsk 42-43 U 6
Čegdomyn 42-43 Z 7
Čechov [SU, Sachalin] 42-43 b 8
Čekanovskogo, kr'až – 42-43 XY 3
Čel'abinsk 42-43 L 6
Čeleken 44-45 G 3
Čeljuskin, Cabo – = mys Čel'uskin 42-43 UV 2
Čeljuskinův mys = mys Čel'uskin 42-43 UV 2
Čelkar 42-43 KL 8
Čel'uskin, mys – 42-43 T-V 2
Čenstochová = Czestochowa 33 J 3
Čepca 38-39 K 4
Čerdyn 38-39 L 3
Čeremchovo 42-43 T 7
Čerepanovo 42-43 P 7
Čerepovec 42-43 F 6
Čerevkovo 38-39 J 3
Čerkassy 38-39 F 6
Čerkessk 38-39 H 7
Čerlak 42-43 N 7
Černá Hora 36-37 H 4
Čern'achovsk 33 K 1
Černatica 36-37 L 4-5
Černé moře 36-37 N 4-P 3
Černigov 38-39 F 5
Černigovka 42-43 Z 9
Černogorsk 42-43 R 7
Černomorskoje 36-37 OP 3
Černorečje = Dzeržinsk 42-43 GH 6
Černovskije Kopi, Čita- 42-43 V 7
Černovskoje 38-39 J 4
Černovtcy 38-39 DE 6
Černyševskij 42-43 V 5
Černyševskoje 33 KL 1
Čerskij 42-43 f 4
Čerskogo, chrebet – 42-43 V 7
Čertež 38-39 L 4
Červen br'ag 36-37 KL 4
Česká republika 42-43 B-E 7
Česká republika 33 F-H 4
Česká Třebova 33 G 4
České Budějovice 33 G 4
České země 33 F-H 4
Českomoravská vrchovina 33 GH 4

Čibit 42-43 Q 7
Čiganak 42-43 N 8-9
Čiili 42-43 M 9
Čimbaj 42-43 KL 9
Čimkent 42-43 M 9
Čina 48-49 E-K 5
Čingischánův val 48-49 LM 2
Čiovo 36-37 G 4
Čirčik 42-43 M 9
Čirpan 36-37 L 4
Čistopol' 42-43 HJ 6
Čita 42-43 V 7
Čiža 42-43 G 4

Čkalov = Orenburg 42-43 JK 7

Čojbalsan = 18 48-49 L 2
Čojbalsangijn Ajmag = Dornod = 18 ◁ 48-49 LM 2
Čokurdach 42-43 cd 3
Čona 42-43 V 5
Čop 38-39 D 6
Čormož 38-39 L 4
Čornaja 38-39 L 2
Čornaja [SU, Tajmyrskaja AO] 42-43 Q 3
Č'orskogo, chrebet – 42-43 a 4-c 5
Čortkov 38-39 E 6
Č'ošskaja guba 42-43 H 4

Ču 42-43 N 9
Čubartau = Baršatas 42-43 O 8
Čudovo 42-43 E 6
Čudskoje ozero 42-43 O 6
Čugujev 38-39 G 6
Čukotskaja Avtonomnaja Oblast' = Autonome Oblast der Tschuktschen 42-43 g-k 4
Čukotské moře 19 BC 35-36
Čukotskij, mys – 42-43 I 5
Čukotskij poluostrov 42-43 kl 4
Čukotský autonomní okruh 42-43 g-j 4
Čulkovo 42-43 Q 5
Čul'man 42-43 XY 6
Čuluut gol 48-49 J 2
Čulym [SU, ~] 42-43 Q 6
Čulym [SU, ●] 42-43 P 6
Čumikan 42-43 Za 7
Čuna [SU ◁ Angara] 42-43 S 6
Čun'a [SU ◁ Podkamennaja Tunguska] 42-43 ST 5
Čuokkarašša 30-31 KL 2
Čurapča 42-43 Z 5
Čurupinsk 36-37 P 2
Čusovaja 38-39 L 4
Čusovoj 42-43 K 6
Čust 44-45 L 2
Čuvašská autonomní republika = 4 ◁ 42-43 H 6
Čuvašskaja Avtonomnaja Sovetskaja Socialističeskaja Respublika = Autonome Republik der Tschuwaschen = 4 ◁ 42-43 H 6

Ch

Chaaltyn gol 48-49 GH 4
Cha-am [T] 52-53 CD 4
Chaba 48-49 F 2
Chabarovo 42-43 L 4
Chabarovsk 42-43 a 8
Chablis 34-35 J 5
Chačmas 38-39 J 7
Chaco 80 D 3
Chaco Austral 80 DE 3
Chaco Boreal 80 DE 2
Chaco Central 80 D 2-E 3
Chaco River 76-77 J 7
Chachapoyas 78-79 D 6
Chāčharān 72-73 K 4
Chachoengsao 52-53 D 4
Chad 60-61 HJ 5
Chadasan 48-49 J 2
Chadchal = Chatgal 48-49 HJ 1
Chadum 64-65 F 6
Chadzaar 48-49 G 4
Chaeryŏng 50-51 EF 3
Chagang-do 50-51 EF 2
Chagan nuur 48-49 L 3
Chaghcharān 44-45 K 4
Chagny 34-35 K 5
Chagos 22-23 N 6
Chagres [PA, ~] 72-73 ab 2
Chagres [PA, ●] 72-73 b 2
Chagres, Brazo del – 72-73 b 2
Chagres, Río – 72-73 bc 2
Chagres Arm = Brazo del Chagres 72-73 b 2
Chahār Burjak 44-45 J 4
Chāhār Burjak = Chahār Burjak 44-45 J 4
Chahār Maḥāl-e Bakhteyārī = 3 ◁ 44-45 G 4
Chahbā = Shahbā' 46-47 G 6
Chāh Bāhār = Bandar-e Chāh Bahār 44-45 HJ 5
Ch'aho 50-51 G 2
Chaidamu Pendi = Tsaidam 48-49 GH 4
Ch'ail-bong 50-51 F 2
Chai Nat 52-53 D 3
Chaîne Pontique 44-45 C-E 2
Chaîne Rocheuse = Rocky Mountains 70-71 L 5-P 9
Chaiya 52-53 C 5
Chajari 80 E 4
Chajdag gol 48-49 EF 3
Chajlar 48-49 M 2
Chajlar = Hailar 48-49 M 2
Chajlar gol = Hailar He 48-49 MN 2
Chajpudyrskaja guba 38-39 LM 2
Chajrchan 48-49 J 2
Chajr'uzovo 42-43 e 6
Chaka Nor = Chöch nuur 48-49 H 4
Chake Chake 63 DE 4
Chāl = Shāl 46-47 N 5
Chala 78-79 E 8
Chalabesa 63 B 5
Cha-lan-tun = Yalu 48-49 N 2
Chalbi Desert 63 D 2
Chalchyn gol 48-49 M 2
Chaleur Bay 70-71 XY 8
Chalhuanca 78-79 E 7
Cha-ling Hu = Kyaring Tsho 48-49 H 5
Chálkē 36-37 M 7
Chalkidikē 36-37 K 3
Chalkis 36-37 K 6
Chal'mer-Ju 42-43 L 4
Chalmer-Sede = Tazovskij 42-43 OP 4
Châlons-sur-Marne 34-35 JK 4
Chalon-sur-Saône 34-35 K 5
Chalosse 34-35 G 7
Chalturin 42-43 H 6
Challapata 78-79 F 8
Challis, ID 76-77 F 3
Cham 33 F 4
Chaman 44-45 K 4
Chamba [EAT] 63 D 5
Chamba [IND] 44-45 M 4
Chambal [IND ◁ Kali Sindh] 44-45 M 5-6
Chambal [IND ◁ Yamuna] 44-45 M 5-6
Chamberlain Lake 74-75 J 1
Chambersburg, PA 74-75 DE 4-5
Chambéry 34-35 K 6
Chambeshi 64-65 H 5
Chamchamāl 46-47 L 5
Chamdo = Chhamdo 48-49 H 5
Chami Choto = Hami 48-49 G 3
Chamo, Lake – = Tyamo 60-61 M 7
Champa [IND] 44-45 N 6
Champa [SU] 42-43 X 5
Champagne 34-35 J 5-K 4
Champagny Islands 56-57 D 3
Champaign, IL 72-73 J 3-4
Champāran = Motihari 44-45 NO 5
Champasak 52-53 DE 4
Champlain, Lake – 72-73 LM 3
Champotón 72-73 H 8
Chanāb = Chenab 44-45 M 4
Chan Bogd 48-49 K 3
Chancay 78-79 D 7
Chanch 48-49 J 1
Chan-chiang = Zhanjiang 48-49 L 7
Chanchoengsao 52-53 D 4
Chānda = Chandrapur 44-45 M 7
Chandalar River 70-71 G 4
Chandeleur Islands 72-73 J 6
Chandigarh 44-45 LM 4
Chandler 70-71 Y 8
Chandler, AZ 76-77 H 9
Chandlers Falls 63 D 2
Chandrapur 44-45 M 7
Chandyga 42-43 a 5
Chang, Ko – [T → Krung Thep] 52-53 D 4
Changai = Shanghai 48-49 N 5
Changaj 48-49 H 2
Changajn nuruu 48-49 HJ 2
Ch'ang-an = Xi'an 48-49 K 5
Changane, Rio – 64-65 H 7
Changara 64-65 H 6
Changbai 50-51 FG 2
Changbai Shan 48-49 O 3
Chang-chia-k'ou = Zhangjiakou 48-49 L 3
Changchih = Changzhi 48-49 L 4
Ch'ang-chih = Changzhi 48-49 L 4
Changchun 48-49 NO 3
Changde 48-49 L 6
Changdu = Chhamdo 48-49 H 5
Chang-hai = Shanghai 48-49 N 5
Changhang 50-51 F 4-5
Changhowŏn 50-51 F 4
Ch'ang-hsing Tao = Changxing Dao 50-51 C 3
Changhŭng 50-51 F 5
Changhŭng-ni 50-51 FG 2
Chang Jiang [TJ, ~ ◁ Dong Hai] 48-49 K 5-6
Changji Huizu Zizhizhou 48-49 FG 3
Changjin 50-51 F 2
Changjin-gang 50-51 F 2
Changjin-ho 50-51 F 2
Changjŏn 50-51 G 3
Changkiakow = Zhangjiakou 48-49 L 3
Chang-kuang-ts'ai Ling = Zhangguangcai Ling 48-49 O 2-3
Changnim-ni 50-51 F 3
Ch'angnyŏng 50-51 G 5
Ch'ang-pai = Changbai 50-51 FG 2
Ch'ang-pai Shan = Changbai Shan 48-49 O 3
Chang-san-ying = Zhangsanying 50-51 AB 2
Changsha 48-49 L 6
Changshu 48-49 N 5
Ch'angsŏng = Chongsŏng 50-51 GH 1
Chang Tang = Jang Thang 48-49 E-G 5
Ch'ang-tê = Anyang 48-49 LM 4
Ch'ang-tê = Changde 48-49 L 6
Changteh = Changde 48-49 L 6
Changting 48-49 M 6
Ch'ang-tu = Chhamdo 48-49 H 5
Changtutsung = Chhamdo 48-49 H 5
Ch'angwŏn 50-51 G 5
Changxing Dao [TJ, Liaodong Wan] 50-51 C 3
Changyeh = Zhangye 48-49 J 4
Changyŏn 48-49 NO 4
Changzhi 48-49 L 4
Changzhou 48-49 M 5
Chaniá 36-37 KL 8
Chaniŏn, Kólpos – 36-37 KL 8
Chanka, ozero – 42-43 Z 9
Chankiang = Zhanjiang 48-49 L 7
Channāb = Chenab 44-45 M 4
Channel Islands [GB] 32 E 7
Channel Islands [USA] 76-77 CD 9
Channel Islands National Monument = Anacapa Island, Santa Barbara Island 76-77 D 9
Channel-Port-aux-Basques 70-71 Z 8
Chanovej 38-39 M 2
Chansi = Shanxi 48-49 L 4
Chantaburi = Chanthaburi 52-53 D 4
Chantada 34-35 CD 7
Chantajka 42-43 PQ 4
Chantajskoje, ozero – 42-43 QR 4
Chanten en Mansen, Nationaal Gebied der – 42-43 L-P 5
Chan Tengri, pik – 44-45 MN 2
Chanthaburi 52-53 D 4
Chantong = Shandong 48-49 M 4
Chantrey Inlet 70-71 RS 4
Chanty-Mansijsk 42-43 M 5
Chanty y los Mansi, Circunscripción Nacional de los – 42-43 L-P 5
Chañar 80 C 4
Chañaral [RCH ↖ Copiapó] 80 B 3
Chañaral, Isla – 80 B 3
Chao'an 48-49 M 7
Chaochow = Chao'an 48-49 M 7
Chao Hu 48-49 M 5
Chao Phraya, Mae Nam – 52-53 CD 3-4
Chaor He 48-49 N 2
Chaotung = Zhaotong 48-49 J 6
Chao-t'ung = Zhaotong 48-49 J 6
Chaoyang [TJ, Guangdong] 48-49 M 7
Chaoyang [TJ, Liaoning] 48-49 MN 3
Ch'ao-yang-chên = Huinan 48-49 O 3
Chapada da Veadeiros, Parque Nacional dos – 78-79 K 7
Chapada Diamantina 78-79 L 7
Chapadinha 78-79 L 5
Chapala, Lago de – 72-73 F 7
Chapčeranga 42-43 V 8
Chapel Hill, NC 74-75 D 7
Chapra 44-45 N 5
Chaqui 78-79 F 8
Chā'r, Jebel – = Jabal Shā'r 46-47 GH 5
Charadai 80 E 3
Charagua 78-79 G 8
Charagua, Cordillera de – 78-79 G 8-9
Char Ajrag 48-49 KL 2
Charaña 78-79 F 8
Charbin = Harbin 48-49 O 2
Chār Burjak 44-45 J 4
Charcas 72-73 F 7
Charcot, Île – 24 C 29
Chārchān 48-49 F 4
Chārchān Darya 48-49 F 4
Char Chorin 48-49 J 2
Char Choto 48-49 J 3
Chardāvol 46-47 M 6
Chardon, OH 74-75 C 4
Charente 34-35 G 6
Char Gov' 48-49 GH 3
Chari 60-61 H 6
Chārīkār 44-45 K 3-4
Char Irčis 48-49 F 2
Charitona Lapteva, bereg – 42-43 Q 3-R 2
Charity 78-79 H 3
Char'kov 38-39 G 5-6
Charleroi 34-35 K 3
Charles, Cape – 72-73 LM 4
Charles Island 70-71 VW 5
Charleston, SC 72-73 KL 5
Charleston, WV 72-73 K 4
Charleston Peak 76-77 F 7
Charlestown 72-73 O 8
Charlesville 64-65 F 4
Charleville [AUS] 56-57 J 5
Charleville-Mézières 34-35 K 4
Charlotte, NC 72-73 KL 4-5
Charlotte Amalie 72-73 O 8
Charlotte Harbor 72-73 K 6
Charlottenberg 30-31 E 8
Charlottesville, VA 72-73 L 4
Charlottetown 70-71 Y 8
Charlottetown = Roseau 72-73 O 8
Charlovka 38-39 G 2
Charlton 58 F 6
Charlton Island 70-71 UV 7
Char Narijn uul 48-49 K 3
Char nuur [MVR] 48-49 G 2
Char nuur [TJ] 48-49 H 4
Charolais, Monts du – 34-35 K 5
Charovsk 42-43 G 6
Charqī, Jebel ech- = Jabal ar-Ruwāq 46-47 G 5-6
Charqiliq 48-49 F 4
Charters Towers 56-57 J 3-4
Chartres 34-35 H 4
Char us nuur 48-49 G 2
Chasan 50-51 H 1
Chasavjurt 38-39 J 7
Chascomús 80 E 5
Chase City, VA 74-75 D 6
Chasŏng 50-51 F 2
Chassahowitzka Bay 74-75 b 2
Chašuri 38-39 H 7
Chatanga 42-43 TU 3
Chatan gol 48-49 K 3
Chatangskij zaliv 42-43 UV 3
Châteaubriant 34-35 G 5
Château-du-Loir 34-35 H 5
Châteaudun 34-35 H 4
Châteaulin 34-35 EF 4
Châteauroux 34-35 H 5
Château-Thierry 34-35 J 4
Châtellerault 34-35 H 5
Chatgal 48-49 HJ 1
Chatham [CDN, New Brunswick] 70-71 XY 8
Chatham [CDN, Ontario] 70-71 U 9
Chatham, NY 74-75 G 3
Chatham, VA 74-75 D 6
Chatham = Isla San Cristóbal 78-79 B 5
Chatham, Îles – 56-57 Q 8
Chatham, Isla – 80 B 8
Chatham Islands 56-57 Q 8
Chatham Strait 70-71 K 6
Châtillon 36-37 B 3
Châtillon-sur-Seine 34-35 K 5
Chatsworth 74-75 C 2
Chāṭṭagām 44-45 P 6
Chattahoochee River 72-73 JK 5
Chattanooga, TN 72-73 J 4
Chattarpur = Chhatarpur 44-45 M 6
Châu Đôc = Châu Phu 52-53 E 4
Chaumont 34-35 K 4
Chaŭn-do 50-51 EF 5
Châu Phu 52-53 E 4
Chautauqua Lake 74-75 D 3
Chaux-de-Fonds, La – 33 C 5
Chavast 44-45 K 2
Chaves 34-35 D 8
Chaves [BR] 78-79 K 5

Chave 169

Chaves, Isla – = Isla Santa Cruz 78-79 AB 5
Chavīb Deh 46-47 N 7
Chaviva 78-79 E 4
Chaya = Drayä 48-49 H 5
Ch'a-yü = Dsayul 48-49 H 6
Chazón 80 D 4

Cheat Mountain 74-75 CD 5
Cheat River 74-75 D 5
Cheb 33 F 3
Chebāyesh, Al- = Al-Jaza'ir 46-47 M 7
Chebir, Uáu el – = Wādī Bay al-Kabīr 60-61 GH 2
Cheboygan, MI 72-73 K 2
Chech, Erg – = 'Irq ash-Shaykh 60-61 D 3-4
Chechaouène = Shifshāwn 60-61 CD 1
Chechenes e Ingush, República Autónoma de los – = 5 ◁ 38-39 J 7
Checheno-Ingush Autonomous Republic = 5 ◁ 38-39 J 7
Chech'on 50-51 G 4
Chedâdî, El- = Ash-Shiddādī 46-47 J 4
Cheektowaga, NY 74-75 DE 3
Cheepie 56-57 HJ 5
Chefoo = Yantai 48-49 N 4
Chefu = Yantai 48-49 N 4
Chegga = Ash-Shaqqāt 60-61 C 3
Chegutu 64-65 GH 6
Chehalis, WA 76-77 B 2
Chehalis River 76-77 B 2
Chehel-e Chashmeh, Kūhhā-ye – 46-47 M 5
Cheikh Aḥmed = Shaykh Ahmad 46-47 J 4
Cheikh Hlâl = Shaykh Hilāl 46-47 G 5
Cheikh Ṣalâḥ = Shaykh Salāh 46-47 J 4
Cheikh Zerâfâ = Zilāf 46-47 G 6
Cheju 48-49 O 5
Cheju-do 48-49 NO 5
Cheju-haehyŏp 48-49 O 5
Chekiang = Zhejiang 48-49 MN 6
Chekkâ, Râs – = Rā's ash-Shikk'ah 46-47 F 5
Chela, Serra da – 64-65 D 6
Chelan, WA 76-77 CD 2
Chelan, Lake – 76-77 C 1
Chélia, Djebel – = Jabal Shīlyah 60-61 F 1
Chê-ling Kuan = Zheling Guan 48-49 L 6
Chełm 33 L 3
Chełmińskre, Pojezierze – 33 J 2
Chełmża 33 J 2
Chelsea, VT 74-75 G 2-3
Cheltenham 32 EF 6
Cheltenham, PA 74-75 F 4
Chelyuskin, Cape – = mys Čel'uskin 42-43 UV 2
Chelleh Khāneh, Kūh-e – 46-47 N 4
Chemawa, OR 76-77 B 3
Chemba 64-65 H 6
Chemehuevi Valley Indian Reservation 76-77 F 8
Chemnitz 33 F 3
Chemulpo = Inch'ŏn 48-49 O 4
Chemult, OR 76-77 C 4
Chenab 44-45 M 4
Ch'ên-ch'i = Chenxi 48-49 L 6
Chên-chiang = Zhenjiang 48-49 M 5
Ch'ên-chou = Yuanling 48-49 L 6
Cheney, WA 76-77 E 2
Chên-fan = Minqin 48-49 J 4
Ch'êng-chiang = Chengjiang 48-49 J 7
Chengde 48-49 M 3
Chengdu 48-49 J 5
Chengjiang 48-49 J 7
Chengkiang = Chengjiang 48-49 J 7
Chengkou 48-49 K 5
Chengmai 48-49 KL 8
Chengteh = Chengde 48-49 M 3
Chengtu = Chengdu 48-49 J 5
Cheng-Xian = Sheng Xian 48-49 N 6
Chengzitan 50-51 D 3
Chên-hsi = Bar Köl 48-49 G 3
Chenkiang = Zhenjiang 48-49 M 5
Chennapaṭṭaṇam = Madras 44-45 N 8
Chensi = Bar Köl 48-49 G 3
Chensi = Shanxi 48-49 L 4
Chentiin nuruu 48-49 K 2
Chentij = 15 ◁ 48-49 L 2
Chenxi 48-49 L 6
Chen Xian 48-49 L 6
Chenyang = Shenyang 48-49 NO 3
Chenyuan = Zhenyuan [TJ, Yunnan] 48-49 J 7
Chên-yüan = Zhenyuan [TJ, Yunnan] 48-49 J 7
Chepes 80 C 4
Cher 34-35 J 5
Cherangani 63 C 2
Cheraw, SC 74-75 CD 7
Cherbourg 34-35 G 4
Cherchen = Chärchän 48-49 F 4
Cheren = Keren 60-61 M 5
Chergui, Chott ech – = Ash-Shaṭṭ ash-Sharqī 60-61 DE 2
Cherlen gol 48-49 KL 2
Cherlen gol = Herlen He 48-49 M 2
Cherrapunj = Cherrapunjee 44-45 P 5
Cherrapunjee 44-45 P 5
Cherry 56-57 N 2
Cherry Creek, NV 76-77 F 6
Cherson 38-39 F 6
Chesapeake, VA 72-73 LM 4
Chesapeake Bay 72-73 L 4
Cheshire, OR 76-77 B 3
Chesley 74-75 C 2
Chester 32 E 5
Chester, CA 76-77 C 5
Chester, MT 76-77 H 1
Chester, PA 74-75 F 5
Chester, SC 74-75 C 7
Chesterfield 32 F 5
Chesterfield, Île – 64-65 K 6
Chesterfield, Îles – 56-57 L 3
Chesterfield Inlet [CDN, ∪] 70-71 ST 5
Chesterfield Inlet [CDN, ●] 70-71 ST 5
Chestertown, MD 74-75 EF 5
Chesuncook Lake 74-75 HJ 1-2
Cheta [SU, ~] 42-43 S 3
Cheta [SU, ●] 42-43 S 3
Chetlat Island 44-45 L 8
Chetumal 72-73 J 8
Chetumal, Bahía de – 72-73 J 8
Cheviot, The – 32 EF 4
Cheviot Hills 32 E 4
Chewelah, WA 76-77 DE 1
Cheyenne, WY 72-73 F 3
Cheyenne River 72-73 F 3

Chhamdo 48-49 H 5
Chhaprā = Chapra 44-45 N 5
Chhārīkār = Chārikār 44-45 K 3-4
Chhatarpur [IND, Madhya Pradesh] 44-45 M 6
Chhattisgarh 44-45 N 6
Chhergundo 48-49 H 5
Chhergundo Zhou = Yushu Zangzu Zizhizhou 48-49 GH 5
Chhibchang Tsho 48-49 G 5
Chhindvāṛā = Chhindwara [IND ← Seoni] 44-45 M 6
Chhindwara [IND ← Seoni] 44-45 M 6
Chhōṭā Andamān = Little Andaman 44-45 P 8
Chhōṭā Nikōbār = Little Nicobar 44-45 P 9
Chhumar 48-49 G 4-5
Chhushul 48-49 FG 6

Chia-hsing = Jiaxing 48-49 N 5
Chia-i 48-49 MN 7
Chia-li = Lharugö 48-49 G 5
Chia-ling Chiang = Jialing Jiang 48-49 K 5
Chia-mu-szŭ = Jiamusi 48-49 P 2
Chi-an = Ji'an [TJ, Jiangxi] 48-49 LM 6
Chi-an = Ji'an [TJ, Jilin] 50-51 EF 2
Chiang-chou = Xinjiang 48-49 L 4
Chiang Dao 52-53 CD 3
Chiange 64-65 D 6
Chiang-hsi = Jiangxi 48-49 LM 6
Chiang Khan 52-53 D 3
Chiang Mai 52-53 CD 3
Chiang Rai 52-53 CD 3
Chiang-su = Jiangsu 48-49 MN 5
Chiapa, Rio – = Rio Grande 72-73 H 8
Chiapas 72-73 H 8
Chiari 36-37 CD 3
Chiávari 36-37 C 3
Chiavenna 36-37 C 2
Chiba 50-51 N 5
Chibabava 64-65 H 7
Chibemba 64-65 DE 6
Chibia 64-65 D 6
Chibinogorsk = Kirovsk 42-43 EF 4
Chibiny 38-39 F 2
Chibougamau 70-71 VW 7-8
Chiburi-jima 50-51 J 5
Chibuto 64-65 H 7
Chicacole = Shrikakulam 44-45 N 7
Chicago, IL 72-73 J 3
Chicapa, Rio – 64-65 F 4
Chic-Chocs, Monts – 70-71 X 8
Chickasha, OK 72-73 G 4-5
Chiclayo 78-79 CD 6
Chico, CA 72-73 B 4
Chico, Rio – [RA, Chubut] 80 C 6
Chico, Rio – [YV] 78-79 F 2
Chico, Rio – [RA, Santa Cruz ◁ Bahía Grande] 80 C 7
Chico, Rio – [RA, Santa Cruz ◁ Rio Gallegos] 80 C 7
Chicoa 64-65 H 6
Chicoana 80 CD 3
Chiconomo 63 CD 6
Chicopee, MA 74-75 G 3
Chicoutimi 70-71 WX 8
Chicualacuala 64-65 H 7
Ch'i-ch = Qiqihar 48-49 N 2
Chichagof Island 70-71 J 6
Chichén Itzá 72-73 J 7
Chichester 32 F 6
Chidley, Cape – 70-71 Y 5
Chi-do 50-51 EF 5
Chiefland, FL 74-75 b 2
Chiehmo = Chärchän 48-49 F 4
Chiemsee 33 F 5
Chien-ch'ang = Jianchang [TJ → Benxi] 50-51 E 2
Chien-ch'ang = Jianchang [TJ ✓ Jinzhou] 50-51 B 2
Ch'ien-chiang = Qianjiang [TJ, Hubei] 48-49 L 5
Chiengi 64-65 G 4
Chiengmai = Chiang Mai 52-53 C 3
Chien-Ho = Jian He [TJ, ~] 50-51 D 2
Chien-ko = Jiange 48-49 JK 5
Chien-ning = Jian'ou 48-49 M 6
Chien-ou = Jian'ou 48-49 M 6
Chien-p'ing = Jianping 50-51 B 2
Chien-shui = Jianshui 48-49 J 7
Ch'ien-wei = Qianwei 50-51 C 2
Chien-yang = Jianyang [TJ, Sichuan] 48-49 JK 5
Chieti 36-37 F 4
Chifeng 48-49 M 3
Chifre, Serra do – 78-79 L 8
Chignik, AK 70-71 E 6
Chigyŏng 50-51 F 3
Chih-chiang = Zhijiang [TJ, Hunan] 48-49 KL 6
Ch'ih-fêng = Chifeng 48-49 M 3
Chih-fu = Yantai 48-49 N 4
Chihkiang = Zhijiang 48-49 KL 6
Chih-li Wan = Bo Hai 48-49 M 4
Chi-hsi = Jixi 48-49 P 2
Chihuahua 72-73 E 6
Chii-san = Chiri-san 50-51 F 5
Chike = Xunke 48-49 O 2
Chikugo 50-51 H 6
Chikwawa 64-65 HJ 6
Chilapa de Alvarez 72-73 G 8
Chilās 44-45 L 3
Chilca 78-79 D 7
Chilcoot, CA 76-77 CD 6
Chile, Cuenca de – 22-23 E 7-F 6
Chile Basin 22-23 EF 6-7
Chilecito [RA, La Rioja] 80 C 3
Chilete 78-79 D 6
Chili 80 B 5-C 2
Chili, Bassin du – 22-23 E 7-F 6
Chilia, Braţul – 36-37 N 3
Chilibekken 22-23 EF 6-7
Chilibre 72-73 b 2
Ch'i-lien Shan = Qilian Shan 48-49 HJ 4
Chilika Hrada = Chilka Lake 44-45 NO 7
Chililabombwe 64-65 G 5
Chi-lin = Jilin [TJ, ●] 48-49 O 3
Chi-lin = Jilin [TJ, ☆] 48-49 N 2-O 3
Chilivani 36-37 C 5
Chilka Lake 44-45 NO 7
Chilko Lake 70-71 M 7
Chiloé, Isla de – 80 AB 6
Chilok 42-43 UV 7
Chilonga 63 B 5-6
Chilongozi 63 BC 6
Chiloquin, OR 76-77 C 4
Chilpancingo de los Bravos 72-73 G 8
Chiltern Hills 32 F 6
Chilung = Kee-lung 48-49 N 6
Chilwa, Lake – 64-65 J 6
Chillán 80 B 5
Chill Chainnigh = Kilkenny 32 C 5
Chillicothe, MO 72-73 H 3-4
Chillicothe, OH 72-73 K 4
Chilly, ID 76-77 FG 3
Chiman tagh 48-49 FG 4
Chimborazo [EC, ▲] 78-79 D 5
Chimbote 78-79 D 6
Chimoio 64-65 H 6
Chimpay 80 C 5
Chimpembe 63 B 5
China, Republiek – 48-49 N 7
China Lake, CA 76-77 E 8
China Meridional, Cuenca de – 52-53 FG 3-4
China Meridional, Mar de – 52-53 E 5-G 3
Chinan 50-51 F 5
Chinan = Jinan 48-49 M 4
Ch'in-an = Qin'an 48-49 K 5
Chinandega 72-73 J 9
China Oriental, Mar de – 48-49 N 6-O 5
Chinapa 76-77 HJ 10
China Point 76-77 D 9
Chinbo 50-51 G 4
Chincoteague, VA 74-75 F 6
Chincoteague Bay 74-75 F 5
Chincha Alta 78-79 D 7
Chin-ch'êng = Jincheng 48-49 L 4
Chinchilla 56-57 K 5
Chinchilla de Monte-Aragón 34-35 G 9
Chinchorro, Banco – 72-73 J 8
Chinchow = Jinzhou 48-49 N 3
Chinde 64-65 J 6
Chin-do [ROK, ⊙] 50-51 EF 5
Chindo [ROK, ●] 50-51 F 5
Chindwin Myit 52-53 C 1-2
Chine 48-49 E-K 5
Chine Méridionale, Mer de – 52-53 E 5-G 3
Chine Orientale, Mer de – 48-49 N 6-O 5
Chinese muur 48-49 K 4
Ching-ch'uan = Yinchuan 48-49 JK 4
Ch'ing Hai = Chöch nuur 48-49 H 4
Chinghai = Qinghai 48-49 GH 4
Ching-ho = Jinghe [TJ, ●] 48-49 E 3
Ch'ing-ho-ch'êng = Qinghecheng 50-51 E 2
Ch'ing-ho-mêng = Qinghemen 50-51 C 2
Ching-ku = Jinggu 48-49 J 7
Ching-ning = Jingning 48-49 K 4
Chingola 64-65 G 5
Chingombe 63 B 6
Ching-po Hu = Jingbo Hu 48-49 O 3
Ching-t'ai = Jingtai 48-49 J 4
Ch'ing-tao = Qingdao 48-49 N 4
Ch'ing-tui-tzŭ = Qingduizi 50-51 D 3
Ching-tung = Jingdong 48-49 J 7
Ch'ing-yang = Qingyang [TJ, Gansu] 48-49 K 4
Ching-yüan = Jingyuan 48-49 JK 4
Ch'ing-yüan = Qingyuan [TJ, Liaoning] 50-51 E 1
Chinhae 50-51 G 5
Chinhae-man 50-51 G 5
Chinhoyi 64-65 GH 6
Chin-hsien = Jin Xian [TJ, Liaoning ↗ Jinzhou] 50-51 C 2
Chin-hsien = Jin Xian [TJ, Liaoning ↑ Lüda] 48-49 N 4
Chinhsien = Jinzhou 48-49 N 3
Chin-hua = Jinhua 48-49 MN 6
Ch'in-huang-tao = Qinhuangdao 48-49 MN 3-4
Chi-ning = Jining [TJ, Nei Monggol Zizhiqu] 48-49 L 3
Chi-ning = Jining [TJ, Shandong] 48-49 M 4
Chinju 48-49 O 4
Chinko 60-61 J 7
Chinle, AZ 76-77 J 7
Chinle Valley 76-77 J 7
Ch'in Ling = Qin Ling 48-49 KL 5
Chin-mên Tao 48-49 M 7
Chinnamp'o = Nampo 48-49 NO 4
Chinon 34-35 H 5
Chino Valley, AZ 76-77 G 8
Chinquião = Zhenjiang 48-49 M 5
Chinsali 64-65 H 5
Chin-sha Chiang = Jinsha Jiang 48-49 J 6
Chinsura 44-45 O 6
Chinwangtao = Qinhuangdao 48-49 MN 3-4
Chinwithetha Pyinnei 52-53 B 2
Ch'in-yang = Qinyang 48-49 L 4
Chinyŏng 50-51 G 5
Chiôco 64-65 H 6
Chióggia 36-37 E 3
Chios [GR, ⊙] 36-37 L 6
Chios [GR, ●] 36-37 M 6
Chipata 64-65 H 5
Chipili 63 B 5
Chipinge 64-65 H 7
Chipoka 63 C 6
Chiporiro 64-65 H 6
Chipre 44-45 C 3
Chiputneticook Lakes 74-75 JK 2
Chiquimula 72-73 HJ 9
Chiquitos, Llanos de – 78-79 G 8
Chira 63 D 2
Chira Bazar 48-49 DE 4
Chiraz = Shīrāz 44-45 G 5
Chiredzi 64-65 H 7
Chirfa 60-61 G 4
Chiricahua National Monument 76-77 J 9-10
Chiricahua Peak 76-77 J 10
Chirikof Island 70-71 EF 6
Chiriquí, Golfo de – 72-73 K 10
Chiriquí, Laguna de – 72-73 K 9-10
Chiri-san 50-51 F 5
Chiromo 64-65 J 6
Chirripó Grande, Cerro – 72-73 K 10
Chirundu 64-65 G 6
Chisamba 64-65 G 5-6
Chisel Lake 70-71 QR 7
Chi-shih Shan = Amnyemachhen Gangri 48-49 HJ 5
Chishtian Mandi = Chishtiyān Maṇḍī 44-45 L 5
Chishtiyān Maṇḍī 44-45 L 5
Chisimaio = Kismaayo 64-65 K 3
Chişinău 38-39 E 6
Chitado 64-65 D 6
Chita-hantō 50-51 L 5
Ch'i-t'ai = Qitai 48-49 FG 3
Chitambo 63 B 6
Chitembo 64-65 E 5
Chitogarh = Chittaurgarh 44-45 L 6
Chitose 50-51 b 2
Chitradurga 44-45 M 8
Chitrāl 44-45 L 3
Chitré 72-73 K 10
Chittagong = Chāṭṭagām 44-45 P 6
Chittaldurga = Chitradurga 44-45 M 8
Chittaorgarh = Chittaurgarh 44-45 L 6
Chittaurgarh 44-45 L 6
Chittoor 44-45 M 8
Chittoor = Chittor 44-45 M 8
Chiuchuan = Jiuquan 48-49 H 4
Chiulezi, Rio – 63 D 5-6
Chiumbe, Rio – 64-65 F 4
Chiume 64-65 F 5-6
Ch'iung-chou Hai-hsia = Qiongzhou Haixia 48-49 KL 7
Chiungshan = Qiongshan 48-49 L 8
Ch'iung-tung = Qionghai 48-49 L 8
Chiuta, Lagoa – 64-65 J 5
Chiva [SU] 42-43 L 9
Chivasso 36-37 B 3
Chivay 78-79 E 8
Chivilcoy 80 DE 4
Chivu 64-65 H 6
Chiwanda 64-65 HJ 5
Chiwefwe 63 B 6
Chiweta 64-65 H 5
Chixoy, Rio – 72-73 H 8

Chjargas 48-49 G 2
Chjargas nuur 48-49 GH 2

Chloride, AZ 76-77 F 8

Chmeiṭīyé = Shmayṭīyah 46-47 H 5
Chmelnickij 38-39 E 6

Chobe 64-65 F 6
Chobe National Park 64-65 FG 6
Chocaya 78-79 F 9
Chocca 78-79 D 7
Chocolate Mountains 76-77 F 9
Chocontá 78-79 E 3
Chochiang = Charqiliq 48-49 F 4
Choch'iwŏn 50-51 F 4
Chöch nuur 48-49 H 4
Chöch Šili 48-49 G 4
Chöch Šili uul 48-49 FG 4
Ch'o-do [Nordkorea] 50-51 E 3-4
Ch'o-do [ROK] 50-51 F 5
Chodžambas 44-45 JK 3
Chodžejli 42-43 K 9
Chodžent = Leninabad 44-45 KL 2-3
Chodzież 33 H 2
Choele-Choel 80 CD 5
Choibalsan = Čojbalsan 48-49 L 2
Choiseul 52-53 j 6
Chojna 33 G 2
Chojnice 33 HJ 2
Chōkai-zan 50-51 MN 3
Chōḷamaṇḍala = Coromandel Coast 44-45 N 7-8
Cholame, CA 76-77 CD 8
Chold = Chuld 48-49 K 2-3
Cholet 34-35 G 5
Cholgwan 50-51 E 3
Cholm 38-39 F 4
Cholmogory 42-43 G 5
Cholmsk 42-43 b 8
Cholodnoje 38-39 N 3
Cholos nuur 48-49 H 4
Ch'ŏlsan 50-51 E 3
Choluteca 72-73 J 9
Chŏlla-namdo 50-51 F 5
Chŏlla-pukto 50-51 F 5
Choma 64-65 G 6
Chomba 63 D 5
Ch'ŏnan 50-51 F 4
Chon Buri 52-53 D 4
Chŏnch'ŏn 50-51 F 2
Chone 78-79 CD 5
Ch'ŏng'chŏn-gang 50-51 EF 2-3
Chongdjin = Ch'ŏngjin 48-49 OP 3
Chŏnggŏ-dong 50-51 E 3
Ch'ŏngha 50-51 G 4
Ch'ŏngjin 48-49 OP 3
Chongjin = Ch'ŏngjin 48-49 OP 3
Chŏngju 48-49 O 4
Chongming 48-49 N 5
Chongor 48-49 L 2
Chongor = Bajan Adraga 48-49 KL 2
Chongor Oboo Sum = Bajandalaj 48-49 J 3
Chongor Tagh = Qungur tagh 48-49 D 4
Ch'ŏngp'yŏngch'ŏn 50-51 FG 4
Chongqing 48-49 K 6
Ch'ŏngsan-do 50-51 F 5
Chongshan = Chongzuo 48-49 K 7
Ch'ongsŏktu-ri 50-51 EF 3
Chongsŏng 50-51 GH 1
Chŏngŭp 50-51 F 5
Ch'ŏngyang [ROK] 50-51 F 4
Chongzuo 48-49 K 7
Chŏnju 48-49 O 4
Chonos, Archipiélago de los – 80 AB 6-7
Chonuu 42-43 b 4
Chooloj Gov' 48-49 H 3
Chop'or 38-39 H 5-6
Chor 42-43 Za 8
Chorasan = Khorāsān 44-45 H 3-4
Chôra Sfakion 36-37 L 8
Chordogoj 42-43 W 5
Chor He 48-49 N 2
Chorinsk 42-43 U 7
Chorog 44-45 L 3
Chorrera, La – Chorrera [PA] 72-73 b 3
Chorsabad = Khorsabad 46-47 K 4
Chŏrwŏn 50-51 F 3
Chŏryŏng-do = Yŏng-do 50-51 G 5
Chorzele 33 K 2
Chorzów 33 J 3
Chosedachard 38-39 L 2
Chōsen-kaikyō 48-49 O 5
Chōshi 50-51 N 5
Chos-Malal 80 BC 5
Chosŏn-man = Tonghan-man 48-49 O 4
Choszczno 33 GH 2
Chota 78-79 D 6
Chota Nāgpur 44-45 NO 6
Choteau, MT 76-77 G 2
Chotin 38-39 E 6
Chou Shan = Zhoushan Dao 48-49 N 5-6
Chou-shan Ch'ün-tao = Zhoushan Qundao 48-49 N 5
Chovd [MVR, ●] 48-49 G 2
Chovd [MVR, ☆ = 3 ◁] 48-49 G 2
Chovd gol 48-49 G 2
Chövsgöl [MVR, ●] 48-49 KL 3
Chövsgöl [MVR, ☆ = 6 ◁] 48-49 J 1
Chövsgöl nuur 48-49 J 1
Chowan River 74-75 E 6
Chowchilla, CA 76-77 C 7

Christchurch [NZ] 56-57 OP 8
Christian Island 74-75 C 2
Christiansburg, VA 74-75 CD 6
Christianshåb = Qasigiánguir 70-71 ab 4
Christie Bay 70-71 O 5
Christmas Creek 56-57 E 3
Christmas Island [AUS] 52-53 E 9
Chromtau 42-43 K 7
Chrudim 33 GH 4
Chrysé 36-37 LM 8
Chrysochûs, Kólpos – 46-47 E 5

Chuang-ho = Zhuanghe 50-51 D 3
Chubb Crater = New Quebec Crater 70-71 VW 5
Chubbuck, CA 76-77 F 8
Chubisgalt = Chövsgöl 48-49 KL 3
Chubsugul = Chövsgöl nuur 48-49 J 1
Chūbu 50-51 LM 4-5
Chubut 80 BC 6
Chubut, Rio – 80 C 6
Chucheng = Zhucheng 48-49 MN 4
Chu-chi = Zhuji 48-49 N 6
Ch'ü-ching = Qujing 48-49 J 6
Ch'ü-chou = Qu Xian 48-49 M 6
Chu-chou = Zhuzhou 48-49 L 6
Chuchow = Zhuzhou 48-49 L 6
Ch'üeh-shan = Queshan 48-49 L 5
Chugach Mountains 70-71 GH 5
Chugoku 50-51 HJ 5
Chūgoku-sammyaku 50-51 JK 5
Chuguchak 48-49 E 2
Chūgūchak = Tarbagataj 48-49 EF 2
Chuhsien = Qu Xian 48-49 M 6
Ch'u-hsiung = Chuxiong 48-49 J 7
Chü-hua Tao = Juhua Dao 50-51 C 2
Ch'uja-do 50-51 F 6
Chukchi Plateau 19 B 35
Chukchi Sea 19 BC 35-36
Chukchos, Circunscripción Nacional de los – 42-43 g-j 4
Chukchos, Dorsal de – 19 B 35
Chukchos, Mar de – 19 BC 35-36
Chuki = Zhuji 48-49 N 6

170 Chave

Chukot Autonomous Area 42-43 g-j 4
Chukudu Kraal 64-65 F 7
Chūl, Gardaneh-ye – 46-47 MN 6
Chulaq Aqqan Su 48-49 G 4
Chula Vista, CA 72-73 C 5
Chuld 48-49 K 2-3
Chulga 38-39 M 3
Chü-liu-ho = Juliuhe 50-51 D 1
Chulp'o 50-51 F 5
Chulucanas 78-79 CD 6
Chulumani 78-79 F 8
Chumbicha 80 C 3
Chum Phae 52-53 D 3
Chumphon 52-53 CD 4
Chumsaeng 52-53 D 3
Chumunjin 50-51 G 4
Ch'unch'ŏn 48-49 O 4
Chungam-ni 50-51 G 5
Ch'ungch'ŏng-namdo 50-51 F 4
Ch'ungch'ŏng-pukto 50-51 FG 4
Chüngges 48-49 E 3
Chunghwa 50-51 EF 3
Ch'ungju 50-51 FG 4
Chungking = Chongqing 48-49 K 6
Ch'ung-ming = Chongming 48-49 N 5
Ch'ungmu 50-51 G 5
Chŭngsan 50-51 E 3
Chungshan = Zhongshan 48-49 L 7
Chung-tien = Zhongdian 48-49 HJ 6
Chüngüj gol 48-49 GH 2
Chung-wei = Zhongwei 48-49 JK 4
Chunya 64-65 H 4
Chuquibamba 78-79 E 8
Chuquicamata 80 C 2
Chuquisaca = Sucre 78-79 FG 8
Chur 33 D 5
Churchill [CDN] 70-71 RS 6
Churchill, ID 76-77 FG 4
Churchill, Cape – 70-71 S 6
Churchill Falls 70-71 XY 7
Churchill Peak 70-71 LM 6
Churchill River [CDN, Manitoba] 70-71 RS 6
Churchill River [CDN ◁ Hamilton Inlet] 70-71 Y 7
Churu 44-45 LM 5
Chusei-hokudō = Ch'ungch'ŏng-pukto 50-51 FG 4
Chusei-nandō = Ch'ungch'ŏng-namdo 50-51 F 4
Chu-shan = Zhushan 48-49 KL 5
Chusistan = Khūzestān 44-45 F 4
Chuska Mountains 76-77 J 7-8
Chust 38-39 D 6
Chutag 48-49 J 2
Chuučnar 48-49 G 5
Chuŭronjang 50-51 GH 2
Chuvash Autonomous Republic = 4 ◁ 42-43 H 6
Chuvashi, República Autónoma de los – = 4 ◁ 42-43 H 6
Chuwārtah 46-47 L 5
Chuxiong 48-49 J 7
Chuxiong Yizu Zizhizhou 48-49 J 6
Chuy 80 F 4
Chu Yang Sin 52-53 E 4
Chužand 44-45 K 2-L 3
Chužir 42-43 U 7
Chvalynsk 38-39 J 5
Chwārta = Chuwārtah 46-47 L 5
Chypre 44-45 C 3

Cs

Csád 60-61 HJ 5
Csangcsou = Changchun 48-49 NO 3
Csecsen-Ingus Autonóm Köztársaság 38-39 J 7
Cseh-erdő 33 F 4
Cseh Közt. 33 FH 4
Cseljuszkin-fok = mys Čel'uskin 42-43 UV 2
Csendesóceáni – – Antarktiszi-hátság 24 D 22-20
Csongrád 33 K 5
Csukcs Autonóm Körzet 42-43 g-k 4
Csukcs-hát 19 B 35
Csukcs-tenger 19 BC 35-36
Csungking = Chongqing 48-49 K 6
Csuvas Autonóm Köztársaság 42-43 H 6
Csuvas Autonóm Köztársaság 38-39 J 4

D

Đa, Sông – 52-53 D 2
Dab'ah 46-47 G 7
Dab'ah, Aḍ- 60-61 K 2
Dab'ah, Rā's aḍ- 62 C 2
Dabakala 60-61 D 7
Daba Shan 48-49 KL 5
Dabas nuur 48-49 H 4
Dabbâ = Jabal Jarbī 46-47 H 5
Dabbah, Ad- 60-61 KL 5
Dabbūsah, Ad- 46-47 J 7
Dabeiba 78-79 D 3
Dabie Shan [TJ, ▲▲] 48-49 M 5
Dabola 60-61 B 6
Daborow 60-61 b 2
Dąbrowa Tarnowska 33 K 3
Dabuxun Hu = Dabas nuur 48-49 H 4
Dacar = Dakar 60-61 A 6
Dacar, Bir ed – = Bi'r ad-Dhikār 60-61 J 3
Dacca = Ḍhāka [BD, ●] 44-45 OP 6
Dachaidan = Tagalgan 48-49 H 4
Dachangshan Dao 50-51 D 3
Dachau 33 E 4
Dachstein 33 F 5
Đac Lăc, Cao Nguyên – 52-53 E 4
Daday 46-47 E 2
Dade City, FL 74-75 b 2
Dadra and Nagar Haveli 44-45 L 6
Dādū 44-45 K 5
Dadu He 48-49 J 5
Daet 52-53 H 4
Dafdaf, Jabal – 62 F 3
Dafīnah, Ad- 44-45 E 6
Dagabur = Degeh Bur 60-61 N 7
Dagana 60-61 AB 5
Dağbaşı 46-47 H 4
Dagelet = Ullŭng-do 48-49 P 4
Dagestan, Autonome Republiek – 38-39 J 7
Dagestan, Autonome Republik 38-39 J 7
Dagestan, Autonomous Republic – 38-39 J 7
Dagestańska Autonomiczna Republika 42-43 T 7-V 6
Daggett, CA 76-77 E 8
Daghestán, République Autonome du – 38-39 J 7
Daghgharah, Ad- 46-47 L 6
Dağlıca 46-47 KL 4
Dagö = Hiiumaa 30-31 JK 8
Dagomba 60-61 D 7
Dagomys, Soči- 38-39 G 7
Dagomys, Soči- 38-39 G 7
Dagua [PNG] 52-53 M 7
Daguestán, República Autónoma del – 38-39 J 7
Dagujia 50-51 E 1
Dagverdharnes 30-31 b 2
Dāhānu 44-45 L 6-7
Daḥī, Nafūd ad- 44-45 EF 6
Dahlak = Dehalak Desēt 60-61 N 5
Dahnā', Ad- 44-45 E 5-F 6
Dahomey = Benin 60-61 E 6-7
Dahrah 60-61 H 3
Dahr Walātah 60-61 C 5
Dahshūr = Minshāt Dahshūr 62 D 3
Dahūk 46-47 K 4
Dahushan 50-51 D 2
Daimiel 34-35 F 9
Daiō zaki 50-51 L 5
Daipingqiao = Taipingshao 50-51 E 2
Dairen = Dalian 48-49 N 4
Dairūṭ = Dayrūṭ 60-61 L 3
Dai-sen 50-51 J 5
Dai-Sengen dake 50-51 ab 3
Dais hōji = Kaga 50-51 L 4
Daisy, WA 76-77 DE 1
Daitō-shima 48-49 P 6
Daitō sima = Daitō-shima 48-49 P 6
Dajarra 56-57 G 4
Dakar 60-61 A 6
Dakawa 63 D 4
Daketa Sheṭ 60-61 N 7
Dakhan = Deccan 44-45 M 6-8
Dākhilah, Wāḥāt ad- 60-61 K 3
Dakhlah, Ad- 60-61 A 4
Dakhla Oasis = Wāḥāt ad-Dākhilah 60-61 K 3
Dakka = Ḍhāka 44-45 OP 6
Dakota Północna = North Dakota 72-73 FG 2
Dakota Południowa = South Dakota 72-73 FG 3
Dakshiṇ Andamān = South Andaman 44-45 P 8
Dakshiṇ Paṭhār = Deccan 44-45 M 6-8
Dala 30-31 bc 2
Dalaba 60-61 B 6
Dalai 48-49 N 2
Dalai Lama Gangri 48-49 GH 5
Dalai Nur 48-49 M 2
Dalaj Nuur = Hulun Nur 48-49 M 2
Dalāk, Kūh-e – 46-47 N 4
Dalälven 30-31 G 7
Dalaman Nehri 46-47 C 4
Dalandzadgad 48-49 JK 3
Dalarna 30-31 EF 7
Da Lat 52-53 E 4
Dalavakasır = Oyalı 46-47 J 4
Dālbandīn 44-45 J 5
Dalby [AUS] 56-57 K 5
Dale 30-31 AB 7
Dale, OR 76-77 D 3
Dale, PA 74-75 D 4
Dalen 30-31 C 8
Dalgaranga, Mount – 56-57 C 5
Dalhousie, Cape – 70-71 KL 3
Dali [TJ, Yunnan] 48-49 HJ 6
Dalian 48-49 N 4
Dalias 34-35 F 10
Dali Baizu Zizhizhou 48-49 HJ 6
Daling He 50-51 C 2
Dalјā' 62 D 4
Ḍalkūt = Kharīfūt 44-45 G 7
Dāllah, 'Ayn – 62 B 4
Dallas, OR 76-77 B 3
Dallas, TX 72-73 G 5
Dall Island 70-71 K 7
Dallol Bosso 60-61 E 5-6
Dalmacia = Dalmacija 36-37 F 3-H 4
Dalmacija 36-37 F 3-H 4
Dalmaj, Hawr – 46-47 L 6
Dalmatia = Dalmacija 36-37 F 3-H 4
Dalmatie = Dalmacija 36-37 F 3-H 4
Dalmatien = Dalmacija 36-37 F 3-H 4
Dal'negorsk 42-43 a 9
Dal'nerečensk 42-43 Za 8
Dal'nerečensk 42-43 Za 8
Dal'nij = Lüda-Dalian 48-49 N 4
Daloa 60-61 C 7
Dalqū 60-61 L 4-5
Dalrymple, Mount – 56-57 J 4
Dalton, GA 72-73 JK 5
Dalton, MA 74-75 G 3
Daltonganj 44-45 N 6
Dalton Ice Tongue 24 C 12-13
Dalton in Furness 32 E 4
Dalvik 30-31 d 2
Dalwhinnie 32 DE 3
Daly City, CA 76-77 B 7
Daly River 56-57 F 2
Daly Waters 56-57 F 3
Damā, Wādī – 62 FG 4
Damān 44-45 L 6
Damanhūr 60-61 L 2
Damaq 46-47 N 5
Damar, Pulau – 52-53 J 8
Damara 60-61 H 8
Damaraland 64-65 E 7
Damas = Dimashq 44-45 D 4
Damasco = Dimashq 44-45 D 4
Damascus, VA 74-75 C 6
Damascus = Dimashq 44-45 D 4
Damaskus = Dimashq 44-45 D 4
Damaszek = Dimashq 44-45 D 4
Damašek = Dimashq 44-45 D 4
Damaszkusz = Dimashq 44-45 D 4
Damaturu 60-61 G 6
Damāvand, Kūh-e – 44-45 G 3
Damāzīn, Ad- 60-61 LM 6
Damba 64-65 DE 4
Dambuki 48-49 S 3-T 2
Dam Dam = South Dum Dum 44-45 OP 6
Damdūm, Bi'r – 62 BC 2
Dāmghān 44-45 GH 3
Damietta = Dumyāṭ 60-61 L 2
Damietta Mouth = Maṣabb Dumyāṭ 62 DE 2
Dāmir, Ad- 60-61 L 5
Damīr Qābū 46-47 JK 4
Dammām, Ad- 44-45 FG 5
Damodar 44-45 O 6
Damot 60-61 b 2
Dampier 56-57 C 4
Dampier, Selat – 52-53 K 7
Dampier Archipelago 56-57 C 4
Dampier Downs OC 56-57 D 3
Dampier Land 56-57 D 3
Dāmūr, Ad- 46-47 F 6
Dan, Kap – 70-71 d 4
Dana, Mount – 76-77 D 7
Đa Năng 52-53 E 3
Danbury, CT 74-75 G 4
Danby Lake 76-77 F 8
Dancharia 34-35 G 7
Dandarah 62 E 4
Dandong 48-49 N 3
Dänemark 30-31 C-E 10
Danemark 30-31 C-E 10
Danemark, Détroit du – 19 C 20-22
Dänemarkstraße 19 C 22-20
Danforth, ME 74-75 JK 2
Danfu 52-53 h 5
Dange, Rio – 64-65 D 4
Dang Raek, Phanom – 52-53 DE 4
Dangraek, Phnom – = Phanom Dang Raek 52-53 DE 4
Dan Guno 60-61 F 6-7
Dania 30-31 CD 10
Dánia 30-31 CD 10
Dánia-szoros 19 C 22-20
Dánia-szoros 30-31 ab 1
Daniel, WY 76-77 H 4
Danilov 42-43 G 6
Danişment 46-47 GH 3
Danissa 63 E 2
Danjo-shotō 50-51 G 6
Dank 44-45 H 6
Danli 72-73 J 9
Dannemora, NY 74-75 FG 2
Dannevirke 56-57 P 8
Dan River 74-75 CD 6
Danshui = Tan-shui 48-49 N 6
Dansia 78-79 H 4
Dánsko 30-31 CD 10
Dánský průliv 19 C 22-20
Dánský pruliv 30-31 ab 1
Dansville, NY 74-75 E 3
Dante, VA 74-75 B 6
Dante = Xaafuun 60-61 c 1
Danube = Dunărea 36-37 M 3
Danubio = Dunărea 36-37 M 3
Danushkodi 44-45 MN 9
Danville, IL 72-73 J 3
Danville, ME 74-75 H 2-3
Danville, VA 72-73 L 4
Dan Xian 48-49 K 8
Danzig = Gdańsk 33 J 1
Danziger Bucht = Zatoka Gdańska 33 J 1
Dao-Timni 60-61 G 4
Daou, Eḍ- = Aḍ-Ḍaw 46-47 G 5
Dapsang = K 2 44-45 M 3
Dapupan 52-53 GH 3
Daqing Shan 48-49 L 3
Daqmā', Ad- 44-45 FG 6
Daquan 48-49 H 3
Dar'ā 46-47 G 6
Darā, Jazīreh – 46-47 N 7
Dārāb 44-45 GH 5
Darabani 36-37 M 1
Darad = Dardistān 44-45 L 3
Darag = Legaspi 52-53 H 4
Daraj 60-61 G 2
Dār al-Bayḍā', Ad- 60-61 BC 2
Darašun = Veršino-Darasunskij 42-43 VW 7
Darašun = Veršino-Darasunskij 42-43 VW 7
Darau = Darāw 62 E 5
Darāw 62 E 5
Darb, Ad- 44-45 E 7
Dār Bādām 46-47 M 6
Darband, Kūh-e – 44-45 H 4
Darbandī Khan, Sadd ad- 46-47 L 5
Darbanga = Darbhanga 44-45 O 5
Darbhanga 44-45 O 5
Darbī = Darvi 48-49 G 2
Darby, MT 76-77 FG 2
Darchan 48-49 K 2
Dardanele = Çanakkale Boğazı 44-45 B 2-3
Dardanele = Çanakkale Boğazı 36-37 M 5
Dardanellák = Çanakkale Boğazi 44-45 B 2-3
Dardanellen = Çanakkale Boğazı 44-45 B 2-3
Dardanelles = Çanakkale Boğazı 44-45 B 2-3
Dardanelos = Çanakkale Boğazı 44-45 B 2-3
Dardanely, úž. - = Çanakkale Boğazı 36-37 M 5
Dardanely, úžina – = Çanakkale boğazı 44-45 B 2-3
Dār Dīshah 46-47 J 5
Dardo = Kangding 48-49 J 5-6
Dār el Beïḍā', ed – = Ad-Dār al-Bayḍā' 60-61 BC 2
Darende 46-47 G 3
Dar es Salaam 64-65 JK 4
Dārfūr 60-61 J 6
Dārfūr 60-61 K 5-6
Dargagā, Jebel ed – = Jabal Ardar Gwagwa 62 F 6
Dargan-Ata 44-45 J 2
Dargaville 56-57 O 7
Dargo 58 H 6
Dar Hu = Dalaj Nur 48-49 M 3
Darien, GA 74-75 C 9
Darién [PA, ≅] 72-73 L 10
Darien [PA, ●] 72-73 b 2
Darien = Dalian 48-49 N 4
Darién, Golfo del – 78-79 D 3
Dārigah 46-47 K 5
Dariganga 48-49 L 2
Darjeeling 44-45 O 5
Dārjiling = Darjeeling 44-45 O 5
Darkhazīneh 46-47 N 7
Darling Downs 56-57 JK 5
Darling Range 56-57 C 6
Darling River 56-57 H 6
Darlington 32 EF 4
Darlington, SC 74-75 CD 7
Darlowo 33 H 1
Darmstadt 33 D 4
Darnah 60-61 J 2
Darnick 56-57 H 6
Darnley, Cape – 24 C 7-8
Daroca 34-35 G 8
Darrington, WA 76-77 C 1
Darsah 44-45 G 8
Dart, Cape – 24 B 24
Dartmoor Forest 32 E 6
Dartmouth [CDN] 70-71 Y 9
Dartuch, Cabo – 34-35 J 9
Daru 52-53 M 8
Darūdāb 60-61 M 5
Daruvar 36-37 G 3
Darvaza 44-45 H 2
Darvi 48-49 G 2
Darwešān 44-45 JK 4
Darwešān 44-45 JK 4
Darwin [AUS] 56-57 F 2
Darwin, CA 76-77 E 7
Darwin, Bahía – 80 AB 7
Dās 44-45 G 5
Dashen Terara, Ras – 60-61 M 6
Dashiqiao 50-51 D 2
Dasht 44-45 J 5
Dasht-e Āzādegān 46-47 N 7
Dashtīārī = Polān 44-45 J 5
Dataran Tinggi Cameron = Tanah Tinggi Cameron 52-53 D 6
Datça = Reşadiye 46-47 B 4
Date 50-51 b 2
Datia 44-45 M 5
Datiyā = Datia 44-45 M 5
D'atkovo 38-39 FG 5
Datong [TJ, Shanxi] 48-49 L 3
Datong He 48-49 J 4
Datu, Tanjung – 52-53 E 6
Datu, Teluk – 52-53 EF 6
Datu Piang 52-53 H 5
Dau'an = Al-Huraybah 44-45 F 7
Daudmannsodden 30-31 hj 5
Daugava 30-31 LM 9
Daugava = Severnaja Dvina 42-43 G 5
Daugavpils 30-31 M 10
Daulagiri = Dhaulāgiri 44-45 N 5
Daule, Rio – 78-79 CD 5
Dauna Parma = Dawa 60-61 M 7-8
Dauphin 70-71 QR 7
Dauphiné 34-35 KL 6
Daurskij chrebet = chrebet Čerskogo 42-43 V 7
Dautlatābād = Malāyer 44-45 F 4
Davalguiri = Dhaulagiri 44-45 N 5
Davao 52-53 J 5
Davao Gulf 52-53 J 5
Davenport, IA 72-73 H 3
Davenport, WA 76-77 D 2
Davenport Downs 56-57 H 4
Davenport Range 56-57 FG 4
Davey, Port – 56-57 HJ 8
David 72-73 K 10
David-Gorodok 38-39 E 5
Davidson Mountains 70-71 H 4
Davis, CA 76-77 BC 6
Davis, WV 74-75 D 5
Davis, Détroit de – 70-71 Z 4-5
Davis, Estrecho de – 70-71 Z 4-5
Davis, Straat – 70-71 Z 4-5
Davisa, Cieśnina – 70-71 Z 4-5
Davis Bay 24 C 14
Davis Creek, CA 76-77 C 5
Davis Dam, AZ 76-77 F 8
Davis Sea 24 C 10
Davis Strait 70-71 Z 4-5
Davisstraße 70-71 Z 4-5
Davis-szoros 70-71 Z 4-5
Davisův průliv 70-71 Z 4-5
Davlekanovo 42-43 JK 7
Davos 33 DE 5
Ḍaw, Aḍ- 46-47 G 5
Dawādimā, Ad- 44-45 EF 6
Dawangjia Dao 50-51 D 3
Dawanle = Dewelē 60-61 N 6
Dawāsir, Wādī ad- 44-45 EF 6
Dawa Weniz 60-61 M 7-8
Dawḥah, Ad- 44-45 G 5
Dawr, Ad- 46-47 KL 5
Dawrah, Baghdād- 46-47 L 6
Dawson 70-71 J 5
Dawson, Isla – 80 BC 8
Dawson Creek 70-71 M 6
Dawson-Lambton Glacier 24 B 33-34
Dawson Range 70-71 J 5
Dawwah 44-45 H 6
Dawwāya = Jamā'at al-Ma'yuf 46-47 M 7
Dax 34-35 G 7
Da Xian 48-49 K 5
Daxue Shan 48-49 J 5-6
Day, FL 74-75 b 1
Dayang Bunting, Pulau – 52-53 C 5
Dayang He 50-51 D 2
Daylesford 58 G 6
Daym Zubayr 60-61 K 7
Dayong 48-49 L 6
Dayr, Ad- 62 E 5
Dayr as-Suryānī 62 CD 2
Dayr az-Zawr 44-45 DE 3
Dayr Ḥāfir 46-47 G 4
Dayr Katrīnah 62 E 3
Dayr Māghar 46-47 H 4
Dayr Mawās 62 D 4
Dayr Samū'īl 62 D 3
Dayrūṭ 60-61 L 3
Dayton, NV 76-77 D 6
Dayton, OH 72-73 K 4
Dayton, WA 76-77 E 2
Daytona Beach, FL 72-73 KL 6
Dayu 48-49 L 6
Da Yunhe [TJ, Jiangsu] 48-49 M 5
Dayville, OR 76-77 D 3
Dazkırı 46-47 CD 4
Dead Indian Peak 76-77 HJ 3
Deadman Bay 74-75 b 2
Dead Sea = Baḥr al-Mayyit 44-45 D 4
Deadwood Reservoir 76-77 F 3
Deal Island 58 cd 1
Deán Funes 80 D 4
Dean River 70-71 L 7
Dearg, Beinn – 32 D 3
Deary, ID 76-77 E 2
Dease Arm 70-71 MN 4
Dease Lake 70-71 KL 6
Dease Strait 70-71 P 4
Death Valley 72-73 C 4
Death Valley, CA 76-77 E 7
Death Valley National Monument 76-77 E 7-8
Deauville 34-35 GH 4
Debar 36-37 J 5
Debark 60-61 M 6
Dębica 33 K 3-4
Dęblin 33 KL 3
Débo, Lac – 60-61 D 5
De Borgia, MT 76-77 F 2
Debre Birhan 60-61 MN 7
Debrecen 33 K 5
Debrecín = Debrecen 33 K 5
Debre Markos 60-61 M 6
Debre Tabor 60-61 M 6
Decamere = Dekemḥarē 60-61 M 5
Decatur, AL 72-73 J 5
Decatur, GA 72-73 K 5
Decatur, IL 72-73 HJ 3-4
Decazeville 34-35 J 6
Decepción, Cabo – = Cape Disappointment 80 J 8-9
Deception 24 C 30
Děčín 33 G 3
Declo, ID 76-77 G 4
Decoto, CA 76-77 BC 7
Děčín 33 G 3
Deda 36-37 L 2
Dedo, Cerro – 80 B 6
Dédougou 60-61 D 6
Dedza 64-65 H 5
Dee [GB, Cambrian Mts.] 32 E 5
Dee [GB, Grampian Mts.] 32 E 3
Deep Creek Range 76-77 G 5-6
Deep River [USA] 74-75 D 7
Deepwater 58 K 2
Deerfield Beach, FL 74-75 cd 3
Deering, Mount – 56-57 E 5
Deer Lodge, MT 76-77 G 2
Deer Lodge Mountains 76-77 G 2
Deer Lodge Pass 76-77 G 3
Deer Park, WA 76-77 E 2
Deeth, NV 76-77 F 5
Deffa, ed – = Aḍ-Ḍiffah 60-61 J 2
Dêge 48-49 H 5
Degeh Bur 60-61 N 7
Deggendorf 33 F 4
De Grey 56-57 CD 4
De Grey River 56-57 CD 4
Dehalak Desēt 60-61 N 5
Dehgolān 46-47 M 5
Dehkhwareqan = Āzar Shahr 46-47 LM 4
Dehlorān 44-45 F 4
Dehna = Ad Dahnā' 44-45 E 5-F 6
Dehna, Ed- = Ad-Dahnā' 44-45 E 5-F 6
Dehōk = Dahūk 46-47 K 4
Dehong Daizu Zizhizhou = D ◁ 48-49 H 6-7
Dehra Dun 44-45 M 4
Deh Shū 44-45 J 4
Deir, Ed – = Ad-Dayr 62 E 5
Deir es-Suryânî = Dayr as-Suryânî 62 CD 2
Deir ez Zôr = Dayr az-Zawr 44-45 DE 3
Deir Ḥâfir = Dayr Ḥāfir 46-47 G 4
Deir Katerîna = Dayr Katrīnah 62 E 3
Deir Mâghar = Dayr Mâghar 46-47 H 4
Deir Mawâs = Dayr Mawâs 62 D 4
Deir Samweil = Dayr Samū'īl 62 D 3
Dej 36-37 K 2
Dejnev, Cap – = mys Dežneva 42-43 lm 4
De Jongs, Tanjung – 52-53 L 8
De-Kastri 42-43 ab 7
Dekemhare 60-61 M 5
Dekese 64-65 F 3
Dekoûa, Tell – = Tall adh-Dhakwah 46-47 G 6
Dél-Afrika 64-65 F-H 8
Delaimiya, Ad- = Ad-Dulaymīyah 46-47 K 6
De Land, FL 74-75 c 2
Delano, CA 76-77 D 8
Delano Peak 72-73 D 4
Delaware 72-73 LM 4

Delaw 171

Filipinas, Cuenca de – 22-23 Q 5
Filipinas, Fosa de – 22-23 Q 5
Filipiny 52-53 H 3-J 5
Filipíny 52-53 H 3-J 5
Filippiás 36-37 J 6
Filippijnen 52-53 H 3-J 5
Filippijnenbekken 22-23 Q 5
Filippijnentrog 22-23 Q 5
Filipstad 30-31 EF 8
Fillmore, CA 76-77 D 8
Fillmore, UT 76-77 G 6
Fimi 64-65 E 3
Finch 74-75 F 2
Findık 46-47 JK 4
Fındıklı 46-47 J 2
Findlay, OH 72-73 K 3
Finger Lakes 72-73 L 3
Fingoè 64-65 H 6
Finike 46-47 D 4
Finisterre, Cabo de – 34-35 BC 7
Finke 56-57 FG 5
Finke River 56-57 G 5
Finland 30-31 L 7-M 4
Finland, Gulf of – 30-31 K 8-M 7
Finlande 30-31 L 7-M 4
Finlande, Golfe de – 30-31 K 8-M 7
Finlandia 30-31 L 7-M 4
Finlandia 30-31 K 7-M 4
Finlandia, Golfo de – 30-31 K 8-M 7
Finlay River 70-71 LM 6
Finnis, Cape – 58 B 4
Finnischer Meerbusen 30-31 K 8-M 7
Finnland 30-31 L 7-M 4
Finnmark 30-31 K 3-N 2
Finnmarksvidda 30-31 KL 3
Finnország 30-31 K 7-M 4
Finnország 30-31 K 7-M 4
Finn-öböl 30-31 L 8-M 7
Finn-öböl 30-31 L 8-M 7
Finnskogene 30-31 E 7
Finnsnes 30-31 GH 3
Finschhafen 52-53 N 8
Finse 30-31 B 7
Finse Golf 30-31 K 8-M 7
Fińska, Zatoka - 30-31 L 8-M 7
Finsko 30-31 K 7-M 4
Finský záliv 30-31 L 8-M 7
Finspång 30-31 FG 8
Finsteraarhorn 33 CD 5
Finsterwalde 33 FG 3
Finṭās, Jabal al- 62 D 6
Fiordland National Park 56-57 N 8-9
Fiqīq 60-61 D 2
Fırat Nehri 44-45 D 3
Firebaugh, CA 76-77 C 7
Firenze 36-37 D 4
Firkessedougou = Ferkéssédougou 60-61 CD 7
Firozabad 44-45 M 5
Fīrūzābād [IR, Fārs] 44-45 G 5
Fīrūzābād [IR, Lorestān] 46-47 MN 6
Fischerhalbinsel = poluostrov Rybačij 42-43 EF 4
Fishermans Island 74-75 F 6
Fisher Strait 70-71 U 5
Fishguard & Goodwick 32 D 5-6
Fishing Point 74-75 F 6
Fish Lake Valley 76-77 DE 7
Fiskåfjället 30-31 F 5
Fiskenæsset = Qeqertarssuatsiaq 70-71 a 5
Fiskivötn 30-31 c 2
Fitchburg, MA 74-75 GH 3
Fitri, Lac – 60-61 H 6
Fitzgerald, GA 74-75 B 9
Fitzmaurice River 56-57 EF 2
Fitz Roy 80 C 7
Fitz Roy, Monte – 80 B 7
Fitzroy Crossing 56-57 DE 3
Fitzroy River [AUS, Queensland] 56-57 JK 4
Fitzroy River [AUS, Western Australia] 56-57 DE 3
Fitzwilliam Strait 70-71 NO 2
Fiume = Rijeka 36-37 F 3
Five Miles Rapids 76-77 D 2
Fizi 64-65 G 3

Flå 30-31 C 7
Flagstaff, AZ 72-73 D 4
Flagstaff Lake 74-75 H 2
Flaherty Island 70-71 U 6
Flakstadøy 30-31 E 3
Flåm 30-31 B 7
Flamand = Arak 60-61 E 3
Flamborough Head 32 FG 4
Fläming 33 F 2-3
Flaming Gorge Reservoir 76-77 J 5
Flamingo, FL 74-75 c 4
Flamingo, Teluk – 52-53 L 8
Flandern = Flandre 34-35 J 3
Flanders = Vlaanderen 34-35 J 3
Flandes = Vlaanderen 34-35 J 3
Flanigan, NV 76-77 D 5
Flannan Isles 32 BC 2
Flatey 30-31 b 2
Flateyri 30-31 ab 1
Flathead Indian Reservation 76-77 FG 2
Flathead Lake 72-73 CD 2
Flathead Mountains = Salish Mountains 76-77 F 1-2
Flathead River 76-77 F 1
Flatow = Złotów 33 H 2
Flattery, Cape – [AUS] 56-57 J 2
Flattery, Cape – [USA] 76-77 A 1
Flat Top Mountain 74-75 C 6
Flèche, la – 34-35 GH 5
Fleetwood 32 E 5
Flekkefjord 30-31 AB 8
Flen 30-31 G 8
Flensburg 33 DE 1
Flers 34-35 G 4
Flesher, MT 76-77 G 2
Fletcher, Seuil – 19 A
Fletcher-hátság 19 A
Fletcherrücken 19 A
Fletcherrug 19 A
Fletcher, Dorsal de – 19 A
Flinders Bay 56-57 BC 6
Flinders Island [AUS, Bass Strait] 56-57 J 7
Flinders Island [AUS, Great Australian Bight] 56-57 F 6
Flinders Ranges 56-57 G 6
Flinders River 56-57 H 3-4
Flin Flon 70-71 Q 7
Flint [GB] 32 E 5
Flint, MI 72-73 K 3
Flora 30-31 A 7
Flora, OR 76-77 E 3
Floreana 78-79 AB 5
Floreana, Isla – 78-79 A 5
Florence, AL 72-73 J 5
Florence, AZ 76-77 H 9
Florence, OR 76-77 A 4
Florence, SC 72-73 L 5
Florence = Firenze 36-37 D 4
Florence = Firenze 36-37 D 4
Florence Junction, AZ 76-77 H 9
Florencia [CO] 78-79 DE 4
Florencia = Firenze 36-37 D 4
Florencja = Firenze 36-37 D 4
Florenz = Firenze 36-37 D 4
Flores [GCA] 72-73 J 8
Flores [RI] 52-53 H 8
Flores, Las – [RA, Buenos Aires] 80 E 5
Flores, Mar de – 52-53 GH 8
Flores, Mer de – 52-53 GH 8
Flores, Morze – 52-53 GH 8
Floreské moře 52-53 GH 8
Flores Sea 52-53 GH 8
Floressee 52-53 GH 8
Floresta Amazônica 78-79 E-H 6
Flores-tenger 52-53 GH 8
Florešty 36-37 MN 2
Floreszee 52-53 GH 8
Florešty 36-37 MN 2
Floriano 78-79 L 6
Florianópolis 80 G 3
Florida [USA] 72-73 K 5-6
Florida [ROU, ●] 80 E 4
Florida, Cape – 74-75 cd 4
Florida, Straits of – 72-73 K 7-L 6
Florida Bay 72-73 K 7
Florida City, FL 74-75 c 4
Florida Island 52-53 jk 6
Florida Keys 72-73 K 6-7
Floride = Florida 72-73 K 5-6
Flórina 36-37 J 5
Floryda = Florida 72-73 K 5-6
Flower Station 74-75 E 2
Floyd, VA 74-75 C 6
Floyd, Mount – 76-77 G 8
Flumendosa 36-37 C 6
Flying Fish, Cape – 24 BC 26
Fly River 52-53 M 8

Foča 36-37 H 4
Foça [TR] 46-47 B 3
Fo-chan = Foshan 48-49 L 7
Fochi 60-61 H 5
Focşani 36-37 M 3
Foča 36-37 H 4
Fóggia 36-37 F 5
Fogo Island 70-71 a 8
Föhr 33 D 1
Foix [F, ≅] 34-35 H 7
Foix [F, ●] 34-35 H 7
Fokváros = Kaapstad 64-65 E 9
Folda [N, Nordland] 30-31 F 4
Folda [N, Nord-Trøndelag] 30-31 D 5
Folégandros 36-37 L 7
Foley Island 70-71 V 4
Folgefonni 30-31 B 7-8
Foligno 36-37 E 4
Folkestone 32 G 6
Folkston, GA 74-75 B 9
Folldal 30-31 CD 6
Folsom, CA 76-77 C 6
Folteşti 36-37 MN 3
Fonda, NY 74-75 F 3
Fond-du-Lac 70-71 PQ 6
Fond du Lac, WI 72-73 J 3
Fond du Lac River 70-71 Q 6
Fondi 36-37 E 5
Fonsagrada 34-35 D 7
Fonseca, Golfo de – 72-73 J 9
Fontainebleau 34-35 J 4
Fonte Boa 78-79 F 5
Fontenelle Reservoir 76-77 HJ 4
Fontur 30-31 fg 1
Fonualei 52-53 c 2
Foochow = Fengdu 48-49 K 5-6
Foochow = Fujian 48-49 MN 6
Foochow = Fuzhou 48-49 MN 6
Foraker, Mount – 70-71 F 5
Forbes 56-57 J 6
Ford, Cape – 56-57 E 2
Ford City, CA 76-77 D 8
Førde 30-31 AB 7
Ford Lake 76-77 F 9
Fords Bridge 56-57 HJ 5
Forécariah 60-61 B 7
Forel, Mont – 70-71 d 4
Forest [CDN] 74-75 B 3
Forestal, La – 80 E 2
Forest City, NC 74-75 BC 7
Forestier Peninsula 58 d 3
Forez, Monts du – 34-35 J 6
Forfar 32 E 3
Forks, WA 76-77 A 1-2
Forlandsundet 30-31 hj 5
Forlì 36-37 DE 3
Formentera 34-35 H 9
Formentor, Cabo – 34-35 J 8
Formiga 78-79 K 9
Formosa [BR, Goiás] 78-79 K 8
Formosa [RA, ●] 80 E 3
Formosa = Republiek China 48-49 N 7
Formosa = Taiwan 48-49 N 7
Formosa = Tajvan 48-49 N 7
Formosa, Estrecho de – = T'ai-wan Hai-hsia 48-49 M 7-N 6
Formosa, Serra – 78-79 HJ 7
Formosa Bay 63 E 3
Formosa Strait = T'ai-wan Hai-hsia 48-49 M 7-N 6
Formosastraße = Taiwan Haihsia 48-49 M 7-N 6
Formose = Taïwan 48-49 N 7
Formose, Détroit de – = T'ai-wan Hai-hsia 48-49 M 7-N 6
Formoza = Tajwan 48-49 N 7
Fornæs 30-31 D 9
Forqlôs = Furqlūs 46-47 G 5
Forrest [AUS] 56-57 E 6
Forrest River Aboriginal Reserve 56-57 E 2-3
Forsayth 56-57 H 3
Forsmo 30-31 G 6
Forssa 30-31 K 7
Forster 58 L 4
Fort Albany 70-71 U 7
Fortaleza [BR, Ceará] 78-79 M 5
Fort Apache Indian Reservation 76-77 HJ 8-9
Fort-Archambault = Sarh 60-61 H 7
Fort Bayard = Zhanjiang 48-49 L 7
Fort Benton, MT 76-77 H 2
Fort Bragg, CA 76-77 AB 6
Fort Bragg, NC 74-75 D 7
Fort Bridger, WY 76-77 HJ 5
Fort Bruce = Pībōr 60-61 L 7
Fort Brussaux = Markounda 60-61 H 7
Fort-Charlet = Jannah 60-61 FG 4
Fort Chimo 70-71 X 6
Fort Chipewyan 70-71 OP 6
Fort Collins, CO 72-73 EF 3
Fort-Crampel = Kaga Bandoro 60-61 HJ 7
Fort-Charlet = Jannah 60-61 FG 4
Fort Chimo 70-71 X 6
Fort Chipewyan 70-71 OP 6
Fort-Dauphin = Faradofay 64-65 L 8
Fort Defiance, AZ 76-77 J 8
Fort-de-France 72-73 O 9
Fort de Kock = Bukittinggi 52-53 CD 7
Fort-de-Possel = Possel 60-61 H 7
Fort Dodge, IA 72-73 GH 3
Fort Duquesne = Pittsburg, Pa. 72-73 KL 3
Fort Edward, NY 74-75 G 3
Fort Erie 74-75 D 3
Fortescue River 56-57 C 4
Fort Fairfield, ME 74-75 JK 1
Fort-Flatters = Burj Flāṭarz 60-61 EF 3
Fort Frances 70-71 S 8
Fort-Gardel = Zaouatallaz 60-61 F 3-4
Fort Good Hope 70-71 L 4
Fort Grey 56-57 H 5
Forth, Firth of – 32 EF 3
Fort Hall, ID 76-77 G 4
Fort Hall = Murang'a 64-65 J 3
Fort Hall Indian Reservation 76-77 GH 4
Fort Hertz = Pūdāō 52-53 C 1
Fort Huachuca, AZ 76-77 H 10
Fort-Charlet = Jannah 60-61 FG 4
Fort Chimo 70-71 X 6
Fort Chipewyan 70-71 OP 6
Fortín Falcón 80 DE 2
Fortín Lavalle 80 D 3
Fortín Madrejón 80 D 2
Fortín Pilcomayo 80 DE 2
Fortín Príncipe de Beira = Príncipe da Beira 78-79 G 7
Fortín Ravelo 78-79 G 8
Fortín Suárez Arana 78-79 G 8
Fortín Uno 80 CD 5
Fort Jameson = Chipata 64-65 H 5
Fort Johnston = Mangoche 64-65 J 5
Fort Jones, CA 76-77 B 5
Fort Kent, ME 74-75 J 1
Fort Klamath, OR 76-77 BC 4
Fort Knox, KY 72-73 J 4
Fort Lami = N'Djamena 60-61 GH 6
Fort-Lamy = N'Djamena 60-61 GH 6
Fort-Laperrine = Tamanrāsat 60-61 EF 4
Fort Lauderdale, FL 72-73 KL 6
Fort Lewis, WA 76-77 B 2
Fort Liard 70-71 M 5
Fort MacDowell Indian Reservation 76-77 H 9
Fort-Mac-Mahon = Burj Ban Būl'īd 60-61 E 3
Fort MacMurray 70-71 O 6
Fort MacPherson 70-71 JK 4
Fort Madison, IA 72-73 H 3
Fort Maguire 64-65 HJ 5
Fort Manning = Mchinji 64-65 H 5
Fort Meade, FL 74-75 bc 3
Fort Mill, SC 74-75 C 7
Fort Mohave Indian Reservation 76-77 F 8
Fort Myers, FL 72-73 K 6
Fort Nassau = Albany, NY 72-73 LM 3
Fort Nelson 70-71 M 6
Fort Nelson River 70-71 M 6
Fort Norman 70-71 L 4-5
Fort Ogden, FL 74-75 c 3
Fort Peck Lake 72-73 E 2
Fort Pierce, FL 72-73 KL 6
Fort Plain, NY 74-75 F 3
Fort Portal 64-65 H 2
Fort Providence 70-71 N 5
Fort Randolph 72-73 b 2
Fort Reliance 70-71 P 5
Fort Resolution 70-71 O 5
Fortress Mountain 76-77 HJ 3
Fort Rock, OR 76-77 C 4
Fort Rosebery = Mansa 64-65 G 5
Fort Ross, CA 76-77 B 6
Fort-Rousset = Owando 64-65 E 3
Fort Rupert 70-71 V 7
Fort-Saint = Burj al-Ḥaṭṭabah 60-61 F 2
Fort Saint James 70-71 M 7
Fort Saint John 70-71 M 6
Fort Sandeman = Apposai 44-45 K 4
Fort Saskatchewan 70-71 NO 7
Fort Selkirk 70-71 JK 5
Fort Sendeman = Apposai 44-45 K 4
Fort Severn 70-71 T 6
Fort Seward, CA 76-77 B 5
Fort Sherman 72-73 ab 2
Fort Sibut = Sibut 60-61 H 7
Fort Simpson 70-71 M 5
Fort Smith 70-71 OP 5
Fort Smith, AR 72-73 H 4
Fort Smith, District of – 70-71 N-P 5
Fort Stockton, TX 72-73 F 5
Fort Thomas, AZ 76-77 HJ 9
Fort-Trinquet = Bīr Umm Qarayn 60-61 B 3
Fortuna, CA 76-77 AB 5
Fortune Bank 64-65 L 3
Fortune Bay 70-71 Z 8
Fort Vermilion 70-71 NO 6
Fort Victoria = Nyanda 64-65 H 6-7
Fort Wayne, IN 72-73 JK 3
Fort Wingate, NM 76-77 J 8
Fort Worth, TX 72-73 G 5
Fort Yukon, AK 70-71 GH 4
Fosforitnaja 38-39 K 4
Foshan 48-49 L 7
Fosheim Peninsula 70-71 U 1-2
Fosna 30-31 CD 6
Fossano 36-37 BC 3
Fossberg 30-31 BC 7
Fosse Norvégienne 30-31 A 8-C 9
Fosse Péruvienne 78-79 C 6-D 7
Fossil, OR 76-77 C 3
Fougamou 64-65 D 3
Fougères 34-35 G 4
Foula 32 E 1
Foul Bay = Khalīj Umm al-Kataf 62 F 6
Foulpointe = Mahavelona 64-65 LM 6
Foulwind, Cape – 56-57 NO 8
Fouman = Fūman 46-47 N 4
Foumban 60-61 G 7
Foum Taṭāouīn = Taṭāwīn 60-61 G 2
Foundiougne 60-61 A 6
Fourât, El- = Al-Furāt 46-47 H 5
Fourcroy, Cape – 56-57 E 2
Fouta Djallon 60-61 B 6
Foveaux Strait 56-57 N 9
Fowler, MT 76-77 H 1
Fowlers Bay 56-57 F 6
Fowling = Fengdu 48-49 K 5-6
Foxe Basin 70-71 UV 4
Foxe Channel 70-71 UV 4-5
Foxe Channel 70-71 UV 4-5
Foxe Channel 70-71 UV 4-5
Foxe Peninsula 70-71 V 5
Fox Islands 19 D 35
Foyle, Lough – 32 C 4
Foyn, Cape – 24 C 30
Foynes 32 B 5
Foynøya 30-31 mn 4
Foz do Aripuanã = Novo Aripuanã 78-79 G 6
Foz do Embira = Envira 78-79 EF 6
Foz do Iguaçu 80 F 3
Foz do Riozinho 78-79 E 6

Fragua, La – 80 D 3
Framnesfjella 24 C 7
Franca [BR, São Paulo] 78-79 K 9
Franca Josifa, zemľ'a – 42-43 H-M 2
Francavilla Fontana 36-37 GH 5
France 34-35 G 4-K 6
Frances Peak 76-77 J 3-4
Franceville 64-65 D 3
Franche-Comté 34-35 KL 5
Francia Guyana 78-79 J 4
Franciaország 34-35 G 4-K 6
Franciczka Józefa, Ziemia – = Zemľ'a Franca-Josifa 42-43 H 2-M 1
Francie 34-35 G 4-K 6
Francis Case, Lake – 72-73 FG 3
Francistown 64-65 G 7
Francja 34-35 G 4-K 6
François Joseph, Chutes – 64-65 E 4
François Joseph, Chutes – 64-65 E 4
François Joseph, Chutes – 64-65 E 4
Francouzská Guyana 78-79 J 4
Francouzské středohoří 34-35 J 6
Francquihaven = Ilebo 64-65 F 3
Frankenwald 33 E 3
Frankfort, KY 72-73 K 4
Frankfurt am Main 33 D 3
Frankfurt/Oder 33 G 2
Fränkische Alb 33 E 3-4
Frankland, Cape – 58 c 1
Franklin, NH 74-75 H 3
Franklin, PA 74-75 D 4
Franklin, VA 74-75 E 6
Franklin, WV 74-75 D 5
Franklin Bay 70-71 L 3-4
Franklin Delano Roosevelt Lake 72-73 C 2
Franklin Island 24 B 17-18
Franklin Mountains [CDN] 70-71 L 4-M 5
Franklin Strait 70-71 R 3
Franklinton, NC 74-75 D 6
Franklinville, NY 74-75 DE 3
Frankreich 34-35 G 4-K 6
Frankrijk 34-35 G 4-K 6
Fransfontein 64-65 DE 7
Frans-Guyana 78-79 J 4
Františka Josefa, Země – = Zemľ'a Franca-Josifa 42-43 H 2-M 1
Franz Joseph, zemľ'a – = zemľ'a Franca Josifa 42-43 H-M 2
Franz-Joseph-Land = Zemľ'a Franca-Josifa 42-43 H-M 2
Französisch-Guyana 78-79 J 4
Frasca, Capo de – 36-37 BC 6
Frascati 36-37 E 5
Fraserburg 64-65 F 9
Fraserburgh 32 EF 3
Fraser Island = Great Sandy Island 56-57 KL 4-5
Fraser Plateau 70-71 M 7
Fraser Range 56-57 D 6
Fraser River 70-71 MN 7
Fraustadt = Wschowa 33 H 3
Fray Bentos 80 E 4
Frederica 30-31 CD 10
Frederic Hills 56-57 G 3
Frederick, MD 74-75 E 5
Fredericksburg, VA 74-75 DE 5
Fredericton 70-71 X 8
Frederikshåb = Pâmiut 70-71 ab 5
Frederikshamn = Hamina 30-31 M 7
Frederikshavn 30-31 D 9
Fredonia, AZ 76-77 G 7
Fredonia, NY 74-75 D 3
Fredonyer Peak 76-77 C 5
Fredrikstad 30-31 D 8
Freel Peak 76-77 CD 6
Freemansundet 30-31 l 5
Freetown 60-61 B 7
Freewater, OR 76-77 D 3
Fregenal de la Sierra 34-35 D 9
Freiberg 33 F 3
Freiburg im Breisgau 33 C 4-5
Freire 80 B 5
Freising 33 E 4
Freistadt 33 G 4
Freiwaldau = Jeseník 33 H 3
Fréjus 34-35 L 7
Fremantle, Perth- 56-57 BC 6
Fremont, CA 76-77 C 7
Fremont, NE 72-73 G 3
Fremont Island 76-77 G 5
Fremont River 76-77 H 6
French Guiana 78-79 J 4
French Island 58 G 7
Frenchman, NV 76-77 D 6
Frenchman Bay 74-75 JK 2
Frenchmans Cap 58 bc 3
French Shore 70-71 Z 7-8
Frentones, Los – 80 D 3
Freshfield, Cape – 24 C 16
Fresno, CA 72-73 BC 4
Freundschaftsinseln = Tonga Islands 22-23 T 6-7
Freycinet Peninsula 56-57 J 8
Fria 60-61 B 6
Fria, La – 78-79 E 3
Friant, CA 76-77 D 7
Frias 80 CD 3
Fribourg 33 C 5
Friday Harbor, WA 76-77 B 1
Friedrichshafen 33 DE 5
Fries, VA 74-75 C 6
Frijoles 72-73 b 2
Frio, Kaap – 64-65 D 6
Frisco Mountain 76-77 G 6
Frisias Occidentales 34-35 KL 2
Frisias Orientales, Islas – 33 C 2
Frisias Septentrionales, Islas – 33 D 1
Frisones Septentrionales, Bassin du – 33 D 1
Frisonnes Orientales, Îles – 33 C 2
Frisonnes Septentrionales, Îles – 33 D 1
Fritjof Nansen Land = zemľ'a Franca Josifa 42-43 H-M 2
Friuli-Venèzia Giulia 36-37 E 2
Friza, proliv – 48-49 S 2
Frobisher Bay [CDN, ∪] 70-71 X 5
Frobisher Bay [CDN, ●] 70-71 X 5
Frohavet 30-31 C 5-6
Frolovo 38-39 H 6
Frome 32 E 6
Frome, Lake – 56-57 GH 6
Frome Downs 56-57 GH 6
Fronteiras 78-79 L 6
Frontera 72-73 H 8
Fronteras 76-77 J 10
Frontignan 34-35 JK 7
Front Range 72-73 E 3-4
Front Royal, VA 74-75 DE 5
Frosinone 36-37 E 5
Frostburg, MD 74-75 D 5
Frostproof, FL 74-75 c 3
Frövi 30-31 F 8
Frøya 30-31 C 6
Frøya, Banc de – 28-29 JK 3
Frøya, Banco de – 28-29 JK 3
Fröyabank 28-29 JK 3
Frøya-pad 30-31 B 6
Frozen Strait 70-71 U 4
Fruita, CO 76-77 J 6
Fruitland, ID 76-77 E 3
Fruitland, UT 76-77 H 5
Fruška gora 36-37 H 3
Fruška gora 36-37 H 3
Fruto, CA 76-77 B 6

Fu'ād, Bi'r – 62 B 2
Fu'an 48-49 MN 6
Fucheu = Fuzhou 48-49 MN 6
Fu-chien = Fujian 48-49 M 6
Fuchin = Fujin 48-49 P 2
Fu-ch'ing = Fuqing 48-49 MN 6
Fuchow = Fuzhou 48-49 MN 6
Fuchskauten 33 CD 3
Fudai 50-51 NO 2-3
Fuego, Tierra del – 80 C 8
Fuego, Volcán de – 72-73 H 9
Fuente de San Esteban, La – 34-35 DE 8
Fuentes de Oñoro 34-35 D 8
Fuentes de Oñoro 34-35 D 8
Fuerte, Río – 72-73 E 6
Fuerte Bulnes 80 B 8
Fuerte Olimpo 80 E 2
Fuerteventura 60-61 B 3
Fugløy, Banc de – 30-31 HJ 2
Fugløy, Banco de – 30-31 HJ 2
Fuglöy Bank 30-31 HJ 2
Fugloybank 30-31 HJ 2
Fugløy-pad 30-31 HJ 2
Fugløy-pad 30-31 HJ 2
Fu-hsien = Fu Xian [TJ, Liaoning] 48-49 N 4
Fu-hsien = Fuxin 48-49 N 3
Fu-hsien Hu = Fuxian Hu 48-49 J 7
Fujairah, Al- = Al-Fujayrah 44-45 H 5
Fujayrah, Al- 44-45 H 5
Fuji 50-51 M 5
Fujian 48-49 M 6
Fu Jiang 48-49 K 5
Fujin 48-49 P 2
Fujinomiya 50-51 M 5
Fujioka 50-51 M 4

176 Filip

Fuji-san 48-49 Q 4-5
Fujisawa 50-51 MN 5
Fuji-Yoshida 50-51 M 5
Fukae = Fukue 50-51 G 6
Fukagawa 50-51 bc 2
Fūkah 62 B 2
Fukien = Fujian 48-49 M 6
Fukuchiyama 50-51 K 5
Fukue 50-51 G 6
Fukue-shima 50-51 G 6
Fukui 48-49 Q 4
Fukuoka [J, Fukuoka] 48-49 OP 5
Fukuoka [J, Iwate] 50-51 N 2
Fukura = Nandan 50-51 K 5
Fukushima [J, Fukushima] 48-49 R 4
Fukushima [J, Hokkaidō] 50-51 b 3
Fukushima [J, Nagano] 50-51 L 5
Fukuyama 50-51 J 5
Fūlah, Al- 60-61 K 6
Fulaikā', Jazīrat — = Jazīrat Faylakah 46-47 N 8
Fulda [D, ~] 33 D 3
Fulda [D, ●] 33 D 3
Fuling 48-49 K 6
Fulton, CA 76-77 B 6
Fulton, NY 74-75 E 3
Fūman 46-47 N 4
Fumban = Foumban 60-61 G 7
Fūmch'ŏn = Kūmch'on 50-51 F 3
Fumel 34-35 H 6
Funabashi 50-51 MN 5
Funagawa = Oga 50-51 M 3
Funatsu = Kamioka 50-51 L 4
Funchal 60-61 A 2
Fundación 78-79 E 2
Fundão 34-35 D 8
Fundão [BR] 78-79 LM 8
Fundy, Bay of — 70-71 X 8-9
Fünfkirchen = Pécs 33 HJ 5
Funhalouro 64-65 HJ 7
Funing [TJ, Jiangsu] 48-49 MN 5
Funtua 60-61 F 6
Fuqing 48-49 MN 6
Furancungo 64-65 H 5
Furano 50-51 c 2
Furāt, Al- 44-45 DE 3
Furāt, Nahr al- 44-45 E 4
Furāt, Shaṭṭ al- 46-47 LM 7
Fūr Ghūrū = Fdayrik 60-61 B 4
Furmanovka [SU, Kazachskaja SSR] 42-43 N 9
Furnas, Represa de — 78-79 K 9
Furneaux Group 56-57 J 7-8
Fúrnoi 36-37 M 7
Furqlūs 46-47 G 5
Fürstenfeld 33 GH 5
Fürstenwalde 33 FG 2
Fürth 33 E 4
Further India 22-23 OP 5
Furubira 50-51 b 2
Furukamappu = Južno-Kuril'sk 42-43 c 9
Furukawa 50-51 N 3
Fury and Hecla Strait 70-71 TU 4
Fusan = Pusan 48-49 OP 4
Fuse = Higasiôsaka 50-51 KL 5
Fushi = Yan'an 48-49 K 4
Fushun 48-49 NO 3
Fushuncheng 50-51 DE 2
Fusien = Fu Xian 48-49 N 4
Fusin = Fuxin 48-49 N 3
Fusong 48-49 O 3
Füssen 33 E 5
Fu-sung = Fusong 50-51 F 1
Futa Djalon = Fouta Djalon 60-61 B 6
Futamata 50-51 L 5
Futaoi-jima 50-51 H 5
Futsing = Fuqing 48-49 MN 6
Futuna 52-53 b 1
Fuwah 62 D 2
Fu Xian [TJ, Liaoning] 48-49 N 4
Fuxian Hu 48-49 J 7
Fuxin 48-49 N 3
Fuyang [TJ, Anhui] 48-49 M 5
Fuyu [TJ, Heilongjiang] 48-49 NO 2
Fuyu [TJ, Jilin] 48-49 NO 2
Fu-yü = Fuyu 48-49 NO 2
Fuyuan 48-49 P 2
Fuzhou [TJ, Fujian] 48-49 MN 6
Fuzhou [TJ, Jianxi] 48-49 M 6
Fuzhoucheng 48-49 N 4

Fülöp-szigetek 52-53 H 3-J 5

Fiji 52-53 ab 2
Fijibekken 22-23 S 7
Fijieilanden = Fiji Islands 52-53 ab 2
Fyn 30-31 D 10
Fyzabad = Faizabad 44-45 N 5

G

Gaalkacyo 60-61 b 2
Gaarowe = Garoowe 60-61 b 2
Gabbac 60-61 c 2
Gabbs Valley 76-77 DE 6
Gabbs Valley Range 76-77 DE 6
Gabela [Angola] 64-65 DE 5
Gaberones = Gaborone 64-65 FG 7
Gabès = Qâbis 60-61 FG 2
Gabilan Range 76-77 C 7
Gabon 64-65 CD 3
Gabón 64-65 CD 3
Gaborone 64-65 FG 7
Gabrovo 36-37 L 4
Gabú 60-61 B 6
Gabun 64-65 CD 3
Gachsārān 44-45 G 4
Gacko 36-37 H 4
Gadap = Karāchī 44-45 K 6
Gäddede 30-31 F 5
Gadīdah, Al- = Al-Jadīdah [MA] 60-61 C 2
Gadra 44-45 L 5
Gadsden, AL 72-73 J 5
Găeşti 36-37 L 3
Gaeta 36-37 E 5
Gaeta, Golfo di — 36-37 E 5
Gaffney, SC 74-75 C 7
Gagarin 38-39 F 4
Gage, NM 76-77 JK 9
Gagliano del Capo 36-37 GH 6
Gagnoa 60-61 C 7
Gagnon 70-71 X 7
Gago Coutinho = Lungala N'Guimbo 64-65 F 5
Gagra 38-39 GH 7
Gahnpa 60-61 C 7
Gaia = Gayā 44-45 NO 5-6
Gail 33 F 5
Gaima 52-53 M 8
Gaimán 80 C 6
Gainesville, FL 72-73 K 6
Gainesville, GA 72-73 K 5
Gainesville, TX 72-73 G 5
Gairdner, Lake — 56-57 G 6
Gai Xian 50-51 CD 2
Gaizina kalns 30-31 LM 9
Gajny 42-43 J 5
Galadi = Geladī 60-61 O 7
Galán, Cerro — 80 C 3
Galana 64-65 JK 3
Galápagos, Dorsal de las — 22-23 E 5
Galápagos, Îles — = Archipiélago de Colón 78-79 AB 5
Galápagos, Islas — = Archipiélago de Colón 78-79 AB 5
Galápagos, Seuil des — 22-23 E 5
Galapagos, Wyspy — = Archipiélago de Colón 78-79 AB 5
Galapagosdrempel 22-23 E 5
Galapagos Eilanden = Archipiélago de Colón 78-79 AB 5
Galápagosinseln = Archipiélago de Colón 78-79 AB 5
Galápagosschwelle 22-23 E 5
Galápagos-szigetek = Archipiélago de Colón 78-79 AB 5
Galapágy = Archipiélago de Colón 78-79 AB 5
Galashiels 32 E 4
Galaţi 36-37 MN 3
Galatina 36-37 H 5
Galax, VA 74-75 C 6
Galbeed = Woqooyi-Galbeed 60-61 a 1
Galdhøpiggen 30-31 BC 7
Galela 52-53 J 6
Galena, AK 70-71 E 4-5
Galera, Punta — [EC] 78-79 C 4
Galera, Punta — [RCH] 80 AB 6
Galera Point 72-73 OP 9
Galesburg, IL 72-73 HJ 3
Galets 32 E 5-6
Galeta, Isla — 72-73 b 2
Galeta Island 72-73 b 2
Galeton, PA 74-75 E 4
Galguduud 60-61 b 2-3
Galič [SU, Rossijskaja SFSR] 42-43 G 6
Galicia 34-35 CD 7
Galicie = Galicia 34-35 CD 7
Galicja 33 J-L 4
Galič [SU, Rossijskaja SFSR] 42-43 G 6
Galilee, Lake — 56-57 HJ 4
Galipoli = Gelibolu 44-45 B 2
Galiuro Mountains 76-77 H 9
Galizien = Galicia 34-35 CD 7
Gälla 44-45 MN 9
Gall'a, ostrov — 42-43 KL 1
Gallabat = Qallābāt 60-61 M 6
Galladi = Geladī 60-61 O 7
Gallatin Gateway, MT 76-77 H 3
Gallatin Peak 76-77 H 3
Gallatin River 76-77 H 3
Galle = Gälla 44-45 MN 9
Gállego, Río — 34-35 G 7
Gallegos, Río — 80 BC 8
Galles, Pays de — 32 E 5-6
Galliate 36-37 C 3
Gallinas, Punta — 78-79 E 2
Gallipoli 36-37 GH 5
Gallipoli = Gelibolu 44-45 B 2
Gallipolis, OH 74-75 B 5
Gällivare 30-31 J 4
Gallo Mountains 76-77 J 8-9
Galloo Island 74-75 E 3
Galloway 32 DE 4
Gallup, NM 72-73 E 4
Galšir 48-49 L 2
Galšir 48-49 L 2
Galt, CA 76-77 C 6
Galveston, TX 72-73 H 6
Galveston Bay 72-73 H 6
Gálvez [RA] 80 D 4
Galway 32 B 5
Galway Bay 32 B 5
Gam, Pulau — 52-53 JK 7
Gamane = Bertoua 60-61 G 8
Gāmāsiyāb, Rūd-e — 46-47 MN 5
Gambaga 60-61 D 6
Gambeila = Gambēla 60-61 L 7
Gambēla 60-61 L 7
Gambell, AK 70-71 BC 5
Gambia 60-61 AB 6
Gambie [~] 60-61 B 6
Gambie [★] 60-61 AB 6
Gambie [★] 60-61 AB 6
Gamboa 72-73 b 2
Gamboma 64-65 E 3
Gambos 64-65 DE 5
Gamerco, NM 76-77 J 8
Game Reserve Number 1 64-65 EF 6
Gamlakarleby = Kokkola 30-31 K 6
Gamleby 30-31 FG 9
Gamo Gofa 60-61 M 7
Gamova, mys — 50-51 H 1
Gamsah = Jamsah 62 E 4
Gamvik 30-31 N 2
Gana = Ghana 60-61 DE 7
Ganaane, Webi — = Webi Juba 60-61 N 8
Ganado, AZ 76-77 J 8
Gananoque 74-75 E 2
Ganāveh 44-45 FG 5
Ganchhendzönga = Gangchhendsönga 44-45 O 5
Gand = Gent 34-35 JK 3
Ganda 64-65 D 5
Gandajika 64-65 FG 4
Gandak 44-45 NO 5
Gander 70-71 a 8
Gandesa 34-35 H 8
Gandia 34-35 GH 9
Ganga 44-45 M 5
Ganga, Mouths of the — 44-45 OP 6
Gan Gan 80 C 6
Ganganagar 44-45 LM 5
Gangchhendsönga 44-45 O 5
Gange, Bouches du — = Mouths of the Ganga 44-45 OP 6
Gange, Vallée sous-marine du — 44-45 O 6-7
Ganges = Ganga 44-45 M 5
Ganges, Boca del — = Mouths of the Ganga 44-45 OP 6
Ganges, Dorsal del — 44-45 O 6-7
Ganges, Mondingen van de — = Mouths of the Ganga 44-45 OP 6
Ganges Canyon 44-45 O 6-7
Gangesgeul 44-45 O 6-7
Gangesmündungen = Mouth of the Ganga 44-45 OP 6
Gangesrinne 44-45 O 6-7
Gangesz-deltavidék = Mouth of the Ganga 44-45 OP 6
Gangesz-hasadék 44-45 O 6-7
Gangīr, Rūdkhāneh ye — 46-47 LM 6
Gangou 50-51 B 2
Gangouzhen = Gangou 50-51 B 2
Gangthog = Gangtok 44-45 O 5
Gangtö Gangri 48-49 G 6
Gangtok 44-45 O 5
Gangtun 50-51 C 2
Gangy, ústí — = Mouth of the Ganga 44-45 OP 6
Gan He 48-49 N 1
Gan Jiang 48-49 LM 6
Gannan Zangzu Zizhizhou 48-49 J 5
Gannett, ID 76-77 FG 4
Gannett Peak 72-73 E 3
Gänsebank 42-43 GH 3
Gansos, Banco de los — 42-43 GH 3
Gansu 48-49 G 3-J 4
Ganta = Gahnpa 60-61 C 7
Gantheaume Bay 56-57 B 5
Gan'uškino 38-39 JK 6
Gan'uškino 38-39 JK 6
Ganxian = Ganzhou 48-49 LM 6
Ganzenbank 42-43 GH 3
Ganzhou 48-49 LM 6
Gao 60-61 D 5
Gao'an 48-49 LM 6
Gaoligong Shan 48-49 H 6
Gaoqiao = Gaoqiaozhen 50-51 C 2
Gaoqiaozhen 50-51 C 2
Gaotai 48-49 H 4
Gaoua 60-61 D 6
Gaoual 60-61 B 6
Gaoxiong = Kaohsiung 48-49 MN 7
Gap 34-35 L 6
Gar, Bir el — = Bi'r al-Qaf 60-61 H 3
Garacad 60-61 bc 2
Garah 58 JK 2
Garamba, Parc national de la — 64-65 GH 2
Garanhuns 78-79 M 6
Gara Samuil 36-37 M 4
Garb, Gebel el — = Jabal Nafusah 60-61 G 2
Garbahaarrey 60-61 N 8
Garba Tula 63 D 2
Garberville, CA 76-77 B 5
Garcias 78-79 J 9
Gard 34-35 K 6-7
Garda 36-37 D 3
Garda, Lago di — 36-37 D 3
Gardelegen 33 E 2
Garden City, KS 72-73 F 4
Garden Grove, CA 76-77 D 9
Garden Valley, ID 76-77 F 3
Gardēz 44-45 K 4
Gardhsskagi 30-31 b 2
Gardiner, ME 74-75 J 2
Gardiner, MT 76-77 H 3
Gardiners Bay 74-75 GH 4
Gardner, MA 74-75 GH 3
Gardnerville, NV 76-77 D 6
Garentsovo moře 38-39 E-J 1
Garfield Heights, OH 74-75 C 4
Garfield Mountain 76-77 G 3
Gargaliánoi 36-37 J 7
Gargano 36-37 FG 5
Gargano, Testa del — 36-37 G 5
Gargar 46-47 L 3
Gargar, Īstgāh-e — 46-47 N 7
Gargia 30-31 K 3
Garian = Gharyān 60-61 G 2
Garibaldi, OR 76-77 B 3
Garies 64-65 E 9
Garissa 64-65 JK 3
Garland, NC 74-75 D 7
Garland, UT 76-77 G 5
Garmashīn, 'Ain — = 'Ayn Jarmashīn 62 CD 5
Garmisch-Partenkirchen 33 E 5
Garmsār 38-39 K 8
Garnet, MT 76-77 G 2
Garonne 34-35 G 6
Garoowe 60-61 b 2
Garopaba 80 G 3
Garoua 60-61 G 7
Garrison, MT 76-77 G 2
Garry Lake 70-71 Q 4
Gartempe 34-35 H 5
Gartog 48-49 E 5
Gartok = Gartog 48-49 E 5
Garua = Garoua 60-61 G 7
Gary, IN 72-73 J 3
Garzan = Zok 46-47 J 3
Garze 48-49 J 5
Garze Zangzu Zizhizhou 48-49 HJ 5
Garzón [CO] 78-79 DE 4
Gasan-Kuli 44-45 G 3
Gascogne 34-35 GH 7
Gascogne, Golfe de — 34-35 EF 6
Gascoyne, Mount — 56-57 C 4
Gascoyne River 56-57 C 5
Gashaka 60-61 G 7
Gasmata 52-53 gh 6
Gasparilla Island 74-75 b 3
Gaspé 70-71 Y 8
Gaspé, Cap de — 70-71 Y 8
Gaspésie, Péninsule de — 70-71 XY 8
Gas-san [J] 50-51 MN 3
Gassaway, WV 74-75 C 5
Gaston, OR 76-77 B 3
Gastonia, NC 72-73 K 4
Gastre 80 C 6
Gašuun Gov' 48-49 G 3
Gašuun nuur 48-49 HJ 3
Gašuun Gov' 48-49 G 3
Gašuun nuur 48-49 HJ 3
Gat = Ghat 60-61 G 3
Gata, Cabo de — 34-35 FG 10
Gata, Sierra de — 34-35 D 8
Gátas, Akrōtḗrion — 46-47 E 5
Gatčina 42-43 DE 6
Gatčina 42-43 DE 6
Gate City, VA 74-75 B 6
Gateshead 32 EF 4
Gateway, CO 76-77 J 6
Gateway, MT 76-77 F 1
Gateway, OR 76-77 C 3
Gâtinais 34-35 J 4
Gâtine, Hauteurs de — 34-35 G 5
Gatooma = Kadoma 64-65 G 6
Gatrun, el- = Al-Qaṭrūn 60-61 GH 4
Gatun 72-73 b 2
Gatun, Barrage de — = Presa de Gatún 72-73 ab 2
Gatún, Brazo de — 72-73 b 2
Gatún, Esclusas de — 72-73 b 2
Gatún, Lago de — 72-73 b 2
Gatún, Presa de — 72-73 ab 2
Gatún, Río — 72-73 b 2
Gatun Arm = Brazo de Gatún 72-73 b 2
Gatuncillo 72-73 b 2
Gatuncillo, Río — 72-73 b 2
Gatun Dam = Presa de Gatún 72-73 ab 2
Gatun Lake = Lago de Gatún 72-73 b 2
Gatun Locks = Esclusas de Gatún 72-73 b 2
Gatvand 46-47 N 6
Gauani = Gewanī 60-61 N 6
Gauhati 44-45 P 5
Gauja 30-31 L 9
Gaula 30-31 D 6
Gauley Mountain 74-75 C 5
Gaurisankar = Jomotsering 44-45 O 5
Gaurīshankar = Jomotsering 44-45 O 5
Gausta 30-31 C 8
Gausvik 30-31 G 3
Gávdos 36-37 L 8
Gave de Pau 34-35 G 7
Gāveh Rūd 46-47 M 5
Gaviota, CA 76-77 C 8
Gävle 30-31 G 7
Gävleborg 30-31 G 6-7
Gavrilov-Jam 38-39 G 4
Gawdezereh 44-45 J 5
Gawler 56-57 G 6
Gawler Ranges 56-57 G 6
Gawso 60-61 D 7
Gaya [DY] 60-61 E 6
Gaya [IND] 44-45 NO 5-6
Gayaza 63 B 3
Gayndah 56-57 K 5
Gaza 64-65 H 7
Gaza = Ghazzah 44-45 C 4
Gazalkent 42-43 MN 9
Gazelle, CA 76-77 B 5
Gazelle Peninsula 52-53 h 5
Gazi 63 D 4
Gaziantep 44-45 D 3
Gaziantep Ovası 46-47 GH 4
Gazibenli = Yahyalı 46-47 F 3
Gaziler 46-47 K 2
Gazi Mağusa 44-45 CD 3
Gazipaşa 46-47 E 4

Gbarnga 60-61 C 7

Gcuwa 64-65 G 9

Gdańsk 33 J 1
Gdańsk, Baie de — = Zatoka Gdańska 33 J 1
Gdańsk, Bocht van — = Zatoka Gdańska 33 J 1
Gdańsk, Golfo de — = Zatoka Gdańska 33 J 1
Gdańska, Zatoka — 33 J 1
Gdánsk Bay = Zatoka Gdańska 33 J 1
Gdingen = Gdynia 33 HJ 1
Gdov 38-39 E 4
Gdynia 33 HJ 1

Gearhart Mountain 76-77 C 4
Geba, Rio — 60-61 AB 6
Gebal = Jubayl 46-47 F 5
Gebe, Pulau — 52-53 J 7
Gebeit = Jubayt 60-61 M 4
Gebiz 46-47 D 4
Gebze 46-47 C 2
Gedaref = Al-Qadārif 60-61 M 6
Gedi 64-65 J 3
Gedid, el — = Sabhah 60-61 G 3
Gedikbulak = Canik 46-47 K 3
Gediz 46-47 C 3
Gediz Nehri 46-47 B 3
Gedlegubē 60-61 NO 7
Gēdo [ETH] 60-61 M 7
Gedo [SP] 60-61 N 8
Gedser 30-31 DE 10
Geelong 56-57 H 7
Geelvink Channel 56-57 B 5
Geelvink Channel 56-57 B 5
Geelvink Channel 56-57 B 5
Geese Bank 42-43 GH 3
Geeveston 56-57 J 8
Géfyra 36-37 K 5
Gegeen gol = Gen He 48-49 N 1
Geidam 60-61 G 6
Geilo 30-31 C 7
Geiranger 30-31 B 6
Geislingen 33 D 4
Geita 64-65 H 3
Gejiu 48-49 J 7
Gela 36-37 F 7
Geladi 60-61 O 7
Gelai 63 D 3
Gelasa, Selat — 52-53 E 7
Gelbes Meer 48-49 N 4
Gelendost 46-47 D 3
Gelendžik 38-39 G 7
Gelendžik 38-39 G 7
Gele Zee 48-49 N 4
Gelibolu 44-45 B 2
Gelsenkirchen 33 C 3
Gemas 52-53 D 6
Gemena 64-65 E 2
Gemerek 46-47 G 3
Gemiyanı = Türkeli 46-47 F 2
Gemlik 46-47 C 2
Gemlik Körfezi 46-47 C 2
Gemona del Friuli 36-37 E 2
Gemsa = Jamsah 62 E 4
Gemu Gofa = Gamu Gofa 60-61 M 7
Genale Weniz 60-61 N 7
Genç 46-47 J 3
Geneina, El- = Al-Junaynah 60-61 J 6
General Acha 80 CD 5
General Acha 80 CD 5
General Acha 80 CD 5
General Alvear [RA, Buenos Aires] 80 DE 5
General Alvear [RA, Mendoza] 80 C 4-5
General Belgrano [Antarktika] 24 B 32-33
General Bernardo O'Higgins 24 C 31
General Conesa [RA, Río Negro] 80 CD 6
General Deheza 80 D 4
General Enrique Mosconi 80 D 2
General Güemes 80 CD 2
General Guido 80 E 5
General Juan Madariaga 80 E 5
General La Madrid 80 D 5
General Lavalle 80 E 5
General Lorenzo Vintter 80 D 6
General Machado = Camacupa 64-65 E 5
General Pico 80 D 5
General Pinedo 80 D 3
General Roca 80 C 5
General San Martín [RA, Chaco] 80 E 3
General Santos 52-53 HJ 5
General Toševo 36-37 N 4
General Toševo 36-37 N 4
General Villamil = Playas 78-79 C 5
General Villegas 80 D 4-5
Gênes = Gènova 36-37 C 3
Genesee, ID 76-77 E 2
Genesee River 74-75 DE 3
Geneseo, NY 74-75 E 3
Geneva, NY 74-75 E 3
Geneva, OH 74-75 C 4
Geneva = Genève 33 C 5
Genève 33 C 5
Genewa = Geneve 33 C 5
Genf = Genève 33 C 5
Genghiz Khan, Wall of — 48-49 LM 2
Gengis Khan, Muralla de — 48-49 LM 2
Gengis Khan, Mur de — 48-49 LM 2
Gen He [TJ, ~] 48-49 N 1
Genhe [TJ, ●] 48-49 N 1
Geničesk 38-39 F 6
Geničesk 38-39 F 6
Genil 34-35 E 10
Genk 34-35 K 3
Genkai nada 50-51 GH 6
Gennargentu, Monti del — 36-37 C 5-6
Genoa 56-57 J 7
Genoa = Gènova 36-37 C 3
Genootschapseilanden 22-23 B 6-7
Gènova 36-37 C 3
Génova = Gènova 36-37 C 3
Gènova, Golfo di — 36-37 C 4
Genovesa, Isla — 78-79 B 4
Genrietty, ostrov — 42-43 ef 2
Gent 34-35 JK 3
Genteng 52-53 E 8
Genua = Gènova 36-37 C 3
Genzan = Wŏnsan 48-49 O 4
Geographe Bay 56-57 BC 6
Geographe Channel 56-57 B 4-5
Geographe Channel 56-57 B 4-5
Geographe Channel 56-57 B 4-5
Geok-Tepe 44-45 H 3
Georga, zemľa — 42-43 F-H 1
George 64-65 F 9
George, Lake — [AUS] 56-57 JK 7
George, Lake — [EAU] 64-65 H 3
George, Lake — [RWA] 63 B 3
George, Lake — [USA, Florida] 74-75 c 2
George, Lake — [USA, New York] 74-75 G 3
George, Rivière — 70-71 X 6
George Gill Range 56-57 F 4
Georgetown [AUS, Queensland] 56-57 H 3
George Town [AUS, Tasmania] 56-57 J 8
Georgetown [CDN, Ontario] 74-75 D 3
Georgetown [GUY] 78-79 H 3
George Town [MAL] 52-53 CD 5
Georgetown, CA 76-77 C 6
Georgetown, DE 74-75 F 5
Georgetown, ID 76-77 H 4
Georgetown, SC 74-75 D 8
George Washington Birthplace National Monument 74-75 E 5
Georgia [★] 38-39 HJ 7
Georgia [☆] 72-73 K 5
Georgia, Strait of — 70-71 M 8
Georgia del Sur = South Georgia 80 J 8

Georg 177

Georgia del Sur, Dorsal de – 24 D 33-E 34
Georgian Bay 70-71 U 8-9
Georgia Południowa = South Georgia 80 J 8
Georgias del Sur, Islas – = South Georgia 80 J 8
Georgië 38-39 HJ 7
Géorgie 38-39 HJ 7
Géorgie du Sud = South Georgia 80 J 8
Géorgie du Sud, Seuil de – 24 D 33-E 34
Georgien 38-39 HJ 7
Georgijevka 42-43 P 8
Georgijevsk 38-39 H 7
Georgijevskoje 38-39 HJ 4
Georgina River 56-57 G 4
Georg von Neumayer 24 B 36
Gera 33 EF 3
Gerais, Chapado dos – 78-79 K 8
Gerais, Chapado dos – 78-79 K 8
Gerais, Chapado dos – 78-79 K 8
Geraldine, MT 76-77 HJ 2
Geraldton [AUS] 56-57 B 5
Geraldton [CDN] 70-71 T 8
Gerasimovka 42-43 N 6
Gercüş 46-47 J 4
Gerdakānehbālā 46-47 M 5
Gerdine, Mount – 70-71 F 5
Gerede 46-47 E 2
Gerede = Beydili 46-47 D 2
Gerede Çayı 46-47 E 2
Gerger 46-47 H 3
Geriş 46-47 D 4
Gerlach, NV 76-77 D 5
Gerlachovský štít 33 JK 4
Gerlachovský štít 33 JK 4
Gêrlogubī = Gedlegubē 60-61 NO 7
Germany 33 D-F 2-4
Germencik 46-47 B 4
Germī 46-47 N 3
Germiston 64-65 G 8
Gerona 34-35 J 8
Gers 34-35 H 7
Gerze 46-47 F 2
Gesellschaftsinseln 22-23 B 6-7
Gestro Weniz, Wabē – 60-61 N 7
Gettysburg, PA 74-75 E 5
Getz Ice Shelf 24 B 23-24
Gevar ovası 46-47 L 4
Gevaş 46-47 K 3
Gevgelija 36-37 K 5
Gewanē 60-61 N 6
Geyik Dağları 46-47 E 4
Geyser, MT 76-77 H 2
Geyser, Banc du – 64-65 L 5
Geysir 30-31 c 2
Geyve 46-47 D 2
Gezira, El – = Al-Jazīrah 60-61 L 6

Ghāb, Al- 46-47 G 5
Ghāb, El- = Al-Ghāb 46-47 G 5
Ghāb, Jabal – 46-47 H 5
Ghadai = Ghaday 46-47 M 8
Ghadāmes = Ghadāmis 60-61 FG 2-3
Ghadāmis 60-61 FG 2-3
Ghaday 46-47 M 8
Ghadūn, Wādī – 44-45 G 7
Ghaghara 44-45 N 5
Ghallah, Bi'r – 62 E 3
Ghana 60-61 DE 7
Ghānim, Jazīrat – 62 E 4
Ghanzi 64-65 F 7
Gharaq as-Sulṭānī, Al- 62 CD 3
Gharbī, Jabal – 46-47 H 5
Gharbīyah, Al- 62 C 3
Ghardaqah, Al- 60-61 L 3
Ghardāyah 60-61 E 2
Ghārib, Jabal – 60-61 L 3
Gharqābād 46-47 NO 5
Gharyān 60-61 G 2
Ghat 60-61 G 3
Ghāṭ'ā', Al- 46-47 J 5
Ghawdex 36-37 F 7
Ghayḍah, Al- [Y ← Sayḥūt] 44-45 FG 7-8
Ghayḍah, Al- [Y ↗ Sayḥūt] 44-45 G 7
Ghazāl, 'Ayn al- [ET] 62 E 5
Ghazāl, Bahr al- [Sudan, ~] 60-61 KL 7
Ghazāl, Bahr al- [Sudan, ☆] 60-61 JK 7
Ghazawāṭ, Al- 60-61 D1
Ghazīr = Jazīr 46-47 F 5
Ghaz köl 48-49 G 4
Ghaznı 44-45 K 4
Ghazzah 44-45 C 4
Ghedo = Gēdo 60-61 M 7
Gheorghe Gheorghiu-Dej 36-37 M 2
Gheorghieni 36-37 LM 2
Gherla 36-37 KL 2
Gherlogubi = Gerlogubī 60-61 NO 7
Ghiedo = Gēdo 60-61 M 7
Ghigner = Gīnīr 60-61 N 7
Ghimbi = Gimbī 60-61 M 7
Ghinah, Wādī al- 46-47 G 7-8
Ghōr, El- = Al-Ghūr 46-47 F 7
Ghuja 48-49 E 3
Ghūr, Al- 46-47 F 7
Ghurdaqa, El – = Al-Ghardaqah 60-61 L 3
Ghūryān 44-45 J 4

Giannitsá 36-37 K 5
Giannutri 36-37 D 4
Giant Mountains 33 GH 3
Gia Rai 52-53 E 5
Giarre 36-37 F 7
Gibbon, OR 76-77 D 3
Gibbonsville, ID 76-77 G 3
Gibeil = Jubayl 62 E 3
Gibeon [Namibia, ●] 64-65 E 8
Gibraltar 34-35 E 10
Gibraltar, Détroit de – 34-35 D 11-E 10
Gibraltar, Estrecho de – 34-35 D 11-E 10
Gibraltar, Straat van – 34-35 D 11-E 10
Gibraltar, Strait of – 34-35 D 11-E 10
Gibraltar, Straße von – 34-35 D 11-E 10
Gibraltári-szoros 34-35 DE 11
Gibraltarska, Cieśn. 34-35 DE 11
Gibraltarský průliv 34-35 DE 11
Gibson Desert 56-57 DE 4
Gīdolē 60-61 M 7
Gien 34-35 J 5
Gießen 33 D 3
Gifu 48-49 Q 4
Giganta, Sierra de la – 72-73 D 6-7
Giglio 36-37 D 4
Gigüela 34-35 F 9
Gihân, Râs – = Rā's al-Bālā'im 62 E 3
Giheina = Juhaynah 62 D 4
Gihu = Gifu 48-49 Q 4
Gijón 34-35 E 7
Gila Bend, AZ 76-77 G 9
Gila Cliff 76-77 J 9
Gila Cliff Dwellings National Monument 76-77 J 9
Gila Desert 72-73 D 5
Gila Mountains 76-77 J 9
Gīlān 44-45 FG 3
Gīlān, Sārāb-e – 46-47 LM 5
Gīlān-e Gharb 46-47 LM 5
Gila River 72-73 D 5
Gila River Indian Reservation 76-77 GH 9
Gilbert River [AUS, ~] 56-57 H 3
Gilbert River [AUS, ●] 56-57 H 3
Gilbués 78-79 K 6
Gilf Kebir Plateau = Haḍbat al-Jilf al-Kabīr 60-61 K 4
Gilgandra 56-57 J 6
Gilgat = Gilgit 44-45 L 3
Gilgil 63 CD 3
Gilgit 44-45 L 3
Gillam 70-71 S 6
Gillen, Lake – 56-57 D 5
Gilles, Lake – 58 C 4
Gilmore, ID 76-77 G 3
Gilroy, CA 76-77 G 7
Giluwe, Mount – 52-53 M 8
Gimbala, Jebel – = Jabal Marrah 60-61 JK 6
Gīmbī 60-61 M 7
Gimma = Jīma 60-61 M 7
Gimpu 52-53 GH 7
Ginebra = Genève 33 C 5
Gineifa = Junayfah 62 E 2
Ginevrabotnen 30-31 kl 5
Gīngiova 36-37 KL 4
Gīnīr 60-61 N 7
Ginyer = Gīnīr 60-61 N 7
Gióia del Colle 36-37 G 5
Giovi, Passo dei – 36-37 C 3
Gippsland 56-57 J 7
Girard, OH 74-75 C 4
Girard, PA 74-75 C 3-4
Girardot 78-79 E 4
Giren = Jīma 60-61 M 7
Giresum 38-39 G 7
Giresun 44-45 D 2
Giresun Dağları 46-47 H 2
Girge = Jirjā 60-61 L 3
Giri 64-65 E 2
Giridih 44-45 O 6
Girilambone 58 H 3
Girishk 44-45 J 4
Girne 46-47 E 5
Gironde 34-35 G 6
Girvan 32 D 4
Girvas 30-31 O 4
Gisborne 56-57 P 7
Gisenyi 64-65 G 3
Gislaved 30-31 E 9
Gisr ash-Shughur 46-47 G 5
Gitega 64-65 GH 3
Giulianova 36-37 EF 4
Giumbo = Jumbo 64-65 K 3
Giùra 36-37 L 6
Giurgiu 36-37 L 4
Givet 34-35 K 3
Gižduvan 42-43 L 9
Gizeh = Al-Jīzah 60-61 KL 3
Gižiga 42-43 f 5
Gižiginskaja guba 42-43 e 5
Gīzmel 46-47 M 5
Gizo 52-53 j 6
Giżycko 33 KL 1
Gižduvan 42-43 L 9
Gižiga 42-43 f 5
Gižiginskaja guba 42-43 e 5
Giżycko 33 KL 1

Gjersvik 30-31 E 5
Gjirokastër 36-37 HJ 5
Gjögurtá 30-31 d 1
Gjøvik 30-31 D 7
Gjuhës, Kepi i – 36-37 H 5

Glace Bay 70-71 YZ 8
Glacier Bay National Monument 70-71 J 6
Glacier National Park [USA] 72-73 CD 2
Glacier Peak 76-77 C 1
Glade Park, CO 76-77 J 6
Gladstone [AUS, Queensland] 56-57 K 4
Gladstone [AUS, South Australia] 56-57 G 6
Glady, WV 74-75 D 5
Gláma 30-31 b 2
Glamis, CA 76-77 F 9
Glasgow 32 DE 4
Glassboro, NJ 74-75 F 5
Glatz = Kłodzko 33 H 3
Glauchau 33 F 3
Glazov 42-43 J 6
Gleeson, AZ 76-77 J 10
Gleisdorf 33 GH 5
Gleiwitz = Gliwice 33 J 3
Glenbrook 58 K 4
Glen Canyon 76-77 H 7
Glencoe [CDN] 74-75 C 3
Glendale, AZ 72-73 D 5
Glendale, CA 72-73 C 5
Glendale, NV 76-77 F 7
Glendale, OR 76-77 B 4
Glenelg River 58 E 6
Glengyle 56-57 GH 4
Glen Innes 56-57 K 5
Glen Lyon, PA 74-75 EF 4
Glen Lyon, PA 74-75 EF 4
Glen More 32 D 3
Glenmorgan 56-57 JK 5
Glenns Ferry, ID 76-77 F 4
Glenore 56-57 H 3
Glens Falls, NY 74-75 G 3
Glenwood, OR 76-77 B 3
Glenwood, WA 76-77 C 2
Glide, OR 76-77 B 4
Glina 36-37 G 3
Glittertind 30-31 C 7
Gliwice 33 J 3
Globe, AZ 72-73 D 5
Glogau = Głogów 33 GH 3
Gloggnitz 33 G 5
Głogów 33 GH 3
Glomfjord 30-31 EF 4
Glomma 30-31 D 7
Glommersträsk 30-31 HJ 5
Glória 78-79 M 6
Gloria, La – [CO] 78-79 E 3
Glorieuses, Îles – 64-65 L 5
Gloucester, MA 74-75 H 3
Gloucester City, NJ 74-75 F 5
Glouchester 32 E 6
Glouster, OH 74-75 BC 5
Gloversville, NY 74-75 F 3
Glubokoje [SU, Belorusskaja SSR] 30-31 M 10
Glubokoje [SU, Kazachskaja SSR] 42-43 P 7
Gluchov 38-39 F 5

Gliwice 33 J 3
Głogów 33 GH 3

Gmünd 33 G 4
Gmunden 33 FG 5

Gnaday 46-47 M 8
Gnesen = Gniezno 33 H 2
Gniezno 33 H 2
Gnowangerup 56-57 C 6

Goa 44-45 L 7
Goageb [Namibia, ●] 64-65 E 8
Goaso = Gawso 60-61 D 7
Goba [ETH] 60-61 N 7
Gobabis 64-65 E 7
Gobernador Gregores 80 BC 7
Gobi 48-49 H-L 3
Gobō 50-51 K 6
Godavari 44-45 N 7
Godavari Delta 44-45 N 7
Goddo 78-79 HJ 4
Goddua = Ghuddawah 60-61 G 3
Godfrey Tank 56-57 E 4
Godhavn = Qeqertarssuq 70-71 Za 4
Godoy Cruz 80 BC 4
Gods Lake [CDN, ●] 70-71 S 7
Gods Lake [CDN, ≈] 70-71 S 7
Godthåb = Nûk 70-71 a 5
Godwin Austen, Mount – = K 2 44-45 M 3
Goede Hoop, Kaap de – 64-65 E 9
Goélands, Lac aux – 70-71 Y 6
Goeree 34-35 J 3
Goffs, CA 76-77 F 8
Goggiam = Gojam 60-61 M 6
Gogland, ostrov – 30-31 M 7
Gogra = Ghaghara 44-45 N 5
Gogrial = Qūqriyāl 60-61 K 7
Goiana 78-79 MN 6
Goiandira 78-79 K 8
Goianésia 78-79 K 8
Goiânia 78-79 JK 8
Goiás [BR, ●] 78-79 JK 8
Goiás [BR, ☆] 78-79 J 8-K 7
Goiás, Serra Geral de – 78-79 K 7
Goiatuba 78-79 JK 8
Gojam 60-61 M 6
Gojjam = Gojam 60-61 M 6
Gökbel 46-47 C 4
Gökçeada 46-47 AB 2
Gökırmak 46-47 F 2
Gökova Körfezi 46-47 BC 4
Göksu [TR, ~] 46-47 FG 4
Göksu [TR, ●] 46-47 K 3
Göksun 46-47 G 3
Göksu Nehri 44-45 C 3
Gök Tepe [TR, ▲] 46-47 C 4
Göktepe [TR, ●] 46-47 E 4
Gokwe 64-65 G 6
Gol 30-31 C 7
Golaja Pristan' 36-37 P 2
Golāshkerd 44-45 H 5
Gölbaşı [TR, Adıyaman] 46-47 G 4
Gölbaşı [TR, Ankara] 46-47 E 3
Golconda, NV 76-77 E 5
Gölcük [TR, Kocaeli] 46-47 CD 2
Gołdap 33 L 1
Gold Beach, OR 76-77 A 4
Goldburg, ID 76-77 G 3
Gold Butte, MT 76-77 H 1
Gold Coast [AUS, ●] 56-57 K 5
Gold Coast [≅] 60-61 D 8-E 7
Gold Coast-Southport 58 LM 1
Golden, ID 76-77 F 3
Goldendale, WA 76-77 C 3
Golden Gate 72-73 B 4
Golden Vale 32 BC 5
Goldfield, NV 76-77 E 7
Gold Hill, UT 76-77 G 5
Goldküste 60-61 D 8-E 7
Gold Point, NV 76-77 E 7
Goldsboro, NC 72-73 L 4-5
Goldsworthy, Mount – 56-57 CD 4
Göle 46-47 K 2
Goléa, El- = Al-Gulī'ah 60-61 E 2
Golec-In'aptuk, gora – = gora In'aptuk 42-43 UV 6
Golec-Longdor, gora – = gora Longdor 42-43 W 6
Golela 64-65 H 8
Goleniów 33 G 2
Goleta, CA 76-77 D 8
Golfe Nuevo 80 D 6
Golfe Persique 44-45 FG 5
Golfito 72-73 K 10
Golfo Aranci 36-37 CD 5
Golfo Dulce 72-73 K 10
Golfo Pérsico 44-45 FG 5
Gölhisar 46-47 C 4
Gölköy 46-47 G 2
Göllü = Çoğun 46-47 F 3
Gölmarmara 46-47 BC 3
Golmo 48-49 GH 4
Golodnaja step' = Betpak-Dala 42-43 MN 8
Golog Zangzu Zizhizhou 48-49 HJ 5
Golog Zizhizhou 48-49 HJ 5
Gölören 46-47 E 4
Golpāyegān 44-45 G 4
Gölpazarı 46-47 D 2
Golspie 32 E 2-3
Gol Tappeh 46-47 L 4
Golungo Alto 64-65 D 4
Golyšmanovo 42-43 MN 6
Golyšmanovo 42-43 MN 6
Gołdap 33 L 1
Goma 64-65 G 3
Gomati 44-45 N 5
Gomba 63 D 5
Gombari 63 B 2
Gombe [EAT] 64-65 H 3
Gombe [WAN] 60-61 G 6
Gomel' 38-39 F 5
Gomera 60-61 A 3
Gómez Palacio 72-73 EF 6
Gonābād 44-45 H 4
Gonaïves 72-73 M 8
Gonam [SU, ~] 42-43 Y 6
Gonam [SU, ●] 42-43 Z 6
Gonâve, Golfe de la – 72-73 M 8
Gonâve, Île de la – 72-73 M 8
Gonbād-e Kavus = Gonbad-e Qābūs 44-45 H 3
Gonbad-e Qābūs 44-45 H 3
Gondar = Gonder 60-61 M 6
Gonder [ETH, ●] 60-61 M 6
Gonder [ETH, ☆] 60-61 M 6
Gönen 46-47 B 2
Gongga Shan 48-49 J 6
Gongjiatun = Gangtun 50-51 C 2
Gongoji, Serra do – 78-79 LM 7-8
Gongola 60-61 G 7
Gongola, River – 60-61 G 6
Gongyingzi 50-51 BC 2
Gongzhuling = Huaide 48-49 NO 3
Goniądz 33 L 2
Gonja 63 D 4
Gono-kawa 50-51 J 5
Gonoura 50-51 G 6
Gonzales, CA 76-77 C 7
Gonzanamá 78-79 D 5
Goodenough, Cape – 24 C 13
Goodenough Island 52-53 gh 6
Good Hope, Cape of – 64-65 E 9
Goodhouse 64-65 E 8
Gooding, ID 76-77 F 4
Goodooga 58 HJ 2
Goolgowi 58 G 4
Goomalling 56-57 C 6
Goona = Guna 44-45 M 6
Goondiwindi 56-57 JK 5
Goonyella 56-57 J 4
Goose Bay [CDN, Newfoundland] 70-71 Y 7
Goose Creek 76-77 FG 4-5
Goose Lake [USA] 72-73 B 3
Go Quao 52-53 DE 5
Gor'ačegorsk 42-43 Q 6
Gor'ačegorsk 42-43 Q 6
Gorakhpoor = Gorakhpur 44-45 N 5
Gorakhpur 44-45 N 5
Gorakpur = Gorakhpur 44-45 N 5
Goram Islands = Kepulauan Seram-Laut 52-53 K 7
Goran, El – = El Ķoran 60-61 N 7
Gördes 46-47 C 3
Gordion 46-47 DE 3
Gordon, GA 74-75 B 8
Gordon, Lake – 58 bc 3
Gordon Downs 56-57 E 3
Gordonsville, VA 74-75 D 5
Gordonvale 56-57 J 3
Gorē [ETH] 60-61 M 7
Gore [NZ] 56-57 N 9
Goré [Tschad] 72-73 H 7
Gore, Isla – 76-77 F 10
Görele 46-47 H 2
Gore Mountain 74-75 H 2
Gorgān 44-45 GH 3
Gorgān, Rūd-e – 44-45 GH 3
Gorgona, Isla – 78-79 D 4
Gorgora 60-61 M 6
Gori Cheboa 63 E 2
Gori Cheboa 63 E 2
Gori Cheboa 63 E 2
Gorizia 36-37 E 3
Gorki [SU, Belorusskaja SSR] 38-39 F 5
Gorki [SU, Rossijskaja SFSR Jamalo-Neneckaja AO] 42-43 M 4
Gorki = Gor'kij 42-43 GH 6
Gor'kij = Nižnij Novgorod 42-43 GH 6
Gor'kovskoje vodochranilišče 42-43 GH 6
Gor'kovskoje vodochranilišče 42-43 GH 6
Görlitz 33 G 3
Gorlovka 38-39 G 6
Gorman, CA 76-77 D 8
Gorna Or'ahovica 36-37 LM 4
Górne, Jezioro – = Lake Superior 72-73 HJ 2
Gornji Milanovac 36-37 J 3
Gorno-Altai Autonomous Region = 9 ◁ 42-43 Q 7
Gorno-Altaj, Oblast Autónoma de – = 9 ◁ 42-43 Q 7
Gorno-Altajsk 42-43 Q 7
Górno-Altajski Obwód Autonomiczny = 8 ◁ 42-43 Q 7
Gorno-Badachšanskaja Autonome Oblast 44-45 L 3
Gorno-Badachšanskaja Autonome Oblast 44-45 L 3
Gorno-Badachšanskaja Autonomnaja Oblast 44-45 L 3
Górnobadachszański Obwód Autonomiczny 44-45 B 3
Gorno-Badachšan, Oblast Autónoma de – 44-45 L 3
Gorno-Badachšan, Oblast Autónoma de – 44-45 L 3
Gorno-Badachšanskaja Autonome Oblast 44-45 L 3
Gorno-Badachšanskaja Autonome Oblast 44-45 L 3
Gorno-Badachšanskaja Autonomnaja Oblast 44-45 L 3
Gorno-Badachšanskaja Avtonomnaja Oblast' = Autonome Oblast der Bergbadachschanen 44-45 L 3
Gorno-Badakhshan Autonomous Region 44-45 L 3
Górnokarabachski, Ob.A - 38-39 J 7-8
Gornozavodsk 42-43 b 8
Górny Egipt = Aṣ-Ṣa'īd 60-61 L 3-4
Gorodok = Zakamensk 42-43 T 7
Goroka 52-53 N 8
Gorom = Gorom-Gorom 60-61 DE 6
Gorom-Gorom 60-61 DE 6
Gorongosa, Serra de – 64-65 HJ 6
Gorontalo 52-53 H 6
Gorrahei = Korahe 60-61 NO 7
Gort 32 B 5
Goryn' 38-39 E 5
Gorzów Wielkopolski 33 GH 2
Gosen [J] 50-51 M 4
Gosford-Woy Woy 56-57 K 6
Goshen, CA 76-77 D 7
Goshen, NY 74-75 F 4
Goshogawara 50-51 MN 2
Goshute Indian Reservation 76-77 F 6
Goslar 33 DE 3
Gospić 36-37 F 3
Gosport 32 F 6
Gostynin 33 J 2
Gosyogahara = Goshogawara 50-51 MN 2
Göta älv 30-31 D 9-E 8
Göta kanal 30-31 EF 8
Götaland 30-31 E-G 9
Göteborg 30-31 D 9
Göteborg och Bohus 30-31 D 8
Gotha 33 E 3
Gotland [S, ⊙] 30-31 H 9
Gotland [S, ☆] 30-31 H 9
Gotland, Fosa de – 30-31 HJ 9
Gotland, Fosse de – 30-31 HJ 9
Gotland Deep 30-31 HJ 9
Gotlanddiep 30-31 HJ 9
Gotland-mélység 30-31 HJ 9
Gotlandtief 30-31 HJ 9
Gotlandzka, Głębia - 30-31 HJ 9
Gotō-rettō 48-49 O 5
Gotska Sandön 30-31 HJ 8
Gōtsu 50-51 HJ 5
Göttingen 33 DE 3
Gottschee = Kočevje 36-37 F 3
Goubangzi 50-51 CD 2
Goubéré 60-61 K 7
Goudiry 60-61 B 6
Goudkust 60-61 D 8-E 7
Gough, GA 74-75 B 8
Gouin, Réservoir – 70-71 VW 8
Goulburn 56-57 J 6
Goulburn Islands 56-57 F 2
Gould Bay 24 B 31-32
Goulimīm = Julimīnā 60-61 BC 3
Goundam 60-61 D 5
Gouré 60-61 G 6
Gourma 60-61 E 6
Gourma Rharous 60-61 D 5
Gouro 60-61 H 5
Gouverneur, NY 74-75 F 2
Gōvā = Goa 44-45 L 7
Gov'altaj = 5 ◁ 48-49 H 3
Gov'altajn nuruu 48-49 H 2-J 3
Govena, mys – 42-43 g 6
Goverla 36-37 L 1
Governador Valadares 78-79 L 8
Gowanda, NY 74-75 D 3
Gower Peninsula 32 DE 6
Goya 80 E 3
Göynücek 46-47 F 2
Göynük [TR, Bingöl] 46-47 J 3
Göynük [TR, Bolu] 46-47 D 2
Goz Beïda 60-61 J 6
Goze Delčev 36-37 KL 5
Goze Delčev 36-37 KL 5
Gozha Tsho 48-49 E 4

Görögország 36-37 J 7-L 5

Graaff-Reinet 64-65 FG 9
Grã-Canária = Gran Canaria 60-61 A 3
Grace, ID 76-77 H 4
Gracias a Dios, Cabo – 72-73 K 8
Gradaús 78-79 J 6
Gradaús, Serra dos – 78-79 JK 6
Gräddö 30-31 H 8
Grafton 56-57 K 5
Grafton, WV 74-75 CD 5
Graham, NC 74-75 D 6-7
Graham, Mount – 72-73 DE 5
Graham Bell, ostrov – = ostrov Greém-Bell 42-43 MN 1
Graham Island 70-71 JK 7
Graham Moore, Cape – 70-71 V-X 3
Grahamstad = Grahamstown 64-65 G 9
Grahamstown 64-65 G 9
Grain Coast 60-61 B 7-C 8
Graines, Côte des – 60-61 B 7-C 8
Grajaú 78-79 K 6
Grajaú, Rio – [BR, Maranhão] 78-79 K 5-6
Grajewo 33 L 2
Grambûsa, Akrōtḗrion – 36-37 K 8
Grámmos 36-37 J 5
Grampian Mountains 32 DE 3
Gran = Esztergom 33 J 5
Granada [E] 34-35 F 10
Granada [NIC] 72-73 JK 9
Granada [WG] 72-73 O 9
Gran Altiplanicie Central 80 BC 7
Gran Atlas 60-61 CD 2
Gran Bahía Australiana = Great Australian Bight 56-57 E 6-G 7
Gran Bajo [RA, Santa Cruz] 80 C 7

178 Georg

Granby 70-71 W 8
Gran Canaria 60-61 AB 3
Gran Chaco 80 D 3-E 2
Gran Chaco 80 D 3-E 2
Grand Bahama Island 72-73 L 6
Grand Baie Australienne = Great Australian Bight 56-57 E 6-G 7
Grand Ballon 34-35 L 5
Grand Bassa = Buchanan 60-61 B 7
Grand-Bassam 60-61 D 7-8
Grand-Bourg 72-73 OP 8
Grand Canal 32 BC 5
Grand Canyon 72-73 D 4
Grand Canyon, AZ 76-77 GH 7
Grand Canyon National Monument 76-77 G 7
Grand Canyon National Park 72-73 D 4
Grand Cayman 72-73 KL 8
Grand Coulee [USA] 76-77 D 2
Grand Coulee, WA 76-77 D 2
Grand Coulee Dam 72-73 BC 2
Grand Coulee Equalizing Reservoir = Banks Lake 76-77 D 2
Grande Comore = Ngazidja 64-65 K 5
Grande Dépression Centrale 64-65 EF 3
Grande Muraille 48-49 K 4
Grande Prairie 70-71 N 6-7
Grand Erg de Bilma 60-61 G 5
Grand Erg Occidental = Al-'Irq al-Kabīr al-Gharbī 60-61 D 3-E 2
Grand Erg Oriental = Al 'Irq al-Kabīr ash-Sharqī 60-61 F 2-3
Grande-Rivière, la – 70-71 V 7
Grande Rivière à la Balleine 70-71 VW 6
Grande Ronde, OR 76-77 B 3
Grande Ronde River 76-77 E 2-3
Grandes Antilles 72-73 K 7-N 8
Grandes Antillas 72-73 K 7-N 8
Gran Desierto 72-73 D 5
Grandes Landes 34-35 G 6-7
Grande Syrte = Khalīj as-Surt 60-61 H 2
Grand Falls [CDN] 70-71 Za 8
Grand Falls [EAK] 63 D 3
Grand Falls [USA] 76-77 H 8
Grand Falls = Churchill Falls 70-71 XY 7
Grandfather Mountain 74-75 C 6
Grand Forks, ND 72-73 G 2
Grandioznyj, pik – 42-43 RS 7
Grand Island [USA, New York] 74-75 D 3
Grand Island, NE 72-73 G 3
Grand Isle 74-75 G 2
Grand Junction, CO 72-73 DE 4
Grand Khingan 48-49 M 3-W 1
Grand-Lahou 60-61 CD 7-8
Grand Lake [USA, Maine] 74-75 K 2
Grand Météor, Banc du – 22-23 H 4
Grândola 34-35 C 9
Grand Paradiso 36-37 B 3
Grand-Popo 60-61 E 7
Grand Rapids, MI 72-73 J 3
Grand River [CDN] 74-75 CD 3
Grand River [USA, South Dakota] 72-73 F 2
Grand River Valley 76-77 J 6
Grand Teton National Park 76-77 H 3-4
Grand Teton Peak 72-73 D 3
Grand Trunk Pacific Railway = Candian National Railways 70-71 PQ 7
Grand View, ID 76-77 EF 4
Grandview, WA 76-77 D 2
Grand Wash Cliffs 76-77 FG 8
Gran Erg Occidental = Al-'Irq al-Kabīr al-Gharbī 60-61 D 3-E 2
Gran Erg Oriental = Al-'Irq al-Kabīr ash-Sharqī 60-61 F 2-3
Granger, WA 76-77 CD 2
Granger, WY 76-77 J 5
Grängesberg 30-31 F 7
Grangeville, ID 76-77 EF 3
Gran Chaco 80 D 3-E 2
Granite, OR 76-77 D 3
Granite Downs 56-57 F 5
Granite Mountains 76-77 F 8
Granite Peak [USA, Montana] 72-73 E 2
Granite Peak [USA, Utah] 76-77 G 5
Granite Range [USA, Nevada] 76-77 D 5
Granite Springs Valley 76-77 D 5
Graniteville, SC 74-75 C 8
Granja 78-79 L 5
Gran Jingán 48-49 M 3-N 1
Gran Lago Salado = Great Salt Lake 72-73 D 3
Gran Malvina = West Falkland 80 D 8
Gran Muralla 48-49 K 4
Gränna 30-31 F 8
Gran Pampa Pelada 78-79 F 9
Gran Sabana, La – 78-79 G 3
Gran San Bernardo 36-37 B 3
Gran Sasso 36-37 E 4
Grant, FL 74-75 c 3
Grant, MT 76-77 G 3
Grant, Mount – [USA, Clan Alpine Mountains] 76-77 DE 6
Grant, Mount – [USA, Wassuk Range] 76-77 D 6
Grant Land 19 A 25-27
Grant Range 76-77 F 6
Grants, NM 72-73 E 4
Grants Pass, OR 76-77 B 4
Grantsville, UT 76-77 G 5
Grantsville, WV 74-75 C 5
Granville 34-35 G 4
Grasse 34-35 L 7
Grass Lake, CA 76-77 B 5
Grass Valley, CA 76-77 C 6
Grass Valley, OR 76-77 C 3
Grassy 56-57 H 7-8
Grassy Knob 74-75 C 5-6
Gratangen 30-31 GH 3
Graudenz = Grudziądz 33 J 2
Gravatá 78-79 M 6
Gravenhage, 's- 34-35 JK 2
Gravenhurst 74-75 D 2
Grave Peak 76-77 F 2
Gravesend 58 JK 2
Gravina di Pùglia 36-37 G 5
Gray 34-35 K 5
Gray, GA 74-75 B 8
Grays Harbor 76-77 AB 2
Graz 33 G 5
Gr'azi 38-39 GH 5
Gr'azovec 38-39 GH 4
Grdelica 36-37 JK 4
Great Abaco Island 72-73 L 6
Great Artesian Basin 56-57 GH 4-5
Great Australian Bight 56-57 E 6-G 7
Great Bahama Bank 72-73 L 6-7
Great Barrier Island 56-57 P 7
Great Barrier Reef 56-57 H 2-K 4
Great Basin 72-73 CD 3-4
Great Bay 74-75 F 5
Great Bear Lake 70-71 MN 4
Great Bear River 70-71 LM 4-5
Great Bend, KS 72-73 FG 4
Great Bitter Lake = Al-Buḥayrat al-Murrat al-Kubrá 62 E 2
Great Dividing Range 56-57 H-K 3-7
Great Driffield 32 FG 4-5
Greater Antilles 72-73 K 7-N 8
Greater Sunda Islands 52-53 E-H 7-8
Great Exuma Island 72-73 L 7
Great Falls [USA] 76-77 H 2
Great Falls, MT 72-73 DE 2
Great Falls, SC 74-75 C 7
Great Inagua Island 72-73 M 7
Great Kei River = Groot Keirivier 64-65 GH 9
Great Khingan Range 48-49 M 3-N 1
Great Lake 56-57 J 8
Great Meteor Seamount 22-23 H 4
Great Namaqua Land = Namaland 64-65 E 8
Great Nicobar 44-45 P 9
Great Northern Pacific Railway 72-73 DE 2
Great Northern Peninsula 70-71 Z 7-8
Great Oyster Bay 58 d 3
Great Peconic Bay 74-75 G 4
Great Plains 72-73 E 2-F 5
Great Ruaha 64-65 J 4
Great Sacandaga Lake 74-75 FG 3
Great Salt Lake 72-73 D 3
Great Salt Lake Desert 72-73 D 3
Great Sandy Desert [AUS] 56-57 DE 4
Great Sandy Desert [USA] 72-73 BC 3
Great Sandy Island 56-57 KL 4-5
Great Slave Lake 70-71 NO 5
Great Smoky Mountains 74-75 B 7
Great Valley 74-75 A 7-F 4
Great Victoria Desert 56-57 EF 5
Great Wall 48-49 K 4
Great Yarmouth 32 GH 5
Grebená 36-37 J 5
Grèboun, Mont – 60-61 F 4-5
Grèce 36-37 J 7-L 5
Grecia 36-37 J 7-L 5
Grecja 36-37 J 7-L 5
Gredos, Sierra de – 34-35 E 8
Greece 36-37 J 7-L 5
Greeley, CO 72-73 F 3
Greely Fiord 70-71 UV 1
Greém-Bell, ostrov – 42-43 MN 1
Green Bay 72-73 J 2-3
Green Bay, WI 72-73 J 3
Greenbrier River 74-75 CD 5-6
Green Cape 58 K 6
Greencastle, PA 74-75 DE 5
Green Cove Springs, FL 74-75 bc 1-2
Greeneville, TN 74-75 B 6
Greenfield, CA 76-77 C 7
Greenfield, MA 74-75 G 3
Greenhorn Mountains 76-77 D 8
Green Island [AUS] 56-57 J 3
Green Islands 52-53 hj 5
Greenland 19 BC 23
Greenland Basin 22-23 JK 2
Greenland Sea 19 B 20-18
Green Mountains [USA, Vermont] 74-75 G 2-3
Greenock 32 D 4
Green Pond, SC 74-75 C 8
Greenport, NY 74-75 G 4
Green River [USA, Wyoming] 72-73 E 3-4
Green River, UT 76-77 H 6
Green River, WY 76-77 J 5
Green River Basin 72-73 DE 3
Greensboro, GA 74-75 B 8
Greensboro, NC 72-73 L 4
Greensburg, PA 74-75 D 4
Green Swamp 74-75 D 7
Greenville 60-61 C 7-8
Greenville, CA 76-77 C 5
Greenville, FL 74-75 b 1
Greenville, IN 74-75 A 4
Greenville, ME 74-75 HJ 2
Greenville, MS 72-73 HJ 5
Greenville, NC 72-73 L 4
Greenville, PA 74-75 C 4
Greenville, SC 72-73 K 5
Greenville, TX 72-73 GH 5
Greenwich, London- 32 FG 6
Greenwood, MS 72-73 HJ 5
Greenwood, SC 72-73 K 5
Greer, ID 76-77 EF 2
Greer, SC 74-75 B 7
Gregory, Lake – 56-57 GH 5
Gregory Downs 56-57 G 3
Gregory Lake 56-57 E 3-4
Gregory Range 56-57 H 3
Gregory River 56-57 G 3
Greifenberg in Pommern = Gryfice 33 G 2
Greifswald 33 F 1
Grein 33 G 4
Greinerville 63 B 4
Greiz 33 EF 3
Gréko, Akrōtērion – 46-47 F 5
Gremicha 42-43 F 4
Grenå 30-31 D 9
Grenada 72-73 O 9
Grenade 72-73 O 9
Grenadines 72-73 O 9
Grenen 30-31 D 9
Grenfell [AUS] 58 HJ 4
Grenivík 30-31 de 2
Grenlandia 19 BC 23
Grenlandzkie, Morze – 19 B 20-18
Grenoble 34-35 KL 6
Grenvill, Cape – 56-57 H 2
Gretna, LA 72-73 HJ 6
Grey Islands 70-71 Za 7
Greylock, Mount – 74-75 G 3
Greymouth 56-57 O 8
Grey Range 56-57 H 5
Greytown = Bluefields 72-73 K 9
Gribingui = Ibingui-Économique 60-61 H 7
Gridley, CA 76-77 C 6
Griechenland 36-37 J 7-L 5
Griekenland 36-37 J 7-L 5
Griekwaland-Wes 64-65 F 8
Griffin, GA 72-73 K 5
Griffith 56-57 J 6
Grigoriopol 36-37 N 2
Grim, Cape – 56-57 H 8
Grimari 60-61 HJ 7
Grimes, CA 76-77 C 6
Grimma 33 F 3
Grimsby 32 FG 5
Grimsby [CDN] 74-75 D 3
Grimsey 30-31 d 1
Grimstad 30-31 C 8
Grímsvötn 30-31 e 2
Grindavík 30-31 b 3
Grindsted 30-31 C 10
Grinnell Land 70-71 UV 1-2
Grinnell Peninsula 70-71 RS 2
Griqualand West = Griekwaland-Wes 64-65 F 8
Grodno 38-39 DE 5
Groenland 19 BC 23
Groenland, Bassin du – 22-23 JK 2
Groenland, Mer du – 19 B 20-18
Groenlandbekken 22-23 JK 2
Groenlandia 19 BC 23
Groenlandia, Cuenca de – 22-23 JK 2
Groenlandia, Mar de – 19 B 20-18
Groenlandzee 19 B 20-18
Grœtavær 30-31 FG 3
Groix, Île de – 34-35 F 5
Groll, Crête de – 22-23 H 6
Grollkuppe 22-23 H 6
Groll-Ondiepte 22-23 H 6
Groll Seamount 22-23 H 6
Groll, Cima de – 22-23 H 6
Grong 30-31 E 5
Groningen [NL] 34-35 L 2
Groningen [SME] 78-79 HJ 3
Grönland 19 BC 23
Grönländisches Becken 22-23 JK 2
Grönlandsee 19 B 20-18
Grónské moře 19 B 20-18
Grónsko 19 BC 23
Groot Barrierif = Great Barrier Reef 56-57 H 1-K 4
Groot Brittannië en Noordierland 32 F-H 4-5
Groot Brukkaros 64-65 E 8
Groote Eylandt 56-57 G 2
Grootfontein 64-65 E 6
Groot-Karasberge 64-65 E 8
Groot-Karoo 64-65 F 9
Groot Keirivier 64-65 GH 9
Groot Visrivier 64-65 E 8
Grosa, Punta – 34-35 H 9
Gros Morne National Park 70-71 Z 8
Großbritannien und Nordirland 32 F-H 4-5
Große Antillen 72-73 K 7-N 8
Große Arabische Wüste = Ar-Rub' al-Hālī 44-45 F 7-G 6
Große Australische Bucht = Great Australian Bight 56-57 E 6-G 7
Große Bahamabank 72-73 L 6-7
Große Mauer 48-49 K 4
Große Meteorbank 22-23 H 4
Großenbrode 33 E 1
Große Nefud = An-Nafūd 44-45 E 5
Große Persische Salzwüste = Dasht-e Kavīr 44-45 GH 4
Großer Arber 33 F 4
Großer Bärensee 70-71 MN 4
Großer Beerberg 33 E 3
Großer Chingan = Großer Khingan 48-49 M 3-N 1
Großer Chingan = Großer Khingan 48-49 M 3-N 1
Großer Fischfluß = Groot Visrivier 64-65 E 8
Großer Chingan = Großer Khingan 48-49 M 3-N 1
Großer Khingan 48-49 M 3-N 1
Großer Salzsee = Great Salt Lake 72-73 D 3
Großer Sklavensee 70-71 NO 5
Große Sandwüste = Great Sandy Desert 56-57 DE 4
Großes Artesisches Becken = Great Artesin Basin 56-57 GH 4-5
Großes Barrierriff = Great Barrier Reef 56-57 H 2-K 4
Große Schüttinsel = Ostrov 33 H 4-5
Große Sundainseln 52-53 E-H 7-8
Großes Wallriff = Great Barrier Reef 56-57 H 2-K 4
Große Syrte = Khalīj as-Surt 60-61 H 2
Grosseto 36-37 D 4
Große Victoriawüste = Great Victoria Desert 56-57 EF 5
Großglockner 33 F 5
Gros Ventre River 76-77 H 4
Grote Antillen 72-73 K 7-N 8
Grote Australische Bocht = Great Australian Bight 56-57 E 6-G 7
Grote Bahamabank 72-73 L 6-7
Grote Ocean 22-23 Q-T 5-6
Grote Sunda-Eilanden 52-53 GH 8
Grote Syrte = Khalīj as-Surt 60-61 H 2
Grote Xingangebergte 48-49 M 3-N 1
Grotli 30-31 BC 6
Groton, NY 74-75 E 3
Grottoes, VA 74-75 D 5
Grouse, ID 76-77 G 4
Grouse Creek, UT 76-77 G 5
Grouse Creek Mountain 76-77 FG 3
Grove City, PA 74-75 CD 4
Groveland, CA 76-77 CD 7
Grover, WY 76-77 H 4
Grover City, CA 76-77 C 8
Grovont, WY 76-77 H 4
Growler, AZ 76-77 FG 9
Growler Mountains 76-77 G 9
Groznyj 38-39 HJ 7
Grönlandi-tenger 19 B 20-18
Grudovo 36-37 M 4
Grudziądz 33 J 2
Grumantbyen 30-31 jk 5
Grumeti 63 C 3
Grumo Appula 36-37 G 5
Grünau [Namibia] 64-65 E 8
Grünberg in Schlesien = Zielona Góra 33 GH 2-3
Grünberg in Schlesien = Zielona Góra 33 GH 2-3
Grünberg in Schlesien = Zielona Góra 33 GH 2-3
Grundarfjördhur 30-31 ab 2
Grundy, VA 74-75 BC 6
Grúzia 38-39 H 7
Gruzie 38-39 H 7
Gruzja 38-39 H 7
Gryfice 33 G 2
Gryllefjord 30-31 G 3
Grytviken 80 J 8
Gṣaiba = Quṣaybah 46-47 J 5
Guacanayabo, Golfo de – 72-73 L 7
Guadalajara [E] 34-35 F 8
Guadalajara [MEX] 72-73 EF 7
Guadalaviar 34-35 G 8
Guadalcanal [Solomon Is.] 52-53 j 6
Guadalcanar Gela = Guadalcanal 52-53 j 6
Guadalete 34-35 DE 10
Guadalimar 34-35 F 9
Guadalope 34-35 G 8
Guadalquivir 34-35 E 10
Guadalupe [E] 34-35 E 9
Guadalupe [MEX, Nuevo León] 72-73 FG 6
Guadalupe, CA 76-77 C 8
Guadalupe, Isla de – 72-73 C 6
Guadalupe, Sierra de – 34-35 E 9
Guadalupe Mountains [USA ↘ Phoenix] 76-77 J 10
Guadalupe Peak 72-73 F 5
Guadarrama, Sierra de – 34-35 EF 8
Guadeloupe 72-73 O 8
Guadeloupe Passage 72-73 O 8
Guadiana 34-35 D 10
Guadiana Menor 34-35 F 10
Guadix 34-35 F 10
Guadur = Gwādar 44-45 J 5
Guafo, Golfo de – 80 B 6
Guafo, Isla – 80 AB 6
Guai 52-53 L 7
Guainía, Río – 78-79 F 4
Guaiquinima, Cerro – 78-79 G 3
Guaitecas, Islas – 80 AB 6
Guajará-Mirim 78-79 FG 7
Guajira, Península de – 78-79 E 2
Gualala, CA 76-77 B 6
Gualaquiza 78-79 D 5
Gualeguay 80 E 4
Gualeguaychu 80 E 4
Gualior = Gwalior 44-45 M 5
Guamblin, Isla – 80 A 6
Guaña 78-79 G 4
Guanahani = San Salvador 72-73 M 7
Guanajutao 72-73 F 7
Guanare 78-79 F 3
Guanarito 78-79 F 3
Guandong Bandao 50-51 C 3
Guane 72-73 K 7
Guang'an 48-49 K 5
Guangchang 48-49 M 6
Guangdong 48-49 L 7
Guanghai 48-49 L 7
Guanghua 48-49 L 5
Guangji 48-49 M 6
Guanglu Dao 50-51 D 3
Guangnan 48-49 JK 7
Guangxi Zhuangzu Zizhiqu 48-49 KL 7
Guangyuan 48-49 K 5
Guangzhou 48-49 LM 7
Guangzhou Wan = Zhanjiang Gang 48-49 L 7
Guano Lake 76-77 D 4
Guanshui 50-51 E 2
Guantánamo 72-73 LM 7-8
Guanyun 48-49 MN 5
Guaña 78-79 G 4
Guapi 78-79 D 4
Guaporé = Rondônia 78-79 G 7
Guaporé, Rio – [BR ◁ Rio Mamoré] 78-79 G 7
Guaqui 78-79 F 8
Guarabira 78-79 MN 6
Guaranda 78-79 D 5
Guarapuava 80 F 3
Guaratinguetá 78-79 KL 9
Guaratuba 80 G 3
Guarayos, Llanos de – 78-79 G 8
Guarayos, Llanos de – 78-79 G 8
Guarda 34-35 D 8
Guardafui = 'Asayr 44-45 G 8
Guardo 34-35 E 7
Guarulhos 78-79 K 9
Guasave 72-73 E 6
Guascama, Punta – 78-79 D 4
Guasdualito 78-79 EF 3
Guasipati 78-79 G 3
Guastalla 36-37 D 3
Guatemala [GCA, ●] 72-73 HJ 9
Guatemala [GCA, ★] 72-73 HJ 8
Guatemala, Bassin du – 22-23 DE 5
Guatemala, Cuenca de – 22-23 DE 5
Guatemala Basin 22-23 DE 5
Guatemalabecken 22-23 DE 5
Guatemalabekken 22-23 DE 5
Guaviare, Río – 78-79 F 4
Guaxupé 78-79 K 9
Guayana = Guyana 78-79 H 3-4
Guayana = Guyana 78-79 H 3-4
Guayana Francesa 78-79 J 4
Guayanas, Cuenca de las – 22-23 G 5
Guayaquil 78-79 CD 5
Guayaquil, Golfo de – 78-79 C 5
Guayaramerin 78-79 F 7
Guaymas = Heroica Guaymas 72-73 D 6
Guba 64-65 G 5
Gubacha 42-43 K 6
Guban 60-61 ab 1
Gubanovo = Vereščagino 42-43 JK 6
Gùbbio 36-37 E 4
Guben 33 G 3
Gučin Us 48-49 J 2
Gučin Us 48-49 J 2
Gūḍalūr = Cuddalore 44-45 MN 8
Gudauta 38-39 GH 7
Gudbrandsdal 30-31 CD 7
Gudenå 30-31 CD 9
Gudermes 38-39 J 7
Güdül 46-47 E 2
Gudur 44-45 MN 8
Gūḍūru = Gudur 44-45 MN 8
Guéckédou 60-61 BC 7
Guelma = Qalmah 60-61 F 1
Guelph 70-71 UV 9
Guéné 60-61 E 6
Guéra, Massif de – 60-61 H 6
Guéréda 60-61 J 6
Guéret 34-35 H 5
Guernsey 32 E 7
Guerrero [MEX, ☆] 72-73 FG 8
G'ueševo 36-37 K 4
G'ueševo 36-37 K 4
Guettara, Aïn El – = El Guettâra 60-61 D 4
Guettâra, El – 60-61 D 4
Guezzam, In – = 'Ayn Qazzān 60-61 EF 5
Gugē 60-61 M 7
Gughe = Gugē 60-61 M 7
Guia 78-79 H 8
Guiana Basin 22-23 G 5
Guiana Brasileira 78-79 G-J 4-5
Guichi 48-49 M 5
Guidder = Guider 60-61 G 6-7
Guide 48-49 J 4
Guider 60-61 G 6-7
Guiding 48-49 K 6
Guiers, Lac de – 60-61 AB 5
Guiglo 60-61 C 7
Guildford 32 F 6
Guilin 48-49 KL 6
Guimarães [P] 34-35 C 8
Guimarães [BR] 78-79 L 5
Guimaras Island 52-53 H 4
Guinan Zhou = Qiannon Zizhizhou 48-49 K 6
Guinea 60-61 B 6-C 7
Guinea, Cuenca de – 22-23 J 5
Guinea, Dorsal de – 22-23 JK 6
Guinea, Golfo de – 60-61 C-F 8
Guinea, Golf von – 60-61 C-F 8
Guinea, Gulf of – 60-61 C-F 8
Guinea Basin 22-23 J 5
Guineabecken 22-23 J 5
Guinea Bissau 60-61 AB 6
Guinea Ecuatorial 60-61 FG 8
Guineai-öböl 60-61 C-F 8
Guinea Rise 22-23 JK 6
Guineaschwelle 22-23 JK 6
Guinee 60-61 B 6-C 7
Guinée 60-61 B 6-C 7
Guinée, Bassin de – 22-23 J 5
Guinée, Golfe de – 60-61 C-F 8
Guinee, Golf van – 60-61 C-F 8
Guinée, Seuil de – 22-23 JK 6
Guineebekken 22-23 J 5
Guinee-Bissau 60-61 AB 6
Guinée-Bissau 60-61 AB 6
Guineedrempel 22-23 JK 6
Guinée-Équatoriale 60-61 FG 8
Guinejský záliv 60-61 C-F 8
Güines [C] 72-73 K 7
Guingamp 34-35 F 4
Guiping 48-49 KL 7
Guiyang [TJ, Guizhou] 48-49 K 6
Guiyang [TJ, Hunan] 48-49 L 6
Guizhou 48-49 JK 6
Gujana 78-79 H 3-4
Gujana Francuska 78-79 J 4
Gujańska, Wyżyna – = Macizo de las Guyanas 78-79 F 3-J 4
Gujarāt 44-45 L 6
Gujerat = Gujarāt 44-45 L 6
Gūjrānwālah 44-45 L 4
Gujrāt 44-45 L 4
Gük Tappah 46-47 L 5
Gulabarga = Gulburga 44-45 M 7
Gul'ajevo, Archangel'sk- 38-39 H 3
Gul'ajpole 38-39 G 6
Gulargambone 58 J 3
Gulbān aṭ-Ṭaiyārāt, Bīr – = Qulbān aṭ-Ṭayyārāt 46-47 JK 5
Gulbene 30-31 M 9
Gulbin Ka 60-61 F 6
Gülek = Çamalan 46-47 F 4
Gulf Coastal Plain 72-73 G 6-J 5
Gulfport, FL 74-75 b 3
Gulfport, MS 72-73 J 5
Gulgong 58 JK 4
Guli'ah, Al- = Al-Qulī'ah 60-61 H 1
Gulīnīm = Jūlmīnā 60-61 BC 3
Gulistan 42-43 M 9
Güllab Dere 46-47 H 4
Gullbringu-Kjósar 30-31 b 2-c 3
Gullfoss 30-31 d 2
Güllük 46-47 B 4
Güllük Körfezi 46-47 B 4
Gülnar 46-47 E 4
Gulrān 44-45 J 3

Gülşehir 46-47 F 3
Gulu 64-65 H 2
Guma Bazar 48-49 D 4
Gumbinnen = Gusev 33 L 1
Gumbiro 63 C 5
Gumma 50-51 M 4
Gumti = Gomati 44-45 N 5
Gümüşane Dağları 46-47 H 2
Gümüşhacıköy 46-47 F 2
Gümüşhane 44-45 D 2
Guna 44-45 M 6
Gunabad = Gonâbâd 44-45 H 4
Günar = Anaypazari 46-47 E 4
Gunchū = Iyo 50-51 J 6
Gündoğmus 46-47 DE 4
Güney 46-47 C 3
Güney = Kırık 46-47 J 2
Güneydoğu Toroslar 44-45 DE 3
Gungu 64-65 E 4
Gunnbjørn Fjeld 70-71 ef 4
Gunnedah 56-57 K 6
Gunnison, CO 72-73 E 4
Gunnison, UT 76-77 H 6
Gunnison Island 76-77 G 5
Gunt 42-43 L 3
Guntakal 44-45 M 7
Guntur 44-45 MN 7
Guṅṭūru = Guntur 44-45 MN 7
Gunungapi, Pulau – 52-53 J 8
Gunungsitoli 52-53 C 6
Gunzan = Kunsan 48-49 O 4
Gūra = Gurha 44-45 L 5
Guragē 60-61 M 7
Guraghe = Guragē 60-61 M 7
Gurd Abū Muḥarrik 60-61 KL 3
Gurdāspur 44-45 M 4
Gurguéia, Rio – 78-79 L 6
Gūrha = Gurha 44-45 L 5
Gurjev 38-39 K 6
Gurjevsk 42-43 Q 7
Gurk 33 G 5
Gurma = Gourma 60-61 E 6
Gürpınar 46-47 K 3
Gurskøy 30-31 A 6
Gurudaspur = Gurdaspur 44-45 M 4
Gurun [MAL] 52-53 D 5
Gürün [TR] 46-47 G 3
Gurupá 78-79 J 5
Gurupá, Ilha Grande de – 78-79 J 5
Gurupi, Rio – 78-79 K 5
Gurupi, Serra do – 78-79 K 5-6
Gurvansajchan 48-49 K 2
Gusau 60-61 F 6
Gus-Chrustal'nyj 38-39 H 4
Gus-Chrustal'nyj 38-39 H 4
Gusev 33 L 1
Gushan 50-51 D 3
Gusher, UT 76-77 J 5
Gushi 48-49 M 5
Gus-Chrustal'nyj 38-39 H 4
Gusinaja, guba – 42-43 cd 3
Gusinaja Zeml'a, poluostrov – 42-43 HJ 3
Gustav Adolf land 30-31 l 5
Gustav V land 30-31 kl 4
Gustine, CA 76-77 C 7
Güstrow 33 EF 2
Gutaj 42-43 U 7-8
Gutenko Mountains 24 B 30
Gütersloh 33 CD 3
Guulin 48-49 H 2
Guvāhāṭī = Gauhati 44-45 P 5
Güyan = Kılaban 46-47 K 4
Guyana 78-79 H 3-4
Guyana, Bergland von – = Macizo de las Guyanas 78-79 F 3-J 4
Guyanabecken 22-23 G 5
Guyanabekken 22-23 G 5
Guyanai-hegyvidék = Macizo de las Guyanas 78-79 F 3-J 4
Guyanas, Macizo de las – 78-79 F 3-J 4
Guyandot River 74-75 BC 5-6
Guyane 78-79 H 3-4
Guyane, Bassin de – 22-23 G 5
Guyane Française 78-79 J 4
Guyanes, Plateau des – = Macizo de las Guyanas 78-79 F 3-J 4
Guyanská vysočina = Macizo de las Guyanas 78-79 F 3-J 4
Guyenne 34-35 G-J 6
Guyi = Miluo 48-49 L 6
Guyra 56-57 K 6
Güzelyurt 46-47 E 5
Güzelyurt Körfezi 46-47 E 5

Gvalior = Gwalior 44-45 M 5
Gvāliyar = Gwalior 44-45 M 5
Gvardejskoje 38-39 F 6

Gwa 52-53 B 3
Gwabegar 56-57 JK 6
Gwādar 44-45 J 5
Gwai 64-65 G 6
Gwalia 56-57 D 5
Gwalior 44-45 M 5
Gwaliyar = Gwalior 44-45 M 5
Gwanda 64-65 G 7
Gwane 64-65 G 2
Gwatemala 72-73 HJ 9
Gwda 33 H 2
Gweru 64-65 G 6
Gwinea 60-61 B 6-C 7
Gwinea Bissau 60-61 AB 6
Gwinea Równikowa 60-61 FG 8
Gwinejska, Zatoka – 60-61 C-F 8
Gwydir River 56-57 J 5

Gyamda Dsong 48-49 G 5
Gyangtse 48-49 FG 6
Gyáros 36-37 L 7
Gyda 42-43 O 3
Gydanskaja guba 42-43 O 3
Gydanskij poluostrov 42-43 OP 3-4
Gympie 56-57 K 5
Gyöngyös 33 J 5
Györ 33 H 5
Gypsum Palace 58 G 4
Gýtheion 36-37 K 7
Gyula 33 K 5

Gy

Gyamda Dsong 48-49 G 5
Gyangtse 48-49 FG 6
Gyáros 36-37 L 7

Gyda 42-43 O 3
Gydanhalbinsel = Gydanskij poluostrov 42-43 OP 3-4
Gydanskaja guba 42-43 O 3
Gydanskij poluostrov 42-43 OP 3-4

Gyezsnyev-fok = mys Dezneva 42-43 lm 4

Gympie 56-57 K 5

Gyöngyös 33 J 5
Györ 33 H 5
Györ-Moson-Sopron 42-43 DE 9

Gypsum Palace 58 G 4

Gyula 33 K 5

H

Haafuun 60-61 c 1
Haafuun, Raas – 44-45 G 8
Haag, Den – = 's-Gravenhage 34-35 JK 2
Haag = Gravenhage, s- 34-35 JK 2
Haakon VII land 30-31 hj 5
Haapajärvi 30-31 LM 6
Haapamäki 30-31 KL 6
Haapsalu 30-31 KL 8
Haardt 33 CD 4
Haarlem 34-35 JK 2
Hābā, Bi'r – 46-47 H 5
Habana, La – [C, ●] 72-73 K 7
Habārūt 44-45 G 7
Habaswein 63 DE 2
Habay 70-71 N 6
Ḥabbānīyah 46-47 K 6
Ḥabbānīyah, Hawr al- 46-47 K 6
Habbārīyah 46-47 JK 6
Habeš = Ethiopie 60-61 MN 7
Ḥabīb, Wādī – 62 DE 4
Haboro 50-51 b 1
Habrat Najid 46-47 K 7
Hacheim, Bir – = Bi'r al-Ḥukayyim 60-61 J 2
Hachijō-jima 48-49 Q 5
Hachinohe 48-49 R 3
Hachiōji 50-51 M 5
Hachirō-gata 50-51 MN 3
Hachita, NM 76-77 J 10
Hacıbektaş 46-47 F 3
Hacıömer 46-47 JK 3
Hacısaklı = Ovacık 46-47 E 4
Hack, Mount – 56-57 G 6
Hackberry, AZ 76-77 G 8
Hadal 'Awāb, Jabal – 62 F 7
Ḥaḍbarāh 44-45 H 7
Ḥadd, Rā's al- 44-45 HJ 6
Haddār, Al- 44-45 EF 6
Hadejia [WAN, ~] 60-61 F 6
Hadejia [WAN, ●] 60-61 G 6
Ḥadēra 46-47 F 6
Hadersleben = Haderslev 30-31 C 10
Haderslev 30-31 C 10
Hadım 46-47 E 4
Ḥadītah, Al- 44-45 F 4
Hadjout = Ḥajut 60-61 E 1
Hadley Bay 70-71 P 3
Hadong [ROK] 50-51 FG 5
Ha Đông [VN] 52-53 E 2
Ḥaḍr, Al- 46-47 K 5
Hadramaut = Ḥaḍramawt 44-45 F 7
Ḥaḍramaut, Wādī – = Wādī al-Musīlah 44-45 FG 7
Ḥaḍramawt 44-45 F 7
Hadseløy 30-31 EF 3
Hadu 64-65 JK 3
Ḥaḍūr Shu'ayb 44-45 EF 7
Haedo, Cuchilla de – 80 E 4
Haeju 48-49 O 4
Haeju-man 50-51 E 4
Haemi 50-51 F 4
Haenam 50-51 F 5
Haengyŏng 50-51 GH 1
Ḥafar al- Bāṭin, Al- 44-45 F 5
Ḥaffah 46-47 FG 5
Hafik 46-47 G 3
Hafızbey 46-47 D 4
Hafnarfjördhur 30-31 bc 2
Haft Gel 44-45 FG 4
Hagadera = Alanga Arba 64-65 JK 2
Haga = Gravenhage, 's- 34-35 JK 2
Håga = Gravenhage, 's- 34-35 JK 2
Hagen 33 C 3
Hagerē Hiwet 60-61 M 7
Hagerman, ID 76-77 F 4
Hagermeister Island 70-71 D 6
Hagerstown, MD 74-75 DE 5
Hagersville 74-75 C 3
Hagfors 30-31 EF 7-8
Hagi [IS] 30-31 b 2
Hagi [J] 50-51 H 5
Hagiá 36-37 K 6
Ha Giang 52-53 DE 2
Hágios Evstrátios 36-37 L 6
Hagiwara 50-51 L 5
Hague, Cap de la – 34-35 G 4
Hague, The – = 's-Gravenhage 34-35 JK 2
Haguenau 34-35 L 4
Hagui = Hagi 50-51 H 5
Hagunia, El – = Al-Haqūnīyah 60-61 B 3
Hai'an [TJ, Guangdong] 48-49 KL 7
Haibei Zangzu Zizhizhou 48-49 H-J 4
Haicheng 50-51 D 2
Ḥaidarābād 44-45 KL 5
Haiderabad = Hyderābād 44-45 M 7
Haiderbad = Ḥaidarābād 44-45 KL 5
Hai Du'o'ng 52-53 E 2
Haifa = Ḥēfa 44-45 CD 4
Haifeng 48-49 M 7
Haifong = Hai Phong 52-53 E 2
Haikang 48-49 KL 7
Haikou 48-49 L 7-8
Haikow = Haikou 48-49 L 7-8
Ḥā'il 44-45 E 5
Hai-la-êrh = Hailar 48-49 M 2
Hailar 48-49 M 2
Hailar He 48-49 MN 2
Hailey, ID 76-77 F 4
Hailong 48-49 O 3
Hailun 48-49 O 2
Hailuoto 30-31 L 5
Haimen [TJ, Jiangsu] 48-49 N 5
Haimen [TJ, Zhejiang] 48-49 N 6
Haimur Wells = Ābār Ḥaymūr 62 EF 6
Hainan = Hainan Dao 48-49 KL 8
Hainán, Estrecho de – = Qiongzhou Haixia 48-49 KL 7
Hainan Dao 48-49 KL 8
Hainanský průliv = Qiongzhou Haixia 48-49 KL 7
Hainan Strait = Qiongzhou Haixia 48-49 KL 7
Hainanstraße = Qiongzhou Haixia 48-49 KL 7
Hai-nan Tao = Hainan Dao 48-49 KL 8
Hainan Zangzu Zizhizhou 48-49 H 5-J 4
Hainan Zizhizhou 48-49 K 8
Hainaut 34-35 JK 3
Haines, AK 70-71 JK 6
Haines, OR 76-77 DE 3
Haines City, FL 74-75 c 2
Haines Junction 70-71 J 5
Hai Phong 52-53 E 2
Ḥais = Ḥays 44-45 E 8
Haitan Dao = Pingtan Dao 48-49 MN 6
Haiti 72-73 M 8
Haïti 72-73 M 8
Haiti = Hispaniola 72-73 MN 8
Haixi Monggolzu Zangzu Kazakzu Zizhizhou 48-49 GH 4
Haiyā = Haiyyā 60-61 M 5
Haiyang Dao 50-51 D 3
Hai-yang Tao = Haiyang Dao 50-51 D 3
Haizhou 48-49 M 5
Ḥajar, Al- [Oman] 44-45 H 6
Ḥajara, Al- = Ṣaḥrā' al-Ḥijārah 46-47 JK 8
Hajdúböszörmény 33 KL 5
Hajdúhadház 42-43 J 9
Ḥājjī Āqa = Bostānābād 46-47 M 4
Hajiki-saki 50-51 M 3
Ḥajīr, Jabal – 44-45 G 8
Ḥājī Sa'īd, Kūh-e – 46-47 M 4
Ḥājj 62 FG 3
Ḥajjah 44-45 E 7
Ḥajjār, Al- 60-61 EF 4
Ḥājjīābād 44-45 H 5
Hajnańska, Cieśnina – = Qiongzhou Haixia 48-49 KL 7
Hajnan-szoros = Qiongzhou Haixia 48-49 KL 7
Hajnówka 33 L 2
Hajo-do 50-51 F 5
Hajut 60-61 E 1
Hakasz Autonóm Terület 42-43 R 7
Hakkâri 46-47 K 4
Hakkâri Dağları 46-47 K 4
Hakken san 50-51 KL 5
Hakodate 48-49 R 3
Hakui 50-51 L 4
Haku-san [J ↗ Ōno] 50-51 L 4
Haku-san [J ↓ Ōno] 50-51 L 5
Ḥalab 44-45 D 3
Ḥalabān 44-45 E 6
Ḥalabcha = Sirwān 46-47 LM 5
Ḥalabīyah 46-47 H 5
Hala Hu = Char nuur 48-49 H 4
Ḥalā'ib = Ḥalāyb 60-61 M 4
Ḥalāib, Jazā'ir – 62 G 6
Halâl, Gebel – = Jabal Hilāl 62 EF 2
Ḥalāyb 60-61 M 4
Ḥalbā 46-47 FG 5
Halberstadt 33 E 3
Halden 30-31 D 8
Haldensleben 33 E 2
Hale, Mount – 56-57 C 5
Haleakala Crater 52-53 ef 3
Ḥaleb = Ḥalab 44-45 D 3
Halfâyah, Al- 46-47 M 7
Halfeti 46-47 GH 4
Ḥalfīn, Wādī – 44-45 H 6
Hal Flood Range 24 B 23
Ḥalī = Khay' 44-45 E 7
Haliburton 74-75 D 2
Halicarnassus = Bodrum 46-47 B 4
Hālidah, Bi'r – 62 B 2
Halifax [CDN] 70-71 Y 9
Halifax, VA 74-75 D 6
Halifax Bay 56-57 J 3
Ḥalīl, Al- 46-47 F 7
Ḥalīl Rūd 44-45 H 5
Hall, MT 76-77 G 2
Hall = A 33 E 5
Hall, ostrov – = ostrov Gall'a 42-43 KL 1
Halland 30-31 E 9
Hallandale, FL 74-75 c 4
Halla-san 50-51 F 6
Halle 33 EF 3
Halleck, NV 76-77 F 5
Hällefors 30-31 F 8
Hallein 33 F 5
Halley Bay 24 B 33-34
Hallingdal 30-31 C 7
Hallingskarvet 30-31 BC 7
Hall Lake 70-71 U 4
Hällnäs 30-31 H 5
Hallowell, ME 74-75 J 2
Hall Peninsula 70-71 X 5
Hallsberg 30-31 F 8
Halls Creek 56-57 E 3
Hallstavik 30-31 H 7-8
Halmahera 52-53 J 6
Halmahera, Laut – 52-53 J 7
Halmeu 36-37 K 2
Halmstad 30-31 E 9
Hälsingland 30-31 F 7-G 6
Haltiatunturi 30-31 J 3
Halvmåneøya 30-31 lm 6
Hâlys = Kızılırmak 44-45 D 3
Hama = Ḥamāâ 46-47 G 5
Ḥamād, Al- 46-47 H 6-J 7
Hamad, Birkat – 46-47 KL 7
Hamada 50-51 HJ 5
Hamadān 44-45 F 3-4
Ḥamāh 44-45 D 3
Hamajima 50-51 L 5
Hamamatsu 48-49 Q 5
Hamamatu = Hamamatsu 48-49 Q 5
Haman = Sarıkaya 46-47 F 3
Hamanaka 50-51 d 2
Hamana ko 50-51 L 5
Hamar 30-31 D 7
Ḥamār, Al- 46-47 M 8
Ḥamar, Dār – 60-61 K 6
Ḥamār, Wādī – 46-47 H 4
Hamas = Ḥamāh 44-45 D 3
Hamasaka 50-51 K 5
Ḥamāṭah, Jabal – 60-61 LM 4
Hama-Tombetsu 50-51 c 1
Hamatonbetu = Hama-Tombetsu 50-51 c 1
Hambergbreen 30-31 k 6
Hamber Provincial Park 70-71 N 7
Hambourg = Hamburg 33 E 2
Hamburg 33 E 2
Hamburg, CA 76-77 B 5
Hamburg, NY 74-75 D 3
Hamburg, PA 74-75 EF 4
Hamburgo = Hamburg 33 E 2
Hamch'ang 50-51 G 4
Ḥamḍ, Wādī al- 44-45 D 5
Ḥamḍah 44-45 E 7
Ḥamdānīyah, Al- 46-47 G 5
Hämeen lääni 30-31 KL 7
Hämeenlinna 30-31 L 7
Hamelin Pool 56-57 B 5
Hameln 33 D 2
Hamersley Range 56-57 C 4
Ham-gang = Namhan-gang 50-51 F 4
Hamgyŏng-namdo 50-51 FG 2-3
Hamgyŏng-pukto 50-51 G 2-H 1
Hamhŭng 48-49 O 3-4
Hami 48-49 G 3
Ḥamīdīyah 46-47 F 5
Hamilton [AUS] 56-57 H 7
Hamilton [Bermuda Islands] 72-73 O 5
Hamilton [CDN] 70-71 V 9
Hamilton [NZ] 56-57 OP 7
Hamilton, MT 76-77 F 2
Hamilton, NY 74-75 F 3
Hamilton, OH 72-73 K 4
Hamilton, WA 76-77 C 1
Hamilton, Mount – 76-77 F 6
Hamilton, The – 56-57 GH 4
Hamilton City, CA 76-77 BC 6
Hamilton Inlet 70-71 Z 7
Hamilton River 56-57 FG 5
Hamilton River = Churchill River 70-71 Y 7
Hamilton Square, NJ 74-75 F 4
Hamina 30-31 M 7
Ḥamīr, Wādī – [IRQ] 46-47 JK 7
Ḥamīr, Wādī – [Saudi-Arabien] 46-47 J 7
Hamitabad = Isparta 44-45 C 3
Hamlet, NC 74-75 D 7
Hamm 33 CD 3
Ḥammāl, Wādī al- = Wādī 'Ajaj 46-47 J 5
Ḥammām = Makhfir al-Ḥammān 46-47 H 5
Ḥammām, Al- 62 C 2
Ḥammāmāt, Khalīj al- 60-61 G 1
Ḥammār, Hawr al- 44-45 F 4
Hammerdal 30-31 F 6
Hammerfest 30-31 KL 2
Hammett, ID 76-77 F 4
Hammond, IN 72-73 J 3
Hammond, OR 76-77 AB 2
Hammonton, NJ 74-75 F 5
Hampton, FL 74-75 bc 2
Hampton, NH 74-75 H 3
Hampton, OR 76-77 C 4
Hampton, SC 74-75 C 8
Hampton, VA 74-75 E 6
Hampton Tableland 56-57 E 6
Ḥamrā', Al- [Saudi-Arabien] 44-45 D 6
Ḥamrā', Al- [SYR] 46-47 G 5
Ḥamrā', Al-Ḥammādat al- 60-61 G 2-3
Ḥamrīn, Jabal – 46-47 KL 5
Hamsah, Bi'r al- = Bi'r al-Khamsah 60-61 K 2
Hams Fork 76-77 H 4-5
Ḥāmūl, Al- 62 D 2
Hamun = Daryācheh Sīstān 44-45 HJ 4
Hamur 46-47 K 3
Ḥamza, Al- = Qawām al-Ḥamzah 46-47 L 7
Hanak = Ortahanak 46-47 K 2
Ḥanākīyah, Al- 44-45 E 6
Hanamaki 50-51 N 3
Hanang 64-65 J 3
Hanazura-oki = Sukumo wan 50-51 J 6
Hancheu = Hangzhou 48-49 MN 5
Hancock, NY 74-75 F 3-4
Handa 50-51 L 5
Handae-ri 50-51 FG 2
Handan 48-49 LM 4
Handaq, Al- = Al-Khandaq 60-61 KL 5
Handeni 64-65 J 4
Handrān 46-47 L 4
Hanford, CA 76-77 D 7
Hanford Works United States Atomic Energy Commission Reservation 76-77 D 2
Hangai = Changajn Nuruu 48-49 HJ 2
Hangchow = Hangzhou 48-49 MN 5
Hangcsou = Hangzhou 48-49 MN 5
Hang-hsien = Hangzhou 48-49 MN 5
Hanging Rock 58 H 5
Hängö 30-31 K 8
Hangu 48-49 M 4
Hangzhou 48-49 MN 5
Hani 46-47 J 3
Ḥanīfah, Wādī – 44-45 F 6
Ḥanīyah, Al- 46-47 LM 8
Ḥank, Al- 60-61 C 3-4
Hanko = Hangö 30-31 K 8
Hankou, Wuhan- 48-49 LM 5
Hankow = Wuhan-Hankou 48-49 LM 5
Hanksville, UT 76-77 H 6
Hanku = Hangu 48-49 M 4
Hann, Mount – 56-57 E 3
Hanna 70-71 O 7
Han-Negev 46-47 F 7
Hannibal, MO 72-73 H 3-4
Hannō 50-51 M 5
Hannover 33 D 2
Hanöbukten 30-31 F 10
Ha Nôi 52-53 DE 2
Hanoi = Ha Nôi 52-53 DE 2
Hanoj = Ha Nôi 52-53 DE 2
Ḥanōt Yōna = Khān Yūnūs 46-47 EF 7
Hanover [CDN] 74-75 C 2
Hanover, NH 74-75 GH 3
Hanover, PA 74-75 E 5
Hanover, VA 74-75 E 6
Hanover, Isla – 80 AB 8
Hansenfjella 24 BC 6
Han Shui 48-49 K 5
Hanson River 56-57 F 4
Hanti-Manszi Autonóm Körzet 42-43 L-P 5
Hanyang, Wuhan- 48-49 L 5
Hanzhong 48-49 K 5
Haoli = Hegang 48-49 OP 2
Haora 44-45 O 6
Haouach, Ouadi – 60-61 J 5
Haparanda 30-31 KL 5
Hapch'ŏn 50-51 FG 5
Happy Camp, CA 76-77 C 5
Ḥaql 44-45 CD 5
Haqūnīyah, Al- 60-61 B 3
Ḥaraḍ 44-45 F 6
Haramachi 50-51 N 4
Haram Dāgh 46-47 M 4
Haranomachi = Haramachi 50-51 N 4
Hara nur = Char nuur 48-49 G 2
Hararděre = Xarardeere 60-61 b 3
Harare 64-65 H 6
Ḥarāsīs, Jiddat al- 44-45 H 6-7
Hara Ulsa nur = Char us nuur 48-49 G 2
Ḥarawa = Harewa 60-61 N 6-7
Harbin 48-49 O 2
Hardangerfjord 30-31 A 8-B 7
Hardangervidda 30-31 BC 7
Hardeeville, SC 74-75 C 8
Hardey River 56-57 C 4
Harding 64-65 GH 9
Hardvār = Hardwar 44-45 M 4
Hardwār = Hardwar 44-45 M 4
Hardwick, VT 74-75 G 2
Hardy, Peninsula – 80 BC 9
Hardy, Rio – 76-77 F 9
Hareidlandet 30-31 A 6
Harer 60-61 N 7
Ḥarergē 60-61 NO 7
Harewa 60-61 N 6-7
Hargeisa = Hargeysa 60-61 a 2
Hargeysa 60-61 a 2
Hari, Batang – 52-53 D 7
Ḥarīb 44-45 EF 7-8
Haridwar = Hardwar 44-45 M 4
Ḥarim 46-47 G 4
Harima nada 50-51 K 5
Harimgye 50-51 G 4
Harīrōd 44-45 J 4
Ḥāritah, Al- 46-47 M 7
Härjedalen 30-31 E 6-F 7
Harkov = Char'kov 38-39 G 5
Harkov = Char'kov 38-39 G 5
Harlem, GA 74-75 B 8
Harlingen 34-35 K 2
Harlingen, TX 72-73 G 6
Harmal, Al- 46-47 G 5
Harmancık = Çardı 46-47 C 3
Harmanli 36-37 LM 5
Harmanli [TR] 46-47 GH 4
Harmony, ME 74-75 J 2
Harney Basin 72-73 BC 3
Harney Lake 76-77 D 4
Härnösand 30-31 GH 6
Haro 34-35 F 7
Haro, Cabo – 72-73 D 6
Harold Byrd Range 24 A 25-22
Haro Strait 76-77 B 1
Harper 60-61 C 8
Harper, OR 76-77 E 4
Harpers Ferry, WV 74-75 DE 5
Harpster, ID 76-77 F 2-3
Harquahala Mountains 76-77 G 9
Harquahala Plains 76-77 G 9
Ḥarrah, Al- [ET] 62 C 3
Ḥarrah, Al- [Saudi-Arabien] 44-45 D 4
Harran [TR] 46-47 H 4
Harrar = Ḥarer 60-61 N 7
Harrawa = Ḥarawa 60-61 N 6-7
Harricana, Rivière – 70-71 V 7-8
Harrington, DE 74-75 F 5
Harrington, WA 76-77 DE 2
Harrington Harbour 70-71 Z 7
Harris 32 C 3
Harris, Dorsal de – = Dorsal de Lomonosov 19 A
Harris, Lake – 58 B 3
Harrisburg, OR 76-77 B 3
Harrisburg, PA 72-73 L 3
Harrismith 64-65 G 8
Harrison, ID 76-77 E 2
Harrison, MT 76-77 H 3
Harrison, Cape – 70-71 Z 7
Harrisonburg, VA 74-75 D 5
Harris Ridge = Lomonosov Ridge 19 A
Harrisrücken = Lomonosowrücken 19 A
Harrisrug = Lomonosovrug 19 A
Harriston 74-75 C 3

180 Gülše

Harrisville, WV 74-75 C 5
Harrogate 32 F 4-5
Harrow, London- 32 F 6
Harsīn 46-47 M 5
Harşit Deresi 46-47 H 2
Harstad 30-31 FG 3
Harsvik 30-31 D 5
Hart, Cape – 58 D 5-6
Hartenggole He = Chaaltyn gol 48-49 GH 4
Hartford, CT 72-73 M 3
Hartlepool 32 F 4
Hartley = Chegutu 64-65 GH 6
Hartline, WA 76-77 D 2
Hart Mountain 76-77 D 4
Harts Range 56-57 FG 4
Hartsrivier 64-65 FG 8
Hartsville, SC 74-75 CD 7
Hartwell, GA 74-75 B 7
Hartwell Lake 74-75 B 7
Harūj al-Aswad, Al- 60-61 H 3
Hārūnābād [IR] 46-47 N 4
Hārūt Rōd 44-45 J 4
Harvard, CA 76-77 E 8
Harvey 56-57 C 6
Harwell 32 F 6
Harwich 32 G 6
Harwich, MA 74-75 HJ 4
Haryana 44-45 M 5
Harz 33 E 3
Ḥāş, Jabal al- 46-47 G 5
'Ḥasā, Al- 44-45 F 5
Ḥasā, Wādī al- [JOR, Al-Karak] 46-47 F 7
Ḥasā, Wādī al- [JOR, Ma'ān] 46-47 G 7
Ḥaṣāheīṣa, El – = Al-Ḥuṣayhīṣah 60-61 L 6
Ḥasakah, Al- 44-45 D 3
Hāsana = Hassan 44-45 M 8
Hasançelebi 46-47 GH 3
Hasan Dağı 46-47 EF 3
Hasankale = Pasinler 46-47 J 2-3
Ḥasb, Sha'īb – 44-45 E 4
Hasêtchê, El- = Al-Hasakah 44-45 D 3
Hashemiya, Al- = Al-Hāshimīyah 46-47 L 6
Hāshimīyah, Al- 46-47 L 6
Hashimoto 50-51 K 5
Hashir 46-47 K 4
Hashtpar 46-47 N 4
Hashtrūd 46-47 M 4
Hashun Shamo = Gašuun Gov' 48-49 G 3
Hasib, Sha'ib – = Sha'īb Ḥasb 44-45 E 4
Haskovo 36-37 L 5
Ḥasmat 'Umar, Bi'r – 62 EF 7
Hassa 46-47 G 4
Hassan 44-45 M 8
Hassayampa River 76-77 G 9
Hassel Sound 70-71 R 2
Hasselt 34-35 K 3
Ḥāssī ar-Raml 60-61 E 2
Hassi-Inifel = Ḥāssī Īnīfīl 60-61 E 2-3
Ḥāssī Īnīfīl 60-61 E 2-3
Ḥāssī Mas'ūd 60-61 F 2
Hassi-Messaoud = Ḥāssī Mas'ūd 60-61 F 2
Hassi-R'Mel = Ḥāssī ar-Raml 60-61 E 2
Hässleholm 30-31 EF 9
Hastings [GB] 32 G 6
Hastings [NZ] 56-57 P 7
Hastings, FL 74-75 c 2
Hastings, NE 72-73 G 3
Hasvik 30-31 JK 2
Ḥaṭab, Wādī al- 62 E 7
Hat'ae-do 50-51 E 5
Haṭāṭibah, Al- 62 D 2
Hatay 44-45 D 3
Hatch, UT 76-77 G 7
Haţeg 36-37 K 3
Hatfield [AUS] 58 F 4
Hathras 44-45 M 5
Hatinohe = Hachinohe 48-49 R 3
Hatip 46-47 E 4
Hatizyō zima = Hachijō-jima 48-49 Q 5
Ha-tongsan-ni 50-51 F 3
Hatteras, NC 74-75 F 7
Hatteras, Cape – 72-73 LM 4
Hatteras Island 72-73 LM 4
Hattfjelldal 30-31 F 5
Hattiesburg, MS 72-73 J 5
Ḥaṭṭīyah 46-47 F 8
Hatton 70-71 P 7
Hatvan 33 JK 5
Hat Yai 52-53 D 5
Hatzfeld = Jimbolia 36-37 J 3
Haud 60-61 NO 7
Haugesund 30-31 A 8
Haukadalur 30-31 c 2
Haukeligrend 30-31 B 8
Haukipudas 30-31 L 5
Haukivesi 30-31 N 6-7
Haukivuori 30-31 M 6-7
Ḥāurā = Haora 44-45 O 6
Ḥaurā = Ḥawrah 44-45 F 7
Ḥaurā, Al- = Al-Ḥawrah 44-45 F 8
Hauraki Gulf 56-57 OP 7
Ḥauṣah = Ḥawṣah 46-47 G 8
Hausruck 33 F 3
Haut-Altaï, Région Autonome du – = 9 ◁ 42-43 Q 7
Haut-Atlas 60-61 CD 2
Haute Egypte = Aṣ-Ṣa'īd 60-61 L 3-4
Haute-Guinée 22-23 JK 5
Haute-Kotto 60-61 J 7
Haute-Mbomou 60-61 K 7
Haute-Sangha 60-61 H 8
Hautes Plateaux = Nijād al-'Alī 60-61 D 2-E 1
Haut Plateau d'Amerique = American Highland 24 B 8
Haut-Zaïre 64-65 G 2
Havajské ostrovy = Hawaiian Islands 52-53 d 3-e 4
Havana = La Habana 72-73 K 7
Havana = La Habana 72-73 K 7
Havane = La Habana 72-73 K 7
Havanna = La Habana 72-73 K 7
Havasu Lake 76-77 FG 8
Havel 33 F 2
Havelock 74-75 DE 2
Havelock, NC 74-75 E 7
Haverfordwest 32 D 6
Haverhill, MA 74-75 H 3
Haverhill, NH 74-75 GH 3
Haverstraw, NY 74-75 FG 4
Havlíčkův Brod 33 G 4
Havlíčkův Brod 33 G 4
Havøysund 30-31 L 2
Havre, MT 72-73 DE 2
Havre, le – 34-35 GH 4
Havre de Grace, MD 74-75 EF 5
Havre-Saint-Pierre 70-71 Y 7
Havsa 46-47 B 2
Havza 46-47 F 2
Hawai = Hawaii 52-53 ef 4
Hawai, Dorsal de las – 22-23 AB 4
Hawai, Islas – = Hawaiian Islands 52-53 d 3-e 4
Hawaii 52-53 ef 4
Hawaï, Dorsale des – 22-23 AB 4
Hawaï, Îles – = Hawaiian Islands 52-53 d 3-e 4
Hawaiian Islands 52-53 d 3-e 4
Hawaiian Ridge 22-23 AB 4
Hawaii-Inseln = Hawaiian Islands 52-53 d 3-e 4
Hawaiirücken 22-23 AB 4
Hawaiirug 22-23 AB 4
Hawaii-szigetek = Hawaiian Islands 52-53 d 3-e 4
Hawaje = Hawaiian Islands 52-53 d 3-e 4
Hawana = La Habana 72-73 K 7
Ḥawashīyah, Wādī – 62 E 3
Ḥawātah, Al- 60-61 LM 6
Ḥawd = Haud 60-61 NO 7
Ḥawḍ, Al- [RIM] 60-61 C 5
Hawera 56-57 OP 7
Hawick 32 E 4
Ḥawīzah, Hawr al- 46-47 M 7
Hawke, Cape – 56-57 K 6
Hawke Bay 56-57 P 7
Hawker 56-57 G 6
Hawkes, Mount – 24 A 32-33
Hawkinsville, GA 74-75 B 8
Ḥawrah 44-45 F 7
Ḥawrah, Al- 44-45 F 8
Ḥawrān, Wādī – 44-45 E 4
Haw River 74-75 D 7
Ḥawṣah 46-47 G 8
Ḥawsh 'Īsā 62 D 2
Ḥawṭah, Al- = Al-Ḥillah 44-45 F 6
Hawthorn, FL 74-75 bc 2
Hawthorne, NV 76-77 D 6
Hay [AUS] 56-57 HJ 6
Haya, La – = 's-Gravenhage 34-35 JK 2
Hayang 50-51 G 5
Haydar Dağı 46-47 DE 4
Hayden, AZ 76-77 H 9
Haye, La – = 's-Gravenhage 34-35 JK 2
Hayes, Mount – 70-71 G 5
Hayes Halvø 70-71 XY 2
Hayes River 70-71 S 6
Hayfork, CA 76-77 B 5
Hay Lake = Habay 70-71 N 6
Haylow, GA 74-75 B 9
Haymana 46-47 E 3
Haymana Yaylâsı 46-47 E 3
Ḥaymūr, Ābār – 62 EF 6
Ḥaymūr, Wādī – 62 E 6
Hayrabolu 46-47 B 2
Hay River [AUS] 56-57 G 4
Hay River [CDN, ~] 70-71 N 6
Hay River [CDN, ●] 70-71 NO 5
Ḥays 44-45 E 8
Hays, KS 72-73 G 4
Ḥayshān, Jabal – 62 C 4
Ḥaysī, Bi'r al- 62 F 3
Haystack Mountain 74-75 G 3
Haystack Peak 76-77 G 6
Hayton's Falls 63 CD 3
Hayward, CA 76-77 BC 7
Ḥayy, Al- 44-45 F 4
Ḥayyā 60-61 M 5
Ḥayy Allāh, Jabal – 62 B 4
Ḥayy Allāh, Jabal – 62 B 4
Ḥayz, Al- 62 C 3-4
Hazak = İdil 46-47 J 4
Hazārān, Kūh-e – = Kūh-e Hezārān 44-45 H 5
Hazard, KY 72-73 K 4
Ḥaẓawẓā' 46-47 GH 7
Hazebrouck 34-35 J 3
Hazen, NV 76-77 D 6
Hazen Strait 70-71 OP 2
Hazīm, Al- 46-47 G 7
Ḥazīmī, Wādī al- 46-47 J 6
Hazlehurst, GA 74-75 B 9
Hazleton, PA 74-75 F 4
Hazlett, Lake 56-57 E 4
Ḥazm, Al- 62 G 3
Hazo = Kozluk 46-47 J 3
Hazro 46-47 J 3
Hazul, Al- = Al-Huzul 46-47 K 8

Headquarters, ID 76-77 F 2
Heads, The – 76-77 A 4
Healdsburg, CA 76-77 B 6
Healesville 58 GH 6
Heard 22-23 N 8
Hearst 70-71 U 8
Hearst Island 24 BC 30-31
Hebei 48-49 LM 4
Heber, UT 76-77 H 5
Hebgen Lake 76-77 H 3
Hebo, OR 76-77 AB 3
Hebreos, Oblast Autónomo de los – 42-43 Z 8
Hébridas = Outer Hebrides 32 B 3-C 2
Hebriden = Outer Hebrides 32 B 3-C 2
Hébrides = Outer Hebrides 32 B 3-C 2
Hebrides, Sea of the – 32 C 3
Hebron [CDN] 70-71 Y 6
Hébron = Al-Halīl 46-47 F 7
Hecate Strait 70-71 K 7
Heceta Head 76-77 A 3
Hechuan 48-49 JK 5
Hecla and Griper Bay 70-71 O 2
Hede 30-31 E 6
He Devil Mountain 76-77 E 3
Hedien = Khotan 48-49 DE 4
Hedjas = Al-Hijāz 44-45 D 5-6
Hedjaz 44-45 D 5-6
Hedmark 30-31 D 6-E 7
Hedzsáz 44-45 D 5-6
Heerlen 34-35 KL 3
Hefei 48-49 M 5
Hegang 48-49 OP 2
Heian-hokudō = P'yŏngan-pukto 50-51 E 2-3
Heian-nandō = P'yŏngan-namdo 50-51 EF 3
Ḥeidarābād = Ḥeydarābād 46-47 L 4
Heide 33 D 1
Heidelberg 33 D 4
Ḥeifa 44-45 CD 4
Hei-ho = Aihui 48-49 O 1
Heijo = P'yŏngyang 48-49 NO 4
Heilar He = Chajlar gol 48-49 N 1-2
Heilbronn 33 D 4
Heiligenbeil = Mamonovo 33 JK 1
Heilong Jiang [TJ, ~] 48-49 O 1
Heilongjiang [TJ, ☆] 48-49 M-P 2
Hei-lung Chiang = Heilong Jiang 48-49 O 1
Hei-lung Chiang = Heilong Jiang 48-49 O 1
Hei-lung Chiang = Heilong Jiang 48-49 O 1
Heilung Kiang = Heilong Jiang 48-49 O 1
Heimaey 30-31 c 3
Heinola 30-31 M 7
Heir, El- = Qaṣr al-Ḥayr 46-47 H 5
Heishan 50-51 CD 2
Ḥeisī, Bīr el- = Bi'r al-Ḥaysī 62 F 3
Hekimdağ 46-47 D 3
Hekimhan 46-47 G 3
Hekla 30-31 d 3
Helagsfjället 30-31 E 6
Helder, Den – 34-35 K 2
Helen, Mount – 76-77 E 7
Helena, AR 72-73 H 5
Helena, GA 74-75 B 8
Helena, MT 72-73 D 2
Helendale, CA 76-77 E 8
Helen Reef 52-53 K 6
Heleysund 30-31 l 5
Helgeland 30-31 E 5-F 4
Helgoland 33 C 1
Helikŏn 36-37 K 6
Heliopolis = Al-Qahīrah-Miṣr al-Jadīdah 62 DE 2
Helix, OR 76-77 D 3
Hella 30-31 c 3
Helleland 30-31 B 8
Hellepoort = Portes de l'Enfer 64-65 G 4
Hellin 34-35 G 9
Hell-Ville 64-65 L 5
Helmand Rōd 44-45 K 4
Helmond 34-35 KL 3
Helmsdale 32 E 2
Helmstedt 33 E 2
Helmville, MT 76-77 G 2
Helong 48-49 O 3
Helper, UT 76-77 H 6
Helsingborg 30-31 DE 9
Helsingfors = Helsinki 30-31 L 7
Helsingør 30-31 DE 9
Helsinki 30-31 L 7
Helska, Mierzeja – 33 J 1
Ḥelwân = Ḥulwān 60-61 L 3
Hemet, CA 76-77 E 9
Hempstead, NY 74-75 G 4
Henan 48-49 L 5
Henares 34-35 F 8
Henashi-saki 50-51 M 2
Henbury 56-57 F 4
Henchow = Hengyang 48-49 L 6
Hendawashi 63 C 3
Hendaye 34-35 FG 7
Hendek 46-47 D 2
Henderson, KY 72-73 J 4
Henderson, NC 74-75 D 6
Henderson, NV 76-77 F 7
Henderson Bay 74-75 E 2-3
Hendersonville, NC 74-75 B 7
Heng'ang = Hengyang 48-49 L 6
Heng-chan = Hengyang 48-49 L 6
Heng-chou = Heng Xian 48-49 K 7
Hengduan Shan 48-49 H 6
Hengelo 34-35 L 2
Henghsien = Heng Xian 48-49 K 7
Hengshan [TJ, Hunan] 48-49 L 6
Hengshan = Hengyang 48-49 L 6
Hengshui 48-49 LM 4
Heng Xian 48-49 K 7
Hengyang 48-49 L 6
Henik Lake = South Henik Lake 70-71 R 5
Henlopen, Cape – 74-75 F 5
Hennebont 34-35 F 5
Hennesberget 30-31 E 4
Henrietta Maria, Cape – 70-71 U 6
Henriette, ostrov – = ostrov Genrietty 42-43 ef 2
Henrique de Carvalho = Saurimo 64-65 F 4
Henry, Cape – 74-75 F 6
Henry, Mount – 76-77 F 1
Henry Kater Peninsula 70-71 XY 4
Henry Mountains 76-77 H 6-7
Henrys Fork 76-77 H 3-4
Henty 58 H 5
Henzada = Hinthāda 52-53 BC 3
Heppner, OR 76-77 D 3
Heppner Junction, OR 76-77 CD 3
Hepu 48-49 K 7
Heraclea 36-37 G 5
Heraclea = Ereğli 44-45 C 2
Héradhsflói 30-31 fg 2
Héradhsvötn 30-31 d 2
Herákleia = Ereğli 44-45 C 2
Herald, ostrov – 19 B 36
Heras, Las – [RA, Santa Cruz] 80 C 7
Herāt 44-45 J 4
Hercegnovi 36-37 H 4
Hereford 32 E 5
Herefoss 30-31 C 8
Hereroland 64-65 EF 7
Herford 33 D 2
Heri Rud = Harī Rūd 44-45 J 4
Herīs 46-47 M 3
Heritage Range 24 B 28-A 29
Herkimer, NY 74-75 F 3
Herlen He 48-49 M 2
Hermanas, NM 76-77 JK 10
Herma Ness 32 F 1
Hermannsburg [AUS] 56-57 F 4
Hermannstadt = Sibiu 36-37 KL 3
Hermansverk 30-31 B 7
Hermel, el- = Al-Harmal 46-47 G 5
Hermidale 58 H 3
Hermiston, OR 76-77 D 3
Hermite, Isla – 80 C 9
Hermit Islands 52-53 N 7
Hermôn = Jabal as-Saykh 46-47 FG 6
Hérmos = Gediz çayı 46-47 C 3
Hermosillo 72-73 D 6
Hernandarias 80 F 3
Herning 30-31 C 9
Heroica Alvarado = Alvarado 72-73 GH 8
Heroica Guaymas 72-73 D 6
Heroica Matamoros = Matamoros 72-73 G 6
Heroica Puebla de Zaragoza = Puebla de Zaragoza 72-73 G 8
Heroica Veracruz = Veracruz 72-73 GH 8
Heron, MT 76-77 F 1
Herrera 34-35 F 7
Herrera del Duque 34-35 E 9
Herrera de Pisuerga 34-35 EF 7
Herrick 56-57 J 8
Herrington Island 74-75 AB 5-6
Herschel Island 70-71 J 3-4
Hertford 32 FG 6
Hertford, NC 74-75 E 6
Hertogenbosch, 's- 34-35 KL 3
Hervey Bay [AUS, ∪] 56-57 K 4-5
Hervey Bay [AUS, ●] 56-57 K 5
Herzogenbusch = 's-Hertogenbosch 34-35 KL 3
Herzogenbusch = 's-Hertogenbosch 34-35 KL 3
Herzog-Ernst-Bucht 24 B 32-33
Heshjīn 46-47 N 4
Hesperia, CA 76-77 E 8
Hessen 33 D 3
Hesteyri 30-31 b 1
Heuglin, Kapp – 30-31 lm 5
Heves 33 K 5
He Xian [TJ, Guangxi Zhuangzu Zizhiqu] 48-49 L 7
Hexigten Qi 48-49 M 3
Ḥeydarābād 46-47 L 4
Heywood [AUS] 58 EF 7
Hezārān, Kūh-e – 44-45 H 5
Heze 48-49 M 4
Hezelton 70-71 L 6

Hialeah, FL 74-75 c 4
Hiawatha, UT 76-77 H 6
Hibbing, MN 72-73 H 2
Hibbs, Point – 58 b 3
Hichiro-wan = zaliv Terpenija 42-43 b 8
Hickory, NC 74-75 C 7
Hickory, Lake – 74-75 C 7
Hidaka 50-51 c 2
Hidaka-sammyaku 50-51 c 2
Hidalgo [MEX, Hidalgo] 72-73 G 7
Hidalgo del Parral 72-73 EF 6
Hida sammyaku 50-51 L 4-5
Hiddensee 33 F 1
Hidzaz, Al – = Al-Hijāz 44-45 D 5-6
Hidžáz = Al-Hijāz 44-45 D 5-6
Hienghène 56-57 MN 4
Hierisós 36-37 KL 5
Hieropolis = Manbij 46-47 GH 4
Hierro 60-61 A 3
Higasiōsaka 50-51 KL 5
High Atlas 60-61 CD 2
Highland, WA 76-77 E 2
Highland Peak 76-77 F 7
High Point, NC 72-73 KL 4
High Prairie 70-71 NO 6
High Rock Lake 74-75 CD 7
High Springs, FL 74-75 b 2
Highwood, MT 76-77 H 2
Highwood Peak 76-77 H 2
Hiiraan 60-61 ab 3
Hiiumaa 30-31 JK 8
Ḥijārah, Ṣaḥrā' al- [IRQ] 46-47 L 7
Ḥijārah, Ṣaḥrā' al- [Saudi-Arabien] 46-47 JK 8
Ḥijāz, Al- 44-45 D 5-6
Ḥijāzah 62 E 5
Hijo = Tagum 52-53 J 5
Hikari 50-51 H 6
Hiko, NV 76-77 F 7
Hikone 50-51 L 5
Hiko-san 50-51 H 6
Hilāl, Jabal – 62 EF 2
Hilālī, Wādī al- 46-47 J 7
Hildesheim 33 DE 2
Hill, MT 76-77 H 1
Ḥillah, Al- [IRQ] 44-45 E 4
Ḥillah, Al- [Saudi-Arabien] 44-45 F 6
Hill City, ID 76-77 F 4
Hillerød 30-31 DE 10
Hillsboro, GA 74-75 B 8
Hillsboro, NC 74-75 D 6
Hillsboro, NH 74-75 H 3
Hillsboro, OR 76-77 B 3
Hillsboro Canal 74-75 c 3
Hillside, AZ 76-77 G 8
Hillston 56-57 HJ 6
Hillsville, VA 74-75 C 6
Hilmänd, Däryā-ye – = Helmand Rōd 44-45 K 4
Hilmar, CA 76-77 C 7
Hilton Head Island 74-75 C 8
Hilts, CA 76-77 B 5
Hilu-Babor = Īlubabor 60-61 LM 7
Hilvan 46-47 H 4
Hilversum 34-35 K 2
Himachal Pradesh 44-45 M 4
Himálaj 48-49 C 5-G 6
Himalája 48-49 C 5-G 6
Himalaja 44-45 L 4-P 5
Himalaje 48-49 C 5-G 6
Himalaya 44-45 L 4-P 5
Himeji 48-49 P 5
Hime-saki 50-51 M 3
Himezi = Himeji 48-49 P 5
Himi 50-51 L 4
Hinai 50-51 N 2
Hinchinbrook Island [AUS] 56-57 J 3
Hinckley, UT 76-77 G 6
Hindenburg = Zabrze 33 J 3
Hindīyah, Al- 46-47 KL 6
Hindūbāgh 44-45 K 4
Hindū Kush 44-45 KL 3
Hindupur 44-45 M 8
Hindupura = Hindupur 44-45 M 8
Hindustan 44-45 M 5-O 6
Hindusztán 44-45 M 5-O 6
Hines, FL 74-75 b 2
Hines, OR 76-77 D 4
Hines Creek 70-71 N 6
Hinesville, GA 74-75 C 9
Hinghwa = Putian 48-49 M 6
Hingjen = Xingren 48-49 K 6
Hingol 44-45 K 5
Hingoli 44-45 M 7
Hınıs 46-47 J 3
Hinkley, CA 76-77 E 8
Hinlopenstretet 30-31 kl 5
Hinna = Īmī 60-61 N 7
Hinnøy 30-31 FG 3
Hinojosa del Duque 34-35 E 9
Hinomi-saki 50-51 J 5
Hinş = Dumlu 46-47 J 2
Hinterindien 22-23 OP 5
Hinterrhein 33 D 5
Hinthāda 52-53 BC 3
Hinton [CDN] 70-71 N 7
Hinton, WV 74-75 C 6
Hınzır Dağı 46-47 FG 3
Hippo Regius = Annābah 60-61 F 1
Hiraan = Hiiraan 60-61 ab 3
Hirado 50-51 G 6
Hirado-shima 50-51 G 6
Hirata 50-51 J 5
Hirato jima = Hirado-shima 50-51 G 6
Hiratori 50-51 c 2
Hireimis, Qârat el- = Qārat Huraymis 46-47 B 7
Hirfanlı Barajı 46-47 E 3
Hirgis Nur = Chjargas nuur 48-49 GH 2
Hîrlău 36-37 M 2
Hirono 50-51 N 4
Hiroo 50-51 c 2
Hirosaki 48-49 QR 3
Hiroshima 48-49 P 5
Hirosima = Hiroshima 48-49 P 5
Hiroszima = Hiroshima 48-49 P 5
Hirota-wan 50-51 NO 3
Hirr, Wādī al- 46-47 K 7
Hirschberg im Riesengebirge = Jelenia Góra 33 GH 3
Hirson 34-35 K 4
Hirtshals 30-31 C 9
Hisaka-jima 50-51 G 6
Hisar 44-45 M 5
Ḥiṣār, Koh-i – 44-45 K 4
Hisarönü 46-47 DE 2
Ḥismā 62 FG 3
Ḥismet 'Umar, Bīr – = Bi'r Ḥasmat 'Umar 62 EF 7
Hispaniola 72-73 MN 8
Hissâr = Hisar 44-45 M 5
Ḥissar, Kūh-e – = Kōh-i Ḥiṣār 44-45 K 4
Hiszpania 34-35 D 7-G 9
Hīt 46-47 K 6
Hita 50-51 H 6
Hitachi 48-49 R 4
Hitachi-Ōta = Hitati-Ōta 50-51 N 4
Hitati = Hitachi 48-49 R 4
Hite, UT 76-77 H 7
Hitoyoshi 50-51 H 6
Hitra 30-31 C 6
Hiuchi-dake 50-51 M 4
Hiuchi-nada 50-51 J 5
Hiw 62 E 4-5
Hiwasa 50-51 K 6
Hizan 46-47 K 3

Hjälmaren 30-31 FG 8
Hjelmelandsvågen 30-31 AB 8
Hjelmsøy 30-31 L 2
Hjørring 30-31 C 9

Hkweibûm 52-53 B 2

Hlaingbwè 52-53 C 3
Hluingbwe = Hlaingbwè 52-53 C 3

Hnežđno = Gniezno 33 H 2

Ho 60-61 E 7
Hoa Binh 52-53 DE 2
Hoai Nho'n 52-53 E 4
Hoangho = Huang He 48-49 L 4
Hoang Sa, Quân Đao – 52-53 F 5
Hoarusib 64-65 D 6
Hoback Peak 76-77 H 4
Hobart 56-57 J 8
Hobbs, NM 72-73 F 5
Hobbs Coast 24 B 23
Hobe Sound, FL 74-75 cd 3
Hobetsu 50-51 bc 2
Hobro 30-31 C 9
Hŏbsögöl Dalay = Chövsgöl nuur 48-49 J 1
Hobyo 60-61 b 2
Hochaltai, Autonome Oblast – = 9 ◁ 42-43 Q 7
Hochgolling 33 FG 5
Hô Chi Minh, Thành Phô – 52-53 E 4
Hochow = Hechuan 48-49 K 5-6
Hochwan = Hechuan 48-49 K 5-6
Hô Chi Minh, Thành Phô – 52-53 E 4
Hoddua = Ghuddawah 60-61 G 3
Hodeida = Al-Hudaidah 44-45 E 8
Ḥōḍein, Wādī – = Wādī Ḥuḍayn 62 F 6
Hodgdon, ME 74-75 JK 1-2
Hodh = Al-Ḥawḍ 60-61 C 5

Hódmezővásárhely 33 K 5
Hodna, Chott el – = Ash-Shaṭṭ al-Hudnah 60-61 EF 1
Hodna, Chott el – = Ash-Shaṭṭ al-Hudnah 60-61 EF 1
Hodna, Chott el – = Ash-Shaṭṭ al-Hudnah 60-61 EF 1
Hoek van Holland, Rotterdam- 34-35 JK 3
Hoengsŏng 50-51 FG 4
Hoeryŏng 50-51 G 1
Hoeyang 50-51 F 3
Hof 33 E 3
Höfdhakaupstadhur 30-31 cd 2
Hofei = Hefei 48-49 M 5
Höfn 30-31 f 2
Hofors 30-31 FG 7
Ḥofrat en Naḥâs = Ḥufrat an-Naḥās 60-61 JK 7
Hofsjökull 30-31 d 2
Hofsós 30-31 d 2
Hōfu 50-51 H 5-6
Hofuf = Al-Hufūf 44-45 FG 5
Höganäs 30-31 E 9
Hogan Island 58 c 1
Hogback Mountain [USA, Montana] 76-77 GH 3
Hoge Atlas 60-61 CD 2
Hog Island [USA, Maryland] 74-75 F 6
Hohe Acht 33 C 3
Hohe Acht 33 C 3
Hohe Acht 33 C 3
Hohensalza = Inowrocław 33 HJ 2
Hoher Atlas 60-61 CD 2
Hohe Tauern 33 F 5
Hohhot = Huhehaote 48-49 L 3
Hoh-kai = Ohōtsuku-kai 50-51 cd 1
Ho-hsien = He Xian [TJ, Guangxi Zhuangzu Zizhiqu] 48-49 L 7
Hô Chí Minh, Thành Phô – 52-53 E 4
Hoifung = Haifeng 48-49 M 7
Hoihong = Haikang 48-49 KL 7
Hoima 64-65 H 2
Hoion = Hai'an 48-49 KL 7
Hokitika 56-57 NO 8
Hokkaidō [J, ⊙] 48-49 RS 3
Hokkaidō [J, ☆] 50-51 bc 2
Hokuoka = Fukuoka 48-49 OP 5
Hokuriku 50-51 L 5-M 4
Holanda = Países Bajos 34-35 K 3-L 2
Holandia 34-35 J 3-L 2
Hólar 30-31 d 2
Holbæk 30-31 D 10
Holbrook 58 H 5
Holbrook, AZ 76-77 HJ 8
Holbrook, ID 76-77 G 4
Holden, UT 76-77 G 6
Holguín 72-73 L 7
Höljes 30-31 E 7
Holland = Netherlands 34-35 K 3-L 2
Holland = Niederlande 34-35 K 3-L 2
Hollandia 34-35 J 3-L 2
Hollandia = Jayapura 52-53 M 7
Hollick-Kenyon Plateau 24 AB 25-26
Hollidaysburg, PA 74-75 D 4
Hollister, CA 76-77 C 7
Hollister, ID 76-77 F 4
Hollmann, Cape – 52-53 gh 5
Holly Hill, FL 74-75 c 2
Holly Hill, SC 74-75 C 8
Holly Ridge, NC 74-75 E 7
Hollywood, FL 72-73 KL 6
Hollywood, Los Angeles-, CA 72-73 BC 5
Holman Island 70-71 NO 3
Hólmavík 30-31 c 2
Holmes, Mount – 76-77 H 3
Holmestrand 30-31 CD 8
Holmsund 30-31 J 6
Holopaw, FL 74-75 c 2
Holroyd River 56-57 H 2
Holsnøy 30-31 A 7
Holstebro 30-31 C 9
Holsteinsborg = Sisimiut 70-71 Za 4
Holston River 74-75 B 6
Holten, Banc de – 30-31 C 5
Holten, Banco de – 30-31 C 5
Holtenbank 30-31 C 5
Holten-pad 30-31 C 5
Holt-tenger = Baḥr al-Mayyit 44-45 D 4
Holtville, CA 76-77 F 9
Holung = Helong 50-51 G 1
Holy Cross, AK 70-71 DE 5
Holyhead 32 D 5
Holyoke, MA 74-75 G 3
Holzminden 33 D 3
Hombori 60-61 D 5
Home, OR 76-77 E 3
Home Bay 70-71 XY 4
Homedale, ID 76-77 E 4
Homer, AK 70-71 F 6
Homer, NY 74-75 E 3
Homerville, GA 74-75 B 9
Homestead 56-57 HJ 4
Homestead, FL 74-75 c 4
Homoine 64-65 HJ 7
Homoljske Planine 36-37 J 3
Ḥomra, Al- = Al-Ḥumrah 60-61 L 6
Homra, Hamada el – = Al-Ḥamādat al-Ḥamrā' 60-61 G 2-3
Homs 44-45 D 4
Ḥomṣ = Al-Khums 60-61 GH 2
Hon, Cu Lao – = Cu Lao Thu 52-53 EF 4
Honai 50-51 J 6
Honan = Henan 48-49 L 5
Honaz dağı 46-47 C 4
Honbetsu 50-51 cd 2
Honda 78-79 E 3
Honda Bay 52-53 G 5
Hondo [J] 50-51 H 6
Hondo = Honshū 48-49 PQ 4
Honduras 72-73 J 9
Honduras, Cabo de – 72-73 JK 8
Honduras, Golfe de – 72-73 J 8
Honesdale, PA 74-75 F 4
Honey Lake 76-77 C 5
Honfleur 34-35 H 4
Hongarije 33 H-K 5
Hongch'ŏn 50-51 FG 4
Hong-do 50-51 E 5
Hong He [TJ, Yunnan] 48-49 J 7
Honghe Hanizu Yizu Zizhizhou 48-49 J 7
Honghu [TJ, ●] 48-49 L 6
Hongjiang 48-49 KL 6
Hong Kong 48-49 LM 7
Hongkong = Hong Kong 48-49 LM 7
Hongluoxian 50-51 C 2
Hongmoxian = Hongluoxian 50-51 C 2
Hongrie 33 H-K 5
Hongshui He 48-49 K 6-7
Hongsŏng 50-51 F 4
Hongū 50-51 K 6
Hongueda, Détroit d' 70-71 XY 8
Honguedo, Détroit de – 70-71 XY 8
Hongwŏn 50-51 FG 2-3
Honiara 52-53 jk 6
Honjo 50-51 MN 3
Honningsvåg 30-31 LM 2
Honshū 48-49 PQ 4
Honshu, Cresta Meridional de – 48-49 R 5-6
Honshūi-hátság 48-49 R 5-6
Honshu Méridional, Seuil de – 48-49 R 5-6
Honsiu, Grzbiet – 48-49 R 5-6
Honsyû = Honshū 48-49 PQ 4
Hood = Isla Española 78-79 B 5
Hood, Mount – 72-73 B 2
Hood Canal 76-77 B 2
Hood Point 56-57 CD 6
Hood River, OR 76-77 C 3
Hoog-Altaj, Autonome Gebied – = 9 ◁ 42-43 Q 7
Hooker, Bi'r – 62 D 2
Hooker Creek 56-57 F 3
Hook Island 56-57 J 4
Hoonah, AK 70-71 JK 6
Hoopa, CA 76-77 B 5
Hoopa Valley Indian Reservation 76-77 AB 5
Hooper, UT 76-77 G 5
Hoover Dam 72-73 D 4
Hopa 46-47 J 2
Hope, AR 72-73 H 5
Hope, AZ 76-77 G 9
Hope, Ben – 32 D 2
Hopedale 70-71 YZ 6
Hopeh = Hebei 48-49 LM 4
Hope Island 74-75 C 2
Hopen 19 B 16
Hopes Advance, Cape – 70-71 X 5
Hopetoun [AUS, Victoria] 56-57 H 7
Hopetoun [AUS, Western Australia] 56-57 D 6
Hopetown 64-65 F 8
Hopewell, VA 74-75 E 6
Hopi Indian Reservation 76-77 H 7-8
Hopkins, Lake – 56-57 E 4
Hopkinsville, KY 72-73 J 4
Hopland, CA 76-77 B 6
Hoppo = Hepu 48-49 K 7
Hopu = Hepu 48-49 K 7
Ho-p'u = Hepu 48-49 K 7
Hoquiam, WA 76-77 AB 2
Hōrān, Wādī – = Wādī Ḥawrān 44-45 E 4
Horasan 46-47 K 2
Hörby 30-31 E 10
Hordaland 30-31 A 8-B 7
Hordio = Hurdiyo 44-45 G 8
Horlick Mountains 24 A 26-27
Hormoz 44-45 H 5
Hormoz, Tangeh – 44-45 H 5
Horn [IS] 30-31 bc 1
Horn, Îles – 52-53 b 1
Hornafjördhur 30-31 f 2
Hornavan 30-31 GH 4
Hörnefors 30-31 H 6
Hornell, NY 74-75 E 3
Horni Egypt = Aṣ-Ṣa'īd 60-61 L 3-4
Horn Mountains [CDN] 70-71 MN 5
Hornos, Cabo de – 80 CD 9
Hornsea 32 FG 5
Hornsund 30-31 jk 6
Hornsundtind 30-31 k 6
Horobetsu 50-51 b 2
Horonobe 50-51 bc 1
Horqueta 80 E 2
Horseheads, NY 74-75 E 3
Horsens 30-31 CD 10
Horse Shoe Bend, ID 76-77 EF 4
Horse Springs, NM 76-77 JK 9
Horsham [AUS] 56-57 H 7
Horská badachšanská autonomní oblast 44-45 B 3
Horten 30-31 D 8
Horton River 70-71 M 4
Horvátország 36-37 F-H 3
Horzum-Armutlu = Gölhisar 46-47 C 4
Hořejší jezero = Lake Superior 72-73 HJ 2
Hoṣeima, el – = Al-Ḥusaymah 60-61 D 1
Ḥoseinābād = Īlām 44-45 F 4
Ḥoseynābād 46-47 M 5
Hoseyniyeh 46-47 MN 6
Hoshingo Mdogo 63 DE 3
Ḥôsh 'Īsá = Ḥawsh 'Īsá 62 D 2
Hospitalet de Llobregat 34-35 J 8
Hospitalet de Llobregat 34-35 J 8
Hosta Butte 76-77 JK 8
Hoste, Isla – 80 C 9
Hot 52-53 C 3
Hotamış Gölü 46-47 E 4
Hotan = Khotan 48-49 DE 4
Hot Creek Valley 76-77 E 6
Hotien = Khotan 48-49 DE 4
Hoting 30-31 G 5
Hot Springs, AR 72-73 H 5
Hot Springs, MT 76-77 F 2
Hot Springs, NC 74-75 B 7
Hot Springs, VA 74-75 D 6
Hottah Lake 70-71 N 4
Houlton, ME 74-75 JK 1
Houma 48-49 L 4
Houma, LA 72-73 H 6
Ḥoumaïmâ, Bîr – = Bi'r Ḥumaymah 46-47 HJ 5
'Houndé 60-61 D 6
Houston, TX 72-73 G 5-6
Houtman Abrolhos 56-57 B 5
Ḥouz Soltān, Daryācheh – 46-47 O 5
Ḥouz Soltān, Karavānsarā-ye – = Daryācheh Ḥouz Soltān 46-47 O 5
Hover, WA 76-77 D 2
Hovrah = Haora 44-45 O 6
Howar = Wādī Huwār 60-61 K 5
Howe, ID 76-77 G 4
Howe, Cape – 56-57 K 7
Howick [CDN] 74-75 G 2
Howrah = Haora 44-45 O 6
Hoy 32 E 2
Høyanger 30-31 B 7
Hôyokaikō = Bungo-suidō 48-49 P 5
Hoyran gölü 46-47 D 3
Höytiäinen 30-31 N 6
Hozat 46-47 H 3

Hpā'an 52-53 C 3
Hpalam 52-53 B 2
Hpyū 52-53 C 3

Hradec Králové 33 GH 3
Hrochei La 48-49 DE 5
Hron 33 J 4
Hrvatska 36-37 F-H 3

Hsay Walad 'Alī Bābī 60-61 B 5
Hsia-ho = Xiahe 48-49 J 4
Hsia-kuan = Xiaguan 48-49 J 6
Hsia-mên = Xiamen 48-49 M 7
Hsi-an 48-49 K 5
Hsi-an = Xi'an 48-49 K 5
Hsiang-kang = Hong Kong 48-49 LM 7
Hsiang-yang = Xiangyang 48-49 L 5
Hsiang-yang-chên = Xiangyangzhen 50-51 E 1
Hsiao-ch'ang-shan Tao = Xiaochang-shan Dao 50-51 D 3
Hsiao-ling Ho = Xiaoling He 50-51 C 2
Hsia-tung = Xiadong 48-49 H 3
Hsi-ch'ang = Xichang [TJ, Sichuan] 48-49 J 6
Hsi Chiang = Xi Jiang 48-49 L 7
Hsi-ch'uan = Xichuan 48-49 L 5
Hsi Chiang = Xi Jiang 48-49 L 7
Hsien-hs'ien = Xian Xian 48-49 M 4
Hsien-yang = Xianyang 48-49 K 5
Hsi-fêng-k'ou = Xifengkou 50-51 B 2
Hsi-hsien = She Xian 48-49 M 5-6
Hsi-hsien = Xi Xian [TJ, Shanxi] 48-49 L 4
Hsi-hu = Wusu 48-49 EF 3
Hsi Chiang = Xi Jiang 48-49 L 7
Hsi-liao Ho = Xar Moron He 48-49 MN 3
Hsin-chiang = Xinjiang Uygur Zizhiqu 48-49 D-F 3
Hsinchu 48-49 N 6-7
Hsing-ch'êng = Xingcheng 50-51 C 2
Hsing-jên = Xingren 48-49 K 6
Hsing-ning = Xingning 48-49 M 7
Hsin-hai-lien = Haizhou 48-49 M 5
Hsin-hsiang = Xinxiang 48-49 LM 4
Hsin-hua = Xinhua 48-49 L 6
Hsi-ning = Xining 48-49 J 4
Hsin-kao Shan = Yu Shan 48-49 N 7
Hsinking = Changchun 48-49 NO 3
Hsin-liao Ho = Xiliao He 48-49 N 3
Hsin-li-t'un = Xinlitun 50-51 CD 1-2
Hsin-lo = Xinle 48-49 LM 4
Hsin-min = Xinmin 50-51 D 1-2
Hsin-pin = Xinbin 50-51 E 2
Hsin-ts'ai = Xincai 48-49 LM 5
Hsin-tu = Xindu 48-49 L 7
Hsin-yang = Xinyang 48-49 LM 5
Hsi-ta-ch'uan = Xidachuan 50-51 FG 2
Hsüan-hua = Xuanhua 48-49 LM 3
Hsüan-wei = Xuanwei 48-49 J 6
Hsuchang = Xuchang 48-49 L 5
Hsü-chou = Xuzhou 48-49 M 5
Hsûmbârâbûm 52-53 C 1
Hsün-hua = Xunhua 48-49 J 4

Hszincsiang-Ujgur = Xinjiang Uygur Zizhiqu 48-49 D-F 3

Htâwei 52-53 C 4

Hua'an 48-49 M 6
Huab 64-65 D 7
Huachi [PE] 78-79 D 5
Huachinera 76-77 J 10
Huacho 78-79 D 7
Huacrachuco 78-79 D 6
Huagaruancha 78-79 DE 7
Hua-hsien = Hua Xian [TJ, Henan] 48-49 LM 4
Huai'an 48-49 MN 5
Huai-chi = Huaiji 48-49 L 7
Huaide 48-49 NO 3
Huai He 48-49 M 5
Huaiji 48-49 L 7
Huainan 48-49 M 5
Huaining = Anqing 48-49 M 5
Huaiyin 48-49 M 5
Huai-yin = Qingjiang 48-49 M 5
Hualian = Hua-lien 48-49 N 7
Hua-lien 48-49 N 7
Huallaga, Río – 78-79 D 6
Huallanca 78-79 D 6
Hualpai Indian Reservation 76-77 G 8
Hualpai Mountains 76-77 G 8
Huambo 64-65 E 5
Hu'a Mu'o'ng 52-53 D 2-3
Huancabamba 78-79 CD 6
Huancané [PE] 78-79 F 8
Huancavelica [PE, ●] 78-79 DE 7
Huancayo 78-79 DE 7
Huanchaca, Serrania de – 78-79 G 7
Huangbai 50-51 F 2
Huang He 48-49 L 4
Huang He = Chatan gol 48-49 K 3
Huang He = Ma Chhu 48-49 J 4
Huangheyan 48-49 H 5
Huang Ho = Chatan gol 48-49 K 3
Huang Ho = Huang He 48-49 L 4
Huang Ho = Ma Chhu 48-49 J 4
Huang-ho-yen = Huangheyan 48-49 H 5
Huang-hsien = Huang Xian 48-49 MN 4
Huanghuadian 50-51 D 2
Huang-hua-tien = Huanghuadian 50-51 D 2
Huangnan Zangzu Zizhizhou 48-49 J 4-5
Huangshi 48-49 LM 5
Huangshijiang = Huangshi 48-49 LM 5
Huang-t'u-liang-tzŭ = Huangtuliangzi 50-51 B 2
Huangtuliangzi 50-51 B 2
Huanguelén 80 D 5
Huang Xian 48-49 MN 4
Huangyuan = Thangkar 48-49 J 4
Huan-jên = Huanren 50-51 E 2
Huanren 50-51 E 2
Huanta 78-79 E 7
Huánuco [PE, ●] 78-79 D 6-7
Huara 80 BC 1-2
Huaráz 78-79 D 6
Huari 78-79 E 8
Huarmey 78-79 D 7
Huascaran = Nevado Huascaran 78-79 D 6
Huascaran, Nevado – 78-79 D 6
Huasco 80 B 3
Hua Shan 48-49 L 5
Huatabampo 72-73 DE 6
Huauchinango 72-73 G 7
Hua Xian [TJ, Henan] 48-49 LM 4
Ḥubâra, Wâdî – = Wādī al-Asyūṭī 62 D 4
Hubbaḷi = Hubli-Dhawad 44-45 M 7
Hubbard, Mount – 70-71 J 5
Hubei 48-49 KL 5
Hubli-Dhawad 44-45 M 7
Huch'ang 50-51 F 2
Hu-chou = Wuxing 48-49 MN 5
Huchuento, Cerro – 72-73 E 7
Ḥudaybū = Ṭamrīdah 44-45 GH 8
Ḥudaydah, Al- 44-45 E 8
Ḥuḍayn, Wādī – 62 F 6
Huddersfield 32 F 5
Hudiksvall 30-31 G 7
Hudnah, Ash-Shaṭṭ al- 60-61 EF 1
Hudson, NY 74-75 FG 3
Hudson, Bahía de – 70-71 S-U 5-6
Hudson, Baie d' 70-71 S-U 5-6
Hudson, Cerro – 80 B 7
Hudson, Détroit d' 70-71 WX 5
Hudson, Estrecho de – 70-71 WX 5
Hudson, Surco del – 74-75 GH 5
Hudson, Vallée sous-marine de l' 74-75 GH 5
Hudsona, Cieśnina – 70-71 WX 5
Hudsona, Zatoka – 70-71 S-U 5-6
Hudsonbai 70-71 S-U 5-6
Hudson Bay 70-71 S-U 5-6
Hudson Canyon 74-75 GH 5
Hudson Falls, NY 74-75 G 3
Hudsongeul 74-75 GH 5
Hudson-hasadék 74-75 GH 5
Hudson Mountains 24 B 27
Hudson-öböl 70-71 S-U 5-6
Hudsonrinne 74-75 GH 5
Hudson River 72-73 M 3
Hudsonský kaňon 70-71 WX 5
Hudson Strait 70-71 WX 5
Hudsonstraße 70-71 WX 5
Hudson-szoros 70-71 WX 5
Hudsonův záliv 70-71 S-U 5-6
Huê 52-53 E 3
Huedin 36-37 K 2
Huelva 34-35 D 10
Huércal-Overa 34-35 FG 10
Huesca 34-35 G 7
Huéscar 34-35 F 10
Ḥufrat an-Naḥās 60-61 JK 7
Hufūf, Al- 44-45 FG 5
Hughenden 56-57 H 4
Huhehaote 48-49 L 3
Huibplato 64-65 E 8
Hŭich'ŏn 48-49 O 3
Hui-chou = She Xian 48-49 M 5-6
Huila [Angola, ●] 64-65 D 6
Huila [Angola, ☆] 64-65 DE 5
Huila, Nevado del – 78-79 D 4
Huinan 48-49 O 3
Hui-tsê = Huize 48-49 J 6
Huittinen 30-31 K 7
Hui Xian 48-49 JK 5
Huixtla 72-73 H 8
Huiyang 48-49 LM 7
Huize 48-49 J 6
Ḥukayyim, Bi'r al- 60-61 J 2
Hûker, Bîr – = Bi'r Hooker 62 D 2
Hŭksan-chedo 50-51 E 5
Hŭksan-jedo = Hŭksan-chedo 50-51 E 5
Hukui = Fukui 48-49 Q 4
Hukuntsi 64-65 F 7
Hukusima = Fukushima 48-49 R 4
Hulan 48-49 O 2
Ḥulayfā' 44-45 E 5
Hull 70-71 V 8
Hull, Kingston upon – 32 FG 5
Hull Mountain 76-77 B 6
Hulu = Ulu 52-53 HJ 6
Huludao 50-51 C 2
Hulun = Hailar 48-49 M 2
Hulun Nur 48-49 M 2
Hu-lu-tao = Huludao 50-51 C 2
Ḥulwân 60-61 L 3
Huma 48-49 O 1
Hu-ma-êrh Ho = Huma He 48-49 NO 1
Huma He 48-49 NO 1
Humahuaca 80 C 2
Humaitá [BR] 78-79 G 6
Humansdorp 64-65 FG 9
Ḥumaydah, Al- 62 F 3
Ḥumaym 44-45 GH 6
Ḥumaymah, Bi'r – 46-47 HJ 5
Humbe 64-65 D 6
Humber 32 G 5
Humberto de Campos 78-79 L 5
Humboldt [CDN] 70-71 PQ 7
Humboldt, AZ 76-77 GH 8
Humboldt, NV 76-77 D 5
Humboldt, Mount – 56-57 N 4
Humboldt Bay 76-77 A 5
Humboldt Gletscher 70-71 Y 2
Humboldtkette 48-49 H 4
Humboldt Range 76-77 D 5
Humboldt River 72-73 C 3
Humboldt Salt Marsh 76-77 DE 6
Hume, Lake – 56-57 J 7
Humedad, Isla – 72-73 a 2
Humenné 33 KL 4
Humpata 64-65 D 6
Humphrey, ID 76-77 GH 3
Humphreys, Mount – 76-77 D 7
Humphreys Peak 72-73 D 4
Humptulips, WA 76-77 B 2
Ḥumrah, Al- 60-61 L 6
Hums, Al- = Al-Khums 60-61 GH 2
Humurgân = Sürmene 46-47 J 2
Hūn 60-61 H 3
Húnaflói 30-31 c 1-2
Hunan 48-49 L 6
Hun Chiang = Hun Jiang 50-51 E 2
Hunchun 48-49 P 3
Hun Chiang = Hun Jiang 50-51 E 2
Hunedoara 36-37 K 3
Hungary 33 H-K 5
Hung-chiang = Hongjiang 48-49 KL 6
Hungerford [AUS] 58 G 2
Hung Ho = Hong He [TJ, Yunnan] 48-49 J 7
Hung Hu = Honghu 48-49 L 6
Hungkiang = Hongjiang 48-49 KL 6
Hŭngnam 48-49 O 4
Hungría 33 H-K 5
Hungry Horse Reservoir 76-77 G 1
Hung-shui Ho = Hongshui He 48-49 K 6-7
Hun He 50-51 D 2
Hun Ho = Hun He 50-51 D 2
Hun Chiang = Hun Jiang 50-51 E 2
Hunjani 64-65 H 6
Hun Jiang [TJ, ~] 50-51 E 2
Hunjiang [TJ, ●] 50-51 F 2
Ḥunkurāb, Rā's – 62 F 5
Hunsrück 33 C 3-4
Hunte 33 D 2
Hunter, Dorsal de – 56-57 OP 4
Hunter, Île – 56-57 O 4
Hunter, Seuil – 56-57 OP 4
Huntera, Grzbiet – 56-57 OP 4
Hunterdrempel 56-57 OP 4
Hunter Island [AUS] 56-57 H 8
Hunter River 58 K 4
Hunters, WA 76-77 DE 1
Hunterschwelle 56-57 OP 4
Hunter-szigeti-hátság 56-57 OP 4
Huntingdon 32 F 5
Huntingdon [CDN] 74-75 FG 2
Huntingdon, PA 74-75 DE 4
Hunting Island 74-75 C 8
Huntington, OR 76-77 E 3
Huntington, UT 76-77 H 6
Huntington, WV 72-73 K 4
Huntington Beach, CA 76-77 DE 9
Huntsville, AL 72-73 J 5
Huntsville, TX 72-73 GH 5
Hunyung 50-51 H 1
Hunzā = Bāltit 44-45 L 3
Huon Gulf 52-53 N 8
Huon Peninsula 52-53 N 8
Hupeh = Hubei 48-49 KL 5
Hûrând 46-47 M 3
Huraybah, Al- 44-45 F 7
Huraymis, Qārat – 62 B 2
Hurd, Cape – 74-75 BC 2
Hurdiyo 60-61 c 1
Hure Qi 48-49 N 3
Huribgah = Khurībgah 60-61 C 2
Hurjādah = Al-Ghardaqah 60-61 L 3
Hurley, NM 76-77 J 9
Hurma Çayı 46-47 G 3
Huron, CA 76-77 C 7
Huron, SD 72-73 G 3
Huron, Jezioro – = Lake Huron 72-73 K 2-3
Huron, Lake – 72-73 K 2-3
Huronsee = Lake Huron 72-73 K 2-3
Huronské jezero = Lake Huron 72-73 K 2-3
Huron-tó = Lake Huron 72-73 K 2-3
Hurricane, UT 76-77 G 7
Húsavík 30-31 e 1
Ḥuṣayhiṣah, Al- 60-61 L 6
Ḥusaymah, Al- 60-61 D 1
Ḥusaynīyah, Al- 44-45 EF 7
Hüseyinli = Kızılırmak 46-47 EF 2
Huşi 36-37 MN 2
Huskisson 58 K 5
Huskvarna 30-31 F 9
Husum 33 D 1
Hutanopan 52-53 CD 6
Hutchinson, KS 72-73 G 4
Hutchinsons Island 74-75 cd 3
Hutch Mountain 76-77 H 8
Huutokoski 30-31 M 6
Hüvek = Bozova 46-47 H 4
Huwar, Wādī – 60-61 K 5
Huy 34-35 K 3
Hüyük 46-47 D 4
Huzgan 46-47 MN 7
Huzhou = Wuxing 48-49 MN 5
Huzi san = Fuji-san 48-49 Q 4-5

182 Hódme

Huzul, Al- 46-47 K 8

Hvalsbakur 30-31 g 2
Hval Sund 70-71 WX 2
Hvammsfjördhur 30-31 bc 2
Hvammstangi 30-31 c 2
Hvar 36-37 G 4
Hveragerdhi 30-31 c 2
Hvitá [IS, Árnes] 30-31 c 2
Hvitá [IS, Mýra] 30-31 c 2
Hvitárvatn 30-31 d 2
Hvolsvöllur 30-31 cd 3

Hwaak-san 50-51 F 3-4
Hwach'ŏn 50-51 F 3
Hwach'ŏn-ni 50-51 FG 3
Hwaian = Huai'an 48-49 MN 5
Ḥwaiza, Hōr al- = Hawr al-Ḥawīzah 46-47 M 7
Hwange 64-65 G 6
Hwanggan 50-51 FG 4
Hwanghae-namdo 50-51 E 3-4
Hwanghae-pukto 50-51 EF 3
Hwangho = Huang He 48-49 L 4
Hwanghsien = Huang Xian 48-49 MN 4
Hwangju 50-51 EF 3
Hwangyuan = Thangkar 48-49 J 4
Hwap'yŏng 50-51 F 2
Hwasun 50-51 F 5
Hweichow = She Xian 48-49 M 5-6
Hweitseh = Huize 48-49 J 6

Hijaz 44-45 D 5-6
Hybla 74-75 E 2
Hyden 56-57 C 6
Hyde Park, VT 74-75 G 2
Hyder, AZ 76-77 G 9
Hyderabad 44-45 M 7
Hyderabad = Ḥaidarābād 44-45 KL 5
Hyères 34-35 L 7
Hyères, Îles d' 34-35 L 7
Hyesanjin 48-49 O 3
Hyltebruk 30-31 E 9
Hyndman, PA 74-75 D 5
Hyndman Peak 76-77 FG 4
Hyōgo 50-51 K 5
Hyŏnch'on 50-51 G 2
Hyŏpch'ŏn = Hapch'ŏn 50-51 FG 5
Hyrra-Banda = Ira Banda 60-61 J 7
Hyrum, UT 76-77 H 5
Hyrynsalmi 30-31 N 5
Hyūga 50-51 H 6
Hyvinkää 30-31 L 7

Ḥzimī, Wādī al- = Wādī al-Ḥazimī 46-47 J 6

Ch

Chaaltyn gol 48-49 GH 4
Cha-am [T] 52-53 CD 4
Chaba 48-49 F 2
Chabarovo 42-43 L 4
Chabarovsk 42-43 a 8
Chabarowsk = Chabarovsk 42-43 a 8
Chablis 34-35 J 5
Chaco 80 D 3
Chaco Austral 80 DE 3
Chaco Boreal 80 DE 2
Chaco Central 80 D 2-E 3
Chaco River 76-77 J 7
Chačmas 38-39 J 7
Chad 60-61 HJ 5
Chadasan 48-49 J 2
Chadchal = Chatgal 48-49 HJ 1
Chadum 64-65 F 6
Chadzaar 48-49 G 4
Chaeryŏng 50-51 EF 3
Chagang-do 50-51 EF 2
Chagan nuur 48-49 L 3
Chaghcharān 44-45 K 4
Chagny 34-35 K 5
Chagos 22-23 N 6
Chagres [PA, ~] 72-73 ab 2
Chagres [PA, ●] 72-73 b 2
Chagres, Brazo del – 72-73 b 2
Chagres, Rio – 72-73 bc 2
Chagres Arm = Brazo del Chagres 72-73 b 2
Chahār Burjak 44-45 J 4
Chāhār Burjak = Chahār Burjak 44-45 J 4
Chahār Maḥāl-e Bakhteyārī = 3 ◁ 44-45 G 4
Chahbâ = Shahbā' 46-47 G 6
Chāh Bāhār = Bandar-e Chāh Bahār 44-45 HJ 5
Ch'aho 50-51 G 2
Chachapoyas 78-79 D 6
Châcharân 72-73 K 4
Chachoengsao 52-53 D 4
Chaidamu Pendi = Tsaidam 48-49 GH 4
Ch'ail-bong 50-51 F 2
Chai Nat 52-53 D 3
Chaîne Pontique 44-45 C-E 2
Chaîne Rocheuse = Rocky Mountains 70-71 L 5-P 9
Chaiya 52-53 C 5
Chajari 80 E 4
Chajdag gol 48-49 EF 3
Chajlar 48-49 M 2
Chajlar = Hailar 48-49 M 2
Chajlar gol = Hailar He 48-49 MN 2
Chajpudyrskaja guba 38-39 LM 2
Chajrchan 48-49 J 2
Chajr'uzovo 42-43 e 6
Chaka Nor = Chöch nuur 48-49 H 4
Chakasische Autonome Oblast 42-43 R 7
Chakasische Autonome Oblast = 9 ◁ 42-43 R 7
Chakàská republika = 9 ◁ 42-43 R 7
Chakaski Obwód Autonomiczny = 9 ◁ 42-43 R 7
Chakasskaja Avtonomnaja Oblast' = Chakasische Autonome Oblast = 9 ◁ 42-43 R 7
Chake Chake 63 DE 4
Chāl = Shāl 46-47 N 5
Chala 78-79 E 8
Chalabesa 63 B 5
Cha-lan-tun = Yalu 48-49 N 2
Chalbi Desert 63 D 2
Chaleur Bay 70-71 XY 8
Chalhuanca 78-79 E 7
Chalchyn gol 48-49 M 2
Cha-ling Hu = Kyaring Tsho 48-49 H 5
Chálkē 36-37 M 7
Chalkidikē 36-37 K 3
Chalkis 36-37 K 6
Challapata 78-79 F 8
Challis, ID 76-77 F 3
Chal'mer-Ju 42-43 L 4
Chalmer-Sede = Tazovskij 42-43 OP 4
Châlons-sur-Marne 34-35 JK 4
Chalon-sur-Saône 34-35 K 5
Chalosse 34-35 G 7
Chalturin 42-43 H 6
Cham 33 F 4
Chaman 44-45 K 4
Chamba [EAT] 63 D 5
Chamba [IND] 44-45 M 4
Chambal [IND ◁ Kali Sindh] 44-45 M 5-6
Chambal [IND ◁ Yamuna] 44-45 M 5-6
Chamberlain Lake 74-75 J 1
Chambersburg, PA 74-75 DE 4-5
Chambéry 34-35 K 6
Chambeshi 64-65 H 5
Chamdo = Chhamdo 48-49 H 5
Chamchamāl 46-47 L 5
Chami Choto = Hami 48-49 G 3
Chamo, Lake – = Tyamo 60-61 M 7
Champa [IND] 44-45 N 6
Champa [SU] 42-43 X 5
Champagne 34-35 J 5-K 4
Champagny Islands 56-57 D 3
Champaign, IL 72-73 J 3-4
Champāran = Motihari 44-45 NO 5
Champasak 52-53 DE 4
Champlain, Lake – 72-73 LM 3
Champotón 72-73 H 8
Chanāb = Chenab 44-45 M 4
Chañar 80 C 4
Chañaral [RCH ↖ Copiapó] 80 B 3
Chañaral, Isla – 80 B 3
Chan Bogd 48-49 K 3
Chancay 78-79 D 7
Chānda = Chandrapur 44-45 M 7
Chandalar River 70-71 G 4
Chandeleur Islands 72-73 J 6
Chandigarh 44-45 LM 4
Chandler 70-71 Y 8
Chandler, AZ 76-77 H 9
Chandlers Falls 63 D 2
Chandrapur 44-45 M 7
Chandyga 42-43 a 5
Chang, Ko – [T → Krung Thep] 52-53 D 4
Changai = Shanghai 48-49 N 5
Changaj 48-49 H 2
Changajn nuruu 48-49 HJ 2
Ch'ang-an = Xi'an 48-49 K 5
Changane, Rio – 64-65 H 7
Changara 64-65 H 6
Changbai 50-51 FG 2
Changbai Shan 48-49 O 3
Changde 48-49 L 6
Changdu = Chhamdo 48-49 H 5
Chang-hai = Shanghai 48-49 N 5
Changhang 50-51 F 4-5
Changhowŏn 50-51 F 4
Ch'ang-hsing Tao = Changxing Dao 50-51 C 3
Changhŭng 50-51 F 5
Changhŭng-ni 50-51 FG 2
Chang-chia-k'ou = Zhangjiakou 48-49 L 3
Changchih = Changzhi 48-49 L 4
Ch'ang-chih = Changzhi 48-49 L 4
Changchun 48-49 NO 3
Chang Jiang [TJ, ~ ◁ Dong Hai] 48-49 K 5-6
Changji Huizu Zizhizhou 48-49 FG 3
Changjin 50-51 F 2
Changjin-gang 50-51 F 2
Changjin-ho 50-51 F 2
Changjŏn 50-51 G 3
Changkiakow = Zhangjiakou 48-49 L 3
Chang-kuang-ts'ai Ling = Zhangguangcai Ling 48-49 O 2-3
Changnim-ni 50-51 F 3
Ch'angnyŏng 50-51 G 5
Ch'ang-pai = Changbai 50-51 FG 2
Ch'ang-pai Shan = Changbai Shan 48-49 O 3
Chang-san-ying = Zhangsanying 50-51 AB 2
Changsha 48-49 L 6
Changshu 48-49 N 5
Ch'angsŏng = Chongsŏng 50-51 GH 1
Chang Tang = Jang Thang 48-49 E-G 5
Ch'ang-tê = Anyang 48-49 LM 4
Ch'ang-tê = Changde 48-49 L 6
Changteh = Changde 48-49 L 6
Changting 48-49 M 6
Ch'ang-tu = Chhamdo 48-49 H 5
Changtutsung = Chhamdo 48-49 H 5
Ch'angwŏn 50-51 G 5
Changxing Dao [TJ, Liaodong Wan] 50-51 C 3
Changyeh = Zhangye 48-49 J 4
Changyŏn 48-49 NO 4
Changzhi 48-49 L 4
Changzhou 48-49 M 5
Chanch 48-49 J 1
Chan-chiang = Zhanjiang 48-49 L 7
Chanchoengsao 52-53 D 4
Chaniá 36-37 KL 8
Chaniṓn, Kólpos – 36-37 KL 8
Chanka, ozero – 42-43 Z 9
Chankiang = Zhanjiang 48-49 L 7
Channāb = Chenab 44-45 M 4
Channel Islands [GB] 32 E 7
Channel Islands [USA] 76-77 CD 9
Channel Islands National Monument = Anacapa Island, Santa Barbara Island 76-77 D 9
Channel-Port-aux-Basques 70-71 Z 8
Chanovej 38-39 M 2
Chansi = Shanxi 48-49 L 4
Chantaburi = Chanthaburi 52-53 D 4
Chantada 34-35 CD 7
Chantajka 42-43 PQ 4
Chantajskoje, ozero – 42-43 QR 4
Chanten en Mansen, Nationaal Gebied der – 42-43 L-P 5
Chan Tengri, pik – 44-45 MN 2
Chanten und Mansen, Autonome Oblast der – 42-43 L-P 5
Chanten und Mansen, Nationalkreis der – 42-43 L-P 5
Chanthaburi 52-53 D 4
Chantong = Shandong 48-49 M 4
Chantrey Inlet 70-71 RS 4
Chantsko-mansijský autonomní okruh 42-43 L-P 5
Chanty-Mansijsk 42-43 M 5
Chanty-Mansijskaja Avtonomnaja Oblast' = Autonome Oblast der Chanten und Mansen 42-43 L-P 5
Chanty-Mansyjski Okręg Autonomiczny 42-43 L-P 5
Chanty y los Mansi, Circunscripción Nacional de los – 42-43 L-P 5
Chao'an 48-49 M 7
Chao Hu 48-49 M 5
Chaochow = Chao'an 48-49 M 7
Chao Phraya, Mae Nam – 52-53 CD 3-4
Chaor He 48-49 N 2
Chaotong = Zhaotong 48-49 J 6
Chao-t'ung = Zhaotong 48-49 J 6
Chaoyang [TJ, Guangdong] 48-49 M 7
Chaoyang [TJ, Liaoning] 48-49 MN 3
Ch'ao-yang-chên = Huinan 48-49 O 3
Chapada da Veadeiros, Parque Nacional dos – 78-79 K 7
Chapada Diamantina 78-79 L 7
Chapadinha 78-79 L 5
Chapala, Lago de – 72-73 F 7
Chapčeranga 42-43 V 8
Chapel Hill, NC 74-75 D 7
Chapra 44-45 N 5
Chaqui 78-79 F 8
Châ'r, Jebel – = Jabal Shā'r 46-47 GH 5
Charadai 80 E 3
Charagua 78-79 G 8
Charagua, Cordillera de – 78-79 G 8-9
Char Ajrag 48-49 KL 2
Charaña 78-79 F 8
Charbin = Harbin 48-49 O 2
Chār Burjak 44-45 J 4
Charcas 72-73 F 7
Charcot, Île – 24 C 29
Chardāvol 46-47 M 6
Chardon, OH 74-75 C 4
Charente 34-35 G 6
Chargehoasen = Al-Wāḥāt al-Khārijah 60-61 KL 3-4
Char Gov' 48-49 GH 3
Chärchän 48-49 F 4
Chärchän Darya 48-49 F 4
Char Chorin 48-49 J 2
Char Choto 48-49 J 3
Chari 60-61 H 6
Chārīkār 44-45 K 3-4
Char Irčis 48-49 F 2
Charitona Lapteva, bereg – 42-43 Q 3-R 2
Charity 78-79 H 3
Char'kov 38-39 G 5-6
Charkow = Char'kov 38-39 G 5-6
Charkow = Char'kov 38-39 G 5-6
Charków = Char'kov 38-39 G 5
Charleroi 34-35 K 3
Charles, Cape – 72-73 LM 4
Charles Island 70-71 VW 5
Charleston, SC 72-73 KL 5
Charleston, WV 72-73 K 4
Charleston Peak 76-77 F 7
Charlestown 72-73 O 8
Charlesville 64-65 F 4
Charleville [AUS] 56-57 J 5
Charleville-Mézières 34-35 K 4
Charlotte, NC 72-73 KL 4-5
Charlotte Amalie 72-73 O 8
Charlotte Harbor 72-73 K 6
Charlottenberg 30-31 E 8
Charlottesville, VA 72-73 L 4
Charlottetown 70-71 Y 8
Charlottetown = Roseau 72-73 O 8
Charlovka 38-39 G 2
Charlton 58 F 6
Charlton Island 70-71 UV 7
Char Narijn uul 48-49 K 3
Char nuur [MVR] 48-49 G 2
Char nuur [TJ] 48-49 H 4
Charolais, Monts du – 34-35 K 5
Charovsk 42-43 G 6
Charqî, Jebel ech- = Jabal ar-Ruwāq 46-47 G 5-6
Charqiliq 48-49 F 4
Charters Towers 56-57 J 3-4
Chartres 34-35 H 4
Chartûm = Al-Kharṭūm 60-61 L 5
Chartum = Al-Kharṭūm 60-61 L 5
Char us nuur 48-49 G 2
Chasan 50-51 H 1
Chasavjurt 38-39 J 7
Chascomús 80 E 5
Chase City, VA 74-75 D 6
Chasŏng 50-51 F 2
Chassahowitzka Bay 74-75 b 2
Chašuri 38-39 H 7
Chatanga 42-43 TU 3
Chatan gol 48-49 K 3
Chatangskij zaliv 42-43 UV 3
Châteaubriant 34-35 G 5
Château-du-Loir 34-35 H 5
Châteaudun 34-35 H 4
Châteaulin 34-35 EF 4
Châteauroux 34-35 H 5
Château-Thierry 34-35 J 4
Châtellerault 34-35 H 5
Chatgal 48-49 HJ 1
Chatham [CDN, New Brunswick] 70-71 XY 8
Chatham [CDN, Ontario] 70-71 U 9
Chatham, NY 74-75 G 3
Chatham, VA 74-75 D 6
Chatham = Isla San Cristóbal 78-79 B 5
Chatham, Îles – 56-57 Q 8
Chatham, Isla – 80 B 8
Chatham Islands 56-57 Q 8
Chatham Strait 70-71 K 6
Châtillon 36-37 B 3
Châtillon-sur-Seine 34-35 K 5
Chatsworth 74-75 C 2
Chāṭṭagām 44-45 P 6
Chattahoochee River 72-73 JK 5
Chattanooga, TN 72-73 J 4
Chattarpur = Chhatarpur 44-45 M 6
Châu Đôc = Châu Phu 52-53 E 4
Chaumont 34-35 K 4
Chaŭn-do 50-51 EF 5
Châu Phu 52-53 E 4
Chautauqua Lake 74-75 D 3
Chaux-de-Fonds, La – 33 C 5
Chavast 44-45 K 2
Chaves 34-35 D 8
Chaves [BR] 78-79 K 5
Chaves, Isla – = Isla Santa Cruz 78-79 AB 5
Chavīb Deh 46-47 N 7
Chaviva 78-79 E 4
Chaya = Drayä 48-49 H 5
Ch'a-yü = Dsayul 48-49 H 6
Chazón 80 D 4

Cheat Mountain 74-75 CD 5
Cheat River 74-75 D 5
Cheb 33 F 3
Chebâyesh, Al- = Al-Jaza'ir 46-47 M 7
Chebir, Uáu el – = Wādī Bay al-Kabīr 60-61 GH 2
Cheboygan, MI 72-73 K 2
Chedâdī, El- = Ash-Shiddādī 46-47 J 4
Cheektowaga, NY 74-75 DE 3
Cheepie 56-57 HJ 5
Chefoo = Yantai 48-49 N 4
Chefu = Yantai 48-49 N 4
Chegga = Ash-Shaqqāt 60-61 C 3
Chegutu 64-65 GH 6
Chehalis, WA 76-77 B 2
Chehalis River 76-77 B 2
Chehel-e Chashmeh, Kūhhā-ye – 46-47 M 5
Chech, Erg – = 'Irq ash-Shaykh 60-61 D 3-4
Chechaouène = Shifshâwn 60-61 CD 1
Chechenes e Ingush, República Autónoma de los – = 5 ◁ 38-39 J 7
Checheno-Ingush Autonomous Republic = 5 ◁ 38-39 J 7
Chech'on 50-51 G 4
Cheikh Aḥmed = Shaykh Ahmad 46-47 J 4
Cheikh Hlâl = Shaykh Hilāl 46-47 G 5
Cheikh Ṣalâḥ = Shaykh Salāh 46-47 J 4
Cheikh Zerâfá = Zilāf 46-47 G 6
Cheju 48-49 O 5
Cheju-do 48-49 NO 5
Cheju-haehyŏp 48-49 O 5
Chekiang = Zhejiang 48-49 MN 6
Chekkâ, Râs – = Rā's ash-Shikk'ah 46-47 F 5
Chela, Serra da – 64-65 D 6
Chelan, WA 76-77 CD 2
Chelan, Lake – 76-77 C 1
Chélia, Djebel – = Jabal Shīlyah 60-61 F 1
Chê-ling Kuan = Zheling Guan 48-49 L 6
Chelleh Khâneh, Kūh-e – 46-47 N 4
Chełm 33 L 3
Chełmińskre, Pojezierze – 33 J 2
Chełmża 33 J 2
Chelsea, VT 74-75 G 2-3
Cheltenham 32 EF 6
Cheltenham, PA 74-75 F 4
Chelyuskin, Cape – = mys Čel'uskin 42-43 UV 2
Chemawa, OR 76-77 B 3
Chemba 64-65 H 6
Chemehuevi Valley Indian Reservation 76-77 F 8
Chemnitz 33 F 3
Chemulpo = Inch'ŏn 48-49 O 4
Chemult, OR 76-77 C 4
Chenab 44-45 M 4
Cheney, WA 76-77 E 2
Chên-fan = Minqin 48-49 J 4
Chengde 48-49 M 3
Chengdu 48-49 J 5
Ch'êng-chiang = Chengjiang 48-49 J 7
Chengjiang 48-49 J 7
Chengkiang = Chengjiang 48-49 J 7
Chengkou 48-49 K 5
Chengmai 48-49 KL 8
Chengteh = Chengde 48-49 M 3
Chengtu = Chengdu 48-49 J 5
Cheng-Xian = Sheng Xian 48-49 N 6
Chengzitan 50-51 D 3
Chên-hsi = Bar Köl 48-49 G 3
Ch'ên-ch'i = Chenxi 48-49 L 6
Chên-chiang = Zhenjiang 48-49 M 5
Ch'ên-chou = Yuanling 48-49 L 6
Chenkiang = Zhenjiang 48-49 M 5
Chennapaṭṭaṇam = Madras 44-45 N 8
Chensi = Bar Köl 48-49 G 3
Chensi = Shanxi 48-49 L 4
Chentiin nuruu 48-49 K 2
Chentij = 15 ◁ 48-49 L 2
Chenxi 48-49 L 6
Chen Xian 48-49 L 6
Chenyang = Shenyang 48-49 NO 3
Chenyuan = Zhenyuan [TJ, Yunnan] 48-49 J 7
Chên-yüan = Zhenyuan [TJ, Yunnan] 48-49 J 7
Chepes 80 C 4
Cher 34-35 J 5
Cherangani 63 C 2
Cheraw, SC 74-75 CD 7
Cherbourg 34-35 G 4
Cheren = Keren 60-61 M 5
Chergui, Chott ech – = Ash-Shaṭṭ ash-Sharqī 60-61 DE 2
Cherchen = Chärchän 48-49 F 4
Cherlen gol 48-49 KL 2
Cherlen gol = Herlen He 48-49 M 2
Cherrapunj = Cherrapunjee 44-45 P 5
Cherrapunjee 44-45 P 5
Cherry 56-57 N 2
Cherry Creek, NV 76-77 F 6
Cherson 38-39 F 6
Chesapeake, VA 72-73 LM 4
Chesapeake Bay 72-73 L 4
Cheshire, OR 76-77 B 3
Chesley 74-75 C 2
Chester 32 E 5
Chester, CA 76-77 C 5
Chester, MT 76-77 H 1
Chester, PA 74-75 F 5
Chester, SC 74-75 C 7
Chesterfield 32 F 5
Chesterfield, Île – 64-65 K 6
Chesterfield, Îles – 56-57 L 3
Chesterfield Inlet [CDN, ∪] 70-71 ST 5
Chesterfield Inlet [CDN, ●] 70-71 ST 5
Chestertown, MD 74-75 EF 5
Chesuncook Lake 74-75 HJ 1-2
Cheta [SU, ~] 42-43 S 3
Cheta [SU, ●] 42-43 S 3
Chetlat Island 44-45 L 8
Chetumal 72-73 J 8
Chetumal, Bahia de – 72-73 J 8
Cheviot, The – 32 EF 4
Cheviot Hills 32 E 4
Chewelah, WA 76-77 DE 1
Cheyenne, WY 72-73 F 3
Cheyenne River 72-73 F 3

Chhamdo 48-49 H 5
Chhaprā = Chapra 44-45 N 5
Chhārīkār = Chārikār 44-45 K 3-4
Chhatarpur [IND, Madhya Pradesh] 44-45 M 6
Chhattisgarh 44-45 N 6
Chhergundo 48-49 H 5
Chhergundo Zhou = Yushu Zangzu Zizhizhou 48-49 GH 5
Chhibchang Tsho 48-49 G 5
Chhindvāṛā = Chhindwara [IND ← Seoni] 44-45 M 6
Chhindwara [IND ← Seoni] 44-45 M 6
Chhōṭā Andamān = Little Andaman 44-45 P 8
Chhōṭā Nikōbār = Little Nicobar 44-45 P 9
Chhumar 48-49 G 4-5
Chhushul 48-49 FG 6

Chia-hsing = Jiaxing 48-49 N 5
Chia-i 48-49 MN 7
Chia-li = Lharugö 48-49 G 5
Chia-ling Chiang = Jialing Jiang 48-49 K 5
Chia-mu-szŭ = Jiamusi 48-49 P 2
Chi-an = Ji'an [TJ, Jiangxi] 48-49 LM 6
Chi-an = Ji'an [TJ, Jilin] 50-51 EF 2
Chiang Dao 52-53 CD 3
Chiange 64-65 D 6
Chiang-hsi = Jiangxi 48-49 LM 6
Chiang-chou = Xinjiang 48-49 L 4
Chiang Khan 52-53 D 3
Chiang Mai 52-53 CD 3
Chiang Rai 52-53 CD 3
Chiang-su = Jiangsu 48-49 MN 5
Chiapa, Rio – = Rio Grande 72-73 H 8
Chiapas 72-73 H 8
Chiari 36-37 CD 3
Chiàvari 36-37 C 3
Chiavenna 36-37 C 2
Chiba 50-51 N 5
Chibabava 64-65 H 7
Chibemba 64-65 DE 6
Chibia 64-65 D 6
Chibinogorsk = Kirovsk 42-43 EF 4
Chibiny 38-39 F 2
Chibougamau 70-71 VW 7-8
Chiburi-jima 50-51 J 5
Chibuto 64-65 H 7
Chicacole = Shrikakulam 44-45 N 7
Chicago, IL 72-73 J 3
Chicapa, Rio – 64-65 F 4
Chic-Chocs, Monts – 70-71 X 8
Chickasha, OK 72-73 G 4-5
Chiclayo 78-79 CD 6
Chico, CA 72-73 B 4
Chico, Rio – [RA, Chubut] 80 C 6
Chico, Rio – [YV] 78-79 F 2
Chico, Rio – [RA, Santa Cruz ◁ Bahia Grande] 80 C 7
Chico, Rio – [RA, Santa Cruz ◁ Rio Gallegos] 80 C 7
Chicoa 64-65 H 6
Chicoana 80 CD 3
Chiconomo 63 CD 6
Chicopee, MA 74-75 G 3
Chicoutimi 70-71 WX 8

Chico 183

Chicualacuala 64-65 H 7
Chidley, Cape — 70-71 Y 5
Chi-do 50-51 EF 5
Chiefland, FL 74-75 b 2
Chiehmo = Chärchän 48-49 F 4
Chiemsee 33 F 5
Chiengi 64-65 G 4
Chiengmai = Chiang Mai 52-53 C 3
Chien-Ho = Jian He [TJ, ~] 50-51 D 2
Chien-ch'ang = Jianchang [TJ → Benxi] 50-51 E 2
Chien-ch'ang = Jianchang [TJ ↙ Jinzhou] 50-51 D 2
Ch'ien-chiang = Qianjiang [TJ, Hubei] 48-49 L 5
Chien-ko = Jiange 48-49 JK 5
Chien-ning = Jian'ou 48-49 M 6
Chien-ou = Jian'ou 48-49 M 6
Chien-p'ing = Jianping 50-51 B 2
Chien-shui = Jianshui 48-49 J 7
Ch'ien-wei = Qianwei 50-51 C 2
Chien-yang = Jianyang [TJ, Sichuan] 48-49 JK 5
Chieti 36-37 F 4
Chifre, Serra do — 78-79 L 8
Chignik, AK 70-71 E 6
Chigyŏng 50-51 F 3
Ch'ih-fêng = Chifeng 48-49 M 3
Chih-fu = Yantai 48-49 N 4
Chih-chiang = Zhijiang [TJ, Hunan] 48-49 KL 6
Chihkiang = Zhijiang 48-49 KL 6
Chih-li Wan = Bo Hai 48-49 M 4
Chi-hsi = Jixi 48-49 P 2
Chihuahua 72-73 E 6
Ch'i-ch = Qiqihar 48-49 N 2
Chichagof Island 70-71 J 6
Chichén Itzá 72-73 J 7
Chichester 32 F 6
Chii-san = Chiri-san 50-51 F 5
Chike = Xunke 48-49 O 2
Chikugo 50-51 H 6
Chikwawa 64-65 HJ 6
Chilapa de Alvarez 72-73 G 8
Chilås 44-45 L 3
Chilca 78-79 D 7
Chilcoot, CA 76-77 CD 6
Chile 80 B 5-C 2
Chile 80 B 5-C 2
Chile, Cuenca de — 22-23 E 7-F 6
Chile Basin 22-23 EF 6-7
Chilebecken 22-23 EF 6-7
Chilecito [RA, La Rioja] 80 C 3
Chilete 78-79 D 6
Chili 80 B 5-C 2
Chili, Bassin du — 22-23 E 7-F 6
Chilia, Braţul — 36-37 N 3
Chilibekken 22-23 EF 6-7
Chilibre 72-73 b 2
Ch'i-lien Shan = Qilian Shan 48-49 HJ 4
Chilika Hrada = Chilka Lake 44-45 NO 7
Chililabombwe 64-65 G 5
Chi-lin = Jilin [TJ, ●] 48-49 O 3
Chi-lin = Jilin [TJ, ☆] 48-49 N 2-O 3
Chilivani 36-37 C 5
Chilka Lake 44-45 NO 7
Chilko Lake 70-71 M 7
Chillán 80 B 5
Chill Chainnigh = Kilkenny 32 C 5
Chillicothe, MO 72-73 H 3-4
Chillicothe, OH 72-73 K 4
Chilly, ID 76-77 FG 3
Chiloé, Isla de — 80 AB 6
Chilok 42-43 UV 7
Chilonga 63 B 5-6
Chilongozi 63 BC 6
Chiloquin, OR 76-77 C 4
Chilpancingo de los Bravos 72-73 G 8
Chiltern Hills 32 F 6
Chilung = Kee-lung 48-49 N 6
Chilwa, Lake — 64-65 J 6
Chiman tagh 48-49 FG 4
Chimbay [EC, ▲] 78-79 D 5
Chimborazo [EC, ▲] 78-79 D 5
Chimbote 78-79 D 6
Chimpay 80 C 5
Chimpembe 63 B 5
China 48-49 E-K 5
China [TJ] 48-49 E-K 5
China, Republiek — 48-49 N 7
China Lake, CA 76-77 E 8
China Meridional, Cuenca de — 52-53 FG 3-4
China Meridional, Mar de — 52-53 E 5-G 3
Chinan 50-51 F 5
Chinan = Jinan 48-49 M 4
Ch'in-an = Qin'an 48-49 K 5
Chinandega 72-73 J 9
China Oriental, Mar de — 48-49 N 6-O 5
Chinapa 76-77 HJ 10
China Point 76-77 D 9
Chinbo 80 C 5
Chincoteague, VA 74-75 F 6
Chincoteague Bay 74-75 F 5
Chinde 64-65 J 6
Chin-do [ROK, ⊙] 50-51 EF 5

Chindo [ROK, ●] 50-51 F 5
Chindwin Myit 52-53 C 1-2
Chine 48-49 E-K 5
Chine Méridionale, Mer de — 52-53 E 5-G 3
Chine Orientale, Mer de — 48-49 N 6-O 5
Chinese muur 48-49 K 4
Ch'ing Hai = Chöch nuur 48-49 H 4
Chinghai = Qinghai 48-49 GH 4
Ching-ho = Jinghe [TJ, ●] 48-49 E 3
Ch'ing-ho-ch'êng = Qinghecheng 50-51 E 2
Ch'ing-ho-mêng = Qinghemen 50-51 C 2
Ching-ch'uan = Yinchuan 48-49 JK 4
Ching-ku = Jinggu 48-49 J 7
Chingola 64-65 G 5
Chingombe 63 B 6
Ching-po Hu = Jingbo Hu 48-49 O 3
Ching-t'ai = Jingtai 48-49 J 4
Ch'ing-tao = Qingdao 48-49 N 4
Ch'ing-tui-tzŭ = Qingduizi 50-51 D 3
Ching-tung = Jingdong 48-49 J 7
Ch'ing-yang = Qingyang [TJ, Gansu] 48-49 K 4
Ching-yüan = Jingyuan 48-49 JK 4
Ch'ing-yüan = Qingyuan [TJ, Liaoning] 50-51 E 1
Chinhae 50-51 G 5
Chinhae-man 50-51 G 5
Chinhoyi 64-65 GH 6
Chin-hsien = Jin Xian [TJ, Liaoning ↗ Jinzhou] 50-51 C 2
Chin-hsien = Jin Xian [TJ, Liaoning ↑ Lüda] 48-49 N 4
Chinhsien = Jinzhou 48-49 N 3
Chin-hua = Jinhua 48-49 MN 6
Ch'in-huang-tao = Qinhuangdao 48-49 MN 3-4
Chincha Alta 78-79 D 7
Chin-ch'êng = Jincheng 48-49 L 4
Chinchilla 56-57 K 5
Chinchilla de Monte-Aragón 34-35 G 9
Chinchorro, Banco — 72-73 J 8
Chinchow = Jinzhou 48-49 N 3
Chi-ning = Jining [TJ, Nei Monggol Zizhiqu] 48-49 L 3
Chi-ning = Jining [TJ, Shandong] 48-49 M 4
Chinju 48-49 O 4
Chinko 60-61 J 7
Chinle, AZ 76-77 J 7
Chinle Valley 76-77 J 7
Chin-mên Tao 48-49 M 7
Chinnamp'o = Nampo 48-49 NO 4
Chinon 34-35 H 5
Chino Valley, AZ 76-77 G 8
Chinquião = Zhenjiang 48-49 M 5
Chinsali 64-65 H 5
Chin-sha Chiang = Jinsha Jiang 48-49 J 6
Chinsura 44-45 O 6
Chinwangtao = Qinhuangdao 48-49 MN 3-4
Chinwithetha Pyinnei 52-53 B 2
Chiny 48-49 E-K 5
Ch'in-yang = Qinyang 48-49 L 4
Chinyŏng 50-51 G 5
Chiôco 64-65 H 6
Chiôggia 36-37 E 3
Chios [GR, ⊙] 36-37 L 6
Chios [GR, ●] 36-37 M 6
Chipata 64-65 H 6
Chipili 63 B 5
Chipinge 64-65 H 7
Chipoka 63 C 6
Chiporiro 64-65 H 6
Chipre 44-45 C 3
Chiputneticook Lakes 74-75 JK 2
Chiquimula 72-73 HJ 9
Chiquitos, Llanos de — 78-79 G 8
Chira 63 D 2
Chira Bazar 48-49 DE 4
Chiredzi 64-65 H 7
Chirfa 60-61 G 4
Chiricahua National Monument 76-77 J 9-10
Chiricahua Peak 76-77 J 10
Chirikof Island 70-71 EF 6
Chiriqui, Golfo de — 72-73 K 10
Chiriquí, Laguna de — 72-73 K 9-10
Chiri-san 50-51 F 5
Chiromo 64-65 J 6
Chirripó Grande, Cerro — 72-73 K 10
Chirundu 64-65 G 6
Chisamba 64-65 G 5-6
Chisel Lake 70-71 QR 7
Chi-shih Shan = Amnyemachhen Gangri 48-49 HJ 5

Chishtian Mandi = Chishtiyān Maṇḍī 44-45 L 5
Chishtiyān Maṇḍī 44-45 L 5
Chisimaio = Kismaayo 64-65 K 3
Chişinău 38-39 E 6
Chitado 64-65 D 6
Chita-hantō 50-51 L 5
Chitambo 63 B 6
Chitembo 64-65 E 5
Chitogarh = Chittaurgarh 44-45 L 6
Chitose 50-51 b 2
Chitradurga 44-45 M 8
Chitrāl 44-45 L 3
Chitré 72-73 K 10
Chittagong = Chāṭṭagām 44-45 P 6
Chittaldurga = Chitradurga 44-45 M 8
Chittaorgarh = Chittaurgarh 44-45 L 6
Chittaurgarh 44-45 L 6
Chittoor 44-45 M 8
Chittoor = Chittor 44-45 M 8
Chiuchuan = Jiuquan 48-49 H 4
Chiulezi, Rio — 63 D 5-6
Chiumbe, Rio — 64-65 F 4
Chiume 64-65 F 5-6
Ch'iung-chou Hai-hsia = Qiongzhou Haixia 48-49 KL 7
Chiungshan = Qiongshan 48-49 L 8
Ch'iung-tung = Qionghai 48-49 L 8
Chiuta, Lagoa — 64-65 J 5
Chiva [SU] 42-43 L 9
Chivasso 36-37 B 3
Chivay 78-79 E 8
Chivilcoy 80 DE 4
Chivu 64-65 H 6
Chiwanda 64-65 HJ 5
Chiwefwe 63 B 6
Chiweta 64-65 H 5
Chixoy, Río — 72-73 H 8
Chjargas 48-49 G 2
Chjargas nuur 48-49 GH 2
Chloride, AZ 76-77 F 8
Chmeiṭiyé = Shmayṭiyah 46-47 H 5
Chmelnickij 38-39 E 6
Chobe 64-65 F 6
Chobe National Park 64-65 FG 6
Chocaya 78-79 F 9
Chocca 78-79 D 7
Chociebuż = Cottbus 33 G 3
Chocolate Mountains 76-77 F 9
Chocontá 78-79 E 3
Ch'o-do [Nordkorea] 50-51 E 3-4
Ch'o-do [ROK] 50-51 F 5
Chodzież 33 H 2
Chodžambas 44-45 JK 3
Chodžejli 42-43 K 9
Chodžent = Leninabad 44-45 KL 2-3
Choele-Choel 80 CD 5
Chochiang = Charqiliq 48-49 F 4
Choch'iwŏn 50-51 F 4
Chöch nuur 48-49 H 4
Chöch Šili 48-49 G 4
Chöch Šili uul 48-49 FG 4
Choibalsan = Čojbalsan 48-49 L 2
Choiseul 52-53 j 6
Chojna 33 G 2
Chojnice 33 HJ 2
Chōkai-zan 50-51 MN 3
Chōlamaṇḍala = Coromandel Coast 44-45 N 7-8
Cholame, CA 76-77 CD 8
Chold = Chuld 48-49 K 2-3
Cholet 34-35 G 5
Cholgwan 50-51 E 3
Chŏlla-namdo 50-51 F 5
Chŏlla-pukto 50-51 F 5
Cholm 33 KL 3
Cholmogory 42-43 G 5
Cholmsk 42-43 b 8
Cholodnoje 38-39 N 3
Cholos nuur 48-49 H 4
Ch'ŏlsan 50-51 E 3
Choluteca 72-73 J 9
Choma 64-65 G 6
Chomba 63 B 6
Ch'ŏnan 50-51 F 4
Chon Buri 52-53 D 4
Chone 78-79 CD 5
Chongdjin = Ch'ŏngjin 48-49 OP 3
Ch'ŏngha 50-51 G 4
Ch'ŏngjin 48-49 OP 3
Chongjin = Ch'ŏngjin 48-49 OP 3
Chongju 48-49 O 4
Ch'ŏngju 48-49 OP 3
Chŏngŭp 48-49 O 4
Chongor = Bajan Adraga 48-49 KL 2
Chongor Oboo Sum = Bajandalaj 48-49 J 3

Chongor Tagh = Qungur tagh 48-49 D 4
Ch'ŏngp'yŏngch'ŏn 50-51 FG 4
Chongqing 48-49 K 6
Ch'ŏngsan-do 50-51 F 5
Chongshan = Chongzuo 48-49 K 7
Ch'ongsŏktu-ri 50-51 EF 3
Chongsŏng 50-51 GH 1
Chŏngŭp 50-51 F 4
Ch'ŏngyang [ROK] 50-51 F 4
Chongzuo 48-49 K 7
Chŏnch'ŏn 50-51 F 2
Chŏnju 48-49 O 4
Chonos, Archipiélago de los — 80 AB 6-7
Chonosarchipel = Archipiélago de los Chonos 80 AB 6-7
Chonuu 42-43 b 4
Choolooj Gov' 48-49 H 3
Chop'or 38-39 H 5-6
Chor 42-43 Za 8
Chorasan = Khorāsān 44-45 H 3-4
Chŏra Sfakion 36-37 L 8
Chordogoj 42-43 W 5
Chor He 48-49 N 2
Chorinsk 42-43 U 7
Chorog 44-45 L 3
Chorrera, La — Chorrera [PA] 72-73 b 2
Chorsabad = Khorsabad 46-47 K 4
Chorvatsko 36-37 F-H 3
Chorwacja 36-37 F-H 3
Chŏrwŏn 50-51 F 3
Chorzele 36-37 K 2
Chorzów 33 J 3
Chosedachard 38-39 L 2
Chōsen-kaikyō 48-49 O 5
Chŏshi 50-51 N 5
Chos-Malal 80 BC 5
Choszczno 33 GH 2
Chota 78-79 D 6
Chota Nāgpur 44-45 NO 6
Chotбuz = Cottbus 33 G 3
Choteau, MT 76-77 G 2
Chotin 38-39 E 6
Chou Shan = Zhoushan Dao 48-49 N 5-6
Chou-shan Ch'ün-tao = Zhoushan Qundao 48-49 N 5
Chovd [MVR, ●] 48-49 G 2
Chovd [MVR, ☆ = 3 ◁] 48-49 G 2
Chovd gol 48-49 G 2
Chövsgöl [MVR, ●] 48-49 KL 3
Chövsgöl [MVR, ☆ = 6 ◁] 48-49 J 1
Chövsgöl nuur 48-49 J 1
Chowan River 74-75 H 6
Chowchilla, CA 76-77 C 7
Christchurch [NZ] 56-57 OP 8
Christian Island 74-75 C 2
Christiansburg, VA 74-75 CD 6
Christianshåb = Qasigiánguir 70-71 a 4
Christie Bay 70-71 O 5
Christmas Creek 56-57 E 3
Christmas Island [AUS] 52-53 E 9
Chromtau 42-43 K 7
Chrudim 33 GH 4
Chrysê 36-37 LM 8
Chrysochûs, Kólpos — 46-47 E 5
Chuang-ho = Zhuanghe 50-51 D 3
Chubb Crater = New Quebec Crater 70-71 VW 5
Chubbuck, CA 76-77 F 8
Chubisgalt = Chövsgöl 48-49 KL 3
Chubsugul = Chövsgöl nuur 48-49 J 1
Chûbu 50-51 LM 4-5
Chubut 80 BC 6
Chubut, Rio — 80 C 6
Ch'üeh-shan = Queshan 48-49 L 5
Chuejská autonomní oblast Ningxia 48-49 JK 3-4
Chugach Mountains 70-71 GH 5
Chugoku 50-51 HJ 5
Chûgoku-sammyaku 50-51 JK 5
Chuguchak 48-49 E 2
Chŭgŭchak = Tarbagataj 48-49 EF 2
Chuhsien = Qu Xian 48-49 M 6
Ch'u-hsiung = Chuxiong 48-49 J 7
Chu-hua Tao = Juhua Dao 50-51 C 2
Chucheng = Zhucheng 48-49 MN 4
Chu-chi = Zhuji 48-49 N 6
Ch'u-ching = Qujing 48-49 J 6
Ch'ü-chou = Qu Xian 48-49 M 6
Chu-chou = Zhuzhou 48-49 L 6
Chuchow = Zhuzhou 48-49 L 6
Ch'uja-do 50-51 F 6

Chukchi Plateau 19 B 35
Chukchi Sea 19 BC 35-36
Chukchos, Circunscripción Nacional de los — 42-43 g-j 4
Chukchos, Dorsal de — 19 B 35
Chukchos, Mar de — 19 BC 35-36
Chuki = Zhuji 48-49 N 6
Chukudu Kraal 64-65 F 7
Chūl, Gardaneh-ye — 46-47 MN 6
Chulaq Aqqan Su 48-49 G 4
Chula Vista, CA 72-73 C 5
Chuld 48-49 K 2-3
Chule 38-39 M 3
Chulucanas 78-79 CD 6
Chulumani 78-79 F 8
Chumbicha 80 C 3
Chum Phae 52-53 D 3
Chumphon 52-53 CD 4
Chumsaeng 52-53 D 3
Chumunjin 50-51 G 4
Chungam-ni 50-51 G 5
Chüngges 48-49 E 3
Chunghwa 50-51 EF 3
Ch'ungch'ŏng-namdo 50-51 F 4
Ch'ungch'ŏng-pukto 50-51 FG 4
Ch'ungju 50-51 FG 4
Chungking = Chongqing 48-49 K 6
Ch'ung-ming = Chongming 48-49 N 5
Ch'ungmu 50-51 G 5
Chüngsan 50-51 E 3
Chungshan = Zhongshan 48-49 L 7
Chung-tien = Zhongdian 48-49 HJ 6
Chüngüj gol 48-49 GH 2
Chung-wei = Zhongwei 48-49 JK 4
Ch'unch'ŏn 48-49 O 4
Chunya 64-65 H 4
Chuquibamba 78-79 E 8
Chuquicamata 80 C 2
Chuquisaca = Sucre 78-79 FG 8
Chur 33 D 5
Churáchándpur 48-49 H 6
Churchill [CDN] 70-71 RS 6
Churchill, ID 76-77 FG 4
Churchill, Cape — 70-71 S 6
Churchill Falls 70-71 XY 7
Churchill Peak 70-71 LM 6
Churchill River [CDN, Manitoba] 70-71 RS 6
Churchill River [CDN ◁ Hamilton Inlet] 70-71 Y 7
Churu 44-45 LM 5
Chusei-hokudō = Ch'ungch'ŏng-pukto 50-51 FG 4
Chusei-nandō = Ch'ungch'ŏng-namdo 50-51 F 4
Chu-shan = Zhushan 48-49 KL 5
Chusistan = Khūzestān 44-45 F 4
Chuska Mountains 76-77 J 7-8
Chust 38-39 D 6
Chutag 48-49 J 2
Chuúčnar 48-49 G 5
Chuúronjang 50-51 GH 2
Chuvash Autonomous Republic = 4 42-43 H 6
Chuvashi, República Autónoma de los — = 4 ◁ 42-43 H 6
Chuwârtah 46-47 L 5
Chuxiong 48-49 J 7
Chuxiong Yizu Zizhizhou 48-49 J 6
Chuy 80 F 4
Chu Yang Sin 52-53 E 4
Chužand 44-45 K 2-L 3
Chužir 42-43 U 7
Chvalynsk 38-39 J 5
Chwârta = Chuwârtah 46-47 L 5
Chypre 44-45 C 3

I

Iaco, Rio — 78-79 EF 7
Iaçu 78-79 L 7
Iakoutie, République Autonome de — 42-43 U-b 4
Ialomiţa 36-37 M 3
Ialu = Yalu Jiang 50-51 EF 2
Iamalo-Nenets, District National des — 42-43 M-O 4-5
Iaşi 36-37 M 2
Iaundé = Yaoundé 60-61 G 8
Iavello = Yabêlo 60-61 M 7-8
Iba [RP] 52-53 G 3
Ibadan 60-61 E 7
Ibagué 78-79 DE 4
Ibar 36-37 J 4
Ibaraki 50-51 M 4
Ibarra 78-79 D 4
Ibarreta 80 E 3
Ibb 44-45 E 8
Iberá, Esteros del — 80 E 3

Iberian Basin 22-23 HJ 3
Iberisch Bekken 22-23 HJ 3
Iberisches Becken 22-23 HJ 3
Iberisches Randgebirge = Sistema Ibérico 34-35 F 7-G 8
Iberville, Lac d' 70-71 W 6
Ibi [WAN] 60-61 F 7
Ibiá 78-79 J 8
Ibib, Wâdî — 62 F 6
Ibicaraí 78-79 M 7-8
Ibicui, Rio — 80 E 3
Ibicuy 80 E 3
Ibingui-Économique 60-61 H 7
Ibipetuba 78-79 KL 7
Ibiza [E, ⊙] 34-35 H 9
Ibiza [E, ●] 34-35 H 9
Ibjillî 60-61 F 3
Ibn Hânî, Ra's — 46-47 F 5
Ibn Şuqayh, 'Uqlat — 46-47 M 8
Ibo 63 E 6
Ibo = Sassandra 60-61 C 7
Ibotirama 78-79 L 7
'Ibrá 44-45 H 6
Ibrâhîm, Jabal — 44-45 E 6
Ibrâhîmîyah, Qanâl al- 62 D 3
'Ibrî 44-45 H 6
Ibsâwî, 'Ayn — 62 B 4
Ibshaway 62 D 3
Ibu 52-53 J 6
Ibusuki 50-51 H 7
Iča [SU] 42-43 e 6
Ica [PE, ⊙] 78-79 D 7
Içá, Rio — 78-79 F 5
Icabarú 78-79 G 4
Içana 78-79 F 4
Içana, Rio — 78-79 F 4
Icatu 78-79 L 7
İçel [TR, ●] 44-45 C 3
İçel [TR, ☆] 46-47 EF 4
Iceland 30-31 c-f 2
Iceland Basin 28-29 CD 4
Iceland Jan Mayen Ridge 28-29 F 2
Ichang = Yichang 48-49 L 5
Ich Chogosoor 48-49 GH 5
Ichibusa-yama 50-51 H 6
Ichihara 50-51 N 5
Ichikawa 50-51 MN 5
Ichinohe 50-51 N 2
Ichinomya 50-51 L 5
Ichinoseki 48-49 QR 4
Ich'ŏn [Nordkorea] 50-51 F 3
Ich'ŏn [ROK] 48-49 O 4
Ichow = Linyi 48-49 M 4
Ichun = Yichun [TJ, Heilongjiang] 48-49 O 2
Ichun = Yichun [TJ, Jiangxi] 48-49 LM 6

Ichang = Yichang 48-49 L 5
Ich Chogosoor 48-49 GH 5
Ichibusa-yama 50-51 H 6
Ichihara 50-51 N 5
Ichikawa 50-51 MN 5
Ichinohe 50-51 N 2
Ichinomya 50-51 L 5
Ichinoseki 48-49 QR 4
Ich'ŏn [Nordkorea] 50-51 F 3
Ich'ŏn [ROK] 48-49 O 4
Ichow = Linyi 48-49 M 4
Ichun = Yichun [TJ, Heilongjiang] 48-49 O 2
Ichun = Yichun [TJ, Jiangxi] 48-49 LM 6

Ida = Kaz dağ 46-47 B 3
Idad, Qârat al — 62 C 3
Idah 60-61 F 7
Idaho 72-73 C 2-D 3
Idaho City, ID 76-77 F 4
Idaho Falls, ID 72-73 D 3
Idanha, OR 76-77 BC 3
Idar-Oberstein 33 C 4
'Idd, Al- 44-45 G 6
'Idd al-Ghanam 60-61 J 6
Idel' 38-39 F 3
Idê Óros 36-37 M 8
Iderijn gol 48-49 HJ 2
Idfû 60-61 L 4
'Idhaim, Nahr al- = Shaṭṭ al-'Uzaym 46-47 L 5
Idi 52-53 C 5-6
Idil 46-47 J 4
Idiofa 64-65 E 4
'Idîsât, El — = Al-'Udaysât 62 E 5
Idkû, Buḥayrat — 62 D 2
Idlib 44-45 D 3
Idrî 60-61 G 3
Idria, CA 76-77 C 7
Idrica 30-31 N 9
Idrija 36-37 EF 2
Ídris Daği 46-47 E 2

Ieper 34-35 J 3
Ierápetra 36-37 L 8
Ierland 32 BC 5
Ierse Zee 32 D 5
Iesi 36-37 E 4

Ifakara 64-65 J 4
Ifalik 52-53 MN 5
Ifanadiana 64-65 L 7
Ife 60-61 EF 7
Iferouâne 60-61 F 5
Iffley 56-57 H 3
Ifnī 60-61 B 3
Iforas, Adrar des – 60-61 E 4-5

Igalula 64-65 H 4
Iganga 64-65 H 2
Igarapava 78-79 K 9
Igarapé-Açu 78-79 K 5
Igarapé-Mirim 78-79 K 5
Igarité 78-79 L 7
Igarka 42-43 Q 4
Iğdır 46-47 KL 3
Ighil-Izane = Ghālizān 60-61 E 1
Ighil M'Goun = Ighil M'Gūn 60-61 C 2
Ighil M'Gūn 60-61 C 2
Igidi, Erg – = Ṣaḥrā' al-Īgīdī 60-61 CD 3
Igielny, Przylądek – 64-65 F 9
Iglau = Jihlava 33 G 4
Iglèsias 36-37 C 6
Iglesiente 36-37 C 6
'Igma, Gebel el- = Jabal al-'Ajmah 60-61 L 3
Ignacio, CA 76-77 B 6
İğneada Burun 46-47 C 2
Igo, CA 76-77 B 5
Igomo 64-65 H 4
Igra 38-39 K 4
Igrim 42-43 L 5
Igrumaro 63 C 4
Iguaçu, Rio – 80 F 3
Igualada 34-35 H 8
Iguala de la Independencia 72-73 G 8
Iguape 80 G 2
Iguatu 78-79 M 6
Iguazú, Cataratas del – 80 F 3
Iguéla 64-65 C 3
Igula 63 C 4

Ihosy 64-65 L 7
İhsangazi 46-47 E 2
İhsaniye 46-47 D 3
I-hsien = Yi Xian [TJ, Liaoning] 50-51 C 2
Ihtiman 36-37 KL 4

Ichang = Yichang 48-49 L 5
Ich Chogosoor 48-49 GH 5
Ichibusa-yama 50-51 H 6
Ichihara 50-51 N 5
Ichikawa 50-51 MN 5
Ichinohe 50-51 N 2
Ichinomya 50-51 L 5
Ichinoseki 48-49 QR 4
Ich'ŏn [Nordkorea] 50-51 F 3
Ich'ŏn [ROK] 48-49 O 4
Ichow = Linyi 48-49 M 4
Ichun = Yichun [TJ, Heilongjiang] 48-49 O 2
Ichun = Yichun [TJ, Jiangxi] 48-49 LM 6

Iida 50-51 L 5
Iida = Suzu 50-51 L 4
Iide-san 50-51 M 4
Iijoki 30-31 LM 5
Iisalmi 30-31 M 6
Iizuka 50-51 H 6

Ijara 64-65 K 3
Ījīdī, Ṣāḥrā' al- 60-61 CD 3
Ijill, Kidyat – 60-61 B 4
IJssel 34-35 KL 2
IJsselmeer 34-35 K 2

Ik 38-39 K 4
Ikaalinen 30-31 K 7
Ikanga 63 D 3
Ikaria 36-37 LM 7
Ikeda [J, Hokkaidō] 50-51 c 2
Ikeda [J, Shikoku] 50-51 JK 5-6
Ikeja 60-61 E 7
Ikela 64-65 F 3
Ikelemba 64-65 E 2
Ikerre 60-61 F 7
Ikhîl 'm Goûn = Ighil M'Gūn 60-61 C 2
Ikhwân, Gezir el- = Jazā'ir al-Ikhwān 62 F 4
Ikhwān, Jazā'ir al- 62 F 4
Iki 50-51 G 6
Iki suidō 50-51 GH 6
Ikitsuki-shima 50-51 G 6
İkizdere 46-47 J 2
Ikkerre 60-61 F 7
Ikoma 64-65 H 3
Ikonde 63 B 4
Ikonium = Konya 44-45 C 3
Ikopa 64-65 L 6
Ikoto = Ikutu 63 C 1
Ikpikpuk River 70-71 F 3-4
Ikr'anoje 38-39 J 6
Ikungi 63 C 4
Ikungu 63 C 4
Ikuno 50-51 K 5
Ikushumbetsu 50-51 bc 2
Ikutha 63 D 3
Ikutu 63 C 1

Ilagan 52-53 H 3
Ilāhābād = Allahabad 44-45 N 5
Īlām 44-45 F 4
Ilan = Yilan 48-49 OP 2
Ilangali 64-65 HJ 4
Ilanskij 42-43 S 6
Ilaro 60-61 E 7
Ilay, Wādī – 62 F 7
Ilchuri Alin = Yilehuli Shan 48-49 NO 1
Ilebo 64-65 F 3
Ileckaja Zaščita = Sol'-Ileck 42-43 JK 7
Ileckaja Zaščita = Sol'-Ileck 42-43 JK 7
Île-de-France 34-35 HJ 4
Ilek [SU, ~] 38-39 K 5
Ileret 63 D 1
Île Royale = Cape Breton Island 70-71 X-Z 8
Îles Anglo-Normandes = Channel Islands 32 E 7
Îles Britanniques 28-29 F 5-G 4
Îles Canaries = Islas Canarias 60-61 A 3
Îles Eoliennes = Ìsole Eòlie o Lipari 36-37 F 6
Ileşha 60-61 EF 7
Îles Ioniennes 36-37 H 6-J 7
'Ilfag = 'Afag 46-47 L 6
Ilford 70-71 RS 6
Ilfracombe 32 D 6
Ilgaz 46-47 E 2
Ilgaz Dağlar 46-47 EF 2
Ilgin 46-47 DE 3
Ilha Grande [BR, Rio de Janeiro] 78-79 L 9
Ilha Grande = Ilha das Sete Quedas 80 EF 2-3
Ilha Grande ou das Sete Quedas 78-79 HJ 9
Ilha Mexiana 78-79 K 4-5
Ilhas Desertas 60-61 A 2
Ílhavo 34-35 C 8
Ilhéus 78-79 M 7
Ili [SU] 42-43 O 8
Ili [TJ] 48-49 E 3
Iliamna Lake 70-71 E 6
Iliamna Volcano 70-71 EF 5
Iliç 46-47 H 3
Iligan 52-53 H 5
Ilihuli Shan = Ilchuri Alin 48-49 NO 1
Ilion 44-45 B 3
Ilion, NY 74-75 F 3
Iljič 42-43 M 9
Iljič'ovsk 36-37 O 2
Iljič 42-43 M 9
Iljič'ovsk 36-37 O 2
Iljinskij [SU ↑ Južno-Sachalinsk] 42-43 b 8
Illampur, Nevado – 78-79 F 8
Illapel 80 B 4
Iller 33 E 4
Illimani, Nevado de – 78-79 F 8
Illinois 72-73 HJ 3
Illinois Peak 76-77 F 2
Illinois River 72-73 HJ 3-4
Illīzī 60-61 F 3
Illubabor = Īlubabor 60-61 LM 7
Il'men', ozero – 42-43 E 6
Ilo 78-79 E 8
Ilo, Rada de – 78-79 E 8
Iloilo 52-53 H 4
Ilorin 60-61 E 7
Il'pyrskij 42-43 f 5-6
Īlubabor 60-61 LM 7
Ilūkste 30-31 LM 9-10
Ilula 63 C 3
Ilwaco, WA 76-77 AB 2
Ilwaki 52-53 J 8
Ilyas Burnu 46-47 AB 2
Ilża 33 K 3

Iłża 33 K 3

Illampur, Nevado – 78-79 F 8
Illapel 80 B 4
Iller 33 E 4
Illimani, Nevado de – 78-79 F 8
Illinois 72-73 HJ 3
Illinois Peak 76-77 F 2
Illinois River 72-73 HJ 3-4
Illīzī 60-61 F 3
Illubabor = Īlubabor 60-61 LM 7

Imabari 50-51 J 5-6
Imabetsu 50-51 N 2
Imagane 50-51 ab 2
Imaichi 50-51 M 4
Imajō 50-51 KL 5
Imandra, ozero – 42-43 E 4
Imari 50-51 GH 6
Imataca, Serrania de – 78-79 G 3
Imatra 30-31 N 7
Imatra vallinkoski 30-31 N 7
Imazu 50-51 KL 5
Imbābah 62 D 2
Imbaimadai 78-79 G 3
Imbros = İmroz 46-47 A 2
Imeri, Serra – 78-79 F 4
Imfal = Imphal 44-45 P 6
Īmī 60-61 N 7
Imilac 80 C 2
Imja-do 50-51 E 5
Imjin-gang 50-51 F 3
Imlay, NV 76-77 DE 5
Immokalee, FL 74-75 c 3
Immyŏng-dong 50-51 G 2
Imnaha River 76-77 E 3
Imo 60-61 F 7
Ìmola 36-37 D 3
Imotski 36-37 G 4
Imperatriz 78-79 K 6
Impèria 36-37 C 4
Imperial, CA 76-77 F 9
Imperial Dam 76-77 F 9
Imperial Valley 72-73 CD 5
Impfondo 64-65 E 2
Imphal 44-45 P 6
Imp'o 50-51 FG 5
İmralı Adası 46-47 C 2
İmranlı 46-47 GH 3
İmroz 46-47 A 2
Imthân 46-47 G 6
Imuruan Bay 52-53 G 4
Imwŏnjin 50-51 G 4

In'a 42-43 b 6
Ina [J] 50-51 LM 5
Inanwatan 52-53 K 7
Iñapari 78-79 EF 7
In'aptuk, gora – 42-43 UV 6
Inari [SF, ●] 30-31 M 3
Inari [SF, ≈] 30-31 MN 3
Inawashiro 50-51 MN 4
Inawashiro ko 50-51 MN 4
Inca 34-35 J 9
İnce Burun 44-45 C 2
İncekum Burnu 46-47 EF 4
İncesu 46-47 F 3
Inch'ŏn 50-51 F 4
İncili = Karasu 46-47 D 2
İncir burun 46-47 G 2
Incudine, l' 36-37 C 5
Indaor = Indore 44-45 M 6
Indaur = Indore 44-45 M 6
Inde [≅] 22-23 NO 4
Inde [★] 44-45 L-N 6
Independence, CA 76-77 D 7
Independence, MO 72-73 H 4
Independence, OR 76-77 B 3
Independence Mountains 76-77 EF 5
Independence Valley 76-77 F 5
Independencia [MEX] 76-77 F 9
Independencia, Islas – 78-79 D 7
Inderagiri, Sungai – 52-53 D 7
Index, WA 76-77 C 2
India 44-45 L-N 6
India, Bassas da – 64-65 JK 7
Indiana 72-73 J 3-4
Indiana, PA 74-75 D 4
Indianapolis, IN 72-73 J 4
Indian Lake [USA, Ohio] 74-75 AB 4
Indian Mountain 76-77 H 4
Indian Ocean 22-23 NO 6-7
Indian Peak 76-77 G 6
Indian River [USA, Florida] 72-73 K 6
Indian Springs, NV 76-77 F 7
Indian Valley, ID 76-77 E 3
Índico Central, Cuenca del – 22-23 NO 6
Índico Central, Dorsal del – 22-23 N 5-7
Índico Meridional, Dorsal de – 22-23 OP 8
Índico Sudoccidental, Cuenca del – 22-23 MN 7
Índico Sudoriental, Cuenca del – 22-23 OP 7
Indie 44-45 L-N 6
Indien 44-45 L-N 6
Indiga 42-43 HJ 4
Indigirka 42-43 bc 4
Indio, CA 76-77 E 9
Indio, Rio – 72-73 c 2
Indios, Cachoeira dos – 78-79 G 4
Indische Oceaan 22-23 NO 6-7
Indischer Ozean 22-23 NO 6-7
Indisch Zuidpolairbekken 22-23 O-Q 8
Indispensable Strait 52-53 k 6
Indo = Sindh 44-45 L 4
Indo, Dorsal de – 44-45 K 6
Indochina 22-23 OP 5
Indonesia 52-53 D-K 7
Indonésie 52-53 D-K 7
Indonesië 52-53 D-K 7
Indonésie 52-53 D-K 7
Indonesien 52-53 D-K 7
Indonézia 52-53 D-K 7
Indonezja 52-53 D-K 7
Indore 44-45 M 6
Indostán 44-45 M 5-O 6
Indramaiu = Indramayu 52-53 E 8
Indramayu 52-53 E 8
Indravati 44-45 N 7
Indre 34-35 H 5
Indre Arna 30-31 AB 7
Indūra = Nizamabad 44-45 M 7
Indus = Sengge Khamba 48-49 DE 5
Indus = Sindh 44-45 L 4
Indus, Vallée sous-marine de l' 44-45 K 6
Indus Canyon 44-45 K 6
Indusgeul 44-45 K 6
Indus-hasadék 44-45 K 6
Indusrinne 44-45 K 6
İnebolu 46-47 E 2
İnegöl 46-47 C 2
Inerie, Gunung – 52-53 H 8
Ineul 36-37 L 2
İnevi = Cihanbeyli 46-47 E 3
In-Ezzane = 'Ayn 'Azzān 60-61 G 4
Infernão, Cachoeira do – 78-79 G 6
I-n-Gall 60-61 F 5
Ingende 64-65 E 3
Ingeniero Jacobacci 80 BC 6
Ingersoll 74-75 C 3
Ingham 56-57 J 3
Inglaterra 32 E-G 5
Ingle, CA 76-77 C 7
Inglefield Bredning 70-71 XY 2
Inglefield Land 70-71 XY 2
Inglewood 56-57 K 5
Inglewood, CA 76-77 D 9
Ingólfshöfdhi 30-31 ef 3
Ingolstadt 33 EF 3
Ingøy 30-31 KL 2
Ingrid Christensen land 24 BC 8
Ingrid Christensen land 24 BC 8
Ingrid Christensen land 24 BC 8
Ingul 36-37 P 2
Ingulec 38-39 F 6
Inhambane [Moçambique, ●] 64-65 J 7
Inhambane [Moçambique, ☆] 64-65 HJ 7
Inhambupe 78-79 M 7
Inhaminga 64-65 HJ 6
Inharrime 64-65 J 7
Inhung-ni 50-51 F 3
Inirida, Rio – 78-79 F 4
Inishowen Peninsula 32 C 4
Injune 56-57 J 5
Inkerman 56-57 H 3
Inkom, ID 76-77 GH 4
Inland Sea = Seto-naikai 48-49 P 5
Inlandsee = Seto-naikai 48-49 P 5
Inn 33 E 5
Innamincka 58 E 1
Innere Mongolei Autonomes Gebiet – 48-49 K 3-M 2
Inner Mongolian Autonomous Region 48-49 K 3-M 2
Inner Sound 32 D 3
Innisfail [AUS] 56-57 J 3
Innoshima 50-51 J 5
Innsbruck 33 E 5
Innymnej, gora – 42-43 kl 4
Ino 50-51 J 6
Inomino-misaki 50-51 J 6
Inongo 64-65 E 3
İnönü 46-47 D 3
Inoucdjouac 70-71 V 6
Inowrocław 33 HJ 2
Inowrocław 33 HJ 2
Inquisivi 78-79 F 8
Inscription, Cape – 56-57 B 5
Insein = Inzein 52-53 C 3
Insterburg = Čern'achovsk 33 K 1
Inta 42-43 KL 4
Interlaken 33 CD 5
Inthanon, Doi – 52-53 C 3
Intiyaco 80 DE 3
Inubō saki 50-51 N 5
Inútil, Bahia – 80 BC 8
Inuvik 70-71 K 4
Inuvik, District of – 70-71 KL 4-5
Invercargill 56-57 NO 9
Inverell 56-57 K 5
Inverleigh 56-57 H 3
Inverness 32 DE 3
Inverness, FL 74-75 b 2
Inverurie 32 EF 3
Inverway 56-57 EF 3
Investigator Group 58 AB 4
Investigator Strait 56-57 FG 7
Inyangani 64-65 H 6
Inyokern, CA 76-77 DE 8
Inyo Mountains 76-77 DE 7
Inza [SU, ●] 42-43 H 7
Inzein 52-53 C 3
Inzia 64-65 E 4

Iñapari 78-79 EF 7

Iōánnina 36-37 J 6
Iō-jima 50-51 H 7
Iokanga 38-39 G 2
Iolotan' 44-45 J 3
Iona, ID 76-77 H 4
Ione, CA 76-77 C 6
Ione, OR 76-77 D 3
Ione, WA 76-77 E 1
Ionian Basin 36-37 GH 7
Ionian Islands 36-37 H 6-J 7
Ionian Sea 36-37 GH 7
Iónioi Nēsoi 36-37 H 6-J 7
Ionisch Bekken 36-37 GH 7
Ionische Inseln 36-37 H 6-J 7
Ionisches Becken 36-37 GH 7
Ionisches Meer 36-37 GH 7
Ionische Zee 36-37 GH 7
Ionti = Joontoy 64-65 K 3
Iony, ostrov – 42-43 b 6
Íos 36-37 L 7
Iosser 38-39 K 3
Iowa 72-73 H 3

Ipadu, Cachoeira – 78-79 F 4
Ipameri 78-79 K 8
Iparia 78-79 E 6
Ipatovo 38-39 H 6
Ipel' 33 J 4
Ipiaú 78-79 M 7
Ipin = Yibin 48-49 JK 6
Ipiranga [BR, Amazonas ↗ Benjamin Constant] 78-79 F 5
Ipixuna 78-79 KL 5
Ipixuna, Rio – [BR ◁ Rio Purus] 78-79 G 6
Ipoh 52-53 D 6
Iporá [BR, Goiás] 78-79 J 8
Ippy 60-61 J 7
İpsala 46-47 B 2
Ipswich [GB] 32 G 5
Ipswich, Brisbane- 56-57 K 5
Ipu 78-79 L 5
Ipueiras 78-79 L 5

Iqlīt 62 E 5
Iquique 80 B 2
Iquitos 78-79 E 5

Ira Banda 60-61 J 7
Iracoubo 78-79 J 3
Irago-suidō 50-51 L 5
Irago-zaki 50-51 L 5
Irāk 44-45 EF 4
Irak 44-45 D-F 4
Irak = Arāk 44-45 F 4
Irala [PY] 80 EF 3
Īrān 44-45 F-H 4
Iran 44-45 F-H 4
Irán 44-45 F-H 4
Iran, Hochland von – 22-23 MN 4
Iran, Hoogland van – 22-23 MN 4
Irán, Meseta de – 22-23 MN 4
Iran, Plateau d' 22-23 MN 4
Iran, Plateau of – 22-23 MN 4
Īrānshāh 46-47 M 4
Īrānshahr 44-45 HJ 5
Irapa 78-79 G 2
Irapuato 72-73 F 7
Iraq 44-45 D-F 4
'Irāq Arabī 46-47 L 6-M 7
Irarrarene = Irharharân 60-61 F 3
Irati 80 F 3
Irawadi = Erāwadī Myit 52-53 C 2
Irazú, Volcán – 72-73 K 9
Irbeni väin 30-31 JK 9
Irbid 44-45 D 4
Irbit 42-43 L 6
Irecê 78-79 L 7
Ireland 32 BC 5
Irene 80 D 5
Irgalem = Yirga 'Alem 60-61 M 7
Irgiz [SU, ~] 38-39 M 6
Irgiz [SU, ●] 42-43 L 8
Irharharân 60-61 F 3
Irhyang-dong 50-51 GH 2
Iri 50-51 F 4-5
Irian, Teluk – = Teluk Cenderawasih 52-53 KL 7
Irian Barat 52-53 K 7-L 8
Irian Jaya 52-53 K 7-L 8
Irian Occidental 52-53 K 7-L 8
Iriba 60-61 J 5
Iriga 52-53 H 4
Iringa 64-65 J 4
Iriomote-jima 48-49 N 7
Iriomote zima = Iriomote-jima 48-49 N 7
Iriri, Rio – 78-79 J 5
Irische See 32 D 5
Irish Sea 32 D 5
Irituia 78-79 K 5
Irkuck = Irkutsk 42-43 TU 7
Irkutsk 42-43 TU 7
Irland 32 BC 5
Irlanda 32 BC 5
Irlanda, Mar de – 32 D 5
Irlanda del Norte 32 CD 4
Irlande 32 BC 5
Irlande, Mer d' 32 D 5
Irlande du Nord 32 CD 4
Irlandia 32 BC 5
Irlandia Północna 32 C 4
Irlandzkie, Morze - 32 D 5
Irmak 46-47 E 3
Irminger, Mar de – 70-71 d-f 5
Irminger, Mer d' 70-71 d-f 5
Irmingersee 70-71 d-f 5
Irminger-tenger 70-71 d-f 5
Irmingerzee 70-71 d-f 5
Iro, Lac – 60-61 HJ 7
Īrōḍ = Erode 44-45 M 8
Iron Baron 58 C 4
Irondequoit, NY 74-75 E 3
Iron Knob 56-57 G 6
Iron Mountain 76-77 G 7
Ironside, OR 76-77 DE 3
Ironton, OH 74-75 B 5
Ironwood, MI 72-73 HJ 2
Iroquois Falls 70-71 U 8
Írország 32 BC 5
Irō saki 50-51 M 5
'Irq, Al- 60-61 J 3
'Irqah 44-45 F 8
'Irq al-Gharbī al-Kabīr, Al- 60-61 D 3-E 2
'Irq ash-Sharqī al-Kabīr, Al- 60-61 F 2-3
Irrawaddy = Erāwadī Myit 52-53 C 2
Irské moře 32 D 5
Irsko 32 BC 5
Ír-tenger 32 D 5
Irtyš 42-43 N 6
Irtyšskoje 42-43 NO 7
Irtyš 42-43 N 6
Irtyšskoje 42-43 NO 7
Irumu 64-65 G 2
Irún 34-35 G 7
Iruya 80 CD 2
Irwin, ID 76-77 H 4
Irwŏl-san 50-51 G 4

Īs, Jabal – 62 F 6
Isabela 52-53 H 5
Isabela, Isla – 78-79 A 5
Isabella, CA 76-77 D 8
Isabella, Cordillera – 72-73 J 9
Isabella Lake 76-77 D 8
Isachsen 70-71 Q 2
Isachsen, Cape – 70-71 OP 2
Ísafjardhardjúp 30-31 b 1
Ísafjördhur 30-31 b 1
Isahara = Isahaya 50-51 GH 6
Isahaya 50-51 GH 6
Isangi 64-65 F 2
Isar 33 F 4
'Isāwīyah, Al- 44-45 D 4
Isâwuwan, 'Irq – 60-61 F 3
Ìschia 36-37 E 5
Ise [J] 50-51 L 5
Iseo 36-37 D 3
Isère 34-35 K 6
Isère, Pointe – 78-79 J 3
Išerim, gora – 42-43 K 5
Isèrnia 36-37 F 5
Iset' 42-43 L 6
Ise-wan 50-51 L 5
Iseyin 60-61 E 7
Isezaki 50-51 M 4
Isfahan = Eşfahān 44-45 G 4
Isfjorden 30-31 j 5
I-shan = Yishan 48-49 K 7
Ishibashi 50-51 N 3
Ishigaki-shima 48-49 NO 7
Ishikari 50-51 b 2
Ishikari gawa 50-51 b 2
Ishikari-wan 50-51 b 2
Ishikawa 50-51 L 4
Ishinomaki 50-51 N 3
Ishinomaki wan 50-51 N 3
Ishioka 50-51 N 4
Ishizuchino san 50-51 J 6
Isigaki sima = Ishigaki-shima 48-49 NO 7
Isigny-sur-Mer 34-35 G 4
Işık Dağı 46-47 E 2
Isil'kul' 42-43 N 7
Išim [SU, ~] 42-43 M 7
Išim [SU, ●] 42-43 M 6
Išimbaj 42-43 K 7
Išimskaja ravnina 42-43 N 6-7
Isiolo 64-65 J 2
Isiro 64-65 G 2
Isisford 56-57 H 4
Isispynten 30-31 mn 5
Iskandar 42-43 M 9
Īskandarīyah, Al- 60-61 KL 2
Iskar 36-37 L 4
Iskardū = Skardū 44-45 M 3
İskele = Karataş 46-47 F 4
İskenderun 44-45 D 3
İskenderun Körfezi 46-47 F 4
İskilip 46-47 F 2
Iskitim 42-43 P 7
Iskushuban 60-61 bc 1
Isla-Cristina 34-35 D 10
İslâhiye 46-47 G 4
Islāmābād 44-45 L 4
Islāmābād = Anantnag 44-45 M 4
Islamorada, FL 74-75 c 4
Island 30-31 c-f 2
Islandbecken 28-29 CD 4
Island City, OR 76-77 E 3
Islande 30-31 c-f 2
Island Falls, ME 74-75 J 1-2
Islandia 30-31 c-f 2
Islandia, Cuenca de – 28-29 CD 4
Island-Jan-Mayen-Rücken 28-29 F 2
Island Lagoon 56-57 G 6
Island Lake [CDN, ≈] 70-71 RS 7
Island Mountain, CA 76-77 B 5
Island Park, ID 76-77 H 3
Island Park Reservoir 76-77 H 3
Island Pond, VT 74-75 GH 2
Islands, Bay of – [NZ] 56-57 OP 7
Isla Nueva 80 C 9
Islas Anglo-Normandas = Channel Islands 32 E 7
Islas Británicas 28-29 F 5-G 4
Islas Jónicas 36-37 H 6-J 7
Islay 32 C 4
Isle 34-35 H 6
Isle au Haut 74-75 J 2-3

Isle 185

Isle Royale 72-73 J 2
Isleton, CA 76-77 C 6
Ismā'īlīyah, Al- 60-61 L 2
Ismetpaşa = Yeşilyurt 46-47 H 3
Isnā 60-61 L 3
Isohama = Ōarai 50-51 N 4
Isoka 64-65 H 5
Ispahân = Eşfahān 44-45 G 4
İsparta 44-45 C 3
Isperih 36-37 M 4
İspir 46-47 J 2
Israel 44-45 CD 4
Israël 44-45 CD 4
Israelite Bay 56-57 DE 6
Issano 78-79 H 3
Issaouane, Erg – = 'Irq Isâwuwan 60-61 F 3
Issoudun 34-35 HJ 5
Issyk-Kul' 44-45 M 2
Issyk-Kul', ozero – 48-49 M 3
Iştabl, Bi'r – 62 B 2
Istâda-Moqur, Ab-e – 44-45 K 4
İstanbul 44-45 BC 2
Istiaia 36-37 K 6
Istiwā'ī, Al- 60-61 KL 7
Istmina 78-79 D 3
Istria 36-37 EF 3
Istria = Istra 36-37 EF 3
Istrie = Istra 36-37 EF 3
Istrien = Istria 36-37 EF 3

Išerim, gora – 42-43 K 5
Išim [SU, ∼] 42-43 M 7
Išim [SU, ●] 42-43 M 6
Išimbaj 42-43 K 7
Išimskaja ravnina 42-43 N 6-7

Itabaianinha 78-79 M 7
Itabaina 78-79 M 6
Itaberaba 78-79 L 7
Itaberai 78-79 JK 8
Itabuna 78-79 M 7
Itacaiúnas, Rio – 78-79 JK 6
Itacaré 78-79 M 7
Itacoatiara 78-79 H 5
Itacolomi, Pico – 78-79 L 9
Itaetê 78-79 L 7
Itaguatins 78-79 K 6
Itaí 80 G 2
Itaipava, Cachoeira – [BR, Rio Araguaia] 78-79 K 6
Itaipava, Cachoeira – [BR, Rio Xingu] 78-79 J 5
Itaituba 78-79 H 5
Itajaí 80 G 3
Itajubá 78-79 K 9
Itajuípe 78-79 LM 7
Itaka 42-43 W 7
Italia 36-37 C 3-F 5
Itálica 34-35 DE 10
Itálie 36-37 C 3-F 5
Italië 36-37 C 3-F 5
Italie 36-37 C 3-F 5
Italien 36-37 C 3-F 5
Italy 36-37 C 3-F 5
Itambé 78-79 L 8
Itany 78-79 J 4
Itaocara 78-79 L 9
Itapaci 78-79 JK 7
Itapajé 78-79 LM 5
Itapebi 78-79 M 8
Itapemirim 78-79 LM 9
Itapetinga 78-79 LM 8
Itapetininga 80 G 2
Itapeva 80 G 2
Itapicuru, Rio – [BR, Bahia] 78-79 M 7
Itapicuru, Rio – [BR, Maranhão] 78-79 L 5
Itapicuru, Serra – 78-79 KL 6
Itapicurumirim 78-79 L 5
Itapipoca 78-79 M 5
Itapira 78-79 K 9
Itaqui 80 E 3
Itarsi 44-45 M 6
Itasca, Lake – 72-73 G 2
Itatuba 78-79 G 6
Itawa = Etawah 44-45 M 5
Itebero 63 AB 3
Itende 63 C 4
Ithaca, NY 72-73 L 3
Ithákē 36-37 J 6
Ithrā = Itrah 46-47 G 7
Itigi 64-65 H 4
Itimbiri 64-65 F 2
Itinoseki = Ichinoseki 48-49 QR 4
Itiquira 78-79 J 8
Itiquira, Rio – 78-79 H 8
Itiruçu 78-79 L 7
Itiúba 78-79 M 7
'Itmâniya, El- = Al-'Uthmānīyah 62 DE 4
Itō 50-51 M 5
Itoigawa 50-51 L 4
Itoikawa = Itoigawa 50-51 L 4
Itrah 46-47 G 7
Itrī, Jabal – 62 F 7
Itsā 62 D 3
Itsjang = Yichang 48-49 L 5
I-tu = Yidu [TJ, Shandong] 48-49 M 4
Ituaçu 78-79 L 7
Itui, Rio – 78-79 E 6
Itula 64-65 G 3
Itumbiara 78-79 K 8
Ituni Township 78-79 H 3
Itupiranga 78-79 JK 6
Ituri 64-65 G 2
Iturup, ostrov – 42-43 c 8
Ituxi, Rio – 78-79 F 6
Itzehoe 33 D 1-2

Iva, SC 74-75 B 7
Ivai, Rio – 80 F 2
Ivajlovgrad 36-37 M 5
Ivalo 30-31 M 3
Ivalojoki 30-31 M 3
Ivangorod 30-31 N 8
Ivanhoe 56-57 H 6
Ivano-Frankovsk 38-39 DE 6
Ivanovka 36-37 O 2
Ivanovo [SU, Rossijskaja SFSR Ivanovo] 42-43 FG 6
Ivanuškova = Koršunovo 42-43 UV 6
Ivanuškova = Koršunovo 42-43 UV 6
Ivaščenkovo = Čapajevsk 42-43 HJ 7
Ivaščenkovo = Čapajevsk 42-43 HJ 7
Ivdel' 42-43 L 5
Ivenec 30-31 M 11
Iversen, Banc d' 42-43 EF 3
Iversen, Banco de – 42-43 EF 3
Iversenbank 42-43 EF 3
Iversen-pad 42-43 EF 3
Ivigtût 70-71 b 5
Ivindo 64-65 D 2
Ivinheima, Rio – 78-79 J 9
Ivohibe 64-65 L 7
Ivoire, Côte d' [≅] 60-61 CD 8
Ivoorkust [≅] 60-61 CD 8
Ivoorkust [★] 60-61 CD 7
Ivrea 36-37 B 3
İvrindi 46-47 B 3
Ivuna 63 C 5

Iwadate 50-51 MN 2
Iwaizumi 50-51 NO 3
Iwaki 50-51 N 4
Iwaki yama 50-51 N 2
Iwakuni 50-51 J 5
Iwamizawa 48-49 R 3
Iwanai 50-51 b 2
Iwanowo = Ivanovo 42-43 FG 6
Iwanuma 50-51 N 3
Iwata 50-51 LM 5
Iwate [J, ●] 50-51 N 3
Iwate [J, ☆] 50-51 N 2-3
Iwate-yama 50-51 N 3
Iwo 60-61 E 7
Iwō-jima = Iō-jima 50-51 H 7
Iwŏn 50-51 G 2

Ixiamas 78-79 F 7
Ixopo 64-65 GH 9
Ixtepec 72-73 G 8

I-yang = Yiyang [TJ, Hunan] 48-49 L 6
Iyo 50-51 J 6
Iyomishima 50-51 J 6
Iyonada 50-51 HJ 6

Izabal, Lago de – 72-73 HJ 8
Izalco 72-73 H 9
Izashiki = Sata 50-51 H 7
Izbat ash-Shaykh 62 C 5
Izberbaš 38-39 J 7
Izberbaš 38-39 J 7
Iževsk 42-43 J 6
Izkī 44-45 H 6
Izland 30-31 c-f 2
Izland 30-31 cd 2
Ižma [SU, ∼] 42-43 J 5
Ižma [SU, ●] 42-43 J 4
Izmail 38-39 E 6
İzmir 44-45 B 3
İzmir Körfezi 46-47 B 3
İzmit = Kocaeli 44-45 BC 2
İzmit Körfezi 46-47 C 2
İznik 46-47 C 2
İznik Gölü 46-47 C 2
Izozog, Bañados de – 78-79 G 8
Izozog, Bañados de – 78-79 G 8
Izra' 46-47 G 6
Izrael 44-45 CD 4
Izu hantō 50-51 M 5
Izuhara 50-51 G 5
Izumi 50-51 H 6
Izumo 50-51 J 5
Izu-shotō 48-49 QR 5
Izu syotō = Izu-shotō 48-49 QR 5
Izvestij CIK, ostrova – 42-43 OP 2

Iževsk 42-43 J 6
Ižma [SU, ∼] 42-43 J 5
Ižma [SU, ●] 42-43 J 4

J

Ja = Dja 60-61 G 8
Jāb, Tall – 46-47 G 6
Jabal, Bahr al- 60-61 L 7
Jabalayn, Al- 60-61 L 6
Jabal Lubnān = 2 [RL, ☆ ◁] 46-47 F 6
Jabalón 34-35 F 9
Jabalpur 44-45 MN 6
Jabjabah, Wādī – 62 E 7
Jablah 46-47 F 5
Jablanica [AL] 36-37 J 5
Jablanica [BG] 36-37 L 4
Jablanica [YU] 36-37 G 4
Jablunkovský průsmyk 33 J 4
Jabung, Tanjung – 52-53 DE 7
Jabuticabal 78-79 K 9
Jaca 34-35 G 7
Jacaré, Rio – [BR, Bahia] 78-79 L 6-7
Jacarei 78-79 K 9
Jáchal = San José de Jáchal 80 C 4
Jachhen 48-49 E 5
Jáchymov 33 F 3
Jaciparaná 78-79 G 6
Jackman Station, ME 74-75 H 2
Jackson, CA 76-77 C 6
Jackson, MI 72-73 JK 3
Jackson, MS 72-73 HJ 5
Jackson, MT 76-77 G 3
Jackson, OH 74-75 B 5
Jackson, TN 72-73 J 4
Jackson, WY 76-77 H 4
Jackson, ostrov – = ostrov Džeksona 42-43 H-K 1
Jackson Head 56-57 N 8
Jackson Lake 76-77 H 4
Jackson Mountains 76-77 D 5
Jacksonville, FL 72-73 KL 5
Jacksonville, NC 74-75 E 7
Jacksonville, OR 76-77 B 4
Jacksonville Beach, FL 74-75 C 9
Jäckvik 30-31 G 4
Jacmel 72-73 M 8
Jacobina 78-79 L 7
Jacob Lake, AZ 76-77 GH 7
Jacques Cortier, Détroit de – 70-71 Y 7-8
Jacuípe, Rio – 78-79 LM 7
Jacumba, CA 76-77 EF 9
Jacundá 78-79 K 5
Jadā, Sha'īb – = Sha'īb al-Judā' 46-47 LM 7-8
Jadaf, Wādī al- 44-45 E 4
Jadaf al-Jadaf 46-47 J 6
Jaddī, Wādī – 60-61 E 2
Jade 33 D 2
Jaderské moře 36-37 E 3-H 5
Jadīda, el – = Al-Jadīdah 60-61 C 2
Jadīdah, Al- [ET] 62 C 5
Jadīdah, Al- [MA] 60-61 G 2
Jadīd Rā's al-Fīl 60-61 K 6
Jadotville = Likasi 64-65 G 5
Jadrin 38-39 J 4
Jādū 60-61 G 2
Jaén 34-35 F 10
Jæren 30-31 A 8
Jaesalmēr = Jaisalmer 44-45 KL 5
Jafa, Tēl Avive – = Tel-Avīv-Yafō 44-45 C 4
Ja'farābād [IR] 44-45 F 3
Jaffa, Cape – 58 D 6
Jaffatin = Jazā'ir Jiftūn 62 EF 4
Jaffna = Yāpanaya 44-45 MN 9
Jafr, Al- [JOR, ∼] 46-47 G 7
Jafr, Al- [JOR, ●] 44-45 D 4
Jafr, El- = Al-Jafr 44-45 D 4
Jafū, Ḥāssī – 60-61 E 2
Jagdalpur 44-45 N 7
Jägerndorf = Krnov 33 HJ 3
Jaghbūb, Al- 60-61 J 3
Jaghiagh, Wādī – 46-47 J 4
Jaghjagh, Ouâdî – = Wādī Jaghiagh 46-47 J 4
Jagodnoje 42-43 cd 5
Jagog Tsho 48-49 F 5
Jagst 33 DE 4
Jagtial 44-45 M 7
Jagua, La – 78-79 E 3
Jaguarão 80 F 4
Jaguarari 78-79 LM 7
Jaguaribe, Rio – 78-79 M 6
Jagüé, Rio del – 80 C 3
Jahrah, Al- 44-45 F 5
Jahrom 44-45 G 5
Jaicós 78-79 L 6
Jailolo 52-53 J 6
Jaipur 44-45 M 5
Jaisalmer 44-45 KL 5
Jaja 42-43 Q 6
Jajah, Al- 62 D 5
Jājarm 44-45 H 3
Jajce 36-37 G 3
Jakan, mys – 42-43 j 4
Jakarta 52-53 E 8
Jakasia, Oblast Autónomo de – = 10 ◁ 42-43 R 7
Jakobshavn = Jlullssat 70-71 ab 4
Jakobstad 30-31 JK 6
Jakoeten Autonome Republiek 42-43 U-b 4
Jakša 42-43 K 5
Jakša 42-43 K 5
Jakuck = Jakutsk 42-43 Y 5
Jakucka Autonomiczna Republika 42-43 U-b 4
Jakut Autonóm Köztársaság 42-43 U-b 4
Jakutische Autonome Republik 42-43 U-b 4
Jakutsk 42-43 Y 5
Jakutská autonomní republika 42-43 U-b 4
Jakutskaja Avtonomnaja Sovetskaja Socialističeskkaja Respublika = Jakutische Autonome Sozialistische Sowjetrepublik 42-43 U-b 4
Jaladah, Al- 44-45 F 7
Jalālābād 44-45 KL 4
Jalālat al-Baḥrīyah, Jabal al- 62 DE 3
Jalālat al-Qiblīyah, Jabal al- 62 E 3
Jalāl Kōt = Jalālābād 44-45 KL 4
Jalāmīd, Al- 46-47 HJ 7
Ja'lan 44-45 H 6
Jalandar = Jullundur 44-45 LM 4
Jalandhar = Jullundur 44-45 LM 4
Jalapa Enríquez 72-73 GH 8
Jalawlā' 46-47 L 5
Jalgāňv = Jālgaon [IND ← Bhusawal] 44-45 M 6
Jālgaon [IND ← Bhusawal] 44-45 M 6
Jalhāk, Al- 60-61 L 6
Jalīb, Maqarr al- 46-47 J 6
Jalībah 46-47 M 7
Jalib Shahab 46-47 M 7
Jalingo 60-61 G 7
Jalisco 72-73 EF 7
Jallekān 46-47 N 6
Jālna 44-45 M 7
Jalon, Rio – 34-35 G 8
Jalo Oasis = Wāḥāt Jālū 60-61 J 3
Jalpug, ozero – 36-37 N 3
Jalta 38-39 F 7
Jalu = Yalu Jiang 50-51 EF 2
Jālū, Wāḥāt – 60-61 J 3
Jamaame 60-61 N 8
Jamaat 48-49 E 2
Jamā'at al-Ma'yuf 46-47 M 7
Jamaica 72-73 L 8
Jamaica Channel 72-73 L 8
Jamaica Channel 72-73 L 8
Jamaica Channel 72-73 L 8
Jamaika 72-73 L 8
Jamaïque 72-73 L 8
Jamajka 72-73 L 8
Jamakhaṇḍī = Jamkhandi 44-45 LM 7
Jamal, poluostrov – 42-43 MN 3
Jamal-Nenets, Circunscripción Nacional de los – 42-43 M-O 4-5
Jamal-Nentsen, Nationaal Gebied der – 42-43 M-O 4-5
Jamal-Nenzen, Nationalkreis der – 42-43 M-O 4
Jamal-Nyenyec Autonóm Körzet 42-43 M-P 4
Jamalsko-něnecký autonomní okruh 42-43 M-P 4-5
Jamalsko-Nieniecki Okręg Autonomiczny 42-43 M-P 4-5
Jamantau, gora – 42-43 K 7
Jamanxim, Rio – 78-79 H 6
Jamari, Rio – 78-79 G 6
Jambi [RI, ●] 52-53 D 7
Jambi [RI, ☆ = 5 ◁] 52-53 D 7
Jambol 36-37 M 4
Jambongan, Pulau – 52-53 G 5
Jambūr 46-47 L 5
Jambuto 38-39 O 2
Jamdena, Pulau – = Pulau Yamdena 52-53 K 8
James, Baie – 70-71 UV 7
James Bay 70-71 UV 7
James Ranges 56-57 F 4
James River [USA ◁ Chesapeake Bay] 72-73 L 4
James River [USA ◁ Missouri River] 72-73 G 2
Jamestown [AUS] 58 D 4
Jamestown, ND 72-73 G 2
Jamestown, NY 72-73 L 3
Jamkhandi 44-45 LM 7
Jamm 30-31 MN 8
Jammerbugt 30-31 C 9
Jammu 44-45 LM 4
Jammu and Kashmir 44-45 LM 3-4
Jamnā = Yamuna 44-45 MN 5
Jāmnagar 44-45 L 6
Jampol' 38-39 E 6
Jāmpūr 44-45 KL 5
Jamsah 62 E 4
Jämsänkoski 30-31 L 7
Jamshedpur 44-45 NO 6
Jamsk 42-43 de 6
Jämtland 30-31 E-G 6
Jämtlands Sikås 30-31 F 6
Jamursba, Tanjung – = Tanjung Yamursba 52-53 K 7
Jana 42-43 Z 4
Janaperi, Rio – 78-79 G 4
Janaúba 78-79 L 8
Janaucu, Ilha – 78-79 JK 4
Janaul 42-43 JK 6
Jandaq 44-45 GH 4
Jandiatuba, Rio – 78-79 F 5-6
Jandowae 56-57 K 5
Janesville, CA 76-77 C 5
Jangarej 42-43 L 4
Jangce = Chang Jiang 48-49 K 5-6
Jangcy = Chang Jiang 48-49 K 5-6
Jangijul' 42-43 M 9
Jang Thang 48-49 E-G 5
Jangtsekiang = Chang Jiang 48-49 K 5-6
Jang-tse-tjiang = Chang Jiang 48-49 K 5-6
Jānī Beyglū 46-47 M 3
Janīn 46-47 F 6
Janina = Iōánnina 36-37 J 6
Jánina = Iōánnina 36-37 J 6
Jan Mayen 19 B 19-20
Jan Mayen, Dorsal de – 28-29 F 2
Jan Mayen, Dorsale de – 28-29 F 2
Jan Mayen, Plataforma de – 28-29 H 1-2
Jan Mayen, Seuil de – 28-29 H 1-2
Jan-Mayendrempel 28-29 H 1-2
Jan Mayen Ridge 28-29 H 1-2
Jan-Mayen-Schwelle 28-29 H 1-2
Jan-Mayen-Schwelle 28-29 H 1-2
Jan-Mayen-Schwelle 28-29 H 1-2
Jannah 60-61 FG 4
Jano-Indigirskaja nizmennost' 42-43 Z-c 3
Janos 76-77 J 10
Jánoshalma 33 J 5
Janov = Gênova 36-37 C 3
Janskij 42-43 Za 4
Janskij zaliv 42-43 Za 3
Jantarnyj 33 J 1
Jantra 36-37 M 4
Januária 78-79 KL 8
Jao-ho = Raohe 48-49 P 2
Jaonpur = Jaunpur 44-45 N 5
Jao-yang Ho = Raoyang He 50-51 D 2
Japán 48-49 Q 5-R 3
Japan 48-49 Q 5-R 3
Japan Basin 50-51 J-L 2
Japangraben 22-23 R 4
Japanisches Becken 50-51 J-L 2
Japanisches Meer 48-49 P 4-Q 3
Japán-medence 50-51 J-L 2
Japans Bekken 50-51 J-L 2
Japan Sea 48-49 P 4-Q 3
Japanse Zee 48-49 P 4-Q 3
Japán-tenger 48-49 P 4-Q 3
Japan Trench 22-23 R 4
Japantrog 22-23 R 4
Japón 48-49 P 5-Q 3
Japon 48-49 P 5-Q 3
Japón, Cuenca del – 50-51 J-L 2
Japón, Fosa del – 22-23 R 4
Japon, Fosse du – 22-23 R 4
Japón, Mar de – 48-49 P 4-Q 3
Japon, Mer du – 48-49 P 4-Q 3
Japonia 48-49 Q 5-R 3
Japonské moře 48-49 P 4-Q 3
Japońskie, Morze – 48-49 P 4-Q 3
Japonsko 48-49 Q 5-R 3
Japurá, Rio – 78-79 F 5
Jara, La – 34-35 E 9
Jarābulus 46-47 GH 4
Jarādah 60-61 D 2
Jaraguari 78-79 HJ 8-9
Jaransk 42-43 H 6
Jarārah, Wādī – 62 F 6
Jarāwī, Al- 46-47 H 7
Jarbah, Jazīrat – 60-61 G 2
Jarbidge, NV 76-77 F 5
Jarcevo [SU, Jenisej] 42-43 R 5
Jarcevo [SU ↗ Smolensk] 38-39 F 4
Jardines de la Reina 72-73 L 7
Jarega 38-39 K 3
Jarensk 42-43 H 5
Jari, Rio – 78-79 J 5
Jarīd, Shaṭṭ al- 60-61 F 2
Jarīr, Wādī – 44-45 E 5-6
Jarkand = Yarkand 48-49 D 4
Jarkov = Char'kov 38-39 G 5-6
Jarkovo 42-43 M 6
Jarmashīn, 'Ayn – 62 CD 5
Jarny 34-35 K 4
Jarocin 33 H 2-3
Jarok, ostrov – 42-43 a 3
Jaroslavl' 42-43 FG 6
Jarosław 33 L 3-4
Jarosław 33 L 3-4
Jarotschin = Jarocin 33 H 2-3
Järpen 30-31 E 6
Jarrāḥī, Rūd-e – 46-47 N 7
Jarroto 38-39 O 2
Jar-Sale 42-43 MN 4
Jartum = Al-Kharṭūm 60-61 L 5
Jaru 78-79 G 7
Järvenpää 30-31 L 7
Jäsk 44-45 H 5
Jašma 38-39 H 2
Jasnyj 42-43 Y 7
Jasonhalvøy 24 C 30-31
Jason Islands 80 D 8
Jasper [CDN, Alberta] 70-71 N 7
Jasper [CDN, Ontario] 74-75 F 2
Jasper, FL 74-75 b 1
Jasper National Park 70-71 N 7
Jaṣṣān 46-47 L 6
Jastrebac 36-37 J 4
Jászberény 33 JK 5
Jašma 38-39 H 2
Jász-Nagykun-Szolnok 42-43 H 9
Jataí [BR ↙ Rio Verde] 78-79 J 8
Jatapu, Rio – 78-79 H 5
Játiva 34-35 G 9
Jatobá 78-79 JK 5
Jat Potī = Kārēz 44-45 K 4
Jaú 78-79 K 9
Jaú, Rio – 78-79 G 5
Jau'aliyāt, Jebel el- = Jabal al-Aḍiriyāt 46-47 G 7
Jauer = Jawor 33 H 3
Jauf, Al- = Al-Jawf 44-45 DE 5
Jauf, El – = Al-Jawf 60-61 J 4
Jauja 78-79 DE 7
Jaunde = Yaoundé 60-61 G 8
Jaunjelgava 30-31 L 9
Jaunpur 44-45 N 5
Jáva 52-53 EF 8
Java [RI] 52-53 EF 8
Java, Fosse de – 22-23 P 6
Java, Mar de – 52-53 EF 8
Java, Mer de – 52-53 EF 8
Java Head = Tanjung Layar 52-53 DE 8
Javaj, poluostrov – 42-43 NO 3
Javalambre 34-35 G 8
Javari, Rio – 78-79 E 6
Java Sea 52-53 EF 8
Javasee 52-53 EF 8
Jáva-tenger 52-53 EF 8
Javatrog 22-23 P 6
Javazee 52-53 EF 8
Javhār = Jawhār 44-45 L 7
Javlenka 42-43 M 7
Javor 36-37 HJ 4
Jávské moře 52-53 EF 8
Jawa 52-53 EF 8
Jawa = Java 52-53 EF 8
Jawa Barat = 11 ◁ 52-53 E 8
Jawajskie, Morze – 52-53 EF 8
Jaw'alīyāt, Jabal al- 46-47 G 7
Jawa Tengah = 12 ◁ 52-53 E 8
Jawa Timur = 14 ◁ 52-53 F 8
Jawf, Al- [LAR] 60-61 J 4
Jawf, Al- [Saudi-Arabien] 44-45 DE 5
Jawf, Al- [Y] 44-45 EF 7
Jawhār 44-45 L 7
Jawhar [ETH] 60-61 ab 3
Jawor 33 H 3
Jaxartes = Syrdarja 44-45 K 2
Jaya, Gunung – 52-53 L 7
Jayapura 52-53 M 7
Jayawijaya, Pegunungan – 52-53 LM 7
Jāyid 46-47 J 6
Jaypur = Jaipur 44-45 M 5
Jaypura = Jeypore 44-45 N 7
Jaza'ir, Al- [DZ] 60-61 E 1
Jaza'ir, Al- [IRQ] 46-47 M 7
Jazīr 46-47 F 5
Jazīra, Al- = Arḍ al-Jazīrah 44-45 E 3-F 4
Jazīrah, Al- [IRQ] 46-47 J 5
Jazīrah, Al- [Sudan] 60-61 L 6
Jazīrah, Arḍ al- 44-45 E 3-F 4
Jāz Mūreyān, Hāmūn-e – 44-45 H 5
Jazzīn 46-47 F 6

Jean, NV 76-77 F 8
Jeanette, ostrov – = ostrov Žanetty 42-43 ef 2
Jebaïl = Jubayl 46-47 F 5
Jebba 60-61 E 7
Jebel, Bahr el – = Bahr al-Jabal 60-61 L 7
Jebelein, El- = Al-Jabalayn 60-61 L 6
Jeblé = Jablah 46-47 F 5
Jécori 76-77 J 1
Jeddah = Jiddah 44-45 D 6
Jędrzejów 33 K 3
Jefferson, MT 76-77 GH 2
Jefferson, OH 74-75 C 4
Jefferson, OR 76-77 B 3
Jefferson, Mount – [USA, Nevada] 76-77 E 6
Jefferson, Mount – [USA, Oregon] 76-77 C 3
Jefferson City, MO 72-73 H 4
Jeffersonville, GA 74-75 B 8
Jeffrey, Abysse de – 56-57 F 7
Jeffrey, Fosa – 56-57 F 7
Jeffrey Depth 56-57 F 7
Jeffreydiep 56-57 F 7
Jeffrey-mélység 56-57 F 7
Jeffreytiefe 56-57 F 7
Jefremov 38-39 G 5
Jeges-tenger 19 AB 32-5
Jegorjevsk 42-43 FG 6
Jegyrjach 42-43 M 5
Jehlam = Jihlam 44-45 L 4
Jehlum = Jihlam 44-45 L 4
Jehol = Chengde 48-49 M 3
Jejsk 38-39 G 6
Jēkabpils 30-31 L 9
Jekaterinburg 42-43 L 6
Jekaterinovka [SU, Primorskij Kraj] 50-51 J 1
Jekubābād 44-45 K 5

Kabo 60-61 H 7
Kabobo 63 B 4
Kaboel = Kabul 44-45 K 4
Kabompo 64-65 F 5
Kabongo 64-65 FG 4
Kaboul = Kabul 44-45 K 4
Kabudārāhang 46-47 N 5
Kābul 44-45 K 4
Kābul = Kābul 44-45 K 4
Kabul = Kābul 44-45 K 4
Kabul = Kābul 44-45 K 4
Kabunda 63 B 6
Kaburuan, Pulau – 52-53 J 6
Kābuwītā 60-61 L 8
Kabwe 64-65 G 5
Kachchh = Kutch 44-45 K 6
Kacheliba 63 C 2
Ka-Chem = Malyj Jenisej 42-43 RS 7
Kachgar = Qāshqār 48-49 CD 4
Kachin Pyinnei 52-53 C 1-2
Kachovka 38-39 F 6
Kachovskoje vodochranilišče 38-39 FG 6
K'achta 42-43 U 7
K XVIII-Rücken 22-23 O 7
Kaçkar Dağı 46-47 J 2
Kačug 42-43 U 7
Kačug 42-43 U 7
Ka-Chem = Malyj Jenisej 42-43 RS 7
Kadaingdi 52-53 C 3
Kadaingti = Kadaingdi 52-53 C 3
Kadan Kyûn 52-53 C 4
Kaḍappa = Cuddapah 44-45 M 8
Kade [GH] 60-61 D 7
Kadéï 60-61 H 8
Kadhdhāb, Sinn al- 62 DE 6
Kadıköy, İstanbul- 46-47 C 2
Kadiköy Deresi 46-47 B 2-3
Kadina 58 CD 4-5
Kadınhanı 46-47 E 3
Kadirli 46-47 FG 4
Kadmat Island 44-45 L 8
Ka-do 50-51 E 3
Kadoma 64-65 G 6
Kadugli = Kāduqlī 60-61 KL 6
Kaduna [WAN, ●] 60-61 F 6
Kāduqlī 60-61 KL 6
Kadykčan 42-43 C 5
Kadykčan 42-43 C 5
Kadyks = Cádiz 34-35 D 10
Kaech'i-ri 50-51 G 2
Kaesŏng 48-49 O 4
Kāf 44-45 D 4
Kāf, Al- 60-61 F 1
Kafan 38-39 J 8
Kafanchan 60-61 F 7
Kafêrévs, Akrōtḗrion – 36-37 L 6
Kaffrine 60-61 AB 6
Kafr ash-Shaykh 62 D 2
Kafr az-Zayyāt 62 D 2
Kafta = Ķeftiya 60-61 M 6
Kafu 64-65 H 2
Kafue [Z, ~] 64-65 G 6
Kafue [Z, ●] 64-65 G 6
Kafue Flats 64-65 G 6
Kafue National Park 64-65 G 5-6
Kafulwa 63 B 5
Kaga 50-51 L 4
Kaga Bandoro 60-61 HJ 7
Kagan 44-45 J 3
Kagawa 50-51 JK 5
Kagera 64-65 H 3
Kagera, Parc national de la – 64-65 H 3
Kagera Magharibi 64-65 H 3
Kagi = Chiayi 48-49 MN 7
Kağızman 46-47 K 2
Kagmâr = Kajmâr 60-61 L 6
Kagoro 60-61 F 7
Kagoshima 48-49 OP 5
Kagoshima wan 50-51 H 7
Kagosima = Kagoshima 48-49 OP 5
Kagul 38-39 E 6
Kahama 64-65 H 3
Kahayan, Sungai – 52-53 F 7
Kahemba 64-65 E 4
Kahia 64-65 G 4
Kâhira = Al-Qāhirah 60-61 KL 2
Kahlā [IR] 46-47 N 5
Kahler Asten 33 D 3
Kahlotus, WA 76-77 D 2
Kahoku-gata 50-51 L 4
Kahoolawe 52-53 e 3
Kahramanmaraş 44-45 D 3
Kâhta 46-47 H 4
Ka-Chem = Malyj Jenisej 42-43 RS 7
Kachovskoje vodochranilišče 38-39 FG 6
Kai, Kepulauan – 52-53 K 8
Kaiama 60-61 E 7
Kaibab Indian Reservation 76-77 G 7
Kaibab Plateau 76-77 G 7
Kaidong = Tongyu 48-49 N 3
Kaieteur Falls 78-79 GH 3
Kaifeng 48-49 LM 5
K'ai-fong = Kaifeng 48-49 LM 5
Kaihwa = Wenshan 48-49 JK 7
Kai Kecil 52-53 K 8
Kaikohe 56-57 O 7
Kaikoura 56-57 O 8
Kailas Gangri = Kailash Gangri 48-49 E 5
Kailash Gangri 48-49 E 5
Kailu 48-49 N 3
Kaimana 52-53 K 7
Kaimon-dake 50-51 H 7
Kainan 50-51 K 5
Kainantu 52-53 N 8
Kainji Dam 60-61 EF 6-7
Kainsk = Kujbyšev 42-43 O 6
Kaipara Harbour 56-57 O 7
Kaiparowits Plateau 76-77 H 7
Kair = Al-Qāhirah 60-61 KL 2
Kairiru 52-53 M 7
Kairó = Al-Qāhirah 60-61 KL 2
Kaïrouan = Al-Qayrawān 60-61 FG 1
Kairuku 52-53 N 8
Kaisariyah = Caesarea 46-47 F 6
Kaiser Peak 76-77 D 7
Kaiserslautern 33 CD 4
Kaiser-Wilhelm II.-Land 24 C 9-10
Kaishū = Haeju 48-49 O 4
Kaitaia 56-57 O 7
Kaitangata 56-57 NO 9
Kaitum älv 30-31 HJ 4
Kaizanchin = Hyesanjin 48-49 O 3
Kajaani 30-31 MN 5
Kajabbi 56-57 H 4
Kajakī 44-45 JK 4
Kajang [RI] 52-53 H 8
Kajiado 64-65 J 3
Kajmán-árok 72-73 KL 8
Kajmański, Rów – 72-73 KL 8
Kajmanský příkop 72-73 KL 8
Kajmār 60-61 L 6
Kajnar [SU, Kazachskaja SSR] 42-43 O 8
Kākā 60-61 L 6
Kakamas 64-65 F 8
Kakamega 64-65 HJ 2
Kakarka = Sovetsk 42-43 H 6
Kakata 60-61 B 7
Kakbil = Karaoğlan 46-47 H 3
Kake 50-51 J 5
Kakegawa 50-51 LM 5
Kakelwe 63 B 4
Kakia 64-65 F 7-8
Kakinada 44-45 N 7
Käkisalmi = Prioz'orsk 42-43 DE 5
Kakogawa 50-51 K 5
Kakonko 63 B 3
Kakšaal-Too, chrebet – 44-45 M 2
Kakšaal-Too, chrebet – 44-45 M 2
Kakuda 50-51 N 4
Kakulu 63 AB 4
Kakuma 64-65 HJ 2
Kakunodate 50-51 N 3
Kala 63 B 5
Kala, El – = Al-Qal'ah 60-61 F 1
Kalabahi 52-53 H 8
Kalabo 64-65 F 6
Kalabrien = Calàbria 36-37 FG 6
Kalábryta 36-37 K 6
Kalābsha 60-61 L 4
Kalač 38-39 H 5
Kalač-na-Donu 38-39 H 6
Kalač 38-39 H 5
Kalač-na-Donu 38-39 H 6
Kaladar 74-75 E 2
Ka Lae 52-53 e 4
Kalahari = Kalahari Desert 64-65 EF 7
Kalahari Desert 64-65 EF 7
Kalahari Gemsbok National Park 64-65 F 8
Kalakan 42-43 W 6
Kalama, WA 76-77 B 2-3
Kalamáta 36-37 JK 7
Kalamazoo, MI 72-73 J 3
Kalambo Falls 64-65 H 4
Kalampáka 36-37 JK 6
Kalan = Tunceli 44-45 DE 3
Kalančak 36-37 P 2
Kalančak 36-37 P 2
Kalangali 63 C 4
Kalannie 56-57 C 6
Kalanshiyu, Sarīr – = Sarīr Qalanshū 60-61 J 3
Kalaotao, Pulau – 52-53 H 8
Kalar 42-43 W 6
Kalaraš 36-37 N 2
Kalaraš 36-37 N 2
Kalasin [RI] 52-53 F 6
Kalasin [T] 52-53 D 3
Kalat = Qalāt 44-45 K 5
Kalāt, Jabal – 62 F 6
Kalâtdlit nunât 70-71 b 2-c 5
Kalāt-i Ghilzay = Qalāt 44-45 K 4
Kal'azin 38-39 G 4
Kale [TR, Antalya] 46-47 CD 4
Kale [TR, Denizli] 46-47 C 4
Kale [TR, Gümüşane] 46-47 H 2
Kalecik 46-47 E 2
Kalecik = Kabahaydar 46-47 H 4
Kalehe 64-65 G 3
Kalemie 64-65 G 4
Kalemma 63 CD 3
Kale Sultanie = Çanakkale 44-45 B 2
Kaletwa 52-53 B 2
Kalevala 42-43 E 4
Kalewa 52-53 BC 2
Kaleybar 46-47 M 3
Kálfafell 30-31 de 2-3
Kálfafellsstadhur 30-31 f 2
Kalgan = Zhangjiakou 48-49 L 3
Kalgoorlie 56-57 D 6
Kalhāt 44-45 H 6
Kali = Sangha 64-65 E 2-3
Kaliakra, nos – 36-37 N 4
Kalibo 52-53 H 4
Kalifornia = California 72-73 B 3-C 5
Kaliforniai-öböl 72-73 D 5-E 7
Kalifornie = California 72-73 B 3-C 5
Kalifornien = California 72-73 B 3-C 5
Kalifornien, Golf von – 72-73 D 5-E 7
Kalifornijska, Zatoka – 72-73 D 5-E 7
Kalifornský záliv 72-73 D 5-E 7
Kalikata = Calcutta 44-45 O 6
Kalima 64-65 G 3
Kalimantan 52-53 F 7-G 6
Kalimantan Barat = 7 ◁ 52-53 F 7
Kalimantan Selatan = 9 ◁ 52-53 G 7
Kalimantan Tengah = 8 ◁ 52-53 F 7
Kalimantan Timur = 10 ◁ 52-53 G 6
Kalinin = Tver' 42-43 EF 6
Kaliningrad 33 K 1
Kalinkoviči 38-39 EF 5
Kalinkoviči 38-39 EF 5
Kalinku 63 C 5
Kalisch = Kalisz 33 J 3
Kalisizo 63 BC 3
Kalispell, MT 72-73 CD 2
Kalisz 33 J 3
Kalisz Pomorski 33 GH 2
Kaliua 64-65 H 3-4
Kalix älv 30-31 JK 4
Kalkan 46-47 C 4
Kalkata = Calcutta 44-45 O 6
Kalkfeld 64-65 E 7
Kalkfontein = Karasburg 64-65 E 8
Kalkrand 64-65 E 7
Kalkuta = Calcutta 44-45 O 6
Kalkutta = Calcutta 44-45 O 6
Kallafo = Ķelafo 60-61 N 7
Kallaste 30-31 M 8
Kallipolis = Gelibolu 44-45 B 2
Kallsjön 30-31 E 6
Kalmar 30-31 G 9
Kalmar län 30-31 FG 9
Kalmarsund 30-31 G 9
Kalmouks, République Autonome des – 38-39 HJ 6
Kalmükische Autonome Republik 38-39 HJ 6
Kalmukken Autonome Republiek 38-39 HJ 6
Kalmyk Autonomous Republic 38-39 HJ 6
Kalmykovo 42-43 J 8
Kaloko 64-65 G 4
Kalola 63 B 5
Kalomo 64-65 G 6
Kalonje 63 B 6
Kalpeni Island 44-45 L 8
Kal Sefīd 46-47 M 5
Kaluga 38-39 G 5
Kalulaui = Kahoolawe 52-53 e 3
Kalundborg 30-31 D 10
Kalundu 63 B 3
Kalungwishi 63 B 5
Kaluš 38-39 D 6
Kaluš 38-39 D 6
Kalutara 44-45 MN 9
Kalvarija 30-31 K 10
Kálymnos 36-37 M 7
Kama [RCB] 64-65 G 3
Kama [SU, ~] 42-43 J 6
Kamae 50-51 HJ 6
Kamaeura = Kamae 50-51 HJ 6
Kamaishi 48-49 R 4
Kamaishi wan 50-51 NO 3
Kamaisi = Kamaishi 48-49 R 4
Kamalampakea 63 B 4
Kaman [TR] 46-47 E 3
Kamarān 44-45 E 7
Kamba [ZRE] 64-65 F 3
Kambalnaja Sopka, vulkan – 42-43 e 7
Kambia 60-61 B 7
Kambing, Pulau – = Pulau Atauro 52-53 J 8
Kambodja 52-53 DE 4
Kambodscha 52-53 DE 4
Kambodža 52-53 DE 4
Kambodža 52-53 DE 4
Kambodzsa 52-53 DE 4
Kambove 64-65 G 5
Kambrisches Gebirge = Cambrian Mountains 32 D 5-E 6
Kamčatka, poluostrov – 42-43 e 6-7
Kamčatskij poluostrov 42-43 fg 6
Kamčatskij zaliv 42-43 f 6
Kamčija 36-37 M 4
Kamczatka = poluostrov Kamčatka 42-43 e 6-7
Kamčatka, poluostrov – 42-43 e 6-7
Kamčatskij poluostrov 42-43 fg 6
Kamčatskij zaliv 42-43 f 6
Kamčija 36-37 M 4
Kamchatka, Peninsula de – = Kamčatka 42-43 e 6-7
Kamcsatka-félsziget = poluostrov Kamčatka 42-43 e 6-7
Kamela, OR 76-77 D 3
Kamenec-Podol'skij 38-39 E 6
Kamenjak, Rt – 36-37 E 3
Kamenka [SU, Rossijskaja SFSR Mezenskaja guba] 42-43 G 4
Kamenka [SU → Tambov] 38-39 H 5
Kamen'-na-Obi 42-43 OP 7
Kamennogorsk 30-31 NO 7
Kamennomostskij 38-39 GH 7
Kamenskoje 42-43 fg 5
Kamensk-Šachtinskij 38-39 GH 6
Kamensk-Šachtinskij 38-39 GH 6
Kamensk-Ural'skij 42-43 LM 6
Kamenz 33 FG 3
Kameoka 50-51 K 5
Kameroen 60-61 G 7-8
Kamerun 60-61 G 7-8
Kameshli = Al-Qāmishlīyah 44-45 E 3
Kāmēt 44-45 M 4
Kamiah, ID 76-77 EF 2
Kamień Pomorski 33 G 2
Kamiiso 50-51 b 3
Kamikawa 50-51 c 2
Kami-Koshiki-shima 50-51 G 7
Kāmil, Al- 44-45 H 6
Kamilīn, Al- 60-61 L 5
Kamina 64-65 FG 4
Kaminokuni 50-51 ab 3
Kaminoshima 50-51 G 5
Kaminoyama 50-51 N 3
Kami-Sihoro 50-51 c 2
Kāmit, Jabal – 62 B 6
Kamitsushima 50-51 G 5
Kamituga 63 AB 3
Kamiyaku 50-51 H 7
Kāmlīn, El- = Al-Kamilīn 60-61 L 5
Kamloops 70-71 MN 7
Kammuri yama 50-51 HJ 5
Kamniokan 42-43 V 6
Kamo [J] 50-51 M 4
Kamoenai 50-51 ab 2
Kamortā Drīp = Camorta Island 44-45 P 9
Kamp 33 G 4
Kampala 64-65 H 2
Kampanien = Campània 36-37 F 5
Kampar 52-53 D 6
Kampemba 63 AB 5
Kamp'o 50-51 G 5
Kampo = Campo 60-61 F 8
Kampolombo, Lake – 64-65 G 5
Kampot 52-53 D 4
Kampucheä = Kambodscha 52-53 DE 4
Kampuchea = Kambodzsa 52-53 DE 4
Kampulu 63 B 5
Kampung Pasir Besar 52-53 D 6
Kamskoje vodochranilišče 42-43 K 6
Kamskoje vodochranilišče 42-43 K 6
Kamtchatka, Presqu'île de – = Kamčatka 42-43 e 6-7
Kamtchatka Peninsula = Kamčatka 42-43 e 6-7
Kamtschatka, Halbinsel – = poluostrov Kamčatka 42-43 e 6-7
Kamtsjatka = Kamčatka 42-43 e 6-7
Kamudi [EAK] 63 D 3
Kamui-misaki 50-51 ab 2
Kāmyārān 46-47 M 5
Kamyšin 38-39 HJ 5
Kamyšlov 42-43 L 6
Kamyšin 38-39 HJ 5
Kamyšlov 42-43 L 6
Kan [SU] 42-43 S 6-7
Kanaal, Het – 32 E 7-F 6
Kanaal-Eilanden = Channel Islands 32 E 7
Kanaaupscow, Rivière – 70-71 VW 7
Kanab, UT 76-77 G 7
Kanab Creek 76-77 G 7
Kanada 70-71 M 5-W 7
Kanadai-medence 19 AB 32-33
Kanadisches Becken 19 AB 32-33
Kanadská pánev 19 AB 32-33
Kanadyjski, Basen – 19 AB 22-33
Kanagawa 50-51 M 5
Kanā'is, Rā's al- 62 BC 2
Kanal, Der – 32 E 7-F 6
Kanala = Canala 56-57 N 4
Kanalinseln = Channel Islands 32 E 7
Kan'ān 46-47 L 6
Kananga 64-65 F 4
Kanarenschwelle 22-23 HJ 4
Kanarische Inseln = Islas Canarias 60-61 A 3
Kanarisches Becken 22-23 HJ 4
Kanári-szigetek = Islas Canarias 60-61 A 3
Kanarraville, UT 76-77 G 7
Kanárské ostrovy = Islas Canarias 60-61 A 3
Kanaryjskie, Wyspy – = Islas Canarias 60-61 A 3
Kanaš 42-43 H 6
Kanaš 42-43 H 6
Kanawha River 74-75 BC 5
Kanazawa 48-49 Q 4
Kanchanaburi 52-53 C 4
Kancheepuram = Kanchepuram 44-45 MN 8
Kanchenjunga = Gangchhendsönga 44-45 O 5
Kanchibia 63 B 5
Kānchipuram = Kanchepuram 44-45 MN 8
Kanchow = Zhangye 48-49 J 4
Kandahār = Qandahār 44-45 K 4
Kandalakša 42-43 EF 4
Kandalakšskij zaliv 42-43 EF 4
Kandalakša 42-43 EF 4
Kandalakšskij zaliv 42-43 EF 4
Kandangan 52-53 FG 7
Kandavu 52-53 a 2
Kandi [DY] 60-61 E 6
Kandıra 46-47 D 2
Kandla 44-45 L 6
Kandos 56-57 JK 6
Kandreho 64-65 L 6
Kandūleh 46-47 M 5
Kandulu 63 D 5
Kandy = Maha Nuwara 44-45 N 9
Kane, PA 74-75 D 4
Kane Basin 70-71 WX 2
Kanem 60-61 H 6
Kanevskaja 38-39 G 6
Kaneyama 50-51 M 4
Kang 64-65 F 7
Kangal 46-47 G 3
Kangar 52-53 D 5
Kangaroo Island 56-57 G 7
Kangāvar 46-47 M 5
Kangding 48-49 J 5-6
Kangean, Pulau – 52-53 G 8
Kangerdlugssuaq [Grønland, ∪] 70-71 ef 4
Kangerdlugssuaq [Grønland, ●] 70-71 ab 4
Kangetet 64-65 J 2
Kanggye 48-49 O 3
Kanggyŏng 50-51 F 4
Kanghwa 50-51 F 4
Kanghwa-do 50-51 EF 4
Kanghwa-man 50-51 E 4
Kangjin 50-51 F 5
Kangnŭng 48-49 OP 4
Kango 64-65 D 2
Kangsŏ 50-51 E 3
Kangwŏn-do [Nordkorea] 50-51 F 3
Kangwŏn-do [ROK] 50-51 G 4
Kan Ho = Gan He 48-49 N 1
Kaniama 64-65 FG 4
Kaniapiskau Lake 70-71 W 7
Kaniet Islands 52-53 N 7
Kānī Masī 46-47 K 4
Kanin, poluostrov – 42-43 GH 4
Kanin Nos [SU, ●] 38-39 H 2
Kanin Nos, mys – 42-43 G 4
Kanireş = Karlıova 46-47 J 3
Kanita 50-51 N 2
Kankakee, IL 72-73 J 3
Kankan 60-61 C 6
Kankō = Hamhŭng 48-49 O 3-4
Kankō = Hŭngnam 48-49 O 4
Kankossa = Kankūssah 60-61 B 5
Kan-kou-chên = Gango 50-51 B 2
Kankūssah 60-61 B 5
Kankyō-hokudō = Hamgyŏng-pukto 50-51 G 2-H 1
Kankyō-nandō = Hamgyŏng-namdo 50-51 FG 2-3
Kannanūr = Cannanore 44-45 LM 8
Kannapolis, NC 74-75 C 7
Kannus 30-31 K 6
Kano [WAN, ●] 60-61 F 6
Kanoji 50-51 J 5
Kanona 63 B 6
Kanosh, UT 76-77 G 6
Kanouri 60-61 G 6
Kanoya 50-51 H 7
Kanpur 44-45 MN 5
Kansas 72-73 FG 4
Kansas City, KS 72-73 GH 4
Kansas City, MO 72-73 H 4
Kansas River 72-73 G 4
Kansk 42-43 S 6
Kansŏng 50-51 G 3
Kansu = Gansu 48-49 G 3-J 4
Kantabrisches Gebirge = Cordillera Cantábrica 34-35 D-F 7
Kantalahti = Kandalakša 42-43 EF 4
Kantara = Al-Qanṭarah 62 E 2
Kantchari 60-61 E 6
Kantō 50-51 MN 4
Kantō sammyaku 50-51 M 4-5
Kanuma 50-51 M 4
Kanuri = Kanouri 60-61 G 6
Kanyākumārī Antarīp = Cape Comorin 44-45 M 9
Kanyama 63 B 2
Kanye 64-65 FG 7-8
Kanzanlı 46-47 F 4
Kao-an = Gao'an 48-49 LM 6
Kao-hsiung 48-49 MN 7
Kaokoveld 64-65 D 6-7
Kaolack 60-61 A 6
Kao-li-kung Shan = Gaoligong Shan 48-49 H 6
Kaosiung = Kao-hsiung 48-49 MN 7
Kaotai = Gaotai 48-49 H 4
Kaouar 60-61 G 5
Kap'a-do 50-51 F 6
Kapagere 52-53 N 8-9
Kapanga 64-65 F 4
Kapatu 63 B 5
Kapbecken 22-23 K 7
Kapčagajskoje vodochranilišče 42-43 O 9
Kapčagajskoje vodochranilišče 42-43 O 9
Kap der Guten Hoffnung 64-65 E 9
Kapela 36-37 F 3
Kapenguria 63 C 2
Kapfenberg 33 G 5
Kapıdağı Yarımadası 46-47 BC 2
Kapinnie 58 B 5
Kapiri Mposhi 64-65 G 5
Kapit 52-53 F 6
Kāpōētā = Kābuwītā 60-61 L 8
Kapona 64-65 G 4
Kapongolo 63 AB 4
Kapos 33 J 5
Kaposvár 33 HJ 5
K'appesel'ga 38-39 F 3
Kapsan 50-51 FG 2
Kapschwelle 22-23 K 8
Kapské Město = Kaapstad 64-65 E 9
Kapsowar 63 CD 2
Kapstadt = Kaapstad 64-65 E 9
Kapsukas 30-31 K 10
Kapsztad = Kaapstad 64-65 E 9
Kapuas, Sungai – [RI, Kalimantan Barat] 52-53 F 6
Kapunda 58 D 5
Kapuskasing 70-71 U 8
Kapustin Jar 38-39 J 6
Kaputar, Mount – 58 JK 3
Kaputir 63 C 2
Kapverde 20-21 H 5
Kapverdenschwelle 22-23 H 4-5
Kapverdische Inseln = Islas Cabo Verde 22-23 H 4-5
Kapverdisches Becken 22-23 GH 4-5
Kara = Ust'-Kara 42-43 LM 4
Kara, Mar de – 42-43 K 3-R 2
Kara, Mer de – 42-43 K 3-R 2
Karaali 46-47 E 3
Karababa Dağı 46-47 FG 3
Karabah-hegyvidéki Autonóm Terület 38-39 J 7-8
Kara-Bau 38-39 K 6
Karabekaul 44-45 JK 3
Karabiga 46-47 B 2
Kara-Bogaz-Gol 38-39 K 7
Kara-Bogaz-Gol, zaliv – 44-45 G 2
Karabük 44-45 C 2
Karaburun [TR] 46-47 B 3
Karabutak 42-43 L 8
Karaca = Şiran 46-47 H 2
Karacabey 46-47 C 2
Karaca Dağ [TR, Ankara] 46-47 E 3
Karacadağ [TR, Konya] 46-47 E 4
Karaçadağ [TR, Sanlı Urfa ▲▲] 46-47 H 4
Karacadağ [TR, Sanlı Urfa ●] 46-47 H 4
Karacaköy 46-47 C 2
Karacasu 46-47 C 4
Karachayevo-Cherkess Autonomous Region = 2 ◁ 38-39 H 7
Karāchī 44-45 K 6
Karaçurun = Hilvan 46-47 H 4
Karaczajsko-Czerkieski, Ob.A. - 38-39 H 7
Karaczi = Karāchī 44-45 K 6
Karačajevsko-čerkeská AR 38-39 H 7
Karáči = Karāchī 44-45 K 6
Karachai y Cherkeses, Oblast Autónoma de los – = 2 ◁ 38-39 H 7
Karachayevo-Cherkess Autonomous Region = 2 ◁ 38-39 H 7
Karachi 44-45 K 6
Karacsáj-Cserkesk Autonóm Terület 38-39 H 7
Karácsony-sziget = Christmas Island 52-53 E 9
Karadağ 46-47 E 4

Karadeniz Boğazı = Boğazici 44-45 BC 2
Karadoğan = Kıbrısak 46-47 DE 2
Karafuto = Sachalin 42-43 b 7-8
Karagajly 42-43 NO 8
Karaganda 42-43 NO 8
Karagije, vpadina – 38-39 K 7
Karaginskij, ostrov – 42-43 fg 6
Karaginskij zaliv 42-43 fg 6
Karagoua 60-61 G 6
Karahallı 44-45 C 3
Karahasanlı 46-47 F 3
Karachai y Cherkeses, Oblast Autónoma de los – = 2 ◁ 38-39 H 7
Karachayevo-Cherkess Autonomous Region = 2 ◁ 38-39 H 7
Karaibskie, Morze – 72-73 K-N 8
Kāraikkāl = Karajkal 44-45 MN 8
Karaisalı = Çeceli 46-47 F 4
Karaj 44-45 G 3
Karajkal 44-45 MN 8
Karak, Al- 44-45 D 4
Karakallı = Özalp 46-47 KL 3
Karakeçi 46-47 H 4
Karakeçili 46-47 E 3
Karakelong, Pulau – 52-53 J 6
Karakoçan 46-47 HJ 3
Karakoram 44-45 L 3-M 4
Karakoram Pass = Qaramurun davan 44-45 MN 3
Kara Korē 60-61 MN 6
Karakorum = Char Chorin 48-49 J 2
Karaköse = Ağrı 44-45 E 3
Karakumskij kanal 44-45 J 3
Karakumy 44-45 HJ 3
Karam = Karin 60-61 O 6
Karaman 44-45 C 3
Karaman = Çameli 46-47 C 4
Karamian, Pulau – 52-53 F 8
Karamürsel 46-47 C 2
Karamyševo 30-31 N 9
Karamyševo 30-31 N 9
Karand 46-47 M 5
Karaoğlan 46-47 H 3
Karapınar 46-47 E 4
Karas, Pulau – 52-53 K 7
Karasburg 64-65 E 8
Kara Sea 42-43 K 3-R 2
Karasee 42-43 K 3-R 2
Kara Shar = Qara Shahr 48-49 F 3
Karasjok 30-31 L 3
Karasjokka 30-31 L 3
Karasu [TR, ~] 46-47 J 3
Karasu [TR, ●] 46-47 D 2
Karasu = Hizan 46-47 K 3
Karasu = Salavat 46-47 F 2
Karasu-Aras Dağları 44-45 E 2-3
Karasuk 42-43 O 7
Karataş 46-47 F 4
Karataş Burnu 46-47 F 4
Karatau 42-43 N 9
Karatau, chrebet – 42-43 MN 9
Kara-tenger 42-43 L 3-Q 2
Kara-tenger 38-39 K-N 1
Karatobe 42-43 J 8
Karatschaier und Tscherkessen, Autonome Oblast der – = 2 ◁ 38-39 H 7
Karatschi = Karāchī 44-45 K 6
Karatsjai-Tsjerkessen Autonome Oblast = 2 ◁ 38-39 H 7
Karatsu 50-51 G 6
Karaul 42-43 P 3
Karaussa Nor = Char us nuur 48-49 G 2
Karawang 52-53 E 8
Karawayn, Bi'r – 62 C 4
Karayazı 46-47 JK 3
Karayün 46-47 G 3
Karažal 42-43 N 8
Karažal 42-43 N 8
Karbalā' 44-45 E 4
Karcag 33 K 5
Kardeljevo 36-37 G 4
Karditsa 36-37 JK 6
Kärdla 30-31 K 8
Kărdžali 36-37 L 5
Kărdžali 36-37 L 5
Kareeberge 64-65 F 9
Kareima = Kuraymah 60-61 L 5
Karél Autonóm Köztársaság 42-43 E 4-5
Karelia 30-31 N 7-O 6
Karėlia 30-31 N 7-O 6
Karelia 28-29 P 2-3
Karelian Autonomous Republic 42-43 E 4-5
Karélie 42-43 E 4-5
Karélie 30-31 N 7-O 6
Karelië 28-29 P 2-3
Karelien 28-29 P 2-3
Karelische Autonome Republiek 42-43 E 4-5
Karelische Autonome Republik 42-43 E 4-5
Karelska Autonomiczna Republika 42-43 E 4-5
Karel'skaja Avtonomnaja Sovetskaja Socialističeskaja Respublika = Karelische Autonome Republik 42-43 E 4-5
Karelstad = Charlesville 64-65 F 4
Karema 64-65 H 4
Karen = Karin Pyinnei 52-53 C 3
Karesuando 30-31 JK 3
Karet = Qārrāt 60-61 C 4
Kārēz 44-45 K 4
Kargamıs 46-47 G 4
Kargapazarı Dağları 46-47 J 2
Kargat 42-43 P 6
Kargi [EAK] 63 D 2
Kargı [TR] 46-47 F 2
Kargopol' 42-43 F 5
Karhula 30-31 M 7
Kariba, Lake – 64-65 G 6
Kariba Dam 64-65 G 6
Kariba Gorge 64-65 GH 6
Kariba-yama 50-51 ab 2
Karibib 64-65 E 7
Karibisches Becken 72-73 MN 8
Karibisches Meer 72-73 K-N 8
Karib-medence 72-73 MN 8
Karibské moře 72-73 K-N 8
Karib-tenger 72-73 K-N 8
Karigasniemi 30-31 LM 3
Karima = Kuraymah 60-61 L 5
Karimata, Kepulauan – 52-53 E 7
Karimata, Selat – 52-53 E 7
Karimunjawa, Kepulauan – 52-53 EF 8
Karin 60-61 O 6
Karin Pyinnei 52-53 C 3
Karis 30-31 KL 7-8
Karische Zee 42-43 K 3-R 2
Karisimbi, Mont – 64-65 G 3
Kariya 50-51 L 5
Karjaa = Karis 30-31 KL 8
Karjepolje 38-39 H 2
Karkaar 60-61 b 2
Karkar Island 52-53 N 7
Karkheh, Rūd-e – 46-47 N 6-7
Karkinitskij zaliv 38-39 F 6
Karkkila 30-31 KL 7
Karkonosze 33 GH 3
Karkonosze 33 GH 3
Karkūk = Kirkūk 44-45 EF 3
Karla-Aleksandra, ostrov – 42-43 H-K 1
Karl Alexander, ostrov – = ostrov Karla Aleksandra 42-43 H-K 1
Karliova 46-47 J 3
Karl-Marx-Stadt = Chemnitz 33 F 3
Karlobag 36-37 F 3
Karlovac 36-37 F 3
Karlovy Vary 33 F 3
Karlsbad = Karlovy Vary 33 F 3
Karlsborg 30-31 F 8
Karlshamn 30-31 F 9
Karlskoga 30-31 F 8
Karlskrona 30-31 FG 9
Karlsruhe 33 D 4
Karlstad 30-31 EF 8
Karlstadt = Karlovac 36-37 F 3
Karmah 60-61 L 5
Karmøy 30-31 A 8
Karnak, Al- 62 E 5
Karnal 44-45 M 5
Karnataka 44-45 M 7-8
Karni-Alpok 33 F 5
Karni-Alpok 36-37 E 2
Karnijskie, Alpi - 33 F 5
Karnijskie, Alpi - 36-37 E 2
Karnische Alpen 36-37 E 2
Karnobat 36-37 M 4
Karnské Alpy 33 F 5
Karnské Alpy 36-37 E 2
Kärnten 33 FG 5
Karnūlu = Kurnool 44-45 M 7
Karoi 64-65 G 6
Karokobe = Karukubī 63 B 2
Karolina Północna = North Carolina 72-73 KL 4
Karolina Południowa = South Carolina 72-73 K 5
Karolina-szigetek = Caroline Islands 52-53 L-O 5
Karolinen = Caroline Islands 22-23 R 5
Karoliny = Caroline Islands 52-53 L-O 5
Karoliny = Caroline Islands 52-53 L-O 5
Karonga 64-65 H 4
Karoonda 58 DE 5
Kārōra = Kārūrah 60-61 M 5
Karosa 52-53 G 7
Karpaşa 46-47 EF 5
Karpaten 36-37 L 2-3
Kárpathos [GR, ⊙] 36-37 M 8
Kárpathos [GR, ●] 36-37 M 8
Karpaty 36-37 L 2-M 3
Karpaty 36-37 L 2-M 3
Karpeddo 63 D 2
Karpenḗsion 36-37 JK 6
Karpentaria, Zatoka – = Gulf of Carpentaria 56-57 GH 2
Karpinsk 38-39 LM 4
Karpinsk = Krasnoturjinsk 42-43 L 5-6
Karrats Fjord 70-71 Za 3
Kars 44-45 E 2
Karsakpaj 42-43 M 8
Kārsava 30-31 MN 9
Karši 44-45 K 3
Karşiyaka, İzmir- 46-47 B 3
Karské moře 42-43 L 3-Q 2
Karské moře 38-39 K-N 1
Karskie, Morze – 42-43 L 3-Q 2
Karskie, Morze - 38-39 K-N 1
Karskije Vorota, proliv – 42-43 J-L 3
Karši 44-45 K 3
Kartal, İstanbul- 46-47 C 2
Kartaly 42-43 KL 7
Karthage 60-61 G 1
Karthago = Qarṭāj 60-61 C 1
Karukubī 63 B 2
Karumba 56-57 H 3
Karumwa 63 C 3
Kārūn, Rūd-e – 44-45 FG 4
Karungi 30-31 K 4-5
Karungu 63 C 3
Kārūrah 60-61 M 5
Karviná 33 J 4
Karwar 44-45 L 8
Karyai 36-37 KL 5
Karymkary 42-43 M 5
Kaş 44-45 BC 3
Kasa = Ui-do 50-51 E 5
Kasaba 63 B 5
Kasaba = Kiği 46-47 J 3
Kasaba = Turgutlu 46-47 BC 3
Kasache 63 C 6
Kasachstan 42-43 J-P 8
Kasai [ZRE] 64-65 E 3
Kasai-Occidental 64-65 EF 3-4
Kasai-Oriental 64-65 FG 3-4
Kasaji 64-65 F 5
Kasama 64-65 H 5
Kasan = Kazan' 42-43 HJ 6
Kasanda 63 BC 2
Kasane 64-65 FG 6
Kasanga 64-65 H 4
Kasaoka 50-51 J 5
Kasba Lake 70-71 Q 5
Kaschau = Košice 33 K 4
Kaseda 50-51 H 7
Kasempa 64-65 FG 5
Kasenga 64-65 G 5
Kasenyi 64-65 GH 2
Kasese 64-65 GH 2-3
Kasha 63 E 3
Kāshān 44-45 G 4
Kashghariya 48-49 DE 4
Kashi 48-49 D 4
Kashi = Qāshqār 48-49 CD 4
Kashima 50-51 GH 6
Kashing = Jiaxing 48-49 N 5
Kashishi 63 B 6
Kashiwazaki 50-51 LM 4
Kashkān, Rūdkhāneh-ye – 46-47 N 6
Kāshmar 44-45 H 3-4
Kashmir 44-45 LM 4
Kashmor 44-45 O 5
Kashqar = Qāshqār 48-49 CD 4
Kash Rūd = Khāsh Rōd 44-45 J 4
Kasigao 63 D 3
Kasimov 42-43 G 7
Kašin 38-39 G 4
Kašira 38-39 G 5
Kasirota = Pulau Kasiruta 52-53 J 7
Kasiruta, Pulau – 52-53 J 7
Kasivobara = Severo-Kuril'sk 42-43 de 7
Kaskinen = Kaskö 30-31 J 6
Kaskö 30-31 J 6
Kasongan 52-53 F 7
Kasongo 64-65 G 3
Kasongo-Lunda 64-65 E 4
Kásos 36-37 M 8
Kaspické moře 44-45 F 1-G 3
Kaspické moře 38-39 J 6-K 8
Kaspijskie, Morze – 44-45 F 1-G 3
Kaspisches Meer 44-45 F 2-G 3
Kaspische Zee 44-45 F 2-G 3
Kasrık = Kirkgeçit 46-47 K 3
Kassai = Kasai 64-65 E 3
Kassa = Ko 33 K 4
Kassa = Košice 33 K 4
Kassa = Košice 33 K 4
Kassalā 60-61 M 5
Kassándra 36-37 K 5-6
Kassel 33 D 3
Kasserine = Al-Qasrayn 60-61 F 1-2
Kastamonu 44-45 CD 2
Kastamum = Kastamonu 44-45 CD 2
Kastéllion 36-37 K 8
Kastellórizon = Mégistē 46-47 C 4
Kastoria 36-37 J 5
Kastornoje 38-39 G 5
Kasulu 64-65 H 3
Kasumiga ura 50-51 N 5
Kasungu 64-65 H 5
Kasungu National Park 63 C 6
Kasur = Qaṣūr 44-45 L 4
Kašin 38-39 G 4
Kašira 38-39 G 5
Kaszpi-tenger 44-45 F 1-G 3
Kaszpi-tenger 38-39 J 7-K 8
Kataba 64-65 FG 6
Katahdin, Mount – 72-73 MN 2
Kaṭaka = Cuttack 44-45 NO 6
Katako-Kombe 64-65 F 3
Katakumba 64-65 F 4
Katalonien = Catalunya 34-35 H 8-J 7
Katami sammyaku 50-51 c 1-2
Katana 63 B 3
Katanga 42-43 T 5-6
Katanga = Shaba 64-65 FG 4
Katangli 42-43 b 7
Katanning 56-57 C 6
Katar 44-45 G 5
Katav-Ivanovsk 42-43 K 7
Katāwāz = Zarghūn Shahr 44-45 K 4
Katchall Island 44-45 P 9
Katenga 64-65 G 4
Katera 63 BC 3
Katerîna, Gebel – = Jabal Katrīnah 60-61 L 3
Katerinē 36-37 K 5
Kates Needle 70-71 KL 6
Katete 64-65 H 5
Kathā 52-53 C 2
Katherine 56-57 F 2
Kāthiāwār 44-45 K 6
Kathlambagebirge = Drakensberge 64-65 G 9-H 8
Kathmandu = Kātmāndu 44-45 NO 5
Kathua 63 D 3
Kati 60-61 C 6
Katif, El- = Al-Qaṭīf 44-45 F 5
Katihar 44-45 O 5
Katiola 60-61 CD 7
Katmai, Mount – 70-71 F 6
Katmai National Monument 70-71 EF 6
Kātmāndu 44-45 NO 5
Katmandu = Kātmāndu 44-45 NO 5
Káto Achaïa 36-37 J 6
Káto Achaïa 36-37 J 6
Káto Achaïa 36-37 J 6
Katomba 56-57 JK 6
Katonga 63 B 2-3
Katoomba 58 JK 4
Katoomba = Blue Mountains 56-57 JK 6
Katowice 33 J 3
Katrancık Dağı 46-47 D 4
Katrīnah, Jabal – 60-61 L 3
Katrineholm 30-31 G 8
Katsina 60-61 F 6
Katsina Ala 60-61 F 7
Katsuda 50-51 N 4
Katsumoto 50-51 G 6
Katsuura 50-51 N 5
Katsuyama 50-51 L 4
Katta = Katsuta 50-51 N 4
Kattakurgan 44-45 K 2-3
Kattegat 30-31 D 9
Katwe 63 B 3
Kau, Teluk – 52-53 J 6
Kauai 52-53 e 3
Kauai Channel 52-53 e 3
Kauai Channel 52-53 e 3
Kauai Channel 52-53 e 3
Kaufbeuren 33 E 5
Kauhajoki 30-31 JK 6
Kaukasus 38-39 HJ 7
Kaukauveld 64-65 F 6
Kaukaz 38-39 HJ 7
Kaukázus 38-39 HJ 7
Kauliranta 30-31 KL 4
Kaulun = Kowloon 48-49 LM 7
Kaunas 30-31 K 10
Kaura Namoda 60-61 F 6
Kautokeino 30-31 KL 3
Kavajë 36-37 H 5
Kavak [TR, Samsun] 46-47 FG 2
Kavak [TR, Sivas] 46-47 G 3
Kaval'kan 42-43 a 6
Kavaratti 44-45 L 8
Kavaratti Island 44-45 L 8
Kavardhā = Kawardha 44-45 N 6
Kavarna 36-37 N 4
Kavieng 52-53 h 5
Kavīr, Dasht-e – 44-45 GH 4
Kavīr-e Lūt 42-43 J 5
Kavirondo Gulf 63 C 3
Kavkaz 38-39 HJ 7
Kavu 63 B 4
Kaw 78-79 J 4
Kawagoe 50-51 M 5
Kawaguchi 50-51 MN 4-5
Kawaharada = Sawata 50-51 M 3-4
Kawamata 50-51 N 4
Kawambwa 64-65 GH 4
Kawanoe 50-51 J 5-6
Kawardha 44-45 N 6
Kawasaki 48-49 QR 4
Kawashiri-misaki 50-51 H 5
Kawewe 63 AB 5
Kawich Range 76-77 E 6-7
Kawimbe 64-65 H 4
Kawlin 52-53 C 2
Kawm Umbū 60-61 L 4
Kawn Ken = Khon Kaen 52-53 D 3
Kawthaung 52-53 C 4
Kaya [HV] 60-61 D 6
Kaya [J] 50-51 K 5
Kaya [RI] 52-53 G 6
Kayadibi = Salmanlı 46-47 F 3
Kayak Island 70-71 H 6
Kayambi 64-65 H 4
Kayā Pyinnei 52-53 C 3
Kaya-san 50-51 G 5
Kayenta, AZ 76-77 H 7
Kayes 60-61 B 6
Kayhaydi 60-61 B 5
Kaymas 46-47 D 2
Kaynar 46-47 G 3
Kaynaslı 46-47 D 2
Kayoa, Pulau – 52-53 J 6
Kaypak 46-47 G 4
Kayseri 44-45 D 3
Kaysville, UT 76-77 GH 5
Kayuagung 52-53 DE 7
Kazachskaja guba 38-39 K 7
Kazachskij melkosopočnik 42-43 M-P 7-8
Kazachstan 42-43 J-P 8
Kazachstan = Aksaj 42-43 J 7
Kazačinskoje [SU, Jenisej] 42-43 R 6
Kazačinskoje [SU, Kirenga] 42-43 U 6
Kazačje 42-43 a 3
Kazačinskoje [SU, Jenisej] 42-43 R 6
Kazačinskoje [SU, Kirenga] 42-43 U 6
Kazačje 42-43 a 3
Kazah-hátság = Kazachskij Melkosopočnik 42-43 M-P 7-8
Kazahsztán 42-43 J-P 8
Kazachskaja Sovetskaja Socialističeskaja Respublika = Kasachstan 42-43 J-P 8
Kazachskij melkosopočnik 42-43 M-P 7-8
Kazachstán 42-43 J-P 8
Kazachstán 38-39 J-L 6
Kazajstán 42-43 J-P 8
Kazakhie, Steppe de – = Kazachskij Melkosopočnik 42-43 M-P 79
Kazakhstan 42-43 J-P 8
Kazamoto = Katsumoto 50-51 G 6
Kazan' [SU, Tatarskaja ASSR] 42-43 HJ 6
Kazan [TR] 46-47 E 2
Kazandağ 46-47 K 3
Kazandžik 44-45 GH 3
Kazandžik 44-45 GH 3
Kazanlak 36-37 L 4
Kazan River 70-71 Q 5
Kazanskoje [SU, Zapadno-Sibirskaja nizmennost'] 42-43 M 6
Kazaskie, Pogórze – = Kazachskij Melkosopočnik 42-43 M-P 7-9
Kazašská plošina = Kazachskij Melkosopočnik 42-43 M-P 7-9
Kazatin 38-39 E 6
Kazbek, gora – 38-39 H 7
Kāzerūn 44-45 G 5
Kazi-Magomed 38-39 J 7
Kāẓimīyah, Baghdād-Al- 46-47 L 6
Kazimoto 63 D 5
Kazincbarcika 33 K 4
Kazumba 64-65 F 4
Kazungula 64-65 G 6
Kazvin = Qazvīn 44-45 FG 3
Kazym 38-39 N 3
Kazym [SU, Chanty-Mansijskaja AO] 42-43 M 5
Kbaisa = Kubaysah 46-47 K 6
Kea 36-37 L 7
Keams Canyon, AZ 76-77 H 8
Kearney, NE 72-73 G 3
Keban 46-47 H 3
Keban Barajı 46-47 H 3
Kebāng 44-45 PQ 5
Kebbi = Sokoto 60-61 EF 6
Kébémer 60-61 A 5
Kebkābiya = Kabkābīyah 60-61 J 6
Kebnekajse 30-31 H 4
Kebumen 52-53 E 8
Keçiborlu 46-47 D 4
Kecskemét 33 J 5
Kėdainiai 30-31 L 10
Keddie, CA 76-77 C 5-6
Kedia d'Idjil = Kidyat Ijjill 60-61 B 4
Kediri 52-53 F 8
Kédougou 60-61 B 6
Keele Peak 70-71 KL 5
Keeler, CA 76-77 E 7
Keele River 70-71 L 5
Keeling, Bassin de – 22-23 OP 6
Keeling, Cuenca de – 22-23 OP 6
Keeling Basin 22-23 OP 6
Keelingbecken 22-23 OP 6
Keelingbekken 22-23 OP 6
Kee-lung 48-49 N 6
Keelung = Kee-lung 48-49 N 6
Keene, NH 74-75 G 3
Keeseville, NY 74-75 G 2
Keetmanshoop 64-65 E 8
Keewatin, District of – 70-71 RS 4-5
Kefa 60-61 M 7
Kefallēnia 36-37 J 6
Kéfalos 36-37 M 7
Kefamenanu 52-53 HJ 8
Kefar Ata = Qiryat-Ata' 46-47 F 6
Keferdiz 46-47 G 4
Kefil, Al- = Al-Kifl 46-47 L 6
Kēfisiá 36-37 KL 6
Keflavík 30-31 b 2-3
Keftiya 60-61 M 6
Kegueur Terbi 60-61 H 4
Kehl 33 CD 4
Kei 63 B 2
Keiki-dō = Kyŏnggi-do 50-51 F 4
Keila 30-31 L 8
Keishō-hokudō = Kyŏngsang-pukto 50-51 G 4
Keishō-nandō = Kyŏngsang-namdo 50-51 FG 5
Keitele 30-31 LM 6
Keith 32 E 3
Keith [AUS] 56-57 GH 7
Keith Arm 70-71 M 4
Keitū = Keytū 46-47 N 5
Kejvy 38-39 G 2
Kék-Nílus = Abay 60-61 M 6
Kelafo 60-61 N 7
Keles 46-47 C 3
Keleti-Erg = Al-'Irq al-Kabīr ash-Sharqī 60-61 F 2-3
Kelet-szibériai-hát 19 B 36-1
Kelet-szibériai-tenger 42-43 d-h 3
Kelford, NC 74-75 E 6
Kelifely, Causse du – 64-65 KL 6
Kelil'vun, gora – 42-43 g 4
Kelkit 46-47 H 2
Kelkit Çayı 46-47 G 2
Kellé 64-65 D 2-3
Keller Lake 70-71 M 5
Kellett, Cape – 70-71 L 3
Kelleys Islands 74-75 B 4
Kellogg, ID 76-77 EF 2
Kelloselkä 30-31 N 4
Kelmė 30-31 K 10
Kélo 60-61 H 7
Kelowna 70-71 N 7-8
Kelso [ZA] 64-65 H 9
Kelso, CA 76-77 F 8
Kelso, WA 76-77 B 2
Kelta-tenger 32 C 6
Keltische See 32 C 6
Keltische Zee 32 C 6
Kelton Pass 76-77 G 5
Kelulun He = Herlen He 48-49 M 2
Kelvin, AZ 76-77 H 9
Kem' [SU, ●] 42-43 E 4
Kemā 48-49 H 6
Kė Macina 60-61 C 6
Kemah 46-47 H 3
Kemaliye 46-47 H 3
Kemaliye = Vakfıbekir 46-47 H 2
Kemalpaşa [TR, Artvin] 46-47 J 2
Kemalpaşa [TR, İzmir] 46-47 B 3
Kemanai = Towada 50-51 N 2
Kembalpur 44-45 L 4
Kembolcha 60-61 MN 6
Kemer [TR, Antalya] 46-47 D 4
Kemer [TR, Burdur] 46-47 D 4
Kemer [TR, Muğla] 46-47 C 4
Kemer = Eskiköy 46-47 D 4
Kemerovo 42-43 PQ 6
Kemi 30-31 L 5
Kemijärvi [SF, ●] 30-31 M 4
Kemijärvi [SF, ≈] 30-31 MN 4
Kemijoki 30-31 L 4-5
Kemijoki = Kem' 42-43 E 4
Kemmerer, WY 76-77 H 5
Kėmo-Ibingui 60-61 H 7
Kemp Land 24 C 6
Kemp Peninsula 24 B 31
Kempsey 56-57 K 6
Kempten 33 E 5
Kemptville 74-75 EF 2
Keňa 64-65 JK 2
Kena = Qinā 60-61 L 3
Kenai, AK 70-71 F 5
Kenai Mountains 70-71 F 6-G 5
Kenai Peninsula 70-71 FG 5
Kenamo 70-71 L 7
Kenansville, FL 74-75 c 3
Kenbridge, VA 74-75 DE 6
Kendal 32 E 4
Kendari 52-53 H 7
Kendawangan 52-53 F 7
Kēndrāpādā = Kendrapara 44-45 O 6
Kendrāpāra 44-45 O 6
Kendrick, ID 76-77 E 2
Kendu 63 C 3
Kenema 60-61 B 7
Kenge 64-65 D 3
Kengtung = Kyöngdön 52-53 CD 2
Kenhardt 64-65 F 8
Kenia 64-65 JK 2
Kéniéba 60-61 B 6
Kenitra = Al-Q'nitrah 60-61 C 2

Kenit 189

Kenmare [IRL, ~] 32 A 6
Kenmare [IRL, ●] 32 B 6
Kenmore, NY 74-75 D 3
Kennebec River 74-75 HJ 2
Kennebunk, ME 74-75 H 3
Kennedy, Mount – 70-71 J 5
Kennedy Channel 70-71 WX 1-2
Kennedy Channel 70-71 WX 1-2
Kennedy Channel 70-71 WX 1-2
Kennewick, WA 76-77 D 2
Kenney Dam 70-71 M 7
Keno Hill 70-71 JK 5
Kenora 70-71 S 8
Kenosha, WI 72-73 J 3
Kenova, WV 74-75 B 5
Kent 32 G 6
Kent, OH 74-75 C 4
Kent, OR 76-77 C 3
Kent, WA 76-77 B 2
Kentau 42-43 M 9
Kent Group 58 cd 1
Kent Peninsula 70-71 P 4
Kentucky 72-73 JK 4
Kentucky Lake 72-73 J 4
Kenya 64-65 JK 2
Kenya, Mount – 64-65 J 2-3
Keokuk, IA 72-73 H 3
Kepce Dağları 46-47 K 4
Kępno 33 J 3
Keppel Bay 56-57 K 4
Kepsut 46-47 C 3
Kerala 44-45 M 8-9
Kerang 56-57 H 7
Kerasûs = Giresun 44-45 D 2
Kerava 30-31 L 7
Kerbi = Poliny-Osipenko 42-43 a 7
Kerby, OR 76-77 B 4
Kerč 38-39 G 6
Kerčel 38-39 M 4
Kerčenskij proliv 38-39 G 6-7
Kerč 38-39 G 6
Kerčel 38-39 M 4
Kerčenskij proliv 38-39 G 6-7
Kerema 52-53 N 8
Kerempe Burnu 46-47 E 1
Keren 60-61 M 5
Kerga 38-39 J 3
Kerguelen 22-23 N 8
Kerguelen, Grande Dorsale des – 22-23 N 8-J 9
Kerguelen, Plataforma de las – 22-23 N 8-J 9
Kerguelen-Gaussberg Ridge 22-23 N 8-J 9
Kerguelen-Gaußberg-Rücken 22-23 N 8-O 9
Kerguelen-Gaussbergrug 22-23 N 8-J 9
Kericho 63 C 3
Kerinci, Gunung – 52-53 D 7
Kerio 63 D 2
Keriske 42-43 Z 4
Keriya 48-49 E 4
Keriya Darya 48-49 E 4
Kerkenna, Îles – = Arkhbīl Qarqannah 60-61 G 2
Kerki 44-45 K 3
Kérkyra [GR, ⊙] 36-37 H 6
Kérkyra [GR, ●] 36-37 H 6
Kerling 30-31 de 2
Kerlingarfjöll 30-31 d 2
Kerma = Karmah 60-61 L 5
Kermadec, Fosse des – 56-57 Q 6-7
Kermadec, Îles – 56-57 PQ 6
Kermadec-árok 56-57 Q 6-7
Kermadecgraben 56-57 Q 6-7
Kermadec Islands 56-57 PQ 6
Kermadecký příkop 56-57 Q 6-7
Kermadec-Tonga, Fosa de – 56-57 Q 6-7
Kermadec-Tonga, Fosse de – 22-23 T 6-7
Kermadec-Tonga-Graben 22-23 T 6-7
Kermadec Tonga Trench 22-23 T 6-7
Kermadec Tongatrog 22-23 T 6-7
Kermadec Trench 56-57 Q 6-7
Kermadectrog 56-57 Q 6-7
Kermân 44-45 H 4
Kerman, CA 76-77 CD 7
Kermânshâh = Bākhtarān 44-45 F 4
Kermânshâhân = 1 ◁ 44-45 F 4
Kerme Körfezi 46-47 B 4
Kern River 76-77 D 8
Kernville, CA 76-77 D 8
Kérouané 60-61 C 7
Kershaw, SC 74-75 C 7
Kerulen = Cherlen gol 48-49 L 2
Keşan 46-47 B 2
Kesânê = Keşan 46-47 B 2
Keşap 46-47 H 2
Kesennuma 50-51 NO 3
Keserű-tavak = Al-Buḥayrat al-Murrat al-Kubrá 62 E 2
Keshan 48-49 O 2
Keshvar, Īstgāh-e – 46-47 N 6
Keskin 46-47 E 3
Keski-Suomen lääni 30-31 L 6
Kestenga 30-31 OP 5
Kesten'ga 42-43 E 4
Keszthely 33 H 5
Ket' 42-43 P 6
Keta 60-61 E 7
Keta, ozero – 42-43 QR 4
Ketapang [RI, Kalimantan] 52-53 EF 7
Ketchikan, AK 70-71 K 6
Ketchum, ID 76-77 F 4
Kete Krachi 60-61 DE 7
Kętrzyn 33 K 1-2
Kettharin Kyûn 52-53 C 4
Kettle Falls, WA 76-77 DE 1
Kettle River Range 76-77 D 1
Ketumbaine 63 D 3
Keulen = Köln 33 C 3
Kevin, MT 76-77 H 1
Kevir = Dasht-e Kavīr 44-45 GH 4
Keweenaw Peninsula 72-73 J 2
Kewir = Dasht-e Kavīr 44-45 GH 4
Kexholm = Prioz'orsk 42-43 DE 5
Key Largo 74-75 cd 4
Key Largo, FL 74-75 c 4
Keyser, WV 74-75 D 5
Keysville, VA 74-75 D 6
Keytū 46-47 N 5
Key West, FL 72-73 K 7
Kežma 42-43 T 6
Kežmarok 33 K 4
Kežma 42-43 T 6
Kežmarok 33 K 4
Khaanzuur, Raas – = Raas Khansiir 60-61 ab 1
Khabīr, Zāb al- = Zāb al-Kabīr 46-47 K 4
Khabra Najid = Habrat Najid 46-47 K 7
Khābūr, Nahr al- 44-45 E 3
Khābūrah, Al- 44-45 H 6
Khādim, Shūshat al- 62 B 3
Khāf, Rūd – = Khvāf 44-45 J 4
Khaibar = Shurayf 44-45 D 5
Khairabad 44-45 N 5
Khakass Autonomous Region = 10 ◁ 42-43 R 7
Khakassie, Région Autonome des – = 10 ◁ 42-43 R 7
Khalafābād 46-47 N 7
Khālda, Bīr – = Bi'r Hālidah 46-47 B 7
Khalīj as-Sintirā', Al- 60-61 A 4
Khalīj-e Fārs, Banāder va Jazāyer-e – = 5 ◁ 44-45 G 5
Khalīl, El- = Al-Halīl 46-47 F 7
Khaliq tau 48-49 E 3
Khāliş, Al- 46-47 L 6
Khalkhāl 46-47 N 4
Khalūf, Al- 44-45 H 6
Kham 48-49 H 5
Khamāsīn, Al- 44-45 EF 6
Khambat = Khambhat 44-45 L 6
Khambhat 44-45 L 6
Khambhāt nī Khādī = Gulf of Cambay 44-45 L 6
Khamir 44-45 E 7
Khāmis, Al-Jandal al- 60-61 L 5
Khampa Dsong 48-49 F 6
Khamsa, Bīr el- = Bi'r al-Khamsah 60-61 K 2
Khamsah, Bi'r al- 60-61 K 2
Khān al-Baghdādī 46-47 K 6
Khānaqīn = Khāniqīn 46-47 L 5
Khān az-Zabīb 46-47 G 7
Khandaq, Al- 60-61 KL 5
Khandaq, El- = Al-Khandaq 60-61 KL 5
Khaṅḍavā = Khandwa 44-45 M 6
Khandwa 44-45 M 6
Khan ez Zābib = Khān az-Zabīb 46-47 G 7
Khangai = Changajn nuruu 48-49 HJ 2
Khāniqīn 44-45 F 4
Khānpūr [PAK, Sindh] 44-45 KL 5
Khanshalah 60-61 F 1
Khansiir, Raas – 60-61 ab 1
Khantan = Kuantan 52-53 D 6
Khanty-Mansi Autonomous Area 42-43 L-P 5
Khanty-Mansis, District National des – 42-43 L-P 5
Khān Yūnūs 62 EF 2
Khanzi 64-65 F 7
Khanzi = Ghanzi 64-65 F 7
Khānzūr, Ras – = Raas Khaanzuur 60-61 ab 1
Kharāb, Al- 44-45 EF 7
Kharagpur [IND, West Bengal] 44-45 O 6
Kharan Kalat = Khārān Qalāt 44-45 K 5
Khārān Qalāt 44-45 K 5
Kharaz, Jabal – 44-45 E 8
Kharbin = Harbin 48-49 O 2
Khârga, El- = Al-Khārijah 60-61 L 3
Khârga, Wâḥât el- = Al-Wāḥāt al-Khārījah 60-61 KL 3-4
Kharīfūt 44-45 G 7
Khārijah, Al- 60-61 L 3
Khārijah, Al-Wāḥāt al- 60-61 KL 3-4
Kharīṭ, Wādī al- 62 EF 5
Kharîṭ, Wâdî el- = Wādī al-Kharīṭ 62 EF 5
Kharj, Al- 44-45 F 6
Khārk, Jazīreh-ye – 44-45 FG 5
Kharkheh, Rūd-e – 46-47 M 6
Kharkov = Char'kov 38-39 G 5-6
Khar Rūd 46-47 N 5
Khartoem = Al-Khartūm 60-61 L 5
Khartoum = Al-Khartūm 60-61 L 5
Khartūm = Al-Khartūm 60-61 L 5
Khartum = Al-Khartūm 60-61 L 5
Kharṭūm, Al- 60-61 L 5
Kharṭūm Baḥrī, Al- 60-61 L 5
Kharṭūm Baḥrī, El- = Al-Kharṭūm Baḥrī 60-61 L 5
Khaṣab, Al- 44-45 H 5
Khashm al-Qirbah 60-61 LM 6
Khâsh Rôd 44-45 J 4
Khaṭâṭba, El- = Al-Haṭāṭibah 62 D 2
Khaṭṭ, Wād al- 60-61 B 3
Khawr al-Amaīyah 46-47 N 8
Khawr al-Fakkān 44-45 H 5
Khawr Rūrī 44-45 G 7
Khay' 44-45 E 7
Khaybar, Ḥarrat – 44-45 DE 5
Khāybar, Kotal – 44-45 L 4
Khayrpūr [PAK, Punjab] 44-45 K 5
Khazhung Tsho 48-49 F 5
Khāzir, Nahr al- 46-47 K 4
Khazir Su = Nahr al-Khāzir 46-47 K 4
Khechmâ = Al-Bogham 46-47 J 5
Khedir, Al- = Khiḍr Dardash 46-47 L 7
Khemarat 52-53 DE 3
Khem Belder = Kyzyl 42-43 R 7
Khenachich, El – 60-61 D 4
Khenchela = Khanshalah 60-61 F 1
Khentei Nuruu = Chentijn Nuruu 48-49 K 2
Khiḍr Dardash 46-47 L 7
Khīrābād = Khairabad 44-45 N 5
Khirr, Wādī al- 44-45 E 4
Khnâchich, El – 60-61 D 4
Khobdo = Chovd 48-49 G 2
Khobso Gol = Chövsgöl nuur 48-49 J 1
Khökh Nuur = Chöch nuur 48-49 H 4
Khökh Schili uul = Chöch Šili uul 48-49 FG 4
Khomâm 46-47 NO 4
Khomas Highland = Khomasplato 64-65 E 7
Khomasplato 64-65 E 7
Khomeyn 46-47 NO 6
Khondâb 46-47 N 5
Khong, Mae Nam – 52-53 D 3
Khong Sedone = Muang Khôngxédon 52-53 E 3
Khon Kaen 52-53 D 3
Khor 38-39 L 9
Khorâsân 44-45 H 3-4
Khorâsân, Kavīre – = Dasht-e Kavīr 44-45 GH 4
Khorat = Nakhon Ratchasima 52-53 D 3-4
Khōrmāl = Hūrmāl 46-47 LM 5
Khorramâbâd [IR, Lorestân] 44-45 FG 4
Khorramâbâd [IR, Mâzandarân] 46-47 O 4
Khorramshahr 44-45 F 4
Khorsabad 46-47 K 4
Khosrovī 46-47 L 5
Khosrowâbâd [IR, Hamadân] 46-47 N 5
Khosrowâbâd [IR, Kordestan] 46-47 M 5
Khotan 48-49 DE 4
Khotan darya 48-49 E 3-4
Khouribga = Khurībqah 60-61 C 2
Khowst 44-45 KL 4
Khūḍdar 44-45 K 5
Khuff 44-45 E 6
Khükhe Noor = Chöch nuur 48-49 H 4
Khums, Al- 60-61 GH 2
Khurasan = Khorāsān 44-45 H 3-4
Khurayṣ 44-45 F 5
Khurībqah 60-61 C 2
Khūrīyā Mūrīyā, Jazā'ir – 44-45 H 7
Khurmah, Al- 44-45 E 6
Khūrmāl 46-47 LM 5
Khurr, Wādī al- = Wādī al-Khirr 46-47 K 7
Khushāb 44-45 L 4
Khūzestān 44-45 F 4
Khvāf 44-45 J 4
Khvoy 44-45 EF 3
Khwāf = Khvāf 44-45 J 4
Khyber Pass = Kotal Khāybar 44-45 L 4
Khyetentshering 48-49 G 5
Kiabakari 63 C 3
Kiama 58 K 5
Kiambi 64-65 G 4
Kiamusze = Jiamusi 48-49 P 2
Kian = Ji'an 48-49 LM 6
Kiangning = Nanjing 48-49 M 5
Kiangsi = Jiangxi 48-49 LM 6
Kiangsu = Jiangsu 48-49 MN 5
Kiantajärvi 30-31 N 5
Kiaohsien = Jiao Xian 48-49 M 4
Kiawah Island 74-75 CD 8
Kiayukwan = Jiuquan 48-49 H 4
Kibaha = Bagamoyo 64-65 J 4
Kibale 63 B 2
Kibali 64-65 GH 2
Kibamba 64-65 G 3
Kibangou 64-65 D 3
Kibau 64-65 HJ 4
Kibaya 64-65 J 4
Kiberashi 63 D 4
Kiberege 64-65 J 4
Kibiti 63 D 4
Kiboko 63 D 3
Kibombo 64-65 G 3
Kibondo 64-65 H 3
Kıbrıscık 46-47 DE 2
Kibungu 64-65 H 3
Kibuye 63 AB 5
Kibwezi 64-65 J 3
Kičevo 36-37 J 5
Kichčik 42-43 de 7
Kicking Horse Pass 70-71 NO 7
Kidal 60-61 E 5
Kidatu 64-65 J 4
Kidepo National Park 64-65 H 2
Kidete 63 D 4
Kidira 60-61 B 6
Kidston 56-57 H 3
Kiel 33 E 1
Kielce 33 K 3
Kieler Bucht 33 E 1
Kiên Hung = Go Quao 52-53 DE 5
Kienning = Jian'ou 48-49 M 6
Kienshui = Jianshui 48-49 J 7
Kierunavaara 30-31 J 4
Kiestinki = Kesten'ga 42-43 E 4
Kieta 52-53 j 6
Kiev = Kijev 38-39 F 5
Kiëv = Kijev 38-39 F 5
Kiew = Kijev 38-39 F 5
Kīfah 60-61 B 5
Kiffa = Kīfah 60-61 B 5
Kifl, Al- 46-47 L 6
Kifrī 46-47 L 5
Kigali 64-65 GH 3
Kiganga 63 C 4
Kiği 46-47 J 3
Kigoma 64-65 G 3
Kigosi 63 B 3
Kıgzı = Gürpinar 46-47 K 3
Kiha = Kwiha 60-61 MN 6
Kihelkonna 30-31 JK 8
Kihindi 63 D 5
Kihnu 30-31 K 8
Kihowera 63 D 5
Kihti = Skiftet 30-31 J 7
Kihurio 63 D 4
Kichčik 42-43 de 7
Kii hantō 48-49 Q 5
Kii sammyaku 50-51 KL 5-6
Kii-suidō 48-49 PQ 5
Kijang 50-51 G 5
Kijev 38-39 F 5
Kijevka [SU, Kazachskaja SSSR] 42-43 N 7
Kijevka [SU, Rossijskaja SFSR] 50-51 J 1
Kijevskoje vodochranilišče 38-39 F 5
Kijevskoje vodochranilišče 38-39 F 5
Kijów = Kyyiv 38-39 F 5
Kikinda 36-37 J 3
Kikládok 36-37 L 6
Kikombo 63 CD 4
Kikonai 50-51 B 3
Kikori 52-53 M 8
Kikwit 64-65 E 4
Kil 30-31 E 8
Kilauea Crater 52-53 ef 4
Kilbuck Mountains 70-71 E 5-D 6
Kilchu 50-51 G 2
Kilcoy 56-57 K 5
Kil'din 38-39 FG 2
Kildinstroj 30-31 PQ 3
Kildonan 64-65 H 6
Kilembe 63 B 2
Kilgore, ID 76-77 GH 3
Kilifi 64-65 JK 3
Kilija 36-37 N 3
Kilimanjaro [EAT, ▲] 64-65 J 3
Kilimanjaro [EAT, ☆] 64-65 J 3
Kilimatinde 64-65 HJ 4
Kilin = Jilin 48-49 N 2-O 3
Kilis 46-47 G 4
Kilkee 32 AB 5
Kilkenny 32 C 5
Kilkis 36-37 K 5
Killarney [IRL] 32 B 5
Killarney [AUS] 58 L 2
Killiecrankie Pass 32 E 3
Killin 32 D 3
Killinek Island 70-71 Y 5
Killington Peak 74-75 G 3
Killybegs 32 B 4
Kilmarnock 32 DE 4
Kil'mez 38-39 K 4
Kilmore 58 G 6
Kilo 63 B 2
Kilombero 64-65 J 4
Ki-long = Chilung 48-49 N 6
Kilonia = Kiel 33 E 1
Kilosa 64-65 J 4
Kilossa = Kilosa 64-65 J 4
Kilpisjärvi 30-31 J 3
Kilrea 32 C 4
Kilrush 32 B 5
Kiltān Island 44-45 L 8
Kilwa 64-65 G 4
Kilwa, Khirbat – 46-47 G 8
Kilwa Kisiwani 64-65 JK 4
Kilwa-Kissiwni = Kilwa Kisiwani 64-65 JK 4
Kilwa Kivinje 64-65 JK 4
Kilwa-Kiwindje = Kilwa Kivinje 64-65 JK 4
Kimaam 52-53 L 8
Kimali 63 C 3
Kimama, ID 76-77 G 4
Kimasozero 30-31 O 5
Kimba 58 C 4
Kimbe 52-53 gh 6
Kimbe Bay 52-53 h 6
Kimberley [AUS] 56-57 E 3
Kimberley [CDN] 76-77 EF 1
Kimberley [ZA] 64-65 FG 8
Kimberly, NV 76-77 F 6
Kimchaek 48-49 OP 3
Kimch'ŏn 48-49 O 4
Kimhandu 63 D 4
Kimje 50-51 F 5
Kimkang = Chengmai 48-49 KL 8
Kimōlos 36-37 L 7
Kimpoku san 50-51 LM 3
Kimry 42-43 F 6
Kimuenza 64-65 E 3
Kina 48-49 E-K 5
Kinabalu, Gunung – 52-53 G 5
Kinchinjunga = Gangchhendsönga 44-45 O 5
Kindersley 70-71 P 7
Kindia 60-61 B 6
Kindu 64-65 G 3
Kinel' 42-43 J 7
Kinešma 42-43 G 6
Kinešma 42-43 G 6
King and Queen Court House, VA 74-75 E 6
Kingchow = Jiangling 48-49 L 5
Kingchwan = Jingchuan 48-49 K 4
King City, CA 76-77 C 7
King Edward VIIIth Gulf 24 C 6-7
King George Vth Land 24 BC 15-16
King George VIth Sound 24 B 29-30
King George Island 24 CD 30-31
King George Sound 56-57 CD 7
King Hill, ID 76-77 F 4
Kingisepp [SU, Luga] 30-31 N 8
Kingisepp [SU, Saaremaa] 30-31 K 8
King Island [AUS] 56-57 H 7
Kingku = Jinggu 48-49 J 7
King Lear 76-77 D 5
King Leopold Ranges 56-57 DE 3
Kingman, AZ 76-77 FG 8
King Mountain [USA, Oregon] 76-77 D 4
Kingoonya 56-57 G 6
King Oscar Land 70-71 TU 2
Kings Canyon National Park 76-77 D 7
Kingscote 56-57 G 7
Kingscourt 32 C 5
Kingsland, GA 74-75 C 9
King's Lynn 32 FG 5
King's Lynn 32 FG 5
Kings Mountain, NC 74-75 C 7
King Sound 56-57 D 3
Kings Peaks 72-73 DE 3
Kingsport, TN 74-75 B 6
Kings River 76-77 CD 7
Kingston [CDN] 70-71 Y 9
Kingston [JA] 72-73 L 8
Kingston [NZ] 56-57 N 9
Kingston, NY 74-75 FG 4
Kingston, PA 74-75 EF 4
Kingston, WA 76-77 B 2
Kingston Peak 76-77 EF 8
Kingston SE 56-57 G 7
Kingston upon Hull 32 FG 5
Kingstown [WV] 72-73 O 9
Kingstown [IRL] 32 CD 5
Kingstree, SC 74-75 D 8
Kingsville, TX 72-73 G 6
King William Island 70-71 R 4
King William's Town 64-65 G 9
Kingwood, WV 74-75 D 5
Kingyang = Qingyang 48-49 K 4
Kingyuan = Yishan 48-49 K 7
Kinhwa = Jinhua 48-49 MN 6
Kınık 46-47 B 3
Kinkala 64-65 D 3
Kinkazan tō 50-51 NO 3
Kinmen Dao = Chin-mên Tao 48-49 M 7
Kinmount 74-75 D 2
Kinnaird's Head 32 F 3
Kinneret, Yam – 44-45 D 4
Kino kawa 50-51 K 5
Kinomoto = Kumano 50-51 L 6
Kinosaki 50-51 K 5
Kinross 32 E 3
Kinsale 32 B 6
Kinshasa 64-65 E 3
Kinsien = Jin Xian 48-49 N 4
Kinston, NC 72-73 L 4
Kintampo 60-61 D 7
Kin-tcheou = Jinzhou 48-49 N 3
Kintinku 63 C 4
Kintop 52-53 G 7
Kintyre 32 D 4
Kinyangiri 63 C 4
Kinyatī 63 C 1
Kioesjoedrempel 48-49 P 6-Q 7
Kios = Gemlik 46-47 C 2
Kioshan = Queshan 48-49 L 5
Kioto = Kyōto 48-49 PQ 4
Kipembawe 64-65 H 4
Kipengere 63 C 5
Kipeta 63 B 5
Kipili 64-65 H 4
Kipini 64-65 K 3
Kiptopeke, VA 74-75 F 6
Kipushi 64-65 G 5
Kirakira 52-53 k 7
Kiraz 46-47 C 3
Kırbaşı 46-47 DE 2-3
Kirenaika = Barqah 60-61 J 2
Kirenga 42-43 U 6
Kirensk 42-43 U 6
Kirghizie 44-45 LM 2
Kirgiezië 44-45 LM 2
Kirgisensteppe = Kazachskij Melkosopočnik 42-43 M-P 7-8
Kirgisien 44-45 LM 2
Kirgis Nor = Chjargas nuur 48-49 GH 2
Kirgizia 44-45 LM 2
Kirgizia 44-45 LM 2
Kirgizia 44-45 LM 2
Kirgiz Kizilsu Zizhizhou 48-49 CD 3-4
Kirgizskaja Sovetskaja Socialističeskaja Respublika = Kirgisien 44-45 LM 2
Kirgizskij chrebet 44-45 LM 2
Kirguizistán 44-45 LM 2
Kiri 64-65 E 3
Kiribati 20-21 S 6
Kiridh 60-61 b 2
Kırık 46-47 J 2
Kırıkhan 46-47 G 4
Kırıkkale 44-45 C 2-3
Kirillov 42-43 F 6
Kirin = Jilin [TJ, ●] 48-49 O 3
Kirin = Jilin [TJ, ☆] 48-49 N 2-O 3
Kirin-do 50-51 E 4
Kirishima-yama 50-51 H 7
Kirit = Jiriid 60-61 O 7
Kiriwina Islands = Trobriand Islands 52-53 h 6
Kırka 46-47 D 3
Kırkağaç 46-47 BC 3
Kirkcaldy 32 E 3
Kirkcudbright 32 DE 4
Kirkenes 30-31 O 3
Kırkgeçit = Kasrık 46-47 K 3
Kirkjuból 30-31 g 2
Kirkland, WA 76-77 BC 2
Kirkland Lake 70-71 U 8
Kırklareli 44-45 B 2
Kirksville, MO 72-73 H 3
Kirkūk 44-45 EF 3
Kirkwall 32 E 2
Kirkwood 64-65 FG 9
Kirman = Kermān 44-45 H 4
Kirmir Çayı 46-47 E 2
Kırobası 46-47 EF 4
Kirongwe 63 DE 4
Kirov [SU ↑ Br'ansk] 38-39 F 5
Kirov = Vjatka 42-43 HJ 6
Kirovabad 38-39 J 7
Kirovakan 38-39 HJ 7
Kirovograd 38-39 F 6
Kirovsk [SU, Rossijskaja SFSR Murmansk] 42-43 EF 4
Kirovskij [SU, Kazachskaja SSR] 42-43 O 9
Kirovskij [SU, Rossijskaja SFSR ↖ Petropavlovsk-Kamčatskij] 42-43 de 7
Kirs 42-43 J 6
Kırşehir 44-45 C 3
Kīrthar, Koh – 44-45 K 5
Kirthar Range = Koh Kīrthar 44-45 K 5
Kirtland, NM 76-77 J 7
Kiruna 30-31 HJ 4
Kiruru 52-53 KL 7
Kiryū 50-51 M 4
Kisa 30-31 F 8-9
Kisaki 63 B 4-5
Kisakata 50-51 M 3
Kisaki 63 D 4
Kisale, Lac – 64-65 G 4
Kisangani 64-65 G 2
Kisangire 64-65 J 4
Kis-Antillák 72-73 N 9-O 8
Kisar, Pulau – 52-53 J 8
Kisarawe 64-65 J 4
Kisarazu 50-51 MN 5
Kisel'ovsk 42-43 Q 7
Kisen = Hŭich'ŏn 48-49 O 3
Kisengwa 64-65 G 4

190 Kenma

Kőrishegy 33 HJ 5
Kőriyama 48-49 QR 4
Korjacký autonomní okruh
42-43 g 5-e 6
Korják Autonóm Körzet
42-43 g 5-e 6
Korjaken, Nationaal Gebied der
– 42-43 g 5-e 6
Korjaken, Nationalkreis der –
42-43 g 5-e 6
Korkino 42-43 L 7
Korkodon 42-43 de 5
Korkuteli = Dösemeatlı
46-47 CD 4
Korla 48-49 F 3
Kornat 36-37 F 4
Kornsjø 30-31 DE 8
Koro [FJI] 52-53 a 2
Köroğlu Dağları 44-45 C 2
Köroğlu Tepesi 46-47 DE 2
Korogwe 64-65 J 4
Koromandelküste = Coromandel
Coast 44-45 N 7-8
Koromandelské pobřeži =
Coromandel Coast 44-45 N 7-8
Koromandelskie, Wybrzeże =
Coromandel Coast 44-45 N 7-8
Koromandelskie, Wybrzeże =
Coromandel Coast 44-45 N 7-8
Koromo = Toyota 50-51 N 5
Korôneia, Limnē – 36-37 K 5
Korong Vale 58 F 6
Koror 52-53 KL 5
Körös 33 K 5
Koro Sea 52-53 ab 2
Korosko = Wādī Kuruskū 62 E 6
Korosten' 38-39 E 5
Koro Toro 60-61 H 5
Korpilombolo 30-31 JK 4
Korppoo 30-31 JK 7
Korsakov 42-43 b 8
Korsika = Corse 36-37 C 4
Korsør 30-31 D 10
Koršunovo 42-43 UV 6
Koršunovo 42-43 UV 6
Körtī = Kūrtī 60-61 L 5
Kortrijk 34-35 J 3
Koruçam Burnu 46-47 E 5
Korumburra 58 GH 7
Koryak Autonomous Area
42-43 g 5-e 6
Korynt = Kórinthos 36-37 K 7
Kós [GR, ⊙] 36-37 M 7
Kós [GR, ●] 36-37 M 7
Kosa 38-39 KL 4
Košaba 38-39 H 4
Koš-Agač 42-43 Q 7-8
Kosaka 50-51 N 2
Kö-saki 50-51 N 2
Koščagyl 44-45 G 1
Kościan 33 H 2
Kościerzyna 33 HJ 1
Kosciusko, Mount – 56-57 J 7
Koščagyl 44-45 G 1
Köse 46-47 H 2
Kösedağ Tepesi 46-47 GH 2
K'o-shan = Keshan 48-49 O 2
K'o-shih = Qäshqär 48-49 CD 4
Koshiki-rettō 50-51 G 7
Köshū = Kwangju 48-49 O 4
Kósi = Aruṇ 44-45 O 5
Kósi = Sapt Kosi 44-45 O 5
Kosī, Sūn – 44-45 O 5
Košice 33 HJ 4
Kosju 42-43 KL 4
Koški [SU] 42-43 M 3
Koslan 42-43 H 5
Köslin = Koszalin 33 H 1
Kosmos, WA 76-77 BC 2
Koso Gol = Chövsgöl nuur
48-49 J 1
Košong [Nordkorea] 48-49 O 4
Kŏsŏng [ROK] 50-51 G 5
Kosŏng-ni 50-51 F 6
Kosovo 36-37 J 4
Kosovo polje 36-37 J 4
Kosovska Mitrovica 36-37 J 4
Kostarika 72-73 JK 9-10
Kostaryka 72-73 JK 9-10
Kosten = Kościan 33 H 2
Kôsti = Kūstī 60-61 L 6
Kostino [SU ↓ Igarka] 42-43 Q 4
Kostnice = Konstanz 33 D 5
Kostroma [SU, ●] 42-43 G 6
Kostrzyn 33 G 2
Koszalin 33 H 1
Kőszeg 33 H 5
Koszyce = Košice 33 K 4
Koszyce = Košice 33 K 4
Košaba 38-39 H 4
Koš-Agač 42-43 Q 7-8
Košice 33 K 4
Kościerzyna 33 HJ 1
Kota [IND] 44-45 M 5
Kotaagung 52-53 D 8
Kota Baharu 52-53 D 5
Kotabaru 52-53 G 7
Kotabaru = Jayapura 52-53 M 7
Kota Belud 52-53 G 5
Kotabumi 52-53 D 6
Kotah = Kota 44-45 M 5
Kota Kinabalu 52-53 FG 5
Kota Kota 64-65 H 5
Kotamubagu 52-53 HJ 6
Kotatengah 52-53 D 6

Kotel 36-37 M 4
Kotel'nič 42-43 H 6
Kotel'nič 42-43 H 6
Kotel'nikovo 38-39 H 6
Kotel'nyj, ostrov – 42-43 Za 2-3
Kotido 64-65 H 2
Kotka 30-31 M 7
Kotlas 42-43 H 5
Kotooka 50-51 N 2
Kotto 60-61 J 7
Kotuj 42-43 T 3
Kotujkan 42-43 U 3
Kotzebue, AK 70-71 D 4
Kotzebue Sound 70-71 CD 4
Kouango 60-61 HJ 7
Kouba = Kelta 60-61 H 5
Koudougou 60-61 D 6
Koufra, Oasis de – = Wāḥāt al
-Kufrah 60-61 J 4
Koufra, Oasis de – = Wāḥāt al-
Kufrah 60-61 J 4
Kouilou 64-65 D 3
Koukdjuak River 70-71 W 4
Koula-Moutou 64-65 D 3
Koulen 52-53 DE 4
Koulikoro 60-61 C 6
Koumass = Kumasi 60-61 D 7
Koumra 60-61 H 7
Koungheul 60-61 B 6
Kounradskij 42-43 O 8
Kou-pang-tzü = Goubangzi
50-51 CD 2
Koupéla 60-61 D 6
Kouriles 48-49 S 3-T 2
Kouriles, Fosse des – 19 D 2-E 3
Kourou 78-79 J 3
Kouroussa 60-61 BC 6
Koutiala 60-61 C 6
Kouvola 30-31 M 7
Kouyou 64-65 DE 3
Kovdor 42-43 DE 4
Kovdozero 30-31 OP 4
Kovel' 38-39 D 5
Kovero 30-31 O 6
Kovik 70-71 V 5
Kovrov 42-43 G 6
Koweit 44-45 F 5
Kowôn 48-49 O 4
Kôyaṃpattūr = Coimbatore
44-45 M 8
Köyceğiz 46-47 C 4
Kôyllikôṭa = Calicut 44-45 LM 8
Koyukuk River 70-71 EF 4
Koyulhisar 46-47 GH 2
Köyyeri 46-47 G 3
Kozaklı 46-47 F 3
Kozan 46-47 F 4
Kozáně 36-37 J 5
Kozara 36-37 G 3
Kozi 63 DE 3
Kozie 33 HJ 3
Kozloduj 36-37 K 4
Kozluk 46-47 J 3
Koz'mino [SU ↘ Nachodka]
50-51 J 1
Koz'modemjansk 38-39 J 4
Kôzu-shima 50-51 M 5
Kožva 42-43 K 4
Kozloduj 36-37 K 4
Közép-afrikai Köztársaság
60-61 HJ 5
Közép-szibériai-fennsík
42-43 R-X 4-5
Kpalimé 60-61 E 7
Kpandu 60-61 DE 7
Kra, Isthme de – = Kho Khot
Kra 52-53 CD 4
Kra, Isthmus von – = Kho Khot
Kra 52-53 CD 4
Kra, Istmo de – = Kho Khot Kra
52-53 CD 4
Kra, Istmus of – = Kho Khot Kra
52-53 CD 4
Kra, Kho Khot – 52-53 CD 4
Kra, Przesmyk – = Kho Khot
Kra 52-53 CD 4
Krabi 52-53 C 5
Kra Buri 52-53 C 4
Kra-földszoros = Kho Khot Kra
52-53 CD 4
Kragerø 30-31 C 8
Kragujevac 36-37 J 3
Krainburg = Kranj 36-37 F 2
Krakatau = Pulau Anak Krakatau
52-53 DE 8
Krakau = Kraków 33 JK 3
Krakkó = Kraków 33 JK 3
Kraków 33 JK 3

Kralendijk 72-73 N 9
Kraljevo 36-37 J 4
Královny Alžběty, ostrovy –
70-71 N-V 2
Kramatorsk 38-39 G 6
Kramfors 30-31 G 6
Kranidion 36-37 K 7
Kranj 36-37 F 2
Krapina 36-37 FG 2
Kras 36-37 EF 3
Krasavino 42-43 GH 5
Kraská šije = Kho Khot Kra
52-53 CD 4
Kraskino 50-51 H 1
Kraslava 30-31 M 10
Kraśnik 33 KL 3
Krasnoarmejsk 38-39 HJ 5
Krasnoarmejsk 38-39 H 6
Krasnodar 38-39 G 6
Krasnograd 38-39 G 6
Krasnogvardejsk 44-45 K 3
Krasnogvardejsk = Gatčina
42-43 DE 6
Krasnoj Armii, proliv –
42-43 ST 1
Krasnojarsk 42-43 R 6
Krasnoje 38-39 H 4
Krasnoje Selo 38-39 NO 8
Krasnokamensk 42-43 W 7-8
Krasnokamsk 42-43 K 6
Krasnookt'abr'skij 38-39 HJ 6
Krasnosel'kup 42-43 OP 4
Krasnoturjinsk 42-43 L 5-6
Krasnoufimsk 42-43 K 6
Krasnoural'sk 42-43 L 6
Krasnousolskij 38-39 L 5
Krasnovišersk 42-43 K 5
Krasnovišersk 42-43 K 5
Krasnovodsk 44-45 G 2-3
Krasnovodskaja guba 38-39 K 8
Krasnovodsko plato 44-45 G 2
Krasnoznamenskoje 42-43 M 7
Krasnyj = Možga 42-43 J 6
Krasnyj Čikoj 42-43 UV 7
Krasnyj Čikoj 42-43 UV 7
Krasnyje džony 36-37 N 2
Krasnyj Jar 38-39 J 6
Krasnyj Luč 38-39 G 6
Krasnyj Liman 38-39 G 6
Krasnyj Luč 38-39 G 6
Krasnystaw 33 L 3
Kraśnik 33 KL 3
Kratié 52-53 E 4
Kraulshavn = Nûgssuaq
70-71 YZ 3
Krawang = Karawang 52-53 E 8
Krečetovo 38-39 G 3
Krečetovo 38-39 G 3
Krefeld 33 BC 3
Kremenčug 38-39 FG 6
Kremenčugskoje vodochranilišče
38-39 F 6
Kremenčug 38-39 FG 6
Kremenčugskoje vodochranilišče
38-39 F 6
Kremnica 33 J 4
Krems 33 G 4
Krenachich, El – = El
Khenachich 60-61 D 4
Krenachich, Oglat – = Oglat
Khenachich 60-61 D 4
Krēñ = Çeşme 46-47 B 3
Kresta, zaliv – 42-43 k 4
Krestcy 38-39 F 4
Krestovaja guba 42-43 H-K 3
Krestovyj, pereval – 38-39 HJ 7
Kreta = Krḗtē 36-37 L 8
Krḗtē 36-37 L 8
Krētské moře 36-37 K 7-M 8
Kreuzburg (Oberschlesien) =
Kluczbork 33 HJ 3
Kribi 60-61 F 8
Kričev 38-39 F 5
Kričev 38-39 F 5
Krim = Krym' 38-39 F 6
Krios, Akrôtḗrion – 36-37 K 8
Krishna 44-45 M 7
Krishna Delta 44-45 N 7
Kristiansand 30-31 BC 8
Kristianstad 30-31 F 9-10
Kristianstads län 30-31 E 9-F 10
Kristiansund 30-31 B 6
Kristiinankaupunki = Kristinestad
30-31 J 6
Kristineberg 30-31 H 5
Kristinehamn 30-31 EF 8
Kristinestad 30-31 J 6
Kriva Palanka 36-37 JK 4
Krivoj Rog 38-39 F 6
Križevci [YU, Bilo gora] 36-37 G 2
Križevci [YU, Bilo gora] 36-37 G 2
Krk 36-37 F 3
Krkonoše 33 GH 3
Krkonoše 33 GH 3
Krkonoše 33 GH 3
Krnov 33 H 3
Kroatien 36-37 F-H 3
Krohnwodoke = Nyaake
60-61 C 8
Kroksfjardharnes 30-31 c 2
Królowej Elżbiety, Wyspy –
70-71 N-V 2
Kronoberg 30-31 EF 9

Kronockaja Sopka, vulkan –
42-43 ef 7
Kronockij, mys – 42-43 f 7
Kronockij zaliv 42-43 f 7
Kronoki 42-43 f 7
Kronprins Christians Land
19 AB 20-21
Kronprins Christians Land
19 AB 20-21
Kronprinsesse Mærtha land
24 B 35-1
Kronprins Frederiks Bjerge
70-71 de 4
Kronprins Christians Land
19 AB 20-21
Kronprins Olav land 24 C 5
Kronprinz-Christian-Land =
Kronprins Christians Land
19 AB 20-21
Kronstadt = Brașov 36-37 L 3
Kroonstad 64-65 G 8
Kropotkin 38-39 H 6
Krosno 33 K 4
Krosno Odrzańskie 33 G 2-3
Krotoschin = Krotoszyn 33 H 3
Krotoszyn 33 H 3
Kruger National Park 64-65 H 7-8
Krugersdorp 64-65 G 8
Krui 52-53 D 8
Kruis, Kaap – 64-65 D 7
Krujë 36-37 HJ 5
Krung Thep 52-53 D 4
Kruševac 36-37 J 4
Kruševo 36-37 J 5
Kruševac 36-37 J 4
Kruševo 36-37 J 5
Krušné hory 33 F 3
Krymsk 38-39 G 6
Krymskije gory 38-39 F 7-G 6
Krynica 33 K 4
Krzyż 33 H 2

Ksar-el-Boukhari = Qaşr al-
Bukharī 60-61 E 1
Ksar el Kebir – = Al-Qşar al-Kabīr
60-61 C 1
Ksar es Souk = Al-Qaşr aş-
Şaghīr 60-61 D 2
Ksar es Souk = Al-Qaşr as-Sūq
60-61 K 2
Ksenjevka 42-43 WX 7
Ksyl-Orda = Kzyl-Orda
42-43 M 8-9
Ktesiphon 46-47 L 6

Kuala Belait 52-53 F 6
Kuala Berang 52-53 D 5-6
Kuala Kangsar 52-53 CD 6
Kualakapuas 52-53 F 7
Kuala Kerai 52-53 D 5
Kualalangsa 52-53 B 6
Kuala Lumpur 52-53 D 6
Kuala Merang 52-53 D 5
Kuala Perlis 52-53 CD 5
Kuala Selangor 52-53 D 6
Kuala Trengganu 52-53 DE 5
Kuancheng 50-51 B 2
Kuandian 50-51 E 2
Kuang-an = Guang'an 48-49 K 5
Kuang-ch'ang = Guangchang
48-49 M 6
Kuangchou = Guangzhou
48-49 L 7
Kuang-chou Wan = Zhanjiang
Gang 48-49 L 7
Kuangcsou = Guangzhou
48-49 LM 7
Kuang-hai = Guanghai 48-49 L 7
Kuang-hsi = Guangxi Zhuangzu
Zizhiqu 48-49 KL 7
Kuang-hsin = Shangrao
48-49 M 6
Kuang-lu Tao = Guanglu Dao
50-51 D 3
Kuang-nan = Guangnan
48-49 JK 7
Kuango = Kwango 64-65 E 3-4
Kuangsi = Guangxi Zhuangzu
Zizhiqu 48-49 KL 7
Kuangtung = Guangdong
48-49 L 7
Kuang-yüan = Guangyuan
48-49 K 5
Kuantan 52-53 D 6
Kuantan, Batang – = Sungai
Inderagiri 52-53 D 7
K'uan-tien = Kuandian 50-51 E 2
K'uang-tung Pan-tao = Guandong
Bandao 50-51 C 3
Kuan-yün = Guanyun 48-49 MN 5
Kuba [C] 72-73 KL 7
Kuba [SU] 38-39 J 7
Kuban 38-39 G 6
Kubango = Rio Cubango
64-65 E 6
Kubaysah 46-47 K 6
Kubbar, Jazīrat – 46-47 N 8
Kubbum 60-61 J 6
Kubokawa 50-51 J 6
Kučevo 36-37 J 3
Kucha 48-49 E 3
Kuche = Kucha 48-49 E 3
Kuchengtze = Qitai 48-49 FG 3
Kuching 52-53 F 6
Kuchinoerabu-jima 50-51 GH 7
Kum = Qom 44-45 G 4

Kuchino-shima 50-51 G 7
Kuçovë 36-37 HJ 5
Küçük Ağrı Dağı 46-47 L 3
Küçüksu = Kotum 46-47 K 3
Küçükyozgat = Elma Dağı
46-47 E 3
Kudamatsu 50-51 H 5-6
Kudat 52-53 G 5
Kuddla = Kandla 44-45 L 6
Kudirkos Naumiestis 30-31 K 10
Kudo = Taisei 50-51 ab 2
Kudūk 60-61 L 6-7
Kudymkar 42-43 JK 6
Kuei-ch'ih = Guichi 48-49 M 5
Kueichou = Guizhou 48-49 JK 6
Kuei-lin = Guilin 48-49 KL 6
Kuei-p'ing = Guiping 48-49 KL 7
Kuei-tê = Guide 48-49 J 4
Kuei-ting = Guiding 48-49 K 6
Kuei-yang = Guiyang [TJ,
Guizhou] 48-49 K 6
Kuei-yang = Guiyang [TJ, Hunan]
48-49 L 6
Kūfah, Al- 46-47 L 6
Kufra = Wāḥāt al-Kufrah
60-61 J 4
Kufra, Al- = Wāḥāt al-Kufrah
60-61 J 4
Kufra, Oasis de – = Wāḥāt al
-Kufrah 60-61 J 4
Kufra, oáza – = Wāḥāt al-Kufrah
60-61 J 4
Kufrah, Wāḥāt al- 60-61 J 4
Kufraoasen = Wāḥāt al-Kufrah
60-61 J 4
Kufra Oasis = Wāḥāt al -Kufrah
60-61 J 4
Kufra-oázis = Wāḥāt al-Kufrah
60-61 J 4
Küfre = Sirvan 46-47 K 3
Kufstein 33 F 5
Kuh dağı = Kazandağ 46-47 K 3
Kūhak 44-45 J 5
Kūhīn 46-47 N 4
Kuhmo 30-31 NO 5
Kuitozero 30-31 O 5
Kuja 42-43 M 8-9
Kujal'nickij liman 36-37 O 2
Kujang-dong 50-51 EF 3
Kujawy 33 J 2
Kujbyšev = Samara 42-43 HJ 7
Kujbyševka-Vostočnaja =
Belogorsk 42-43 YZ 7
Kujbyšev = Samara 38-39 K 5
Kujbyšev = Samara 38-39 K 5
Kujbyševskoje vodochranilišče
42-43 HJ 7
Kujbyšev 42-43 O 6
Kujbyšev = Samara 42-43 HJ 7
Kujbyševka-Vostočnaja =
Belogorsk 42-43 YZ 7
Kujbyšev = Samara 38-39 K 5
Kujbyšev = Samara 38-39 K 5
Kujbyševskoje vodochranilišče
42-43 HJ 7
Kuji 48-49 R 3
Kujto, ozero – 42-43 E 5
Kujumba 42-43 S 5
Kujū-san 50-51 H 6
Kukarka = Sovetsk 42-43 H 6
Kukawa 60-61 G 6
Kuke 64-65 F 7
Kula [BG] 36-37 K 4
Kula [TR] 46-47 C 3
Kula [YU] 36-37 H 3
Kul'ab 44-45 K 3
Kulagino 38-39 K 6
Kulal 63 D 2
Kulaly, ostrov – 38-39 J 7
Kulambangra = Kolombangara
52-53 j 6
Kulanjin 48-49 N 5
Kular, chrebet – 42-43 Z 4
Kulaura 44-45 P 6
Kuldiga 30-31 J 9
Kulebaki 38-39 H 4
Kulgera 56-57 F 6
Kulha Gangri 48-49 G 6
Kulhakangri = Kulha Gangri
48-49 G 6
Kulikoro = Koulikoro 60-61 C 6
Kulja = Ghulja 48-49 E 3
Kullen 30-31 E 9
Kullorsuaq = Guanyun 48-49 MN 5
Küllük = Güllük 46-47 B 4
Kulmbach 33 E 3
Kulmsee = Chełmża 33 J 2
Kulp 46-47 J 3
Kul'sary 42-43 J 8
Kulu 46-47 E 3
Kulumadau 52-53 h 6
Kulunda 42-43 OP 7
Kulundinskaja ravnina 42-43 O 7
Kulwin 58 F 5
Kum = Qom 44-45 G 4

Kuma 38-39 J 6-7
Kuma [J] 50-51 J 6
Kumagaya 50-51 M 4
Kumai, Teluk – 52-53 F 7
Kumaishi 50-51 ab 2
Kumalar Dağı 46-47 D 3
Kumamba, Kepulauan –
52-53 LM 7
Kumamoto 48-49 P 5
Kumano 50-51 L 6
Kumano-nada 50-51 L 5-6
Kumanovo 36-37 JK 4
Kumasi 60-61 D 7
Kumaun 44-45 M 4
Kumayt, Al- 46-47 M 6
Kumba 60-61 F 8
Kumbakonam 44-45 MN 8
Kumbe 52-53 LM 8
Kŭmch'on 50-51 F 5
Kŭmch'ŏn = Kimch'ŏn 48-49 O 4
Kumertau 42-43 K 7
Kŭm-gang 50-51 F 4
Kŭmgang-san 50-51 FG 3
Kŭmhwa 50-51 F 3
Kumini-dake 50-51 H 6
Kŭmje = Kimje 50-51 F 5
Kumla 30-31 F 8
Kumluca 46-47 D 4
Kŭmnyŏng 50-51 FG 5
Kŭmo-do 50-51 FG 5
Kumo-Manyčskaja vpadina
38-39 HJ 6
Kumo-Manyčskaja vpadina
38-39 HJ 6
Kumon Range = Kūmūn
Taungdan 52-53 C 1
Kumphawapi 52-53 D 3
Kŭmsan 51-51 F 4
Kumul = Hami 48-49 G 3
Kūmūn Taungdan 52-53 C 1
Kunašir, ostrov – 42-43 c 9
Kunašir, ostrov – 42-43 c 9
Kunayt, Al- 46-47 M 6
Kunda 30-31 M 8
Kundabwika Falls 63 B 5
Kundapura = Condapoor
44-45 L 8
Kundelungu 64-65 G 4-5
Kundelungu, Parc National de –
63 AB 5
Kundiawa 52-53 M 8
Kundur, Pulau – 52-53 D 6
Kunduz 44-45 K 3
Kunene 64-65 DE 6
K'ung'o-Ala-Too, chrebet –
42-43 O 9
Kungrad 44-45 H 3
Kungsbacka 30-31 DE 9
Kungu 64-65 E 2
Kungur 42-43 K 6
Kung-ying-tsü = Gongyingzi
50-51 BC 2
Kunie = Île des Pins 56-57 N 4
Kunjirap Daban 48-49 D 4
Kunkŭr 60-61 L 7
Kūnlôn 52-53 C 2
Kunlun Shan 48-49 D-H 4
Kunming 48-49 J 6
Kunovat 38-39 N 3
Kunsan 48-49 O 4
Kunsan-man 50-51 F 4
Kuntillâ, Al- 62 F 3
K'unyŏnp'yŏng-do = Tae-
yŏnp'yŏng-do 50-51 E 4
Kuolajarvi 38-39 EF 2
Kuopio 30-31 M 6
Kupa 36-37 FG 3
Kupang 52-53 H 9
Kup'ansk 38-39 G 6
Kupino 42-43 O 7
Kupiškis 30-31 L 10
Kupiškis 30-31 L 10
Kupreanof Island 70-71 K 6
Kura 38-39 J 8
Kurahashi-jima 50-51 J 5
Kurashiki 50-51 J 5
Kuraymah 60-61 L 5
Kurayoshi 50-51 JK 5
Kurchahan Hu = Chagan nuur
48-49 L 3
Kurdistan = Kordestān 44-45 F 3
Kurdufán 60-61 K 5-L 6
Kure [J] 48-49 P 5
Küre [TR] 46-47 E 2
Kurejka [SU, ~] 42-43 QR 4
Kurejka [SU, ●] 42-43 PQ 4
Kurgan 42-43 M 6
Kurganinsk 38-39 GH 6-7
Kurgan-T'ube 44-45 KL 3
Kuria Muria Island = Jazā'ir
Khūriyā Mūriyā 44-45 H 7
Kurikka 30-31 JK 6
Kuril-árok 19 D 2-E 3
Kurilen 48-49 S 3-T 2
Kurilengraben 19 D 2-E 3
Kuriles, Fosa de las – 19 D 2-E 3
Kuril Islands 48-49 S 3-T 2
Kuril'sk 42-43 c 8
Kuril'skije ostrova 48-49 S 3-T 2
Kuril-szigetek 48-49 S 3-T 2
Kuril Trench 19 D 2-E 3
Kurily 19 E 3-4

Kürkcü = Sarıkavak 46-47 E 4
Kurkur 62 E 6
Kurland 30-31 JK 9
Kurlandzkie, Wzn. - 30-31 JK 9
Kurle = Korla 48-49 F 3
Kurleja 42-43 WX 7
Kurmuk 60-61 L 6
Kurnool 44-45 M 7
Kurobe 50-51 L 4
Kuroishi 50-51 N 2
Kuromatsunai 50-51 b 2
Kuronsko 30-31 JK 9
Kurosawajiri = Kitakami 50-51 N 3
Kuro-shima 50-51 G 7
Kuršėnai 30-31 K 9-10
Kursī 46-47 J 4
Kursk 38-39 G 5
Kurskaja kosa 33 K 1
Kurskij zaliv 33 K 1
Kuršumlija 36-37 J 4
Kurşunlu [TR, Çankırı] 46-47 E 2
Kuršėnai 30-31 K 9-10
Kuršumlija 36-37 J 4
Kurtalan 46-47 J 4
Kurthasanlı 46-47 E 3
Kūrtī 60-61 L 5
Kurtoğlu Burnu 46-47 C 4
Kurucaşile 46-47 E 2
Kuruçay 46-47 H 3
Kuruman 64-65 F 8
Kurume [J, Kyūshū] 50-51 H 6
Kurumkan 42-43 V 7
Kuruṇegala 44-45 MN 9
Kurun-Ur'ach 42-43 a 6
Kurupukari 78-79 H 4
Kuruskū, Wādī – 62 E 6
Kuryle 19 E 3-4
Kuryongp'o 50-51 G 5
Kurzeme 30-31 JK 9
Kuşadası 46-47 B 4
Kuşadası Körfezi 46-47 B 4
Kusakaki-shima 50-51 G 7
Kusatsu 50-51 KL 5
Kusaybah, Bi'r – 60-61 K 4
Kušč'ovskaja 38-39 GH 6
Kuş Gölü 46-47 BC 2
Ku-shan = Gushan 50-51 D 3
Kushih = Gushi 48-49 M 5
Kushikino 50-51 GH 7
Kushima 50-51 H 7
Kushimoto 50-51 K 6
Kushiro 48-49 RS 3
Kūshkak 46-47 NO 5
Kushui 48-49 G 3
Kusiro = Kushiro 48-49 RS 3
Kuška 44-45 J 3
Kuskokwim Bay 70-71 D 6
Kuskokwim Mountains 70-71 EF 5
Kuskokwim River 70-71 DE 5
Kuşluyan = Gölköy 46-47 G 2
Kušmurun 42-43 LM 7
Kusnezk = Kuzneck 42-43 H 7
Kusŏng 50-51 E 2-3
Kustanaj 42-43 LM 7
K'ustendil 36-37 K 4
Küstenkanal 33 CD 2
Kūstī 60-61 L 6
Küstrin = Kostrzyn 33 G 2
Kusu 50-51 H 6
Kušum 38-39 K 5
K'us'ur 42-43 Y 3
Kušva 42-43 K 6
Kušč'ovskaja 38-39 GH 6
Kuška 44-45 J 3
Kušmurun 42-43 LM 7
Kušum 38-39 K 5
Kušva 42-43 K 6
Kūt, Al- 44-45 F 4
Kut, Ko – 52-53 D 4
Kūt 'Abdollāh 46-47 N 7
Kütahya 44-45 BC 3
Kutai 52-53 G 6
Kutaisi 38-39 H 7
Kut-al-Imara = Al-Kūt 44-45 F 4
Kutaradja = Banda Aceh 52-53 BC 5
Kutch 44-45 K 6
Kutch, Gulf of – 44-45 KL 6
Kutch, Rann of – 44-45 KL 6
Kutchan 50-51 b 2
Kutcharo-ko 50-51 d 2
Kutina 36-37 G 3
Kutno 33 J 2
Kutsing = Qujing 48-49 J 6
Kutu 64-65 E 3
Kutum 60-61 J 6
Kutunbul, Jabal – 44-45 E 7
Kuusalu 30-31 L 8
Kuusamo 30-31 N 5
Kuusankoski 30-31 M 7
Kuvait 44-45 F 5
Kuvajt 44-45 F 5
Kuvandyk 42-43 K 7
Kuwait 44-45 F 5
Kuwana 50-51 L 5
Kuwayt, Al- 44-45 F 5
Kuwejt 44-45 F 5
Kūysanjaq 46-47 L 4
Kuyucak 46-47 C 4
Kuz'movka 42-43 QR 5
Kuzneck 42-43 H 7
Kuzneckij Alatau 42-43 Q 6-7
Kuzneck-Sibirskij = Novokuzneck 42-43 Q 7
Kuznetsk = Kuzneck 42-43 H 7
Kuzomen' 42-43 F 4
Kuzucubelen 46-47 EF 4
Kvænangen 30-31 J 2
Kvaløy 30-31 KL 2
Kvalsund 30-31 KL 2
Kvalvågen 30-31 k 6
Kvarken 30-31 J 6
Kvarner 36-37 F 3
Kvarnerić 36-37 F 3
Kverkfjöll 30-31 ef 2
Kvigtind 30-31 EF 5
Kvikne 30-31 D 6
Kvitøya 30-31 no 4
Kwa 64-65 E 3
Kwair, Al- = Al-Quwayr 46-47 K 4
Kwakhanai 64-65 F 7
Kwale 63 D 4
Kwamouth 64-65 E 3
Kwa Mtoro 63 CD 4
Kwandang 52-53 H 6
Kwangan = Guang'an 48-49 K 5
Kwangando 63 D 3
Kwangchang = Guangchang 48-49 M 6
Kwangch'on 50-51 F 4
Kwangchow = Guangzhou 48-49 L 7
Kwangju 48-49 O 4
Kwango 64-65 E 3-4
Kwangsi = Guangxi Zhuangzu Zizhiqu 48-49 KL 7
Kwangtung = Guangdong 48-49 L 7
Kwangyuan = Guangyuan 48-49 K 5
Kwania, Lake – 63 C 2
Kwanmo-bong 50-51 G 2
Kwanto = Kantō 50-51 MN 4
Kwanyun = Guanyun 48-49 MN 5
Kwanza, Rio – 64-65 E 4-5
Kwara 60-61 E 6-F 7
Kwatta 44-45 K 4
Kwazulu [ZA, ≅] 64-65 H 8
Kweiang = Guiyang 48-49 K 6
Kweichih = Guichi 48-49 M 5
Kweichow = Fengjie 48-49 K 5
Kweichow = Guizhou 48-49 JK 6
Kweichu = Guiyang 48-49 K 6
Kweilin = Guilin 48-49 KL 6
Kweiping = Guiping 48-49 KL 7
Kweiteh = Shangqiu 48-49 LM 5
Kweiyang = Guiyang 48-49 K 6
Kwekwe 64-65 G 6
Kwenge 64-65 E 4
Kwenlun = Kunlun Shan 48-49 D-H 4
Kwesang-bong 50-51 G 2
Kwethluk, AK 70-71 DE 5
Kwidzyn 33 J 2
Kwigillingok, AK 70-71 D 6
Kwiha 60-61 MN 6
Kwilu 64-65 E 3
Kwinana 56-57 BC 6
Kwonghoi = Guanghai 48-49 L 7
Kyaiktō 52-53 C 3
Kyaka 63 B 3
Kyancutta 56-57 G 6
Kyaring Tsho [TJ, Qinghai] 48-49 H 5
Kyaring Tsho [TJ, Xizang Zizhiqu] 48-49 F 5
Kyaukhsī 52-53 C 2
Kyaukse = Kyaukhsī 52-53 C 2
Kydōniai = Ayvacık 46-47 B 3
Kyebang-san 50-51 G 4
Kyezīmanzan 52-53 C 2
Kykladen 36-37 L 7
Kykládes 36-37 L 7
Kykládes Nēsoi 36-37 L 7
Kyklady 36-37 L 6
Kyle of Lochalsh 32 D 3
Kyllēnē 36-37 J 7
Kýmē 36-37 L 6
Kymen lääni 30-31 MN 7
Kymijoki 30-31 M 7
Kynuna 56-57 H 4
Kyoga, Lake – 64-65 H 2
Kyōga-saki 50-51 K 5
Kyogle 58 L 2
Kyŏmip'o = Songnim 48-49 O 4
Kyŏngan-ni 50-51 F 4
Kyŏngdôn 52-53 CD 2
Kyŏnggi-do 50-51 F 4
Kyonghŭng 50-51 H 1
Kyŏngju 48-49 OP 4
Kyŏngnyŏlbi-yŏlto 50-51 E 4
Kyŏngsan 50-51 G 5
Kyŏngsang-pukto 50-51 G 4
Kyŏngsan-namdo 50-51 FG 5
Kyŏngsŏng 50-51 GH 2
Kyŏngsŏng = Sŏul 48-49 O 4
Kyŏngwŏn 50-51 H 1
Kyōto 48-49 PQ 4
Kyparissia 36-37 J 7
Kyparissiakòs Kólpos 36-37 J 7
Kypr 44-45 C 3
Kypr 38-39 F 8
Kyrá Panagia 36-37 KL 6
Kyrgyzstán 44-45 LM 2
Kyrksæterøra 30-31 C 6
Kyrkslätt 30-31 L 7
Kyrönjoki 30-31 K 6
Kyštovka 42-43 O 6
Kyštym 42-43 L 6
Kyštovka 42-43 O 6
Kyštym 42-43 L 6
Kýthēra 36-37 K 7
Kythēron, Stenòn – 36-37 K 7-8
Kýthnos 36-37 L 7
Kytyl-Žura 42-43 Y 5
Kytyl-Žura 42-43 Y 5
Kyūgôk 52-53 C 2
Kyuschuschwelle 48-49 P 6-Q 7
Kyūshū 48-49 P 5
Kyushu, Seuil des – 48-49 P 6-Q 7
Kyūshūi-hátság 48-49 P 6-Q 7
Kyushu Ridge 48-49 P 6-Q 7
Kyūshū sammyaku 50-51 H 6
Kyūsyū = Kyūshū 48-49 P 5
Kywong 58 H 5
Kyzyl 42-43 R 7
Kyzyl-Kija 44-45 L 2-3
Kyzylkum 42-43 LM 9
Kyzyl-Mažalyk 42-43 QR 7
Kyzyl-Mažalyk 42-43 QR 7
Kyzyl-Suu 44-45 L 3
Kzyl-Orda 42-43 M 9

L

Laa 33 H 4
La'ā', Al- = Al-Lu'ā'ah 46-47 L 7
Laascaanood 60-61 b 2
Laasqoray 60-61 b 1
Laas Warwar 60-61 bc 2
La Barge, WY 76-77 HJ 4
Labbezanga 60-61 E 5-6
Labe 33 G 3
Labé [Guinea] 60-61 B 6
La Belle, FL 74-75 c 3
Labiau = Polessk 33 K 1
Labin 36-37 F 3
Labinsk 38-39 H 7
Labis 52-53 D 6
La Blanquilla, Isla – 78-79 G 2
Laboulaye 80 D 4
Labrador, Bassin du – 22-23 G 3
Labrador, Coast of – 70-71 YZ 6-7
Labrador, Cuenca del – 22-23 G 3
Labrador, Mar del – 70-71 Y-a 5-6
Labrador, Mer du – 70-71 Y-a 5-6
Labrador Basin 22-23 G 3
Labradorbecken 22-23 G 3
Labradorbekken 22-23 G 3
Labrador City 70-71 X 7
Labrador Peninsula 70-71 V 6-Y 7
Labrador Sea 70-71 Y-a 5-6
Labradorsee 70-71 Y-a 5-6
Labradorskie, Morze – 70-71 Y-a 5-6
Labrador-tenger 70-71 Y-a 5-6
Labradorzee 70-71 Y-a 5-6
Lábrea 78-79 G 6
Labuan 52-53 FG 5
Labuan, Pulau – 52-53 FG 5
Labuha 52-53 J 7
Labuhan 52-53 E 8
Labuhanbajo 52-53 GH 8
Labuhanbilik 52-53 CD 6
Labytnangi 42-43 M 4
Lača, ozero – 38-39 G 3
Laccadive Islands 44-45 L 9
Lacepede Islands 56-57 D 3
Lacey, WA 76-77 B 2
Lachlan River 56-57 HJ 6
Lacio = Latium 36-37 E 4-5
Lackawanna, NY 74-75 D 3
Lacolle 74-75 G 2
Lacombe 70-71 O 7
Laconia, NH 74-75 H 3
Lacoochee, FL 74-75 b 2
Lacq 34-35 G 7
Lacrosse, WA 76-77 E 2
La Crosse, WI 72-73 H 3
Lac Superior = Lake Superior 72-73 HJ 2
Lača, ozero – 38-39 G 3
Ladakh 44-45 M 4
Ladakh Range 44-45 M 3-4
Lâdhiqīyah, Al- 44-45 CD 3
La Digue Island 64-65 N 3
Lâdik 46-47 FG 2
Ladiqiya, El- = Al-Lādhiqīyah 44-45 CD 3
Ladismith 64-65 F 9
Ladožskoje ozero 42-43 E 5
Ladožskoje ozero 42-43 E 5
L'ady 30-31 N 8
Ladybrand 64-65 G 8
Lady Franklinfjord 30-31 k 4
Lady Newnes Ice Shelf 24 B 18-17
Ladysmith [ZA] 64-65 G 8
Lae 52-53 N 8
La Encantada, Cerro de – 72-73 C 5
Lærdalsøyri 30-31 BC 7
Læsø 30-31 D 9
Lafayette, IN 72-73 J 3
Lafayette, LA 72-73 H 5-6
Lafia 60-61 F 7
Lafiagi 60-61 EF 7
Lagan 30-31 E 9
Lagarfljót 30-31 f 2
Lagarterito 72-73 b 2
Lagarto = Palmas Bellas 72-73 a 2
Lågen 30-31 CD 7
Laghouat = Al-Aghwāṭ 60-61 E 2
Lågneset 30-31 j 6
Lago Argentino 80 B 8
Lagodei, El- = Qardho 44-45 F 9
Lago Maggiore 36-37 C 2-3
Lagonegro 36-37 FG 5
Lago Novo 78-79 J 4
Lagos [P] 34-35 C 10
Lagos [WAN] 60-61 E 7
Lagosa 64-65 GH 4
Lagos Amorgas = Al-Buḥayrat al-Murrat al-Kubrá 62 E 2
Lagos de Moreno 72-73 F 7
Lago Superior = Lake Superior 72-73 HJ 2
Lagowa, El – = Al-Laqawah 60-61 K 6
Lågøya 30-31 k 4
La Grande, OR 76-77 D 3
Lagrange 56-57 D 3
La Grange, GA 72-73 JK 5
La Grange, NC 74-75 E 7
Laguna [BR] 80 G 3
Laguna, La – [PA ↑ Panamá] 72-73 b 2
Laguna, La – [PA ← Panamá] 72-73 b 3
Laguna Beach, CA 76-77 DE 9
Laguna Dam 76-77 FG 9
Laguna Mountains 76-77 E 9
Lagunas [PE] 78-79 DE 6
Lagunas [RCH] 80 BC 2
Laguna Superior 72-73 H 8
Laguna Yema 80 D 2
Lahad Datu 52-53 G 5-6
Laham [RI] 52-53 G 6
Lahat 52-53 D 7
Lāhawr 44-45 L 4
Lahewa 52-53 C 6
Laḥij 44-45 EF 8
Lāhījān 44-45 FG 3
Lahn 33 D 3
Laholm 30-31 E 9
Laholms bukten 30-31 E 9
Lahontan Reservoir 76-77 D 6
Lahore = Lāhawr 44-45 L 4
Lahti 30-31 LM 7
Laï 60-61 H 7
Laibach = Ljubljana 36-37 F 2
Lai Châu 52-53 D 2
Lai Châu 52-53 D 2
Laidley 58 L 1
Lai HKa = Lechā 52-53 C 2
Lai Châu 52-53 D 2
Lailá = Laylā 44-45 F 6
Lailān = Laylān 46-47 L 5
Laingsburg 64-65 EF 9
Laipo = Lipu 48-49 KL 7
Laisamis 63 D 2
Laiyuan 48-49 LM 4
Lai-yüan = Laiyuan 48-49 LM 4
Lajā', Al- 46-47 G 6
Lajes [BR, Rio Grande do Norte] 78-79 M 6
Lajes [BR, Santa Catarina] 80 F 3
Lajkovac 36-37 HJ 3
La Jolla, CA 76-77 E 9
Lajtamak 42-43 M 6
La Junta, CO 72-73 F 4
Lake, WY 76-77 H 3
Lake Bolac 58 F 6
Lake Butler, FL 74-75 b 1
Lake Cargelligo 56-57 J 6
Lake Charles, LA 72-73 H 5
Lake City, FL 74-75 b 1
Lake City, SC 74-75 D 8
Lake Charles, LA 72-73 H 5
Lakefield [AUS] 56-57 H 2-3
Lake George, NY 74-75 FG 3
Lake Grace 56-57 C 6
Lake Harbour 70-71 WX 5
Lake Havasu City, AZ 76-77 F-G 8
Lake Charles, LA 72-73 H 5
Lake King 56-57 CD 6
Lakeland, FL 72-73 K 6
Lakeland, GA 74-75 B 9
Lake Mead National Recreation Area 76-77 FG 7-8
Lake Oswego, OR 76-77 B 3
Lake Placid, FL 74-75 c 3
Lake Placid, NY 72-73 M 3
Lake Pleasant, NY 74-75 F 3
Lakeport, CA 76-77 B 6
Lake Range 76-77 D 5
Lakes Entrance 58 HJ 6
Lakeside, AZ 76-77 J 8
Lakeside, OR 76-77 A 4
Lakeside, UT 76-77 G 5
Lakeside, VA 74-75 E 6
Lake Toxaway, NC 74-75 B 7
Lakeview, MI 74-75 A 3
Lakeview, OR 76-77 C 4
Lake Wales, FL 74-75 c 3
Lakewood, NJ 74-75 F 4
Lakewood, NY 74-75 D 3
Lakewood, OH 74-75 BC 4
Lake Worth, FL 72-73 KL 6
Lakhadsweep 44-45 L 8
Lakhnaū = Lucknow 44-45 MN 5
Lakōnikòs Kólpos 36-37 K 7
Laksefjord 30-31 M 2
Lakselv 30-31 L 2
Lakṣhadvīp = Lakshadweep 44-45 L 8
Lâlapaşa 46-47 B 2
Lalaua 64-65 J 5
Lālī 46-47 N 6
Lalībela 60-61 M 6
La Manche, průliv - 32 E 7-F 6
Lambaréné 64-65 D 3
Lambasa 52-53 a 2
Lambayeque [PE, ●] 78-79 CD 6
Lambert Glacier 24 B 8
Lambi Kyûn 52-53 C 4
Lambton, Cape – 70-71 M 3
Lāmding = Lumding 44-45 P 5
Lamé 60-61 G 7
Lamego 34-35 D 8
La Mesa, CA 76-77 E 9
Lamèzia Terme 36-37 FG 6
Lamia 36-37 K 6
L'amin 42-43 N 5
Lamo = Lamu 64-65 K 3
Lamoille, NV 76-77 F 5
La Moine, CA 76-77 B 5
Lamona, WA 76-77 D 2
Lamon Bay 52-53 H 4
Lamont, CA 76-77 D 8
Lamont, ID 76-77 H 3-4
Lamotrek 52-53 N 5
Lampa [PE] 78-79 EF 8
Lampang 52-53 C 3
Lampedusa 36-37 E 8
Lampedusa, Ìsola – 60-61 G 1
Lampi Island = Lambi Kyûn 52-53 C 4
Lampung 52-53 DE 7
Lamu [EAK] 64-65 K 3
Lanai 52-53 e 3
Lanao, Lake – 52-53 HJ 5
Lancang Jiang 48-49 HJ 7
Lancaster 32 E 4
Lancaster, CA 76-77 DE 8
Lancaster, NH 74-75 H 2
Lancaster, PA 74-75 EF 4
Lancaster, SC 74-75 C 7
Lancaster Sound 70-71 TU 3
Lancheu = Lanzhou 48-49 JK 4
Lanchou = Lanzhou 48-49 JK 4
Lanchow = Lanzhou 48-49 JK 4
Lanciano 36-37 F 4
Lancun 48-49 N 4
Landau 33 D 4
Landeck 33 E 5
Landego 30-31 EF 4
Landerneau 34-35 E 4
Lander River 56-57 F 4
Landrum, SC 74-75 B 7
Landsberg am Lech 33 E 4
Landsberg (Warthe) = Gorzów Wielkopolski 33 GH 2
Land's End 32 CD 6
Land's End [CDN] 70-71 LM 2
Landshut 33 F 4
Landskrona 30-31 E 10
Landsort, Fosa de – 30-31 H 8
Landsort, Fosse du – 30-31 H 8
Landsort, Głębia – 30-31 H 8
Landsortdiep 30-31 H 8
Landsorttief 30-31 H 8
Langchhen Khamba 48-49 DE 5
Langchung = Langzhong 48-49 JK 5
Langeland 30-31 D 10
Langerūd 46-47 O 4
Langjökull 30-31 cd 2
Langkawi, Pulau – 52-53 C 5
Langlois, OR 76-77 A 4
Langon 34-35 G 6
Langøy 30-31 F 3
Langres 34-35 K 5
Langres, Plateau de – 34-35 K 5
Langsa 52-53 C 6
Lang Shan = Char Narijn uul 48-49 K 3
Lang So'n 52-53 E 2
Langtans udde 24 C 31
Languedoc 34-35 J 7-K 6
Langzhong 48-49 JK 5
Lanín, Volcán – 80 B 5
Lannion 34-35 F 4
Lansdale, PA 74-75 F 4
Lansing, MI 72-73 K 3
Lan-ts'ang Chiang = Lancang Jiang 48-49 HJ 7
Lan-ts'ang Chiang = Lancang Jiang 48-49 HJ 7
Lan-ts'ang Chiang = Lancang Jiang 48-49 HJ 7
Lan-ts'un = Lancun 48-49 N 4
Lanusei 36-37 C 6
Lan Yü 48-49 N 7
Lanzarote 60-61 B 3
Lanzhou 48-49 JK 4
Laoag 52-53 GH 3
Laodicea = Al-Lādhiqīyah 44-45 CD 3
Laoha He 50-51 B 2
Lao-ha Ho = Laoha He 50-51 B 2
Laohekou = Guanghua 48-49 L 5
Laohushan 50-51 BC 2
Lao Kay 52-53 D 2
Laon 34-35 J 4
Laora 52-53 H 7
Laos 52-53 D 2-3
Laoshan 48-49 N 4
Laosz 52-53 D 2-E 3
Lao-t'ieh-shan-hsi Chiao = Laotieshanxi Jiao 50-51 C 3
Lao-t'ieh-shan-hsi Chiao = Laotieshanxi Jiao 50-51 C 3
Lao-t'ieh-shan-hsi Chiao = Laotieshanxi Jiao 50-51 C 3
Lapa 80 FG 3
La Panza Range 76-77 CD 8
La Paz, Bahía de – 72-73 DE 7
Laperuza, proliv – 42-43 b 8
Lápēthos = Lapta 46-47 E 5
Lapine, OR 76-77 C 4
Lapin lääni 30-31 L-N 4
Lapinlahti 30-31 MN 6
Lapland 30-31 F 5-N 3
Laplandskij zapovednik 30-31 OP 4
La Plata, MD 74-75 E 5
Laponia 30-31 F 5-N 3
Laponia 30-31 F 5-N 3
Laponie 30-31 F 5-N 3
Laponsko 30-31 F 5-N 3
Laporte, PA 74-75 E 4
Lapovo 36-37 J 3
Lappajärvi 30-31 KL 6
Lappeenranta 30-31 N 7
Lappföld 30-31 F 5-N 3
Lappföld 30-31 F 5-N 3
Lappi 30-31 L 5
Lappland 30-31 F 3-N 5
Laprida [RA, Buenos Aires] 80 D 5
Lâpseki 46-47 B 2
Lapta 46-47 E 5
Laptev, Mar de – 42-43 V 2-a 3
Laptev, Mer du – 42-43 V 2-a 3
Laptev Sea 42-43 V 2-a 3
Laptěvů, moře – 42-43 V 2-Z 3
Laptevzee 42-43 V 2-a 3
Laptewsee 42-43 V 2-a 3
Laptyev-tenger 42-43 V 2-Z 3
Lapua 30-31 K 6
Lapush, WA 76-77 A 2
Łapy 33 L 2
Laqawah, Al- 60-61 K 6
Lāqīyat 60-61 K 4
Lār [IR] 44-45 G 5
Larache = Al-'Arā'ish 60-61 C 1
Laramie, WY 72-73 EF 3
Laramie Range 72-73 E 3
Laranjeiras do Sul 80 F 3
Larantuka 52-53 H 8
Larat, Pulau – 52-53 K 8
Lärbro 30-31 H 9
Lare 63 D 2
Laredo, TX 72-73 G 6
Lārestān 44-45 GH 5
Largeau = Faya-Largeau 60-61 H 5
Largo, FL 74-75 b 3
Largo Remo, Isla – 72-73 b 2
Largo Remo Island 72-73 b 2
Lariang 52-53 G 7
Larino 36-37 F 5
Lárisa 36-37 K 6
Laristan = Lārestān 44-45 GH 5
Larjak 42-43 OP 5
Lāṛkānah 44-45 K 5
Larnaca = Lárnax 44-45 C 4
Lárnax 44-45 C 4
Larne 32 D 4
Larrey Point 56-57 C 3
Larrimah 56-57 F 3
Lars Christensen land 24 BC 7
Lars Christensen land 24 BC 7
Larsen is-shelf 24 C 30-31
Lars Christensen land 24 BC 7
Larvik 30-31 D 8
Lasa = Lhasa 48-49 G 6
La Sal, UT 76-77 J 6
Las Aves, Islas – 78-79 F 2
Las Cruces, NM 72-73 E 5
Lāsgird = Lāsjerd 44-45 G 3
Lāshe lowayn 44-45 J 4
Lashio = Lāshō 52-53 C 2
Lashkar = Gwalior 44-45 M 5
Lashkar Gāh 44-45 JK 4
Lashkar Satma 48-49 F 4
Lāshō 52-53 C 2
La Silveta, Cerro – 80 B 8
Lasíthion 36-37 L 8
Lāsjerd 44-45 G 3
Las Minas, Bahía – 72-73 b 2
Lasolo, Teluk – 52-53 H 7
Lassance 78-79 KL 8
Lassen Peak 72-73 B 3
Lassen Volcanic National Park 76-77 C 5
Lastoursville 64-65 D 3
Lastovo 36-37 G 4
Las Vegas, NM 72-73 EF 4
Las Vegas, NV 72-73 C 4
Las Vegas Bombing and Gunnery Range 76-77 EF 7
Latacunga 78-79 D 5
Latady Island 24 BC 29
Latakia = Al-Lādhiqīyah 44-45 CD 3
Late 52-53 c 2
Latina 36-37 E 5

Latin 193

Latium = Lázio 36-37 E 4-5
La Tortuga, Isla – 78-79 FG 2
Latrobe 58 c 2
Latrobe, PA 74-75 D 4
Latvia 30-31 K-M 9
Lauban = Lubań 33 G 3
Lauderdale 58 c 3
Lauenburg/Elbe 33 E 2
Lauenburg in Pommern = Lębork 33 H 1
Laughlan Islands 52-53 h 6
Lau Group 52-53 b 2
Launceston [AUS] 56-57 J 8
Launceston [GB] 32 D 6
Laura 56-57 H 3
Laurel, DE 74-75 F 5
Laurel, MD 74-75 E 5
Laurel, MS 72-73 J 5
Laurel, OH 74-75 A 5
Laurel Hill 74-75 D 4-5
Laurens, SC 74-75 BC 7
Laurentides, Parc provincial des – 70-71 W 8
Laurie Island 24 C 32
Laurinburg, NC 74-75 D 7
Lauritsala 30-31 N 7
Lausanne 33 C 5
Lausitzer Gebirge 33 G 3
Laut, Pulau – [RI, Kepulauan Natuna] 52-53 E 6
Laut, Pulau – [RI, Selat Makasar] 52-53 G 7
Laut Kecil, Kepulauan – 52-53 G 7-8
Lautoka 52-53 a 2
Lava Bads 76-77 JK 8
Lava Beds [USA, Oregon ↘ Cedar Mountains] 76-77 E 4
Lava Beds [USA, Oregon ← Harney Basin] 76-77 C 4
Lava Beds [USA, Oregon ↘ Steens Mountain] 76-77 D 4
Lava Beds National Monument 76-77 C 5
Laval [CDN] 70-71 VW 8
Laval [F] 34-35 G 4
Lavapié, Punta – 80 AB 5
Laveaga Peak 76-77 C 7
Lavelanet 34-35 HJ 7
La Verkin, UT 76-77 G 7
Laverton 56-57 D 5
Lavongai = New Hanover 52-53 gh 5
Lavonia, GA 74-75 B 7
Lavrador = Labrador Peninsula 70-71 V 6-Y 7
Lavras 78-79 L 9
Lávrion 36-37 KL 7
Lawa 78-79 J 4
Lawen, OR 76-77 D 4
Lawers, Ben – 32 DE 3
Lawit, Gunung – [RI] 52-53 F 6
Lawowa 52-53 H 7
Lawqah 46-47 K 8
Lawra 60-61 D 6
Lawrence, MA 74-75 H 3
Lawrence, NY 74-75 G 4
Lawrenceburg, OH 74-75 A 5
Lawrenceville, VA 74-75 E 6
Laws, CA 76-77 D 7
Lawton, OK 72-73 G 5
Lawz, Jabal al- 44-45 D 5
Laxå 30-31 F 8
Lāyalpūr = Faisalābād 44-45 L 4
Layar, Tanjung – 52-53 DE 8
Laylā 44-45 F 6
Laylān 46-47 L 5
Layton, UT 76-77 G 5
Lazarev 42-43 ab 7
Lazarevskoje, Soči- 38-39 G 7
Lazarevskoje, Soči- 38-39 G 7
Lázio 36-37 E 4-5

Lead, SD 72-73 F 3
Leadore, ID 76-77 G 3
Leaksville, NC 74-75 D 6
Leamington, UT 76-77 GH 6
Leavenworth, WA 76-77 C 2
Leavitt Peak 76-77 D 6
Łeba 33 H 1
Lebádeia 36-37 K 6
Lebam, WA 76-77 B 2
Lebanon 48-49 D 4
Lebanon, NH 74-75 GH 3
Lebanon, OR 76-77 B 3
Lebanon, PA 74-75 E 4
Leb'ažje [SU, Kazachskaja SSR] 42-43 O 7
Leb'ažje [SU, Rossijskaja SFSR] 42-43 M 6
Leb'ažje [SU, Kazachskaja SSR] 42-43 O 7
Leb'ažje [SU, Rossijskaja SFSR] 42-43 M 6
Lebedin 38-39 F 5
Lebesby 30-31 M 2
Lébithia 36-37 M 7
Lebo 64-65 F 2
Lèbôn 52-53 B 2
Lębork 33 H 1
Lebrija 34-35 DE 10
Lebú 80 B 5
Lecce 36-37 H 5
Lecco 36-37 C 3
Lech 33 E 4
Lechâ 52-53 C 2
Lectoure 34-35 H 7
Leduc 70-71 O 7
Lee, MA 74-75 G 3
Leeds 32 F 5
Leer 33 C 2
Leesburg, FL 74-75 bc 2
Leesburg, ID 76-77 FG 3
Leesburg, VA 74-75 E 5
Leeton 56-57 J 6
Leeuwarden 34-35 KL 2
Leeuwin, Cape – 56-57 B 6
Leeuwin, Dorsal de – 56-57 A 8-B 7
Leeuwin, Seuil – 56-57 A 8-B 7
Leeuwindrempel 56-57 A 8-B 7
Leeuwin-hát 56-57 A 8-B 7
Leeuwin Rise 56-57 A 8-B 7
Leeuwinschwelle 56-57 A 8-B 7
Lee Vining, CA 76-77 D 7
Leeward Islands 72-73 O 8
Lefini 64-65 E 3
Lefka 46-47 E 5
Lefroy, Lake – 56-57 D 6
Legaspi 52-53 H 4
Legaupi = Legaspi 52-53 H 4
Leghorn = Livorno 36-37 CD 4
Legnica 33 GH 3
Le Grand, Cape – 56-57 D 6
Leh 44-45 M 4
Lehi, UT 76-77 GH 5
Lehliu 36-37 M 3
Lehrte 33 DE 2
Lehututu 64-65 F 7
Leiah = Leya 44-45 L 4
Leibnitz 33 G 5
Leicester 32 F 5
Leichhardt Range 56-57 J 4
Leichhardt River 56-57 GH 3
Lei-chou Pan-tao = Leizhou Bandao 48-49 L 7
Leiden 34-35 K 2
Leie 34-35 J 3
Leigh Creek 56-57 G 6
Leikanger 30-31 A 6
Leine 33 D 3
Leinster 32 C 5
Leipsói 36-37 M 7
Leipzig 33 F 3
Leiranger 30-31 F 4
Leiria 34-35 C 9
Leisler, Mount – 56-57 EF 4
Leitha 33 H 5
Leith Harbour 80 J 8
Leitmeritz = Litoměřice 33 G 3
Leiyang 48-49 L 6
Leizhou Bandao 48-49 L 7
Lejâ'a, El- = Al-Lajā' 46-47 G 6
Lek 34-35 K 3
Leka 30-31 D 5
Lekef = Al-Kāf 60-61 F 1
Lekemti = Nekemtē 60-61 M 7
Leksand 30-31 F 7
Leksozero 30-31 O 6
Leksula 52-53 J 7
Lel = Lēh 44-45 M 4
Leland Elk Rapids, MI 74-75 A 2
Leleque 80 B 6
Lelingluang 52-53 K 8
Lemahabang 52-53 E 8
Léman 33 C 5
Le Marie, Estrecho de – 80 C 9-D 8
Lembale 63 BC 4
Lemesós 44-45 C 4
Lemhi, ID 76-77 G 3
Lemhi Range 76-77 G 3
Lemhi River 76-77 G 3
Lemju 38-39 K 3
Lemland 30-31 J 8
Lemmenjoen kansallispuisto 30-31 LM 3
Lemmon, Mount – 76-77 H 9
Lêmnos 36-37 L 6
Lemoore, CA 76-77 CD 7
Lemvig 30-31 C 9
Lena [SU] 42-43 W 5-6
Lena, OR 76-77 D 3
Lençóis 78-79 L 7
Lenda 63 B 2
Lendery 42-43 E 5
Lenger 42-43 MN 9
Lengerskij = Georgijevka 42-43 P 8
Lengua de Vaca, Punta – 80 B 4
Lengyelország 33 H-L 3
Lenina, pik – 44-45 L 3
Leninabad 44-45 KL 2-3
Leninakan 38-39 H 7
Leningrad = Sankt-Peterburg 42-43 E 5-6
Lenino = Leninsk-Kuzneckij 42-43 Q 6-7
Leninogorsk 42-43 P 7
Leninsk-Kuzneckij 42-43 Q 6-7
Leninskoje 38-39 J 4
Lenkoran 38-39 J 8
Lennep, MT 76-77 H 2
Lennox, Isla – 80 C 9
Lenoir, NC 74-75 C 7
Lens 34-35 J 3
Lensk 42-43 V 5
Lentini 36-37 F 7
Léo 60-61 D 6
Leoben 33 G 5
Leominster, MA 74-75 GH 3
León [MEX] 72-73 F 7
León [NIC] 72-73 J 9
León [E, ≅] 34-35 E 7-8
León [E, ●] 34-35 E 7
León, Cerro del – 72-73 G 8
Leon, Montes de – 34-35 D 7
León, Pays de – 34-35 E 4
Leonardtown, MD 74-75 E 5
Leonardville 64-65 E 7
Leongatha 58 G 7
Leonídion 36-37 K 7
Leonora 56-57 D 5
Léopold II, Lac – = Mai Ndombe 64-65 E 3
Léopoldville = Kinshasa 64-65 E 3
Leovo 36-37 MN 2
Lepar, Pulau – 52-53 E 7
Lepel 38-39 E 5
Leper Colony = Balboa Heights 72-73 b 3
Lephepe 64-65 FG 7
Lépi = Caála 64-65 DE 5
Leping 48-49 M 6
Lepsy 42-43 O 8
Leptis magna 60-61 GH 2
Lequeitio 34-35 F 7
Lêr = Līr 60-61 KL 7
Léré [Tschad] 60-61 G 7
Lérida 34-35 H 8
Lérida [CO, Vaupés] 78-79 E 4
Lerma 34-35 F 7-8
Léros 36-37 M 7
Le Roy, MI 74-75 A 2
Le Roy, NY 74-75 DE 3
Le Roy, WY 76-77 H 5
Lerwick 32 F 1
Lésbos 36-37 L 6
Leščevo = Charovsk 42-43 G 6
Leshan 48-49 J 6
Lesistyje Karpaty 33 KL 4
Leskovac 36-37 J 4
Leslie, ID 76-77 G 4
Lesnoj [SU, Vjatka] 42-43 J 6
Lesnoj = Umba 42-43 J 6
Lesnoj Umba 42-43 EF 4
Lesosibirsk 42-43 R 6
Lesotho 64-65 G 8
Lesozavodsk 42-43 Za 8
Lesozavodskij 30-31 P 4
Lesser Antilles 72-73 N 9-O 8
Lesser Sunda Islands 52-53 GH 8
Lešukonskoje 42-43 H 5
Leszno 33 H 3
Leščevo = Charovsk 42-43 G 6
Lešukonskoje 42-43 H 5
Letaba [ZA, ~] 64-65 H 7
Lethbridge 70-71 O 8
Lethem 78-79 H 4
Leti, Kepulauan – 52-53 J 8
Letiahau 64-65 F 7
Leticia 78-79 EF 5
Letland 30-31 K-M 9
Letnij bereg 38-39 G 2-3
Letonia 30-31 K-M 9
Letpadan = Letpandan 52-53 C 3
Letpandan 52-53 C 3
Lettland 30-31 K-M 9
Lettonie 30-31 K-M 9
Lettország 30-31 K-M 9
Leuser, Gunung – 52-53 C 6
Leuven 34-35 K 3
Levan, UT 76-77 H 6
Levanger 30-31 D 6
Levant, Bassin du – 44-45 BC 4
Levantei-medence 44-45 BC 4
Levantine Basin 44-45 BC 4
Levantisches Becken 44-45 BC 4
Levantské moře 46-47 C 5
Levantské moře 36-37 NO 8
Levantijns Bekken 44-45 BC 4
Lévanzo 36-37 DE 6
Levent 46-47 G 3
Leveque, Cape – 56-57 D 3
Leverett Glacier 24 A 24-22
Leverkusen 33 C 3
Levice 33 J 4
Levick, Mount – 24 B 16-17
Levin 56-57 P 8
Lévis 70-71 W 8
Levittown, PA 74-75 F 4
Lévka = Lefka 46-47 E 5
Levká Órē 36-37 KL 8
Levkás [GR, ⊙] 36-37 J 6
Levkás [GR, ●] 36-37 J 6
Levkōsia 44-45 C 3
Levski 36-37 L 4
Levskigrad 36-37 L 4
Lewes, DE 74-75 F 5
Lewis, Butt of – 32 C 2
Lewis, Isle of – 32 C 2
Lewisburg, PA 74-75 E 4
Lewisburg, WV 74-75 C 6
Lewis Pass 56-57 O 8
Lewis Range 72-73 D 2
Lewis River 76-77 BC 2
Lewiston, ID 72-73 C 2
Lewiston, ME 72-73 MN 3
Lewiston, UT 76-77 H 5
Lewistown, PA 74-75 DE 4
Lexington, KY 72-73 K 4
Lexington, NC 74-75 CD 7
Lexington, VA 74-75 D 6
Lēxúrion 36-37 J 6
Leyah 44-45 L 4
Leydsdorp 64-65 H 7
Leyte 52-53 J 4
Leżajsk 33 L 3
Lezhë 36-37 H 5
Leżajsk 33 L 3

L'gov 38-39 G 5

Lha Ri 48-49 E 5
Lharugö 48-49 G 5
Lhasa 48-49 G 6
Lhasza = Lhasa 48-49 G 6
Lhatse Dsong 48-49 F 6
Lhokkruet 52-53 BC 6
Lhokseumawe 52-53 C 5
Lhunpo Gangri 48-49 EF 5-6

Liangjiadian 50-51 CD 3
Liangshan Yizu Zizhizhou 48-49 J 6
Liangshan Zizhizhou 48-49 J 6
Liang Xiang 48-49 LM 4
Liangxiangzhen 48-49 LM 4
Lianhua 48-49 L 6
Lianjiang [TJ, ● Guangdong] 48-49 KL 7
Lianping 48-49 LM 7
Lianshanguan 50-51 D 2
Lianyungang 48-49 MN 5
Liaocheng 48-49 LM 4
Liao-chung = Liaozhong 50-51 D 2
Liaodong Bandao 48-49 N 4
Liaodong Wan 48-49 MN 3-4
Liao He 50-51 D 1
Liao Ho = Liao He 50-51 D 1
Liaoning 48-49 MN 3
Liaosi = Liaoxi 48-49 N 3
Liaotung = Liaodong Bandao 48-49 N 4
Liaoxi 48-49 N 3
Liaoyang 48-49 N 3
Liaoyuan 48-49 NO 3
Liaoyuan = Shuangliao 48-49 N 3
Liard River 70-71 M 5
Liaunim = Liaoning 48-49 MN 3
Liban 48-49 D 4
Liban 44-45 D 4
Libano 48-49 D 4
Libanon 48-49 D 4
Libau = Liepāja 30-31 J 9
Libby, MT 76-77 F 1
Libby Reservoir 76-77 F 1
Libebe = Andara 64-65 F 6
Libenge 64-65 E 2
Liberal, KS 72-73 F 4
Liberec 33 G 3
Libéria 60-61 BC 7
Libéria 60-61 BC 7
Liberia 60-61 BC 7
Liberia, Ramal de – 22-23 J 5
Libéria, Seuil du – 22-23 J 5
Liberia Basin 22-23 J 5
Liberiadrempel 22-23 J 5
Liberiaschwelle 22-23 J 5
Libérie 60-61 BC 7
Liberty, NY 74-75 F 4
Liberty, OH 74-75 A 5
Liberty, WA 76-77 C 2
Libia 60-61 G-J 3
Libia 60-61 G-J 3
Libiai-sivatag 60-61 J 3-L 4
Libië 60-61 G-J 3
Libijska, Pustynia – 60-61 J 3-L 4
Libische Woestijn 60-61 J 3-L 4
Libourne 34-35 GH 6
Libreville 64-65 CD 2
Libya 60-61 G-J 3
Libyan Desert 60-61 J 3-L 4
Libye 60-61 G-J 3
Libye 60-61 G-J 3
Libye, Désert de – 60-61 J 3-L 4
Libyen 60-61 G-J 3
Libyjská poušť 60-61 J 3-L 4
Libysche Wüste 60-61 J 3-L 4
Licantén 80 B 4
Licata 36-37 E 7
Lice 46-47 J 3
Lichangshan Liedao 50-51 D 3
Li-ch'ang-shan Lieh-tao = Lichangshan Liedao 50-51 D 3
Li-chiang = Lijiang 48-49 J 6
Lichinga 64-65 J 5
Lichtenburg 64-65 FG 8
Licosa, Punta – 36-37 F 5
Lida 38-39 E 5
Lida, NV 76-77 E 7
Lidām, Al- = Al-Khamāsīn 44-45 EF 6
Lidingö 30-31 H 8
Lidinon, Akrōtḗrion – 36-37 L 8
Lidköping 30-31 E 8
Lido di Ostia, Roma- 36-37 DE 5
Liechtenstein 33 D 5
Liège 34-35 K 3
Liegnitz = Legnica 33 GH 3
Lieja = Liège 34-35 K 3
Lieksa 30-31 NO 6
Lielupe 30-31 KL 9
Lielvārde 30-31 L 9
Lienartville 64-65 G 2
Lien-chiang = Lianjiang [TJ, Guangdong] 48-49 KL 7
Lien-hua = Lianhua 48-49 L 6
Lienhwa = Lianhua 48-49 L 6
Lien-shan-kuan = Lianshanguan 50-51 D 2
Lienyunkang = Lianyungang 48-49 MN 5
Lienz 33 F 5
Liepāja 30-31 J 9
Liezen 33 FG 5
Lifi Mahuida 80 C 6
Lifīyah, Al- 46-47 K 7
Lifou, Île – 56-57 N 4
Lifu = Île Lifou 56-57 N 4
Lifubu 63 B 5
Liganga 63 C 5
Light, Cape – 24 B 30-31
Lightning Ridge 58 HJ 2
Ligonha, Rio – 64-65 J 6
Ligua, La – 80 B 4
Ligùria 36-37 B 4-C 3
Liguria, Mar de – 36-37 BC 4
Ligurian Sea 36-37 BC 4
Ligurie = Ligùria 36-37 B 4-C 3
Ligurien = Ligùria 36-37 B 4-C 3
Ligurisches Meer 36-37 BC 4
Ligurische Zee 36-37 BC 4
Ligurské moře 36-37 C 4
Liguryjskie, Morze - 36-37 C 4
Lihir Group 52-53 h 5
Lihua = Litang 48-49 J 5
Lihula 30-31 K 8
Lichtenštejnsko 33 D 5
Lijepaja = Liepāja 30-31 J 9
Lijiang 48-49 J 6
Likasi 64-65 G 5
Likati 64-65 F 2
Likely, CA 76-77 C 5
Likiang = Lijiang 48-49 J 6
Likoma Island 64-65 HJ 5
Likoto 64-65 F 3
Likouala [RCB ◁ Sangha] 64-65 E 2
Likouala [RCB ◁ Zaïre] 64-65 E 2
Likuala = Likouala [RCB ◁ Sangha] 64-65 E 2
Likuala = Likouala [RCB ◁ Zaïre] 64-65 E 2
Likupang 52-53 J 6
Liland 30-31 G 3
Lille 34-35 J 3
Lille Bælt 30-31 CD 10
Lille-Ballangen 30-31 G 3
Lillehammer 30-31 D 7
Lillesand 30-31 C 8
Lillestrøm 30-31 D 7-8
Lilongwe [MW, ~] 63 C 6
Lilongwe [MW, ●] 64-65 H 5
Lilydale 58 c 2
Lim 36-37 H 4
Lima [P] 34-35 C 8
Lima, MT 76-77 G 3
Lima, OH 72-73 K 3
Lima [PE, ●] 78-79 D 7
Lima = Dsayul 48-49 H 6
Limão, Cachoeira do – 78-79 J 6
Lima Reservoir 76-77 GH 3
Limassol = Lemesós 44-45 C 4
Limay, Rio – 80 C 5
Limay Mahuida 80 C 5
Limbang 52-53 FG 6
Limbaži 30-31 L 9
Limbe 60-61 F 8
Limburg 33 D 3
Limchow = Hepu 48-49 K 7
Limeira 78-79 K 9
Limerick 32 B 5
Limfjorden 30-31 D 9
Limia 34-35 C 8-D 7
Li Miao Zhou = Hainan Zangzu Zizhizhou 48-49 K 8
Liminka 30-31 L 5
Limkong = Lianjiang 48-49 KL 7
Limmen Bight 56-57 G 2
Limnē 36-37 K 6
Limoges 34-35 H 6
Limoges [CDN] 74-75 F 2
Limón 72-73 K 9-10
Limón, Bahía – 72-73 b 2
Limon Bay 72-73 b 2
Limousin 34-35 HJ 6
Limoux 34-35 J 7
Limpia, Laguna – [RA ↖ Resistencia] 80 DE 3
Limpopo 64-65 G 7
Lin 36-37 J 5
Linan = Jianshui 48-49 J 7
Linares [CO] 78-79 D 4
Linares [E] 34-35 F 9
Linares [MEX] 72-73 G 7
Linares [RCH] 80 B 5
Lincang 48-49 HJ 7
Lin-chiang = Linjiang [TJ, Jilin] 48-49 O 3
Lin-ch'ing = Linqing 48-49 M 4
Linchow = Hepu 48-49 K 7
Linchuan = Fuzhou 48-49 MN 6
Lincoln [GB] 32 F 5
Lincoln [RA] 80 D 4
Lincoln, CA 76-77 C 6
Lincoln, ME 74-75 J 2
Lincoln, NE 72-73 G 3
Lincoln, NH 74-75 GH 2
Lincoln Sea 19 A 24-25
Lincolnton, NC 74-75 C 7
Lind, WA 76-77 D 2
Lindau 33 D 5
Linde [SU] 42-43 X 4
Lindesberg 30-31 F 8
Lindesnes 30-31 B 9
Lindi [EAT] 64-65 J 4-5
Lindi [ZRE] 64-65 G 2
Lindian 48-49 NO 2
Lindos 36-37 N 7
Lindsay 74-75 D 2
Lindsay, CA 76-77 D 7
Linea, La – 34-35 E 10
Linec = Linz 33 EF 4
Linfen 48-49 L 4
Lingao 48-49 K 8
Lingayen Gulf 52-53 GH 3
Linge [BUR] 52-53 C 2
Lingeh = Bandar-e Lengeh 44-45 GH 5
Lingen 33 C 2
Lingga, Kepulauan – 52-53 DE 7
Lingga, Pulau – 52-53 DE 7
Lingling 48-49 L 6
Lingmar 48-49 F 5-6
Linguère 60-61 AB 5
Lingyuan 50-51 B 2
Ling-yüan = Lingyuan 50-51 B 2
Lingyun 48-49 K 7
Linhai 48-49 N 6
Linhares 78-79 LM 8
Linh Cam 52-53 E 3
Linhe 48-49 K 3
Lin-ho = Linhe 48-49 K 3
Lin-hsi = Linxi 48-49 M 3
Lin-hsia = Linxia 48-49 J 4
Lini = Linyi [TJ ↗ Xuzhou] 48-49 M 4
Linjiang [TJ, Jilin] 48-49 O 3
Linköping 30-31 FG 8
Linkou 48-49 OP 2
Linkow = Linkou 48-49 OP 2
Linli 48-49 L 6
Linn, Mount – 76-77 B 5
Linné, Kapp – 30-31 j 5
Linnhe, Loch – 32 D 3
Linosa 36-37 E 8
Linosa, Ìsola – 60-61 G 1
Linqing 48-49 M 4
Lins 78-79 JK 9
Linsia = Linxia 48-49 J 4
Linsin = Linxia 48-49 J 4
Lintan 48-49 J 5
Lintao 48-49 J 4
Lintien = Lindian 48-49 NO 2
Lintsing = Linqing 48-49 M 4
Linxi 48-49 M 3
Linxia 48-49 J 4
Linxia Huizu Zizhizhou = A ◁ 48-49 J 4
Linyanti 64-65 F 6
Linyi [TJ, Shandong ↗ Xuzhou] 48-49 M 4
Linyu = Shanhaiguan 50-51 BC 2
Linz 33 FG 4
Lion, Golf du – 34-35 JK 7
Liouesso 64-65 DE 2
Lipari 36-37 F 6
Lipawa = Liepāja 30-31 J 9
Lipeck 38-39 G 5
Lipez, Cordillera de – 78-79 F 9
Lipin Bor 38-39 G 3
Liping 48-49 K 6
Ripljan 36-37 J 4
Lipno 33 J 2
Lipova 36-37 J 2
Lippe 33 C 3
Lippstadt 33 D 3
Lipsk = Leipzig 33 F 3
Lipsko = Leipzig 33 F 3
Lipu 48-49 KL 7
Līr 60-61 KL 7
Lira 64-65 H 2
Liranga 64-65 E 3
Lisabon = Lisboa 34-35 C 9
Lisala 64-65 F 2
Līsār 46-47 N 3
Lisboa 34-35 C 9
Lisbon, OH 74-75 C 4
Lisbon = Lisboa 34-35 C 9
Lisbonne = Lisboa 34-35 C 9
Lisburn 32 CD 4
Lisburne, Cape – 70-71 C 4
Lishi 48-49 L 4
Lishih = Lishi 48-49 L 4
Lishui [TJ, Zhejiang] 48-49 MN 6
Lisičansk 38-39 G 6
Lisičansk 38-39 G 6
Lisieux 34-35 H 4
Lisle, NY 74-75 EF 3
Lismore [AUS] 56-57 K 5
Lismore [IRL] 32 C 5
Lissa = Leszno 33 H 3
Lissabon = Lisboa 34-35 C 9
Lisszabon = Lisboa 34-35 C 9
Lista 30-31 B 8
Lister, Mount – 24 B 17
Listowel 74-75 C 3
Listowel 32 B 5
Litan 48-49 J 5
Litang 48-49 K 7
Līṭānī, Nahr al- 46-47 F 6
Litauen 30-31 KL 10
Litchfield, CA 76-77 CD 5
Līth, Al- 44-45 E 6
Lithgow 56-57 JK 6
Lithuania 30-31 KL 10
Litke 42-43 ab 7
Litóchōron 36-37 K 5

194 Latiu

Litoměřice 33 G 3
Litoměřice 33 G 3
Litomyšl 33 GH 4
Litomyšl 33 GH 4
Litouwen 30-31 KL 10
Litovko 42-43 Za 8
Little Andaman 44-45 P 8
Little Belt Mountains 76-77 H 2
Little Cayman 72-73 KL 8
Little Colorado River 72-73 DE 5
Little Desert, The – 58 E 6
Little Falls, NY 74-75 F 3
Littlefield, AZ 76-77 G 7
Little Humboldt River 76-77 E 5
Little Lake, CA 76-77 E 8
Little Mecatina River 70-71 YZ 7
Little Minch 32 C 3
Little Nicobar 44-45 P 9
Little Pee Dee River 74-75 D 7-8
Little Rock, AR 72-73 H 5
Littlerock, CA 76-77 DE 8
Little Rock, WA 76-77 B 2
Little Rock Mountains 76-77 J 1-2
Little Ruaha 63 C 4-5
Little Smoky Valley 76-77 F 6
Little Snake River 76-77 J 5
Littleton, NC 74-75 DE 6
Littleton, NH 74-75 H 2
Little Valley, NY 74-75 D 3
Little Wood River 76-77 FG 4
Lituania 30-31 KL 10
Lituanie 30-31 KL 10
Litunde 63 D 6
Litva 30-31 KL 10
Litvánia 30-31 K-M 10
Litwa 30-31 KL 10
Liu-chia-tzū = Liujiazi 50-51 C 2
Liuchow = Liuzhou 48-49 K 7
Liuhe [TJ, Jilin] 50-51 E 1
Liu-ho = Liuhe [TJ, Jilin] 50-51 E 1
Liujiazi 50-51 C 2
Liurbao 50-51 D 2
Liuwa Plain 64-65 F 5
Liuzhou 48-49 K 7
Live Oak, FL 74-75 b 1
Livermore, CA 76-77 C 7
Livermore, Mount – 72-73 F 5
Livermore Falls, ME 74-75 HJ 2
Liverpool 32 E 5
Liverpool Bay [CDN] 70-71 L 3-4
Liverpool Range 56-57 JK 6
Livingston, MT 76-77 H 3
Livingstone 64-65 G 6
Livingstone Memorial 64-65 GH 5
Livingstone Mountains 64-65 H 4-5
Livingstone 63 C 5
Livingstonia = Chiweta 64-65 H 5
Livingston Island 24 CD 30
Livland 30-31 L 9-M 8
Livno 36-37 G 4
Livny 38-39 G 5
Livonia 30-31 L 9-M 8
Livonie 30-31 L 9-M 8
Livonsko 30-31 L 9-M 8
Livonsko 30-31 L 9-M 8
Livorno 36-37 CD 4
Livourne = Livorno 36-37 CD 4
Liwale 64-65 J 4
Lī Yūbū 60-61 K 7
Lizarda 78-79 K 6
Lizard Head Peak 76-77 J 4
Lizard Point 32 D 7
Lizbona = Lisboa 34-35 C 9

Ljubljana 36-37 F 2
Ljungan 30-31 G 6
Ljungby 30-31 E 9
Ljusdal 30-31 FG 7
Ljusnan 30-31 F 6-7
Ljusne 30-31 G 7

Llamellin 78-79 D 6
Llandrindod Wells 32 E 5
Llanes 34-35 E 7
Llangefni 32 D 5
Llano 76-77 H 10
Llano Estacado 72-73 F 5
Llanquihue, Lago – 80 B 6
Llata 78-79 D 6
Llerena 34-35 DE 9
Lleyn Peninsula 32 D 5
Llobregat 34-35 H 7-8
Llorena, Punta – = Punta San Pedro 72-73 K 10
Lloyd Bay 56-57 H 2
Lloydminster 70-71 OP 7
Llullaillaco, Volcán – 80 C 2-3

Loa, UT 76-77 H 6
Loa, Río – 80 BC 2
Loange 64-65 F 3-4
Loango 64-65 D 3
Lobata 52-53 H 7
Lobatse 64-65 FG 8
Lobaye 60-61 H 8
Loberia [RA, Buenos Aires] 80 E 5
Lobito 64-65 D 5
Lob nuur 48-49 G 3
Lobstick Lake 70-71 Y 7
Lobva 38-39 LM 4
Loche, La – 70-71 P 6
Loch Garman = Wexford 32 C 5
Lochgilphead 32 D 3
Lo-ch'ing = Yueqing 48-49 N 6
Lochnagar 32 E 3
Lochsa River 76-77 F 2
Lock 58 BC 4
Lockes, NV 76-77 F 6
Lockhart 58 H 5
Lockhart River Aboriginal Reserve 56-57 H 2
Lock Haven, PA 74-75 E 4
Lockport, NY 74-75 D 3
Lôc Ninh 52-53 E 4
Locri 36-37 G 6
Lod 46-47 F 7
Lodejnoje Pole 38-39 FG 3
Lodi 36-37 C 3
Lodi, CA 76-77 C 6
Lodi = Aynı 46-47 JK 4
Lødingen 30-31 F 3
Lodja 64-65 F 3
Lodsch = Łódź 33 J 3
Lodwar 64-65 J 2
Łódź 33 J 3
Loei 52-53 D 3
Lofa River 60-61 B 7
Lofocki, Basen - 30-31 A-C 2
Lofotbecken 28-29 JK 1
Lofoten 30-31 E 3-4
Lofoten, Bassin des – 28-29 JK 1
Lofoten, Cuenca de las – 28-29 JK 1
Lofoten Basin 28-29 JK 1
Lofotenbekken 28-29 JK 1
Lofthus 30-31 B 7
Lofty Range, Mount – 56-57 G 6
Lofusa = Lufusā 63 C 2
Logan, OH 74-75 B 5
Logan, UT 72-73 D 3
Logan, WV 74-75 BC 6
Logan, Mount – [CDN, Yukon Territory] 70-71 HJ 5
Logandale, NV 76-77 F 7
Logan Mountains 70-71 L 5
Logansport, IN 72-73 J 3
Loge, Rio – 64-65 D 4
Logojsk 30-31 M 10
Logone 60-61 H 7
Logroño 34-35 F 7
Logroño 34-35 F 7
Løgstør 30-31 C 9
Lohardaga 44-45 N 6
Lōhārdaggā = Lohardaga 44-45 N 6
Lōhit = Luhit 44-45 Q 5
Lohja 30-31 KL 7
Lohtaja 30-31 K 5
Lohumbo 63 C 3
Loibl 33 G 5
Loikaw = Lûykau 52-53 C 3
Loimaa 30-31 K 7
Loir 34-35 G 5
Loire 34-35 H 5
Loiya 63 C 2
Loja [E] 34-35 E 10
Loja [EC, ●] 78-79 D 5
Loji 52-53 J 7
Lo-jung = Luorong 48-49 K 7
Loka = Lūkā 63 B 1
Lokan tekojärvi 30-31 MN 3
Lokichoggio 63 C 1
Lokila = Lukilā 63 C 1
Lokitaung 64-65 HJ 2
Lokka 30-31 MN 4
Lokoja 60-61 F 7
Lokolo 64-65 EF 3
Loksa 30-31 LM 8
Loks Land 70-71 Y 5
Lŏl, Nahr – = Nahr Lūl 60-61 K 7
Lola, Mount – 76-77 C 6
Loleta, CA 76-77 A 5
Lolgorien 63 C 3
Loliondo 63 C 3
Lol Laikumaiki 63 D 4
Lolland 30-31 D 10
Lolmuryoi 63 D 4
Lolo 64-65 D 3
Lolo, MT 76-77 F 2
Lolobau 52-53 h 5
Loloda 52-53 J 6
Lolui 63 C 3
Lom [BG] 36-37 K 4
Lom [RFC] 60-61 G 7
Loma, MT 76-77 H 1-2
Lomadi 52-53 C 3
Lomami 64-65 FG 3
Loma Mountains 60-61 B 7
Lomas [PE] 78-79 E 8
Lombard, MT 76-77 H 2
Lombardei = Lombardia 36-37 C 3-D 2
Lombardia 36-37 C 3-D 2
Lombardie = Lombardia 36-37 C 3-D 2
Lomblem = Pulau Lomblen 52-53 H 8
Lomblen, Pulau – 52-53 H 8
Lombok, Pulau – 52-53 G 8
Lombok, Selat – 52-53 G 8
Lomé 60-61 E 7
Lomela [ZRE, ~] 64-65 F 3
Lomela [ZRE, ●] 64-65 F 3
Lomié 60-61 G 8
Lomitas, Las – 80 D 2
Lomond, Ben – [AUS] 58 cd 2
Lomond, Loch – 32 D 3
Lomonosov 38-39 E 4
Lomonosov, Dorsal de – 19 A
Lomonosovka 42-43 M 7
Lomonosov Ridge 19 A
Lomonosovrug 19 A
Lomonosovův hřbet 19 A
Lomonosowrücken 19 A
Lomonossov, Crête de – 19 A
Lomonoszov-hátság 19 A
Lompoc, CA 76-77 C 8
Lom Sak 52-53 D 3
Łomża 33 L 2
Loncoche 80 B 5
Londen = London 32 G 6
Londlani 63 C 3
London [CDN] 70-71 UV 9
London [GB] 32 G 6
Londonderry 32 C 4
Londonderry, Cape – 56-57 E 2
Londonderry, Islas – 80 B 9
Londres = London 32 G 6
Londrina 80 FG 2
Londýn = London 32 G 4
Londyn = London 32 G 4
Lone Mountain 76-77 E 7
Lone Pine, CA 76-77 DE 7
Lonerock, OR 76-77 D 3
Lonetree, WY 76-77 H 5
Longa [Angola] 64-65 E 5
Longa, proliv – 42-43 j 3-4
Long Bay 72-73 L 5
Long Beach, CA 72-73 BC 5
Longboat Key 74-75 b 3
Long Branch, NJ 74-75 FG 4
Longchuan [TJ, Dehong Daizu Zizhizhou] 48-49 H 7
Long Creek, OR 76-77 D 3
Longdor, gora – 42-43 W 6
Long Eddy, NY 74-75 F 4
Longford 56-57 J 8
Longford 32 BC 5
Longhua 48-49 M 3
Longido 63 D 3
Longiram 52-53 G 6-7
Long Island [BS] 72-73 LM 7
Long Island [CDN] 70-71 UV 7
Long Island [PNG] 52-53 N 7-8
Long Island [USA] 72-73 M 3-4
Long Island Sound 74-75 G 4
Longjing 50-51 G 1
Longling 48-49 H 7
Longmalinau 52-53 G 6
Longmire, WA 76-77 C 2
Longnan 48-49 LM 7
Longnawan 52-53 FG 6
Longonot 63 D 3
Long Point [CDN, Ontario] 74-75 CD 3
Long Point Bay 74-75 CD 3
Longqi = Zhangzhou 48-49 M 7
Longquan 48-49 M 6
Long Range Mountains 70-71 Z 7-8
Longreach 56-57 H 4
Longs Peak 72-73 E 3
Long Valley [USA, California] 76-77 D 7
Long Valley [USA, Nevada] 76-77 D 5
Longview, TX 72-73 GH 5
Longview, WA 72-73 B 2
Longxi 48-49 J 4-5
Long Xuyên 52-53 DE 4
Longyearbyen 30-31 jk 5
Longyou 48-49 M 6
Longzhen 48-49 O 2
Lonja 36-37 G 3
Lønsdal 30-31 F 4
Lons-le-Saunier 34-35 K 5
Lookout, Cape – [USA, North Carolina] 72-73 L 5
Lookout, Cape – [USA, Oregon] 76-77 A 3
Lookout Mountain 76-77 E 3
Lookout Mountains [USA, Washington] 76-77 BC 2-3
Lookout Pass 76-77 F 2
Loolmalasin 63 CD 3
Loongana 56-57 E 6
Loop Head 32 A 5
Lopatina, gora – 42-43 b 7
Lopatino = Volžsk 42-43 H 6
Lopatka, mys – 19 D 3
Lop Buri 52-53 D 4
Loperot 63 C 2
Lopez, Cap – 64-65 C 3
López Collada 76-77 FG 10
Loping = Leping 48-49 M 6
Lop Noor = Lob nuur 48-49 G 3
Lopori 64-65 F 2
Lopphavet 30-31 JK 2
Lopt'uga 38-39 J 3
Lopydino 38-39 K 3
Lōra, Hāmūn-e – 44-45 JK 5
Lora Creek 56-57 FG 5
Lora del Río 34-35 E 10
Lorain, OH 72-73 K 3
Loralai = Lorālāy 44-45 K 4
Lorālāy 44-45 K 4
Lorca 34-35 G 10
lorda Hovea, práh – 56-57 M 5-7
Lord Howe Island 56-57 LM 6
Lord Howe Islands = Ontong Java Islands 52-53 j 6
Lord Howe Rise 56-57 M 5-7
Lord Mayor Bay 70-71 ST 4
Lordsburg, NM 76-77 J 9
Lorena 78-79 KL 9
Lorengau 52-53 N 7
Lorestān 44-45 F 4
Loreto [BOL] 78-79 G 8
Loreto [BR, Maranhão] 78-79 K 6
Loreto [CO] 78-79 EF 5
Loreto [MEX, Baja California Norte] 72-73 D 6
Lorian Swamp 64-65 JK 2
Lorica 78-79 D 3
Lorı dere 46-47 HJ 2
Lorient 34-35 F 5
Loris, SC 74-75 D 7
Lorne, Firth of – 32 CD 3
Loro 78-79 F 4
Loros, Los – 80 BC 3
Lörrach 33 C 5
Lorraine 34-35 KL 4
Lorugumu 63 C 2
Los Alamos, CA 76-77 C 8
Los Alamos, NM 72-73 E 4
Los Angeles, CA 72-73 BC 5
Los Angeles Aqueduct 76-77 DE 8
Los Banos, CA 76-77 C 7
Los Gatos, CA 76-77 C 7
Lošinj 36-37 F 3
Los Molinos, CA 76-77 BC 5
Los Monjes, Islas – 78-79 EF 2
Los Roques, Islas – 78-79 F 2
Lossiemouth 32 E 3
Los Testigos, Islas – 78-79 G 2
Lost Hills, CA 76-77 D 8
Lost River Range 76-77 FG 3-4
Lost Trail Pass 76-77 G 3
Lošinj 36-37 F 3
Lot 34-35 H 6
Lota 80 B 5
Lotagipi Swamp 64-65 HJ 2
Lotaryngia 34-35 KL 4
Lothair, MT 76-77 H 1
Lotharingen 34-35 KL 4
Lotharingia 34-35 KL 4
Lothringen 34-35 KL 4
Lotmozero 30-31 NO 3
Lotrinsko 34-35 KL 4
Lotta 38-39 EF 2
Lotyšsko 30-31 K-M 9
Lötzen = Giżycko 33 KL 1
Louang Namtha 52-53 D 2
Louangphrabang 52-53 D 3
Loubnân, Jabal – = Jabal Lubnān [RL, ▲▲] 46-47 FG 5-6
Loubomo 64-65 D 3
Louchi 42-43 E 4
Loudéac 34-35 F 4
Loudonville, OH 74-75 BC 4
Louga 60-61 A 5
Lougheed Island 70-71 PQ 2
Louisa, VA 74-75 DE 5
Louisbourg 70-71 Z 8
Louisburg, NC 74-75 D 6
Louisiade, Archipel de – 52-53 h 7
Louisiade Archipelago 52-53 h 7
Louisiana 72-73 H 5
Louis Trichardt 64-65 GH 7
Louisville, GA 74-75 B 8
Louisville, KY 72-73 JK 4
Loulan = Loulanyiyi 48-49 F 3
Loulanyiyi 48-49 F 3
Loulé 34-35 C 10
Loup River 72-73 G 3
Lourdes 34-35 G 7
Lourenço Marques = Maputo 64-65 H 8
Lourenço Marques, Baia de – = Baía do Maputo 64-65 H 8
Lousia, KY 74-75 B 5
Louth 32 FG 5
Louth [AUS] 56-57 HJ 6
Louvain = Leuven 34-35 K 3
Louviers 34-35 H 4
Lovászi 33 H 5
Lovat' 38-39 F 4
Loveč 36-37 L 4
Loveč 36-37 L 4
Lovelock, NV 76-77 D 5
Lovenia, Mount – 76-77 H 5
Loviisa = Lovisa 30-31 M 7
Lovingston, VA 74-75 D 6
Lovisa 30-31 M 7
Lovl'a 38-39 JK 4
Lovozero 38-39 G 2
Lóvua 64-65 F 5
Low, Cape – 70-71 T 5
Lowa 64-65 G 3
Lowell, ID 76-77 F 2
Lowell, MA 72-73 M 3
Lowell, OR 76-77 B 4
Lower California 76-77 F 10
Lower Guinea 22-23 K 5-6
Lower Hutt 56-57 OP 8
Lower Lake 76-77 CD 5
Lower Lake, CA 76-77 B 6
Lower Lough Erne 32 BC 4
Lower Peninsula 72-73 JK 3
Lower Woolgar 56-57 H 3
Lowestoft 32 GH 5
Łowicz 33 J 2
Lowlands 32 D 4-E 3
Lowman, ID 76-77 F 3
Low Rocky Point 58 b 3
Lowville, NY 74-75 F 3
Loxton 58 E 5
Loyalton, CA 76-77 C 6
Loyang = Luoyang 48-49 L 5
Loyauté, Îles – 56-57 N 4
Lozanna = Lausanne 33 C 5
Lozère 34-35 J 6
Loznica 36-37 H 3
Lozva 38-39 M 3-4

Lu'ā'ah, Al- 46-47 L 7
Luacano 64-65 F 5
Luachimo 64-65 F 4
Luala 64-65 G 4
Lualaba 64-65 G 4
Luama 64-65 G 3
Luambe 63 C 6
Lu'an 48-49 M 5
Luanda 64-65 D 4
Luando, Rio – 64-65 E 5
Luang, Khao – [T ← Nakhon Si Thammarat] 52-53 CD 5
Luang, Thale – 52-53 D 5
Luanginga, Rio – 64-65 F 5
Luangue, Rio – 64-65 E 4
Luangwa 64-65 H 5
Luangwa Valley Game Reserve 64-65 H 5
Luanping 48-49 M 3
Luanshya 64-65 G 5
Luan Xian 48-49 M 4
Luapula 64-65 G 5
Luarca 34-35 D 7
Luatizi, Rio – 63 D 6
Luau 64-65 F 5
Lubań 33 G 3
Lubānas ezers 30-31 M 9
Lubandaye 63 B 4
Lubang Islands 52-53 G 4
Lubango 64-65 D 5
Lubbock, TX 72-73 F 5
L'ubča 38-39 E 5
L'ubča 38-39 E 5
Lübeck 33 E 2
Lubefu [ZRE, ~] 64-65 F 3
Lubefu [ZRE, ●] 64-65 F 3
Lubeka = Lübeck 33 E 2
L'ubercy 38-39 G 4
Lubero 64-65 G 3
Lubika 63 B 4
Lubilash 64-65 F 4
Lubin 33 H 3
L'ubinskij 42-43 N 6
Lublana = Ljubljana 36-37 F 3
Lublaň = Ljubljana 36-37 F 3
Lublin 33 L 3
Lubliniec 33 J 3
Lublinitz = Lubliniec 33 J 3
Lubnān, Jabal – 46-47 FG 5-6
Lubnān al-Janūbī = 3 ◁ 3 46-47 F 6
Lubnān ash-Sharqī, Jabal – 46-47 G 5-6
Lubnān ash-Shimālī = 1 ◁ 1 46-47 G 5
Lubny 38-39 F 5-6
L'ubotin 38-39 G 6
Lubudi [ZRE, ~] 64-65 FG 4
Lubudi [ZRE, ●] 64-65 G 4
Lubukklinggau 52-53 D 7
Lubuksikaping 52-53 CD 6
Lubumbashi 64-65 G 5
Lubutu 64-65 G 3
Lubwe 63 B 5
Lucania, Mount – 70-71 HJ 5
Lucas, Punta – = Cape Meredith 80 D 8
Lucca 36-37 D 4
Lucemburk = Luxembourg 34-35 KL 4
Lucembursko 34-35 KL 4
Lucena [E] 34-35 E 10
Lucena [RP] 52-53 H 4
Lučenec 33 J 4
Lucera 36-37 F 5
Lucerne Lake 76-77 E 8
Lucerne Valley, CA 76-77 E 8
Lucheringo 63 CD 6
Lu-chou = Hefei 48-49 M 5
Luchow = Lu Xian 48-49 K 6
Luchuan 48-49 KL 7
Luchwan = Luchuan 48-49 KL 7
Lucia, CA 76-77 C 7
Lucin, UT 76-77 G 5
Lucipara, Kepulauan – 52-53 J 8
Lucira 64-65 D 5
Luck 38-39 DE 5
Luckenwalde 33 F 2
Lucknow [IND] 44-45 MN 5
Lučenec 33 J 4
Lüderitz [Namibia] 64-65 DE 8
Lüderitzbaai 64-65 DE 8
Ludhiana 44-45 M 4
Ludhiyānā = Ludhiana 44-45 M 4
L'udinovo 38-39 F 5
Ludlow, CA 76-77 EF 8
Ludogorie 36-37 M 4
Ludowici, GA 74-75 C 9
Luduş 36-37 KL 2
Ludvika 30-31 F 7
Ludwigsburg 33 D 4
Ludwigshafen 33 CD 4
Ludwigslust 33 E 2
Ludza 30-31 M 9
Luebo 64-65 F 4
Luele, Rio – 64-65 F 4
Luemba 63 B 3
Luembe, Rio – 64-65 F 4
Luena 64-65 F 5
Luena, Rio – 64-65 F 5
Luena Flats 64-65 F 5
Lufeng 48-49 M 7
Lufira 64-65 G 4-5
Lufkin, TX 72-73 H 5
Lufusā 63 C 2
Luga [SU, ~] 42-43 D 6
Luga [SU, ●] 42-43 D 6
Lugano 33 D 5
Luganville 56-57 N 3
Lugard's Falls 63 D 3
Lugela 64-65 J 6
Lugenda, Rio – 64-65 J 5
Lugh Ferrandi = Luuq 60-61 N 8
Lugo [E] 34-35 D 7
Lugo [I] 36-37 D 3
Lugoj 36-37 JK 3
Luhayyah, Al- 44-45 E 7
Luhit 44-45 Q 5
Luhsien = Lu Xian 48-49 K 6
Luiana, Rio – 64-65 F 6
Luichow = Haikang 48-49 KL 7
Luik = Liège 34-35 K 3
Luilaka 64-65 F 3
Luimneach = Limerick 32 B 5
Luirojoki 30-31 M 4
Luís Correira 78-79 L 5
Luishia 64-65 G 5
Luiza 64-65 F 4
Luizjana = Louisiana 72-73 H 5
Luján [RA, Buenos Aires] 80 E 4
Lujenda = Rio Lugenda 64-65 J 5
Lujiapuzi 50-51 D 2
Lūkā 63 B 1
Lukanga 63 B 6
Lukanga Swamp 64-65 G 5
Lukašek 42-43 Z 7
Lukašek 42-43 Z 7
Lukenie 64-65 E 3
Lukenie Supérieure, Plateau de la – 64-65 F 3
Lukilā 63 C 1
Lukimwa 63 D 5
Lukolela 64-65 E 3
Lukovit 36-37 L 4
Łuków 33 L 3
Luksemburg 34-35 KL 4
Luksemburg = Luxembourg 34-35 KL 4
Lukuga 64-65 G 4
Lukuledi 63 D 5
Lukulu 63 B 6
Lukusashi 63 B 6
Lūl, Nahr – 60-61 K 7
Luleå 30-31 JK 5
Lule älv 30-31 J 4-5
Lülebargas = Lüleburgaz 46-47 B 2
Lüleburgaz 46-47 B 2
Lulonga 64-65 E 2
Lulua 64-65 F 4
Luluabourg = Kananga 64-65 F 4
Luma 63 D 6
Lumbala 64-65 F 5
Lumber River 74-75 D 7
Lumberton, NC 72-73 L 5
Lumbo 64-65 K 5-6
Lumding 44-45 P 5
Lumege = Cameia 64-65 F 5
Lumeje 64-65 F 5
Lumu 52-53 G 7
Lumut 52-53 D 5
Lün 48-49 K 2
Luna, NM 76-77 J 9
Lund 30-31 E 10
Lund, NV 76-77 F 6
Lund, UT 76-77 G 6-7
Lunda 64-65 EF 4
Lundazi [Z, ~] 63 C 6
Lundazi [Z, ●] 64-65 H 5
Lundenburg = Břeclav 33 H 4
Lundi [ZW, ~] 64-65 H 7
Lundi [ZW, ●] 64-65 H 7
Lundy 32 D 6
Lüneburg 33 E 2
Lüneburger Heide 33 DE 2
Lunenburg 70-71 Y 9
Lunéville 34-35 L 4
Lunga [Z] 64-65 G 5
Lunga Game Reserve 64-65 FG 5
Lungala N'Guimbo 64-65 EF 5
Lung-chên = Longzhen 48-49 O 2
Lung-chiang = Qiqihar 48-49 N 2
Lung-ching-ts'un = Longjing 50-51 G 1
Lung-chuan = Suichuan 48-49 L 6
Lung-hsi = Longxi 48-49 J 4-5
Lung-hua = Longhua 50-51 AB 2
Lunglē = Lungleh 44-45 P 6
Lungleh 44-45 P 6
Lungling = Longling 48-49 H 7
Lung-nan = Longnan 48-49 LM 7
Lungsi = Longxi 48-49 J 4-5
Lunguè-Bungo, Rio – 64-65 F 5
Lungyu = Longyou 48-49 M 6
Luni [IND, ~] 44-45 L 5
Luninec 38-39 E 5
Lunsemfwa 64-65 GH 5
Luntai = Buquq 48-49 E 3
Luofu 63 B 3

Luofu 195

Makat 42-43 J 8
Makedonia 36-37 JK 5
Makedonie 36-37 JK 5
Makedonija 36-37 JK 5
Makejevka 38-39 G 6
Make-jima 50-51 H 7
Makeni 60-61 B 7
Makgadikgadi Salt Pan 64-65 FG 7
Makhfir al-Ḩammân 46-47 H 5
Makhiruq, Wâdî el- = Wâdî al-Makhrûq 46-47 G 7
Makhmûr 46-47 K 5
Makhrûq, Khashm al- 46-47 J 7
Makhrûq, Wâdî al- 46-47 G 7
Makian, Pulau – 52-53 J 6
Makîlî, Al- 60-61 J 2
Makinsk 42-43 MN 7
Makinson Inlet 70-71 UV 2
M'akit 42-43 d 5
Makka = Makkah 44-45 DE 6
Makkah 44-45 DE 6
Makkaur 30-31 O 2
Mak-Klintoka, ostrov – 42-43 H-K 1
Maklakovo 42-43 R 6
Maklakovo = Lesosibirsk 42-43 R 6
Makó 33 K 5
Makoko 63 C 4
Makokou 64-65 D 2
Makoua 64-65 DE 2-3
Makounda = Markounda 60-61 H 7
Makragéfyra = Uzunköprü 46-47 B 2
Makran = Mokrân 44-45 HJ 5
Makrâna 44-45 L 5
Makrónêsos 36-37 L 7
Maks al-Baḩrî, Al- 62 CD 5
Maks al-Qiblî, Al- 60-61 L 4
Maks el-Baharî = Al-Maks al-Baḩrî 62 CD 5
Makteir = Maqtayr 60-61 BC 4
Mâkû 46-47 L 3
Mâkû Chây 46-47 L 3
Mâkû Chây 46-47 L 3
Mâkû Chây 46-47 L 3
Makumbako 63 C 5
Makumbi 64-65 EF 4
Makurazaki 50-51 GH 7
Makurdi 60-61 F 7
Makuyuni 63 D 3
Mala = Malaita 52-53 k 6
Malabar, Côte de – = Malabar Coast 44-45 L 8-M 9
Malabar Coast 44-45 L 8-M 9
Malabarküste = Malabar Coast 44-45 L 8-M 9
Malabár-part = Malabar Coast 44-45 L 8-M 9
Malabarské pobřeží = Malabar Coast 44-45 L 8-M 9
Malabarskie, Wybrzeże – = Malabar Coast 44-45 L 8-M 9
Malabo 60-61 F 8
Malacca = Malaiische Halbinsel 52-53 C 5-D 6
Malacca, Détroit de – 52-53 CD 6
Malacca, Estrecho de – 52-53 CD 6
Malacca, Peninsule de – 52-53 C 5-D 6
Malacca, Strait of – 52-53 CD 6
Malacký průliv 52-53 C 5-D 6
Malad City, ID 76-77 G 4
Maladeta 34-35 H 7
Málaga 34-35 E 10
Málaga [CO] 78-79 E 3
Malagarasi [EAT, ~] 64-65 H 3
Malagarasi [EAT, ●] 63 B 4
Malaiische Halbinsel 52-53 C 5-D 6
Malaiischer Archipel 22-23 O 5-Q 6
Malaija = Melayu 52-53 D 6
Malaita 52-53 k 6
Malaja In'a 42-43 c 5
Malaja Ob' 42-43 M 5-L 4
Malaja Višera 42-43 E 6
Malaja Višera 42-43 E 6
Maláj-félsziget 52-53 C 5-D 6
Malajsie 52-53 D-F 6
Malajski, Półwysep – 52-53 C 5-D 6
Malajský poloostrov 52-53 C 5-D 6
Malajzia 52-53 D-F 6
Malakâl 60-61 L 7
Mâlâkanḍ 44-45 L 4
Malaka-szoros 52-53 C 5-D 6
Malakka 52-53 C 5-D 6
Malakka, Cieśnina – 52-53 C 5-D 6
Malakka, Straat – 52-53 CD 6
Malakkastraße 52-53 C 5-D 6
Mala Krsna 36-37 J 3
Malalaling 64-65 F 8
Malang 52-53 F 8
Malange 64-65 E 4
Malangen 30-31 H 3
Mälaren 30-31 G 8
Malargüe 80 C 5
Malartic 70-71 V 8
Malasia 52-53 D-F 6
Malaspina 80 C 6-7
Malaspina Glacier 70-71 H 5-6
Malatia = Malatya 44-45 D 3
Malatya 44-45 D 3
Malatya Dağları 46-47 G 4-H 3
Malâvî 46-47 MN 6
Malavi = Malawi 64-65 HJ 5
Malawi 64-65 HJ 5
Malawi, Lake – 64-65 H 5
Malayagiri 44-45 O 6
Malayalam Coast = Malabar Coast 44-45 L 8-M 9
Malaya Parvata = Eastern Ghats 44-45 M 8-N 7
Malay Archipelago 22-23 O 5-Q 6
Malâyer 44-45 F 4
Malâyer, Rûdkhâneh-ye – 46-47 N 5
Malay Peninsula 52-53 C 5-D 6
Malaysia 52-53 D-F 6
Malayu = Melayu 52-53 D 6
Malazgirt 46-47 K 3
Malbon 56-57 H 4
Malbooma 58 AB 3
Malbork 33 J 1-2
Malcèsine 36-37 D 3
Malden, MA 74-75 H 3
Maldivas 22-23 N 5
Maldive Islands 22-23 N 5
Maldives 22-23 N 5
Maldonado [ROU, ●] 80 F 4
Maldonado, Punta – 72-73 FG 8
Male 20-21 N 5
Malé Antily 72-73 N 9-O 8
Maléas, Akrōtérion – 36-37 K 7
Malebo, Pool – 64-65 E 3
Malediven 22-23 N 5
Mâlêgânv = Malegaon 44-45 LM 6
Mâlegaon = Malegaon 44-45 LM 6
Maleise Archipel 22-23 O 5-Q 6
Maleisië 52-53 D-F 6
Male Karpaty 33 H 4
Malek Kandî 46-47 M 4
Malekula 56-57 N 3
Malela 64-65 G 3
Malema 64-65 J 5
Malen'ga 38-39 G 3
Malé Otroči jezero = Lesser Slave Lake 70-71 NO 6
Malé Sundy 52-53 GH 8
Malezja 52-53 D-F 6
Malghîr, Shaṭṭ – 60-61 F 2
Malgrat 34-35 J 8
Malḩah 46-47 K 5
Malheur Lake 76-77 D 4
Malheur River 76-77 E 4
Mali [RMM] 60-61 C 6-D 5
Malije Derbety 38-39 HJ 6
Malik, Qûr al- 62 BC 5
Malik, Wâdî al- 60-61 KL 5
Malıköy 46-47 E 3
Mali Kyûn 52-53 C 4
Malimba, Monts – 63 B 4
Malin 38-39 E 5
Malin, OR 76-77 C 4
Malinau = Longmalinau 52-53 G 6
Malindi 64-65 K 3
Malines = Mechelen 34-35 K 3
Malin Head 32 C 4
Malinyi 63 CD 5
Malipo 48-49 J 7
Malita 52-53 HJ 5
Malkara 46-47 B 2
Małkinia Górna 33 L 2
Mallacoota Inlet 58 JK 6
Mallaig 32 D 3
Mallakastër 36-37 HJ 5
Mallapunyah 56-57 G 3
Mallawî 62 D 4
Mallès Venosta 36-37 D 2
Mallicolo = Malekula 56-57 N 3
Mallît 60-61 K 6
Mallorca 34-35 J 9
Mallow 32 B 5
Malmberget 30-31 J 4
Malmedy 34-35 L 3
Malmesbury [ZA] 64-65 E 9
Malmö 30-31 E 10
Malmöhus 30-31 E 9-10
Malmyž 38-39 JK 4
Malmyž 38-39 JK 4
Maloca 78-79 H 4
Malojaroslavec 38-39 FG 4
Maloje Karmakuly 42-43 HJ 3
Malole 63 B 5
Malombe, Lake – 64-65 J 5
Malone, NY 74-75 F 2
Malonga 64-65 F 5
Malouines, Îles – = Falkland Islands 80 DE 8
Malovata 36-37 N 2
Måløy 30-31 A 7
Malpelo, Isla – 78-79 C 4
Málta 36-37 ab 2
Malta 36-37 EF 8
Málta 36-37 EF 8
Malta, ID 76-77 G 4
Maltahöhe 64-65 E 7
Malte 36-37 EF 8
Maltepe = Manyas 46-47 B 2
Malu 52-53 k 6
Maluku = 22 ◁ 52-53 J 7
Maluku-szigetek 52-53 J 6-8
Maluku-tenger 52-53 HJ 7
Ma'lûlâ 46-47 G 6
Malumba 64-65 G 3
Malumteken 52-53 h 5
Malung 30-31 E 7
Malût 60-61 L 6
Malvan 44-45 L 7
Malvinas = Falkland Islands 80 DE 8
Malviny = Falkland Islands 80 DE 8
Malwa 44-45 M 6
Malwinas, Islas – = Falkland Island 80 DE 8
Malwinen = Falkland Islands 80 DE 8
Malwiny = Falkland Islands 80 DE 8
Malya 63 C 3
Malý Atlas 60-61 D 2-E 1
Malyj Jenisej 42-43 RS 7
Malyj Kavkaz 38-39 HJ 7
Malyj L'achovskij, ostrov – 42-43 bc 3
Malyj Nimnyr 42-43 Y 6
Malyj Tajmyr, ostrov – 42-43 UV 2
Malyj Uzen' 38-39 J 6
Małe Antyle 72-73 N 9-O 8
Małe Jezioro Niewolnicze 70-71 NO 6
Małe Sundajskie, Wyspy – 52-53 GH 8
Małkinia Górna 33 L 2
Mały Nefud = Ad-Dahnâ 44-45 E 5-F 6
Mama 42-43 V 6
Mamahatun = Tercan 46-47 J 3
Mamasa 52-53 G 7
Mambasa 64-65 G 2
Mamberamo, Sungai – 52-53 L 7
Mambere = Carnot 60-61 H 8
Mambirima Falls 63 B 6
Mambone = Nova Mambone 64-65 J 7
Mamfe 60-61 F 7
Mâmî, Râ's – 44-45 GH 8
Màmmola 36-37 G 6
Mammoth, AZ 76-77 H 9
Mammoth Hot Springs, WY 76-77 H 3
Mamonovo 33 JK 1
Mamoré, Rio – 78-79 FG 7-8
Mamou 60-61 B 6
Mampawah 52-53 E 6
Mampi = Sepopa 64-65 F 6
Mampong 60-61 D 7
Mamry, Jezioro – 33 K 1
Mamuju 52-53 G 7
Man [CI] 60-61 C 7
Man, Isle of – 32 DE 4
Mana 78-79 J 3
Manaas 48-49 F 3
Manacapuru 78-79 G 5
Manacor 34-35 J 9
Manado 52-53 H 6
Managua 72-73 J 9
Managua, Lago de – 72-73 J 9
Manakara 64-65 L 7
Manâmah, Al- 44-45 G 5
Manambaho 64-65 KL 6
Manambolo 64-65 K 6
Manam Island 52-53 N 7
Manamo, Caño – 78-79 G 3
Manamo, Caño – 78-79 G 3
Mananara [RM, ~] 64-65 L 7
Mananara [RM, ●] 64-65 L 6
Mananjary 64-65 L 7
Manantenina 64-65 L 7
Manantiales 80 BC 8
Manapouri, Lake – 56-57 N 9
Manâqil, Al- 60-61 L 6
Manâr, Jabal al- 44-45 EF 8
Manârský záliv = Gulf of Mannar 44-45 M 9
Manas, gora – 42-43 N 9
Mânasârovar = Mapham Tsho 48-49 E 5
Manâșif, Al- 46-47 J 5
Manasquan, NY 74-75 FG 4
Manaus 78-79 H 5
Man'aung Kyûn 52-53 B 3
Manavgat 46-47 D 4
Manbij 46-47 G 4
Mancha, La – 34-35 F 9
Manchan 48-49 G 2
Manche 32 E 7-F 6
Manche, La – 32 E 7-F 6
Manche, La- 32 E 7-F 6
Manchester [GB] 32 EF 5
Manchester, CT 74-75 G 4
Manchester, NH 72-73 MN 3
Manchester, VT 74-75 G 3
Manchouli = Manzhouli 48-49 M 2
Manchuria = Manzhou 48-49 N-P 2
Máncora 78-79 C 5
Máncora = Puerto Máncora 78-79 C 5
Mancos, CO 76-77 J 7
Mancha, Canal de la – 32 E 7-F 6
Manchuria 48-49 N-P 2
Mand, Rûd-e – = Rûd-e Mond 44-45 G 5
Manda [EAT, Iringa] 64-65 HJ 5
Manda [EAT, Mbeya] 63 C 4
Mandab, Bâb al- 44-45 E 8
Mandabe 64-65 K 7
Mandal 30-31 B 8-9
Mandal [MVR] 48-49 K 2
Mandalay = Mandale 52-53 C 2
Mandale 52-53 C 2
Mandalgov' 48-49 JK 2
Mandalî 46-47 L 6
Mandal Ovoo 48-49 JK 3
Mandalya Körfezi 46-47 B 4
Mandalyat = Selimiye 46-47 B 4
Mandaon 52-53 H 4
Mandar 52-53 G 7
Mandar, Teluk – 52-53 G 7
Mandara, Monts – 60-61 G 6-7
Màndas 36-37 C 6
Mandasor 44-45 LM 6
Mândavî = Mandvi 44-45 K 6
Mandchourie 48-49 N-P 2
Mandeb, Bab al- = Bâb al-Mandab 44-45 E 8
Mandeb, Bab el – = Bâb al-Mandab 44-45 E 8
Mandi 44-45 M 4
Mandidzudzure 64-65 H 6-7
Mandimba 64-65 J 5
Mandingues, Monts – 60-61 C 6
Mandioli, Pulau – 52-53 J 7
Mandla 44-45 N 6
Mandria 46-47 E 5
Mandritsara 64-65 L 6
Manḍsaor = Mandsaur 44-45 LM 6
Mandsaur 44-45 LM 6
Mandschurei 48-49 N-P 2
Mandui = Mândvi 44-45 K 6
Mandurah 56-57 BC 6
Mandùria 36-37 G 5
Mandvi [IND, Gujarat ↙ Bhuj] 44-45 K 6
Mandžusko 48-49 N-P 2
Mandżuria 48-49 N-P 2
Mandzsu-medence 48-49 N-P 2
Mânesht, Kûh-e – 46-47 M 6
Manfalûṭ 62 D 4
Manfredònia 36-37 FG 5
Manfredònia, Golfo di – 36-37 FG 5
Manga [BR] 78-79 L 7
Manga [RN] 60-61 G 6
Mangabeiras, Chapada das – 78-79 K 6-L 7
Mangabeiras, Chapada das – 78-79 K 6-L 7
Mangabeiras, Chapada das – 78-79 K 6-L 7
Mangai 64-65 E 3
Mangalia 36-37 N 4
Mangalmé 60-61 HJ 6
Mangalore 44-45 L 8
Mangaḷūru = Mangalore 44-45 L 8
Mangas, NM 76-77 J 8
Manggar 52-53 E 7
Manggyŏng-dong 50-51 GH 1
Mangi 64-65 G 2
Mangkalihat, Tanjung – 52-53 GH 6
Manglares, Cabo – 78-79 CD 4
Mango 60-61 E 6
Mangoche 64-65 J 5
Mangoky 64-65 K 7
Mangole, Pulau – 52-53 J 7
Mangoli = Pulau Mangole 52-53 J 7
Mangrove, Punta – 72-73 F 8
Mangueigne 60-61 J 6
Mangueira, Lagoa – 80 F 4
Mangueni, Plateau de – 60-61 G 4
Mangui 48-49 O 1
Manguinho, Ponta do – 78-79 M 7
Mangyai 48-49 G 4
Mangyšlak, plato – 44-45 G 2
Mangyšlakskij zaliv 38-39 J 6-K 7
Mangyšlak, plato – 44-45 G 2
Mangyšlakskij zaliv 38-39 J 6-K 7
Manhattan, KS 72-73 G 4
Manhattan, MT 76-77 H 3
Manhattan, NV 76-77 E 6
Manhattan Beach, CA 76-77 D 9
Manhuaçu 78-79 L 9
Mani [CO] 78-79 E 4
Mani [TJ] 48-49 F 5
Mânî', Wâdî al- 46-47 J 5-6
Mania 64-65 L 7
Maniamba 64-65 HJ 5
Manica [Moçambique, ●] 64-65 H 6
Manica [Moçambique, ☆] 64-65 H 6-7
Manicaland 64-65 H 6
Manicoré 78-79 G 6
Manicouagan, Rivière – 70-71 X 7-8
Maniema 63 AB 4
Manika, Plateau de la – 64-65 G 4-5
Manila 52-53 H 3-4
Manila, UT 76-77 HJ 5
Manila Bay 52-53 GH 4
Manilla 58 K 3
Manipur [IND, ☆] 44-45 P 5-6
Manipur = Imphal 44-45 P 6
Manisa 44-45 B 3
Manislee River 74-75 A 2
Manitoba 70-71 Q-S 6
Manitoba, Lake – 70-71 R 7
Manitoulin Island 70-71 U 8
Manitouwadge 70-71 T 8
Manitowoc, WI 72-73 J 3
Manîtsoq 70-71 Za 4
Maniwaki 70-71 V 8
Manizales 78-79 D 3
Manja 64-65 K 7
Manjacaze 64-65 H 7-8
Manjîl 46-47 N 4
Manjimup 56-57 C 6
Manjra 44-45 M 7
Mankato, MN 72-73 H 3
Mankono 60-61 C 7
Mankoya 64-65 F 5
Manna 52-53 D 7
Mannahill 58 DE 4
Mannar, Golfe de – 44-45 M 9
Mannar, Golf von – = Gulf of Mannar 44-45 M 9
Mannar, Gulf of – 44-45 M 9
Mannar, Zatoka – = Gulf of Mannar 44-45 M 9
Mannari-öböl = Gulf of Mannar 44-45 M 9
Mannâr Khârî = Gulf of Mannar 44-45 M 9
Mannheim 33 D 4
Manning, SC 74-75 CD 8
Mannington, WV 74-75 C 5
Man'niyah, Al- = Al-Ma'anîyah 44-45 E 4
Manokwari 52-53 K 7
Manombo 64-65 K 7
Manono 64-65 G 4
Manp'ojin 50-51 F 2
Manqalah 60-61 L 7
Manresa 34-35 HJ 8
Mans, le – 34-35 H 4-5
Mansa [ZRE] 64-65 G 5
Mansalar = Pulau Mursala 52-53 C 6
Mansaya = Masaya 72-73 J 9
Mansel Island 70-71 U 5
Manseriche, Pongo de – 78-79 D 5
Mansfield [AUS] 58 H 6
Mansfield [GB] 32 F 5
Mansfield, OH 72-73 K 3
Mansfield, PA 74-75 E 4
Mansfield, WA 76-77 D 2
Manso, Rio – 78-79 J 7-8
Manșûrâbâd = Mehrân 46-47 M 6
Manșûrah, Al- [ET] 60-61 L 2
Manșûrîyah, Al- 46-47 L 5
Manta 78-79 C 5
Manta, Bahia de – 78-79 C 5
Mantalingajan, Mount – 52-53 G 5
Mantaro, Rio – 78-79 E 7
Manteca, CA 76-77 C 7
Manteco, El – 78-79 G 3
Manteo, NC 74-75 F 7
Mantes-la-Jolie 34-35 H 4
Manti, UT 76-77 H 6
Mantiqueira, Serra da – 78-79 KL 9
Mantoue = Mantova 36-37 D 3
Mantova 36-37 D 3
Mantsjoerije 48-49 N-P 2
Mänttä 30-31 L 6
Mantua = Mantova 36-37 D 3
Mantung 58 E 5
Manturovo 38-39 HJ 4
Mäntyharju 30-31 M 7
Mäntyluoto 30-31 J 7
Mantzikert = Malazgirt 46-47 K 3
Manû 78-79 E 7
Manuelito, NM 76-77 J 8
Manuelzinho 78-79 HJ 6
Manuk, Pulau – 52-53 K 8
Mânûk, Tall – 46-47 H 6
Manukau 56-57 OP 7
Manukau Harbour 56-57 O 7
Manus 52-53 N 7
Manyara, Lake – 64-65 J 3
Manyas 46-47 B 2
Manyč 38-39 H 6
Manyč 38-39 H 6
Manyonga 63 C 3-4
Manyoni 64-65 H 4
Manzanares [E, ~] 34-35 F 8
Manzanares [E, ●] 34-35 F 9
Manzanillo [C] 72-73 L 7
Manzanillo [MEX] 72-73 EF 8
Manzanillo, Punta – 72-73 L 9-10
Manzanza 63 B 4
Manzay 44-45 KL 4
Manzhouli 48-49 M 2
Manzikert = Malazgirt 46-47 K 3
Manzilah, Al- 62 DE 2
Manzilah, Buḩayrat al- 62 DE 2
Manzini 64-65 H 8
Manzovka = Sibircevo 42-43 Z 9
Mao [Tschad] 60-61 H 6
Maoka = Cholmsk 42-43 b 8
Maoke, Pegunungan – 52-53 LM 7
Maoming 48-49 L 7
Mapaga 52-53 G 7
Mapai 64-65 H 7
Mapare 64-65 NO 6
Mapham Tsho 48-49 E 5
Mapham Yumtsho = Mapham Tsho 48-49 E 5
Mapi 52-53 L 8
Mapia, Kepulauan – 52-53 KL 6
Mapichi, Serrania de – 78-79 F 3-4
Mapimi, Bolsón de – 72-73 F 6
Ma-p'ing = Liuzhou 48-49 K 7
Mapinhane 64-65 HJ 7
Mapire 78-79 G 3
Mapiripan, Salto – 78-79 E 4
Mapleton, OR 76-77 AB 3
Mapoon Aboriginal Reserve 56-57 H 2
Mappi = Mapi 52-53 L 8
Maprik 52-53 M 7
Mapuera, Rio – 78-79 H 5
Mapula 63 D 6
Maputo [Moçambique, ●] 64-65 H 8
Maputo, Baía do – 64-65 H 8
Ma'qalâ' 44-45 F 5
Ma'qil, Al- 46-47 M 7
Maqinchao 80 C 6
Maqnâ 62 F 3
Maqtayr 60-61 BC 4
Maquan He = Tsangpo 48-49 EF 6
Maquela do Zombo 64-65 DE 4
Maqueze 64-65 H 7
Maqwa', Al- 46-47 M 8
Mar, Serra do – 80 G 2-3
Mara [EAT, ~] 64-65 H 3
Mara [EAT, ●] 63 C 3
Mara [EAT, ☆] 64-65 HJ 3
Maraã 78-79 F 5
Marabá 78-79 K 6
Marabitanas 78-79 F 4
Maracá, Ilha – 78-79 G 4
Maracá, Ilha de – 78-79 JK 4
Maracaibo 78-79 E 2
Maracaibo, Lago de – 78-79 E 2-3
Maracaju 78-79 H 9
Maracaju, Serra de – 78-79 H 9-J 8
Maracanã [BR, Pará] 78-79 K 5
Maracay 78-79 F 2
Marâdah 60-61 H 3
Maradi 60-61 F 6
Mar Adriático 36-37 E 3-H 5
Ma'rafây, Jabal – 62 F 6
Mara Game Reserve 64-65 HJ 3
Marâghah, Al- 62 D 4
Marâgheh 44-45 F 3
Marahuaca, Cerro – 78-79 FG 4
Marajó, Baia de – 78-79 K 4-5
Marajó, Ilha de – 78-79 JK 5
Marâkand 46-47 L 3
Maralal 64-65 J 2
Maral Bashi 48-49 D 3-4
Maralinga 56-57 F 6
Mar Amarillo 48-49 N 4
Maramasike 52-53 k 6
Maramba = Livingstone 64-65 G 6
Marambaia, Restinga da – 78-79 L 9
Marampa 60-61 B 7
Maran [MAL] 52-53 D 6
Mârân = Mohâjerân 46-47 N 5
Marana, AZ 76-77 H 9
Maranboy 56-57 F 2
Marand 46-47 L 3
Marandellas = Marondera 64-65 H 6
Maranguape 78-79 M 5
Maranhão 78-79 KL 5-6
Maranoa River 56-57 J 5
Marañón, Rio – 78-79 DE 5
Marañón, Rio – 78-79 DE 5
Mar Arábigo 44-45 JK 7
Mar Argentino 80 D 7-E 5
Maraş = Kahramanmaraş 44-45 D 3
Maraşalçakmak = Ovacıg 46-47 H 3
Mărășești 36-37 M 3
Maratha = Maharashtra [IND, ≅] 44-45 M 7
Maratha = Maharashtra [IND, ☆] 44-45 L 7-M 6
Marathón 36-37 KL 6
Marathon [CDN] 70-71 T 8
Marathon, FL 74-75 c 4
Maratua, Pulau – 52-53 G 6
Marau [RI] 52-53 F 7
Marauni 52-53 k 7
Maraviě = Morava 33 G-J 4
Marawî 60-61 L 5
Mar'ayt 44-45 G 7
Mar Báltico 30-31 G 10-J 8
Marbella 34-35 E 10
Mar Blanco 42-43 FG 4
Marble Bar 56-57 CD 4
Marble Canyon, AZ 76-77 H 7
Marble Gorge 76-77 H 7
Marble Hall 64-65 G 8
Marburg 33 D 3
Marburg = Maribor 36-37 F 2
Marcali 33 H 5
Marcaria 36-37 D 3
Marcas = Marche 36-37 E 4

Marca 197

Mar Caspio 44-45 F 2-G 3
Marcelino 78-79 F 5
Marcellus, WA 76-77 D 2
Marcha [SU, ~] 42-43 W 5
Marcha [SU, ●] 42-43 X 5
Marche 34-35 HJ 5
Marche 36-37 E 4
Marchena 34-35 E 10
Marchena, Isla – 78-79 AB 4
Marches = Marche 36-37 E 4
Mar Chiquita, Laguna – 80 D 4
Marcoule 34-35 K 6
Marcus Baker, Mount – 70-71 G 5
Marcus-Necker, Dorsal de – 22-23 R 4-T 5
Marcus Necker, Dorsale de – 22-23 R 4-T 5
Marcus Necker Ridge 22-23 R 4-T 5
Marcus-Necker-Rücken 22-23 R 4-T 5
Marcus Neckerrug 22-23 R 4-T 5
Marcy, Mount – 74-75 FG 2-3
Mar Chiquita, Laguna – 80 D 4
Mardân 44-45 L 4
Mar del Norte 32 F-J 3
Mar del Plata 80 E 5
Mardin 44-45 E 3
Mardin Dağları 46-47 J 4
Maré, Île – 56-57 N 4
Mare, Muntele – 36-37 K 2
Marebe = Mā'rib 44-45 F 7
Maree, Loch – 32 D 3
Mareeba 56-57 HJ 3
Mareeg = Mereeg 60-61 b 3
Mar Egeo 36-37 L 5-M 7
Maremma 36-37 D 4
Maréna 60-61 B 6
Marengo, WA 76-77 DE 2
Marengo = Ḥajut 60-61 E 1
Marèttimo 36-37 DE 7
Marfa', Al- = Al-Maghayrā' 44-45 G 6
Marfil, Costa de – [≅] 60-61 CD 8
Margarita 80 D 3
Margarita, Isla de – 78-79 G 2
Margeride, Monts de la – 34-35 J 6
Margherita 63 B 2
Margherita = Jamaame 64-65 K 2
Margherita, Lake – = Abaya 60-61 M 7
Margilan 44-45 L 2
Mārgo, Dasht-i – 44-45 J 4
Margoh, Dasht-e – = Dasht-e Marg 44-45 J 4
Marguerite, Baie – 24 C 29-30
Mar Chiquita, Laguna – 80 D 4
Mari, Autonome Republik der – = 3 ◁ 42-43 H 6
Mari, República Autónoma de los – = 3 ◁ 42-43 H 6
Maria Chiquita 72-73 b 2
María Chiquita 72-73 b 2
María Elena 80 BC 2
María Enrique, Altos de – 72-73 bc 2
Maria Chiquita 72-73 b 2
Maria Island [AUS, Northern Territory] 56-57 G 2
Maria Island [AUS, Tasmania] 56-57 J 8
Mariakani 63 D 3
María Madre, Isla – 72-73 E 7
María Magdalena, Isla – 72-73 E 7
Mariana Basin 22-23 R 5
Marianao 72-73 K 7
Marianas, Cuenca de las – 22-23 R 5
Marianas, Fosa de las – 22-23 R 5
Mariana Trench 22-23 R 5
Marianenbecken 22-23 R 5
Marianenbekken 22-23 R 5
Marianengraben 22-23 R 5
Marianentrog 22-23 R 5
Mariannes, Bassin des – 22-23 R 5
Mariannes, Fosse des – 22-23 R 5
Mariano Machado = Ganda 64-65 D 5
Mariánské Lázně 33 F 4
Marías, Islas – 72-73 E 7
Marias Pass 72-73 D 2
Marias River 76-77 H 1
Mari Autonome Republiek = 3 ◁ 42-43 H 6
Mari Autonóm Köztársaság 42-43 H 6
Mari Autonomous Republic = 3 ◁ 42-43 H 6
Maria van Diemen, Cape – 56-57 O 6
Mariazell 33 G 5
Mā'rib 44-45 F 7
Maribor 36-37 F 2
Marica [BG, ~] 36-37 L 4
Marica [BG, ●] 36-37 LM 4
Maricopa, AZ 76-77 G 9
Maricopa, CA 76-77 D 8
Maricopa Indian Reservation 76-77 G 9
Maricourt 70-71 W 5
Marīdī 60-61 KL 8
Mariê, Rio – 78-79 F 5
Marie-Galante 72-73 OP 8
Mariehamn 30-31 HJ 7
Marie Louise Island 64-65 MN 4
Marienburg = Feldioara 36-37 L 3
Marienburg (Westpreußen) = Malbork 33 J 1-2
Mariental 64-65 E 7
Marienwerder = Kwidzyn 33 J 2
Mariestad 30-31 E 8
Marietta, GA 72-73 K 5
Marietta, OH 74-75 C 5
Mariinsk 42-43 Q 6
Marii Prončiščevoj, buchta – 42-43 VW 2
Marii Prončiščevoj, buchta – 42-43 VW 2
Mariis, République Autonome des – = 3 ◁ 42-43 H 6
Marijská autonomní republika 42-43 H 6
Marijskaja Avtonomnaja Sovetskaja Socialističeskaja Respublika = Autonome Republik der Mari = 3 ◁ 42-43 H 6
Marília 78-79 JK 9
Marina, Île – = Santo 56-57 MN 3
Marina di Gioiosa Iònica 36-37 G 6
Marinduque Island 52-53 H 4
Marinette, WI 72-73 J 2
Maringa [ZRE] 64-65 F 2
Mar Interior = Seto-naikai 48-49 P 5
Marion 24 E 4
Marion, MT 76-77 F 1
Marion, NC 74-75 BC 7
Marion, SC 74-75 D 7
Marion, VA 74-75 C 6
Marion, Lake – 74-75 C 8
Marion Island 24 E 4
Maripa 78-79 FG 3
Maripasoula 78-79 J 4
Mariposa, CA 76-77 D 7
Marīr, Jazīrat – 62 FG 6
Mariscal Estigarribia 80 D 2
Marismas, Las – 34-35 D 10
Marīwān 46-47 M 5
Mārīyah, Al- 44-45 G 6
Marj, Al- 60-61 J 2
Marjaayoûn = Marj'uyūn 46-47 F 6
Märjamaa 30-31 L 8
Marjan = Wāza Khwā 44-45 K 4
Marjevka 42-43 M 7
Mar Jónico 36-37 GH 7
Marj'uyūn 46-47 F 6
Marka [SP] 60-61 NO 8
Markādā' 46-47 J 5
Markazī 44-45 E 3-F 4
Markdale 74-75 C 2
Marken = Marche 36-37 E 4
Markham 74-75 D 3
Markham, WA 76-77 AB 2
Markham, Mount – 24 A 15-16
Markkēri = Mercara 44-45 M 8
Markleeville, CA 76-77 CD 6
Markounda 60-61 H 7
Markovo [SU, Čukotskaja AO] 42-43 gh 5
Marktredwitz 33 EF 3-4
Marlborough [AUS] 56-57 JK 4
Marlinton, WV 74-75 CD 5
Marlo 58 J 6
Marmagab 44-45 L 7
Marmande 34-35 H 6
Marmara Adası 44-45 B 2
Marmara Denizi 44-45 B 2
Marmarâs = Marmaris 46-47 C 4
Marmarica = Barqat al-Baḥrīyah 60-61 JK 2
Marmaris 46-47 C 4
Mar Mediterraneo 28-29 J 8-O 9
Marmelos, Rio dos – 78-79 G 6
Mar Menor 34-35 G 10
Marmet, WV 74-75 C 5
Marmolada 36-37 DE 2
Mar Muerto = Baḥr al-Mayyit 44-45 D 4
Marne 34-35 JK 4
Marne au Rhin, Canal de la – 34-35 K 4
Maroantsétra 64-65 LM 6
Maroc 60-61 C 3-D 2
Marokkó 60-61 C 3-D 2
Marokko 60-61 C 3-D 2
Maroko 60-61 C 3-D 2
Marondera 64-65 H 6
Maroni 78-79 J 3-4
Maroona 58 F 6
Maros [RI] 52-53 GH 7-8
Marosvasarhely = Tîrgu Mureş 36-37 L 2
Maroua 60-61 G 6
Marovoay 64-65 L 6
Marowijne [SME, ~] 78-79 J 3-4
Marqat Bazar 48-49 D 4
Marquesas Keys 74-75 b 4
Marquette, MI 72-73 J 2
Marrah, Jabal – 60-61 JK 6
Marrâkech = Marrākush 60-61 C 2
Marrākush 60-61 C 2
Marrawah 56-57 H 8
Marree 56-57 G 5
Mar Rojo 44-45 D 5-7
Marromeu 64-65 J 6
Marruecos 60-61 C 3-D 2
Marrupa 64-65 J 5
Marsá 'Alam 62 F 5
Marsá al-Burayqah 60-61 HJ 2
Marsabit 64-65 J 2
Marsabit Game Reserve 63 D 2
Marsala 36-37 E 7
Marsá Sha'b 60-61 M 4
Marsa Sūsa = Sūsah 60-61 J 2
Marseille 34-35 K 7
Marsfjället 30-31 F 5
Marshall, NC 74-75 B 7
Marshall, TX 72-73 H 5
Marshall, Fosse des – 22-23 S 5
Marshall, Îles – 22-23 S 5
Marshall, Mount – 74-75 D 5
Marshallgraben 22-23 S 5
Marshallinseln 22-23 S 5
Marshall Trench 22-23 S 5
Marshalltrog 22-23 S 5
Marshall, Fosa de las – 22-23 S 5
Marshfield = Coos Bay, OR 72-73 AB 3
Mars Hill, ME 74-75 JK 1
Marsing, ID 76-77 E 4
Marstrand 30-31 D 9
Marsylia = Marseille 34-35 K 7
Martaban = Mōktama 52-53 C 3
Martensøya 30-31 l 4
Marthaguy Creek 58 H 3
Martha's Vineyard 72-73 MN 3
Martigny 33 C 5
Martigues 34-35 K 7
Martim Vaz, Ilhas – 78-79 O 9
Martin 33 J 4
Martinik = Martinique 72-73 OP 9
Martinique 72-73 OP 9
Martin Peninsula 24 B 25-26
Martin Point 70-71 H 3
Martinsburg, WV 74-75 DE 5
Martinsdale, MT 76-77 H 2
Martins Ferry, OH 74-75 C 4
Martinsville, VA 74-75 D 6
Mar Tirreno 36-37 D-F 6
Marton [NZ] 56-57 OP 8
Martos 34-35 EF 10
Martre, Lac la – 70-71 MN 5
Martuk 42-43 K 7
Martwe, Morze – = Baḥr al-Mayyit 44-45 D 4
Marua = Maroua 60-61 G 6
Marugame 50-51 J 5
Marui 52-53 M 7
Maruim 78-79 M 7
Marungu 64-65 GH 4
Marvão 34-35 D 9
Mārvāṛ = Marwar [IND, ≅] 44-45 L 5
Mārvāṛ = Marwar [IND, ●] 44-45 L 5
Marvine, Mount – 76-77 H 6
Marwar [IND, ≅] 44-45 L 5
Marwar [IND, ●] 44-45 L 5
Marx 38-39 J 5
Mary 44-45 J 3
Maryborough [AUS, Queensland] 56-57 K 5
Maryborough [AUS, Victoria] 56-57 HJ 7
Maryjska Autonomiczna Republika 42-43 H 6
Mary Kathleen 56-57 GH 4
Maryland [USA] 72-73 L 4
Mary Rvier 56-57 F 2
Marysvale, UT 76-77 GH 6
Marysville, WA 76-77 BC 1
Maryūt, Buḥayrat – 62 CD 2
Maryvale 56-57 HJ 3
Maryville, CA 76-77 C 6
Marzo, Cabo – 78-79 D 3
Marzu, Kūh-e – 46-47 M 6
Marzūq 60-61 G 3
Marzūq, Ṣaḥrā' – 60-61 G 3-4
Masai Mara Game Reserve 63 C 3
Masai Steppe 64-65 J 3
Masaka 64-65 H 3
Masalembu Besar, Pulau – 52-53 FG 8
Masampo = Masan 48-49 O 4-5
Masan 48-49 O 4-5
Masandam, Rā's – 44-45 H 5
Maṣarah, Al- 62 C 5
Masardis, ME 74-75 J 1
Masasi 64-65 J 5
Masavi 78-79 G 8
Masaya 72-73 J 9
Masbat = Masbate 52-53 H 4
Masbate 52-53 H 4
Mascara = Mū'askar 60-61 E 1
Mascareignes, Bassin des – 22-23 M 6
Mascarene Basin 22-23 M 6
Mascarene Islands 64-65 M 7-O 6
Mascarene Plateau 22-23 MN 6
Mascareñas, Cuenca de las – 22-23 M 6
Mascareñas, Dorsal de las – 22-23 MN 6
Mascate = Masqaṭ 44-45 H 6
Maserti = Ömerli 46-47 J 4
Maseru 64-65 G 8
Mashala 64-65 F 3-4
Mashash, Bīr – = Bi'r Mushāsh 46-47 G 7
Mashhad 44-45 HJ 3
Mashike 50-51 b 2
Māshkel, Hāmūn-i – 44-45 J 5
Mashonaland North 64-65 GH 6
Mashonaland South 64-65 GH 6
Mashrā' ar-Raqq 60-61 K 7
Mashraqī Bangāl 44-45 O 5-P 6
Mashrūkah, Qārat al- 62 C 2
Mashū-ko 50-51 d 2
Mašigina, guba – 42-43 HJ 3
Masīlah, Wādī al- 44-45 F 7
Masi-Manimba 64-65 E 3
Masin 52-53 L 8
Masindi 64-65 H 2
Maṣīrah, Jazīrat al- 44-45 HJ 6
Maṣīrah, Khalij al- 44-45 H 6-7
Masisi 63 B 3
Masjed Soleymān 44-45 FG 4
Maskanah 46-47 GH 4-5
Maskarenenbecken 22-23 M 6
Maskarenenbekken 22-23 M 6
Maskarenenrücken 22-23 MN 6
Maskarenenrug 22-23 MN 6
Maskat = Masqat 44-45 H 6
Maskate = Masqaṭ 44-45 H 6
Masoala, Cap – 64-65 M 6
Mason, WY 76-77 HJ 4
Mason City, IA 72-73 H 3
Masqaṭ 44-45 H 6
Maṣr el-Gedîda = Al-Qahirah-Miṣr al-Jadīdah 62 D 2
Massa 36-37 D 3
Massachusetts 72-73 M 3
Massachusetts Bay 72-73 MN 3
Massakori = Massakory 60-61 H 6
Massakory 60-61 H 6
Massa Marittima 36-37 D 4
Massangena 64-65 H 7
Massango 64-65 E 4
Massangulo 63 C 6
Massasi = Masasi 64-65 J 5
Massaua = Mitsiwa 60-61 MN 5
Massena, NY 74-75 F 2
Massenya 60-61 H 6
Masset 70-71 K 7
Massif Central 34-35 J 6
Massillon, OH 74-75 C 4
Massina = Macina 60-61 CD 6
Massinga 64-65 J 7
Masson Island 24 C 10
Mastabah 44-45 D 6
Masterton 56-57 P 8
Mastung 44-45 K 5
Mastūrah 44-45 D 6
Masuda 50-51 H 5
Māsūleh 46-47 N 4
Maṣyāf 46-47 G 5
Masyw Centralny 34-35 J 6
Mašigina, guba – 42-43 HJ 3
Maszkat = Masqat 44-45 H 6
Matabeleland 64-65 G 6-7
Mata da Corda, Serra da – 78-79 K 8
Matadi 64-65 D 4
Matagalpa 72-73 J 9
Matagami 70-71 V 8
Matagamon, ME 74-75 J 1
Matagorda Bay 72-73 GH 6
Matagorda Island 72-73 G 6
Maṭâi = Maṭāy 62 D 3
Mataj 42-43 O 8
Matala 64-65 E 5
Matam 60-61 B 5
Matamoros [MEX, Coahuila] 72-73 F 6
Matamoros [MEX, Tamaulipas] 72-73 G 6
Matancillas 80 B 4
Matandu 63 D 5
Matane 70-71 X 8
Matanzas 72-73 K 7
Matão, Serra do – 78-79 J 6
Matapalo, Cabo – 72-73 K 10
Mataporquera 34-35 E 7
Mātara [CL] 44-45 N 9
Mataram 52-53 G 8
Matarani 78-79 E 8
Mataranka [AUS] 56-57 F 2
Mataró 34-35 J 8
Matatiele 64-65 G 9
Maṭāy 62 D 3
Mategua 78-79 G 7
Matehuala 72-73 F 7
Matemo 63 E 6
Matera 36-37 G 5
Mátészalka 33 KL 4-5
Matetsi 64-65 G 6
Mâţeur = Māṭir 60-61 FG 1
Mather, CA 76-77 D 7
Mathews, VA 74-75 E 6
Mathura 44-45 M 5
Mati 52-53 J 5
Matías Hernández 72-73 bc 2
Matimana 63 D 5
Matimbuka 64-65 J 5
Matinicus Island 74-75 J 3
Māṭir 60-61 FG 1
Maṭlā', Al- 46-47 M 8
Matlock, WA 76-77 B 2
Matočkin Šar 42-43 KL 3
Matočkin Šar, proliv – 42-43 KL 3
Matočkin Šar 42-43 KL 3
Matočkin Šar, proliv – 42-43 KL 3
Mato Grosso [BR, Mato Grosso] 78-79 HJ 7
Mato Grosso, Planalto do – 78-79 HJ 7
Mato Grosso do Sul 78-79 HJ 8-9
Matombo 63 D 4
Matope 64-65 HJ 6
Matopo Hills 64-65 G 7
Matosinhos 34-35 C 8
Mátra 33 JK 5
Matra = Mathura 44-45 M 5
Maṭraḥ 44-45 H 6
Maṭrūḥ 60-61 K 2
Maṭrūḥ = Marsá Maṭrūḥ 60-61 K 2
Maṭrūḥ, Marsá – 62 B 2
Matsue 48-49 P 4
Matsumae 50-51 ab 3
Matsumoto 50-51 LM 4
Matsunami = Suzu 50-51 L 4
Matsusaka 50-51 KL 5
Ma-tsu Tao 48-49 MN 6
Matsuyama 50-51 J 6
Mattagami River 70-71 U 7-8
Mattamuskeet Lake 74-75 EF 7
Mattawamkeag, ME 74-75 JK 2
Matterhorn [USA] 76-77 F 5
Matthew, Île – 56-57 O 4
Matthews Peak 64-65 J 2
Maṭṭī, Sabkhat – 44-45 G 6
Matua 52-53 F 7
Matucana 78-79 D 7
Matue = Matsue 48-49 P 4
Matuku 52-53 ab 2
Matumoto = Matsumoto 48-49 Q 4
Matundu 64-65 F 2
Matura = Mathura 44-45 M 5
Maturín 78-79 G 2-3
Matuyama = Matsuyama 48-49 P 5
Maúa [Moçambique] 64-65 J 5
Maubeuge 34-35 JK 3
Maud, Banc de – 24 C 1
Maud, Wzniesienie – 24 C 1
Maudbank 24 C 1
Maude 58 G 5
Maud-fenékhegy 24 C 1
Maudlow, MT 76-77 H 2
Maud Seamount 24 C 1
Maués 78-79 H 5
Maués-Açu, Rio – 78-79 H 5
Mauhan 52-53 C 2
Maui 52-53 e 3
Maulamyaing 52-53 C 3
Maullín 80 B 6
Maumere 52-53 H 8
Maun [RB] 64-65 F 6
Mauna Kea 52-53 e 4
Mauna Loa 52-53 e 4
Maungdaw 52-53 B 2
Maunoir, Lac – 70-71 M 4
Maupin, OR 76-77 C 3
Mauretania 60-61 BC 4
Mauretanien 60-61 BC 4-5
Maurice 64-65 N 7
Maurice, Lake – 56-57 EF 5
Mauricio 64-65 N 7
Mauricius 64-65 N 7
Mauritánia 60-61 BC 4
Mauritania 60-61 BC 4-5
Mauritánie 60-61 BC 4
Mauritanië 60-61 BC 4-5
Mauritanie 60-61 BC 4-5
Mauritius 64-65 N 7
Maury Mountains 76-77 C 3
Mausil = Al-Mūṣil 44-45 E 3
Mava 52-53 M 8
Mavago 64-65 J 5
Mavinga 64-65 EF 6
Mawa 64-65 G 2
Mawhūb 62 C 5
Mawhun = Mauhan 52-53 C 2
Mawson 24 C 7
Maximo 63 D 6
Maxville 74-75 F 2
Maxville, MT 76-77 G 2
Maxwell, CA 76-77 B 6
May, ID 76-77 G 3
Maya, Pulau – 52-53 E 7
Mayādīn 46-47 J 5
Mayaguana Island 72-73 M 7
Mayagüez 72-73 N 8
Mayama 64-65 DE 3
Maya Mountains 72-73 J 8
Mayang-do 50-51 G 2-3
Mayanja 63 BC 2
Mayapán 72-73 J 7
Maydān 46-47 L 5
Maydān Ikbis 46-47 G 4
Maydena 56-57 J 8
Maydh 60-61 b 1
Maydī 44-45 E 7
Mayenne [F, ~] 34-35 G 4-5
Mayenne [F, ●] 34-35 G 4
Mayer, AZ 76-77 G 8
Mayesville, SC 74-75 C 7-8
Mayfield, ID 76-77 F 4
Maymana 44-45 JK 3
Maymyo = Memyō 52-53 C 2
Maynard, WA 76-77 B 2
Maynas 78-79 DE 5
Mayo, FL 74-75 b 1-2
Mayodan, NC 74-75 CD 6
Mayo Landing 70-71 JK 5
Mayor, El – 76-77 F 9
Mayotte 64-65 K 5
Mayoumba 64-65 CD 3
May Point, Cape – 74-75 F 5
Mayrhofen 33 EF 5
Maysarī, Al- 46-47 H 7
Maysville, NC 74-75 E 7
Mayu, Pulau – 52-53 J 6
Mayunga 64-65 G 3
Mayville, NY 74-75 D 3
Mayyit, Baḥr al- 44-45 D 4
Mazabuka 64-65 G 6
Mazagan = Al-Jadīdah 60-61 C 2
Mazagão 78-79 J 5
Mazáka = Kayseri 44-45 D 3
Mazamet 34-35 J 7
Mazan = Villa Mazán 80 C 3
Māzandarān 44-45 GH 3
Mazār, Al- 46-47 F 7
Mazara del Vallo 36-37 DE 7
Mazār-i-Sharīf 44-45 K 3
Mazarrón 34-35 G 10
Mazarrón, Golfo de – 34-35 G 10
Mazar tagh 48-49 D 4
Mazatenango 72-73 H 9
Mazatlán 72-73 E 7
Mazatzal Peak 76-77 H 8
Mazedonien 36-37 JK 5
Mažeikiai 30-31 K 9
Mazgirt 46-47 H 3
Mazhafah, Jabal – = Jabal Buwārah 62 F 3
Mazıdağı 46-47 J 4
Mazirbe 30-31 JK 9
Mazoco 63 C 5
Mazr'a, Al- 46-47 F 7
Māzū 46-47 N 6
Mazurskie, Pojezierze – 33 K 2-L 1
Mažeikiai 30-31 K 9

Mbabane 64-65 H 8
Mbaikī 60-61 H 8
Mbala 64-65 H 4
Mbalabala 64-65 GH 7
Mbale 64-65 H 2
M'Balmayo 60-61 G 8
Mbamba Bay 63 C 5
Mbandaka 64-65 E 2-3
Mbanga 60-61 FG 8
Mbanza Congo 64-65 D 4
Mbanza Ngungu 64-65 D 3-4
Mbarangandu [EAT, ~] 63 D 5
Mbarangandu [EAT, ●] 63 D 5
Mbarara 64-65 H 3
Mbari 60-61 J 7
M'Bé 64-65 E 3
Mbemkuru 64-65 JK 4
Mbenkuru 63 D 5
Mbeya [EAT, ▲] 63 C 5
Mbeya [EAT, ●] 64-65 H 4
M'Bigou 64-65 D 3
Mbin 60-61 F 8
M'Binda 64-65 D 3
Mbindera 63 D 5
Mbinga 63 C 5
Mbini 60-61 G 8
Mbizi 64-65 H 7
Mbogo's 63 C 4
Mbomou 60-61 J 7-8
M'Boro 63 AB 2
Mbour 60-61 A 6
Mbozi 63 C 5
Mbud 60-61 B 5
Mbuji-Mayi 64-65 F 4
Mbulu 63 C 3
Mburu 63 C 5
Mburucuyá 80 E 3

Mcensk 38-39 G 5
Mchinga 64-65 JK 4
Mchinji 64-65 H 5

Mdaina, Al- = Al-Madīnah 46-47 M 7
Mdandu 63 C 5

Meacham, OR 76-77 D 3
Mead, WA 76-77 E 2
Mead, Lake – 72-73 D 4
Meade Peak 76-77 H 4
Meadow Lake 70-71 P 7
Meadow Valley Range 76-77 F 7
Meadow Valley Wash 76-77 F 7
Meadville, PA 74-75 CD 4
Meaford 74-75 C 2
Mealy Mountains 70-71 Z 7
Meandro = Büyük Menderes Nehri 46-47 B 4
Mearim, Rio – 78-79 L 5
Meaux 34-35 J 4
Mebote 64-65 H 7
Mebreije, Rio – = Rio Mebridege 64-65 D 4
Mebridege, Rio – 64-65 D 4
Meca = Makkah 44-45 DE 6
Meca, La – = Makkah 44-45 DE 6
Mecca, CA 76-77 EF 9
Mecca = Makkah 44-45 DE 6
Mechanicsburg, PA 74-75 E 4

Mechanicville, NY 74-75 G 3
Meched = Mashhad 44-45 HJ 3
Mechelen 34-35 K 3
Méchéria = Mīshrīyah 60-61 DE 2
Mecidiye 46-47 B 3
Meçitözü 46-47 F 2
Mecklenburg 33 EF 2
Mecklenburger Bucht 33 EF 1
Mecque, la – = Makkah 44-45 DE 6
Mecsek 33 J 5
Mecúfi 64-65 K 5
Mecula 64-65 J 5
Medan 52-53 C 6
Médanos [RA, Buenos Aires ●] 80 D 5
Medanosa, Punta – 80 CD 7
Mededsia 44-45 C 3
Medellín [CO] 78-79 D 3
Medellín [RA] 80 D 3
Medelpad 30-31 FG 6
Medenîn = Madanīyīn 60-61 FG 2
Medford, MA 74-75 H 3
Medford, OR 72-73 B 3
Medgidia 36-37 N 3
Mediano 34-35 H 7
Mediaş 36-37 L 2
Medical Lake, WA 76-77 DE 2
Medicanceli 34-35 F 8
Medicine Bow Peak 72-73 EF 3
Medicine Hat 70-71 O 7
Medina, OH 74-75 BC 4
Medina = Al-Madīnah 44-45 DE 6
Medina del Campo 34-35 E 8
Medina de Rioseco 34-35 E 8
Medina-Sidonia 34-35 DE 10
Médine = Al-Madīnah 44-45 DE 6
Medinipur 44-45 O 6
Mediolan = Milano 36-37 C 3
Mediterranean Sea 28-29 J 8-O 9
Medjdel, El- = Ashqĕlōn 46-47 F 7
Mednogorsk 42-43 K 7
Mednyi, ostrov – 19 D 2
Médoc 34-35 G 6
Medvedica 38-39 H 5-6
Medvědí ostrov 19 B 16-17
Medve-sziget 19 B 16-17
Medvežij ostrova 42-43 f 3
Medvežjegorsk 42-43 EF 5
Medvežij ostrova 42-43 f 3
Medvežjegorsk 42-43 EF 5
Medyna = Al-Madīnah 44-45 DE 6
Meekatharra 56-57 C 5
Meerut 44-45 M 5
Mēga [ETH] 60-61 M 8
Mega [RI] 52-53 K 7
Mégalē Prëspa, Límnē – 36-37 J 5
Megalópolis 36-37 JK 7
Megálo Sofráno 36-37 M 7
Mégantic 74-75 H 2
Mégara 36-37 K 6-7
Meghalaya 44-45 P 5
Megion 42-43 O 5
Mégistē 46-47 C 4
Megler, WA 76-77 B 2
Megrega 42-43 E 5
Mehadia 36-37 K 3
Mehdia = Mahdīyah 60-61 E 1
Meherrin River 74-75 E 6
Mehrabān 46-47 M 3-4
Mehrān 46-47 M 6
Mehsāna 44-45 L 6
Meia Ponte, Rio – 78-79 K 8
Meighen Island 70-71 RS 1
Meihekou = Shanchengzhen 50-51 EF 1
Meikhtīlā 52-53 BC 2
Meiktila = Meikhtīlā 52-53 BC 2
Meiling Guan = Xiaomei Guan 48-49 LM 6
Meiningen 33 E 3
Meißen 33 F 3
Mei Xian 48-49 M 7
Mejicana, Cumbre de – 80 C 3
Mejillones 80 B 2
Mejnypil'gyno 42-43 j 5
Meka Galla 63 D 2
Mekambo 64-65 D 2
Mekelē 60-61 M 6
Mekerrhane, Sebkra – = Sabkhat Mukrān 60-61 E 3
Mekka = Makkah 44-45 DE 6
Meknès = Miknās 60-61 C 2
Mekong = Lancang Jiang 48-49 HJ 7
Mekran = Mokrān 44-45 HJ 5
Mékrou 60-61 E 6
Meksyk 72-73 E 6-G 8
Meksykańska, Zatoka – 72-73 G-J 7
Meksykański, Basen – 72-73 HJ 6
Melagénai 30-31 M 10
Melaḥ, Yam ham – 46-47 F 7
Melaka [MAL, ●] 52-53 D 6
Melaka, Selat – 52-53 CD 6
Melanesia 22-23 Q 5-S 6
Melanesië 22-23 Q 5-S 6
Mélanésie 22-23 Q 5-S 6
Melanesien 22-23 Q 5-S 6
Mělas 36-37 L 7
Melayu 52-53 D 6
Melba, ID 76-77 E 4
Melbourne [AUS] 56-57 H 7
Melbourne, FL 74-75 c 2
Melbu 30-31 F 3
Melchers, Kapp – 30-31 m 6
Melchor, Isla – 80 AB 7
Melchor Múzquiz 72-73 F 6
Meldrim, GA 74-75 C 8
Melendiz Dağları 46-47 F 3
Melenki 38-39 H 4
Mélèzes, Rivière aux – 70-71 W 6
Melfi 36-37 F 5
Melfi [Tschad] 60-61 H 6
Melfort 70-71 Q 7
Melik, Wadi el – = Wādī al-Malik 60-61 KL 5
Melili 63 CD 6
Melilia = Melilla 60-61 D 1
Melilla 60-61 D 1
Melimoyu, Monte – 80 B 6
Melinde = Malindi 64-65 K 3
Melipilla 80 B 4
Melitene = Malatya 44-45 D 3
Melito di Porto Salvo 36-37 FG 7
Melitopol' 38-39 FG 6
Melk 33 G 4
Mellerud 30-31 E 8
Mellīt = Mallīt 60-61 K 6
Mellizo Sur, Cerro – 80 B 7
Mělník 33 G 3
Mel'nikovo [SU ← Tomsk] 42-43 P 6
Melo [ROU] 80 F 4
Meloco 63 D 6
Melrhir, Chott – = Shaṭṭ Malghīr 60-61 F 2
Melrhir, Chott – = Shaṭṭ Malghīr 60-61 F 2
Melrhir, Chott – = Shaṭṭ Malghīr 60-61 F 2
Melrhir, Schott – = Shaṭṭ Malghīr 60-61 F 2
Melrose, MT 76-77 G 3
Melsetter = Mandidzudzure 64-65 H 6-7
Meltaus 30-31 L 4
Melton Mowbray 32 F 5
Meluco 63 D 6
Melun 34-35 J 4
Melunga 64-65 E 6
Melūṭ = Malūṭ 60-61 L 6
Melville, MT 76-77 HJ 2
Melville, Cape – 56-57 HJ 2
Melville, Lake – 70-71 YZ 7
Melville Bay 56-57 G 2
Melville Bugt 70-71 X-Z 2
Melville Hills 70-71 M 4
Melville Island [AUS] 56-57 F 2
Melville Island [CDN] 70-71 N-P 2
Melville Peninsula 70-71 U 4
Melville Sound = Viscount Melville Sound 70-71 O-Q 3
Memala 52-53 F 7
Memba 64-65 K 5
Memboro 52-53 G 8
Memel = Klaipėda 30-31 J 10
Memmingen 33 DE 5
Memphis 60-61 L 3
Memphis, TN 72-73 HJ 4
Memphremagog, Lac – 74-75 GH 2
Memuro 50-51 c 2
Memyō 52-53 C 2
Menado = Manado 52-53 H 6
Ménaka 60-61 E 5
Menam = Mae Nam Chao Phraya 52-53 CD 3-4
Menan Khong 52-53 D 3
Menarandra 64-65 KL 7-8
Menard, MT 76-77 H 3
Menbij = Manbij 46-47 G 4
Mende 34-35 J 6
Mendez [EC] 78-79 D 5
Mendī [ETH] 60-61 M 7
Mendi [PNG] 52-53 M 8
Mendocino, CA 76-77 AB 6
Mendocino, Cape – 72-73 AB 3
Mendocino, Fractura de – 22-23 BC 4
Mendocino, Gradin de – 22-23 BC 4
Mendocino Fracture Zone 22-23 BC 4
Mendocino Range 76-77 AB 5
Mendocinostufe 22-23 BC 4
Mendocinotrap 22-23 BC 4
Mendol, Pulau – 52-53 D 6
Mendong Gonpa 48-49 F 5
Mendota, CA 76-77 C 7
Mendoza [PA] 72-73 b 2
Mendoza [RA, ●] 80 C 4
Mènè 64-65 E 2
Mene de Mauroa 78-79 E 2
Menemen 46-47 B 3
Mengen [TR] 46-47 E 2
Mengene Dağı 46-47 KL 3
Menggala 52-53 E 7
Mengkoka, Gunung – = Pulau Penyeler 52-53 H 7
Mengtze = Mengzi 48-49 J 7
Mengulek, gora – 42-43 Q 7
Mengzi 48-49 J 7
Menindee 56-57 H 6
Menindee Lake 58 EF 4
Menongue 64-65 E 5
Menorca 34-35 K 8
Men'šikova, mys – 42-43 KL 3
Men'šikova, mys – 42-43 KL 3
Mentakab 52-53 D 6
Mentawai, Kepulauan – 52-53 CD 7
Mentok 52-53 DE 7
Menton 34-35 L 7
Menzelinsk 38-39 K 4
Menzies 56-57 D 5
Menzies, Mount – 24 B 6-7
Meoqui 72-73 E 6
Meponda 63 C 6
Meppel 34-35 KL 2
Meppen 33 C 2
Meqdādiya, Al- = Al-Miqdādīyah 46-47 L 6
Mequinenza 34-35 GH 8
Mer Adriatique 36-37 E 3-H 5
Meramangye, Lake – 56-57 F 5
Merano 36-37 D 2
Merapoh 52-53 D 6
Mēraṭh = Meerut 44-45 M 5
Meratus, Pegunungan – 52-53 G 7
Merauke 52-53 LM 8
Mer Baltique 30-31 G 10-J 8
Merbein 58 EF 5
Mer Blanche 42-43 FG 4
Merca = Marka 64-65 KL 2
Mercan Dağları 46-47 H 3
Mercara 44-45 M 8
Mer Caspienne 44-45 F 2-G 3
Merced, CA 72-73 BC 4
Mercedario, Cerro – 80 BC 4
Mercedes [RA, Buenos Aires] 80 DE 4
Mercedes [RA, Corrientes] 80 E 3
Mercedes [RA, San Luis] 80 C 4
Mercedes [ROU] 80 E 4
Mercedes, Las – 78-79 F 3
Merced River 76-77 C 7
Mer Celtique 32 C 6
Mercimekkale 46-47 J 3
Mercy, Cape – 70-71 Y 5
Merdenik = Göle 46-47 K 2
Meredit, Cabo – = Cape Meredith 80 D 8
Meredith, Cape – 80 D 8
Mereeg 60-61 b 3
Mer Egee 36-37 L 5-M 7
Meregh = Mareeg 64-65 L 2
Meregh = Mereeg 60-61 b 3
Merena = Santo 56-57 MN 3
Merga = Nukhaylah 60-61 K 5
Mergui = Myeik 52-53 C 4
Mergui, Archipelag – = Myeik Kyûnzu 52-53 C 4
Merguï, Archipel de – = Myeik Kyûnzu 52-53 C 4
Mergui, Archipiélago de – = Myeik Kyûnzu 52-53 C 4
Mergui-Archipel = Myeik Kyûnzu 52-53 C 4
Mergui-szigetek = Myeik Kyûnzu 52-53 C 4
Mergujské souostroví = Myeik Kyûnzu 52-53 C 4
Meriç = Büyük Doğanca 46-47 B 2
Meriç Nehri 46-47 B 2
Merida [E] 34-35 D 9
Mérida [MEX] 72-73 J 7
Mérida [YV] 78-79 E 3
Mérida, Cordillera de – 78-79 EF 3
Meriden, CT 74-75 G 4
Meridian, ID 76-77 E 4
Meridian, MS 72-73 J 5
Merimbula 58 JK 6
Meringur 56-57 H 6
Mer Intérieure = Seto-naikai 48-49 P 5
Mer Ionienne 36-37 GH 7
Merir 52-53 K 6
Mer Jaune 48-49 N 4
Merke [SU] 42-43 N 9
Merket Bazar = Marqat Bazar 48-49 D 4
Mer Ligurienne 36-37 BC 4
Merlin, OR 76-77 B 4
Merluna 56-57 H 2
Mer Méditeranée 28-29 J 8-O 9
Mermer 46-47 J 3
Mer Morte = Baḥr al-Mayyit 44-45 D 4
Merna, WY 76-77 H 4
Mer Noire 38-39 E-G 7
Merowē = Marawī 60-61 L 5
Merq, el- = Al-Marj 60-61 J 2
Merredin 56-57 C 6
Merrick 32 D 4
Merrill, OR 76-77 C 4
Merrimack River 74-75 H 3
Merrit 70-71 M 7
Merriwa 58 JK 4
Mer Rouge 44-45 D 5-7
Merseburg 33 EF 3
Mersin = İçel 44-45 C 3
Mersing 52-53 D 6
Mers-les-Bains 34-35 H 3
Merthyr Tydfil 32 DE 6
Merthyr Tydfil 32 DE 6
Merti 63 D 2
Mer Tyrrhénienne 36-37 D-F 6
Mertz Glacier 24 C 15
Mer Tyrrhénienne 36-37 D-F 6
Meru [EAK] 64-65 J 2-3
Meru [EAT] 64-65 J 3
Meru National Park 63 D 2
Merv 44-45 J 3
Merv = Mary 44-45 J 3
Merwar = Marwar 44-45 L 5
Merzifon 46-47 F 2
Mesa, AZ 72-73 D 5
Mesabi Range 72-73 H 2
Mesa Central = Mesa de Anáhuac 72-73 FG 7-8
Mesagne 36-37 GH 5
Mesarya 46-47 E 5
Mesa Verde National Park 76-77 J 7
Mescit Dağı 46-47 J 2
Mescit Dağları 46-47 J 2
Mescitli = Söylemez 46-47 JK 3
Meščura 38-39 K 3
Meseta del Norte 72-73 F 6
Meshhed = Mashhad 44-45 HJ 3
Meshkīn Shar 46-47 M 3
Meshra' er Req = Mashrā' ar-Raqq 60-61 K 7
Meskené = Maskanah 46-47 GH 4-5
Mesmiyé = Al-Mismīyah 46-47 G 6
Mesolóngion 36-37 J 6
Mesopotamia 44-45 E 3-F 4
Mesopotamia [RA] 80 E 3-4
Mesopotamië 44-45 E 3-F 4
Mésopotamie 44-45 E 3-F 4
Mesopotamien 44-45 E 3-F 4
Mesquite, NV 76-77 F 7
Messalo, Rio – 64-65 J 5
Messēnē [GR, ●] 36-37 JK 7
Messēnē [GR, ∅] 36-37 J 7
Messēniakòs Kólpos 36-37 JK 7
Messina 36-37 F 6
Messina [ZA] 64-65 GH 7
Messina, Stretto di – 36-37 F 6-7
Messinge 63 C 5
Messojacha 42-43 O 4
Mestre, Venézia- 36-37 E 3
Mesudiye 46-47 G 2
Meščura 38-39 K 3
Meta, Rio – 78-79 E 3
Meta Incognita Peninsula 70-71 X 5
Metairie, LA 72-73 H 6
Metalici, Munţii – 36-37 K 2
Metaline Falls, WA 76-77 E 1
Metán 80 D 3
Metangula 64-65 HJ 5
Metaponto 36-37 G 5
Metarica 63 D 6
Metema 60-61 M 6
Meteor, Abysse – 22-23 HJ 8
Meteor, Banco del – 22-23 H 4
Meteor, Fosa de – 22-23 HJ 8
Meteōra 36-37 J 6
Meteorbank 22-23 H 4
Meteor Crater 76-77 H 8
Meteor Depth 22-23 HJ 8
Meteordiep 22-23 HJ 8
Meteortiefe 22-23 HJ 8
Methow River 76-77 CD 1
Mê Thuôt = Ban Me Thuôt 52-53 E 4
Mēthymna 36-37 LM 6
Metinic Island 74-75 J 3
Metkovič 36-37 GH 4
Metlakatla, AK 70-71 KL 6
Metlaouî, El – = Al-Mitlawī 60-61 F 2
Metolius, OR 76-77 C 3
Metorica 63 D 6
Métsobon 36-37 J 6
Metter, GA 74-75 B 8
Mēṭṭur Kuḷam = Stanley Reservoir 44-45 M 8
Metuge 63 E 6
Mĕtulla 46-47 F 6
Metundo 63 E 5
Metz 34-35 L 4
Meulaboh 52-53 C 6
Meureudu 52-53 C 5
Meuse 34-35 K 4
Mexcala, Río – = Río Balsas 72-73 F 8
Mexicaans Bekken 72-73 HJ 6
Mexicali 72-73 C 5
Mexican Hat, UT 76-77 J 7
Mexická pánev 72-73 HJ 6
Mexický záliv 72-73 G-J 7
Mexico 72-73 E 6-G 8
México 72-73 E 6-G 8
Mexico, ME 74-75 H 2
México [MEX, ●] 72-73 G 8
Mexico, Fosa de – 22-23 DE 5
México, Golfo de – 72-73 HJ 7
Mexico, Gulf of – 72-73 HJ 7
Mexico Basin 72-73 HJ 6
Mexico Bay 74-75 E 3
México City = México 72-73 G 8
Mexicotrog 72-73 HJ 7
Mexikanisches Becken 72-73 HJ 6
Mexikó 72-73 E 6-G 8
Mexiko 72-73 E 6-G 8
Mexiko, Golf von – 72-73 G-J 7
Mexikograben 22-23 DE 5
Mexikói-medence 72-73 HJ 6
Mexikói-öböl 72-73 J 7
Mexique 72-73 E 6-G 8
Mexique, Bassin du – 72-73 HJ 6
Mexique, Golfe du – 72-73 HJ 7
Meyādīn = Mayādīn 46-47 J 5
Meyāndowāb = Mīāndowāb 46-47 M 4
Meyāneh 44-45 F 3
Meyāneh, Kūreh-ye – 46-47 M 5
Meydān Dāgh 46-47 MN 4
Meydān-e Naftūn 46-47 N 7
Meyersdale, PA 74-75 D 5
Mezdra 36-37 KL 4
Meždurečenskij 42-43 MN 6
Meždušarskij, ostrov – 42-43 HJ 3
Mezen' [SU, ~] 42-43 H 5
Mezen' [SU, ●] 42-43 GH 4
Mézenc, Mont – 34-35 JK 6
Mezenskaja guba 42-43 G 4
Mežirečje 36-37 L 1
Mezőkövesd 33 K 5
Mezopotámia 44-45 E 3-F 4
Mezopotamia 44-45 E 3-F 4
Mezopotámie 44-45 E 3-F 4
Meždurečenskij 42-43 MN 6
Meždušarskij, ostrov – 42-43 HJ 3
Mežirečje 36-37 L 1
Mfūlū 60-61 KL 7
Mfwanganu 63 C 3
Mia, Wed – = Wādī Miyāh 60-61 EF 2
Miagas, Pulau – 52-53 J 5
Miajadas 34-35 E 9
Miajlar 44-45 KL 5
Miami, AZ 76-77 H 9
Miami, FL 72-73 K 6
Miami Beach, FL 72-73 KL 6
Miami Canal 72-73 K 6
Miami Shores, FL 74-75 cd 4
Mīāndou Āb = Mīāndowāb 46-47 M 4
Miandrivazo 64-65 L 6
Mianma 52-53 BC 2
Mianwali = Miyānwālī 44-45 L 4
Mian Xian 48-49 K 5
Mianyang [TJ, Sichuan] 48-49 J 5
Miaodao Qundao 48-49 N 4
Miao Liedao = Miaodao Qundao 48-49 N 4
Miass [SU, ●] 42-43 L 7
Miastko 33 H 1-2
Miasto Ho Chi Minha = Thản Phô Ho Chi Minh 52-53 E 4
Miasto Ho Chi Minha = Thản Phô Ho Chi Minh 52-53 E 4
Miaws, Bi'r – 62 F 6
Micay 78-79 D 4
Michajlovka 38-39 J 6
Michajlovskij 42-43 OP 7
Michalitsion = Karacabey 46-47 C 2
Michalovce 33 KL 4
Michelson, Mount – 70-71 GH 4
Michigan 72-73 J 2-K 3
Michigan, Jezioro – = Lake Michigan 72-73 J 2-3
Michigan, Lake – 72-73 J 2-3
Michigansee = Lake Michigan 72-73 J 2-3
Michigan-tó = Lake Michigan 72-73 J 2-3
Michipicoten Island 70-71 T 8
Michoacán 72-73 F 8
Micronesia [⊙] 22-23 R-T 5
Micronesia [★] 52-53 MN 5
Micronesië [⊙] 22-23 R-T 5
Micronésie [⊙] 22-23 R-T 5
Micronesië [★] 52-53 MN 5
Micronésie [★] 52-53 MN 5
Mičurin 36-37 MN 4
Mičurinsk 38-39 GH 5
Mičurin 36-37 MN 4
Mičurinsk 38-39 GH 5
Mida 63 DE 3
Midáeion = Eskişehir 44-45 C 2-3
Midai, Pulau – 52-53 E 6
Midas, NV 76-77 E 5
Mid Atlantic Ridge 22-23 H 5-3
Middelburg [ZA, Kaapland] 64-65 FG 9
Middelburg [ZA, Transvaal] 64-65 GH 8
Middelfart 30-31 CD 10
Middellandse Zee 28-29 J 8-O 9
Midden Atlas = Al-Aṭlas al-Mutawassiṭ 60-61 CD 2
Midden Siberisch Bergland 42-43 R-W 4-5
Middle Alkali Lake 76-77 CD 5
Middle America Trench 22-23 DE 5
Middle Andaman 44-45 P 8
Middle Atlas = Al-Aṭlas al-Mutawassiṭ 60-61 CD 2
Middlebury, VT 74-75 G 2
Middle East, The – 22-23 NO 4
Middle Fork John Day River 76-77 D 3
Middle Fork Salmon River 76-77 F 3
Middleport, OH 74-75 B 5
Middlesboro, KY 72-73 JK 4
Middlesbrough 32 F 4
Middleton, ID 76-77 E 4
Middleton Island 70-71 GH 6
Middleton Reef 56-57 L 5
Middletown, NY 74-75 F 4
Middletown, NJ 74-75 F 4
Middle West 72-73 F-J 3
Midhdharidhrah, Al- 60-61 A 5
Midhsandur 30-31 c 2
Midia = Midye 46-47 C 2
Mid Indian Basin 22-23 NO 6
Midland 74-75 CD 2
Midland, CA 76-77 F 9
Midland, TX 72-73 F 5
Midnapore = Medinipur 44-45 O 6
Midnapur = Medinipur 44-45 O 6
Midongy-atsimo 64-65 L 7
Midsayap 52-53 HJ 5
Midvale, ID 76-77 E 3
Midvale, UT 76-77 H 5
Midville, GA 74-75 B 8
Midyān II 62 F 3
Midyat 46-47 J 4
Midžor 36-37 K 4
Midžor 36-37 K 4
Mie 50-51 L 5
Międzyrzec Podlaski 33 L 3
Mielec 33 K 3
Mienhsien = Mian Xian 48-49 K 5
Mien-yang = Mianyang [TJ, Sichuan] 48-49 J 5
Miercurea-Ciuc 36-37 L 2
Mieres 34-35 DE 7
Mīēso 60-61 N 7
Mifflintown, PA 74-75 E 4
Migamuwa 44-45 M 9
Migdal Ashqĕlōn = Ashqĕlōn 46-47 F 7
Migdal Gad = Ashqĕlōn 46-47 F 7
Mīghān, Kavīr-e – 46-47 N 5
Migole 63 CD 4
Miguel Alves 78-79 L 5
Miguel Calmon 78-79 LM 7
Mihajlovgrad 36-37 K 4
Mihalgazi 46-47 D 2
Mihalıççık 46-47 D 3
Mihara 50-51 J 5
Miho wan 50-51 J 5
Michiganské jezero = Lake Michigan 72-73 J 2-3
Mīīto = Moyto 60-61 H 6
Mijares 34-35 G 8-9
Mijriyyah, Al- 60-61 B 5
Mikata 50-51 K 5
Mikawa wan 50-51 L 5
Miki 50-51 K 5
Mikindani 64-65 K 5
Mikkaichi = Kurobe 50-51 L 4
Mikkeli 30-31 M 7
Miknās 60-61 C 2
Mikronesien, ≅ 22-23 R-T 5
Mikronesien, ★ 52-53 MN 5
Mikumi 63 D 4
Mikumi National Park 63 D 4
Mikun' 42-43 HJ 5
Mikuni 50-51 KL 4
Mila = Mīlah 60-61 F 1
Milaan = Milano 36-37 C 3
Milagro, El – 80 C 4
Mīlah 60-61 F 1
Milāḥah, Wādī – 62 E 4
Mīlājerd 46-47 N 5
Milan, WA 76-77 E 2
Milan = Milano 36-37 C 3
Milán = Milano 36-37 C 3
Milán = Milano 36-37 C 3
Milano 36-37 C 3
Milánó = Milano 36-37 C 3
Milas 46-47 B 4
Milazzo 36-37 F 6
Milbridge, ME 74-75 K 2
Mildura 56-57 H 6
Mīleh, Kūh-e – 46-47 M 6
Milepa 63 D 5
Miles 56-57 JK 5
Miles, WA 76-77 D 2
Miles City, MT 72-73 E 2
Milet 46-47 B 4
Miletos = Milet 44-45 B 3
Miletus = Milet 44-45 B 3
Milford, CA 76-77 C 5
Milford, DE 74-75 F 5
Milford, MA 74-75 H 3
Milford, NH 74-75 H 3
Milford, PA 74-75 F 4
Milford, UT 76-77 G 6
Milford Sound [NZ, ◡] 56-57 N 8
Milgis 63 D 2
Milḥ, Qurayyāt al- 46-47 G 7
Milicz 33 H 3
Miling 56-57 C 6
Militsch = Milicz 33 H 3
Milk, Wādī el – = Wādī al-Malik 60-61 KL 5
Mil'kovo 42-43 ef 7
Milk River 72-73 E 2
Millau 34-35 J 6
Mill City, OR 76-77 B 3
Milledgeville, GA 74-75 B 8
Millegan, MT 76-77 H 2
Mille Lacs Lake 72-73 H 2
Millen, GA 74-75 C 8
Millerovo 38-39 H 6

Mille 199

Montewideo = Montevideo 80 EF 4-5
Montezuma Castle National Monument 76-77 H 8
Montfort 34-35 FG 4
Montgomery, AL 72-73 J 5
Montgomery, WV 74-75 C 5
Montgomery = Sāhīwāl 44-45 L 4
Montgomery Pass 76-77 D 6
Monticello, FL 74-75 b 1
Monticello, GA 74-75 B 8
Monticello, NY 74-75 F 4
Monticello, UT 72-73 DE 4
Monticello Reservoir = Lake Berryessa 76-77 B 6
Montijo 34-35 D 9
Montilla 34-35 E 10
Mont-Laurier 70-71 V 8
Montluçon 34-35 J 5
Montmorillon 34-35 H 5
Monto 56-57 K 4
Montoro 34-35 E 9
Montpelier, ID 76-77 H 4
Montpelier, VT 72-73 M 3
Montpellier 34-35 JK 7
Montréal [CDN] 70-71 VW 8
Montreuil [F → Berck] 34-35 H 3
Montreuil [F → Paris] 34-35 J 4
Montreux 33 C 5
Montrose 32 EF 3
Montrose, CO 72-73 E 4
Montrose, PA 74-75 F 4
Montross, VA 74-75 E 5
Mont-Saint-Michel, le – 34-35 FG 4
Monts Cantabriques = Cordillera Cantabrica 34-35 D-F 7
Montseny 34-35 J 8
Montserrat 34-35 H 8
Montserrat [West Indies] 72-73 O 8
Monts Ibériques = Cordillera Iberica 34-35 F 7-G 9
Montsinéry 78-79 J 4
Mont Tremblant Provincial Park = Parc provincial de la Montagne Tremblante 70-71 VW 8
Mont Wright 70-71 X 7
Monument, OR 76-77 D 3
Monument Valley 76-77 H 7
Monza 36-37 C 3
Monze 64-65 G 6
Monzón 34-35 H 8
Mookhorn 74-75 F 6
Moolawatana 58 DE 2-3
Moomba 58 E 2
Moonaree 58 B 3
Moonda Lake 56-57 H 5
Moonie 58 K 1
Moonie River 58 J 1
Moon National Monument, Craters of the – 76-77 G 4
Moonta 56-57 G 6
Moora 56-57 C 6
Moore, ID 76-77 G 4
Moore, Cape – 24 BC 17
Moore, Lake – 56-57 C 5
Mooresville, NC 74-75 C 7
Moorhead, MN 72-73 G 2
Moose, WY 76-77 H 4
Moosehead Lake 74-75 J 2
Moose Jaw 70-71 P 7
Moose Lake [CDN, ≈] 70-71 R 7
Mooselookmeguntic Lake 74-75 H 2
Moose River [CDN, ~] 70-71 U 7
Moosonee 70-71 U 7
Mopeia 64-65 J 6
Mopipi 64-65 FG 7
Moppo = Mokp'o 48-49 O 5
Mopti 60-61 D 6
Moquegua [PE, ●] 78-79 E 8
Moqur 44-45 K 4
Mora [E] 34-35 EF 9
Mora [RFC] 60-61 G 6
Mora [S] 30-31 F 7
Morača 36-37 H 4
Morača 36-37 H 4
Moradabad 44-45 MN 5
Morafenobe 64-65 K 6
Moraleda, Canal de – 80 B 6-7
Moramanga 64-65 L 6
Moran, WY 76-77 H 4
Morás, Punta de – 34-35 D 6-7
Moratalla 34-35 FG 9
Morava [CS] 33 H 4
Morava [YU] 36-37 J 3
Moravia = Morava 33 G-J 4
Moravie = Morava 33 G-J 4
Morawa 56-57 C 5
Morawhanna 78-79 H 3
Moray Firth 32 DE 3
Morcenx 34-35 G 6
Mordāb = Mordāb-e Pahlavī 46-47 N 4
Mordāb-e Pahlavī 46-47 N 4
Mordağı 46-47 L 4
Mordovian Autonomous Republic = 5 ◁ 42-43 H 7
Mordovskaja Avtonomnaja Sovetskaja Socialističeskaja Respublika = Mordwinische Autonome Republik = 5 ◁ 42-43 H 7
Mordvanos, República Autònoma de los – = 5 ◁ 42-43 H 7
Mordves, République Autonome des – = 5 ◁ 42-43 H 7
Mordvin Autonóm Köztársaság 42-43 H 7
Mordvinen Autonome Republiek = 5 ◁ 42-43 H 7
Mordvinská autonomní republika = 5 ◁ 42-43 H 7
Mordwinische Autonome Republik = 5 ◁ 42-43 H 7
Mordwińska Autonomiczna Republika = 5 ◁ 42-43 H 7
More, Ben – [GB, Mull] 32 C 3
More, Ben – [GB, Outer Hebrides] 32 C 3
More Assynt, Ben – 32 DE 2
Morecambe Bay 32 E 4-5
Moree 56-57 J 5
Morehead City, NC 74-75 E 7
Moreland, ID 76-77 G 4
Morelia 72-73 F 8
Morella 34-35 GH 8
Morella [AUS] 56-57 H 4
Morelos [MEX, ☆] 72-73 G 8
Morenci, AZ 76-77 J 9
Moreno [BR] 78-79 M 6
Møre og Romsdal 30-31 BC 6
Moresby Island 70-71 K 7
Moreton Bay 58 L 1
Moreton Island 56-57 K 5
Morgan 56-57 GH 6
Morgan Hill, CA 76-77 C 7
Morganton, NC 74-75 C 7
Morgantown, WV 74-75 CD 5
Morgat 34-35 E 4
Mori [J] 50-51 b 2
Mori [RI] 52-53 H 7
Mori = Kusu 50-51 H 6
Moriah, Mount – 76-77 FG 6
Morioka 48-49 R 4
Morisset 58 K 4
Morizane = Yamakuni 50-51 H 6
Morjärv 30-31 K 4
Morkoko 42-43 V 4
Morlaix 34-35 F 4
Mormon Range 76-77 F 7
Mornington, Isla – 80 A 7
Mornington Island 56-57 G 3
Moro, OR 76-77 C 3
Morobe 52-53 N 8
Morocco 60-61 C 3-D 2
Morogoro 64-65 J 4
Moro Gulf 52-53 H 5
Morokwen = Morokweng 64-65 F 8
Morokweng 64-65 F 8
Morombe 64-65 K 7
Morón [C] 72-73 L 7
Mörön [MVR] 48-49 J 2
Morón [RA] 80 E 4
Morona, Río – 78-79 D 5
Morondava 64-65 K 7
Morón de la Frontera 34-35 E 10
Moroni 64-65 K 5
Moroni, UT 76-77 H 6
Mörönus 48-49 G 5
Morotai, Pulau – 52-53 J 6
Moroto [EAU, ▲] 63 C 2
Moroto [EAU, ●] 64-65 H 2
Morozovsk 38-39 H 6
Morpeth 32 F 4
Morphou = Mórfu 46-47 E 5
Morrinsville 56-57 OP 7
Morrisburg 74-75 F 2
Morris Jesup, Kap – 19 A 19-23
Morristown, TN 72-73 K 4 -
Morro, Punta – 80 B 3
Morro Grande 78-79 HJ 5
Morros [BR, Maranhão] 78-79 L 5
Morrosquillo, Golfo de – 78-79 D 2-3
Morrumbala 64-65 J 6
Morrumbene 64-65 J 7
Mors 30-31 C 9
Moršansk 38-39 H 5
Moršansk 38-39 H 5
Mortara 36-37 C 3
Morteros 80 D 4
Mortlake 58 F 7
M'ortvij Kultuk 38-39 K 6
Morundah 58 GH 5
Moruya 56-57 K 7
Morvan 34-35 K 5
Morven 56-57 J 5
Morwell 56-57 J 7
Moržovec, ostrov – 42-43 GH 4
Moržovec, ostrov – 42-43 GH 4
Mosambický průliv 64-65 K 7-5
Mosambik 64-65 H 7-J 5
Moščnyj, ozero – 30-31 MN 8
Moscou = Moskva 42-43 F 6
Moscow, ID 72-73 C 2
Moscow = Moskva 42-43 F 6
Moscù = Moskva 42-43 F 6
Mosel 33 C 4
Moselle 34-35 L 4
Mosera = Jazirat al-Maṣīrah 44-45 H 6
Moses Lake 76-77 D 2
Moses Lake, WA 76-77 D 2
Moshi [EAT] 64-65 J 3
Mosi-Oa-Toenja 64-65 FG 6
Mosjøen 30-31 E 5
Moskal'vo 42-43 b 7
Moskau = Moskva 42-43 F 6
Moskenesøy 30-31 EF 4
Moskou = Moskva 42-43 F 6
Moskva [SU, ~] 38-39 G 4
Moskva [SU, ●] 42-43 F 6
Moskwa = Moskva 38-39 G 4
Mosonmagyaróvár 33 HJ 5
Mosquera 78-79 D 4
Mosquitia 72-73 K 8
Mosquito Lagoon 74-75 c 2
Mosquitos, Costa de – 72-73 K 9
Mosquitos, Golfe de los – 72-73 K 10
Moss 30-31 D 8
Mossaka 64-65 E 3
Mosselbaai 64-65 F 9
Mossendjo 64-65 D 3
Mossi 60-61 D 6
Mossman 56-57 HJ 3
Mossul = Al-Mūṣil 44-45 E 3
Moss Vale 56-57 JK 6
Most 33 F 3
Mostaganem = Mustaghānam 60-61 DE 1
Mostar 36-37 GH 4
Mostardas 80 D 4
Mosty 30-31 L 11
Mosŭlp'o 50-51 EF 6
Moščnyj, ozero – 30-31 MN 8
Moszkva = Moskva 42-43 F 6
Moszkva = Moskva 38-39 G 4
Moszul = Al-Mūṣil 44-45 E 3
Moṭa 60-61 M 6
Motaba 64-65 E 2
Motala 30-31 F 8
Motherwell and Wishaw 32 DE 4
Motīhāri 44-45 NO 5
Motoichiba = Fuji 50-51 M 5
Motomiya 50-51 N 4
Motovskij zaliv 30-31 PQ 3
Motril 34-35 F 10
Mottinger, WA 76-77 D 2-3
Motul de Felipe Carillo Puerto 72-73 J 7
Motygino 42-43 RS 6
Motyklejka 42-43 c 6
Mouila 64-65 D 3
Mouka 60-61 J 7
Moulamein 56-57 HJ 6-7
Moulamein Creek 56-57 HJ 7
Mould Bay 70-71 MN 2
Moulins 34-35 J 5
Moulmein = Maulamyaing 52-53 C 3
Mouloûya, Oued – = Wādī al-Mūlūyah 60-61 D 2
Moultrie, GA 72-73 K 5
Moultrie, Lake – 74-75 C 8
Moundou 60-61 H 7
Moundsville, WV 74-75 C 5
Moung 52-53 D 4
Mountain City, NV 76-77 F 5
Mountain City, TN 74-75 BC 6
Mountain Home, ID 76-77 F 4
Mountains, Gates of the – 76-77 H 2
Mountain Village, AK 70-71 D 5
Mount Airy, NC 74-75 C 6
Mount Barker 56-57 C 6
Mount Cambriens = Cambrian Mountains 32 D 6-E 5
Mount Carmel, PA 74-75 E 4
Mount Carmel, UT 76-77 G 7
Mount Darwin 64-65 H 6
Mount Desert Island 74-75 JK 2
Mount Dora, FL 74-75 c 2
Mount Dutton [AUS] 58 BC 1
Mount Elliot = Selwyn 56-57 H 4
Mount Elliot = Selwyn 56-57 H 4
Mount Forest 74-75 C 2-3
Mount Gambier 56-57 GH 7
Mount Garnet 56-57 HJ 3
Mount Hagen 52-53 M 8
Mount Hebron, CA 76-77 BC 5
Mount Holly, NJ 74-75 F 4-5
Mount Hope [AUS, New South Wales] 58 GH 4
Mount Hope [AUS, South Australia] 56-57 FG 6
Mount Hope, WV 74-75 C 6
Mount Isa 56-57 G 4
Mount Kenya National Park 63 D 3
Mount MacKinley National Park 70-71 FG 5
Mount Magnet 56-57 C 5
Mount Manara 56-57 HJ 6
Mount Morgan 56-57 K 4
Mount Morris, NY 74-75 E 3
Mount Olive, NC 74-75 D 7
Mount Perry 56-57 K 5
Mount Pleasant, UT 76-77 H 6
Mount Rainier National Park 76-77 C 2
Mount Shasta, CA 76-77 B 5
Mount Swan 56-57 G 4
Mount Union, PA 74-75 E 4
Mount Vernon, GA 74-75 B 8
Mount Vernon, IL 72-73 J 4
Mount Vernon, NY 74-75 G 4
Mount Vernon, OR 76-77 D 3
Mount Vernon, WA 76-77 BC 1
Mount Willoughby 56-57 F 5
Moura 34-35 D 9
Moura [AUS] 56-57 JK 4
Moura [BR] 78-79 G 5
Mourão 34-35 D 9
Mourdi, Dépression du – 60-61 J 5
Mourdiah 60-61 C 6
Mourmansk, Seuil de – 42-43 EF 2
Mouslimiyé = Muslimīyah 46-47 G 4
Moussoro 60-61 H 6
Moutiers 34-35 L 6
Moutohora 56-57 P 7
Moutong 52-53 H 6
Moutsamoudou = Mutsamudu 64-65 KL 5
Mowich, OR 76-77 BC 4
Mowming = Maoming 48-49 L 7
Moxico 64-65 EF 5
Moyale 64-65 J 2
Moyamba 60-61 B 7
Moyen Atlas = Al-Aṭlas al-Mutawassiṭ 60-61 CD 2
Moyie Springs, ID 76-77 E 1
Moyo [EAU] 63 B 2
Moyo = Pulau Moyo 52-53 G 8
Moyo, Pulau – 52-53 G 8
Moyobamba 78-79 D 6
Moyock, NC 74-75 EF 6
Moyowosi 63 B 3-4
Møysalen 30-31 FG 3
Moyto 60-61 H 6
Mozambicki, Basen – 64-65 K 5
Mozambicki, Kanał – 64-65 K 7-5
Mozambik 64-65 H 7-J 5
Mozambiki-csatorna 64-65 K 7-5
Mozambiki-medence 64-65 K 5
Mozambique 64-65 H 7-J 5
Mozambique = Moçambique [Moçambique, ●] 64-65 K 5-6
Mozambique, Bassin de – 64-65 K 5
Mozambique, Canal de – 64-65 K 7-5
Mozambique, Cuenca de – 64-65 K 5
Mozambique, Estrecho de – 64-65 K 7-5
Mozambique, Straat – 64-65 K 7-5
Mozambique Basin 64-65 K 5
Mozambiquebekken 64-65 K 5
Mozambique Channel 64-65 K 7-5
Mozambique Channel 64-65 K 7-5
Mozambique Channel 64-65 K 7-5
Mozdok 38-39 H 7
Možga 42-43 J 6
Mozyr' 38-39 E 5
Možga 42-43 J 6

Mpampáeski = Babaeski 46-47 B 2
Mpanda 64-65 H 4
Mpepo 64-65 H 5
Mpika 64-65 H 5
Mporokoso 64-65 GH 4
M'Pouya 64-65 E 3
Mpulungu 64-65 H 4
Mpurakasese 64-65 J 5
Mpwapwa 63 D 4

M'rāītī, Al- 60-61 C 4
Mrayyah, Al- 60-61 C 5
Mreïti, El – = Al-M'rāītī 60-61 C 4
Mrtvé moře = Baḥr al-Mayyit 44-45 D 4

Msagali 64-65 J 4
Msai'īda = Musā'idah 46-47 M 7
Msasa 63 B 3
Msta [SU, ~] 42-43 E 6
Mswega 63 D 5

Mtakuja 64-65 H 4
Mtama 63 D 5
Mtimbo 63 D 5
Mtito Andei 63 D 3
Mtowabaga 63 C 3
Mtwara 64-65 K 5

Mualama 64-65 J 6
Muan 50-51 F 5
Muang Khammouan 52-53 E 3
Muang Không 52-53 E 4
Muang Khôngxédon 52-53 E 3
Muang Paksé 52-53 DE 3-4
Muang Pakxan 52-53 D 3
Muang Xaignabouri 52-53 D 3
Muar 52-53 D 6
Muaraaman 52-53 D 7
Muaraancalong 52-53 G 6
Muaraenim 52-53 D 7
Muaralesan 52-53 G 6
Muarasiberut 52-53 C 7
Muaratebo 52-53 D 7
Muaratembesi 52-53 D 7
Muaratewe 52-53 FG 7
Mū'askar, Al- 60-61 E 1
Mubārak, Jabal – 46-47 F 8
Mubende 64-65 H 2
Mubi 60-61 G 6
Mucajaí, Rio – 78-79 G 4
Mucajaí, Serra do – 78-79 G 4
Muchinga Mountains 63 BC 5
Mučkapskij 38-39 H 5
Mucojo 64-65 K 5
Muconda 64-65 F 5
Mucuburi, Rio – 63 D 6
Mucur 46-47 F 3
Mucuri 78-79 M 8
Mucuri, Rio – 78-79 L 8
Mucuripe, Ponta de – 78-79 M 5
Mucusso 64-65 F 6
Mučkapskij 38-39 H 5
Mudanjiang 48-49 OP 3
Mudanya 46-47 C 2
Mudawwarah, Al- 44-45 D 5
Mudaysīsāt, Jabal – 46-47 G 7
Muddo Gashi = Mado Gashi 64-65 J 2
Muddus-nationalpark 30-31 J 4
Muddy Creek 76-77 H 6
Muddy Gap, WY 76-77 K 4
Muddy Peak 76-77 F 7
Mudgee 56-57 JK 6
Mudīruyat esh Shimāliya = Ash-Shimālīyah 60-61 KL 5
Mud Lake 76-77 E 7
Mudôn 52-53 C 3
Mûdros 36-37 L 6
Mudug 60-61 b 2
Mudurnu 46-47 D 2
Muecate 64-65 J 5
Mueda 64-65 J 5
Muendaze 63 E 6
Mufulira 64-65 G 5
Mughayrā', Al- 46-47 G 8
Mugi 50-51 K 6
Mugila, Monts – 64-65 G 4
Muğla 44-45 B 3
Mugodžary, gory – 42-43 K 8
Mugodžary, gory – 42-43 K 8
Mugombazi 63 B 4
Muḥammad, Rā's – 60-61 LM 4
Muḥammadī, Wādī – 46-47 K 6
Muḥammad Ṭulayb 62 D 5
Muhammed, Ras – = Rā's Muḥammad 60-61 LM 4
Muhārī, Al- 46-47 L 7
Muhārī, Sha'īb al- 46-47 KL 7
Muhembo 64-65 F 6
Muhinga = Muyinga 64-65 GH 3
Mühlbach = Sebeş 36-37 K 2-3
Mühldorf 33 F 4
Mühlhausen 33 E 3
Mühlig-Hoffmann-Gebirge 24 B 1-2
Muhu 30-31 K 8
Muhuwesi 63 D 5
Muirite 63 D 6
Muja = Ust'-Muja 42-43 W 6
Mujezerskij 42-43 E 5
Mujlad, Al- 60-61 K 6
Mujnak 42-43 K 9
Muju 50-51 F 4-5
Mujunkum = peski Mojynkum 42-43 MN 9
Muka = Mouka 60-61 J 7
Mukač'ovo 38-39 D 6
Mukač'ovo 38-39 D 6
Mukah 52-53 F 6
Mukallā, Al- 44-45 FG 8
Mukawa 50-51 b 2
Mukawwa', Jazīrat – 62 FG 6
Mukdahan 52-53 D 3
Mukden = Shenyang 48-49 NO 3
Mukebo 63 AB 4
Mukhā, Al- 44-45 E 8
Mukhalid = Nětanya 46-47 F 6
Mukinbudin 56-57 C 6
Mukoko 63 BC 3
Mukomuko 52-53 D 7
Mukrān, Sabkhat – 60-61 E 3
Mukry 44-45 K 3
Mukumbi = Makumbi 64-65 F 4
Mulainagiri 44-45 LM 8
Mulan 48-49 O 2
Mulanje 64-65 J 6
Mulanje, Mount – 64-65 J 6
Mūlayit Taung 52-53 C 3
Muldoon, ID 76-77 G 4
Muleba 63 BC 3
Mule Creek, NM 76-77 J 9
Mulgubi 50-51 G 2
Mulhacén 34-35 F 10
Mülhausen = Mulhouse 34-35 L 5
Mülhausen = Mulhouse 34-35 L 5
Mulhouse 34-35 L 5
Muli = Vysokogornyj 42-43 ab 7
Mulka 58 D 2
Mull 32 CD 3
Mullan, ID 76-77 EF 2
Mullan Pass 72-73 D 2
Mullens, WV 74-75 C 6
Muller, Pegunungan – 52-53 F 6
Müllerberg 30-31 l 6
Mullewa 56-57 C 5
Mullingar 32 C 5
Mullins, SC 74-75 D 7
Mulobezi 64-65 FG 6
Multān 44-45 L 4
Mulu, Gunung – 52-53 FG 6
Mulucas 52-53 J 6-8
Mulula, Wed – = Wādī al-Mūlūyah 60-61 D 2
Mulūṣī, Bi'r al- 46-47 J 6
Mulūṣī, Shādir al- 46-47 HJ 6
Mūlūyah, Wādī al- 60-61 D 2
Muluzia 63 B 5
Mulymja 42-43 LM 5
Mumbaī = Bombay 44-45 L 7
Mumbwa 64-65 G 6
Mumeng 52-53 N 8
Mumpu, Mount – 63 B 6
Mumra 38-39 J 6
Mun, Mae Nam – 52-53 D 3
Muna [SU] 42-43 W 4
Muna, Pulau – 52-53 H 8
Munasarowar Lake = Mapham Tsho 48-49 E 5
Munayjah, Bi'r – 62 F 6
München 33 EF 4
Munch'ŏn 50-51 F 3
Muncie, IN 72-73 JK 3
Münden 33 D 3
Mundiwindi 56-57 CD 4
Mundo, Río – 34-35 F 9
Mundrabilla 56-57 E 6
Mundubbera 56-57 JK 5
Mungallala Creek 56-57 J 5
Mungana 56-57 H 3
Mungari 64-65 H 6
Mungbere 64-65 G 2
Munger 44-45 O 5
Mungindi 56-57 J 5
Munhango 64-65 E 5
Munich = München 33 EF 4
Munkács = Mukacevo 33 L 4
Munkfors 30-31 EF 8
Munksund 30-31 JK 5
Muñoz Gamero, Península – 80 B 8
Munsan 50-51 F 4
Munsfjället 30-31 F 5
Münster [D] 33 C 2-3
Munster [IRL] 32 B 5
Munte 52-53 G 6
Muntok = Mentok 52-53 DE 7
Muñoz Gamero, Península – 80 B 8
Muodoslompolo 30-31 K 4
Mu'o'ng Khoua 52-53 D 2
Mu'o'ng Pak Beng 52-53 D 2-3
Muong Plateau = Cao Nguyên Trung Phân 52-53 E 4
Mu'o'ng Sen, Đeo – 52-53 DE 3
Muonio 30-31 KL 4
Muonio älv 30-31 K 4
Mup'vŏng-ni = Chŏnch'ŏn 50-51 F 2
Muqayshit 44-45 G 6
Muqayyar, Al- = Ur 44-45 F 4
Muqdisho 60-61 O 8
Muqsim, Jabal – 62 EF 6
Muqur = Moqur 44-45 K 4
Mur 33 FG 5
Mura 36-37 FG 2
Murādābād = Moradabad 44-45 MN 5
Muradiye [TR, Manisa] 46-47 B 3
Muradiye [TR, Van] 46-47 KL 3
Murakami 50-51 M 3
Murallón, Cerro – 80 B 7
Mūrān [IR] 46-47 N 7
Murang'a 64-65 J 3
Mur'anyo = Bandar Murcaayo 60-61 bc 1
Muraši 42-43 H 6
Muraši 42-43 H 6
Murat Dağı 44-45 B 3
Murat Dağları = Şerafettin Dağları 46-47 J 3
Murathüyügü = Musabeyli 46-47 G 4
Murat Nehri 44-45 E 3
Muravera 36-37 CD 6
Murayama 50-51 N 3
Muraywad, Al- 46-47 L 8
Murchison, Cape – 70-71 S 3
Murchison Falls = Kabelega Falls 64-65 H 2
Murchison Falls National Park = Kabelega Falls National Park 64-65 H 2
Murchisonfjord 30-31 k 4-5
Murchisonfjorden 30-31 kl 4
Murchison River 56-57 C 5
Murcia [E, ≅] 34-35 G 9-10
Murcia [E, ●] 34-35 G 9-10
Murdochville 70-71 XY 8
Murdock, FL 74-75 b 3
Mureş 36-37 K 2-3
Murfreesboro, NC 74-75 E 6
Murfreesboro, TN 72-73 J 4
Murgab [SU, ~] 44-45 J 3
Murgab [SU, ●] 44-45 L 3
Murge 36-37 G 5
Murghāb Rōd 44-45 JK 3-4
Murgon 56-57 K 5
Muriaé 78-79 L 9
Müritz 33 F 2
Murmansk 42-43 EF 4
Murmansk, Plataforma de – 42-43 EF 2
Murmanskij bereg 38-39 G 2
Murmansk Rise 42-43 EF 2
Murmanskschwelle 42-43 EF 2
Murmaši 42-43 E 4
Murmaši 42-43 E 4
Muro, Capo di – 36-37 C 5
Muro Lucano 36-37 FG 5
Murom 42-43 G 6
Muromcevo 42-43 O 6
Muroran 48-49 R 3
Muros 34-35 C 7
Muroto 50-51 JK 6

Murot 201

Muroto zaki 50-51 K 6
Murphy, ID 76-77 E 4
Murphy, TN 74-75 A 7
Murr, Bi'r – 62 D 6
Murrat al-Kubrá, Al-Buḥayrat al- 62 E 2
Murrat el-Kubrá, Buḥeiret el – = Al-Buḥayrat al-Murrat al-Kubrá 62 E 2
Murray, Fosse de – 22-23 BC 4
Murray, Fractura de – 22-23 BC 4
Murray, Lake – [PNG] 52-53 M 8
Murray, Lake – [USA] 74-75 C 7
Murraybreukzone 22-23 BC 4
Murray Bridge 58 D 5
Murray-Bruchzone 22-23 BC 4
Murray Fracture Zone 22-23 BC 4
Murray River [AUS] 56-57 H 6-7
Murrumbidgee River 56-57 HJ 6
Murrumburrah 58 J 5
Mursala, Pulau – 52-53 C 6
Murtaf'āt Tāsīlī 60-61 F 3
Murtoa 58 F 6
Murupara 56-57 P 7
Murupu 78-79 G 4
Murvārā = Murwara 44-45 N 6
Murwara 44-45 N 6
Murwillumbah 56-57 K 5
Murzūq = Marzūq 60-61 G 3
Murzūq, Edeien el- = Ṣaḥrā' Marzūq 60-61 G 3-4
Mürzzuschlag 33 G 5
Muş 44-45 E 3
Mūsā, Khūr-e – 46-47 N 7-8
Muṣa Ali Terara 60-61 N 6
Musabeyli 46-47 G 4
Musā'idah 46-47 M 7
Musala 36-37 K 4
Musan 48-49 OP 3
Mūsā Qal'a 44-45 JK 4
Musay'īd 44-45 G 5-6
Musayyib, Al- 46-47 L 6
Musazade = Arhavi 46-47 J 2
Muscat = Masqaṭ 44-45 H 6
Muscongus Bay 74-75 J 3
Musgrave 56-57 H 2
Musgrave Ranges 56-57 F 5
Mūshā 62 D 4
Mushāsh, Bi'r – 46-47 G 7
Mushie 64-65 E 3
Mushkābād = Ebrāhīmābād 46-47 O 5
Mushora = Mushūrah 46-47 K 4
Mushūrah 46-47 K 4
Musi, Air – 52-53 D 7
Mūṣil, Al- 44-45 E 3
Musinia Peak 76-77 H 6
Musisi 63 C 4
Mūsiyān 46-47 M 6
Muskat = Masqaṭ 44-45 H 6
Muskegon, MI 72-73 J 3
Muskingum River 74-75 BC 5
Muskogee, OK 72-73 GH 4
Muskoka, Lake – 74-75 D 2
Muslimīyah 46-47 G 4
Musmâr = Mismâr 60-61 M 5
Musoma 64-65 H 3
Musoshi 63 AB 5
Muş ovası 46-47 J 3
Mussali, Mount – = Muṣa Ali 60-61 N 6
Mussanāt, Al- 46-47 M 8
Mussau 52-53 N 7
Musselburgh 32 E 4
Musselshell River 72-73 E 2
Mussende 64-65 E 5
Mussuma 64-65 F 5
Mustafa Kemalpaşa 46-47 C 2-3
Mustaghānam 60-61 DE 1
Musters, Lago – 80 BC 7
Mustla 30-31 L 8
Mustvee 30-31 M 8
Musu-dan 50-51 GH 2
Muswellbrook 56-57 K 6
Mûṭ [ET] 60-61 K 3
Mut [TR] 46-47 E 4
Muta 63 A 3
Mutankiang = Mudanjiang 48-49 OP 3
Mutare 64-65 H 6
Muthanna, Al- 46-47 L 7
Mu'tiq, Jabal – 62 E 4
Mutis, Gunung – 52-53 H 8
Mutki 46-47 J 3
Muṭlah = Al-Maṭlā' 46-47 M 8
Mutsamudu 64-65 KL 5
Mutshatsha 64-65 F 5
Mutsu 50-51 N 2
Mutsu-wan 50-51 N 2
Muttra = Mathurā 44-45 M 5
Muwaffaqīyah, Al- 46-47 L 6
Muwayḥ, Al- 44-45 E 6
Muwayliḥ, Al- 62 F 4
Muxima 64-65 D 4
Muyinga 64-65 GH 3
Muyumba 64-65 G 4
Muẓaffarābād 44-45 LM 4
Muẓaffargaṛh 44-45 L 4-5
Muzaffarnagar 44-45 M 5
Muzaffarpur 44-45 NO 5
Muži 42-43 L 4
Muz tagh 48-49 E 4
Muz tagh ata 48-49 D 4
Muži 42-43 L 4

Mvôlô = Mvūlū 60-61 KL 7
Mvuma 64-65 GH 6

Mwali 64-65 K 5
Mwambwa 63 C 5
Mwanamundia 63 DE 3
Mwanza [EAT] 64-65 H 3
Mwanza [ZRE] 64-65 G 4
Mwatate 63 D 3
Mwaya 64-65 H 4
Mwazya 63 BC 5
Mweka 64-65 F 3
Mwene-Ditu 64-65 F 4
Mwenga 64-65 G 3
Mwenzo 63 C 5
Mweru, Lake – 64-65 G 4
Mweru Swamp 64-65 G 4
Mwingi 63 D 3
Mwinilunga 64-65 FG 5
Mwitikira 63 C 4

Myan'aung 52-53 BC 3
Myeik 52-53 C 4
Myeik Kyûnzu 52-53 C 4
Myingyan 52-53 BC 2
Myitkyīnā 52-53 C 1
Mykēnai 36-37 K 7
Mýkonos 36-37 L 7
Myla 38-39 K 2
Mymensingh = Maimansingh 44-45 OP 6
Mynämäki 30-31 JK 7
Mynaral 42-43 N 8
Myohyang-sanmaek 50-51 E 3-F 2
Myōkō-zan 50-51 LM 4
Myŏngch'ŏn 50-51 GH 2
Mýra 30-31 c 2
Myrdal 30-31 B 7
Mýrdalsjökull 30-31 d 3
Mýrdalssandur 30-31 d 3
Myre 30-31 F 3
Mýrina 36-37 L 6
Myrthle 74-75 D 2
Myrtle Beach, SC 74-75 D 8
Myrtle Creek, OR 76-77 B 4
Myrtleford 58 H 6
Myrtle Point, OR 76-77 AB 4
Mysen 30-31 D 8
mys Kriljon 42-43 b 8
Myślenice 33 JK 4
Mysovsk = Babuškin 42-43 U 7
Mys Vchodnoj 42-43 QR 3
Mys Želanija 42-43 MN 2
Mys Želanija 42-43 MN 2
Myślenice 33 JK 4
My Tho 52-53 E 4
Mytilēnē 36-37 M 6
Myton, UT 76-77 HJ 5
Mývatn 30-31 e 2

Mziha 64-65 J 4
Mzimba 64-65 H 5
Mzuzu 63 C 5

N

Naab 33 F 4
Na'âg, Gebel – = Jabal Ni'âj 62 E 6
Na'âm, Bi'r an- 46-47 G 7
Na'âm, Maqarr an- 46-47 HJ 7
Nā'am Zarqat 62 F 6
Naantali 30-31 JK 7
Naas 32 C 5
Näätämöjoki 30-31 MN 3
Naauwpoort = Noupoort 64-65 FG 9
Nābah, Bi'r – 62 E 7
Nabč 48-49 G 4
Nabč 48-49 G 4
Nâbeul = Nābul 60-61 G 1
Nabiac 58 L 4
Nabilatuk 63 C 2
Nabire 52-53 L 7
Nabīsar 44-45 KL 5-6
Nabk, An- [Saudi-Arabien] 46-47 G 7
Nabk, An- [SYR] 44-45 D 4
Nāblus = Nābulus 46-47 F 6
Nabq 62 F 3
Nābul 60-61 G 1
Nābulus 46-47 F 6
Nacaca 63 D 5
Naçala 64-65 K 5
Nacfa = Nakfa 60-61 M 5
Naches, WA 76-77 C 2
Nachičevan' 38-39 J 8
Nachičevan, Autonome Republik – = 10 ◁ 38-39 J 8
Nachiczewańska 38-39 J 8
Nachingwea 64-65 J 5
Nachitsjevan Autonome Republiek = 10 ◁ 38-39 J 8
Nachodka 42-43 Z 9
Nachrači = Kondirskoje 42-43 M 6
Nacka 30-31 H 8
Naco, AZ 76-77 HJ 10
Nacololo 63 D 6
Nacozari de Gracia 72-73 DE 5
Nachičevan, República Autónoma de – = 10 ◁ 38-39 J 8

Nadelkap 64-65 F 9
Nådendal = Naantali 30-31 JK 7
Nadeždinsk = Serov 42-43 L 6
Nadeždinsk = Serov 42-43 L 6
Nadhatah, An- 46-47 J 6
Nadiād 44-45 L 6
Nadjaf, An- = An-Najaf 44-45 E 4
Nadjd = Najd 44-45 E 5-6
Nădlac 36-37 J 2
Nadoa = Dan Xian 48-49 K 8
Nadqān 44-45 G 6
Nadvoicy 38-39 F 3
Nadym 38-39 O 2
Næstved 30-31 DE 10
Nafada 60-61 G 6
Nafīshah 62 DE 2
Nafṭ, Āb i – 46-47 L 6
Naft-e Sefīd 46-47 N 7
Naft-e Shāh 46-47 L 5-6
Nafṭ Hānah 46-47 L 5
Nafṭ Khāna = Nafṭ Hānah 46-47 L 5
Nafūd, An- 44-45 E 5
Nafusah, Jabal – 60-61 G 2
Naga 52-53 H 4
Nagahama [J, Ehime] 50-51 J 6
Nagahama [J, Shiga] 50-51 L 5
Nagai 50-51 MN 3
Nagaland 44-45 P 5
Nagano 48-49 Q 4
Naganohara 50-51 M 4
Nagaoka 48-49 Q 4
Nāgaor = Nagaur 44-45 L 5
Nagapattinam 44-45 MN 8
Naga Pradesh = Nagaland 44-45 P 5
Nagara gawa 50-51 L 5
Nagar Aveli = Dadra and Nagar Haveli 44-45 L 6
Nāgarkōyil = Nāgercoil 44-45 M 9
Nagar Pārkar 44-45 KL 6
Nagasaki 48-49 O 5
Naga-shima [J, ⊙] 50-51 GH 6
Nagashima [J, ●] 50-51 L 5
Nagato 50-51 H 5
Nagaur 44-45 L 5
Nag Chhu 48-49 G 5
Nagchhu Dsong 48-49 G 5
Nagchhukha = Nagchhu Dsong 48-49 G 5
Nag Chhu 48-49 G 5
Nāgercoil 44-45 M 9
Nag Chhu 48-49 G 5
Nāgīshōt = Nāqīshūt 60-61 L 8
Nagorno-Karabag, Oblast Autónoma de – = 9 ◁ 38-39 J 7-8
Nagorno-Karabagh, Région Autonome de – = 9 ◁ 38-39 J 7-8
Nagorno-Karabagh Autonome Oblast = 9 ◁ 38-39 J 7-8
Nagorno-Karabagh Autonomous Region = 9 ◁ 38-39 J 7-8
Nagornyj 42-43 Y 6
Nagoya 48-49 Q 4
Nagpur 44-45 M 6
Nagura, Ras en – = Rā's an-Naqurah 46-47 F 6
Naguun Mörön 48-49 NO 1-2
Nagykanizsa 33 H 5
Nagykőrös 33 JK 5
Nagyvárad = Oradea 36-37 JK 2
Nagy-Antillák 72-73 K 7-N 8
Nagy-Ausztráliai-öböl = Great Australian Bight 56-57 E 6-G 7
Nagy-Bahama-pad 72-73 L 6-7
Nagy-Britannia és Észak-Írország 32 F-H 4-5
Nagy Fal 48-49 K 4
Nagy-Hingan 48-49 M 3-N 1
Nagy-korallzátony = Great Barrier Reef 56-57 H 2-K 4
Nagy-Medve-tó 70-71 MN 4
Nagy-Rabszolga-tó 70-71 NO 5
Nagy-Sóstó = Great Salt Lake 72-73 D 3
Nagyszeben = Sibiu 36-37 L 3
Nagy-Szunda-szigetek 52-53 GH 8
Naha 48-49 O 6
Nahanni National Park 70-71 LM 5
Nahari 50-51 JK 6
Nahariya = Nahariyya 46-47 F 6
Nahariyya 46-47 F 6
Nahāvand 46-47 N 5
Nahicsevání Autonóm Köztársaság 38-39 J 8
Nāhid, Bi'r – 62 C 2
Nahoní Karabašská AR 38-39 J 7-8
Nahuel Huapi, Lago – 80 B 6
Nahungo 63 D 5
Nahunta, GA 74-75 BC 9
Nachičevan' 38-39 J 8
Nachičevan, Autonome Republik – = 10 ◁ 38-39 J 8
Nachičevan', Autonome Sozialistische Sowjetrepublik – = 10 ◁ 38-39 J 8
Nachičevan, República Autónoma de – = 10 ◁ 38-39 J 8
Nachičevanská AR 38-39 J 8
Nachrači = Kondirskoje 42-43 M 6

Nain [CDN] 70-71 Y 6
Nā'īn [IR] 44-45 G 4
Naindi 52-53 a 2
Naini Tal 44-45 M 5
Nain Singh Range = Nganglong Gangri 48-49 E 5
Nairn 32 E 3
Nairobi 64-65 J 3
Naissaar 30-31 L 8
Naivasha 64-65 J 3
Najaf, An- 44-45 E 4
Najafābād 44-45 G 4
Najd 44-45 E 5-6
Naj' Ḥammādī 62 DE 4-5
Najin 48-49 P 3
Najran 44-45 E 7
Naju 50-51 F 5
Nakadōri-shima 50-51 G 6
Naka gawa 50-51 K 6
Nakajō 50-51 M 3
Nakaminato 50-51 N 4
Nakamura 50-51 J 6
Nakamura = Sōma 50-51 N 4
Nakano 50-51 M 4
Nakano-shima 50-51 J 4
Nakano-umi 50-51 J 5
Nakasato 50-51 N 2
Naka-Shibetsu 50-51 d 2
Nakasongola 63 C 2
Nakatane 50-51 H 7
Nakatsu 50-51 H 6
Nakatsugawa 50-51 L 5
Nakatsukawa = Nakatsugawa 50-51 L 5
Nakatu 50-51 H 6
Nakel = Nakło nad Notecią 33 H 2
Nakfa 60-61 M 5
Nakhichevan, Autonomous Republic = 10 ◁ 38-39 J 8
Nakhichevan, République Autonome de – = 10 ◁ 38-39 J 8
Nakhīlī, Bi'r – 46-47 K 5
Nakhl 62 E 3
Nakhlāy, Bi'r – 62 D 6
Nakhon Lampang = Lampang 52-53 C 3
Nakhon Pathom 52-53 CD 4
Nakhon Phanom 52-53 D 3
Nakhon Ratchasima 52-53 D 3-4
Nakhon Sawan 52-53 CD 3
Nakhon Si Thammarat 52-53 CD 5
Nakina 70-71 T 7
Nakło nad Notecią 33 H 2
Nakło nad Notecią 33 H 2
Naknek, AK 70-71 E 6
Nakonde 63 C 5
Nakskov 30-31 D 10
Naktong-gang 50-51 G 5
Nakuru 64-65 J 3
Nāl 44-45 K 5
Nalajch 48-49 K 2
Nal'čik 38-39 H 7
Nal'čik 38-39 H 7
Nallıhan 46-47 D 2
Nālūt 60-61 G 2
Namacurra 64-65 J 6
Na'mah, An- 60-61 C 5
Namak, Daryācheh – 44-45 G 4
Namak-e Mīghan, Kavīre – 44-45 H 4
Namakwaland 64-65 E 8
Namakzār-e Khwāf 44-45 HJ 4
Namaland 64-65 E 8
Na'mân, Jazīrat an – = Jazīrat an-Nu'mān 62 F 4
Namanga 64-65 J 3
Namangan 44-45 L 2
Na'mānīyah, An- 46-47 L 6
Namanyere 64-65 H 4
Namapa 64-65 JK 5
Namarrói 64-65 J 6
Namasagali 64-65 H 2
Namasakata 63 D 5
Namatanai 52-53 h 5
Namatele 63 D 5
Nambanje 63 D 5
Nam Bô 52-53 DE 5
Nambour 56-57 K 5
Năm Căn 52-53 D 5
Nam Choed Yai = Kra Buri 52-53 C 4
Namch'ŏnjŏm 50-51 F 3
Namcy 42-43 Y 5
Nam Choed Yai = Kra Buri 52-53 C 4
Nam Đinh 52-53 E 2-3
Namerikawa 50-51 L 4
Nametil 64-65 JK 6
Nam-gang 50-51 F 3
Namhae-do 50-51 G 5
Namhan-gang 50-51 F 4
Namhoi = Foshan 48-49 L 7
Nam Choed Yai = Kra Buri 52-53 C 4
Namib = Namibwoestyn 64-65 D 6-E 8
Namib Desert = Namibwoestyn 64-65 D 6-E 8
Namibia 64-65 E 7
Namibia 64-65 E 7
Namibie 64-65 E 7
Namib-Naukluft Park 64-65 DE 7

Namib-sivatag = Namib woestijn 64-65 D 6-E 8
Namibwoestyn 64-65 D 6-E 8
Namjabarba Ri 48-49 H 6
Namlea 52-53 J 7
Namling Dsong 48-49 FG 6
Namoi River 56-57 J 6
Namous, Oued en – = Wādī an-Nāmus 60-61 D 2
Nampa, ID 72-73 C 3
Nampala 60-61 C 5
Nampo 48-49 NO 4
Namp'ot'ae-san 50-51 G 2
Nampula 64-65 JK 6
Namsen 30-31 E 5
Namsi 50-51 E 3
Namsos 30-31 DE 5
Nam Tsho 48-49 G 5
Namuli, Serra – 64-65 J 6
Namuling Zong = Namling Dsong 48-49 FG 6
Namulo 63 D 6
Namuno 63 D 6
Namur 34-35 K 3
Nāmūs, Wādī an- 60-61 D 2
Namus, Wau en – = Wāw an-Nāmūs 60-61 H 4
Nāmūs, Waw an- 60-61 H 4
Namutoni 64-65 E 6
Namwala 64-65 G 6
Namwŏn 50-51 F 5
Nan 52-53 D 3
Nan, Mae Nam – 52-53 D 3
Nana Candungo 64-65 F 5
Nanae 50-51 b 3
Nanaimo 70-71 M 8
Nanam 50-51 GH 2
Nana-Mambéré 60-61 GH 7
Nanango 56-57 K 5
Nanao [J] 50-51 L 4
Nanao wan 50-51 L 4
Nanau 63 E 1
Nanay, Rio – 78-79 E 5
Nancha 48-49 O 2
Nanchang 48-49 LM 6
Nanchang = Nanchong 48-49 JK 5
Nancheng 48-49 M 6
Nan-ching = Nanjing [TJ, Jiangsu] 48-49 M 5
Nanchino = Nanjing 48-49 M 5
Nanchong 48-49 JK 5
Nanchung = Nanchong 48-49 JK 5
Nancy 34-35 L 4
Nanda Devi 44-45 MN 4
Nandan 50-51 K 5
Nanded 44-45 M 7
Nandeir = Nanded 44-45 M 7
Nandi 52-53 a 2
N'andoma 42-43 G 5
Nandurbār 44-45 L 6
Nandyal 44-45 M 7
Nangade 63 DE 5
Nanga Eboko 60-61 G 8
Nangah Pinoh 52-53 F 7
Nan-gang = Nam-gang 50-51 F 3
Nānga Parbat 44-45 LM 3-4
Nangatayap 52-53 F 7
Nang'-ch'ien = Nangqian 48-49 H 5
Nangnim-sanmaek 50-51 F 2
Nangqian 48-49 H 5
Nan Hai 48-49 L 8-M 7
Nanhai = Foshan 48-49 L 7
Nan-hsiung = Nanxiong 48-49 LM 6
Nanjing [TJ, Jiangsu] 48-49 M 5
Nankhu 48-49 G 3
Nankin = Nanjing 48-49 M 5
Nanking = Nanjing 48-49 M 5
Nankoku 50-51 JK 6
Nanlaoye Ling 50-51 E 2-F 1
Nan Ling [TJ, ▲▲] 48-49 L 6-7
Nanling [TJ, ●] 48-49 M 5
Nanning 48-49 K 7
Nannup 56-57 C 6
Nanpan Jiang 48-49 JK 7
Nanping [TJ, Fujian] 48-49 M 6
Nanping [TJ, Hubei] 48-49 L 6
Nanripo 63 D 6
Nansei-shotō 48-49 NO 6-7
Nansei syotō = Nansei-shotō 48-49 NO 6-7
Nansen Sound 70-71 ST 1
Nan Shan 48-49 HJ 4
Nansio 64-65 H 3
Nantai-san 50-51 M 4
Nan-tch'ang = Nanchang 48-49 LM 6
Nan-tch'eng = Nancheng 48-49 M 6
Nan-tch'ong = Nanchong 48-49 JK 5
Nantes 34-35 G 5
Nanticoke, PA 74-75 EF 4
Nantong 48-49 N 5
Nantsang = Nanchang 48-49 LM 6
Nantucket, MA 74-75 HJ 4
Nantucket Island 72-73 N 3
Nantucket Sound 74-75 H 4
Nantung = Nantong 48-49 N 5
Nanty Glo, PA 74-75 D 4
Nanuque 78-79 LM 8

Nanusa, Kepulauan – 52-53 J 6
Nanxiong 48-49 LM 6
Nanyang 48-49 L 5
Nanyi = Nancha 48-49 O 2
Nanyuki 64-65 J 2
Nanzheng = Hanzhong 48-49 K 5
Nao, Cabo de la – 34-35 H 9
Naoconane Lake 70-71 W 7
Naoetsu 50-51 LM 4
Naōgata = Nōgata 50-51 H 6
Naoli He 48-49 P 2
Nao-li Ho = Naoli He 48-49 P 2
Naos, Isla – 72-73 bc 3
Naouâ = Nawā 46-47 FG 6
Napa, CA 76-77 B 6
Napaku 52-53 G 6
Napanee 74-75 E 2
Napanwainami 52-53 L 7
Napas 42-43 P 6
Nape 52-53 DE 3
Napels = Nàpoli 36-37 EF 5
Napier [NZ] 56-57 P 7
Napier, Mount – 56-57 EF 3
Napier Mountains 24 C 6
Naples, FL 72-73 K 6
Naples, NY 74-75 E 3
Naples = Nàpoli 36-37 EF 5
Napo, Rio – 78-79 E 5
Nápoles = Nàpoli 36-37 EF 5
Nàpoli 36-37 E 5
Nàpoli, Golfo di – 36-37 EF 5
Nápoly = Nàpoli 36-37 EF 5
Naqāda = Naqādah 62 E 5
Naqādah 62 E 5
Naqadeh 46-47 L 4
Nāqīshūt 60-61 L 8
Naqūrah, Rā's an- 46-47 F 6
Nara [J] 50-51 KL 5
Nārā [PAK] 44-45 K 5
Nara [RMM] 60-61 C 5
Naracoorte 56-57 GH 7
Naradham 58 GH 4
Naranjas, Punta – 78-79 C 3
Narathiwat 52-53 DE 5
Narāyanganj 44-45 OP 6
Narbadā = Narmada 44-45 LM 6
Narbonne 34-35 J 7
Nardò 36-37 GH 5
Narembeen 56-57 C 6
Narew 33 K 2
Nārī 44-45 K 5
Narinda, Helodranon'i – 64-65 L 5
Narjan-Mar 42-43 JK 4
Narlı 46-47 G 4
Narmada 44-45 LM 6
Narman 46-47 JK 2
Narodnaja, gora – 42-43 L 5
Naro-Fominsk 38-39 FG 4
Narok 64-65 J 3
Narooma 56-57 JK 7
Narrabri 56-57 JK 6
Narragansett Bay 74-75 H 4
Narrandera 56-57 J 6
Narran Lake 58 H 2
Narran River 58 H 2
Narrogin 56-57 C 6
Narromine 56-57 J 6
Narrows, OR 76-77 D 4
Narrows, VA 74-75 C 6
Narssaq 70-71 bc 5
Narssarssuaq 70-71 bc 5
Narugo 50-51 N 3
Narungombe 63 D 5
Naru-shima 50-51 G 6
Naruto 50-51 K 5
Narva [SU, ~] 30-31 M 8
Narva [SU, ●] 42-43 D 6
Narva laht 30-31 M 8
Narvik 30-31 G 3
Narvskoje vodochranilišče 30-31 N 8
Narvskoje vodochranilišče 30-31 N 8
Narwa = Narva 42-43 D 6
Narym 42-43 P 6
Naryn [SU, Kirgizskaja SSR ~] 44-45 L 2
Naryn [SU, Kirgizskaja SSR ●] 44-45 M 2
Naryn [SU, Rossijskaja SFSR] 42-43 S 7
Naryn = Taš-Kumyr 44-45 L 2
Narynkol 44-45 MN 2
Nasafjell 30-31 F 4
Nasarawa [WAN, Plateau] 60-61 F 7
Nasaret = Naẓerat 46-47 F 6
Năsăud 36-37 L 2
Naschitti, NM 76-77 J 7
Nāshik = Nasik 44-45 L 6-7
Nashua, NH 74-75 H 3
Nashville, GA 74-75 B 9
Nashville, TN 72-73 J 4
Našice 36-37 H 3
Näsijärvi 30-31 KL 7
Nasik 44-45 L 6-7
Nāṣir, An- 60-61 L 7
Nasir, Jabal an- 60-61 F 4
Nāṣirīyah [IRQ] 44-45 F 4
Nasīyah, Jabal – 62 E 6
Nasondoye 64-65 FG 5
Naṣr 62 D 2
Naṣr, An- 62 E 5
Naṣr, Khazzan an- 60-61 L 4

202 Murot

Nāṣrīyah 46-47 G 6
Nassarawa = Nasarawa 60-61 F 7
Nassau [BS] 72-73 L 6
Nassau, Bahia – 80 C 9
Nassau Sound 74-75 c 1
Nässjö 30-31 F 9
Nass River 70-71 L 6-7
Nastapoka Islands 70-71 V 6
Našice 36-37 H 3
Nata 64-65 G 7
Na-ta = Dan Xian 48-49 K 8
Natagaima 78-79 DE 4
Natal [BR, Rio Grande do Norte] 78-79 MN 6
Natal [RI] 52-53 C 6
Natal [ZA] 64-65 GH 8
Natal, Bassin de – 22-23 LM 7
Natal, Cuenca de – 22-23 LM 7
Natal, Ramal de – 64-65 J 9
Natal, Seuil de – 64-65 J 9
Natal Basin 22-23 LM 7
Natalbecken 22-23 LM 7
Natalbekken 22-23 LM 7
Nataldrempel 64-65 J 9
Natali-hátság 64-65 J 8-9
Natal Ridge 64-65 J 9
Natalschwelle 64-65 J 8-9
Natanya = Nětanya 46-47 F 6
Natash, Wādī – 62 EF 5
Natashquan River 70-71 Y 7
Natchez, MS 72-73 H 5
Natchitoches, LA 72-73 H 5
Nathorst land 30-31 jk 6
National City, CA 76-77 E 9
National Park 74-75 B 7
National Reactor Testing Station 76-77 G 4
Natitingou 60-61 E 6
Natividade 78-79 K 7
Nätong Dsong 48-49 G 6
Natron, Lake – 64-65 J 3
Naṭrūn, Wādī an- 62 CD 2
Natrun Lakes = Wādī an-Naṭrūn 62 CD 2
Natuna, Kepulauan – 52-53 E 6
Natuna Besar, Pulau – 52-53 E 6
Natural Bridges National Monument 76-77 HJ 7
Naturaliste, Cape – 56-57 B 6
Naturita, CO 76-77 J 6
Nauja Vilejka, Vilnius- 30-31 LM 10
Naukurr 56-57 FG 2
Naulavaraa 30-31 N 6
Naulila 64-65 DE 6
Nā'ūr 46-47 F 7
Nauru 20-21 S 6
Náusa 36-37 JK 5
Nauški 42-43 U 7
Nauški 42-43 U 7
Nauta 78-79 E 5
Nauvo 30-31 JK 7
Nava de Ricomalillo, La – 34-35 E 9
Navajo, AZ 76-77 J 8
Navajo Indian Reservation 76-77 HJ 7-8
Navajo Mountain 76-77 H 7
Navan 32 C 5
Navangar = Jāmnagar 44-45 L 6
Navarin, mys – 42-43 jk 5
Navarino, Isla – 80 C 9
Navarra 34-35 G 7
Navassa Island 72-73 LM 8
Naver 32 D 2
Navia 34-35 D 7
Navoi 42-43 M 9
Navojoa 72-73 E 6
Navolato 72-73 E 7
Návpaktos 36-37 JK 6
Návplion 36-37 K 7
Navrongo 60-61 D 6
Navşar = Şemdinli 46-47 L 4
Navy Board Inlet 70-71 U 3
Nawá 46-47 FG 6
Nawa = Naha 48-49 O 6
Nawābshāh 44-45 K 5
Nawādhību 60-61 A 4
Nawākshūt 60-61 A 5
Nawari = Nahari 50-51 JK 6
Nawāṣīf, Ḥarrat – 44-45 E 6
Nawfalīyah, An- 60-61 H 2
Naws, Rā's – 44-45 H 7
Naxos [I] 36-37 F 7
Náxos [GR, ⊙] 36-37 L 7
Náxos [GR, ●] 36-37 L 7
Nayarit 72-73 EF 7
Nāy Band [IR, Banāder va Jazāyer-e Khalīj-e Fārs] 44-45 G 5
Nāy Band [IR, Khorāsān] 44-45 H 4
Nāy Band, Ra's-e – 44-45 G 5
Nayoro 50-51 c 1
Nayoro = Gornozavodsk 42-43 b 8
Nazaré 34-35 C 9
Nazaré [BR, Amazonas] 78-79 F 4
Nazaré [BR, Bahia] 78-79 M 7
Nazarê = Naẓerat 46-47 F 6
Nazareth = Naẓerat 46-47 F 6
Nazareth Bank 64-65 O 5
Nazca 78-79 DE 7
Nazca, Dorsal de – 22-23 E 7-F 6
Nazca, Seuil de – 22-23 E 7-F 6
Nazca Ridge 22-23 F 7-E 6
Nazcarug 22-23 E 7-F 6
Nazcaschwelle 22-23 E 7-F 6
N'azepetrovsk 38-39 LM 4
Naẓerat 46-47 F 6
Nazija 38-39 F 4
Nazilli 46-47 C 4
Nazimiye 46-47 HJ 3
Nazimovo = Novonazimovo 42-43 QR 6
Nazino 42-43 OP 5-6
Nāzlū Rūd 46-47 L 4
Nazombe 63 D 5
Nazrēt 60-61 M 7
Nazwá 44-45 H 6
Nazyvajevsk 42-43 N 6
Nazzah 62 D 4

Nchanga 63 AB 6
Nchelenge 63 B 5

Ndabala 63 B 6
N'daghāmshah, Sabkhat – 60-61 AB 5
Ndai 52-53 k 6
Ndala 63 C 4
Ndalatando 64-65 DE 4
Ndali 60-61 E 7
Ndélé 60-61 J 7
N'Dendé 64-65 D 3
Ndeni 52-53 l 7
N'djamena 60-61 GH 6
N'Djolé [Gabun] 64-65 CD 3
Ndola 64-65 G 5
Nduye 63 B 2
Ndye 63 B 2
Ndzuwani 64-65 KL 5

Neagh, Lough – 32 C 4
Neah Bay, WA 76-77 A 1
Neale, Lake – 56-57 F 4
Neales, The – 56-57 G 5
Neapel = Nàpoli 36-37 E 5
Neápolis [GR, Grámmos] 36-37 J 5
Neápolis [GR, Pelopónnēsos] 36-37 K 7
Neapol = Nàpoli 36-37 EF 5
Neapol = Nàpoli 36-37 EF 5
Near Islands 19 D 1
Nebek, En- = An-Nabk 44-45 D 4
Nebine Creek 56-57 J 5
Nebit-Dag 44-45 GH 3
Neblina, Pico da – 78-79 FG 4
Nebo, Mount – 76-77 H 6
Nebraska 72-73 FG 3
Nebrodie, Monti – 36-37 F 7
Nechako Plateau 70-71 L 7
Neckar 33 D 4
Necochea 80 E 5
Neder-Californië 76-77 F 10
Neder-Guinee 22-23 K 5-6
Nederland 34-35 K 3-L 2
Needle Peak 76-77 E 8
Needles, CA 76-77 F 8
Neepawa 70-71 R 7
Nefoussa, Djebel – = Jabal Nafusah 60-61 G 2
Neftejugansk 42-43 NO 5
Nefud = An-Nafūd 44-45 E 5
Nefud, En- = An-Nafūd 44-45 E 5
Negade = Naqādah 62 E 5
Negapatam = Nagapattinam 44-45 MN 8
Negara 52-53 FG 8
Negeb = Han-Negev 46-47 F 7
Negēlē 60-61 MN 7
Negerpynten 30-31 l 6
Neggio = Nejo 60-61 M 7
Neghilli = Negēlē 60-61 MN 7
Negoiu 36-37 L 3
Negomane 63 D 5
Negombo = Mīgamuwa 44-45 M 9
Negotin 36-37 K 3
Negribreen 30-31 k 5
Negros 52-53 H 5
Negru Vodă 36-37 N 4
Negueve = Han-Negev 46-47 F 7
Nehalem, OR 76-77 B 3
Nehbandān 44-45 HJ 4
Nehe 48-49 NO 2
Neiafu 52-53 c 2
Nei-chiang = Neijiang 48-49 JK 6
Neihart, MT 76-77 H 2
Neijiang 48-49 JK 6
Neikiang = Neijiang 48-49 JK 6
Nei Menggu = Nei Monggol Zizhiqu 48-49 K 3-M 2
Neimenggu, Région Autonome – 48-49 K 3-M 2
Neineva 46-47 JK 5
Neiße 33 G 3
Neisse = Nysa 33 H 3
Neiva 78-79 DE 4
Neja 42-43 G 6
Nejd = Najd 44-45 E 5-6
Nejo 60-61 M 7
Nejto 38-39 NO 1-2
Nekemtē 60-61 M 7
Nekropolis 62 E 5
Neksø 30-31 F 10
Nelidovo 38-39 F 4
Nel'kan 42-43 Za 6
Nellore 44-45 MN 8
Nellūru = Nellore 44-45 MN 8
Nel'ma 42-43 ab 8
Nelson [CDN] 70-71 N 8
Nelson [NZ] 56-57 O 8
Nelson [RA] 80 DE 4
Nelson, AZ 76-77 G 8
Nelson, CA 76-77 C 6
Nelson, Estrecho – 80 AB 8
Nelson Forks 70-71 M 6
Nelson Island 70-71 C 5
Nelson River 70-71 RS 6
Nelsonville, OH 74-75 B 5
Nelspruit 64-65 H 8
Nemah, WA 76-77 B 2
Neman 30-31 J 10
Ne'māniya, An- = An-Na'mānīyah 46-47 L 6
Německo 33 C-F 2-4
Nemenčinė 30-31 L 10
Nemenčinė 30-31 L 10
Nemira, Muntele – 36-37 M 2
Nemours = Ghazawat 60-61 D 1
Nemrut Daği 46-47 JK 3
Nemunas 30-31 K 10
Nemuro 48-49 S 3
Nemuro-kaikyō 50-51 d 1-2
Nemuro wan 50-51 d 2
Nenagh 32 BC 5
Nenana, AK 70-71 FG 5
Něnecký autonomní okruh 42-43 J-L 4
Nenets, Circunscripción Nacional de los – 42-43 J-L 4
Nenets, District National des – 42-43 J-L 4
Nenets Autonomous Area 42-43 J-L 4
Nen Jiang [TJ, ~] 48-49 N 2
Nenjiang [TJ, ●] 48-49 O 2
Nen Jiang = Naguun Mörön 48-49 NO 1-2
Nentsen, Nationaal Gebied der – 42-43 J-L 4
Nenzen, Nationalkreis der – 42-43 J-L 4
Neola, UT 76-77 H 5
Neosho River 72-73 G 4
Nepa 42-43 U 6
Nepál 44-45 NO 5
Nepal 44-45 NO 5
Nephi, UT 76-77 GH 6
Nephin 32 B 4
Nepoko 64-65 G 2
Nérac 34-35 H 6
Nerbudda = Narmada 44-45 LM 6
Nerča 42-43 W 7
Nerčinsk 42-43 W 7
Nerčinskij Zavod 42-43 W 7
Nerča 42-43 W 7
Nerčinsk 42-43 W 7
Nerčinskij Zavod 42-43 W 7
Nerechta 38-39 H 4
Neretva 36-37 H 4
Neriquinha = N'Riquinha 64-65 F 6
Neris 30-31 L 10
Ñermete, Punta – 78-79 C 6
Nerojka, gora – 42-43 KL 5
Nerskoje ploskogorje 42-43 c 5
Ner'ungri 42-43 XY 6
Nes' 38-39 HJ 2
Nesebâr 36-37 MN 4
Neskaupstadhur 30-31 fg 2
Nesna 30-31 E 4
Ness, Loch – 32 D 3
Néstos 36-37 L 5
Nesttun, Bergen- 30-31 AB 7
Nesviž 30-31 M 11
Nesviž 30-31 M 11
Nětanya 46-47 F 7
Nethanya = Nětanya 46-47 F 7
Netherdale 56-57 J 4
Netherlands 34-35 K 3-L 2
Nettilling Lake 70-71 W 4
Neubrandenburg 33 F 2
Neubraunschweig = New Brunswick 70-71 X 8
Neuchâtel 33 C 5
Neuchâtel, Lac de – 33 C 5
Neue Hebriden = Vanuatu 56-57 N 2-O 3
Neuengland = New England 72-73 M 3-N 2
Neufchâteau [B] 34-35 K 4
Neufchateau [F] 34-35 KL 4
Neufchâtel-en-Bray 34-35 H 4
Neufundland = Newfoundland 70-71 Za 8
Neufundlandbank 22-23 G 3
Neufundlandbecken 22-23 GH 3
Neufundlandschwelle 22-23 G 3-H 4
Neuguinea 52-53 L 7-M 8
Neuguineaschwelle 52-53 M 5-6
Neuhebridenbecken 56-57 MN 3
Neuhebridengraben 56-57 N 3-4
Neukaledonien 58-59 MN 3
Neukastilien = Castilla la Nueva 34-35 E 8-F 7
Neumarkt 33 E 4
Neumünster 33 DE 1
Neunkirchen [A] 33 H 5
Neunkirchen [D] 33 C 4
Neupommern-Bougainville-Graben 52-53 h 6
Neuquén [RA, ●] 80 C 5
Neuruppin 33 F 2
Neusatz = Novi Sad 36-37 HJ 3
Neuschottland = Nova Scotia 70-71 X 9-Y 8
Neuschwabenland 24 B 36-2
Neuseeland 56-57 N 8-O 7
Neuseelandschwelle 56-57 M 5-7
Neuse River 74-75 E 7
Neusibirische Inseln = Novosibirskije ostrova 42-43 Z-f 2
Neusiedler See 33 H 5
Neustettin = Szczecinek 33 H 2
Neustrelitz 33 F 2
Neu-Ulm 33 E 4
Neuwied 33 CD 3
Neva 38-39 F 4
Nevada 72-73 CD 4
Nevada City, CA 76-77 C 6
Nevado, Cerro el – 80 C 5
Nevado, Sierra del – 80 C 5
Neve, Serra da – 64-65 D 5
Nevel' 38-39 EF 4
Never 42-43 XY 7
Nevers 34-35 J 5
Nevinnomyssk 38-39 H 7
Nevis 72-73 O 8
Nevis, Ben – 32 D 3
Nevjansk 42-43 KL 6
Nevşehir 44-45 C 3
Newala 64-65 J 5
New Albany, IN 72-73 J 4
New Amsterdam 78-79 H 3
Newark [GB] 32 F 5
Newark, DE 74-75 F 5
Newark, NJ 72-73 M 3
Newark, NY 74-75 E 3
Newark, OH 74-75 B 4
New Bedford, MA 72-73 MN 3
Newberg, OR 76-77 B 3
New Bern, NC 72-73 L 4
Newberry, CA 76-77 E 8
Newberry, SC 74-75 C 7
New Boston, OH 74-75 B 5
New Braunfels, TX 72-73 G 6
New Britain 52-53 gh 6
New Britain, CT 74-75 G 4
New Britain Bougainville Trench 52-53 h 6
New Brunswick 70-71 X 8
New Brunswick, NJ 74-75 F 4
Newburgh [CDN] 74-75 E 2
Newburgh, NY 74-75 F 4
Newbury 32 F 6
Newburyport, MA 74-75 H 3
New Caledonie 56-57 MN 3
Newcastel Creek 56-57 F 3
New Castile = Castilla la Nueva 34-35 E 9-F 8
Newcastle [AUS] 56-57 K 6
Newcastle [GB] 32 D 4
Newcastle [ZA] 64-65 GH 8
New Castle, OH 74-75 A 5
New Castle, PA 74-75 C 4
Newcastle, VA 74-75 C 6
Newcastle Bay 56-57 H 2
Newcastle upon Tyne 32 EF 4
Newcastle upon Tyne 32 EF 4
Newcastle Waters 56-57 F 3
Newcomb, NM 76-77 J 7
Newcomerstown, OH 74-75 C 4
Newdale, ID 76-77 H 4
Newdegate 56-57 CD 6
New Delhi 44-45 M 5
New England [USA] 72-73 M 3-N 2
New England Range 56-57 K 5-6
Newenham, Cape – 70-71 D 6
Newfane, VT 74-75 G 3
Newfondland Basin 22-23 GH 3
Newfoundland [CDN, ⊙] 70-71 Za 8
Newfoundland [CDN, ☆] 70-71 Y 6-Z 8
Newfoundland Bank 22-23 G 3
Newfoundlandbekken 22-23 GH 3
Newfoundlanddrempel 22-23 G 3-H 4
Newfoundland-Ondiepte 22-23 G 3
Newfoundland Ridge 22-23 G 3-H 4
New Georgia 52-53 j 6
New Georgia Group 52-53 j 6
New Georgia Sound = The Slot 52-53 j 6
New Glasgow 70-71 Y 8
New Guinea 52-53 L 7-M 8
New Guinea Rise 52-53 M 5-6
Newhalem, WA 76-77 C 1
Newhall, CA 76-77 D 8
New Hampshire 72-73 M 3
New Hanover [PNG] 52-53 gh 5
Newhaven [GB] 32 G 6
New Haven, CT 72-73 M 3
New Hebrides 56-57 N 2-O 3
New Hebrides Basin 56-57 MN 3
New Hebrides Trench 56-57 N 3-4
New Iberia, LA 72-73 H 5-6
New Ireland 52-53 h 5
New Jersey 72-73 M 3
New Kensington, PA 74-75 D 4
New Kowloon 48-49 LM 7
New Lexington, OH 74-75 BC 5
New Liskeard 70-71 UV 8
New London, CT 74-75 GH 4
Newman, CA 76-77 C 7
Newmarket [CDN] 74-75 D 2
New Martinsville, WV 74-75 C 5
New Meadows, ID 76-77 E 3
New Mexico 72-73 EF 5
New Norfolk 56-57 J 8
New Orleans, LA 72-73 HJ 5-6
New Philadelphia, OH 74-75 C 4
New Pine Creek, OR 76-77 C 4
New Plymouth 56-57 O 7
Newport [GB, I. of Wight] 32 F 6
Newport [GB, Severn] 32 E 6
Newport, KY 72-73 K 4
Newport, ME 74-75 J 2
Newport, NH 74-75 GH 3
Newport, OR 76-77 A 3
Newport, RI 74-75 H 4
Newport, TN 74-75 B 6-7
Newport, VT 74-75 GH 2
Newport, WA 76-77 E 1
Newport News, VA 72-73 L 4
New Providence Island 72-73 L 6-7
Newquay 32 D 6
New Rochelle, NY 74-75 G 4
Newry 32 CD 4
New Siberian Islands = Novosibirskije ostrova 42-43 Z-f 2
New Smyrna Beach, FL 74-75 c 2
New South Wales 56-57 H-K 6
Newton, KS 72-73 G 4
Newton, MA 74-75 H 3
Newton, NC 74-75 C 7
Newton, NJ 74-75 F 4
Newton Falls, NY 74-75 F 2
Newtontoppen 30-31 k 5
Newtownards 32 D 4
New Westminster 70-71 MN 8
New York 72-73 LM 3
New York, NY 72-73 M 3-4
New York Mountains 76-77 F 8
New Zealand 56-57 N 8-O 7
Neyed = Najd 44-45 E 5-6
Neyrīz 44-45 G 5
Neyshābūr 44-45 H 3
Nezametnyj = Aldan 42-43 XY 6
Nežin 38-39 F 5
Nezperce, ID 76-77 EF 2
Nez Perce Indian Reservation 76-77 EF 2
Nežin 38-39 F 5

Ngabang 52-53 EF 6
Ngamdo Tsonag Tsho 48-49 G 5
Ngami, Lake – 64-65 F 7
Nganghouei = Anhui 48-49 M 5
Nganglaring Tso = Ngangla Ringtsho 48-49 EF 5
Nganglong Gangri 48-49 E 5
Ngangtha Ringtsho 48-49 EF 5
Ngangtse Tsho 48-49 F 5
Ngan-yang = Anyang 48-49 LM 4
Ngao 52-53 CD 3
Ngaoundéré 60-61 G 7
Ngara 63 B 3
Ngau 52-53 a 2
Ngaumdere = Ngaoundéré 60-61 G 7
Ngaundere = Ngaoundéré 60-61 G 7
Ngazidja 64-65 K 5
Ngerengere 63 D 4
Ngiro, Ewaso – 64-65 J 3
Ngiva 64-65 E 6
Ngoc Linh 52-53 E 3
Ngoko 64-65 E 2
Ngomba 63 C 5
Ngong 64-65 J 3
Ngoring Tsho 48-49 H 4-5
Ngorongoro Crater 64-65 HJ 3
N'Gounié 64-65 D 3
Ngoura 60-61 H 6
Ngouri 60-61 H 6
Ngourti 60-61 G 5
Ngoywa 64-65 H 4
Ngozi 63 B 3
Nguigmi 60-61 G 6
Ngulu 52-53 L 5
Ngunza 64-65 D 5
N'Guri = Ngouri 60-61 H 6
Nguru 60-61 G 6

Nha Trang 52-53 EF 4
Nhecolândia 78-79 H 8
Nhi Ha, Sông – 52-53 D 2
Nhill 56-57 H 7

Niafounké 60-61 D 5
Niagara Falls 72-73 KL 3
Niagara Falls, NY 72-73 L 3
Niagara River 74-75 D 3
Niah 52-53 F 6
Ni'āj, Jabal – 62 E 6
Niamey 60-61 E 6
Niangara 64-65 G 2
Nia-Nia 64-65 G 2
Nianqingtanggula Shan = Nyanchhenthanglha 48-49 G 5-6
Nias, Pulau – 52-53 C 6
Niassa 64-65 J 5
Niassa = Malawi 64-65 HJ 5
Nibāk 44-45 G 6
Nibe 30-31 C 9
Niblinto 80 B 5
Nicaragua 72-73 JK 9
Nicaragua, Lago de – 72-73 JK 9
Nicaro 72-73 L 7
Nice 34-35 L 7
Nicea = Nice 34-35 L 7
Nichinan 50-51 H 7
Nicholson [AUS] 56-57 E 3
Nicholson River 56-57 G 3
Nickel = Nikel' 42-43 E 4
Nickol Bay 56-57 C 4
Nicobar Islands 44-45 P 9
Nicolás, Canal – 72-73 KL 7
Nicomedia = İzmit 44-45 BC 2
Nico Pérez 80 EF 4
Nicosia 36-37 F 7
Nicosia = Levkōsia 44-45 C 3
Nicosie = Levkōsia 44-45 C 3
Nicoya 72-73 J 9
Nicoya, Golfo de – 72-73 J 9
Nicoya, Península de – 72-73 J 9-10
Nida 33 K 3
Nī Dillī = New Delhi 44-45 M 5
Nido, El – 52-53 G 4
Niebüll 33 D 1
Niedere Tauern 33 FG 5
Niederguinea 22-23 K 5-6
Niederkalifornien 68 K 6-7
Niederlande 34-35 K 3-L 2
Niederösterreich 33 GH 4
Niedersachsen 33 C-E 2
Niedźwiedzia, Wyspa – 19 B 16-17
Niemba [ZRE, ~] 63 B 4
Niemba [ZRE, ●] 63 B 4
Niemcy 33 C-F 2-4
Nienburg 33 D 2
Nienchentangla = Nyanchhenthanglha 48-49 F 6-G 5
Nieniecki Okręg Autonomiczny 42-43 J-L 4
Nieuw Amsterdam [SME] 78-79 HJ 3
Nieuw-Antwerpen = Nouvelle-Anvers 64-65 EF 2
Nieuw-Caledonië 56-57 MN 3
Nieuw-Castillië = Castilla la Nueva 34-35 E 9-F 8
Nieuwe Hebriden 56-57 N 2-O 3
Nieuwe Hebriden Bekken 56-57 MN 3
Nieuwe Hebridentrog 56-57 N 3-4
Nieuw-Guinea 52-53 L 7-M 8
Nieuw Guineadrempel 52-53 M 5-6
Nieuw Nickerie 78-79 H 3
Nieuwoudtville 64-65 E 9
Nieuwsiberische Eilanden = Novosibirskije ostrova 42-43 Z-f 2
Nieuw-Zeeland 56-57 N 8-O 7
Nieuw-Zeelandrug 56-57 M 5-7
Nieves = Nevis 72-73 O 8
Niewolnicza, Rzeka – 70-71 O 5-6
Niewolnicze, Wybrzeże – 60-61 E 7
Niffur = Nippur 46-47 L 6
Nifīsha = Nafīshah 62 DE 2
Niğde 44-45 CD 3
Niger [RN, ★] 60-61 FG 5
Niger [RN, ☆] 60-61 F 7
Niger, Bouches du – 60-61 F 8
Niger, Mouths of the – 60-61 F 7-8
Niger, River – 60-61 E 6
Nigéria 60-61 E-G 7
Nigérie 60-61 E-G 7
Nighthawk, WA 76-77 D 1
Nigrita 36-37 K 5
Nihah 46-47 J 2
Nihonmatsu = Nihommatsu 50-51 N 4
Niigata 48-49 Q 4
Niihama 50-51 J 5-6
Niihau 52-53 de 3
Niimi 50-51 J 5
Nii-shima 50-51 M 5
Niitsu 50-51 M 4
Nijād al-'Alī 60-61 D 2-E 1
Nijamābād = Nizamabad 44-45 M 7
Nijmegen 34-35 KL 3
Nikaragua 72-73 JK 9
Nikel' 42-43 E 4
Nikēphorion = Ar-Raqqah 44-45 DE 3
Nikhaib, An- = Nukhayb 44-45 E 4
Nikheila, En – = An Nuhaylah 62 D 4
Nikito-Ivdel'skoje = Ivdel' 42-43 L 5
Nikki 60-61 E 6-7
Nikolajev 38-39 F 6
Nikolajevsk = Pugač'ov 42-43 HJ 7
Nikolajevskij 38-39 J 5
Nikolajevsk-na-Amure 42-43 b 7
Nikol'sk [SU, Severnyje uvaly] 42-43 H 6
Nikol'skij 42-43 M 8
Nikol'skoje [SU, Komandorskije ostrova] 42-43 fg 6
Nikomēdeia = İzmit 44-45 BC 2

Nikom 203

Nikonga 63 B 3-4
Nikopol 36-37 L 4
Nikopol' 38-39 F 6
Nikosia = Levkōsia 44-45 C 3
Nikōsie = Levkōsia 44-45 C 3
Nikozja = Levkōsia 44-45 C 3
Nīk Pey 46-47 N 4
Niksar 46-47 G 2
Nikšić 36-37 H 4
Nil = Baḥr an-Nīl 60-61 L 3-4
Nīl, Baḥr an- 60-61 L 3-4
Nila, Pulau – 52-53 JK 8
Nīlagiri = Nilgiri Hills 44-45 M 8
Nīl al-Abyaḍ, An- 60-61 L 6
Nīl al-Azraq, An- 60-61 L 6
Niland, CA 76-77 F 9
Nil Błękitny = Abay 60-61 M 6
Nile = Baḥr an-Nīl 60-61 L 3-4
Nile Bleu = Abay 60-61 M 6
Niles, OH 74-75 C 4
Nilo = Baḥr an-Nīl 60-61 L 3-4
Nīlus = Baḥr an-Nīl 60-61 L 3-4
Nimba, Mont – 60-61 C 7
Nimega = Nijmegen 34-35 KL 3
Nimègue = Nijmegen 34-35 KL 3
Nîmes 34-35 JK 7
Nimmitabel 58 J 6
Nimnyrskij = Malyj Nimnyr 42-43 Y 6
Nimrod, MT 76-77 G 2
Nimūli 60-61 L 8
Nimwegen = Nijmegen 34-35 KL 3
Nimwegen = Nijmegen 34-35 KL 3
Nīnawā 46-47 JK 5
Nīnawā = Ninive 46-47 K 4
Nindigully 58 J 2
Nine Degree Channel 44-45 L 9
Nine Degree Channel 44-45 L 9
Nine Degree Channel 44-45 L 9
Nineve = Ninive 44-45 E 3
Ninfas, Punta – 80 D 6
Ning'an 48-49 OP 3
Ningbo 48-49 N 6
Ningcheng 50-51 B 2
Ningde 48-49 M 6
Ningdu 48-49 M 6
Ningguo 48-49 M 5
Ninghsia, Autonomes Gebiet 48-49 H 3-K 4
Ning-hsiang = Ningxiang 48-49 L 6
Ninghsien = Ning Xian 48-49 K 4
Ninghszia-Huj 48-49 JK 3-4
Ninghua 48-49 M 6
Ninghwa = Ninghua 48-49 M 6
Ning-po = Ningbo 48-49 N 6
Ningsia, Autonomes Gebiet – 48-49 JK 3-4
Ningsia Autonomous Region 48-49 JK 3-4
Ningteh = Ningde 48-49 M 6
Ninguta = Ning'an 48-49 OP 3
Ningxia 48-49 H 3-K 4
Ningxia, Region Autónoma de – 48-49 JK 3-4
Ningxiahui, Région Autonome – 48-49 JK 3-4
Ningxiahui, Region autonomiczny – 48-49 JK 3-4
Ningxia Huizu Zizhiqu 48-49 JK 3-4
Ning Xian 48-49 K 4
Ningxiang 48-49 L 6
Ninh Binh 52-53 E 2
Ninh Hoa [VN ↑ Nha Trang] 52-53 EF 4
Ninigo Group 52-53 M 7
Ninive 44-45 E 3
Ninjintangla Shan = Nyanchhenthanglha 48-49 G 5-6
Ninnis Glacier 24 C 16-15
Ninua = Ninive 44-45 E 3
Niobrara River 72-73 F 3
Niokolo Koba, Parc national du – 60-61 B 6
Nioro du Rip 60-61 A 6
Nioro du Sahel 60-61 C 5
Niort 34-35 G 5
Nipawin 70-71 Q 7
Nipepe 63 D 6
Nipigon 70-71 T 8
Nipigon, Lake – 70-71 ST 8
Nipissing, Lake – 70-71 UV 8
Nippur 46-47 L 6
Nipton, CA 76-77 F 8
Niquelândia 78-79 K 7
Nīr 46-47 N 4
Nirasaki 50-51 M 5
Niriz, Daryācheh i – = Daryācheh Bakhtegān 44-45 G 5
Niš 36-37 JK 4
Nişāb 44-45 E 5
Nişâb, An – = Anşāb 44-45 F 8
Nišava 36-37 K 4
Niscemi 36-37 F 5
Nisch = Niš 36-37 JK 4
Nishinomiya 50-51 K 5
Nishinoomote 50-51 H 7
Nishino shima 50-51 J 4
Nishio 50-51 L 5
Nishisonoki hantō 50-51 G 6

Nishiyama 50-51 M 4
Nishtawn 44-45 G 7
Nishtūn = Nishtawn 44-45 G 7
Nisia Floresta 78-79 MN 6
Nisibin = Nusaybin 44-45 E 3
Nisibis = Nusaybin 44-45 E 3
Nisko 33 KL 3
Nissan 30-31 E 9
Nisser 30-31 C 8
Nisutlin Plateau 70-71 K 5
Nisyros 36-37 M 7
Nisz = Niš 36-37 JK 4
Nisz = Niš 36-37 JK 4
Niš 36-37 JK 4
Nišava 36-37 K 4
Niťaure 30-31 L 9
Niterói 78-79 L 9
Nitra 33 J 4
Nitro, WV 74-75 C 5
Niuafo'ou 52-53 b 2
Niuatoputapu 52-53 c 2
Niva 30-31 P 4
Nivelles 34-35 K 3
Nivernais 34-35 J 5
Nivskij 42-43 E 4
Niya Bazar 48-49 E 4
Nizamabad 44-45 M 7
Nizamghāṭ 44-45 Q 5
Nizam Sagar 44-45 M 7
Nizip 46-47 G 4
Nizke Tatry 33 JK 4
Nizkij, mys – 42-43 hj 5
Nižn'aja Kamenka 38-39 JK 2
Nižn'aja Peša 42-43 H 4
Nižn'aja Tunguska 42-43 TU 5
Nižn'aja Tura 42-43 K 6
Nižneangarsk 42-43 UV 6
Nižneilimsk 42-43 T 6
Nižneimbatskoje 42-43 QR 5
Nižnekamsk 42-43 J 7
Nižneleninskoje 42-43 Z 8
Nižneudinsk 42-43 S 7
Nižnevartovsk 42-43 O 5
Nižnije Sergi 38-39 L 4
Nižnij Lomov 38-39 H 5
Nižnij Novgorod 42-43 GH 6
Nižnij Tagil 42-43 KL 6
Nižnij Trajanov val 36-37 N 3
Nizozemsko 34-35 J 3-L 2
Nizza = Nice 34-35 L 7
Nižn'aja Kamenka 38-39 JK 2
Nižn'aja Peša 42-43 H 4
Nižn'aja Tunguska 42-43 TU 5
Nižn'aja Tura 42-43 K 6
Nižneangarsk 42-43 UV 6
Nižneilimsk 42-43 T 6
Nižneimbatskoje 42-43 QR 5
Nižnekamsk 42-43 J 7
Nižneleninskoje 42-43 Z 8
Nižneudinsk 42-43 S 7
Nižnevartovsk 42-43 O 5
Nižnije Sergi 38-39 L 4
Nižnij Lomov 38-39 H 5
Nižnij Novgorod 42-43 GH 6
Nižnij Tagil 42-43 KL 6
Nižnij Trajanov val 36-37 N 3
Njala = Mono 60-61 E 7
Njardhvik 30-31 b 2
Njassa = Lake Malawi 64-65 H 5
Njombe [EAT, ~] 64-65 H 4
Njombe [EAT, ●] 64-65 HJ 4
Nkata Bay = Nkhata Bay 64-65 H 5
Nkhata Bay 64-65 H 5
Nkiôna 36-37 K 6
Nkongsamba 60-61 FG 8
Nkréko, Ákra – = Akrōtérion Gréko 46-47 F 5
Nkululu 63 C 4

Nṁetország 33 C-F 2-4

Noanama 78-79 D 4
Noatak, AK 70-71 D 4
Noatak River 70-71 DE 4
Nobeoka 48-49 P 5
Nockatunga 58 F 1
Nófilia, en – = An-Nawfalīyah 60-61 H 2
Nogajskaja step' 38-39 J 7
Nogal = Nugal 44-45 F 9
Nogales [MEX] 76-77 J 10
Nogales, AZ 72-73 D 5
Nogales Heroica 72-73 D 5
Nogat 33 J 1
Nōgata 50-51 H 6
Noginsk 38-39 H 4
Nogoyá 80 DE 4
Noheji 50-51 N 3
Noir, Isla – 80 B 8
Noirmoutier, Île de – 34-35 F 5
Nojima-saki 50-51 MN 5
Nojon 48-49 J 3
Nokia 30-31 K 7
Nola [RCA] 60-61 H 8
Nolinsk 42-43 H 6
Nomamisaki 50-51 GH 7
Nome, AK 70-71 C 5
No-min Ho = Nuomin He 48-49 N 2
Nõmme, Tallinn- 30-31 L 8
Nomo-saki 50-51 G 6

Nong'an 48-49 NO 3
Nong Khai 52-53 D 3
Nongoma 64-65 H 8
Nonni = Nen Jiang 48-49 O 1-2
Nonsan 50-51 F 4
Noonan 30-31 F 4
Noord-Amerika 22-23 DE 3
Noordatlantische Rug 22-23 H 5-3
Noordaustralisch Bekken 56-57 C 2
Noordbandabekken 52-53 HJ 7
Noordelijke IJszee 19 AB 32-5
Noord-Ierland 32 CD 4
Noord-Korea 48-49 O 3-4
Noordossetische Autonome Republiek = 4 ◁ 38-39 H 7
Noordpacifisch Bekken 22-23 AB 3-4
Noordwestaustralisch Bekken 22-23 OP 6
Noordwestpacifisch Rug 22-23 S 3-4
Noordzee 32 F-J 3
Noormarkku 30-31 J 6
Noors Bekken 22-23 JK 2
Noorse Geul 30-31 A 8-C 9
Noorvik 30-31 D 4
Noorweegse Zee 19 C 19-B 17
Noorwegen 30-31 C 7-L 2
Nootka Island 70-71 L 8
Noqui 64-65 D 4
Nora 30-31 C 7
Norah 60-61 MN 5
Nord, Canal du – 32 CD 4
Nord, Mer du – 32 F-J 3
Nordalbanische Alpen = Alpet e Shqipërisë 36-37 HJ 4
Nordamerika 22-23 DE 3
Nordamerikanisches Becken 22-23 FG 4
Nordatlantischer Rücken 22-23 H 5-3
Nordaustlandet 30-31 k-m 5
Nordaustralisches Becken 56-57 C 2
Nordbandabecken 52-53 HJ 7
Nordborneo = Sabah 52-53 G 5
Nordcross, GA 74-75 A 8
Norden 33 C 2
Nordenškel'da, archipelag – 42-43 RS 2
Nordenškel'da, zaliv – 42-43 JK 2
Nordenskiøldbukta 30-31 l 4
Nordenskiøld land 30-31 jk 6
Nordenškel'da, archipelag – 42-43 RS 2
Nordenškel'da, zaliv – 42-43 JK 2
Nord-Fidschibecken 56-57 O 3
Nordfjord 30-31 AB 7
Nordfjorden 30-31 j 5
Nordfriesische Inseln 33 D 1
Nordfriesische Inseln 33 D 1
Nordhausen 33 E 3
Nordhorn 33 C 2
Nordhur-Ísafjardhar 30-31 b 1-2
Nordhur-Múla 30-31 f 2
Nordhur-Thingeyjar 30-31 ef 1-2
Nordirland 32 CD 4
Nordkanal = North Channel 32 CD 4
Nordkapp [N] 30-31 LM 2
Nordkapp [Svalbard] 30-31 k 4
Nordkinn 30-31 MN 2
Nordkjosbotn 30-31 HJ 3
Nordkorea 48-49 O 3-4
Nordland 30-31 E 5-G 3
Nördliche Dwina = Severnaja Dvina 42-43 G 5
Nördlicher Ural = Severnyj Ural 42-43 K 5-6
Nördlingen 33 E 4
Nord-Marianen 20-21 RS 5
Nordos Çayı 46-47 K 3
Nordossetische Autonome Republik = 4 ◁ 38-39 H 7
Nordostrundingen 19 A 18-20
Nord-Ostsee-Kanal 33 D 1-2
Nord-Ouest, Territoire du – Northwest Territories 70-71 M-U 4
Nord-Ouest Australien, Bassin du – 22-23 OP 6
Nord-Ouest Indien, Dorsale du – 22-23 N 5-6
Nordpazifisches Becken 22-23 AB 3-4
Nordpolarmeer 19 AB 32-5
Nordre Kvaløy 30-31 H 2
Nordre Strømfjord 70-71 a 4
Nordre Trøndelag 30-31 DE 5
Nordvik 42-43 V 3
Nordwestaustralisches Becken 22-23 OP 6
Nordwest-Westfalen 33 CD 3
Nordrhodesien = Sambia 64-65 G 6-J 5
Nordsee 32 F-J 3
Nord-Trøndelag 30-31 DE 5
Nordvik 42-43 V 3
Nordwestindischer Rücken 22-23 N 5-6

Nordwestindische Rug 22-23 N 5-6
Nordwestpazifischer Rücken 22-23 S 3-4
Nordwestpazifisches Becken 22-23 ST 3-4
Nordwest-Territorien = Northwest Territories 70-71 M-U 4
Nore 30-31 C 7
Norfolk, NE 72-73 G 3
Norfolk, VA 72-73 LM 4
Norfolk, Dorsal de – 56-57 N 6-7
Norfolk, Grzbiet – 56-57 C 2
Norfolk, Seuil – 56-57 N 6-7
Norfolkdrempel 56-57 N 6-7
Norfolk-hátság 56-57 N 6-7
Norfolk Island 56-57 N 5
Norfolk Ridge 56-57 N 6-7
Norfolkschwelle 56-57 N 6-7
Norheimsund 30-31 AB 7
Nori 42-43 N 4
Norikura dake 50-51 L 4
Noril'sk 42-43 Q 4
Norische Alpen 33 FG 5
Norlina, NC 74-75 D 3
Norman, OK 72-73 G 4
Normanby 32 F 4
Normanby Island 52-53 h 7
Normandie 34-35 GH 4
Normannische Inseln = Channel Islands 32 E 7
Norman River 56-57 H 3
Normanton [AUS] 56-57 H 3
Norman Wells 70-71 KL 4
Noroeste, Territorios del – = Northwest Territories 70-71 M-U 4
Norquinçó 80 B 6
Norra Bergnäs 30-31 H 4
Norra Storfjället 30-31 FG 5
Norrbotten [S, ≡] 30-31 J 5-K 4
Norrbotten [S, ✫] 30-31 G-K 4
Nørresundby, Ålborg- 30-31 CD 9
Norris, MT 76-77 H 3
Norristown, PA 74-75 F 4
Nörrköping 30-31 G 8
Norrland 30-31 F-J 5
Norrtälje 30-31 H 8
Norseman 56-57 D 6
Norsk 42-43 Y 7
Norská pánev 38-39 A 1-2
Norské moře 19 C 19-B 17
Norsko 30-31 C 8-L 2
Norský příkop 30-31 A 8-C 9
Norte, Cabo – 78-79 K 4
Norte, Canal del – = North Channel [GB] 32 CD 4
Norte, Canal do – 78-79 JK 4
Norte, Punta – 80 D 6
Norte, Serra do – 78-79 H 7
North, SC 74-75 C 8
North, Cape – [CDN, Nova Scotia] 70-71 YZ 8
North Adams, MA 74-75 G 3
Northallerton 32 F 4
Northam [AUS] 56-57 C 6
Northam [ZA] 64-65 G 8
North America 22-23 DE 3
North American Basin 22-23 FG 4
Northampton 32 FG 5
Northampton [AUS] 56-57 B 5
Northampton, MA 74-75 G 3
North Andaman 44-45 P 8
North Arm 70-71 NO 5
North Augusta, SC 74-75 BC 8
North Australian Basin 56-57 C 2
North Banda Basin 52-53 HJ 7
North Bay 70-71 UV 8
North Belcher Islands 70-71 U 6
North Bend, OR 76-77 B 3
North Bend, WA 76-77 C 2
Northbrook, ostrov – = ostrov Nortbruk 42-43 GH 2
North Bruny Island 58 cd 3
North Canadian River 72-73 FG 4
North Cape [NZ] 56-57 O 6
North Caribou Lake 70-71 ST 7
North Carolina 72-73 KL 4
North Channel 32 CD 4
North Channel [CDN] 70-71 U 8
North Charleston, SC 74-75 D 8
Northcliffe 56-57 C 6
North Creek, NY 74-75 FG 3
North Dakota 72-73 FG 2
North East, PA 74-75 CD 3
North East Carry, ME 74-75 HJ 2
North Eastern 64-65 K 2-3
Northeast Providence Channel 72-73 L 6
Northeast Providence Channel 72-73 L 6
Northeast Providence Channel 72-73 L 6
Northeim 33 DE 3
Northern [MW] 63 C 5-6
Northern Ireland 32 CD 4
Northern Pacific Railway 72-73 EF 2

Northern Territory 56-57 FG 3-4
Northfield, VT 74-75 G 2
North Fiji Basin 56-57 O 3
North Foreland 32 GH 6
North Fork, CA 76-77 D 7
North Fork, ID 76-77 FG 3
North Fork Clearwater River 76-77 D 2
North Fork Feather River 76-77 C 5-6
North Fork Humboldt River 76-77 F 5
North Fork John Day River 76-77 D 3
North Fork Mountain 74-75 D 5
North Fork Payette River 76-77 E 3
North Horr 64-65 J 2
North Island 56-57 N 5
North Channel 32 CD 4
North Channel [CDN] 70-71 U 8
North Charleston, SC 74-75 D 8
North Island [NZ] 56-57 P 7
North Island [USA] 76-77 D 8
North Korea 48-49 O 3-4
North Las Vegas, NV 76-77 F 7
North Little Rock, AR 72-73 H 4-5
North Miami, FL 74-75 cd 4
North Minch 32 C 3-D 2
North New River Canal 74-75 c 3
North Ossetian Autonomous Republic = 4 ◁ 38-39 H 7
North Pacific Basin 22-23 AB 3-4
North Palisade 72-73 C 4
North Pass 72-73 J 6
North Platte, NE 72-73 F 3
North Platte River 72-73 F 3
North Powder, OR 76-77 DE 3
North Rona 32 D 2
North Ronaldsay 32 EF 2
North Santiam River 76-77 B 3
North Saskatchewan River 70-71 OP 7
North Sea 32 F-J 3
North Stradbroke Island 56-57 K 5
North Stratford, NH 74-75 H 2
North Taranaki Bight 56-57 O 7
North Tonawanda, NY 74-75 D 3
North Truchas Peak 72-73 E 4
North Uist 32 BC 3
Northumberland Islands 56-57 JK 4
Northumberland Strait 70-71 Y 8
North Umpqua River 76-77 B 4
Northwest Australian Basin 22-23 OP 6
North West Cape 56-57 B 4
North Western 64-65 FG 5
North-West-Frontier 44-45 L 3-4
Northwest Highlands 32 D 2-3
Northwest Indian Ridge 22-23 N 5-6
Northwest Pacific Basin 22-23 ST 3-4
Northwest Pacific Ridge 22-23 S 3-4
Northwest Passage 70-71 J-L 3
Northwest Territories 70-71 M-U 4
North Wilkesboro, NC 74-75 C 6
North York 74-75 D 3
Norton, VA 74-75 B 6
Norton Sound 70-71 D 5
Noruega 30-31 C 7-L 2
Noruega, Canal de – 30-31 A 8-C 9
Noruega, Cuenca de – 22-23 JK 2
Noruega, Mar de – 19 C 19-B 17
Norvège 30-31 C 7-L 2
Norvège, Mer de – 19 C 19-B 17
Norvègia 30-31 C 8-L 2
Norvegia, Kapp – 24 B 34-35
Norvegia 30-31 C 8-L 2
Norveška, Rynna – 30-31 A 8-C 9
Norwegie, Morze – 19 C 19-B 17
Norweskie, Morze – 30-31 B 5-J 2
Norwich 32 G 5
Norwich [CDN] 74-75 C 3
Norwich, CT 74-75 GH 3
Norwich, NY 74-75 F 3
Norwood, NC 74-75 CD 7
Norwood, NY 74-75 F 2
Noshiro 48-49 QR 3
Nosiro = Noshiro 48-49 QR 3
Nossob 64-65 E 7
Nosy-Bé 64-65 L 5
Nosy-Varika 64-65 L 7
Notch Peak 76-77 G 6
Noteć 33 G 2
Noto 36-37 F 7

Noto [J] 50-51 L 4
Notodden 30-31 C 8
Noto hantō 48-49 Q 4
Noto-jima 50-51 L 4
Notoro-ko 50-51 d 1
Notre Dame, Monts – 70-71 WX 8
Notre Dame Bay 70-71 Z 8-a 7
Nottawasaga Bay 74-75 C 2
Nottaway, Rivière – 70-71 V 7
Nottingham 32 F 5
Nottingham Island 70-71 VW 5
Nottoway River 74-75 E 6
Nouadhibou = Nawādhību 60-61 A 4
Nouakchott = Nawākshūt 60-61 A 5
Nouméa 56-57 N 4
Noupoort 64-65 FG 9
Nouveau Brunswick = New Brunswick 70-71 X 8
Nouveau-Québec 70-71 V-X 6
Nouveau-Québec, Cratère du – 70-71 VW 5
Nouvelle Amsterdam 22-23 NO 7
Nouvelle Angleterre = New England 72-73 M 3-N 2
Nouvelle-Anvers 64-65 EF 2
Nouvelle-Calédonie 56-57 MN 3
Nouvelle-Castille = Castilla la Nueva 34-35 E 9-F 8
Nouvelle-Ecosse = Nova Scotia 70-71 X 9-Y 8
Nouvelle-Guinée 52-53 L 7-M 8
Nouvelle-Guinée, Seuil de – 52-53 M 5-6
Nouvelle-Hébrides, Bassin de – 56-57 MN 3
Nouvelle-Hébrides, Fosse des – 56-57 N 3-4
Nouvelles-Hébrides 56-57 N 2-3
Nouvelle Sibérie, Îles – – Novosibirskije ostrova 42-43 Z-f 2
Nouvelle-Zélande 56-57 N 8-O 7
Nouvelle-Zemble, Gouttière de la – 42-43 K 3-L 2
Nová Anglie = New England 72-73 M 3-N 2
Novabad 44-45 L 3
Nova Chaves = Muconda 64-65 F 5
Nova Cruz 78-79 MN 6
Nova Chaves = Muconda 64-65 F 5
Nova Freixo = Cuamba 64-65 J 5
Nova Gaia 64-65 E 4-5
Nova Gradiška 36-37 GH 3
Nova Gradiška 36-37 GH 3
Nová Guinea 52-53 L 7-M 8
Nova Chaves = Muconda 64-65 F 5
Nova Iguaçu 78-79 L 9
Novaja Buchara = Kagan 44-45 J 3
Novaja Kazanka 38-39 J 6
Novaja L'al'a 38-39 M 4
Novaja Odessa 36-37 OP 2
Novaja Pis'm'anka = Leninogorsk 42-43 J 7
Novaja Sibir', ostrov – 42-43 de 3
Novaja Zeml'a 42-43 J 3-L 2
Novaja Zemlja-hasadék 42-43 K 3-L 2
Nová Kaledonie 56-57 MN 3
Nova Lamego = Gabú 60-61 B 6
Nova Lima 78-79 L 8-9
Nova Lisboa = Huambo 64-65 E 5
Nova Lusitânia 64-65 H 6
Nova Mambone 64-65 J 7
Novara 36-37 J 3
Nova Sofala 64-65 HJ 7
Nova Scotia 70-71 X 9-Y 8
Novaya Zemlya Trough 42-43 K 3-L 2
Nova Zagora 36-37 LM 4
Nova Zemblageul 42-43 K 3-L 2
Nové Hebridy = Vanuatu 56-57 N 2-O 3
Nové Skotsko = Nova Scotia 70-71 X 9-Y 8
Nové Zámky 33 J 4
Novgorod 42-43 EF 5
Novgorod-Severskij 38-39 F 5
Novigrad 36-37 E 3
Novi Bečej 36-37 J 3
Novi Bečej 36-37 J 3
Novi Pazar [BG] 36-37 M 4
Novi Pazar [YU] 36-37 M 4
Novi Sad 36-37 HJ 3
Novoagansk 42-43 O 5
Novoaleksandrovskaja 38-39 H 6
Novoaltajsk 42-43 PQ 7
Novoanninskij 38-39 H 5
Novobiril'ussy 42-43 QR 6
Novobogatinskoje 38-39 K 6
Novočerkassk 38-39 GH 6
Novočerkassk 38-39 GH 6
Novograd-Volynskij 38-39 E 5
Novogrudok 38-39 E 5
Novo Hamburgo 80 FG 3
Novojerudinskij 42-43 RS 6

Novokazalinsk 42-43 L 8
Novokujbyševsk 38-39 JK 5
Novokujbyševsk 38-39 JK 5
Novokuzneck 42-43 Q 7
Novolazarevskaja 24 B 1
Novo-Mariinsk = Anadyr' 42-43 j 5
Novo Mesto 36-37 F 3
Novomoskovsk 38-39 GH 5
Novonazimovo 42-43 QR 6
Novonikolajevsk = Novosibirsk 42-43 P 6-7
Novo Redondo = N'Gunza Kabolo 64-65 D 5
Novorossijk 38-39 G 7
Novošachtinsk 38-39 G 6
Novosibirsk 42-43 P 6-7
Novosibirskije ostrova 42-43 Z-f 2
Novosibiřské ostrovy = Novosibirskije ostrova 42-43 Z-f 2
Novosokol'niki 38-39 EF 4
Novos'olovo 42-43 R 6
Novošachtinsk 38-39 G 6
Novotroick 42-43 K 7
Novo-Troickij Promysel = Balej 42-43 W 7
Novoukrainka 38-39 F 6
Novo-Urgenč = Urgenč 42-43 L 9
Novo-Urgenč = Urgenč 42-43 L 9
Novouzensk 38-39 J 5
Novozybkov 38-39 F 5
Novska 36-37 G 3
Nový Brunšvik = New Brunswick 70-71 X 8
Novyj Bor 38-39 K 2
Novyj Bug 38-39 F 6
Novyje Karymkary 42-43 MN 5
Novyj Karymkary = Karymkary 42-43 M 5
Novyj Margelan = Fergana 44-45 L 2-3
Novyj Port 42-43 MN 4
Novyj Tevriz 42-43 O 6
Nový Zéland 56-57 N 8-O 7
Nowa Anglia = New England 72-73 M 3-N 2
Nowa Fundlandia = Newfoundland 70-71 Za 8
Nowa Gwinea 52-53 L 7-M 8
Nowaja-Semlja-Rinne 42-43 K 3-L 2
Nowa Kaledonia 56-57 MN 3
Nowa Sól 33 G 3
Nowa Szkocja = Nova Scotia 70-71 X 9-Y 8
Nowa Szkocja = Nova Scotia 70-71 X 9-Y 8
Nowa Zelandia 56-57 N 8-O 7
Nowbarān 46-47 N 5
Nowe 33 J 2
Nowe Hebrydy = Vanuatu 56-57 N 2-O 3
Nowgorod = Novgorod 42-43 E 6
Nowkash 46-47 MN 6
Nowogwinejski, Rów – 52-53 M 5-6
Nowogwinejskie, Morze – 52-53 NO 7
Nowohebrydzki, Basen – 56-57 MN 3
Nowohebrydzki, Rów – 56-57 N 3-4
Nowosyberyjskie, Wyspy – Novosibirskije ostrova 42-43 Z-f 2
Nowozelandzki, Grzbiet – 56-57 M 5-6
Nowra 56-57 K 6
Now Shar 38-39 K 8
Nowy Brunszwik = New Brunswick 70-71 X 8
Nowy Jork = New York, NY 72-73 M 3-4
Nowy Jork = New York, NY 72-73 M 3-4
Nowy Korczyn 33 K 3
Nowy Sącz 33 K 4
Nowy Targ 33 K 4
Noxon, MT 76-77 F 1-2
Noya 34-35 C 7
Noyon 34-35 J 4

N'Riquinha = Lumbala 64-65 F 6

Nsanje 64-65 J 6
Nsefu 63 BC 6
Nsukka 60-61 F 7

Ntcheu 64-65 HJ 5

Nuanetsi = Mwenezi 64-65 GH 7
Nūbah, An- 60-61 K-M 4-5
Nūbah, Jibāl an- 60-61 KL 6
Nubia, Desierto de – 60-61 LM 4
Núbiai-sivatag 60-61 LM 4
Nubie, Désert de – 60-61 LM 4
Nubieber, CA 76-77 C 7
Nubijska, Pustynia – 60-61 LM 4
Nubijská poušť 60-61 LM 4
Nubische Woestijn 60-61 LM 4
Nubische Wüste 60-61 LM 4
Nūbiya = An-Nubah 60-61 K-M 4-5
Nu Chiang = Nag Chhu 48-49 G 5
Nu Chiang = Nag Chhu 48-49 G 5

Nueces River 72-73 G 6
Nueltin Lake 70-71 R 5
Nueva Antioquia 78-79 EF 3
Nueva Bretaña-Bougainville, Fosa de – 52-53 h 6
Nueva Caledonia 56-57 MN 3
Nueva Casas Grandes 72-73 E 5
Nueva Delhi = New Delhi 44-45 M 5
Nueva Escocia = Nova Scotia 70-71 X 9-Y 8
Nueva Germania 80 E 2
Nueva Guinea 52-53 L 7-M 8
Nueva Guinea, Dorsal de – 52-53 M 5-6
Nueva Inglaterra = New England 72-73 M 3-N 2
Nueva Providencia 72-73 b 2
Nueva Rosita 72-73 F 6
Nueva San Salvador 72-73 HJ 9
Nuevas Hébridas 56-57 N 2-O 3
Nuevas Hébridas, Cuenca de – 56-57 MN 3
Nuevas Hébridas, Fosa de – 56-57 N 3-4
Nueva Siberia, Islas de – – Novosibirskije ostrova 42-43 Z-f 2
Nueva York = New York, NY 72-73 M 3-4
Nueva Zelanda 56-57 N 8-O 7
Nueva Zelanda, Dorsal de – 56-57 M 5-7
Nueva Zembla, Dorsal de – 42-43 K 3-L 2
Nueve de Julio [RA, Buenos Aires] 80 D 5
Nuevo Chagres 72-73 ab 2
Nuevo Chagres 72-73 ab 2
Nuevo Emperador 72-73 b 2
Nuevo Chagres 72-73 ab 2
Nuevo Laredo 72-73 FG 6
Nuevo León 72-73 F 7-G 6
Nuevo Rocafuerte 78-79 D 5
Nuevo San Juan 72-73 b 2
Nuffar = Nippur 46-47 L 6
Nugaal 60-61 b 2
Nugruş, Gebel = – Jabal Nuqruş 62 F 5
Nûgssuaq 70-71 YZ 3
Nûgssuaq Halvø 70-71 a 3
Nuguria Islands 52-53 hj 5
Nuhaylah, An- 62 E 4
Nuhu Cut 52-53 K 8
Nuhûd, An- 60-61 K 6
Nuhurowa = Kai Kecil 52-53 K 8
Nuhu Rowa = Kai Kecil 52-53 K 8
Nuhu Tjut = Nuhu Cut 52-53 K 8
Nuhu Yut = Nuhu Cut 52-53 K 8
Nui Đeo 52-53 E 2
N'uja [SU, ~] 42-43 V 5
N'uja [SU, ●] 42-43 W 5
Nujiang Lisuzu Zizhizhou = C ◁ 48-49 H 6
Nûk 70-71 a 5
Nukey Bluff 58 BC 4
Nukhayb 44-45 E 4
Nukhaylah 60-61 K 5
Nukheila, Bîr – = Nukhaylah 60-61 K 5
Nukumanu Islands 52-53 jk 5
Nukus 42-43 KL 9
N'ukža 42-43 X 6-7
N'ukža 42-43 X 6-7
Nulato, AK 70-71 E 5
Nullagine 56-57 D 4
Nullarbor 56-57 EF 6
Nullarbor Plain 56-57 EF 6
Num, Meos – 52-53 KL 7
Numan 60-61 G 7
Nu'mân, Jazîrat an- 62 F 4
Numancia 34-35 F 8
Numata [J, Gunma] 50-51 M 4
Numata [J, Hokkaidō] 50-51 bc 2
Numazu 50-51 M 5
Numedal 30-31 C 7-8
Numeia = Nouméa 56-57 N 4
Numero 1 Station = Maḥaṭṭat 1 62 D 7
Numero 2 Station = Maḥaṭṭat 2 62 DE 7
Numero 3 Station = Maḥaṭṭat 3 62 DE 7
Numero 4 Station = Maḥaṭṭat 4 62 E 7
Numfoor, Pulau – 52-53 KL 7
Numto 42-43 MN 5
Numurkah 58 G 6
Nun Chiang = Nen Jiang 48-49 O 1-2
Nun Chiang = Nen Jiang 48-49 O 1-2
Nundle 58 K 3
Nungan = Nong'an 48-49 NO 3
Nungo 64-65 J 5
Nun Chiang = Nen Jiang 48-49 O 1-2
Nunivak Island 70-71 C 6
Nuomin He 48-49 N 2
Nuoro 36-37 C 5
Nuqrat as-Salmān = As-Salmān 46-47 L 7

Nuqruş, Jabal – 62 F 5
Nura 48-49 HJ 5
Nuratau, chrebet – 42-43 M 9
N'urba 42-43 W 5
Nur Dağları 46-47 G 4
Nûrestân 44-45 KL 3-4
Nurhak Dağı 46-47 G 3
Nurmes 30-31 N 6
Nürnberg 33 E 4
Nusa Tenggara Barat = 16 ◁ 52-53 G 8
Nusa Tenggara Timur = 17 ◁ 52-53 H 8
Nusaybin 44-45 E 3
Nuşf, Bi'r an- 62 B 2
Nushagak River 70-71 E 5-6
Nu Shan 48-49 H 6
Nûshki 44-45 K 5
Nutrias = Puerto de Nutrias 78-79 EF 3
Nutzotin Mountains 70-71 H 5
Nuwara Eliya 44-45 N 9
Nuwaybi' al-Muzayyinah 62 F 3
Nuweiba' = Nuwaybi' al-Muzayyinah 62 F 3
Nuyts Archipelago 56-57 F 6

Nxai Pan National Park 64-65 FG 6

Ny

Nyaake 60-61 C 8
Nya Chhu = Yalong Jiang 48-49 HJ 5
Nya Chhu = Yalong Jiang 48-49 HJ 5
Nyahanga 64-65 H 3
Nya Chhu = Yalong Jiang 48-49 HJ 5
Nyakahanga 64-65 H 3
Nyâlâ 60-61 J 6
Ny Ålesund 30-31 hj 5
Nyalikungu 63 C 3
Nyamandhlovu 64-65 G 6
Nyambiti 64-65 H 3
Nyâmlîl 60-61 K 7
Nyamtumbu 64-65 J 5
Nyanchhenthanglha [TJ, ▲▲] 48-49 F 6-G 5
Nyanchhenthanglha [TJ, ⇆] 48-49 G 5-6
Nyanga 64-65 D 3
Nyanji 63 BC 6
Nyanza [EAK] 64-65 H 2-3
Nyanza [RU] 63 B 4
Nyanza [RWA] 63 B 3
Nyasa = Lake Malawi 64-65 H 5
Nyaunglebin 52-53 C 3
Nyawalu 63 AB 3
Nyborg 30-31 D 10
Nybro 30-31 F 9
Nyda 42-43 N 4
Nyenchentanglha = Nyanchhenthanglha 48-49 F 6-G 5
Nyenyec Autonóm Körzet 42-43 J-L 4
Nyeri [EAK] 64-65 J 3
Nyeri [EAU] 63 B 2
Ņermete, Punta – 78-79 C 6
Ny Friesland 30-31 k 5
Nyika Plateau 64-65 H 4-5
Nyira Gonga 63 B 3
Nyîrbátor 33 KL 5
Nyíregyháza 33 K 5
Nyiri Desert 63 D 3
Nyiro, Uoso – = Ewaso Ngiro 64-65 J 3
Nyiru, Mount – 64-65 J 2
Nyîtra = Nitra 33 J 4
Nykarleby 30-31 K 6
Nykøbing Falster 30-31 DE 10
Nykøbing Mors 30-31 C 9
Nykøbing Sjælland 30-31 D 9-10
Nyköping 30-31 G 8
Nyland = Uusimaa 30-31 KL 7
Nylstroom 64-65 G 7
Nymagee 58 H 4
Nymboida 58 L 2
Nymburk 33 G 3
Nynäshamn 30-31 GH 8
Nyngan 56-57 J 6
Nyong 60-61 G 8
Nyonga 64-65 H 4
Nyrud 30-31 N 3
Nysa 33 H 3
Nysa Kłodzka 33 H 3
Nysa Kłodzka 33 H 3
Nysa Łużycka 33 F 3
Nyslott = Savonlinna 30-31 N 7
Nyssa, OR 76-77 E 4
Nystad = Uusikaupunki 30-31 J 7
Nytva 42-43 JK 6
Nyûdô-saki 50-51 M 2
Nyugat-európai-medence
Nyugati-Erg = Al-'Irq al-Kabîr al-Gharbî 60-61 D 3-E 2
Nyugati-Fríz-szk. 30-31 KL 7
Nyugat-Szahara 60-61 A 4-B 3
Nyunzu 64-65 G 4

Nzega 64-65 H 3
Nzérékoré 60-61 C 7
N'Zeto 64-65 D 4
Nzoia 63 C 2
Nzoro 63 B 2

O

Oahe, Lake – 72-73 F 2
Oahu 52-53 e 3
Oakbank 56-57 H 6
Oak City, UT 76-77 G 6
Oakdale, CA 76-77 C 3
Oakey 56-57 K 5
Oak Harbor, WA 76-77 B 1
Oak Hill, FL 74-75 c 2
Oak Hill, WV 74-75 C 5-6
Oakland, CA 72-73 B 4
Oakland, MD 74-75 D 5
Oakland, OR 76-77 B 4
Oaklands 58 GH 5
Oakley, ID 76-77 FG 4
Oakover River 56-57 D 4
Oakridge, OR 76-77 B 4
Oamaru 56-57 O 9
Ōarai 50-51 N 4
Oasis, CA 76-77 DE 7
Oasis, NV 76-77 F 5
Oates Land 24 B 16-17
Oatlands [AUS] 58 cd 3

Oatman, AZ 76-77 F 8
Oaxaca 72-73 G 8
Oaxaca de Juárez 72-73 GH 8
Ob' 42-43 NO 5
Oba [Vanuatu] 56-57 N 3
Obama 50-51 K 5
Oban 32 D 3
Oban [NZ] 56-57 N 9
Obara = Ōchi 50-51 J 5
Obdorsk = Salechard 42-43 M 4
Obeidh, El- = Al-Ubayyiḍ 60-61 KL 6
Oberá 80 F 3
Oberägypten = Aş-Şa'îd 60-61 L 3-4
Oberer See = Lake Superior 72-73 HJ 2
Oberer Trajanswall = Verchnij Trajanov val 36-37 N 2
Obere Tunguska = Angara 42-43 S 6
Oberguinea 22-23 JK 5
Oberhausen 33 C 3
Oberösterreich 33 F-H 4
Oberpfälzer Wald 33 F 4
Oberstdorf 33 E 5
Obi, Pulau – 52-53 J 7
Óbidos [BR] 78-79 HJ 5
Obihiro 48-49 R 3
Objačevo 42-43 H 5
Objačevo 42-43 H 5
Obkeik, Jebel – = Jabal 'Ubkayk 60-61 M 4
Oblačnaja, gora – 42-43 Za 9
Oblačnaja, gora – 42-43 Za 9
Oblučje 42-43 Z 8
Oblučje 42-43 Z 8
Obo 60-61 K 7
Oboa 63 C 2
Obock 60-61 N 6
Obojan 38-39 G 5
Obok = Obock 60-61 N 6
Obonai = Tazawako 50-51 N 3
Oboz'orskij 38-39 H 3
Obra 33 G 2
Obrenovac 36-37 HJ 3
Obrian Peak = Trident Peak 76-77 D 5
Obrovac 36-37 F 3
Obruk = Kizören 46-47 E 3
Obruk Yaylâsı 46-47 E 3
Obšćij Syrt 42-43 H-K 7
Obskaja guba 42-43 N 3-4
Obšćij Syrt 42-43 H-K 7
Obuasi 60-61 D 7
Obuchi = Rokkasho 50-51 N 2

Očakov 36-37 O 2
Ōchë 36-37 L 6
Ochiai = Dolinsk 42-43 b 8
Ochogbo = Oshogbo 60-61 EF 7
Óch'ŏng-do 50-51 E 4
Och'onjang 50-51 G 2
Ochota 42-43 b 6
Ochotsk 42-43 b 6
Ochotsk, Zee van – 42-43 b-d 6-7
Ochockie, Morze – 42-43 b-d 6-7
Ochogbo = Oshogbo 60-61 EF 7
Óch'ŏng-do 50-51 E 4
Och'onjang 50-51 G 2
Ochota 42-43 b 6
Ochotsk 42-43 b 6
Ochotsk, Mar de – 42-43 b-d 6-7

Ochotsk, Zee van – 42-43 b-d 6-7
Ochotskij Perevoz 42-43 a 5
Ochotskisches Meer 42-43 b-d 6-7
Ocilla, GA 74-75 B 9
Ockelbo 30-31 C 7
Ocmulgee National Monument 74-75 B 8
Ocmulgee River 74-75 B 8-9
Oconee River 74-75 B 8
Ocotlán 72-73 F 7
Ocracoke Island 74-75 F 7
Oda [GH] 60-61 D 7
Ôda [J] 50-51 J 5
Ôda, Hör – = Hawr Awdah 46-47 M 7
'Ôda, Jebel – – = Jabal 'Udah 60-61 M 4
Ódádhahraun 30-31 e 2
Ôdaejin 50-51 GH 2
Ôdate 50-51 N 2
Odawara 50-51 M 5
Odaym 46-47 M 7
Odda 30-31 B 7
Odemira 34-35 C 10
Ödemis 46-47 BC 3
Odendaalsrus 64-65 G 8
Odense 30-31 D 10
Odenwald 33 D 4
Oder 33 G 2
Oderzo 36-37 E 3
Odessa [SU] 38-39 F 6
Odessa, TX 72-73 F 5
Odessa, WA 76-77 D 2
Odiénné 60-61 C 7
Odioñgan 52-53 H 4
Odioñgan 52-53 H 4
Ôdomari = Korsakov 42-43 b 8
Odorheiul Secuiesc 36-37 L 2
Odra 33 H 3
Odum, GA 74-75 B 9
Odweeyne = Oodweyne 60-61 b 2
Odzala 64-65 DE 2
Oedmoerten Autonome Republiek = 2 ◁ 42-43 J 6
Oeganda 64-65 H 2
Oekraine 38-39 E-G 6
Oelan Bator = Ulaanbaatar 48-49 K 2
Oels = Oleśnica 33 H 3
Oenpelli 56-57 F 2
Oeral 28-29 V 3-U 4
Oe-raro-do 50-51 F 5
Oermiameer = Urmia 44-45 F 3
Oest-Orda-Boerjaten, Nationaal Gebied der = 11 ◁ 42-43 T 7
Oeyön-do 50-51 F 4
Oezbekistan 44-45 J 2-K 3
Of 46-47 J 2
Öfanto 36-37 F 5
Offenbach 33 D 4
Offenburg 33 CD 4
Ofooué 64-65 D 3
Ofotfjord 30-31 G 3
Öfunato 50-51 NO 3
Oga 50-51 M 3
Ôgada 50-51 J 6
Ogadên 60-61 NO 7
Oga hantô 50-51 M 3
Ôgaki 50-51 L 5
Ogasawara 54 RS 7
Ogasawara, Fosa de – 22-23 R 4
Ogashi 50-51 N 3
Ogashi tôge 50-51 MN 3
Ôgawara 50-51 N 3
Ogawara ko 50-51 N 2
Ogbomosho 60-61 E 7
Ogden, UT 72-73 D 3
Ogdensburg, NY 72-73 LM 3
Ogeechee River 74-75 BC 8
Ogi 50-51 M 4
Ogida = Hinai 50-51 N 2
Ogilby, CA 76-77 F 9
Ogilvie Mountains 70-71 J 4-5
Òglio 36-37 CD 3
Ognista, Ziemia – 80 C 8
Ognon 34-35 KL 5
Ôgnut = Göynük 46-47 J 3
Ogoja 60-61 F 7
Ogoki River 70-71 T 7
Ogon'ok 42-43 ab 6
Ogooué 64-65 D 3
Ogr = 'Uqr 60-61 K 6
Ogre 30-31 L 9
Ogué = Ogooué 64-65 D 3
Ogulin 36-37 F 3
Ogun 60-61 E 7
Ogurčinskij, ostrov – 44-45 G 3
Ogurčinskij, ostrov – 44-45 G 3
Oğuzeli 46-47 G 4

Ohakune 56-57 P 7
Ohata 50-51 N 1
Ôhata 50-51 N 2
Ohazama 50-51 N 3
O'Higgins [RCH] 80 BC 2
Ohio 72-73 J 4
Ohio River 72-73 J 4
Ohňová země 80 C 8
Ohopoho 64-65 D 6
Ohře 33 F 4
Ohrid 36-37 J 5
Ohridsko Ezero 36-37 J 5
Ohře 33 G 3
Ôhuam 60-61 H 7
Ôhunato 50-51 NO 3
Ocha 42-43 b 7

Östliches Indisches Südpolarbecken 22-23 O-Q 8
Ostpazifischer Rücken 22-23 D 6-7
Ostpazifisches Südpolarbecken 22-23 DE 8-9
Ostrau = Ostrava 33 J 4
Ostrava 33 J 4
Ostróda 33 JK 2
Ostrołęka 33 KL 2
Ostrołęka 33 KL 2
Ostrov [CS] 33 H 4-5
Ostrov [SU] 38-39 E 4
Ostrowiec Świętokrzyski 33 KL 3
Ostrowiec Świętokrzyski 33 KL 3
Ostrów Mazowiecka 33 KL 2
Ostrów Wielkopolski 33 HJ 3
Ostryna 30-31 L 11
Ostsee 30-31 G 10-J 8
Ostsibirische Schwelle 19 B 36-1
Ostsibirische See 42-43 d-h 3
Ostsibirische Schwelle 19 B 36-1
Ostsibirische Schwelle 19 B 36-1
Osttirol 33 F 5
Ostuni 36-37 G 5
O'Sullivan Reservoir = Potholes Reservoir 76-77 D 2
Osum 36-37 J 5
Ōsumi-kaikyō 48-49 P 5
Ōsumi-shotō 48-49 OP 5
Ōsumisyotō = Ōsumi-shotō 48-49 OP 5
Osuna 34-35 E 10
Osveja 30-31 N 10
Oswego, NY 72-73 L 3
Oswego = Lake Oswego, OR 76-77 B 3
Oświęcim 33 J 3-4
Oš [SU] 44-45 L 2
Ošarovo 42-43 S 5
Ošm'any 30-31 LM 10
Oświęcim 33 J 3-4
Ōta 50-51 M 4
Ōta = Mino-Kamo 50-51 L 5
Otago Peninsula 56-57 O 9
Ōtahara = Ōtawara 50-51 N 4
Ōtake 50-51 HJ 5
Otaki 56-57 OP 8
Ōtakine yama 50-51 N 4
Otar 42-43 O 9
Otare, Cerro – 78-79 E 4
Otaru 48-49 QR 3
Otaru-wan = Ishikari-wan 50-51 b 2
Otavalo 78-79 D 4
Otavi 64-65 E 6
Otawi = Otavi 64-65 E 6
Otgon Tenger uul 48-49 H 2
Othello, WA 76-77 D 2
Othōnoi 36-37 H 6
Óthrys 36-37 K 6
Oti 60-61 E 7
Otis, OR 76-77 B 3
Otish Mountains 70-71 W 7
Otjekondo 64-65 E 6
Otjiwarongo 64-65 E 7
Otlukbeli Dağları 46-47 H 3-J 2
Otobe 50-51 b 2-3
Otofuke 50-51 c 2
Otoineppu 50-51 c 1
Otpor = Zabajkal'sk 42-43 W 8
Otra 30-31 B 8
Otranto 36-37 H 5
Otranto, Canale d' 36-37 H 5-6
Otroči pobřeží 60-61 E 7
Ōtsu [J, Hokkaidō] 50-51 c 2
Ōtsu [J, Shiga] 50-51 KL 5
Ōtsuchi 50-51 NO 3
Otta 30-31 C 7
Ottawa 70-71 V 8
Ottawa Islands 70-71 U 6
Ottawa River 70-71 V 8
Ottenby 30-31 G 9
Otter, Peaks of – 74-75 D 6
Otter Creek, FL 74-75 b 2
Otter Lake 74-75 D 2
Ottumwa, IA 72-73 H 3
Oturkpo 60-61 F 7
Otuzco 78-79 D 6
Otway, Bahía – 80 AB 8
Otway, Cape – 56-57 H 7
Otway, Seno – 80 B 8
Otwock 33 K 2
Ötztaler Alpen 33 E 5
Ouachita Mountains 72-73 GH 5
Ouachita River 72-73 H 5
Ouadda 60-61 J 7
Ouaddaï 60-61 HJ 6
Ouagadougou 60-61 D 6
Ouahigouya 60-61 D 6
Ouahran = Wahrān 60-61 D 2
Ouaka 60-61 J 7
Oualata = Walātah 60-61 C 5
Oua n'Ahaggar, Tassili – = Murtaf'āt Tāsīlī 60-61 E 5-F 4
Ouanda Djallé 60-61 J 7
Ouango = Kouango 60-61 HJ 7
Ouangolodougou 60-61 C 7
Ouargla = Warqlā 60-61 F 2
Oubangui 64-65 E 2
Oud-Castilië = Castilla la Vieja 34-35 E 8-F 7
Oudmourtes, République Autonome des – = 2 ◁ 42-43 J 6
Oudtshoorn 64-65 F 9
Oued, El- = Al-Wād 60-61 F 2
Oued Zem = Wād Zam 60-61 C 2
Oueïta 60-61 J 5
Ouémé [DY, ~] 60-61 E 7
Ouessant, Île d' 34-35 E 4
Ouesso 64-65 E 2
Ouest Européen Bassin de l' 22-23 HJ 3
Ouezzân = Wazzān 60-61 C 2
Ouganda 64-65 H 2
Ouham-Pendé 60-61 H 7
Ouidah 60-61 E 7
Ouina 60-61 G 7
Oûjda = Ūjdah 60-61 D 2
Oulainen 30-31 L 5
Oulan Bator = Ulaanbaatar 48-49 K 2
Oulu 30-31 LM 5
Oulujärvi 30-31 M 5
Oulujoki 30-31 M 5
Oum-Chalouba 60-61 J 5
Oum-Chalouba 60-61 J 5
Oum er Rbia, Ouèd – = Wād Umm ar-Rabīyah 60-61 C 2
Oum Hadjer 60-61 H 6
Oum-Chalouba 60-61 J 5
Oumm ed Drouss, Sebkra – = Sabkhat Umm ad-Durūs 60-61 B 4
Ounasjoki 30-31 L 4
Ounastunturi 30-31 KL 3
Ounasvaara 30-31 LM 4
Ounianga Kébir 60-61 J 5
Oupu 48-49 O 1
Oural 28-29 V 3-U 4
Ouray, UT 76-77 J 5
Ourém 78-79 K 5
Ouri 60-61 H 4
Ourinhos 78-79 K 9
Ourique 34-35 C 10
Ouro Preto [BR, Minas Gerais] 78-79 L 9
Oûroum eș Șoughrá = Urūm aș-Șuğrah 46-47 G 4
Ours, Grand Lac de l' 70-71 MN 4
Ours, Île aux – 19 B 16-17
Ourthe 34-35 K 3
Ōu sammyaku 50-51 N 2-4
Ouse 32 FG 5
Oust 34-35 F 5
Outardes, Rivière aux – 70-71 X 7-8
Outer Hebrides 32 B 3-C 2
Outjo 64-65 E 7
Ouvéa, Île – 56-57 N 4
Ouyen 56-57 H 6-7
Ouzbékie 44-45 J 2-K 3
Ovacık [TR, Elâzığ] 46-47 H 3
Ovacık [TR, İcel] 46-47 E 4
Ovalau 52-53 a 2
Ovalle 80 B 4
Ovamboland 64-65 DE 6
Ovando, MT 76-77 G 2
Ovar 34-35 C 8
Överkalix 30-31 K 4
Overton, NV 76-77 F 7
Övertorneå 30-31 K 4
Ovidiopol 36-37 O 2
Oviedo 34-35 DE 7
Oviedo, FL 74-75 c 2
Ovo 63 B 2
Övörchangaj = 10 ◁ 48-49 J 2
Övre Soppero 30-31 J 3
Ovruč 38-39 E 5
Ovruč 38-39 E 5
Owando 64-65 E 3
Ōwani 50-51 N 2
Owase 50-51 L 5
Owashi = Owase 50-51 L 5
Owego, NY 74-75 E 3
Oweîqila, Ma'țan – = Ma'ātin 'Uwayqilah 46-47 C 7
Owendo 64-65 C 2
Owen Falls Dam 64-65 DE 3
Owensboro, KY 72-73 J 4
Owens Lake 76-77 E 7
Owen Sound 70-71 U 9
Owens River 76-77 D 7
Owens River Valley 76-77 D 7
Owen Stanley Range 52-53 N 8-9
Owerri 60-61 F 7
Owo 60-61 F 7
Owyhee, Lake – 76-77 E 4
Owyhee Range 76-77 E 4
Owyhee River 72-73 C 3
Oxapampa 78-79 DE 7
Oxelösund 30-31 G 8
Oxford 32 F 6
Oxford [NZ] 56-57 O 8
Oxford, NC 74-75 D 6
Oxford Peak 76-77 GH 4
Oxley 56-57 H 6
Oxnard, CA 72-73 BC 5
Oxus = Amudarja 44-45 J 2
Oyalı 46-47 J 4
Oyama [J] 50-51 MN 4
Oyem 64-65 D 2
Øyeren 30-31 D 8
Oyo [WAN, ☆] 60-61 E 7
Øyrlandet 30-31 jk 6
Oysterville, WA 76-77 A 2
Oyuklu = Yavı 46-47 J 3
Özalp 46-47 KL 3
Ozamiz 52-53 H 5
Ozark Plateau 72-73 H 4
Ozarks, Lake of the – 72-73 H 4
Ózd 33 K 4
Ozernoj, mys – 42-43 fg 6
Ozernoj, zaliv – 42-43 f 6
Ozette Lake 76-77 A 1
Ozieri 36-37 C 5
Ozinki 38-39 J 5
Ozorków 33 J 3
Oz'ornyj [SU → Orsk] 42-43 L 7
Oz'ory 38-39 G 5

Ö

Ödemis 46-47 BC 3
Ödenburg = Sopron 33 H 5
Öjöngö Nuur = Ojorong nuur 48-49 F 2
Öland 30-31 G 9
Öldzijt 48-49 J 2
Ölegey = Ölgij 48-49 FG 2
Ölgij 48-49 FG 2
Ölinseln = Chagos 22-23 N 6
Ölön = Lün 48-49 K 2
Öls nuur 48-49 G 4
Ömerli 46-47 J 4
Ömnödelger 48-49 KL 2
Ömnögov' = 14 ◁ 48-49 K 3
Öndörchaan 48-49 L 2
Öræfajökull 30-31 e 2
Örbyhus 30-31 G 7
Ördene 48-49 L 3
Ördög-sziget = Île du Diable 78-79 J 3
Örebro [S, ●] 30-31 F 8
Örebro [S, ☆] 30-31 F 8
Öregrund 30-31 H 7
Ören [TR] 46-47 BC 4
Örencik 46-47 C 3
Öresund 30-31 E 10
Örményország 38-39 HJ 7
Örnsköldsvik 30-31 H 6
Ösel = Saaremaa 30-31 K 8
Österbotten = Pohjanmaa 30-31 K 6-M 5
Österdalälven 30-31 E 7
Östergötland 30-31 F 8-9
Österreich 33 E-G 5
Österreich 33 E-G 5
Östersund 30-31 F 6
Östhammar 30-31 GH 7
Östlicher Großer Erg = Al-'Irq ash-Sharqī al-Kabīr 60-61 F 2-3
Östlicher Sajan = Vostočnyj Sajan 42-43 R 6-T 7
Östliches Indisches Südpolarbecken 22-23 O-Q 8
Östliches Indisches Südpolarbecken 22-23 O-Q 8
Ötztaler Alpen 33 E 5
Överkalix 30-31 K 4
Övertorneå 30-31 K 4
Övörchangaj = 10 ◁ 48-49 J 2
Övre Soppero 30-31 J 3
Özalp 46-47 KL 3

P

Pa = Chongqing 48-49 K 6
Paan = Batang 48-49 H 6
Paan = Hpā'an 52-53 C 3
Paarl 64-65 E 9
Paasdrempel 22-23 C-E 7
Paaseiland 22-23 D 7
Pabianice 33 JK 3
Pacajus 78-79 M 5
Pacaraima, Serra – 78-79 G 4
Pacasmayo 78-79 CD 6
Pachači 42-43 gh 5
Pāchenār 46-47 N 4
Pachino 36-37 F 7
Pachu = Maral Bashi 48-49 D 3-4
Pachuca de Soto 72-73 G 7
Pa'ch'unjang 50-51 F 3
Pacific, CA 76-77 C 6
Pacific Grove, CA 76-77 BC 7
Pacific Ocean 22-23 Q-T 5-6
Pacifico Central, Cuenca del – 22-23 BC 5
Pacífico Noroccidental, Cuenca del – 22-23 R 4
Pacífico Noroccidental, Dorsal del – 22-23 S 3-4
Pacifico Norte, Cuenca del – 22-23 AB 3-4
Pacífico Oriental, Dorsal del – 22-23 D 6-7
Pacifico Sur, Cuenca del – 24 D 21-19
Pacifico Sur, Dorsal del – 24 D 22-C 20
Pacifique-Antartique, Bassin du – 22-23 DE 8-9
Pacifique Central, Bassin du – 22-23 BC 5
Pacifique Méridional, Bassin du – 24 D 21-19
Pacifique Méridional, Dorsale du – 24 D 22-C 20
Pacifique Nord, Bassin du – 22-23 AB 3-4
Pacifique Oriental, Dorsale du – 22-23 D 6-7
Pacifique Ouest Septentrional, Bassin du – 22-23 R 4
Pacifique Ouest Septentrional, Dorsale du – 22-23 S 3-4
Pacifisch-Zuidpolairbekken 22-23 DE 8-9
Pacitan 52-53 F 8
Packwood, WA 76-77 BC 2
Pacoval 78-79 J 5
Pactriu = Chachoengsao 52-53 D 4
Pacu, Cachoeira do – 78-79 J 9
Padang 52-53 CD 7
Padang, Pulau – 52-53 D 6
Padang Endau 52-53 D 6
Padangsidimpuan 52-53 CD 6
Padauiri, Rio – 78-79 G 4
Padcaya 78-79 FG 9
Paden City, WV 74-75 C 5
Paderborn 33 D 3
Padibe 63 C 2
Padilla 78-79 G 8
Padoue = Pádova 36-37 DE 3
Pàdova 36-37 DE 3
Padre Island 72-73 G 6
Padstow 32 D 6
Padua = Pàdova 36-37 DE 3
Paducah, KY 72-73 J 4
Padwa = Padova 36-37 DE 3
Paek-san 50-51 F 3
Paektu-san = Baitou Shan 50-51 FG 2
Paengnyŏng-do 50-51 DE 4
Paeroa 56-57 P 7
Paestum 36-37 F 5
Páfos 46-47 E 5
Pafûri 64-65 H 7
Pag 36-37 F 3
Pagadian 52-53 H 5
Pagai, Kepulauan – 52-53 CD 7
Pagai Selatan, Pulau – 52-53 CD 7
Pagai Utara, Pulau – 52-53 C 7
Pagasētikós Kólpos 36-37 K 6
Page, AZ 76-77 H 7
Page, WA 76-77 D 2
Pagėgiai 30-31 JK 10
Pageh = Kepulauan Pagai 52-53 CD 7
Pageland, SC 74-75 C 7
Pager 63 C 2
Paget, Mount – 80 J 8
Pagi 52-53 M 7
Pagi = Kepulauan Pagai 52-53 CD 7
Pago Pago = Fagatogo 52-53 c 1
Pahäjärvi 30-31 K 7
Pahandut = Palangkaraya 52-53 F 7
Pahaska, WY 76-77 J 3
Pahokee, FL 74-75 c 3
Pahranagat Range 76-77 F 7
Pahrock Range 76-77 F 6-7
Pahrump, NV 76-77 K 6
Pahsien = Chongqing 48-49 K 6
Pahute Peak 76-77 F 7
Pachači 42-43 gh 5
Paiçandu, Cachoeira – 78-79 J 5
Pai-ch'êng = Bai 48-49 E 3
Paicheng = Taoan 48-49 N 2
Paide 30-31 L 8
P'ai-hsien = Pei Xian 48-49 M 5
Päijänne 30-31 L 7
Paimbœuf 34-35 F 5
Paimpol 34-35 F 4
Painan 52-53 CD 7
Paine, Cerro – 80 B 8
Painesville, OH 74-75 C 4
Painganga = Penganga 44-45 M 7
Painted Desert 76-77 H 7-8
Painted Rock Reservoir 76-77 G 9
Paintsville, KY 74-75 B 6
Paises Bajos 34-35 K 3-L 2
Paisley 32 D 4
Paisley, OR 76-77 C 4
Paita 78-79 C 5-6
Pai-t'ou Shan = Baitou Shan 50-51 FG 2
Pai-t'u-ch'ang-mên = Baituchangmen 50-51 CD 2
Paiute Indian Reservation [USA, California] 76-77 D 7
Paiute Indian Reservation [USA, Utah] 76-77 FG 6
Paiva Couceiro = Gambos 64-65 DE 5
Paja = Bâjâ 63 C 1-2
Pajala 30-31 K 4
Pajares 34-35 E 7
Pájaros, Punta – 80 B 3
Paj-Choj 42-43 L 4
Paj-Choj 42-43 L 4
Pajer, gora – 42-43 L 4
Paj-Choj 42-43 L 4
Paka [MAL] 52-53 D 6
Pakanbaru = Pekanbaru 52-53 D 6
Pak Beng = Mu'o'ng Pak Beng 52-53 D 2-3
Pakch'ŏn 50-51 E 3
Pakhoi = Beihai 48-49 K 7
Pákistán 44-45 K 5-L 4
Pakistan 44-45 K 5-L 4
Pakistán 44-45 K 5-L 4
Pakisztán 44-45 K 5-L 4
Pak Lay 52-53 D 3
Pakrac 36-37 G 3
Paks 33 J 5
Paksane = Muang Pakxan 52-53 D 3
Pakse = Muang Paksé 52-53 DE 3-4
P'akupur 42-43 NO 5
Pakwach 63 B 2
Pala [Tschad] 60-61 H 7
Palagruža 36-37 G 4
Palagruža 36-37 G 4
Palaiochōra 36-37 KL 8
Palaiokastritsa 36-37 H 6
Pālakkāț = Palghat 44-45 M 8
Palāmū = Daltonganj 44-45 N 6
Palana [AUS] 58 c 1
Palana [SU] 42-43 ef 6
Palandöken Dağı 46-47 J 3
Palanga 30-31 J 10
Palangkaraya 52-53 F 7
Pālanpur 44-45 L 6
Palapye 64-65 G 7
Palatka 42-43 d 5
Palatka, FL 74-75 c 2
Palau 52-53 KL 5
Pálau [I] 36-37 C 5
Palau, Dorsal de las – 48-49 Q 8-P 9
Palau, Grzbiet – 48-49 Q 8-P 9
Palau, Seuil de – 48-49 Q 8-P 9
Palaudrempel 48-49 Q 8-P 9
Palaui-hátság 48-49 Q 8-P 9
Palau Islands 52-53 K 5
Palauk 52-53 C 4
Palau Ridge 48-49 Q 8-P 9
Palauschwelle 48-49 Q 8-P 9
Palauský práh 48-49 Q 8-P 9
Palaw 52-53 C 4
Palawan 52-53 G 4-5
Palawan Passage 52-53 G 4-5
Palazzolo Acrèide 36-37 F 7
Paldiski 30-31 KL 8
Paleleh 52-53 H 6
Palembang 52-53 DE 7
Palencia 34-35 E 7
Palenque [MEX] 72-73 H 8
Palermo 36-37 E 6
Palermo, CA 76-77 C 6
Palestine, TX 72-73 GH 5
Palghat 44-45 M 8
Palgrave, Mount – 56-57 C 4
Palisade, NV 76-77 EF 5
Paljakka 30-31 MN 5
Palk Strait 44-45 MN 8-9
Pallapalla 78-79 E 7
Pallastunturi 30-31 KL 3
Palliser, Cape – 56-57 P 8
Palma 34-35 J 9
Palma [Moçambique] 64-65 JK 5
Palma, Bahía de – 34-35 J 9
Palma, La – [E] 60-61 A 3
Palmares 78-79 M 6
Palmares do Sul 80 FG 4
Palmas = Pulau Miagas 52-53 J 5
Palmas, Cape – 60-61 C 8
Palmas, Las – = Las Palmas de Gran Canaria 60-61 AB 3
Palmas, Rio las – 76-77 E 9
Palmas Bellas 72-73 a 2
Palmas de Gran Canaria, Las – 60-61 AB 3
Palma Soriano 72-73 LM 7
Palm Beach, FL 72-73 KL 6
Palmdale, CA 76-77 DE 8
Palmdale, FL 74-75 c 3
Palmeira 80 FG 3
Palmeira dos Índios 78-79 M 6
Palmeirais 78-79 L 6
Palmeirinhas, Ponta das – 64-65 D 4
Palmer 24 C 30
Palmer, AK 70-71 G 5
Palmer, Cape – 24 B 27
Palmer River [AUS, Northern Territory] 56-57 F 4-5
Palmer River [AUS, Queensland] 56-57 H 3
Palmerston [CDN] 74-75 C 3
Palmerston [NZ] 56-57 O 9
Palmerston = Darwin 56-57 F 2
Palmerstone, Cape – 56-57 JK 4
Palmerston North 56-57 OP 8
Palmerton, PA 74-75 F 4
Palmerville 56-57 H 3
Palmetto, FL 74-75 b 3
Palmi 36-37 F 6
Palmira [CO, Valle del Cauca] 78-79 D 4
Pālmīrās Antarīp = Palmyras Point 44-45 O 6
Palm Islands 56-57 J 3
Palm Springs, CA 76-77 E 9
Palmyra [SYR] 44-45 D 4
Palmyra, NY 74-75 E 3
Palmyras Point 44-45 O 6
Palo Alto, CA 76-77 B 7
Paloh [RI] 52-53 E 6
Paloma, La – [ROU, Rocha] 80 F 4
Palomani 78-79 EF 7
Palomar Mountain 72-73 C 5
Palomós 34-35 J 8
Palos, Cabo de – 34-35 G 10
Palos de la Frontera 34-35 D 10
Palo Seco 72-73 b 3
Palouse, WA 76-77 E 2
Palouse Falls 76-77 D 2
Palouse River 76-77 DE 2
Pältsa 30-31 J 3
Palu [RI] 52-53 G 7
Palu [TR] 46-47 H 3
Pam 56-57 M 4
Pama 60-61 E 6
Pamanukan 52-53 E 8
Pamanzi-Bé, Île – 64-65 L 5
Pam'ati 13 Borcov 42-43 R 6
Pamba 63 B 5
Pamiers 34-35 HJ 7
Pamir 44-45 L 3
Pâmiut 70-71 ab 5
Pamlico River 74-75 E 7
Pamlico Sound 72-73 L 4
Pampa, TX 72-73 F 4
Pampa Grande [BOL] 78-79 G 8
Pampa Húmeda 80 D 4-5
Pampas [PE, Huancavelica] 78-79 DE 7
Pampas [RA] 80 D 4-5
Pampa Seca 80 CD 4-5
Pampilhosa 34-35 C 8
Pamplona 34-35 G 7
Pamplona [CO] 78-79 E 3
Pan, Tierra del – 34-35 DE 7-8
Panaca, NV 76-77 F 7
Panag'urište 36-37 KL 4
Panag'urište 36-37 KL 4
Panaitan, Pulau – 52-53 DE 8
Panaji 44-45 L 7
Panama 72-73 KL 10
Panamá [PA, ●] 72-73 bc 3
Panamá [PA, ★] 72-73 KL 10
Panamá [PA, ☆] 72-73 a 3-b 2
Panamá, Bahía de – 72-73 bc 3
Panamá, Canal de – 72-73 b 2
Panama, Canal de – = Canal de Panamá 72-73 b 2
Panamá, Golfo de – 72-73 L 10
Panamá, Istmo de – 72-73 L 9-10
Panama Canal = Canal de Panamá 72-73 b 2
Panama City, FL 72-73 JK 5-6
Panama-csatorna 72-73 b 2
Panamakanal = Canal de Panamá 72-73 b 2
Panamá Viejo 72-73 c 2
Panamint Range 76-77 E 7
Panamint Valley 76-77 E 7-8
Panamski, Kanał – = Canal de Panamá 72-73 b 2
Panamský průplav = Canal de Panamá 72-73 b 2
Panao 78-79 D 6
Panaon Island 52-53 HJ 5
Pana Tinani 52-53 h 7
Panay 52-53 H 4
Pancake Range 76-77 EF 6
Pančevo 36-37 J 3
Panda 64-65 H 7
Pandharpur 44-45 LM 7
Pandie Pandie 56-57 GH 5
Pándormos = Bandırma 44-45 B 2
P'andž 44-45 K 3
P'andž 44-45 K 3
Panenské ostrovy 72-73 NO 8
Panevėžys 30-31 KL 10
Panevėžys 30-31 KL 10
Panfilov 42-43 OP 9
Pangaion 36-37 KL 5
Pangala 64-65 BC 2
Pangalanes, Canal des – 64-65 L 6-7
Pangani [EAT, ~] 64-65 J 3
Pangani [EAT, ● Morogoro] 63 D 4
Pangani [EAT, ● Tanga] 63 C 5
Pangbei = Erlian 48-49 L 3
Pangeo 52-53 J 6
Pangi 64-65 G 3
Pangkajene 52-53 G 7
Pangkalpinang 52-53 E 7
Pangnirtung 70-71 XY 4
Panguitch, UT 76-77 G 7
Pangutaran Group 52-53 GH 5
Panhandle 70-71 JK 6
Paniai, Danau – 52-53 L 7
Panié, Mount – 56-57 M 4
Pänj = P'andž 44-45 K 3

Panjāb 44-45 K 4
Panjāb = Punjab [IND] 44-45 LM 4
Panjāb = Punjab [PAK] 44-45 L 4
Panjang 52-53 E 8
Panjang, Hon – 52-53 D 5
Panjgūr 44-45 J 5
Panjim = Panaji 44-45 L 7
Panjwīn 46-47 L 5
Pankshin 60-61 FG 7
Panlı 46-47 E 3
P'anmunjŏm 50-51 F 3-4
Panna 44-45 N 6
Panoche, CA 76-77 C 7
Pānó Lévkara 46-47 E 5
Panshan 50-51 D 2
Pantanal Mato-Grossense 78-79 H 8
Pantano, AZ 76-77 H 9-10
Pantar, Pulau – 52-53 H 8
Pantelleria [I, ⊙] 36-37 E 7
Pantelleria [I, ●] 36-37 DE 7
Pantoja 78-79 DE 5
Pantokrátōr 36-37 H 6
Pánuco, Río – 72-73 G 7
Panyu = Guangzhou 48-49 LM 7
Pao, El – [YV, Bolívar] 78-79 G 3
Paochi = Baoji 48-49 K 5
Pao-ching = Baojing 48-49 K 6
Pao-ch'ing = Shaoyang 48-49 L 6
Paoki = Baoji 48-49 K 5
Pàola 36-37 FG 6
Paoning = Langzhong 48-49 JK 5
Paoshan = Baoshan [TJ, Yunnan] 48-49 HJ 6
Paoteh = Baode 48-49 L 4
Pao-ting = Baoding 48-49 LM 4
Paotow = Baotou 48-49 KL 3
Paotsing = Baojing 48-49 K 6
Paotsing = Baoqing 48-49 P 2
Paoying = Baoying 48-49 M 5
P'aozero 38-39 EF 2
Pápa 33 H 5
Papagayo, Golfo del – 72-73 J 9
Papago Indian Reservation 76-77 GH 9-10
Papantla de Olarte 72-73 G 7
Papatoetoe 56-57 OP 7
Paphos = Páfos 46-47 E 5
Pa-pien Chiang = Babian Jiang 48-49 J 7
Pa-pien Chiang = Babian Jiang 48-49 J 7
Pa-pien Chiang = Babian Jiang 48-49 J 7
Papíkion 36-37 L 5
Papilė 30-31 K 9
Papouasie et Nouvelle-Guinée 52-53 MN 7-8
Papua, Gulf of – 52-53 MN 8
Papua-Neuguinea 52-53 MN 7-8
Papua New Guinea 52-53 MN 7-8
Papua-Nieuw-Guinea 52-53 MN 7-8
Papua-Nová Guinea 52-53 MN 7-8
Papua-Nowa Gwinea 52-53 MN 7-8
Papúa-Nueva Guinea 52-53 MN 7-8
Pápua Új-Guinea 52-53 MN 7-8
Pâques, Île de – 22-23 D 7
Pará [BR] 78-79 J 5
Pará = Belém 78-79 K 5
Pará, Dorsal de – 22-23 GH 5
Pará, Rio do – 78-79 JK 5
Para, Seuil de – 22-23 GH 5
Parabel' 42-43 P 6
Paraburdoo 56-57 C 4
Paracale 52-53 H 4
Paracas, Península – 78-79 D 7
Paracatu 78-79 K 8
Paracels, Îles – – = Quân Đao Tây Sa 52-53 EF 3
Parachilna 58 D 3
Paraćin 36-37 J 4
Paracuru 78-79 M 5
Parada, Punta – 78-79 D 8
Paraday, Montes de – 28-29 C 5-6
Paraday Seamount Group 28-29 C 5-6
Paradise, CA 76-77 C 6
Paradise, MT 76-77 F 2
Paradise, NV 76-77 F 7
Paradise Valley, NV 76-77 E 5
Parádrempel 22-23 GH 5
Paragould, AR 72-73 H 4
Paragua, La – 78-79 G 3
Paraguá, Río – [BOL] 78-79 G 7
Paragua, Río – [YV] 78-79 G 3
Paraguai, Rio – 78-79 H 9
Paraguaipoa 78-79 E 2
Paraguaná, Península de – 78-79 F 2
Paraguarí [PY, ●] 80 E 3
Paraguay 80 DE 2
Paraguay, Río – 80 E 2
Paragwaj 80 DE 2
Paraíba 78-79 M 6
Paraíba, Rio – 78-79 M 6
Parainen = Pargas 30-31 K 7
Paraiso [PA] 72-73 b 2
Parakou 60-61 E 7
Paramaribo 78-79 HJ 3
Paramirim 78-79 L 7
Paramonga 78-79 D 7
Paramušir, ostrov – 42-43 de 7
Paramušir, ostrov – 42-43 de 7
Paraná [RA] 80 DE 4
Paraná [BR, ●] 78-79 K 7
Paraná [BR, ☆] 80 FG 2
Paraná, Río – [RA] 80 E 3-4
Paraná, Rio – [BR ◁ Rio de la Plata] 78-79 J 9
Paranã, Rio – [BR ◁ Rio Tocantins] 78-79 K 7
Paranaguá 80 G 3
Paranaíba 78-79 J 8
Paranaíba, Rio – 78-79 JK 8
Paranapanema, Rio – 78-79 J 9
Paranapiacaba, Serra do – 78-79 G 2-3
Paranavaí 80 F 2
Parandak, Īstgâh-e – 46-47 O 5
Paranjang 50-51 F 4
Parapol'skij dol 42-43 fg 5
Pará Rise 22-23 GH 5
Paráschwelle 22-23 GH 5
Parata, Pointe della – 36-37 BC 5
Paratinga 78-79 L 7
Paraúna 78-79 JK 8
Parbati 44-45 M 5
Parbatipur 44-45 O 5
Parbig 42-43 P 6
Parchim 33 EF 2
Parc national de la Komoé 60-61 D 7
Parczew 33 L 3
Pardo, Rio – [BR, Planalto Brasileiro] 78-79 L 8
Pardo, Rio – [BR ◁ Rio Paraná] 78-79 J 9
Pardubice 33 GH 3
Pardubitz = Pardubice 33 GH 3
Parecis, Campos dos – 78-79 H 7
Parecis, Chapada dos – 78-79 GH 7
Parecis, Chapada dos – 78-79 GH 7
Parecis, Chapada dos – 78-79 GH 7
Parelhas 78-79 M 6
Pare Mountains 63 D 3-4
Parentis-en-Born 34-35 G 6
Parepare 52-53 G 7
Parga 36-37 J 6
Pargas 30-31 K 7
Paria, Golfo de – 78-79 G 2
Paria, Península de – 78-79 G 2
Pariaman 52-53 CD 7
Paria River 76-77 H 7
Paricutín, Volcán – 72-73 F 8
Parika 78-79 H 3
Parima, Sierra – 78-79 G 4
Pariñas, Punta – 78-79 C 5
Parintins 78-79 H 5
Pariñas, Punta – 78-79 C 5
Parīpārit Kyûn 52-53 B 4
Paris 34-35 J 4
Paris, ID 76-77 H 4
Paris, TX 72-73 GH 5
París = Paris 34-35 J 4
Párisz = Paris 34-35 I 4
Parkano 30-31 K 6
Park City, UT 76-77 H 5
Parkdale, OR 76-77 C 3
Parker, AZ 76-77 FG 8
Parker Dam, CA 76-77 F 8
Parkersburg, WV 72-73 K 4
Parkes 56-57 J 6
Park Range 72-73 E 3-4
Park Valley, UT 76-77 G 5
Parlākimidi 44-45 NO 7
Parma 36-37 D 3
Parma, ID 76-77 E 4
Parma, OH 74-75 C 4
Parnaguá 78-79 L 7
Parnaíba 78-79 L 5
Parnaíba, Rio – 78-79 L 5
Parnassós 36-37 K 6
Párnēs 36-37 K 6
Párnōn 36-37 K 7
Pärnu [SU, ∼] 30-31 L 8
Pärnu [SU, ●] 30-31 KL 8
Paromaj 42-43 b 7
Parona = Fındık 46-47 JK 4
Paroo Channel 56-57 H 6
Paroo Channel 56-57 H 6
Paroo Channel 56-57 H 6
Paroo River 58 G 2
Páros 36-37 L 7
Parowan, UT 76-77 G 7
Parr, SC 74-75 C 7
Parral 80 B 5
Parramore Island 74-75 F 6
Parras de la Fuente 72-73 F 6
Parry, Cape – 70-71 M 3
Parry Bay 70-71 U 4
Parry Island 74-75 C 2
Parry Islands 70-71 M-R 2
Parryøya 30-31 kl 4
Parsa = Persepolis 44-45 G 5
Parsnip River 70-71 M 6-7
Parsons, KS 72-73 G 4
Parsons, WV 74-75 D 5
Parṭa Jebel 36-37 J 3
Pårtefjällèt 30-31 GH 4
Parthenay 34-35 GH 5
Parti-Atlasz 60-61 D 2-E 1
Partinico 36-37 E 6
Partizansk 42-43 Z 9
Paru, Rio – [BR] 78-79 J 5
Pārvatī = Parbati 44-45 M 5
Parvatipurom 44-45 N 7
Parijs = Paris 34-35 J 4
Paryż = Paris 34-35 I 4
Paříž = Paris 34-35 J 4
Pasadena, CA 72-73 C 5
Pasadena, TX 72-73 GH 6
Pasaje 78-79 D 5
Pasajes de San Juan 34-35 FG 7
Pascagoula, MS 72-73 J 5
Paşcani 36-37 M 2
Pasco, WA 76-77 D 2
Pascua, Isla de – 22-23 D 7
Pascua, Plataforma de la isla de – 22-23 C-E 7
Pasewalk 33 FG 2
Pashâwar 44-45 KL 4
Pashchimī Bangāl = West Bengal 44-45 O 6
Pashid Haihsia 48-49 N 7
P'asina 42-43 QR 3
Pasinler 46-47 J 2-3
P'asino, ozero – 42-43 QR 4
P'asinskij zaliv 42-43 PQ 3
Pasir Besar = Kampung Pasir Besar 52-53 D 6
Paskenta, CA 76-77 B 6
Pasley, Cape – 56-57 D 6
Pašman 36-37 F 4
Pasnī 44-45 J 5
Paso, El – 78-79 E 3
Paso de Indios 80 BC 6
Paso de los Libres 80 E 3
Paso de los Toros 80 EF 4
Paso Robles, CA 76-77 C 8
Pasov = Passau 33 F 4
Passau 33 F 4
Pàssero, Capo – 36-37 F 7
Passo Fundo 80 F 3
Passos 78-79 K 9
Pastaza, Río – 78-79 D 5
Pasto 78-79 D 4
Pastora Peak 76-77 J 7
Pasvalys 30-31 KL 9
Pasvikelv 30-31 NO 3
Pašman 36-37 F 4
Patagonia 80 B 8-C 6
Patagonia, AZ 76-77 H 10
Patagonia, Plataforma de – 22-23 FG 8
Patagonian Shelf 22-23 FG 8
Patagónica, Cordillera – 80 B 8-5
Patagonischer Schelf 22-23 FG 8
Patagonisch Plat 22-23 FG 8
Patagonischer Schelf 22-23 FG 8
Patagonischer Schelf 22-23 FG 8
Pātan [Nepal] 44-45 NO 5
Patane = Pattani 52-53 D 5
Patang = Batang 48-49 H 6
Patargān, Daqq-e – 44-45 J 4
Patchewollock 58 EF 5
Patchogue, NY 74-75 G 4
Paternò 36-37 F 7
Pateros, WA 76-77 D 1-2
Paterson, NJ 74-75 F 4
Paterson, WA 76-77 D 2-3
Pathum Thani 52-53 CD 4
Patía, Río – 78-79 D 4
Patiala 44-45 M 4
Patience Well 56-57 E 4
P'atigorsk 38-39 H 7
Paṭiyālā = Patiala 44-45 M 4
Pátmos 36-37 M 7
Patna 44-45 O 5
Patnos 46-47 K 3
Patomskoje nagorje 42-43 V 6-W 6
Patos [BR, Paraíba] 78-79 M 6
Patos, Lagoa dos – 80 F 4
Patquía 80 C 4
Pátrai 36-37 J 6
Patraïkòs Kólpos 36-37 J 6-7
Pátra = Pátrai 36-37 JK 6
Patreksfjördhur 30-31 ab 2
Patricia [CDN, ≅] 70-71 S-U 7
Patricio Lynch, Isla – 80 A 7
Patricio Lynch, Isla – 80 A 7
Patrocínio 78-79 K 8
Patta Island 64-65 K 3
Pattani 52-53 D 5
Patten, ME 74-75 J 2
Patterson, CA 76-77 C 7
Patterson, GA 74-75 B 9
Patti 36-37 F 6
Pattiá 78-79 D 4
Patton, PA 74-75 D 4
Patu 78-79 M 6
Patuca, Punta – 72-73 K 8
Patuca, Río – 72-73 J 9-K 8
Patung = Badong 48-49 KL 5
Pau 34-35 G 7
Pau d'Arco 78-79 K 6
Pauillac 34-35 G 6
Paulina, OR 76-77 D 3
Paulina Mountains 76-77 C 4
Paulis = Isiro 64-65 G 2
Paulista [BR, Pernambuco] 78-79 MN 6
Paulista [BR, Zona litigiosa] 78-79 L 8
Paulistana 78-79 L 6
Paulo Afonso, Cachoeira de – 78-79 M 6
Paungde = Paungdī 52-53 BC 3
Paungdī 52-53 BC 3
Pavant Mountains 76-77 G 6
Pavēh 46-47 M 5
Pavia 36-37 C 3
Pavino 38-39 J 4
Pavlodar 42-43 O 7
Pavlovac 36-37 G 3
Pavlovo 38-39 H 4
Pavlovskaja 38-39 GH 6
Pavo, GA 74-75 B 9
Pavullo nel Frignano 36-37 D 3
Pavuvu = Russell Islands 52-53 j 6
Pavy 30-31 N 8-9
Pawleys Island, SC 74-75 D 8
Pawtucket, RI 74-75 H 4
Páxoi 36-37 J 6
Payakumbuh 52-53 D 7
Payette, ID 76-77 E 3
Payette River 76-77 E 3-4
Payne, Lac – 70-71 W 6
Payne Bay = Bellin 70-71 WX 5
Paynes Creek, CA 76-77 BC 5
Paysandú [ROU, ●] 80 E 4
Pays-Bas 34-35 K 3-L 2
Payson, AZ 76-77 H 8
Payson, UT 76-77 GH 5
Payún, Cerro – 80 BC 5
Paz, La – [MEX, Baja California Sur] 72-73 DE 7
Paz, La – [RA, Entre Ríos] 80 DE 4
Paz, La – [RA, Mendoza] 80 C 4
Paz, La – [BOL, ●] 78-79 F 8
Paž'a 38-39 L 3
Pazar 46-47 J 2
Pazar = Şorba 46-47 E 2
Pazarbası Burnu 46-47 D 2
Pazarcık 46-47 G 4
Pazarcık = Pazaryeri 46-47 C 2-3
Pazardžik 36-37 KL 4
Pazardžik 36-37 KL 4
Pazaryeri [TR, Bilecik] 46-47 C 2-3
Pazifischer Ozean 22-23 Q-T 5-6
Paž'a 38-39 L 3
Pčinja 36-37 J 4-5
Pčinja 36-37 J 4-5
Peace River [CDN, ∼] 70-71 MN 6
Peace River [CDN, ●] 70-71 N 6
Peach Springs, AZ 76-77 G 8
Peacock Bay 24 B 26-27
Peake Creek 58 B 1-2
Peak Hill [AUS, New South Wales] 58 J 4
Peak Hill [AUS, Western Australia] 56-57 C 5
Peale, Mount – 72-73 DE 4
Pearce, AZ 76-77 J 10
Pearl Harbor 52-53 e 3
Pearl River 72-73 H 5
Pearson, GA 74-75 B 9
Peary Channel 70-71 R 2
Peary Channel 70-71 R 2
Peary Channel 70-71 R 2
Peary Land 19 A 21-23
Pebane 64-65 J 6
Pebas 78-79 E 5
Peć 36-37 J 4
Peças, Ilha das – 80 G 3
Pečenga [SU, ●] 42-43 E 4
Pechabun = Phetchabun 52-53 CD 3
Pechawar = Pashâwar 44-45 KL 4
Pêcheurs, Presqu'île des – = poluostrov Rybačij 42-43 EF 4
Pečora [SU, ∼] 42-43 K 5
Pečora [SU, ●] 42-43 K 4
Pecoraro, Monte – 36-37 FG 6
Pečorskaja guba 42-43 JK 4
Pečorskaja magistral' 42-43 JK 5
Pečory 30-31 M 9
Pecos, TX 72-73 F 5
Pecos River 72-73 F 5
Pécs 33 HJ 5
Pecs = Pécs 33 HJ 5
Pečenga [SU, ●] 42-43 E 4
Pečora [SU, ∼] 42-43 K 5
Pečora [SU, ●] 42-43 K 4
Pečorskaja guba 42-43 JK 4
Pečorskaja magistral' 42-43 JK 5
Pečory 30-31 M 9
Pedder, Lake – 58 bc 3
Pedee, OR 76-77 B 3
Pedernales [EC] 78-79 CD 4
Pedernales [YV] 78-79 G 3
Pederneira, Cachoeira – 78-79 FG 6
Pedra Azul 78-79 L 8
Pedras Negras 78-79 G 7
Pedregal [PA] 72-73 c 2
Pedreiras 78-79 KL 5
Pedrera, La – 78-79 EF 5
Pedro, Point – = Pēduru Tuḍuwa 44-45 N 9
Pedro Afonso 78-79 K 6
Pedro Cays 72-73 L 8
Pedro de Valdivia 80 BC 2
Pedro II 78-79 L 5
Pedro Juan Caballero 80 E 2
Pedro Miguel 72-73 b 2
Pedro Miguel, Esclusas de – 72-73 b 3
Pedro Miguel Locks = Esclusas de Pedro Miguel 72-73 b 2
Pedro R. Fernández 80 E 3
Pēduru Tuḍuwa [CL, ∧] 44-45 N 9
Peebinga 56-57 H 6
Peebles 32 E 4
Pee Dee River 72-73 L 5
Peekskill, NY 74-75 G 4
Peel River 70-71 JK 4
Peel Sound 70-71 R 3
Peene 33 F 2
Peera Peera Poolanna Lake 56-57 G 5
Pegasus Bay 56-57 O 8
Pegram, ID 76-77 H 4
Pēgū 52-53 C 3
Pehpei = Beipei 48-49 K 6
Pehuajó 80 D 5
Peian = Bei'an 48-49 O 2
Pei-chên = Beizhen 50-51 C 2
Peighambar Dāgh = Peyghambar Dāgh 46-47 N 4
Pei-hai = Beihai 48-49 K 7
P'ei-hsien = Pei Xian 48-49 M 5
Peine 33 E 2
Pei-ngan = Bei'an 48-49 O 2
Peipei = Beipei 48-49 K 6
Pei-p'iao = Beipiao 50-51 C 2
Peiping = Beijing 48-49 LM 3-4
Peiraiévs 36-37 K 7
Pei Shan = Bei Shan 48-49 GH 3
Peixe 78-79 K 7
Pei Xian [TJ ↖ Xuzhou] 48-49 M 5
Pejpus, Jezioro – – = Čudskoje ozero 42-43 O 6
Pekalongan 52-53 EF 8
Pekan 52-53 D 6
Pekanbaru 52-53 D 6
Pekin = Beijing 48-49 LM 3-4
Pekín = Beijing 48-49 LM 3-4
Pékin = Beijing 48-49 LM 3-4
Peking = Beijing 48-49 LM 3-4
Pekul'nej, chrebet – 42-43 hj 4
Peleaga 36-37 K 3
Peleduj 42-43 V 6
Pelée, Montagne – 72-73 O 8
Pelēnaion 36-37 LM 6
Peleng, Pulau – 52-53 H 7
Pēlion 36-37 K 6
Pelješac 36-37 G 4
Pelješac 36-37 G 4
Pelkosenniemi 30-31 MN 4
Pello 30-31 L 4
Pelly Bay 70-71 S 4
Pelly Mountains 70-71 K 5
Pelly River 70-71 K 5
Peloncillo Mountains 76-77 J 9
Pelopónnēsos 36-37 JK 7
Peloritani, Monti – 36-37 F 6-7
Pelotas 80 F 4
Pelotas, Rio – 80 F 3
Pelusium 62 E 2
Pelusium, Bay of – = Khalīj aṭ-Ṭīnah 62 E 2
Pelvoux 34-35 L 6
Pelym [SU, ∼] 42-43 L 5
Pelym [SU, ●] 42-43 L 6
Pemadumcook Lake 74-75 J 2
Pemalang 52-53 EF 8
Pemangkat 52-53 E 6
Pematangsiantar 52-53 C 6
Pemba [EAT] 64-65 JK 4
Pemba [Moçambique] 64-65 K 5
Pemba [Z] 64-65 G 6
Pemberton [AUS] 56-57 C 6
Pembina 70-71 NO 7
Pembroke 32 D 6
Pembroke [CDN] 72-73 L 2
Pembroke, GA 74-75 C 8
Peña, Sierra de la – 34-35 G 7
Peñafiel 34-35 EF 8
Peñagolosa 34-35 G 8
Peña Negra, Punta – 78-79 C 5
Peña Nevada, Cerro – 72-73 FG 7
Penang = George Town 52-53 CD 5
Peñarroya 34-35 G 8
Peñarroya-Pueblonuevo 34-35 E 9
Peñas, Cabo de – 34-35 E 7
Peñas, Golfo de – 80 AB 7
Peñas, Punta – 78-79 G 2
Penawawa, WA 76-77 E 2
Penck, Cape – 24 C 9
Pendembu 60-61 B 7
Pender Bay 56-57 D 3
Pendjab = Punjab [IND] 44-45 LM 4
Pendjab = Punjab [PAK] 44-45 L 4
Pendleton, OR 72-73 C 2
Pend Oreille Lake 76-77 E 1-2
Pend Oreille River 76-77 E 1
Pendroy, MT 76-77 GH 1
Pendžikent 44-45 K 3
Pendžikent 44-45 K 3
Pēneiós 36-37 K 6
Penetanguishene 74-75 CD 2
Penganga 44-45 M 7
Penge [ZRE, Haut-Zaïre] 63 AB 2
Penge [ZRE, Kasai-Oriental] 64-65 FG 4
Penghu Liedao = Penghu Lieh-tao 48-49 M 7
Penghu Lieh-tao 48-49 M 7
Penglai 48-49 N 4
Pengra Pass 76-77 BC 4
Pengze 48-49 M 6
Penida, Nusa – 52-53 FG 8
Península Malaya 52-53 C 5-D 6
Peñíscola 34-35 H 8
Penitente, Serra do – 78-79 K 6
Penki = Benxi 48-49 N 3
Penmarch, Pointe de – 34-35 E 5
Penne 36-37 EF 4
Penn Hills, PA 74-75 D 4
Pennine Chain 32 E 4-F 5
Pennine Chain 32 E 4-F 5
Pennine Chain 32 E 4-F 5
Pennsylvania 72-73 KL 3
Penn Yan, NY 74-75 E 3
Penny Highland 70-71 X 4
Penny Strait 70-71 R 2
Penobscot Bay 74-75 J 2
Penobscot River 74-75 J 2
Penong 56-57 F 6
Penrith 32 E 4
Pensa = Penza 42-43 GH 7
Pensacola, FL 72-73 J 5
Pensacola Mountains 24 A 33-34
Pentecost Island 56-57 N 3
Pentecost River 56-57 E 3
Penticton 70-71 N 8
Pentland Firth 32 E 2
Penyu, Kepulauan – 52-53 J 8
Penza 42-43 GH 7
Penzance 32 CD 6
Penžina 42-43 g 5
Penžinskaja guba 42-43 f 5
Penžina 42-43 g 5
Penžinskaja guba 42-43 f 5
Peña, Sierra de la – 34-35 G 7
Peñafiel 34-35 EF 8
Peñagolosa 34-35 G 8
Peña Negra, Punta – 78-79 C 5
Peña Nevada, Cerro – 72-73 FG 7
Peñarroya 34-35 G 8
Peñarroya-Pueblonuevo 34-35 E 9
Peñas, Cabo de – 34-35 E 7
Peñas, Golfo de – 80 AB 7
Peñas, Punta – 78-79 G 2
Peñíscola 34-35 H 8
Peoria, AZ 76-77 G 9
Peoria, IL 72-73 HJ 3
Pepel 60-61 B 7
Peperkust 60-61 B 7-C 8
Pepřonosné pobřeží 60-61 B 7-C 8
Pequeni, Río – 72-73 bc 2
Pequeñas Antillas 72-73 N 9-O 8
Pequop Mountains 76-77 F 5
Perälä 30-31 JK 6
Perche 34-35 H 4
Percival Lakes 56-57 DE 4
Perdido, Monte – 34-35 GH 7
Pereguete, Río – 72-73 b 3
Pereira 78-79 D 4
Pereira, Cachoeira – 78-79 H 5
Pereira d 'Eça = N'Giva 64-65 E 6
Perekop 38-39 F 6
Perelik 36-37 L 5
Peremul Par 44-45 L 8
Pereslavl'-Zalesskij 38-39 G 4
Perevoz [SU ↗ Bodajbo] 42-43 W 6
Pergamino 80 D 4
Pergamon 46-47 B 3
Pergamos = Pergamon 46-47 B 3
Perhonjoki 30-31 KL 6
Péribonca, Rivière – 70-71 W 7-8
Perico 80 CD 2
Périgord 34-35 H 6
Perigoso, Canal – 78-79 K 4
Périgueux 34-35 H 6
Perija, Sierra de – 78-79 E 2-3
Perim Island = Barīm 44-45 E 8
Periquito, Cachoeira do – 78-79 G 6
Peri Suyu 46-47 J 3
Perito Moreno 80 BC 7
Perlas, Archipiélago de las – 72-73 KL 10
Perlas, Punta de – 72-73 K 9
Perm' 42-43 K 6
Permskoje = Komsomol'sk-na-Amure 42-43 a 7
Pernambuco 78-79 LM 6
Pernambuco = Recife 78-79 N 6
Pernik 36-37 K 4
Péronne 34-35 J 4
Peron Peninsula 56-57 B 5
Pérou 78-79 D 5-E 7
Pérou, Bassin du – 22-23 E 6
Pérouse, proliv la – = proliv Laperuza 42-43 b 8
Perovsk = Kzyl-Orda 42-43 M 9
Perpignan 34-35 J 7
Perrégaux = Muḥammadīyah 60-61 DE 1
Perrine, FL 74-75 c 4
Perris, CA 76-77 E 9
Perry, FL 74-75 b 1
Perry, NY 74-75 DE 3
Perse = Iran 44-45 F-H 4

208 Panjā

Perşembe 46-47 G 2
Persepolis 44-45 G 5
Perseveranta 78-79 G 7
Persia = Iran 44-45 F-H 4
Persian Gulf 44-45 FG 5
Persie = Iran 44-45 F-H 4
Persien = Iran 44-45 F-H 4
Persischer Golf 44-45 FG 5
Persja = Iran 44-45 F-H 4
Perska, Zatoka – 44-45 FG 5
Perský záliv 44-45 FG 5
Pertek 46-47 H 3
Perth [AUS, Tasmania] 58 c 2
Perth [AUS, Western Australia]
   56-57 BC 6
Perth [CDN] 74-75 E 2
Perth [GB] 32 E 3
Perth Amboy, NJ 74-75 F 4
Peru [CDN] 74-75 E 2
Peru 78-79 D 5-E 7
Perú 78-79 D 5-E 7
Perú [RA] 80 D 5
Perú, Cuenca del – 22-23 E 6
Perú, Fosa del – 78-79 C 6-D 7
Peru, Rów – 78-79 C 6-D 7
Peru Basin 22-23 E 6
Perubecken 22-23 E 6
Perubekken 22-23 E 6
Peru Chile Trench 78-79 C 6-D 7
Peru Chile Trench 78-79 C 6-D 7
Perúgia 36-37 E 4
Perugraben 78-79 C 6-D 7
Peru Chile Trench 78-79 C 6-D 7
Perui-árok 78-79 C 6-D 7
Peruibe 80 G 2
Perutrog 78-79 C 6-D 7
Pervari = Hashir 46-47 K 4
Perveri 46-47 GH 4
Pervomajsk 38-39 EF 6
Pervoural'sk 42-43 KL 6
Pervyj Kuril'skij proliv 42-43 de 7
Perzië = Iran 44-45 F-H 4
Perzische Golf 44-45 FG 5
Perzsa-öböl 44-45 FG 5
Perzsia = Irán 44-45 F-H 4
Pèsaro 36-37 E 4
Pescadero, CA 76-77 B 7
Pescadores = Penghu Lieh-tao
   48-49 M 7
Pesčanyj, ostrov – 42-43 WX 3
Pescara 36-37 F 4
Pèschici 36-37 FG 5
Pesčanyj, ostrov – 42-43 WX 3
Peshawar = Pashāwar 44-45 KL 4
Peshwar = Pashāwar 44-45 KL 4
Peštera 36-37 KL 4
Peštera 36-37 K 4
Petah Tiqua = Pètah Tiqwa
   46-47 F 6
Pètah Tiqwa 46-47 F 6
Petalión, Kólpos – 36-37 L 7
Petaluma, CA 76-77 B 6
Petauke 64-65 H 5
Petén, El – 72-73 H 8
Peterborough 32 FG 5
Peterborough [AUS, South
   Australia] 56-57 GH 6
Peterborough [AUS, Victoria]
   58 F 7
Peterborough [CDN] 70-71 V 9
Peterborough, NH 74-75 GH 3
Peterhead 32 F 3
Petermann Ranges 56-57 E 4-F 5
Peter Pond Lake 70-71 P 6
Petersburg, AK 70-71 K 6
Petersburg, VA 72-73 L 4
Petersburg, WV 74-75 D 5
Petersburg = Sankt-Peterburg
   42-43 E 5-6
Pétikostelí = Pécs 33 HJ 5
Petilia Policastro 36-37 G 6
Petitjean = Sīdī Qāsim
   60-61 CD 2
Petit Manan Point 74-75 K 2
Petitot River 70-71 M 5-6
Peto 72-73 J 7
Petorca 80 B 4
Petra [JOR] 46-47 F 7
Petra, ostrova – 42-43 VW 2
Petra I, ostrov – 24 C 27
Petra Velikogo, zaliv – 42-43 Z 9
Petre, Point – 74-75 E 3
Petřič 36-37 K 5
Petrič 36-37 K 5
Petrified Forest National
   Monument 76-77 J 8
Pétriou = Chachoengsao
   52-53 D 4
Petroaleksandrovsk = Turtkul'
   42-43 L 9
Petrodvorec 30-31 O 8
Petrohrad = Sankt-Peterburg
   42-43 E 5-6
Petrohrad = Sankt-Peterburg
   42-43 E 5-6
Petrohrad = Peterburg, St.-
   38-39 F 3
Petrolándia 78-79 M 6
Petrólea 78-79 E 3
Petrolia, CA 76-77 A 5
Petrolina [BR, Pernambuco]
   78-79 M 6
Petropavlovka 42-43 TU 7
Petropavlovsk 42-43 MN 7

Petropavlovsk-Kamčatskij
   42-43 ef 7
Petropavlovsk-Kamčatskij
   42-43 ef 7
Petrópolis 78-79 L 9
Petroşeni 36-37 K 3
Petroskoi = Petrozavodsk
   42-43 EF 5
Petrovaradin 36-37 HJ 3
Petrovka [SU, Vladivostok]
   50-51 J 1
Petrovsk 38-39 J 5
Petrovskij Zavod = Petrovsk-
   Zabajkal'skij 42-43 U 7
Petrovsk-Zabajkal'skij 42-43 U 7
Petrozavodsk 42-43 EF 5
Petrun 38-39 LM 2
Pettau = Ptuj 36-37 FG 2
Petuchovo 42-43 M 6
Peumo 80 B 4
Pevek 42-43 gh 4
Peyghambar Dāgh 46-47 N 4
Peza 38-39 J 2
Pézenas 34-35 J 7

Pfaffenhofen 33 E 4
Pfarrkirchen 33 F 4
Pfefferküste 60-61 B 7-C 8
Pforzheim 33 D 4

Phalodi 44-45 L 5
Phaltan 44-45 LM 7
Phangan, Ko – 52-53 CD 5
Phanggong Tsho 48-49 DE 5
Phan Rang 52-53 EF 4
Phan Thiet 52-53 E 4
Phatthalung 52-53 D 5
Phaykkhaphum Phisai 52-53 D 3
Phelps Lake 74-75 E 7
Phenix City, AL 72-73 J 5
Phenjan = P'yŏngyang
   48-49 NO 4
Phetchabun 52-53 CD 3
Phetchaburi 52-53 C 4
Philadelphia [ET] 62 D 3
Philadelphia, PA 72-73 LM 3-4
Philip Island 56-57 N 5
Philippe-Thomas = Al-Mittawī
   60-61 F 2
Philippeville 34-35 K 3
Philippeville = Sakīkdah
   60-61 F 1
Philippi, WV 74-75 CD 5
Philippine Basin 22-23 Q 5
Philippinen 52-53 H 3-J 5
Philippinenbecken 22-23 Q 5
Philippinengraben 22-23 Q 5
Philippines 52-53 H 3-J 5
Philippines, Bassin des –
   22-23 Q 5
Philippines, Fosse des –
   22-23 Q 5
Philippine Trench 22-23 Q 5
Philipsburg, MT 76-77 G 2
Philipsburg, PA 74-75 D 4
Philip Smith Mountains
   70-71 HJ 4
Phillipi, Lake – 56-57 G 4
Phillip Island 58 G 7
Phillippines 52-53 H 3-J 5
Phillips, ME 74-75 H 2
Phillipsburg, NJ 74-75 F 4
Phillips Mountains 24 B 22-23
Phippsøya 30-31 kl 4
Phitsanulok 52-53 CD 3
Phnom Penh 52-53 D 4
Phnum Pénh = Phnom Penh
   52-53 D 4
Pho, Laem – 52-53 D 5
Phoenix, AZ 72-73 D 5
Phoenix, Fosse des – 22-23 AB 6
Phoenixgraben 22-23 AB 6
Phoenix Trench 22-23 AB 6
Phoenixtrog 22-23 AB 6
Phoenixville, PA 74-75 EF 4
Phôngsaly 52-53 D 2
Phosphate Hill 56-57 GH 4
Phra Chedi Sam Ong 52-53 C 3-4
Phra Chedi Sam Ong 52-53 C 3-4
Phra Chedi Sam Ong 52-53 C 3-4
Phra Nakhon Si Ayutthaya
   52-53 D 4
Phu Diên Châu 52-53 E 3
Phu Diên Châu 52-53 E 3
Phu Diên Châu 52-53 E 3
Phuket 52-53 C 5
Phuket, Ko – 52-53 C 5
Phu Ly 52-53 E 2
Phu Ly 52-53 E 2
Phum Rovieng 52-53 E 4
Phunakha 44-45 OP 5
Phu Quôc, Dao – 52-53 D 4
Phu Tho 52-53 DE 2

Piacá 78-79 K 6
Piacenza 36-37 C 3
Piangil 56-57 H 7
Pianosa, Ìsola – 36-37 D 4
Piaseczno 33 K 2
Piatra 36-37 L 3
Piatra-Neamţ 36-37 M 2
Piauí 78-79 L 6
Piauí, Rio – 78-79 L 6
Piave 36-37 E 2
Piazza Armerina 36-37 F 7

Pïbŏr = Bïbŭr 60-61 L 7
Pïbŏr, Nahr – = Nahr Bïbŭr
   60-61 L 7
Picabo, ID 76-77 F 4
Picacho, AZ 76-77 H 9
Picacho, CA 76-77 F 9
Picardie 34-35 HJ 4
Pichanal 80 CD 2
Pichi Ciego 80 C 4
Pichieh = Bijie 48-49 K 6
Pichilemú 80 B 4
Pichtovka 42-43 P 6
Pickens, SC 74-75 B 7
Pickle Crow 70-71 ST 7
Pico, El – 78-79 G 8
Picola 58 G 5
Picos 78-79 L 6
Pico Truncado 80 C 7
Picton [CDN] 74-75 E 2-3
Picton [NZ] 56-57 O 8
Picton, Mount – 58 bc 3
Picuí 78-79 M 6
Picún Leufú 80 BC 5
Pide de Palo 80 C 4
Piedmont 72-73 K 5-L 4
Piedmont, SC 74-75 B 7
Piedmont, WV 74-75 D 5
Piedra del Águila 80 BC 6
Piedras 78-79 D 8
Piedras, Rio – [PA] 72-73 b 2
Piedras, Rio de las – 78-79 E 7
Piedras Negras 72-73 F 6
Pieksämäki 30-31 M 6
Pielinen 30-31 N 6
Piemonte 36-37 BC 3
Pieprzowe, Wybrzeże –
   60-61 B 7-C 8
Pierce, ID 76-77 F 2
Piercy, CA 76-77 B 6
Pierre, SD 72-73 F 3
Pierson, FL 74-75 c 2
Pidurutalâgala 44-45 N 9
Pie de Palo 80 C 4
Pietarsaari = Jakobstad
   30-31 JK 6
Pietermaritzburg 64-65 H 8
Pietersburg 64-65 G 7
Pietrasanta 36-37 CD 4
Pietrosul [R ✓ Borşa] 36-37 L 2
Pietrosul [R ✓ Vatra Dornei]
   36-37 L 2
Pigailoe 52-53 N 5
Pigeon Point 76-77 B 7
Pigüm-do 50-51 E 5
Pihtipudas 30-31 LM 6
Pihyŏn 50-51 E 2
Piippola 30-31 M 5
Pija, Sierra de – 72-73 J 8
Pikelot 52-53 N 5
Pikes Peak 72-73 F 4
Piketberg 64-65 E 9
Pikeville, KY 74-75 B 6
Pikou 50-51 D 3
Piła 33 H 2
Pilão Arcado 78-79 L 7
Pilar [PY] 80 E 3
Pilares de Nacozari 76-77 J 10
Pilas Group 52-53 H 5
Pilawa 33 K 3
Pilcaniyeu 80 BC 6
Pilcomayo, Rio – [BR] 80 D 2
Pil'gyn 42-43 jk 4
Pilica 33 K 3
Pillar, Cape – 56-57 J 8
Pillau = Baltijsk 33 J 1
Pilot Mountain, NC 74-75 C 6
Pilot Peak [USA, Absaroka Range]
   76-77 HJ 3
Pilot Peak [USA, Gabbs Valley
   Range] 76-77 E 6
Pilot Peak [USA, Toano Range]
   76-77 FG 5
Pilot Rock, OR 76-77 D 3
Pilsen = Plzeň 33 F 4
Piltene 30-31 JK 9
Pilzno = Pizen 33 F 4
Piła 33 H 2
Pim 42-43 N 5
Pimba 56-57 G 6
Pimenta Bueno 78-79 G 7
Pimienta, Costa de la –
   60-61 B 7-C 8
Piña [PA] 72-73 a 2
Pinaleno Mountains 76-77 HJ 9
Pinamelayan 52-53 H 4
Pinang = George Town
   52-53 CD 5
Pinar = Ören 46-47 BC 4
Pınarbaşı 46-47 G 3
Pinar del Rio 72-73 K 7
Pınarhisar 46-47 B 2
Pîncota 36-37 J 2
Pindaré, Rio – 78-79 K 5
Pindos Óros 36-37 J 5-6
Pine, ID 76-77 F 4
Pine Bluff, AR 72-73 H 5
Pine City, WA 76-77 E 2
Pine Creek [AUS] 56-57 F 2
Pine Creek [USA] 74-75 E 5
Pinedale, WY 76-77 J 4
Pine Forest Mountains 76-77 D 5
Pinega 42-43 G 5
Pine Hills 72-73 J 5
Pine Island 74-75 b 3

Pine Island Bay 24 B 26
Pine Islands 74-75 c 4
Pine Point 70-71 O 5
Pinerolo 36-37 B 3
Pine Valley Mountains 76-77 G 7
Ping, Mae Nam – 52-53 C 3
P'ing-ch'üan = Pingquan
   50-51 C 2
Pingdong = Ping-tung 48-49 N 7
Pinggree, ID 76-77 G 4
Pingree, ID 76-77 G 4
Pingrup 56-57 C 6
Pingsiang = Pingxiang 48-49 L 6
Pingtan Dao 48-49 MN 6
Ping-tung 48-49 N 7
Pingwu 48-49 J 5
Pingxiang [TJ, Guangxi Zhuangzu
   Zizhiqu] 48-49 K 7
Pingxiang [TJ, Jiangxi] 48-49 L 6
Pinhal 78-79 K 9
Pinheiro 78-79 KL 5
Pini, Pulau – 52-53 C 7
Pinjarra 56-57 C 6
Pinkiang = Harbin 48-49 O 2
Pinnacles National Monument
   76-77 C 7
Pinnaroo 56-57 H 7
Pinón, Monte – 72-73 b 2
Pinos, Mount – 76-77 D 8
Pinos, Point – 76-77 BC 7
Pinrang 52-53 G 7
Pins, Îles de – 56-57 N 4
Pins, Pointe aux – 74-75 C 3
Pinsk 38-39 E 5
Pinta, Isla – 78-79 A 4
Pintada [BR, Rio Grande do Sul]
   80 F 4
Pintados 80 BC 2
Pintas, Sierra de – 76-77 F 10
Pinto [RA] 80 D 3
Piña [PA] 72-73 a 2
Pioche, NV 76-77 F 7
Piombino 36-37 D 4
Pioneer Mountains 76-77 G 3
Pioner, ostrov – 42-43 QR 2
Pionki 33 K 3
Piorini, Lago – 78-79 G 5
Piorini, Rio – 78-79 G 5
Piotrków Trybunalski 33 J 3
Pipérion 36-37 L 6
Pipinas 80 E 5
Piquetberg = Piketberg
   64-65 E 9
Piquiri, Rio – 80 F 2
Piracanjuba 78-79 JK 8
Piraçununga 78-79 K 9
Piracuruca 78-79 L 5
Piraeus = Peiraiévs 36-37 K 7
Piraí do Sul 80 G 2
Pirajuí 78-79 K 9
Pïr 'Alï Emāmzādeh 46-47 N 6
Piran 36-37 E 3
Piran = Dicle 46-47 J 3
Piranê 80 E 3
Piranhas 78-79 M 6
Piranhas, Rio – [BR, Rio Grande
   do Norte] 78-79 M 6
Pirapora 78-79 L 8
Pir'atin 38-39 F 5
Piratuba 80 F 2
Pirāus = Peiraiévs 36-37 K 7
Pirêe, le – = Peiraiévs 36-37 K 7
Pireneje 34-35 GH 10
Pireneusok 34-35 G-J 7
Pireo, El – = Peiraiévs 36-37 K 7
Pireus = Peiraiévs 36-37 K 7
Pireus = Peiraiévs 36-37 K 7
Pireusz = Peiraiévs 36-37 K 7
Pirin 36-37 K 5
Pirinçlik 46-47 H 4
Pirineos 34-35 G-J 7
Piripiri 78-79 L 5
Pirmasens 33 C 4
Pirna 33 F 3
Piro-bong 50-51 G 3
Pirot 36-37 K 4
Pirpintos, Los – 80 D 3
Pirtleville, AZ 76-77 J 10
Piru 52-53 J 7
Pisa 36-37 D 4
Pisagua 80 B 1
Pisco 78-79 D 7
Pisco, Bahia de – 78-79 D 7
Pisek 33 G 4
Pisgah, Mount – 76-77 C 3
Pishan = Guma Bazar 48-49 D 4
P'i-shan = Guma Bazar 48-49 D 4
Pisticci 36-37 G 5
Pistóia 36-37 D 3-4
Pistol River, OR 76-77 A 4
Pisuerga 34-35 E 7
Pisz 36-37 K 2
Pita 60-61 B 6
Pite 30-31 J 5

Pite älv 30-31 HJ 5
Piteşti 36-37 L 3
Pit-Gorodok 42-43 RS 6
Pithara 56-57 C 6
Piti, Cerro – 80 C 2
Pitigliano 36-37 D 4
Pitiquito 76-77 G 10
Pitk'ajarvi 30-31 NO 3
Pit River 76-77 BC 5
Pitt Island [CDN] 70-71 KL 7
Pitt Island [NZ] 56-57 Q 8
Pittsboro, NC 74-75 D 7
Pittsburg, CA 76-77 C 6
Pittsburg, KS 72-73 H 4
Pittsburgh, PA 72-73 KL 3
Pittsfield, MA 74-75 G 3
Pittsfield, ME 74-75 J 2
Pittston, PA 74-75 F 4
Pittsworth 58 K 1
Pite älv 30-31 HJ 5
Piuka = Bifuka 50-51 c 1
Piura [PE, ●] 78-79 CD 6
Piute Peak 76-77 D 8
Piva 36-37 H 4
Pivka 36-37 F 3
Pizzo 36-37 FG 6

Pjagina, poluostrov – 42-43 de 6

Placentia Bay 70-71 Za 8
Placerville, CA 76-77 C 6
Placetas 72-73 L 7
Plácido de Castro 78-79 F 7
Plains, MT 76-77 F 2
Plainview, TX 72-73 F 5
Planada, CA 76-77 CD 7
Planaltina 78-79 K 8
Planalto Brasileiro 78-79 KL 8
Plantation, FL 74-75 c 3
Plant City, FL 74-75 b 2-3
Plasencia 34-35 D 8
Plaster City, CA 76-77 EF 9
Plastun 42-43 a 9
Plata, Isla de la – 78-79 C 5
Plata, Isla – 78-79 A 4
Plata, La – [CO] 78-79 D 4
Plata, La – [RA] 80 E 5
Plata, Rio de la – 80 EF 5
Plateau 60-61 F 7
Plateau Central = Cao Nguyên
   Trung Phân 52-53 E 4
Plateau Continental Patagonien
   22-23 FG 8
Platen, Kapp – 30-31 lm 4
Platinum, AK 70-71 D 6
Platte Island 64-65 N 4
Platte River [USA, Nebraska]
   72-73 FG 3
Plattsburgh, NY 72-73 LM 3
Plauen 33 F 3
Plavno = Plauen 33 F 3
Playas 78-79 C 5
Playas, La – 80 C 5
Plaza Huincul 80 BC 5
Pleasant, Mount – 74-75 D 6
Pleasant Grove, UT 76-77 H 5
Pleasant Valley, OR 76-77 E 3
Pleasanton, WA 76-77 DE 2
Pleasantville, NJ 74-75 FG 5
Pleihari 52-53 F 7
Pleiku 52-53 E 4
Plenita 36-37 K 3
Plenty, Bay of – [NZ, ∪] 56-57 P 7
Pleseck 42-43 G 5
Pleß = Pszczyna 33 J 3-4
Pleszew 33 H 2
Pleven 36-37 L 4
Plitvice 36-37 F 3
Plitvička Jezera 36-37 FG 3
Plitvička Jezera 36-37 FG 3
Pljevlja 36-37 H 4
Płock 33 JK 2
Ploiești 36-37 LM 3
Plomo, El – 72-73 GH 10
Plovdiv 36-37 L 4
Plumas, Las – 80 C 6
Plummer, ID 76-77 E 2
Plumtree 64-65 G 7
Plunge 30-31 J 10
Plush, OR 76-77 D 4
Plymouth 32 DE 6
Plymouth, CA 76-77 C 6
Plymouth, MA 74-75 H 4
Plymouth, NC 74-75 D 7
Plymouth, NH 74-75 GH 3
Plymouth, PA 74-75 EF 4
Plzeň 33 F 4

Płock 33 JK 2

Po 36-37 D 3
Pô [HV] 60-61 D 6
Pobè 60-61 E 7
Pobeda, pik – 42-43 c 4
Pobedino 42-43 b 8
Pobedy, pik – 44-45 MN 2
Pobřeží Slonoviny 60-61 CD 8
Pobřeží Slonoviny = Côte
   d'Ivoire 60-61 CD 7
Pocatello, ID 72-73 D 3
P'och'ŏn 50-51 F 4
Pochval'nyj 42-43 cd 4
Pocklington Reef 52-53 j 7
Poções 78-79 LM 7
Pocomoke City, MD 74-75 F 5
Pocomoke Sound 74-75 EF 6

Poconé 78-79 H 8
Poços de Caldas 78-79 K 9
Poczdam = Potsdam 33 F 2
Podborovje 38-39 FG 4
Podgorica 36-37 H 4
Podgornoje 42-43 P 6
Podkamennaja Tunguska
   42-43 R 6
Podkova 36-37 L 5
Podol'sk 38-39 G 4
Podor 60-61 AB 5
Podporožje 42-43 EF 5
Podporožje 42-43 EF 5
Podravska Slatina 36-37 GH 3
Podtesovo 42-43 R 6
Po-êrh-t'a-la Chou = Bortala
   Monggol Zizhizhou 48-49 E 2-3
Po-êrh-t'a-la Chou = Bortala
   Monggol Zizhizhou 48-49 E 2-3
Po-êrh-t'a-la Chou = Bortala
   Monggol Zizhizhou 48-49 E 2-3
Pofadder 64-65 EF 8
Poggibonsi 36-37 D 4
Pogibi 42-43 b 7
Pogyndeno 42-43 fg 4
Po Hai = Bo Hai 48-49 M 4
Po-hai Hai-hsia = Bohai Haixia
   48-49 N 4
P'ohang 48-49 OP 4
Pohjanmaa 30-31 K 6-M 5
Pohjois-Karjalan lääni 30-31 N 6
Pohsien = Bo Xian 48-49 LM 5
Point Arena, CA 76-77 AB 6
Pointe-à-Pitre 72-73 O 8
Pointe-Noire 64-65 D 3
Point Harbor, NC 74-75 F 6
Point Lake 70-71 O 4
Point Marion, PA 74-75 D 5
Point Pleasant, NJ 74-75 FG 4-5
Point Pleasant, WV 74-75 BC 5
Point Roberts, WA 76-77 B 1
Poitevin, Marais – 34-35 G 5
Poitiers 34-35 H 5
Poitou 34-35 GH 5
Poivre, Côte du – = Malabar
   Coast 44-45 L 8-M 9
Poix 34-35 HJ 4
Pojarkovo 42-43 Y 8
Pokataroo 58 J 2
Pokhara 44-45 N 5
Poko 64-65 G 2
Pokrovsk 42-43 Y 5
Pokrovsk-Ural'skij 42-43 K 5
Polacca Wash 76-77 H 8
Pola de Siero 34-35 E 7
Polán [IR] 44-45 J 5
Poland 33 H-L 3
Pol'arnoje 42-43 c 3
Polarny, Płaskowyz – 24 A 31-6
Pol'arnyj 38-39 F 2
Pol'arnyj Ural 42-43 LM 4
Polar Plateau 25 A 31-6
Polathane = Akçaabat 46-47 H 2
Polatli 44-45 D 3
Polcirkeln 30-31 J 4
Polen 33 H-L 3
Polesje 38-39 DE 5
Poleskoj 38-39 M 4
Polessk 33 K 1
Pŏlgyo 50-51 F 5
Poli 60-61 G 7
Poli = Boli 48-49 P 2
Policastro, Golfo di – 36-37 F 5-6
Polillo Islands 52-53 H 3-4
Polinesia 22-23 A 5-6
Poliny Osipenko 42-43 a 7
Pólis 46-47 E 5
Polk, PA 74-75 CD 4
Pollino 36-37 G 6
Pollock, ID 76-77 E 3
Polmak 30-31 N 2
Polock 38-39 E 4
Pologi 38-39 G 6
Pologne 33 H-L 3
Polonezköy 46-47 C 2
Polonia 33 H-L 3
Polonio, Cabo – 80 F 4
Polousnyj kr'až 42-43 bc 4
Polousnyj kr'až 42-43 bc 4
Polska 33 H-L 3
Polsko 33 H-L 3
Polson, MT 76-77 FG 2
Poltava 38-39 F 6
Poltorack = Ašchabad
   44-45 HJ 3
Pŏltsamaa 30-31 LM 8
Poluj 42-43 M 4
Poluj = Pospelnj 42-43 MN 4
Polunočnoje 42-43 L 5
Polunočnoje 42-43 L 5
Polýaigos 36-37 L 7
Polýchnitos 36-37 LM 6
Polýgyros 36-37 K 5
Polynesia 22-23 A 5-6
Polynesie 22-23 A 5-6
Polynésie 22-23 A 5-6
Polynesien 22-23 A 6-7
Pomorne, Morze – 32 F-J 3
Północnoaustralijski, Basen –
   56-57 C 2
Północnofidżyjski, Basen –
   56-57 O 3

Półno   209

Puerto de Chorrera 72-73 b 3
Puerto de Chorrera 72-73 b 3
Puerto de Chorrera 76-77 b 3
Puerto de Lobos 76-77 G 10
Puerto del Rosario 60-61 B 3
Puerto de Nutrias 78-79 EF 3
Puerto de Santa Maria, El – 34-35 D 10
Puerto Deseado 80 CD 7
Puerto Elvira 80 E 2
Puerto Esperidião 78-79 H 8
Puerto Estrella 78-79 E 2
Puerto Frey 78-79 G 7
Puerto Grether 78-79 FG 8
Puerto Harberton 80 C 8
Puerto Heath 78-79 F 7
Puerto Chicama 78-79 CD 6
Puerto Iguazú 80 EF 3
Puerto Isabel 78-79 H 8
Puerto Juárez 72-73 J 7
Puerto La Cruz 78-79 G 2
Puerto Leguízamo 78-79 E 5
Puertollano 34-35 EF 9
Puerto Lobos [RA] 80 C 6
Puerto Madryn 80 E 2
Puerto Maldonado 78-79 EF 7
Puerto México = Coatzacoalcos 72-73 H 8
Puerto Montt 80 B 6
Puerto Natales 80 B 8
Puerto Nuevo [CO] 78-79 F 3
Puerto Ordaz, Ciudad Guayana- 78-79 G 3
Puerto Páez 78-79 F 3
Puerto Pilón 72-73 b 2
Puerto Pinasco 80 E 2
Puerto Pirámides 80 D 6
Puerto Piritu 78-79 FG 2-3
Puerto Pizarro 78-79 E 5
Puerto Plata 72-73 M 8
Puerto Portillo 78-79 E 6
Puerto Prado 78-79 DE 7
Puerto Princesa 52-53 G 5
Puerto Quellón 80 B 6
Puerto Quellón = Quellón 80 B 6
Puerto Ramírez 80 B 6
Puerto Real 34-35 DE 9
Puerto Rico [BOL] 78-79 F 7
Puerto Rico [Puerto Rico] 72-73 N 8
Puerto Rico, Fosa de – 22-23 FG 4
Puerto-Rico-Graben 22-23 FG 4
Puerto Rico Trench 22-23 FG 4
Puerto Ricotrog 22-23 FG 4
Puerto Rondón 78-79 E 3
Puerto San Julián 80 C 7
Puerto Santa Cruz 80 C 8
Puerto Santa Cruz = Santa Cruz 80 C 8
Puerto Sastre 80 E 2
Puerto Suárez 78-79 H 8
Puerto Supe 78-79 D 7
Puerto Tejada 78-79 D 4
Puerto Trinidad 72-73 b 3
Puerto Victoria [PE] 78-79 DE 6
Puerto Wilches 78-79 E 3
Puerto Williams 80 C 9
Pueyrredón, Lago – 80 B 7
Pugač'ov 42-43 HJ 7
Pugač'ov 42-43 HJ 7
Puget Sound 76-77 B 2
Puglia 36-37 FG 5
Pugwash 70-71 Y 8
Pujehun 60-61 B 7
Pujõn-ho 50-51 FG 2
Pukchin 50-51 E 2
Pukch'ŏng 48-49 O 3
Puket = Ko Phuket 52-53 C 5
Pukhan-gang 50-51 F 3-4
Puksa 38-39 H 3
Puksubæk-san = Ch'ail-bong 50-51 F 2
Pula 36-37 E 3
Pulacayo 78-79 F 9
Pulandian = Xinjin 50-51 CD 3
Pulap 52-53 N 5
Pular, Volcán – 80 C 2
Pulaski, NY 74-75 EF 3
Pulaski, VA 74-75 C 6
Puławy 33 L 3
Puli = Tash Qurghan 48-49 D 4
Pullmann, WA 76-77 E 2
Pulo Anna 52-53 K 6
Pulog, Mount – 52-53 H 3
Pulozero 30-31 PQ 3
Pułtusk 33 K 2
Pülümür 46-47 HJ 3
Pu-lun-t'o Hai = Ojorong nuur 48-49 F 2
Pulusuk 52-53 NO 5
Puluwat 52-53 NO 5
Puławy 33 L 3
Pułtusk 33 K 2
Puná [EC] 78-79 CD 5
Puna = Pune 44-45 L 7
Puná, Isla – 78-79 C 5
Puna Argentina 80 C 2-3
Punäkha = Phunakha 44-45 OP 5
Punata 78-79 F 8
Pune 44-45 L 7
Puneń = Pune 44-45 L 7
P'ungnam-ni 50-51 F 5
P'ungnyu-ri 50-51 F 2

P'ungsan 50-51 FG 2
Punia 64-65 G 3
Punjab [IND] 44-45 LM 4
Punjab [PAK] 44-45 L 4
Puno = San Carlos de Puno 78-79 EF 8
Punta Arenas [RCH, ●] 80 BC 8
Punta Baja [MEX, Baja California Norte] 72-73 C 5
Punta Delgada [RCH] 80 C 8
Punta Delgada [RA, ●] 80 D 6
Punta de Diaz 80 BC 3
Punta Gorda [BH] 72-73 J 8
Punta Gorda, FL 74-75 bc 3
Punta Mala 72-73 L 10
Punta Negra [PE] 78-79 C 6
Punta Norte del Cabo San Antonio 80 E 5
Punta Rasa 80 E 5
Puntarenas 72-73 K 9-10
Puntas Negras, Cerro – 80 C 2
Punta Sur del Cabo San Antonio 80 E 5
Puntilla, La – 78-79 C 5
Punxsutawney, PA 74-75 D 4
Punyu = Guangzhou 48-49 LM 7
Puolanka 30-31 MN 5
Pup'yŏng-dong 50-51 G 2
Puqi 48-49 L 6
Puquio 78-79 E 7
Puquios [RCH ↗ Arica] 80 C 1
Pur 42-43 O 4
Purcell Mountains 70-71 N 7-8
Puri 44-45 O 7
Purnea = Purnia 44-45 O 5
Purnia 44-45 O 6
Purniyā = Purnia 44-45 O 5
Pursat 52-53 D 4
Purukcahu 52-53 F 7
Purulia 44-45 O 6
Puruliya = Purulia 44-45 O 6
Purus, Rio – 78-79 F 6
Purwakarta 52-53 E 8
Purwaredja = Purworejo 52-53 EF 8
Purwokerto 52-53 EF 8
Purworejo 52-53 EF 8
Puryŏng 50-51 GH 1-2
Pusan 48-49 OP 4
Puškin 42-43 DE 6
Puškino 38-39 J 5
Püspökladány 33 K 5
Puškin 42-43 DE 6
Puškino 38-39 J 5
Putao = Pūdaö 52-53 C 1
Put'atina, ostrov – 50-51 J 1
Puthein 52-53 B 3
Putien 48-49 M 6
Putien = Putian 48-49 M 6
Puting, Tanjung – 52-53 F 7
Putnam 63 B 2
Putorana, plato – 42-43 RS 4
Puttalam = Puttalama 44-45 M 9
Puttalam 44-45 M 9
Puttgarden 33 E 1
Puttuchcheri = Pondicherry 44-45 MN 8
Putumayo [CO, ●] 78-79 D 4-5
Putumayo, Rio – 78-79 E 5
Pütürge = Imron 46-47 H 3
Putuskum = Potiskum 60-61 G 6
Puulavesi 30-31 M 7
Puy, le – 34-35 J 6
Puyallup, WA 76-77 B 2
Puyehue [RCH, ●] 80 B 6
Puyo 78-79 D 5
Pwani 64-65 J 4
Pweto 64-65 G 4
Pwllheli 32 D 5

Pyhäjärvi 30-31 L 6
Pyhäjoki 30-31 L 5-6
Pyhäranta 30-31 JK 7
Pyhätunturi 30-31 M 4
Pyin 52-53 C 3
Pyinmanā 52-53 C 3
Pýlos 36-37 J 7
Pymatuning Reservoir 74-75 C 4
Pyŏktong 50-51 E 2
P'yŏngam-ni 50-51 F 5
P'yŏngan-namdo 50-51 EF 3
P'yŏngan-pukto 50-51 E 2-3
P'yŏngch'ang 50-51 G 4
P'yŏnggang 50-51 F 3
P'yŏnggok-themen 50-51 G 4
P'yŏnghae 50-51 G 4
P'yŏngnamjin 50-51 F 2
P'yŏngt'aek 50-51 F 4
P'yŏngyang 48-49 NO 4
Pyramid, NV 76-77 D 5
Pyramid Lake 72-73 C 4
Pyramid Lake Indian Reservation 76-77 D 6
Pyrenäen 34-35 G-J 7
Pyreneeën 34-35 G-J 7
Pyrenees 34-35 G-J 7
Pyrénées 34-35 G-J 7
Pyreneje 34-35 G-J 7
Pyrgion 36-37 LM 6
Pýrgos [GR, Pelopónnesos] 36-37 J 7
Pýrgos [GR, Sámos] 36-37 M 7
Pyritz = Pyrzyce 33 G 2

Pyrzyce 33 G 2
Pyšma 38-39 M 4
Pyšma 38-39 M 4
Pytalovo 38-39 E 4
Pyu = Hpyu 52-53 C 3

Q

Qa'āmiyāt, Al- 44-45 F 7
Qa'ara, Al- = Al-Qa'rah 46-47 J 6
Qābes = Qābis 60-61 FG 2
Qābis 60-61 FG 2
Qābis, Khalīj – 60-61 G 2
Qabīt, Wādī – = Wādī Qitbīt 44-45 G 7
Qabr Hūd 44-45 FG 7
Qaḍārif, Al- 60-61 M 6
Qadīmah, Al- 44-45 DE 6
Qādir Karam 46-47 L 5
Qādisiyah, Al- 46-47 L 7
Qâ'en 44-45 H 4
Qaf, Bi'r al- 60-61 H 3
Qafşah 60-61 F 2
Qāhirah, Al- 60-61 KL 2
Qā'im, Al- 46-47 J 5
Qairouân, El – = Al-Qayrawān 60-61 FG 1
Qairwan = Al-Qayrawān 60-61 FG 1
Qaisā = Qaysā' 44-45 G 8
Qal'ah, Al- 60-61 F 1
Qal'äh-ye Shaharak = Shaharak 44-45 J 4
Qal'a-i-Bist = Lashkar Gāh 44-45 JK 4
Qal'a Shahr 44-45 K 3
Qalāt [AFG] 44-45 K 4
Qalāt [PAK] 44-45 K 4
Qal'at al-'Azlam 62 F 4
Qal'at al-'Uwainid = Qal'at al-'Azlam 62 F 4
Qal'at Bishah 44-45 E 6-7
Qal'at Dīzakh 46-47 L 4
Qal'at eḍ Ḍab'a = Ḍab'ah 46-47 J 8
Qal'at Flâtarz 60-61 EF 3
Qal'at Makmāhūn 60-61 E 3
Qal'at Ṣāliḥ 46-47 M 7
Qal'at Sekar = Qal'at Sukkar 46-47 LM 7
Qal'at Sukkar 46-47 LM 7
Qal'at 'Uneizah = 'Unayzah 46-47 FG 7
Qalb ar-Rīshāt 60-61 B 4
Qal'eh, Kūh-e – 46-47 N 6
Qal'eh Chāy 46-47 LM 4
Qal'eh Chāy 46-47 LM 4
Qal'eh Darreh 46-47 M 6
Qal'eh Chāy 46-47 LM 4
Qal'eh Sahar 46-47 N 7
Qalib Bākūr 46-47 L 8
Qalībīyah 60-61 G 1
Qallābāt 60-61 M 6
Qalmah 60-61 F 1
Qalqīlyah 46-47 F 6
Qaltat Zammūr 60-61 B 3
Qalyūb 62 D 2
Qamar, Ghubbat al- 44-45 G 7
Qamar, Jabal al- 44-45 G 7
Qāmishlīyah, Al- 44-45 E 3
Qânâq 70-71 WX 2
Qandahār 44-45 K 4
Qandala 60-61 b 1
Qanṭarah, Al- [ET] 62 E 2
Qaqortoq 70-71 b 5
Qara Dāgh 46-47 L 5
Qara Dong 48-49 E 4
Qa'rah, Al- [IRQ] 46-47 J 6
Qārah, Al- [Saudi-Arabien] 46-47 J 8
Qarah Dāgh 46-47 K 4
Qaramai 48-49 EF 2
Qaramurun davan 44-45 MN 3
Qarānqū, Rūd-e – 46-47 M 4
Qara Qash Darya 48-49 E 3
Qara Qorām = Karakoram 44-45 L 3-4
Qara Shahr 48-49 F 3
Qara Tappa 46-47 L 5
Qardho 60-61 b 2
Qareh Āghāj 46-47 M 4
Qareh Būteh 46-47 M 4
Qareh Chāy 46-47 M 3
Qareh Chāy 46-47 M 3
Qareh Dāgh 44-45 F 2
Qareh Dāgh 46-47 M 3
Qareh Diyā' ad-Dīn 46-47 L 3
Qareh Sū [IR, Bākhtarān] 46-47 M 5
Qareh Sū [IR, Tehrān] 46-47 N 5
Qarghaliq 48-49 D 4
Qarn at-Tays, Jabal – 62 E 6
Qarnayt, Jabal – 44-45 E 6
Qarqannah, Arkhbīl – 60-61 G 2
Qārrāt Ṣaḥrā' al-Igīdi 60-61 C 4-D 3
Qārūn, Birkat – 60-61 KL 3
Qaryah 44-45 E 7
Qaryatayn, Al- 46-47 G 5

Qaṣab 46-47 K 4
Qaṣab = Al-Khaṣab 44-45 H 5
Qaṣab, Wādī – 62 E 4
Qaṣab, Wādī al- 46-47 K 4-5
Qaṣabah, Rá's – 62 E 4
Qaṣabeh 46-47 M 3
Qāshqar darya 48-49 CD 4
Qasigiánguit 70-71 ab 4
Qaṣīm, Al- 44-45 E 5
Qaṣīr as-Sirr, Bi'r – 62 B 2
Qaṣr, Al- [ET] 60-61 K 3
Qaṣr al-Bukharī 60-61 E 1
Qaṣr al-Burqú 46-47 GH 6
Qaṣr al-Ḥayr 46-47 H 5
Qaṣr al-Khubbāz 46-47 JK 6
Qaṣr 'Amīj 46-47 J 6
Qaṣrayn, Al- 60-61 F 1-2
Qaṣr Bilāl 46-47 M 8
Qaṣr-e Shīrīn 46-47 LM 5
Qaṣrīn, El – = Al-Qaṣrayn 60-61 F 1-2
Qaṣūr 44-45 L 4
Qaṭanā 46-47 G 6
Qatar 44-45 G 5
Qaṭīf, Al- 44-45 FG 5
Qaṭrānah, Al- 46-47 FG 6
Qaṭrāni, Bi'r al – 62 B 2
Qaṭrānī, Jabal – 62 D 3
Qaṭrūn, Al- 60-61 GH 4
Qaṭṭār, Jabal – 62 E 5
Qaṭṭārah, 'Ayn – 60-61 K 2
Qaṭṭārah, Munḥafaḍ al- 60-61 K 2-3
Qawām al-Hamzah 46-47 L 7
Qawz Rajab 60-61 M 5
Qay'īyah, Al- 44-45 E 6
Qayrawān, Al- 60-61 FG 1
Qaysā' 44-45 G 8
Qayṣūhmah, Al- 44-45 F 5
Qaysūm, Jazā'ir – 62 EF 4
Qayyārah 60-61 K 5
Qazvīn 44-45 FG 3

Qiongzhou, Détroit de – = Qiongzhou Haixia 48-49 KL 7
Qiongzhou Haixia 48-49 KL 7
Qiqihar 48-49 N 2
Qiraiya, Wādī – = Wādī Qurayyah 62 F 2
Qiryat Āta' 46-47 F 6
Qiryat Shēmóna 46-47 F 6
Qishm = Qeshm [IR, ⊙] 44-45 H 5
Qishm = Qeshm [IR, ●] 44-45 H 5
Qishn 44-45 G 7
Qishrān 44-45 D 6
Qislah 46-47 N 8
Qitai 48-49 FG 3
Qitbīt, Wādī – 44-45 G 7
Qizan = Jīzān 44-45 E 6
Qizil Uzun = Rūd-e Qezel Owzan 44-45 F 3
Qohord 46-47 N 5
Qojūr 46-47 N 5
Qom 44-45 G 4
Qom Rūd 46-47 O 6
Qomul = Hami 48-49 G 3
Qonqirāl = Qūqriāl 60-61 K 7
Qōratū = Qurayṭū 46-47 L 5
Qorweh 46-47 M 5
Qoseir, El- = Al-Quṣayr 60-61 L 3
Qōsh, Al- = Alqūsh 46-47 K 4
Qotbeh, Kūh-e – 46-47 M 6
Qoṭūr 44-45 E 3
Qoṭūr Chāy 46-47 L 3
Qoṭūr Chāy 46-47 L 3
Qoṭūr Chāy 46-47 L 3
Qoubayât, El- = Al-Qubayyāt 46-47 G 5
Qousair, El- = Al-Quṣayr 46-47 G 5
Qōz Regeb = Qawz Rajab 60-61 M 5
Qṣar al-Kabīr, Al- 60-61 C 1
Qṣar as-Sūq = Ar-Rashidīyah 60-61 D 2
Quabbin Reservoir 74-75 G 3
Quakenbrück 33 CD 2
Quakertown, PA 74-75 F 4
Quambatook 58 F 5
Quangbinh = Đông Ho'i 52-53 E 3
Quang Ngai 52-53 EF 3-4
Quang Tri 52-53 E 3
Quang Yên 52-53 E 2
Quanhsian = Quanzhou 48-49 KL 6
Quanxian = Quanzhou 48-49 KL 6
Quanzhou [TJ, Fujian] 48-49 MN 6-7
Quanzhou [TJ, Guangxi Zhuangzu Zizhiqu] 48-49 KL 6
Qu'Appelle River 70-71 Q 7
Quartu Sant'Elena 36-37 C 6
Quartzsite, AZ 76-77 G 9
Qubayyāt, Al- 46-47 G 5
Qūchān 44-45 H 3
Qūchghār 44-45 K 3
Quchaq Bai 48-49 D 4
Quds, Al- 46-47 F 7
Quealy, WY 76-77 J 5
Queanbeyan 56-57 JK 7
Québec [CDN, ●] 70-71 W 8
Quebec [CDN, ☆] 70-71 V-Y 7
Quebracho 80 E 2
Quedal, Cabo – 80 AB 6
Quedlinburg 33 E 3
Queen Alexandra Range 24 A 17-15
Queen Charlotte 70-71 K 7
Queen Charlotte Islands 70-71 K 7
Queen Charlotte Sound 70-71 KL 7
Queen Charlotte Strait 70-71 L 7
Queen Charlotte 70-71 K 7
Queen Charlotte Islands 70-71 K 7
Queen Charlotte Sound 70-71 K 7
Queen Charlotte Strait 70-71 L 7
Queen Elizabeth Islands 70-71 N-U 2
Queen Elizabeth National Park = Ruwenzori National Park 64-65 EF 3
Queen Charlotte 70-71 K 7
Queen Charlotte Islands 70-71 KL 6-7
Queen Charlotte Sound 70-71 KL 7
Queen Charlotte Strait 70-71 L 7
Queen Mary Coast = Queen Mary Land 24 C 10
Queen Mary Land 24 C 10
Queen Maud Gulf 70-71 Q 4
Queen Maud Land = Dronning Maud Land 24 B 36-4
Queen Maud's Range = Dronning Maud fjellkjede 24 A
Queens Channel 56-57 E 2
Queenscliff 58 G 7

Queens Channel 56-57 E 2
Queens Channel 56-57 E 2
Queensland 56-57 G-J 4
Queenstown [AUS] 56-57 HJ 8
Queenstown [NZ] 56-57 N 8
Queenstown [ZA] 64-65 G 9
Queets, WA 76-77 A 2
Quela 64-65 J 6
Quelimane 64-65 J 6
Quelpart = Cheju-do 48-49 NO 5
Quemado, NM 76-77 H 7
Quemoy = Chin-mén Tao 48-49 M 7
Que Que = Kwekwe 64-65 G 6
Queras, Río – 72-73 a 3
Quercy 34-35 H 6
Querétaro 72-73 FG 7
Querobabi 76-77 H 10
Quesada 34-35 F 10
Queshan 48-49 L 5
Quesnel 70-71 M 7
Quetta = Kwatta 44-45 K 4
Quezaltenango 72-73 H 9
Quezon City 52-53 H 4
Quffah, Wādī al- 62 E 6
Quiaca, La – 80 CD 2
Quiansu = Jiangsu 48-49 LM 6
Quibala 64-65 DE 5
Quibaxe 64-65 D 4
Quibdó 78-79 D 3
Quiberon 34-35 F 5
Quijotoa, AZ 76-77 GH 9
Quilcene, WA 76-77 B 2
Quilimari 80 B 4
Quillacollo 78-79 F 8
Quillagua 80 BC 2
Quill Lakes 70-71 Q 7
Quillota 80 B 4
Quilon 44-45 M 9
Quilpie 56-57 H 5
Quimbele 64-65 E 4
Quimili 80 D 3
Quimper 34-35 E 4-5
Quimperle 34-35 F 5
Quinault, WA 76-77 B 2
Quinault Indian Reservation 76-77 AB 2
Quince Mil 78-79 EF 7
Quincy, CA 76-77 C 6
Quincy, IL 72-73 H 4
Quincy, MA 74-75 H 3
Quincy, WA 76-77 D 2
Quines 80 C 4
Qui Nho'n 52-53 EF 4
Quinn River 76-77 E 5
Quinn River Crossing, NV 76-77 DE 5
Quintanar de la Orden 34-35 F 9
Quintana Roo 72-73 J 7-8
Quiongdong = Quionghai 48-49 L 8
Quirima 64-65 E 5
Quirimba, Ilhas – 64-65 K 5
Quirindi 58 K 3
Quissanga 64-65 K 5
Quissico 64-65 HJ 7
Quiterajo 63 E 3
Quitman, GA 74-75 B 9
Quito 78-79 D 5
Quitovac 76-77 G 10
Quixadá [BR, Ceará] 78-79 M 5
Quixeramobim 78-79 M 5-6
Quijiang = Shaoguan 48-49 L 6-7
Qūlāshgird = Golāshkerd 44-45 H 5
Qulay'ah, Rá's al- 46-47 H 5
Qulayb, Bi'r – 62 EF 5
Qulbān aṭ-Ṭayyārāt 46-47 JK 5
Qulbān Layyah 46-47 M 8
Quleib, Bīr – = Bi'r Qulayb 62 EF 5
Qūlonjī 46-47 L 4
Qum = Qom 44-45 G 4
Qum darya 48-49 F 3
Qum Köl 48-49 F 4
Qum tagh 48-49 G 4
Qumush 48-49 F 3
Qunāytirah 46-47 FG 6
Qunduz = Kunduz 44-45 K 3
Qunfudhah, Al- 44-45 DE 7
Qungur tagh 48-49 D 4
Quoram = Korem 60-61 M 6
Quorn [AUS] 56-57 G 6
Qūqriāl 60-61 K 7
Qurayṭū 46-47 L 5
Qurayyah, Al- 44-45 GH 6
Qurayyah, Wādī – 62 F 2
Qurbah 60-61 M 1
Qurdūd 60-61 KL 6-7
Qūréná = Shaḥḥāt 60-61 J 2
Qurnah, Al- 46-47 M 7
Quruq Tagh 48-49 G 4
Qūş 62 E 5
Quṣ'ir, Al- 44-45 G 7-8
Quṣayr, Al- [ET] 60-61 L 3
Quṣayr, Al- [IRQ] 46-47 L 7
Quṣayr, Al- [SYR] 46-47 G 5
Qushrān 44-45 H 5
Qushui = Chhushul 48-49 FG 6
Qūşīyah, Al- 62 D 4
Qusṭanṭīn 60-61 F 1
Quṭayfah, Al- 46-47 G 6

Quwārib, Al- 60-61 A 5
Quwaymât, Al- 46-47 GH 6
Quwayr, Al- 46-47 K 4
Quwayrah, Al- 46-47 F 8
Quwaysinā 62 D 2
Qu Xian 48-49 M 6
Qūyūn, Jazīreh – 46-47 L 4

R

Raab 33 G 5
Raab = Győr 33 H 5
Raahe 30-31 L 5
Ra'an, Ar- 46-47 J 8
Raanes Peninsula 70-71 T 2
Raas, Pulau – 52-53 FG 8
Rab 36-37 F 3
Raba 33 H 5
Raba [RI] 52-53 G 8
Rabaçal 34-35 D 8
Rabat [M] 36-37 F 7
Rabat = Ar-Ribâṭ 60-61 C 2
Rabaul 52-53 h 5
Ráb = Györ 33 H 5
Rāb = Györ 33 H 5
Rāb'i, Al-Jandal ar – 60-61 L 5
Rābigh 44-45 D 6
Rabszolga-part 60-61 E 7
Rabun Bald 74-75 B 7
Raccoon Mountains = Sand Mountains 72-73 J 5
Race, Cape – 70-71 a 8
Râchayâ = Râshayyâ 46-47 FG 6
Rach Gia 52-53 DE 4-5
Rachov 38-39 D 6
Racht = Rasht 44-45 FG 3
Racibórz 33 J 3
Racine, WI 72-73 J 3
Radā' [Y] 44-45 EF 8
Radama, Nosy – 64-65 L 5
Rădăuți 36-37 L 2
Radford, VA 74-75 C 6
Radīsīyat Baḥrī, Ar- 62 E 5
Radkersburg 33 GH 5
Radom 33 K 3
Radomsko 33 JK 3
Radøy 30-31 A 7
Radstock, Cape – 58 AB 4
Rae 70-71 NO 5
Rae Bareli 44-45 N 5
Raeford, NC 74-75 D 7
Rae Isthmus 70-71 T 4
Rae Strait 70-71 RS 4
Rafaela 80 D 4
Rafael del Encanto 78-79 E 5
Rafai 60-61 J 7-8
Rafḥah 44-45 E 5
Rafsanjān 44-45 H 4
Raft River 76-77 G 4
Raft River Mountains 76-77 G 5
Rāgā = Rājā 60-61 K 7
Ragaing Pyinnei 52-53 B 2
Ragaing Yōma 52-53 B 2-3
Ragged Island 74-75 J 3
Ragozino = Novyj Tevriz 42-43 O 6
Ragunda 30-31 FG 6
Ragusa 36-37 F 7
Ragusa = Dubrovnik 36-37 GH 4
Raha 52-53 H 7
Rahāb, Ar- = Ar-Rihāb 46-47 L 7
Rahad, Ar- 60-61 L 6
Rahad, Nahr ar- 60-61 L 6
Rahad al-Bardī 60-61 J 6
Rahaeng = Tak 52-53 C 3
Rahaṭ, Ḥarrat – 44-45 DE 6
Raḥḥālīyah, Ar- 46-47 K 6
Rāhjerd 46-47 O 5
Raḥmat, Āb-e – 46-47 N 6
Raiâitît, Wâdî – = Wâdî Rayâytît 62 F 6
Raichur 44-45 M 7
Raidat aṣ Ṣai'ar = Raydat aṣ-Ṣay'ar 44-45 F 7
Raidestós = Tekirdağ 44-45 B 2
Raigarh 44-45 N 6
Railroad Pass 76-77 E 6
Railroad Valley 76-77 F 6-7
Rainbow 58 EF 5
Rainbow Bridge National Monument 76-77 H 7
Rainier, OR 76-77 B 2
Rainier, Mount – 72-73 BC 2
Rainy Lake 72-73 H 2
Raippaluoto 30-31 J 6
Raipur [IND, Madhya Pradesh] 44-45 N 6
Rājā 60-61 K 7
Rajada 78-79 L 6
Rajahmundry 44-45 N 7
Rajakoski 30-31 N 3
Rājamahēndri = Rajahmundry 44-45 N 7
Rajang [RI, ~] 52-53 F 6
Rajapalaiyam 44-45 M 9
Rājapālayam = Rajapalaiyam 44-45 M 9
Rajasthan 44-45 LM 5
Rajčichinsk 42-43 YZ 8
Rajčichinsk 42-43 YZ 8
Rajeputana = Rajasthan 44-45 LM 5
Rajkot 44-45 L 6
Rajputāna = Rajasthan 44-45 LM 5
Rājshāhī 44-45 O 6
Rakaia 56-57 O 8
Rakasdal 48-49 E 5
Rakata = Pulau Anak Krakatau 52-53 DE 8
Rakhshān 44-45 JK 5
Rakiura = Stewart Island 56-57 N 9
Rakops 64-65 F 7
Rakousko 33 E-G 5
Rakovník 33 F 3
Raksakiny 42-43 NO 5
Rakvere 30-31 M 8
Raleigh, NC 72-73 L 4
Raleigh Bay 74-75 EF 7
Râm, Jabal – 46-47 F 8
Ramādī, Ar- 44-45 E 4
Ramah 70-71 Y 6
Ramah, NM 76-77 J 8
Ramalho, Serra do – 78-79 KL 7
Râm Allâh 46-47 F 7
Râm Allâh 46-47 F 7
Raman [TR] 46-47 J 4
Ramapo, Abysse de – 48-49 R 5
Ramapo, Fosa de – 48-49 R 5
Ramapo Deep 48-49 R 5
Ramapodiep 48-49 R 5
Ramapotiefe 48-49 R 5
Rambi 52-53 b 2
Rambrè 52-53 B 3
Rambrè Kyûn 52-53 B 3
Ramḍā', Ar- 46-47 L 8
Rāmhormoz 46-47 N 7
Rami, 'Ayn ar- 62 B 2
Ramla 46-47 F 7
Ramona, CA 76-77 E 9
Rampur [IND, Uttar Pradesh] 44-45 MN 5
Ramree = Rambrè 52-53 B 3
Ramree Island = Rambrè Kyûn 52-53 B 3
Ramseur, NC 74-75 D 7
Ramsey 32 DE 4
Ramsgate 32 G 6
Ramthā, Ar- 46-47 FG 6
Ramu River 52-53 N 8
Raṇ, Mōṭuṇ – = Rann of Kutch 44-45 KL 6
Rancagua 80 BC 4
Rānchi 44-45 O 6
Ranco, Lago – 80 B 6
Rand 58 H 5
Randazzo 36-37 F 7
Randers 30-31 CD 9
Randijaur 30-31 HJ 4
Randolph, UT 76-77 H 5
Randsburg, CA 76-77 DE 8
Randsfjord 30-31 D 7
Rāṇēbanūra = Ranibennur 44-45 M 8
Rāṇēbanūru = Ranibennur 44-45 M 8
Ranebennur = Ranibennur 44-45 M 8
Rangárvalla 30-31 cd 3
Rangeley, ME 74-75 H 2
Rangely, CO 76-77 J 5
Rangiora 56-57 O 8
Rangôn = Yangôn 52-53 BC 3
Rangôn Taing 52-53 C 3
Rangoon = Yangôn 52-53 BC 3
Rangsang, Pulau – 52-53 D 6
Rangûn = Yangôn 52-53 BC 3
Rangun = Yangôn 52-53 BC 3
Ranibennur 44-45 M 8
Rānīyah 46-47 L 4
Rank 60-61 L 6
Rankins Spring 56-57 J 6
Ransiki 52-53 K 7
Rantau, Pulau – 52-53 D 6
Rantauprapat 52-53 CD 6
Rānya = Rānīyah 46-47 L 4
Ranyah, Wādī – 44-45 E 6
Raohe 48-49 P 2
Raoui, Erg er – = 'Irq ar-Rawī 60-61 D 3
Raoyang He 50-51 D 2
Rapallo 36-37 C 3
Raper, Cape – 70-71 XY 4
Rapid City, SD 72-73 F 3
Räpina 30-31 M 8
Rapla 30-31 L 8
Rappahannock River 74-75 E 6
Rapti [IND] 44-45 N 5
Raqqah, Ar- 44-45 DE 3
Rāqūbah 60-61 H 3
Raquette Lake 74-75 F 3
Raquette River 74-75 F 2
Raša 36-37 EF 3
Rā's al-'Ayn 46-47 J 4
Rā's al-Ḥikmah 62 BC 2
Rā's al-Khaymah 44-45 GH 5
Ra's al-Wād 60-61 E 1
Rā's an-Naqb 44-45 D 4-5
Rasappa = Riṣāfah 46-47 H 5
Rā's as-Sidr 62 E 3
Rā's at-Tannūrah 44-45 G 5
Rā's Ba'labakk 46-47 G 5
Rā's Duqm 44-45 H 7
Raseiniai 30-31 K 10
Râs el 'Aïn = Rā's al-'Ayn 46-47 J 4
Rā's Ghārib 62 E 3
Rashād 60-61 L 6
Rāshayyā = Abū Adī 46-47 FG 6
Rashīd 62 D 2
Rashīd, Maṣabb – 62 D 2
Rāshidah, Ar- 62 C 5
Rāshīdīyah, Ar- 60-61 D 2
Rashin = Najin 48-49 P 3
Rasht 44-45 FG 3
Raška 36-37 J 4
Rason Lake 56-57 D 5
Rass, Ar- 44-45 E 5
Rass-el-Oued = Ra's al-Wād 60-61 E 1
Rasskazovo 38-39 H 5
Rastatt 33 D 4
Rastenburg = Kętrzyn 33 K 1-2
Rastigaissa 30-31 LM 3
Rasu, Monte – 36-37 C 5
Râs Za'farâna = Az-Za'farânah 62 E 3
Raša 36-37 EF 3
Raška 36-37 J 4
Rata, Ilha – 78-79 N 5
Ratchaburi 52-53 C 4
Rathenow 33 F 2
Rathlin Island 32 C 4
Ratibor = Racibórz 33 J 3
Rätische Alpen 33 DE 5
Rat Islands 19 D 1
Ratka, Wādī ar- = Wādī ar-Ratqah 46-47 J 5-6
Ratlam 44-45 LM 6
Ratnagiri [IND, Maharashtra] 44-45 L 7
Raton, NM 72-73 F 4
Ratqah, Wādī ar- 46-47 J 5-6
Rättvik 30-31 F 7
Ratyzbona = Regensburg 33 EF 4
Raualpindi = Rāwalpindī 44-45 L 4
Rauch 80 E 5
Raudhamelur 30-31 bc 2
Raudhatayn 46-47 M 8
Raufarhöfn 30-31 f 1
Rauma 30-31 J 7
Raumo = Rauma 30-31 J 7
Raurkela = Rourkela 44-45 NO 6
Rausu 50-51 d 1-2
Ravalli, MT 76-77 F 2
Ravalpindi = Rāwalpindī 44-45 L 4
Ravānsar 46-47 M 5
Rāvar 44-45 H 4
Rava-Russkaja 38-39 DE 5
Ravena = Ravenna 36-37 E 3
Ravendale, CA 76-77 CD 5
Ravenna 36-37 E 3
Ravenna, OH 74-75 C 4
Ravenne = Ravenna 36-37 E 3
Ravensburg 33 D 5
Ravenshoe 56-57 HJ 3
Ravensthorpe 56-57 D 6
Ravenswood, WV 74-75 C 5
Rāvī 44-45 L 4
Rāwah 46-47 JK 5
Rāwalpindī 44-45 L 4
Rawa Mazowiecka 33 K 3
Rawāndūz 46-47 L 4
Rawḍah, Ar- 62 D 4
Rawenna = Ravenna 36-37 E 3
Rawī, 'Irq ar- 60-61 D 3
Rawicz 33 H 3
Rawitsch = Rawicz 33 H 3
Rawlinna 56-57 E 6
Rawlins, WY 72-73 E 3
Rawlinson Range 56-57 E 4-5
Rawson [RA, Chubut] 80 CD 6
Rawwāfah, Ar- 62 G 4
Ray, Cape – 70-71 Z 8
Raya, Bukit – 52-53 F 7
Rayachuru = Raichur 44-45 M 7
Rayāq 46-47 G 6
Rāyāt 46-47 L 4
Rayāytīt, Wādī – 62 F 6
Rāy Barēlī = Rae Bareli 44-45 N 5
Raydat aṣ-Ṣay'ar 44-45 F 7
Rāygaṛh = Raigarh 44-45 N 6
Raymond, CA 76-77 D 7
Raymond, WA 76-77 B 2
Raymond Terrace 58 KL 4
Raymondville, TX 72-73 G 6
Ray Mountains 70-71 F 4
Raynesford, MT 76-77 H 2
Rayong 52-53 D 4
Rāypur = Raipur [IND, Madhya Pradesh] 44-45 N 6
Raz, Pointe du – 34-35 E 4
R'azan' 38-39 GH 5
Rāzān [IR, Bākhtarān] 46-47 N 5
Razan [IR, Lorestān] 46-47 N 6
Razazah, Hawr ar- 46-47 KL 6
Razdel'naja 38-39 F 6
Razdolinsk 42-43 R 6
Razeh 46-47 N 6
Razelm, Lacul – 36-37 N 3
Razgrad 36-37 M 4
R'ažsk 38-39 H 5
R'ažsk 38-39 H 5
R'dayif, Ar- = Ar-Rudayyif 60-61 F 2
Ré, Île de – 34-35 G 5
Reading [GB] 32 F 6
Reading, PA 72-73 L 3
Read Island 70-71 O 4
Real del Castillo 76-77 E 9-10
Realicó 80 CD 4-5
Réam 52-53 D 4
Rebbenesøy 30-31 GH 2
Rebecca, Lake – 56-57 D 6
Rebia, Umm er – = Nahr Umm ar-Rabī' 60-61 C 2
Rebiána = Ribyānah 60-61 J 4
Reboledo 80 EF 4
Reboly 38-39 F 3
Rebun-jima 48-49 QR 2
Recalde 80 D 5
Recherche, Archipelago of the – 56-57 D 6
Recherche, Archipel de la – 56-57 D 6
Rechŏ Taung 52-53 C 4
Recht = Rasht 44-45 FG 3
Rečica 38-39 EF 5
Recife 78-79 N 6
Reconquista 80 DE 3
Recreo [RA, La Rioja] 80 CD 3
Rečica 38-39 EF 5
Reḡā'iyeh = Orūmīyeh 44-45 EF 3
Reḡā'iyeh, Daryācheh – = Urmia 44-45 F 3
Red Bank, NJ 74-75 F 4
Red Bluff, CA 72-73 B 3
Red Butte 76-77 GH 8
Redcliffe, Brisbane- 56-57 K 5
Red Cliffs 58 F 5
Red Deer 70-71 O 7
Red Deer River [CDN, Alberta] 70-71 O 7
Reddick, FL 74-75 b 2
Redding, CA 72-73 B 3
Redeyef, Er – = Ar-R'dayif 60-61 F 2
Red Hill 56-57 HJ 7
Red Hills [USA, Alabama] 72-73 J 5
Red House, NV 76-77 E 5
Red Lake [USA] 72-73 G 2
Red Lake [CDN, ●] 70-71 S 7
Redlands, CA 76-77 E 8-9
Red Lion, PA 74-75 E 5
Redmond, OR 76-77 C 3
Red Mountain [USA, California] 76-77 B 5
Red Mountain [USA, Montana] 76-77 G 2
Red Mountain, CA 76-77 E 8
Rednitz 33 E 4
Redon 34-35 F 5
Redonda, Ponta – 78-79 M 5
Redondela 34-35 C 7
Redondo Beach, CA 76-77 D 9
Red River 72-73 H 5
Red River of the North 72-73 G 2
Redrock, AZ 76-77 H 9
Redrock, NM 76-77 J 9
Red Rocks Point 56-57 E 6
Red Sea 44-45 D 5-7
Red Springs, NC 74-75 D 7
Red Tank 72-73 b 2
Reḡvandeh 46-47 N 4
Redwood City, CA 76-77 B 7
Redwood Valley, CA 76-77 B 6
Ree, Lough – 32 C 5
Reed City, MI 74-75 A 3
Reedley, CA 76-77 D 7
Reedsport, OR 76-77 AB 4
Reefton 56-57 O 8
Reese River 76-77 E 6
Refā'ī, Ar- = Ar-Rifā'ī 46-47 M 7
Refaniye 46-47 H 3
Regen 33 F 4
Regência 78-79 M 8
Regência, Ponta de – 78-79 M 8
Regensburg 33 EF 4
Reggane = Rijān 60-61 E 3
Règgio di Calàbria 36-37 FG 6
Règgio nell'Emilia 36-37 D 3
Regina [CDN] 70-71 Q 7
Régina [Französisch-Guyana] 78-79 J 4
Registan = Rīgestān 44-45 JK 4
Registro 80 G 2
Regresso, Cachoeira – 78-79 HJ 5
Reguengos de Monsaraz 34-35 D 9
Reh 48-49 M 3
Rehoboth 64-65 E 7
Rehoboth Beach, DE 74-75 F 5
Rěḥōvōt 46-47 F 7
Rei = Rey 46-47 O 5
Reichenberg = Liberec 33 G 3
Reichle, MT 76-77 G 3
Reid 56-57 E 6
Reidsville, NC 74-75 D 6
Reigate 32 FG 6
Reihoku 50-51 GH 6
Reims 34-35 JK 4
Reina Adelaida, Archipiélago – 80 AB 8
Reina Isabel, Islas de la – 70-71 N-U 2
Reina Maud, Banco de la – 24 C 1
Reindeer Lake 70-71 Q 6
Reine Elizabeth, Îles de la – 70-71 N-U 2
Reinosa 34-35 E 7
Reino Unido de Gran Bretaña e Irlanda del Norte 32 F-H 4-5
Reinøy 30-31 H 2-3
Reisa 30-31 J 3
Rejaf = Rijāf 63 B 1
Relem, Cerro – 80 B 5
Reliance, WY 76-77 J 5
Rélizane = Ghālizān 60-61 E 1
Remansão 78-79 JK 5
Remanso 78-79 L 6
Remarkable, Mount – 56-57 G 6
Remédios [BR, Fernando de Noronha] 78-79 N 5
Remeshk 44-45 H 5
Remington, VA 74-75 E 5
Rèmire 78-79 J 3-4
Remiremont 34-35 KL 4
Remote, OR 76-77 B 4
Rems 33 D 4
Remscheid 33 C 3
Remsen, NY 74-75 F 3
Rena 30-31 D 7
Renascença 78-79 F 5
Rendova Island 52-53 j 6
Rendsburg 33 DE 1
Rénéia 36-37 L 7
Rengat 52-53 D 7
Reni 38-39 E 6
Reniferowe, Jezioro – 70-71 Q 6
Renk = Al-Rank 60-61 L 6
Renmark 56-57 H 6
Rennell Island 52-53 k 7
Rennes 34-35 G 4
Rennick Glacier 24 C 16-17
Reno [I] 36-37 DE 3
Reno, ID 76-77 G 3
Reno, NV 72-73 C 4
Renos, Lago de los – 70-71 Q 6
Renoville, CA 76-77 EF 8
Renovo, PA 74-75 E 4
Renqiu 48-49 M 4
Rensselaer, NY 74-75 FG 3
Rénszarvas-tó 70-71 Q 6
Rentiersee 70-71 Q 6
Renton, WA 76-77 B 2
Reo 52-53 H 8
Republic, WA 76-77 D 1
República Centroafricana 60-61 HJ 7
República Checa 33 F-H 4
República Dominicana 72-73 MN 7-8
República Checa 33 F-H 4
Republican River 72-73 G 3
République Centrafricaine 60-61 HJ 7
République Dominicaine 72-73 MN 7-8
République Tchèque 33 F-H 4
Repulse Bay [AUS] 56-57 JK 4
Repulse Bay [CDN, ◡] 70-71 T 4
Repulse Bay [CDN, ●] 70-71 TU 4
Repunshiri = Rebun-jima 50-51 b 1
Requena 34-35 G 9
Requena [PE] 78-79 E 6
Reşadiye [TR, Bitlis] 46-47 K 3
Reşadiye [TR, Muğla] 46-47 B 4
Reşadiye [TR, Tokat] 46-47 G 2
Reşadiye Yarımadası 46-47 BC 4
Reşāfé, Er- = Riṣāfah 46-47 H 5
Resa'iya = Orūmīyeh 44-45 EF 3
Reschenpaß 33 E 5
Reserve, NM 76-77 J 9
Resht = Rasht 44-45 FG 3
Resistencia 80 DE 3
Reşiţa 36-37 J 3
Resolute 70-71 S 3
Resolution Island 70-71 Y 5
Rethel 34-35 K 4
Réthymnon 36-37 L 8
Reunion 64-65 N 7
Réunion 64-65 N 7
Reus 34-35 H 8
Reuss 33 D 5
Reut 36-37 N 2
Reutlingen 33 D 4
Revā = Narmada 44-45 LM 6
Reval = Tallinn 42-43 CD 5
Revda [SU, Srednij Ural] 42-43 KL 6
Revelstoke 70-71 N 7
Revillagigedo, Islas de – 72-73 D 8
Revillagigedo Island 70-71 KL 6
Rěvīvīm 46-47 F 7
Revoil-Beni-Ounif = Banī Wanīf 60-61 D 2
Rewā = Narmada 44-45 LM 6
Rewda = Revda 42-43 KL 6
Rex, Mount – 24 B 29
Rexburg, ID 76-77 H 4
Rexford, MT 76-77 F 1
Rey, Isla del – 72-73 L 10
Reyes, Point – 76-77 B 6-7
Reyhanlı 46-47 G 4
Reykhólar 30-31 b 2
Reykholt 30-31 c 2
Reykjanes 30-31 b 3
Reykjanes, Dorsal de – 22-23 H 2-3
Reykjanes, Seuil de – 22-23 H 2-3
Reykjanes Ridge 22-23 H 2-3
Reykjanesrücken 22-23 H 2-3
Reykjanesrug 22-23 H 2-3
Reykjavík 30-31 bc 2
Reynolds, ID 76-77 E 4
Reynolds Range 56-57 F 4
Reynoldsville, PA 74-75 D 4
Reynosa 72-73 G 6
Rezā'iyeh = Orūmīyeh 44-45 EF 3
Rēzekne 30-31 M 9
Rezina 36-37 N 2

Rhein 33 C 3
Rheine 33 C 2
Rheinland-Pfalz 33 CD 3-4
Rhin = Rhein 33 C 3
Rhine = Rhein 33 C 3
Rhino Camp 64-65 H 2
Rhode Island [USA, ⊙] 74-75 H 4
Rhode Island [USA, ☆] 72-73 MN 3
Rhodopē 36-37 KL 5
Rhodope 36-37 KL 5
Rhodope Mountains 36-37 KL 5
Rhodopen 36-37 KL 5
Rhön 33 DE 3
Rhondda 32 E 6
Rhone [CH] 33 C 5
Rhône [F] 34-35 K 6
Rhône au Rhin, Canal du – 34-35 L 4-5

Riaad = Ar-Riyāḍ 44-45 F 6
Riachão 78-79 K 6
Riad = Ar-Riyāḍ 44-45 F 6
Riad, Er- = Ar-Riyāḍ 44-45 F 6
Riang 44-45 P 5
Riau = 4 ◁ 52-53 D 6
Riau, Kepulauan – 52-53 DE 6
Ribacsij-félsziget = poluostrov Rybačij 42-43 EF 4
Ribadeo 34-35 D 7
Ribas do Rio Pardo 78-79 J 9
Ribaṭ, Ar- 60-61 C 2
Ribatejo 34-35 C 9
Ribaué 64-65 J 5-6
Ribe 30-31 C 10
Ribeira 34-35 C 7
Ribeirão [BR, Pernambuco] 78-79 MN 6
Ribeirão [BR, Rondônia] 78-79 FG 7
Ribeirão Preto 78-79 K 9
Ribeiro Gonçalves 78-79 KL 6
Riberalta 78-79 F 7
Ribyānah 60-61 J 4
Ribyānah, Ṣaḥrā' – 60-61 J 4
Riccione 36-37 E 3-4
Rice, CA 76-77 F 8
Riceboro, GA 74-75 C 9
Rice Lake 74-75 DE 2
Richard's Bay 64-65 H 8
Richardson Mountains 70-71 J 4
Richfield, ID 76-77 FG 4
Richfield, UT 76-77 GH 6
Richford, VT 74-75 G 2
Richgrove, CA 76-77 D 8
Richland, WA 72-73 C 2
Richland Balsam 74-75 B 7
Richlands, VA 74-75 C 6
Richmond [AUS] 56-57 H 4
Richmond [ZA, Kaapland] 64-65 F 9
Richmond [ZA, Natal] 64-65 G 9-H 8
Richmond, CA 72-73 B 4
Richmond, IN 72-73 JK 3-4
Richmond, VA 72-73 L 4
Richmond Gulf 70-71 V 6
Richmond Hill, GA 74-75 C 9
Richwood, WV 74-75 C 5
Ridder = Leninogorsk 42-43 P 7
Riddle, ID 76-77 EF 4
Riddle, OR 76-77 B 4
Rideau Lake 74-75 E 2
Ridgecrest, CA 76-77 E 8
Ridgeland, SC 74-75 C 8
Ridgetown 74-75 C 3
Ridgeway, SC 74-75 C 7
Ridgway, PA 74-75 D 4
Riding Mountain National Park 70-71 Q 7
Ridīsiya, Er- = Ar-Radīsīyat Baḥrī 62 E 5
Ridvan = Alenz 46-47 J 4
Riesa 33 F 3
Riesco, Isla – 80 B 8
Riesengebirge 33 GH 3
Riesi 36-37 F 7
Rietfontein 64-65 F 8
Rieth, OR 76-77 D 3
Rieti 36-37 E 4
Rīf = Ar-Rīf 60-61 CD 1-2
Rīf, Ar- 60-61 CD 1-2
Rīf, er – = Ar-Rīf 60-61 CD 1-2
Rifā'ī, Ar- 46-47 M 7
Rifstangi 30-31 ef 1
Rift Valley 64-65 J 2
Riga 30-31 KL 9
Riga, Golfe d' = Rīgas Jūŗas Līcis 30-31 KL 9

212 Quwār

Riga, Golfo de – = Rīgas Jūŗas Līcis 30-31 KL 9
Riga, Golf van – = Rīgas Jūŗas Līcis 30-31 KL 9
Riga, Gulf of – = Rīgas Jūŗas Līcis 30-31 KL 9
Rigaer Bucht = Rīgas Jūŗas Līcis 30-31 KL 9
Rīgas Jūŗas Līcis 30-31 KL 9
Rigby, ID 76-77 H 4
Rigestān 44-45 JK 4
Riggins, ID 76-77 E 3
Rigo 52-53 N 8
Rigolet 70-71 Z 7
Rihāb, Ar- 46-47 L 7
Riihimäki 30-31 L 7
Riiser-Larsen halvøy 24 C 4-5
Rijād = Ar-Riyāḍ 44-45 F 6
Rijadh = Ar-Riyāḍ 44-45 F 6
Rijāf 63 B 1
Rijān 60-61 E 3
Rijeka 36-37 F 3
Rijpfjord 30-31 I 4
Rikeze = Zhigatse 48-49 F 6
Rikorda, ostrov – 50-51 H 1
Riksgränsen 30-31 GH 3
Rikubetsu 50-51 c 2
Rikuzen-Takada 50-51 NO 3
Rila 36-37 K 4-5
Rīm, Bi'r – 62 B 2
Rimah, Wādī ar- 44-45 E 5
Rimāl, Ar- = Ar-Rub' al-Khālī 44-45 F 7-G 6
Rimini 36-37 E 3
Rîmnicu Sărat 36-37 M 3
Rîmnicu Vîlcea 36-37 L 3
Rimouski 70-71 X 8
Rim Rocky Mountains 76-77 C 4
Rîm = Roma 36-37 E 5
Rin = Rhein 33 C 3
Rinca, Pulau – 52-53 G 8
Rinconada 80 C 2
Rin'gang = Riāng 44-45 P 5
Ringerike-Hønefoss 30-31 CD 7
Ringkøbing 30-31 BC 9
Ringling, MT 76-77 H 2
Ringvassøy 30-31 H 3
Riñihue [RCH, ●] 80 B 5-6
Rinjani, Gunung – 52-53 G 8
Riñihue [RCH, ●] 80 B 5-6
Rio Abajo 72-73 bc 2
Riobamba 78-79 D 5
Rio Blanco [BR] 78-79 G 7
Rio Branco [BR, Amazonas] 78-79 F 6
Rio Branco [BR, Rio Branco] 78-79 G 4-5
Rio Bravo del Norte 72-73 E 5-F 6
Rio Chico [RA, Santa Cruz ●] 80 C 7
Rio Claro [TT] 72-73 O 9
Rio Claro [BR, Goiás ◁ Rio Araguaia] 78-79 J 8
Rio Claro [BR, Goiás ◁ Rio Paranaíba] 78-79 J 8
Rio Cuarto [RA, ●] 80 D 4
Rio Chico [RA, Santa Cruz ●] 80 C 7
Rio de Janeiro [BR, ●] 78-79 L 9
Rio de Janeiro [BR, ☆] 78-79 LM 9
Rio do Sul 80 G 3
Rioekioetrog 48-49 O 7-P 6
Rio Grande [BR, Minas Gerais] 78-79 K 8-9
Rio Grande [BR, Rio Grande do Sul] 80 F 4
Rio Grande [MEX] 72-73 H 8
Rio Grande [RA, Tierra del Fuego ●] 80 C 8
Rio Grande [USA, Texas] 72-73 FG 6
Rio Grande [BOL, ~] 78-79 G 8
Rio Grande [NIC, ~] 72-73 JK 9
Rio Grande, Ramal de – 22-23 GH 7
Rio Grande, Seuil du – 22-23 GH 7
Rio Grande de Santiago 72-73 F 7
Rio Grande do Norte 78-79 M 6
Rio Grande do Norte = Natal 78-79 MN 6
Rio Grande do Sul 80 F 3-4
Rio Grandedrempel 22-23 GH 7
Rio Grande Rise 22-23 GH 7
Rio-Grande-Schwelle 22-23 GH 7
Rio-Grande-Schwelle 22-23 GH 7
Rio-Grande-Schwelle 22-23 GH 7
Riohacha 78-79 E 2
Rio Chico [RA, Santa Cruz ●] 80 C 7
Rioja [PE] 78-79 D 6
Rioja, La – [E] 34-35 F 7
Rioja, La – [RA, ●] 80 C 3
Rio Largo 78-79 MN 6
Rio Mayo [RA, ●] 80 BC 7
Rio Mulatos 78-79 F 8
Rio Muni = Mbini 60-61 G 8
Rio Negro [BR, Amazonas] 78-79 G 5
Rio Negro [BR, Mato Grosso] 78-79 H 8
Rio Negro [BR, Paraná ●] 80 F 3
Rio Negro [RA, Rio Negro ~] 80 D 5-6
Rio Negro [RA, Rio Negro ☆] 80 C 6
Rio Negro [ROU, ~] 80 EF 4
Rio Negro, Embalse del – 80 E 4
Rio Negro, Pantanal do – 78-79 H 8
Rio Pardo de Minas 78-79 L 8
Rio Primero [RA, ●] 80 D 4
Rio Real 78-79 M 7
Rio Sonora 72-73 D 6
Riosucio [CO, ●] 78-79 D 3
Rio Tercero [RA, ●] 80 D 4
Riou-Kiou, Fosse des – 48-49 O 7-P 6
Riouw Archipel = Kepulauan Riau 52-53 DE 6
Rio Verde [BR, Goiás ●] 78-79 J 8
Rio Verde [MEX, Oaxaca] 72-73 G 8
Rio Verde [PY] 80 E 2
Rio Verde [RCH] 80 B 8
Rio Verde [BR, Goiás ◁ Represa de São Simão] 78-79 J 8
Rio Verde [BR, Mato Grosso ◁ Rio Paraná] 78-79 J 9
Rio Verde [BR, Mato Grosso ◁ Rio Teles Pires] 78-79 H 7
Rio Verde de Mato Grosso 78-79 HJ 8
Riparia, WA 76-77 DE 2
Ripley, CA 76-77 F 9
Ripley, NY 74-75 D 3
Ripley, WV 74-75 C 5
Ripoll 34-35 J 7
Riṣāfah 46-47 H 5
Rīsām 'Anayzah 62 E 2
Riṣānī, Ar- 60-61 D 2
Risasi 64-65 G 3
Rishiri suidō 50-51 b 1
Rishiri tō 48-49 QR 2
Ri'shōn Lĕẕiyyōn 46-47 F 7
Rising Sun, OH 74-75 A 5
Risiri 50-51 b 1
Risle 34-35 H 4
Risør 30-31 C 8
Ristikent 30-31 O 3
Ritscherhochland 24 B 36
Ritter, Mount – 72-73 C 4
Rittman, OH 74-75 BC 4
Ritzville, WA 76-77 D 2
Riukiu = Ryūkyū 48-49 N 7-O 6
Riu-Kiu, Fosa de – 48-49 O 7-P 6
Riukiu, Rów – 48-49 O 7-P 6
Riva 36-37 D 3
Rivadavia [RA, Buenos Aires] 80 D 5
Rivadavia [RA, Salta] 80 D 2
Rivadavia [RCH] 80 B 3
Rivalensundet 30-31 mn 5
Rivera [RA] 80 D 5
Rivera [ROU, ●] 80 E 4
Riverbank, CA 76-77 C 7
River Cess 60-61 BC 7
Riverdale, CA 76-77 D 7
Riverhead, NY 74-75 G 4
Riverina 56-57 HJ 6-7
Rivers 60-61 F 7-8
Riversdal 64-65 F 9
Riversdale = Riversdal 64-65 F 9
Riverside, CA 72-73 C 5
Riverside, OR 76-77 DE 4
Riverton [AUS] 56-57 G 6
Riviera Beach, FL 74-75 cd 3
Rivière-du-Loup 70-71 WX 8
Rivoli 36-37 B 3
Rivungo 64-65 F 6
Riyad = Ar-Riyāḍ 44-45 F 6
Riyāḍ, Ar- 44-45 F 6
Rize 44-45 E 2
Rize Dağları 46-47 J 2
Rizzuto, Cabo – 36-37 G 6
Rjukan 30-31 C 8
R'kîz, Ar- 60-61 AB 5
R'kîz, Lac – = Ar-R'kîz 60-61 AB 5
Roan Cliffs 76-77 J 6
Roanne 34-35 K 5
Roanoke, VA 72-73 KL 4
Roanoke Island 74-75 F 7
Roanoke Rapids, NC 74-75 E 6
Roanoke River 72-73 L 4
Roatán, Isla de – 72-73 J 8
Robāṭ 46-47 M 5
Robbins Island 58 b 2
Robe [NZ] 58 D 6
Robe, Mount – 58 E 3
Roberts, ID 76-77 GH 4
Roberts Creek Mountain 76-77 E 6
Robertsfors 30-31 J 5
Robertson, WY 76-77 HJ 5
Robertson Bay 24 BC 17-18
Robertsons øy 24 C 31
Robertsport 60-61 B 7
Robertstown 58 D 4
Roberval 70-71 W 8
Robinette, OR 76-77 E 3
Robinson Crusoe 69 C 6
Robinson Island 24 C 30
Robinson Range 56-57 C 5
Robinson River 56-57 G 3
Robinvale 56-57 H 6
Robla, La – 34-35 E 7
Robson, Mount – [CDN, ▲] 70-71 N 7
Roca, Cabo da – 34-35 C 9
Roçadas = Xangongo 64-65 E 6
Roçalgate = Rās al-Ḥadd 44-45 HJ 6
Rocamadour 34-35 HJ 6
Rocas, Atol das – 78-79 N 5
Rocas Negras = Black Rock 80 H 8
Rocha [ROU, ●] 80 F 4
Rochefort 34-35 G 5-6
Rochelle, la – 34-35 G 7
Rochester, MN 72-73 H 3
Rochester, NH 74-75 H 3
Rochester, NY 72-73 L 3
Roche-sur-Yon, la – 34-35 G 5
Rock, The – 58 H 5
Rockall 28-29 EF 4
Rockall Plateau 28-29 E 4
Rockallplateau 28-29 E 4
Rockall, Ramal de – 28-29 E 4
Rock Creek, OR 76-77 CD 3
Rock Creek [USA ◁ Clark Fork River] 76-77 G 2
Rockefeller Plateau 24 AB 23-24
Rockford, IL 72-73 HJ 3
Rockhampton 56-57 JK 4
Rock Hill, SC 72-73 K 4-5
Rockingham [AUS] 56-57 BC 6
Rockingham, NC 74-75 CD 7
Rockingham Bay 56-57 J 3
Rock Island, IL 72-73 HJ 3
Rock Island, WA 76-77 CD 2
Rock Lake 76-77 E 2
Rockland, ID 76-77 G 4
Rockland, ME 74-75 J 2-3
Rocklands Reservoir 56-57 H 7
Rockport, WA 76-77 C 1
Rock Springs, AZ 76-77 GH 8
Rock Springs, WY 72-73 E 3
Rockstone 78-79 H 3
Rockville, MD 74-75 E 5
Rockville, OR 76-77 E 4
Rockwood, PA 74-75 D 5
Rocky Mount, NC 74-75 E-6-7
Rocky Mount, VA 74-75 D 6
Rocky Mountain 76-77 G 2
Rocky Mountain National Park 72-73 EF 3
Rocky Mountains 70-71 L 5-P 9
Rocky Mountain Trench 70-71 L 6-N 7
Rocky Point [USA, California] 76-77 A 5
Rôḍā, Er- = Ar-Rawḍah 62 D 4
Roda, la – 34-35 F 9
Rodalquilar 34-35 FG 10
Rødberg 30-31 C 7
Rødby Havn 30-31 D 10
Rode Bekken = Sichuan Pendi 48-49 JK 5-6
Rodeo 80 BC 4
Rodeo, NM 76-77 J 10
Rodez 34-35 J 6
Rode Zee 44-45 D 5-7
Rodezja i Niasa = Zambia 64-65 G 6-H 5
Rodney 74-75 C 3
Rodópes 36-37 KL 5
Rodopy 36-37 KL 5
Rodopy 36-37 KL 5
Ródos [GR, ⊙] 36-37 N 7
Ródos [GR, ●] 36-37 N 7
Rodosto = Tekirdağ 46-47 B 2
Rodosto = Tekirdağ 44-45 B 2
Rodrigues [Mascarene Islands] 22-23 N 6-7
Rodrigues [MS] 64-65 O 6
Roebourne 56-57 C 4
Roebuck Bay 56-57 D 3
Roemelië = Rumelija 36-37 LM 4
Roemenië 36-37 K-M 2
Roermond 34-35 K 3
Roeselare 34-35 J 3
Roe's Welcome Sound 70-71 T 4-5
Rogač'ov 38-39 EF 5
Rogač'ov 38-39 EF 5
Rogagua, Lago – 78-79 F 7
Rogaland 30-31 B 8
Rogerson, ID 76-77 F 4
Rogersville, TN 74-75 B 6
Rognan 30-31 F 4
Rogoaguado, Lago – 78-79 F 7
Rogue River 76-77 A 4
Rogue River Mountains 76-77 AB 4
Roha-Lalibela = Lalībela 60-61 M 6
Rohan 34-35 F 4
Rohrī 44-45 K 5
Rohtak 44-45 M 5
Rojas 80 D 4
Rokkasho 50-51 N 2
Rokugō-saki = Suzu misaki 50-51 L 4
Rolla 30-31 G 3
Rolla, MO 72-73 H 4
Rolleston 56-57 J 4
Rolvsøy 30-31 K 2
Rom 30-31 B 8
Rom [EAU] 63 C 2
Rom = Roma 36-37 E 5
Roma 36-37 E 5
Roma [AUS] 56-57 J 5
Romain, Cape – 74-75 D 8
Romaine, Rivière – 70-71 Y 7
Roman 36-37 M 2
Romana, La – 72-73 J 8
Romanche Deep 22-23 J 6
Romanchediep 22-23 J 6
Romancherinne 22-23 J 6
Romang, Pulau – 52-53 J 8
Români = Rummānah 62 E 2
Romania 36-37 K-M 2
Románia 36-37 K-M 2
Romano, Cape – 74-75 bc 4
Romano, Cayo – 72-73 L 7
Romanovka [SU, Bur'atskaja ASSR] 42-43 V 7
Romans-sur-Isère 34-35 K 6
Roman Wall 32 E 4
Romanzof, Cape – 70-71 C 5
Róma = Roma 36-37 E 5
Romblon 52-53 H 4
Rome, GA 72-73 J 5
Rome, NY 72-73 LM 3
Rome, OR 76-77 E 4
Rome = Roma 36-37 E 5
Romilly-sur-Seine 34-35 J 4
Romney, WV 74-75 D 5
Romny 38-39 F 5
Rømø 30-31 C 10
Romsdal 30-31 BC 6
Romsdalfjord 30-31 B 6
Ronan, MT 76-77 FG 2
Roncador, Serra do – 78-79 J 7
Roncador Reef 52-53 j 6
Roncesvalles 34-35 G 7
Ronceverte, WV 74-75 C 6
Ronda 34-35 E 10
Rondane 30-31 C 7
Rondón = Puerto Rondón 78-79 E 3
Rondônia [BR, ●] 78-79 G 7
Rondônia [BR, ☆] 78-79 G 7
Rondonópolis 78-79 HJ 8
Ronge, la – 70-71 P 6
Ronge, Lac la – 70-71 Q 6
Rongui 63 E 5
Ron Ma, Mui – 52-53 E 3
Rønne 30-31 F 10
Ronne Bay 24 B 29
Ronneby 30-31 F 9
Roof Butte 76-77 J 7
Roosendaal en Nispen 34-35 K 3
Roosevelt, UT 76-77 HJ 5
Roosevelt, WA 76-77 C 3
Roosevelt, Rio – 78-79 G 6-7
Roosevelt Island 24 AB 20-21
Roper River 56-57 F 2
Roper Valley 56-57 F 2-3
Ropi 30-31 J 3
Roquefort-sur-Soulzon 34-35 J 7
Roraima 78-79 GH 4
Roraima, Mount – 78-79 G 3
Røros 30-31 D 6
Rørvik 30-31 D 5
Rosa 64-65 H 4
Rosalia, WA 76-77 E 2
Rosamond, CA 76-77 D 8
Rosamond Lake 76-77 DE 8
Rosário [BR] 78-79 L 5
Rosario [RA, Santa Fe] 80 DE 4
Rosario, Rio del – 76-77 F 10
Rosario de la Frontera 80 D 3
Rosario del Tala 80 E 4
Rosário do Sul 80 EF 4
Rosário Oeste 78-79 HJ 7
Rosarito [MEX, Baja California Norte ↓ Tijuana] 76-77 E 9
Rosas 34-35 J 7
Roscoe, NY 74-75 F 4
Roscoff 34-35 EF 4
Roscommon 32 BC 5
Roseau 72-73 O 8
Rosebery 56-57 HJ 8
Roseboro, NC 74-75 D 7
Roseburg, OR 76-77 B 4
Roșeireș, Er- = Ar-Ruṣayriṣ 60-61 LM 6
Rosengarten 19 C 19-20
Rosenheim 33 EF 5
Rose River 56-57 G 2
Rosetown 70-71 P 7
Rosetta = Rashīd 62 D 2
Rosetta Mouth = Maṣabb Rashīd 62 D 2
Rosette = Rashīd 62 D 2
Rose Wood 58 L 1
Rosignano Marittimo 36-37 CD 4
Rosignol 78-79 H 3
Roșiori-de-Vede 36-37 L 3-4
Rosja 42-43 L-g 4
Roskilde 30-31 E 10
Roslavl' 38-39 F 5
Roslyn, WA 76-77 C 2
Ross 56-57 O 8
Ross, Mar de – = Ross Sea 24 B 20-18
Ross, Mer de – = Ross Sea 24 B 20-18
Rossa, Morze – = Ross Sea 24 B 20-18
Rossano 36-37 G 6
Rossel Island 52-53 hi 7
Ross Ice Shelf 24 AB 20-17
Rossijskaja Sovetskaja Federativnaja Socialističeskaja Respublika = Rußland 42-43 L-g 4
Ross Island [Antarktika, Ross Sea] 24 B 17-18
Ross Island [Antarktika, Weddell Sea] 24 C 31
Ross Island [CDN] 70-71 R 7
Rosslare 32 CD 5
Rossmeer = Ross Sea 25 B 20-18
Rosso 60-61 A 5
Rossoš' 38-39 GH 5
Rossoš' 38-39 GH 5
Rossovo moře = Ross Sea 24 B 20-18
Ross River 70-71 K 5
Ross Sea 24 B 20-18
Ross-Schelfeis = Ross Ice Shelf 24 AB 20-17
Ross-tenger = Ross Sea 24 B 20-18
Røssvatn 30-31 E 5
Røssvik 30-31 FG 4
Rossville 56-57 HJ 3
Rostock 33 F 1
Rostov 42-43 FG 6
Rostov-na-Donu 38-39 GH 6
Roswell, NM 72-73 F 5
Rota 34-35 D 10
Rote, Pulau – 52-53 H 9
Rotes Becken = Sichuan Pendi 48-49 JK 5-6
Rotes Meer 44-45 D 5-E 7
Rothaargebirge 33 D 3
Rothbury 32 EF 4
Rothenburg 33 DE 4
Rothesay 32 D 4
Roto 56-57 J 6
Rotondo, Mont – 36-37 C 4
Rotorua 56-57 P 7
Rotterdam 34-35 JK 3
Rotti = Pulau Rote 52-53 H 9
Roubaix 34-35 J 3
Rouen 34-35 H 4
Roulers = Roeselare 34-35 J 3
Roumanie 36-37 K-M 2
Roumélie = Rumelija 36-37 LM 4
Round Island 64-65 N 6
Round Mountain 56-57 K 6
Round Mountain, NV 76-77 E 6
Round Valley Indian Reservation 76-77 B 6
Rounga, Dar – 60-61 J 6-7
Rourkela 44-45 NO 5
Rousay 32 E 2
Rouses Point, NY 74-75 G 2
Roussillon 34-35 J 7
Rouṭbé, El- = Ar-Ruṭbah 46-47 G 6
Rouyn 70-71 V 8
Rovaniemi 30-31 L 4
Rovdino 38-39 H 3
Rovereto 36-37 D 3
Rovigo 36-37 D 3
Rovinj 36-37 E 3
Rovkuly 30-31 O 5
Rovníková Guinea 60-61 FG 8
Rovno 38-39 E 5
Rovuma, Rio – 64-65 J 5
Rowley Island 70-71 UV 4
Rowley Shoals 56-57 C 3
Rowuma = Rio Rovuma 64-65 J 5
Rox, NV 76-77 F 7
Roxas 52-53 H 4
Roxboro, NC 74-75 D 6
Roxburgh [NZ] 56-57 N 9
Roy, UT 76-77 G 5
Royal Canal 32 C 5
Royal Society Range 24 B 15-16
Royan 34-35 G 6
Royaume-Uni 32 F-H 4-5
Røykenvik 30-31 D 7
Royston, GA 74-75 B 7
Rozewie, Przylądek – 33 J 1
Rožňava 33 K 4
Roztocze 33 L 3
Roztoky = Rostock 33 F 1-2
Rožňava 33 K 4
Rtiščevo 38-39 H 5
Rtiščevo 38-39 H 5
Ruacana Falls 64-65 DE 6
Ruaha National Park 63 C 4
Ruanda = Rwanda 64-65 GH 3
Ruapehu 56-57 P 7
Rubā'ī, Ash-Shallāl ar- = Al-Jandal ar-Rāb'i 60-61 L 5
Rub al Chali, Pustynia – = Ar-Rub' al-Khālī 44-45 F 7-G 6
Rub al-Chālí, poušť – = Ar-Rub' al-Hālī 44-45 F 7-G 6
Rub al Chali, Pustynia – = Ar-Rub' al-Khālī 44-45 F 7-G 6
Rub' al-Khālī = Ar-Rub'ai-Khālī 44-45 F 7-G 6
Rub' al-Khālī, Ar- 44-45 F 7-G 6
Rubcovsk 42-43 P 7
Rubeho 63 D 4
Rubesibe 50-51 c 2
Rubi 64-65 G 2
Rubia, La – 80 D 4
Rubondo 63 BC 3
Ruby, AK 70-71 EF 5
Ruby Lake 76-77 F 5
Ruby Mountains 76-77 F 5
Ruby Range [USA] 76-77 G 3
Ruby Valley 76-77 F 5
Ruchlovo = Skovorodino 42-43 XY 7
Rudall 58 BC 4
Rudayyif, Ar- 60-61 F 2
Rūdbār 46-47 N 4
Rudé moře 44-45 D 5-7
Rudensk 30-31 M 11
Rudewa 63 C 5
Rudnaja Pristan' 42-43 a 9
Rudnyj 42-43 L 7
Rudog 48-49 D 5
Rudol'fa, ostrov – 42-43 JK 1
Rūd Sar 46-47 O 4
Rudyard, MT 76-77 H 1
Ruffec 34-35 GH 5
Rufiji 64-65 J 4
Rufino 80 D 4
Rufisque 60-61 A 5-6
Rufunsa 64-65 GH 6
Rugao 48-49 N 5
Rugby 32 F 5
Rügen 33 FG 1
Rugozero 38-39 F 3
Ruhnu 30-31 K 9
Ruhr 33 D 3
Ruhudji 63 D 5
Ruhuhu 63 C 5
Ruijin 48-49 M 6
Ruivo, Pico – 60-61 A 2
Ruiz, Nevado del – 78-79 DE 4
Rujewa 63 C 5
Rūjiena 30-31 L 9
Rujm Tal'at al-Jamā'ah 46-47 F 7
Rukhaimiyah, Ar- = Ar-Rukhaymīyah 46-47 L 8
Rukhaymīyah, Ar- 46-47 L 8
Ruki 64-65 E 2-3
Rukungiri 63 B 3
Rukuru 63 C 5
Rukwa 64-65 H 4
Rukwa, Lake – 64-65 H 4
Rum 32 C 3
Ruma 36-37 H 3
Rumāh, Ar- 44-45 F 5
Rumahui 52-53 k 7
Rumania 36-37 K-M 2
Rumänien 36-37 K-M 2
Rumaylah, Ar- 46-47 M 7
Rumaythah, Ar- 46-47 L 7
Rumbalara 56-57 FG 5
Rumberpon, Pulau – 52-53 KL 7
Rumbīk 60-61 K 7
Rum Cay 72-73 M 7
Rumelia = Rumelija 36-37 LM 4
Rumelien = Rumelija 36-37 LM 4
Rumelija 36-37 LM 4
Rumford, ME 74-75 H 2
Rummānah 62 E 2
Rummelsburg in Pommern = Miastko 33 H 1-2
Rumoe = Rumoi 50-51 b 2
Rumoi 48-49 R 3
Rumorosa 76-77 EF 9
Rumpi 63 C 5
Rumula 56-57 HJ 3
Rumunia 36-37 K-M 2
Rumunsko 36-37 K-M 2
Rumuruti 63 CD 2
Rundu 64-65 E 6
Runga, Dar – = Dar Rounga 60-61 J 6-7
Rungu 63 AB 2
Rungwa [EAT, ~] 63 C 4
Rungwa [EAT, ●] 64-65 H 4
Rungwa East 63 BC 4
Rungwe Mount 64-65 H 4
Runton Range 56-57 D 4
Ruo Shui 48-49 HJ 3
Ruoxi 48-49 M 6
Rupat, Pulau – 52-53 D 6
Rupert, ID 76-77 G 4
Rupert, Rivière de – 70-71 VW 7
Rupert House = Fort Rupert 70-71 V 7
Ruppert Coast 24 B 21-22
Ruq'ī, Ar- 46-47 M 8
Rūrkalā = Rourkela 44-45 NO 5
Rurrenabaque 78-79 F 7
Rusanovo 38-39 KL 1
Rusanovo 42-43 JK 3
Rusape 64-65 H 6
Ruṣayriṣ, Ar- 60-61 LM 6
Ruse 36-37 LM 4
Rușetu 36-37 M 3
Rusia 42-43 L-g 4
Rusko 42-43 L-g 4
Rusland 42-43 L-g 4
Russas 78-79 M 5
Russell [NZ] 56-57 OP 7
Russell Island 70-71 R 3
Russell Islands 52-53 j 6
Russell Range 56-57 D 6
Russenes 30-31 L 2
Russia 42-43 L-g 4
Russian River 76-77 B 6
Russie 42-43 L-g 4
Russisi = Ruzizi 64-65 G 3
Russkij, ostrov – [SU, p-ov Tajmyr] 42-43 RS 2

Russk 213

Russkij, ostrov – [SU, Vladivostok] 42-43 Z 9
Russkij Zavorot, mys – 42-43 JK 4
Rußland 42-43 L-g 4
Rustâq, Ar- 44-45 H 6
Rustavi 38-39 HJ 7
Rustenburg 64-65 G 8
Ruston, LA 72-73 H 5
Rûṣû = Al-Quwārib 60-61 A 5
Rusufa = Riṣāfah 46-47 H 5
Rusumu, Chutes – 63 B 3
Rusumu, Chutes – 63 B 3
Rusumu, Chutes – 63 B 3
Rutana 64-65 GH 3
Rutanzige 64-65 G 3
Ruṭbah, Ar- [IRQ] 44-45 DE 4
Ruṭbah, Ar- [SYR] 46-47 G 6
Ruth, NV 76-77 F 6
Rutherfordton, NC 74-75 C 7
Ruthin 32 E 5
Rutland, VT 72-73 M 3
Rutshuru 64-65 G 3
Ruvo di Pùglia 36-37 G 5
Ruvu [EAT, ~] 64-65 J 4
Ruvu [EAT, ●] 63 D 4
Ruvu = Pangani 64-65 J 3
Ruvuma [EAT, ~] 63 C 5
Ruvuma [EAT, ☆] 64-65 J 5
Ruvuvu 63 B 3
Ruwâq, Jabal ar- 46-47 G 5-6
Ruwenzori 64-65 G 2
Ruwenzori National Park 64-65 GH 3
Ruwu = Pangani 64-65 J 3
Ruzajevka 42-43 GH 7
Ruzizi 64-65 G 3
Ružomberok 33 J 4
Ružomberok 33 J 4

Rwanda 64-65 GH 3
Rwashamaire 63 B 3

Ryanggang-do 50-51 FG 2
Rybačij 33 K 1
Rybačij, poluostrov – 42-43 EF 4
Rybacki, Półwysep – = poluostrov Rybačij 42-43 EF 4
Rybačij 33 K 1
Rybačij, poluostrov – 42-43 EF 4
Rybinsk 42-43 F 6
Rybinskoje vodochranilišče 42-43 FG 6
Rybinskoje vodochranilišče 42-43 FG 6
Rybnica 38-39 E 6
Rybnik 33 J 3
Ryderwood, WA 76-77 B 2
Rye Patch Reservoir 76-77 D 5
Ryke Yseøyane 30-31 m 6
Rijn = Rhein 33 C 3
Ryōtsu 50-51 M 3
Rypin 33 J 2
Ryškany 36-37 M 2
Ryškany 36-37 M 2
Ryūkyū 48-49 N 7-O 6
Ryūkyū, příkop – 48-49 O 7-P 6
Ryūkyū-árok 48-49 Q 7-P 6
Ryūkyūgraben 48-49 O 7-P 6
Ryukyu Trench 48-49 O 7-P 6

Rzeszów 33 KL 3
Ržev 38-39 FG 4
Rzym = Roma 36-37 E 5

Ržev 38-39 FG 4

Ř

Řecko 36-37 J 7-L 5
Řezno = Regensburg 33 EF 4

S

Sá [BR] 78-79 L 8
Saale 33 E 3
Saalfeld 33 E 3
Saar 33 C 4
Saarbrücken 33 C 4
Saaremaa 30-31 K 8
Saargemünd = Sarreguemines 34-35 L 4
Saarijärvi 30-31 L 6
Saariselkä 30-31 MN 3
Saarland 33 C 4
Saarlouis 33 C 4
Saaz = Žatec 33 F 3
Saba 72-73 O 8
Sabaa, Gebel es – = Qārat as-Sab'ah 60-61 H 3
Šabac 36-37 H 3
Sabadell 34-35 J 8
Sabae 50-51 KL 5
Sabah 52-53 G 5
Sab'ah, Qārat as- 60-61 H 3
Sabaki = Galana 64-65 JK 3
Sābālān, Kūhhā-ye – 46-47 M 3
Sabana, Archipiélago de – 72-73 KL 7
Sabanalarga [CO, Atlántico] 78-79 DE 2
Sabang [RI, Aceh] 52-53 C 5
Şabanözü 46-47 E 2
Sabari 44-45 N 7
Şabāyā, Jabal – 44-45 E 7
Sab' Biyār 46-47 G 6
Şabbūrah 46-47 G 5
Sabbah 60-61 G 3
Sabhah, As- 46-47 H 5
Sabi 64-65 H 7
Sabile 30-31 K 9
Sabinas 72-73 F 6
Sabinas Hidalgo 72-73 F 6
Sabine land 30-31 k 5
Sabine Peninsula 70-71 OP 2
Sabine River 72-73 H 5
Sabini, Monti – 36-37 E 4
Şābirīyah, Aş- 46-47 M 8
Şabīyah, Qaşr aş- 46-47 N 8
Sable 56-57 M 3
Sable, Cape – [CDN] 70-71 XY 9
Sable, Cape – [USA] 72-73 K 6
Sable Island [CDN] 70-71 Z 9
Sable Island [PNG] 52-53 hj 5
Sables-d'Olonne, les – 34-35 FG 5
Saboûrâ = Şabbūrah 46-47 G 5
Sabrina Land 24 C 12-13
Sabun 42-43 P 5
Sabuncu 46-47 D 3
Sabuncupınar = Sabuncu 46-47 D 3
Şabyā', Aş- 44-45 E 7
Sābzawār = Shīndand 44-45 J 4
Sabzewār 44-45 H 3
Sacaba 78-79 F 8
Sacaca 78-79 F 8
Sacajawea Peak 76-77 E 3
Sacami, Lac – 70-71 V 7
Sacanta 80 D 4
Sacedi-Arabië 44-45 D 5-F 6
Sachalin 42-43 b 7-8
Sachalinskij zaliv 42-43 b 7
Sach'ang-ni 50-51 F 2
Sacharvan 38-39 KL 2
Sachigo River 70-71 S 6-7
Šachrisabz 44-45 K 3
Sachsen 33 FG 3
Šachtinsk 42-43 N 8
Šachty 38-39 H 6
Šachunja 42-43 GH 6
Šack 38-39 H 5
Sackets Harbor, NY 74-75 EF 3
Saco, ME 74-75 H 3
Sacramento, CA 72-73 B 4
Sacramento, Pampa del – 78-79 D 6
Sacramento Mountains 72-73 EF 5
Sacramento River 72-73 B 3-4
Sacramento Valley 72-73 B 3-4
Sa'dah 44-45 E 7
Sada-misaki 50-51 HJ 6
Sadani 64-65 J 4
Saddle Mountain 76-77 G 4
Saddle Mountains 76-77 CD 2
Saddle Peak 76-77 H 3
Sa Đec 52-53 E 4
Sadıkali = Karahasanlı 46-47 F 3
Sādis, Al-Jandal as- 60-61 L 5
Sadiya 44-45 Q 5
Sa'dīyah, As- 46-47 L 5
Sa'dīyah, Hawr as- 46-47 M 6
Sado 34-35 C 10
Sado 48-49 Q 4
Şadr, Wādī – 62 F 3
Šadrinsk 42-43 LM 6
Sæby 30-31 D 9
Saeki = Saiki 50-51 HJ 6
Şafā, Aş- 46-47 G 6
Şafā, Tulūl aş- 46-47 G 6
Safad = Ẕefat 44-45 D 4
Şafah, Aş- 46-47 J 4
Safājā 60-61 L 3
Safājā, Jazīrat – 62 F 4
Safaji Island = Jazīrat Safājah 62 F 4
Şafāqis 60-61 FG 2
Şafayn, 'Ard – 46-47 H 5
Safēd Kōh, Selselae – 44-45 JK 4
Şaff, Aş- 62 D 3
Saffāf, Birkat as- 46-47 M 7
Saffāf, Hōr as- = Birkat as-Saffāf 46-47 M 7
Saffānīyah 44-45 F 5
Şaffār Kalay 44-45 J 4
Säffle 30-31 E 8
Safford, AZ 76-77 J 9
Saffron Walden 32 G 5-6
Şāfī 60-61 C 2
Säfīd, Kūh-e – = Kūh-e Sefīd 46-47 M 5-N 6
Säfīd Kuh = Selselae Safēd Kōh 44-45 JK 4
Säfīd Rūd = Sefīd Rūd 46-47 N 4
Safīrah 46-47 G 4
Şāfītā' 46-47 G 5
Safranbolu 46-47 E 2
Saga 48-49 P 5
Sagae 50-51 MN 3
Sagaing = Sitkaing 52-53 D 2
Sagaing = Sitkaing Taing 52-53 B 2-C 7
Sagami nada 48-49 Q 4-R 5
Saganoseki 50-51 HJ 6
Šagany, ozero – 36-37 NO 3
Sagar [IND, Maharashtra] 44-45 M 6
Sagara 50-51 M 5
Saga-ri 50-51 F 5
Sagarmatha 48-49 F 6
Sagavanirktok River 70-71 G 3-4
Sage, WY 76-77 H 5
Sage Zong = Sakha Dsong 48-49 F 6
Şaghīr, Zāb aş- 46-47 K 5
Saghru, Jebel – = Jabal Sārū 60-61 C 2
Sagī', Har – 46-47 F 7
Saginaw, MI 72-73 K 3
Saginaw Bay 72-73 K 3
Sagiz 42-43 JK 8
Šagonar 42-43 R 7
Sagra 34-35 F 10
Sagra, La – 34-35 EF 8
Sagres 34-35 C 10
Saguaro National Monument 76-77 H 9
Saguenay, Rivière – 70-71 WX 8
Sagunto 34-35 GH 9
Sahagún 34-35 E 7
Sahand, Kūh-e – 46-47 M 4
Sahara 60-61 C-K 4
Sahara-Atlas 60-61 D 2-F 1
Saharan Atlas 60-61 D 2-F 1
Saharanpur 44-45 M 4
Sahara Occidental 60-61 A 4-B 3
Sahara Well 56-57 D 4
Sahara Zachodnia 60-61 A 4-B 3
Saharský Atlas 60-61 D 2-F 1
Saharunpore = Saharanpur 44-45 M 4
Şahbā', Wādī aş- 44-45 F 6
Sahel = Sâhil 60-61 BC 5
Šahḥāt = Shaḥḥāt 60-61 J 2
Sâḥil 60-61 BC 5
Sâhīwāl 44-45 L 4
Şaḥn, Aş- 46-47 K 7
Şaḥneh 46-47 M 5
Şaḥrā', Bi'r – 62 C 6
Şaḥrā, Jabal – 62 EF 4
Şaḥrā' al-Gharbīyah, Aş- 62 BC 4
Sahuarita, AZ 76-77 H 10
Sahuayo de José Maria Morelos 72-73 F 7-8
Sahyādri = Western Ghats 44-45 L 6-M 8
Saibai Island 52-53 M 8
Sai Buri 52-53 D 5
Saiburi = Alor Setar 52-53 CD 5
Şa'īd, Aş- 60-61 L 3-4
Saïd, Es- = Aş-Şa'īd 60-61 L 3-4
Şaïdâ = Şaydā [RL] 44-45 CD 4
Sa'īdābād = Sīrjān 44-45 H 5
Saidaiji 50-51 JK 5
Sa'īd Bundās 60-61 JK 7
Saigō 50-51 J 4
Saigon = Thành Phô Hô Chi Minh 52-53 E 4
Saigón = Thàn Phô Hô Chi Minh 52-53 E 4
Saiḥūt = Sayḥūt 44-45 G 7
Saijo 50-51 J 6
Saikai National Park = Gotō-rettō 50-51 G 6
Saiki 50-51 HJ 6
Šaim 42-43 L 5
Saima 50-51 E 2
Saimaa 30-31 MN 7
Sai-ma-chi = Saima 50-51 E 2
Saimbeyli 46-47 FG 3
Sā'īn Dezh 46-47 M 4
Sainjang 50-51 E 3
Sāīn Qal'eh = Shāhīn Dezh 46-47 M 4
Saint Albans, VT 74-75 G 2
Saint Albans, WV 74-75 BC 5
Saint-Amand-Mont-Rond 34-35 J 5
Saint-André, Cap – 64-65 K 6
Saint Andrews, SC 74-75 CD 8
Saint Anthony 70-71 Za 7
Saint Anthony, ID 76-77 H 4
Saint Arnaud 58 F 6
Saint Augustin, Baie de – 64-65 K 7
Saint-Augustine, FL 72-73 KL 6
Saint Austell 32 D 6
Saint-Avold 34-35 L 4
Saint Barthélemy 72-73 O 8
Saint-Boniface 70-71 R 8
Saint-Brieuc 34-35 F 4
Saint Catharines 70-71 UV 9
Saint Catherines Island 74-75 C 9
Saint Charles, ID 76-77 H 4
Saint Charles, MO 72-73 H 4
Saint Charles, Cape – 70-71 Za 7
Saint Christopher és Nevis 72-73 O 8
Saint Christopher i Nevis 72-73 O 8
Saint Christopher-Nevis 72-73 O 8
Saint Clair, Lake – 70-71 U 9
Saint Clairsville, OH 74-75 C 4
Saint Cloud, FL 74-75 c 2
Saint Cloud, MN 72-73 H 2
Saint Croix 72-73 O 8
Saint Charles, ID 76-77 H 4
Saint Charles, MO 72-73 H 4
Saint Charles, Cape – 70-71 Za 7
Saint Christopher y Nevis 72-73 O 8
Saint David Islands = Kepulauan Mapia 52-53 KL 6
Saint David's Head 32 CD 6
Saint-Denis [F] 34-35 J 4
Saint-Denis [Réunion] 64-65 N 7
Saint-Dié 34-35 L 4
Saint-Dizier 34-35 K 4
Sainte-Agathe-des-Monts 70-71 VW 8
Saint Elias, Mount – 70-71 H 5
Saint Elias Mountains 70-71 J 5-6
Saint-Élie 78-79 J 3-4
Sainte-Lucie 72-73 O 8
Sainte-Marie [CDN] 74-75 H 1
Sainte-Marie [Gabun] 64-65 D 3
Sainte-Marie [Martinique] 72-73 O 9
Sainte-Marie, Cap – 64-65 L 8
Sainte-Marie, Île – = Nosy Boraha 64-65 M 6
Saintes 34-35 G 6
Saint-Étienne 34-35 JK 6
Saint-Flour 34-35 J 6
Saint Francis, ME 74-75 J 1
Saint Francis River 72-73 H 4
Saint François, Lac – 74-75 H 2
Saint Francois Island 64-65 M 4
Saint-Gaudens 34-35 H 7
Saint George [AUS] 56-57 J 5
Saint George, GA 74-75 B 9
Saint George, SC 74-75 C 8
Saint George, UT 76-77 G 7
Saint George, Point – 76-77 A 5
Saint-Georges [Französisch-Guyana] 78-79 J 4
Saint George's [WG] 72-73 O 9
Saint-Georges, Canal – = Saint George's Channel 32 C 6-D 5
Saint George's Channel 32 C 6-D 5
Saint George's Channel [PNG] 52-53 h 5-6
Saint George's Channel 32 C 6-D 5
Saint George's Channel [PNG] 52-53 h 5-6
Saint George's Channel 32 C 6-D 5
Saint George's Channel [PNG] 52-53 h 5-6
Saint-Gilles-sur-Vie 34-35 FG 5
Saint-Girons 34-35 H 7
Saint Govan's Head 32 D 6
Saint Helena 66 F 10
Saint Helena, CA 76-77 B 6
Saint Helena Bay = Sint Helenabaai 64-65 E 9
Saint Helena Range 76-77 B 6
Saint Helena Sound 74-75 CD 8
Saint Helens 32 E 5
Saint Helens [AUS] 58 d 2
Saint Helens, OR 76-77 B 3
Saint Helens, WA 76-77 B 2
Saint Helens, Mount – 76-77 BC 2
Saint Helens Point 58 d 2
Saint Helier 32 E 7
Saint-Hyacinthe 70-71 W 8
Saint Charles, ID 76-77 H 4
Saint Charles, MO 72-73 H 4
Saint Charles, Cape – 70-71 Za 7
Saint Christopher és Nevis 72-73 O 8
Saint Christopher i Nevis 72-73 O 8
Saint Christopher-Nevis 72-73 O 8
Saint Christopher-Nevis = Saint Kitts und Nevis 72-73 O 8
Saint Christopher y Nevis 72-73 O 8
Saint Ignatius, MT 76-77 FG 2
Saint James, Cape – 70-71 K 7
Saint-Jean 70-71 W 8
Saint-Jean, Lac – 70-71 W 8
Saint-Jean-de-Luz 34-35 FG 7
Saint Joe River 76-77 E 2
Saint John [CDN] 70-71 X 8
Saint John, Lake – = Lac Saint Jean 70-71 W 8
Saint John River 70-71 X 8
Saint John's [CDN] 70-71 a 8
Saint John's [West Indies] 72-73 O 8
Saint Johns, AZ 76-77 J 8
Saint Johns = Saint-Jean 70-71 W 8
Saint Johnsbury, VT 74-75 G 2
Saint Johns River 74-75 c 1-2
Saint Joseph, MO 72-73 GH 4
Saint Joseph, Lake – 70-71 ST 7
Saint-Joseph-d'Alma = Alma 70-71 W 8
Saint Joseph Island [SY] 64-65 M 4
Saint-Junien 34-35 H 6
Saint Kilda 32 B 3
Saint Laurent 70-71 W 8
Saint-Laurent, Fleuve – 70-71 W 8-9
Saint-Laurent, Golfe du – = Gulf of Saint Lawrence 70-71 Y 8
Saint Lawrence [AUS] 56-57 J 4
Saint Lawrence, Gulf of – 70-71 Y 8
Saint Lawrence Island 70-71 BC 5
Saint Lawrence River 70-71 X 8
Saint-Lô 34-35 G 4
Saint-Louis [SN] 60-61 A 5
Saint Louis, MO 72-73 H 4
Saint Lucia 72-73 O 9
Saint Lucia, Lake – = Sint Luciameer 64-65 H 8
Saint Magnus Bay 32 EF 1
Saint-Malo 34-35 FG 4
Saint Maries, ID 76-77 E 2
Saint-Marin 36-37 E 4
Saint Martin [⊙] 72-73 O 8
Saint Martins Bay 74-75 A 1-2
Saint Mary Lake 76-77 G 1
Saint Mary Peak 56-57 G 6
Saint Marys [AUS] 56-57 J 8
Saint Mary's [CDN, Ontario] 74-75 C 3
Saint Marys, GA 74-75 C 9
Saint Marys, PA 74-75 D 4
Saint Marys, WV 74-75 C 5
Saint Marys River [USA] 72-73 K 2
Saint Mathieu, Pointe – 34-35 E 4
Saint Matthew 42-43 l 5
Saint Matthew Island 70-71 B 5
Saint Matthew Island = Zādetkyī Kyūn 52-53 C 5
Saint Matthews, SC 74-75 C 8
Saint Matthias Group 52-53 NO 7
Saint-Maurice, Rivière – 70-71 W 8
Saint Michael, AK 70-71 D 5
Saint Michaels, AZ 76-77 J 8
Saint-Nazaire 34-35 F 5
Saint-Omer 34-35 HJ 3
Saintonge 34-35 G 6
Saint Paul [CDN] 70-71 O 7
Saint Paul [Saint Paul] 22-23 NO 7
Saint Paul, MN 72-73 H 2
Saint Paul, VT 74-75 B 6
Saint Paul River 60-61 BC 7
Saint Pauls, NC 74-75 D 7
Saint Peter Port 32 E 7
Saint Petersburg, FL 72-73 K 6
Saint-Pierre et Miquelon 70-71 Za 8
Saint Pierre Island 64-65 LM 4
Saint-Quentin 34-35 J 4
Saint-Raphaël 34-35 L 7
Saint Regis, MT 76-77 F 2
Saint-Sébastien, Cap – 64-65 L 5
Saint Simons Island 74-75 C 9
Saint Simons Island, GA 74-75 C 9
Saint Stephens, SC 74-75 D 8
Saint Thomas [CDN] 74-75 C 3
Saint Thomas [Westindien] 72-73 NO 8
Saint-Tropez 34-35 L 7
Saint Vincent 72-73 O 9
Saint Vincent, Gulf – 56-57 G 6-7
Saint Vincent en de Grenadinen 72-73 O 9
Saio = Dembī Dolo 60-61 LM 7
Saishū = Cheju-do 50-51 F 6
Saitama 50-51 M 4
Saiteli = Kadinhanı 46-47 E 3
Saito 50-51 H 6
Sai'wun = Say'ūn 44-45 F 7
Sajak 42-43 O 8
Sajama, Nevado de – 78-79 F 8
Sajano-Šušenskoje vodochranilišče 44-45 R 7
Sajano-Šušenskoje vodochranilišče 44-45 R 7
Sajarī, Bi'r – 46-47 H 6
Sajgon = Thành Phô Ho Chi Minh 52-53 JK 4
Saji-dong 50-51 G 2
Šajmak 44-45 L 3
Sajnšand 48-49 KL 3
Sajnšand 48-49 KL 3
Sajo 33 K 4
Sajram nuur 48-49 DE 3
Saka 63 D 3
Sakai 48-49 Q 5
Sakaide 50-51 JK 5
Sakaiminato 50-51 J 5
Sakākah 44-45 E 4-5
Sakakawea, Lake – 72-73 F 2
Sakamachi = Arakawa 50-51 M 3
Sakania 64-65 G 5
Sakarya 44-45 C 2
Sakarya Nehri 44-45 C 2
Sakata 48-49 Q 4
Sakavi = Mercimekkale 46-47 J 3
Sakawa 50-51 J 6
Sakchu 50-51 E 2
Saketa 52-53 J 7
Sakha Dsong 48-49 F 6
Sakht-Sar 46-47 O 4
Saki 38-39 F 6
Sakīkdah 60-61 F 1
Sakinohama 50-51 K 6
Sakishima-guntō 48-49 NO 7
Sakisima guntō = Sakishima-guntō 48-49 NO 7
Sâkkâne, 'Erg I-n- 60-61 D 4
Sakon Nakhon 52-53 B 3
Sakonnet Point 74-75 H 4
Sakovlevskoje = Privolžsk 42-43 N 5
Sakrivier [ZA, ●] 64-65 EF 9
Sal 38-39 H 6
Sala 30-31 G 8
Salacgrīva 30-31 KL 9
Sala Consilina 36-37 F 5
Salada, Laguna – [MEX] 76-77 F 9
Saladillo [RA, Buenos Aires] 80 DE 5
Salado, Río – [RA, Santa Fe] 80 D 3
Salado, Valle del – 72-73 F 7
Salaga 60-61 D 7
Salah, In- = 'Ayn Şālih 60-61 E 3
Salāhuddīn 46-47 KL 5
Salair 42-43 PQ 7
Salairskij kr'až 42-43 PQ 7
Salairskij kr'až 42-43 PQ 7
Salajar = Pulau Selayar 52-53 H 8
Salal 60-61 H 6
Şalālah 44-45 G 7
Salālah, Jabal – 62 F 7
Salamanca 34-35 E 8
Salamanca, NY 74-75 D 3
Salamat, Bahr – 60-61 H 6-7
Salāmatābād 46-47 M 5
Salamaua 52-53 N 8
Salamis 36-37 K 7
Salamīyah 46-47 G 5
Salamon-medence 52-53 h 6
Salamon-szigetek, ⊙ 52-53 h 6-k 7
Salamon-szigetek, ★ 52-53 kl 7
Salamon-tenger 52-53 hj 6
Salang = Ko Phuket 52-53 C 5
Salantai 30-31 J 9
Salatan, Cape – = Tanjung Selatan 52-53 F 7
Salatiga 52-53 F 8
Salavat 42-43 K 7
Salaverry 78-79 D 6
Salawati, Pulau – 52-53 K 7
Salazar = Ndalatando 64-65 DE 4
Saldanha [ZA] 64-65 E 9
Saldus 30-31 K 9
Sale [AUS] 56-57 J 7
Salé = Slā 60-61 C 2
Salé, Grand Lac – = Great Salt Lake 72-73 D 3
Salechard 42-43 M 4
Saleh, Teluk – 52-53 G 8
Şāleḥābād [IR ↖ Hamadān] 46-47 N 5
Şāleḥābād [IR ↙ Īlām] 46-47 M 6
Salem [IND] 44-45 M 8
Salem, FL 74-75 b 2
Salem, MA 74-75 H 3
Salem, NJ 74-75 F 5
Salem, OH 74-75 C 4
Salem, OR 72-73 B 2
Salem, VA 74-75 C 6
Salem, WV 74-75 C 5
Salemi 36-37 E 7
Sälen 30-31 E 7
Salentina 36-37 GH 5
Salerno 36-37 F 5
Salerno, Golfo di – 36-37 F 5
Salford 32 E 5
Salgótarjan 33 J 4
Salgueiro 78-79 M 6
Salibabu, Pulau – 52-53 J 6
Salida, CO 72-73 E 4
Şalīf, Aş- 44-45 E 7
Şāliḥīyah, Aş- [ET] 62 DE 2
Şāliḥīyah, Aş- [SYR] 46-47 J 5
Salihli 46-47 C 3
Salima 64-65 HJ 5
Şalīmah, Wāḥat – 60-61 K 4
Salina, KS 72-73 G 4
Salina, UT 76-77 H 6
Salina, Ìsola – 36-37 F 6
Salina, La – 76-77 G 10
Salina Cruz 72-73 G 8
Salinas [BR] 78-79 L 8
Salinas [EC] 78-79 C 5
Salinas, CA 72-73 B 4
Salinas, Cabo de – 34-35 J 9
Salinas, Punta de – 78-79 D 7
Salinas Grandes [RA ↖ Córdoba] 80 C 4-D 3
Salinas River 76-77 C 7-8
Saline Valley 76-77 E 7
Salinópolis 78-79 K 4-5
Salisbury 32 EF 6
Salisbury, CT 74-75 G 3-4
Salisbury, MD 72-73 LM 4
Salisbury, NC 72-73 KL 4
Salisbury = Harare 64-65 H 6
Salisbury, ostrov – = ostrov Salsberi 42-43 HJ 1
Salisbury Island 70-71 VW 5
Salish Mountains 76-77 F 1-2
Saljany 38-39 J 8
Šalkar 38-39 K 5
Šalkar, ozero – 38-39 K 5
Şalkhad 46-47 G 6
Salkum, WA 76-77 B 2
Salla 30-31 N 4
Salley, SC 74-75 C 8
Sallyana 44-45 N 5

214 Russk

Sal'm, ostrov − 42-43 KL 2
Salmah, Jabal − 44-45 E 5
Salmán, As- 46-47 L 7
Salmanlı 46-47 F 3
Salmanlı = Kaymas 46-47 D 2
Salmás 46-47 L 3
Salmi 42-43 E 5
Salmon, ID 76-77 FG 3
Salmon Creek Reservoir
76-77 F 4
Salmon Falls 76-77 F 4
Salmon Falls Creek Lake
76-77 F 4
Salmon Gums 56-57 D 6
Salmon River [USA, Idaho]
72-73 CD 2
Salmon River Mountains
72-73 C 3-D 2
Salo 30-31 K 7
Salomón [⊙] 52-53 h 6-k 7
Salomón [★] 52-53 kl 7
Salomon, Bassin des − 52-53 h 6
Salomon, Cuenca de las −
52-53 h 6
Salomon, Îles − [⊙] 52-53 h 6-k 7
Salomon, Îles − [★] 52-53 kl 7
Salomon, Mar de las − 52-53 hj 6
Salomon, Mer des − 52-53 hj 6
Salomona, Morze − 52-53 hj 6
Salomona, Wyspy − [⊙]
52-53 h 6-k 7
Salomona, Wyspy − [★]
52-53 kl 7
Salomonbekken 52-53 h 6
Salomonen, ⊙ 52-53 h 6-k 7
Salomonen, ★ 52-53 kl 7
Salomonenbecken 52-53 h 6
Salomonensee 52-53 hj 6
Salomonseilanden [⊙]
52-53 h 6-k 7
Salomonseilanden [★] 52-53 kl 7
Salomonzee 52-53 hj 6
Salonga 64-65 F 3
Salonga Nord, Parc national de la
− 64-65 F 3
Salonga Sud, Parc national de la
− 64-65 F 3
Salònica = Thessaloníkē
36-37 K 5
Salonika = Thessaloníkē
36-37 K 5
Saloniki = Thessaloníkē
36-37 K 5
Salonique = Thessaloníkē
36-37 K 5
Salonta 36-37 JK 2
Salor 34-35 D 9
Salpausselkä 30-31 L-O 7
Salsacate 80 CD 4
Salsberi, ostrov − 42-43 HJ 1
Sal'sk 38-39 H 6
Salso 36-37 E 7
Salsomaggiore Terme 36-37 C 3
Sal╪, As- 46-47 F 6
Salta [RA, ●] 80 CD 2
Salten 30-31 F 4-G 3
Saltfjord 30-31 EF 4
Salt Flat, TX 72-73 EF 5
Saltillo 72-73 FG 6
Salt Lake, NM 76-77 J 8
Salt Lake City, UT 72-73 D 3
Salt Lakes 56-57 D 5
Salt Marsh = Lake MacLeod
56-57 B 4
Salto [RA] 80 DE 4
Salto [ROU, ●] 80 E 4
Salto, El − 72-73 E 7
Salto da Divisa 78-79 LM 8
Salto Grande, Embalse − 80 E 4
Saltoluokta 30-31 H 4
Salton, CA 76-77 F 9
Salton Sea 72-73 CD 5
Salt River [USA, Arizona]
72-73 D 5
Salt River Indian Reservation
76-77 H 9
Saltspring Island 76-77 B 1
Saltville, VA 74-75 C 6
Saluda, SC 74-75 BC 7-8
Saluen 48-49 H 6
Saluen = Thanlwin Myit
52-53 C 2-3
Saluin = Thanlwin Myit
52-53 C 2-3
Salûm, As- 60-61 K 2
Saluzzo 36-37 B 3
Salvador 72-73 J 3
Salvador 78-79 M 7
Salwá Baḥrī 62 E 5
Salwador 72-73 J 9
Salween = Thanlwin Myit
52-53 C 2-3
Salwin = Thanlwin Myit
52-53 C 2-3
Salyání = Sallyana 44-45 N 5
Salzach 33 F 4-5
Salzbrunn 64-65 E 7
Salzburg [A, ●] 33 F 5
Salzburg [A, ☆] 33 F 5
Salzgitter 33 E 2-3
Salzwedel 33 E 2
Sam 38-39 L 6
Sama de Langreo 34-35 E 7

Samâh, Bi'r − 46-47 L 8
Samâlût 62 D 3
Samaná, Bahía de − 72-73 N 8
Samânalkanda 44-45 N 9
Samandağı 46-47 F 4
Samangân 44-45 K 3
Samani 48-49 R 3
Samar 52-53 J 4
Samara [SU, Rossijskaja SFSR ~]
42-43 J 7
Samara [SU, Rossijskaja SFSR ●]
42-43 HJ 7
Samarai 52-53 gh 7
Samarga 42-43 ab 8
Samarinda 52-53 G 7
Samarkand 44-45 K 3
Samarkand = Temirtau 42-43 N 7
Sâmarrâ' 44-45 E 4
Samâwah, As- 44-45 EF 4
Sambala 64-65 H 4
Sambaliung 52-53 G 6
Sambalpore = Sambalpur
44-45 N 6
Sambas 52-53 E 6
Sambava 64-65 M 5
Sambhal 44-45 M 5
Sambia 64-65 G 6-H 5
Samboja 52-53 G 7
Sambongi = Towada 50-51 N 2
Sambor 38-39 D 6
Sambor [K] 52-53 E 4
Samborombón, Bahía − 80 E 5
Sambre 34-35 K 3
Samch'ôk 48-49 OP 4
Samch'ônp'o 50-51 FG 5
Samdûng 50-51 F 3
Same [EAT] 64-65 J 3
Samfya 63 B 5
Samḥah 44-45 G 8
Samîm, Umm as- 44-45 H 6
Samnagjin 50-51 G 5
Samoa 52-53 c 1
Samoa, CA 76-77 A 5
Samoa, Îles − = Samoa Islands
52-53 c 1
Samoa, Wyspy − = Samoa
Islands 52-53 c 1
Samoainseln = Samoa Islands
52-53 c 1
Samoa Islands 52-53 c 1
Samora = Zamora de Hidalgo
72-73 F 7-8
Sámos [GR, ⊙] 36-37 M 7
Sámos [GR, ●] 36-37 M 7
Samosir, Pulau − 52-53 C 6
Samothráki 36-37 L 5
Sampacho 80 D 4
Sampang 52-53 F 8
Samper de Calanda 34-35 G 8
Sampit [SU] 52-53 F 7
Sampit, Teluk − 52-53 F 7
Samrah = Mazıdağı 46-47 J 4
Samrong 52-53 D 4
Samsø 30-31 D 10
Samsu 50-51 G 2
Samsun 44-45 D 2
Samter = Szamotuly 33 H 2
Samui, Ko − 52-53 D 5
Samur 38-39 J 7
Samutlu = Temelli 46-47 E 3
Samut Prakan 52-53 D 4
San 33 L 3
San [RMM] 60-61 CD 6
Sanâ [Y, Hadramawt] 44-45 FG 7
Şan'â' [Y, Tihâmah] 44-45 EF 7
Sana [YU] 36-37 G 3
Sanaag 60-61 b 2
Sânabâd 46-47 N 4
Şanabû 62 D 4
SANAE 24 b 36-1
Şanâfir, Jazîrat − 62 F 4
Sanaga 60-61 C 7
San Agustín [RA, Buenos Aires]
80 E 5
San Agustin, Cape − 52-53 J 5
Sanâm, As- 44-45 G 6
Sanâm, Jabal − 46-47 M 7
San Ambrosio 69 C 5
Sanana, Pulau − 52-53 J 7
Sanandaj 44-45 F 3
San Andreas, CA 76-77 C 6
San Andrés [CO, ⊙] 72-73 KL 9
San Andres Mountains 72-73 E 5
San Andres Tuxtla 72-73 GH 8
San Angel 78-79 E 2-3
San Angelo, TX 72-73 FG 5
San Anselmo, CA 76-77 B 7
San Antonio [RCH] 80 B 4
San Antonio, TX 72-73 G 6
San Antonio, Cabo − [C]
72-73 K 7
San Antonio de Caparo 78-79 E 3
San Antonio del Mar 76-77 E 10
San Antonio de los Cobres 80 C 2
San Antonio Oeste 80 CD 4
San Antonio Peak 76-77 E 8
San Ardo, CA 76-77 C 7
Sanâw 44-45 G 7
Sanbalpur = Sambalpur
44-45 N 6
San Benedetto del Tronto
36-37 EF 4

San Benedicto, Isla − 72-73 DE 8
San Benito, TX 72-73 G 6
San Benito Mountain 76-77 C 7
San Bernardino, CA 72-73 CD 5
San Bernardino Mountains
76-77 E 8
San Bernardo [RCH] 80 BC 4
San Blas, Cape − 72-73 J 6
San Blas, Cordillera de −
72-73 L 10
San Blas, Punta − 72-73 L 10
San Borja 78-79 F 7
San Buenaventura = Ventura, CA
76-77 D 8
San Carlos [RCH] 80 B 5
San Carlos [RP, Luzón]
52-53 GH 3
San Carlos [RP, Negros]
52-53 H 4
San Carlos [YV, Cojedes]
78-79 F 3
San Carlos, AZ 76-77 H 9
San Carlos, Estrecho de − =
Falkland Sound 80 DE 8
San Carlos Bay 74-75 bc 3
San Carlos de Bariloche 80 B 6
San Carlos de Bolívar 80 D 5
San Carlos de Puno 78-79 EF 8
San Carlos de Río Negro
78-79 F 4
San Carlos de Zulia 78-79 E 3
San Carlos Indian Reservation
76-77 HJ 9
San Carlos Lake 76-77 H 9
San Clemente, CA 76-77 E 9
San Clemente Island 72-73 BC 5
San Cristóbal [CO] 78-79 E 5
San Cristóbal [RA] 80 D 4
San Cristóbal [Solomons]
52-53 k 7
San Cristóbal [YV] 78-79 E 3
San Cristóbal, Isla − 78-79 B 5
San Cristóbal de las Casas
72-73 H 8
San Cristobal Wash 76-77 G 9
San Cristoval = San Cristóbal
52-53 k 7
Sancti-Spiritus [C] 72-73 L 7
Sand 30-31 AB 8
Sandai 52-53 F 7
Sandakan 52-53 G 5
Sandane 30-31 AB 7
Sandanski 36-37 K 5
Sanday 32 EF 2
Sandefjord 30-31 D 8
Sanders, AZ 76-77 J 8
Sandersville, GA 74-75 B 8
Sandfontein 64-65 EF 7
Sandhornøy 30-31 EF 4
Sandia 78-79 F 7
San Diego, CA 72-73 C 5
San Diego, Cabo − 80 CD 8
San Diego Aqueduct 76-77 E 9
Sandıklı 46-47 CD 3
Sand Key 74-75 b 3
Sand Mountains 72-73 J 5
Sandnes 30-31 A 8
Sandoa 64-65 F 4
Sandomierz 33 K 3
San Donà di Piave 36-37 E 3
Sandover River 56-57 FG 4
Sandpoint, ID 76-77 E 2
Sandringham 56-57 G 4
Sandstone 56-57 C 5
Sand Tank Mountains 76-77 G 9
Sandur 30-31 ab 2
Sandveld [Namibia] 64-65 EF 7
Sandviken 30-31 G 7
Sandwich del Sud, Fosse du −
24 D 34
Sandwich Południowy, Rów −
24 D 34
Sandwich del Sur, Dorsal de las
− 24 D 34
Sandy, NV 76-77 F 8
Sandy Cape [AUS, Queensland]
56-57 K 4
Sandy Cape [AUS, Tasmania]
58 ab 2
Sandy City, UT 72-73 D 3
Sandy Creek 76-77 J 4-5
Sandy Hills 72-73 GH 5
Sandy Hook 74-75 G 4
Sandy Key 74-75 c 4
Sandy Lake [CDN, ≈ Ontario]
70-71 S 7
Sandy Ridge 74-75 B 6
Sandy River 76-77 BC 3
San Estanislao 80 E 2
San Esteban de Gormaz
34-35 F 8
San Felipe [CO] 78-79 F 4
San Felipe [RCH] 80 B 4
San Felipe [YV] 78-79 F 2
San Felipe, Punta − 76-77 D 10
San Felipe de Puerto Plata =
Puerto Plata 72-73 M 8
San Felix de Guixols 34-35 J 8
San Félix [Desventurados] 69 B 5
San Félix [RCH] 69 BC 5
San Fernando [E] 34-35 D 10
San Fernando [RA] 80 E 4
San Fernando [RCH] 80 B 4

San Fernando [TT] 72-73 L 9
San Fernando [YV] 78-79 F 3
San Fernando, CA 76-77 D 8
San Fernando [RP ↘ Baguio]
52-53 GH 3
San Fernando [RP ↘ Manila]
52-53 H 3
San Fernando de Atabapo
78-79 F 4
San Fernando del Valle de
Catamarca 80 C 3
Sånfjället 30-31 E 6
Sanford, FL 72-73 K 6
Sanford, ME 74-75 H 3
Sanford, NC 74-75 D 7
San Francisco [RA] 80 D 4
San Francisco, CA 72-73 AB 4
San Francisco Bay 76-77 B 7
San Francisco de la Caleta
72-73 bc 3
San Francisco del Oro 72-73 E 6
San Francisco del Parapetí
78-79 G 8-9
San Francisco de Macorís
72-73 MN 8
San Francisco Peaks 76-77 GH 8
San Francisco Plateau
72-73 D 4-E 5
San Francisco River 76-77 J 9
San Francisco Solano, Punta −
78-79 D 3
Sangá 52-53 C 2
Sanga = Sangha 64-65 E 2-3
Sangagchhö Ling 48-49 G 6
Sangaly 38-39 H 3
Sangar 42-43 Y 5
Sangários = Sakarya Nehri
44-45 C 2
Sangasår 46-47 L 4
Sangay 78-79 D 5
Sangeang, Pulau − 52-53 GH 8
Sanger, CA 76-77 D 7
Sangha 64-65 E 2-3
Sanghaj = Shanghai 48-49 N 5
Sang-i Mâsha 44-45 K 4
Sangir, Kepulauan − 52-53 J 6
Sangir, Pulau − 52-53 J 6
Sangju 50-51 G 4
Sangkulirang 52-53 G 6
Sangkulirang, Teluk − 52-53 G 6
Sângli 44-45 LM 7
Sangmélima 60-61 G 8
Sangonera, Río − 34-35 G 10
Sangre, La − 76-77 H 10
Sangre de Cristo Range 72-73 E 4
Sangre Grande 72-73 OP 9
Sangue, Rio do − 78-79 H 7
Sangymgort 42-43 M 5
Sanibel Island 74-75 b 3
San Ignacio [PY] 80 E 3
San Ignacio [BOL ↗ La Paz]
78-79 F 7
San Ignacio [BOL ↗ Santa Cruz]
78-79 G 8
Saniquellie 60-61 C 7
San Isidro [RA] 80 E 4
Sanitatas 64-65 D 6
Saniyah, Hawr as- 46-47 M 7
San Jacinto, CA 76-77 E 9
San Jacinto Mountains 76-77 E 9
San Javier [BOL, Santa Cruz]
78-79 G 8
San Javier [RA, Misiones] 80 EF 3
San Jerónimo, Serranía de −
78-79 D 3
Sanjô 50-51 M 4
San Joaquín [BOL] 78-79 FG 7
San Joaquin River 72-73 BC 4
San Joaquin Valley 72-73 BC 4
San Jorge, Canal de − = Saint
George's Channel 32 C 6-D 5
San Jorge, Golfo − 80 CD 7
San Jorge, Golfo de − 34-35 H 8
San José [CR] 72-73 K 9-10
San Jose, UT 72-73 D 3
San José [GCA] 72-73 H 9
San José [PA] 72-73 b 3
San José [RP] 52-53 H 3
San Jose, CA 72-73 B 4
San José [ROU, ●] 80 E 4
San José, Isla − [MEX]
72-73 DE 6
San José, Isla − = Weddell
Island 80 DE 8
San José de Buenavista 52-53 H 4
San José de Chiquitos 78-79 G 8
San José de Chiquitos 78-79 G 8
San José de Jáchal 80 C 4
San José de las Salinas 80 CD 4
San José del Guaviare 78-79 E 4
San José de Ocuné 78-79 E 4
San Juan [PE] 78-79 DE 8
San Juan [Puerto Rico] 72-73 N 8
San Juan [RA, ●] 80 C 4
San Juan, Cabo − [Guinea
Ecuatorial] 60-61 F 8
San Juan, Cabo − [RA] 80 D 8

San Juan, Río − [NIC] 72-73 K 9
San Juan Archipelago 76-77 B 1
San Juan Bautista 34-35 H 9
San Juan Bautista 80 E 3
San Juan Bautista =
Villahermosa 72-73 H 8
San Juan de Guia, Cabo de −
78-79 DE 2
San Juan del Norte = Bluefields
72-73 K 9
San Juan del Norte, Bahía de −
72-73 K 9
San Juan de los Morros 78-79 F 3
San Juan Mountains 72-73 E 4
San Juan River 72-73 E 4
Sankisen 50-51 cd 2
Sankt Gallen 33 D 5
Sankt Georgs-Kanal = Saint
George's Channel 32 C 6-D 5
Sankt Gotthard 33 D 5
Sankt Michel = Mikkeli
30-31 MN 7
Sankt Moritz 33 DE 5
Sankt Pölten 33 G 4
Sankt-Peterburg 42-43 E 5-6
San Lázaro, Cabo − 72-73 D 7
Şanlı Urfa 44-45 D 3
San Lorenzo [EC] 78-79 D 4
San Lorenzo [PY] 80 E 3
San Lorenzo [RA, Santa Fe]
80 D 4
San Lorenzo [YV, Zulia] 78-79 E 3
San Lorenzo [BOL ↙ Riberalta]
78-79 F 7
San Lorenzo [BOL ↑ Tarija]
78-79 FG 9
San Lorenzo, Cabo de −
78-79 C 5
San Lorenzo, Cerro − 80 B 7
San Lorenzo, Isla − [PE]
78-79 D 7
San Lorenzo, Sierra de −
34-35 F 7
Sanlúcar de Barrameda
34-35 D 10
San Lucas, CA 76-77 C 7
San Lucas, Cabo − 72-73 E 7
San Luis [RA, ●] 80 C 4
San Luis, Sierra de − [YV]
78-79 EF 2
San Luis Obispo, CA 72-73 B 4
San Luis Obispo Bay 76-77 C 8
San Luís Potosí 72-73 FG 7
San Manuel, AZ 76-77 H 9
San Marco, Capo − 36-37 BC 6
San Marcos [RCH] 80 B 4
San Marcos, TX 72-73 G 6
San Marino [RSM, ●] 36-37 E 4
San Marino [RSM, ★] 36-37 E 4
San Martín [BOL] 78-79 G 8
San Martín [RA, La Rioja] 80 C 3
San Martín, Lago − 80 B 7
San Martín, Río − 78-79 G 8
San Mateo, CA 72-73 B 4
San Mateo Peak 72-73 E 5
San Matías, Golfo − 80 D 6
San-mên-hsia = Sanmenxia
48-49 L 5
Sanmenxia 48-49 L 5
San Miguel [ES] 72-73 J 9
San Miguel [MEX] 76-77 H 10
San Miguel, AZ 76-77 H 10
San Miguel, Río − [BOL]
78-79 G 7-8
San Miguel de Huachi 78-79 F 8
San Miguel del Monte 80 E 5
San Miguel de Tucumán 80 CD 3
San Miguel Island 76-77 C 8
San Miguelito [PA] 72-73 bc 3
San Miguel River 76-77 JK 6-7
Sannâr 60-61 L 6
San Narciso 52-53 GH 3
San Nicolás de los Arroyos 80 D 4
San Nicolas Island 72-73 BC 5
Sannikova, proliv − 42-43 ab 3
Sanniquellie = Saniquellie
60-61 C 7
Sannohe 50-51 N 2
Sannûr, Wâdî − 62 D 3
Sanok 33 L 4
San Pablo [RP] 52-53 H 4
San Pablo Bay 76-77 B 6
San Pedro [RA, Buenos Aires]
80 E 4
San Pedro [RA, Santiago del
Estero] 80 C 3
San Pedro [PY, ●] 80 E 2
San Pedro [BOL, Santa Cruz ↗
Santa Cruz] 78-79 G 8
San Pedro [BOL, Santa Cruz ↑
Trinidad] 78-79 G 7
San Pedro, Punta − [CR]
72-73 K 10
San Pedro, Sierra de − 34-35 D 9
San Pedro, Volcán − 78-79 F 9
San Pedro Channel 76-77 D 9
San Pedro de las Colonias
72-73 F 6
San Pedro de Macorís 72-73 N 8
San Pedro Channel 76-77 D 9

San Pedro Mártir, Sierra −
72-73 CD 5
San Pedro River 76-77 H 9
San Pedro Sula 72-73 J 8
San Pietro 36-37 BC 6
San Quintin, Cabo − 72-73 C 5
San Rafael [RA] 80 C 4
San Rafael, CA 72-73 B 4
San Rafael, Río − 76-77 EF 10
San Rafael del Encanto 78-79 E 5
San Rafael Mountains 76-77 CD 8
San Rafael River 76-77 H 6
San Rafael Swell 76-77 H 6
San Ramón de la Nueva Orán
80 CD 2
San Remo 36-37 BC 4
San Román, Cabo − 78-79 EF 2
San Rosendo 80 B 5
San Salvador [BS] 72-73 M 7
San Salvador [ES] 72-73 HJ 9
San Salvador, Isla − 78-79 A 5
San Salvador de Jujuy 80 CD 2
Sansanding 60-61 CD 6
Sansanné-Mango = Mango
60-61 E 6
San Sebastián 34-35 FG 7
San Sebastián [RA] 80 C 8
San Sebastián de la Gomera
60-61 A 3
San Severo 36-37 F 5
Sansibar = Zanzibar 64-65 JK 4
San Silvestre [YV] 78-79 EF 3
San Simeon, CA 76-77 C 8
San Simon, AZ 76-77 J 9
Sansing = Yilan 48-49 OP 2
Santa Ana [CO, Guainía] 78-79 F 4
Santa Ana [ES] 72-73 HJ 9
Santa Ana [MEX] 72-73 D 5
Santa Ana, CA 72-73 C 5
Santa Ana [BOL ↘ Trinidad]
78-79 F 7
Santa Ana Mountains 76-77 E 9
Santa Bárbara [MEX] 72-73 E 6
Santa Bárbara [RCH] 80 B 5
Santa Barbara, CA 72-73 BC 5
Santa Bárbara [YV ↙ Maturín]
78-79 G 3
Santa Bárbara [YV → San
Cristóbal] 78-79 E 3
Santa Bárbara [YV → San
Fernando de Atabapo]
78-79 F 4
Santa Bárbara, Serra de −
78-79 J 9
Santa Barbara Channel
76-77 CD 8
Santa Barbara Channel
76-77 CD 8
Santa Barbara Channel
76-77 CD 8
Santa Barbara Island 76-77 D 9
Santa Catalina [RA, Jujuy] 80 C 2
Santa Catalina = Catalina 80 C 3
Santa Catalina, Gulf of −
76-77 DE 9
Santa Catalina Island 72-73 BC 5
Santa Catarina 80 FG 3
Santa Catarina, Ilha de − 80 G 3
Santa Catarina, Valle de −
76-77 EF 10
Santa Clara [C] 72-73 KL 7
Santa Clara [CO] 78-79 EF 5
Santa Clara, CA 72-73 B 4
Santa Cruz [BR, Rio Grande do
Norte] 78-79 M 6
Santa Cruz [RA, Santa Cruz]
80 BC 7
Santa Cruz, CA 72-73 B 4
Santa Cruz [BOL, ●] 78-79 G 8
Santa Cruz, Îles − = Santa Cruz
Islands 52-53 l 7
Santa Cruz, Isla − [EC]
78-79 AB 5
Santa Cruz, Wyspy − = Santa
Cruz 52-53 l 7
Santa Cruz Cabrália 78-79 M 8
Santa Cruz de Barahona =
Barahona 72-73 M 8
Santa Cruz de la Palma 60-61 A 3
Santa Cruz de Tenerife 60-61 A 3
Santa Cruz do Sul 80 F 3
Santa-Cruz-Inseln = Santa Cruz
Islands 52-53 l 7
Santa Cruz Island 72-73 BC 5
Santa Cruz Islands 52-53 l 7
Santa Cruz Mountains 76-77 BC 7
Santa Cruz River 76-77 H 9
Santa Cruz-szigetek = Santa
Cruz Islands 52-53 l 7
Santa Elena [BOL] 78-79 G 9
Santa Elena [PE] 78-79 E 5
Santa Elena, Cabo − 72-73 K 9
Santa Elena de Uairén 78-79 G 4
Santa Fe, NM 72-73 E 4
Santa Fe [RA, ●] 80 D 4
Santa Fé do Sul 78-79 J 9
Santa Fe Pacific Railway 72-73 F 4
Santa Filomena 78-79 K 5
Santa Genoveva = Cerro las
Casitas 72-73 E 7
Santa Helena [BR, Maranhão]
78-79 K 5
Santa Helena [BR, Pará]
78-79 H 5-6
Santai 48-49 JK 5

Santa Inés [BR, Bahia] 78-79 LM 7
Santa Inés, Isla – 80 B 8
Santa Isabel [RA, La Pampa] 80 C 5
Santa Isabel [Solomon Is.] 52-53 jk 6
Santa Isabel = Malabo 60-61 F 8
Santa Isabel, Ilha Grande de – 78-79 L 5
Santa Isabel, Sierra – 76-77 F 10
Santa Isabel do Araguaia 78-79 K 6
Santa Isabel do Morro 78-79 J 7
Santa Lucia 72-73 O 8
Santa Lucia Range 76-77 C 7-8
Santaluz [BR, Bahia] 78-79 M 7
Santa Margarita, CA 76-77 C 8
Santa Margarita, Isla – 72-73 D 7
Santa Margherita Ligure 36-37 C 3
Santa Maria [BR, Amazonas] 78-79 H 5
Santa Maria [BR, Rio Grande do Sul] 80 EF 3
Santa Maria [PE, Loreto] 78-79 E 5
Santa Maria [RA] 80 C 3
Santa Maria [Vanuatu] 56-57 N 2
Santa Maria [Z] 63 B 5
Santa Maria, CA 72-73 B 5
Santa Maria, Cabo de – 34-35 CD 10
Santa Maria, Cabo de – = Cap Sainte-Marie 64-65 L 8
Santa María Asunción Tlaxiaco 72-73 G 8
Santa Maria das Barreiras 78-79 JK 6
Santa Maria de Ipire 78-79 F 3
Santa Maria di Leuca, Capo – 36-37 H 6
Santa Marta [CO] 78-79 DE 2
Santa Marta, Sierra Nevada de – 78-79 E 2
Santa Monica, CA 72-73 BC 5
Santana 78-79 L 7
Santana, Coxilha da – 80 E 3-F 4
Santana, Ilha de – 78-79 L 5
Santana do Livramento 80 EF 4
Santander 34-35 F 7
Santander [CO, Cauca] 78-79 D 4
Sant'Antioco [I, ⊙] 36-37 BC 6
Sant'Antioco [I, ●] 36-37 BC 6
Santañy 34-35 J 9
Santañy 34-35 J 9
Santa Paula, CA 76-77 D 8
Santa Pola, Cabo de – 34-35 GH 9
Santarém [BR] 78-79 J 5
Santarem [P] 34-35 C 9
Santaren Channel 72-73 L 7
Santaren Channel 72-73 L 7
Santaren Channel 72-73 L 7
Santa Rita [BR, Paraíba] 78-79 MN 6
Santa Rita [YV, Zulia] 78-79 E 2
Santa Rita, NM 76-77 E 3
Santa Rita do Araguaia 78-79 J 8
Santa Rito do Weil 78-79 F 5
Santa Rosa [BR, Acre] 78-79 EF 6
Santa Rosa [BR, Rio Grande do Sul] 80 F 3
Santa Rosa [CO, Guainía] 78-79 EF 4
Santa Rosa [PE] 78-79 E 5
Santa Rosa [RA, La Pampa] 80 CD 5
Santa Rosa [RA, Mendoza] 80 C 4
Santa Rosa [RA, San Luis] 80 C 4
Santa Rosa, CA 72-73 B 4
Santa Rosa [BOL, Beni ↘ Riberalta] 78-79 F 7
Santa Rosa de Copán 72-73 J 9
Santa Rosa del Palmar 78-79 G 8
Santa Rosa Island [USA, California] 72-73 B 5
Santa Rosalía [MEX] 72-73 D 6
Santa Rosa Range 76-77 E 5
Santa Rosa Wash 76-77 GH 9
Šantarskije ostrova 42-43 a 6-7
Santa Sylvina 80 DE 3
Santa Tecla = Nueva San Salvador 72-73 HJ 9
Santa Vitória do Palmar 80 F 4
Santa Ynez, CA 76-77 CD 8
Santee River 74-75 D 8
San Telmo 76-77 DF 10
Sant'Eufémia, Golfo di – 36-37 FG 6
Santiago [BR] 80 EF 3
Santiago [DOM] 72-73 M 7
Santiago [PA] 72-73 K 10
Santiago de Chile 80 B 4
Santiago de Chuco 78-79 D 6
Santiago de Cuba 72-73 L 7-8
Santiago de Chile 80 B 4
Santiago de Chuco 78-79 D 6
Santiago de Chile 80 B 4
Santiago de Chuco 78-79 D 6
Santiago del Estero [RA, ●] 80 CD 3
Santiago di Compostela 34-35 CD 7
Santiago Ixcuintla 72-73 EF 7
Santiagoma 78-79 H 8
Santiago Papasquiaro 72-73 EF 6-7

Santiam Pass 76-77 BC 3
Santigi 52-53 H 6
Santo 56-57 MN 3
Santo Amaro 78-79 M 7
Santo André 78-79 K 9
Santo André – Isla de San Andrés 72-73 KL 9
Santo Ângelo 80 EF 3
Santo António [São Tomé e Príncipe] 60-61 F 8
Santo Antônio, Cachoeira – [BR, Rio Madeira] 78-79 FG 6
Santo António de Jesus 78-79 LM 7
Santo António do Zaire = Soyo 64-65 D 4
Santo Corazón 78-79 H 8
Santo Domingo [DOM] 72-73 MN 8
Santo Domingo, Rio – [MEX] 72-73 G 8
Santo Domingo de Guzmán = Santo Domingo 72-73 MN 8
Santo Domingo Tehuantepec 72-73 G 8
Santoña 34-35 F 7
Santoña 34-35 F 7
Santoríni = Thếra 36-37 L 7
Santos 78-79 K 9
Santo Tomás [PE] 78-79 E 7
Santo Tomás, Punta – 76-77 E 10
Santo Tomé [RA, Corrientes] 80 E 3
Sanup Plateau 76-77 G 8
San Valentín, Cerro – 80 B 7
San Vicente 72-73 O 9
San Vicente [ES] 72-73 J 9
San Victor 80 E 4
San Vito, Capo – 36-37 E 6
San Xavier Indian Reservation 76-77 H 9-10
Sanya = Ya Xian 48-49 KL 8
San Yanaro 78-79 EF 4
San Ysidro, CA 76-77 D 8
Sanza Pombo 64-65 E 4
São Bernardo 78-79 L 5
São Borja 80 EF 3
São Carlos [BR, São Paulo] 78-79 K 9
São Domingos [Guiné-Bissau] 60-61 A 6
São Félix do Xingu 78-79 J 6
São Filipe 78-79 M 7
São Francisco, Rio – [BR, Pernambuco] 78-79 LM 6
São Francisco do Sul 80 G 3
São Gabriel 80 EF 4
São Gotardo 78-79 KL 8
Sao Hill 63 C 5
São Jerónimo, Serra de – 78-79 J 8
Sao João, Ilhas de – 78-79 L 5
São João do Piauí 78-79 L 6
São José do Rio Preto [BR, São Paulo] 78-79 JK 9
São José dos Campos 78-79 KL 9
São Luís 78-79 L 5
São Marcos, Baía de – 78-79 L 5
São Mateus [BR, Espírito Santo] 78-79 M 8
São Miguel do Araguaia 78-79 JK 7
São Miguel do Tapuio 78-79 L 6
Saona, Isla – 72-73 N 8
São Paulo [BR, ⊙] 20-21 H 5
São Paulo [BR, ☆] 78-79 JK 9
São Paulo de Olivença 78-79 F 6
São Raimundo Nonato 78-79 L 6
São Romão [BR, Amazonas] 78-79 F 6
São Romão [BR, Minas Gerais] 78-79 KL 8
São Roque, Cabo de – 78-79 N 6
São Sebastião, Ilha de – 78-79 KL 9
São Sebastião, Ponta – 64-65 J 7
São Simão, Represa de – 78-79 K 8
São Tomé [São Tomé e Príncipe] 60-61 F 8
São Tomé, Cabo de – 78-79 LM 9
São Tomé, Ilha – 60-61 F 8-9
São Tomé and Príncipe 60-61 F 8-9
São Tomé en Príncipe 60-61 F 8-9
São Tomé és Príncipe 60-61 F 8
São Tomé e Príncipe 60-61 F 8-9
São Tomé und Príncipe 60-61 F 8-9
São Tomé y Príncipe 60-61 F 8-9
Saoúira, eş – = Aş-Şawîrah 60-61 BC 2
Saoura, Ouèd – = Wâdî as-Sâwrah 60-61 D 2-3
São Vicente [BR, São Paulo] 78-79 K 9
São Vicente, Cabo de – 34-35 C 10
Sápai 56-57 L 5
Sapanjang, Pulau – 52-53 G 8
Sapateiro, Cachoeira do – 78-79 H 5
Sape [RI] 52-53 G 8

Sapele 60-61 EF 7
Sapelo Island 74-75 C 9
Šaphane Dağı 46-47 C 3
Sapiéntza 36-37 J 7
Saposoa 78-79 D 6
Sapphire Mountains 76-77 G 2-3
Sappho, WA 76-77 AB 1
Sapporo 48-49 QR 3
Sapri 36-37 F 5
Sapt Kosi 44-45 O 5
Sapudi, Pulau – 52-53 FG 8
Sapulpa, OK 72-73 G 4
Sapwe 63 B 5
Saqasiq, Es- = Az-Zaqazîq 60-61 KL 2
Sâqîyat al-Ḥamrâ', As- 60-61 B 3
Saqqârah 62 D 3
Saqqez 44-45 F 3
Sarab 38-39 K 9
Sarâb [IR, Ādharbayejân-e Khâvarî] 46-47 M 4
Saraburi 52-53 D 4
Sarafutsu 50-51 c 1
Saragossa = Zaragoza 34-35 G 8
Saragossa 78-79 D 5
Sarajevo 36-37 H 4
Sarala 42-43 Q 7
Saramati 44-45 P 5
Saran' [SU, Kazachskaja SSR] 42-43 N 8
Saranac Lake, NY 74-75 F 2
Saranda 63 C 4
Sarandë 36-37 HJ 6
Sarandi del Yí 80 EF 4
Sarangani Bay 52-53 HJ 5
Sarangani Islands 52-53 HJ 5
Saranlay = Sarinleey 60-61 N 8
Saranpaul' 42-43 L 5
Saransk 42-43 GH 7
Saránta Ekklēsíes = Kırklareli 44-45 B 3
Sarapul 42-43 J 6
Sarapul'skoje 42-43 a 8
Sararât Sayyâl, Bi'r – 62 F 6
Sarâksand = Hashtrûd 46-47 M 4
Sarasota, FL 72-73 K 6
Saratoga Springs, NY 72-73 M 3
Saratov 38-39 HJ 5
Saratovskoje vodochranilišče 38-39 J 5
Saratovskoje vodochranilišče 38-39 J 5
Sarâvân [IR] 44-45 J 5
Saravan [LAO] 52-53 E 3
Sarawak 52-53 F 6
Saray 46-47 B 2
Sarâyah 46-47 F 5
Sarayköy 46-47 C 4
Sarayönü 46-47 E 3
Sarayú = Ghaghara 44-45 N 5
Sâr Cham 46-47 MN 4
Sâr Cham 46-47 MN 4
Sardaigne = Sardegna 36-37 C 5
Sardalas 60-61 G 3
Sardarshahar = Sardârshahr 44-45 L 5
Sardârshahr 44-45 L 5
Sar Dasht [IR, Khûzestân] 46-47 N 6
Sar Dasht [IR, Kordestân] 46-47 L 4
Sardegna 36-37 C 5
Sardes 46-47 C 3
Sardinia = Sardegna 36-37 C 5
Sardinien = Sardegna 36-37 C 5
Sardis, GA 74-75 BC 8
Sard Rûd 46-47 LM 3
Sare 63 C 3
Sarek nationalpark 30-31 GH 4
Sarektjåkko 30-31 G 4
Sar-e Pol-e Dhahâb 46-47 LM 5
Sare Pul 44-45 K 5
Sargasové moře 72-73 N-P 6
Sargasses, Mer des – 72-73 N-P 6
Sargasso Sea 72-73 N-P 6
Sargassosee 72-73 N-P 6
Sargasso-tenger 72-73 N-P 6
Sargassowe, Morze – 72-73 N-P 6
Sargassozee 72-73 N-P 6
Sárga-tenger 48-49 N 4
Sargazos, Mar de los – 72-73 N-P 6
Sargho, Djebel – = Jabal Şaghrû 60-61 C 2
Sargoda = Sargodhā 44-45 L 4
Sargodhā 44-45 L 4
Sargon, Dur – = Khorsabad 46-47 K 4
Sarh 60-61 H 7
Sarḩadd 44-45 L 3
Şarhrö', Jbel – = Jabal Şaghrû' 60-61 C 2
Sâr Cham 46-47 MN 4
Sârî 44-45 G 3
Sariá 36-37 M 8
Sâric 76-77 H 10
Sarıgöl 46-47 C 3
Sarıkamış 46-47 K 2
Sarıkavak 46-47 E 4
Sarıkavak = Kumluca 46-47 D 4

Sarıkaya 46-47 F 3
Sarıkaya = Gömele 46-47 D 2
Sarikei 52-53 F 6
Sarina 56-57 J 4
Sarinleey 60-61 N 8
Sarıoğlan 46-47 FG 3
Sarir 60-61 J 3
Sarī Tappah 46-47 KL 5
Sariwŏn 48-49 O 4
Sariyar Barajı 46-47 D 2
Sarıyer, İstanbul- 46-47 C 3
Sarız = Köyyeri 46-47 G 3
Şarja 42-43 H 6
Sarjū = Ghaghara 44-45 N 5
Sark 32 E 7
Sarki-fennsik 24 A 31-6
Sarkî Karaağaç 46-47 D 3
Şarkışla 46-47 G 3
Šarkovščina 30-31 MN 10
Šarkovskij 38-39 F 4
Sarlat 34-35 H 6
Sarmi 52-53 L 7
Sarmiento 80 BC 7
Sär mörön 48-49 MN 3
Särna 30-31 E 7
Sarneh 46-47 M 6
Sarnen 36-37 C 3
Sarnia 70-71 U 9
Sarolangun 52-53 D 7
Saroma-ko 50-51 c 1
Saronikós Kólpos 36-37 K 7
Saros Körfezi 46-47 B 2
Sarpa 38-39 J 6
Šar Planina 36-37 J 4-5
Sarpsborg 30-31 D 8
Sar Qal'ah 46-47 L 5
Sarrah, Ma'tan as- 60-61 J 4
Sarre, la – 70-71 V 8
Sarrebourg 34-35 L 4
Sarreguemines 34-35 L 4
Sarria 34-35 D 7
Sarro, Djebel – – = Jabal Şaghrû 60-61 C 2
Šar Süm = Altay 48-49 F 2
Sartang 42-43 Z 4
Sartène 36-37 C 5
Sarthe 34-35 G 5
Sârû, Jabal – 60-61 C 2
Saruhan = Manisa 44-45 B 2
Saruhanlı 46-47 B 3
Sârûq Chây 46-47 M 4
Sârûq Chây 46-47 M 4
Sârûq Chây 46-47 M 4
Saruyama-zaki 50-51 L 4
Sarvar 46-47 J 4
Sarvestân 46-47 N 7
Sarych, mys – 38-39 F 7
Sarych, mys – 38-39 F 7
Saryesik-Atyrau 42-43 O 8
Sarykamyšskaja kotlina 38-39 L 7
Sarykamyšskaja kotlina 38-39 L 7
Sâryngol 48-49 K 2
Saryozek 42-43 O 9
Sarysu 42-43 M 8
Saryšagan 42-43 N 8
Sarytaš 38-39 K 7
Sary-Taš [SU, Tadžikskaja SSR] 44-45 L 3
Sarytaš 38-39 K 7
Sary-Taš [SU, Tadžikskaja SSR] 44-45 L 3
Sasebo 48-49 O 5
Saskatchewan 70-71 PQ 6-7
Saskatchewan River 70-71 Q 7
Saskatoon 70-71 P 7
Saskylach 42-43 VW 3
Sason 46-47 J 3
Sasovo 38-39 H 5
Sassafras Mountain 74-75 B 7
Sassandra [CI, ~] 60-61 C 7
Sassandra [CI, ●] 60-61 C 7-8
Saşşnitz 33 FG 1
Sastobe 42-43 MN 9
Sasyk, ozero – 36-37 NO 3
Sasykkol', ozero – 42-43 P 8
Sata 50-51 H 5
Satadougou 60-61 B 6
Satakunta 30-31 JK 7
Sata-misaki 48-49 OP 5
Satara 44-45 L 7
Satawal 52-53 N 5
Satilla River 74-75 C 9
Satipo 78-79 DE 7
Satırlar = Yeşilova 46-47 C 4
Satka 42-43 KL 6
Satlaj 44-45 L 5
Satlaj = Langchhen Khamba 48-49 DE 5
Sátoraljaújhely 33 K 4
Satpura Range 44-45 L-N 6
Satsuma-hantō 50-51 GH 7
Sattahip 52-53 D 4
Satna 44-45 N 5
Saţţaţ 60-61 C 2
Satu Mare 36-37 K 2
Sâr Cham 46-47 MN 4
Sauce [RA] 80 E 3-4
Sauda 30-31 B 8
Sauda, Jebel el – = Jabal as-Sawdâ 60-61 GH 3
Saûde 78-79 L 7
Saudhárkrókur 30-31 d 2
Saudi-Arabia 44-45 D 5-F 6
Saudi-Arabien 44-45 D 5-F 6

Saúdská Arábie 44-45 D 5-F 6
Saugeen River 74-75 C 2
Saugerties, NY 74-75 FG 3
Saugor = Sagar 44-45 M 6
Sáújbolágh = Mahâbâd 44-45 F 3
Saukorem 52-53 K 7
Saûl 78-79 J 4
Saul'der 42-43 M 9
Sault-Sainte-Marie 70-71 U 8
Sault Sainte Marie, MI 72-73 JK 2
Saumlaki 52-53 K 8
Saumur 34-35 G 5
Şauqirah, Ghubbat – = Dawḥat as-Sawqirah 44-45 H 7
Saura, Wed – = Wâdî Sâwrah 60-61 D 2-3
Saurâshtra 44-45 KL 6
Saurimo 64-65 F 4
Sausalito, CA 76-77 B 7
Sautar 64-65 E 5
Sauzal, El – 76-77 E 10
Sava 36-37 J 3
Savage River 58 b 2
Savai'i 52-53 c 1
Savalou 60-61 E 7
Savannah, GA 72-73 KL 5
Savannah Beach, GA 74-75 C 8
Savannah River 72-73 K 5
Savannakhêt 52-53 DE 3
Savari = Sabari 44-45 N 7
Savaştepe 46-47 B 3
Savè [DY] 60-61 E 7
Save [F] 34-35 H 7
Save, Rio – 64-65 H 7
Sâveh 44-45 G 3-4
Savigliano 36-37 BC 3
Savo 30-31 M 6-7
Savoie 34-35 L 5-6
Sâvojbolâgh = Mahâbâd 44-45 F 3
Savona 36-37 C 3
Savonlinna 30-31 N 7
Savu = Pulau Sawu 52-53 H 9
Savu, Mer de – 52-53 H 8
Savukoski 30-31 N 4
Savur 46-47 J 4
Savu Sea 52-53 H 8
Savu, Pulau – 52-53 H 9
Sawahlunto 52-53 D 7
Sawâb, Wâdî aş- 46-47 J 5
Sawâkin 60-61 M 5
Sawara 50-51 N 5
Sawata 50-51 M 3-4
Sawdâ, Jabal as- 60-61 GH 3
Sawdirî 60-61 K 6
Sawḥaṭ 60-61 H 3
Şawîrah, Aş- 60-61 BC 2
Sawknah 60-61 GH 3
Sawqirah 44-45 H 7
Sawqirah, Dawḥat as- 44-45 H 7
Şawrah, Aş- 62 F 4
Sâwrah, Wâdî – 60-61 D 2-3
Sawtooth Mountains 76-77 FG 3-4
Sawtooth Range 76-77 C 1-2
Sawu, Mar de – 52-53 H 8
Sawu, Morze – 52-53 H 8
Sawu, Pulau – 52-53 H 9
Sawusee 52-53 H 8
Sawuské moře 52-53 H 8
Sawu-tenger 52-53 H 8
Sawuzee 52-53 H 8
Şawwân, 'Ard aş- 46-47 G 7
Saxton, PA 74-75 DE 4
Say 60-61 E 6
Sayaboury = Muang Xaignabouri 52-53 D 3
Saya de Malha Bank 64-65 O 5
Şaydâ [RL] 44-45 CD 4
Sayhût 44-45 G 7
Saykh, Jabal aş- 46-47 FG 6
Sayn Shanda = Sajnšand 48-49 KL 3
Sayo = Dembî Dolo 60-61 LM 7
Şayq, Wâdî – 44-45 F 8
Sayre, PA 74-75 E 4
Say'ün 44-45 F 7
Sazanit 36-37 H 5
Sâzîn 46-47 N 5
Sba, Wad – = Nahr Sîbû 60-61 CD 2
S'bû, Wâd – = Nahr Sîbû 60-61 CD 2
Scafell Pike 32 E 4
Scalloway 32 F 1
Scandinavie 28-29 K 4-N 1
Scandinavie 28-29 K 4-N 1
Scapa Flow 32 E 2
Scappoose, OR 76-77 B 3
Scarborough 32 FG 4
Scarborough [TT] 72-73 OP 9
Ščeglovsk = Kemerovo 42-43 PQ 6
Scerpeddi, Punta – 36-37 C 6
Schaffhausen 33 D 5
Schäßburg = Sighişoara 36-37 L 2
Schaulen = Šiauliai 30-31 K 10
Schebschi Mountains 60-61 G 7
Schefferville 70-71 X 7

Schelde 34-35 J 3
Schell Creek Range 76-77 F 6
Schemnitz = Banská Štiavnica 33 J 4
Schenectady, NY 72-73 LM 3
Schiza 36-37 J 7
Schlawe in Pommern = Sławno 33 H 1
Schlesien 33 G-J 3
Schleswig 33 DE 1
Schleswig-Holstein 33 D 1-E 2
Schlüchtern 33 DE 3
Schmidt Island = ostrov Šmidta 42-43 QR 1
Schneekoppe = Sniežka 33 GH 3
Schneidemühl = Piła 33 H 2
Schotland 32 D 3-E 4
Schottland 32 D 3-E 4
Schouten Island 58 d 3
Schouwen 34-35 J 3
Schrag, WA 76-77 D 2
Schroda = Środa Wielkopolska 33 HJ 2
Schuckmannsburg 64-65 F 6
Schurz, NV 76-77 D 6
Schüttenhofen = Sušice 33 F 4
Schwabach 33 E 4
Schwäbische Alb 33 D 5-E 4
Schwäbisch Gmünd 33 DE 4
Schwäbisch Hall 33 DE 4
Schwandorf 33 F 4
Schwaner, Pegunungan – 52-53 F 7
Schwarze Elster 33 FG 3
Schwarzer Volta = Black Volta 60-61 D 7
Schwarzes Meer 38-39 E-G 7
Schwarzwald 33 D 4-5
Schwatka Mountains 70-71 EF 4
Schweden 30-31 F 9-J 10
Schweidnitz = Świdnica 33 H 3
Schweinfurt 33 E 3
Schweitzergletscher 24 B 32-33
Schweiz 33 CD 5
Schweizer Land 70-71 d 4
Schwerin 33 E 2
Schwerin (Warthe) = Skwierzyna 33 G 2
Schwetz = Świecie 33 HJ 2
Schwiebus = Świebodzin 33 K 2
Schwyz 33 D 5
Sciacca 36-37 E 7
Scicli 36-37 F 7
Scilly, Isles of – 32 C 7
Scipio, UT 76-77 G 6
Scone 58 K 4
Scoresby Land 19 B 21
Scoresby Sund [Grønland, ∪] 19 B 20-21
Scoresbysund [Grønland, ●] 19 B 20-21
Scotia, CA 76-77 AB 5
Scotia, Dorsal del – 22-23 G 8
Scotia, Seuil de la – 22-23 G 8
Scotia Ridge 22-23 G 8
Scotiarücken 22-23 G 8
Scotiarug 22-23 G 8
Scotland 32 D 3-E 4
Scotland Neck, NC 74-75 E 6
Scotstown 74-75 H 2
Scott 24 B 17-18
Scott, Cape – 70-71 L 7
Scott, Mount – [USA → Crater Lake] 72-73 B 3
Scott, Mount – [USA ↓ Pengra Pass] 76-77 BC 4
Scott Glacier [Antarktika, Dronning Maud fjellkjede] 24 A 21-23
Scott Glacier [Antarktika, Knox Land] 24 C 11
Scott Inlet 70-71 WX 3
Scott Island 24 C 19
Scott Range 24 C 5-6
Scott Reef 56-57 E 2
Scottsbluff, NE 72-73 F 3
Scottsdale 56-57 J 8
Scottsville, VA 74-75 D 6
Scranton, PA 72-73 LM 3
Ščučě = 38-39 N 7
Ščučinsk 42-43 MN 7
Scunthorpe 32 FG 5
Scutari = İstanbul-Üsküdar 44-45 BC 2
Scythopolis = Bet-Shēan 46-47 F 6

Schaffhausen 33 D 5
Scalloway 32 F 1
Schelde 34-35 J 3
Schell Creek Range 76-77 F 6
Schenectady, NY 72-73 LM 3
Schíza 36-37 J 7
Schleswig 33 DE 1
Schleswig-Holstein 33 D 1-E 2
Schlüchtern 33 DE 3
Schmidt Island = ostrov Šmidta 42-43 QR 1
Schotland 32 D 3-E 4
Schouten Island 58 d 3
Schouwen 34-35 J 3
Schrag, WA 76-77 D 2
Schuckmannsburg 64-65 F 6
Schurz, NV 76-77 D 6

Schwabach 33 E 4
Schwäbische Alb 33 D 5-E 4
Schwäbisch Gmünd 33 DE 4
Schwäbisch Hall 33 DE 4
Schwandorf 33 F 4
Schwaner, Pegunungan – 52-53 F 7
Schwarze Elster 33 FG 3
Schwarzer Volta = Black Volta 60-61 D 7
Schwarzes Meer 38-39 E-G 7
Schwarzwald 33 D 4-5
Schwatka Mountains 70-71 EF 4
Schweinfurt 33 E 3
Schweitzergletscher 24 B 32-33
Schweizer Land 70-71 d 4
Schwerin 33 E 2
Schwyz 33 D 5

Seaford, DE 74-75 F 5
Seaham 32 F 4
Sea Islands 72-73 K 5
Sea Lake 58 F 5
Sea Lion Islands 80 E 8
Seal River 70-71 R 6
Searchlight, NV 76-77 F 8
Searles Lake 76-77 E 8
Searsport, ME 74-75 J 2
Seaside, CA 76-77 C 7
Seaside, OR 76-77 B 3
Seaside Park, NJ 74-75 FG 5
Seattle, WA 72-73 B 2
Sebâ', Gebel es- = Qârat as-Sab'ah 60-61 H 3
Sebago Lake 74-75 H 3
Sebangau, Teluk – 52-53 F 7
Sebangka, Pulau – 52-53 DE 6
Sebastian, FL 74-75 c 3
Sebastian, Cape – 76-77 A 4
Sebastián Vizcaíno, Bahía – 72-73 CD 6
Sebastopol, CA 76-77 B 6
Sebatik, Pulau – 52-53 G 6
Seben 46-47 D 2
Sebeş 36-37 K 2-3
Sebes Körös 33 K 5
Sebḥa = Sabhah 60-61 G 3
Şebinkarahisar 46-47 H 2
Sebring, FL 74-75 c 3
Sebta = Ceuta 60-61 CD 1
Sebuku, Pulau – 52-53 G 7
Sebuku, Teluk – 52-53 G 6
Seburi-yama 50-51 H 6
Secen Chaan = Öndörchaan 48-49 L 2
Secen Chaan = Öndörchaan 48-49 L 2
Secen Chaan = Öndörchaan 48-49 L 2
Sechuan = Sichuan 48-49 J 5-6
Sechura 78-79 C 6
Sechura, Bahía de – 78-79 C 6
Secunderabad 44-45 M 7
Sedan 34-35 K 4
Sedan [AUS] 56-57 G 6
Seddonville 56-57 O 8
Sedel'nikovo 42-43 O 6
Sédhiou 60-61 AB 6
Šedok 38-39 H 7
Sĕdōm 46-47 F 7
Sedona, AZ 76-77 H 8
Sedov, Fosse – 19 A
Sedova, pik – 42-43 J 3
Sedovdiep 19 A
Sedow, Fosa de – 19 A
Sedow-mélység 19 A
Sedowtiefe 19 A
Seeheim [Namibia] 64-65 E 8
Seeis 64-65 E 7
Seeley Lake, MT 76-77 G 2
Şefaatli 46-47 F 3
Sefadu = Koidu-Sefadu 60-61 B 7
Seferihisar 46-47 B 3
Sefīd, Kūh-e – 46-47 M 5-N 6
Sefīd Rūd 46-47 N 4
Sefton, Restinga de – 69 BC 6
Segedin = Szeged 33 J 5
Segedín = Szeged 33 J 5
Segendy 38-39 K 7
Segesta 36-37 E 7
Segesvár = Sighişoara 36-37 L 2
Segeža 42-43 EF 5
Segeža 42-43 EF 5
Segguedim = Séguédine 60-61 G 4
Sego, UT 76-77 J 6
Segorbe 34-35 G 9
Ségou 60-61 C 6
Šegovary 38-39 H 3
Segovia 34-35 E 8
Segovia, Río – = Río Coco 72-73 K 9
Segozero 38-39 F 3
Segré 34-35 G 5
Segre, Río – 34-35 H 8
Segu = Ségou 60-61 C 6
Séguédine 60-61 G 4
Séguéla 60-61 C 7
Seguin, TX 72-73 G 6
Segura, Río – 34-35 G 9
Segura, Sierra de – 34-35 F 9-10
Sehirköy = Şarköy 46-47 B 2
Sehit Nusretbey 46-47 H 4
Seiland 30-31 K 2
Seinäjoki 30-31 K 6
Seine 34-35 H 4
Seine, Baie de la – 34-35 G 4
Seishin = Ch'ŏngjin 48-49 OP 3
Seishū = Ch'ŏngju 48-49 O 4
Seistan = Sīstān 44-45 J 4
Seiyit, Sararāt – = Bi'r Sararāt Sayyāl 62 F 6
Sejm 38-39 F 5
Sejmčan 42-43 d 5
Sejmčan 42-43 d 5
Sejny 33 L 1
Sejrī, Bīr – = Bi'r Sajarī 46-47 H 6
Seke 64-65 F 2
Sekenke 64-65 H 3
Šeki 38-39 J 7
Sekiu, WA 76-77 A 1
Sekondi-Takoradi 60-61 D 7-8
Šelagskij, mys – 42-43 gh 3
Selah, WA 76-77 C 2
Sēlam = Salem 44-45 M 8
Selaru, Pulau – 52-53 K 8
Selatan, Tanjung – 52-53 F 7
Selawik, AK 70-71 DE 4
Selawik Lake 70-71 DE 4
Selayar, Pulau – 52-53 H 8
Selbu 30-31 D 6
Selby 32 F 5
Seldovia, AK 70-71 F 6
Selemdža 42-43 YZ 7
Selemdža 42-43 YZ 7
Selemiyé = Salamīyah 46-47 G 5
Selendi 46-47 C 3
Selenge [MVR, ●] 48-49 J 2
Selenge [MVR, ☆ = 11 ◁] 48-49 K 2
Selenge mörön 48-49 J 2
Selenn'ach 42-43 a 4
Selenodolsk = Zelenodol'sk 42-43 HJ 6
Sélestat 34-35 L 4
Seletyteniz, ozero – = ozero Siletiteniz 42-43 N 7
Seleucia = Silifke 44-45 C 3
Seleucia Pieria = Samandağ 46-47 F 4
Selĕvkeia = Silifke 44-45 C 3
Selfoss 30-31 c 3
Šelichova, zaliv – 42-43 e 5-6
Seliger, ozero – 38-39 F 4
Seligman, AZ 76-77 G 8
Selim 46-47 K 2
Selīma, Wâḥat es – = Wāḥat Şalīmah 60-61 K 4
Selimiye 46-47 B 4
Seling Tsho 48-49 FG 5
Selinus 36-37 E 7
Seliphug Gonpa 48-49 E 5
Seljord 30-31 C 8
Selkirk [CDN] 70-71 R 7
Selkirk Mountains 70-71 N 7-8
Selleck, WA 76-77 C 2
Sells, AZ 76-77 H 10
Selma, AL 72-73 J 5
Selma, CA 76-77 D 7
Selma, NC 74-75 D 7
Selous Game Reserve 64-65 J 4
Selukwe 64-65 H 6
Selva 80 D 3
Selvagens, Ilhas – 60-61 A 2
Selvas 69 DE 3
Selway River 76-77 F 2
Selwyn 56-57 H 4
Selwyn Mountains 70-71 KL 5
Selwyn Range 56-57 GH 4
Seman 36-37 H 5
Semarang 52-53 F 8
Semau, Pulau – 52-53 H 9
Sembodja = Samboja 52-53 G 7
Şemdinli 46-47 L 4
Semenanjung 52-53 K 7
Semeru, Gunung – 52-53 F 8
Semeuluë, Pulau – = Pulau Simeulue 52-53 BC 6
Semeyen = Simēn 60-61 M 6
Semipalatinsk 42-43 OP 7
Semirara Islands 52-53 H 4
Semka = Sangā 52-53 C 2
Semmering 33 GH 5
Semnān [IR, ●] 44-45 G 3
Semnan [IR, ☆] 44-45 GH 3
Semois 34-35 K 4
Šemonaicha 42-43 P 7
Sem'onov 38-39 H 4
Semu 63 C 3
Senador Pompeu 78-79 LM 6
Senaisla = Sunaysilah 46-47 J 5
Sena Madureira 78-79 F 6
Şenanga 64-65 F 6
Šenber 42-43 M 8
Sendai [J, Kagoshima] 50-51 GH 7
Sendai [J, Miyagi] 48-49 R 4
Sene = Pru 60-61 D 7
Seneca, OR 76-77 D 3
Seneca, SC 74-75 B 7
Seneca Falls, NY 74-75 E 3
Seneca Lake 74-75 E 3
Senegal 60-61 AB 6
Sénégal 60-61 AB 6
Sénégal [SN, ~] 60-61 B 5
Sénégal [SN, ★] 60-61 AB 6
Sengejskij, ostrov – 42-43 HJ 4
Sengge Khamba 48-49 DE 5
Sengilej 38-39 J 5
Sengwe 64-65 G 6
Senhor do Bonfim 78-79 L 7
Senigállia 36-37 E 4
Senījān 46-47 N 5
Senirkent 46-47 D 3
Senj 36-37 F 3
Senja 30-31 G 3
Senjang = Shenyang 48-49 NO 3
Senkaku-shotō 48-49 N 6
Senkaku syotō = Senkaku-shotō 48-49 N 6
Šenkursk 42-43 G 5
Senlis 34-35 J 4
Senmonorom 52-53 E 4
Sennār = Sannār 60-61 L 6
Seno 52-53 DE 3
Sens 34-35 J 4
Senta 36-37 HJ 3
Sentery 64-65 G 4
Sentinel, AZ 76-77 G 9
Sentinel Range 24 B 28
Sento-Sé 78-79 L 6
Şenyurt 46-47 J 4
Seo de Urgel 34-35 H 7
Seoni 44-45 M 6
Seoul = Sŏul 48-49 O 4
Separ, NM 76-77 J 9
Separation Well 56-57 D 4
Separ Shāhābād 46-47 MN 5
Šepetovka 38-39 E 5
Sepik River 52-53 M 7
Sepone 52-53 E 3
Sepopa 64-65 F 6
Sep'o-ri 50-51 F 3
Sept-Îles 70-71 X 7-8
Sequim, WA 76-77 B 1
Sequoia National Park 72-73 C 4
Serachs 44-45 J 3
Şerafettin Dağları 46-47 J 3
Seram [RI] 52-53 JK 7
Seram, Mar de – 52-53 JK 7
Seram, Mer de – 52-53 JK 7
Seram, Morze – 52-53 J 7
Seram-Laut, Kepulauan – 52-53 K 7
Serampore 44-45 O 6
Seramsee 52-53 J 7
Seramské moře 52-53 J 7
Seram-tenger 52-53 J 7
Seramzee 52-53 JK 7
Serang 52-53 E 8
Serâyâ = Sarāyah 46-47 F 5
Serbia 36-37 H 3-J 4
Serbia 36-37 H 3-J 4
Serbie 36-37 H 3-J 4
Serbien 36-37 H 3-J 4
Serbka 36-37 O 2
Serdar = Kaypak 46-47 G 4
Serdéles = Sardalas 60-61 G 3
Serdobsk 38-39 HJ 5
Serebr'ansk 42-43 P 8
Serefiye 46-47 G 2
Şereflikoçhişar 46-47 E 3
Seremban 52-53 D 6
Serena, La – [E] 34-35 E 9
Serena, La – [RCH] 80 B 3
Serengeti National Park 64-65 HJ 3
Serengeti Plain 63 C 3
Serenje 64-65 GH 5
Sergeja Kirova, ostrova – 42-43 QR 2
Sergijev Posad 42-43 F 6
Serginskij 42-43 LM 5
Sergiopolis = Riṣāfah 46-47 H 5
Sergipe 78-79 M 7
Seria 52-53 F 6
Seribu, Kepulauan – 52-53 E 7-8
Sérifos 36-37 L 7
Serik 46-47 D 4
Seringa, Serra da – 78-79 J 6
Şerkaly 42-43 M 5
Šerlovaja Gora 42-43 W 7
Sermata, Pulau – 52-53 J 8
Sermilik 70-71 d 4
Serov 42-43 L 6
Serowe 64-65 G 7
Serpa 34-35 D 10
Serpa Pinto = Menongue 64-65 E 5
Serpeddì, Punta – 36-37 C 6
Serpiente, Boca de la – 78-79 G 2-3
Serpuchov 38-39 G 5
Serra Geral [BR, Santa Catarina] 80 F 3
Serra Geral [BR, Rio Grande do Sul ↖ Porto Alegre] 80 F 3
Sérrai 36-37 K 5
Serrana Bank = Banco Serrana 78-79 CD 2
Serra Talhada 78-79 M 6
Serrezuela 80 C 4
Serrinha [BR ↑ Feira de Santana] 78-79 M 7
Sertânia 78-79 M 6
Sertão 78-79 L 7-M 6
Serua, Pulau – 52-53 K 8
Serule 64-65 G 7
Serxü 48-49 H 5
Sese Islands 64-65 H 3
Sesepe 52-53 J 7
Sesfontein 64-65 D 6
Sesheke 64-65 FG 6
Sesimbra 34-35 C 9
Sessa Aurunca 36-37 EF 5
Sestroreck 42-43 DE 5
Seszele 64-65 CD 3
Setana 48-49 Q 3
Sète 34-35 J 7
Sētēia 36-37 M 8
Sete Quedas, Salto das – [BR, Rio Teles Pires] 78-79 H 6
Setermoen 30-31 H 3
Setesdal 30-31 B 8
Sétif = Saṭīf 60-61 F 1
Seto 50-51 L 5
Seto-naikai 48-49 P 5
Seṭṭāt = Saṭṭāt 60-61 C 2
Setté Cama 64-65 C 3
Sette-Daban, chrebet – 42-43 a 5
Setúbal 34-35 C 9
Setúbal, Baía de – 34-35 C 9
Seuil Neo-zélandais 56-57 M 5-7
Seuil Sibérien Oriental 19 B 36-1
Seul = Sŏul 48-49 O 4
Seul, Lac – 70-71 S 7
Sevan 38-39 H 7
Sevan, ozero – 38-39 J 7
Sevastopol' 38-39 F 7
Seven Emu 56-57 G 3
Seven Islands = Sept-Îles 70-71 X 7-8
Severn 32 E 6
Severnaja 42-43 QR 4
Severnaja Dvina 42-43 G 5
Severnaja Semlja = Severnaja Zeml'a 42-43 ST 1-2
Severnaja Sos'va 42-43 L 5
Severnaja Zeml'a 42-43 ST 1-2
Severní Borneo = Sabah 52-53 G 5
Severní Irsko 32 C 4
Severní ledový oceán 19 AB 32-5
Severní moře 32 F-J 3
severní pól 19 A
Severní Rhodésie = Zambie 64-65 G 6-H 5
Severní středoatlantský hřbet 56-57 C 2
Severnoje [SU ↑ Samara] 42-43 O 6
Severn River 70-71 T 6-7
Severnyj 42-43 LM 4
Severnyj čink = Donyztau 42-43 K 8
Severnyj čink = Donyztau 42-43 K 8
Severnyje uvaly 42-43 HJ 5-6
Severnyj Ural 42-43 K 5-6
Severobajkal'sk 44-45 UV 6
Severo-Bajkal'skoje nagorje 42-43 UV 6
Severodoneck 38-39 GH 6
Severodvinsk 42-43 FG 5
Severofidžijská pánev 56-57 O 3
Severofríské o-vy 33 D 1
Severo-Jenisejskij 42-43 RS 5
Severo-Kuril'sk 42-43 de 7
Severoosetinská AR 38-39 H 7
Severo-Sibirskaja nizmennost' 42-43 P-X 3
Severouralsk 38-39 LM 3
Severozápadní teritoria = Northwest Territories 70-71 M-U 4
Sevier Desert 76-77 G 6
Sevier Lake 76-77 G 6
Sevier River 72-73 D 4
Sevierville 74-75 B 7
Sevilla 34-35 E 10
Sevlievo 36-37 L 4
Sèvre 34-35 G 5
Sevsib 42-43 M 6
Sewa 60-61 B 7
Seward, AK 70-71 G 5-6
Seward Peninsula 70-71 CD 4
Sewell, Lake – = Canyon Ferry Reservoir 76-77 H 2
Sewilla = Sevilla 34-35 E 10
Seychellen 64-65 L-N 4
Seychellen 64-65 L-N 4
Seychelles 66 M 8
Seychelle-szigetek 64-65 LM 4
Seychelles 64-65 L-N 4
Seydhisfjördhur 30-31 fg 2
Seydişehir 46-47 D 4
Seyhan = Adana 44-45 D 3
Seyhan Nehri 44-45 D 3
Seychely 64-65 LM 4
Seyitgazi 46-47 D 3
Seyla' = Saylac 60-61 N 6
Seymour [AUS] 58 G 6
Seymour, IN 72-73 JK 4
Seyne-sur-Mer, la – 34-35 K 7
Sezze 36-37 E 5

Sfax = Şafāqis 60-61 FG 2
Sfîntu Gheorghe 36-37 LM 3
Sfîntu Gheorghe, Braţul – 36-37 N 3
Sfîre = Safīrah 46-47 G 4
Sfoûk = Sufūq 46-47 J 4

Sha Alam 52-53 D 6
Shaanxi 48-49 K 4-5
Shaba 64-65 FG 4
Shabakah, Ash- [IRQ, ≅] 46-47 K 7
Shabakah, Ash- [IRQ, ●] 46-47 K 7
Shabani = Zvishavane 64-65 GH 7
Shabb, Ash- 62 C 6
Shabeelle, Webi – 60-61 N 8
Shabellaha Dhexe = 5 ◁ 60-61 b 3
Shabellaha Hoose = 3 ◁ 60-61 b 3
Shabēlle, Webi – = Wabē Shebelē Weniz 60-61 N 7
Shabunda 64-65 G 3
Shabwah 44-45 F 7
Shackleton Ice Shelf 24 C 10
Shackleton Inlet 24 A 19-17
Shackleton Range 24 A 35-1
Shādegān 46-47 N 7
Shafter, CA 76-77 D 8
Shafter, NV 76-77 F 5
Shag Rocks 80 H 8
Shaguotun 50-51 C 2
Shāh, Godār-e – 46-47 MN 5
Shahabad [IND, Maisuru] 44-45 M 7
Shaḥāmī 46-47 H 6
Shāhān, Kūh-e – 46-47 LM 5
Shaḥan, Wādī – = Wādī Shiḥan 44-45 G 7
Shahbā 46-47 G 6
Shahbā', Ḥarrat ash- 46-47 G 6-7
Shahdād 44-45 H 4
Shahdād, Namakzār-e – 44-45 H 4
Shāhī 44-45 G 3
Shāhī 38-39 K 8
Shahidulla Mazar 48-49 D 4
Shahpura 44-45 L 5
Shahrak 44-45 J 4
Shahr-e Bābak 44-45 GH 4
Shahredā 44-45 G 4
Shahr-e Kord 44-45 G 4
Shahrestānbāla 46-47 NO 4
Shāh Rūd [IR, ~] 46-47 NO 4
Shāhrūd [IR, ●] 44-45 GH 3
Shāhzand 46-47 N 6
Shā'ib al-Banāt, Jabal – 60-61 L 3
Sha'īt, Wādī – 62 E 5
Shajahanpur 44-45 MN 5
Shajianzi 50-51 E 2
Shaka, Ras – 63 E 3
Shakar Bolāghī = Qara Būteh 46-47 M 4
Shakh yar 48-49 E 3
Shaki 60-61 E 7
Shakir, Jazīrat – 60-61 LM 3
Shakotan misaki 50-51 b 2
Shāl 46-47 N 5
Shalaamboot 60-61 N 8
Shala Hayik 60-61 M 7
Shalar, Nahr – 46-47 L 5
Shalar Rūd = Nahr Shalar 46-47 L 5
Shallāl, Ash- [ET, ~] 60-61 L 3
Shallāl, Ash- [ET, ●] 60-61 L 3
Shallotte, NC 74-75 D 7-8
Shāmah, Ash- = Al-Ḥarrah 46-47 GH 7
Shamālī, Ash- 60-61 KL 5
Shāmbā 60-61 L 7
Shāmīyah, Ash- 46-47 L 7
Shammar, Jabal – 44-45 E 5
Shamo = Gobi 48-49 H-K 3
Shamokin, PA 74-75 E 4
Shamrock, FL 74-75 b 2
Shāmshīr = Pāveh 46-47 M 5
Shamva 64-65 H 6
Sha'nabī, Jabal ash- 60-61 F 1-2
Shanchengzhen 50-51 EF 1
Shandan 48-49 J 4
Shandī 60-61 L 5
Shandish, MI 74-75 AB 3
Shandong 48-49 M 4
Shandong Bandao 48-49 MN 4
Shangani 64-65 G 6
Shangbangcheng 50-51 B 2
Shang-chia-ho = Shangjiahe 50-51 E 2
Shang-ch'iu = Shangqiu 48-49 LM 5
Shangchuan Dao 48-49 L 7
Shangcigang = Beijingzi 50-51 DE 3
Shanghai 48-49 N 5
Shanghang 48-49 M 6-7
Shanghsien = Shang Xian 48-49 KL 5
Shangjao = Shangrao 48-49 M 6
Shangjiahe 50-51 E 2
Shangkiu = Shangqiu 48-49 LM 5
Shangqiu 48-49 LM 5
Shangrao 48-49 M 6
Shang Xian 48-49 KL 5
Shangzhi 48-49 O 2
Shanhaiguan 48-49 MN 3
Shan-hai-kuan = Shanhaiguan 50-51 BC 2
Shan-hsi = Shaanxi 48-49 L 4-5
Shaniko, OR 76-77 C 3
Shannon 32 B 5
Shannon Airport 32 B 5
Shannon Ø 19 B 20
Shannontown, SC 74-75 CD 8
Shan Pyinnei 52-53 C 2
Shanshan 48-49 G 3
Shansi = Shanxi 48-49 L 4
Shan-tan = Shandan 48-49 J 4
Shantou 48-49 M 7
Shantow = Shantou 48-49 M 7
Shantung = Shandong 48-49 M 4
Shanwa 63 C 3
Shanxi 48-49 L 4
Shanyin 48-49 L 4
Shaoguan 48-49 L 6-7
Shaohsing = Shaoxing 48-49 N 5-6
Shaotze = Wan Xian 48-49 K 5
Shaowu 48-49 M 6
Shaoxing 48-49 N 5-6
Shaoyang 48-49 L 6
Shaqlāwah 46-47 L 4
Shaqqar 60-61 C 3
Shaqrā' 44-45 F 5
Shār, Jabal – [Saudi-Arabien] 62 F 4
Shā'r, Jabal – [SYR] 46-47 GH 5
Sharafkhāneh 46-47 LM 3
Sharāh, Ash- 46-47 F 7
Sharbithāt, Rā's ash- 44-45 H 7
Sharbot Lake 74-75 E 2
Shari 50-51 d 2
Shari = Chari 60-61 H 6
Shārī', Bahr ash- = Buhayrat Shārī 46-47 L 5
Shārī, Buhayrat – 46-47 L 5
Sharī'ah, Nahr ash- 46-47 F 6-7
Shārib, Ma'tan – 62 C 2
Shari-dake 50-51 d 2
Shāriqah, Ash- 44-45 GH 5
Shark Bay 56-57 B 5
Sharmah, Ash- 62 F 3-4
Sharmah, Wādī ash- = Wādī Şadr 62 F 3
Sharm ash-Shaykh 62 F 4
Sharm esh-Sheikh = Sharm ash-Shayh 62 F 4
Shar Mörön = Chatan gol 48-49 K 3
Sharon, PA 72-73 KL 3
Sharqāṭ, Ash- 46-47 K 5
Sharqī, Ash- 60-61 GH 6
Sharqī, Ash-Shaṭṭ ash- 60-61 DE 2
Sharqi, Jebel esh- = Jabal Lubnān ash-Sharqī 46-47 G 5-6
Sharrukīn, Dur – = Khorsabad 46-47 K 4
Shāsh, 'Irq ash- 60-61 D 3-4
Shashemenē 60-61 M 7
Shashi 48-49 L 5-6
Shasta, Mount – 72-73 B 3
Shasta Lake 76-77 B 5
Shaṭrah, Ash- 46-47 LM 7
Shau = Wādī Huwār 60-61 K 5
Shaubak, Esh- = Ash-Shawbak 46-47 F 7
Shawatun = Shaguotun 50-51 C 2
Shawbak, Ash- 46-47 F 7
Shawinigan Sud 70-71 W 8
Shawnee, OK 72-73 G 4
Shaw River 56-57 C 4
Shāwshāw, Jabal – 62 C 5
Shawville 74-75 E 2
Sha Xian 48-49 M 6
Shaykh Aḥmad 46-47 J 4
Shaykh Hilāl 46-47 G 5
Shaykh Sa'd 46-47 M 6
Shaykh Şalāh 46-47 J 4
Shaykh 'Uthmān, Ash- 44-45 EF 8
Shayōg = Shyog 44-45 M 3-4
Shāzī, Wādī ash- 46-47 J 7
Shea 78-79 H 4
She'aiba, Ash- = Ash-Shu'aybah 46-47 M 7
Sheaville, OR 76-77 E 4
Shebelē Weniz, Webī – 60-61 N 7
Sheboygan, WI 72-73 J 3
Sheenjek River 70-71 H 4
Sheep Peak 76-77 F 7
Sheep Range 76-77 F 7
Sheffield [AUS] 58 c 2
Sheffield [GB] 32 F 5
Shefoo = Yantai 48-49 N 4
Sheḥamī = Shaḥāmī 46-47 H 6
Shê-hsien = She Xian [TJ, Anhui] 48-49 M 5-6
Shekhar Dsong 48-49 F 6
Shelār 46-47 N 6
Shelburne [CDN, Ontario] 74-75 CD 2
Shelburne Bay 56-57 H 2
Shelby, MT 76-77 H 1
Shelby, NC 72-73 K 4
Shelikof Strait 70-71 EF 6
Shell Creek [USA, Colorado] 76-77 J 5
Shelley, ID 76-77 GH 4
Shellharbour, Wollongong- 56-57 K 6
Shelter Cove, CA 76-77 A 5
Shelton, WA 76-77 B 2
Shenāfiya, Ash- = Ash-Shinātīyah 46-47 L 7
Shenandoah, PA 74-75 EF 4
Shenandoah, VA 74-75 D 5
Shenandoah Mountains 74-75 D 5
Shenandoah National Park 74-75 DE 5
Shenandoah River 74-75 DE 5
Shendam 60-61 FG 7

Shend 217

Sinai = Sīnā' 60-61 L 3
Sinai, Peninsula de − − Sīnā' 60-61 L 3
Sinaï, Presqu'île du − = Sīnā' 60-61 L 3
Sinaihalbinsel = Sīnā' 60-61 L 3
Sinai Peninsula = Sīnā' 60-61 L 3
Sinaj, poloostrov − = Sīnā' 60-61 L 3
Sinaloa 72-73 E 6-7
Sinan 48-49 K 6
Sinanju 50-51 E 3
Sinanpaşa 46-47 CD 3
Sinaüen = Sināwan 60-61 G 2
Sināwan 60-61 G 2
Sinbillâwayn, As- 62 DE 2
Sincan 46-47 GH 3
Sincanlı = Sinanpaşa 46-47 CD 3
Sincelejo 78-79 DE 3
Sinch'ang 50-51 G 2
Sinch'ang-ni 50-51 F 3
Sincheng = Xingren 48-49 K 6
Sinch'ŏn 50-51 E 3
Sincik 46-47 H 3
Sinclair, Lake − 74-75 B 8
Sind 44-45 M 5
Sind = Sindh 44-45 K 5
Sinda = Sindh 44-45 K 5
Sindangbarang 52-53 E 8
Sindelfingen 33 D 4
Sindh 44-45 K 5
Sındıran = Yenice 46-47 E 3
Sındırğı 46-47 C 3
Sin-do 50-51 D 1-2
Šindy = Sajmak 44-45 L 3
Sinelnikovo 38-39 G 6
Sines 34-35 C 10
Sines, Cabo de − 34-35 C 10
Singah = Sinjah 60-61 L 6
Si-ngan = Xi'an 48-49 K 5
Singapore 52-53 DE 6
Singapore, Strait of − 52-53 DE 6
Singapour 52-53 DE 6
Singapur 52-53 DE 6
Singaraja 52-53 E 8
Singatoka 52-53 a 2
Sing Buri 52-53 D 3-4
Singen 33 D 5
Singida 64-65 H 3
Singkawang 52-53 E 6
Singkep, Pulau − 52-53 DE 7
Singkil 52-53 C 7
Singleton 56-57 K 6
Singleton, Mount − 56-57 F 4
Singora = Songkhla 52-53 D 5
Sin'gosan 50-51 F 3
Singtai = Xingtai 48-49 L 4
Sin'gye 50-51 F 3
Sińhbhūm = Singhbhum 44-45 NO 6
Sin-hiang = Xinxiang 48-49 LM 4
Sinhsien = Xin Xian 48-49 L 4
Sining = Xining 48-49 J 4
Siniscola 36-37 CD 5
Sinjah 60-61 L 6
Sinjai 52-53 GH 8
Sinjär 46-47 J 4
Sinjār, Jabal − 46-47 JK 4
Sin-kalp'ajin 50-51 F 2
Sinkât 60-61 M 5
Sinkiang = Xinjiang 48-49 L 4
Sinkiang = Xinjiang Uygur Zizhiqu 48-49 D-F 3
Sinkiang, Autonomes Gebiet − = Xinjiang Uygur Zizhiqu 48-49 D-F 3
Sinlo = Xinle 48-49 LM 4
Sinmak 50-51 F 3
Sinmi-do 50-51 E 3
Sinmin = Xinmin 50-51 D 1-2
Sinnamary [Französisch-Guyana, ●] 78-79 J 3
Sinneh = Sanandaj 44-45 F 3
Sińnhabhūm = Singhbhum 44-45 NO 6
Sinnûris 62 D 3
Sinnyŏng = Sillyŏng 50-51 G 4
Sinoe = Greenville 60-61 C 7-8
Sinola = Chinhoyi 64-65 GH 6
Sinop 44-45 D 2
Sinope = Sinop 44-45 D 2
Sinoquipe 76-77 H 10
Sin'p'o 48-49 O 3-4
Sinquim = Xi'an 48-49 K 5
Sinsiang = Xinxiang 48-49 LM 4
Sintang 52-53 F 6
Sint Eustatius 72-73 O 8
Sint Helenabaai 64-65 E 9
Sintjiang = Xinjiang Uygur Zizhiqu 48-49 D-F 3
Sint Luciameer 64-65 H 8
Sintra 34-35 C 9
Sintra [BR] 78-79 G 6
Sintsai = Xincai 48-49 LM 5
Sinwŏn-ni 50-51 E 3
Sinyang = Xinyang 48-49 LM 5
Sinzyô = Shinjô 48-49 QR 4
Sió 33 J 5
Sioma 64-65 F 6
Sion 33 C 5
Sioux City, IA 72-73 GH 3
Sioux Falls, SD 72-73 G 3
Sioux Lookout 70-71 S 7
Šipčenski prohod 36-37 LM 4
Siphaqeni 64-65 GH 9

Siping 48-49 N 3
Sipitang 52-53 G 5-6
Siple, Mount − 24 B 24
Sipolilo = Chiporiro 64-65 H 6
Sipora, Pulau = Pulau Sipura 52-53 C 7
Sip Sông Châu Thai 52-53 D 2
Sip Sông Châu Thai 52-53 D 2
Sip Sông Châu Thai 52-53 D 2
Sipura, Pulau − 52-53 C 7
Siquijor Island 52-53 H 5
Siquisique 78-79 F 2
Šira [SU] 42-43 QR 7
Sira [N, ~] 30-31 B 8
Sira [N, ●] 30-31 B 8
Siracuas 36-37 D 2
Siracusa 36-37 F 7
Šir'ajevo 36-37 O 2
Siran 46-47 H 2
Sir Edward Pellew Group 56-57 G 3
Siret [R, ~] 36-37 M 3
Siret [R, ●] 36-37 M 2
Sirhān, Wādī as- 44-45 D 4
Siria 44-45 D 4
Sirirskaja ravnina 42-43 L-P 5-6
Sir James MacBrien, Mount − 70-71 KL 5
Sīrjän 44-45 H 5
Sırkıntı 46-47 F 4
Şırnak 46-47 K 4
Sirr, Nafūd as- 44-45 E 5-F 6
Sirsa 44-45 LM 5
Sirte = Khalīj Surt 60-61 H 2
Sirte, Gulf of − = Khalīj Surt 60-61 H 2
Sir Thomas, Mount − 56-57 EF 5
Sirtica = As-Surt 60-61 H 2-3
Şirvan 46-47 K 3
Sīrvän, Rūd-e − 46-47 M 5
Sirwän 46-47 LM 5
Sirwän, Ābi − 46-47 L 5
Sirya = Zeytinlik 46-47 JK 2
Sisak 36-37 G 3
Si Sa Ket 52-53 D 3-4
Sishen 64-65 F 8
Sisimiut 70-71 Za 4
Siskiyou, OR 76-77 B 4
Siskiyou Mountains 76-77 B 4-5
Sisophon 52-53 D 4
Sīstän 44-45 J 4
Sīstän, Daryācheh − 44-45 HJ 4
Sīstän va Balūchestān 44-45 H 4-J 5
Sistema Iberico 34-35 F 7-H 8
Sisteron 34-35 K 6
Sisters, OR 76-77 C 3
Sithônia 36-37 K 5-6
Sitio da Abadia 78-79 K 7
Sitka, AK 70-71 J 6
Sitkaing 52-53 C 2
Sitkaing Taing 52-53 B 2-C 1
Šitkino 42-43 S 6
Sittwe 52-53 B 2
Siunī = Seoni 44-45 M 6
Siuslaw River 76-77 B 4
Siut = Asyūt 60-61 L 3
Sivaki 42-43 Y 7
Sīvand 44-45 G 4
Sivas 44-45 D 3
Sivaslı 46-47 C 4
Šiveluč, vulkan − 42-43 f 6
Siverek 46-47 H 4
Sivrice 46-47 H 3
Sivrihisar 46-47 D 3
Sivučij, mys − 42-43 fg 6
Sivučij, mys − 42-43 fg 6
Sīwah, Wāhat − 60-61 K 3
Siwālik Range 44-45 M 4-N 5
Siwni = Seoni 44-45 M 6
Siyäh Chaman 46-47 M 4
Siyäh Chaman 46-47 M 4
Siyäh Chaman 46-47 M 4
Siyäl, Jazā'ir − 62 G 6
Siyälkot 44-45 LM 4
Sizilien = Sicilia 36-37 EF 7
Sjam = Tajlandia 52-53 CD 3
Sjöbo 30-31 EF 10
Sjøvegan 30-31 GH 3
Sjuøyane 30-31 I 4
Skadarsko jezero 36-37 H 4
Skadovsk 36-37 P 2
Skagafjardhar 30-31 d 2
Skagafjördhur 30-31 c 1-d 2
Skagen 30-31 D 9
Skagerrak 30-31 B 9-D 8
Skagit River 76-77 C 1
Skagway, AK 70-71 JK 6
Skaland 30-31 G 3
Skålar 30-31 f 1
Skálholt 30-31 cd 2
Skaliste, Góry − = Rocky Mountains 70-71 L 5-P 9
Skalistyi Golec, gora − 42-43 WX 6
Skalnaté hory = Rocky Mountains 70-71 L 5-P 9
Skanderborg 30-31 CD 8
Skandinavien 28-29 K 4-N 1
Skåne 30-31 E 10
Skanör 30-31 E 10
Skara 30-31 E 8

Skaraborg 30-31 EF 8
Skardü 44-45 M 3
Skarżysko-Kamienna 33 K 3
Skarżysko-Kamienna 33 K 3
Skeena Mountains 70-71 L 6
Skeena River 70-71 L 6
Skegness 32 G 5
Skeidharársandur 30-31 e 3
Skellefteå 30-31 J 5
Skellefte älv 30-31 H 5
Skelleftehamn 30-31 JK 5
Skene 30-31 E 9
Skerki, Banco − 36-37 D 7
Skerki, Iavice - 36-37 D 7
Skerkibank 36-37 D 7
Ski 30-31 D 8
Skiathos 36-37 K 6
Skidaway Island 74-75 C 9
Skien 30-31 C 8
Skierniewice 33 K 3
Skikda = Sakīkdah 60-61 F 1
Skipskjølen 30-31 NO 2
Skive 30-31 C 9
Skjalfandafljót 30-31 e 2
Skjálfandi 30-31 e 1
Skjervøy 30-31 J 2
Skjold 30-31 H 3
Sklad 30-31 M 4
Sklavenflußl 70-71 O 5-6
Sklavenküste 60-61 E 7
Skobelev = Fergana 44-45 L 2-3
Skócia 32 D 3-E 4
Skógafoss 30-31 cd 3
Skolpen, Banc de − 42-43 F 3
Skolpen, Banco de − 42-43 F 3
Skolpenbank 42-43 F 3
Skolpen Bank 42-43 F 3
Skolpen-pad 42-43 F 3
Skolpen-pad 30-31 Q 2
Skönvik 30-31 G 6
Skópelos 36-37 K 6
Skopin 38-39 G 5
Skopje 36-37 J 4-5
Skotsko 32 D 3-E 4
Skövde 30-31 EF 8
Skovorodino 42-43 XY 7
Skowhegan, ME 74-75 J 2
Skukuza 64-65 H 8
Skul'any 36-37 M 2
Skull Valley, AZ 76-77 G 8
Skull Valley Indian Reservation 76-77 G 5
Skuodas 30-31 JK 9
Skuratova, mys − 42-43 LM 3
Skutari, İstanbul- = İstanbul-Üsküdar 44-45 BC 2
Skutskär 30-31 GH 7
Skwierzyna 33 G 2
Skye 32 C 3
Skykomish, WA 76-77 C 2
Skyring, Seno − 80 B 8
Skyrópula 36-37 KL 6
Skýros 36-37 L 6
Slå 60-61 C 2
Slagelse 30-31 D 10
Slagnäs 30-31 H 5
Slancy 30-31 N 8
Slänic 36-37 L 3
Slatina 36-37 L 3
Slatoust = Zlatoust 42-43 K 6
Slav'anka 50-51 H 1
Slav'ansk 38-39 G 6
Slav'ansk-na-Kubani 38-39 G 6
Slave 70-71 O 5-6
Slave Coast 60-61 E 7
Slavenkust 60-61 E 7
Slave River 70-71 O 5-6
Slavgorod [SU, Rossijskaja SFSR] 42-43 O 7
Slavkov u Brna 33 H 4
Slavonija 36-37 GH 3
Slavonska Požega 36-37 GH 3
Slavonska Požega 36-37 GH 3
Slavonski Brod 36-37 GH 3
Sławno 33 H 1
Sleetmute, AK 70-71 E 5
Slezsko 33 GH 3
Slide Mountain 74-75 F 3
Sliema 36-37 F 8
Sligeach = Sligo 32 B 4
Sligo 32 B 4
Slite 30-31 H 9
Sliten = Zlītan 60-61 GH 2
Sliven 36-37 M 4
Slivnica 36-37 K 4
Slobodčikovo 38-39 J 3
Slobodčikovo 38-39 J 3
Slobodskoj 42-43 HJ 6
Slobodzeja 36-37 NO 2
Slobozia 36-37 M 3
Slonim 38-39 E 5
Slot, The − 52-53 j 6
Slough 32 F 5
Sloūk = Sulūk 46-47 H 4
Slovákia 33 JK 4
Slovakia 33 JK 4
Slovaquie 33 JK 4
Slovenia 36-37 F 3-G 2
Slovénie 36-37 F 3-G 2
Slovenské rudohorie 33 JK 4
Slovensko 33 JK 4
Slovenija 36-37 F 3-G 2

Slovinsko 36-37 F 3-G 2
Slowaakse Republiek 33 H-K 4
Slowakei 33 JK 4
Slowenien 36-37 F 3-G 2
Sluck 38-39 E 5
Sl'ud'anka 42-43 T 7
Slunj 36-37 F 3
Słupsk 33 H 1
Sławno 33 H 1
Słowacka Republika 33 JK 4
Słowenia 36-37 F 2
Słupsk 33 H 1
Småland 30-31 EF 9
Small, ID 76-77 G 3
Small Point 74-75 J 3
Smallwood Rèservoir 70-71 Y 7
S'marah 60-61 B 3
Smederevo 36-37 J 3
Smedjebacken 30-31 G 7
Smela 38-39 F 6
Smeru = Gunung Semeru 52-53 F 8
Smethport, PA 74-75 D 4
Šmidta, ostrov − 42-43 QR 1
Smiley, Cape − 24 B 29
Smiltene 30-31 LM 9
Smith [CDN] 70-71 O 6-7
Smith Arm 70-71 M 4
Smithers 70-71 L 7
Smithfield, NC 74-75 D 7
Smithfield, UT 76-77 H 5
Smithfield, VA 74-75 E 6
Smith Island [CDN] 70-71 V 5
Smith Island [USA] 74-75 E 8
Smith River 76-77 H 2
Smith River, CA 76-77 A 5
Smiths Creek Valley 76-77 E 6
Smith's Falls 70-71 V 9
Smiths Ferry, ID 76-77 EF 3
Smith Sound 70-71 W 2
Smithton 56-57 HJ 8
Smithtown 58 L 3
Smoke Creek Desert 76-77 D 5
Smoky Bay 58 A 4
Smoky Cape 58 L 3
Smoky Hill River 72-73 FG 4
Smoky Mountains 76-77 F 4
Smoky River 70-71 N 7
Smøla 30-31 B 6
Smol'an 36-37 L 5
Smolensk 38-39 F 5
Smólikas 36-37 J 5
Smoot, WY 76-77 H 4
Smyrna = İzmir 44-45 B 3
Smyrne = İzmir 44-45 B 3
Snaefell [GB] 32 D 4
Snæfell [IS] 30-31 f 2
Snæfellsjökull 30-31 ab 2
Snæfellsnes 30-31 b 2
Snag 70-71 HJ 5
Snake Range 76-77 F 6
Snake River [USA ◁ Columbia River] 72-73 C 2
Snake River Canyon 76-77 E 3
Snake River Plains 72-73 D 3
Snake Valley 76-77 G 6
Snåsa 30-31 E 5
Šniardwy, Jezioro − 33 K 2
Sniezka 33 GH 3
Snieżka 33 GH 3
Snigir'ovka 38-39 F 6
Snøhetta 30-31 C 6
Snohomish, WA 76-77 BC 2
Snoqualmie Pass 76-77 C 2
Snota 30-31 C 6
Snøtind 30-31 E 4
Snowdon 32 DE 5
Snowdrift 70-71 OP 5
Snowflake, AZ 76-77 H 8
Snow Hill, MD 74-75 F 5
Snow Hill Island 24 C 31
Snow Road 74-75 E 2
Snowshoe Peak 76-77 F 1
Snowtown 58 CD 4
Snowville, UT 76-77 G 5
Snowy, Mount − 74-75 F 3
Snowy River 58 J 6
Snyder, TX 72-73 F 5

Soalala 64-65 KL 6
Soanierana-Ivongo 64-65 LM 6
Soan-kundo 50-51 E 3
Soap Lake, WA 76-77 D 2
Soasiu 52-53 J 6
Soavinandriana 64-65 L 6
Sôbât, Nahr − = As-Sūbāt 60-61 L 7
Sobi jezero 70-71 Q 6
Sobolevo [SU, p-ov Kamčatka] 42-43 e 7
Sobo-zan 50-51 H 6
Sobozo 60-61 GH 4
Sobrado [BR] 78-79 J 6
Sobral [BR, Ceará] 78-79 L 5
Socha 78-79 E 3
Sochaczew 33 K 2
Soche = Yarkand 48-49 D 4
Sôch'ŏn 50-51 F 4
Sochor, gora − 42-43 TU 7
Soči 38-39 G 7

Sociedad, Islas de la − 22-23 B 6-7
Société, Îles de la − 22-23 B 6-7
Society Islands 22-23 B 6-7
Socompa, Volcán − 80 C 2
Socorro [CO] 78-79 E 3
Socorro, Isla − 72-73 DE 8
Socoto = Sokoto 60-61 EF 6
Socotra = Suqutrā' 44-45 G 8
Socuéllamos 34-35 F 9
Sôdá, Gebel es − = Jabal as-Sawdā' 60-61 GH 3
Soda Lake 76-77 F 8
Sodankylä 30-31 LM 4
Soda Springs, ID 76-77 H 4
Soddu = Sodo 60-61 M 7
Söderhamn 30-31 G 7
Söderköping 30-31 G 8
Södermanland 30-31 G 8
Södertälje 30-31 GH 8
Södirî = Sawdirī 60-61 K 6
Sodo 60-61 M 7
Sodom = Sĕdôm 46-47 F 7
Sodus, NY 74-75 E 3
Soedan [≅] 60-61 C-K 6
Soedan [★] 60-61 J-L 6
Soekmekaar 64-65 G 7
Soest 33 D 3
Sofala, Baia de − 64-65 HJ 7
Sofia 64-65 L 6
Sofia = Sofija 36-37 G 3
Sofia = Sofija 36-37 K 4
Sofie = Sofija 36-37 K 4
Sofija 36-37 K 4
Sofijsk 42-43 Z 7
Sofporog 30-31 O 5
Soga 63 D 4
Sogamoso 78-79 E 3
Soğanlı Çayı 46-47 E 2
Sogndalstrand 30-31 B 8
Sognefjord 30-31 AB 7
Sogn og Fjordane 30-31 AB 7
Sogwip'o 50-51 F 6
Sôhâg = Sawhāj 60-61 L 3
Sôhan-man 48-49 NO 4
Sohano 52-53 h 6
Sohar = Şuḩār 44-45 H 6
So-hüksan-do 50-51 E 5
Soissons 34-35 J 4
Sôja 50-51 J 5
S'ojacha 38-39 NO 1
S'ojacha [SU, ●] 42-43 N 3
Šojna [SU] 42-43 G 4
Sôjosôn-man = Sôhan-man 48-49 NO 4
Šokal'skogo, ostrov − 42-43 NO 3
Šokal'skogo, proliv − 42-43 RS 2
Söke 44-45 B 3
Sokhna = Sawknah 60-61 GH 3
Sokodé 60-61 E 7
Sokol 42-43 G 6
Sokolo 60-61 C 6
Sokółka 33 L 2
Sokółka 33 L 2
Sokołów Podlaski 33 L 2
Sokołów Podlaski 33 L 2
Sokoto [WAN, ~] 60-61 E 6
Sokoto [WAN, ●] 60-61 EF 6
Sokotra = Suqutrā' 44-45 G 8
Sôkpâ 52-53 C 3
Sôk-to 50-51 E 3
Sol, Costa del − 34-35 E 10
Solai 64-65 J 2-3
Solaklı − Of 46-47 J 2
Solapur 44-45 M 7
Soledad 78-79 DE 2
Soledad, CA 76-77 C 7
Soledad, Isla − = East Falkland 80 E 8
Solesmes 34-35 G 5
Soleymān, Takht-e − 46-47 O 4
Solfonn 30-31 B 8
Solhan 46-47 J 3
Solihull 32 F 5
Solikamsk 42-43 K 6
Sol'-Ileck 42-43 JK 7
Solimões, Rio − 78-79 G 5
Solingen 33 C 3
Sollefteå 30-31 G 6
Sóller 34-35 J 9
Sollum = As-Salūm 60-61 K 2
Sol-Iun = Solon 48-49 N 2
Solna 30-31 H 8
Solo = Surakarta 52-53 F 8
Sologne 34-35 HJ 5
Šologoncy 42-43 VW 4
Solok 52-53 D 7
Solomon Basin 52-53 h 6
Solomon Islands [☉] 52-53 h 6-k 7
Solomon Sea 52-53 hj 6
Solon 48-49 N 2
Solončak Šalkarteniz 42-43 L 8
Solončak Šalkarteniz 42-43 L 8
Solong Cheer = Sulan Cheer 48-49 K 3
Solong Cheer = Sulan Cheer 48-49 K 3
Solong Cheer = Sulan Cheer 48-49 K 3

Solor, Pulau − 52-53 H 8
Solothurn 33 C 4
Soloveckije ostrova 42-43 F 4
Šolta 36-37 G 4
Solţānābād = Arāk 44-45 F 4
Solţānīyeh 46-47 N 4
Soltau 33 DE 2
Soluch = Sulūq 60-61 J 2
Solun 48-49 N 2
Soluň = Thessaloníkē 36-37 K 5
Solvay, NY 74-75 E 3
Sölvesborg 30-31 F 9
Sol'vyčegodsk 42-43 H 5
Sol'vyčegodsk 42-43 H 5
Solway Firth 32 DE 4
Solwezi 64-65 G 5
Sôma [J] 50-51 S 5-6
Soma [TR] 46-47 B 3
Somabhula 64-65 G 6
Somalia 60-61 N 8-O 7
Somalia, Cuenca de − 22-23 M 5-6
Somali Basin 22-23 M 5-6
Somalibecken 22-23 M 5-6
Somaliebekken 22-23 M 5-6
Somalië 60-61 N 8-O 7
Somalie 60-61 N 8-O 7
Somalies, Bassin des − 22-23 M 5-6
Somálsko 60-61 N 8-O 7
Sombor 36-37 H 3
Sombrero, El − [YV] 78-79 F 3
Şomcuta Mare 36-37 K 2
Somero 30-31 K 7
Somers, MT 76-77 F 1
Somerset, PA 74-75 D 4-5
Somerset East = Somerset-Oos 64-65 FG 9
Somerset Island 70-71 S 3
Somerset-Oos 64-65 FG 9
Somersworth, NH 74-75 H 3
Somerton, AZ 76-77 F 9
Somerville, MA 74-75 H 3
Somerville, NJ 74-75 F 4
Someş 36-37 K 2
Somesbar, CA 76-77 B 5
Somme 34-35 H 3
Somuncurá, Meseta de − 80 C 6
Son [IND] 44-45 N 6
Sônch'ôn 50-51 E 3
Sonda, Fosa de la − 22-23 P 6
Sonda, Grandes islas de la − 52-53 E-H 7-8
Sonda, Pequeñas islas de la − 52-53 GH 8
Sonde, Grandes Îles de la − 52-53 E-H 7-8
Sonde, Îles de la − 22-23 O 5-Q 6
Sonde, Petites Îles de la − 52-53 GH 8
Sønderborg 30-31 CD 10
Sonderburg = Sønderborg 30-31 CD 10
Sondershausen 33 E 3
Søndre Kvaløy 30-31 GH 3
Søndre Strømfjord 70-71 a 4
Søndre Strømfjord = Kangerlugssuaq 70-71 ab 4
Sóndrio 36-37 CD 2
Sôngch'on 50-51 F 3
Songea 64-65 J 5
Songhua Hu 48-49 O 3
Songhua Jiang 48-49 O 2
Sônghwan 50-51 F 4
Songjiang 48-49 N 5
Songjiangzhen 50-51 F 1
Sôngjin = Kim Chak 48-49 OP 3
Songjông-ni 50-51 F 5
Songkhla 52-53 D 5
Songkla = Songkhla 52-53 D 5
Sôngnae-ri = Inhung-ni 50-51 F 3
Songnim 48-49 O 4
Songo 64-65 H 5
Songpan 48-49 J 5
Songwe 63 C 5
Sonhat 44-45 N 6
Sonkovo 42-43 F 6
Sonmiani = Sonmiyāni 44-45 K 5
Sonmiyāni 44-45 K 5
Sonmiyāni, Khalīj − 44-45 J 6-K 5
Sonneberg 33 E 3
Sono, Rio do − [BR, Goiás] 78-79 K 6-7
Sonoma, CA 76-77 B 6
Sonoma Range 76-77 E 5
Sonora 72-73 D 3
Sonora, AZ 76-77 H 9
Sonora, CA 76-77 C 6-7
Sonora Peak 76-77 D 6
Sonoyta, Rio − 76-77 G 10
Sonqor 46-47 M 5
Sonsón 78-79 DE 3
Sonsonate 72-73 HJ 9
Sonsorol 52-53 K 5
Soperton, GA 74-75 B 8
Sôp'o-ri 50-51 FG 2
Sopot 33 J 1
Sopron 33 H 5
Sor 34-35 C 9
Sôrak-san 50-51 G 3
Sora 36-37 E 5
Sôrak-san 50-51 G 3
Šôrath = Jûnâgadh 44-45 KL 5
Sorau = Žary 33 G 3
Sorbas 34-35 FG 10
Sorel 70-71 W 8

Sorell 58 cd 3
Sorell, Cape – 56-57 HJ 8
Sorell, Lake – 58 c 2
Soren Arwa = Selat Yapen 52-53 L 7
Sørfonna 30-31 lm 5
Sòrgono 36-37 C 5
Sorgun = Büyük Köhne 46-47 F 3
Sörhād = Sarhade Wākhān 44-45 L 3
Soria 34-35 F 8
Sørkapp 30-31 k 6
Sørkapp land 30-31 k 6
Sørkjosen 30-31 J 3
Sorø 30-31 D 10
Sorocaba 80 G 2
Soročinsk 42-43 J 7
Soročinsk 42-43 J 7
Soroka = Belomorsk 42-43 EF 5
Sorol 52-53 M 5
Sorong 52-53 K 7
Soroti 64-65 H 2
Sørøy 30-31 K 2
Sørøysund 30-31 K 2
Sorraia 34-35 C 9
Sorrento 36-37 F 5
Sør-Rondane 24 B 2-3
Sorsele 30-31 G 5
Sorsogon 52-53 HJ 4
Sortavala 42-43 E 5
Sortland 30-31 F 3
Sør-Trøndelag 30-31 CD 6
Sørvågen 30-31 E 4
Sõrve 30-31 JK 9
Sŏsan 50-51 F 4
Sosnogorsk 42-43 JK 5
Sosnovka 38-39 H 5
Sosnovo 30-31 NO 7
Sosnovo-Oz'orskoje 42-43 V 7
Sosnowiec 33 J 3
Šostka 38-39 F 5
Sōsura 50-51 H 1
Sos'va 38-39 M 4
Sos'va [SU, Chanty-Mansijskaja AO] 42-43 L 5
Sos'va [SU ↘ Serov] 42-43 L 6
So-tch'ê = Yarkand 48-49 D 4
Sotkamo 30-31 N 5
Sotra 30-31 A 7
Souanké 64-65 D 2
Şoûâr = Aş-Şuwār 46-47 J 5
Soubré 60-61 C 7
Soudan 56-57 G 4
Soudan [≅] 60-61 C-K 6
Soudan [★] 60-61 J-L 6
Soufrière 72-73 O 9
Souillac 34-35 H 6
Souk-Ahras = Sūq Aḥrās 60-61 F 1
Sŏul 48-49 O 4
Sources, Mont aux – 64-65 G 8
Soure [BR] 78-79 K 5
Souris River 70-71 Q 8
Sousa 78-79 M 6
Soûssa = Sūssah 46-47 J 5
Sousse = Sūsah 60-61 G 1
South Africa 64-65 F-H 8
South Alligator River 56-57 F 2
South Alligator River 56-57 F 2
South America 22-23 FG 6
Southampton [GB] 32 F 6
Southampton, NY 74-75 GH 4
Southampton Island 70-71 TU 5
South Andaman 44-45 P 8
South Aulatsivik Island 70-71 YZ 6
South Australia 56-57 E-G 5-6
South Australia Basin 22-23 PQ 8
South Banda Basin 52-53 J 8
South Bend, IN 72-73 JK 3
South Bend, WA 76-77 B 2
South Boston, VA 74-75 D 6
South Branch Potomac River 74-75 D 5
South Bruny Island 58 cd 3
South Carolina 72-73 K 5
South Charleston, WV 74-75 BC 5
South China Basin 52-53 FG 3-4
South China Sea 52-53 E 5-G 3
South Charleston, WV 74-75 BC 5
South China Basin 52-53 FG 3-4
South China Sea 52-53 E 5-G 3
South Dakota 72-73 FG 3
South Dum Dum 44-45 OP 6
South East Cape 56-57 J 8
Southeast Indian Basin 22-23 OP 7
South East Point 58 H 7
Southend [CDN] 70-71 PQ 6
Southend-on-Sea 32 G 6
Southern [Z] 64-65 G 6
Southern Alps 56-57 NO 8
Southern Cross 56-57 CD 6
Southern Indian Lake 70-71 R 6
Southern Pacific Railway 72-73 EF 5
Southern Pine Hills = Pine Hills 72-73 J 5
Southern Pines, NC 74-75 D 7
Southern Uplands 32 DE 4
South Fiji Basin 56-57 OP 4-5
South Fork Clearwater River 76-77 F 3
South Fork Flathead River 76-77 G 2
South Fork John Day River 76-77 D 3
South Fork Mountains 76-77 B 5
South Fork Owyhee River 76-77 E 4-5
South Fork Salmon River 76-77 F 3
South Gate, CA 76-77 DE 9
South Georgia 80 J 8
South Georgia Ridge 24 D 33-E 34
South Henik Lake 70-71 R 5
South Hill, VA 74-75 D 6
South Honshu Ridge 48-49 R 5-6
South Horr 64-65 J 2
South Charleston, WV 74-75 BC 5
South China Basin 52-53 FG 3-4
South China Sea 52-53 E 5-G 3
South Indian Ridge 22-23 OP 8
South Island 56-57 OP 8
South Korea 48-49 OP 4
South Mountain 74-75 E 4-5
South Nahanni River 70-71 LM 5
South Ogden, UT 76-77 H 5
South Orkneys 24 C 32
South Ossetian Autonomous Region = 7 ◁ 38-39 H 7
South Pacific Basin 24 D 21-19
South Pacific Ridge 24 D 22-C 20
South Paris, ME 74-75 H 2
South Pass [USA, Louisiana] 72-73 J 6
South Pass [USA, Wyoming] 72-73 E 3
South Plate River 72-73 F 3
Southport [AUS] 58 c 3
Southport, NC 74-75 DE 7-8
South Portland, ME 74-75 HJ 3
South Ronaldsay 32 EF 2
South Sandwich Islands 24 CD 34
South Sandwich Trench 24 D 34
South Saskatchewan River 70-71 OP 7
South Shetlands 24 C 30
South Shields 32 F 4
South Taranaki Bight 56-57 O 7
South Tent 76-77 H 6
South Tyrol 36-37 D 2
South Tyrol 36-37 D 2
South Uist 32 BC 3
South Umpqua River 76-77 B 4
Southwest Africa = Namibia 64-65 E 7
South West Cape [AUS] 58 bc 3
Southwest Cape [NZ] 56-57 N 9
Southwest Cay 72-73 KL 9
Southwest Indian Basin 22-23 MN 7
Southwest Pass [USA, Mississippi River Delta] 72-73 J 6
South Williamsport, PA 74-75 E 4
Soutpansberge 64-65 GH 7
Souzel 78-79 J 5
Sovetsk 33 K 1
Sovetsk [SU, Vjatka] 42-43 H 6
Sovetskaja Gavan' 42-43 ab 8
Sōya [J, Hokkaidō] 50-51 b 1
Sōya-kaikyō 48-49 R 2
Sōya misaki 50-51 bc 1
Söylemez 46-47 JK 3
Soyo 64-65 D 4
Sozopol 36-37 MN 4
Spain 34-35 D 7-G 9
Spalato = Split 36-37 G 4
Spalding 32 FG 5
Spalding [AUS] 58 D 4
Spalding, ID 76-77 E 2
Spangle, WA 76-77 E 2
Spanien 34-35 D 7-G 9
Spanish Fork, UT 76-77 H 5
Spanish Head 32 D 4
Spanish Town 72-73 L 8
Spanje 34-35 D 7-G 9
Spanta, Akrōtḗrion – 36-37 KL 8
Spanyolország 34-35 D 7-G 9
Sparbu 30-31 D 6
Sparks, GA 74-75 B 9
Sparks, NV 76-77 D 6
Sparta, GA 74-75 B 8
Sparta, NC 74-75 C 6
Sparta = Spártē 36-37 K 7
Spartanburg, SC 72-73 K 4-5
Spártē 36-37 K 7
Spartivento, Capo – [I, Calàbria] 36-37 G 7
Spartivento, Capo – [I, Sardegna] 36-37 G 6
Spassk = Spassk-Dal'nij 42-43 Z 9
Spassk-Dal'nij 42-43 Z 9
Speke Gulf 64-65 H 3
Spencer, ID 76-77 G 3
Spencer, NC 74-75 C 7
Spencer, WV 74-75 C 5
Spencer, Cape – [AUS] 56-57 G 7
Spencer Gulf 56-57 G 6
Spessart 33 D 3-4
Spétsai 36-37 K 7
Spey 32 E 3
Speyer 33 D 4
Spèzia, La – 36-37 C 3
Spezzano Albanese 36-37 G 6
Spicberky 30-31 k
Spicer Islands 70-71 UV 4
Spilimbergo 36-37 E 2
Spīn Buldak 44-45 K 4
Spirit Lake, ID 76-77 E 1-2
Spirit Lake, WA 76-77 BC 2
Spitsbergen 30-31 k 6-o 5
Spittal 33 F 5
Spitzberg = Svalbard 34-35 k-m 6
Spitzbergen 30-31 k 6-o 5
Split 36-37 G 4
Splügen 33 D 5
Spojené arabské emiráty 44-45 GH 6
Spojené státy americké 72-73 C-K 4
Spokane, WA 72-73 C 2
Spokane Indian Reservation 76-77 DE 2
Spokane River 76-77 DE 2
Spokojnyj 42-43 YZ 6
Špola 38-39 F 6
Spoleto 36-37 E 4
Sporaden 36-37 M 6-8
Sporades 36-37 M 6-8
Sporady 36-37 M 6-7
Sporady 36-37 M 6-7
Sporyj Navolok, mys – 42-43 M-O 2
Spotted Range 76-77 F 7
Sprague, WA 76-77 DE 2
Sprague River 76-77 C 4
Sprague River, OR 76-77 C 4
Spratly Islands = Quần Đao Hoang Sa 52-53 F 5
Spray, OR 76-77 D 3
Spree 33 G 3
Spreewald 33 F 2-G 3
Spremberg 33 G 3
Sprengisandur 30-31 de 2
Spring Bay 76-77 G 5
Springbok 64-65 E 8
Springdale, MT 76-77 HJ 3
Springdale, NV 76-77 E 7
Springdale, UT 76-77 G 7
Springdale, WA 76-77 DE 1
Springerville, AZ 76-77 J 8
Springfield, GA 74-75 C 8
Springfield, ID 76-77 G 4
Springfield, IL 72-73 HJ 4
Springfield, MA 72-73 M 3
Springfield, MO 72-73 H 4
Springfield, OH 72-73 K 3-4
Springfield, OR 76-77 B 3
Springfield, VT 74-75 G 3
Spring Hope, NC 74-75 DE 7
Spring Mountains 76-77 F 7
Springs 64-65 G 8
Springsure 56-57 J 4
Spring Valley [USA] 76-77 F 6
Springville, NY 74-75 D 3
Springville, UT 76-77 H 5
Spruce Knob 72-73 KL 4
Spruce Mountain 76-77 F 5
Spruce Pine, NC 74-75 BC 6-7
Spry, UT 76-77 G 7
Spur Lake, NM 76-77 J 8-9
Squaw Valley, CA 72-73 BC 4
Squillace, Golfo di – 36-37 G 6
Srbsko 36-37 H 3-J 4
Srbija 36-37 H 3-J 4
Sredinnyj chrebet 42-43 f 6-e 7
Sredna gora 36-37 L 4
Srednekolymsk 42-43 d 4
Sredne-Sibirskoje ploskogorje 42-43 R-W 4-5
Srednij Ural 42-43 KL 6
Sredsib 42-43 L 7-P 7
Srem 33 H 2
Sremska Mitrovica 36-37 H 3
Sremska Rača 36-37 H 3
Sremska Rača 36-37 H 3
Sretensk 42-43 W 7
Srê Umbell 52-53 D 4
Sri Jayawardanapura 44-45 N 9
Srikakulam 44-45 M 7
Sri Lanka 44-45 N 9
Sri Lanka 44-45 N 9
Srinagar 44-45 LM 4
Srirangam 44-45 M 8
Srivardhan 44-45 L 7
Środa Wielkopolska 33 HJ 2
Sseu-p'ing = Siping 48-49 N 3
Ssongea = Songea 64-65 J 5
Staateninsel = Isla de los Estados 80 D 8
Staaten River 56-57 H 3
Stachanov 38-39 G 6
Stack Skerry 32 D 2
Stade 33 D 2
Städjan 30-31 E 7
Stadlandet 30-31 A 6
Stafford 32 E 5
Staked Plain = Llano Estacado 72-73 F 5
Stalina, pik – = pik Kommunizma 44-45 L 3
Stalinabad = Dušanbe 44-45 K 3
Stalino = Ošarovo 42-43 S 5
Stalinsk = Novokuzneck 42-43 Q 7
Stalowa Wola 33 L 3
Stambul = İstanbul 44-45 BC 2
Stambuł = İstanbul 44-45 BC 2
Stamford [AUS] 56-57 H 4
Stamford, CT 74-75 G 4
Stampriet 64-65 E 7
Stamsund 30-31 EF 3
Stanbury Mountains 76-77 G 5
Standerton 64-65 GH 8
Stanford, MT 76-77 H 2
Stanislaus River 76-77 C 6-7
Stanke Dimitrov 36-37 K 4
Stanley [AUS] 58 b 2
Stanley [Falkland Islands] 80 E 8
Stanley, ID 76-77 F 3
Stanley, Mount – 56-57 F 4
Stanley Pool = Pool Malebo 64-65 E 3
Stanley Reservoir 44-45 M 8
Stanleyville = Kisangani 64-65 G 2
Stann Creek 72-73 J 8
Stanovoj chrebet 42-43 X-Z 6
Stanovoje nagorje 42-43 VW 6
Stanthorpe 58 KL 2
Stanwood, WA 76-77 B 1
Stany Zjednoczone 72-73 C-K 4
Stapi 30-31 b 2
Star, NC 74-75 D 7
Starachowice 33 K 3
Staraja Buchara = Buchara 44-45 JK 3
Staraja Russa 42-43 E 6
Stara Pazova 36-37 J 3
Stara Zagora 36-37 L 4
Stargard Szczeciński 33 G 2
Stargard Szczeciński 33 G 2
Starigrad 36-37 F 3
Starke, FL 74-75 bc 2
Starkey, ID 76-77 E 3
Starnberg 33 E 4-5
Starnberger See 33 E 5
Starobel'sk 38-39 G 6
Starogard Gdański 33 HJ 2
Staroizborsk 30-31 MN 9
Starokonstantinov 38-39 E 6
Starominskaja 38-39 G 6
Starotitarovskaja 38-39 G 6-7
Staryj Oskol 38-39 G 5
Staßfurt 33 E 3
Staszów 33 K 3
State College, PA 74-75 DE 4
Staten Island 74-75 FG 4
Statenville, GA 74-75 B 9
Statesboro, GA 74-75 C 8
Statesville, NC 72-73 K 4
Stauffer, OR 76-77 C 4
Staunton, VA 72-73 KL 4
Stavanger 30-31 A 8
Stavern 30-31 CD 8
Stavropol' 38-39 H 6
Stavropol' = Togliatti 42-43 H 7
Stavrós 36-37 K 5
Stawell 56-57 H 7
Steamboat, NV 76-77 D 6
Steele Island 24 B 30-31
Steelpoort 64-65 GH 7
Steelton, PA 74-75 E 4
Steenkool = Bintuni 52-53 K 7
Steensby Inlet 70-71 V 3
Steens Mountain 76-77 D 4
Steenstrups Gletscher 70-71 Za 2
Steep Point 56-57 B 5
Ştefăneşti 36-37 M 2
Stefansson Island 70-71 OP 3
Steflești 36-37 K 3
Stege 30-31 E 10
Steiermark 33 G 5
Steinbrück = Zidani most 36-37 F 2
Steinen, Rio – 78-79 J 7
Steinhatchee, FL 74-75 b 2
Steinkjer 30-31 DE 5
Steinnest 30-31 m 6
Steins, NM 76-77 J 9
Stellaland 64-65 F 8
Stellenbosch 64-65 EF 9
Stendal 33 E 2
Stensele 30-31 G 5
Stepanakert 38-39 J 8
Stephanie, Lake – = Thew Bahir 60-61 M 8
Stephenville 70-71 YZ 8
Stepn'ak 42-43 N 7
Sterkstroom 64-65 G 9
Sterling, CO 72-73 F 3
Sterlitamak 42-43 K 7
Sternberg = Torzym 33 G 2
Štětín = Szczecin 33 G 2
Stettin = Szczecin 33 G 2
Steubenville, OH 72-73 K 3
Stevenson, WA 76-77 BC 3
Stevenson, The – 56-57 FG 5
Stevensville, MT 76-77 FG 2
Stewart, AK 70-71 KL 6
Stewart, NV 76-77 D 6
Stewart, Isla – 80 B 8-9
Stewart Island 56-57 N 9
Stewart Islands 52-53 k 6
Stewart River [CDN, ~] 70-71 JK 5
Stewart River [CDN, ●] 70-71 J 5
Steyr 33 G 4
Stikine Mountains = Cassiar Mountains 70-71 KL 6
Stikine Plateau 70-71 K 6
Stikine River 70-71 KL 6
Stillwater Mountains 76-77 DE 6
Stimson, Mount – 76-77 G 1
Stinear Nunataks 24 BC 7
Štip 36-37 K 5
Stirling City, CA 76-77 C 6
Stirling Range 56-57 C 6
Stites, ID 76-77 EF 2
Stjernøy 30-31 K 2
Stjørdalshalsen 30-31 D 6
Stobi 36-37 J 5
Stockerau 33 G 4
Stockett, MT 76-77 H 2
Stockholm 30-31 GH 8
Stockholm, ME 74-75 JK 1
Stockholms län 30-31 GH 8
Stockport 32 E 5
Stocks, Cima de – 78-79 N 7
Stocks, Crête de – 78-79 N 7
Stocks-fenèkhegy 78-79 N 7
Stockskuppe 78-79 N 7
Stocks-Ondiepte 78-79 N 7
Stocks Seamount 78-79 N 7
Stockton, CA 72-73 BC 4
Stockton on Tees 32 F 4
Stojba 42-43 Z 7
Stoke on Trend 32 EF 5
Stokes Point 58 ab 2
Stokkseyri 30-31 c 3
Stokksnes 30-31 f 2
Stolac 36-37 GH 4
Stolbcy 30-31 M 11
Stolbovoj, ostrov – 42-43 Za 3
Stolp = Słupsk 33 H 1
Ston 36-37 G 4
Stonehaven 32 EF 3
Stonehenge 32 EF 6
Stonehenge [AUS] 56-57 H 4
Stone Mountains 74-75 C 6
Stoner, CO 76-77 J 7
Stonington 24 C 30
Stonington, ME 74-75 J 2-3
Stony Creek, VA 74-75 E 6
Stonyford, CA 76-77 B 6
Stony Point [USA] 74-75 E 3
Stony River 70-71 EF 5
Stopnica 33 K 3
Stora Lulevatten 30-31 HJ 4
Stora Sjöfallet 30-31 H 4
Stora-Sjöfallets nationalpark 30-31 GH 4
Storavan 30-31 H 5
Stord 30-31 A 8
Store Bælt 30-31 D 10
Støren 30-31 CD 6
Storfjord 30-31 B 6
Storfjordbotn 30-31 LM 2
Storfjorden 30-31 k 6
Storlien 30-31 E 6
Storm Bay 56-57 J 8
Stornorrfors 30-31 HJ 6
Stornoway 32 CD 2
Storøya 30-31 n 4
Storoževsk 42-43 J 5
Storoževsk 42-43 J 5
Storsjön 30-31 E 6
Storuman [S, ●] 30-31 G 5
Storuman [S, ≈] 30-31 G 5
Stosch, Isla – 80 A 7
Straatsburg = Strasbourg 34-35 L 4
Strabane 32 C 4
Straight Cliffs 76-77 H 7
Strakonice 33 FG 4
Stralsund 33 F 1
Strand 64-65 E 9
Stranda 30-31 c 1-2
Stranraer 32 D 4
Strasbourg 34-35 L 4
Strasbourg = Brodnica 33 J 2
Strasburk = Strasbourg 34-35 L 4
Straßburg = Strasbourg 34-35 L 4
Stratford [AUS] 58 H 7
Stratford [CDN] 70-71 U 9
Stratford, CA 76-77 D 7
Stratford, CT 74-75 G 4
Stratford on Avon 32 F 5
Strathgordon 58 bc 3
Strathmore 32 E 3
Strathroy 74-75 C 3
Stratonis Turris = Caesarea 46-47 F 6
Stratton, ME 74-75 H 2
Straubing 33 F 4
Strawberry Mountains 76-77 D 3
Strawberry River 76-77 H 5
Streaky Bay [AUS, ∪] 56-57 F 6
Streaky Bay [AUS, ●] 56-57 FG 6
Středozemní moře 36-37 C 7-M 8
Streich Mound 56-57 D 6
Strelka-Čun'a 42-43 T 5
Strelka-Čun'a 42-43 T 5
Strelna 38-39 G 2
Strenči 30-31 LM 9
Strenči 30-31 LM 9
Stresa 36-37 C 3
Strevell, ID 76-77 G 4
Strickland River 52-53 M 8
Stroeder 80 D 6
Strofádes 36-37 J 7
Strómboli 36-37 F 6
Strömstad 30-31 D 8
Strömsund 30-31 F 6
Ströms Vattudal 30-31 F 5-6
Stronsay 32 EF 2
Stroud 32 EF 6
Stroudsburg, PA 74-75 F 4
Struer 30-31 C 9
Strugi Krasnyje 30-31 M 8
Struma 36-37 K 5
Strumica 36-37 K 5
Stryj 38-39 D 6
Strymón 36-37 K 5
Strzelecki Creek 58 E 2
Strzelno 33 HJ 2
Středosibiřská vysočina 42-43 R-X 4-5
Střední Atlas = Al-Aṭlas al-Mutawassiṭ 60-61 CD 2
Středoafrická republika 60-61 HJ 7
Střelkový mys 64-65 F 9
Stuart, FL 74-75 c 3
Stuart, VA 74-75 C 6
Stuart Island 70-71 D 5
Stuart Lake 70-71 M 7
Stuart Range 56-57 FG 5
Stubbenkammer 33 FG 1
Studenica 36-37 J 4
Stumpy Point, NC 74-75 F 7
Stung Treng 52-53 E 4
Stupino 38-39 G 4-5
Stura di Demonte 36-37 B 3
Sturge Island 24 C 17
Sturt, Mount – 56-57 H 5
Sturt Creek 56-57 E 3
Sturt Desert 56-57 H 5
Sturt Plain 56-57 F 3
Stutterheim 64-65 G 9
Stuttgart 33 D 4
Stykkishólmur 30-31 b 2
Stylis 36-37 K 6
Styr' 38-39 E 5
Sūākin = Sawākīn 60-61 M 5
Suan 50-51 F 3
Süanhua = Xuanhua 48-49 LM 3
Suanhwa = Xuanhua 48-49 LM 3
Su-ao 48-49 N 7
Su'ao = Su-ao 48-49 N 7
Suazi 64-65 H 8
Šubarkuduk 42-43 K 8
Sûbâț, Nahr as- 60-61 L 7
Subayhah 46-47 H 7
Subiaco 36-37 E 5
Sublett, ID 76-77 G 4
Subotica 36-37 HJ 2
Subugo 63 C 3
Suceava 36-37 LM 2
Suchaj nuur 48-49 GH 4
Suchana 42-43 W 4
Süchbaatar [MVR, ●] 48-49 JK 1
Süchbaatar [MVR, ☆ = 17] 48-49 L 2
Sucheng = Su Xian 48-49 M 5
Su-chia-t'un = Sujiatun 50-51 D 2
Su-ch'ien = Suqian 48-49 M 5
Suchiniči 38-39 FG 5
Suchoj Liman 36-37 O 2
Suchona 42-43 G 6
Suchou = Xuzhou 48-49 M 5
Su-chou = Yibin 48-49 JK 6
Suchow = Xuzhou 48-49 M 5
Suchow = Yibin 48-49 JK 6
Suchumi 38-39 H 7
Sucre [BOL] 78-79 FG 8
Sucuaro 78-79 F 4
Sucunduri, Rio – 78-79 H 6
Sucuriú, Rio – 78-79 J 8
Süd = As-Sudd 60-61 L 7
Sudáfrica, República de – 64-65 F-H 8
Südafrika 64-65 F-H 8
Südamerika 22-23 FG 6
Sudan, ≅ 60-61 C-K 6
Sudan, ★ 60-61 KL 6
Sudán [≅] 60-61 C-K 6
Sûdân [≅] 60-61 C-K 6
Súdán [★] 60-61 J-L 6
Sudán [★] 60-61 J-L 6
Südantillenbecken 22-23 G 8
Südatlantischer Rücken 22-23 J 6-8
Südaustralisches Becken 22-23 PQ 8
Sudayr 44-45 EF 5
Südbandabecken 52-53 J 8
Sudbury [CDN] 70-71 U 8
Südchinesisches Becken 52-53 FG 3-4
Südchinesisches Meer 52-53 E 5-G 2
Sudd, As- 60-61 L 7
Suddie 78-79 H 3
Sud-Est Indien, Bassin du – 22-23 OP 7
Sud-Est Indien, Dorsale du – 22-23 OP 8
Süd-Fidschibecken 56-57 OP 4-5
Südgeorgien = South Georgia 80 J 8
Südgeorgienschwelle 24 D 33-E 34
Sudhavik 30-31 b 1
Süd-Honschu-Rücken 48-49 R 5-6
Sudhur-Múla 30-31 f 2
Sudhur-Thingeyjar 30-31 ef 2

220 Sorel

Südindischer Rücken 22-23 OP 8
Sudirman, Pegunungan – 52-53 L 7
Südkorea 48-49 OP 4
Südlicher Ural = Južnyj Ural 42-43 K 7-L 6
Sudong-ni = Changhang 50-51 F 4-5
Südossetische Autonome Oblast = 7 ◁ 46-47 H 7
Südostindisches Becken 22-23 OP 7
Sud-Ouest Indien, Bassin du – 22-23 MN 7
Südpazifischer Rücken 24 D 22-C 20
Südpazifisches Becken 24 D 21-19
Sudr = Râ's as-Sidr 62 E 3
Sudr, Wâdī – = Wâdī Sidr 62 E 3
Südsandwichgraben 24 CD 34
Südtirol 36-37 D 2
Südwestafrika = Namibia 64-65 E 7
Südwestindisches Becken 22-23 MN 7
Sue = Nahr Sūī 60-61 K 7
Sueca 34-35 G 9
Suecia 30-31 F 9-J 10
Suède 30-31 F 9-J 10
Sueski, Kanał = Qanat as-Suways 60-61 L 2
Suez = As-Suways 60-61 L 3
Sūfân, Qulbân as- 46-47 H 8
Sūfeyân 46-47 LM 3
Suffolk, VA 74-75 E 6
Suflion 36-37 LM 5
Sufu = Qäshqär 48-49 CD 4
Sufūq 46-47 J 4
Šuga 42-43 N 4
Sugarloaf Mountain 74-75 HJ 2
Sugiyasu 50-51 H 6
Suğla Gölü 46-47 DE 4
Suguta 63 D 2
Sūhāj = Sawhaț 60-61 L 3
Șuḥār 44-45 H 6
Suhelīpāḍ = Suheli Par 44-45 L 8
Suheli Par 44-45 L 8
Suhl 33 E 3
Su-hsien = Su Xian 48-49 M 5
Șuhut 46-47 D 3
Suchiniči 38-39 FG 5
Suichuan 48-49 L 6
Sui-chung = Suizhong 50-51 C 2
Suichwan = Suichuan 48-49 L 6
Suide 48-49 KL 4
Suifenhe 48-49 OP 3
Suihsien = Sui Xian [TJ, Hubei] 48-49 L 5
Suihua 48-49 O 2
Suihwa = Suihua 48-49 O 2
Suilai = Manaas 48-49 F 3
Suir 32 C 5
Suisse 33 CD 5
Suiteh = Suide 48-49 KL 4
Sui Xian [TJ, Hubei] 48-49 L 5
Suiyuan 48-49 K 4-L 3
Sui-yüan = Suiyuan 48-49 K 4-L 3
Suiza 33 CD 5
Suizhong 50-51 C 2
Šuja [SU, Ivanovo] 42-43 G 6
Sujiatun 50-51 D 2
Sukabumi 52-53 E 8
Sukadana 52-53 EF 7
Sukagawa 50-51 MN 4
Sukaraja = Marau 52-53 F 7
Sukch'ŏn 50-51 E 3
Sukhe Bator = Süchbaatar 48-49 JK 1
Șukhnah, Aș- 46-47 H 5
Sūki, As- 60-61 L 6
Sukkertoppen = Manîtsoq 70-71 Za 4
Sukses 64-65 E 7
Sukulu 63 C 2
Sukumo 50-51 J 6
Sukumo wan 50-51 J 6
Sul, Canal do – 78-79 K 4-5
Sula, MT 76-77 FG 3
Sula [SU, ~] 38-39 F 6
Sula [SU, ●] 38-39 K 2
Sula, Kepulauan – 52-53 HJ 7
Sulak 38-39 J 7
Sulakyurt 46-47 E 2
Sulan Cheer 48-49 K 3
Sulan Cheer 48-49 K 3
Sulan Cheer 48-49 K 3
Sula Sgeir 32 C 2
Sulawesi 52-53 G 7-H 6
Sulawesi Selatan = 21 ◁ 52-53 G 7
Sulawesi Tengah = 19 ◁ 52-53 H 6
Sulawesi Tenggara = 20 ◁ 52-53 H 7
Sulawesi Utara = 18 ◁ 52-53 H 6
Sulaymân, Kohistân – 44-45 KL 4-5
Sulaymânīyah 44-45 EF 3
Sulaymīyah, As- 44-45 F 6
Sulayyil, As- 44-45 F 6
Șulb, Aș- 44-45 F 5
Sul'ca 38-39 J 3
Sule He 48-49 H 4
Sule Skerry 32 D 2
Süleymanlı 46-47 G 4
Sulima 60-61 B 7
Sulina 36-37 N 3
Sulina, Braţul – 36-37 N 3
Sulitjelma [N, ▲] 30-31 G 4
Sulitjelma [N, ●] 30-31 FG 4
Šuljereckoje 38-39 F 3
Sullana 78-79 C 5
Šul'mak = Novabad 44-45 L 3
Sulmona 36-37 E 4-5
Su-lo Ho = Sule He 48-49 H 4
Sulphur, NV 76-77 D 5
Sulphurdale, UT 76-77 G 6
Sultanabad = Arâk 44-45 F 4
Sultandağı 46-47 D 3
Sultan Dağları 46-47 D 3
Sultan Hamud 63 D 3
Sultanhisar 46-47 C 4
Sultanpur [IND, Uttar Pradesh] 44-45 N 5
Sulu, Mar de – 52-53 GH 5
Sulu, Mer de – 52-53 GH 5
Sulu, Morze – 52-53 GH 5
Sulu Archipelago 52-53 H 5
Suluca = Suluova 46-47 F 2
Sulūk 46-47 H 4
Sülüklü 46-47 E 3
Sul'ukta 44-45 KL 3
Suluova 46-47 F 2
Sulūq 60-61 J 2
Sulu Sea 52-53 GH 5
Sulusee 52-53 GH 5
Suluské moře 52-53 GH 5
Sulu-tenger 52-53 GH 5
Suluzee 52-53 GH 5
Sulzberger Bay 24 B 21-22
Šumadija 36-37 J 3-4
Sūmār 46-47 L 6
Sumas, WA 76-77 BC 1
Sumatera = Sumatra 52-53 C 6-D 7
Sumatera Barat = 3 ◁ 52-53 D 7
Sumatera Selatan = 6 ◁ 52-53 D 7
Sumatera Tengah = Riau = 4 ◁ 52-53 D 6
Sumatera Utara = 2 ◁ 52-53 C 6
Sumatra 52-53 C 6-D 7
Sumaúma 78-79 G 6
Sumba [RI] 52-53 G 9
Sumba, Selat – 52-53 GH 8
Sumbawa 52-53 G 8
Sumbawa Besar 52-53 G 8
Sumbawanga 64-65 H 4
Sumbe 63 C 3
Sümber 48-49 K 2
Sumbu 63 B 5
Sumbu Game Reserve 63 B 5
Sumburgh Head 32 F 2
Šumen 36-37 M 4
Šumerl'a 38-39 J 4
Sumgait 38-39 JK 7
Šumicha 42-43 L 6
Sumisu-jima 48-49 R 5
Sumisu zima = Sumisu-jima 48-49 R 5
Șummân, Aș- [Saudi-Arabien ↑ Ar-Rīyâḍ] 44-45 F 5
Șummân, Aș- [Saudi-Arabien ↘ Ar-Rīyâḍ] 44-45 F 6
Summer Lake 76-77 C 4
Summer Lake, OR 76-77 C 4
Summerville, SC 74-75 CD 8
Summerville, WV 74-75 C 5
Summit 72-73 b 2
Summit, CA 76-77 E 8
Summit, OR 76-77 B 3
Summit Lake Indian Reservation 76-77 D 5
Summit Mountain 76-77 E 6
Sumoto 50-51 K 5
Šumperk 33 H 3-4
Sumprabum = Hsûmbârabûm 52-53 C 1
Sumpter, OR 76-77 DE 3
Sumter, SC 72-73 KL 5
Sumy 38-39 FG 5
Suna [EAT] 63 C 4
Sunagawa 50-51 b 2
Sunan 50-51 E 3
Sunato 63 DE 6
Sunaysilah 46-47 J 5
Sunburst, MT 76-77 H 1
Sunbury, PA 74-75 E 4
Suncho Corral 80 D 3
Sunch'ŏn [Nordkorea] 50-51 E 3
Sunch'ŏn [ROK] 48-49 O 4-5
Sunchow = Guiping 48-49 KL 7
Suncook, NH 74-75 H 3
Sunda, Selat – 52-53 E 8
Sundagraben 22-23 P 6
Sundar Ban = Sundarbans 44-45 OP 6
Sundarbans 44-45 OP 6
Sunda Trench 22-23 P 6
Sundbyberg 30-31 G 8
Sunderbunds = Sundarbans 44-45 OP 6
Sunderland 32 F 4
Sunderland [CDN] 74-75 D 2
Sündiken Dağları 46-47 D 2-3
Sundown [AUS] 56-57 F 5
Sundsvall 30-31 GH 6
Sungaidareh 52-53 D 7
Sungai Patani 52-53 CD 5
Sungaipenuh 52-53 D 7
Sungari 48-49 N 2-O 3
Sungari Reservoir = Songhua Hu 48-49 O 3
Sung-chiang = Songjiang 48-49 N 5
Sung hua Chiang = Songhua Jiang 48-49 N 2-O 3
Sung hua Chiang = Songhua Jiang 48-49 N 2-O 3
Sung hua Chiang = Songhua Jiang 48-49 N 2-O 3
Süngjibaegam 50-51 G 2
Sungkiang = Songjiang 48-49 N 5
Sungu 64-65 E 3
Sungurlu 46-47 F 2
Sunhwa = Xunhua 48-49 J 4
Súnion, Atrōtērion – 36-37 KL 7
Sunke = Xunke 48-49 O 2
Sunnagyn, chrebet – = Aldano-Učurskij chrebet 42-43 Y 6
Sunndalsøra 30-31 C 6
Sunniland, FL 74-75 c 3
Sunnūris = Sinnūris 62 D 3
Sunnyside, UT 76-77 H 6
Sunnyside, WA 76-77 CD 2
Sunnyvale, CA 76-77 B 7
Suno saki 50-51 M 5
Sun River 76-77 GH 2
Sunset Country 58 E 5
Suntar 42-43 W 5
Suntar-Chajata, chrebet – 42-43 ab 5
Suntar-Chajata, chrebet – 42-43 ab 5
Suntar-Chajata, chrebet – 42-43 ab 5
Suntsar 44-45 J 5
Sun Valley, ID 76-77 F 4
Sunyani 60-61 D 7
Suojarvi 42-43 E 5
Suojarvi 38-39 F 3
Suokonmäki 30-31 KL 6
Suolahti 30-31 LM 6
Suomen selkä 30-31 K-N 6
Suomussalmi 30-31 N 5
Suō nada 50-51 H 6
Suonenjoki 30-31 M 6
Supai, AZ 76-77 G 7
Superior, AZ 76-77 H 9
Superior, MT 76-77 F 2
Superior, WI 72-73 H 2
Superior, Lake – 72-73 HJ 2
Suphan Buri 52-53 CD 4
Süphan Dağı 46-47 K 3
Supiori 52-53 KL 7
Sup'ung-chŏsuji 50-51 E 2
Supung Hu 48-49 NO 3
Šupunskij, mys – 42-43 f 7
Sūq Aḥrâs 60-61 F 1
Suq ash-Shuyūkh 46-47 M 7
Suqian 48-49 M 5
Suquṭrā' 44-45 G 8
Șūr [Oman] 44-45 H 6
Șūr [RL] 46-47 F 6
Sur, Point – 76-77 BC 7
Sura, Raas – = Raas Surud 60-61 b 1
Šurab 44-45 L 2
Surabaia = Surabaya 52-53 F 8
Surabaya 52-53 F 8
Surakarta 52-53 F 8
Șūrân 46-47 G 5
Surat [AUS] 56-57 J 5
Surat [IND] 44-45 L 6
Surate = Surat 44-45 L 6
Surat Thani 52-53 CD 5
Sūrdâsh 46-47 L 5
Surf, CA 76-77 C 8
Surgut [SU, Chanty-Mansijskaja AO] 42-43 N 5
Surgut [SU, Samara] 42-43 J 7
Surguticha 42-43 PQ 5
Surigao 52-53 J 5
Surin 52-53 D 4
Surinam 78-79 HJ 4
Surinam 78-79 HJ 4
Suriname 78-79 HJ 4
Sürmene 46-47 J 2
Surnadalsøra 30-31 C 6
Surprise Valley 76-77 CD 5
Surt 60-61 H 2
Surt, Khalīj – 60-61 H 2
Surt, Ṣaḥrā' – 60-61 H 2-3
Surtsey 30-31 C 3
Sürüç 46-47 H 4
Surud, Raas – 60-61 b 1
Suruga wan 50-51 M 5
Surulangun 52-53 D 7
Šuryškary 42-43 M 4
Susa 36-37 B 3
Susa [IR] 46-47 N 6
Susa [J] 50-51 H 5
Susa = Sūsah 60-61 G 1
Sušac 36-37 G 4
Sūsah [LAR] 60-61 J 2
Sūsah [TN] 60-61 G 1
Susaki 50-51 J 6
Susami 50-51 K 6
Susan = Susa 46-47 N 6
Susanville, CA 72-73 B 3
Suşehri 46-47 GH 2
Sušice 33 F 4
Susitna River 70-71 FG 5
Susquehanna, PA 74-75 EF 4
Susquehanna River 74-75 E 5
Susques 80 C 2
Sūssah 46-47 J 5
Sussey 32 FG 6
Susuman 42-43 cd 5
Susurluk 46-47 C 3
Sušac 36-37 G 4
Sušice 33 F 4
Sütçüler 46-47 D 4
Sutherland [ZA] 64-65 EF 9
Sutherlin, OR 76-77 B 4
Sutlej = Satlaj 44-45 L 4
Sutsien = Suqian 48-49 M 5
Sutter Creek, CA 76-77 C 6
Sutton, WV 74-75 C 5
Suttsu 50-51 ab 2
Suur väin 30-31 K 8
Suva 52-53 a 2
Suvorovo 36-37 N 3
Suwa 50-51 M 4
Suwa-ko 50-51 M 4-5
Suwałki 33 L 1
Suwałki 33 L 1
Suwannee River 74-75 b 2
Suwannee Sound 74-75 b 2
Șuwâr, Aș- 46-47 J 5
Suwaybit, As- 46-47 H 6
Suwaydā', As- 44-45 D 4
Suwayḥ 44-45 HJ 6
Suwayqīyah, Hawr as- 46-47 LM 6
Șuwayr 46-47 J 7
Șuwayrah, Aș- 46-47 L 6
Suways, As- 60-61 L 2-3
Suways, Khalīj as- 60-61 L 3
Suways, Qanat as- 60-61 L 2
Suweis, Es- = As-Suways 60-61 L 2-3
Suweis, Khalîg es – = Khalīj as-Suways 60-61 L 3
Suweis, Qanât es- = Qanat as-Suways 60-61 L 2
Suwŏn 48-49 P 4
Șuwwān, 'Arḍ eș- = 'Arḍ aș-Șawwān 46-47 G 7
Su Xian 48-49 M 5
Suxima = Tsushima 50-51 G 5
Sūy, Nahr – 60-61 K 7
Suzaka 50-51 M 4
Suzhou 48-49 N 5
Suzu 50-51 L 4
Suzuka 50-51 L 5
Suzu misaki 50-51 L 4
Svájc 33 CD 5
Svalbard 30-31 k 6-n 5
Svalbard 30-31 k 6-o 5
Svappavaara 30-31 J 4
Svartenhuk Halvø 70-71 Za 3
Svartisen 30-31 EF 4
Svatá Lucie 72-73 O 9
Sv'atoj Nos, mys – 42-43 ab 3
Svatovo 38-39 G 6
Svatý Kryštof a Nevis 72-73 O 8
Svatý Tomaš 60-61 F 8
Svatý Vincenc 72-73 O 9
Svay Rieng 52-53 E 4
Svazijsko 64-65 H 8
Sveagruva 30-31 k 6
Svealand 30-31 E-G 7
Svedala 30-31 E 10
Svédország 30-31 F 9-K 4
Svedorszag 30-31 F 9-K 4
Sveg 30-31 F 6
Svelvik 30-31 CD 8
Švenčionėliai 30-31 M 10
Svendborg 30-31 D 10
Svenskøya 30-31 mn 5
Šventoji 30-31 L 10
Sverdlovsk = Jekaterinburg 42-43 L 6
Sverdrup, ostrov – 42-43 O 3
Sverdrup Islands 70-71 P-T 2
Sverofríské o-vy 30-31 C 10
Svetac 36-37 F 4
Svetlaja 42-43 a 8
Svetlograd 38-39 H 6
Svetlyj [SU → Orsk] 42-43 L 7
Svetozarevo 36-37 J 3-4
Svilengrad 36-37 LM 5
Svir 30-31 M 10
Svir [SU, ~] 42-43 EF 5
Svirsk 42-43 T 7
Svištov 36-37 L 4
Svištov 36-37 L 4
Svobodnyj [SU ↑ Belogorsk] 42-43 YZ 7
Svolvær 30-31 F 3
Swaib, As- = Ash-Shuwayyib 46-47 MN 7
Swaibit, As- = As-Suwaybit 46-47 H 6
Swain Reefs 56-57 K 4
Swainsboro, GA 74-75 B 8
Șwaira, Aș- = Aș-Șuwayrah 46-47 L 6
Swakopmund 64-65 D 7
Swale 32 F 4
Swallow Islands 52-53 l 7
Swanage 32 F 6
Swan Hill 56-57 H 7
Swan Hills 70-71 N 7
Swan Range 76-77 G 2
Swan River [CDN, ●] 70-71 Q 7
Swansea 32 DE 6
Swansea, SC 74-75 C 8
Swans Island 74-75 J 2-3
Swanton, VT 74-75 G 2
Swartberge 64-65 F 9
Swasiland 64-65 H 8
Swât 44-45 L 3-4
Swatow = Shantou 48-49 M 7
Swaziland 64-65 H 8
Sweden 30-31 F 9-J 10
Sweetgrass, MT 76-77 GH 1
Sweet Home, OR 76-77 B 3
Sweetwater, TX 72-73 FG 5
Swellendam 64-65 F 9
Świdnica 33 H 3
Świdwin 33 GH 2
Świebodzin 33 G 2
Świecie 33 HJ 2
Swift Current 70-71 P 7-8
Swinburne, Cape – 70-71 R 3
Swindon 32 F 6
Swinemünde = Swinoujście 33 G 2
Swinoujście 33 G 2
Swinoujście 33 G 2
Switzerland 33 CD 5
Sybaris 36-37 G 6
Syberia 42-43 O-X 5
Sybin = Sibiu 36-37 L 3
Sychem = Nâbulus 46-47 F 6
Syczuańska, Kotlina – = Sichuan Pendi 48-49 JK 5-6
Sydney [AUS] 56-57 K 6
Sydney [CDN] 70-71 Y 8
Syene = Aswân 60-61 L 4
Syjamska, Zatoka – 52-53 D 4-5
Syktyvkar 42-43 J 5
Sylarna 30-31 E 6
Sylhet = Silhat 44-45 P 6
Sylt 33 D 1
Sylva, NC 74-75 B 7
Sylvania, GA 74-75 C 8
Sylvan Pass 76-77 H 3
Sylvester, GA 74-75 B 9
Sym 42-43 Q 5
Sýmē 36-37 M 7
Synaj, Półwysep – = Sīnā' 60-61 L 3
Syndassko 42-43 UV 3
Syowa 24 C 4-5
Syracuse, NY 72-73 LM 3
Syracuse = Siracusa 36-37 F 7
Syrakus = Siracusa 36-37 H 7
Syrakuzy = Siracusa 36-37 F 7
Syrdarja 42-43 M 9
Syria 44-45 D 4
Syriam = Thanlyin 52-53 C 3
Syrian Desert 44-45 DE 4
Sýrie 42-43 D 4
Syrië 44-45 D 4
Syrie 44-45 D 4
Syrie, Désert de – 44-45 DE 4
Syrien 44-45 D 4
Syrische Woestijn 44-45 DE 4
Syrische Wüste 44-45 DE 4
Syrjanowsk = Zyr'anovsk 42-43 PQ 8
Sýrna 36-37 M 7
Sýros 36-37 L 7
Syrská poušť 44-45 DE 4
Syryjska, Pustynia – 44-45 DE 4
Sysert' 38-39 M 4
Sysladobsis Lake 74-75 JK 2
Sysola 38-39 K 3
Sysran = Syzran' 42-43 N 7
Sytynja 42-43 YZ 4
Syzran' 42-43 N 7
Szamos 36-37 K 2
Szamotuły 33 H 2
Szawle = Šiauliai 30-31 KL 10
Szawle = Šiauliai 30-31 KL 10
Szczecin 33 G 2
Szczecinek 33 H 2
Szczytno 33 K 2
Szechuan = Sichuan 48-49 J 6-K 5
Szeged 33 JK 5
Székesfehérvár 33 J 5
Szekszárd 33 J 5
Szemao = Simao 48-49 J 7
Szeming = Xiamen 48-49 M 7
Szentes 33 K 5
Szeping = Siping 48-49 N 3
Szeskie Wzgórza 33 L 1
Szkocja 32 D 3-E 4
Szolnok 33 K 5
Szombathely 33 H 5
Sztokholm = Stockholm 30-31 H 8
Szū-mao = Simao 48-49 J 7
Szumawa 33 F 4
Szū-p'ing = Siping 48-49 N 3
Szū-tao-kou = Sidaogou 50-51 F 2
Szwajcaria 33 CD 5
Szwecja 30-31 F 9-K 4

Š

Šabac 36-37 H 3
Šack 38-39 H 5
Šadrinsk 42-43 LM 6
Šagany, ozero – 36-37 NO 3
Šagonar 42-43 R 7
Šaḥḥât = Shaḥḥât 60-61 J 2
Šachrisabz 44-45 K 3
Šachtinsk 42-43 N 8
Šachty 38-39 H 6
Šachunja 42-43 GH 6
Šaim 42-43 L 5
Šajmak 44-45 L 3
Šalkar 38-39 K 5
Šalkar, ozero – 38-39 K 5
Šalomounovy ostrovy [⊙] 52-53 h 6-k 7
Šalomounovy ostrovy [★] 52-53 kl 7
Šangaly 38-39 H 3
Šantarskije ostrova 42-43 a 6-7
Šarja 42-43 H 6
Šarkovskij 38-39 F 4
Šarkovščina 30-31 MN 10
Šar Süm = Altay 48-49 F 2
Šaryngol 48-49 K 2
Šaul'der 42-43 M 9
Ščeglovsk = Kemerovo 42-43 PQ 6
Ščuč'a 38-39 N 2
Ščučinsk 42-43 MN 7
Šedok 38-39 H 7
Šegovary 38-39 H 3
Šeki 38-39 J 7
Šelagskij, mys – 42-43 gh 3
Šelichova, zaliv – 42-43 e 5-6
Šemonaicha 42-43 P 7
Šenber 42-43 M 8
Šenkursk 42-43 G 5
Šepetovka 38-39 E 5
Šerkaly 42-43 M 5
Šerlovaja Gora 42-43 W 7
Šibenik 36-37 FG 4
Šichrany = Kanaš 42-43 H 6
Šilega 42-43 GH 5
Šilka 42-43 W 7
Šilkan 42-43 c 6
Šilutė 30-31 J 10
Šimanovsk 42-43 Y 7
Šindy = Sajmak 44-45 L 3
Šipčenski prohod 36-37 LM 4
Šira [SU] 42-43 QR 7
Šir'ajevo 36-37 O 2
Šitkino 42-43 S 6
Šiveluč, vulkan – 42-43 f 6
Šjauljaj = Šiauliai 30-31 KL 10
Šmidta, ostrov – 42-43 QR 1
Šojna [SU] 42-43 G 4
Šokal'skogo, ostrov – 42-43 NO 3
Šokal'skogo, proliv – 42-43 RS 2
Šologoncy 42-43 VW 4
Šolta 36-37 G 4
Šostka 38-39 F 5
Španělsko 34-35 D 7-G 9
Špola 38-39 F 6
Štětín = Szczecin 33 G 2
Štip 36-37 K 5
Štýr.Hradec = Graz 33 G 5
Šubarkuduk 42-43 K 8
Šuga 42-43 N 4
Šuja [SU, Ivanovo] 42-43 G 6
Šuljereckoje 38-39 F 3
Šul'mak = Novabad 44-45 L 3
Šumava 33 F 4
Šumen 36-37 M 4
Šumerl'a 38-39 J 4
Šumicha 42-43 L 6
Šumperk 33 H 3-4
Šupunskij, mys – 42-43 f 7
Šurab 44-45 L 2
Šuryškary 42-43 M 4
Švédsko 30-31 F 9-K 4
Švenčionėliai 30-31 M 10
Švýcarsko 33 CD 5

Ś

Śląsk 33 GH 3
Śląsk 33 GH 3
Śniardwy, Jezioro – 33 K 2
Śrem 33 H 2
Środa Wielkopolska 33 HJ 2
Środkowoafrykańska, Republika – 60-61 HJ 7
Środkowosyberyjska, Wyżyna – 42-43 R-X 4-5
Środkowy Zachód = Middle West 72-73 F-J 3

Środk 221

Śródziemne, Morze -
36-37 C 7-M 8
Świdnica 33 H 3
Świdwin 33 GH 2
Świebodzin 33 G 2
Świecie 33 HJ 2
Świetego Wawrzyńca, Zatoka -
= Gulf of Saint Lawrence
70-71 Y 8

Sz

Szahara 60-61 C-K 4
Szaharai-Atlasz 60-61 D 2-F 1
Szaloniki = Thessaloníkē
36-37 K 5
Szamarkand = Samarkand
44-45 JK 3
Szambolcs-Szatmár-Bereg
42-43 JK 8
Szamoa 52-53 c 1
Szamoa-szigetek = Samoa
Islands 52-53 c 1
Szamos 36-37 K 2
Szamotuly 33 H 2
Szárazér-Porgányi-főcsatorna
42-43 H 10
Szaúd-Arábia 44-45 D 5-F 6
Szawle = Šiauliai 30-31 KL 10

Szczecin 33 G 2
Szczecinek 33 H 2
Szczytno 33 K 2

Szechuan = Sichuan
48-49 J 6-K 5
Szeged 33 JK 5
Székesfehérvár 33 J 5
Szekszárd 33 J 4
Szemao = Simao 48-49 J 7
Szeming = Xiamen 48-49 M 7
Szenegál 60-61 AB 6
Szentes 33 K 5
Szeping = Siping 48-49 N 3
Szerbia 36-37 H 3-J 4
Szeskie Wzgórza 33 L 1

Sziám = Thaiföld 52-53 CD 3
Sziámi-öböl 52-53 D 4-5
Szibéria 42-43 O-X 5
Sziklás-hegység = Rocky
Mountains 70-71 L 5-P 9
Szilézia 33 GH 3
Színai-félsziget = Sínā' 60-61 C 3
Szingapur 52-53 DE 6
Sziria 44-45 D 4
Szir-sivatag 44-45 DE 4

Szkocja 32 D 3-E 4

Szlovénia 36-37 F 3-G 2

Szmirna = İzmir 44-45 B 3
Szmirna = İzmir 36-37 M 6

Szófia = Sofija 36-37 K 4
Szolnok 33 K 5
Szomália 60-61 N 8-O 7
Szombathely 33 H 5

Szpárti = Spártē 36-37 K 7
Szporádok 36-37 M 6-7

Sztokholm = Stockholm
30-31 H 8

Szudán [≅] 60-61 C-K 6
Szudán [★] 60-61 KL 6
Szuez = As-Suways 60-61 L 3
Szü-mao = Simao 48-49 J 7
Szumátra 52-53 C 6-D 7
Szumawa 33 F 4
Szü-p'ing = Siping 48-49 N 3
Szü-tao-kou = Sidaogou
50-51 F 2

Szváziföld 64-65 H 8

Szwajcaria 33 CD 5
Szwecja 30-31 F 9-K 4

T

Ta = Da Xian 48-49 K 5
Tabaco 52-53 H 4
Tābah, Bi'r - 62 F 3
Tabajé, Ponta - 78-79 LM 5
Tabankort 60-61 D 5
Tabarka = Ṭabarqah 60-61 F 1
Ṭabarqah 60-61 F 1
Ṭabas 44-45 H 4
Tabasco 72-73 H 8
Tăbašino 38-39 J 4
Tabašino 38-39 J 4
Tabatinga [BR, Amazonas]
78-79 F 5
Taber 70-71 O 7
Taberg 30-31 EF 9
Tablas Island 52-53 H 4

Table, Île de la - = Đao Cai Ban
52-53 E 2
Table Mountain 76-77 G 3
Taboga 72-73 b 3
Taboga, Isla - 72-73 bc 3
Taboguilla, Isla - 72-73 bc 3
Tábor 33 G 4
Tabora 64-65 H 4
Tabor City, NC 74-75 D 7
Tabory 38-39 M 4
Tabou 60-61 C 8
Tabris = Tabrīz 44-45 F 3
Tabrīz 44-45 F 3
Tabu-dong 50-51 G 4
Tabūk 44-45 D 5
Tăby 30-31 GH 8
Tabyn-Bogdo-Ola = gora Tavan
Bogdo Ula 48-49 F 2
Tacau = Kaohsiung 48-49 MN 7
Ta-ch'ang-shan Tao =
Dachangshan Dao 50-51 D 3
T'a-ch'ěng = Chuguchak
48-49 E 2
Tachia 48-49 MN 7
Tachibana-wan 50-51 GH 6
Tachikawa 50-51 M 5
Ta-ch'ing Shan = Daqing Shan
48-49 L 3
Tachnoj 42-43 TU 7
Tachta 42-43 a 7
Tachta-Bazar 44-45 J 3
Tachtabrod 42-43 M 7
Tachtojamsk 42-43 de 5
Ta-ch'üan = Daquan 48-49 H 3
Tacloban 52-53 HJ 4
Tacna [PE, ●] 78-79 E 8
Tacoma, WA 72-73 B 2
Taconic Range 74-75 G 3-4
Tacora, Volcán - 80 C 1
Tacuarembó [ROU, ●] 80 EF 4
Tadami gawa 50-51 M 4
Tademaït, Plateau du - =
Hadbah Tādmayt 60-61 E 3
Tâḍipatri = Tadpatri 44-45 M 7-8
Tadjikie 44-45 KL 3
Tadjoura 60-61 N 6
Tadjoura, Golfe de - 60-61 N 6
Tâdmâyt, Ḥaḅdah - 60-61 E
Tadmur 44-45 D 4
Tadoussac 70-71 X 8
Tadpatri 44-45 M 7-8
Tadschikistan 44-45 KL 3
Tadum = Tradum 48-49 E 6
Tadžikistán 44-45 KL 3
Tadžikistan 44-45 KL 3
Tádžikistán 44-45 KL 3
Tadžikskaja Sovetskaja
Socialističeskaja Respublika =
Tadschikistan 44-45 KL 3
Tadžykistan 44-45 KL 3
Tadzsikisztán 44-45 KL 3
T'aean 50-51 E 3
T'aebaek-san 50-51 G 4
T'aebaek-sanmaek 48-49 O 4
Taebu-do 50-51 F 4
T'aech'ŏn 50-51 E 3
Taech'ŏng-do 50-51 E 4
Taedong-gang 50-51 EF 3
Taegu 48-49 O 4
Tae-hüksan-do 50-51 E 5
Taehwa-do 50-51 E 3
Taejŏn 48-49 O 4
Taejŏng 50-51 EF 6
Tae-muŭi-do 50-51 EF 4
Ta-êrh Hu = Dalaj Nur 48-49 M 3
T'aet'an 50-51 E 3
Tae-yŏnp'yŏng-do 50-51 E 4
Tafalla 34-35 G 7
Tafaraut = Ṭarfāyah 60-61 B 3
Tafassasat, Wâdî - 60-61 F 4
Tafassasat, Ouèd - = Wâdî
Tafâssasat 60-61 F 4
Tafassasset, Ténéré du -
60-61 FG 4
Tafdasat 60-61 F 3-4
Ṭafilah, Aṭ- 46-47 F 7
Tafi Viejo 80 C 3
Tafresh 46-47 N 5
Tafresh, Kūh-e - 46-47 NO 5
Taft, CA 76-77 D 8
Taftân, Kūh-e - 44-45 J 5
Tagalgan 48-49 H 4
Taganrog 38-39 G 6
Taganrogskij zaliv 38-39 G 6
Tăgau 52-53 C 2
Tagawa = Takawa 50-51 H 6
Tagbilaran 52-53 H 5
Tag-Dheer = Togdheer 60-61 b 2
Tâghît 60-61 D 2
Tagil 38-39 M 4
Tagiüra = Tâjûrâ' 60-61 G 2
Tâgu = Taegu 48-49 O 4
Taguatinga [BR, Distrito Federal]
78-79 K 8
Taguatinga [BR, Goiás] 78-79 K 7
Tagula 52-53 h 7
Tagum 52-53 J 5
Tahan, Gunung - 52-53 D 6
Tahara 50-51 L 5
Tahat 60-61 F 4
Tahoe, Lake - 72-73 BC 4
Tahoe City, CA 76-77 C 6
Tahoe Valley, CA 76-77 CD 6

Tahola, WA 76-77 A 2
Tahoua 60-61 F 6
Taḥrīr, At- 62 CD 2
Ta-hsien = Da Xian 48-49 K 5
Ta-hsüeh Shan = Daxue Shan
48-49 J 5-6
Ṭaḥṭā 60-61 J 5
Tahtacı = Borlu 46-47 C 3
Tahtalı Dağı 46-47 D 4
Tahtali Dağlar 46-47 F 4-G 3
Ta-hu = Tachia 48-49 MN 7
Tahulandang, Pulau - 52-53 J 6
Tahuna 52-53 HJ 6
Ta-hu-shan = Dahushan
50-51 D 2
Taï 60-61 C 7
Tai'an [TJ, Liaoning] 50-51 D 2
Tai'an [TJ, Shandong] 48-49 M 4
Taibai Shan 48-49 K 5
Taibei = Taipei 48-49 N 6-7
Taichū = Taichung 48-49 MN 7
Taichung 48-49 MN 7
T'ai-chung = Taichung
48-49 MN 7
Taiden = Taejŏn 48-49 O 4
Taidong = Taitung 48-49 N 7
Ṭā'if, Aṭ- 44-45 E 6
Taigu 48-49 L 4
Taihang Shan 48-49 LM 4
Taihe [TJ, Jiangxi] 48-49 L 6
Taihei yō 50-51 K 7-O 3
Taihing = Taixing 48-49 N 5
Taiho = Taihe [TJ, Jiangxi]
48-49 L 6
Taihoku = Tai-pei 48-49 N 6-7
Tai Hu [TJ, ≈] 48-49 MN 5
Taiki 50-51 c 2
Taiku = Taegu 48-49 O 4
Tailai 48-49 N 2
T'ai-lai = Tailai 48-49 N 2
Tailem Bend 56-57 GH 7
Taim 80 F 4
Tain 32 D 3
Tai-nan 48-49 MN 7
T'ai-nan = Tai-nan 48-49 MN 7
Tainaro, Akrōtērion - 36-37 K 7
Taipale 30-31 N 6
Taipeh = Tai-pei 48-49 N 6-7
Tai-pei 48-49 N 6-7
Taiping [MAL] 52-53 CD 5-6
Taipingshao 50-51 E 2
Taiping Yang 48-49 O 8-R 5
Taipinsan = Miyako-jima
48-49 O 7
Taisei 50-51 ab 2
Taisha 50-51 J 5
Taishun 48-49 MN 6
Ta'iss = Ta'izz 44-45 E 8
Taitao, Cabo - 80 A 7
Taitao, Península de - 80 AB 7
T'ai-tchong = Tai-chung
48-49 MN 7
Taitō = Tai-tung 48-49 N 7
Tai-tung 48-49 N 7
T'ai-tzŭ Ho = Taizi He 50-51 D 2
Taivalkoski 30-31 N 5
Taivassalo 30-31 JK 7
Taiwa 50-51 N 3
Taiwan 48-49 N 7
Taiwán 48-49 N 7
Taiwan 48-49 N 7
T'ai-wan Hai-hsia 48-49 M 7-N 6
Taiwan Haixia = T'ai-wan Hai-hsia
48-49 M 7-N 6
T'ai-wan Shan 48-49 N 7
Taiwanský průliv = Taiwan
Haihsia 48-49 M 7-N 6
Taixing 48-49 N 5
T'ai-yüan = Taiyuan 48-49 L 4
Taizhong = Taichung 48-49 MN 7
Taizhou 48-49 MN 5
Taizi He 50-51 D 2
Ta'izz 44-45 E 8
Tâj, At- 60-61 J 4
Tajarhī 60-61 G 4
Tajdžinar nuur 48-49 GH 4
Tajdžinar nuur 48-49 GH 4
Tajga 42-43 PQ 6
Tajgonos, mys - 42-43 ef 5
Tajgonos, poluostrov - 42-43 f 5
Tajima 50-51 M 4
Tajis 44-45 G 8
Tajitos 76-77 G 10
Tajlandia 52-53 CD 3
Tajmír (Dolgan-Nyenyec)
Autonóm Körzet 42-43 P-U 3
Tajmura 42-43 ST 5
Tajmyr, Circunscripción Nacional
de - 42-43 P-U 3
Tajmyr, ozero - 42-43 TU 3
Tajmyr, poluostrov - 42-43 R-U 2
Tajmyrský (Dolgansko-něnecký)
autonomní okruh 42-43 P-U 3
Tajo 34-35 F 8
Tajsir 48-49 F 2
Tajšet 42-43 S 6
Tajumulco, Volcán de -
72-73 H 8
Tajuña 34-35 F 8
Tajuña 34-35 F 8

Tajūrā' 60-61 G 2
Tajvan 48-49 N 7
Tajvani-szoros = Taiwan Haihsia
48-49 M 7-N 6
Tajwan 48-49 N 7
Tajwańska, Cieśnina - = Taiwan
Haihsia 48-49 M 7-N 6
Tak 52-53 C 3
Takâb 46-47 M 4
Takaba 63 E 2
Takachiho = Mitai 50-51 H 6
Takada 48-49 Q 4
Takada = Bungotakada 50-51 H 6
Takada = Rikuzen-Takata
50-51 NO 3
Takahagi 50-51 N 4
Takahashi 50-51 J 5
Takahashi-gawa 50-51 J 5
Takahe, Mount - 24 B 25-26
Takalar 52-53 G 8
Takamatsu 48-49 PQ 5
Takamatu = Takamatsu
48-49 PQ 5
Takamori 50-51 H 6
Takanabe 50-51 H 6
Takao = Kao-hsiung 48-49 MN 7
Takaoka 48-49 Q 4
Takapuna 56-57 O 7
Takasaki 48-49 Q 4
Takataka 52-53 k 6
Takawa 50-51 H 6
Takayama 50-51 L 4
Takefu 50-51 KL 5
Takemachi = Taketa 50-51 H 6
Takengon 52-53 C 6
Takéo 52-53 D 4
Take-shima [J, Ōsumi shotō]
50-51 H 7
Take-shima [J ↖ Oki] 50-51 HJ 4
Taketa 50-51 H 6
Takhīs, Bi'r - 62 CD 6
Ta Khmau 52-53 DE 4
Takht-e Jämshīd = Persepolis
44-45 G 4
Takikawa 50-51 b 2
Takinoue 50-51 c 1
Takla Lake 70-71 O 4
Takla Makan 48-49 D-F 4
Takla Makan Chöli 48-49 D-F 4
Takla Makan Chöli 48-49 D-F 4
Takla Makan Chöli 48-49 D-F 4
Tako-bana 50-51 J 5
Takoma Park, MD 74-75 E 5
Takua Pa 52-53 C 5
Takyu = Taegu 48-49 O 4
Talā [ET] 62 D 2
Talacasto 80 C 4
Talaimannar = Taleimannarama
44-45 MN 9
Talak 60-61 EF 5
Tálaqān 46-47 O 4
Talara 78-79 C 5
Talas 44-45 G 8
Talasea 52-53 gh 6
Talaud, Kepulauan - 52-53 J 6
Talavera de la Reina 34-35 E 8-9
Talawdī 60-61 L 6
Talbingo 58 J 5
Talbot, Cape - 56-57 E 2
Talbot, Mount - 56-57 E 5
Talcahuano 80 AB 5
Taldy-Kurgan 42-43 OP 8
Taleimannarama 44-45 MN 9
Talent, OR 76-77 B 4
Tale Sap = Thale Luang
52-53 D 5
Tali = Dali [TJ, Yunnan]
48-49 HJ 6
Taliabu, Pulau - 52-53 HJ 7
Talica 38-39 M 4
Ta-lien = Dalian 48-49 N 4
Talimā 78-79 H 4
Ta-ling Ho = Daling He 50-51 G 2
Taliwang 52-53 G 8
Talju, Jabal - 60-61 K 6
Talkeetna Mountains 70-71 G 5
Talkheh Rūd 46-47 M 3
Talladega, AL 72-73 J 5
Tall 'Afar 46-47 K 4
Tallahassee, FL 72-73 K 5
Tall al-Abyad 46-47 H 4
Tall as-Sam'ān 46-47 H 4
Tall Bisah 46-47 G 5
Tall Ḥalaf 46-47 HJ 4
Tall Kalakh 46-47 G 5
Tall Kayf 46-47 K 4
Tall Kujik 46-47 JK 4
Tall Tāmir 46-47 J 4
Tall 'Uwaynāt 46-47 K 4
Tal'menka 42-43 PQ 7
Talo = Nantong 48-49 N 5
Talŏdī = Talawdī 60-61 L 6
Talovaja 38-39 GH 5
Talsi 30-31 K 9
Taltal 80 B 3
Taltson River 70-71 O 5

Talvār, Rūdkhāneh - 46-47 MN 5
Talvik 30-31 K 2
Talwood 58 J 2
Tamādah 60-61 E 4
Tamale 60-61 D 7
Tamana [J] 50-51 H 6
Tamano 50-51 JK 5
Tamanrasset 60-61 EF 4
Tamanrâsat, Wâdī - 60-61 E 4
Tamaqua, PA 74-75 F 4
Tamarugal, Pampa del - 80 C 1-2
Tamási 33 J 5
Tamatave = Toamasina
64-65 LM 6
Tamaulipas 72-73 G 6-7
Tamayama 50-51 N 3
Tambach 63 CD 2
Tambacounda 60-61 B 6
Tambaqui 78-79 G 6
Tambej 42-43 N 3
Tambo 56-57 J 4
Tambo, El - [CO, Cauca]
78-79 D 4
Tambo, Río - [PE ◁ Río Ucayali]
78-79 E 7
Tambohorano 64-65 K 6
Tambora, Gunung - 52-53 G 8
Tamboritha, Mount - 58 H 6
Tambov 38-39 H 5
Tamč 48-49 G 2
Tam Cag Bulak = Tamsagbulag
48-49 M 2
Tamč 48-49 G 2
Tamdybulak 42-43 L 9
Tâmega 34-35 D 8
Tâmesis = Thames 32 G 6
Tamgak, Monts - 60-61 F 5
Tamiahua, Laguna de -
72-73 G 7
Tamiami Canal 74-75 c 4
Tamil Nadu 44-45 M 8-9
Ta'mīn, At- 46-47 KL 5
Tâmir'z'qīd 60-61 AB 5
Tamise = Thames 32 G 6
Tâmīyah 62 D 3
Tamiza = Thames 32 G 6
Tam Ky 52-53 E 3
Tammerfors = Tampere
30-31 K 7
Tammisaari = Ekenäs 30-31 K 7
Tampa, FL 72-73 K 6
Tampa Bay 72-73 K 6
Tampelan, Kepulauan -
52-53 E 6
Tampere 30-31 KL 7
Tampico 72-73 G 7
Tampin 52-53 D 6
Tampoketsa, Plateau du - =
Causse du Kelifely 64-65 KL 6
Tamrīdah 44-45 G 8
Tamsagbulag 48-49 M 2
Tâmshikiţ 60-61 BC 5
Tamud = Thamūd 44-45 F 7
Tamworth [AUS] 56-57 K 6
Tamyang 50-51 F 5
Tana [EAK] 64-65 JK 3
Tana [Vanuatu] 56-57 N 3
Tana [N, -] 30-31 M 2-3
Tana [N, ●] 30-31 N 2
Tanabat 52-53 C 6
Tanabe 50-51 K 6
Tanabu = Mutsu 50-51 N 2
Tanacross, AK 70-71 H 5
Ta-n-Adar 60-61 F 5
Tanafjord 30-31 N 2
Tanaga Island 19 D 36-1
Tanágra 36-37 K 6
Tana Hayiķ 60-61 M 6
Tanahbala, Pulau - 52-53 C 7
Tanahgrogot 52-53 G 7
Tanahjampea, Pulau - 52-53 H 8
Tanahkadukung 52-53 H 9
Tanahmasa, Pulau - 52-53 C 6-7
Tanah Menah 52-53 D 5
Tanahmerah 52-53 LM 8
Tanakeke, Pulau - 52-53 G 8
Tanami 56-57 E 3
Tanami Desert 56-57 F 3
Tanana, AK 70-71 F 4
Tananarive = Antananarivo
64-65 L 6
Tanana River 70-71 G 5
Tân Âp 52-53 E 3
Tânaro 36-37 B 3
Ṭanburah 60-61 K 7
Tanchavur = Thanjavur
44-45 MN 8
Tanch'ŏn 50-51 G 2
Tanchow = Dan Xian 48-49 K 8
Tancitaro, Pico de - 72-73 F 8
Tandag 52-53 J 5
Tandaho = Tendaho 60-61 N 6
Tandil 80 E 5
Tandou Lake 58 EF 4
Tandža = Ṭanjah 60-61 C 1
Tanega-shima 48-49 P 5
Tanega sima = Tanega-shima
48-49 P 5
Tanew 33 L 3
Tanezrouft = Tânîzruft
60-61 DE 4
Tanf, Jabal at- 46-47 H 6
Tanga 64-65 J 4

Tangail = Ṭāngâyal 44-45 O 6
Tanga Islands 52-53 h 5
Tanganyika, Lake -
64-65 G 3-H 4
Tangar = Thangkar 48-49 J 4
Tangâyal 44-45 O 6
T'ang-chan = Tangshan
48-49 M 4
Tanger = Ṭanjah 60-61 C 1
Ṭanggela Youmu Hu = Thangra
Yumtsho 48-49 EF 5
Tanggu 48-49 M 4
Tangier Sound 74-75 EF 5-6
Tangjin 50-51 F 4
Tang La [TJ, Himalaya ⇆]
48-49 F 6
Tang La [TJ, Tanglha] 48-49 G 5
Tangla = Tanglha 48-49 FG 5
Tanglha 48-49 FG 5
Tangshan 48-49 M 4
Tangshancheng 50-51 DE 2
Tanguj 42-43 T 6
Tangyuan 48-49 O 2
Tanhsien = Dan Xian 48-49 K 8
Tanimbar, Kepulauan - 52-53 K 8
Taninthâri 52-53 C 4
Taninthâri Taing 52-53 C 4
Tânîzruft 60-61 DE 4
Ṭanjah 60-61 C 1
Tanjay 52-53 H 5
Tanjong Malim 52-53 D 6
Tanjor = Thanjavur 44-45 MN 8
Tanjung 52-53 G 7
Tanjungbalai 52-53 CD 6
Tanjungkarang 52-53 DE 8
Tanjungkarang-Telukbetung =
Bandar Lampung 52-53 DE 8
Tanjungpandan 52-53 E 7
Tanjungpinang 52-53 DE 6
Tanjungredep 52-53 G 6
Tanlovo 42-43 NO 4
Tännäs 30-31 E 6
Tannûmah, At- 46-47 MN 7
Tannu-Ola, chrebet - 42-43 R 7
Tanoé 60-61 D 7
Tanoút 60-61 F 6
Tanque, AZ 76-77 J 9
Tansania 64-65 HJ 4
Tan-shui 48-49 N 6
Tansîft, Wâdī - 60-61 C 2
Ṭan-šan 48-49 C-G 3
Ṭanṭā 60-61 KL 2
Tanyang 50-51 G 4
Tanyeri 46-47 HJ 3
Tanzania 64-65 HJ 4
Tanzania 64-65 HJ 4
Tanzanie 64-65 HJ 4
Tanzanie 64-65 HJ 4
Taoan 48-49 N 2
Tao'an = Baicheng 48-49 N 2
T'ao-chou = Lintan 48-49 J 5
Taormina 36-37 F 7
Taos, NM 72-73 E 4
Taoudenni 60-61 D 4
Taourirt = Tâwrīrt 60-61 D 2
Tapa 30-31 L 8
Tapachula 72-73 H 9
Tapajós, Rio - 78-79 H 5
Tapaktuan 52-53 C 6
Ta-pa Shan = Daba Shan
48-49 KL 5
Tapat, Pulau - 52-53 J 7
Tapauá 78-79 FG 6
Tapauá, Rio - 78-79 F 6
Tapepo 63 B 4
Taperoá [BR, Bahia] 78-79 M 7
Tapeta 60-61 C 7
Tâpî = Tapti 44-45 M 6
Ta-pieh Shan = Dabie Shan
48-49 LM 5
Tapini 52-53 N 8
Tapirapecó, Sierra - 78-79 FG 4
Tappahannock, VA 74-75 E 5-6
Tappi-saki 50-51 MN 2
Tappita = Tapeta 60-61 C 7
Tapti 44-45 M 6
Tapuaenuku 56-57 O 8
Tapuruquara 78-79 FG 5
Ṭaqṭaq 46-47 L 5
Tara 36-37 H 4
Tara [AUS] 56-57 K 5
Tara [N, -] 42-43 O 6
Tara [SU, ●] 42-43 N 6
Taram Darya = Tarim darya
48-49 E 3
Taran, mys - 33 JK 1
Tarangire National Park 63 D 3-4
Táranto 36-37 G 5
Táranto, Golfo di - 36-37 G 5

Tarapoto 78-79 D 6
Taraquá 78-79 F 4
Tarare 34-35 K 6
Tarascon 34-35 K 7
Tarasovo 38-39 J 2
Tarat, Ouèd – = Wādī Tarāt 60-61 F 3
Tarāt, Wādī – 60-61 F 3
Tarauacá 78-79 E 6
Tarauacá, Rio – 78-79 E 6
Tarayfāwī 46-47 J 7
Tarazona 34-35 G 8
Tarbagataij, chrebet – 42-43 PQ 8
Tarbagataj 48-49 EF 2
Tarbaj 63 E 2
Tarbes 34-35 H 7
Tarboro, NC 74-75 E 7
Tarchankut, mys – 36-37 OP 3
Tarcoola 56-57 FG 6
Tarcoon 58 H 3
Tardoire 34-35 H 6
Tardoki-Jani, gora – 42-43 a 8
Taree 56-57 K 6
Tareja = Ust'-Tareja 42-43 R 3
Tärendö 30-31 JK 4
Tarent = Taranto 36-37 G 5
Tarente = Tàranto 36-37 G 5
Tarento = Tàranto 36-37 G 5
Tareraimbu, Cachoeira – 78-79 J 6
Ṭarfā', Wādī aṭ- 62 D 3
Ṭarfāwī, Bi'r – [ET] 62 C 6
Ṭarfāwī, Bi'r – [IRQ] 46-47 K 5
Ṭarfāyah [MA, ●] 60-61 B 3
Ṭarfāyah, Qārat aṭ- 62 BC 2
Tarfāyah, Rā's – 60-61 B 3
Targhee Pass 76-77 H 3
Târgovište 36-37 M 4
Târgovište 36-37 M 4
Tarhit = Tāghīt 60-61 D 2
Tarhūnah [DZ] 60-61 G 2
Tarian Ganga = Dariganga 48-49 L 2
Tarīf 44-45 G 6
Tarifa 34-35 E 11
Tarifa, Punta de – 34-35 DE 10
Tarija [BOL, ●] 78-79 G 9
Tarīm 44-45 F 7
Tarim darya 48-49 E 3
Tarime 63 C 3
Tarkio, MT 76-77 F 2
Tarko-Sale 42-43 O 5
Tarkwa 60-61 D 7
Tarlac 52-53 H 3
Ṭārmīyah, Aṭ- 46-47 KL 6
Tarn 34-35 H 7
Tärna 30-31 F 5
Tarnów 33 K 3
Ṭārom 44-45 GH 5
Taroom 56-57 JK 5
Târoûdânt = Tārūdānt 60-61 C 2
Tarpon Springs, FL 74-75 b 2
Tarquinia 36-37 D 4
Tarragona 34-35 H 8
Tarrakoski 30-31 J 3
Tar River 74-75 E 7
Tarso = Tarsus 46-47 F 4
Tarso Emissi = Kégueur Terbi 60-61 H 4
Tarsus 46-47 F 4
Tarsusırmağı 46-47 F 4
Tartagal [RA, Salta] 80 D 2
Tartār, Wādī at- 46-47 K 5
Tartaria, Estrecho de – 42-43 b 7-a 8
Tartaria, República Autònoma de – = 6 ◁ 42-43 J 6
Tartarie, Manche de – 42-43 b 7-a 8
Tartas [SU] 42-43 O 6
Ṭartīn, Bi'r – 46-47 J 5
Tartu 30-31 M 8
Ṭarṭūs 44-45 D 4
Tārūdant 60-61 C 2
Tarūfāwī, Bi'r – 46-47 K 6
Tarumizu 50-51 H 7
Tarutino 36-37 N 2
Tarutung 52-53 C 6
Tarvisio 36-37 E 2
Tašauz 42-43 K 9
Tasāwah 60-61 G 3
Taşçı = Bakırdağı 46-47 F 3
Tasejevo 42-43 RS 6
Taşeli Yaylâsı 46-47 E 4
Tashichhö Dsong = Thimbu 44-45 OP 5
Tashigong = Zhaxigang 48-49 DE 5
Tashi Gonpa 48-49 G 5
Ta-shih-ch'iao = Dashiqiao 50-51 D 2
Tashijong Dsong 44-45 P 5
Tashilhumpo = Zhaxilhünbo 48-49 F 6
Ṭashk, Daryācheh – 44-45 GH 5
Tash Qurghan 48-49 D 4
Tasikmalaja 52-53 E 8
Taškent 42-43 M 9
Tasköprü 46-47 F 2
Tasköprü = Hekimdağ 46-47 D 3
Taš-Kumyr 44-45 L 2
Tas-Kystabyt 42-43 bc 5
Taşlıcay 46-47 K 3
Tasman, Mar de – 56-57 K-N 7
Tasman, Mer de – 56-57 K-N 7
Tasmana, Morze – 56-57 K-N 7
Tasman Bay 56-57 O 8
Tasman Head 58 cd 3
Tasmania 56-57 HJ 8
Tasmania, Dorsal de – 22-23 R 8
Tasmánie = Tasmania 56-57 HJ 8
Tasmanie = Tasmania 56-57 HJ 8
Tasmanie, Seuil de – 22-23 R 8
Tasmanien = Tasmania 56-57 HJ 8
Tasmanischer Rücken 22-23 R 8
Tasman Land 56-57 D 3-E 2
Tasmanovo moře 56-57 K-N 7
Tasman Peninsula 58 d 3
Tasman Rise 22-23 R 8
Tasmanrug 22-23 R 8
Tasman Sea 56-57 K-N 7
Tasmansee 56-57 K-N 7
Tasman-tenger 56-57 K-N 7
Tasmanzee 56-57 K-N 7
Taşova 46-47 G 2
Tassili n'Ajjer = Murtaf'āt Tāsīlī 60-61 F 3
Taštagol 42-43 Q 7
Taštyp 42-43 Q 7
Tasūj 46-47 L 3
Tašauz 42-43 K 9
Taškent 42-43 M 9
Taš-Kumyr 44-45 L 2
Taštagol 42-43 Q 7
Taštyp 42-43 Q 7
Tata 33 J 5
Tatabánya 33 HJ 5
Tatár Autonóm Köztársaság 42-43 J 6
Tatar Autonomous Region = 6 ◁ 42-43 J 6
Tatarbunary 36-37 N 3
Tataren Autonome Republiek = 6 ◁ 42-43 J 6
Tatarensont 42-43 b 7-a 8
Tatarische Autonome Republik = 6 ◁ 42-43 J 6
Tatarischer Sund 42-43 b 7-a 8
Tatars, République Autonome des – = 6 ◁ 42-43 J 6
Tatarsk 42-43 NO 6
Tatarska, Cieśnina – 42-43 b 7-a 8
Tatarska Autonomiczna Republika 42-43 J 6
Tatarskaja Avtonomnaja Sovetskaja Socialističeskaja Respublika = Tatarische Autonome Republik = 6 ◁ 42-43 J 6
Tatarský průliv 42-43 b 7-a 8
Tatarstán 42-43 J 6
Tatar Strait 42-43 b 7-a 8
Tatár-szoros 42-43 b 7-a 8
Tātā'ū, Rūd-e – 46-47 LM 4
Taṭāwīn 60-61 G 2
Tateoka = Murayama 50-51 N 3
Tateyama 50-51 M 5
Tateyamahōjō = Tateyama 50-51 M 5
Tathlina Lake 70-71 N 5
Tathlīth 44-45 E 7
Tathlīth, Wādī – 44-45 E 6-7
Tatlīt = Tathlīth 44-45 E 7
Tatnam, Cape – 70-71 ST 6
Ta-t'ong = Datong 48-49 L 3
Tatran 48-49 EF 4
Tatry 33 JK 4
Tatsaitan = Tagalgan 48-49 H 4
Tatsuno 50-51 K 5
Tatta = Ṭhaṭṭha 44-45 K 6
Tatung = Datong [TJ, Shanxi] 48-49 L 3
Ta-t'ung Ho = Datong He 48-49 J 4
Tatvan 46-47 K 3
Tau 30-31 AB 8
Tauá 78-79 L 6
Taubaté 78-79 KL 9
Tauberbischofsheim 33 DE 4
Taujskaja guba 42-43 cd 6
Taukum 42-43 O 9
Taumarunui 56-57 OP 7
Taumaturgo 78-79 E 6
Taungdwingyī 52-53 BC 2-3
Taunggyī 52-53 C 2
Taungngū 52-53 C 3
Taunton 32 E 6
Taunton, MA 74-75 H 4
Taunus 33 D 3
Taupo 56-57 P 7
Taupo, Lake – 56-57 P 7
Taurage 30-31 JK 10
Tauranga 56-57 P 7
Taurirt = Tāwrīrt 60-61 D 2
Tauro 44-45 C 3
Taurogi = Taurage 30-31 K 10
Taurovo 42-43 N 6
Taurus 44-45 C 3
Taurus Mountains 44-45 C 3
Taus = Domažlice 33 F 4
Taushqan Darya = Kök shal 48-49 D 3
Tauz 38-39 J 7
Ṭavālesh, Kūhha-ye – 46-47 MN 3
Tavan Bogdo Ula, gora – 48-49 F 2
Tavares, FL 74-75 c 2
Tavas 46-47 C 4
Tavastehus = Hämeenlinna 30-31 L 7
Tavda [SU, ~] 42-43 L 6
Tavda [SU, ●] 42-43 M 6
Taveta 64-65 J 3
Taveuni 52-53 b 2
Tavira 34-35 D 10
Tavolara 36-37 CD 5
Tavoliere 36-37 F 5
Tavoy = Htāwei 52-53 C 4
Tavoy Island = Mali Kyūn 52-53 C 4
Tavşanlı 46-47 C 3
Tavua 52-53 a 2
Ta-wa = Dawa 50-51 D 2
Ta-wang-chia Tao = Dawangjia Dao 50-51 D 3
Tawau 52-53 G 6
Ṭawīl, Bi'r – 60-61 L 4
Ṭawīl, Sabkhat aṭ- 46-47 J 5
Ṭawīlah, Juzur – 62 EF 4
Tawile Island = Juzur Ṭawīlah 62 EF 4
Tawi-tawi Island 52-53 GH 5
Ṭawkar 60-61 M 5
Tāwrīrt 60-61 D 2
Ṭāwūq 46-47 L 5
Ṭāwūq Chāy 46-47 L 5
Ṭāwūq Chāy 46-47 L 5
Ṭāwūq Chāy 46-47 L 5
Tāwurghā', Sabkhat – 60-61 H 2
Tawzar 60-61 F 2
Taxco de Alarcón 72-73 FG 8
Tay 32 E 3
Tay, Firth of – 32 E 3
Tayabamba 78-79 D 6
Tayan 52-53 F 7
Ta-yang Ho = Dayang He 50-51 D 2
Ṭayb al-Fāl 46-47 J 5
Tayeeglow 60-61 ab 3
Taÿgetos 36-37 K 7
Tayishan = Guanyun 48-49 MN 5
Taylorsville, NC 74-75 C 6-7
Taymā' 44-45 D 5
Tayna 63 B 3
Tây Ninh 52-53 E 4
Ṭayr, Jabal aṭ- 44-45 E 7
Tây Sa, Quân Đao – 52-53 EF 3
Taytay 52-53 GH 4
Ta-yü = Dayu 48-49 L 6
Tayung = Dayong 48-49 L 6
Taz 42-43 OP 4
Tazādīt 60-61 B 4
Tāzah 60-61 D 2
Tazarbū 60-61 J 3
Tāzārīn 60-61 CD 2
Tazarine = Tāzārīn 60-61 CD 2
Tazawako 50-51 N 3
Tázerbó = Tazarbū 60-61 J 3
Tazewell, VA 74-75 C 6
Tazovskaja guba 42-43 NO 4
Tazovskij 42-43 OP 4
Tazovskij poluostrov 42-43 NO 4
Tbilisi 38-39 H 7
Tbiliszi = Tbilisi 38-39 H 7
Tchad 60-61 HJ 5
Tchad, Lac – 60-61 G 6
Tch'ang-cha = Changsha 48-49 L 6
Tchang-kia-k'eou = Zhangjiakou 48-49 L 3
Tch'ang-tch'ouen = Changchun 48-49 NO 3
Tchan-kiang = Zhanjiang 48-49 L 7
Tchéliouskine, Cap – = mys Čel'uskin 42-43 UV 2
Tch'eng-tö = Chengde 48-49 M 3
Tch'eng-tou = Chengdu 48-49 J 5
Tcherkesses, Région Autonome des – = 2 ◁ 38-39 H 7
Tchertchen = Chārchān 48-49 F 4
Tchetcheno-Ingouches, République Autonome des – = 5 ◁ 38-39 J 7
Tchibanga 64-65 D 3
Tchien = Zwedru 60-61 C 7
Tchin Tabaraden 60-61 F 5
Tchong King = Chongqing 48-49 K 6
Tchouktchis, District National des – 42-43 g-j 4
Tchouktchis, Mer des – 19 BC 35-36
Tchouktchis, Seuil des – 19 B 35
Tchouvaches, République Autonome des – = 4 ◁ 42-43 H 6
Tczew 33 J 1
Te Anau, Lake – 56-57 N 9
Teano 36-37 F 5
Tea Tree 56-57 F 4
Te Awamutu 56-57 OP 7
Tebas = Thēbai 36-37 K 6
Tebas = Thēbai [ET] 60-61 L 3
Tebessa = Tibissah 60-61 F 1
Tebingtinggi [RI, Sumatera Selatan] 52-53 D 7
Tebingtinggi [RI, Sumatera Utara] 52-53 CD 6
Tebulosmta, gora – 38-39 J 7
Teby = Thebai 36-37 K 6
Tecate 72-73 C 5
Tecer Dağları 46-47 G 3
Techis 48-49 E 3
Tecka 80 B 6
Tecomán 72-73 F 8
Tecuala 72-73 E 7
Tecuci 36-37 M 3
Tedeini, In – = 'Ayn Tādīn 60-61 E 4
Tedžen 44-45 J 3
Tedžen 44-45 J 3
Tees 32 EF 4
Tefé 78-79 G 5
Tefé, Rio – 78-79 F 5
Tefedest = Tafdasat 60-61 F 3-4
Tefenni 46-47 C 4
Tegal 52-53 E 8
Tégerḥi = Tajarḥī 60-61 G 4
Tegernsee 33 EF 5
Teguantepeque = Santo Domingo Tehuantepec 72-73 G 8
Tegucigalpa 72-73 J 9
Tegul'det 42-43 Q 6
Tehachapi, CA 76-77 D 8
Tehachapi Mountains 76-77 D 8
Tehachapi Pass 76-77 D 8
Tehama, CA 76-77 B 5
Tehek Lake 70-71 R 4
Teheran = Tehrān 44-45 G 3
Teherán = Tehrān 44-45 G 3
Téhéran = Tehrān 44-45 G 3
Tehrān 44-45 G 3
Tehuacán 72-73 G 8
Tehuantepec, Golfo de – 72-73 GH 8
Tehuantepec, Istmo de – 72-73 GH 8
Teide, Pico de – 60-61 A 3
Teixeira da Silva = Bailundo 64-65 E 5
Tejkovo 38-39 H 4
Tejo 34-35 C 9
Tejon Pass 72-73 C 4-5
Tekağaç Burun 46-47 B 4
Te Kao 56-57 O 6
Teke [TR, ≅] 46-47 CD 4
Teke [TR, ●] 46-47 C 2
Teke Burnu 46-47 B 3
Tekeli 42-43 O 9
Tekeli Dağı 46-47 G 2
Tekirdağ 44-45 B 2
Tekman 46-47 J 3
Tekoa, WA 76-77 E 2
Tekouiât, Ouèd – = Wādī Tākwayat 60-61 E 4
Teksas = Texas 72-73 FG 5
Te Kuiti 56-57 OP 7
Tel 44-45 N 6
Tela 72-73 J 8
Tēla = Tel 44-45 N 6
Telanaipura = Jambi 52-53 D 7
Telavi 38-39 J 7
Telefomin 52-53 M 8
Telegraph Creek 70-71 K 6
Telegraph Point 58 L 3
Telemark 30-31 BC 8
Telemsès = Tlemcès 60-61 EF 5
Teleneštу 36-37 N 2
Teleneštу 36-37 N 2
Teleno, El – 34-35 D 7
Telescope Peak 76-77 E 7
Teles Pires, Rio – 78-79 H 6
Telford 32 E 5
Télig 60-61 D 4
Telijn nuur 48-49 F 2
Télimélé 60-61 B 6
Teljō, Jebel – = Jabal Talju 60-61 K 6
Tell Abyad = Tall al-Abyaḍ 46-47 H 4
Tellatlas 60-61 D 2-C 1
Tell Atlas 60-61 D 2-E 1
Tell Bīs = Tall Bisah 46-47 G 5
Teller, AK 70-71 CD 4
Tell Ḥalaf = Tall Ḥalaf 46-47 HJ 4
Tell Kalakh = Tall Kalakh 46-47 G 5
Tell Kôttchak = Tall Kujik 46-47 JK 4
Tell Sem'ân = Tall as-Sam'ān 46-47 H 4
Telocaset, OR 76-77 E 3
Telok Anson = Teluk Intan 52-53 CD 6
Telok Betong = Bandar Lampung 52-53 DE 8
Teloloapan 72-73 FG 8
Tēlos 36-37 M 7
Tel'posiz, gora – 42-43 K 5
Telsen 80 C 6
Telšiai 30-31 K 10
Telšiai 30-31 K 10
Telukbetung = Tanjungkarang 52-53 DE 8
Telukdalam 52-53 C 6
Teluk Intan 52-53 CD 6
Tema 60-61 DE 7
Temassinine = Burj 'Umar Idrīs 60-61 EF 3
Tembellaga = Timboulaga 60-61 F 5
Tembenči 42-43 S 4
Tembenči 42-43 S 4
Tembilahan 52-53 D 7
Temblor Range 76-77 D 8
Temecula, CA 76-77 E 9
Temelli 46-47 E 3
Temesvár = Timişoara 36-37 J 3
Términos, Laguna de – 72-73 H 8
Temir 42-43 K 8
Temirtau [SU, Kazachskaja SSR] 42-43 N 7-8
Temirtau [SU, Rossijskaja SFSR] 42-43 Q 7
Témiscaming 70-71 V 8
Temnikov 42-43 G 7
Temora 56-57 J 6
Témpē 36-37 K 6
Tempe, AZ 76-77 GH 9
Tempe, Danau – 52-53 GH 7
Témpio Pausânia 36-37 C 5
Temple, TX 72-73 G 5
Temple Bay 56-57 H 2
Temporal, Cachoeira – 78-79 J 7
Temuco 80 B 5
Temže = Thames 32 G 6
Tena [CO] 78-79 D 5
Tenabo, NV 76-77 E 5
Tenabo, Mount – 76-77 E 5
Tenali 44-45 N 7
Tenasserim = Taninthārī 52-53 C 4
Tenasserim = Taninthārī Taing 52-53 C 4
Tenda, Colle di – 36-37 B 3
Tendaho 60-61 N 6
Ten Degree Channel 44-45 P 8
Ten Degree Channel 44-45 P 8
Ten Degree Channel 44-45 P 8
Tendrovskaja kosa 36-37 OP 2
Tendūf 60-61 C 3
Tendürek Dağı 46-47 KL 3
Tenedos = Bozcaada 46-47 AB 3
Ténéré 60-61 FG 4-5
Tenerife [E] 60-61 A 3
Ténès = Tanas 60-61 E 1
Tenf, Jebel – = Jabal at-Tanf 46-47 H 6
Tenga, Kepulauan – 52-53 G 8
Tengarong 52-53 G 7
Tengchong 48-49 H 6-7
Tengchung = Tengchong 48-49 H 6-7
Tenggeli Hai = Nam Tsho 48-49 G 5
Tenghsien = Teng Xian 48-49 M 4
Tengiz, ozero – 42-43 M 7
Tengréla = Tingrèla 60-61 C 6
Tengri Nuur = Nam Tsho 48-49 G 5
Teng Xian 48-49 M 4
Teniente, El – 80 BC 4
Teniente Matienzo 24 C 30-31
Tenino, WA 76-77 B 2
Tenke 64-65 G 5
Tenkodogo 60-61 DE 6
Tennant, CA 76-77 C 5
Tennant Creek 56-57 FG 3
Tennessee 72-73 JK 4
Tennessee River 72-73 J 4-5
Tennille, GA 74-75 B 8
Tēnos 36-37 L 7
Tenosique de Pino Suárez 72-73 H 8
Tenryū gawa 50-51 L 5
Tensīft, Ouèd – = Wad Tansīft 60-61 C 2
Ten Sleep 76-77 K 3-4
Tenterfield 56-57 K 5
Ten Thousand Islands 72-73 K 6
Tenyueh = Tengchong 48-49 H 6-7
Teocaltiche 72-73 F 7
Teófilo Otoni 78-79 L 8
Teotepec, Cerro – 72-73 FG 8
Tepa 52-53 J 8
Tepasto 30-31 L 3-4
Tepatitlán de Morelos 72-73 F 7
Tepe = Karakoçan 46-47 HJ 3
Tepeköy = Torbalı 46-47 B 3
Tepic 72-73 EF 7
Teplice 33 E 3
Tepoca, Bahía de – 76-77 G 10
Tepoca, Cabo – 76-77 G 10
Teques, Los – 78-79 F 2
Těqūma 46-47 F 7
Ter 34-35 J 8
Tēra 60-61 E 6
Tera 34-35 D 8
Teradomari 50-51 M 4
Terai 44-45 NO 5
Terang 58 F 7
Terangan = Pulau Trangan 52-53 K 8
Tercan 46-47 J 3
Terek 38-39 J 7
Terengganu, Kuala – 52-53 DE 5
Teresina 78-79 L 6
Teresinha 78-79 J 4
Teressa Island 44-45 P 9
Terhazza [RMM, ≅] 60-61 CD 4
Terhazza [RMM, ∅] 60-61 CD 4
Teriberka [SU, ●] 42-43 F 4
Termas, Las – 80 CD 3
Terme 46-47 G 2
Termet = Termit 60-61 G 5
Termez 44-45 K 3
Tèrmini Imerese 36-37 E 7-F 6
Termit 60-61 G 5
Tèrmoli 36-37 F 4-5
Ternate 52-53 J 6
Ternej 42-43 a 8
Terni 36-37 E 4
Ternopol' 38-39 E 6
Terpenija, mys – 42-43 bc 8
Terpenija, zaliv – 42-43 b 8
Terrace 70-71 L 7
Terracina 36-37 E 5
Terråk 30-31 E 5
Terranova = Newfoundland 70-71 Za 8
Terranova, Banco de – 22-23 G 3
Terranova, Cuenca de – 22-23 GH 3
Terranova, Ramal de – 22-23 G 3-H 4
Terrassa 34-35 HJ 8
Terrebonne, OR 76-77 C 3
Terre Clarie 24 C 14
Terre Haute, IN 72-73 J 4
Terrell, TX 72-73 G 5
Terre-Neuve = Newfoundland 70-71 Za 8
Terre-Neuve, Banc de – 22-23 G 3
Terre-Neuve, Bassin de – 22-23 GH 3
Terre-Neuve, Seuil de – 22-23 G 3-H 4
Terreton, ID 76-77 G 4
Tersakan Gölü 46-47 E 3
Terskej Ala-Too, chrebet – 44-45 M 2
Terst = Trieste 36-37 E 3
Teruel 34-35 G 8
Terutao, Ko – 52-53 C 5
Terytoria Północno-Zachodnie = Northwest Territories 70-71 M-U 4
Tesaua = Tasāwah 60-61 G 3
Teseney 60-61 M 5-6
Teshekpuk Lake 70-71 F 3
Teshikaga 50-51 d 2
Teshio 48-49 R 3
Teshio dake 50-51 c 2
Teshio-gawa 50-51 bc 1
Teshio-santi 50-51 bc 1
Tesijn gol 48-49 H 2
Tesino = Ticino 33 D 5
Tesio = Teshio 48-49 R 3
Teslin 70-71 K 5
Teslin Lake 70-71 K 5
Teslin River 70-71 K 5
Tessalit 60-61 E 4
Tessaoua 60-61 F 6
Tessin = Ticino 33 D 5
Teste, la – 34-35 G 6
Tetas, Punta – 80 B 2
Tete [Moçambique, ●] 64-65 H 6
Tete [Moçambique, ☆] 64-65 H 6
Tětěrě 42-43 T 5
Teterev 38-39 E 5
Teteven 36-37 L 4
Tetonia, ID 76-77 H 4
Teton Mountains 76-77 H 3-4
Teton River 76-77 H 2
Tetouan = Tiṭwān 60-61 CD 1
Tetovo 36-37 J 4-5
Tetschen = Děčin 33 G 3
Tetuán = Tiṭwān 60-61 CD 1
Tet'uche-Pristan' = Rudnaja Pristan' 42-43 a 9
Tet'uši 42-43 H 6-7
Tet'uši 38-39 J 5
Tet'uši 42-43 H 6-7
Tet'uši 38-39 J 5
Teuco, Rio – 80 D 2-3
Teufelsinsel = Île du Diable 78-79 J 3
Teulada 36-37 C 6
Teun, Pulau – 52-53 J 8
Teuri-tō 50-51 b 1
Teutoburger Wald 33 C 2-D 3
Tèvere 36-37 E 4
Těverya 46-47 F 6
Tevriz 42-43 N 6
Texarkana, AR 72-73 H 5
Texarkana, TX 72-73 GH 5
Texas [AUS] 56-57 K 5
Texas [USA] 72-73 FG 5
Texas City, TX 72-73 GH 6
Texel 34-35 K 2
Texoma, Lake – 72-73 G 5
Tezaua = Tasāwah 60-61 G 3
Teziutlán 72-73 G 7-8
Tezpur 44-45 P 5
Thabazimbi 64-65 G 7
Thabt, Gebel eth – = Jabal ath-Thabt 62 EF 3
Thabt, Jabal ath- 62 EF 3
Thadôn [BUR, Karin Pyinnei] 52-53 C 3
Thaiföld 52-53 CD 3
Thailand 52-53 CD 3
Thailand, Golf van – 52-53 D 4-5
Thailand, Golf von – 52-53 D 4-5
Thailand, Gulf of – 52-53 D 4-5

Thail 223

Thaïlande 52-53 CD 3
Thaïlande, Golfe de – 52-53 D 4-5
Thailandia 52-53 CD 3
Thailandia, Golfo de – 52-53 D 4-5
Thaj, Ath- 44-45 F 5
Thajsko 52-53 CD 3
Thajský záliv 52-53 D 4-5
Thakhek 52-53 DE 3
Thâkurgâon 44-45 O 5
Thal [PAK] 44-45 L 4
Thâlith, Al-Jandal ath- 60-61 KL 5
Thallon 58 J 2
Thalmann, GA 74-75 C 9
Thames 32 G 6
Thames [NZ] 56-57 P 7
Thames River 74-75 C 3
Thamūd 44-45 F 7
Thandwe 52-53 B 3
Thangkar 48-49 J 4
Thangool 56-57 K 4
Thangra Tsho = Thangra Yumtsho 48-49 EF 5
Thangra Yumtsho 48-49 EF 5
Thanh Hoa 52-53 E 3
Thanjavur 44-45 MN 8
Thanlwin Myit 52-53 C 2-3
Thanlyin 52-53 C 3
Thapsacus = Dibsah 46-47 GH 5
Thar 44-45 L 5
Thar, Dhāṭ yā = Great Indian Desert 44-45 L 5
Thargomindah 56-57 H 5
Tharsis 34-35 D 10
Tharthâr, Bahr ath – = Munkhafad ath-Tharthâr 44-45 E 4
Tharthâr, Munkhafad ath- 44-45 E 4
Tharthâr, Wādī ath- 46-47 K 5
Tharwāniyah = Ath-Tharwāniyah 44-45 GH 6
Tharwāniyah, Ath- 44-45 GH 6
Thásos [GR, ⊙] 36-37 L 5
Thásos [GR, ●] 36-37 L 5
Thatcher, AZ 76-77 HJ 9
Thaton = Thadôn 52-53 C 3
Thaṭṭhah 44-45 K 6
Thayne, WY 76-77 H 4
Thāzī 52-53 C 2
Thbeng 52-53 DE 4
Thbeng Meanchey 52-53 DE 4
Thêbai [ET] 60-61 L 3
Thêbai [GR] 36-37 K 6
Thèba = Thebai 36-37 K 6
Thebe = Thêbai 60-61 L 3
Theben = Thêbai 36-37 K 6
Thebes = Thêbai 36-37 K 6
Thèbes = Thêbai 36-37 K 6
Thebes = Thêbai [ET] 60-61 L 3
Théby = Thebai 36-37 K 6
The Dalles, OR 76-77 C 3
Theems = Thames 32 G 6
Thelon Game Sanctuary 70-71 PQ 5
Thelon River 70-71 Q 5
Themse = River Thames 32 G 6
Theodore 56-57 JK 4-5
Theodore Roosevelt Lake 76-77 H 9
The Pas 70-71 Q 7
Thêra 36-37 L 7
Thermaïkòs Kólpos 36-37 K 5-6
Thermopýlai 36-37 K 6
Theron Range 24 AB 34-36
Theronsville = Pofadder 64-65 EF 8
Thessalía 36-37 JK 6
Thessalonikē 36-37 K 5
Thetford 32 G 5
Thetford Mines 70-71 W 8
Thiel Mountains 24 A
Thielsen, Mount – 76-77 BC 4
Thiers 34-35 J 6
Thiès 60-61 A 6
Thika 63 D 3
Thikombia 52-53 b 2
Thimbu 44-45 OP 5
Thingvallavatn 30-31 c 2
Thingvellir 30-31 c 2
Thio 56-57 N 4
Thionville 34-35 KL 4
Thisted 30-31 C 9
Thistilfjördhur 30-31 f 1
Thistle, UT 76-77 H 5-6
Thistle Island 56-57 G 7
Thjórsá 30-31 d 2
Thlêta Madârî, Berzekh – = Râ's ash-Shūkât ath-Thalâtha 60-61 D 1
Thlewiaza River 70-71 R 5
Thmail = Thumayl 46-47 K 6
Thogdoragpa 48-49 F 5
Thogjalung 48-49 E 5
Thomas, WV 74-75 D 5
Thomasville, GA 72-73 K 5
Thomasville, NC 74-75 C 7
Thompson 70-71 R 6
Thompson, UT 76-77 HJ 6
Thompson Falls, MT 76-77 F 2
Thompson Peak [USA, Colorado] 76-77 B 5
Thompson Peak [USA, Montana] 76-77 F 2
Thompson's Falls 63 D 2-3
Thomson, GA 74-75 B 8
Thomson, Abysse de – 56-57 K 6
Thomson, Fosa – 56-57 K 6
Thomson Deep 56-57 K 6
Thomsondiep 56-57 K 6
Thomsontiefe 56-57 K 6
Thon Buri, Krung Thep- 52-53 CD 4
Thong Pha Phum 52-53 C 4
Thonon-les-Bains 34-35 L 5
Thoreau, NM 76-77 JK 8
Thørisvatn 30-31 de 2
Thorn = Toruń 33 J 2
Thornton, WA 76-77 E 2
Thorp, WA 76-77 C 2
Thórshöfn 30-31 f 1
Thousand Islands 74-75 EF 2
Thousand Islands = Kepulauan Seribu 52-53 E 7-8
Thousand Spring Creek 76-77 F 5
Thowa 64-65 J 3
Thrákē 36-37 LM 5
Three Creek, ID 76-77 F 4
Three Forks, MT 76-77 H 3
Three Hummock Island 58 bc 2
Three Kings Islands 56-57 O 6
Threemile Rapids 76-77 F 3
Three Pagodas Pass = Phra Chedi Sam Ong 52-53 C 3-4
Three Points, Cape – 60-61 D 8
Three Rivers = Trois-Rivières 70-71 W 8
Three Sisters [USA] 76-77 C 3
Three Springs 56-57 BC 5
Thu, Cu Lao – 52-53 EF 4
Thubby = Abū Ẓabī 44-45 G 6
Thule = Qânâq 70-71 W-X 2
Thumayl 46-47 K 6
Thumb, WY 76-77 H 3
Thun 33 C 5
Thunder Bay [CDN] 70-71 ST 8
Thuqb al-Ḥājj 46-47 L 8
Thüringen 33 E 3
Thüringer Wald 33 E 3
Thurloo Downs 58 F 2
Thurso 32 E 2
Thurston Island 24 BC 26-27
Thyatera = Akhisar 46-47 BC 3
Thyatira = Akhisar 46-47 BC 3
Thykkvibær 30-31 c 3
Thysville = Mbanza-Ngungu 64-65 D 4
Tiahuanacu 78-79 F 8
Tianguá 78-79 L 5
Tianjin 48-49 M 4
Tian Shan 48-49 C-G 3
Tianshui 48-49 JK 5
Tianzhuangtai 50-51 CD 2
Tiaret = Tiyārat 60-61 E 1
Tiassalé 60-61 CD 7
Tib 60-61 G 1
Ṭīb, Râ's aṭ- = Râ's Âdhār 60-61 G 1
Tibaji 80 F 2
Tibastī, Sarīr – 60-61 H 4
Tibati 60-61 G 7
Ṭīb el Fâl = Ṭayb al-Fâl 46-47 J 5
Tibell, Wādī – = Wādī at-Tubal 46-47 J 6
Tiber = Tèvere 36-37 E 4
Tíber = Tèvere 36-37 E 4
Tiberias = Ṭêverya 46-47 F 6
Tibesti 60-61 H 4
Tibet = Xizang 48-49 E-H 5
Tibet, Autonomes Gebiet – 48-49 E-H 5
Tibet, Plateau of – = Jang Thang 48-49 E-G 5
Tibet, Región Autónoma del – 48-49 E-H 5
Tibetská autonomní oblast 48-49 E-G 5
Tibissah 60-61 F 1
Tibnī 46-47 H 5
Tibooburra 56-57 H 5
Tibre = Tevere 36-37 E 4
Tiburón, Isla – 72-73 D 6
Tichborne 74-75 E 2
Tichitt = Tîshît 60-61 C 5
Tichon'kaja Stancija = Birobidžan 42-43 Z 8
Tichoreck 38-39 GH 6
Tichvin 42-43 E 6
Ticino 33 D 5
Ticonderoga, NY 74-75 G 3
Ticul 72-73 J 7
Tidaholm 30-31 EF 8
Tidikelt = Tidikilt 60-61 E 3
Tidioute, PA 74-75 D 4
Tidjikja = Tijiqjah 60-61 B 5
Tidore, Pulau – 52-53 J 6
Tidra, Île – 60-61 A 5
Tiechang 50-51 EF 2
T'ieh-ling = Tieling 50-51 DE 1
Tieling 50-51 DE 1
T'ien-chia-an = Huainan 48-49 M 5
T'ien-chin = Tianjin 48-49 M 4
T'ien-chouei = Tianshui 48-49 JK 5
T'ien-chuang-t'ai = Tianzhuangtai 50-51 CD 2
Tiencsin = Tianjin 48-49 M 4
Tienkiaan = Huainan 48-49 M 5
Tien-san 48-49 C-G 3
Tien Schan 48-49 C-G 3
Tien Shan 48-49 C-G 3
Tienshui = Tianshui 48-49 JK 5
Tien Schan 48-49 C-G 3
Tien Schan 48-49 C-G 3
Tiensjan 48-49 C-G 3
Tienszan 48-49 C-G 3
Tientsin = Tianjin 48-49 M 4
Tiên Yên 52-53 E 2
Tierp 30-31 G 7
Tierra Blanca [MEX, Veracruz] 72-73 G 8
Tiétar 34-35 E 8
Tieton, WA 76-77 C 2
Tifariti = Atfârītī 60-61 B 3
Tiffany Mountain 76-77 CD 1
Tiflis = Tbilisi 38-39 H 7
Tifore, Pulau – 52-53 J 6
Tifton, GA 74-75 B 9
Tigieglo = Tayeegle 64-65 K 2
Tigil' 42-43 e 6
Tigra = Tigrē 60-61 MN 6
Tigray 60-61 MN 6
Tigre = Nahr Dijlah 44-45 E 3
Tigrē = Tigray 60-61 MN 6
Tigre, Dent du – = Đông Voi Mêp 52-53 E 3
Tigre, El – [MEX] 76-77 J 10
Tigre, El – [YV] 78-79 G 3
Tigre, Rio – [EC] 78-79 D 5
Tigris = Nahr Dijlah 44-45 E 3
Tigui 60-61 H 5
Tīh, Jabal at- 60-61 L 3
Tīh, Ṣaḥrā' at- 60-61 L 2
Tiham = Tihāmah 44-45 D 6-E 8
Tihāmah 44-45 D 6-E 8
Ti-hua = Ürümchi 48-49 F 3
Tihwa = Ürümchi 48-49 F 3
Tiirismaa 30-31 L 7
Tijiqjah 60-61 B 5
Tijoca 78-79 K 5
Tijuana 72-73 C 5
Tikal 72-73 J 8
Tikopia 56-57 N 2
Tikrīt 46-47 K 5
Tiksi 42-43 Y 3
Tikšozero 30-31 OP 4
Tikšozero 30-31 OP 4
Tilamuta 52-53 H 6
Tilbeşar ovası 46-47 G 4
Tilburg 34-35 K 3
Tilcara 80 CD 2
Tilemsès 60-61 EF 5
Tilemsi 60-61 E 5
Tiličiki 42-43 g 5
Tiličiki 42-43 g 5
Tilimsân 60-61 D 2
Tillabéry 60-61 E 6
Tillamook, OR 76-77 B 3
Tillamook Bay 76-77 AB 3
Tillery, Lake – 74-75 CD 7
Tillia 60-61 E 5
Tillsonburg 74-75 C 3
Tilpa 56-57 H 6
Tilsit = Sovetsk 33 K 1
Ṭīmā 62 D 4
Timaná 78-79 D 4
Timanskij kr'až 42-43 J 5-H 4
Timanskij kr'až 42-43 J 5-H 4
Timar 46-47 K 3
Timaru 56-57 O 8
Timaševsk 38-39 G 6
Timassah 60-61 H 3
Timassanin = Burj 'Umar Idrīs 60-61 EF 3
Timaševsk 38-39 G 6
Timbédra = Tinbadghah 60-61 C 5
Timber, OR 76-77 B 3
Timber Mountain 76-77 F 6
Timbo [Guinea] 60-61 B 6
Timboulaga 60-61 F 5
Timia 60-61 F 5
Timimoun = Tīmīmūn 60-61 E 3
Tīmīmūn 60-61 E 3
Timiş 36-37 J 3
Timişoara 36-37 J 3
Ti-m-Merhsoï, Oued – 60-61 F 5
Timmins 70-71 U 8
Timmonsville, SC 74-75 D 7
Timmoudi = Tīmmūdī 60-61 D 3
Timon 78-79 L 6
Timor 52-53 H 9-J 8
Timor, Fosa de – 52-53 J 8
Timor, Fosse de – 52-53 J 8
Timor, Mar de – 56-57 E 2
Timor, Mer de – 56-57 E 2
Timor, Morze – 52-53 E 2
Timor-árok 52-53 J 8
Timorgraben 52-53 J 8
Timor Sea 56-57 E 2
Timorsee 56-57 E 2
Timorské moře 52-53 E 2
Timorski, Rów – 52-53 J 8
Timorský kaňon 52-53 J 8
Timor-tenger 56-57 E 2
Timor Timur = 23 ◁ 52-53 J 8
Timortrog 52-53 J 8
Timor Trough 52-53 J 8
Timorzee 56-57 E 2
Timošino 38-39 FG 3
Timošino 38-39 FG 3
Timpahute Range 76-77 F 7
Timsâḥ, Buḥayrat at- 62 E 2
Ṭīnah, Khalīj aṭ- 62 E 2
Tinakula 52-53 kl 7
Ti-n-Asselak 60-61 E 5
Tinbadghah 60-61 C 5
Tindouf = Tindūf 60-61 C 3
Tindouf, Sebkra de – = Sabkhat Tindūf 60-61 C 3
Tindūf 60-61 C 3
Tindūf, Sabkhat – 60-61 C 3
Tineo 34-35 D 7
Tin Essalak = Ti-n-Asselak 60-61 E 5
Tingha 58 K 2-3
Tinghīrt, Hammadat – = Ḥammādat Tinrīrt 60-61 FG 3
Ting-hsi = Dingxi 48-49 J 4
Ting-hsin = Dingxin 48-49 H 3
Tingling Shan = Qin Ling 48-49 KL 5
Tingo María 78-79 D 6
Tingréla 60-61 C 6
Tingri Dsong 48-49 F 6
Tingsryd 30-31 F 9
Tinguipaya 78-79 F 8
Tingvoll 30-31 BC 6
Tingwon 52-53 g 5
Ting-yüan-ying = Bajan Choto 48-49 JK 4
Tinjil, Pulau – 52-53 E 8
Tinkisso 60-61 BC 6
Tinnevelly = Tirunelveli 44-45 M 9
Tinnīn, 'Ayn – 62 C 4
Tinogasta 80 C 3
Tinrhert, Hamada de – = Ḥammādat Tinrīrt 60-61 FG 3
Tinrīrt, Ḥammādat – 60-61 FG 3
Tinsukia 44-45 Q 5
Tīn Tarābīn, Wādī – 60-61 F 4
Tintina 80 D 3
Tintinara 58 E 5
Tio, El – 80 D 4
Tioman, Pulau – 52-53 DE 6
Tionesta, CA 76-77 C 5
Tionesta, PA 74-75 D 4
Tipperary 32 BC 5
Tipton, CA 76-77 D 7
Tipton, Mount – 76-77 F 8
Tiracambu, Serra de – 78-79 K 5
Tīrān, Jazīrat – 62 F 4
Tirana = Tiranë 36-37 HJ 5
Tiranë 36-37 HJ 5
Tiraspol' 38-39 EF 6
Tirbande Turkestân 44-45 JK 3
Tire 46-47 B 3
Tirebolu 46-47 H 2
Tiree 32 C 3
Tiree Passage 32 C 3
Tîrgovişte 36-37 L 3
Tîrgu Cărbuneşti 36-37 KL 3
Tîrgu Jiu 36-37 K 3
Tîrgu Mureş 36-37 L 2
Tîrgu Neamţ 36-37 LM 2
Tirich Mīr 44-45 L 3
Tirikuṇāmalaya 44-45 N 9
Tirl'anskij 38-39 L 5
Tirnabos 36-37 K 6
Tirol 33 EF 5
Tirol 33 EF 5
Tirso 36-37 C 6
Tiruchchendur = Tiruchendur 44-45 M 9
Tiruchchirāppalli = Tiruchirapalli 44-45 M 8
Tiruchendur 44-45 M 9
Tiruchirapalli 44-45 M 8
Tirukkunamalai = Tirikuṇāmalaya 44-45 N 9
Tirunelveli 44-45 M 9
Tirupati 44-45 M 8
Tiruvanatapuram = Trivandrum 44-45 M 9
Tisa 36-37 J 3
Tisdale 70-71 Q 7
Tishīt 60-61 C 5
Tishlah 60-61 AB 4
Tīs Isat Fwafwatē 60-61 M 6
Tismana 36-37 K 3
Tisza 33 K 5
Tisza-tó 42-43 H 9
Tiszaújváros 42-43 HJ 9
Tit-Ary 42-43 Y 3
Titemsi 60-61 E 5
Titicaca, Lago – 78-79 F 8
Titov Veles 36-37 JK 5
Titran 30-31 C 6
Titu [EAK] 63 D 2
Titule 64-65 FG 2
Titusville, FL 74-75 c 2
Titusville, PA 74-75 D 4
Tiṭwān 60-61 CD 1
Tivaouane 60-61 A 5
Tiverton 32 E 6
Tivoli 36-37 E 5
Tiyārat [DZ] 60-61 E 1
Tizimín 72-73 J 7
Tizi-Ouzou = Tīzī Wazū 60-61 E 1
Tīzī Wazū 60-61 E 1
Tiznīt 60-61 C 3
Tjeggelvas 30-31 GH 4
Tjendana, Pulau – = Sumba 52-53 G 9
Tjertjen = Chärchän 48-49 F 4
Tjirebon = Cirebon 52-53 E 8
Tjörn [IS] 30-31 c 2
Tjörn [S] 30-31 D 8-9
Tjörnes 30-31 e 1
Tjøtta 30-31 E 5
Tjumen = T'umen' 42-43 M 6
Tjuvfjorden 30-31 l 6
Tlaquepaque 72-73 F 7
Tlaxcala 72-73 G 8
Tlaxcala de Xicoténcatl 72-73 G 8
Tlemcen = Tilimsân 60-61 D 2
Tlemcès = Tilemsès 60-61 EF 5
Tmessa = Timassah 60-61 H 3
Toamasina 64-65 LM 6
Toano, VA 74-75 E 6
Toano Range 76-77 F 5
Toba [J] 50-51 L 5
Toba, Danau – 52-53 C 6
Tobago 72-73 OP 9
Tobalai, Pulau – 52-53 J 7
Tobar, NV 76-77 F 5
Tobarra 34-35 G 9
Tobelo 52-53 J 6
Tobermorey 56-57 G 4
Tobermory [CDN] 74-75 BC 2
Tobi 52-53 K 6
Tobin, Mount – 76-77 E 5
Tobi-shima 50-51 M 3
Tobo 52-53 JK 7
Toboali 52-53 E 7
Tobol [SU, ~] 42-43 M 6
Tobol [SU, ●] 42-43 L 7
Toboli 52-53 H 7
Tobol'sk 42-43 MN 6
Tobruch = Ṭubruq 60-61 J 2
Tobruk = Ṭubruq 60-61 J 2
Tobseda 42-43 J 4
T'ob'ulech 42-43 b 3
Tocantínia 78-79 K 6
Tocantinópolis 78-79 K 6
Tocantins, Rio – 78-79 K 5-6
Toccoa, GA 74-75 B 7
Tochigi 50-51 MN 4
Tochio 50-51 M 4
Toch'o-do 50-51 E 5
Toco [RCH] 80 C 2
Tocopilla 80 B 2
Tocorpuri, Cerro de – 78-79 F 9
Tocqueville = Ra's al-Wād 60-61 E 1
Tocra = Tūkrah 60-61 HJ 2
Tocumen, Rio – 72-73 c 2
Tocuyo, El – 78-79 F 3
Todeli 52-53 H 7
Todenyang 63 C 1
Tödi [CH] 33 D 5
Todi [I] 36-37 E 4
Todmorden [AUS] 56-57 FG 5
Todness 78-79 H 3
To-dong 50-51 H 4
Todo-saki 50-51 O 3
Todos os Santos, Baía de – 78-79 M 7
Todos os Santos-öböl = Baía de Todos os Santos 78-79 M 7
Todos Santos [BOL, Cochabamba] 78-79 F 8
Todos Santos [MEX] 72-73 D 7
Todos Santos, Islas de – 76-77 E 10
Todro 63 B 2
T'oejo 50-51 FG 3
Toerkmenistan 44-45 HJ 2-3
Toeva Autonome Republiek 42-43 RS 7
Togdheer 60-61 b 2
Togi 50-51 L 4
Togian, Kepulauan – 52-53 H 7
Togo 60-61 E 7
Togochale = Togotyalē 60-61 N 7
Togotyalē 60-61 N 7
Togtoh = Tugt 48-49 L 3-4
Togye-dong 50-51 G 4
Tŏgyu-sen 50-51 FG 5
Tohatchi, NM 76-77 J 8
Tohma Çayı 46-47 G 3
Tohoku 50-51 N 2-4
Toiama = Toyama 48-49 Q 4
Toijala 30-31 K 7
Toili 52-53 H 7
Toi-misaki 50-51 H 7
Toiyabe Range 76-77 E 6
Tokachi-dake 50-51 c 2
Tokachi-gawa 50-51 c 2
Tokai 50-51 LM 5
Tokaj 33 K 4
Tōkamachi 50-51 M 4
Ṭōkar = Ṭawkar 60-61 M 5
Tokara-kaikyō 48-49 O 5-P 6
Tokara-rettō 48-49 OP 6
Tokat 44-45 D 2
Tŏkchŏk-kundo 50-51 EF 4
Tŏkch'ŏn 50-51 F 3
Toki 50-51 L 5
Tokiō = Tōkyō 48-49 QR 4
Tokio = Tōkyō 48-49 QR 4
Tokitsu = Toki 50-51 L 5
Tokko 42-43 WX 6
Tok-kol 50-51 GH 2
Tokmak [SU, Kirgizskaja SSR] 42-43 O 9
Tokolimbu 52-53 H 7
Tokoro 50-51 cd 1
Tokosun = Toksun 48-49 F 3
Tokra = Tūkrah 60-61 HJ 2
Toksun 48-49 F 3
Tokuno-shima 48-49 O 6
Tokuno sima = Tokuno-shima 48-49 O 6
Tokushima 48-49 PQ 5
Tokusima = Tokushima 48-49 PQ 5
Tokuyama 50-51 HJ 5
Tōkyō 48-49 QR 4
Tōkyō wan 50-51 M 5
Tola, La – 78-79 D 4
Tolar Grande 80 C 2
Tolbuhin = Dobrič 36-37 MN 4
Toledo [E] 34-35 EF 9
Toledo, OH 72-73 K 3
Toledo, OR 76-77 B 3
Toledo, Montes de – 34-35 E 9
Tolga = Tūljā 60-61 EF 2
Toliary 64-65 K 7
Tolitoli 52-53 H 6
Toljatti 42-43 H 7
Toll'a, zaliv – 42-43 ST 2
Tolleson, AZ 76-77 G 9
Tolloche 80 D 3
Tolo, Teluk – 52-53 H 7
Tolosa 34-35 FG 7
Tolox, Sierra de – 34-35 E 10
Tolsan-do 50-51 FG 5
Tolstoj, mys – 42-43 e 6
Toltén 80 B 5
Toluca, Nevado de – 72-73 FG 8
Toluca de Lerdo 72-73 FG 8
To-lun = Doloon Nuur 48-49 LM 3
Toma, La – 80 C 4
Tomakomai 48-49 R 3
Tomamae 50-51 b 1
Tomaniive 52-53 a 2
Tomar 34-35 C 9
Tomar [BR] 78-79 G 5
Tomarza 46-47 F 3
Tomaszów Lubelski 33 L 3
Tomaszów Mazowiecki 33 K 3
Tombador, Serra do – [BR, Mato Grosso] 78-79 H 7
Tombē = Ṭumbī 60-61 L 7
Tombigbee River 72-73 J 5
Tomboco 64-65 D 4
Tombouctou 60-61 D 5
Tombstone, AZ 76-77 HJ 10
Tomé 80 B 5
Tömek = Aşağı Pınarbaşı 46-47 E 3
Tomelilla 30-31 EF 10
Tomelloso 34-35 F 9
Tomini 52-53 H 6
Tomini, Teluk – 52-53 H 7
Tomioka 50-51 N 4
Tomkinson Ranges 56-57 E 5
Tommot 42-43 Y 6
Tomo 78-79 F 4
Tomo, Rio – 78-79 F 3
Tompo 42-43 a 5
Tom Price 56-57 C 4
Tomra 30-31 B 6
Tomsk 42-43 PQ 6
Toms River, NJ 74-75 FG 5
Tomtabakken 30-31 EF 9
Tonalá 72-73 H 8
Tonalea, AZ 76-77 H 7
Tonami 50-51 L 4
Tonantins 78-79 F 5
Tonasket, WA 76-77 D 1
Tonbai Shan 48-49 L 5
Tonbridge 32 G 6
Tonda 52-53 M 8
Tønder 30-31 C 10
Tondern = Tønder 30-31 C 10
Tondi 44-45 M 9
Tone-gawa 50-51 N 5
Tonekābon 44-45 G 3
Tonga [AUS] 58 F 3
Tonga [Tonga] 52-53 bc 2
Tŏngā = Ṭūnjah 60-61 L 7
Tonga, Fosa de – 52-53 c 2
Tonga, Fosse des – 52-53 c 2
Tonga, Rów – 52-53 c 2
Tonga-árok 52-53 c 2
Tongagraben 52-53 c 2
Tongaland 64-65 H 8
Tonga Trench 52-53 c 2
Tongatrog 52-53 c 2
Tongch'ang 50-51 EF 2
T'ongch'ŏn 50-51 FG 3
Tongchuan 48-49 K 4
Tongguan [TJ, Shaanxi] 48-49 L 5
Tonghan-man 48-49 O 4
Tonghua 48-49 O 3
Tongjosŏn-man = Tonghan-man 48-49 O 4
Tongliao 48-49 N 3
Tongling 48-49 M 5
Tonglu 48-49 M 5-6
Tongmun'gŏ-ri 50-51 F 2
Tongoy 80 B 4
Tongphu 48-49 H 5
Tongpu = Tongphu 48-49 H 5
Tongren 48-49 K 6
Tong Xian 48-49 M 3-4
Tongyang 50-51 F 3
T'ŏngyŏng = Ch'ungmu 50-51 G 5
Tongyu 48-49 N 3
Tonk 44-45 M 5

224 Thaïl

Tonkin = Bac Bô 52-53 DE 2
Tonkin = Băc Bô 52-53 DE 2
Tonkin, Golfe du – 52-53 E 2-3
Tonkin, Golfo de – 52-53 E 2-3
Tonkin, Golf van – 52-53 E 2-3
Tonkin, Golf von – 52-53 E 2-3
Tonkin, Gulf of – 52-53 E 2-3
Tonking = Bac Bô 52-53 D 2
Tonkini-öböl 52-53 E 2-3
Tonkińska, Zatoka – 52-53 E 2-3
Tonkinský záliv 52-53 E 2-3
Tonlé Sap 52-53 D 4
Tonneins 34-35 GH 6
Tonopah, NV 72-73 C 4
Tønsberg 30-31 CD 8
Tonstad 30-31 B 8
Tonya 46-47 H 2
Tonžský příkop 52-53 c 2
Tooele, UT 72-73 D 3
Tooligie 58 B 4
Toompine 58 G 1
Toora 58 H 7
Toora-Chem 42-43 S 7
Toora-Chem 42-43 S 7
Toora-Chem 42-43 S 7
Toowoomba 56-57 K 5
Topeka, KS 72-73 G 4
Topki 42-43 PQ 6
Topko, gora – 42-43 a 6
Toplița 36-37 L 2
Topock, AZ 76-77 F 8
Topolobampo 72-73 E 6
Topolovgrad 36-37 M 4
Topozero 42-43 E 4
Toppenish, WA 76-77 C 2
Toprakkale 46-47 FG 4
Ṭoqra = Tūkrah 60-61 HJ 2
Toqsun = Toksun 48-49 F 3
Toquepala 78-79 E 8
Toquerville, UT 76-77 G 7
Toquima Range 76-77 E 6
Tor 60-61 L 7
Tora 63 B 2
Torbalı 46-47 B 3
Torbat-e Heydarīyeh 44-45 HJ 3-4
Torbat-e Jām 44-45 J 3
Torbat-e Sheikh Jām = Torbat-e Jām 44-45 J 3
Torbay 32 E 6
Tordesillas 34-35 E 8
Töre 30-31 K 5
Torekov 30-31 E 9
Torellbreen 30-31 j 6
Torell land 30-31 k 6
Torgau 33 F 3
Toriñana, Cabo – 34-35 C 7
Torino 36-37 BC 3
Toriñana, Cabo – 34-35 C 7
Tôrît = Tūrīt 60-61 L 8
Torkamān 46-47 M 4
Tormes 34-35 D 8
Torneå = Tornio 30-31 L 5
Torne älv 30-31 K 4
Torneträsk 30-31 H 3
Torngat Mountains 70-71 Y 6
Tornio 30-31 L 5
Tornquist 80 D 5
Toro 34-35 E 8
Toro [EAU] 63 B 2
Toro, Cerro del – 80 C 3
Torodi 60-61 E 6
Torokina 52-53 hj 6
Toronto 70-71 UV 9
Toro Peak 76-77 E 9
Toropec 38-39 F 4
Tororo 64-65 H 2
Toros dağları 44-45 C 3
Toros-hegység 44-45 C 3
Torrance, CA 76-77 D 9
Torre del Greco 36-37 F 5
Torre de Moncorvo 34-35 D 8
Torrelaguna 34-35 F 8
Torrelavega 34-35 E 7
Torrens, Lake – 56-57 G 6
Torrens Creek 56-57 HJ 4
Torrente 34-35 G 9
Torreón 72-73 F 6
Torres 80 G 3
Torres, Détroit de – 56-57 H 2
Torres, Îles – 56-57 N 2
Torres Islands 56-57 N 2
Torres Martinez Indian Reservation 76-77 E 9
Torres Strait 56-57 H 2
Torres Vedras 34-35 C 9
Torrevieja 34-35 G 10
Torrijos 34-35 E 8-9
Torrington, CT 74-75 G 4
Torsås 30-31 FG 9
Torsby 30-31 E 7
Tortola 72-73 O 8
Tortolì 36-37 C 6
Tortona 36-37 C 3
Tortosa 34-35 H 8
Tortosa, Cabo de – 34-35 H 8
Tortue, Île de la – 72-73 M 7
Tortum 46-47 J 2
Ṭorūd 44-45 H 3
Torugart Davan 44-45 L 2
Torul 46-47 H 2
Toruń 33 J 2
Tõrva 30-31 L 8
Tory 32 B 4
Tory Hill 74-75 DE 2
Toržok 42-43 E 6
Torzym 33 G 2
Toržok 42-43 E 6
Tosan = Chūbu 50-51 L 5-M 4
Tosashimizu 50-51 J 6
Tosa-wan 50-51 J 6
Toscana 36-37 D 4
Toscane = Toscana 36-37 D 4
To-shima 50-51 M 5
Toskana = Toscana 36-37 D 4
Tosno 38-39 F 4
Tos nuur 48-49 H 4
T'o-so Hu = Tos nuur 48-49 H 4
Tosoncengel 48-49 H 2
Tostado 80 D 3
Toston, MT 76-77 H 2
Tosu 50-51 H 6
Tosya 44-45 C 2
Totana 34-35 G 10
Toteng 64-65 F 7
Totes Meer = Baḥr al-Mayyit 44-45 D 4
Tot'ma 42-43 G 5-6
Totonicapán 72-73 HJ 8-9
Totora [BOL, Cochabamba] 78-79 FG 8
Totoya 52-53 ab 2
Totta 42-43 a 6
Tottan Range 24 B 35-36
Totten Glacier 24 C 12
Tottenham [AUS] 56-57 J 6
Tottenham [CDN] 74-75 CD 2-3
Tottenham, London- 32 FG 6
Tottori 48-49 P 4
Ṭouâl 'Abâ = Ṭuwāl 'Abā' 46-47 H 4
Touamotoubekken 22-23 BC 7
Touat = At-Tuwāt 60-61 DE 3
Touba [CI] 60-61 C 7
Touba [SN] 60-61 A 6
Toubqâl, Jbel – = Jabal Tubqāl 60-61 C 2
Toudao Jiang 50-51 F 1-2
Tougan 60-61 D 6
Touggourt = Tūjurt 60-61 EF 2
Touho 56-57 N 4
Toukley 58 KL 4
Toukoto 60-61 BC 6
Toul 34-35 K 4
Toulépleu 60-61 C 7
Toulon 34-35 KL 7
Touloûl, Dîret et- = Dīrat at-Tulūl 46-47 G 6
Touloûl eș Șafâ = Tulūl aș-Șafā 46-47 G 6
Toulouse 34-35 HJ 7
Toummo 60-61 G 4
Toumodi 60-61 CD 7
Toungoo = Taungngū 52-53 C 3
Toûnis = Tūnis 60-61 FG 1
Touraine 34-35 H 5
Tourane = Đa Năng 52-53 E 3
Tournai 34-35 J 3
Tournon 34-35 K 6
Touros 78-79 MN 5-6
Tours 34-35 H 5
Tous les Saints, Baie de – = Baia de Todos os Santos 78-79 M 7
Toussidé, Pic – 60-61 H 4
T'ou-tao Chiang = Toudao Jiang 50-51 F 1-2
T'ou-tao Chiang = Toudao Jiang 50-51 F 1-2
T'ou-tao Chiang = Toudao Jiang 50-51 F 1-2
Touva, République Autonome des – 42-43 RS 7
Töv = 12 ◁ 48-49 K 2
Tovarkovskij 38-39 G 5
Tovqussaq 70-71 a 5
Towada 50-51 N 2
Towada-ko 50-51 N 2
Towanda, PA 74-75 E 4
Townes Pass 76-77 E 7
Townsend, GA 74-75 C 9
Townsend, MT 76-77 H 2
Townshend Island 56-57 K 4
Townsville 56-57 J 3
Towori, Teluk – 52-53 H 7
Towot 60-61 L 7
Towson, MD 74-75 E 5
Towuti, Danau – 52-53 H 7
Tōya-ko 50-51 b 2
Toyama 48-49 Q 4
Toyama-wan 48-49 Q 4
Toyohara = Južno-Sachalinsk 42-43 bc 8
Toyohashi 48-49 Q 5
Toyohasi = Toyohashi 48-49 Q 5
Toyoma 50-51 N 3
Toyonaka 50-51 K 5
Toyooka 50-51 K 5
Toyota 50-51 L 5
Toyotama 50-51 G 5
Tôzeur = Tawzar 60-61 F 2
Törökország 44-45 B-E 3
Törökország 36-37 M-O 6
Trabzon 44-45 DE 2
Trachéia = Silifke 44-45 C 3
Tra Cu 52-53 E 5
Tracy, CA 76-77 C 7
Tradum 48-49 E 6
Træna 30-31 DE 4
Trafalgar, Cabo de – 34-35 D 10
Trafâwî, Bi'r – 46-47 H 4
Trail 72-73 N 8
Trajan, Mur inferior de – = Nižnij Trajanov val 36-37 N 3
Trajan, Mur superior de – = Verchnij Trajanov val 36-37 N 2
Trajano Meridional, Muro de – = Nižnij Trajanov val 36-37 N 3
Trajano Septentrional, Muro de – = Verchnij Trajanov val 36-37 N 2
Trajanova vrata 36-37 L 4
Trajan's Wall = Verchnij Trajanov val 36-37 N 2
Trakai 30-31 L 10
Trakya 46-47 AB 2
Tralee 32 B 5
Tranås 30-31 F 8
Trancas [RA] 80 CD 3
Trangan, Pulau – 52-53 K 8
Trani 36-37 G 5
Trân Ninh, Cao Nguyên – 52-53 D 3
Trans Canada Highway 70-71 P 7
Transhimálaj 48-49 EF 5
Transhimalaje 48-49 EF 5
Transhimalaya 48-49 EF 5
Transilvania 36-37 KL 2
Transit istasyonu = Doğubayazıt 46-47 KL 3
Transkasp 44-45 H 3
Transsib 42-43 L 6
Transsylvanie 36-37 KL 2
Transturan 42-43 K 7
Transvaal 64-65 GH 7
Transylvánie 36-37 K-M 2
Transylvanie 36-37 KL 2
Transylwania 36-37 K-M 2
Transzhimalája 48-49 EF 5
Trâpani 36-37 E 6-7
Trapezunt = Trabzon 44-45 DE 2
Trapezûs = Trabzon 44-45 DE 2
Trapper Peak 76-77 F 3
Traralgon 56-57 H 7
Trarza = At-Trārzah 60-61 AB 5
Trârzah, At- 60-61 AB 5
Trasimeno, Lago – 36-37 DE 4
Trás-os-Montes 34-35 D 8
Trás-os-Montes = Cucumbi 64-65 E 5
Trat 52-53 D 4
Traunstein 33 F 5
Trautenau = Trutnov 33 GH 3
Trava, Cachoeira – 78-79 H 5
Traverse City, MI 72-73 JK 2-3
Tra Vinh 52-53 E 5
Trbovle 36-37 F 2
Treasury = Mono Island 52-53 j 6
Třebič 33 G 4
Trebinje 36-37 H 4
Trebisonda = Trabzon 44-45 DE 2
Trébizonde = Trabzon 44-45 DE 2
Trechado, NM 76-77 J 8
Trefâouî, Bîr – = Bi'r Trafâwī 46-47 H 4
Trego, MT 76-77 F 1
Trégorrois 34-35 F 4
Treinta y Tres [ROU, ●] 80 F 4
Trelew 80 C 6
Trelleborg 30-31 E 10
Tremadoc Bay 32 D 5
Trèmiti, Ìsole – 36-37 F 4
Tremonton, UT 76-77 G 5
Tremp 34-35 H 7
Tren, El – 76-77 G 10
Trenčín 33 J 4
Trencsén = Trenčín 33 J 4
Trencsén = Trenčín 33 J 4
Trencsén = Trenčín 33 J 4
Trenque Lauquen 80 D 5
Trentino-Alto Àdige 36-37 D 2
Trentino-Südtirol = Trentino-Alto Adige 36-37 D 2
Trento 36-37 D 2
Trenton 74-75 E 2
Trenton, FL 74-75 b 2
Trenton, NJ 72-73 M 3-4
Tréport, le – 34-35 H 3
Tres Arroyos 80 DE 5
Três Corações 78-79 KL 9
Tres Esquinas 78-79 DE 4
Tres Forcas, Cap – = Rā's Wūruq 60-61 D 1
Tres Irmãos, Pontas dos – 78-79 M 6-N 5
Treska 36-37 J 5
Três Lagoas 78-79 J 9
Tres Lagos 80 B 7
Tres Montes, Peninsula – 80 A 7
Tres Picos, Cerro – 80 B 6
Tres Puntas, Cabo – 80 CD 7
Três Rios 78-79 L 9
Tres Virgenes, Las – 72-73 D 6
Treuburg = Olecko 33 L 1
Treuer River = Macumba 56-57 G 5
Treungen 30-31 C 8
Treviglio 36-37 C 3
Treviño 34-35 F 7
Treviño 34-35 F 7
Treviso 36-37 E 3
Treze Quedas 78-79 H 4
Triabunna 58 c 3
Triangle, ID 76-77 E 4
Tribuga, Golfo de – 78-79 D 3
Trichaty 36-37 O 2
Trichônis, Límnē – 36-37 J 6
Trichur 44-45 M 8
Trida 56-57 H 6
Tridell, UT 76-77 J 5
Trident Peak 76-77 D 5
Trident = Trento 36-37 D 2
Trient = Trento 36-37 D 2
Trier 33 C 4
Triest = Trieste 36-37 E 3
Triëst = Trieste 36-37 E 3
Trieste 36-37 E 3
Trieszt = Trieste 36-37 E 3
Trikala 36-37 JK 6
Trincheras, Las – 78-79 FG 3
Trincomalee = Tirikuṇāmalaya 44-45 N 9
Trincomali = Tirikuṇāmalaya 44-45 N 9
Trindade = Trinidad [BOL] 78-79 G 7
Trindade = Trinidad [TT] 72-73 O 9
Trindade, Ilha da – 78-79 NO 9
Trinidad [BOL, Beni] 78-79 G 7
Trinidad [C] 72-73 KL 7
Trinidad [CO] 78-79 E 3
Trinidad [PY] 80 E 3
Trinidad [ROU] 80 E 4
Trinidad [TT] 72-73 O 9
Trinidad, CA 76-77 A 5
Trinidad, CO 72-73 F 4
Trinidad, WA 76-77 CD 2
Trinidad = Ilha da Trindade 78-79 NO 9
Trinidad, Bahia – 72-73 b 2
Trinidad, Isla – 80 D 5
Trinidad, Rio – 72-73 b 3
Trinidad and Tobago 72-73 O 9-10
Trinidad a Tobago 72-73 O 9-10
Trinidad en Tobago 72-73 O 9-10
Trinidad és Tobago 72-73 O 9-10
Trinidad und Tobago 72-73 O 9-10
Trinidad y Tobago 72-73 O 9-10
Trinité et Tobago 72-73 O 9-10
Trinity Bay 70-71 a 8
Trinity Center, CA 76-77 B 5
Trinity Islands 70-71 F 6
Trinity Mountains 76-77 B 5
Trinity Range 76-77 D 5
Trinity River [USA, California] 76-77 B 5
Trinity River [USA, Texas] 72-73 G 5
Tripoli = Ṭarābulus al-Gharb 60-61 G 2
Tripolis 36-37 K 7
Tripolis = Ṭarābulus al-Gharb 60-61 G 2
Tripolitaine = Ṭarābulus 60-61 GH 2
Tripolitánia = Ṭarābulus 60-61 GH 2
Tripolitania = Ṭarābulus 60-61 G 2
Tripolsko = Ṭarābulus 60-61 GH 2
Tripura 44-45 P 6
Trishshivaperūr = Trichur 44-45 M 8
Trivandrum 44-45 M 9
Trnava 33 H 4
Trobriand Islands 52-53 h 6
Trofors 30-31 E 5
Trogir 36-37 FG 4
Troglav 36-37 G 4
Tròia [I] 36-37 F 5
Troick [SU ↓ Čel'abinsk] 42-43 L 7
Troickoje [SU, Rossijskaja SFSR] 42-43 a 8
Troicko-Pečorsk 42-43 K 5
Troicko-Pečorsk 42-43 K 5
Troickosavsk = K'achta 42-43 U 7
Trois-Rivières 70-71 W 8
Trojan 36-37 L 4
Trojanski prohod 36-37 L 4
Troki = Trakai 30-31 L 10
Trollhättan 30-31 E 8
Trolltindan 30-31 B 6
Trombetas, Rio – 78-79 H 5
Tromelin, Île – 64-65 M 6
Troms 30-31 G-J 3
Tromsø 30-31 H 3
Tron 30-31 D 6
Trona, CA 76-77 E 8
Tronador, Monte – 80 B 6
Trondheim 30-31 D 6
Trondheimfjord 30-31 CD 6
Tróodos 44-45 C 4
Tropic, UT 76-77 GH 7
Troppau = Opava 33 H 4
Trosa 30-31 G 8
Trotus 36-37 M 2
Troûmbâ = Turumbah 46-47 J 4
Trout Creek 76-77 D 4
Trout Creek, MT 76-77 EF 2
Trout Creek, UT 76-77 G 6
Trout Lake [CDN, Northwest Territories] 70-71 MN 5
Trout Lake [CDN, Ontario] 70-71 S 7
Trouwers Island = Pulau Tinjil 52-53 E 8
Trowbridge 32 EF 6
Troy, AL 72-73 J 5
Troy, ID 76-77 E 2
Troy, MT 76-77 F 1
Troy, NC 74-75 D 7
Troy, NY 72-73 M 3
Troy, OR 76-77 E 3
Troy, PA 74-75 E 4
Troyes 34-35 K 4
Truckee, CA 76-77 CD 6
Truckee River 76-77 D 6
Trudante = Tārūdānt 60-61 C 2
Trujillo [E] 34-35 DE 9
Trujillo [Honduras] 72-73 J 8
Trujillo [PE] 78-79 CD 6
Trujillo [YV] 78-79 EF 3
Trumbull, Mount – 76-77 G 7
Trung Bô 52-53 D 3-E 4
Trung Phân, Cao Nguyên – 52-53 E 4
Trung Phân, Plateau de – = Cao Nguyên Trung Phân 52-53 E 4
Truro 32 D 6
Truro [CDN] 70-71 Y 8
Trutnov 33 GH 3
Truva 44-45 B 3
Truxilho = Trujillo 72-73 J 8
Trydent = Trento 36-37 D 2
Trynidad i Tobago 72-73 O 9-10
Trypolis = Ṭarābulus al-Gharb 60-61 GH 2
Trypolitania = Ṭarābulus 60-61 GH 2
Trysil 30-31 DE 7
Trysilelv 30-31 DE 7
Třebíč 33 G 4
Tsabong 64-65 F 8
Tsaidam 48-49 GH 4
Tsai-Dam = Tsaidam 48-49 GH 4
Tsala Apopka Lake 74-75 bc 2
Tsamkong = Zhanjiang 48-49 L 7
Tsangpo 48-49 EF 6
Tsangwu = Wuzhou 48-49 L 7
Tsaratanana [RM, ▲] 64-65 L 5
Tsaratanana [RM, ●] 64-65 L 6
Tsau 64-65 F 7
Tsavo [EAK, ~] 63 D 3
Tsavo [EAK, ●] 64-65 J 3
Tsavo National Park 64-65 J 3
Tschad 60-61 HJ 5
Tschechei 33 F-H 4
Tscheljuskin, Kap – = mys Čel'uskin 42-43 UV 2
Tschenstochau = Częstochowa 33 JK 3
Tschetschenen und Inguschen, Autonome Republik der – = 5 ◁ 38-39 J 7
Tschinggis-Khan-Wall 48-49 LM 2
Tschuktschen, Nationalkreis der – 42-43 g-j 4
Tschuktschenschwelle 19 B 35
Tschuktschensee 19 BC 35-36
Tschuwaschen, Autonome Republik der – = 4 ◁ 42-43 H 6
Ts'ê-lo = Chira Bazar 48-49 DE 4
Tses 64-65 E 8
Tsethang 48-49 G 6
Tsetserlig = Cecerleg 48-49 J 2
Tshaidam 48-49 GH 4
Tshela 64-65 D 3-4
Tshikapa 64-65 EF 4
Tshimbo 63 B 4
Tshing Hai = Chöch nuur 48-49 H 4
Tshipa = Katakumba 64-65 F 4
Tshofa 64-65 FG 4
Tsho Ngonpo = Chöch nuur 48-49 H 4
Tshopo 64-65 G 2
Tshuapa 64-65 F 3
Tshungu, Chutes – 64-65 FG 2
Tshungu, Chutes – 64-65 FG 2
Tshungu, Chutes – 64-65 FG 2
Tshwane 64-65 F 7
Tsiafajavona 64-65 L 6
Tsienkiang = Qianjiang 48-49 L 5
Tsihombe 64-65 KL 8
Tsinan = Jinan 48-49 M 4
Tsincheng = Jincheng 48-49 L 4
Tsinchow = Tianshui 48-49 JK 5
Tsinghai = Qinghai 48-49 GH 4
Tsinghu = Jinghe 48-49 E 3
Tsingkiang = Qingjiang [TJ, Jiangsu] 48-49 M 5
Tsingkiang = Qingjiang [TJ, Jiangxi] 48-49 M 6
Tsingtau = Qingdao 48-49 N 4
Tsining = Jining 48-49 M 4
Tsining = Xining 48-49 J 4
Tsinyang = Qinyang 48-49 L 4
Tsiroanomandidy 64-65 L 6
Tsitsihar = Qiqihar 48-49 N 2
Tsivory 64-65 L 7
Tsjaad 60-61 HJ 5
Tsjakassen, Autonome Oblast der – = 10 ◁ 42-43 R 7
Tsjechiesche Republiek 33 F-H 4
Tsjeljoeskin, Kaap – = mys Čel'uskin 42-43 UV 2
Tsjetsen-Ingoesjen Autonome Republiek = 5 ◁ 38-39 J 7
Tsjoektsjen, Nationaal Gebied der – 42-43 g-j 4
Tsjoektsjendrempel 19 B 35
Tsjoektsjenzee 19 BC 35-36
Tsjoevasjen, Autonome Republiek = 4 ◁ 42-43 H 6
Tsorlû = Çorlu 46-47 B 2
Tsu 48-49 Q 5
Tsubame 50-51 M 4
Tsuchiura 50-51 N 4
Tsugaru kaikyō 48-49 R 3
Tsukigata 50-51 b 2
Tsukumi 50-51 H 6
Tsuma = Saito 50-51 H 6
Tsumeb 64-65 E 6
Tsungming = Chongming 48-49 N 5
Tsuno-shima 50-51 H 5
Tsunyi = Zunyi 48-49 K 6
Tsuruga 50-51 KL 5
Tsurugi san 50-51 JK 6
Tsurumi-zaki 50-51 J 6
Tsuruoka 50-51 M 3
Tsurusaki 50-51 HJ 6
Tsushima 48-49 O 5
Tsushima-kaikyō 48-49 OP 5
Tsuyama 50-51 JK 5
Tsuyung = Chuxiong 48-49 J 7
Tu = Tibesti 60-61 H 4
Tu = Tsu 48-49 Q 5
Tua 34-35 D 8
Tuamotu, Bassin des – 22-23 BC 7
Tuamotu, Cuenca de las – 22-23 BC 7
Tuamotu Basin 22-23 BC 7
Tuamotubecken 22-23 BC 7
Tuapse 38-39 G 7
Tubac, AZ 76-77 H 10
Tuba City, AZ 76-77 H 7
Tubal, Wādī at- 46-47 J 6
Tuban 52-53 F 8
Tubarão 80 G 3
Tubau 52-53 F 6
Ṭubayq, Jabal aṭ- 44-45 D 5
Tübingen 33 D 4
Tubmanburg 60-61 B 7
Tubqāl, Jabal – 60-61 C 2
Ṭubruq 60-61 J 2
Tubutama 76-77 H 10
Tucacas 78-79 F 2
Tucano 78-79 M 7
Tucavaca 78-79 H 8
Tucholskie, Bory – 33 HJ 2
Tucker Bay 24 B 18
Tuckerton, NJ 74-75 FG 5
Tucson, AZ 72-73 D 5
Tucson Mountains 76-77 H 9
Tucumán = San Miguel de Tucumán 80 CD 3
Tucumcari, NM 72-73 F 4
Tucunuco 80 C 4
Tucupita 78-79 G 3
Tucuruí 78-79 K 5
Tudela 34-35 G 7
Tuela 34-35 D 8
Tufanbeyli 46-47 G 3
Tufi 52-53 N 8
Tugaru kaikyō = Tsugaru-kaikyō 48-49 R 3
Tugela [ZA, ~] 64-65 H 8
Tuggurt = Tūjurt 60-61 EF 2
Tugh Fafan = Fafen 60-61 N 7
Tughghūrt = Tūjurt 60-61 EF 2
Tugt 48-49 L 3-4
Tuguegarao 52-53 H 3
Tugur 42-43 a 7
Tuht = Yaprakli 46-47 E 2
Tujmazy 42-43 JK 7
Tūjurt 60-61 EF 2
T'ukalinsk 42-43 N 6
Tukangbesi, Kepulauan – 52-53 H 8
Tukayyid 46-47 L 8
Tūkrah 60-61 HJ 2
Tuktoyaktuk 70-71 JK 4
Tukums 30-31 K 9
Tukuyu 64-65 H 4
Tula [EAK] 63 D 3
Tulagi 52-53 jk 6
Tulancingo 72-73 G 7
Tulare, CA 72-73 C 4
Tulare Lake 72-73 C 4
Tulare Lake Area 76-77 D 8
Tularosa Mountains 76-77 J 9
Tulcán 78-79 D 4
Tulcea 36-37 N 3
Tul'čin 38-39 E 6
Tul'čin 38-39 E 6
Tuléar = Toliary 64-65 K 7
Tulelake, CA 76-77 C 5
Tule River 76-77 D 7
Tule River Indian Reservation 76-77 D 7-8
T'ul'gan 42-43 K 7
Tuli 64-65 G 7
Tūljā 60-61 EF 2
Tūl Karm 46-47 F 6
Tullamore 58 H 4
Tulle 34-35 HJ 6
Tullibigeal 58 GH 4
Tully 56-57 J 3

Tully 225

Tuloma 38-39 F 2
Tulon = Toulon 34-35 KL 7
Tulpan 42-43 K 5
Tulsa, OK 72-73 G 4
Tulsa = La Barge, WY 76-77 HJ 4
Tuluá 78-79 D 4
Tulufan = Turpan 48-49 F 3
Tulūl, Dīrat at- 46-47 G 6
Tulūl ash-Shaḥm 46-47 FG 8
Tulun 42-43 ST 7
Tuluza = Toulouse 34-35 HJ 7
Tuma 38-39 H 4
Tumacacori National Monument 76-77 H 10
Tumaco 78-79 D 4
Tumaco, Rada de – 78-79 CD 4
Tuman-gang 50-51 G 1
Tumany 42-43 e 5
Tumba, Lac – 64-65 E 3
Tumbarumba 56-57 J 7
Tumbes [EC, ●] 78-79 C 5
Ṭumbī 60-61 L 7
Tumboni 64-65 J 3
Tumby 58 C 5
T'umen' [SU] 42-43 M 6
Tumen [TJ] 48-49 O 3
Tumen Jiang 50-51 G 1
Tumkur 44-45 M 8
Tumkūru = Tumkur 44-45 M 8
Ṭummō, Jabal – 60-61 G 4
Tumpat 52-53 D 5
Tumu 60-61 D 6
Tumucumaque, Serra do – 78-79 HJ 4
Tumureng 78-79 G 3
Tumut 58 J 5
Tunaydah 62 C 5
Tunceli 44-45 DE 3
Tuncelin 46-47 H 3
Tünchel 48-49 K 2
Tundrino 42-43 N 5
Tunduma 64-65 H 4
Tunduru 64-65 J 5
Tundža 36-37 M 4
Tundža 36-37 M 4
Tunesië 60-61 F 1-G 2
Tunesien 60-61 F 1-G 2
Tunézia 60-61 F 1-G 2
Tunezja 60-61 F 1-G 2
T'ung 42-43 W 4
Tungaru = Tunqarū 60-61 L 6
Tung-chou = Nantong 48-49 N 5
Tungchow = Nantong 48-49 N 5
T'ung-ch'uan = Tongchuan 48-49 K 4
Tungchwan = Huize 48-49 J 6
Tungchwan = Santai 48-49 JK 5
Tung-fang = Dongfang 48-49 K 8
Tung Hai = Dong Hai 48-49 NO 5-6
Tunghsien = Tong Xian 48-49 M 3-4
Tunghua = Tonghua 48-49 O 3
Tungjen = Tongren 48-49 K 6
Tung-kuan = Dongguan 48-49 LM 7
T'ung-kuan = Tongguan 48-49 L 5
T'ung-liao = Tongliao 48-49 N 3
Tunglu = Tonglu 48-49 M 5-6
T'ung-p'u = Tongphu 48-49 H 5
Tungshan = Xuzhou 48-49 M 5
Tung-shêng = Dongsheng 48-49 K 4
Tungtai = Dongtai 48-49 N 5
Tung-t'ing Hu = Dongting Hu 48-49 L 6
Tun-hua = Dunhua 48-49 O 3
Tun-huang = Dunhuang 48-49 GH 3
Tunhwang = Dunhuang 48-49 GH 3
Tunicia 60-61 F 1-G 2
Tūnis 60-61 FG 1
Tunisi, Canale di – 36-37 D 7
Tunisia 60-61 F 1-G 2
Tunisie 60-61 F 1-G 2
Tunisko 60-61 F 1-G 2
Tunj 60-61 K 7
Tunja 78-79 E 3
Tūnjah 60-61 L 7
Tunkhannock, PA 74-75 EF 4
Tunnsjø 30-31 E 5
Tunqarū 60-61 L 6
Tunuyan, Sierra de – 80 C 4
Tunxi 48-49 M 6
Tuoketuo = Tugt 48-49 L 3
Tuokexun = Toksun 48-49 F 3
Tuolumne, CA 76-77 CD 7
Tuolumne River 76-77 CD 7
Tuoppajärvi = Topozero 42-43 E 4
Tuosuo Hu = Tos nuur 48-49 H 4
Tupã 78-79 JK 9
Tūp Āghāj 46-47 M 4
Tupanciretã 80 F 3
Tupelo, MS 72-73 J 5
Tupik 38-39 F 4
Tupik [SU ↑ Mogoča] 42-43 WX 7
Tupinambaranas, Ilha – 78-79 H 5
Tupiza 78-79 F 9
Tupper Lake, NY 74-75 F 2
Tupungato, Cerro – 80 BC 4
Tuque, la – 70-71 W 8
Túquerres 78-79 D 4
Ṭūr, Aṭ- 60-61 L 3
Tura [SU, ∼] 42-43 L 6
Tura [SU, ●] 42-43 ST 5
Turabah 44-45 E 6
Turan 42-43 R 7
Turan = Turanskaja nizmennost' 42-43 K 9-L 8
Turanskaja nizmennost' 42-43 K 9-L 8
Ṭurayf 44-45 D 4
Turbat 44-45 J 5
Turbi 63 D 2
Turbio, El – 80 B 8
Turbo 78-79 D 3
Turcja 44-45 B-E 3
Turda 36-37 K 2
Turecko 44-45 B-E 3
Turecko 36-37 M-O 6
Ṭūreh 46-47 N 5
Turek 33 J 2
Turgaj [SU, ∼] 42-43 L 8
Turgaj [SU, ●] 42-43 L 8
Turgajskaja ložbina 42-43 L 7
Turgajskaja ložbina 42-43 L 7
Türgen Echin uul 48-49 FG 2
Türgen Echin uul 48-49 FG 2
Türgen Echin uul 48-49 FG 2
Turgut 46-47 DE 3
Turgutlu 46-47 BC 3
Turhal 46-47 G 2
Türi 30-31 L 8
Turia 34-35 G 9
Turiaçu 78-79 K 5
Turiaçu, Baía de – 78-79 KL 5
Turij Rog 42-43 Z 8
Turin = Torino 36-37 BC 3
Turin = Torino 36-37 BC 3
Turinsk 42-43 L 6
Turín = Torino 36-37 BC 3
Tūrīt 60-61 L 8
Turka 33 L 4
Turkana 63 C 2
Turkana, Lake – 64-65 J 2
Türkei 44-45 B-E 3
Türkeli 46-47 F 2
Turkestan 42-43 M 9
Turkey 44-45 B-E 3
Turkiestan 44-45 K-O 3
Turkistan 42-43 K-O 3
Turkistan 48-49 B-F 4
Türkmen Dağı 46-47 D 3
Turkménie 44-45 HJ 2-3
Turkmenistan 44-45 HJ 2-3
Turkmenistán 44-45 HJ 2-3
Turkmenistán 44-45 HJ 2-3
Turkmen-Kala 44-45 J 3
Turkmenskaja Sovetskaja Socialističeskaja Respublika = Turkmenistan 44-45 HJ 2-3
Türkoğlu 46-47 G 4
Turksib 42-43 P 7
Turks Islands 72-73 M 7
Turku 30-31 K 7
Turkwel 64-65 J 2
Turkije 44-45 B-E 3
Turlock, CA 76-77 C 7
Turneffe Islands 72-73 J 8
Turner, WA 76-77 E 2
Turnhout 34-35 K 3
Turnu Măgurele 36-37 L 4
Turnu Rosu, Pasul – 36-37 KL 3
Turo 63 DE 3
Tuross Head 58 K 6
Turpan 48-49 F 3
Turquino, Pico – 72-73 L 8
Turquestán 42-43 M 9
Turquia 44-45 B-E 3
Turquie 44-45 B-E 3
Tursāq 46-47 L 6
Turtkul' 42-43 L 9
Turuchansk 42-43 Q 4
Turugart = Torugart Davan 44-45 L 2
Turumbah 46-47 J 4
Turun ja Poorin lääni 30-31 K 6-7
Turut = Ṭorūd 44-45 H 3
Turijn = Torino 36-37 BC 3
Turyn = Torino 36-37 BC 3
Tuscaloosa, AL 72-73 J 5
Tuscarora, NV 76-77 E 5
Tusenøyane 30-31 l 6
Tu Shan = Du Shan [TJ, ▲] 50-51 B 2
Tuside = Pic Toussidé 60-61 H 4
Tusima = Tsushima 48-49 O 5
Tusima kaikyō = Tsushima-kaikyō 48-49 OP 5
Tussey Mountain 74-75 DE 4-5
Tustna 30-31 B 6
Tutak 46-47 K 3
Tuticorin 44-45 M 9
Tutončana 42-43 R 4
Tutončana 42-43 R 4
Tutrakan 36-37 M 3-4
Tuttlingen 33 D 4-5
Tūttukkuḍi = Tuticorin 44-45 M 9
Tutubu 63 C 4
Tutuila 52-53 c 1
Tutupaca, Volcán – 78-79 E 8
Tuul gol 48-49 JK 2
Tuva 42-43 RS 7
Tuva, República Autónoma de los – 42-43 RS 7
Tuva Autonomous Republic 42-43 RS 7
Tuvai Autonóm Köztársaság 42-43 RS 7
Tuvinskaja Avtonomnaja Sovetskaja Socialističeskaja Respublika = Tuwinische Autonome Republik 42-43 RS 7
Ṭuwāl 'Aba' 46-47 H 4
Tuwāt, At- 60-61 DE 3
Ṭuwayq, Jabal – 44-45 F 6
Ṭuwaythah 60-61 K 6
Tuwinische Autonome Republik 44-45 RS 7
Tuwińska Autonomiczna Republika 42-43 RS 7
Tuwut 60-61 L 7
Tuxpan [MEX, Nayarit] 72-73 E 7
Tuxpán de Rodriguez Cano 72-73 G 7
Tuxtla Gutiérrez 72-73 H 8
Tûy 34-35 C 7
Tuy An 52-53 E 4
Tuy Hoa 52-53 EF 4
Tūyserkān 46-47 N 5
Tuyun = Duyun 48-49 K 6
Tuz Gölü 44-45 C 3
Ṭuz Khurmātū 46-47 L 5
Tuzla 36-37 H 3
Tuzla [TR] 46-47 F 4
Tuzluca 46-47 K 2
Tūzlū Gol = Kavīr-e Mīghān 46-47 N 5
Tuzly 36-37 O 3

Tŭ-fok 64-65 F 9
Türkmenisztán 44-45 HJ 2-3
Tűzföld 80 C 8

Tvedestrand 30-31 C 8
Tver' 42-43 EF 6

Tweed 74-75 E 2
Tweed 32 E 4
Tweedsmuir Provincial Park 70-71 L 7
Twentynine Palms, CA 76-77 EF 8
Twilight Cove 56-57 E 6
Twin Bridges, MT 76-77 GH 3
Twin Falls, ID 72-73 CD 3
Twin Heads 56-57 E 4
Twin Islands 70-71 UV 7
Twin Peaks 76-77 F 3
Twodot, MT 76-77 HJ 2
Two Harbors, MN 72-73 HJ 2

Tyamo Hayiḳ 60-61 M 7
Tybet 48-49 E-G 5
Tyborøn 30-31 BC 9
Tyentya 60-61 M 7
Tyew Bahir 60-61 M 8
Tygda 42-43 Y 7
Tygh Valley, OR 76-77 C 3
Tygrys = Nahr Dijlah 44-45 E 3
Tyler, TX 72-73 GH 5
Tylösand 30-31 E 9
Tym 42-43 P 6
Tymfrēstós 36-37 JK 6
Tymovskoje 42-43 b 7
Tympákion 36-37 L 8
Tynda 42-43 XY 6
Tynemouth 32 F 4
Tynset 30-31 D 6
Tyōsen kaikyō = Chōsen-kaikyō 48-49 O 5
Tyrell, Lake – 56-57 H 7
Tyrhénské moře 36-37 D-F 6
Tyrifjord 30-31 CD 7
Tyrma 42-43 Z 7
Tyrol = Tirol 33 EF 5
Tyrol du Sud 36-37 D 2
Tyrolsko = Osttirol 36-37 E 2
Tyrone, PA 74-75 D 4
Tyros = Ṣūr 46-47 F 6
Tyrrell, Lake – 58 F 5
Tyrreńskie, Morze - 36-37 D-F 6
Tyrrheense Zee 36-37 D-F 6
Tyrrhenian Sea 36-37 D-F 6
Tyrrhenisches Meer 36-37 D-F 6
Tysnesøy 30-31 A 7-8

Tzaneen 64-65 H 7
Tzechung = Zizhong 48-49 JK 5-6
Tzekung = Zigong 48-49 JK 6
Tzŭ-hu = Bajan Choto 48-49 JK 4
Tzŭ-kung = Zigong 48-49 JK 6

Ty

Tyamo Hayiḳ 60-61 M 7

Tybet 48-49 E-G 5
Tyborøn 30-31 BC 9

Tyentya 60-61 M 7
Tyew Bahir 60-61 M 8

Tygda 42-43 Y 7
Tygh Valley, OR 76-77 C 3
Tygrys = Nahr Dijlah 44-45 E 3

Tyler, TX 72-73 GH 5
Tylösand 30-31 E 9

Tym 42-43 P 6

Tymfrēstós 36-37 JK 6
Tymovskoje 42-43 b 7
Tympákion 36-37 L 8

Tynda 42-43 XY 6
Tynemouth 32 F 4
Tynset 30-31 D 6

Tyōsen kaikyō = Chōsen-kaikyō 48-49 O 5

Tyrell, Lake – 56-57 H 7
Tyrhénské moře 36-37 D-F 6
Tyrifjord 30-31 CD 7
Tyrma 42-43 Z 7
Tyrnau = Trnava 33 H 4
Tyrol = Tirol 33 EF 5
Tyrol du Sud 36-37 D 2
Tyrolsko = Osttirol 36-37 E 2
Tyrone, PA 74-75 D 4
Tyros = Ṣūr 46-47 F 6
Tyrrell, Lake – 58 F 5
Tyrreńskie, Morze - 36-37 D-F 6
Tyrrheense Zee 36-37 D-F 6
Tyrrhenian Sea 36-37 D-F 6
Tyrrhenisches Meer 36-37 D-F 6
Tyrrhenisches Meer 36-37 D-F 6

Tysnesøy 30-31 A 7-8

U

Uaçari, Serra – 78-79 H 4
Uaco Cungo 64-65 E 5
Uaddân = Waddān 60-61 H 3
Uadi-Halfa = Wādī Ḥalfā 60-61 L 4
Uagadugu = Ouagadougou 60-61 D 6
Ualega = Welega 60-61 LM 7
Uancheu = Wenzhou 48-49 N 6
Uanle Uen = Wanleweeyn 64-65 K 2
Uarangal = Warangal 44-45 MN 7
Uaso Nyiro 63 D 2
Uaso Nyiro 63 D 2
Uatumã, Rio – 78-79 H 5
Uauá 78-79 M 6
Uáu en-Nâmûs = Wāw an-Nāmūs 60-61 H 4
Uaupés 78-79 F 5
Uaupés, Rio – 78-79 F 4
Uaxactún 72-73 J 8

Ubá 78-79 L 9
Ubá, Salto do – 80 F 2
Ubaitaba 78-79 M 7
Ubangi 64-65 E 2
Ubangi-Schari = Zentralafrikanische Republik 60-61 HJ 7
Ubari = Awbārī 60-61 G 3
'Ubāri, Edeien- = Ṣaḥrā' Awbārī 60-61 G 3
Ubari, Edeyin – = Ṣaḥrā' Awbārī 60-61 G 3
Ubaye 34-35 L 6
'Ubaylah, Al- 44-45 G 6
Ubayyiḍ, Al- 60-61 KL 6
Ubayyid, Bi'r al- 62 BC 4
Ubayyiḍ, Wādī al- 46-47 K 6
Ube 48-49 P 5
Úbeda 34-35 F 9
Ubekendt Ø 70-71 a 3
Uberaba 78-79 K 8
Uberlândia 78-79 K 8
Ubiña, Peña – 34-35 DE 7
Ubiña, Peña – 34-35 DE 7
'Ubkayk, Jabal – 60-61 M 4
Ubsa Nur = Uvs nuur 48-49 G 1
Ubundu 64-65 FG 3

Učaly 38-39 LM 5
Ucami 42-43 S 5
Ucayali, Río – 78-79 D 6
Uchiko 50-51 J 6
Uchinoko = Uchiko 50-51 J 6
Uchinoura 50-51 H 7
Uchiura-wan 50-51 b 2
Uchta [SU, Komi ASSR] 42-43 J 5
Uchta = Kalevala 42-43 E 4
Üchturpan 48-49 DE 3
Ucrania 38-39 E-G 6
Učur 42-43 Z 6

Učaly 38-39 LM 5
Učur 42-43 Z 6

Uchiko 50-51 J 6
Uchinoko = Uchiko 50-51 J 6
Uchinoura 50-51 H 7
Uchiura-wan 50-51 b 2
Uchta [SU, Komi ASSR] 42-43 J 5
Uchta = Kalevala 42-43 E 4

Uda [SU ◁ Čuna] 42-43 S 7
Uda [SU ◁ Selenga] 42-43 UV 7
Uda [SU ◁ Udskaja guba] 42-43 Z 7
Ūdah, Jabal – 60-61 M 4
Udaipur [IND ↗ Ahmadabad] 44-45 L 6
'Udaysāt, Al- 62 E 5
Udbina 36-37 FG 3
Uddevalla 30-31 DE 8
Uddjaur 30-31 GH 5
Ūdine 36-37 E 2
Udipi 44-45 L 8
Udīsā = Orissa 44-45 N 7-O 6
Udjidji = Ujiji 64-65 G 3-4
Udmurcka Autonomiczna Republika = 2 ◁ 42-43 J 6
Udmurt Autonóm Köztársaság 42-43 J 6
Udmurt Autonomous Republic = 2 ◁ 42-43 J 6
Udmurtische Autonome Republik 42-43 J 6
Udmurtos, República Autónoma de los – = 2 ◁ 42-43 J 6
Udmurtská autonomní republika = 2 ◁ 42-43 J 6
Udmurtskaja Avtonomnaja Sovetskaja Socialističeskaja Respublika = Udmurtische Autonome Republik = 2 ◁ 42-43 J 6
U-do 50-51 F 6
Udon Thani 52-53 D 3
Udskaja guba 42-43 a 7
Udupi 44-45 L 8
Udža 42-43 W 3
Udža 42-43 W 3

Uebonti 52-53 H 7
Ueda 50-51 M 4
Uele 64-65 F 2
Uėlen 70-71 BC 4
Uelzen 33 E 2
Uengan, mys – 42-43 LM 3
Ueno 50-51 L 5
Uere 64-65 G 2

Ufa [SU, ∼] 42-43 K 6
Ufa [SU, ●] 42-43 K 7

Ugalla 64-65 H 4
Uganda 64-65 H 2
Uglič 42-43 F 6
Uglič 42-43 F 6
Ugljan 36-37 F 3
Ugogo 64-65 HJ 4
Ugol'nyj = Beringovskij 42-43 j 5
Ugoma 63 B 3-4
Uguay 80 E 3
Uğurludağ 46-47 F 2

Uha 64-65 H 3
Uha-dong 48-49 O 3
Uhrichsville, OH 74-75 C 4

Uchiko 50-51 J 6
Uchinoko = Uchiko 50-51 J 6
Uchinoura 50-51 H 7
Uchiura-wan 50-51 b 2
Uchta [SU, Komi ASSR] 42-43 J 5
Uchta = Kalevala 42-43 E 4

Ui-do 50-51 E 5
Uige 64-65 DE 4
Uijŏngbu 50-51 F 4
Uiju 50-51 E 2
Uil 38-39 K 6
Uil [SU, ●] 42-43 J 8
Uintah and Ouray Indian Reservation [USA ↓ East Tavaputs Plateau] 76-77 J 6
Uintah and Ouray Indian Reservation [USA ↓ Uinta Mountains] 76-77 HJ 5
Uinta Mountains 72-73 DE 3
Uisŏng 50-51 G 4
Uitenhage 64-65 FG 9

Uj 42-43 L 7
Ujandina 42-43 b 4
Új-Anglia = New England 72-73 M 3-N 2
Ujar 42-43 R 6
Új-Britannia – – Bougainville-árok 52-53 h 6
Ujda = Ujdah 60-61 D 2
Ujdah 60-61 D 2
Új-Delhi = New Delhi 44-45 M 5
Ujedinenija, ostrov – 42-43 OP 2
Új-Foundland = Newfoundland 70-71 M 3-N 2
Új-Guinea 52-53 L 7-M 8
Új-Guinea-hátság 52-53 M 5-6
Ujgurská autonomní oblast Xinjiang = Xinjiang Uygur Zizhiqu 48-49 D-F 3
Új-Hebridák = Vanuatu 56-57 N 2-O 3
Új-Hebridák-árok 56-57 N 3-4
Új-Hebridák-medence 56-57 MN 3
Uji-guntō 50-51 G 7
Ujiji 64-65 G 3-4
Ujjaen = Ujjain 44-45 M 6
Ujjain 44-45 M 6
Új-Kaledónia 56-57 MN 3
Új-Skócia = Nova Scotia 70-71 X 8-Y 9
Új-szibériai-szigetek = Novosibirskije ostrova 42-43 Z-f 2
Ujung Pandang 52-53 G 8
Ujvidék = Novi Sad 36-37 HJ 3
Új-Zéland 56-57 N 8-O 7
Új-Zéland-hátság 56-57 M 5-7
Ukara 63 C 3
'Ukāsh, Wādī – 46-47 J 5-6
Ukerewe Island 64-65 H 3
Ukiah, CA 72-73 B 4
Ukiah, OR 76-77 D 3
Ukimbu 64-65 H 4
Ukmergė 30-31 L 10
Ukonongo 64-65 H 4
Ukraina 38-39 E-G 6
Ukraine 38-39 E-G 6
Ukrajina 38-39 E-G 6
Ukrajna 38-39 E-G 6
Ukumbi 64-65 H 4
Uku-shima 50-51 G 6
Ukwama 63 C 5

Ula 46-47 C 4
'Ulā', Al- 44-45 D 5
Ulaanbaatar 48-49 K 2
Ulaan Choto = Ulan Hot 48-49 N 2
Ulaan Choto = Ulan Hot 48-49 N 2
Ulaangom 48-49 G 1-2
Ulaan Choto = Ulan Hot 48-49 N 2
Ulaan mörön [TJ ◁ Dre Chhu] 48-49 G 5
Ulaan uul 48-49 G 5
Ulala = Gorno-Altajsk 42-43 Q 7
Ulamba 64-65 F 4
Ulan = Dulaan Chijd 48-49 H 4
Ulánbátar = Ulaanbaatar 48-49 K 2
Ulánbátor = Ulaanbaatar 48-49 K 2
Ulan Bator = Ulaanbaatar 48-49 K 2
Ulán Bator = Ulaanbaatar 48-49 K 2
Ulan-Burgasy, chrebet – 42-43 UV 7
Ulan Gom = Ulaangom 48-49 G 1-2
Ulan Hot 48-49 N 2
Ulankom = Ulaangom 48-49 G 1-2
Ulan-Udė 42-43 U 7
Ulapes 80 C 4
Ulaş 46-47 G 3
Ulastai = Uljastaj 48-49 H 2
Ulawa 52-53 k 6
Ul'ba 42-43 P 7
Ulchin 50-51 G 4
Ulcinj 36-37 H 5
Uldza = Bajan Uul 48-49 L 2
Üldzejt = Öldzijt 48-49 J 2
Uldz gol 48-49 L 2
Uleåborg = Oulu 30-31 L 5
Ule Lhee 52-53 C 5
Ulete 64-65 J 4
Ulety 42-43 V 7
Ulhasnagar 44-45 L 7
Uliassutai = Uliastaj 48-49 H 2
Uliastaj 48-49 H 2
Ulijasutai = Uliastaj 48-49 H 2
Ulindi 64-65 G 3
Ulingan 52-53 N 7
Ulja 42-43 b 6
Uljinskij chrebet 42-43 ab 6
Ulladulla 56-57 K 7
Ullsfjord 30-31 HJ 3
Ullŭng-do 48-49 P 4
Ullyul 50-51 E 3
Ulm 33 D 4
Ulm, MT 76-77 H 2
Ulmarra 58 L 2
Uløy 30-31 J 3
Ulsan 48-49 OP 4
Ulster 32 C 4
Ulster Canal 32 C 4
Ulu [RI] 52-53 J 6
Ulu [SU] 42-43 Y 5
Ulúa, Río – 72-73 J 8
Uluabat Gölü 46-47 C 2
Ulubey 46-47 C 3
Ulubey 46-47 G 2
Ulubey [TR, Ordu] 46-47 G 2
Uluborlu 46-47 D 3
Uluçınar 46-47 FG 4
Uludağ 46-47 C 2-3
Ulugh Muz tagh 48-49 F 4
Uluguru Mountains 64-65 J 4
Ulukışla 46-47 F 4
Ulus 46-47 E 2
Ulutau, gora – 42-43 M 8
Ulverstone 58 bc 2
'Ulyā, Qaryat al- 44-45 F 5
Ulyastai = Uliastaj 48-49 H 2
Ulytau 42-43 M 8

Ułan Bator = Ulaanbaatar 48-49 K 2

Ulladulla 56-57 K 7
Ullsfjord 30-31 HJ 3
Ullŭng-do 48-49 P 4
Ullyul 50-51 E 3

Umala 78-79 F 8
Umal'tinskij 42-43 Z 7
Uman' 38-39 F 6
Umanak = Umának 70-71 ab 3
Umanak Fjord 70-71 Za 3
Umának 70-71 ab 3
'Umarī, Qā'al – 46-47 G 7

226 Tulom

Umatilla Indian Reservation 76-77 D 3
Umatilla River 76-77 D 3
Umba [SU, ●] 42-43 J 6
Umboi 52-53 N 8
Úmbria 36-37 DE 4
Umbrien = Úmbria 36-37 DE 4
Umbu [TJ] 48-49 F 5
Umeå 30-31 HJ 6
Ume älv 30-31 H 5
Umm ad-Durūs, Sabkhat – 60-61 B 4
Umm al-'Abīd 60-61 H 3
Umm al-Kataf, Khalīj – 62 F 6
Umm al-Qaywayn 44-45 GH 5
Umm ar-Rabī', Nahr – 60-61 C 2
Umm aṭ-Ṭuyūr al-Fawqānī, Jabal – 62 F 6
Umm aṭ-Ṭūẓ 46-47 K 5
Umm Badr 60-61 K 6
Umm Ball 60-61 K 6
Umm Bishtīt, Bi'r – 62 FG 6
Umm Bujmah 62 E 3
Umm Durmān 60-61 L 5
Umm el-'Abid 60-61 H 3
Umm Hajer = Om Hajer 60-61 M 6
Umm Ḥibāl, Bi'r – 62 E 6
Umm 'Inab, Jabal – 62 E 4
Umm Kaddādah 60-61 K 6
Umm Karār, Tall – 46-47 H 6
Umm Keddāda = Umm Kaddādah 60-61 K 6
Umm Lağğ = Umm Lajj 44-45 D 5
Umm Lajj 44-45 D 5
Umm Naqqāṭ, Jabal – 62 EF 5
Umm Qaṣr 46-47 M 7
Umm Quṣur, Jazīrat – 62 F 3-4
Umm Rashrash = Ėlat 44-45 C 4
Umm Ruwābah 60-61 L 6
Umm Sa'īd, Bi'r – 62 EF 3
Umm Shāghir, Jabal – 62 D 6
Umnak Island 19 D 35-36
Umniati 64-65 G 6
Umpqua River 76-77 AB 4
'Umshaymin, Al- 46-47 H 6
Ŭmsŏng 50-51 F 4
Umtali = Mutare 64-65 H 6
Umtata 64-65 G 9
Umvuma = Mvuma 64-65 H 6
Umzimvubu 64-65 GH 9

Una 36-37 G 3
Una [BR] 78-79 M 8
'Unāb, Wādī el- = Wādī al-'Unnāb 46-47 G 7-8
Unac 36-37 G 3
Unadilla, GA 74-75 AB 8
Unai 78-79 K 8
'Unaizah = 'Unayzah 44-45 E 5
Unalakleet, AK 70-71 D 5
Unalaska Island 19 D 35
Unango 63 C 6
'Unayzah [JOR] 46-47 FG 7
'Unayzah [Saudi-Arabien] 44-45 E 5
'Unayzah, Jabal – 44-45 DE 4
Uncia 78-79 F 8
Uncompahgre Peak 72-73 E 4
Uncompahgre Plateau 76-77 JK 6
Underbool 58 E 5
Undurkhan = Öndörchaan 48-49 L 2
Uneča 38-39 F 5
Uneča 38-39 F 5
Uneiuxi, Rio – 78-79 F 5
Unga Island 70-71 D 6
Ungarn 33 H-K 5
Ungava 70-71 V-X 6
Ungava, Péninsule d' 70-71 VW 5
Ungava Bay 70-71 X 6
Ungava Crater = New Quebec Crater 70-71 VW 5
Ungeny 36-37 MN 2
Unggi 50-51 H 1
Ungvár = Užgorod 33 L 4
Ungvár = Užgorod 33 L 4
União 78-79 L 5
União dos Palmares 78-79 MN 6
Unib, Khawr – 62 F 7
Unije 36-37 EF 3
Unimak Island 19 D 35
Unini, Rio – 78-79 G 5
Unión [RA] 80 C 5
Union, OR 76-77 E 3
Union, SC 74-75 C 7
Union, WV 74-75 C 6
Unión, La – 34-35 G 10
Unión, La – [ES] 72-73 J 9
Unión, La – [PE, Huánuco] 78-79 D 6-7
Unión, La – [RCH] 80 B 6
Union, Mount – 76-77 G 8
Union City, PA 74-75 CD 4
Union Creek, OR 76-77 B 4
Union Pacific Railway 72-73 E 3
Union Point, GA 74-75 B 8
Uniontown, PA 74-75 D 5
Unionville, NV 76-77 DE 5
United Arab Emirates 44-45 G 6-H 5
United Kingdom 32 F-H 4-5
United Provinces = Uttar Pradesh 44-45 MN 5
United States 72-73 D-K 4
United States Atomic Energy Commission Reservation = National Reactor Testing Station 76-77 G 4
Unity, ME 74-75 J 2
University Heights, OH 74-75 C 4
Unjamwesi = Unyamwezi 64-65 H 3-4
'Unnāb, Wādī al- 46-47 G 7-8
Unsan 50-51 E 2-3
Unsan-ni 50-51 EF 3
Unst 32 F 1
Unstrut 33 E 3
Unterer Trajanswall = Nižnij Trajanov val 36-37 N 3
Unyamwezi 64-65 H 3-4
Ünye 46-47 G 2
Unža 38-39 H 4
Unže Pavinskaja 38-39 MN 4
Unža 38-39 H 4
Unže Pavinskaja 38-39 MN 4

Uolkitte = Welkītē 60-61 M 7
Uollega = Welega 60-61 LM 7
Uozu 50-51 L 4

Upanda, Serra – 64-65 DE 5
Upemba, Lac – 64-65 G 4
Upemba, Parc national de l' 64-65 G 4
Upernavik 70-71 Z 3
Upington 64-65 F 8
Upolokša 30-31 O 4
Upolokša 30-31 O 4
Upolu 52-53 c 1
Upper Darby, PA 74-75 F 4-5
Upper Egypt = Aṣ-Ṣa'īd 60-61 L 3-4
Upper Guinea 22-23 JK 5
Upper Klamath Lake 76-77 BC 4
Upper Lake 76-77 C 5
Upper Lake, CA 76-77 B 6
Upper Peninsula 72-73 J 2
Upper Seal Lake = Lac d'Iberville 70-71 W 6
Uppland 30-31 G 7-H 8
Uppsala [S, ●] 30-31 G 8
Uppsala [S, ☆] 30-31 GH 7
Upstart Bay 56-57 J 3

'Uqaylah, Al- 60-61 H 2
'Uqayr, Al- 44-45 FG 5
Uqṣur, Al- 60-61 L 3

Ur 44-45 F 4
Ur, Wādī – 62 D 6-7
Urabá, Golfo de – 78-79 D 3
Urabá, Isla – 72-73 bc 3
Urakawa 50-51 c 2
Ural, MT 76-77 F 1
Ural [SU, ~] 42-43 J 8
Ural [SU, ▲▲] 28-29 V 3-U 4
Urales 28-29 V 3-U 4
Uralla 58 K 3
Uralmed'stroj = Krasnoural'sk 42-43 L 6
Urals 28-29 V 3-U 4
Ural'sk 42-43 J 7
Urana 58 GH 5
Urandangi 56-57 G 4
Urandi 78-79 L 7
Uranium City 70-71 P 6
Uraricoera, Rio – 78-79 G 4
Ura-T'ube 44-45 K 3
Uravan, CO 76-77 J 6
Urawa 48-49 QR 4
'Uray'irah 44-45 F 5
'Urayyiḍah, Bi'r – 62 DE 3
Urbana, La – 78-79 F 3
Urbino 36-37 E 4
Urbión, Picos de – 34-35 F 8
Urcos 78-79 E 7
Urda 38-39 J 6
Urdžar 42-43 P 8
Urdžar 42-43 P 8
Uren' 38-39 J 4
Ureparapara 56-57 N 2
Ures 72-73 DE 6
'Urf, Jabal al- 62 E 4
Urfa = Sanlı Urfa 44-45 D 3
Urfa Yaylâsı 46-47 H 4
'Urf Umm Rashīd 62 F 5
Urga 42-43 K 9
Urga = Ulaanbaatar 48-49 K 2
Urgenč 42-43 L 9
Urgenč 42-43 L 9
Ürgüp 46-47 F 3
Uribe 78-79 E 4
Uribia 78-79 E 2
Urickij [SU, Kazachskaja SSR] 42-43 M 7
Urim = Ur 44-45 F 4
Urīsā = Orissa 44-45 N 7-O 6
Urla 44-45 B 3
Urmannyj 42-43 M 5
Urmia 44-45 F 3
Urmia = Reḍā'īyeh 44-45 EF 3
Urmia, Jezioro – = Daryācheh Orūmīyeh 44-45 F 3
Urmia, Lac – = Urmia 44-45 F 3
Urmia, Lago de – = Urmia 44-45 F 3
Urmiasee = Daryācheh Orūmīyeh 44-45 F 3
Urmia-tó = Daryācheh Orūmīyeh 44-45 F 3
Urmijské jezero = Daryācheh Orūmīyeh 44-45 F 3
Ursatjevskaja = Chavast 44-45 K 2
Ursine, NV 76-77 F 6-7
Urt Mörön = Chadzaar 48-49 G 4
Uruaçu 78-79 K 7
Uruana 78-79 JK 8
Uruapan del Progreso 72-73 F 8
Urubamba 78-79 E 7
Urubamba, Río – 78-79 E 7
Urucará 78-79 H 5
Uruçuí 78-79 L 6
Uruçuí, Serra do – 78-79 K 7-L 6
Urucurituba 78-79 H 5
Uruguai, Rio – 80 F 3
Uruguaiana 80 E 3
Uruguay 80 EF 4
Uruguay, Río – [RA ◁ Río de la Plata] 80 E 3
Uruguay, Salto Grande del – 80 F 3
Urugwaj 80 EF 4
Urūm aṣ-Ṣuğrah 46-47 G 4
Urumbi 78-79 F 4
Ürümchi 48-49 F 3
Urumchi = Ürümchi 48-49 F 3
Urundi = Burundi 64-65 GH 3
Urunga 58 L 3
Ur'ung-Chaja = Jur'ung-Chaja 42-43 VW 3
Ur'ung-Chaja = Jur'ung-Chaja 42-43 VW 3
Ur'ung-Chaja = Jur'ung-Chaja 42-43 VW 3
Urup, ostrov – 48-49 S 2
Uruppu = ostrov Urup 42-43 cd 8
'Urūq al-Mu'tariḍah, Al- 44-45 G 6-7
Uruša 42-43 X 7
Uruša 42-43 X 7
Uruyén 78-79 G 3
Urville, Île d' 24 C 31
Urville, Mer d' 24 C 14-15
Urziceni 36-37 M 3
Uržum 42-43 HJ 6
Uržum 42-43 HJ 6

Usa 42-43 K 4
Usagara 64-65 J 4
Uşak 44-45 B 3
Usakos 64-65 DE 7
Ušakova, ostrov – 42-43 OP 1
Usambara Mountains 63 D 4
Usango 63 C 4
Usbekistan 44-45 J 2-K 3
Usborne, Mount – 80 E 8
Usedom 33 F 1-G 2
Usengo 63 B 4
Usetsu = Noto 50-51 L 4
Usevia 63 B 4
'Usfān 44-45 D 6
Ushero 63 BC 4
Ushibuka 50-51 GH 6
Ushirombo 63 BC 3
Ushuaia 80 C 8
Usk, WA 76-77 E 1
Üsküdar, İstanbul- 44-45 BC 2
Usman' 38-39 GH 5
Usoke 63 C 4
Usolje = Usolje-Sibirskoje 42-43 T 7
Usolje-Sibirskoje 42-43 T 7
Usolje-Solikamskoje = Berezniki 42-43 JK 6
Ussagara = Usagara 64-65 J 4
Ussuri = Wusuli Jiang 48-49 P 2
Ussurijsk 42-43 Z 9
Ussurijskij zaliv 50-51 HJ 1
Ust'-Abakanskoje = Abakan 42-43 R 7
Ust'-Barguzin 42-43 UV 7
Ust'-Bol'šereck 42-43 de 7
Ust'-Bol'šereck 42-43 de 7
Ust'-Čaun 42-43 h 4
Ust'-Cil'ma 42-43 J 4
Ust'-Čižapka 42-43 OP 6
Ust'-Čaun 42-43 h 4
Ust'-Čižapka 42-43 OP 6
Ustica 36-37 E 6
Ust'-Ilimsk 42-43 T 6
Ust'-Ilyč 38-39 L 3
Ust'-Ilyč 38-39 L 3
Ústi nad Labem 33 FG 3
Ust'-Išim 42-43 N 6
Ust'-Išim 42-43 N 6
Ustje-Agapy = Agapa 42-43 Q 3
Ust'-Juribej 42-43 MN 4
Ustka 33 H 1
Ust'-Kamčatsk 42-43 f 6
Ust'-Kamčatsk 42-43 f 6
Ust'-Kamenogorsk 42-43 OP 7-8
Ust'-Kan 42-43 PQ 7
Ust'-Kara 42-43 G 4
Ust'-Karabula 42-43 S 6
Ust'-Karsk 42-43 W 7
Ust'-Kulom 42-43 JK 5
Ust'-Kut 42-43 U 6
Ust'-Luga 38-39 E 4
Ust'-Maja 42-43 Z 5
Ust'-Muja 42-43 W 6
Ust'-Nem 38-39 KL 3
Ust'-Nera 42-43 b 5
Uštobe 42-43 O 8
Ust'-Orda = Ust'-Ordynskij 42-43 TU 7
Ust-Orda-Burjaten, Nationalkreis der – = 10 ◁ 42-43 T 7
Ust-Orda-Burjaten, Nationalkreis der – = 11 ◁ 42-43 T 7
Ust'-Ordyński Buriacki Okręg Autonomiczny = 10 ◁ 42-43 T 7
Ust'-Ordynskij 42-43 TU 7
Ust'-ordynský burjatský okruh = 10 ◁ 42-43 T 7
Ust-Ordynsky-Buryat Autonomous Area = 11 ◁ 42-43 T 7
Ust'-Oz'ornoje 42-43 Q 6
Ust'-Port 42-43 PQ 4
Ust'-Ščug'or 42-43 K 5
Ust Sysolsk = Syktyvkar 42-43 J 5
Ust'-Ščug'or 42-43 K 5
Ust'-Tareja 42-43 R 3
Ust'-Tatta 42-43 Za 5
Ust'-Tym 42-43 OP 6
Ust'-Tym 42-43 OP 6
Ust'-Ulagan 42-43 Q 7
Ust'-Ura 38-39 HJ 3
Ust'urt, plato – 42-43 K 9
Ust'-Usa 42-43 K 4
Ust'-Vym' 38-39 K 3
Usu-dake 50-51 b 2
Usuki 50-51 HJ 6
Usule 63 C 4
Usumacinta, Río – 72-73 H 8
Usumbura = Bujumbura 64-65 G 3
Usure 63 C 4
Usuyŏng 50-51 EF 5
Usu zan 50-51 b 2

Ušakova, ostrov – 42-43 OP 1
Uštobe 42-43 O 8

Uszty-Ordinszkij Burját Autonóm Körzet 42-43 T 7

Utah 72-73 DE 4
Utah Lake 72-73 D 3
Utasinai 50-51 c 2
Utegi 63 C 3
Ute Mountain Indian Reservation 76-77 J 7
Utena 30-31 L 10
Utengule 63 C 5
Ute Peak 76-77 J 7
Utete 64-65 J 4
'Uthmānīyah, Al- 62 DE 4
U Thong 52-53 C 4
Utiariti 78-79 H 7
Utica, NY 72-73 LM 3
Utica, OH 74-75 B 4
Utiel 34-35 G 9
Utiura-wan 48-49 R 3
Utrecht 34-35 K 2
Utrera 34-35 E 10
Utrillas 34-35 G 8
Utsjoki 30-31 M 3
Utsunomiya 48-49 QR 4
Uttaradit 52-53 D 3
Uttar Andamān = North Andaman 44-45 P 8
Uttar Pradesh 44-45 MN 5
Utunomiya = Utsunomiya 48-49 QR 4
Utupua 52-53 l 7

Uu = Wuhu 48-49 M 5
Uudenmaan lääni 30-31 K-M 7
Uusikaarlepyy = Nykarleby 30-31 K 6
Uusikaupunki 30-31 J 7
Uusimaa 30-31 KL 7

Uva 38-39 K 4
Uvalde, TX 72-73 G 6
Uvarovo 38-39 H 5
Uvat 42-43 M 6
Uvéa 52-53 b 1
Uvea = Île Ouvéa 56-57 N 4
Uvel'skij 38-39 M 5
Uvinza 64-65 H 3-4
Uvira 64-65 G 3
Uvs = 2 ◁ 48-49 G 2
Uvs nuur 48-49 G 1

Uwajima 48-49 P 5
'Uwayjā', Al- 44-45 G 6
Uwayl 60-61 K 7
'Uwaynāt, Jabal al- 60-61 K 4
'Uwaynidhīyah, Jazīrat al- 62 FG 4
'Uwayqilah, Ma'ātin – 62 BC 2
'Uwayriḍ, Ḥarrat al- 44-45 D 5
Uwaysit 46-47 GH 7
Uwazima = Uwajima 48-49 P 5
Uwimbi 64-65 HJ 4
Uwinsa = Uvinza 64-65 H 3-4

Uxbridge 74-75 D 2
Uxmal 72-73 J 7

Uyowa 63 BC 4
Uyuni 78-79 F 9
Uyuni, Salar de – 78-79 F 9

Už 38-39 E 5
'Uzaym, Shaṭṭ al- 46-47 L 5
'Uzayr, Al- 46-47 M 7
Uzbekistan 44-45 J 2-K 3
Uzbekistán 44-45 J 2-K 3
Uzbekskaja Sovetskaja Socialističeskaja Respublika = Usbekistan 44-45 J 2-K 3
Uzboj 44-45 H 2-3
Uzgen 44-45 L 2
Užgorod 38-39 D 6
Užice 36-37 HJ 4
Uzlovaja 38-39 G 5
Uzunköprü 46-47 B 2
Uzun Yaylâ 46-47 G 3
Užur 42-43 QR 6

Už 38-39 E 5
Užgorod 38-39 D 6
Užice 36-37 HJ 4
Užur 42-43 QR 6

Ü

Üchturpan 48-49 DE 3

Üldzejt = Öldzijt 48-49 J 2

Ünye 46-47 G 2

Ürgüp 46-47 F 3
Ürümchi 48-49 F 3

Üsküdar, İstanbul- 44-45 BC 2

Üzbegisztán 44-45 J 2-K 3

V

Vääkiö 30-31 N 5
Vaala 30-31 M 5
Vaaldam 64-65 G 8
Vaal River = Vaalrivier 64-65 G 8
Vaalrivier 64-65 G 8
Vaalwater 64-65 G 7
Vaasa 30-31 J 6
Vác 33 J 5
Vacamonte, Punta – 72-73 b 3
Vacaria 80 F 3
Vacaville, CA 76-77 BC 6
Vach [SU] 42-43 O 5
Vachš 44-45 K 3
Vader, WA 76-77 B 2
Vadheim 30-31 A 7
Vadhvān = Wadhwan 44-45 L 6
Vadodara 44-45 L 6
Vadsø 30-31 NO 2
Vadstena 30-31 F 8
Vaduz 33 D 5
Værøy 30-31 E 4
Vafs 46-47 N 5
Vaga 38-39 H 3
Vagaj 42-43 M 6
Vågåmo 30-31 C 7
Vaggeryd 30-31 EF 9
Vågsfjord 30-31 G 3
Váh 33 H 4
Vachš 44-45 K 3
Vaigat 70-71 a 3
Vajdaguba 30-31 OP 3
Vajgač 38-39 LM 1
Vajgač, ostrov – 42-43 KL 3
Vajgač 38-39 LM 1
Vajgač, ostrov – 42-43 KL 3
Vakaga 60-61 J 7
Vakfıkebir 46-47 H 2
Valachia 36-37 LM 3
Valachie 36-37 LM 3
Valadim = Mavago 64-65 J 5
Valais 33 C 5
Valaquia 36-37 LM 3
Valašsko 36-37 K-M 3
Valcheta 80 C 6
Valdagno 36-37 D 3
Valdajskaja vozvyšennost' 38-39 F 4
Valdajskaja vozvyšennost' 38-39 F 4
Val d'Aosta 36-37 B 3
Valdemārpils 30-31 JK 9
Valdemarsvik 30-31 G 8
Valdepeñas 34-35 F 9
Valdepeñas 34-35 F 9
Valderaduey 34-35 E 7-8
Valdés, Peninsula – 80 D 6
Valdesa, La – 72-73 b 3
Valdez, AK 70-71 G 5
Valdia = Weldya 60-61 M 6
Valdivia [RCH] 80 B 5
Val-d'Or 70-71 V 8
Valdosta, GA 72-73 K 5
Valdres 30-31 C 7
Vale, OR 76-77 E 3-4
Valea-lui-Mihai 36-37 K 2
Vålebru 30-31 D 7
Valença 34-35 C 7-8
Valença [BR, Bahia] 78-79 M 7
Valença = Valencia 78-79 F 2
Valença do Piauí 78-79 L 6
Valence 34-35 K 6
Valencia [YV] 78-79 F 2
Valencia [E, ≅] 34-35 G 8-9
Valencia [E, ●] 34-35 GH 9
Valencia, Golfo de – 34-35 H 9
Valencia, Lago de – 78-79 F 2
Valencia de Alcántara 34-35 D 9
Valencia de Don Juan 34-35 E 7
Valenciennes 34-35 J 3
Valentim, Serra do – 78-79 L 6
Valentin 42-43 Za 9
Valenza 36-37 C 3
Valera 78-79 E 3
Valga 30-31 M 9
Valier, MT 76-77 G 1
Valjevo 36-37 H 3
Valka 30-31 LM 9
Valkeakoski 30-31 L 7
Valladolid 34-35 E 8
Valladolid [MEX] 72-73 J 7
Valle, AZ 76-77 G 8
Vallecito Mountains 76-77 E 9
Valle de la Pascua 78-79 FG 3
Valledupar 78-79 E 2
Valle Grande [BOL] 78-79 G 8
Valle Hermoso [MEX] 72-73 G 6
Vallejo, CA 72-73 B 4
Vallenar 80 B 3
Valletta 36-37 F 8
Valley, WY 76-77 J 3
Valley Falls, OR 76-77 C 4
Valleyfield 70-71 VW 8
Valley Pass 76-77 FG 5
Valls 34-35 H 8
Valmiera 30-31 L 9
Valmy, NV 76-77 E 5
Valnera 34-35 F 7
Vals, Tanjung – 52-53 L 8
Valsbaai [ZA, Kaapland] 64-65 E 9
Valsetz, OR 76-77 B 3
Valujki 38-39 G 5
Valverde [E] 60-61 A 3
Valverde del Camino 34-35 D 10
Vamizi 63 E 5
Vammala 30-31 K 7
Van 44-45 E 3
Vanavara 42-43 T 5
Van Buren, ME 74-75 JK 1
Vanceboro, ME 74-75 K 2
Vanceboro, NC 74-75 E 7
Vancouver 70-71 M 8
Vancouver, WA 72-73 B 2
Vancouver Island 70-71 L 8
Vandemere, NC 74-75 E 7
Vandenberg Air Force Base 76-77 C 8
Vanderlin Island 56-57 G 3
Van Diemen, Cape – 56-57 EF 2
Van Diemen Gulf 56-57 F 2
Vāndrā = Bandra 44-45 L 7
Vänern 30-31 E 8
Vänersborg 30-31 E 8
Vanga = Shimoni 64-65 JK 3
Vangaindrano 64-65 L 7
Van Gölü 44-45 E 3
Vangunu 52-53 j 6
Vanikoro Islands 52-53 l 7
Vanimo 52-53 M 7
Vankarem 42-43 k 4
van Keulenfjord 30-31 jk 6
van Mijenfjord 30-31 jk 6
Vännäs 30-31 HJ 6
Vannes 34-35 F 5
Vannøy 30-31 HJ 2
Vánoční ostrov = Christmas Island 52-53 E 9
Vanrhynsdorp 64-65 EF 9
Vanrook 56-57 H 3
Vansbro 30-31 EF 7
Vansittart Bay 56-57 E 2
Vansittart Island 70-71 U 4
Vanua Lava 56-57 N 2
Vanua Levu 52-53 b 2
Vanuatu 56-57 N 2-O 3
Vanwyksvlei 64-65 F 9
Vanzevat 42-43 M 5
Vanžil'-Kynak 42-43 P 5
Vanžil'-Kynak 42-43 P 5
Varakļāni 30-31 M 9
Vārānasi 44-45 N 5
Vārangal = Warangal 44-45 MN 7
Varangerbotn 30-31 N 2
Varangerfjord 30-31 NO 2-3
Varanger halvøya 30-31 NO 2
Varaždin 36-37 FG 2
Varazze 36-37 C 3
Varberg 30-31 DE 9
Vardar 36-37 K 5
Varde 30-31 C 10
Vardhā = Wardha [IND, ~] 44-45 M 6
Vardhā = Wardha [IND, ●] 44-45 M 6
Vardø 30-31 O 2
Varella, Cap – = Mui Dièu 52-53 EF 4
Vareš 36-37 H 3
Varese 36-37 C 3
Vareš 36-37 H 3
Varfolomejevka 42-43 Z 9
Varginha 78-79 K 9
Varillas 80 B 2
Varillas, Las – 80 D 4
Varjegan = Novoangarsk 42-43 O 5
Varkaus 30-31 MN 6
Värmland 30-31 E 8
Värmlandsnäs 30-31 E 8

Värml 227

Varna 36-37 MN 4
Värnamo 30-31 F 9
Varnek 42-43 KL 4
Varnville, SC 74-75 C 8
Varsinais Suomi 30-31 JK 7
Varšipel'da 38-39 G 3
Varsovia = Warszawa 33 KL 2
Varsovie = Warszawa 33 KL 2
Varsó = Warszawa 33 K 2
Varšava = Warszawa 33 K 2
Varšipel'da 38-39 G 3
Varto 46-47 J 3
Varvarovka 36-37 O 2
Varzuga 38-39 G 2
Vasa = Vaasa 30-31 J 6
Vaşcău 36-37 K 2
Vashon Island 76-77 B 2
Vasknarva 30-31 M 8
Vaskojoki 30-31 LM 3
Vaslui 36-37 MN 2
Vassar 74-75 B 3
Vastan = Gevaş 46-47 K 3
Västerås 30-31 FG 8
Västerbotten [S, ≅] 30-31 H 6-J 5
Västerbotten [S, ☆] 30-31 F-J 5
Västerdalälven 30-31 EF 7
Västergötland 30-31 E 9-F 8
Västernorrland 30-31 GH 6
Västervik 30-31 G 9
Västmanland 30-31 FG 8
Vasto 36-37 F 4
Vas'ugan 42-43 O 6
Vas'uganje 42-43 N 5-O 6
Vasvár 33 H 5
Vaté, Île – = Efate 56-57 N 3
Vaticaanstad 36-37 DE 5
Vatican 36-37 DE 5
Vatican City 36-37 DE 5
Vaticano, Ciudad del – 36-37 DE 5
Vatikán 36-37 DE 5
Vatikán 36-37 DE 5
Vatikanstadt 36-37 DE 5
V'atka 42-43 H 6
V'atka = Kirov 42-43 HJ 6
Vatnajökull 30-31 e 2
Vatomandry 64-65 LM 6
Vatra Dornei 36-37 L 2
V'atskije Pol'any 42-43 HJ 6
Vättern 30-31 F 8
Vaughn, MT 76-77 H 2
Vaupés, Río – 78-79 E 4
Vava'u Group 52-53 c 2
Växjö 30-31 F 9
V'azemskij 42-43 Za 8
V'az'ma 38-39 F 4

Veadeiros, Chapada dos – 78-79 K 7-8
Veadeiros, Chapada dos – 78-79 K 7-8
Veadeiros, Chapada dos – 78-79 K 7-8
Vedea 36-37 L 3
Vedia 80 D 4
Vega 30-31 D 5
Vega, La – [DOM] 72-73 MN 8
Vega de Granada 34-35 EF 10
Vegreville 70-71 O 7
Veis = Veys 46-47 N 7
Vejer de la Frontera 34-35 DE 10
Vejle 30-31 C 10
Veka Vekalla = Vella Lavella 52-53 j 6
Vela, Cabo de la – 78-79 E 2
Vela de Coro, La – 78-79 F 2
Velay 34-35 JK 6
Velebit 36-37 F 3
Velence = Venèzia 36-37 E 3
Vélez-Málaga 34-35 EF 10
Velhas, Rio das – 78-79 L 8
Velho = Mágoè 64-65 H 6
Velikaja 38-39 E 4
Velikaja [SU ◁ Anadyrskij zaliv] 42-43 h 5
Velikaja Aleksandrovka 36-37 P 2
Velikaja Ičinskaja sopka = vulkan Ičinskaja Sopka 42-43 e 6
Velikaja Ičinskaja sopka = vulkan Ičinskaja Sopka 42-43 e 6
Velikaja Kambalnaja sopka = vulkan Kambalnaja Sopka 42-43 e 7
Velikaja Kl'učevskaja sopka = vulkan Kl'učevskaja Sopka 42-43 f 6
Velikaja Kl'učevskaja sopka = vulkan Kl'učevskaja Sopka 42-43 f 6
Velikaja Kor'akskaja sopka = vulkan Kor'akskaja Sopka 42-43 ef 7
Velikaja Kronockaja sopka = vulkan Kronockaja Sopka 42-43 ef 7
Velikije Luki 38-39 EF 4
Velikij Šiveluč = vulkan Šiveluč 42-43 f 6
Velikij Šiveluč = vulkan Šiveluč 42-43 f 6
Velikij Ust'ug 42-43 GH 5
Veliko Târnovo 36-37 L 4
Velíž 38-39 F 4
Velíž 38-39 F 4
Velká bahamská lavice 72-73 L 6-7
Velká Británie a severní Irsko 32 F-H 4-5
Velká čínská zeď' 48-49 K 4
Velká Syrta, záliv – = Khalīj as-Surt 60-61 H 2
Velká útesová bariéra = Great Barrier Reef 56-57 H 2-K 4
Velké Antily 72-73 K 7-N 8
Velké Hořké jezero = Al-Buhayrat al-Murrat al-Kubrá 62 E 2
Velké Medvědí jezero 70-71 MN 4
Velké Otročí jezero 70-71 NO 5
Velké Solné jezero = Great Salt Lake 72-73 D 3
Velké Sundy 52-53 E-H 7-8
Velkomstpynten 30-31 j 5
Velký australský záliv = Great Australian Bight 56-57 E 6-G 7
Velký Chingan 48-49 M 3-N 1
Velký východní Erg = Al-'Irq al-Kabīr ash-Sharqī 60-61 F 2-3
Velký západní Erg = Al-'Irq al-Kabīr al-Gharbī 60-61 D 3-E 2
Vella Lavella 52-53 j 6
Velletri 36-37 E 5
Vellore 44-45 M 8
Velluga 42-43 H 6
Velmerstot 33 D 3
Vel'sk 42-43 G 5
Vēlūr = Vellore 44-45 M 8
Vemdalen 30-31 EF 6
Venado, Isla – 72-73 b 3
Venado Tuerto 80 D 4
Venator, OR 76-77 DE 4
Vendas Novas 34-35 C 9
Vendée 34-35 G 5
Vendôme 34-35 H 5
Venecia = Venèzia 36-37 E 3
Venedig = Venèzia 36-37 E 3
Veneta, OR 76-77 B 3-4
Venetie, AK 70-71 G 4
Venetië = Venèzia 36-37 E 3
Veneto 36-37 DE 3
Venèzia 36-37 E 3
Venèzia, Golfo di – 36-37 E 3
Venezuela 78-79 FG 3
Venezuela, Golfo de – 78-79 E 2
Vēngangā = Wainganga 44-45 MN 6-7
Vengerovo 42-43 O 6
Vengurla 44-45 L 7
Vēṅgurlēṅ = Vengurla 44-45 L 7
Venice, FL 74-75 b 3
Venice = Venèzia 36-37 E 3
Venise = Venèzia 36-37 E 3
Venosa 36-37 F 5
Venta 30-31 K 9
Venta de Baños 34-35 E 8
Venta de Baños 34-35 E 8
Ventana, Sierra de la – 80 D 5
Ventnor 32 F 6
Ventoux, Mont – 34-35 K 6
Ventspils 30-31 J 9
Ventuari, Río – 78-79 F 3
Ventura, CA 76-77 D 8
Vera [RA] 80 D 3
Vera, La – 34-35 E 8
Verá, Laguna – 80 E 3
Veracruz [MEX, ●] 72-73 GH 8
Veracruz [MEX, ☆] 72-73 G 7-8
Veranópolis 80 F 3
Verāval 44-45 KL 6
Vercelli 36-37 C 3
Verchn'aja Amga 42-43 Y 6
Verchn'aja Salda 38-39 M 4
Verchn'aja Tojma 42-43 GH 5
Verchnedvinsk 30-31 MN 10
Verchneimbatsk 42-43 QR 5
Verchneje Adimi 50-51 H 1
Verchne Ozernaja 42-43 f 6
Verchneudinsk = Ulan-Udè 42-43 U 7
Verchneural'sk 42-43 KL 7
Verchneusinskoje 42-43 RS 7
Verchnevil'ujsk 42-43 X 5
Verchnij Baskunčak 38-39 J 6
Verchnij Trajanov val 36-37 N 2
Verchnij Ufalej 42-43 KL 6
Verchojansk 42-43 Za 4
Verchojanskij chrebet 42-43 Y 4-Z 5
Verdalsøyra 30-31 DE 6
Verden 33 D 2
Verde River 76-77 H 8
Verdi, NV 76-77 CD 6
Verdon 34-35 L 7
Verdon-sur-Mer, le – 34-35 G 6
Verdun 34-35 K 4
Vereeniging 64-65 G 8
Vereinigte Arabische Emirate 44-45 GH 6
Vereinigte Staaten 72-73 C-K 4
Vérendrye, Parc provincial de la – 70-71 V 8
Verenigde Arabische Emiraten 44-45 G 6-H 5
Verenigde Staten 72-73 D-K 4
Vereščagino [SU ↓ Igarka] 42-43 QR 5
Vereščagino [SU ← Krasnokamsk] 42-43 JK 6
Vereščagino [SU ↓ Igarka] 42-43 QR 5
Vereščagino [SU ← Krasnokamsk] 42-43 JK 6
Verchnij Baskunčak 38-39 J 6
Verín 34-35 D 8
Verkola 38-39 J 3
Verlegenhuken 30-31 jk 4
Vermilion 70-71 O 7
Vermilion Cliffs 76-77 G 7
Vermillion, OH 74-75 B 4
Vermont 72-73 M 3
Vernal, UT 76-77 J 5
Vernon 34-35 H 4
Vernon [CDN, British Colombia] 70-71 N 7
Vernon, AZ 76-77 J 8
Vernon, NV 76-77 D 5
Vernon, TX 72-73 FG 5
Vernon = Onaqui, UT 76-77 G 5
Vernonia, OR 76-77 B 3
Vernyj = Alma-Ata 42-43 O 9
Vero Beach, FL 74-75 cd 3
Verona 36-37 D 3
Versailles 34-35 HJ 4
Versailles, OH 74-75 A 5
Versec = Vršac 36-37 J 3
Versec = Vršac 36-37 J 3
Veršino-Darasunskij 42-43 VW 7
Veršino-Darasunskij 42-43 VW 7
Verviers 34-35 KL 3
Vervins 34-35 JK 4
Vescovato 36-37 C 4
Veselí nad Lužnicí 33 G 4
Veselí nad Lužnicí 33 G 4
Veselinovo 36-37 O 2
Vesjegonsk 42-43 F 6
Vesoul 34-35 KL 5
Vest-Agder 30-31 B 8
Vesterålen 30-31 FG 3
Vestfjorden 30-31 E 4-F 3
Vestfold 30-31 CD 8
Vestfonna 30-31 l 4
Vestmannaeyjar 30-31 c 3
Vestspitsbergen 30-31 j-l 5
Vestur-Bardhastrandar 30-31 ab 2
Vestur-Húnavatn 30-31 cd 2
Vestur-Ísafjardhar 30-31 b 1-2
Vestur-Skaftafell 30-31 de 3
Vestvågøy 30-31 EF 3
Vesúvio 36-37 F 5
Veszprem 33 HJ 5
Vetlanda 30-31 F 9
Vetralla 36-37 DE 4
Vevay, OH 74-75 A 5
Veynes 34-35 K 6
Veyo, UT 76-77 G 7
Veys 46-47 N 7
Vézère 34-35 H 6
Vezirköprü 46-47 F 2

Viacha 78-79 F 8
Viana [BR, Maranhão] 78-79 K 5
Viana del Bollo 34-35 D 7
Viana do Castelo 34-35 C 8
Viangchan 52-53 D 3
Vianópolis 78-79 K 8
Viarèggio 36-37 CD 4
Viborg 30-31 C 9
Viborg = Vyborg 42-43 DE 5
Vibo Valentia 36-37 FG 6
Vic 34-35 J 8
Vicente, Point – 76-77 D 9
Vicenza 36-37 D 3
Vichada, Río – 78-79 F 4
Vichy 34-35 J 5
Vicksburg, AZ 76-77 FG 9
Vicksburg, MS 72-73 HJ 5
Victor, ID 76-77 H 4
Victor, MT 76-77 F 2
Victor Harbor 56-57 G 7
Victoria [AUS] 56-57 HJ 7
Victoria [CDN] 70-71 M 8
Victoria [HK] 48-49 LM 7
Victoria [RA] 80 DE 4
Victoria [RCH, Araucania] 80 B 5
Victoria [SY] 64-65 MN 3
Victoria [ZW] 64-65 H 7
Victoria, TX 72-73 G 6
Victoria = Labuan 52-53 FG 5
Victoria, Île – = Victoria Island 70-71 O-Q 3
Victoria, Lake – [AUS] 58 E 4
Victoria, Lake – [≈] 64-65 H 3
Victoria, Mount – 52-53 N 8
Victoria, Mount – = Tomaniive 52-53 a 2
Victoria and Albert Mountains 70-71 VW 1-2
Victoria de Durango 72-73 F 7
Victoria de las Tunas 72-73 L 7
Victoria Island [CDN] 70-71 O-Q 3
Victoria Land 24 B 17-15
Victoria Point = Kawthaung 52-53 C 4
Victoria River 56-57 EF 3
Victoria River Downs 56-57 F 3
Victoria Strait 70-71 QR 4
Victoria-Wes 64-65 F 9
Victoria West = Victoria-Wes 64-65 F 9
Victorica 80 C 5
Victorino 78-79 F 4
Victorville, CA 76-77 E 8
Vičuga 42-43 G 6
Vičuga 42-43 G 6
Vidal, CA 76-77 F 8
Vidalia, GA 74-75 B 8
Videň = Wien 33 H 4
Vidim 42-43 T 6
Vidin 36-37 K 3-4
Vidio, Cabo – 34-35 DE 7
Vidisha 44-45 M 6
Vidra 36-37 M 3
Viedma 80 D 6
Viedma, Lago – 80 B 7
Vieille Castille = Castilla la Vieja 34-35 E 8-F 7
Viejo, Cerro – 76-77 G 10
Viena = Wien 33 H 4
Vienna, GA 74-75 B 8
Vienna, WV 74-75 C 5
Vienna = Wien 33 H 4
Vienne [F, ~] 34-35 H 5
Vienne [F, ●] 34-35 K 6
Vienne = Wien 33 H 4
Vientiane = Viangchan 52-53 D 3
Vientos, Los – 80 BC 2
Vientos, Paso de los – 72-73 M 7-8
Vieques 72-73 N 8
Vierges, Îles – 72-73 NO 8
Vierwaldstätter See 33 D 5
Vierzon 34-35 J 5
Viesīte 30-31 L 9
Vieste 36-37 G 5
Viêt Tri 52-53 E 2
Vigan 52-53 GH 3
Vigia 78-79 K 5
Vigía, El – 78-79 E 3
Vignola 36-37 D 3
Vigo 34-35 C 7
Vihren 36-37 K 5
Viipuri = Vyborg 42-43 DE 5
Viitasaari 30-31 LM 6
Vijāpur = Bijapur 44-45 LM 7
Vijayanagaram = Vizianagaram 44-45 NO 7
Vijayawada 44-45 N 7
Vik 30-31 d 3
Vika 30-31 M 4
Viking 70-71 O 7
Vikna 30-31 D 5
Vikøyri 30-31 B 7
Vila [Vanuatu] 56-57 N 3
Vila Arriaga = Bibala 64-65 D 5
Vila Artur de Paiva = Cubango 64-65 E 5
Vila Bela da Santissima Trindade 78-79 H 7-8
Vila Cabral = Lichinga 64-65 J 5
Vila Coutinho 64-65 H 5
Vila da Maganja 64-65 J 6
Vila de Aljustrel = Cangamba 64-65 E 5
Vila de Aviz = Oncócua 64-65 D 6
Vila de João Belo = Xai Xai 64-65 H 8
Vila de Manica = Manica 64-65 H 6
Vila de Sèna 64-65 HJ 6
Vila Fontes = Caia 64-65 J 6
Vila Franca de Xira 34-35 C 9
Vila Gouveia = Catandica 64-65 H 6
Vila Henrique de Carvalho = Saurimo 64-65 F 4
Vilaine 34-35 F 5
Vila João de Almeida = Chibia 64-65 D 6
Vilaller 34-35 H 7
Vila Macedo do Cavaleiros = Andulo 64-65 E 5
Vila Marechal Carmona = Uige 64-65 E 4
Vila Mariano Machado = Ganda 64-65 D 5
Vilanculos 64-65 J 7
Viļāni 30-31 M 9
Vila Norton de Matos = Balombo 64-65 D 5
Vila Nova do Seles 64-65 D 5
Vila Paiva Couceiro = Gambos 64-65 DE 5
Vila Pereira d'Eça = Ngiva 64-65 E 6
Vila Pery = Manica 64-65 H 6
Vila Real 34-35 D 8
Vila Real de Santo António 34-35 D 10
Vilar Formoso 34-35 D 8
Vila Salazar = Ndalatando 64-65 DE 4
Vila Teixeira da Silva = Bailundo 64-65 E 5
Vila Teixeira de Sousa = Luau 64-65 EF 5
Vila Velha [BR, Espírito Santo] 78-79 LM 9
Vila Viçosa 34-35 D 9
Vilcabamba, Cordillera – 78-79 E 7
Vil'čeka, zeml'a – 42-43 L-N 1
Vil'čeka, zeml'a – 42-43 L-N 1
Vilejka 38-39 E 5
Vil'gort = Vyl'gort [SU, Syktyvkar] 42-43 HJ 5
Vilhelmina 30-31 G 5
Vilhena 78-79 G 7
Vilija 38-39 E 5
Viljandi 30-31 L 8
Vil'kickogo, ostrov – [SU, Gydanskij p-ov] 42-43 NO 3
Vil'kickogo, ostrov – [SU, Novosibirskije o-va] 42-43 de 2
Vil'kickogo, proliv – 42-43 S-U 2
Villa Abecia 78-79 FG 9
Villa Ángela 80 D 3
Villa Bella 78-79 F 7
Villablino 34-35 D 7
Villacañas 34-35 F 9
Villacarillo 34-35 F 9
Villach 33 F 5
Villacidro 36-37 C 6
Villa Cisneros = Ad-Dakhlah 60-61 A 4
Villada 34-35 E 7
Villa de Cura 78-79 F 2-3
Villa de María 80 D 3
Villa Dolores 80 C 4
Villa Federal = Federal 80 E 4
Villafranca del Bierzo 34-35 D 7
Villafranca de los Barros 34-35 DE 9
Villafranca del Penedès 34-35 H 8
Villa Frontera 72-73 F 6
Villagarcia de Arosa 34-35 C 7
Villàgio Duca degli Abruzzi = Joowhar 64-65 L 2
Villaguay 80 E 4
Villahermosa [MEX] 72-73 H 8
Villajoyosa 34-35 GH 9
Villa María 80 D 4
Villa Mazán 80 C 3
Villamil 78-79 A 5
Villa Montes 78-79 G 9
Villanova i la Geltrú 34-35 HJ 8
Villanueva de Córdoba 34-35 E 9
Villanueva de la Serena 34-35 E 9
Villa Ocampo [RA] 80 DE 3
Villaodrid 34-35 D 7
Villa Ojo de Agua 80 D 3
Villarreal de los Infantes 34-35 GH 9
Villarrica [PY] 80 E 3
Villa San Martín 80 D 3
Villa Unión [RA, La Rioja] 80 C 3
Villa Valeria 80 CD 4
Villavicencio [CO] 78-79 E 4
Villaviciosa 34-35 E 7
Villavieja de Yeltes 34-35 D 8
Villefranche-sur-Saône 34-35 K 5-6
Villena 34-35 G 9
Villeneuve-Saint-Georges 34-35 J 4
Villeneuve-sur-Lot 34-35 H 6
Villeurbanne 34-35 K 6
Villingen-Schwenningen 33 D 4
Villingen-Schwenningen 33 D 4
Villmanstrand = Lappeenranta 30-31 N 7
Vilnius 30-31 L 10
Vilnjus = Vilnius 30-31 L 10
Vilos, Los – 80 B 4
Vil'uj 42-43 W 5
Vil'ujsk 42-43 X 5
Villacañas 34-35 F 9
Villingen-Schwenningen 33 D 4
Vimmerby 30-31 FG 9
Vina, CA 76-77 BC 6
Viña, La – [PE] 78-79 D 6
Viña, La – [RA] 80 C 3
Viña del Mar 80 B 4
Vinalhaven, ME 74-75 J 2-3
Vinaroz 34-35 H 8
Vincennes, IN 72-73 J 4
Vincennes Bay 24 C 11
Vindelälven 30-31 H 5
Vindeln 30-31 HJ 5
Vindhya Range 44-45 L-N 6
Vineland, NJ 74-75 F 5
Vineyard Sound 74-75 H 4
Vinh = Xa-doai 52-53 E 3
Vinh Lo'i 52-53 E 5
Vinh Long 52-53 E 4
Vinho, País do – 34-35 CD 8
Vinje 30-31 B 8
Vinkovci 36-37 H 3
Vinnica 38-39 E 6
Vinson, Mount – 24 B 28
Vinton, VA 74-75 D 6
Viña, La – [PE] 78-79 D 6
Viña, La – [RA] 80 C 3
Viña del Mar 80 B 4
Vipya Mountains 63 C 5
Virac 52-53 H 4
Viramgam 44-45 L 6
Viramgaon = Viramgam 44-45 L 6
Viranşehir 46-47 H 4
Virbalis 30-31 K 10
Virden, NM 76-77 J 9
Vire 34-35 G 4
Virgenes, Cabo – 80 C 8
Virgenes, Islas – 72-73 NO 8
Virginia [USA] 72-73 KL 4
Virginia, MN 72-73 H 2
Virginia Beach, VA 74-75 EF 6
Virginia City, MT 76-77 GH 3
Virginia City, NV 76-77 D 6
Virginia Mountains 76-77 D 6
Virgin Islands 72-73 NO 8
Virgin Mountains 76-77 FG 7
Virgin River 76-77 FG 7
Virgin-szigetek 72-73 NO 8
Virihaure 30-31 G 4
Virovitica 36-37 G 3
Virtaniemi 30-31 MN 3
Virtsu 30-31 K 8
Virunga, Parc national – 64-65 G 2-3
Vis 36-37 G 4
Visagapatão = Vishākhapatnam 44-45 NO 7
Visakhapaṭṭaṇam = Vishakhapatnam 44-45 NO 7
Visalia, CA 76-77 D 7
Visayan Sea 52-53 H 4
Visby 30-31 GH 9
Viscount Melville Sound 70-71 O-Q 3
Višegrad 36-37 H 4
Višera 38-39 L 3
Viseu 34-35 D 8
Viseu [BR] 78-79 K 5
Vişeu-de-Sus 36-37 L 2
Vishākhapatnam = Vishakhapatnam 44-45 NO 7
Vishanpur = Bishenpur 44-45 P 6
Viso, Monte – 36-37 B 3
Vista Reservoir 76-77 F 5
Vistula = Wisła 33 K 3
Vistule = Wisła 33 K 3
Višera 38-39 L 3
Vit 36-37 L 4
Vitebsk 38-39 EF 4
Viterbo 36-37 DE 4
Vitiaz Strait 52-53 N 8
Vitichi 78-79 F 9
Viti Levu 52-53 a 2
Vitim 42-43 V 6
Vitimskoje ploskogorje 42-43 V 7
Vitja, Fosa de – 48-49 S 3
Vitjas, Abysse de – 48-49 S 3
Vitjaz Deep 48-49 S 3
Vitoria [BR, Espírito Santo] 78-79 LM 9
Vitoria [E] 34-35 F 7
Vitória da Conquista 78-79 L 7
Vitoša Planina 36-37 K 4
Vitoša Planina 36-37 K 4
Vitré 34-35 G 4
Vitry-le-François 34-35 K 4
Vitshumbi 63 B 3
Vittangi 30-31 JK 4
Vittòrio d'Africa = Shalanbod 64-65 KL 2
Vittòrio Vèneto 36-37 E 2
Vitu Islands 52-53 g 5
Vityaz-mélység [Iturup] 48-49 S 3
Vivarais, Monts du – 34-35 K 6
Vivario 36-37 C 4
Vivero 34-35 D 7
Vivi 42-43 S 4
Vivi, ozero – 42-43 R 4
Vivoratá 80 E 5
Vivsta 30-31 G 6
Vižajskij zavod = Krasnovišersk 42-43 K 5
Vižas 38-39 J 2
Vizcachas, Meseta de las – 80 B 8
Vizcaíno, Sierra – 72-73 D 6
Vizcaya, Golfo de – 34-35 EF 6
Vizcayai-öböl 34-35 EF 6
Vize 46-47 B 2
Vize, ostrov – 42-43 O 2
Vizianagaram 44-45 NO 7
Vizinga 42-43 HJ 5
Vižajskij zavod = Krasnovišersk 42-43 K 5
Vižas 38-39 J 2

Vjatka 42-43 HJ 6
Vjosë 36-37 HJ 5

Vlaanderen 34-35 J 3
Vladimir 42-43 FG 6
Vladivostok 42-43 Z 9
Vlasenica 36-37 H 3
Vlasotince 36-37 K 4
Vlissingen 34-35 J 3
Vlorë 36-37 H 5
Vltava 33 G 4

Vnitřní Mongolsko, Autonomní oblast – 48-49 K 3-M 2

Vodla 38-39 G 3
Vodlozero 38-39 G 3
Vœune Sai 52-53 E 4
Vogelkop = Cenderawasih 52-53 K 7
Vogelsberg 33 D 3
Vogesen 34-35 L 4-5
Vogézek 34-35 L 4-5
Vogezen 34-35 L 4-5
Vogézy 34-35 L 4-5
Voghera 36-37 C 3
Vohémar = Vohimarina 64-65 M 5
Vohibinany 64-65 LM 6
Vohimarina 64-65 M 5
Vohipeno 64-65 L 7
Voi [EAK, ~] 63 D 3
Voi [EAK, ●] 64-65 J 3
Voinjama 60-61 BC 7
Voiron 34-35 K 6
Vojejkov šelfovyj lednik 24 C 12-13
Vojejkov šelfovyj lednik 24 C 12-13

228 Varna

Vojnica 38-39 EF 2
Vojvodina 36-37 HJ 3
Voj-Vož 38-39 KL 3
Voj-Vož 38-39 KL 3
Volcano Islands 54 RS 7
Volchov 38-39 F 4
Volchov [SU, ●] 42-43 E 5-6
Volchovstroj = Volchov 42-43 E 5-6
Volda 30-31 B 6
Volga [SU, ~] 42-43 F 6
Volgo-Baltijskij kanal 38-39 G 3
Volgodonsk 38-39 H 6
Volgograd 38-39 H 6
Volgogradskoje vodochranilišče 38-39 J 5
Volgogradskoje vodochranilišče 38-39 J 5
Volha = Volga 42-43 F 6
Volkovysk 38-39 DE 5
Volksrepublik China = China 48-49 E-K 5
Volksrepublik China = China 48-49 E-K 5
Volksrepublik China = China 48-49 E-K 5
Volnovacha 38-39 G 6
Voločanka 42-43 R 3
Voločanka 42-43 R 3
Volodarsk 38-39 H 4
Vologda 42-43 FG 6
Volosovo 30-31 N 8
Vol'sk 42-43 H 7
Volta [GH] 60-61 E 7
Volta, Lake – 60-61 DE 7
Volta Noire 60-61 D 6
Voltera 36-37 D 4
Voltti 30-31 K 6
Volturino, Monte – 36-37 F 5
Volturno 36-37 F 5
Volubilis 60-61 C 2
Volžsk 42-43 H 6
Volžskij 38-39 HJ 6
Volžsk 42-43 H 6
Volžskij 38-39 HJ 6
Vona = Perşembe 46-47 G 2
Von Martius, Salto – 78-79 J 7
von Otterøya 30-31 l 5
Voor-Indië 22-23 NO 4
Vopnafjördhur [IS, ∪] 30-31 fg 2
Vopnafjördhur [IS, ●] 30-31 F 2
Vorarlberg 33 DE 5
Vorderindien 22-23 NO 4
Vorderrhein 33 D 5
Vordingborg 30-31 D 10
Vorjapaul' 42-43 L 5
Vorkuta 42-43 L 4
Vormsi 30-31 K 8
Vorogovo 42-43 QR 5
Voroncovo [SU, Dudinka] 42-43 PQ 3
Voronež 38-39 GH 5
Voronež 38-39 GH 5
Voronino 38-39 HJ 4
Voronja 38-39 G 2
Vorošilov = Ussurijsk 42-43 Z 9
Vorošilovgrad 38-39 GH 6
Vorošilov = Ussurijsk 42-43 Z 9
Vorošilovgrad 38-39 GH 6
Vorskla 38-39 G 5
Võrtsjärv 30-31 LM 8
Võru 30-31 M 9
Vosges 34-35 L 4-5
Vosgos 34-35 L 4-5
Voss 30-31 B 7
Vostočnyj Sajan 42-43 R 6-T 7
Vostočnyj Sajan 42-43 R 6-T 7
Vostok [Antarktika] 24 B 11
Vostychoj = Jegyrjach 42-43 M 5
Votice 33 G 4
Votkinsk 42-43 J 6
Votkinskoje vodochranilišče 42-43 JK 6
Votkinskoje vodochranilišče 42-43 JK 6
Vouga 34-35 C 8
Vožgora 38-39 J 3
Voznesensk 38-39 F 6
Voznesensk-Ivanovo = Ivanovo 42-43 FG 6
Vozroždenija, ostrov – 42-43 KL 9
Vozroždenija, ostrov – 42-43 KL 9
Vozvraščenija, gora – 42-43 b 8
Vozvraščenija, gora – 42-43 b 8
Vožgora 38-39 J 3
Vörös-medence = Sichuan Pendi 48-49 JK 5-6
Vörös-tenger 44-45 D 5-E 7
Vraca 36-37 K 4
Vrangel'a, ostrov – 42-43 hj 3
Vranje 36-37 J 4
Vratislav = Wrocław 33 H 3
Vratislav = Wrocław 33 H 3
Vrbas [YU, ~] 36-37 G 3
Vrbas [YU, ●] 36-37 H 3
Vreed-en-Hoop 78-79 H 3
Vršac 36-37 J 3
Vršac 36-37 J 3
Vryburg 64-65 F 8
Vryheid 64-65 H 8
Vsetín 33 J 4
Vukovar 36-37 H 3
Vulcano, Ìsola – 36-37 F 6
Vulture, Monte – 36-37 F 5
Vuotso 30-31 M 3
Vuria 63 D 3
Vuurland 80 C 8
Vyborg 42-43 DE 5
Vyčegda 42-43 J 5
Vyčegda 42-43 J 5
Východní novozemský příkop 42-43 K 3-L 2
Východočínské moře 48-49 N 6-O 5
Východofríské o-vy 30-31 B 11
Východofríské o-vy 33 C 2
Východosibiřské moře 42-43 d-h 3
Vyksa 42-43 G 6
Vyl'gort 42-43 HJ 5
Vyrica 38-39 F 4
Vyšnij Voloč'ok 42-43 EF 6
Vysokaja, gora – 42-43 a 8
Vysokogornyj 42-43 ab 7
Vysoký Atlas 60-61 CD 2
Vyšnij Voloč'ok 42-43 EF 6
Vytegra 42-43 F 5

W

W, Parcs nationaux du – 60-61 E 6
Wa 60-61 D 6
Waajid 60-61 a 3
Waal 34-35 K 3
Waar, Meos – 52-53 KL 7
Wabag 52-53 M 8
Wabana 70-71 a 8
Wabasca River 70-71 NO 6
Wabash River 72-73 J 3
Wabuska, NV 76-77 D 6
Waccamaw, Lake – 74-75 D 7
Waccasassa Bay 74-75 b 2
Wachan = Wākhān 44-45 L 3
Waco, TX 72-73 G 5
Wād, Al- 60-61 F 2
Wadah, Al- 62 F 6
Wād an-Nayl 60-61 LM 6
Wadayama 50-51 K 5
Wād Bandah 60-61 K 6
Waddān 60-61 H 3
Waddington, Mount – 70-71 LM 7
Wadesboro, NC 74-75 C 7
Wād Ḥāmid 60-61 L 5
Wadhwān 44-45 L 6
Wādī, Bi'r al – 46-47 K 6
Wādī Ḥalfā 60-61 L 4
Wādī Jimāl, Jazīrat – 62 F 5
Wādī Zam 60-61 C 2
Wadley, GA 74-75 B 8
Wād Madanī 60-61 L 6
Wadsworth, NV 76-77 D 6
Waegwan 50-51 G 4-5
Wa-fang-tien = Fu Xian 48-49 N 4
Wagal-bong = Maengbu-san 50-51 F 2
Wageningen [SME] 78-79 H 3
Wager Bay 70-71 T 4
Wagga Wagga 56-57 J 7
Wagin 56-57 C 6
Wagina 52-53 j 6
Wagontire, OR 76-77 D 4
Wągrowiec 33 H 2
Wāḥah 60-61 H 3
Wahai 52-53 J 7
Wahlbergøya 30-31 k 5
Wahlenbergfjord 30-31 kl 5
Wahrān 60-61 D 1
Wah Wah Mountains 76-77 G 6
Waidhofen an der Thaya 33 G 4
Waidhofen an der Ybbs 33 G 5
Waigama 52-53 JK 7
Waigeo, Pulau – 52-53 K 6
Waikabubak 52-53 G 8
Waikerie 56-57 GH 6
Waimate 56-57 O 8
Wainganga 44-45 MN 6-7
Waingapu 52-53 GH 8
Waini Point 78-79 H 3
Wainwright, AK 70-71 DE 3
Wairoa 56-57 P 7
Waitaki River 56-57 O 8
Waitara 56-57 OP 7
Waitsap = Huaiji 48-49 L 7
Waitsburg, WA 76-77 D 2
Waitzen = Vác 33 J 5
Waiyeung = Huiyang 48-49 LM 7
Wajh, Al- 44-45 D 5
Wajima 50-51 L 4
Wak, El – 64-65 K 2
Waka 64-65 F 3
Wakamatsu = Aizu-Wakamatsu 50-51 M 4
Wakamatsu-shima 50-51 G 6
Wakasa 50-51 K 5
Wakasa-wan 50-51 K 5
Wakayama 48-49 Q 5
Wake Forest, NC 74-75 D 7
Wakeham = Maricourt 70-71 W 5
Wākhān 44-45 L 3
Wākhjīr, Kotāle – 44-45 LM 3
Wakinosawa 50-51 N 2
Wakkanai 48-49 R 2
Wakool 58 G 5
Wākṣa = Wāqiṣah 46-47 K 7
Wakunai 52-53 j 6
Walachei 36-37 LM 3
Walachije 36-37 LM 3
Wa'lan 60-61 E 4
Walapai, AZ 76-77 G 8
Walātah 60-61 C 5
Wałbrzych 33 H 3
Walcha 58 KL 3
Walcheren 34-35 J 3
Wałcz 33 H 2
Waldenburg (Schlesien) = Wałbrzych 33 H 3
Waldenburg (Schlesien) = Wałbrzych 33 H 3
Waldenburg (Schlesien) = Wałbrzych 33 H 3
Waldo, FL 74-75 bc 2
Waldport, OR 76-77 A 3
Walencja = Valencia 34-35 H 9
Wales 32 E 5-6
Wales, AK 70-71 C 4
Wales Island 70-71 T 4
Walfischbucht = Walvisbaai 64-65 D 7
Walfischrücken 22-23 K 7
Walgett 56-57 J 6
Walgreen Coast 24 B 26
Walhalla, SC 74-75 B 7
Walia = Wales 32 E 5-6
Waligiro 63 DE 3
Walikale 64-65 G 3
Walker Lake [USA] 72-73 C 4
Walker Mountain 74-75 C 6
Walker Mountains 24 B 26-27
Walker River Indian Reservation 76-77 D 6
Walkerton 74-75 C 2
Walkerville, MT 76-77 G 2
Walkite = Welkītē 60-61 M 7
Wallace 74-75 DE 2
Wallace, ID 76-77 EF 2
Wallace, NC 74-75 DE 7
Wallal Downs 56-57 D 3-4
Wallangarra 58 KL 2
Wallaroo 56-57 G 6
Wallasey 32 E 5
Walla Walla, WA 72-73 C 2
Wallel = Tulu Welēl 60-61 LM 7
Wallīj, Sha'īb al- 46-47 H 6
Wallingford, CT 74-75 G 4
Wallis = Valais 33 D 5
Wallis, Îles – 52-53 b 1
Wallowa, OR 76-77 E 3
Wallowa Mountains 76-77 E 3
Wallowa River 76-77 E 3
Wallula, WA 76-77 D 2
Walney 32 E 4
Walnut Canyon National Monument 76-77 H 8
Walnut Cove, NC 74-75 C 6
Walpole 56-57 NO 4
Walpole, NH 74-75 G 3
Walsall 32 F 5
Walterboro, SC 74-75 C 8
Walton, NY 74-75 F 3
Walvisbaai [ZA, ●] 64-65 D 7
Walvisbaai, Dorsale de – 22-23 K 7
Walvis Bay = Walvisbaai [ZA, ●] 64-65 D 7
Walvis Ridge 22-23 K 7
Walvisrug 22-23 K 7
Wałbrzych 33 H 3
Wałcz 33 H 2
Wamba [EAK] 63 D 2
Wamba [WAN] 60-61 F 7
Wamba [ZRE, Bandundu] 64-65 E 4
Wamba [ZRE, Haut-Zaïre] 64-65 G 2
Wami 64-65 J 4
Wamlana 52-53 J 7
Wanaaring 56-57 H 5
Wān Ahjār, Tāsīlī – 60-61 F 3
Wān al-Hajjār, Tāsīlī – = Murtaf'āt Tāsīlī 60-61 E 5-F 4
Wanapiri 52-53 L 7
Wanchuan = Zhangjiakou 48-49 L 3
Wanda Shan 48-49 P 2
Wan-do 50-51 F 5
Wandoan 56-57 JK 5
Wanfu 50-51 D 2
Wanganella 58 G 5
Wanganui 56-57 OP 7
Wangaratta 56-57 J 7
Wangary 58 B 5
Wangi 63 E 3
Wangpang Yang 48-49 N 5
Wangyemiao = Ulan Hot 48-49 N 2
Wanhsien = Wan Xian [TJ, Sichuan] 48-49 K 5
Wankie = Hwange 64-65 G 6
Wankie National Park 64-65 G 6
Wanlaweyn 60-61 NO 8
Wanning 48-49 L 8
Wan-ta Shan-mo = Wanda Shan 48-49 P 2
Wantsai = Wanzai 48-49 LM 6
Wanzai 48-49 LM 6
Wapato, WA 76-77 C 2
Waqbā, Al- 46-47 L 8
Waqf, Al- 62 E 4
Wāqif, Jabal al- 62 D 6
Wāqiṣah 46-47 K 7
Waqooyi-Galbeed = Woqooyi-Galbeed 60-61 a 1
War, WV 74-75 C 6
Warān 60-61 BC 4
Warangal 44-45 MN 7
Waratah 58 b 2
Waratah Bay 58 GH 7
Warburton 58 G 6
Warburton, The – 56-57 G 5
Warburton Aboriginal Reserve = Central Australia Aboriginal Reserve 56-57 E 4-5
Wardān, Wādī – 62 E 3
Warden, WA 76-77 D 2
Wardere = Werdēr 60-61 O 7
Wardha [IND, ~] 44-45 M 6
Wardha [IND, ●] 44-45 M 6
Ward Hunt, Cape – 52-53 N 8
Ware 70-71 LM 6
Ware, MA 74-75 GH 3
Waren 33 F 2
Waren [RI] 52-53 L 7
Wari'ah, Al- 44-45 F 5
Warialda 56-57 K 5
Warin Chamrap 52-53 DE 3
Warin Chamrap 52-53 DE 3
Warin Chamrap 52-53 DE 3
Warjalah 60-61 F 2
Warland, MT 76-77 F 1
Warmbad [ZA] 64-65 G 7-8
Warmbad [Namibia, ●] 64-65 E 8
Warmsprings, MT 76-77 G 2
Warm Springs, OR 76-77 C 3
Warm Springs, NV [USA ↓ Cherry Creek] 76-77 F 6
Warm Springs, NV [USA → Tonopah] 76-77 EF 6
Warm Springs Indian Reservation 76-77 C 3
Warm Springs Valley 76-77 C 5
Warna = Varna 36-37 MN 4
Warnemünde, Rostock- 33 F 1
Warner Range 72-73 B 3
Warner Robins, GA 72-73 K 5
Warner Valley 76-77 CD 4
Warnes [BOL] 78-79 G 8
Waropko 52-53 LM 8
Warqlā = Warjalah 60-61 F 2
Wārqzīz, Jabal – 60-61 C 3
Warra 56-57 K 5
Warracknabeal 58 F 6
Warragul 58 G 7
Warrego River 56-57 J 5
Warren [AUS] 58 HJ 3
Warren, AZ 76-77 J 10
Warren, ID 76-77 F 3
Warren, OH 72-73 K 3
Warren, PA 74-75 D 4
Warrenton 64-65 FG 8
Warrenton, GA 74-75 B 8
Warrenton, NC 74-75 DE 6
Warrenton, OR 76-77 AB 2
Warrenton, VA 74-75 E 5
Warri 60-61 F 7
Warriner Creek 58 BC 2
Warrnambool 56-57 H 7
Warsaw, NC 74-75 DE 7
Warsaw, NY 74-75 DE 3
Warsaw = Warszawa 33 K 2
Warschau = Warszawa 33 KL 2
Warszawa 33 K 2
Warta 33 HJ 2
Warwick 32 EF 5
Warwick [AUS] 56-57 K 5
Warwick, RI 74-75 H 4
Wasatch, UT 76-77 H 5
Wasatch Range 72-73 D 3-4
Wasco, CA 76-77 D 8
Wasco, OR 76-77 C 3
Wash, The – 32 G 5
Washago 74-75 D 2
Washburn Lake 70-71 PQ 3
Washington [USA] 72-73 BC 2
Washington, DC 72-73 LM 4
Washington, GA 74-75 B 8
Washington, NC 74-75 E 7
Washington, PA 74-75 C 4
Washington, Mount – 72-73 M 3
Washita River 72-73 G 4-5
Washm, Al- 44-45 EF 5-6
Wash Shahri 48-49 F 4
Wasior 52-53 KL 7
Wāsiṭ 46-47 L 6
Wāsiṭah, Al- 60-61 L 3
Wassamu 50-51 c 1-2
Wassuk Range 76-77 D 6
Wasum 52-53 g 6
Watampone 52-53 GH 7
Watansopeng 52-53 G 7
Waterberg 64-65 E 7
Waterbury, CT 74-75 G 4
Wateree River 74-75 C 7
Waterford 32 C 5
Waterford [CDN] 74-75 C 3
Waterford, CA 76-77 C 7
Waterloo [AUS] 56-57 EF 3
Waterloo [B] 34-35 K 3
Waterloo [CDN, Ontario] 74-75 C 3
Waterloo, IA 72-73 H 3
Waterloo, MT 76-77 G 3
Waterloo, NY 74-75 E 3
Watertown, NY 72-73 LM 3
Watertown, SD 72-73 G 2
Waterville, ME 72-73 N 3
Waterville, WA 76-77 CD 2
Waterways 70-71 OP 6
Watkins Glen, NY 74-75 E 3
Watkinsville, GA 74-75 B 8
Watlam = Yulin 48-49 L 7
Watling Island = San Salvador 72-73 M 7
Watsa 64-65 G 2
Watson, UT 76-77 J 6
Watson Lake 70-71 L 5
Watsonville, CA 76-77 BC 7
Watt, Point – 56-57 E 5
Watubela, Kepulauan – 52-53 K 7
Watykan 36-37 DE 5
Wau 52-53 N 8
Wauchope 58 L 3
Wauchula, FL 74-75 bc 3
Wau el Kebir = Wāw al-Kabīr 60-61 H 3
Waukarlycarly, Lake – 56-57 D 4
Waukeenah, FL 74-75 ab 1
Wausau, WI 72-73 J 2-3
Wave Hill 56-57 F 3
Waverly, NY 74-75 E 3
Waverly, VA 74-75 E 6
Wāw [Sudan] 60-61 K 7
Waxell Ridge 70-71 H 5
Way, Lake – 56-57 D 5
Wayan, ID 76-77 H 4
Waycross, GA 72-73 K 5
Wayland, KY 74-75 B 6
Wayne, WV 74-75 B 5
Waynesboro, GA 74-75 BC 8
Waynesboro, PA 74-75 E 5
Waynesboro, VA 74-75 D 5
Waynesburg, PA 74-75 CD 5
Waynesville, NC 74-75 B 7
Waza 60-61 G 6
Wāzakhwā 44-45 K 4
Wāzīrābād = Balkh 44-45 K 3
Wazz, Al- 60-61 L 5
Wazzān 60-61 C 2
We, Pulau – 52-53 BC 5
Weaverville, CA 76-77 B 5
Webbe Shibeli = Wābi Shebelē 60-61 N 7
Webster, MA 74-75 GH 3
Webster Springs, WV 74-75 C 5
Weda 52-53 J 6
Weddell, Mer de – = Weddell Sea 24 BC 32-34
Weddella, Morze – = Weddell Sea 24 BC 32-34
Weddell Island 80 D 8
Weddellmeer = Weddell Sea 24 BC 32-34
Weddellovo moře = Weddell Sea 24 BC 32-34
Weddell Sea 24 BC 32-34
Weddell-tenger = Weddell Sea 24 BC 32-34
Weddellzee = Weddell Sea 24 BC 32-34
Weddell, Mar de – = Weddell Sea 24 BC 32-34
Wedel Jarlsberg land 30-31 j 6
Weed, CA 76-77 B 5
Weedon Centre 74-75 H 2
Weedville, PA 74-75 D 4
Weeksbury, KY 74-75 B 6
Weenusk = Winisk 70-71 T 6
Wee Waa 56-57 J 6
Wegener-Inlandeis 24 B 36-1
Węgry 33 H-K 5
Wehlau = Znamensk 33 K 1
Weichang 48-49 M 3
Weichsel = Wisła 33 K 3
Weiden 33 EF 4
Weifang 48-49 MN 4
Weihai 48-49 N 4
Wei He [TJ ◁ Hai He] 48-49 M 4
Wei He [TJ ◁ Huang He] 48-49 K 5
Weihnachtsinsel = Christmas Island 52-53 E 9
Weilmoringle 58 H 2
Weimar 33 E 3
Weining 48-49 JK 6
Weipa 56-57 H 2
Weirton, WV 74-75 C 4
Weiser, ID 76-77 E 3
Weiser River 76-77 E 3
Weißbrunn = Veszprem 33 HJ 5
Weiße Elster 33 F 3
Weißenfels 33 E 3
Weißer Volta = White Volta 60-61 D 7
Weißes Meer 42-43 FG 4
Weißes Meer 42-43 FG 4
Weißkirchen = Bela Crkva 36-37 J 3
Weiss Knob 74-75 D 5
Weißrußland 38-39 EF 5
Weiyang = Huiyang 48-49 LM 7
Wejh = Al-Wajh 44-45 D 5
Welbourn Hill 56-57 F 5
Welch, WV 74-75 C 6
Weldon, NC 74-75 E 6
Weldya 60-61 M 6
Welega 60-61 LM 7
Welel, Tulu – 60-61 LM 7
Welkītē 60-61 M 7
Welkom 64-65 G 8
Welland [CDN] 74-75 D 3
Welland Canal 74-75 D 3
Wellesley Islands 56-57 GH 3
Wellington [AUS] 56-57 JK 6
Wellington [CDN] 74-75 E 3
Wellington [NZ] 56-57 OP 8
Wellington, NV 76-77 D 6
Wellington, OH 74-75 B 4
Wellington, Isla – 80 AB 7
Wellington Channel 70-71 S 2-3
Wellington Channel 70-71 S 2-3
Wells, NV 72-73 C 3
Wells, Lake – 56-57 D 5
Wellsboro, PA 74-75 E 4
Wellsford 56-57 OP 7
Wells Gray Provincial Park 70-71 MN 7
Wells next the Sea 32 G 5
Wellston, OH 74-75 B 5
Wellsville, NY 74-75 E 3
Wellton, AZ 76-77 FG 9
Welo 60-61 MN 6
Wels 33 FG 4
Welshpool 32 E 5
Wellington Channel 70-71 S 2-3
Wembere 64-65 H 3-4
Wenatchee, WA 72-73 BC 2
Wenatchee Mountains 76-77 C 2
Wenchow = Wenzhou 48-49 N 6
Wendel, CA 76-77 CD 5
Wendell, ID 76-77 F 4
Wendell, NC 74-75 D 7
Wenden, AZ 76-77 G 9
Wendling, OR 76-77 B 3
Wendover, UT 76-77 FG 5
Wenecja = Venècia 36-37 E 3
Wenen = Wien 33 H 4
Wenezuela 78-79 FG 3
Wenshan 48-49 JK 7
Wenshan Zhuangzu Miaozu Zizhizhou 48-49 JK 7
Wên-su = Aqsu 48-49 E 3
Wentworth 56-57 H 6
Wenzhou 48-49 N 6
Wepener 64-65 G 8
Werdēr [ETH] 60-61 O 7
Wernecke Mountains 70-71 JK 5
Wernigerode 33 E 3
Werona = Verona 36-37 D 3
Werra 33 D 3
Werribee, Melbourne- 58 FG 6
Werris Creek 56-57 K 6
Werschetz = Vršac 36-37 J 3
Wesel 33 C 3
Weser 33 D 2
Weserbergland 33 D 2-3
Wesleyville, PA 74-75 CD 3
Wessel, Cape – 56-57 G 2
Wessel Islands 56-57 G 2
Westall, Point – 58 AB 4
Westaustralian Basin 22-23 P 7
Westaustralisch Bekken 22-23 P 7
Westaustralisches Becken 22-23 P 7
West Bengal 44-45 O 6
Westbrook, ME 74-75 H 3
West Butte 76-77 H 1
West Caroline Basin 22-23 QR 5
West-Carolinenbekken 22-23 QR 5
West Columbia, SC 74-75 C 8
Westerland 33 D 1
Westerly, RI 74-75 H 4
Western [EAK] 64-65 H 2
Western [Z] 64-65 F 6
Western Australia 56-57 C-E 4-5
Western Dvina = Daugava 30-31 LM 9
Western Ghats 44-45 L 6-M 8
Western Port 56-57 HJ 7
Westernport, MD 74-75 D 5
Western Sahara 60-61 A 4-B 3
Western Shoshone Indian Reservation 76-77 E 4-5
Westerschelde 34-35 J 3
Westerwald 33 CD 3
Westeuropäisches Becken 22-23 HJ 3
West European Basin 22-23 HJ 3
Westeuropees Bekken 22-23 HJ 3
West Falkland 80 D 8
Westfall, OR 76-77 E 3-4
Westfield, MA 74-75 G 3
Westfield, NY 74-75 D 3
Westfield, PA 74-75 E 4
Westfriesische Inseln 34-35 KL 2
West Frisian Islands 34-35 KL 2
Westgate 56-57 J 5
Westham, London- 32 FG 6
West Haven, CT 74-75 G 4
West Ice Shelf 24 C 9
West-Indië 72-73 LM 7
Westindien 72-73 L-O 7
West Indies 72-73 LM 7
West Irian 52-53 K 7-L 8
Westirian 52-53 K 7-L 8
West Jefferson, NC 74-75 C 6
West-Karolinenbecken 22-23 QR 5
Westlake, OR 76-77 A 4

Westl 229